T0389586

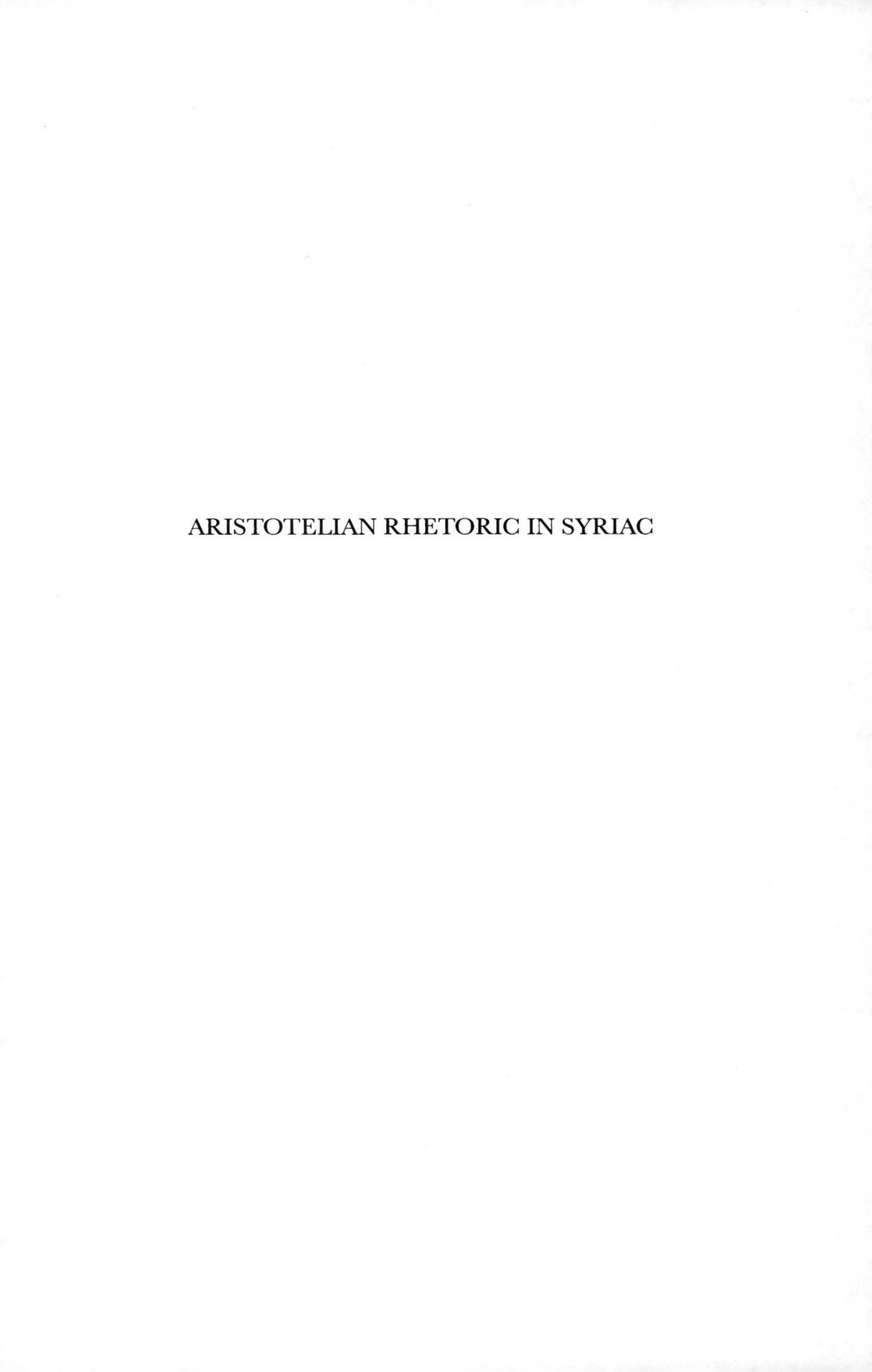

ARISTOTELIAN RHETORIC IN SYRIAC

# ARISTOTELES SEMITICO-LATINUS

*founded by H.J. Drossaart Lulofs*

is prepared under the supervision of the ROYAL NETHERLANDS ACADEMY OF ARTS AND SCIENCES as part of the CORPUS PHILOSOPHORUM MEDII AEVI project of the UNION ACADÉMIQUE INTERNATIONALE.

The Aristoteles Semitico-Latinus project envisages the publication of the Syriac, Arabic and Hebrew translations of Aristotle's works, of the Latin translations of those translations, and of the mediaeval paraphrases and commentaries made in the context of this translation tradition.



VOLUME 18

# ARISTOTELIAN RHETORIC IN SYRIAC

*Barhebraeus,* Butyrum Sapientiae, *Book of Rhetoric*

BY

JOHN W. WATT

WITH ASSISTANCE OF

DANIEL ISAAC, JULIAN FAULTLESS, AND AYMAN SHIHADEH

BRILL
LEIDEN · BOSTON
2005

This book is printed on acid-free paper

**Library of Congress Cataloging-in-Publication Data**

A C.I.P. record for this book is available from the Library of Congress.

ISSN 0927-4103
ISBN 90 04 14517 6



PRINTED IN THE NETHERLANDS

CONTENTS

# PREFACE

This volume presents a critical edition of the *Book of Rhetoric* from the *Cream of Wisdom* of the 13th century Syriac polymath Gregory Abū al-Faraj commonly known as Bar Hebraeus. The suggestion that I might undertake the work came from Professor Hans Daiber, and it has been a privilege to be associated with his group in Frankfurt and to share problems and insights with its other members. The volume takes its place alongside those of Hidemi Takahashi and Peter Joosse as a contribution from the realm of Syriac studies to 'Aristoteles Semitico-Latinus'.

In a perfect world, this work would have been undertaken by someone with equal facility in Syriac, Greek, and Arabic, but such paragons are hard to find. Like a great number of my fellows, I am not in equal command of all three languages. I am therefore very grateful to the late Dr. Daniel Isaac, to Dr. Julian Faultless, and to Dr Ayman Shihadeh for the invaluable help they have given me in the interpretation of the Arabic text of Ibn Sīnā's *Book of Rhetoric* in the *Shifā'*. It is no exaggeration to say that without their assistance, the present volume would not have been possible. They bear no responsibility for the use made of Ibn Sīnā in the elucidation here of Bar Hebraeus—and certainly not for any errors or oversights in that use—but it is right that their vital contribution to this volume should be recognised on its title-page. This collaborative aspect of the project was supported by a Small Research Grant from the British Academy, for which we here express our thanks. The Arabic side of the work also had the benefit of the important publications of Renate Würsch (on Ibn Sīnā), Maroun Aouad (on Ibn Rushd), and Malcolm Lyons (on the Arabic version of Aristotle's *Rhetoric*). To Dr. Aouad I am very grateful for illuminating personal discussions over a number of years on the interpretation of the *Rhetoric* by the Arabic philosophers, and to Prof. Lyons for the gift of a copy of his indispensable edition of the *Rhetoric* when it was hard to obtain.

I wish to express my thanks here also to Prof. Herman Teule, the peer reviewer appointed by the Royal Netherlands Academy, for his valuable suggestions; to Daniel King and Julian Faultless for help in checking the glossaries; to Douglas Watt for assistance in IT matters, particularly the construction of a multilingual database and a program to generate from it the trilingual glossary; to the general editors of the series, Hans Daiber and Remke Kruk, for their acceptance of the volume; and to Trudy Kamperveen at Brill for expert guidance in the preparation of camera-ready copy.

## ABBREVIATIONS

Titles of works referred to here and throughout by a short form are given in full in the Bibliography of cited works at the end of the volume

| | |
|---|---|
| Aouad | M. Aouad, *Averroès (Ibn Rušd). Commentaire moyen à la Rhétorique d'Aristote* |
| AR | Aristotle, *Rhetoric* (54a-99b = 1354a-1399b, 00a- 20b = 1400a-1420b) |
| ARar | Aristotle, *Rhetoric*, extant Arabic Version (ed. Lyons) |
| ARsyr | Aristotle, *Rhetoric*, Syriac Version (not extant) |
| BH | Bar Hebraeus, *The Book of Rhetoric* |
| *BrLex* | Carl Brockelmann, *Lexicon Syriacum* |
| IR | Ibn Rushd, *Commentaire moyen à la Rhétorique* (ed. Aouad) |
| IS | Ibn Sīnā, *Al-Shifā', La Logique VIII—Rhétorique* (*Al-Khaṭāba*) (ed. Salem) |
| Lyons | M. C. Lyons, *Aristotle's* Ars Rhetorica (references are to vol. 1 unless indicated to the contrary) |
| *ThesSyr* | R. Payne Smith, *Thesaurus Syriacus* |
| Würsch | R. Würsch, *Avicennas Bearbeitungen der aristotelischen Rhetorik* |

## NOTE ON FONTS AND TRANSLITERATIONS

The software design community has achieved remarkable results in the production of multilingual programs for personal use, but as with designs of all sorts, products sometimes have a residual flaw or two. The one flaw in the Syriac font used here is its inability clearly to distinguish ܪ from ܪ̈ when followed by ܐ (ܪܐ is singular, ܪ̈ܐ plural). From the translation or the context, the reader will, it is hoped, be able to discern which is intended on each occasion. The multilingual word processor used to produce the Commentary suffers from an insufficient and unreliable set of diacritics. In the Commentary—but only in the Commentary—Arabic personal names have therefore been written without the customary diacritics. In the small number of cases in the Commentary of transliteration of Arabic or Syriac words, a circumflex has been used where the program refused to accept a macron, and *ḩ* and *ch* used for Arabic *ḥ* (ح) and Syriac *ḥ* (ܚ) respectively. The author begs the indulgence of the reader in the matter of these few inconsistencies.

# INTRODUCTION

# INTRODUCTION

## ARISTOTLE'S *RHETORIC* IN THE ORIENT

The *Rhetoric* of Aristotle is widely esteemed in our day as the greatest and most important treatise of classical, or at least Greek, rhetoric. This, however, is very much a modern evaluation, and the influence of the work over the years since its composition has often been much less than this evaluation would suppose. Cicero and Quintilian were certainly familiar with the treatise, but already in the Roman period the attention of rhetors was increasingly focused on the ideas of Hermagoras, and by around the sixth century of our era a corpus of works attributed rightly or wrongly to Hermogenes had emerged as the foundation of Greek rhetorical theory. Further developments occurred primarily through the composition of commentaries on the books of this corpus, and Aristotle's treatise was rarely cited or drawn upon in this tradition. Only from the tenth century and later do we find evidence among Greek rhetors of an interest in Aristotle's *Rhetoric*. From the tenth century the great manuscript *Parisinus Graecus* 1741 contains the *Rhetoric* (and the *Poetics*) in its collection of rhetorical works, and from the twelfth there are extant two commentaries on Aristotle's treatise.[1]

The work was potentially of interest, however, not only to rhetors but also to philosophers. It is registered, within the section devoted to *organika* ('instrumental treatises'), in all three of the old catalogues of Aristotle's works, where Book Three may have appeared as a separate treatise ('*On Style*'). No commentaries on the *Rhetoric* are extant from the Aristotelian commentators of late antiquity, but they undoubtedly knew of it (as also of the *Poetics*). The commentators of the late phase of the Alexandrian School explain how Aristotle (according to their interpretation of his works) treated sophistical, rhetorical, and poetical syllogisms (i.e. syllogisms whose premisses are more false than true, equally true or false, and utterly false respectively) in addition to the apodeictic and dialectical

[1] Cf. e.g. Kennedy, *Greek Rhetoric under Christian Emperors*, 52-132, 317-320; idem, *Aristotle* On Rhetoric, 305-309.

(whose premisses are respectively true and more true than false). From this it is clear that their corpus of Aristotelian logical works (known later in the West as the *Organon*) included not only the six treatises later grouped together as such in the Greek and Western traditions (*Categories, On Interpretation, Prior Analytics, Posterior Analytics, Topics,* and *Sophistical Refutations*), but also the *Rhetoric* and the *Poetics*. The first four of these were held to be devoted to the apodeictic syllogism, the last four to the dialectical, sophistical, rhetorical, and poetical respectively.[2]

The eight- or nine-volume version of the *Organon*, rather than the six- or seven-volume version (the *Eisagoge* of Porphyry often being placed at the front as an introduction to the whole), was the one that found favour in the Orient, no doubt due to the influence of the Alexandrian School. The earliest evidence of this is found in a letter of the Catholicus Timothy I (died 823) requesting the priest Pethion to enquire at the monastery of Mar Mattai 'whether there is some commentary or scholia by anyone, whether in Syriac or not, to the *Topica*, or to the *Refutation of the Sophists*, or to the *Rhetorica*, or to the *Poetica*'.[3] This letter does not prove that a Syriac version of the *Rhetoric* existed at that time,[4] but it indicates that in Timothy's view the *Rhetoric* and the *Poetics* belonged in the same collection of Aristotle's works as the *Topics* and the *Sophistical Refutations*. The matter appears, however, in a much fuller light in the writings of al-Fārābī, who wrote several works on the *Rhetoric* and also took over the theories of the late Alexandrian commentators on the five sorts of syllogisms (premisses) and the co-ordination of these with the eight treatises of the *Organon*.[5] In his programmatic work *On the Philosophy of Aristotle* he asserted that after Aristotle had dealt with 'the certain science', he 'afterwards gave an account of the powers and arts by which man comes to possess the faculty for instructing

[2] Cf. Walzer, 'Zur Traditionsgeschichte der aristotelischen Poetik', 5-14; Moraux, *Les listes anciennes des ouvrages d'Aristote*, 96-104, 172-183.

[3] Brock, 'Two Letters of the Patriarch Timothy', 236 with commentary 241-242.

[4] It seems that Ḥunain did not know the text of the *Poetics*, or at any rate Aristotle's definition of tragedy; cf. Schrier, 'Aristotle's *Poetics*', 264-265. The case of the *Rhetoric*, however, is different, as will be argued below. This letter of Timothy testifies to a translation from Syriac to Arabic of the *Topics* by Timothy himself and Abū Nūḥ (cf. Brock, 'Two Letters of the Patriarch Timothy', 235-236 with commentary 240-241). Syriac versions of the six treatises *Categories* to *Sophistical Refutations* were all in existence at this time (cf. below, n. 9).

[5] Cf. Walzer, 'Zur Traditionsgeschichte der aristotelischen Poetik', 5-14.

whoever is not to use the science of logic or to be given the certain science'. These arts (although al-Fārābī does not actually name them) are rhetoric, which 'enables man to persuade the multitude regarding all theoretical things and those practical things in which it is customary to confine oneself to using persuasive arguments based on particular examples drawn from men's activities when conducting their public business', and poetics, which 'enables man to project images of the things that became evident in the certain demonstrations in the theoretical arts'.[6] In addition to confirming that al-Fārābī viewed the *Rhetoric* and the *Poetics* as the final two treatises of the corpus of Aristotle's logical writings, this work thus also reveals that he perceived the function of the *Rhetoric* to be that of a political tool designed to influence the public towards the good, not merely a device to 'protect' philosophers from the potential errors of non-apodeictic syllogisms.[7] Whereas in the few statements of the late antique Alexandrian philosophers about the work the *Rhetoric* appears merely to be a prophylactic against logical error,[8] in the thought of al-Fārābī it seems to have regained its vital connection with ancient rhetoric as a treatise on public discourse.

Bridging the gap between the Alexandrian commentators and al-Fārābī are two related factors: the translation of the *Rhetoric*, and indeed the entire *Organon*, into Arabic, and the transmission of Greek, particularly Aristotelian, thought to the Orient. During the sixth to tenth centuries, commencing with Sergius of Reshaina, Syriac scholars were of decisive importance in this process. In the early phase and the Umayyad period Syriac translations of Aristotle's logical works and Syriac commentaries upon them were confined to the first few books of the *Organon*, but by the time of al-Fārābī in the tenth century A.D. the entire *Organon* had been translated into Syriac and Arabic.[9] Al-Fārābī himself was attached for a while to the Baghdad School of philosophers, which was dominated

---

[6] *Falsafat Arisṭūṭālīs*, ed. Mahdi, 84-85; tr. Mahdi, *Alfarabi's Philosophy of Plato and Aristotle*, 92-93.

[7] Cf. Watt, 'The Syriac Reception of Platonic and Aristotelian Rhetoric', 580-582.

[8] Cf. Gutas, 'Paul the Persian', 242 and nn. 24-25.

[9] Cf. Brock, 'The Syriac Commentary Tradition', 3-18; Hugonnard-Roche, 'L'*Organon*. Tradition syriaque et arabe', 502-528; Aouad, 'La *Rhétorique*. Tradition syriaque et arabe', 455-459 and 'Compléments' 219-220; Goulet, 'La *Poétique*', 448-449 and Hugonnard-Roche, 'Compléments', 208-211.

by Syriac-speaking Christians. Its head was the Nestorian philosopher Abū Bishr Mattā, who translated (*inter alia*) the *Posterior Analytics* and the *Poetics* from Syriac into Arabic.[10] In the well known (if tendentious) account of the history of philosophy 'from Alexandria to Baghdad' attributed to al-Fārābī, the author tells how, going beyond the previous end of the curriculum at the assertoric figures (*Prior Analytics* 1.7), he read to the end of the *Posterior Analytics* with his teacher Yūḥannā b. Ḥaylān.[11] While there is no direct evidence of a Syriac translation of the *Rhetoric* before the time of al-Fārābī,[12] and no direct evidence that Syriac-speaking Aristotelians had an interest in it, such a translation and such an interest do therefore seem quite likely at least by that time, given the interest of the Baghdad School and al-Fārābī in the complete Alexandrian *Organon* and Abū Bishr Mattā's translation of the *Poetics*. The likelihood that a Syriac translation of the *Rhetoric* was in existence well before that time also emerges from the evidence now to be presented concerning the Old Arabic version and the text used by Bar Hebraeus.

The *Fihrist* of Ibn al-Nadīm registers the existence of three (Arabic) translations of the *Rhetoric*, as well as the commentary of al-Fārābī. These three translations are the 'Old' version—i.e., in the technical terminology of the time, one produced before the activity of Ḥunain—; a translation made by Isḥāq b. Ḥunain; and one made by Ibrahīm b. 'Abdallāh.[13] Only one manuscript of the Arabic *Rhetoric* is extant, namely MS. Paris, Bibliothèque Nationale, Arabe

[10] On Abū Bishr, cf. *K. al-Fihrist*, ed. Flügel (Leipzig, 1871), 263-264, tr. Dodge, *The Fihrist of al-Nadīm*, 630-631; Meyerhof, 'Von Alexandrien nach Bagdad', 415-416.

[11] Ibn Abī Uṣaibi'a, ed. Müller (Cairo/Königsberg, 1882/4), II, 135. Cf. Meyerhof, 'Von Alexandrien nach Bagdad', 405; Rosenthal, *The Classical Heritage in Islam*, 51; Zimmermann, *Al-Fārābī's Commentary and Short Treatise*, cv-cviii. The assertion in this tendentious account that study of anything beyond the assertoric figures was forbidden by church authorities is now generally dismissed as without any historical foundation, even though in fact it is likely that the first few books of the *Organon* were the only ones much studied in the earlier period of Syriac Aristotelianism; cf. ibid., cvii and above, n. 9.

[12] For long it was widely thought that such a Syriac version was presupposed in a letter of Severus Sebokt from the seventh century, but this is not the case, as has been shown by Reinink, 'Severus Sebokts Brief an den Periodeutes Jonan', 97-107. ܐܘܡܢܘܬܐ ܡܠܠܝܬܐ in the letter refers to logic (τέχνη λογική), not rhetoric. Cf. also Brock, 'Two Letters of the Patriarch Timothy', 241-242.

[13] *K. al-Fihrist*, ed. Flügel, 250, tr. Dodge, 601-602.

2346, and there is no doubt that its text is a witness of the Old Arabic version, being much inferior to, and different in lexical characteristics from, the translations produced from the time of Ḥunain. Subsequently, Arabic commentaries on the work were written by Ibn Sīnā and Ibn Rushd, and they both used a text of the same type as that of the Paris manuscript, i.e. the Old Arabic version.[14]

In the body, and especially at the end, of the text in the Paris manuscript there are several notes providing information on the provenance of the text. Unfortunately, some of these are difficult to read or interpret. For our purpose here, however, it is sufficient to observe that the scribe of the manuscript states that the text was transcribed from the handwriting of Ibn al-Samḥ, and that this latter in turn had noted in his copy that where his exemplar was defective he relied upon a second Arabic copy, and where that too was defective he had recourse to a Syriac manuscript. Where Ibn al-Samḥ felt that the Syriac manuscript was sound, he produced an Arabic version to match it, and where he felt it too to be defective, he entered it in his copy with a mark. From this we learn that a Syriac version of the *Rhetoric* certainly existed by the time of Ibn al-Samḥ, although given the many uncertainties in the interpretation of these notes and the date of the said Ibn al-Samḥ, we cannot draw any definite conclusions about its age.[15] In general it is of course a quite likely supposition that the Old Arabic version was translated from the Syriac, and in the commentary added to his edition of the Arabic *Rhetoric* Lyons made numerous suggestions concerning possible Syriac intermediaries which could account for surprising or erroneous readings in the Arabic. However, on the basis of the notes in the Paris manuscript, it remains possible that the translation in these cases is that made by Ibn al-Samḥ from his Syriac manuscript, rather than that of the Old Arabic translator himself.[16] Simply on the basis of this manuscript, therefore, a direct translation of the bulk of it from the Greek (with individual Syriac to Arabic renderings by Ibn al-Samḥ) or a complete translation from a prior Syriac version are both possibilities.

No Syriac manuscript of the *Rhetoric* has survived, and only one Syriac commentary on it is known, namely that by Bar Hebraeus ed-

---

[14] Cf. Lyons i.

[15] Ibid. ii-vi.

[16] Cf. Heinrichs, *Zeitschrift für Geschichte der Arabisch-Islamischen Wissenschaften* 1 (1984), 314.

ited here for the first time. As will be explained later at greater length,[17] Bar Hebraeus' commentary is a paraphrase of the text of Aristotle interwoven with that of the Arabic paraphrase by Ibn Sīnā. Here the question concerns what text of Aristotle Bar Hebraeus had before him: Greek, Syriac, or Arabic? The interweaving of Aristotle and Ibn Sīnā in his exposition makes this question more complicated than would otherwise have been the case, but still there remain sufficient passages where Bar Hebraeus is manifestly paraphrasing the former (manifest, for example, because Ibn Sīnā passes over a section of Aristotle without comment) to enable us to answer with some confidence that he was using a Syriac version. This Syriac version, however, was much closer to the Old Arabic than to any Greek recension known to us, yet quite frequently it uses the very same Greek (loan) words as are present in the Greek text of Aristotle, where the Old Arabic (and Ibn Sīnā) use a native Arabic term.[18] If we can therefore rule out the possibility (in any case remote on *a priori* grounds) that this Syriac version was translated from the Arabic, we must assume either that the Old Arabic was translated from the Syriac, or that both of them were made from very similar Greek texts. A conflation of these last two is also possible, and not at all unlikely: the Old Arabic translator might have worked from a Greek manuscript but also employed as an aid the pre-existing Syriac version, which was later used by Bar Hebraeus. Thus although the letter of Severus Sebokt formerly used to support an early Syriac translation of the *Rhetoric* has nothing to do with the work,[19] it is still very probable that the Syriac *Rhetoric* does indeed come from the time before Ḥunain, given that it is older than, or at the very least contemporary with, the Old Arabic.

From what was said at the outset above concerning the differing levels of interest expressed in Aristotle's *Rhetoric* by rhetors and philosophers, it is natural to suppose that the Syriac version was produced out of the desire of philosophers to have the entire *Organon* available in Syriac, rather than a wish to use it for instruction in rhetoric in Syriac. This supposition may be thought to be strengthened by the request of the Catholicus Timothy I mentioned above,[20]

[17] Cf. below, pp. 20-23.
[18] The evidence for these statements is presented below, pp. 22-29.
[19] Cf. above, n. 12.
[20] Above, p. 4.

and also to the circumstance that Ibn al-Samḥ indicated that 'not many students of the art of logic have arrived at a study of this book or have investigated it satisfactorily'.[21] However, it is not out of the question that Syriac teachers of rhetoric might also have had an interest in the work, and that Ibn al- Samḥ's remark about its few readers among the logicians could be taken not to imply that only logicians (and few of them at that) would have been interested in it, but that with so few 'pure logicians' expressing interest in it the impetus to translation might have come not from logicians alone, but also from rhetors. Greek rhetorical practice was frequently imitated in Syriac, and the large treatise on rhetoric by Antony of Tagrit—an author of uncertain date, but usually ascribed to the ninth century on the authority of Bar Hebraeus[22]—as also its epitome in Jacob bar Shakko's *Book of Dialogues* (thirteenth century), is evidence that some Syrians were also interested in rhetorical theory.[23] It was noted above[24] that in al-Fārābī—and the same applies to Ibn Sīnā and Ibn Rushd[25]—Aristotle's *Rhetoric* regained its original connection with political life and public discourse, and was not restricted to a prophylactic role in logic, as apparently seems to be the case with the Alexandrian commentators. For the latter, of course, as Greeks of late antiquity, the authority on rhetoric was not Aristotle but Hermogenes, but there is no hint anywhere that the corpus of Hermogenes migrated eastwards. In al-Fārābī rhetoric, as taught by Aristotle, is a political instrument at the disposal of the philosopher-king, and the same linkage between rhetoric and political philosophy can be seen in Antony of Tagrit. Although Antony's *Rhetoric* exhibits little or no influence of Aristotle's treatise, this linkage nevertheless shows that al-Fārābī's concept of the 'true philosopher'—the

[21] Lyons iii. No doubt Abū Bishr Mattā translated the *Poetics* from Syriac into Arabic precisely to complete the Arabic *Organon*; cf. Heinrichs, *Arabische Dichtung und griechische Poetik*, 119-120. It seems to me quite possible, furthermore, that al-Fārābī's interpretation of the *Poetics* as a theory of religious discourse, parallel to that of the *Rhetoric* as a theory of political discourse, may represent the thinking of the Baghdad School; cf. my 'Strategy of the Baghdad Philosophers'.

[22] Cf. Watt, *The Fifth Book of the Rhetoric of Antony of Tagrit*, Version, v-x.

[23] Cf. Watt, 'The Syriac Reception', 579-601; idem, 'Syriac Rhetorical Theory and the Syriac Tradition of Aristotle's *Rhetoric*', 243-260.

[24] Above, pp. 4-5.

[25] For Ibn Sīnā, cf. Würsch 140-143 and 180 n. 21. In general, see Butterworth, 'The Rhetorician and his Relationship to the Community', 111-136.

philosopher, that is, who recognises his public obligation to lead the populace to goodness and happiness by non-apodeictic but persuasive means, i.e. by rhetoric[26] —may have come from Syriac teachers, specifically in al-Fārābī's case the Syriac Aristotelian philosophers of the Baghdad School.[27] Richard Walzer plausibly suggested that such a tradition might go back to 'the circle of Themistius'.[28] If this Platonic-Aristotelian amalgam, embracing politics and rhetoric along with philosophy, and familiar to us from late antiquity in the person of Themistius, was indeed a feature of some Hellenophile Syriac groups,[29] then choosing between rhetoric and philosophy as the motivating force behind a Syriac translation of the *Rhetoric* may be a false dichotomy.

Al-Fārābī wrote a lengthy commentary on the *Rhetoric*, of which only the beginning is preserved, in a Latin version by Hermannus Alemannus, and also a shorter commentary in his *Abridgement of the Organon*.[30] These works were known to and utilised by Ibn Sīnā, who wrote on part of the *Rhetoric* in his early *Al-ḥikma al-'arūḍiyya*,[31] and on the whole of it at greater length in his *Shifā'* (كتاب الشفاء, '*The Cure*').[32] The *Shifā'* is divided into four sections (Logic, Physics, Mathematics, and Metaphysics), and the section on logic follows in its nine Books the nine-volume structure of the Alexandrian *Organon* (including the *Eisagoge*). The *Book of Rhetoric* (كتاب الخطابة) therefore forms the eighth part of the first section (Logic, المنطق). Ibn Sīnā's *Book of Rhetoric* is itself divided into four chapters (مقالات), and the chapters subdivided into sections (فصول).

Ibn Sīnā considered himself a Peripatetic philosopher. For him, Aristotle, 'the First Teacher', was the first to have discovered and taught the fundamental principles of knowledge, and the Peripatetic

---

[26] The 'false philosopher' (of al-Fārābī) who does not recognise this obligation and therefore considers philosophy a purely 'private' matter is the figure to which I referred above as a 'pure logician', i.e. one not interested in public discourse.

[27] Cf. the references above, nn. 21, 23.

[28] Cf. Walzer, 'Aspects of Islamic Political Thought', 55.

[29] Cf. Watt, 'From Themistius to al-Fārābī', 17-41.

[30] Al-Fārābī, *Deux ouvrages inédits sur la réthorique*. For a general survey of Arabic commentaries on the *Rhetoric*, cf. Aouad, 'La Rhétorique. Tradition syriaque et arabe', 455-472 and 'Compléments', 219-223; idem, IR I, 1-9.

[31] Ed. Salem (Cairo, 1953).

[32] Ed. Salem (Cairo, 1954). German translation of the first of the four chapters in Würsch.

tradition, in Arabic represented especially by al-Fārābī, 'the Second Teacher', was the only one worthy of serious attention. At the same time, however, he regarded himself as occupying a special position within that tradition as a reformer, and as Aristotle was limited like any other human being by the circumstances of his time and place, Ibn Sīnā did not consider him above criticism on particular matters, and claimed himself to have inaugurated a new stage in the ongoing acquisition of knowledge.[33] By the time he came to write the *Shifā'*, therefore, his intention, according to his disciple Juzjānī, was not to offer a close textual analysis and commentary of Aristotle, but to compose a work setting forth what in his own opinion was valid in the Aristotelian philosophical tradition.[34] The *Shifā'*, therefore, while a compendium of Aristotelian philosophy (and some other matters, e.g. Mathematics), is nevertheless one stamped with Ibn Sīnā's own understanding of the subjects under consideration. In the matter of the *Rhetoric*, especially in his elaboration in Chapter One of *Rhetoric* 1.1-2, he was greatly influenced by al-Fārābī, but here too he did not hesitate to modify and develop the contributions of 'the Second Teacher'.[35]

Just as he did not feel himself bound to precedent in matters of substance, so neither did Ibn Sīnā feel himself under restriction when it came to the literary form of his exposition. In the *Shifā'* he created a running exposition of the philosophical sciences as he considered it appropriate, a method which differed sharply from that of the contemporary Baghdad Peripatetics, whose procedure stood much closer to the old Alexandrian tradition and its Syriac and Christian Arabic offshoot of glosses and notes.[36] The form of the *Book of Rhetoric* in the *Shifā'* is neither an epitome of Aristotle's text (a 'short commentary'), nor the citation of a portion of text followed by an explanation (a 'long commentary'), but an expository paraphrase of Aristotle reflecting Ibn Sīnā's own understanding of the subject under consideration. In the traditional nomenclature, derived particularly from Ibn Rushd, of 'short', 'middle', and 'long' commentaries,

[33] Cf. Gutas, *Avicenna and the Aristotelian Tradition*, 286-296.

[34] Cf. ibid., 101, and Peters, *Aristotle and the Arabs*, 89-91.

[35] Cf. Würsch 12, 213-216, and index 236 s.v. 'Avicenna, seine Abhängigkeit von Farabi'.

[36] Cf. Gutas, 'Aspects of Literary Form and Genre in Arabic Logical Works', 44-48.

Ibn Sīnā's work is therefore a 'middle commentary',[37] though it is doubtful if this classification is of much relevance in his case.[38] His disciple Juzjānī claimed that the *Shifā'* arose from a request to the master for a commentary (شرح) on the books of Aristotle;[39] Ibn Sīnā himself, however, in his later Prologue to the work, referred to it as a compendium (جملة).[40]

Both the stamp of Ibn Sīnā's own conception of the subject, as well as his adherence to the genre of a running paraphrase of Aristotle's text, can be seen in the *Book of Rhetoric*, most dramatically in the contrast between Chapter One and the remainder. Chapter One covers only *Rhetoric* 1.1-2; Chapter Two by contrast covers the remainder of *Rhetoric* Book One, and Chapters Three and Four *Rhetoric* Books Two and Three. Since all four of Ibn Sīnā's Chapters are of approximately equal length, it will already be clear that his treatment of *Rhetoric* 1.1-2 is quite different from that of the rest of Aristotle's treatise. In Chapter One he develops at considerable length his views on the logical foundations of rhetoric by means of a free elaboration on *Rhetoric* 1.1-2, while in the remaining Chapters the rest of Aristotle's treatise is paraphrased (in the manner of a 'middle commentary' described above), with additions and modifications to, and omissions from, the text of Aristotle (in the Old Arabic version), but in much closer adherence to that text than in Chapter One.[41]

To a considerable extent Ibn Sīnā succeeded in his aim of having his own philosophical writings supersede those of Aristotle. His independence from the text of Aristotle and associated conception of his own status as the most accurate communicator of philosophy grew throughout his lifetime.[42] In subsequent centuries the logical texts which formed the basis of study and commentary in Eastern Islam were predominantly Ibn Sīnā's, not those of Aristotle himself,[43] while encyclopaedic exposition in the manner of the *Shifā'*, rather

[37] Cf. Würsch 12.

[38] Cf. Gutas, 'Aspects of Literary Form and Genre in Arabic Logical Works', 41-42, 50-52.

[39] Cf. above, n. 34.

[40] Cf. Gutas, *Avicenna and the Aristotelian Tradition*, 51, 103.

[41] Cf. Würsch 11-13.

[42] Cf. Gutas, *Avicenna and the Aristotelian Tradition*, 288-296.

[43] Cf. Peters, *Aristotle and the Arabs*, 192-200; Gutas, 'Aspects of Literary Form and Genre in Arabic Logical Works', 56-64.

than commentary on an individual treatise of Aristotle, became the principal medium for the diffusion of the new Aristotelianism.[44] In Western Islam, however, in the work of Ibn Rushd, there was a return to the text of Aristotle himself and the older style commentaries on it, with a corresponding movement away from the heritage of Ibn Sīnā.[45] Ibn Rushd in fact differentiated between 'satisfactory' and 'unsatisfactory' commentaries on the *Rhetoric*, envisaging thereby those of al-Fārābī and Ibn Sīnā respectively.[46] On the Christian (Arabic) side, a commentary on the *Rhetoric* may have been written by Ibn Sīnā's contemporary Ibn al-Ṭayyib, but nothing of this has survived.[47]

Ibn Sīnā's legacy was subject to criticism not only from within the Aristotelian fold, but also from outside it by the theologians, particularly in the area of metaphysics. Even so, so influential was his reformulation of Aristotelian logic that it underpinned their attacks on him, not least the well known one of al-Ghazālī.[48] In the thirteenth century both al-Rāzī (d. 1209) and al-Ṭūsī (d. 1274) were profoundly influenced by Ibn Sīnā, though the former was ostensibly a critic, the latter a defender.[49] By this time Syriac Aristotelianism could no longer thrive simply as a direct offshoot of the late antique Greek tradition, but had to engage with the Islamic philosophers. The leading figures of the Jacobite 'Syriac Renaissance' of the twelfth and thirteenth centuries were familiar with older Syriac and Christian Arabic contributions to philosophy, but they were also concerned to learn from newer Islamic representatives of the tradition. Michael the Syrian, Jacobite Patriarch of Antioch from 1166 to 1199 and author of the chronicle which bears his name, had discussions in 1172 with the Muslim philosopher Kamāl al-Dīn ibn Yūnus (d.1242),[50] a polymath teacher in Mosul who became well known as an exegete of al-Rāzī and among whose pupils were both al-Ṭūsī and

---

[44] Cf. Peters, *Aristotle and the Arabs*, 104-120.

[45] Cf. ibid., 215-220; Gutas, 'Aspects of Literary Form and Genre in Arabic Logical Works', 53-56; Schoeler, 'Averroes' Rückwendung zu Aristoteles', 294-301.

[46] Cf. Aouad and Rashed, 'Commentateurs "satisfaisants" et "non satisfaisants",' 83-124; Aouad, IR I, 20-50.

[47] Cf. Aouad, 'La Rhétorique. Tradition syriaque et arabe', 462; idem, IR I, 5-6.

[48] Cf. Peters, *Aristotle and the Arabs*, 185-192; Gutas, 'Aspects of Literary Form and Genre in Arabic Logical Works', 57-60.

[49] Cf. Peters, *Aristotle and the Arabs*, 194-198.

[50] Cf. ibid., 277; Baumstark, *Geschichte der syrischen Literatur*, 299.

the Syriac author Jacob (or Severus) Bar Shakko (d. 1241). In addition to a theological *summa* Bar Shakko composed a philosophical encyclopaedia, the *Book of Dialogues*, which, even at some considerable remove, nevertheless stands in the tradition of encyclopaedism inaugurated by Ibn Sīnā.[51] The *Book of Dialogues* is in two parts, the first in three sections devoted to grammar, rhetoric, and poetics, the second in two dedicated to logic and philosophy.[52] The sections on rhetoric and poetics are largely an epitome of Books One and Five of the *Rhetoric* of Antony of Tagrit,[53] but in the section on poetics Jacob cites verbatim Aristotle's discussion of tragedy in *Poetics* 1449b24-1450a9.[54] This is the only lengthy passage from the *Rhetoric* or *Poetics* explicitly transmitted as deriving from Aristotle whose wording is known in a Syriac version, namely that from which Abū Bishr Mattā made his Arabic version of the *Poetics* three centuries earlier.[55] The greatest figure, however, in the Syriac Renaissance of the thirteenth century was al-Ṭūsī's contemporary Bar Hebraeus.

## BAR HEBRAEUS AND THE *CREAM OF WISDOM*

The outer course of Bar Hebraeus' life is well known from the autobiographical passages in his historical works.[56] He was born in Melitene in 1225/6, the son of a physician named Aaron, who treated the Mongol general Yasa'ur during his attack on Melitene in 1243/4, after which the family fled to Antioch. In Tripoli, like Antioch under Crusader rule at the time, he studied logic (ܡܠܝܠܘܬܐ) and medicine under an East Syrian ('Nestorian') teacher by the name of Jacob,[57] and shortly thereafter, in 1246, he was ordained to the episcopate, first of Gubas, subsequently of Laqabin, and then of Aleppo. He was elected Maphrian in 1264 and in this capacity travelled extensively;

[51] Cf. Peters, *Aristotle and the Arabs*, 104-108.

[52] Cf. Baumstark, *Geschichte der syrischen Literatur*, 311-312 and the literature cited there n. 32.

[53] Cf. Bendrat, 'Der Dialog über die Rhetorik des Jacob Bar Shakko', 19-26; Watt, *The Fifth Book of the Rhetoric of Antony of Tagrit*, Text, xviii-xx.

[54] Cf. Margoliouth, *Analecta Orientalia*, ٧٧-٧٩.

[55] *K. al-Fihrist*, ed. Flügel, 250, tr. Dodge, 602; Schrier, 'Aristotle's *Poetics*', 264-268. Three words are explicitly transmitted from the *Rhetoric*; cf. below, pp. 28-29.

[56] *Chronicon ecclesiasticum*, ed. Abbeloos and Lamy, III, 431-467 (486).

[57] Ibid., II, 667.

his preferred residence was Mosul or the nearby monastery of Mar Mattai, but among the many other places he resided he especially favoured Tabriz and Maragha. Maragha no doubt particularly appealed to him as a centre of learning, and there he may well have known al-Ṭūsī, the Director of the Observatory under the patronage of the Mongol rulers. He died there in 1286, where a funeral service was held for him attended not only by members of his own West Syrian confession, but also by 'Nestorians, Armenians, and Greeks'. His body was later transferred to Mar Mattai.[58]

Some insight into the course of his inner development may be gleaned from an autobiographical passage in his *Book of the Dove*.[59] There he wrote of his zeal for 'Greek wisdom' and his subsequent dissatisfaction and spiritual crisis, until he found fulfilment through study of the writings of Evagrius of Pontus and others. The similarity of this account to that of al-Ghazālī describing his illumination may point to a degree of literary stylisation, but it is likely that there is nevertheless some historical substance to the narrative. Unlike al-Ghazālī, however, Bar Hebraeus did not turn against philosophy, but continued to pursue it to the end of his life. While his mystical writings bear the impress of al-Ghazālī, his philosophical ones exhibit that of Ibn Sīnā.

Bar Hebraeus' literary production is enormous; apart from theological and philosophical works, it includes, *inter alia*, medicine, law, grammar, astronomy, historiography, stories, and poems. He wrote in both Syriac and Arabic, and his *oeuvre* also includes translations from Arabic into Syriac.[60] Much of his output is a reworking of material taken from earlier writers, and he drew easily on Syriac, Arabic, and Persian sources. No other Syriac author was so conversant as he with Muslim Arabic literature, but he was also thoroughly familiar with earlier and more recent Syriac literature. In many of his writings he works in material from two or more sources, often taking one as a framework and incorporating material from the others, producing at the end a concise and coherent exposition which is

---

[58] Cf. the recent study of his life and bibliography of his works in Takahashi, *Bio-Bibliography*, Part I, and Teule, 'Barhebraeus and his Time', 21-43. There is an older bibliography (up to 1986) in Fiey, 'Esquisse', 279-312.

[59] A. J. Wensinck, *Bar Hebraeus' Book of the Dove*, 60-62. Cf. Takahashi, *Bio-Bibliography*, Sections I.1.9-10.

[60] Cf. Fiey, 'Esquisse', 284-312; Takahashi, *Bio-Bibliography*, Section I.2.5.

more easily readable than that offered by his predecessors.[61] Since the dominant impression to emerge from his work is that of a compiler or cross-cultural 'translator', he has often been compared to figures in the Western tradition of whom the same might be said, such as Isidore of Seville, Albertus Magnus, or Thomas Aquinas. A recent and apt comparison is that with Cicero.[62] Precisely why he was so greatly concerned to 'recapitulate' in his own Syriac writings both the preceding Syriac tradition and what he considered of value in the Muslim Arabic contribution cannot be answered with any certainty from our sources. There seems little doubt that he perceived the fall of Baghdad to the Mongols in 1258 as a watershed in world history,[63] and it is possible that viewing it in a sombre light he sensed therein a catastrophe for the Syrians and resolved to create a literary memorial for a dying culture.[64] However, a case can also be made for supposing that he regarded the Mongol conquest as a new and great opportunity for Christians in the region, towards whom the Mongols seemed more favourably disposed than to Muslims, and that his work was therefore conceived not as a monument to a dying culture, but as the inauguration of a bright new chapter in its long history.[65]

In Bar Hebraeus' *Chronography* (*Chronicon syriacum*), the 'Tenth Series', that of 'the Kings of the Arabs', begins with Heraclius and Muhammad and ends with the Mongol capture of Baghdad. Bar Hebraeus therefore saw himself living at the end of a period which began with the Arab conquest. What it was that the Arabs had to contribute is aptly summed up in a passage in his account of that conquest:

> There arose among (the Arabs) philosophers, mathematicians, and physicians, who surpassed the ancients in subtlety of understanding. While they built on no foundation other than those of the Greeks, they constructed greater scientific edifices by means of a more elegant style and more studious researches, with the result that although they had received

[61] Cf. Drossaart Lulofs, *De plantis*, 39-40.
[62] Takahashi, *Bio-Bibliography*, Section I.2.6.
[63] Cf. the sectional divisions in his *Chronography* discussed immediately below.
[64] Cf. Drossaart Lulofs, *De plantis*, 38.
[65] Takahashi, *Bio-Bibliography*, Section I.2.6.

the wisdom from us through translators, all of whom were Syrians, now we find it necessary to seek wisdom from them.[66]

Ever since the fifth or sixth century, from the days of Sergius of Reshaina, 'philosophy' had signified for the Syrians—as indeed for the Greeks—principally the philosophy of Aristotle, albeit sometimes with 'the divine Plato' as the further and ultimate goal. The predominant, indeed usually exclusive, position of Aristotle and the Peripatetics within the realm of philosophy was confirmed and reinforced in the Orient by the work of the Baghdad School of Abū Bishr Mattā and the subsequent Muslim representatives of the Aristotelian tradition. In the view of Bar Hebraeus, the ancient wisdom of the Greeks, systematically formulated as it was by Aristotle, had to be interpreted with the aid of the Arab philosophers, especially al-Fārābī and, above all, Ibn Sīnā.[67] In his opinion, the latter, 'when he took Aristotle's talent, added to it not only five but more than fifty talents' (cf. *Matthew* 25, 14-22).[68] The culmination of Aristotle's thinking was thus to be found in the new Aristotelianism of Ibn Sīnā, and the inspiration and model of Bar Hebraeus' great philosophical encyclopaedia, the *Cream of Wisdom*, is the *Shifā'* of Ibn Sīnā.

The *Cream of Wisdom* (frequently designated by its Latin title *Butyrum sapientiae*) is Bar Hebraeus' philosophical *magnum opus*, an exposition of Aristotelian philosophy which has fairly been called 'the grandest compendium of Aristotelian philosophy ever adumbrated in Syriac'.[69] It was composed near the end of his life, being completed, according to the oldest extant manuscript of the work, on 8th February, 1286.[70] Like the *Shifā'* it is divided into four major

---

[66] *Gregorii Barhebraei Chronicon syriacum*, ed. Bedjan, 98.

[67] Cf. Bar Hebraeus, *Ta'rīkh mukhtaṣar al-duwal*, ed. Ṣālḥānī, 93: 'Aristotle was the one who organised and formulated these sciences and established their methods ... Everyone who translated his words from Greek to another language altered them and speculated as to their right (meaning). Those who got closest to understanding him were al-Fārābī and Ibn Sīnā, for they interpreted his doctrine according to the intended purpose.'

[68] *Gregorii Barhebraei Chronicon syriacum*, ed. Bedjan, 219. Cf. Barsoum, *The Scattered Pearls*, 179 n.1 and 471.

[69] Baumstark, *Geschichte der syrischen Literatur*, 316.

[70] Laur. Or. 83, fol. 227r. Cf. below, p. 36 and Takahashi, *Aristotelian Meteorology*, 9.

parts, but whereas those of the *Shifā'* are Logic, Physics, Mathematics, and Metaphysics, those of the *Cream* are Logic, Physics, Metaphysics, and Practical Philosophy. Bar Hebraeus may have omitted Mathematics because, apart from Astronomy, he was not greatly interested in the subject,[71] but more likely is the supposition that he intended thereby to bring his work into closer correspondence with the corpus of Aristotle's writings.[72] If this is so, already in the overall structure we can see what further analysis of the individual parts amply confirms, that Bar Hebraeus wished to 'leaven' the framework provided by Ibn Sīnā with older Graeco-Syriac Aristotelian material. The framework, however, of the division on Practical Philosophy, absent from the *Shifā'*, was not taken from these older sources, but from the very recent *Naṣirean Ethics* of al-Ṭūsī.[73]

Within the four major divisions of the *Cream*, there are a total of twenty-two Books (ܟܬܒ̈ܐ): nine under Logic (ܡܠܝܠܘܬܐ), and thirteen under the other three. The nine Books of Logic are those of the Aristotelian *Organon* (i.e. including Porphyry's *Eisagoge*), as in the *Shifā'*. Bar Hebraeus' *Book of Rhetoric* (ܟܬܒܐ ܕܪܝܛܘܪܝܩܐ) is therefore the eighth of Logic (ܬܡܝܢܝܐ ܕܡܠܝܠܘܬܐ), as Ibn Sīnā's كتاب الخطابة the eighth of المنطق. Whereas the Books of the *Shifā'* are divided by مقالة and فصل, those of the *Cream* have a further subdivision. Bar Hebraeus' ܩܦܠܐܘܢ (chapter) and ܦܘܣܩܐ (section) are comparable to the مقالة and فصل of Ibn Sīnā,[74] but he makes a further subdivision into ܬܐܘܪܝܐܣ (theories). The pattern of a triple division was probably inspired by al-Ṭūsī's *Naṣirean Ethics*, which is divided by مقالة, قسم, and فصل.[75]

In general, the Books of the *Cream* consist of a paraphrase of the corresponding Books of the *Shifā'*[76] (or in the case of Practical Philosophy, of al-Ṭūsī's *Naṣirean Ethics*), but they also incorporate material from other sources, especially Greek writers. Bar Hebraeus'

---

71 The note in the Florence manuscript cited below (p. 36) appears to indicate that he wrote about mathematics in another treatise. Cf. Takahashi, *Aristotelian Meteorology*, 9 ; Fiey, 'Esquisse d'une bibliographie de Bar Hébraeus', 309.

72 Cf. Zonta, *Fonti greche e orientali*, 4; Takahashi, *Aristotelian Meteorology*, 11-12.

73 Cf. Zonta, *Fonti greche e orientali*, 10-19, 49-106; idem, 'Structure and Sources', 280-284; Joosse, *A Syriac Encyclopaedia*, 1-12 and *passim*.

74 For the correspondences in the *Rhetoric*, see below, p. 20.

75 Cf. Zonta, 'Structure and Sources', 280 n. 4.

76 In the (Arabic) terminology of 'short', 'middle', and 'long' commentaries, the *Cream*, therefore, like the *Shifā'*, is a 'middle' commentary.

adaptation of his main source is on the whole intelligently thought out. As many scholars of previous generations have pointed out, he was certainly no great original thinker, but Drossaart Lulofs has rightly observed that 'in our own days the charge of not being original sounds much less vituperative than in the first half of (the twentieth) century. Above all else, the existence of different ways of being dependent on others ought to be acknowledged ... Both the selection and the arrangement of the 'theories' are well-considered, so that the Syriac text does not betray any disorder; on the contrary, Bar Hebraeus' arrangements make a perfectly natural impression. And so it cannot be maintained that he was an *Avicenna dimidiatus*, for often, in giving the essentials his expositions are more succint and sometimes clearer than those of Ibn Sīnā himself.'[77] To this one might add the admission of Furlani that his translations from Arabic are always felicitous.[78] Drossaart Lulofs further noted that 'passages from ... the *Shifā'* are freely translated from Arabic into Syriac, but Bar Hebraeus quotes the Syriac version of Nicolaus (of Damascus, *Compendium of Aristotelian Philosophy*) very literally.'[79] *Mutatis mutandis*, these comments on the *Book of Plants* are applicable to the *Cream* as a whole. It therefore not only offers us an intelligent and interesting reformulation of the Aristotelianism of Ibn Sīnā, but also lays before us other sources, particularly Greek ones, in Syriac dress. In addition to Nicolaus' *Compendium* noted in the *Book of Plants*, as also in the *Books of Mineralogy and Meteorology*,[80] Bar Hebraeus is known to have used among Greek authors Theo of Alexandria,[81] Polemo,[82] Aristotle *On the Cosmos*,[83] and Aristotle *On the Soul*.[84] In all these cases it is clear that he did not make his own translation from a Greek original, but used a Syriac version, and it is in fact quite unlikely that he knew Greek or had access to Greek manuscripts.[85]

[77] Drossaart Lulofs, *De plantis*, 39-40. Cf. also Joosse, *A Syriac Encyclopaedia*, 3, and Teule, 'Barhebraeus and his Time', 30-33.

[78] Ibid. 39; Furlani, 'Di tre scritti in lingua siriaca', 308.

[79] Drossaart Lulofs, *De plantis*, 35.

[80] Takahashi, *Aristotelian Meteorology*, 51-53 and *passim*.

[81] Ibid., 56-57.

[82] Zonta, *Fonti greche e orientali*, 28-47; Joosse, *A Syriac Encyclopaedia*, 118-121 (*Book of Economy* 3.1.1 and 3.1.4).

[83] Takahashi, *Aristotelian Meteorology*, 55.

[84] Furlani, 'La psicologia di Barhebreo', 32 nn. 3-4, 33 n. 5, 51.

[85] Takahashi, *Bio-Bibliography*, Section I.1.6b; Teule, 'Barhebraeus and his Time', 22-24.

For the Syrians Aristotle had always been above all else the logician, and it is therefore hardly surprising that in the Logic section of the *Cream* Bar Hebraeus had recourse to the text of Aristotle himself, not least in the case of the *Rhetoric* and the *Poetics*, of which no summaries or epitomes are known from late antiquity. In the *Book of Poetics* he used, in addition to the *Shifā'*, the Syriac version of Aristotle's *Poetics*, of which we have a fragment quoted by Jacob Bar Shakko.[86] In the *Book of Rhetoric*, as we shall see below, he relied both on Ibn Sīnā and on the lost Syriac version of Aristotle's *Rhetoric*.

## THE *BOOK OF RHETORIC*

The structure of Bar Hebraeus' *Book of Rhetoric*, like the other books of the *Cream*, owes much to the equivalent book in the *Shifā'*, but is not slavishly dependent upon it. Bar Hebraeus adapted it in an intelligent manner, paying due attention to the subject matter and often giving more emphasis to the text of Aristotle. The following structural outline may help to make this clear:[87]

| *AR* | *IS* | *BH* | *Subject Matter* |
|---|---|---|---|
| | 1.1 | 1.1 | Usefulness of Rhetoric |
| 1.1-2 | 1.2-7 | 1.2-7 | Logical Foundations of Rhetoric |
| 1.3 | 2.1(a) | 1.8 | Three Species of Rhetoric |
| 1.4-8 | 2.1(b)-3 | 2 | Deliberative Rhetoric |
| 1.9 | 2.4 | 3 | Epideictic Rhetoric |
| 1.10-15 | 2.5-9 | 4 | Judicial Rhetoric |
| 2.1-18 | 3.1-5 | 5 | Pathos and Ethos |
| 2.18-26 | 3.6-8 | 6 | Forms of Logical Argument |
| 3 | 4 | 7 | Style and Arrangement |

[86] Cf. above, p. 14; Schrier, 'Aristotle's *Poetics*', 273-274.

[87] Hereafter the abbreviations AR, ARar, ARsyr, IS, and BH are employed in the interests of economy; see the list of Abbreviations at the beginning of the volume. There is a detailed Concordance of Passages at the end of the volume.

Bar Hebraeus' *Book of Rhetoric* is a paraphrase of these two sources, Ibn Sīnā's *Book of Rhetoric* and Aristotle's *Rhetoric*. Ibn Sīnā's is of course itself a paraphrase of (the Old Arabic version of) Aristotle, but while Bar Hebraeus' exposition is on the whole more heavily weighted towards Ibn Sīnā, he nevertheless frequently works in material specific to Aristotle (whom he calls ܪܒܢ,'our master'). Often this consists of a word or a phrase recognisable as coming from AR because IS differs, but sometimes the Aristotelian origin is manifest through the fact that the passage in question has been ignored by IS. Not infrequently BH mentions Aristotle's examples from Greek literature or history where IS omits them.[88]

Bar Hebraeus' dependence upon Ibn Sīnā is evident on every page of his *Book of Rhetoric*. It is particularly obvious in his first chapter (ܦܠܐܘܣ), which in general is a paraphrase of Ibn Sīnā's first chapter (مقالة) rather than of AR 1.1-3, IS 1 being a quite free elaboration of AR 1.1-2.[89] Also in the remaining chapters the close relationship of BH to IS is clear throughout, even though there IS adheres much more closely to AR.[90]

Especially from BH 2 onwards the reader may easily locate (with the aid of the Commentary if so desired) many instances of the direct use of AR, albeit frequently interwoven with IS. Since, however, the use of AR is less blatantly manifest than that of IS, it may be useful to mention a few examples here. At 2.4.7 IS merely states that he 'does not understand the examples in the First Teaching', but BH quotes these examples. A similar case occurs at 4.5.1 where IS omits a whole section which BH duly paraphrases. On a smaller scale, at 1.7.3, 1.8.3, 2.1.7, 2.2.3, 2.2.6-8, 2.4.1, and 2.4.4 IS excludes points in AR which BH includes.[91] Cases of BH combining statements

---

[88] For example, at 1.7.3 (Peisistratus and Theagenes); 1.8.3 (Achilles and Patroclus); 2.4.1 (men and women); 2.4.7 (the Olympic victor, etc.); 4.6.3 (Homer, Solon, etc.); 5.4.7 (Ajax). Cf. also below, n. 92.

[89] Cf. above, p. 12. IS 1 is translated and examined in detail by Würsch, *passim*. BH's paraphrase considerably abbreviates IS's original. AR 1.3 is paraphrased by Ibn Sīnā at the start of IS 2, but by Bar Hebraeus at the end of BH 1.

[90] Cf. Würsch, 109. The reader who wishes rapidly to convince himself that BH's dependence upon IS extended beyond Chapter One may look, for example, at BH 7, which in general is very clearly much closer to IS 4 than to AR 3.

[91] 1.7.3: the examples of tyrants taken from AR; 1.8.3: mention of Achilles and Patroclus; 2.1.7: comparison with noses; 2.2.3: ܡܣܟܢܘܬܗ not بنكاء; 2.2.6-8: references to Perudiqus, athletes, and old age; 2.4.1: men being greater than women; 2.4.4: mention of Aphnus.

from both IS and AR within the same pericope may be found, for example, (not only in some of those just cited, but also) at 3.2.1 and 3.2.3-4. In the first, the remarks about lamentation, etc., are derived from IS, but the ܐܬܠܣܐ is from AR ἆθλα; in the second the statement about shame is from IS, the reference to the Lacedaemonians from AR. In 3.3.3 the argument about fearlessness and praiseworthiness is from IS, but the specification of particular groups (Athenians, philosophers, etc.) from AR. In 3.3.4 the first part is based on IS, but the following example on AR quoting 'the saying of Iphicrates'. In 3.4.2 BH quotes a passage of AR ('Hippolochos, Barmodes, and Aristogiton') passed over by IS, though the whole pericope is based principally on IS. In 4.3.1-2 the exposition is based primarily on AR but includes elements from IS. In 4.5.1 (mentioned above) the opening statement is taken from IS, but the rest (omitted by IS) comes from AR.

From some of the examples adduced above, it will already be clear that the text of Aristotle lying before Bar Hebraeus was not that of any extant Greek recension, but was much closer to ARar. In 2.4.7 one of the examples declared incomprehensible by Ibn Sīnā and passed over by him but quoted by Bar Hebraeus (that of 'the victor in the race', and cf. also 'the third armed man') is not found in any extant Greek manuscript, but is present in ARar. In 4.5.1 both BH and ARar read 'Antigone said to Sophocles' at 73b9 (AR 'Sophocles' Antigone') and omit the negative in 73b15 ('[not] just for some'); both passages are omitted by IS. In 4.4.6, again omitted by Ibn Sīnā, the 'island of Demogelone' appears in both BH and ARar for 73a22 'Aenesidemus to Gelon'. In 4.3.1 'sex, taste, smell, and incense' accord not with the Greek of 70a23-24 but with ARar. In 4.6.3, most of which is not found in IS, a whole set of striking differences from the Greek text of Aristotle is in agreement with ARar. In 3.3.4 the 'Saturannoi' of BH and ARar (here also of Ibn Sīnā, but he construes the passage differently) come from the mis-division of 67b20 τ'οὖσα τυράννων. In 3.4.2 the statement concerning Hippolochos, Harmodius and Aristogiton, omitted by IS, is closer to what stands in ARar than to the Greek. This list could be greatly extended, but rather than so doing, it would seem better, following Aristotle's example (*Rhetoric* 3.11), to set before the readers' eyes the evidence in full for one of the cases mentioned above, illustrative of both points— that BH sometimes used AR rather than IS, and that his Aristotle was not the Greek Aristotle, but the Syriac or Arabic (ARsyr or ARar). The following passage will make this evident:

AR 65a24-30 (Greek)

Hence also the epigram on the Olympian victor, 'Formerly, having on my shoulders a rough yoke, I used to carry fish from Argos to Tegea.' And Iphicrates lauded himself, speaking of what he had come from. And the self-generated rather than the acquired (τοῦ ἐπικτήτου), for it is harder. Hence the poet says, 'Self-taught am I'.

BH 2.4.7

Hence, too, we may add what is written on the Olympian victor, who had on his shoulders a patchwork and carried fish from Argos, and threw it on the ground. But now he was victorious in the race, (that is,) in the contest, as they were bent down by revelling. And the third armed man, Iphicrates, was lying on the ground when praising and describing these by which these came, with the sudden growth of Epictetus, which was harder. On this account the poet said, 'Self-taught am I'.

ARar (ed. Lyons 38.17-39.3; cf. 263-264)

Hence that which is added and written on the Olympian victor, that first on his shoulders he had a load and carried a portion of the fish called Arghus, and threw it on the ground. Then he now won in the running, that is, in the race, as they were desisting from toil. And the third armed man, Iphicrates, was cast down on the ground when praising and describing what was done by them, together with the revelation (?) of Fiqtitus, suddenly, which was more difficult and harder. Hence the poet says, 'I am self-taught', that is, intelligent by nature.

IS 2.3 (81.5)

In the First Teaching he presented examples which I did not understand.
(After this IS proceeds to the paraphrase of AR 65a30-65b19.)

There can therefore be no doubt that Bar Hebraeus made use of a Syriac or Arabic version of the *Rhetoric*, not the Greek.[92] To estab-

[92] The examples adduced above to demonstrate that Bar Hebraeus used a Syriac or Arabic version of the *Rhetoric* in addition to the commentary of Ibn Sīnā are all taken from *Rhetoric* Book 1 (Bar Hebraeus chapters 1 to 4). Numerous examples from the other two Books could easily be added, and are frequently noted in the Commentary. The reader who wishes, however, to see many examples from a later Book within a short compass may look, for example, at BH 6.4.2 to 6.5.13, the paraphrase of AR 2.22-23, enthymemes and topics. Bar Hebraeus gives many more of Aristotle's examples than does Ibn Sīnā, but throughout it is clear that his text of Aristotle is on the whole much closer to ARar than to AR.

lish conclusively one rather than the other, however, is more difficult. It is true that we can point to differences between BH and ARar, but in principle these could be explained either as stemming from Bar Hebraeus himself or from one of the other two Arabic versions mentioned by the *Fihrist* but unknown to us. Nevertheless, it seems certain that it was indeed a Syriac version that lay before him. The evidence is primarily internal, but is confirmed by one piece of external evidence.[93] The internal evidence lies mainly in the Greek loanwords which he used. While the use of a Greek loanword current in Syriac proves nothing of itself, when that loanword is the very word in the Greek text of Aristotle, and the Arabic texts (ARar and IS) in the same passage use a native Arabic term (or do not give it at all), that strongly suggests that the loanword lay before Bar Hebraeus in a Syriac version of the *Rhetoric*. Of course, if this happened only on a few occasions, the coincidence of the Greek and BH could be put down to chance, but the number of occurrences and the uncommon character of some of the words strongly suggest otherwise.

In view of the importance of this conclusion, it seems desirable to present the evidence *in extenso*. What follows, therefore, is a list of those differences between the Arabic texts (ARar and IS) and the Syriac of BH which point in the direction of a Syriac version of the *Rhetoric*. While some of these are different readings or Syriac terms closer in meaning to the Greek than are the Arabic, most are Syriac loanwords from Greek, where the same Greek term appears in the corresponding passage of Aristotle and the Arabic terms are different. In this tabulation I quote the Syriac of BH, the Greek of AR, and the Arabic first of ARar and then of IS. Here the relevant words are merely listed, but discussion of the passages from which they come will often be found in the Commentary.

| | | | | |
|---|---|---|---|---|
| 1.2.2 | ܐܟܣܝܣ | ἕξις | قتية راسخة | ملكة |
| 1.3.5 | ܡܬܘܕܘܣ | μέθοδος | هيلة أو صناعة | صناعة |
| 1.3.6 | ܕܝ̈ܩܢܝܩܐ | διϰανιϰά | التشاجر | تشاجرية |
| 1.4.3 | ܐܣܛܪܛܝܓܘܬܐ | στρατηγία | سلطان | بسالة |

[93] Cf. below, pp. 28-29.

| | | | | |
|---|---|---|---|---|
| 1.5.4 | ܪܘܟܒܐ ܡܕܡ | παραφυές τι | بمنزلة تركيب | مركبة |
| 2.1.1 | ܢܝܫܐ | σκοπός | الم ( ܢܝܫܐ ?) | غرض |
| 2.1.6 | ܕܐܦܐܢܝ | δαπανή | بذل ? | حاصل ? |
| 2.1.8 | ܛܘܪܢܝܐ | τυραννίς | فتنة | تغلبية |
| 2.2.1 | ܒܣܝܡܘܬܐ | εὐδαιμονία | صلاح الحال | صلاح الحال |
| 2.2.2 | ܒܘܒܢܝܗ̇ | αὐτόχθονες | بنكا | بنكاء |
| 2.2.2 | ܗܓܡܘܢܐ | ἡγεμόνας | رؤساء | رؤساء |
| 2.2.9 | BH and AR: brothers; | | ARar and IS: others | |
| 2.3.6 | BH and AR: Corinthians, Simonides; | | ARar and IS: omit | |
| 2.4.7 | BH and AR: Argos a place name; | | ARar: Argos the name of a fish; | IS: omits |
| 3.2.1 | ܐܬܠܣܐ | ἆθλα | جهاد | omits |
| 3.3.3 | ܩܝܢܕܘܢܘܛܝܩܐ | κινδυνευτικός | خطر شديد | differs |
| 3.3.5 | ܐܟܣܝܣܝܬܐ | τῆς ἕξεως | على الفعال | ملكة |
| 3.3.5 | ܗܝܡܢܝܢ | πιστεύοιμεν | تيقنا | تيقنا |
| 4.3.2 | ܦܢܛܣܝܐ | φαντασία | تخيل | تخيل |
| 4.3.4 | ܗܪܝܣܛܝܩܝܬܐ | ἐριστική | مشاغبة | مشاغبة |
| 4.3.5 | ܦܢܛܣܝܐ | φαντασία | تخيل او توهم | يتخيل |
| 4.3.5 | ܦܢܛܣܝܐ | φαντασία | [يتخيل] | يتخيل |
| 4.4.2 | ܕܝܘܣܝܣ | δίωσις | حيف or جنف | حيف |
| 4.4.3 | ܛܘܪܢܐ | τυραννίς | فتنة وهرج | فتنة او وقوع هرج |
| 4.5.1 | ARar and IS omit 73b16-17, in which BH has ܐܘܪܘܡܕܘܢܛܘܣ for εὐρυμέδοντος, ܐܬܝܪ for αἰθήρ, ܐܘܓܝ for αὐγή. | | | |
| 4.5.2 | ܐܣܛܪܛܝܐ | στρατευόμενος | الدخول في الشرطة | بيعة or زحف |
| 4.5.7 | ܥܒ̈ܕܝ ܢܘ̈ܣܐ | ναοποιοί | صانعى المحاريب | differs |
| 5.1.1 | ܡܠܝܣܛܐ | μάλιστα | لا سيما | خصوضا |
| 5.1.5 | ܡܠܝܣܛܐ | ἔτι μᾶλλον | اكثر من ذلك | خصوصا |
| 5.2.4 | ܩܝܢܕܘܢܘܣ | κίνδυνος | خطر | هول |
| 5.2.7 | ܩܝܢܕܘܢܘ | κινδύνοις | هول | مخوف |
| 5.2.7 | ܟܝ̈ܡܘܢܘܗܝ | χειμῶνος | هيج الامواج | omits |
| 5.3.6 | ܩܛܓܪܘܬܐ | κατηγορίας | شكايات | شكاية |
| 5.4.2 | ܡܬܕܒܪܢ | ἀγομένῳ | جلد | omits |
| 5.4.3 | ܠܒܪ ܡܢ ܐܟܣܝܐ | παρὰ τὴν ἀξίαν | هارجا من الطبيعة | غير مستحقه |
| 5.4.6 | ܙܘ̈ܓܐ ܫܢ̈ܝܐ | γάμοι διαφέροντες | التخليط فى النكاح | omits |
| 5.4.7 | ܙܐܘܣ | Ζεύς | المشترى | omits |
| 5.4.7 | ܙܕܝܩܐ | δικαίῳ | ناسك | ناسك |
| 5.5.1 | ܐܦܪ̈ܘܕܝܛܝܣܝܬܐ | ἀφροδίσια | الزهرة | الزهرة |
| 5.5.5 | ܣܒܪܝܢ | οἴονται | جربوا | يجربوا |
| 5.5.10 | ܣܠܐܩܘܢܣ | σαλάκωνες | ذوى فخر | omits |
| 5.5.10 | ܣܘܠܘܩܘ | σόλοικοι | صلف | صلفون |
| 6.2.1 | ܦܪܐܒܘܠܐ ܐܘܟܝܬ ܡܬܠܐ | παραβολή | مثل | مثل |
| 6.2.2 | ܐܬܠܝܛ̈ܐ | ἀθληταί | صراع ( صارع ?) | omits |
| 6.2.2 | ܡܥܒܕ ܐܓܘܢܐ | ἀγωνίζεσθαι | يصطرعو | مصارعة |
| 6.3.3 | ܛܛܝܓܓܣ ܐܘܟܝܬ ܨܘܪ̈ܨܝܬܐ | τέττιγες | خطاطيف | خطاطيف |
| 6.3.3 | ܢܪ̈ܢ | ᾄδωσιν | توزوز | تؤذوا |

| | | | |
|---|---|---|---|
| 6.3.4 ܐܢܘܐܠܝܘܣ ܛܪܘܐ | ξυνὸς ´Ενυάλιος | ولناس | omits |
| 6.3.5 ܓܝܘܪܐ | πάροικος | lost by damage | omits |
| 6.3.7 ܐܦܘܦܢܛܝܩܐ | ἀποφαίνεσθαι | يصير | يصير |
| 6.5.5 ܠܐ ܗܘܐ | ἥκιστα | omits | omits |
| 6.5.6 ܐܝܗܪܘܢ | ἱερόν | كاهن | omits |
| 6.5.6 ܐܝܐܪܝܐ ܘܟܘܡܪܬܐ | ἱέρεια | ايارية | omits |
| 6.5.9 ܐܐܣ | ἐκ τοῦ Αἴαντος | فى ادوسوس | omits |
| 6.5.10 ܕܝܘܩܠܣ | Joh. Diac. Διοκλῆς | Androcles | omits |
| 6.5.11 ܫܚܝܪܬܐ | ἀνομολογούμενα | differs (cf. Lyons 354) | |
| | | | omits |
| 6.6.1 ܐܦܘܣ | ἔπος | شعر | شعر |
| 6.6.3 ܦܘܠܝܛܝܐ | πολιτεία | تدبير | omits |
| 6.6.4 ܗܪܝܣܛܝܩܐ | οἱ ἐριστικοί | مشاغبى | جدلى |
| 6.6.4 ܗܦܐܓܠܡܐ | ἐπάγγελμα | سنة | omits |
| 6.7.1 and 7.9.11 ܗܢܣܛܣܝܣ | ἔνστασις | مقاومة | مقاومة |
| 6.7.2 ܦܪܘܠܘܓܝܙܡܢܐ | παραλογιζόμενος | تقديم الكلام | omits |
| 7.1.1 ܦܪܓܡܐܛܘܬܝܢܐ | πραγματευθῆναι | صناعة | omits |
| 7.1.1 ܒܐܘܟܣܝܐ ܘܐܪܝܐ | ὀξείᾳ καὶ βαρείᾳ | omits | omits |
| 7.1.2 ܐܬܠܣܐ | ἆθλα | ذوو المنازعة | منازعون |
| 7.1.2 ܐܓܘܢܐ | ἀγωνες | منازعة | منازعة |
| 7.1.3 ܐܘܦܩܪܛܝܐ | ὑποκριτή | الانقر اطية | omits |
| 7.1.3 ܠܟܣܝܩܝܐ | (διὰ τὴν) λέξιν | مقالة | لفظ |
| 7.1.4 ܐܟܣܝܘܡܐ | ἀξίωμα | مجاوز للقدر الذى يستوجب | درجة? |
| 7.2.1 ܐܟܣܢܝܐ | ξένος | غريب | غريب |
| 7.2.2 ܕܝܐܠܩܛܘܣ | δίαλεκτος | كلام | omits |
| 7.2.3 ܠܟܣܝܣ | λέξις | كلام | لغات |
| 7.2.4 ܐܦܝܬܗܛܐ | ἐπιθετα | موضوعات | omits |
| 7.2.4 ܠܣܛܝܐ | λησταί | لصوص | لص |
| 7.2.4 ܥܦܝܪܢ ܦܘܪܣܐ | ποϱισταί | محتالون | محتال |
| 7.2.5 ܫܘܝܢ ܒܕܡܘܬܐ | ὁμοειδῆ | منقارب فى الصورة | مناسبة |
| 7.3.5 ܣܟܪܐ | ἀσπίδα | ? (Ibn Rushd مجن) | حربة |
| 7.4.1 ܚܡܫ | πέντε | omits | omits |
| 7.4.1 ܟܣܝܐ | ἀσαφές | ليس محققا | لحن |
| 7.4.2 ܗܠܘܣ | ῞Αλυν | الراس [السِ?] | omits |
| 7.5.1 ܕܝܐܦܛܘܟ̈ܐ ܐܘܟܝܬ ܬܪܝܢ ܐܦ̈ܐ | διαπτυχαί | ذوات وجهين | لها وجهان |
| 7.5.4 ܐܪܡܘܢܝܐ | [ἁρμονία] | [توصيل] | ايقاعى |
| 7.6.3 ܐܓܘܪܣܐ | ἀγρόν | خراج/قراه | omits |
| 7.7.1 ܠܟܣܝܣ | λέξις | المقالات | عبارة |
| 7.7.2 ܐܢܛܝܬܗܣܝܣ | ἀντιθέσεως | وضع بالخلاف | مطابقات المتقابلات |
| 7.7.3 ܐܘܡܘܢܘܡܝܐ | ὁμωνυμία | اتفاق الاسم | اتفاق الاسم |
| 7.8.2 ܗܕܝܘܛܝܩ | ἰδιωτικοί | IR لا يجيدون | لا يجيدون |
| 7.8.2 ܐܓܘܢܐ | ἀγών | IR منازعة | منازعات |
| 7.8.2 ܐܓܘܢܝܣܛܝܩܘܬܐ | ἀγωνιστική | IR خصومات | ------ |
| 7.8.4 ܦܪܘܠܘܓܝܣܡܘܣ | παραλογισμός | IR صدر | تصدير |
| 7.8.4 ܐܓܘܢܝܣܛܐ | ἀγών | lacuna | اولياء |

| | | | |
|---|---|---|---|
| 7.9 ܛܘܟܣܐ | τάξις | IR نظام | ترتيب/نظم |
| 7.9.1 ܦܪܘܒܠܡܐ | πρόβλημα | lacuna | omits |
| 7.9.1 ܐܢܛܝܦܪܐܒܘܠܝ | ἀντιπαραβολή | lacuna | omits |
| 7.9.1 ܐܦܐܢܘܕܘܣ | ἐπάνοδος | lacuna | omits |
| 7.9.5 ܦܪܘܐܘܡܝܐܣܛܘܬܐ ܥܒܕܝܢ | προοιμιάζονται | يفعلون تقديم الكلام | differs |
| 7.10.2 ܣܘܡܦܪܣܡܐ | συμπέρασμα | نتيجة | نتيجة |
| 7.10.2 ܐܓܘ̈ܢܐ | ἀγῶνες | منازعات | اوقات الضرورة |

Cumulatively, the evidence that BH did not use ARar is compelling. It is true, to be sure, that not every case listed above proves the point without question. The omission of 73b16-17 in ARar, for example, might be an error simply of the Paris manuscript, and BH 4.5.1 might have read it in an Arabic manuscript which was free of this error. But on the other hand it is hardly credible that, say, the coincidence of BH 2.1.6 ܕܐܦܐܢ and AR 60a12 δαπανή against ARar بذل and IS حاصل is a matter of chance, or that of BH 4.4.2 ܕܝܘܣܝܣ and AR 72a33 and 35 δίωσις against Arabic جنف or جيف, or that of BH 7.1.1 ܦܪ̈ܓܡܐܛܘܬܐ and AR 03a34 and b6 πραγματευθῆναι against Arabic صناعة. Nor is it very likely that BH used one of the two later Arabic versions mentioned by the *Fihrist*,[94] for quite apart from the fact that he would then have been the only known user of these later versions, and the improbability that a later, post-Ḥunain version would concur with Old Arabic readings in so many striking divergences from the Greek, the tendency of versions from the school of Ḥunain was to replace Greek loanwords by pure Arabic terms, not introduce fresh loanwords.[95] But neither is it credible, as was shown above, that BH used the Greek, and that, for example, both BH 3.3.4 and ARar independently read 67b20 τ'οὖσα τυράννων as 'Saturannoi', or 73a22 'Aenesidemus to Gelon' as 'the island of Demogelone' (BH 4.4.6). The one hypothesis that does justice to all the evidence is that he used a Syriac version similar to the Old Ara-

[94] Cf. above, pp. 6-7.

[95] Cf. Strohmaier, 'Ḥunain ibn Isḥāq', 169-170; Endress, 'The Circle of al-Kindī', 58-60. It is true that Yaḥyā ibn 'Adī sometimes replaced a native Arabic term by a Greek loanword; cf. for example his substitution of الطراغوذية ('tragedy') for the صناعة المديح ('the art of eulogy') of Abū Bishr Mattā's version of *Poetics* 1449b24-27 (cf. Schrier, 'Aristotle's *Poetics*', 266-270). But Yaḥyā ibn 'Adī was making the substitution from the *Syriac*, not the Greek, this substitution is as much a correction as a stylistic variant, and the technique of the Baghdad Syriac-to-Arabic translators around Abū Bishr was in any case different from that of the Greek-to-Syriac/Arabic translators around Ḥunain.

bic, but a Syriac version, made directly from the Greek, that contained more Greek loanwords than those subsequently adopted by the Old Arabic. The Old Arabic (pre-Ḥunain) translator must have either translated directly from the Syriac, or at least worked in dependence upon it.[96] This conclusion is consistent with that of Zonta in his study of the Syriac version of Polemo used in the *Cream*: 'The Syriac translation employed by Bar Hebraeus proves to be the direct ancestor of the Arabic one, and the most ancient witness to the Oriental tradition of Polemo's treatise: it might be traced back to 7th-8th centuries.'[97] It is also consistent with that of Schrier in his study of the commentary on the *Poetics* in the *Cream*: 'Barhebraeus leaned heavily on Avicenna, but many details in his text prove that he had the Syriac translation also on his desk'.[98] And it is consistent, too, with the use of the Syriac version of Nicolaus' *Compendium* in the sections of the *Cream* on *Plants*[99] and *Mineralogy and Meteorology*.[100]

A passage from Bar Hebraeus' *Book of Splendours* (his large treatise on grammar) puts beyond all doubt that he knew a Syriac version of the *Rhetoric* and used it. He refers there to the fact that 'he who translated the *Book of Rhetoric* from Greek to Syriac said ܗܠܝܢ ܕܡܬܦܘ̈ܕܝܢ ܠܡܬܪܨܘ ("to correct the things which are done wrongly") with *waw*, but it is clear that he should have said ܕܡܬܦܕ̈ܕܝܢ with doubling of the *dālath*.'[101] The *Book of Rhetoric* is that of Aristotle, and despite the brevity of the passage it can be identified: 82b23-24, ( ... ) ὅσα ἁμαρτάνουσιν ἐπανορθώσασθαι (μὴ ἐνδέχεται), '(All fearful things are the more fearful) which things they do wrong (it is impossible) to correct'. In BH 5.2.5 this appears paraphrased as: ܘܗܢ ܥܒ̈ܕܐ ܦܠܓ ܕܣܢ̈ܝܐ ܗܠܝܢ ܕܠܐ ܡܬܬܪܨܐ

[96] Cf. above, p. 8.

[97] Zonta, *Fonti greche e orientali*, 117-118. Cf. also Janssens, 'Bar Hebraeus' *Book of the Pupils of the Eye*', 41-43 on the use of a Syriac version of Porphyry's *Eisagoge*.

[98] Schrier, 'Aristotle's *Poetics*', 274. While Ibn Sīnā used the Old Arabic version of the *Rhetoric*, he seems not to have used Abū Bishr's translation of the *Poetics*, but a second translation, presumably that of Yaḥyā ibn 'Adī, which goes back to the same Syriac; cf. ibid., 266-273.

[99] Cf. Drossaart Lulofs, *De plantis*, 35-36, 40.

[100] Cf. Takahashi, *Aristotelian Meteorology in Syriac*, 37-39, 51-53, 60-61.

[101] *Splendours* 100, 1 (Moberg, *Splendeurs*, p. 100, *Strahlen* I, p. 216). Cf. *ThesSyr* 3036.

ܠܡܬܪܨܘ ܦܘܕ̈ܝܗܘܢ, 'Among things greatly feared are those, the errors of which it is impossible to correct'. Bar Hebraeus therefore knew ARsyr and used it, paraphrasing the (ܗܠܝܢ ܕܡܬܦܕ̈ܝܢ ܠܡܬܪܨܘ ܠܐ ܡܨܝܐ ?) of the Syriac version by ܠܡܬܪܨܘ ܦܘܕ̈ܝܗܘܢ (ܠܐ ܡܨܝܐ). That particular formulation could not have been derived from IS[102] or ARar,[103] and the Syriac version he quotes in the *Book of Splendours* is clearly made from the Greek (as he says), not ARar.

Bar Hebraeus' treatise therefore depends on two sources, the lost Syriac version of Aristotle's *Rhetoric*, and Ibn Sīnā's commentary on (the Old Arabic version of) the *Rhetoric* in the *Shifā'*. No other lengthy sources can be traced. While he may generally have endeavoured to use as many sources as he could find, Bar Hebraeus was quite often content with just two. For example, in the treatise *On Plants* he relied on Nicolaus' *Compendium* and the *Shifā'*.[104] While there and in the *Mineralogy* and *Meteorology* he used Nicolaus' *Compendium* rather than a text of Aristotle himself,[105] we know of no epitome of Aristotle's *Rhetoric*, in Greek or Syriac, and we may assume that he knew of none either.

Bar Hebraeus thus envisaged his *Book of Rhetoric* as an exposition of that part of the Aristotelian tradition, not as a manual of rhetoric. He did, however, know of such a manual in Syriac, namely the *Rhetoric* of Antony of Tagrit.[106] In the *Book of Splendours* he referred more frequently to Antony (always to his *Rhetoric*) than to any other Syriac author apart from Ephraim,[107] and also placed it first in the list of books on 'secular teachings' (ܡܠܦܢ̈ ܒܪ̈ܝܐ) to be read in the schools, preceding the *Organon* (including the *Rhetoric*) of Ar-

---

[102] 139.7: 'Among things feared is what is not easy to catch by preventing it' (ما لا يسهل يداركه بمنعه). From IS, however, BH evidently took the very beginning of the sentence ('among things feared ...').

[103] اذا كان الفساد فيها مما لا يستطاع اصلاحه وتلافيه, 'if the error in them is something, the correction and remedy of which cannot be done (Lyons 98.20-21).

[104] Cf. Drossaart Lulofs, *De plantis*, 35.

[105] Ibid. 40 and Takahashi (as above, n. 80) for the *Mineralogy and Meteorology*.

[106] Cf. above, p. 9.

[107] Cf. *Book of Splendours*, transl. Moberg, *Buch der Strahlen* I, 180-182, index C; Strothmann, 'Die Schrift des Anton von Tagrit über die Rhetorik', 199-201, 206-207, also noting the mention of Antony by Bar Hebraeus in his *Chronicon ecclesiasticum*, I, 361-364.

istotle.[108] It is therefore quite likely that he viewed the kind of rhetorical instruction imparted in Antony's treatise as belonging to 'general (pre-philosophical) education' (the *enkyklios paideia* of antiquity), whereas his exposition of Aristotelian rhetoric in the *Cream* belonged to the study of philosophical logic.[109] There are some points of contact between statements made in Antony's *Rhetoric* and here by Bar Hebraeus,[110] but in general the two works are quite different. Jacob Bar Shakko, however, had no objection to interweaving Aristotelian material with that of the 'encyclical' or 'propaideutic' rhetorical tradition, for his citation of Aristotle's definition of tragedy in *Poetics* 1449b24-1450a9[111] occurs within the context of his treatment of poetics derived otherwise almost entirely from Book Five of Antony's *Rhetoric*.[112]

Being therefore an exposition of Aristotle's *Rhetoric* within the context of the entire sweep of Aristotelian philosophy, contacts with other treatises of the corpus are only to be expected. Allusions partly stemming from Bar Hebraeus himself, albeit often picking up something said by Ibn Sīnā, are made to the *Categories* in 6.5.3, *Prior Analytics* in 1.3.4, 1.6.3, and 1.7.2, *Topics* in 1.6.1, 6.5.4, 6.5.13, and 7.9.10, and *Nicomachean Ethics* in 2.1.8, 2.3.3, and 3.1.1. 'Doing good to friends and evil to enemies' in 1.5.2 and 3.3.3 may come from *Rhetoric* 63a20-21, although that is not the passage under paraphrase in either, or may be a (direct or indirect) reminiscence of Plato (*Republic* 332D, similarly in Antony of Tagrit). No other allusion to Plato, however, is present in Bar Hebraeus' *Rhetoric*. It is possible that his copy of ARsyr was furnished with scholia which provided Syriac terms for some Greek loanwords, and perhaps some occasional comments. Thus in 5.5.10 his elaboration of 91a11-12 ('the wise wait at the doors of the rich'), explaining that 'the wise man knows that for the sustenance of his body he needs anything which the rich man has, but the rich man ... does not know that for the sustenance of his soul he needs anything which the wise man

---

[108] *Nomocanon Gregorii Barhebraei*, ed. Bedjan, 106.

[109] Cf. Watt, 'Syriac Rhetorical Theory', 253-260; idem, 'Grammar, Rhetoric, and the Enkyklios Paideia', 55-68.

[110] Cf. the Commentary on 1.1.1, 1.1.3, 1.2.1, 1.5.1, 3.3.3, 6.6.2, 7.3.2, and 7.5.6.

[111] Cf. above, p. 14.

[112] Cf. *The Fifth Book of the Rhetoric of Antony of Tagrit*, Edition, xviii-xix. Jacob's citation of *Poetics* 1449b24-1450a9 follows his account of ridicule ('comedy') taken from Antony, ibid., 80-81 (Version, 68-69).

has', may betray a knowledge of the celebrated response of Aristippus (Diogenes Laertius 2.69), 'Philosophers know what they need, the rich do not'. The attribution of a saying to Diocles rather than Androcles in 6.5.10 might also come from a scholion in ARsyr, since the same attribution appears in a commentary of John the Deacon on Hermogenes. However the possibility of straightforward error in this case cannot be ruled out (ܐܢܕܪܘܩܠܝܣ to ܕܝܘܩܠܝܣ). This has occurred with the mention of 'Phriton' (Chriton, reading Arabic ف for ق from IS) in 2.2.3.[113]

As in Ibn Sīnā's paraphrase of the *Rhetoric* there are scattered indications that the author is a Muslim addressing Muslims,[114] so too in Bar Hebraeus' there are a few Christian touches. In this work he quotes or alludes to the following passages from the Bible: *Genesis* 7, 19-20; *2 Samuel* 12, 1-4; *Job* 14, 5; 13-14; *Psalm* 69, 1; *Song of Songs* 4, 2; 5; 6, 6; 7, 3; *Matthew* 7, 3-5/*Luke* 6, 41-42; *Matthew* 7, 13-14; *Titus* 1, 12; *Hebrews* 12, 1. *Titus* 1, 12 is the famous proverb of Epimenides, 'Cretans are liars', which BH 6.3.5 adds to AR 95a18 'an Attic neighbour/foreigner'. The poetic metaphors from *Song of Songs* in BH 7.3.4 replace the 'frigid epithets' of Alcidamas cited in AR 06a18-32. AR 14a2-3, a citation of *Iliad* 2.671-674 ('Nireus ... the most handsome') is transmuted in IS into 'the praise of God who gives strength to his friends and destroys his enemies', while BH 7.8.4 refers to a 'glorification of God who crowns the runners' (cf. *Hebrews* 12, 1) and 'has fixed for man the limit of his temporal life' (cf. *Job* 14, 5; 13-14). IS replaces the several Greek citations in AR 15a15-18 with two Arabic proverbs, BH 7.9.3 with citations from *Genesis* and *Psalms*. Paraphrasing AR 74b29-30 on 'the greater wrong', IS alludes to what 'the hermit did to the weasel',[115] BH 4.5.7 to the rich man who seized the poor man's one ewe lamb (*2 Samuel* 12, 1-4). BH 1.3.7 adds to AR 55a15-17 ('humans have a natural disposition for the true ...') an allusion to *Matthew* 7, 13-14 ('strait is the gate and narrow the way ...'), picking up IS's addition, 'but the way to it is hard ...'. In BH 3.4.2, however, the allusion to *Matthew* 7, 3-5 ('they see the chip in their brother's eye, but not the plank in their own eyes') comes directly from IS, who, like many

[113] Cf. the Commentary on 5.5.10, 6.5.10, and 2.2.3.
[114] Cf. Würsch, 127-130.
[115] Cf. Würsch, 118.

Muslim authors, evidently knew this passage.[116] In addition to these passages, there may be reminiscences of *Colossians* 2, 17 and *Hebrews* 8, 5; 10, 1 in BH 1.3.7, and of *Romans* 12, 15 in BH 5.1.5.

Despite these biblical touches, Bar Hebraeus was not concerned to present his exposition of Aristotelian rhetoric as an explicitly Christian work.[117] Neither, however, despite his dependence upon Ibn Sīnā, did he want it to appear as a Muslim one. Thus even when following Ibn Sīnā in the main, he was careful to eliminate any comments and remarks of a specifically Islamic character. In 1.3.6 IS's phrase 'except for resistance and war' is dropped, and in 1.8.3 IS's 'those fighting in the cause of God may be killed, thrown out, and stripped' is replaced by 'the slaughter of martyrs for piety (and) persecution for true confession'.[118] In 2.4.1 an example in IS concerning the Qur'ān and the Prophet is not taken over by BH, and in 3.3.3 while IS declares that an orator must adopt the appropriate praise according to countries, peoples, and *confessions* (ملل), BH has places, peoples, and *professions* (ܐܘ̈ܡܢܐ), thus eliminating the reference to the Islamic *milla.* In 4.6.5 he removes IS's reference to 'the Book' (i.e. the Qur'ān) and reverts to 'law(s)', in accordance with AR 76b15-19, in 6.3.4 he removes IS's reference to the wrongfulness of temporary marriage (متعة), and in 6.5.10 that to Islamic infidelity (كفر الملة). In 2.4.1 he transforms IS's 'not exactly orthodox conception'[119] that 'wisdom is better than worship' into 'wisdom is better than abstinence'. It is noteworthy that in 6.5.6 while IS substitutes the singular for AR 99a24 'gods', BH keeps to the plural; and while at the end of the treatise IS has an Islamic epilogue with reference to God the Merciful, BH 7.10.3 keeps to the epilogue of AR 20b3. Generally, in fact, BH is less concerned than IS to introduce a religious perspective into the Aristotelian exposition. Thus in 4.5.3 there is no parallel to IS's statement that 'the legislator is not supported from heaven but is imposed artificially', in 4.6.6 no reference to IS's

[116] Cf. Würsch, 128 referring to Goldziher, 'Matth. VII. 5 in der muhammedanischen Literatur'.

[117] This is not deny, however, that he considered the whole of the wisdom which he presented in the *Cream* to be of divine origin; cf. Takahashi, *Aristotelian Meteorology*, 4-7.

[118] Cf. similarly the replacement in 7.8.4 of IS's 'the praise of God who gives strength to his friends and destroys his enemies' by an allusion to *Hebrews* 12, 1, cited above.

[119] Würsch, 128.

'there is no contract in disobedience to God', and in 2.4.5 no mention (among other things) of IS's remark on the superiority of theology to physiognomy.[120]

Traces of popular Arabic culture have also been left out or transformed by Bar Hebraeus when taking over the general thrust of Ibn Sīnā's exposition, notably in the substitution of biblical sayings or stories for Arabic proverbs. The biblical allusions mentioned above to *2 Samuel* (the poor man's one ewe lamb), *Titus* (Epimenides' 'Cretans are liars'), *Psalms* ('the waters have reached the soul'), and *Genesis* ('the flood has covered the top of the mountain') appear in BH 4.5.7, 6.3.5, and 7.9.3 in place of IS's references to the Arabic proverbs 'the hermit and the weasel', 'dogs to cattle', 'the torrent has reached the brim', and 'fatten your dog and he will eat you'.[121] In BH 1.4.3 there is no mention of the Arabic proverb cited by IS, 'iron is cleft with iron',[122] and in BH 1.5-7 'Socrates' replaces the proverbial 'Zayd' of IS. In 6.6.2 BH keeps the Greek examples of AR 01b9-20 and makes no mention of the Persian one introduced in their place by IS.[123] Strangely, however, in 7.7.5 he preserves IS's reference to Persian *khusrawāniyyāt*, but in his discussion in that pericope of Greek metres—which were no doubt as mysterious to him as to IS—he did not make with IS the Muslim confession that 'God knows best'.[124] He was nevertheless capable of correcting a clear error in IS: in 2.1.8 IS's erroneous 'Socratic' is replaced by the correct 'aristocratic'.[125] In place of Arabic, he takes the opportunity now and then to introduce aspects of Syriac language and rhetoric alongside Aristotle's remarks on Greek. Thus in 7.3.2, while IS substituted an Arabic example of his own for the 'frigid glosses' of AR 06a6-10 (which he omitted), BH both kept AR's examples and added a couple of Syriac ones (from Antony of Tagrit); in 7.3.3 like IS he dropped AR 06a12 'white milk' and in place of IS's Arabic example offered as an over-long word 'Nebuchadnezzar'. In 7.4.3 he made some brief remarks about the Syriac accents, in 7.4.4 Syriac syntax, and in 7.5.6 assonance and balance in Syriac rhetoric.

---

[120] See the similar assessment by Teule of Bar Hebraeus' procedure in other works; cf. 'La Critique du prince', 289, 291-292 and 'Avicenna's *k. al-ishārāt*'.

[121] Cf. Würsch, 118-120; Aouad, IR III, 297.

[122] Cf. Würsch, 156 and 196 n. 79.

[123] Cf. ibid., 120.

[124] Cf. ibid., 115, 121-122.

[125] Cf. ibid., 192.

These individual touches of the author do not alter the fact that in the main the work is a compilation of two sources, Aristotle (in Syriac) and Ibn Sīnā, and it is in the way these two are woven together that its principal interest lies. Bar Hebraeus did not feel obliged to reproduce either of them exactly, although where he followed Aristotle he seems to have adhered more closely to the wording of ARsyr than when following Ibn Sīnā to that of IS, which of course he had to translate from Arabic. Aristotle was his master (ܪܒ), Ibn Sīnā the master's disciple who multiplied the master's talent fifty times.[126] Bar Hebraeus drew upon Ibn Sīnā not because he felt that he adapted Aristotle to conditions closer to his own time,[127] but because he believed that he often understood the intention of the master quite correctly and made clear what in Aristotle's (Syriac) text was ambiguous or obscure. He therefore felt free to draw on both as he saw fit, frequently preferring the master himself—particularly when Ibn Sīnā omitted passages, especially examples from Greek literature or history, many of which Bar Hebraeus retained—but also like the master's servant omitting many passages which he found incomprehensible, yet incorporating much material from the servant's exposition that elaborates or expands upon the master's text. In the preface to the whole *Cream* Bar Hebraeus declared it to be a presentation of 'the Peripatetic sayings and declaratory words, in which I have brought together, fully and clearly, the techniques of logic and the opinions of theoretical and practical philosophy, and in which I have expounded, manifestly and plainly, how vigilant minds may acquire correct teachings through them.'[128] In this part of the work he achieved his aim by his selection from and integration of these two sources.

[126] Cf. above, p. 17.

[127] The lack of concern to apply the text to the contemporary situation distinguishes BH's work from that of the Islamic commentators, particularly Ibn Rushd. The different situation of Christians in a Muslim society is a relevant consideration here.

[128] Cf. Takahashi, *Aristotelian Meteorology*, 4-5.

# THE MANUSCRIPTS

Six manuscripts of the *Cream* presently available contain the *Rhetoric*. One of these, however, Laurenz. Or. 8, was copied in the 16th. or 17th. century from Laurenz. Or. 69, the oldest of the other five, by Antonius Sionita. It has no independent value and has therefore not been used here.[129] This edition is therefore based on five manuscripts.

**F** = Florence, Biblioteca Medicea Laurenziana, Or. 69 (formerly 186). West Syrian (serto), 1340 A.D. 25 to 30 lines per page in two columns. Copied by Najm b. Shams b. Abū al-Faraj of Mardin. Many marginal and inter-column annotations in Arabic. Together with Laurenz. Or. 83 (formerly 187), with which it once formed a single whole, it contains the whole *Cream*. *Rhetoric* on fols. $214r^{b}$-$272r^{b}$.

Literature: Takahashi, *Aristotelian Meteorology*, 15-16; Joosse, 'Bar Hebraeus' *Butyrum Sapientiae*', 450-452; Drossaart Lulofs, *De plantis*, 43, 730; Margoliouth, *Analecta orientalia*, 39-43; Assemani, *Laurentianae catalogus*, 328-329.

**L** = London, British Library, Or. 4079. East Syrian, vocalised, 1809 A.D. 40 lines per page in two columns. Copied by George b. Yaqo b. Dusho of Alqosh. Contains the whole *Cream*. *Rhetoric* on fols. $118r^{a}$-$150v^{a}$.

Literature: Takahashi, *Aristotelian Meteorology*, 16; Joosse, 'Bar Hebraeus' *Butyrum Sapientiae*', 453-455; Drossaart Lulofs, *De plantis*, 46-47; Margoliouth, *Descriptive List*, 24-25.

**V** = Vatican, Syr. 604. East Syrian, vocalised, 1826 A.D. or 1886 A.D. 26 lines per page. Together with Vat. Syr. 603 covers the logic section of the *Cream*. *Rhetoric* on fols. 75r-139v.

Literature: Takahashi, *Aristotelian Meteorology*, 22-23 (cf. 27-28); Joosse, 'Bar Hebraeus' *Butyrum Sapientiae*', 448-450; Drossaart Lulofs, *De plantis*, 45-46; Macomber, 'New Finds', 481 n. 52; van Lantschoot, *Inventaire*, 135-136, 145; Scher, 'Notice sur les manuscrits syriaques', 81.

**R** = Manchester, John Rylands University Library, Syr. 56. West Syrian (serto), copied from an East Syrian exemplar with vocalisation, 1887 A.D. 29 lines per page in two columns. Copied by Matthew b. Paulos in Mosul. Contains the logic section of the *Cream*. *Rhetoric* on fols. $140v^{b}$-$176r^{a}$.

---

[129] Assemani, *Laurentianae catalogus*, 332-325 asserted that the group of manuscripts to which it belonged (Or. 37, 10, 6, and 8) was a translation of Aristotle by Ḥunain. This is quite incorrect. Cf. Margoliouth, *Analecta orientalia*, 40; Takahashi, *Aristotelian Meteorology*, 21.

Literature: Takahashi, *Aristotelian Meteorology*, 23; Joosse, 'Bar Hebraeus' *Butyrum Sapientiae*', 447-448; Coakley, 'A Catalogue of the Syriac MSS. in the John Rylands Library', 181-183.

l = London, British Library, Or. 9380. East Syrian, vocalised, 1892 A.D. 28 lines per page. Copied by 'Isa b. Isaiah b. Cyriacus in Alqosh. Contains the whole *Cream*. *Rhetoric* on fols. 231r-296r.

Literature: Takahashi, *Aristotelian Meteorology*, 18; Joosse, 'Bar Hebraeus' *Butyrum Sapientiae*', 455-457; Drossaart Lulofs, *De plantis*, 47.

The manuscript tradition of the whole *Cream* has been examined and described recently by Drossaart Lulofs,[130] Joosse,[131] and Takahashi.[132] Takahashi has identified three families (A-C).[133] F is the principal manuscript of his family 'A', LVR belong to his family 'C', and l belongs predominantly to 'C' but with some traits of 'A'.

F is the oldest and certainly the most important manuscript of the *Cream*. According to the notes on folio 191v and 227r of its 'other half', Or. 83, it was copied from the author's autograph.[134] Being completed (according to the second of these notes) on 8th May 1651 A.G. (1340 A.D.), only fifty-four years after the author's death and fifty-five after the composition of the *Cream*, it is at any rate much closer in time to the autograph than the surviving witnesses of the other family. In the great majority of instances it manifestly presents the best reading, but it is by no means perfect, and on quite a few occasions the reading of group 'C' is preferable.[135]

The Arabic glosses and marginalia of this manuscript, found in some abundance in this as in the other Books of the *Cream*, are thought by Takahashi to stem from two hands. One set, consisting mostly of Arabic translations of the chapter and section headings, may be from the scribe of the main Syriac text, the other from Daniel Rabbanus, who purchased the manuscript in 1367.[136] The second

[130] *De plantis*, 42-48.

[131] 'Bar Hebraeus' *Butyrum Sapientiae*', 417-458.

[132] *Aristotelian Meteorology*, 15-35, with texts and translations of the colophons 585-600.

[133] Ibid., 33-35.

[134] See the reproduction of the notes and their interpretation in Margoliouth, *Analecta Orientalia*, 41-42 and Takahashi, *Aristotelian Meteorology*, 16, 586-587.

[135] Cf. the similar evaluation of Drossaart Lulofs, *De plantis*, 47-48 and Takahashi, *Aristotelian Meteorology*, 74.

[136] According to a note on fol. 1r; cf. Takahashi, ibid., 16.

(and much larger) group appears to be taken from corresponding passages in Ibn Sīnā's *Shifā'*, sometimes in closer agreement with the text of Bar Hebraeus than is the extant Arabic text of Ibn Sīnā.[137]

The manuscripts of the East Syrian group 'C', namely L, V, and R, form a tightly knit family. While R and especially V have some readings of their own, there are very few examples of them combining against L. There are three such cases of omission by parablepsis in the *Rhetoric* (1.5.3 and two in 7.9.6), two of singular and plural involving the Syriac ܕ/ܪ (4.1.2 and 6.7.1), and five other trivial, easily made errors (4.2.1, 5.1.5, 5.1.6, 6.5.5, 6.6.4). This evidence is consistent with the hypothesis that V and R are both copies of L. L was written in 1809 A.D.; in 1889 it was sold by its then owner, John Elijah Mellus, after he had made a copy of it, to Wallis Budge. Mellus was the copyist, in Mosul in 1887, of Vat. Syr. 613-615, a companion to V containing another part of the *Cream*, and Vat. Syr. 613-615 appears to be a collation of L and Mingana Syr. 310. Mellus may therefore have copied V from L, if the date of V is 1886 (Scher's reading of the colophon); if the date is 1826 (the reading of van Lantschoot), it is still possible that V is a copy of L (by another copyist).[138] R was copied in Mosul in 1887 by Matthew bar Paulos. Since the glossary of terms at its beginning and the colophon at its end are identical or similar to those of L, it is quite likely that it was copied from L.[139] It is therefore possible, but hardly certain, that readings supported by LVR, LV, or LR are in effect simply those of L. If L is not itself the ancestor of R and V, an unknown ancestor of all three will have been the source of their many common variants over against F.[140]

Manuscript l is also associated with Wallis Budge, having been produced at his request in Alqosh in 1892 A.D. Being a recent East Syrian manuscript, one would expect it to be similar to LVR, and indeed it is closer to them than to F. However, on many occasions, usually occurring in clusters, it sides with F against LVR. An electronic count of variant readings in the *Rhetoric* supported by Ll or Fl yielded a ratio of approximately three to one, confirming that while l is predominantly a member of the 'C' group, there is a substantial

[137] Cf. ibid., 602-604; Drossaart Lulofs, *De plantis*, 43.
[138] Cf. Takahashi, *Aristotelian Meteorology*, 22-23, 27-28.
[139] Cf. ibid., 23.
[140] Cf. ibid., 74.

element of 'A' in its profile. In three cases (6.2.1, 6.2.4, and 6.3.6) a reading of l alone against FLVR has been judged original and used in the text. The last of these is the most important of them, a twelve word addition to the other witnesses possibly caused by parablepsis in FLVR (cf. the Commentary on 6.3.6). It seems likely, therefore, that the copyist of l made use of more than one exemplar.[141] External circumstances add to the improbability of l being derived solely from L. L was purchased by Budge in 1889, and it seems unlikely that he would have commissioned l in 1892 if it were merely a copy of L. Budge later lent l to Jessie Payne Margoliouth, who employed it in working on the *Supplement* to the *Thesaurus Syriacus*.[142]

## TEXT, TRANSLATION, COMMENTARY, GLOSSARIES

The Text of this edition is based principally on manuscript F, the oldest and best by far of the five. However, as indicated above, it is by no means free of error, and readings from the East Syrian group have been adopted in a considerable number of cases. There are a few editorial conjectures (*scripsi*). Diacritic punctuation, sporadic in F but fuller in the East Syrian group, has been reduced to the 'necessary points'; interpunctuation, sporadic in all manuscripts, is that of the editor. Well-known orthographic variants in common Syriac words, particularly *plene* and *defectiva* forms and those with or without *yōdh* or *ālaph*, are not registered in the apparatus, but variant forms of Greek names and of less common Greek loanwords are noted.

The seven chapters of the *Book of Rhetoric* are found in each of the manuscripts as follows:

| | F | L | V | R | l |
|---|---|---|---|---|---|
| 1 | 214r$^b$1 | 118r$^a$18 | 75r8 | 140v$^b$11 | 231r26 |
| 2 | 220v$^b$19 | 122r$^a$24 | 83r4 | 145r$^b$4 | 239v5 |
| 3 | 227v$^b$6 | 125v$^b$6 | 90r19 | 149r$^b$21 | 247r1 |
| 4 | 230v$^b$21 | 127r$^b$39 | 93v11 | 151r$^b$4 | 250r24 |
| 5 | 239v$^b$7 | 132r$^a$14 | 102v11 | 156r$^b$11 | 259r21 |

[141] Takahashi, ibid., comes to the same conclusion on account of occasional references to variants in its margin.

[142] Cf. *ThesSyr, Supplement*, vii, x.

| | | | | | |
|---|---|---|---|---|---|
| 6 | 251v$^{b}$5 | 138r$^{a}$29 | 114v11 | 163r$^{a}$16 | 271r25 |
| 7 | 260v$^{b}$16 | 143v$^{a}$5 | 125v2 | 168v$^{a}$24 | 282r9 |

Like his ancient predecessors, the modern translator is faced with the tension between *interpres* and *expositor*: whether to produce an accurate 'image' of the form of the original in the medium of the target language, or to grasp its meaning and represent that in a form natural to the language of the translation. As is common in translations accompanying a text, that offered here is an attempt to do both in some measure. The aim has been a version sufficiently close in form to the original to enable the reader familiar with Syriac to compare the two with ease, yet comprehensible and not stylistically too 'offensive' to the English reader. A feature of this work, however, not regularly encountered in the translation of ancient or medieval texts, is that the Syriac is itself a paraphrase of a text (or rather, of a translation of a text) which will no doubt be familiar to many readers in a modern rendering. Furthermore, the main interest of it for most of them will be its relationship to the text of Aristotle, both the similarities and the differences. It is therefore clearly advantageous to have an English rendering which can be compared with English or other modern versions of the *Rhetoric*, and which will enable the reader easily to recognise the Aristotelian passage being paraphrased where the paraphrase is sufficiently close to Aristotle for such recognition to be appropriate. At the same time, the translator's obligation is to the Syriac text of Bar Hebraeus, not the Greek of Aristotle. It is an unwarranted assumption that Bar Hebraeus read Aristotle in a Greek text familiar to us—as argued in an earlier part of this Introduction,[143] he read it not in Greek, but in a Syriac version—or that he intended to say exactly what Aristotle said. In fact, as also indicated earlier, he frequently followed Ibn Sīnā's paraphrase rather than Aristotle himself, and sometimes he said something different from either. The translation should not therefore mirror a modern translation of Aristotle where it is not appropriate,[144] or obscure real differences which exist between the two. However, the reader does need to know what passage of the *Rhetoric* (AR) is being paraphrased at any

[143] Cf. above, pp. 22-29.

[144] The English version to which I have had recourse for such assimilation where it is appropriate has generally been that of Kennedy, *Aristotle* On Rhetoric.

point, and this, together with a reference to the corresponding passage of Ibn Sīnā (IS), is provided in a footnote to each paragraph ('theory').

Within this general problematic area, the rendering of technical or special terms represents a particular case. The *interpres* tends towards consistency throughout, the *expositor* is more attuned to the different connotations of words in varying contexts. In most cases I have not felt obliged always to translate a Syriac special term by the same English word, since the semantic range of a word in one language does not necessarily correspond to that in another, but the Select Glossary details the English words used in the rendering of each Syriac term listed there. A special problem presented by this text is the appropriate rendering of a Syriac word which clearly corresponds to a Greek one in Aristotle's text, but of which the normal or only attested meaning does not coincide with that of the Greek word in the context of the *Rhetoric*.[145] In many cases Bar Hebraeus' intention emerges fairly clearly from the context in which he employs the word, and this meaning may or may not be the same as the corresponding Greek in Aristotle. In some instances, however, it is difficult or impossible to tell whether or to what extent the Syriac word had a connotation for the author or his readers different from its normal usage and consistent with that of the corresponding Greek in Aristotle. Sometimes it has seemed best not to translate a special term by an English word, but to transliterate the corresponding Greek. This applies in particular to two words of frequent occurrence, *haymānūthā* (in Syriac usually 'faith', but here regularly corresponding to Aristotle's *pistis*[146]) and *'athrā* ('place', but here the regular equivalent of *topos*, 'place of an argument').[147]

A concrete example may clarify some of these points. AR 60b14-17 can be translated rather literally: 'Let happiness (*eudaimonia*) be well-being (*eupraxia*) with virtue, or self-sufficiency (*autarkia*) of life, or the most pleasant life with security, or abundance of possessions and bodies with the ability to protect and use these things'. The corresponding passage in Bar Hebraeus (2.2.2) has been rendered here: 'Prosperity (*kahīnūthā*) is virtuous good conduct

[145] *Mutatis mutandis*, the same applies where Bar Hebraeus is clearly translating the Arabic of Ibn Sīnā.

[146] Cf. the Commentary on 1.1.1.

[147] The corresponding terms in Arabic are تصديق and موضع.

(*shappīrūth sā'ūrūthā*), sufficiency of secure life in a pleasant living with love and honour from men, with abundance of possessions, and the ability to protect and use these things'. We may assume that *kahīnūthā* and *shappīrūth sā'ūrūthā* stood in ARsyr for *eudaimonia* and *eupraxia*, and that ARsyr took these Greek terms in the alternative senses of 'prosperity' and 'good conduct'. To render Bar Hebraeus' paraphrase with 'happiness' and 'well-being' would clearly be unjustified, for it is more likely that ARsyr took the Greek words in the 'wrong' sense and they were subsequently so read in Syriac, than that the Syriac of this passage was read in the 'right' Greek sense against the normal sense of these Syriac words.[148] ARar replaces 'bodies' with 'legal title' (عقد?, Lyons 23.3-4 and 247), and it is likely that ARsyr did likewise.[149] Ibn Sīnā's paraphrase of the passage on the whole takes more liberties with it than does Bar Hebareus, but it is from Ibn Sīnā (65.9)[150] that Bar Hebraeus has derived the phrase 'with love and honour from men'.

The reader of this work should have to hand the normal Greek text of Aristotle's *Rhetoric* (AR), either in the original or a modern version. The principal purpose of the Commentary is, so far as the evidence allows, to elucidate the process leading from the Greek *Rhetoric* to this paraphrase by Bar Hebraeus, particularly where that differs markedly from the Aristotelian original. Where Bar Hebraeus' exposition (BH) can easily be understood by reference to AR, it may require no special comment, but where the reader will be puzzled on comparing BH with Aristotle, the Commentary is intended to provide some explanation. As the work is essentially a tapestry woven from the lost Syriac version of the *Rhetoric* (ARsyr) and Ibn Sīnā's paraphrase in the *Shifā'* (IS) of the Old Arabic (ARar), the Commentary aims to present whatever evidence from these texts is necessary to

---

148 The terms in ARar are صلاح الحال and حسن الفعال. They are used by IR (Aouad II 39, in the latter حسن الفعل) and translated by Aouad 'le bon état' and 'le bel acte'.

149 No doubt because it could make no sense of 'bodies' here, often rendered 'slaves'. Kennedy, *Aristotle* On Rhetoric, 57 has 'live bodies' and a note (n. 95), 'probably meaning both slaves and free men and women in a house or on an estate'. Grimaldi, *Aristotle,* Rhetoric *I*, 106, however, renders it '(a thriving state of property and) body'.

150 بمحبة القلوب وتوفر الكرامة من الناس, 'with love of hearts and abundance of honour from men'.

understand BH. Throughout, therefore, there are frequent conjectures as to the readings of the lost ARsyr, conjectures based on AR, ARar, and BH himself. The critical reader will appreciate that some of these are more securely based than others; in some cases the conjecture may be no more than plausible, in others highly probable. If BH is constructed from ARsyr and IS, then where it differs from AR and IS, or from ARar and IS, a conjecture concerning ARsyr will often be appropriate. One which differs significantly from AR but is supported by ARar, or vice-versa, will evidently have a great deal more weight than one lacking that support, but in the absence of any manuscript of ARsyr it remains a conjecture, however probable. In order to present the linguistic information likely to be desired by the philological reader, it has been necessary to pepper the Commentary with a liberal sprinkling of words and phrases in Greek, Syriac, and Arabic, but it is hoped that enough has been provided in the way of accompanying brief renderings in English to make the evidence intelligible to those unfamiliar with one or more of the three languages.

The Select Glossary provides a profile of the lexical connections between significant terms across the three texts: the Greek of Aristotle, the Arabic of Ibn Sīnā, and the Syriac of Bar Hebraeus. It should be remembered, however, that none of these is simply a version of any other, but that Ibn Sīnā is a paraphrase of the Old Arabic version of Aristotle, Bar Hebraeus a paraphrase of (the Syriac version of) Aristotle and Ibn Sīnā. Consequently, linking under one heading words of different languages from these three texts presupposes a greater degree of editorial judgement than would normally be the case in a multilingual glossary of a text and its version(s). Where a Greek or Arabic word with a reference to a paragraph ('theory') of Bar Hebraeus appears under a Syriac heading, that does not imply that it will necessarily be found in Aristotle or Ibn Sīnā in the identical context and grammatical form as the Syriac term(s) in that paragraph. It does indicate, however, that it will be found somewhere within the Greek or Arabic passage identified (in the footnotes to the Translation and synoptically in the Concordance of Passages[151]) as parallel to this paragraph of Bar Hebraeus—and also that, in the opinion of the editor, it corresponds (or, if accompanied by a ques-

[151] See the Concordance of Passages at the end of the volume.

tion mark, might correspond) to the Syriac term, even if the precise context within the flow of text or the grammatical form (e.g. verb against noun, singular against plural) is different from that in Bar Hebraeus.[152] For this reason, the entries are aggregated to include the various words belonging to the same root or word-group, and grammatical variations such as number, gender, or tense are not separately recorded.

The two additional reverse glossaries (Aristotle-Bar Hebraeus and Ibn Sīnā-Bar Hebraeus) show how the selected terms in the Greek and Arabic authors are transferred into the Syriac terminology of Bar Hebraeus. They should be used in conjunction with the main trilingual glossary, which alone gives the references to the text of Bar Hebraeus and provides information from all three texts together. As in the main glossary, the entries should be viewed primarily as indications of correspondences between word-groups or roots, not necessarily individual words or grammatical forms. Whether Bar Hebraeus derived a term from Aristotle or Ibn Sīnā can only be investigated by use of the main glossary along with the additional bilingual ones (and also, of course, by reference to the texts themselves). The two possibilities are, however, in many cases not strict alternatives. To take a couple of obvious examples, the cases—mentioned above in connection with the Translation—of *pistis* and *topos*, Bar Hebraeus evidently knew very well that what he meant by ܗܝܡܢܘܬܐ or ܐܬܪܐ corresponded both to the equivalent terms in Aristotle and to تصديق and موضع in Ibn Sīnā. Therefore even in a passage where he was following Ibn Sīnā and included the term because it appeared there and not in Aristotle, his 'translation' of it from Ibn Sīnā was not his own coinage, but the term he knew from the Syriac version of Aristotle.

[152] E.g., ܐܓܘܢܐ 3.2.2 corresponds to ἀγωνιᾶν 3.2.2 and اجتهاد 3.2.2, although the Syriac and Arabic are singular nouns, the Greek a verb (plural participle). BH 3.2.2 corresponds to AR 67a6-18 and IS 86.16-87.14. The plural participle of the Greek verb is at AR 67a15, the Arabic noun at IS 87.12. Aristotle means, 'Also (honourable are those things) for which *(people) contend* (ἀγωνιῶσι) without fear'; Ibn Sīnā, 'All of that issued from a queen who had been formed by exercise and *effort*' (اجتهاد); Bar Hebraeus, 'This whole happening pointed to the habit which by exercise and *discipline* (ܐܓܘܢܐ) had been fastened into her soul'. In ARar, and in all likelihood ARsyr, 67a15 is wrongly attached to the preceding quotation (on Sappho) and rendered 'about which she was *endeavouring*' (تجاهد, Lyons 45.1 and 269).

Since Bar Hebraeus read Aristotle in the lost Syriac version of the *Rhetoric*, the Greek-Syriac glossary is likely to reflect to a considerable degree that version's rendering of the Greek text. The list above[153] covers those cases in which his use of the terminology of this version seems clear, given that he did not employ the Greek itself and could hardly have hit on the terms in question from the Arabic either of Aristotle or Ibn Sīnā. It would be strange, therefore, if throughout the text, and not just in these particular instances, he did not make use of the language of this version. In other cases where, in contrast to the situation here with the *Rhetoric*, a Syriac version is extant of an Aristotelian work he paraphrased, it is clear that he largely used the vocabulary of his Syriac *Vorlage*, which he frequently quoted quite literally.[154] Of course, he could also have varied the terminology, using alternative terms either on account of scholarly preference or for literary effect. It would be rash, therefore, invariably to conclude that the word-group or root appearing in any passage is that of the lost Syriac version of the corresponding passage of Aristotle, but it is nevertheless quite likely that this will often be so.[155] As an example, the case of one of the most interesting terms may show the sort of conclusion which might reasonably be drawn from the evidence, as well as some of the inherent difficulties.

The Greek term φαντασία (*phantasia*, 'imagination', 'presentative faculty') occurs in the following places in Aristotle, with correspondences in BH, IS, and ARar:

| | | | | | |
|---|---|---|---|---|---|
| 70a28 | 4.3.2 | ܦܢܛܣܝܐ | 100.10 | تخيل | تخيل |
| ------ | 4.3.2 | ܡܬܗܓܝܢܘܬܐ | 101.2 | تخيل | ------- |
| 70b33 | 4.3.4 | --------- | -------- | | شهوة |
| 71a9 | 4.3.5 | ܦܢܛܣܝܐ | 102.6 | يتخيل | تخيل او توهم |
| 19 | 4.3.5 | ܦܢܛܣܝܐ | 102.13 | يتخيل | [يتخيل] |
| 78b9 | 5.1.2 | ܗܓܝܐ | -------- | | وهم |
| 82a21 | 5.2.4 | ܡܬܗܓܝܢܘܬܐ | 138.5 | تخيل | تخيل |
| 83a17 | 5.2.6 | --------- | --------- | | تخيل او توهم |
| 84a23 | 5.3.3 | ܡܬܗܓܝܢܘܬܐ | 143.11 | يوهم | omits |
| 04a11 | 7.1.1 | ܡܗܓܝܢܘܬܐ | 197.9 | تخييل | متخيل او متوهم |
| 04a11 | 7.1.2 | ܡܗܓܝܢܘܬܐ | 199.14 | تخييل | متخيل او متوهم |

[153] Above, pp. 24-27.

[154] Above, pp. 19, 28; Takahashi, *Aristotelian Meteorology*, 60.

[155] Cf. the case of 82b23-24 (above, pp. 28-29), where we have the wording of ARsyr (from the *Book of Splendours*) and BH's paraphrase: ܗܠܝܢ ܕܡܬܦܩܕܢ ܠܡܬܚܪܝܘ for the former, ܠܡܬܚܪܝܘ ܦܘܩܕܢܗܘܢ for the latter.

In addition to the second appearance of تخيّل at IS 101.2 and that of ܡܬܗܓܓܢܘܬܐ at BH 4.3.2, where φαντασία is not present in Aristotle, forms of ܗܓܓ and forms of خيل appear in BH 1.4.2, 4.2.1, 4.3.6, 5.1.3, 5.5.8, 6.3.3, 7.1.1, 7.1.3, 7.1.4, 7.2.2, 7.2.3, 7.2.6, 7.5.1, 7.5.2, 7.5.4, 7.6.2, and 7.9.4 and the corresponding passages in IS, in none of which is φαντασία present in Aristotle. It is therefore quite clear that Bar Hebraeus normally rendered forms of خيل in Ibn Sīnā by those of Syriac ܗܓܓ, and this may or may not have been because ARsyr frequently rendered φαντασία in this way. It is, however, extremely improbable that Bar Hebraeus himself decided on three occasions to vary this by substituting ܦܢܛܣܝܐ instead, and these three occasions just happen to coincide with three occasions on which φαντασία is present in AR. Regarding ARsyr, therefore, it seems natural to conclude that in all probability in these three passages (70a28, 71a9 and 19) the Greek term was rendered by the loanword ܦܢܛܣܝܐ, but that it remains an open question as to whether the same applies in any of the other passages (in which case BH would have substituted a form of ܗܓܓ), or whether forms of the Syriac root were also used in ARsyr. In the case of ἀγῶν and its cognates,[156] they are usually rendered in BH by ܐܓܘܢܐ and its cognates, but in 5.5.13 = 91b18 (πολιτικοὶ) ἀγῶνες is rendered by ܡܬܟܬܫ̈ܢܐ, and in 2.2.3 = 61a4 and b21 (δύναμις) ἀγωνιστική by ܬܟܬܘܫܐ and ܬܟܬܘܫܢܐ. Taking a term with a related meaning but not passing into Syriac as a loanword, ἀμφισβητεῖν and its cognates are rendered by forms of ܚܪܐ in 6.3.3 = 94b27, 6.5.4 = 98b1, and 7.9.9 = 17b22, but by forms of ܕܘܢ or ܚܪܝܢܐ in 4.6.4 = 76a24, 4.6.5 = 76b2, 5.2.3 = 82a18, 5.5.13 = 91b13, 6.5.10 = 99b31, and 6.5.11 = 00a15. Bar Hebraeus' paraphrase therefore gives us an indication as to what is likely to have been the terminology of ARsyr in general, without necessarily pointing unambiguously to what was employed in a particular passage.

[156] Cf. above, n. 152.

## OUTLINE: CHAPTER AND SECTION TITLES

Both Ibn Sīnā and Bar Hebraeus adhere to the flow of text in Aristotle's *Rhetoric*. Apart from Ibn Sīnā's independent elaboration (IS 1) of *Rhetoric* 1.1-2 followed in BH 1.1-7, and the repetition of 67b28-68a10 at 16b29 in (ARsyr and) ARar, the sequence of ideas in Bar Hebraeus' *Book of Rhetoric* will therefore not cause any surprise to the reader familiar with Aristotle's treatise. Ibn Sīnā and Bar Hebraeus, however, both introduced divisions and divisional titles, which serve as a useful pointer to their interpretation of the text which lay before them. Many of Bar Hebraeus' titles are taken from Ibn Sīnā and are not therefore original, but Bar Hebraeus only took over (or suitably adapted) that with which he agreed, and also introduced divisions and titles additional to that which he found in Ibn Sīnā. An overview of Bar Hebraeus' titles thus offers a general insight into his understanding of the method and subject matter of Aristotelian rhetoric, and may be found useful together with the broad structural divisions outlined above[157] and the detailed concordance below of passages in the three texts.[158]

### CHAPTER ONE
### ON THE INTRODUCTION

1. On the Usefulness of Rhetoric
2. On the Fact that Rhetoric has an Inner Pillar and Outer Aids
3. On the Points which are Particular to Orators and their Nature
4. On the Commonalities and Differences of Rhetoric and other Arts
5. On the Definition of Rhetoric and the Kinds of *Pisteis*
6. On the Pillar or Verification and its Divisions
7. On Necessity and Rhetorical Possibles
8. On the Fact that the Principal Species of Rhetoric are Three

[157] Cf. above, p. 20.

[158] Cf. the Concordance of Passages at the end of the volume.

## CHAPTER TWO
## ON THE DELIBERATIVE SPECIES OF RHETORIC

1. On Deliberations on Great Subjects
2. On Deliberations on Private Subjects
3. On Things which are Expedient
4. On the Greater and the Lesser

## CHAPTER THREE
## ON THE DEMONSTRATIVE SPECIES OF RHETORIC

1. On the Species of Virtue and Vice
2. On the Causes and Signs of Virtue
3. On Tropical Praises
4. On the Partnership of Praise with Advice

## CHAPTER FOUR
## ON THE JUDICIAL SPECIES OF RHETORIC

1. On the Definition of Injustice, the Cause of Accusation and Defence
2. On the Division of Actions to which Injustice Adheres
3. On the Causes of the Pleasure (which is) the Cause of Injustice
4. On the Reasons why Someone Does Wrong Readily
5. On the Magnitude of Wrongdoing and its Triviality According to the Law
6. On the *Pisteis* which Do not Come by Art

## CHAPTER FIVE
## ON CHARACTER AND PASSIONS OF THE SOUL

1. On the Inducement of a Judge and the Kinds of Scorning, the Cause of Anger
2. On the Species of Friendship, Fear, and Confidence
3. On Shame, Shamelessness, and Kindness
4. On Pity, Envy, Indignation, Emulation, and Contempt

5. On the Diversity of People in Character

CHAPTER SIX
ON SUBJECTS WHICH ARE COMMON TO ALL THREE RHETORICAL SPECIES

1. On the Possible and Impossible, Past and Future, and Amplification and Diminution
2. On Rhetorical Paradigms
3. On the Rhetorical Maxim
4. On the Difference between Rhetorical and Dialectical Premisses
5. On the Species of Enthymeme
6. On Slanted Enthymemes Accepted or Rejected in Rhetoric
7. On *Enstasis*

CHAPTER SEVEN
ON RHETORICAL WORDS AND THEIR ARRANGEMENTS

1. On Delivery
2. On Metaphor and Transference of Speech
3. On the Inelegant Words called Frigidities
4. On the Beauty of Rhetorical Speech
5. On What is Appropriate for Poetry and Inappropriate for Rhetoric
6. On the Metre of Rhetorical Speech
7. On Pleasantness of Style
8. On Retorts which are Comely in Utterances and Retorts which are Comely in Letters
9. On the Parts of a Rhetorical Speech and their Arrangement in the Three Species
10. On Rhetorical Interrogation and its Correct Manner, and on Response

# SIGLA

| | |
|---|---|
| F | Laur. Or. 69, 1340 A.D. |
| L | Lond. Or. 4079, 1809 A.D. |
| V | Vat. Syr. 604, 1826 A.D. or 1886 A.D. |
| R | Rylands Syr. 604, 1887 A.D. |
| l | Lond. Or. 9380, 1892 A.D. |

| | |
|---|---|
| add. | add(s) |
| om. | omits(s) |
| trp. | transpose(s) |
| rep. | repetition |
| sg. | singular |
| pl. | plural |
| i. | initial letter |
| f. | final letter |
| codd. | codices (FLVRl) |

# TEXT AND TRANSLATION

ܟܬܒܐ ܕܕܝܠܓܘܣܐ
ܕܐܝܬܘܗܝ، ܬܡܚܝܢܐ ܕܡܠܠܘܬܐ
ܡܢ ܟܬܒܐ ܕܚܐܘܬ ܚܡܫܡܝܬܐ[1]
ܘܗܘ ܐܝܬ ܩܦ̈ܠܐܐ ܫܒܥܐ

ܩܦܠܐܘܢ ܩܕܡܝܐ
ܡܛܠ ܦܪܘܬܐܘܪܝܐ
ܘܗܘ ܐܝܬ ܦܣܘ̈ܩܐ ܬܡܢܝܐ

ܦܣܘܩܐ ܩܕܡܝܐ
ܡܛܠ ܝܘܬܪܗ ܕܦܝܠܣܘܦܘܬܐ
ܬܠܬ ܦܐܪ̈ܘܬܐ

ܡܕܝܢܬܐ. ܝܕ̈ܥܬܐ ܥܠ ܗܝܡܢܘܬܐ ܐܝܟܢܐ ܕܡܕܡ ܐܬܝܗܘ، ܐܡܪܬ ܡܢ ܚܕܐ ܐܝܬܝܗܝܢ. ܒܐܡܪܬ ܣܛܪ ܡܢ ܦܝܠܘܣܘܦܝܐ. ܘܐܝܬܝܗ، ܬܘܒ ܕܦܝܠܘܣܘܦܝܐ ܠܡܕܥܐ ܦܘܫܩܗ. ܠܐ ܠܡܦܩܐ ܝܘܬܪܗ ܡܬܝܠܦܐ.[1] ܘܒܦܝܠܘܣܘܦܝܐ ܒܝܕ ܝܬܝܪ ܚܟ̈ܝܡܐ. ܘܐܡܪܬܘܗܝ[2] ܐܦ ܒܚܟ̈ܝܡܐ ܒܗ، ܕܒܚܟܡܬܐ ܕܐܦܘܕܝܩܛܝܩܐ ܐܦܢ ܚܠܝܐ ܘܪܒܝܒܐ. ܐܠܐ ܒܚܟܡܬܐ ܕܚܟ̈ܝܡܐ ܚܠܝܬܐ ܘܐܡܘܢܝܐ ܘܡܫܡܥܐ. ܚܝܠܐ ܡܕܝܢ ܗܘ ܕܠܚܟ̈ܝܡܐ ܡܦܝܣ. ܘܠܡܗܝܡܢܘ ܗܘ ܡܢܐ ܕܗܠܝܢ ܕܢܐܡܝܢ ܢܟܝܢ. ܠܗ ܗ̇ܘ ܗܘ ܗ̣ܘ ܕܒܡ ܚܝܠܗ ܡܬܚܟܡ ܘܒܦܣܘܩܐ ܠܡܕܥܬܗ ܡܚܟܡ ܘܐܡܬܝܗ، ܗ̇ܘ ܪܗܛܘܪܐ.[3]

ܕܬܬܠܡܝܢ. ܡܛܠ ܓܒܪ ܕܒܢ ܚܝܠܐ ܒܪܢܫܐ ܗܘ. ܘܟܠ ܒܪܢܫܐ ܐܘ ܡܝܘܕܥܬ ܐܘ ܡܕܝܢܬ. ܝܘܕܥܬܐ ܕܝܢ ܐܠܐ ܒܐܦܘܕܝܩܛܝܩܐ ܠܐ ܡܬܗܝܡܢ. ܗܕܝܢܬܐ ܕܝܢ ܐܠܐ ܒܪܗܛܘܪܝܩܐ ܠܐ ܡܬܗܝܡܢ. ܐܘܣ̈ܝܢܬܐ ܡܕܝܢ ܕܠܘܬ ܗܝܡܢܘܬܐ ܢܩܫܝܢ ܗܠܝܢ ܬܬܠܡܝ ܐܝܟ. ܘܕܐܦܘܕܝܩܛܝܩܐ ܠܘܬ ܐܘܪܬܐ ܕܐܡܪܬܐ ܡܬܝܪܐ. ܘܗܝܡܢܘܬܐ ܐܝܟ ܕܒܓܒܪܐ ܒܕܝ ܡܫܝܚܐ. ܐܠܐ ܓܝܪ ܥܠ ܗܝܡܢܘܬܐ ܬܪܝܨܬܐ ܗܘ ܣܦܩܬ. ܠܬܪ̈ܝܢܗܘܢ ܐܦܘܕܝܩܛܝܩܐ ܠܐ ܙܪܝܬ. ܘܟܠ ܥܠܡܘܬܗ ܕܦܫܝܛܐ ܕܗܝܡܢܘܬܐ ܕܗܝܡܢܗ ܠܐ ܗܦܟܬ.

---

Titulus [1] pl. RLl
1 [1] om. RVLl [2] add. ܡܬܚܟܡܐ RLl; add. ܡܬܚܟܡܝܢ V [3] ܪܗܛܘܪܐ F

# THE BOOK OF RHETORIC
# BEING THE EIGHTH (TREATISE OF) LOGIC
# FROM THE BOOK OF THE CREAM OF WISDOM
# SEVEN CHAPTERS

## CHAPTER ONE
## ON THE INTRODUCTION
## EIGHT SECTIONS

### SECTION ONE
### On the Usefulness of Rhetoric
### Three Theories

ONE.[1] The sciences concerned with *pistis*, as was previously demonstrated, are four out of the five—that is, without poetics. It was also shown that sophistic is taught to repel its (own) damage, not increase its usefulness. In dialectic the wise have less profit, and likewise the populace, because although in comparison to apodeixis (dialectic) is feeble and defective, nevertheless in comparison to (the capacity of) the populace it is overpowering, technical, and hard. Therefore the address which persuades the populace, and leads it to have *pistis* in that in which it ought to have *pistis*, is that which is adjusted to its capacity, (which it) is able to comprehend with ease, and (that) is rhetorical.

TWO.[2] Because the addressee is a man, and every man is either learned or unlearned, (and) the learned has *pistis* only through apodeixis, the unlearned only through rhetoric, the arts which are useful for *pistis* are therefore these two. Dialectic helps towards a speaker's victory (in debate), but *pistis*, maybe, is only gained (through it) by chance. For if (dialectic) were concerned about genuine *pistis*, it would not establish two opposites, but for the sake

[1] **1.1.1** IS 1.1 (1.5-2.13).
[2] **1.1.2** IS 1.1 (2.14-3.11).

ܕܬܠܬ. ܬܠܬܐ ܐܢܘܢ ܠܘܩܒܠ ܠܡܘܬܐ ܐܢܫܐ. ܒܠܝܐ[1] ܕܫܒܝܚܬܐ ܗܢܘܢ ܕܠܡܐܡܪܐ[2] ܐܠܗܝܐ ܘܡܘܒܠܐ ܒܠܫܢ ܡܬܪܒܝܢ. ܡܛܠܬܐ ܕܗܢܘܢ ܕܒܬܚܘܡܐ ܬܚܝܬܐ ܕܒܫܡܝܐ ܠܚܘܒܐ ܠܐ ܡܫܟܚܝܢ ܘܠܪܘܡܐ ܕܕܪܓ ܡܕܒܪܬܐ ܠܡܬܬܠܝܘ ܠܐ ܡܫܟܚܝܢ ܘܡܩܒܠܝܢ[3] ܠܒܢܝܐ ܡܫܬܡܠܝܢ. ܘܬܢܝܬܐ ܕܒܬܚܬܝܐ ܗܢܘܢ ܕܒܬܘܪܓܡܐ[4] ܡܦܫܩܢܐ ܡܬܒܪܝܢ. ܘܡܛܠ ܕܬܪܝܗܘܢ ܠܘܩܒܠ ܡܕܒܪܢܐ ܘܬܪܝܢܐ ܕܗܘܝܢ ܡܫܝܚܐ ܐܢܘܢ. ܘܡܢ ܗܢܐ ܬܠܝܬܝܐ ܒܡܥܒܕܐ ܡܠܐ ܒܠܥܕܐ. ܢܗܘܬܪ ܦܪܘܣܐ ܐܝܪܐ ܢܦܠ ܡܢ ܕܐܦܘܕܝܩܛܝܩܐ ܘܕܠܝܩܛܝܩܐ ܚܕܐ ܘܬܪܬܝܢ.

ܦܣܘܩܐ ܬܪܝܢܐ

ܡܛܠܗ̇ ܕܕܝܠܩܛܝܩܐ ܒܡܘܕܐ ܐܝܬ ܠܗܘܢ ܘܡܚܕܕܢܐ ܒܪܝܐ
ܬܘܪܐܣ ܐܪܒ

ܡܕܝܢܬܐ. ܡܫܘܬܦ ܓܝܪ ܕܕܝܠܩܛܝܩܐ ܘܪܝܛܘܪܝܩܐ ܒܗ̇ ܕܒܠܚܘܕܐ ܡܢܗܘܢ ܘܒܗܬܐ ܒܒܢܝܐ ܒܒܝܢܬܐ. ܗ̇ ܓܝܪ ܒܡܠܝܬܐ[1] ܗܕܐ ܕܝܢ ܒܥܘܦܪܐ. ܘܒܗ̇ ܬܘܒ ܕܠܝܬ ܘܠܐ ܚܕܐ ܡܢܗܘܢ ܗ̇ܘ ܕܫܝܡ ܕܠܝܕܐ. ܐܠܐ ܒܟܠ ܓܒܘ ܕܝܠܝܗ̇ ܚܐܦܐ ܢܫܩܝ ܡܬܟܠܠܝܢ. ܦܪܫܝܢ[2] ܕܝܢ ܒܗ̇، *ܕܥܘܪܝܐ ܕܬܪܬܝܗܘܢ[3] ܐܚܝܕܐ. ܐܦ ܡܐܡܪܐ ܐܢܘܢ ܠܒܢܝܐ. ܒܪܡ ܠܒܢܝ ܕܕܝܠܩܛܝܩܐ ܫܬܝܬܐ ܐܢܘܢ. ܘܕܪܝܛܘܪܝܩܐ ܡܫܬܒܪܢܐ.

ܕܬܪܬܝܢ. ܒܐܘܡܢܘܬܐ ܓܝܪ ܗܕܐ ܒܠܚܘܕ ܡܬܚܫܒ. ܒܗ ܒܠܚܘܕ ܗ̇ܘܝܐ ܕܒܡܠܘܫ ܘܒܓܢܐ. ܘܒܡܦܪܓ ܘܒܦܘܩ ܪܘܚܐ. ܘܒܠܒܠ ܘܒܫܓܘܪ. ܒܗ ܐܚܝܕ ܓܝܪ ܒܐܟܡܐ ܕܒܗ ܒܚܕܐ ܗܘܢܝܢ ܗܠܝܢ. ܒܠܚܕ ܡܕܒܬܐ ܕܡܘܩܕܐ ܒܠܚܝܐ. ܘܒܠܗܕܐ ܒܠܚܘܕ ܗ̇ܘ ܡܢܐ ܕܗܘܢܝܢ ܠܐ ܡܕܒܝܢ. ܐܚܝܕ ܕܝܢ ܐܘܡܢܘܬܐ ܒܡܕܒܬܐ ܕܡܘܩܕܐ. ܐܚܪܢܐ ܕܝܢ ܗܘܡܐܝܬ ܠܐ ܒܚܕܐ ܐܦܠܐ ܒܡܕܒܬܐ. ܘܐܝܟܢܐ ܕܒܗ ܐܟܡܐ ܒܡܕܒܬܐ ܐܘܡܢܘܬܐ ܬܘܒ ܦܟܐ. ܗܘܢܘ ܕܡܫܠܡ ܒܡܕܒܬܐ ܗܕܐ ܕܠܗܘܢܐ. ܘܐܟܡܐ ܒܡܕܒܬܐ ܒܠܚܘܕܗ̇. ܐܦ ܡܡܪܐ. ܐܠܐ ܠܐ ܠܒܢܐܝܬ.

3 [1] ܠܒܠܝܐ RVLl [2] om. RVLl [3] i. ܕ RVL [4] ܕܒܬܘܪܓܡܐ F
1 [1] i. add. ܕ RVLl [2] ܦܪܝܫܝܢ F [3*] ܕܥܘܪܝܐ RVL

of delivering a reply it is not concerned with the foundation of its argument.

THREE.[3] There are three orders of human beings: the highest (one) of the wise who assent only to premisses whose acceptance is necessary; the middle (one) of those who refuse to be in the lowest rank of the populace but are not able to rise to the height of the grade of the knowledgeable and (who) benefit by reputable arguments; and the lowest (one) of the populace who are helped by persuasive expositions. Because two of the orders, the first and the second, are small in number, but the world is full to the brim with the third, the utility of rhetoric, therefore, more than apodeixis or dialectic, is general and abundant.

## SECTION TWO
### On the Fact that Rhetoric has an Inner Pillar and Outer Aids
### Four Theories

ONE.[4] Dialectic and rhetoric are associated (both) because each of them seeks a victory in parley, the former by compulsion, the latter by complaisance, and because neither of them has a special subject, but speak on anything to which they take a desire. At the same time they are separate, because the starting points of the two of them (are separate). Although the premisses (of both) are reputable, the reputable (premisses) of dialectic are true, but (those) of rhetoric are based on opinion.

TWO.[5] Everyone may make use of this art, for everyone seeks to praise or blame, accuse or defend, and persuade or dissuade. Because some do these things by habit which they have acquired by familiarity, without knowledge of the universal rules, they do not understand the cause of what they do. Some (however do it) by art with knowledge of the rules, (yet) others (do it) vainly, neither by familiarity nor by knowledge. The one who is successful in this

---

[3] **1.1.3** IS 1.1 (3.12-16; 5.8-14; 6.8).
[4] **1.2.1** AR 1.1.54a1-3; IS 1.2 (6.11-7.12).
[5] **1.2.2** AR 1.1.54a3-11; IS 1.2 (7.16-8.8).

ܕܬܠܬ. ܐܡܪ ܓܝܪ ܐܢܐ. ܕܩܕ̈ܝܫܐ[1] ܠܟ ܗܘܘ ܕܐܘܡܢܘܬ ܟ̈ܠܗ ܐܚܪܢܐ
ܐܟܡܐ ܚܕܝܘܬܐ ܟܠܝܘܡ. ܡܢ ܗܘܘ ܘܦܝܠܣܘܦܐ[2] ܕܐܟܡܐ ܐܘܡܢܘܬܐ ܠܐ
ܕܒܢܝܢ ܐܬܒܪܝܘ ܗܘܐ ܠܗܘܢ. ܘܒܠܗܘܕܐ ܠܥܒܕܐ ܒܠܝܘܡ. ܕܠܒܪ ܡܢ
ܕܡܢܝܢ̇ ܕܗܝܘܠܝܘܬܐ ܐܬܘܪܝܣܐ ܒܒܢܝܢ. ܠܗܕܐ ܓܝܪ ܒܡܢܝܢܐ ܐܝܬ
ܕܟܠܗܘܢ، ܗܡܢܝܢ ܒܢܝܢ̇[3] ܘܡܕܒܪܢܐ ܒܪܝܐ. ܒܡܢܝܢܐ ܡܢ ܐܝܬܝܗܘܢ،
ܡܐܡܪܐ ܕܒܢܝܗ ܘܠܗ ܡܫܬܟܚ ܕܡܒܢܝܢ ܠܒܢܝܢܬܐ. ܘܒܢܝܢܐ ܐܚܪܢܐ.
ܡܐܡܪܐ[4] ܕܒܗ ܗܘܐ ܡܢܝܢܘܬܐ ܡܫܬܟܚܢܐܝܬ. ܡܕܒܪܢܐ ܕܝܢ
ܐܝܬܝܗܘܢ ܐܝܟ ܚ̈ܝܠܐ ܢܦܫܢ̈ܝܐ. ܡܪܢܝܢܘܬܐ ܒܢܝܬ ܘܪܡܐ ܘܦܠܓܐ.
ܐܝܟ ܡܕܒܪܢܘܬ ܡܒܠܠܐ ܒܥܘܪܐ ܘܬܘܒܢܐ ܒܡܦܠܓܘܬܐ ܘܫܘܬܦܘܬܐ
ܒܥܠܡܐ. ܘܡܫܬܡܠܝܢܘܬܗ ܕܗܝܘܠܐ ܒܐܣܟܡܐ ܡܫܡܠܝܐ. ܘܥܡܪܐ
ܐܚܪܢܐ ܕܠܐ ܠܝܬ ܗܡܢܝܘܬܐ ܐܠܐ ܠܝܘܠܦܢܘܬ ܫܡܥ̈ܐ ܡܬܬܬܝܢ.

ܐܡܪܢ. ܐܠܘ ܟܠܗܘܢ[1] ܗܝܘܠܐ ܒܟܠܗܝܢ ܡܕ̈ܝܢܬܐ ܠܡܕܒܪܢܐ ܒܪܝܐ
ܐܫܠܝܘ ܘܒܡܒܘܕܐ ܒܠܝܘܡ. ܐܬܚܝܘ.[2] ܐܟܡܐ ܕܒܝܘܡ ܣܒ̈ܝܢܬܐ ܡܢ
ܡܕ̈ܝܢܬܐ ܒܝܘܡܗ ܕܝܘܡ. ܗܢܘ ܗܘܐ ܒܡܠܠܐ ܕܗܝܘܠܐ ܩܕ̈ܝܫܐ. ܠܐ ܕܝܢ
ܗܝܘܠܐ. ܐܠܐ ܒܝܘܡ ܡܢ ܐܬܪ̈ܘܬܐ. ܐܟܡܐ ܕܒܡܘܬ ܕܐܝܟ ܕܐܪܝܣܛܘ
ܦܠܛܘܢ ܒܐܬܚܝܘܬܗ. ܘܟܠ ܡܐܡܪܐ ܡܦܫܝܐ. ܒܡܢܝܢܐ ܠܓܘܐ.
ܘܡܕܒܪܢܐ ܒܪܝܐ ܡܬܚܫܚܝܢ ܗܘܘ. ܘܒܗܘܢ ܘܡܕܒܪܢܝܗܘܢ ܠܐ ܗܘܐ
ܒܡܫܡܠܝܘܬ ܐܠܐ ܬܪܝܨܐܝܬ ܡܬܦܪܫܝܢ ܗܘܘ.

ܦܣܘܩܐ ܬܠܝܬܝܐ
ܡܛܠ ܒ̈ܢܝܐ ܕܕܝܠܝܢ ܠܗ̈ܝܘܠܐ[1] ܘܐܡܝܢܘܬܗܘܢ
ܬܐܘܪܝܡܐ ܚܕ

ܡܕܡܝܢܘܬܐ. ܟܠ ܗܝܘܠܐ ܕܒܥܪܒܐ ܡܬܬܠܝܐ ܡܛܠܠ ܗܢܘܢ ܗܘ ܕܢܣܒܐ
ܠܡܩܒܠܢܐ ܕܐܝܬܘܗܝ، ܐܘ ܠܐ ܐܝܬܘܗܝ. ܒܐܝܢܐ ܕܗܐܡ ܐܘ ܕܒܛܪ ܐܘ
ܕܒܬܪ. ܕܒܐܝܢ ܕܝܢ ܐܘ ܒܟܠ ܐܘ ܡܫܬܪ̈ܝܢ ܐܘ ܡܫܟܚܢ ܐܘ ܡܛܠ ܐܘ
ܥܒܕ. ܒܗܢ ܡܢ ܐܝܟܢܐ ܠܗ. ܒܗܢ ܕܝܢ ܠܐ. ܐܝܟܢܐ ܓܝܪ ܕܗܐܡ ܢܬܗܦܟܐ
ܕܪܪ ܒܐܝܟܢܘܬ ܡܕܡ ܐܘ ܒܠܘܬܗ. ܠܗ ܢܦܩ ܗܝܘܠܐ. ܘܐܝܟܢܐ[1] ܕܠܐ ܫܘ.
ܠܕܝܢܐ ܢܒܥܘܢ[2] ܥܘܪܪܗ. ܘܐܢ ܘܢܣܒ ܕܝܢܐ. ܗܢܝܢ ܐܝܟܢܐ *ܠܬܪ̈ܝܗܘܢ
ܡܬܒܪ̈ܝܢܐ[3] ܕܡܕܡܗ، ܢܚܘܢ ܘܐܝܟܢܐ ܕܦܫܛܐ ܚܕܐ ܠܗ ܒܗܝܘܠܘܬܗ
ܢܦܩ ܕܒܘܬܐ.

3 [1] i. add. ܕ RVLl [2] pl. F [3] om. F [4] add. ܗܘ̇ RVLl
4 [1] om. RVLl [2] f. om. RVLl
Titulus [1] sg. RVL
1 [1] ܘܐܝܟܢܐ RVL; ܘܐܡܟܐ l [2] ܢܒܥܘܢ F [3]* ܠܡܬܒܪ̈ܝܢܐ F

branch of logic is he who along with the familiar habit also possesses the artistic habit. The familiar habit by itself, even if it succeeds, does not (do so) confidently.

THREE.[6] Our master said that the predecessors who had composed the art of speeches possessed only the familiar habit, and the type of the artistic habit had still not been explored by them. They therefore constructed theories only for matters outside the pillar of rhetoric, for it has a pillar on which its building depends, and outer aids. The pillar is discourse, by which by itself (one should) opine to conclude with the desired (result); or (to put it) in another way, discourse through which *pistis* comes about in the manner of opinion. Aids are, for example, passions of the soul like slander, compassion and anger; preface at the beginning, narrative in the middle and epilogue at the end; the dressing up of an orator in an acceptable outward appearance; and other matters which have nothing to do with *pistis* but which are brought (to bear) for the inducement of the audience.

FOUR.[7] If all orators in all cities had rejected the outer aids and only employed the pillar, as in some cities in the time of our master, the work of those predecessors would have been pointless; but it was not so. However in some places, as in the court of Areopagus at Athens, both every persuasive discourse—the inner pillar—and outer aid were used, and by them their affairs were administered not crookedly, but justly.

## SECTION THREE
### On the Points which are Particular to Orators and their Nature
### Seven Theories

ONE.[8] Every orator who speaks about particular matters needs to show whether a thing is or is not, in the present, past or future; but (to show) that it is just or unjust, advantageous or harmful, honourable or disgraceful, is sometimes necessary for him, but sometimes not. For where the lawmaker has established the justice or injustice

[6] **1.2.3** AR 1.1 54a11-18; IS 1.2 (8.9-15; 12.5-14).
[7] **1.2.4** AR 1.1 54a18-26; IS 1.2 (12.15-13.6).
[8] **1.3.1** AR 1.1 54a26-31; IS 1.3 (13.9-14.9).

ܕܬܪ̈ܬܝܢ. ܚܕܐ ܐܢܫ ܗܘܐ ܒܡ̈ܠܝܟܐ ܠܒܗܘܢ ܕܒܐܢܘܬ ܡܕܡ ܘܠܐ ܒܐܢܘܬܗ ܠܕܝܢܐ ܡܫܬܟܚ[1] ܠܡܦܩܘ. ܘܢܘܬܪܗ ܘܫܘܠܛܢܗ ܠܗܪܟܐ. ܘܫܪ̈ܟܐ ܒܗܘܢܐ ܕܒܢܐ ܕ̈ܒܢܝܢ ܠܦ̈ܘܩܕܢܐ ܐܢܘܢ. ܒܗ̇ܝ ܕܐܘ ܡܡܠܠܘܬܗܘܢ[2] ܕܠܘܬ ܡܘܬܪܐ ܘܡܘܠܟܢܐ ܕܙܠܝܩ ܠܟܠܢܐ. ܐܘ ܡܡܠܠܘܬܗܘܢ ܕܠܘܬ ܡܘܬܪܐ ܘܡܘܠܟܢܐ ܕܒܫܝܢ ܒܫܢܐ. *ܐܘ ܡܡܠܠܘܬܗܘܢ ܕܠܘܬ ܡܘܬܪܐ ܘܡܘܠܟܢܐ ܕܙܠܝܩ ܒܫܢܐ[3]. ܐܘ ܡܡܠܠܘܬܗܘܢ ܕܠܘܬ ܡܘܬܪܐ ܘܡܘܠܟܢܐ ܕܒܫܝܢ ܠܟܠܢܐ. ܘܒܦܠܣܘܦܐ ܡܕܡܝܐ ܕܐܝܬܘܗܝ, ܐܘ ܠܐ ܐܝܬܘܗܝ, ܡܕܡ ܒܠܚܘܕ ܐܠܝܨܐ ܠܗܪܟܐ ܕܢܫܘܐ. ܘܒܬܠܬܐ ܐܝܬ̈ܝܐ ܒܗ̇ ܗ̇ܝ ܕܐܝܬܝܗܘܢ ܐܘ ܠܐ ܐܝܬܝܗܘܢ ܠܗ̇ܘ ܕܒܥܐ ܒܗܘܢ ܣܢܝܩ ܗܘ ܠܡܬܠܠ. ܘܠܕܝܢܐ ܦܫܪ ܡܢ ܕܢܗܘܐ ܥܒܘܪܗ ܐܘ ܥܒܘܪܗ ܕܒܠܒܘܗ ܘܠܐ ܣܢܝܐ[4] ܐܝܬ ܕܢܗܘܐ.

ܕܬܠܬ. ܡܕܒܪ̈ܢܐ ܒܢ̈ܝܐ ܒܫܪ̈ܟܐ ܡܬܬܐܝܐ ܒܠܚܘܕ ܡܬܝܬܝܢ. ܘܡܫܪܪܐ ܕܦܣܩܐ ܒܠܒܢܐ ܢܦܘܩ ܕܦܩܬ ܥܡܘܕܐ ܒܠܒܝܐ ܡܦܣܩܢܐ ܠܐ ܡܗܘܝܐ. ܒܕ ܡܢ ܣܓܝ̈ܐ ܢܦܝ̈ܫܝܢ ܐܢܫܝܢ ܕܠܒܠܐ ܒܠܚܘܕ ܡܬܬܚܕܒܝܢ. ܠܦܣܩܐ ܡܕܝܢ ܒܠܒܢܐ ܦܐܡ ܢܦܘܫܐ ܢܒܢܐ ܐܘ ܡܒܝܢܒܐ ܦܠܐ ܕܢܡܕܘܡ ܢܣܒܐ ܘܬܢܝܡ[1] ܘܠܕܘܟܪܢܐ ܡܬ̈ܠܐ ܒܡܢ̈ܝܢܐ ܒܠܒܢܐ ܕܢܒܐ ܢܦܘܫ. ܒܗ̇ܝ ܕܐܡܒܕܐ ܕܕܢ̈ܝܐ ܠܡܘܡܝܬ ܢܦܘܫܐ ܠܐ ܦܩܘܦܢ. ܐܦܠܐ ܦܩܝܪ ܢܦܘܫܐ ܠܡܦܩܘܒ ܥܪ̈ܒܐ ܡܬܬܠܐ ܕܠܐ ܦܘܦ ܦܩܘܦܢ.

ܕܐܪܒܥ. ܬܠܬܐ ܐܢܐ ܐܝܬܝܗܘܢ ܢܬܪܐ. ܡܕܡܝܐ ܗ̇ܝ ܕܐܝܬܘܗܝ, ܡܕܡ ܐܘ ܠܐ ܐܝܬܘܗܝ. ܬܪܝܢܐ ܕܝܢ ܦܣܩܐ ܒܠܒܢܐ. ܘܬܠܝܬܝܐ ܕܒܪܐ ܡܬܬܠܐ ܒܡܘܢܐ ܒܠܒܢܐ. ܘܡܛܠ ܕܒܡܕܡܝܐ ܒܠܒܢܐ ܒܥܪܝܢ[1] ܦܘܪܫܐ ܡܦܣܩܢܐ ܐܝܟ ܦܘܪܘܫܝܗܘܢ ܘܬܘܪ̈ܝܐ ܘܥܪܒܐ[2] ܕܢܬܦܩ ܥܩܡܒܐ. ܕܗܪܟܐ ܕܠܗܘܢ ܒܠܒܘܕܢܗܘܢ ܣܓܝܦܝܢ ܒܗܘ ܕܡܦܒܪܐ ܒܡܠܠܐ ܡܬܝܚܝܢ ܘܠܐ ܡܕܡ ܐܢܫܝܢ ܡܬܬܠܟܝܢ ܦܫܪ ܡܢ ܗ̇ܝ, ܕܠܕܝܢܐ ܠܡܘܣܒܘ ܦܣܩܘܢܐ ܡܪܒܝܢ[3]. ܘܡܫܝܢ ܡܫܠܘܬܐ ܒܡܕܡܝܐ ܐܘܡܢܘܬ ܡܬܪܢܘܬܐ ܒܠܒܢܐ ܡܫܬܠܚܐ. ܕܡܒܢܐ ܕܝܢ ܐܝܬܝܗ̇ ܡܢܐ ܒܐܢܠܘܓܝܣܡܐ[4] ܠܦܬ. ܘܗܪܟܐ ܬܘܒ ܒܬܪ ܦܠܝܠ ܢܠܦ ܐܢܫ.

2 [1] add. ܗ̇ܘܝ RVLl [2] ܗܬ- F [3*] om. F [4] ܣܢܝ RVLl
3 [1] ܐܘ ܢܬܝܡ RVLl
4 [1] ܒܥܪܝܢ F [2] i. ܕ F [3] ܡܪܒܝܢ F [4] ܒܐܢܠܘܓܝܣܡܐ RL; ܒܐܢܘܠܓܝܣܡܐ

of something, the orator should agree, and where he has not shown (it), leave its establishment to the judge. But if a ruling is lacking, then it is necessary for both of the contenders to dispute before him, and he who persuades him by his oratory gains the victory.

TWO.[9] The custom prevailed in all climes that the justice or injustice of something were left to the judge to decide, but its advantage or harm to the orator. In this way, matters are of four types: because either their effectuation of evident advantage or harm is evident; or their effectuation of hidden advantage or harm is hidden; or their effectuation of evident advantage or harm is hidden; or their effectuation of hidden advantage or harm is evident. In the first type it is only necessary for the orator to show that something is or is not, but in the other three, together with the fact that (things) are or are not, he must succeed in revealing what is hidden in them. For the judge there is no other duty apart from declaring that he or his opponent has established his (case).

THREE.[10] Outer aids are only advantageous in particular matters, and the inducement of the audience by persuasive techniques is not beneficial in the establishment of universal decisions, because only some few individuals are affected by the passions of the soul. Therefore it is fitting that a lawmaker, prophet or wise man should preconsider and define the universal decisions, but a judge should administer particular customs according to the universal rules; because just as judges are not fit for legislation, neither are lawmakers able to cover the unlimited particular cases.

FOUR.[11] The points are therefore three. First, that something is or is not; second, the universal decision; and third, the particular custom within the universal rule. Because persuasive devices like proemium, narrations, and other enticements of the audience are of use only in the first, orators who pay attention only to them are bringing together in words the outside of the subject and gaining nothing other than inclining the judge to have *pistis* in their argument, but the acquisition of *pistis* is to be expected only through the pillar or en-

---

[9] **1.3.2** AR 1.1 54a31-b4; IS 1.3 (14.9-15.15).
[10] **1.3.3** AR 1.1 54b5-16; IS 1.3 (16.8-17.9).
[11] **1.3.4** AR 1.1 54b16-22; IS 1.3 (17.10-18.6).

ܕܝܨܒ. ܒܗ ܡܬܝܚܕܢܘܬܐ ܐܝܬܘܗܝ ܒܚܕܘܕܐ. ܐܠܗܐ ܕܗܘ، ܒܗ ܗܘ، ܬܗܘܐ ܡܬܕܘܣ ܕܪܗܛܘܪܘܬܐ. ܐܘܟܝܬ ܦܫܝܛܘܬܗ ܒܡܪ̈ܟܒܐ ܬܘܟ̈ܒ ܬܘܪܓܡܐ. ܡܦܫܩܢܐ ܐܝܟ ܡܠܦ̈ܢܐ ܕܓܪܘܓܐ ܘܫܘܓܪܐ[1] ܘܢܝܫ̈ܐ[2] ܕܛܘܓܪܐ ܘܡܦܩ ܒܪܘܫܐ. ܒܕܒܠ[3] ܡܬܝܚܕܢܘܬܐ ܡܫܬܡܫܝܢ ܠܗܘܢ. ܘܦܘܪܫܐ ܢܓܘ̈ܕܐ ܒܟܡܝܘܬܐ ܠܐ ܬܘܪܓܡܢܘܬܐ *ܕܡܫܡܥܐ ܘܡܬܠܐ[4] ܒܒܪ ܒܕܝܢ. ܒܕܡܝ̈ܘܬܐ ܗܢܝܢ ܕܒܫܪ̈ܒܐ ܗܠܠܝܢܝܣܘܬܐ ܕܗܘܝܢ ܒܝܬ ܒܒܠܐ ܕܡܕܝܢܬܐ ܠܒܒܠܐ ܕܐܣܛܪܬܐ ܐܘ ܒܢ̈ܝܢ ܕܝܢ̈ܐ ܕܣܕܐ ܡܕܝܢܬܐ ܒܗ ܡܢ ܗ̇، ܕܒܦܘܪܫܐ ܢܬܬ̈ܠܠܝܢ ܒܢ̈ܝܐ ܪ̈ܒܝܢ ܘܡܠܠ̈ܝܢ. ܒܬܘܪܓܡܐ ܒܠܫܢܐ ܡܫܬ̈ܪܝܢ. ܘܦܘܪܫܐ ܒܢ̈ܝܐ ܡܬܕܪܐ ܐܝܟ. ܒܬܪܝܨܘܬ[5] ܡܬܠܠܐ ܒܪ ܥܦܪܐ ܡܬܝܚܕܢܘܬܐ ܘܡܬܪܘܪܒ ܫܪܒܐ ܕܥܘܗܕܢܐ.

ܕܫܬ. ܬܘܪܓܡܐ ܠܒܝܘܬܐ ܒܗ̇ܘ ܕܫܠܡ ܡܫܬܘܬܦ. ܐܒܡܐ ܕܒܫܒܪ، ܒܢ̈ܬܐ ܪܗܛܪܐ ܗ̇ܝ[1] ܠܒܣܡ ܒܪܫܐ ܕܗ̇ܠܐ ܡܬܪܓܡ ܘܡܦܫܩ.[2] ܕܢܝܪܐ ܕܝܢ ܠܗ̇، ܕܐܢ ܒܡܠܘܬܐ ܗ، ܦܣܘܪܘܬܐ ܐܘ ܠܐ. ܐܝܟ ܕܡܕܡ ܢܡܫܘܚܐ ܐܘ ܬܘܕܝܬܐ ܕܡܘܕܐ ܦܣܩ. ܘܡܛܠ ܕܒܫܪ̈ܒܐ ܡܠܦ̈ܢܐ ܦܢ̈ܝܐ ܢܡܛܘܝܐ ܠܗ ܗܟܢ ܣܢܝܛܝܢ. ܒܠܚܘܕ ܡܬܪܓܡܐ ܕܢܬܠܘܢ ܘܒܠ ܗܕܐ ܡܫܕܐ *ܕܒܗܘܢ ܕܐܢ[3] ܕܢܝܪܐ ܢܕܒܝܢ ܐܢܫܐ ܐܢ ܒܐܝܢ ܐܘ ܒܘܠ. ܒܗ̇، ܕܠܫܪ̈ܒܐ ܒܢ̈ܬܐ ܕܠܒܠܫ ܢܕܒܝܢ ܕܐܢ. ܠܗ *ܕܝܢ ܗܒܝܢܐ[4] ܒܗܠܝܢ ܕܐܝܡܐܝܬܝܐ. ܒܗ̇، ܕܠܫܪ̈ܒܐ ܢܒܪ̈ܝܐ ܒܦܢ̈ܝܐ ܢܡܛܘܝܐ ܕܠܗ ܒܠܫܘܕܘܗܝ، ܢܕܒܝܢ ܕܐܢ ܘܗܘ ܢܡܛܘܝܐ ܚܠܦ ܠܗ[5] ܕܠܒܪ ܡܢ ܒܠܬܐ ܢܐܡܪ. ܘܒܠ ܗܕܐ ܠܐ ܠܒܠܫ ܡܬܕܒܪ ܕܢܒܗ ܐܢ ܒܐܝܢ ܐܘ ܒܘܠ.

ܕܫܒܥ. ܡܢ ܗܠܝܢ ܢܕܒܝܢܐ ܕܒܣܝܡ ܗܢܝܢܐ ܕܒܢ̈ܝܐ ܘܐܠܝܓܐ ܚܝܦܘܬ ܡܬܕܘܣ ܗܕܐ ܐܘܡܢܘܬܐ. ܡܟܝܢܐ ܗܝܡܢܘܬܐ ܒܣܠܘܓܝܣܡܘܣ ܫܦܝܪ ܪܕܝܐ ܕܡܬܝܚܕܢܘܬܐ ܡܫܬܡܫܐ ܘܐܦܘܕܝܩܛܝܩܐ[1] ܡܫܬܪܪ. ܒܗ̇، ܕܕܐܦܘܕܝܩܛܝܩܐ ܡܢ ܡܩܕ̈ܡܬܐ *ܕܫܪ̈ܝܪܢ ܗܘܝܐ. ܘܐܦܘܕܝܩܛܝܩܐ ܡܢ ܡܩܕ̈ܡܬܐ ܫܪ̈ܝܪܬܐ.[2] *ܘܬܐܘܪܝܐ ܕܡܩܕ̈ܡܬܐ ܕܫܪ̈ܝܪܬܐ ܘܡܩܕ̈ܡܬܐ ܫܪ̈ܝܪܬܐ[3] ܕܐܘܡܢܘܬܐ ܡܠܠܬܐ ܐܝܬܘܗܝ. ܐܝܟ ܕܐܦ ܬܐܘܪܝܐ ܕܫܪܝܪܐ ܐܦܘܕܝܩܛܝܩܐ *ܘܡܩܕ̈ܡܬܐ ܕܐܦܘܕܝܩܛܝܩܐ ܕܠܗ̇ ܕܐܘܡܢܘܬܐ ܡܠܠܬܐ ܐܝܬܘܗܝ. ܒܗ ܓܝܪ ܐܦܘܕܝܩܛܝܩܐ[4] ܗ̇، ܗ، ܒܫܪܪܐ ܡܠܠܬܐ ܘܐܦܘܕܝܩܛܝܩܐ ܕܡܒܝܢܐ ܠܗ̇ ܒܗ̇، ܕܡܚܘܝܢܐ ܠܫܪܪܐ ܡܗܝܡܢ. ܘܚܘܝܐ ܐܢܫܐ ܠܫܪܪܐ ܢܦܩ ܘܠܗ ܫܢܝܐ. ܒܪܡ ܦܠܝܢ ܬܪܬܐ ܘܐܠܝܓܐ ܐܘܪܚܢܐ ܕܠܗܘܬܗ ܡܒܟܠܐ. ܘܕܠܬ̈ܠܐ ܠܗ ܡܠܝܢ ܘܡܛܪ̈ܝܐ ܠܛܠܠܘܬܗ ܒܠܫܘܕ ܡܬܡܠܝܢ.

5 [1] ܘܣܘܓܪܐ RVLl [2] sg. F [3] ܒܕܒܠ RVLl [4*] pl.F [5] ܒܬܪܝܨܘܬ RVLl
6 [1] om. RVL [2] _ ܘܡܦܫܩ RVL [3*] ܕܒܗܘܢ RVLl [4*] om. F [5] om. RVL
7 [1] ܘܐܦܘܕܝܩܛܝܩܐ FV [2] om. VLl [2*] om. R [3*] om. F; ܘܬܐܘܪܝܐ ܕܡܩܕ̈ܡܬܐ ܫܪ̈ܝܪܬܐ R [4*] om. F

thymeme. You have learnt what this is in the *Analytics*, and here you will shortly learn (it) again.

FIVE.[12] Since the enthymeme is the pillar, it is necessary that the method of rhetoric should be the same (in all cases); that is, its precepts in matters requiring exposition - (by which) I mean (matters) like deliberative ones of exhortation and dissuasion - and (its precepts in) contentious ones of prosecution and defence (should be the same), because all of them are based on the enthymeme. The inducing devices may be useful in a non-expository commercial conflict. (However) because conflicts which arise over matters of state between the people of one state and the people of another, or between the governors of one state, are elevated and exalted above admixture with the outer devices, they are only resolved by expositions. The outer devices are (merely) adornments, for by polishing the speech the enthymeme becomes bright and the matter of the sign is magnified.

SIX.[13] Exposition may share a subject with dispute. For example, an orator may make an exposition and explain that it is necessary to exact a punishment on evil-doers. A judge, however, decides whether an action is an injustice or not as the law declares or (according to) the belief he professes. Because in deliberative matters legal rules are for the most part not prescribed, everyone is allowed to give advice, and people therefore know immediately when a judge makes a judgement on these whether it is just or unjust, because he judges familiar matters which are known to everyone. That is not so, however, in judicial (matters), because he judges alien matters by legal rules which are known only to him, and the law itself forbids him to speak outside the book. Therefore whether his decision is just or unjust is not known to everyone.

SEVEN.[14] From this it is evident that the advantage of the outer (devices) is slight and cultivation of the artistic method is necessary, (which) gives possession of *pistis* by a syllogism lacking the major (premiss) which is called an enthymeme and is opined (to be) dialec-

---

[12] **1.3.5** AR 1.1 54b22-28; IS 1.3 (18.6-19.3).
[13] **1.3.6** AR 1.1 54b28-55a3; IS 1.3 (19.5-8; 20.12-15; 20.2-7).
[14] **1.3.7** AR 1.1 55a3-18; IS 1.3 (21.3-21.15).

## ܦܣܘܩܐ ܬܪܝܢܐ
## ܡܛܠ ܫܘܬܦܘܬܐ ܘܦܘܪܫܢܐ ܕܙܘܓܘܬܐ ܘܐܘܡܢܘܬܐ ܐܢ̈ܫܝܬܐ
## ܬܐܘܪ̈ܝܐ ܚܕܐ

ܡܕܝܢܬܐ. ܪܒ ܗܘ ܓܒ ܡܢܬܗ̇ ܕܙܘܓܘܬܐ. ܒܗ̇ ,*ܕܦܘܫܩܐ ܐܢܫܐ ܥܪ̈ܝܢܐ[1]
ܒܥܪ̈ܒܐ ܡܬܝܠܐ ܠܒ̈ܢܝܐ ܘܫܦܝܪܐ ܒܒܢܝܐ ܡܬܝܬܝܢ ܘܒܗܘܢ. ܫܢܝܐ ܐܢ̈ܫܐ
ܥܒܕܝܢ ܡܬܕܒܪܝܢ. ܘܐܡܬܐ ܕܥܪ̈ܒܐ ܠܒ̈ܢܝܐ ܕܐܦܘܕܝܩܛܝܩܐ ܡܥܬܪܝܢ
ܒܢܦ̈ܫܬܐ ܡܕܒܪ̈ܢܘܬܐ ܠܗ ܒܗ̇. ܐܠܐ ܒܕܝܘܛܝܩܐ ܡܬܕܒܪܝܢ.[2] ܗܟܢܐ ܐܦ
ܥܒ̈ܕܐ ܡܬܝܠܐ ܕܒܡܚܡܘܬܐ[3] ܫܬܝܬܬܐ ܡܬܕܒܪܝܢ ܒܢܦ̈ܫܬܐ ܦܪ̈ܫܬܐ ܠܗ
ܒܗ̇ ܐܠܐ ܒܕܝܘܛܝܩܐ ܡܫܬܬܝܢ. ܘܡܕܒܪܐ[4] ܬܘܒ ܗܟܢܐ ܕܠܡܠܬ
ܣܘܡܟܘܬܐ ܡܠܦܢܘܬܐ ܒܗ̇ܘ ܗܢܐ ܕܗ̇ܠܝܢ ܠܡܕܡܐ ܘܠܡܡܟܟ. ܠܐ ܟܪܐ.
ܒܗ̇ܘ ܡܢܐ ܕܢܦܘܪ ܠܗ ܡܢ ܡܐܡܪܐ ܡܫܝܢܐ[5] ܘܡܡܟܟ ܗܘ ܠܗܘܬܗ ܘܒܝܬ,
ܠܡܫܘܚܬܗ ܘܡܚܝܐ ܚܝܠܐ ܠܡܕܒܪܗ ܦܫܩܐ ܢܚܒ. ܠܗ.

ܕܬܪ̈ܬܝܢ. ܐܡܟܢܐ ܕܕܝܘܛܝܩܘܣ ܠܬܪ̈ܬܝܗܘܢ ܡܫܡ̈ܫܢܝܬܐ ܡܫܠܛܫ.[1] ܪܘܫܐ
ܬܘܒ ܠܬܪ̈ܬܝܗܘܢ ܡܫܡ̈ܫܢܝܬܐ ܡܫܩܫ. ܠܘ ܕܠܗ̇ܘ ܡܢܐ ܕܒ̈ܢܝܐ ܡܦܩܝܢ ܗ̇ܟܢ.
ܐܠܐ ܡܢܐ ܕܐܝܟܢ ܠܗ ܒܐܝܠܝܢ ܬܫܡܫ ܒܟ̈ܠܐ ܘܐܡܪ. ܕܕܚܠ ܠܟ ܒܟܠ
ܘܦܐܝܐ ܘܡܟܠܠ. ܗ̇ܘ ܕܠܡܫ̈ܡܫܢܝܬܗ ܢܚܣ ܕܢܥܒܕ. ܠܝܬ ܓܝܪ ܘܠܐ ܚܕܐ
ܐܘܡܢܘܬܐ ܡܫܡܫܢܝܬܐ[2] ܡܫܠܛܢܘܬܐ[3] ܚܒܝܪܐ ܦܛܪ ܡܢ ܕܕܝܘܛܝܩܐ
ܘܪܫܘܡܝܐ. ܐܦܘܕܝܩܛܝܩܐ ܓܝܪ ܠܚܕ ܒܠܚܘܕ ܓܒܐ ܟܐܢܐ ܡܥܪܪܐ.[4]
ܘܡܫܦܫܛܝܩܐ ܠܗ ܕܬܦܫܘܛ ܐܠܐ ܕܬܫܠܛܐ ܡܦܩܐ. ܘܦܘܐܝܛܝܩܐ
ܡܫܠܛܢܘܬܐ ܗ̇ܝ. ܠܐ ܡܬܗܢܝܢܬܐ.

---

1 ¹* sg. F ² ܡܬܡܕܒܪܝܢ F ³ ܕܒܣܡܝܡܘܬܐ RVL ⁴ scripsi; ܘܡܕܒܪܢܐ F; ܘܡܬܕܒܪܢܐ RVLl; cf. Ibn Sina 23, 3 المدبر ⁵ ܡܫܬܩܐ RVL

2 ¹ ܡܫܠܛ RVLl ² pl. RVLl ³ ܡܫܠܛܢܘܬܐ RVLl ⁴ i. add. ܘ F

tical, because dialectic comes from reputable (premisses) which are true, rhetoric from opined reputable (premisses). The theory of true reputable (premisses) and that of opined reputable (premisses) belongs to the (one) logical art, as also the theory of the true—the apodeictical—and of the reputable—the dialectical—belongs to the same logical art, even though apodeixis is truly logic and dialectic is (only) similar to it because the reputable resembles the true. Human nature is disposed to the truth and may hit on it, but narrow is the gate and hard is the way which leads to it, and few attain to it and many only attain to its shadow.

## SECTION FOUR
## On the Commonalities and Differences of Rhetoric and other Arts
### Five Theories

ONE.[15] The usefulness of rhetoric is very great, because true decisions for just and fair particular matters are naturally best and by them human life is governed fairly. And just as universal matters (which are the province) of apodeixis are not established in unlearned souls by (apodeixis) itself, but are driven in by dialectic, so also particular matters which are (properly) made known by exact wisdom are not implanted in simple souls by it, but by rhetoric. When he who is governed does not grasp a scholarly word of wisdom about what he ought to acknowledge and do, by premisses based on opinion we may persuade him about that which is appropriate for him, acceptable to him, akin to his capacity, and possible for his understanding.

TWO.[16] As a dialectician may argue syllogistically for two opposites, so too an orator may argue persuasively for two opposites; not to turn round and break down that which he builds up, but when another uses arguments unjustly and says, 'Such and such is just, or proper, or praiseworthy,' we should be able to establish their opposites. No art apart from dialectic and rhetoric produces a syllogistic opposite, for apodeixis proves only one side (to be) the just, sophistic

[15] **1.4.1** AR 1.1 55a20-29; IS 1.4 (22.3-23.7).
[16] **1.4.2** AR 1.1 55a29-36; IS 1.4 (23.8-24.8).

ܕܬܠܬ. ܒܪܘܚܢܘܬܐ ܗܝ ܐܦ ܫܘܡ̈ܠܝܐ ܡܫܬܪܪܝܢ. ܐܠܐ ܗܘ ܕܠܓܒܐ
ܡܫܬܪܐ ܡܬܓܠܝܐ ܘܡܬܐܡܪܐ ܕܬܡܢ ܡܫܘܚܬܢ ܡܬܚܫܚܐ ܬܡܢ[1]
ܡܫܬܪܐ ܒܟܝܢܐ. ܐܝܟ ܕܐܦ ܒܪܢܫܐ ܐܦ ܠܡܫܝܚܐ ܕܡܫܝܚܘܬܐ ܘܐܠܗܘܬܐ
ܡܟܝܢ ܗܕ̈ܡܘܗܝ، ܘܠܐܠܗܘܬܐ ܘܡܫܝܚܘܬܐ ܡܚܬܕܝܢ ܚܝ̈ܠܘܗܝ. ܐܠܐ ܡܫܬܪܘܬܐ
ܠܐܠܗܘܬܐ ܠܚܘܕ ܐܝܬܝܗ̇. ܘܗܘܝܢ ܕܗܦܟ ܡܢ ܡܫܬܪܘܬܐ ܐܝܟ ܚܝܠܐ
ܘܫܘܠܡܐ ܘܡܘܬܪܐ ܘܐܫܬܦܠܓܘܬܐ ܠܒܪܢܫܘܬܐ ܬܘܒ[2] ܢܣܒܢ. ܘܠܐܠܗܘܬܐ
ܗܝ ܡܫܠܛܢܘܬܗ̇ ܒܟܝܢ. ܠܒܪܢܫܘܬܐ ܕܝܢ ܠܘ ܡܫܠܛܢܘܬܗ̇ ܐܠܐ ܡܫܠܛ ܗܘ، ܕܠܒܪܢܫܘܬܐ
ܐܝܬܝܗ̇ ܟܕ ܗܝ ܢܣܝܒܐ ܘܡܬܝܗܒ. ܘܐܦ ܒܪܢܫܐ ܒܪܢܫܐ ܗܘ̣ ܕܠܐܠܗܘܬܐ ܠܐ
ܡܬܚܠܠܬܐ ܡܫܬܚܠܦ ܒܗܘ̣ ܡܫܬܚܠܦ ܕܒܕܪ ܢܬܗ. ܒܗܝ ܕܐܬܬܪܐ ܢܐܐ ܠܗ
ܕܡܬܚܙܐ ܚܝܠܐ ܠܡܒܕܪܘ ܡܘܚܗ ܒܗܘ ܡܐ ܕܕܡܠܝ ܠܚܝܘܗܝ. ܘܐܬܬܘܗܝ،
ܐܘܪܚܘܢ ܗܢܐ ܕܠܥܠܐ. ܕܒܗ ܡܥܡܕ ܕܒܕܪ ܒܐܢܫܘܬ ܘܢܗܦܟ ܒܗܠܐܬ
ܘܢܬܐܒ ܐܦ ܒܟܝܢ.

ܕܐܪܒܥ. ܐܝܟܢܐ ܕܐܫܟܚ ܠܐ ܚܕ ܗܘ[1] ܕܢܫܬܡܠ ܟܠ ܒܪܘܚܐ ܡܢ ܟܠ
ܒܪܘܚܐ. ܐܠܐ ܠܦܘܬ ܡܫܬܡܠܝܢܘܬܐ ܐܢܫܝܬܐ. ܐܝܟܢܐ ܕܟܠ ܫܡܠܬܗ ܟܕ
ܫܐܒ ܠܗ ܦܘܕܗ[2] ܬܗܘܐ[3] ܐܠܐ ܒܫܘܡܠܝܗ ܕܒܪܘܚܐ ܘܠܐ ܡܘܒܠ
ܡܘܒܠܐ ܠܫܘܠܡܐ. ܗܟܢܐ ܐܦ ܪܘܚܐ ܚܕ ܗܘ ܠܡܬܠܐ ܒܡܕܪܐ
ܘܦܘܪܫܐ[4] ܡܬܡܚܝܢܐ[5] ܒܟܠ ܥܒܕ. ܘܐܝܟ ܡܕܡ ܡܢ ܢܦܫܬܐ ܠܥܪܒܐ ܡܕܡ
ܒܠܐܬ ܐܘ ܠܐ ܗܘܝ ܡܬܦܫܩܢ. ܠܘ ܫܒܩܐ ܗܠܐ ܠܡܫܟܚ ܠܗܦܟܐ.

ܕܚܡܫ. ܐܝܟܢܐ ܕܒܕܠܝܦܘܬܐ ܫܘܠܡܝܗܘܢ ܐܝܬ ܚܝܠܬܐ
ܘܫܘܠܡܝܗܘܢ ܡܫܬܒܪܢܐ. ܒܪܘܚܢܘܬܐ ܬܘܒ ܡܬܐܡܪܐ ܐܝܬ ܗܘ
ܡܫܡܠܝܢܐ ܕܡܫܬܒܪܢܐ ܗܘ ܫܬܝܬܐ ܘܡܬܐܡܪܐ ܕܕܥܐ *ܠܡܫܡܠܝܢܐ ܒܗ̇،
ܕܕܥܐ[1] ܠܡܫܬܒܪܢܐ. ܦܘܪܫ ܗܘ[2] ܡܫܬܒܪܢܐ ܫܬܝܬܐ ܡܢ ܠܐ ܫܬܝܬܐ. ܟܕ
ܠܗܘ ܗܝ ܡܫܝܚܐ ܕܡܬܕܒܪ ܢܓܠܐ ܡܫܒܪܐ ܕܫܡܠܝܐ.[3] ܒܗܢܐ ܕܝܢ ܡܫܝܚܐ
ܕܡܬܕܒܪ ܚܦܪ ܫܡܠܝܐ. ܘܗܦܟܘܬܐ ܗܝ ܒܪ ܠܗ ܟܠ ܒܗܝܡܢܐ ܕܫܪܪܐ
ܐܠܐ ܒܠܗ، ܕܬܦܫܘ ܚܘܦܐ. ܐܦ ܡܐܡܪܐ ܕܡܬܢ ܠܡܫܪܝܐ ܒܐܠܝܢ ܒܗ̇.
ܘܗܢܐ ܡܢܗ ܗܝ ܠܦܘܬ ܫܘܡܠܝܬܐ ܗܘܝܐ. ܡܢܗ ܕܝܢ ܐܝܟ ܕܠܡܬܠܝܘ
ܡܓܝܢܐ. ܐܝܟܢܐ ܕܕܠܝܦܘܬܐ ܗܝ ܒܡܫܬܡܠܝܢܘܬ ܚܝܠܐ ܕܫܪܪܐ
ܘܒܫܘܠܡ ܗܘܝܐ. ܘܡܫܬܡܠܝܢܘܬܐ ܕܝܢ ܒܡܕܒܪܢܘܬ[4] ܕܠܓܠ ܒܥܝܪܐ ܒܒܫܝܢܬ
ܡܓܝܢܐ.

3 [1] ܗ̣܆ RVLl [2] om. F
4 [1] ܗܘܐ RVLl [2] ܦܘܪܗ RVLl [3] ܗܘܐ F [4] _ ܘܦܘܪ RL; ܘܦܘܪܫܢܐ V [5] sg. RVL
5 [1*] om. F [2] ܕܝܢ RVLl [3] pl. RVLl [4] ܒܡܕܒܪܢܘܬ ? F

endeavours not to persuade but to mislead, and poetics is productive of imagination, not *pistis*.

THREE.[17] Although opposites may be established by rhetoric, nevertheless that which leans to the better side and employs propositions which are more persuasive is naturally more virtuous; just as (with) a man, although his (bodily) members are endowed with what is needed for pleasure and pain and his (mental) faculties are equipped for good and evil, nevertheless virtue belongs only to the good, and those things apart from virtue like strength, health, wealth, and military strategy they may also use for evil. The good we desire for its own sake, evil, however, not for its own sake, but in order to drive out and banish another evil by it. If a man is compelled to help himself in those ways which he has in common with irrational animals, how much more does it befit him to have mastery of the faculty to help himself by that which is special to his nature, namely the organ of speech, by which he can help justly and harm wrongfully, do good and do evil.

FOUR.[18] Just as a doctor is not required to heal every patient of every illness, but (to act) according to what is humanly possible, so that when he is defeated the reason for his failure should not be an error of his but the severity of the illness and the resistance of the condition to recovery, so also an orator is required to bring the pillar and the devices possible (to bring to bear) on every matter, and if some souls are persuaded of some matters (only) with difficulty or not at all, it is not right to consider the orator at fault.

FIVE.[19] Just as in dialectic there may be a true syllogism and a syllogism (based) on opinion, so too in rhetoric there may be a persuasive premiss (based) on opinion which is true, and a premiss which resembles the persuasive because it resembles that (based) on opinion. The true (based) on opinion is different from the untrue, because the opinion of the listener inclines to the one immediately it becomes known, but immediately the other becomes known, the listener rejects (it). Although rhetoric is not concerned with the test of

---

[17] **1.4.3** AR 1.1 55a36-b7; IS 1.4 (24.9-25.5).
[18] **1.4.4** AR 1.1 55b10-14; IS 1.4 (25.8-25.13).
[19] **1.4.5** AR 1.1 55b15-21; IS 1.4 (25.14-27.9).

ܦܘܫܩܐ ܚܡܝܫܝܐ

ܡܛܠ ܬܫܡܫܬܗ̇ ܕܪܗܛܘܪܘܬܐ ܘܥܠ ܗܝܡܢܘܬܐ[1]

ܬܐܘܪ̈ܝܐ ܦ ܚܡܫ

ܡܕܝܢܬܐ. ܪܗܛܘܪܘܬܐ ܕܝܢ ܐܝܬܝܗ̇ ܚܝܠܐ ܡܦܝܣܢܐ ܒܡܠܐ ܕܡܨܝܐ ܒܟܠܚܕ ܡܢ ܫܪ̈ܟܐ ܡܬܠ̈ܬܐ. ܘܚܝܠܐ ܕܝܢ ܐܡܝܢܐ ܒܗ̇، ܕܐܘܡܢܘܬܐ ܗܝ، ܘܒܠ ܐܘܡܢܘܬܐ ܐܚܪܬܐ ܗܝ، ܢܦܫܝܬܐ ܕܝܠܗ̇ ܡܕܒܪ̈ܢܘܬܐ ܕܢܦ̈ܫܢ ܡܢܝܢܬܐ. ܒܡܠܐ ܕܡܨܝܐ ܕܝܢ ܐܡܝܢܐ ܒܗ̇، ܕܠܡܦܝܣܘ ܪܗܛܘܪܝܩܐ ܡܢ ܐܢ ܕܒܡܠܐ ܪܗܛܘܪܐ. ܠܐ ܚܕ ܕܠܒܠ ܫܪܟܐ ܦܣܩܐ ܢܒܒ܀ ܐܠܐ ܠܡܨܝܐ ܡܘܒܠܐ ܠܫܘܪ܀ ܘܒܟܠܚܕ ܡܢ ܫܪ̈ܟܐ ܡܬܠ̈ܬܐ ܐܡܝܢܐ ܒܗ̇، ܕܗ̇ܘ ܕܢܣܒ ܡܬܝܗܒܐ ܠܗ ܡܢܗ. ܐܠܐ ܒܟܠ ܨܒܘ ܕܡܢ ܐܡܪܐ ܕܝ، ܡܠܐܟܘܬܐ ܚܐܦܐ ܢܣܒܐ ܕܬܦܫܘ. ܠܘ ܡܢܝܐ ܐܣܘܬܐ ܕܡܛܠ ܫܘܠܛܢ ܦܪܘܫܐ ܐܝܟܢܐ ܒܠܫܘ ܡܦܝܣܐ. ܦܣܝܩܘܡܪܝܐ ܡܛܠ ܒܕ̈ܝܐ ܒܝܢܝܐ ܕܒܢܘܬܐ. ܘܐܪܬܡܛܝܩܐ ܡܛܠ ܡܢܝܢܐ.

ܕܬܪ̈ܬܝܢ. ܗܡܢܘܬܐ ܪܗܛܘܪܝܩܝܬܐ ܐܘ ܠܐ ܐܘܡܢܝܢ ܐܘ ܐܘܡܢܝܢ. ܘܕܠܐ ܐܘܡܢܘ ܕܝܢ ܐܬܝܗܝܢ ܗܢܝܢ ܕܠܘ ܡܢ ܟܬܒܐ ܘܦܘܪ̈ܣܐ ܕܠܝ ܗܘܝܢ. ܐܠܐ ܒܝܕ ܣܗ̈ܕܐ ܐܘ ܫܛܪ̈ܐ ܐܘ ܟܬܒܐ ܘܥܒܕܐ. ܕܐܘܡܢܘ ܕܝܢ ܐܬܝܗܝܢ ܗܢܝܢ ܕܒܡܡܠܠܐ ܡܬܦܪܣܝܢ ܕܢܦܩ ܠܗܬ[1] ܡܗܝܡܢܘܬܐ ܐܒܣܩܣܝܬܐ. ܕܟܢ ܠܐܬܪ̈ܘܬܐ ܘܐܒܕ̈ܐ ܪܗܛܘܪܐ ܣܓܝܐܝܢ. ܘܗܢܘܢ ܦܘܪ̈ܣܐ ܐܘ ܡܕܝܢ ܡܬܕܝܢ ܠܣܥܘܪ̈ܘܬܐ. ܐܝܟ ܐܬܪ̈ܘܬܐ ܕܡܢܗܘܢ ܘܡܠܟܝܫܟܐ[2] ܡܬܪ̈ܒܝܢ. ܐܘ ܡܢ ܐܘܦܟ̈ܣܐ ܘܡܢܘ̈ܬܐ ܕܕܝܢܝܢ ܒܗܝܢ ܒܢܝܢܐ ܡܬܬܚܝܢ ܠܝ. ܐܒܝܟܐ ܕܒܕ ܡܟܝܢ ܕܝܢܐ ܠܫܘܩܐ ܡܢ ܗܘܘܒܠܝܐ ܠܐܚܪܝܢܐ. ܢܐܡܪ. ܐܝܟܢܐ ܕܦܪܝܣܘܣ ܕܐܝܬܘܗܝ،[3] ܗܢܐܝܟ ܥܘܠܐ ܕܬܫܟܚܘܗܝ، ܘܡܦܪܣܦ ܕܐܝܬܘܗܝ، ܪܫܝܟ ܥܘܠܐ ܕܬܒܪܝܘܗܝ، ܠܗܢܐ ܓܒܪ ܒܕ ܠܐ ܡܟܬܒ ܗܘܐ[4] ܠܝ. ܡܢ ܩܢܘܢܐ ܗܘ ܕܠܪ̈ܫܡܐ ܦܠܐ ܠܡܛܠܐܒܘ ܘܠܫܢܝܐ ܠܡܒܥܐܘ ܐܒܥܝܢܗܝ،.

---

Titulus [1] sg. RVLl

2 [1] ܠܗܘܬ RVLl [2] sg. RVL [3] i. om. RVL [4] i. add. ܕ RVLl

truth but with persuading, premisses resembling the opined may also enter into it. So a part of it may arise in accordance with wisdom, but another part with the intention to mislead, as dialectic is for the faculty of verification or refutation, but sophistic in truth for false imitation with evil intent.

## SECTION FIVE
### On the Definition of Rhetoric and the Kinds of *Pisteis*
### Five Theories

ONE.[20] Rhetoric is a faculty persuasive as far as is possible on every one of the particular matters. It is called 'faculty' because it is an art, and every art is a habit of the soul from which voluntary actions arise. 'As far as is possible' is mentioned because when an orator speaks according to rhetorical rules, he is not required to effect persuasion on every matter, but only on those possible to accept. 'Every one of the particular matters' is mentioned because (rhetoric) does not have a defined subject, but may take a desire to persuade on everything from any category whatever. Medicine is not like this, being persuasive only about the health of the human body, nor geometry (which is only) about the natural contingencies of magnitude, nor arithmetic (which is only) about numbers.

TWO.[21] Rhetorical *pisteis* are either non-artistic or artistic. Lacking art are those which come not from our own techniques and devices, but by witnesses, tortures, contracts, and so forth. With art are those which we devise in a speech to persuade according to the habitual method, in which we invent rhetorical *topoi* and species. Those devices are either prepared beforehand for our use, like the *topoi* from which syllogisms are composed, or at the time of the parley they are obtained by us from elements and rules which we (already) know. For example, when we wish to change the decision from an opposite to the other, we may say, 'If it is fitting to do harm to Crescus (?) who is your enemy, it is fitting to be helpful to Socrates who is your friend', for although it was not prepared for us, we have obtained this from the rule that it is right to do good to friends and evil to enemies.

[20] **1.5.1** AR 1.2 55b25-35; IS 1.5 (28.11-30.2).
[21] **1.5.2** AR 1.2 55b35-56a1; IS 1.5 (32.4-33.5).

ܕܬܠܬ. ܬܠܬܐ ܐܢܘܢ ܙܢ̈ܝܐ ܕܡܫܘ̈ܚܬܐ ܐܘܡܢ̈ܘܬܐ[1] ܕܒܝܕ ܡܡܠܠܐ ܡܬܦܪ̈ܫܢ. ܚܕ ܡܢ ܒܡܘܕܐ ܐܘܡܢܘܬ ܫܘܪܪܐ. ܕܬܪܝܢ ܕܝܢ ܐܘܡܢܝܘܬ ܐܡܘܪܐ.[2] ܒܐܣܟܡܗ ܓܝܪ ܠܡܬܗܡܢܘ ܒܗ ܢܗܘܐ ܙܗܐ ܘܡܫܝܚܢ ܘܚܪܝܦ ܘܗܕܝܪ ܘܡܚܝܬܪ. ܠܡ̈ܠܐ ܓܝܪ ܡܗܝܡܢܝܢ ܡܠܘܢ ܘܒܟܠ. ܘܕܬܠܬܐ ܬܘܒ ܢܓܘܕܘܬ ܫܡ̈ܥܬܐ. ܘܫܪܪܐ ܒܗܝ *ܡ̣ܢ ܠܫܡܥܐ ܗ̇ܘܐ. ܒܗܝ[3] ܕܝܢ ܠܡܕܪ̈ܫܐ. ܐܒܕܢܐ ܕܡܣܟܢܐ ܡܫܬܪܝܘܬܗ ܕܠܗ ܘܫܦܝܘܬܐ ܕܒܠܕܝܢܗ. ܘܦܐܝܘܬ ܐܣܟܡܗ ܕܐܡܘܪܐ ܒܫܪ̈ܟܐ ܕܒܕܘ ܒܕܪܐ. ܒܠܘܓܪܐ ܘܦܠܝܪܘܦܘܪܝܐ ܘܡܘܠܛܘܬܐ ܘܓܘܢܝܐ. ܠܐ ܒܗܘܢ ܕܒܬܕܝܢ ܐܝܟ ܕܒܠܘܟܠܐ ܘܫܘܓܪܐ. *ܒܕ ܗܘܕܪܘܬ[4] ܐܡܘܪܐ ܠܡܬܡܨܝܢܐ ܠܐ ܒܒܕܐ[5] ܐܠܨܐ. ܘܢܓܘܕܘܬ ܫܡ̈ܥܬܐ ܒܡܐܡܪܐ ܐܬܦܝܣܐ ܕܣܢ̈ܝܐ ܢܦ̈ܫܬܐ ܡܒܝܕܝܢ ܗܘܝܐ.

ܕܐܪܒܥ. ܪܗܛܘܪܝܩܐ ܠܕܝܠܝܩܛܝܩܐ[1] ܘܠܣܘܦܣܛܝܩܘܢ ܕܒܢ̈ܝܐ ܡܬܝܬܪܐ ܘܕܘܒܪܐ ܡܕܝ̈ܢܝܐ ܫܒܒܐ. ܡܫܬܘܦܐ ܠܕܝܠܝܩܛܝܩܐ ܡܢ ܒܗ̇ ܕܠܦܘܪ̈ܣܐ ܕܒܠܕܝܢܗ ܐܝܟ ܕܣܘܓܐܐ ܡܦܘܪܣܐ. ܘܕܒܠܬ ܗܝܡܢܘܬܐ ܕܡܣܝܢܐ ܠܗ ܫܪܝܪܘܬ ܡܐܡܪܗ ܗ̣ܘ. ܐܠܐ ܦܨܝܚܘܬ ܠܒܢ̈ܝܗ̇. ܠܦܘܠܝܛܝܩܘܢ ܕܝܢ ܒܗ̇ ܕܐܦ ܠܒܢ̈ܝܐ ܘܣܓ̈ܝܐ ܢܦ̈ܫܬܐ ܐܝܟ ܚܕܘܬܐ ܘܒܣܝܡܘܬܐ ܘܪܚܡܬܐ ܘܫܝܢܘܬܐ ܣܦܩܐ. ܘܒܠܗܕܐ ܡܫܬܟܚܐ ܕܘܒܪܐ[2] ܡܕܝܢ ܗ̣ܘ ܠܕܝܠܝܩܛܝܩܐ ܘܠܦܘܠܝܛܝܩܘܢ ܘܡܕܝܢܝܢ ܡܕܒܪܢܐ. ܒܕ ܠܗ ܡܕܒܪܐ ܗܘ. ܠܐ ܓܝܪ ܡܬܪܒܝܐ[3] ܐܘܡܢܘܬܐ ܡܢ ܡܕܝ̈ܢܬܐ ܕܐܚܪܬܐ. ܐܠܐ ܒܗ̇ܘ ܕܣܝܡ ܒܠܚܘܕ ܡܬܬܦܩ. ܐܝܟ ܕܐܬܚܙܝ ܒܐܦܘܕܝܩܛܝܩܐ.

ܕܚܡܫ. ܗܪܟܐ ܐܡ̣ܪ ܐܢܐ ܕܐܝܠܝܢ ܠܟ ܕܐܚܝܕܝܢ ܒܪܗܛܘܪܘܬܐ ܠܕܪ̈ܫ ܡܠܦܢܘܬܐ ܕܒܠܝܢ ܐܝܟ ܦܠܝܛܐ ܠܐ ܦܪܣ. ܘܐܘܪܚܗ̇ ܠܐ ܕܪܫܘ. ܡܢܗܘܢ ܡܢ ܡܛܠ ܠܐ ܙܪܝܙܘܬܗܘܢ. ܡܢܗܘܢ ܕܝܢ ܡܛܠ ܚܘܬܪܐ ܘܡܫܟܠܠܘܬܐ ܐܒܕܢ ܕܡܡܠܠܐ ܡܠܬܗܘܢ ܡܢ ܗ̇ܝ ܕܦܫܝܩܐܝܬ ܬܬܕܪܟ. ܘܡܢܗܘܢ ܕܝܢ[1] ܡܛܠ ܚܝ̈ܐ ܡܕܡ ܐܚܪ̈ܢܐ ܐܝܟ ܫܘܚܠܦܐ ܘܣܦܪ.

3 [1] ܐܘ ܐܘܡܢܘܬܐ F [2] pl. RL; f. ܗ V [3*] om. RV [4*] ܒܗܘܕܪܘܬ RVL [5] f. om. F

4 [1] ܠܕܝܠܝܩܛܝܩܐ RVLl [2] scripsi; ܕܘܒܪ̈ܐ codd. [3] om. RVLl

5 [1] ܬܘܒ RVLl

THREE.[22] The kinds of artistic *pisteis* which are devised through speech are three. One is the pillar or verification. The second is the character of the speaker. (A speaker) is *pistis*-worthy by his manner when he is honourable, submissive, acute, agreeable, and virtuous, for we accord *pistis* to good men to a greater degree and more readily. The third is the inducement of the audience. Verification is sometimes of the subject, but sometimes of the aids, as when (a speaker) demonstrates his own virtue or the folly of his adversary. The fair manner of a speaker is helpful on matters which are past—in accusation or excuse, praise or blame—not in those which are future—as in inciting or restraining—since the attractiveness of a speaker does not make the possible necessary, and the inducement of the audience comes about by moral propositions which arouse the passions of the soul.

FOUR.[23] Rhetoric (is related) to dialectic and to politics, which discerns virtuous behaviour and civic government. It has in common with dialectic that it mostly uses the devices of an adversary (in dialectic), and that the cause of the *pistis* which that imparts is not the truth of its premiss, but the abundance of its techniques. (It has in common) with politics, however, that it is also concerned with behaviour and passions of the soul like joy or sadness, and love or hate. Therefore it is supposed to be some compound of dialectic and politics and to be compounded from them, although that is not (really) so, for the art is not compounded from parts of another (art), but they only share (some) subject matter, as has been shown with apodeixis.

FIVE.[24] Our master said here that those who hold sway over rhetoric have not observed proper teaching (practice) towards it as they ought, nor have they trod its way, partly from ignorance, partly on account of pride and haughtiness as if their reason was too exalted for you to understand (it) easily, and partly from some human passions, like jealousy and the rest.

---

[22] **1.5.3** AR 1.2 56a1-25; IS 1.5 (33.6-34.5).
[23] **1.5.4** AR 1.2 56a25-35; IS 1.5 (34.9-34.15).
[24] **1.5.5** AR 1.2 56a28-30; IS 1.5 (35.6-35.9).

## ܦܣܘܩܐ ܫܬܝܬܝܐ
## ܡܛܠ ܒܡܘܕܪܐ ܐܘܚܕܢ ܫܪܪܐ ܘܦܘܠܚܢܗ̈ܝ
## ܬܐܘܪ̈ܝܣ ܐܪܒܥ

ܘܕܡܝܢܘܬܐ. ܡܐܡܪܐ ܕܝܢ ܫܪܪܐ ܘܡܬܪܢܝܢܘܬܐ ܘܡܬܚܫܒܢܘܬܐ
ܘܡܫܘܚܘܬܐ. ܘܫܪܪܐ ܗ̇ܝ ܐܝܬܘܗ̇ܝ ܡܐܡܪܐ ܡܦܫܩܢܐ ܕܒܗ
ܡܬܗܓܝܢܐ ܬܘܒ. ܘܠܟܠܗܘܢ ܗܢܘܢ ܕܫܪܟܐ ܢ̈ܦܫ. ܘܗ̣ܘ ܗܘܐ
ܡܐܡܪܐ. ܐܢ ܫܦܝܪܐ ܗܘ ܒܗ ܪܒܬܐ ܡܬܪܢܝܢܘܬܐ ܡܬܦܪܫܐ. ܘܐܝܟܢܐ ܕܕܒܝܪܐ
ܒܗ ܪܒܬܐ ܡܬܚܫܒܢܘܬܐ ܡܬܚܫܚܗ̇[1]. ܘܡܫܘܚܘܬܐ ܡܬܐܡܪܐ ܗܪܟܐ ܠܟܠ
ܬܫܡܫܬܐ ܡܟܕܘܢܝܫܬ ܢܝܫܐ ܪܘܚܢܝܬ. ܘܐܟܡܐ ܕܕܝܐܠܝܩܛܝܩܐ
ܒܣܘܠܘܓܝܣܡܘܣ ܘܡܦܩܦܝܩܐ ܡܬܚܫܚܐ. ܪܝܛܘܪܝܩܐ ܒܡܬܪܢܝܢܘܬܐ[2]
ܘܦܪܕܝܓܡܐ ܡܬܚܫܚܐ. ܒܪܡ ܕܐܦܘܕܝܩܛܝܩܐ ܒܣܘܠܘܓܝܣܡܘܣ ܬܪܬܝ ܐܘ
ܒܡܦܩܦܝܩܐ ܡܬܚܫܚܐ. ܦܘܐܝܛܝܩܐ ܕܝܢ ܒܦܪܕܝܓܡܐ ܬܪܬܝ ܡܢ
ܒܡܬܪܢܝܢܘܬܐ[3] ܡܬܚܒܪܐ. *ܒܪ ܬܫܡܫܬܐ[4] ܒܡܐ̈ܪܐ ܕܢ̈ܫܐ ܘܢܘܗܪܐ ܗܘܐ.
ܘܡܬܪܢܝܢܘܬܐ ܒܪ ܣܘܠܘܓܝܣܡܘܣ ܗ̇ܝ، ܕܫܘ̈ܐܠܐ[5] ܡܬܠܒܟܐ ܡܢ ܒܒ̈ܢܝܐ
ܐܝܟ ܕܒܣܘܠܓܝܐ ܟܠܗ̇ ܡܬܬܪܒܝܢ. ܘܫܘܝ ܦܣܘܩܐ ܡܢ ܡܬܠܬܐ
ܠܗܘܢܐ ܕܕܢ̈ܚܐ ܠܗ ܢܝܪ܆ ܒܒ̈ܢܝܐ ܗܘ ܘܡܬܚܠ.

ܕܬܪ̈ܬܝܢ. ܬܫܡܫܬܐ ܘܡܬܪܢܝܢܘܬܐ ܡܫܬܘ̈ܕܥܢ ܡܢ ܒܗ̇، ܕܟܠ ܚܕܐ ܡܢܗܘܢ
ܦܣܘܩܐ ܒܒܪܐ. ܘܐܡܪܐ ܕܡܚܕܐ ܒܝ[1] ܡܫܬܡܠܝܐ ܡܦܫܩܐ ܗ̇ܝ، ܡܫܬܘܚܕܢܐ.
ܘܡܢ ܚܕܕ̈ܐ ܘܡܢ ܟܠܗ ܘܦܠܓܐ. ܘܗ̇ܝ، ܘܕܡܝܢܘܬܐ ܠܐ ܡܫܬܘܚܕܢܘܬܐ ܗ̇ܝ،
ܘܕܠܐ ܣܘܦ ܘܠܐ ܡܫܬܘܚܕܢܘܬܐ ܘܠܐ ܡܦܢܝܢܘܬܐ. ܒܕܟܠܝܫ ܐܝܟ ܢܝܫܐ
ܘܫܪܐ ܕܦܠܐ ܡܫܬܟܚ. ܘܗ̇ܝ، ܕܬܪ̈ܬܝܢ ܗ̣ܝ، ܡܫܬܘܚܕܢܐ ܒܦܠܓܘܬܐ. ܐܦ ܗ̇ܝ،
ܒܪ ܐܝܟ ܕܕܝܐܠܝܩܛܝܩܐ *ܠܘ ܒܡܫܬ̈ܚܠܦܬܐ[2] ܗܘܝܢ ܕܠܦܘܬ ܓܢܝܐ ܚܕܕܐ
ܡܬܚܫܚܐ. ܒܪܡ ܕܐܦܘܕܝܩܛܝܩܐ ܡܢ ܒܗ̇، ܕܡܫܬܘ̈ܚܕܢܘܬܐ[3] ܕܚܕܕܐ، ܡܢܗܘܢ
ܗܘܝܐ ܠܗܘܢ. ܦܘܐܝܛܝܩܐ ܕܝܢ ܠܘ ܡܫܬܘܚܕܢܝܬܐ ܒܒܪܐ ܒܗܘܢ. ܐܠܐ
ܕܡܫܬ̈ܚܠܦܬܐ ܡܫܬܪ̈ܝܢ ܒܠܚܘܕ ܫܘܡܐ ܠܗ̇.

---

1 [1] f. add. ܐ RVLI [2] i. ܘ RVL [3] i. add. ܕ RVLI [4*] ܒܬܫܡܫܬܐ RVL; ܘܬܫܡܫܬܐ I [5] i. om. RLI; ܕ ܫܘ̈ܐܠܐ V

2 [1] ܒܗ RVLI [2*] ܘܡܫܬ̈ܚܠܦܬܐ RVLI [3] ܕܡܫܬܘ̈ܚܕܢܘܬܐ RVLI

## SECTION SIX
### On the Pillar or Verification and its Divisions
### Four Theories

ONE.[25] One speaks of *verification, enthymeme, thought,* and *demonstration. Verification* is a persuasive statement by which *pistis* is created in the desired conclusion, and it encompasses all the others. As for the statement, if the major (premiss) is lacking in it, it is called an *enthymeme*, but if the major (premiss) is mentioned in it, it is termed a *thought. Demonstration* is used here for every paradigm which shows forth the aim quickly. As dialectic uses *syllogism* and *induction*, rhetoric uses *enthymeme* and *paradigm.* However dialectic benefits more by syllogism than by induction, but rhetoric is helped more by *paradigm* than by enthymeme, because an paradigm comes about through clear and evident things, but an enthymeme, being a syllogism, is that to which questions of 'Why?' are usually called out by the populace. The transfer of a decision from a particular to another which is similar to it is (however) pleasing and acceptable to the populace.

TWO.[26] Paradigm and enthymeme have in common that each of them produces persuasion. The reputable is that which is persuasive immediately it is heard, by some individuals or by the whole populace. The former is undefined, unlimited, unknowable, and unstable, because everyone gives credit according to the purpose and passion which he has. The second is used wisely in rhetoric, for like dialectic it too does not use those (premisses) reputable according to individual choice. However, dialectic needs them because it makes syllogisms from them. Rhetoric, however, does not effect a syllogistic (proof) with them, but it is sufficient for it merely that (its) reputable (premisses) are based on opinion.

THREE.[27] The reputation of true reputable (premisses) does not depart after investigation and consideration. If ever by way of untruth it does depart, what is concealed in them departs, but (it is) not the

---

[25] **1.6.1** AR 1.2 56a35-b24; IS 1.6 (35.12-36.5; 37.6-14).
[26] **1.6.2** AR 1.2 56b26-57a1; IS 1.6 (38.15; 39.4-40.4).
[27] **1.6.3** AR 1.2 57a1-13; IS 1.6 (41.7-12; 42.2-14).

ܕܬܠܬ. ܡܫܬܡܫܢܘܬܐ ܚܕ̈ܬܬܐ ܒܬܪ ܒܡܘܫܐ ܘܒܢܡܘܣܐ ܠܐ ܣܦܩܐ ܡܫܡܫܢܘܬܗܝܢ. ܘܐܢ ܣܦܩ ܣܦܩܐ ܒܦܘܪܣ ܕܓܠܘܬܐ. ܕܒܗܢܐ ܒܗܝܢ ܣܦܩܐ. ܘܠܗܕܐ ܓܝܪ ܠܐ ܡܣܦܩܐ ܐܠܐ ܡܠܬܦܩܐ ܒܡܢܝܢ. ܘܒܠܗܕܐ ܠܘܬܗܘܢ ܒܠܚܘܕ ܠܐ ܡܫܚ̈ܠܦܬܐ ܗܘ̈ܝ. ܘܡܫܬܚܠܦܢܘܬܐ ܡܫܬܒܪܢܘܬܐ[1] ܒܕ ܡܬܒܥܝܢ. ܣܦܩܐ ܡܫܡܫܢܘܬܗܝܢ ܠܐ ܒܦܘܪܣ ܕܓܠܘܬܗܝܢ ܒܠܚܘܕ. ܐܠܐ ܕܒܦܘܪܬܗܝܢ ܬܘܒ. ܪܗܛܪܐ ܐܪܐ ܒܡܫܬܚܠܦܢܘܬܐ ܚܕ̈ܬܬܐ ܠܐ ܒܗ̇[2] ܕܚܕ̈ܬܢ. ܐܠܐ ܒܗ̇ ܕܡܬܚܙܝܐ ܥܒܝܕܘܬܗܝܢ. ܘܡܢ ܒܕ ܐܬܒܢܝܘ ܐܢ̈ܫܐ ܠܡܗܝܡܢܘܬܗܝܢ. ܡܬܚܫܒ ܠܐ ܡܘܕܐܝܬ ܐܝܟ *ܬܪܝܢ ܬܪܝܢ[3] ܡܦܩܦܩܢܘܬܐ ܒܐܣܟܡܐ ܬܪܝܢܐ. ܒܕܝܢܗ ܕܡ ܒܗܢܐ ܕܠܐܘܒܒܐ ܡܣ̈ܝܢܐ ܠܐ ܡܫܒܪ ܡܛܠ ܐܘܪܚܐ. ܐܦ ܕܝܢܐ ܡܛܠ ܕܦܫܝܛ ܠܐ ܡܫܬܟܚ ܠܡܚܙܝܘܢ. ܘܠܐ ܡܬܬܕ̈ܪܢܐ ܒܦܫܡܗ ܐܢܘܢ.

ܐܘܟܒ. ܠܫܪܟܐ ܐܢ̈ܫܐ ܕܒܠܝܢ ܒܝܪ ܦܒܪ ܪܝܫܦܘܪ. ܐܠܐ ܐܝܟ ܕܒܓܙܪܐ ܒܦܪ ܒܕ. ܟܠ ܣܡܘܪ̈ܬܐ ܕܕܝܫ̈ܘܬܐ ܡܦܝܣ ܘܐܡܪ. ܦܠܝ ܠܐ ܪܫܡ ܬ̈ܓܠܓܠܬܐ ܒܗܢܐ ܕܡܝܬܪܘܬ[1] ܢܦܘܩܬܐ ܡܢܐ. ܘܦܠܝ ܡܢ ܐܠܗܐ ܠܐ ܕܢܠ ܒܗܢܐ ܕܒܚܝܠܬ ܡܝ̈ܬܬܐ ܠܐ ܡܗܕܪܐ. ܡܚܠܠ ܕܝܢ ܠܬܪܐܝܬ ܒܫܪ̈ܟܐ ܡܬܡܚܝ̈ܢܐ. ܐܝܟ ܡܠܒܝ̈ܢܐ ܡܡܠ̈ܠܢܐ ܕܗܘܐ ܘܠܐ ܗܘܐ ܒܪܒܢܐ ܕܒܬܝܒ. ܫܘܬܐܝܬ. ܘܒܠܗܕܐ ܦܫܩܐ ܒܠܝܢܐ ܚܝ ܡܚܝܢܘܢ ܕܠܐܢܝܬ ܠܐ ܡܡܚܠ. ܐܝܟ ܕܐܡܪ. ܦܠܝ ܐܒܠܘܪܓܐ ܕܣܦܘܪܛܣ ܒܗ̇ ܕܡܠܝܫ ܗܘܐ ܒܐܕܢܝ ܥܠܝܦܐ ܒܕ ܐܣܘܪܗ. ܘܗܘܝܐ ܓܝܪ ܐܢ ܡܕܡ ܐܚܪܝܢ ܠܐ ܢܣܦ ܒܒܪ ܡܦܝܣ. ܘܐܢܘܢ ܕܠܬܒܬܐ ܒܠܝܢܬܐ ܡܦܘܪܫ[2] ܒܕܓܠܘܬܗ ܒܪ ܥܒܕܗ ܡܪܓܢ ܥܒܘܕܐ.

ܦܣܘܩܐ ܚܡܝܫܝܐ

ܡܛܠ ܐܢܫܐ[1] ܘܡܬܕܡܪ̈ܢܐ ܪܗܛܪ̈ܐ

ܬܐܘܪܝܦܐ ܐܪܟܒ

ܡܕܡܝܢܬܐ. ܗܘܝ ܕܝܢ ܡܬܪܢܫܘܬܐ ܠܗ ܒܠܚܘܕ ܡܢ ܡܬܕܡܪ̈ܢܐ ܥܒ̈ܕܐ ܐܪܥ̈ܐ ܐܠܐ ܐܦ ܡܢ ܐܢܫ̈ܐ. ܘܗܢܝܢ ܗܠܝܢ ܐܘ ܡܢ ܡܫܬܚܠܦܢܐ ܚܕ̈ܬܬܐ ܗܘ̈ܝ. ܐܝܟ ܣܦܘܪܛܣ ܣܚܝܡ ܘܗܘܐ ܢܦܝܩ. ܘܡܣܝܒܪܢܐ ܗܘܐ ܢܦܫܐ ܠܦܠܚܢܐ ܗܘ

3 [1] i. add. ܘ RVLl [2] ܒܗܝܢ F [3] ܬܪ̈ܬܝܢ RVLl
4 [1] ܕܒܡܝܬܪܘܬܐ RVLl [2] ܡܦܘܪܫܝܢ RVLl
Titulus [1] ܐܢܫܐ RL; ܐܢ̈ܫܐ l

populace but the studious (who) investigate this, and therefore to them alone do they become non-reputable. (By contrast), when opined reputable (premisses) are investigated, their reputation may depart not only by way of their untruth, but also (by way) of their renunciation. Now an orator (uses) true reputable (premisses) not because they are true, but because their existence is apparent. Because men are used to giving *pistis* to them, he may use (them) uncanonically, like two affirmatives in the Second Figure, because his converse (is) with the populace, which does not endure the canonical arrangements on account of (their) length. Even a judge is not compelled to take note of them, because he is simple-minded, and at his level they are not acknowledged.

FOUR.[28] An orator deals little with necessary things which are universal, but may by chance (do so) when persuading about righteous actions and saying, 'So and so is not lustful as long as he possesses the virtue of temperance,' or, 'So and so does not fear God as long as he does not confess the resurrection of the dead.' But he speaks rather more about possible things, like deliberative (ones) equally capable of coming into being or not at a future time, and therefore no universal decision may properly be taken from them, as (when) he says, 'So and so slandered Socrates, because he whispered in the ears of the ruler when he bound him.' If he does not do anything bigger (than this), he may perhaps persuade, but if he openly expresses a universal major (premiss), the listener may immediately perceive his falsehood.

## SECTION SEVEN
### On Necessity and Rhetorical Possibles
### Four Theories

ONE.[29] Enthymemes may be generated not only from even possibles, but also from necessaries. These latter are either from true reputable (premisses)—for example, 'Socrates is wise and his soul is noble; a wise man noble of soul is blessed in the world to come'—or

---

[28] **1.6.4** AR 1.2 57a13-19; 22 - 57b1; IS 1.6 (42.14-43.7).

[29] **1.7.1** AR 1.2 57a19-b3; IS 1.6 (43.10-44.5; 45.1-4).

ܒܫܠܡܐ ܕܫܠܡ.. ܐܘ ܡܢ ܫܘܕ̈ܥܐ.[1] ܐܝܟ ܗܕܐ ܦܠܛܬܐ ܠܕܕ. ܡܕܝܢ ܡܚܘܝܢܬܐ ܗܝ. ܘܗܪܟܐ ܠܕܕ ܫܘܕܥܐ ܗܘ ܫܪܝܪܐ ܕܡܚܘܝܢܘܬܐ.[2] ܘܐܬܪ̈ܗܘܢ ܗܠܝܢ ܙܘ̈ܓܐ ܒܐܣܟܡܐ ܩܕܡܝܐ ܐܝܟ ܘܟܠܗܕܐ[3] ܐܠܝܢ. ܗܘ̈ܝ ܕܝܢ ܡܬܗܦܟܢܘܬܐ ܘܡܢ ܡܬܚܡ̈ܢܐ ܕܐܝܟ[4] ܕܩܛܓܘܪܝܐ. ܘܗܢܝܢ ܗܠܝܢ ܐܘ ܡܢ ܡܫܬܟ̈ܚܢܐ ܚܬܝ̈ܬܐ ܗܘ̈ܝ. ܐܝܟ ܣܘܩܪܛܝܣ ܚܝ ܘܡܗܠܟ. ܡܕܝܢ ܪܫܝܡ. ܐܘ ܡܢ ܫܘܕ̈ܥܐ. ܐܝܟ ܣܘܩܪܛܝܣ ܐܢܫ ܒܐܫܬܐ. ܡܕܝܢ ܪܗܛ ܘܠܒܐ ܕܢܦܫܗ. ܘܕܪܘܦܣ ܠܒ̈ܘܬܐ ܐܠܡܦ̈ܬܐ ܠܒܐ. ܡܕܝܢ ܐܦܘܢܐ ܡܠܠܐ ܠܒܐ.

ܕܬܪ̈ܬܝܢ. ܐܝܬܐ ܟܝܢܝܐ ܡܢ ܫܘܕ̈ܥܐ. ܒܗܠܝܢ ܕܬܪ̈ܝܢ ܠܐܢܢܩܝܐ ܗܘܝܐ. ܒܬܪܝܢܐ ܡ̇ܢ ܐܝܟ ܗܕܐ ܐܝܬܝܐ ܢܦܫܐ ܒܪܫܗ. ܡܕܝܢ ܦܠܛܐ. ܘܗܪܟܐ ܡ̇ܢ ܟܕ ܡܫܡܥܢܐ ܡܢ ܡܫܪ ܟܠ ܐܚܘܪܐ. ܘܟܐ ܕܝܢ ܟܠ ܡܫܡܥܢܐ ܒܟܠ ܠܐ ܡܫܪ. ܟܕ ܠܘ ܟܠ ܕܢܦܫܐ ܒܪܫܗ ܦܠܛܐ. ܠܘ ܒܐܣܟܡܐ ܩܕܡܝܐ ܗ̇ܘܐ ܪܘܟܒܐ ܐܠܐ ܒܬܠܝܬܝܐ. ܐܝܟ ܗܕܐ[1] ܐܝܬܝܐ ܢܦܫܐ ܒܪܫܗ. ܘܦܠܛܬܐ ܢܦܫܐ ܒܪܫܗ. ܡܕܝܢ ܗܕܐ ܐܝܬܝܐ ܦܠܛܐ. ܘܒܬܠܝܬܝܐ ܕܝܢ ܐܝܟ ܚܟܝ̈ܡܬܐ ܒܐܢܫ ܒܗ̇، ܕܣܘܩܪܛܝܣ ܚܟܝܡܐ ܒܐܢܫ. ܘܗܪܟܐ ܟܕ ܟܠ ܡܫܡܥܢܐ ܕܐܝܬܘܗܝ،[2] ܐܝܬ ܡܫܪ ܪܟܐ. ܟܠ ܐܚܘܪܐ ܕܝܢ ܒܟܠ ܡܫܪ ܡܫܡܥܢܐ. ܟܕ ܠܘ ܟܠ ܚܟܝܡܐ ܣܘܩܪܛܝܣ[3] ܐܝܬܘܗܝ، ܠܘ ܒܐܣܟܡܐ ܩܕܡܝܐ ܗ̇ܘܐ ܪܘܟܒܐ ܐܠܐ ܒܬܠܝܬܝܐ. ܐܝܟ ܣܘܩܪܛܝܣ ܚܟܝܡܐ. ܘܣܘܩܪܛܝܣ ܒܐܢܫܐ.[4] ܡܕܝܢ ܟܠ ܚܟܝܡܐ ܒܐܢܫܐ. ܗܘܝܐ ܕܝܢ ܐܝܬ ܘܡܢ ܕܬܪ̈ܝܢ ܠܡܬܚܡ̈ܢܐ. ܕܐܝܟ ܕܒܐܣܟܡܐ ܒܬܠܝܬܝܐ ܡܢ ܐܝܟ ܣܘܩܪܛܝܣ ܪܗܛ ܘܠܒܐ ܕܢܦܫܗ. ܡܕܝܢ ܐܢܫ ܒܐܫܬܐ. ܒܬܠܝܬܝܐ ܕܝܢ ܐܝܟ *ܫܦܝܪܐ ܕܢܦܩ[5] ܟܕ ܢܦܩ ܫܦܝܪ *ܗܘܐ ܘܢܦܩ.[6] ܗܠܝܢ ܡܢ ܬܠܝܬܝܐ ܕܐܝܢ̈ܐ ܕܡܬܗܦܟܢܘܬܐ ܪܗܛܢܝܬܐ.

ܕܬܠܬ. ܡܢ ܡܬܗܦܟܢܘܬܐ ܫܘ̈ܝܐ ܗܝܕܝܢ ܗܘܝܐ ܡܬܚܫܒܢܘܬܐ ܡܢܐ ܕܬܚܘܡܐ ܡܫܡܥܢܐ ܐܝܬ ܕܬܪ̈ܝܗܘܢ ܐܢܛܝܦܐܣܝܐ ܗܘܐ. ܘܐܢ ܚܕ ܟܠ ܠܐ ܟܠ ܠܐ ܡܠܝܐ ܠܗ ܢܦܩܐ. ܐܝܟ ܕܣܘܦܣܛܣ[1] ܐܢܛܝܦܐܣܝܐ[2] ܫܩܠ ܠܦܠܛܘܬܗ. ܡܕܝܢ ܡܒܘܕܘܬܐ ܡܬܗܦܟܐ. ܟܕ ܪܟܒܬ ܒܐܣܟܡܐ ܬܪܝܢܐ. ܡܒܘܕܐ ܐܢܛܝܦܐܣܝܐ ܫܩܠܢ ܠܦܠܛܘܬܐ. ܐܝܬܘܗܝ. ܘܗܪܟܐ ܫܩܠܬ ܐܢܛܝܦܐܣܝܐ ܐܟܚܕܐ ܕܐܝܬܝܗ̇ ܗܝ ܕܡܒܘܕܘܬܐ ܐܝܬܝܗ̇ ܗܝ ܬܦܘܩ ܕܠܐ ܡܒܘܕܘܬܐ. ܒܕܚܕ ܡܢ ܢܦܩ ܚܠܐ *ܘܐܬܟܠ. ܐܚܪܢܐ ܕܝܢ ܢܦܩ ܚܠܐ[3] ܘܠܐ ܐܬܟܠ. ܠܗ̇، ܩܕܡܝܬܐ ܡܕܝܢ ܠܐ ܡܗܝܡܢ ܫܡܘܥܐ ܒܒܐ ܕܠܐ ܚܝܘܐ[4] ܪܗܛܢܐ ܕܣܘܦܣܛܣ[5] ܐܦ ܬܠܡܣܘܣ ܒܡܠܟܘܬܐ ܘܐܣܪܢܐ ܒܕܘܟ̈ܝܬܐ ܐܣܝܪܬܐ ܟܕ ܢܦܩܘ ܦܠܣܛܐ ܠܦܪܣܐ ܗܘܘ. ܘܗܢܐ ܬܘܒ ܐܠܐ ܬܫܒܘܚܬܐ ܕܡܬܚܫܒܢܘܬܐ ܪܗܛܢܝܬܐ.

1 [1] sg. RVLl [2] i. ܘ RVL [3] ܘܟܠܗܝ، RVLl [4] i. om. RVLl

2 [1] om. RVLl [2] ܡܢ ܐܝܬܘܗܝ، F [3] om. RVL [4] ܒܐܢܫ RVLl [5*] sg. RVLl [6*] ܗܘ ܐܘ ܢܦܩ RVLl

3 [1] ܕܣܘܦܝܣܛܝܣ R; ܕܣܘܦܣܛܝܣ VLl [2] i. add. ܠ RL [3*] om. Fl [4] ܚܝܘܬܐ RVL [5] i. ܘ F

from signs—for example, 'This girl has given birth; therefore she is a married woman.' Here the birth is a certain sign of matrimony. Both of these are combinations in the First Figure and therefore necessary. But enthymemes are mostly from possibles, and these are either from true reputable (premisses)—for example, 'Socrates is quiet and meek; therefore he is loved'—or from signs—for example, 'Socrates is gripped by fever; therefore his pulse is fast', and 'Dorieus has won Olympic victories; therefore he has won a contest with a crown'.

TWO.[30] An index is inferior to a sign, because it belongs among (the premisses) similar to the necessary. In the Second (Figure), for example, 'This woman has a swollen belly; therefore she is pregnant'. Here although the middle (term) is certainly (attached) to the minor, the major is not certainly (attached) universally to the middle. Because not everyone whose belly is swollen is pregnant, the combination is not in the First Figure but in the Second, as (follows in full): 'This woman has a swollen belly; a pregnant woman has a swollen belly; therefore this woman is pregnant.' In the Third (Figure), for example, 'Wise men are just, because Socrates the wise man is just.' Here, although the major is certainly (attached) to the middle, which is the index, the middle is not certainly (attached) universally to the minor. Because not every wise man is Socrates, the combination is not in the First Figure but in the Third, as (follows in full): 'Socrates is a wise man; Socrates is a just man; therefore every wise man is a just man.' An index also belongs among (the premisses) similar to the possible, mostly in the Second (Figure), as for example, 'Socrates has a rapid pulse; therefore he is gripped by a fever'; but (also) in the Third, as for example, 'The noble are modest, because Joseph was noble and modest.' These are eight modes of rhetorical enthymemes.

THREE.[31] An enthymeme is generated from even possibles when the middle term is an index of both opposites, and if one side is not stronger, the soul does not incline to it. For example, 'Dionysius asks for warriors for his protection; therefore he is planning a tyranny.' Because the major (term) is in the Second Figure—'Tyrants ask for warriors for protection'—here the request for warriors is as

---

[30] **1.7.2** AR 1.2 57b3-25; IS 1.6 (44.12-16; 8-12; 45.4-8).
[31] **1.7.3** AR 1.2 57b25-58a2; IS 1.7 (45.11-47.9).

ܕܐܝܟܢ. ܪܗܛܘܪܘܬܐ ܕܝܢ ܠܡܡܠܠܘܬܐ ܐܚܪܢܝܬܐ ܕܡܢܗܘܢ ܕܝܢ ܥܡܢܢ ܡܢܗܘܢ ܕܝܢ ܠܐ ܒܕܒܠ ܡܢܟܝܢ. ܒܗܿܘ ܕܗܘܐ ܡܫܬܘܕܥܐ. ܘܒܠܚܘܕܐ ܠܒܝܫ ܘܡܛܠ ܥܘܠܦܐ ܕܟܝܢܐ *ܡܬܝܪܫܢܘܬܐ[1] ܪܗܛܘܪܘܬܐ[2] ܠܫܘܠܡܠܦܢܘܬܗ ܕܐܡܘܡܠܠܘܬܐ ܕܥܘܪܒܐ. ܘܐܠܝܢ ܠܡܦܪܥܘܬܗܘܢ. ܐܦ ܠܒܪ ܘܐܬܪ̈ܘܬܐ ܠܡ̈ܠܐ ܕܐܬܦܪܣܐ ܘܕܕܐܠܦܠܘܣܐ[3] ܗܢܘ ܡܦܠܣܝܢ ܡܢ ܕܠܟ̈ܠܐ ܕܐܠܗܐ ܡܢܗܘܢ. ܒܫܒܝܠܐ ܓܒܪ ܡܢܗܘܢ ܡܛܠ ܫܪ̈ܟܐ ܐܬܩܢܐ ܬܘܒ ܘܒܢ̈ܝܢܐ ܘܦܘܠܦ̈ܠܝܣܐ ܗܘܐ ܢܛܝܪܬܐ. ܐܝܟ ܐܬܪ̈ܘܬܐ ܕܐܬܪܐ ܘܒܝܬܪܐ. ܘܒܠܚܕܐ[4] ܡܢܗܘܢ ܕܢܣܒ ܒܢܝܐ ܕܠܝܠܐ ܒܐܠܝܢ. ܠܟܠܗܘܢ ܐܝܪ ܗܠܝܢ ܦܘܪܫܐ ܘܐܕ̈ܫܐ ܘܐܬܪ̈ܘܬܐ ܪܗܛܘܪܐ ܦܠܐ ܠܡܕܪ. ܘܐܕ̈ܫܐ ܕܝܢ ܗܠܝܢ ܐܝܢ ܕܒܪ̈ܝܐ ܡܬܢܐ ܕܪܗܛܘܪܘܬܐ ܡܬܬܘܪܝܢ. ܐܬܪ̈ܘܬܐ ܕܝܢ ܗܠܝܢ ܠܡ̈ܠܐ ܡܬܕ̈ܪܐ.[5]

## ܦܘܣܩܐ ܬܡܝܢܝܐ
## ܡܛܠܗ̇ ܕܬܠܬܐ ܐܝܢ ܐܕ̈ܫܐ ܟ̈ܠܝܐ ܕܪܗܛܘܪܘܬܐ
## ܬܐܘܪ̈ܝܐ ܐܝܟܢ

ܡܕܡܝܢܘܬܐ. ܚܙܝ *ܗ̇ܝ ܕܐܝܟܢ ܐܬܝܠܗ̇ ܡܕܡ ܐܘ ܠܐ[1] ܐܬܝܠܗ̇ ܠܟܠܗܘܢ ܒܢ̈ܝܐ ܪܗܛܘܪ̈ܐ ܠܗܘܢ. ܒܕܠܝܠܘܬ ܦܘܪܫܐ ܕܝܢ ܗܘܟܢܐ ܕܒܢ̈ܝܐ ܒܡܟܬܒܢܐ ܠܥܕ̈ܬܐ ܕܠܦܢ ܐܘ ܒܢ̈ܝܢ ܢܦܫܢ. ܘܗܘܝܢ ܗܠܝܢ ܐܘ ܡܢ ܒܪܢܫܐ ܡܫܬܠܡܝܢ. ܘܗܘܝܢ ܒܢܝܐ ܡܠܟܠܟܐ ܘܡܣܦܪܐ. ܐܘ ܠܒܪܢܫܐ ܐܝܟ ܡܬܠܡܕܝܢ. ܘܗܘܝܢ ܒܢܝܐ ܡܬܠܡܝܢܐ[2] ܘܡܬܩܢܝܢܐ. ܐܘ ܡܢ ܒܪܢܫܐ ܐܝܟ ܗܘܝܢ. ܘܗܘܝܢ ܒܢܝܐ ܕܡܫܬܥܠܝܢܘܬܐ[3] ܘܕܡܦܩ ܒܪܘܚܐ. ܬܠܬܐ ܐܝܟܐ ܐܝܢ ܐܕ̈ܫܐ ܟ̈ܠܝܐ ܕܪܗܛܘܪܘܬܐ. ܡܕܡܝܢܐ ܕܝܢ ܡܠܟܢܝܐ ܘܠܒܢܝܐ ܕܒܬܪ ܒܢܝܗ̇ ܒܕ ܡܫܬܟܢܝܐ ܗܘ ܒܗ ܢܛܐ. ܕܬܪܝܢ ܕܝܢ ܡܣܘܚܝܢܐ[4] ܘܠܒܢܝܐ ܕܡܐܡ ܥܒܕܝܢ ܒܕ ܠܗ ܒܠ ܠܒܠܬܐ ܘܡܒܥܝܐ ܕܠܐ ܐܬܝܠܗܘܢ ܡܬܩܠܫ ܐܘ ܡܬܠܒܢܐ ܐܝܟ ܐܠܐ ܒܠ ܗܢܝܢ ܕܡܒܢܝܢ ܠܗ ܘܡܬܠܒܢ. ܘܬܠܬܐ ܕܡܫܬܝܫܝܐ ܐܘܡܢܘܬ ܡܫܘܬܦܢܐ ܘܠܒܢܝܐ ܕܒܪ ܐܝܬ ܒܗ. ܒܠ ܒܢܝܐ ܕܢܝ ܒܗܘ ܗܘܬ ܡܬܩܦܠܝܢ ܐܘ ܢܦܩ ܪܘܚܐ ܒܪܘܚܐ.

---

4 [1] ܡܬܝܪܫܢܝܘܬܐ RVLI [2*] pl. RVLI [3] ܘܕܐܠܦܠܘܣܐ RVLI [4] i. ܕ RVLI [5] sg. RVLI

1 [1*] ܗܕܐ ܡܕܡ ܐܬܝܠܗ̇ ܘܠܐ RVLI [2] ܡܬܠܡܝܢܐ RVLI [3] ܕܡܫܬܥܠܝܢܘܬܐ RVLI [4] ܡܣܘܚܝܢܐ RVLI

much an index of tyranny as an index of non-tyranny, because one (person) may seize power and act deceitfully, but another seize power and not act deceitfully. The listener does not therefore give *pistis* to the former as long as the orator does not show that Peisistratus and Theagenes in Megara and others in other places were tyrants when they seized office. This, then, is the ninth mode of rhetorical enthymemes.

FOUR.[32] Rhetoric shares (its) subject matter with other arts, some of which are in existence, while others are not yet known, and therefore the difference between a rhetorical enthymeme and syllogisms of the rest of the arts is concealed and obscure. It is (however) necessary to distinguish them, for also the common *topoi* of rhetoric and dialectic are more abundant than the specific (ones) of each of them. Use is made of many of them, like the *topoi* of the more and the less, in ethical, physical, and political questions, and they enter into each of the five in a specific way. It is therefore necessary to know all these distinctions and rhetorical species and *topoi*. 'Species' are those which are useful in the particular questions of rhetoric, *topoi* those of common utility.

## SECTION EIGHT
### On the Fact that the Principal Species of Rhetoric are Three
### Four Theories

ONE.[33] Dispute as to whether something is or is not is common to all rhetorical parleys, but the specific distinction of popular parleys is that the majority relate to matters which are good or evil. These are either awaited from someone, this being a parley of exhortation and dissuasion; or they are devised for someone, this being a parley of praise and blame; or they have been done by someone, this being a parley of prosecution and defence. The principal species of rhetoric are therefore three: first, the deliberative, which is appropriate to the future time, because the end is awaited in it; secondly, the demonstrative, which is close to the present time, because a person is not praised or blamed for a good or evil which do not exist, but for those

[32] **1.7.4** AR 1.2 58a2-35; IS 1.7 (47.12-49.4).
[33] **1.8.1** AR 1.3 58b6-20; IS 2.1 (53.5-54.5; 54.18-55.1).

ܕܐܬܬܝܼܢ. ܬܠܬܐ ܐܝܬܝܗܘܢ[1] ܛܟ̈ܣܐ ܕܒܗܘܢ ܡܫܬܡܠܝܐ ܡܕܒܪܢܘܬܐ
ܪܘܚܢܝܬܐ.[2] ܐܦܪܐ ܘܡܐܡܪܐ ܘܡܫܡ̈ܥܢܐ. ܘܗܠܝܢ ܡܫܡ̈ܥܢܐ ܬܠܬܐ
ܐܝܠܝܢ. ܒܠܕܝܢܐ ܘܕܝܢܐ ܘܣܪܝܐ. ܘܕܝܢܐ ܕܒܬܪܝܬܐ ܗ̇ܝ ܪܕܝܐ ܡܕܝܢܢܐ
ܕܒܝܫܐ ܦܠܐ ܠܡܗܘܐ. ܕܗܠܝܢ ܕܗ̇ܘ، ܕܝܢ ܡܢ ܒܢܝܢܐ ܡܚܣܝܢܐ. ܘܣܪܝܐ
ܫܠܝܘܬ ܣܪ. ܡܢ ܡܬܬܕܝܢܢܐ ܘܫܡܥܬܗ ܕܐܣܝܐ ܒܠܫܢܗ ܣܝܡ. ܘܠܒܠܫ.
ܡܢ ܒܢܝܢܐ ܪܘܚܢܝܐ ܢܝܫܐ ܐܝܬ ܕܠܝܢܐ. ܠܡܠܘܟܐ ܗ̇ܝ ܕܢܠܒܟ ܒܠ
ܡܕܒܪܢܘܬܐ ܕܦܓܪܐ ܘܒܠܟܐ ܡܢ ܗ̇ܝ، ܕܡܩܦܠܐ. ܠܡܣܒܪܢܐ[3] ܕܝܢ ܕܒܠܘܫ
ܠܡܫܬܐ ܘܢܦܫܐ ܠܣܘܦܝܐ. ܘܠܒܪܝܐ ܬܘܒ ܕܢܦܬܚ ܠܟܠܝܐ ܕܐܟܘܠ
*ܘܢܘܦ ܙܘܥܐ ܕܗ̇ܘ ܕܠܐ ܐܟܘܠ. ܐܘ ܕܐܟܘܠ[4] ܒܝܘܡ ܒܕܠܐ ܢܟܐ ܐܘ ܒܪ.
ܢܟܐ ܒܝܘܡ ܡܛܠ ܗ̇ܝ، ܕܢܘܬܪ.

ܕܬܠܬ. ܡܠܘܟܐ ܐܝܬ ܐܡܒܐ ܕܗܠܝܢ ܕܢܦܫ̈ܐ ܘܐܦ ܠܐ ܦܘܬܚ ܐܠܐ
ܡܠܘ ܡܦܩܦܩ ܚܠܝܡ. ܘܗܘܝܐ ܗ̇ܘ ܕܡܠܘܟ ܘܡܩܕܢܐ ܠܗ ܒܐܡܬܗ ܠܗܘܬ
ܗ̇ܘ ܡܢ ܕܡܬܘܪ ܐܘ ܡܦܩܦܩ ܚܝܪ. ܒܡܢܐ ܐܟܡܝܢ ܓܒܪ ܗ̇ܘ ܕܡܦܩܦܩ
ܡܬܠܘܠܘ. ܐܝܟ ܡܠܟܐ ܕܫܡ̈ܥܐ ܣܠܩ ܥܡܘܪܬ ܕܫܠܬܐ ܘܪܕܘܦܝܐ ܕܒܠ ܐܟ̣ܙ
ܬܘܕܝܬܐ ܬܘܪܓܡܐ ܗ̇ܘ ܕܢܣܠܩ ܪܣܡܗ ܢܥܠܡ ܐܝܟ ܢܦܫܗ. ܡܬܠܘܠܘ ܓܒܪ
ܐܒܠܒܘܘ[1] ܒܪ ܕܪܗ ܗܘܐ ܠܦܪܘܦܠܘܘ ܣܒܪܗ[2] ܘܒܕܒ ܕܡܛܠܬܗ
ܡܐܬ. ܠܗܘܐ ܓܒܪ ܒܪ ܗ̇ܝ، ܕܢܝܚܐ ܡܬܐܪܐ ܗܘܬ ܡܬܘܬܐ ܥܦܪ ܠܗ.

ܕܐܪܒܥ. ܦܠܘܣܡܘܣ ܪܘܚܢܝܐ ܐܡܒܐ ܡܬܪܓܡܢܘܬܐ ܒܪ ܐܝܟ
ܕܐܬܝܘܗܝ، ܐܘ ܡܢ[1] ܡܫܬܦ̈ܫܝܢܘܬܐ ܗ̇ܘܐ ܐܘ ܫܒܘܕܒܐ ܗܘ ܐܘ ܐܬܐ.
ܐܠܝܢܐ ܠܪܘܦܐ ܕܢܣܒܠ ܢܬܕܗܘܢ، ܦܪ̈ܘܦܣܘܣ ܡܬܪܓܡܢܘܬܐ ܒܒܠܗܘܢ[2]
ܢܬܒܐ ܚܠܝܡ. ܘܡܛܠ[3] ܕܠܚܪ̈ܒܐ ܐܢܩܒܐ ܠܐ ܠܡܒܪܐ ܐܦܠܐ ܠܡܒܢܐ ܢܦܩ

2 [1] ܐܢܘܢ RVLl [2] ܕܪܘܚܢܝܘܬܐ RVL [3] ܠܡܣܒܪܢܘܬܐ RLl [4*] om. RVLl
3 [1] ܐܒܠܒܘܣ RVL; ܐܒܠܒܘܣ l [2] ܣܒܪܗ RVLl
4 [1] om. RVLl [2] i. ܘ RVLl [3] i. om. RVL

which are present in him and to hand; and thirdly, the judicial or adversarial, which is related to the past time, because a person is prosecuted or mounts a defence on account of an evil which has already occurred.

TWO.[34] The things by which rhetorical practice is accomplished are three: the speaker, the speech, and the hearers. Now these (last), the hearers, are three (in kind): an adversary, a judge, and spectators. A governing ruler of the assembly must be a judge of things to come, an examining arbitrator (?) (a judge) of things past, while spectators only look out for ability in one of those being judged and the defeat of the other. To each of the rhetorical parleys there is a special end: to the deliberative that it should exhort to an action which is expedient and dissuade from one which is harmful; to the demonstrative that it should praise the excellent and blame the deficient; and to the adversarial that it should prosecute him who has done wrong and defend him who has not done wrong, or him who has done wrong (either) unintentionally or intending to be of help.

THREE.[35] A deliberative (orator) sometimes advises things which are honourable even though they are not expedient, but on the contrary are harmful, and similarly he who praises and blames does not habitually look to what is advantageous or harmful, for on many occasions that which causes harm is praised, like the slaughter of martyrs for piety, persecution for true confession, and a man giving his life for his friend. For Achilles was praised when he went to the aid of his companion Patroclus and knew that because of him he would die, for to him, although to live was advantageous, death was honourable.

FOUR.[36] Since the rhetorical syllogism, the enthymeme, is, as has been shown, either from reputable (premisses) or a sign or an index, it is necessary for an orator to lay up for himself premisses useful in all these areas. And because no one is concerned either to gain or repel necessary things, rhetorical deliberations may be specified only

[34] **1.8.2** AR 1.3 58a37-b6; 20-29; IS 2.1 (55.2-6; 9-14).
[35] **1.8.3** AR 1.3 58b29-59a6; IS 2.1 (55.14-56.6).
[36] **1.8.4** AR 1.3 59a6-29; IS 2.1 (56.6-57.3).

ܒܪܢܫܐ. ܡܠܟ̈ܐ ܪܗܛܘܪ̈ܐ ܕܡܫܬܥܝ̈ܢܐ ܒܠܚܘܕ ܡܬܕܠܠܝܢ. ܘܒܠܘܗܝ ܦ̇ܠܐ
ܠܪܗܛܘܪܐ ܡܠܘܟܐ ܠܡܟܬܒܘ ܦܪ̈ܘܣܛܓܡܐ ܡܫܪ̈ܪܢܝܬܐ[4] ܗ̇ܝ ܕܡܫܬܥܝܢܐ ܗܘ
ܥܒܕܐ ܐܘ ܠܐ ܡܫܬܥܝܢܐ. ܘܕܗ̇ܘܐ ܐܘ ܠܐ ܗ̇ܘܐ. ܘܐܝܬܘܗܝ ܗܘܐ
ܐܘ ܠܐ ܐܝܬܘܗܝ[5] ܗܟܢ. ܐܦ ܓܒܪ ܘܒܢܬܝܪܐ ܘܡܣܥܝܪܐ ܛܒ ܡܬܒܕܪ
ܡܠܘܟܐ ܘܡܫܘܚܢܐ ܘܕܘܣܐܣܝܢܐ ܒܝ. ܐܢܫ. ܕܒܗܝܢܐ ܠܡ ܥܒܕܐ ܘܚܬܪܢܐ
ܐܝܬ ܐܘ ܫܘܦܥܝܢܐ[6]. ܪܒܐ ܐܘ ܙܥܘܪܐ. ܘܗܕܐ ܫܥܒܘܕܬܐ ܠܥܒܕܬܐ ܗ̇ܝ
ܐܘ ܒܥܕܬܐ. ܠܬܪܬܐ ܐܘ ܒܥܪܝܬܐ. ܘܗܟܢܐ ܒܒܪܐ ܒܐܝܟ ܐܘ ܒܟܠ. ܡܢ
ܐܘ ܡܠܟ.

---

[4] sg. RL; ܡܬܕܢܝܬܐ ܡܫܪ̈ܪܢܝܬܐ V [5] RVLI [6] add. ܐܘ RVLI

of possibles. Therefore it is necessary for the deliberative orator to prepare premisses establishing that a thing is possible or impossible, that it will or will not happen, or was or never was. Also the deliberative, demonstrative, or judicial (orator) may be greatly helped by 'the greater or lesser' when he says: 'With this thing, there is advantage or harm, great or small,' or, 'This action is good or evil, greater or lesser,' and, 'This deed is just or unjust, much or little.'

ܩܦܠܐܘܢ ܬܪܝܢܐ

ܡܛܠ *ܐܕܫܐ ܡܠܟܝܐ[1] ܕܪܗܛܪܘܬܐ

ܘܒܗ ܐܝܬ ܦܣܘ̈ܩܐ ܐܪܒܥܐ

ܦܣܘܩܐ ܩܕܡܝܐ

ܡܛܠ ܡܠܟ̈ ܥܒ̈ܪܐ ܪ̈ܘܪܒܐ

ܬܐܘܪ̈ܝܣ ܬܡܢܝܐ

ܩܕܡܝܬܐ. ܡܛܠ ܓܝܪ ܕܡܠܟܐ ܠܘܬ ܚܫܐ ܡܕܡ ܛܒܐ ܚܐܪ. ܐܠܓܐ ܕܢܣܒ
ܡܠܘܟܐ ܠܛܒܬܐ ܓܘܐܝܬ ܘܠܦܠ̈ܓܘܬܗ ܕܝܠܢܐܝܬ. ܘܓܠܝܐ ܕܒܛ̈ܒܬܐ
ܘܒܝ̈ܫܬܐ ܕܐܢܫܐܝܬ ܩܘܡ ܠܝܬ ܡܠܟܐ. ܟܕ ܡܠܟܐ ܡܐܡܪܐ ܗܘ ܡܕܝܢܐ
ܕܡܓܒܝܢܐ ܠܘܬ ܩܫܝܐ ܕܛܒܬܐ ܘܢܘܗܪܐ ܕܡܢ ܒܫܝܬܐ. ܘܗܘ ܕܐܢܣ ܡܢ ܟܠ
ܦܘܪܣ ܗܘܐ. ܐܢ ܢܨܒܐ *ܐܢܫ ܘܐܢ ܠܐ ܢܨܒܐ.[1] ܛܒܬܐ ܡܕܡ ܡܠܟܢܝܬܐ
ܡܬܡܨܝܢܘܬܐ ܗܝ. ܘܠܐ ܟܠ ܡܬܡܨܝܢܘܬܐ ܐܝܟ ܗܢܝ ܗ̇ܘ ܕܐܢܫ ܒܐܫܬܐ
ܒܡܨܒܐ ܕܪܘܚܐ[2] ܒܓܪܐ ܘܗܢܝ ܡܪܐ ܡܣܩܐ ܪܘܚܐ ܒܫܡܬܐ ܕܡܫܚܐ
ܡܘܪܓܗ ܘܡܦܫܫܐ ܪܘܚܗ. ܠܐ ܡܬܡܨܝ̈ܢܘܬܐ ܕܡܓܒܝܢ ܡܫܬܡ̈ܥܢ ܐܘ
ܡܬܚܦܩ. ܘܗܢܐ ܥܒܪܐ ܓܘܢܐ ܕܢܦܫ ܡܠܟܐ.

ܕܬܪ̈ܝܢ. ܠܦܘ̈ܠܓ ܛܒܬܐ ܕܝܢ ܕܝܠܢܐܝܬ ܐܘܟܝܬ ܠܐܕ̈ܫܝܗ̇ ܦ̇ܠܐ ܠܡܒܥܝܐ
ܠܐ ܒܝܢܐ ܚܝܘܬܐ ܕܡܘܡܘܬܐ. ܐܠܐ ܒܡܣܬܒܪܢܘܬܐ ܒܠܚܘܕ. ܒܗ̇
ܕܪܗܛܪܘܬܐ ܠܘ ܠܒܪܪܐ ܚܦܝܐ. ܐܠܐ ܐܘܡܢܘܬܐ ܡܕܡ ܗ̇ܝ. ܕܒܗ̇
ܐܘܡܢܘܬܐ ܣܘܠܘܓܝܣܛܝܩܘܬܐ ܒܗܘ̈ܠܘܣ ܦܘܠܝܛܝܩܘܬܐ[1] ܡܬܝܕܥܐ.
ܘܗܢܘܢ ܦܘ̈ܠܓܝܢ ܡܠܟܐ ܕܥܝܪ̈ܐ ܗܠܝܢ ܐܢܘܢ. ܣܛܪ ܡܢܗܘܢ ܕܡܬܒ̈ܥܝܐ
ܕܠܐ ܡܣܬܒܝܢ. ܚܡܫܐ ܐܝܬܝܗܘܢ. ܩܕܡܝܐ ܡܪ̈ܗܛܐ. ܕܬܪ̈ܝܢ ܩܪܒܐ
ܘܥܢܝܐ. ܕܬܠܬܐ ܢܛܘܪܬܐ ܕܡܕܝܢܬܐ. ܕܐܪܒܥܐ ܬܠ̈ܠܬܐ ܘܦܩ̈ܕܬܐ. ܕܚܡܫܐ
ܡܣܡܟܬ ܢܡܘܣܐ.

ܕܬܠܬܐ. ܪܗܛܪܐ ܕܡܛܠ ܡܪ̈ܗܛܐ ܥܠܝܟ ܪܕܦ ܠܗ ܕܢܣܒ ܒܦ̈ܣܝܗ
ܕܡܕܝܢܬܐ ܕܡܠܟܐ ܐܝܟܢ ܘܡܠܟܐ ܐܝܟܢ. ܐܡܝܢܐ ܕܒܗܘܢ ܠܐܦܣܘ̈ܩܝܬܐ
ܢܦܘܩ. ܘܠܛܠܝܐ ܕܠܐ ܪܒܐ ܐܝܕܗ ܒܐܘܡܢܘܬܐ ܕܡܘܬܪܐ ܠܡܕܝܢܬܐ

Titulus [1]* pl. RVL

1 [1]* om. R; ܐܢܫ ܘܠܐ ܢܨܒܐ V [2] i. add. ܕ RVL

2 [1] ܦܘܠ̈ܝܛܝܘܬܐ RVLl

## CHAPTER TWO
## ON THE DELIBERATIVE SPECIES OF RHETORIC
## FOUR SECTIONS

### SECTION ONE
### On Deliberations on Great Subjects
### Eight Theories

ONE.[1] Since deliberation aims towards some good goal, the deliberative (orator) must know the good in general and its divisions specifically. It is clear that there is no deliberation on good or bad (things) which necessarily come to pass, because deliberation is speech causing motion of the will towards the attainment of good and warning of bad, and that which is necessary will come to pass anyway, whether someone wishes (it) or not. Therefore the good to be deliberated is (limited to) the possible, and not (even) every possible, like someone gripped by fever (being affected) by the blowing of a northerly wind, or someone having a windy convulsion (being affected) by anger which raises his temperature and dissipates his wind, (things) impossible to be effected or avoided by our will. So much for the general subject matter of the goal of deliberation.

TWO.[2] It is not necessary, however, to enumerate the divisions of the good specifically—that is, its species—in the accurate manner of wisdom, but only in (the manner of) opinion, because rhetoric is not concerned with truth, but is some (sort of) art, (namely) that in which syllogistic art is stamped with political materials. The divisions of deliberation on the greatest subjects—excluding those which are private, which are unbounded—are five. First is finances; second, war and peace; third, defence of the city; fourth, imports and exports; and fifth, legislation.

---

[1] **2.1.1** AR 1.4 59a30-b2; 5 60b4-5; IS 2.1 (57.7-58.3).
[2] **2.1.2** AR 1.4 59b2-23; IS 2.1 (58.3-10).

ܢܛܪܘ܂ ܘܠܐܢܫܐ ܕܡܢ ܒܬܘܠܬܐ ܒܪܝܢ ܘܡܫܡܠܝܐ ܡܫܡܫܢܐ ܢܦܪܘܫ܂ ܒܗ̇[1] ܠܗ ܒܗ̇ ܡܫܡܫܝܢ ܟܠ ܢܒܩܫܘܢ ܒܬܪܝܢ ܣܘܓܐܐ ܐܠܐ ܘܒܗ̇ ܡܢ ܢܦܩܬܐ ܡܬܚܙܝܢ܂ ܠܕܐܝܟ ܗܠܝܢ ܦܠܐ ܕܐܝܟ ܡܠܘܟܐ܂ ܘܠܐ ܒܠܚܘܕ ܡܢ ܡܢܐ ܕܒܡܘܡܗ ܢܗܘ ܡܬܒܪܐ܂ ܐܠܐ ܘܡܢ ܛܘܒܝ ܥܒܕܐ ܕܐܣܝܘܬܐ ܣܘܓܐܐ[2] ܡܢܐ ܕܐܠܦ܂[3]

ܕܐܪܒܥ܂ ܘܡܠܘܟܐ ܕܪܘܚܐ ܘܚܫܝܫܐ ܠܗܘܢ ܦܢ ܚܠ ܗܘܒܪܢܐ ܕܐܬܘܗܝ܆ ܒܠܬܗ ܕܪܘܚܐ ܢܣܝܐ܂ ܘܐܦ ܠܐ ܪܒ ܟܠ ܚܫܝܫܐ ܢܚܠܘܡ܂ ܒܗ̇ ܦܣܝܩܘܬ ܕܪܘܚܐ ܫܛܪ ܡܢ ܢܦܫܐ ܕܒܠܒܒܐ ܒܣܡܐ܂ ܒܠܬ ܗܢܝܢ ܕܝܢ ܦܠܐ ܕܝܕܥ ܚܠܐ ܕܡܬܒܬܒܢܐ ܒܗܘܢܐ ܘܒܪܐ܂ ܕܐܝܠܝܢ ܗܟܢ ܡܬܒܠܝܢ ܘܕܕܐܝܠܝܢ ܫܛܪ ܡܬܚܫܝܢ ܘܡܠܬܪ ܐܝܬܝܗܘܢ܂ ܘܐܦ ܡܫܬܠܐ ܠܡܕܝܢܬܗ ܒܡܕܝܢܐ ܡܢ ܕܘܟ܂ ܘܢܗܘܐ ܡܦܩ ܒܪܝܐ ܕܡܪܝܒܐ ܕܝܠܗ̇ ܕܡܕܝܢܬܐ ܘܕܒܢ̈ܝ ܐܘܣܝܐ̈ܗ̇ ܘܡܒܕ̈ܩܢܗ̇܂ ܘܡܕܒܪܢܘܗܝ ܘܫܪܬܗܘܢ ܠܒܬܐ ܘܒܝܫܬܐ ܕܪܝܒܘܗܝ܂ ܢܦܫ ܕܝܢ ܐܡܒܐܝܬ ܚܝܠܐ ܕܒܪܝܐ ܒܢܝܠܐ ܕܓܘܫܡܐ܂ ܐܝܟ ܕܡܢ ܠܫܪܕܐ܂ ܘܠܐ ܢܦܩܘܢ ܠܗ ܢܦܫܐ ܕܝܕܥܐ ܕܒܓܪ ܒܗ̇ ܡܦܠܐ ܠܒܘܪܐ ܣܘܓܐܐ ܚܒܪ̈ܐ *ܘܠܡܣܬܟܠܐ ܚܝ̈ܠܘܬܐ܂[1]

ܕܫܒܥ܂ ܘܒܝܠܦܘܪܬܗ̇ ܕܡܕܝܢܬܐ ܦܠܐ ܕܝܕܥ ܪܗܛܪܐ ܐܕܫ̈ܢܗ̇ ܕܝܠܦܘܪܬܐ ܠܗܘܬ ܥܘܬܪܐ ܕܫܡܝܐ ܦܣܛܘܢܐ ܘܦܠܘܪܐ ܘܡܫܝܚܐ ܘܡܡܢܝܢܐ܂ ܝܕܥ ܗܘܐ ܘܠܕܘܒܪ̈ܬܐ ܕܪ̈ܘܫܐ ܘܒܫܠܐܝܐ ܕܒܢܝܗܘܢ ܐܝܟ ܕܒܡܘܠܐܐ ܡܕܝܢܬܐ ܡܬܡܢܝܢ܂ ܘܡܬܣܡܐ ܕܝܠܦܘܪܐ ܚܫܡ ܐܢܫ܂ ܘܠܫܩ̈ܠܐ[1] ܒܬܚ̈ܠܐ ܢܣܒ܂ ܗܕܐ ܓܝܪ ܡܫܡܫܢܐ ܘܐܦ ܠܐ ܢܗܘܐ ܥܡܠ ܢܦܫܗ ܕܐܬܬܐ ܒܝܕܝܐ܂

ܕܬܫܥ܂ ܘܡܛܠ ܬܘܪܣܝܐ ܗܘܐ ܦܠܐ ܕܝܕܥ ܒܒܝܐ ܕܐܦܠܝܢ[1] ܣܦܩܐ ܠܡܕܝܢܬܐ܂ ܘܟܠ ܐܝܠܝܢ ܩܝܣܝܐ ܕܬܬܡܒܪܘܢ ܠܗ̇[2] ܡܢ ܠܒܪ܂ ܘܐܝܠܝܢ ܙܕܩ ܠܡܥܕܪܘ ܒܝܬܗ̇ ܠܦܢܝܬܐ ܐܚܪܬܐ ܐܝܟ ܕܠܬܓܘܪܬܐ܂ ܒܗ̇ ܩܝܒܪ̈ܬܐ ܘܠܒܢ̈ܝܐ ܘܦܠܘܪܐ ܕܫܡܠܝܐ ܥܒܝܬܐ ܒܗ̇ ܡܬܓܒܝܢ܂ ܒܣܝܐܬ ܡܬܦܪܬܐ ܡܕܝܢܬܐ܂ ܢܚܠܘܡ ܕܝܢ ܘܐܡܒܝܢܘܬ ܩܘܡܒܐ[3] ܒܐܢܫ̈ܐ ܡܬܝܢܐ ܘܐܘܪ̈ܚܐ ܒܬܪܐ ܕܒܗܘܢ ܡܬܬܠܝܢ ܚܫ̈ܘܬܐ ܕܡܕܝܢܬܐ܂

3 [1] ܒܗ̇ RVL [2] ܣܘ̈ܓܐܬܐ RVLl [3] ܠܡܐܠܦ RVL
4 [1*] om. RVL
5 [1] ܘܠܒܥ̈ܠܐ RVLl
6 [1] ܕܐܦܠܝܢ F; ܕܐܦܝܢ V [2] f. ܗ RVLl [3] pl. RVLl

THREE.[3] The orator who advises on finances should know what and how great are the resources of the city, so that he may balance wages with them, expel the idle (man) who does not put his hand to an art which is useful to the city, and establish a moderate level for him who is brought down from (his) wealth. Because many become wealthy not (only) when they add to their resources but also when they cut down on expenditures, the deliberative (orator) should pay attention to such things, and profit not only from what he has experienced in person, but also be able to learn from the accounts of the matters by many others.

FOUR.[4] An adviser on war and peace will first consider the strength of the affair which is the cause of war, and if it is not great will advise peace, because the danger of war is more grievous than the enemy's imposition. After this he should know the strength of the combatants, those of his own side and the aliens, which are more warlike, which has a greater number and wealth of arms, and whether from some point or other his city has an advantage. He should be acquainted with the deeds of the warriors of his own city and of those living on its borders and its neighbours, their customs, and the good or bad outcome of their wars. He should constantly compare the strength of the aliens with the strength of his own people, (to see) if they are similar to each other. The experience of the past is not sufficient for him, for the course (of time) may make the few many and the weak strong.

FIVE.[5] On the defence of the city, the orator must know the sorts of defence corresponding to the varieties of lowland and mountainous, inland and coastal setting. He should also know the locations of surprises and ambushes from which cities are usually attacked, strengthen them by an increase in the garrison, and replace the treacherous with the trustworthy. This is possible even if his experience of the place is not based on sight.

---

[3] **2.1.3** AR 1.4 59b23-33; IS 2.1 (58.11-59.4).
[4] **2.1.4** AR 1.4 59b33-60a6; IS 2.1 (59.5-60.6).
[5] **2.1.5** AR 1.4 60a6-11; IS 2.1 (60.7-14).

ܕܥܒܕ. ܘܣܘܡܘܬ ܢܡܘܣܐ ܡܢ ܦ̈ܘܬܐ ܐܝܬܝܗ̇ ܪܘܪ̈ܒܬܐ ܘܚܝܠܐ ܪܗܛܪܐ ܕܐܬܝܪ ܒܫܢܝܪܐ ܒܚܒܝܐ. ܒܡܕܒܪܐ ܚܘܪܒ ܐܠܝܐ ܕܢܒܝܐ ܗܦܟ ܢܡܘܣܐ ܡܢܝܢ ܐܪ̈ܙܐ ܕܡܕܝܢܘܬܐ ܘܙ̈ܢܝܐ ܕܙ̈ܘܒܒܐ ܫܘ̈ܠܛܢܐ ܕܡܬܠܕܝܢ ܡܢܗܘܢ. ܘܕܐܢܐ ܫܘܬܦܘܬܐ ܠܟܠ ܐܘܡܬܐ[1] ܠܫܡܐ. ܘܒܐܠܝܢ ܡܬܛܦܪܐ ܡܕܝܢܘܬܐ ܛܒܘܬܐ. ܘܒܐܠܝܢ ܡܬܝܚܠܐ. ܡܢ ܒܬܠܬܐ ܓܘ̈ܢܐ *ܐܘ ܡܢ[2] ܗܘ̈ܦܠܝܐ ܒܪ̈ܢܐ. ܢܒܥ[3] ܕܝܢ ܣܘܟܠܐ ܡܢܗ̇ ܕܡܕܝܢܘܬܐ ܒܟܠܝܠܘܬ ܕܗܘܢܗ̇. ܟܕ ܪܦܝܘܬܗ ܡܪܥܠܬܐ ܕܕܝܢܐ ܐܘ ܡܥܝܘܬܗ ܠܒܝܫܬܐ. ܗ̇ܝ ܕܠܐ ܪܥܝܘܬܐ ܥܒܕܐ. ܐܟܡܐ ܕܚܘܪܒܘܬܐ ܘܦܓܥܘܬܐ ܒܡܬܚܫܒܘܬܗܘܢ ܡܬܝܕܥܬܐ ܠܗ̇, ܕܐܟܠܐ ܐܝܬ ܢܫܪܐ ܗܟܢ ܗܒܝܢ[4] ܠܫܢܝܐ. ܡܕܒܪ̈ܢܐ ܕܝܢ ܡܬܝܕܥܐܝܬ ܠܗ̇ ܡܠܟܐ[5] *ܗܠܝܢ ܢܡܘ̈ܣܐ[6] ܕܐܫܬܥܝܬܐ[7] ܕܡܬܠܬܝܢ ܘܟܠ ܗܘܦܟܐ ܡܕ̈ܝܢܬܐ[8] ܡܕܒܪ̈ܢ.

ܕܐܬܚ̈ܡܐ. ܙ̈ܢܝܐ ܕܕܘܒܪܐ ܡܕܝܢ̈ܝܐ ܥܒܕ ܐܢܘܢ. ܡܕܒܪܢܐ ܓܝܪ ܕܘܒܪܐ ܠܫܘܕܥܐ ܗܘ ܕܛܘܪܣܢܐ ܗܘܒ ܡܬܒܥܐ. ܟܕ ܪܫܝܥܐ ܕܒܡܗ ܫܘܬܦܘܬܐ ܒܕܘܒܪܐ ܠܐ ܡܥܦ ܕܢܣܒܠ ܐܝܟ ܕܒܫܘܠܛܢܐ ܒܡܛܝܪܐ ܫܛܦ ܠܗ ܡܠܟܘܬܐ. ܘܡܛܠ ܡܢ ܗ̇ܝ, ܕܠܫܢܘܗ ܥܒܕ ܘܠܣܓܝܐܐ ܢܒܕܒ ܠܐ ܡܕܡ ܪܢܐ. ܕܬܪ̈ܬܝܢ ܕܝܢ ܕܗܘܪ ܠܛܒܘܬܐ. ܟܕ ܪܫܝܥܐ ܠܫܘܛܪ ܘܡܛܠܝܐ ܚܪܦ ܕܢܡܘܣܗ̇, ܒܠܒܘܪ ܘܢܬܕܒܪܢܘܬܗ̇. ܕܬܠܬ ܕܘܒܪ ܫܛܝܘܬܐ ܘܡܘܪܘܬܐ. ܟܕ ܪܫܝܥܐ ܒܕ̈ܝܢܐ ܪܡ ܠܗ ܡܠܟܘܬܐ. *ܘܫܛܝܘܬܐ ܡܢ ܐܬܒܪ ܒܗ̇, ܕܐܟܠܐ ܒܫܘܦܐ ܐܘ ܢܬܪܘܬܐ ܠܐ ܡܬܩܢܝܐ[1a] ܡܠܟܘܬܐ[1]. ܕܒܡܘܪܘܬܐ ܕܝܢ ܒܗ̇,[2] ܕܒܡܘܪ; ܡܣܝܢܐ ܐܘܢ ܒܬܪܐ ܘܒܬܪ ܥܘܠܦܢܐ. ܕܐܪܒܥ ܕܘܒܪ ܥܠܡܘܬܐ. ܡܐ ܕܒܡܕܝܢܐ[3] ܥܒ̈ܕ ܠܦܫܐ ܢܗܘܘܢ ܘܠܣܒ[4] ܡܢܗܘܢ ܢܠܡܘܢ ܦܘܪܫܢܐ ܓܒܠܐ. ܘܡܚܐ[5] ܕܝܢ ܢܠܦܘܢܗܘܢ, ܘܗܢܐ ܕܡܗܘܡܦܠܝܐ ܡܬܥܬܗ. ܕܡܫܥܐ[6] ܕܗܘܐ ܛܘܪܣܢܐ. ܡܐ ܕܗܘܐ ܐܬܪܐ ܙܒܢ̈ܝ[7] ܦܘܠܚܢܘܬܐ ܕܡܫܡܠܝܐ ܘܕܬܢܐ ܗܘܘ ܘܠܡܫܬܐ ܕܟܠܗܘܢ ܢܟܠܗܘܢ ܟܠܗܘܢ. ܠܐ ܒܡܛܝܪܐ ܐܠܐ ܒܫܐܪܘܬܗܘܢ. ܕܫܬܐ ܕܗܘܪܐ ܡܠܟܝܐ. ܟܕ ܗܘ ܡܕܒܪܢܐ ܒܪܗ ܕܡܬܝܪܘܬܐ ܗܘܡܪܬܐ ܕܡܫܝܪܘܬܐ ܕܬܘܪܛܢܘܬܐ ܕܗܘܬ ܠܗ. ܘܬܪ̈ܝܗܘܢ ܗܠܝܢ ܕܐܡܪܐ[8] ܐܪܣܛܘܛܠܝܐ[9] ܡܬܘܪܝ.

7 [1] ܐܕܘܡܬܐ ?R [2*] ܘܡܢ RVLl [3] ܢܒܠ F [4] ܗܢܒܝܢ RVLl [5] pl. RVLl [6*] ܗܠܘܢܢܡܘ̈ܣܐ RVLl [7] i. om. RVLl [8] i. add. ܕ RVLl

8 [1*] om. F [1a] scripsi; ܡܬܩܘܪܐ RVLl [2] om. RVL [3] ܕܒܡܕ̈ܝܢܐ RVL [4] i. om. RVLl [5] ܘܡܒܐ RV[corr.] Ll [6] ܕܡܫܠܐ RVLl [7] i. add. ܘ RVLl [8] add. ܐܪܣܛܐ RVLl [9] ܐܪܣܛܘܛܠܐ R

SIX.[6] Concerning provisions, it is necessary to know how much expenditure is adequate for the city, both for what needs to be imported into it from outside, and what it should export to another region for trade. Since when food, clothing, and the preparations of the seasons are cut off, the city is preserved (only) with difficulty, he may also give advice on the kind of support through virtuous men and wealthy artisans by whom the needs of the city may be met.

SEVEN.[7] Legislation is also one of the great things, and a rhetorical faculty which is especially expert will seek (to engage in it). But first it is necessary that the legislator should know the number of the forms of civic government and the kinds of mixed constructions which are generated from them, what association is suitable to each nation, by what an excellent government is preserved and by what it is corrupted, by its own members or external opponents. Corruption arises from within the city itself through ruination of its governance by slack weakness of a judge or his wrathful severity, which results in anarchy; just as being flat-nosed or snub-nosed, by their excessive distension, make a nose into that which is not a nose at all. Legal (matters) in written stories are very helpful for deliberation and provide information on former affairs.

EIGHT.[8] The kinds of civic government are six. First is that sole government which is also called tyranny, when a ruler who does not agree to accept a partner with him in government usually seizes a kingdom by force for himself, and pays heed to nothing apart from having enslaved his fellow and enslaving the free. Second is government of graciousness, when a ruler cares for the advantage of the populace so that they honour only him and exalt him. Third is government of vileness and minority, when for a price a ruler buys a kingdom for himself. It is called (government of) vileness because a kingdom can only be (genuinely) acquired by sword or inheritance, but (it is called government) of minority because the rich who buy power are few in number. Fourth is government of unanimity, when the inhabitants are equal in rank, entrust the administration of the community to one of them, and replace him when they wish. This is

---

[6] **2.1.6** AR 1.4 60a12-17; IS 2.1 (60.14-61.7).
[7] **2.1.7** AR 1.4 60a17-37; IS 2.1 (61.8-15; 64.4).
[8] **2.1.8** AR 1.4 60a20-21,37-38; 8 65b29-66a2; IS 2.1 (62.1-63.10).

ܦܘܫܩܐ ܬܪܝܢܐ
ܡܛܠ ܡ̈ܠܝ ܫܪ̈ܪܐ ܡܗ̈ܝܡܢܬܐ
ܬܐܘܪܝܗ ܬܠܬ

ܡܕܡܝܢܘܬܐ. ܐܬܘ̈ܪܝܬܐ ܕܝܢ ܡܠܝܬܐ ܗܠܝܢ ܕܠܦܘܬ ܫܪ̈ܪܐ ܡܗ̈ܝܡܢܐ ܐܝܟ
ܠܐ ܡܫܬܡܗܝܢ. ܒܪܡ ܒܠܚܘܕ ܐܡܝܢܐ *ܒܡܠܬ̈ ܒܗܝܡܢܘܬܐ[1] ܡܫܬܘܕܥܝܢ
ܫܘܬܦܘܬܐ ܗܘܬ ܐܘ ܡܫܬܘܕܥܢܘܬܐ. ܒܕܠܚܘܕ ܦܠܐ ܕܢܣܒܐ ܡܢܗ ܗܝ
ܒܗܝܡܢܘܬܐ ܘܡܢ ܐܝܠܝܢ ܐܕ̈ܫܐ ܐܘ ܡܠܘ̈ܬܐ ܗܘܝܐ. ܐܡܝܢܐ ܕܡܢܗܝܢ
ܐܬܘ̈ܪܝܬܐ[2] ܡܠܝ̈ܬܐ[3] ܡܠܘܟܐ ܢܛܪ.. ܘܗܪܟܐ ܐܦ̈ܝ ܪܒܝܢ ܕܡܕܒ̈ܪܢܐ ܗ̇ܢ
ܠܐܠܝܨܘܬ ܙܘܘܕܐ[4] ܘܘܡܒܪܐ ܘܡܘܗܒܬܐ ܕܡܢ ܗܠܝܢ ܕܡܣܬ̈ܟܠܝܢ
ܠܡܠܒܫܘܬܐ ܘܡܬܠ̈ܠܢ ܠܡܦܫܩܘܬܐ ܡܒܪܘ. ܘܠܗܠܝܢ ܕܒܗܝܢ ܗ̇ܘܐ
ܙܘܘܕܐ[4] ܘܘܡܒܪܐ ܘܡܬܡܒܠ ܢܫܡ ܕܪܗܛܐ ܘܡܬܬܒܥܐ ܡܦܫܩܘܬܗ
ܠܐ ܡܒܪܘ. ܚܝܢ ܕܝܢ ܠܗ ܗܘܢܐ. ܐܠܐ ܠܒܠܒܡ ܠܡܠܒܫܗ ܢܠܦ.[5]

ܕܬܪ̈ܬܝܢ. ܒܗܝܡܢܘܬܐ ܐܬܬܢܝܗ̇ ܫܦܝܪܘܬ ܡܣܒܪܢܘܬܐ ܡܬܬܪ̈ܬܐ ܘܡܦܫܩܬܐ ܕܢܝܪܐ
ܘܗܝܪܐ ܒܡܘܡܪܐ ܗܢܝܐܐ ܒܡ ܙܗܝܡܘܬܐ ܘܐܡܝܪܐ[1] ܡܢ ܒܒܢܝ̈ܢܐ.
ܡܒܛܪܬܝܘܬ ܢܒܩܐ ܘܡܬܡܟܝܢܘܬ ܣܠܩܐ ܠܦܘܪܐ ܒܢܬ ܘܗܡܒܘܪܐ ܕܗܠܝܢ.
ܗܕܐ ܗܝ ܓܝܪ[2] ܒܗܝܡܢܘܬܐ. ܐܘ ܠܡܘܪܟܐ ܕܡܢܗ̇.[3] ܐܝܟ ܡܫܒܪܢܘܬ ܓܒܐ.
*ܡܬܪ̈ܘܬܗ ܓܝܪ[4] ܐܬܬܢܝܗܝܢ ܫܦܝܪܘܬ ܠܦܘܡܒܐ. ܡܓܒܝܐܘܬ ܐܒܪ̈ܐ ܘܒܢ̈ܝܐ
ܘܐܢ̈ܫܡܐ. ܒܡܘܬܪܐ. ܡܪܒܝܢܘܬ[5] ܠܒܡܘܬܐ ܒܐܢ̈ܫܐ.[6] ܡܫܒܘܬ̈ܐ ܠܒܬܐ.
ܣܘܠܒܢܐ ܘܫܘܦܪܐ ܘܡܣܒܪܢܐ. ܪܒܘܬ ܠܓܒܝܐ. ܒܓܒܝܐ. ܫܒܝܚܐ.
ܐܝܘܪܐ ܘܓܒܝܘܬܐ. ܐܕ̈ܫܐ ܡܬܝܪܘܬܐ ܐܝܟ ܒܪܚܡܘܬܐ.[7] ܓܒܪܘܬܐ.
ܢܚܦܘܬܐ. ܘܕܘܡܝܐ. ܗܠܝܢ ܓܝܪ ܡܢܗܝܢ *ܡܢ ܦܠܓܘܬܝܢ. ܡܢܗܝܢ ܕܝܢ ܢܦܩܝܢ.
ܘܡܢܗܝܢ[8] ܗܘܒ ܒܢ̈ܝܢ. ܐܝܟ ܠܦܘܡܒܐ. ܪ̈ܚܡܐ.[9] ܒܗܘܬܪܐ. ܐܝܘܪܐ.[10] ܘܟܠ
ܕܗܠܝܢ ܣܢܐ ܒܕܒܪܐ ܠܡܪܬܐ ܢܣܐ.[11] ܗܘܘ ܓܒܐ[12] ܠܗܘܬ ܡܘܠܦܢܐ.

ܕܬܠܬ. ܫܦܝܪ ܠܦܘܡܒܐ ܗ̇ܘ ܗܘ ܕܡܢ[1] ܓܒܫܐ ܗܘ ܕܒܡܒܝܢܗ̇ ܕܡܒܕܢܘܬܐ
ܘܡܬܝܩܢܗ̇. ܐܘ ܡܢ ܣܓܝܒܐ ܗܓܒ̈ܘܢܐ ܢܝ̈ܬܢܐ ܡܓܢ̈ܝܐܐ ܣܐܪܐ
ܕܡܦܫܪ̈ܬܐ ܫܦܝܪܬܐ ܢܫܡܝܢ. ܘܗܘ ܗܢܐ ܡܢ ܬܪ̈ܝܗܘܢ ܓܘܪ̈ܒܐ ܕܕܪܐ
ܘܢ̈ܠܐ ܡܫܬܪܒ. ܘܡܗܝܡܢܘܬ[2] ܒܢ̈ܝܐ ܒܡܓܐܘܬܐ ܘܪܒܘܬܐ ܘܫܘܦܪܐ
ܘܡܒܫܐ ܘܢܝܠܐ ܠܬܬܒܫܐ[3] ܘܡܦܩܬܐ ܘܓܒܪܘܬܐ ܗܘܝܐ. ܐܝܠܐ
ܠܟܠ ܒܢܫܐ ܒܠܒܗ ܙܓܬܐ ܐܝܟ[4] ܕܠܝܢܬܐ. ܒܕ ܠܗܢܐ ܡܢ *ܫܦܘܪܗ ܓܦܪ.

1 [1*] ܒܡܒܪ̈ܕܘܬܐ F [2] i. add. ܕ RVLl [3] ܡܠܬ̈ܐ RVLl [4] ܙܘܒܕܐ RL [5] ܢܠܦ̇ RVLl
2 [1] i. om. RVLl [2] om. F [3] i. om. F [4*] ܡܒ̈ܝܬܐ ܕܝܢ RVLl [5] i. add. ܘ RVLl [6] sg. RVLl [7] ܪܚܡܘܬܐ RVL [8*] om. RVLl [9] sg. RVLl [10] i. add. ܘ RVLl [11] om. RVLl [12] ܓܒܐ RVL
3-4 [1] i. om. RVL [2] ܘܡܗܝܡܢܘܬ RVL [3] ܠܬܬܒܫܐ RVL [4] ܐܝܟ RVL

called democracy. Fifth is government of pre-eminence, when the inhabitants are desirous of present and future well-being and cause the best of all of them to rule over them, not by force but with their freedom. Sixth is royal government, when a ruler with practical virtue acquires theoretical virtue. Both of these governments are called aristocratic.

## SECTION TWO
### On Deliberations on Private Subjects
### Nine Theories

ONE.[9] Although the deliberative *topoi* on personal subjects are unbounded, nevertheless all of them together have in common deliberations on prosperity, be it true or opined. Therefore it is necessary that we show what prosperity is, and from what species or parts it exists, so that the deliberative (orator) may prepare deliberative *topoi* from them. Our master said here that the predecessors indeed dealt with the necessity of amplification and diminution and gave warning of those things which destroy order and nullify persuasion, but they did not deal with the things by which there is amplification and diminution, the goal of the orator destroyed, and his persuasion impeded. We, however, will not (act) in this way, but we will teach everything in its (proper) order.

TWO.[10] Prosperity is virtuous good conduct, sufficiency of secure life in a pleasant living with love and honour from men, with abundance of possessions, and the ability to protect and use these things. For according to the common opinion, this is what prosperity is, or nearly so. Its parts are: good birth, a multitude of kinsmen, children and friends, wealth, kindness to others, a good old age, health, beauty, strength, bodily stature, prowess, glory, honour, good luck, the species of virtue—like prudence, courage, temperance, justice. Some of these are bodily, some mental, and some external, such as birth, friends, wealth, and honour. Everyone who lives such a life up to the end is fortunate according to the populace.

---

[9] **2.2.1** AR 1.5 60b4-14; IS 2.2 (64.11-65.7).
[10] **2.2.2** AR 1.5 60b14-31; IS 2.2 (65.8-66.1).

ܠܗܘܢܐ ܕܝܢ ܕܒܪܘܬܗ ܘܠܗܘܢܐ ܗܘܬ ܢܒܝܘܬܗ. ܘܠܢܒܝܘܬܐ ܡܝܬܪܘܬܐ
ܐܝܬ ܕܠܝܬܝܗ. ܒܦܓܪܐ ܡܢ ܫܘܦܪܐ ܘܪܒܘܬܐ. ܒܢܦܫܐ ܕܝܢ ܢܟܦܘܬܐ
ܘܐܘܡܢܘܬ ܒܟܠܐ ܘܪܚܡܬ ܒܟܠܐ. ܘܐܢܫܝܢ ܡܢ ܐܝܟ ܠܡܕܒܪܢܘܬܐ ܟܠ
ܢܘܒܠܘܬܐ ܒܠܫܢܐ ܐܠܗܝܢ ܢܥܢܘܢ. ܘܡܬܐܡܪܐ ܕܐܦܪܘܛܘܢ ܫܘܡܗܐ
ܕܒܬܠ̈ܐ ܕܝܨܒܬܐ ܡܢܗܘܢ ܗܘ.

ܕܐܪܒܥ. ܘܡܢܝܢܬ ܒܡܬܪܐ ܐܝܬܝܗܝܢ ܫܟܝܚܐܝܬ ܕܕܪ̈ܒܢܐ ܘܐܪ̈ܒܥܬܐ
ܘܡܘܪ̈ܝܐ ܘܡܢܝ̈ܢܐ ܘܒܠܗܝܢ ܦܘܩܕܢ̈ܐ ܕܡܫܝܚܐ ܘܬܡܢ̈ܝܢ ܘܪܘܚܢܐܝܬ
ܡܬܝܠܦ̈ܢ ܘܠܡܬܚܒܢܘ ܒܗܘܢ ܐܝܟ ܙܢܝܬܐ ܕܢܫ̈ܝܢ. ܘܐܪ̈ܒܥܬܐ ܗܘܬ ܕܕܠܐ
ܒܟܠܐ ܡܬܩ̈ܠܦܝܢ ܦܐܪ̈ܝܗܝܢ ܘܓ̈ܠܠܬܐ ܕܡܬܪ̈ܐ[5] ܡܬܦܪ̈ܬܗܝܢ. ܗܢܝܢ ܐܢܝܢ
ܗܢܝܐܬܐ ܠܡܫܝ̈ܚܝܢ.[6] ܡܠܝܢ ܕܝܢ ܡܟܐ ܕܠܐ ܕܢܠܐ ܘܗܦܟ ܡܢ ܫܩ̈ܝܬܐ
ܡܬܢܝܚܐ ܢܬܗܦܟܝܢ ܒܗܘܢ ܡܢܗܘܢ. ܒܪ ܢ̈ܫܐ ܠܡܗܝܡܢܐ ܐܘ ܠܡܒܪܢܘ ܒܥܘܒܐ
ܐܘ ܙܘܒܢܐ. ܘܡܒܐܝܬ ܠܡܐܡܪ. ܗ̇ܝ ܕܠܡܬܚܙܪ ܒܗ̇ܝ ܕܐܬܝܚܕ ܐܬܝܗ̇. ܠܐ
ܒܗ̇ܝ ܕܢܦܫܐ ܘܢܦܪ.

ܕܚܡܫ.[0] ܥܒܕܢܐ ܕܝܢ ܐܝܬܘܗܝ ܦܘܠܚܢܗ̇ ܒܝܬܝܐ ܪܘܚܢܐܝܬ ܙܕܝܩܐ
ܘܫܒܝܪܘܬ ܫܘܒܚܢܐ. ܗܕܐ ܗ̇ܝ ܒܢ ܡܫܝܚܘܬܐ ܠܘܬ ܡܦܠܚܢܐ ܘܠܗ̇,
ܡܬܐܡܪܝܢ ܫܘܒ̈ܚܐ. ܘܐܝܩܪܐ ܗܘܐ ܠܥܒܕܘܬ ܫܘܒܪܘܬܐ ܢܦܫ. ܘܗ̇ܘ
ܐܝܩܪܐ *ܐܘ ܒܐܝܩܪܬܐ[1] ܗ̇ܘܐ ܐܝܟ ܕܠܗܕܪ̈ܐ[2] ܥܒܝܪܬܐ. ܐܘ ܠܗ ܒܐܝܩܪܬܐ
ܐܝܟ ܕܠܗܘܢ[3] ܕܡܚܝܢ ܠܡܗܕܪ ܠܒ̈ܢܝܐ ܘܠܐ ܒܗ. ܡܚܝܠ[4] ܗܘܝܢ. ܐܝܟ
ܡܠܟܐ ܘܡܬܪܐ ܘܡܕܝ̈ܢܬܐ ܕܡܬܡܠܟܝܢ. ܡܛܠ ܗ̇ܝ ܕܡܚܝܢ ܠܡܥܒܕܗ[5] ܕܐܝܟ
ܐܘ ܡܠܟܘܬܐ ܐܘ ܦܘܪܢܣܐ ܡܢ ܫܘܠܛܢܐ. ܡܠܘ̈ܐܬܗ ܕܝܢ ܕܐܝܩܪܐ.
ܕܥܒܕܐ ܠܟܠܐ. ܕܒܣܝܐ ܥܠܡܐ. ܘܥܒܕܐ ܡܗܝܡܢܐ. ܙܒܘܬ[6] ܡܬܢܬܐ. ܕܫܢ̈ܐ
ܕܠܗܘܢ ܐܚܝܢ ܒܠܫܢܐ ܡܢ ܡܬܠ ܡܫܝܚܘܬܐ. ܢܦܫܐ ܕܝܢ ܡܛܠܠܗ̇, ܕܕܒܢܐ
ܥܒܕ̈ܒܐ ܗܘ ܕܐܝܩܪܐ. ܘܒܬܪ ܒܡܢܝܢܐ ܗܘܐ ܒܫ̈ܦܝܐ. ܡܠܦ̈ܢܐ[7]
ܕܡܬܬܦܝܣܝܢ. ܬܘܪܣܝܐ ܓܢܝܐ ܐܝܟ ܢܒܗܘܢ ܙܒܢܐ ܘܙܢܐ.

ܕܫܬ.[0] ܡܫܬܪ̈ܬܐ ܕܝܢ ܕܦܓܪܐ ܫܘܠܛܢܐ ܢܝܫܒܐ. ܒܗ̇ܝ ܕܐܒܕܒܐ
ܕܦܘܪܕܩܘܣ ܐܒܕܪ ܐܝܬ ܡܢ ܕܠܐ ܚܝܠ ܦܘܒܐ ܒܥܘܬܗ ܒܪ ܠܒܪܢܫܐ
ܕܬܒܐ ܒܫܘܠܛܢܗ. ܡܫܬܘܠܦ ܕܝܢ ܫܘܠܛܢܐ ܠܦܘܬ ܡܘܬ̈ܒܐ. ܒܪ ܥܒܘܪܬ
ܫܘܠܛܢ ܦܠܠܐ ܡܢ[1] ܗ̇, ܗ, ܕܠܘܬ ܪܘܚܐ[2] ܘܒܥܘܬܢܐ ܠܐ ܢܗܘܐ ܢܚܝܫ.
ܕܠܝܠܡܐ ܕܝܢ ܗ̇, ܕܠܘܬ ܦܠܠܘܬܐ ܘܬܬܒܥܐ ܢܗܘܐ ܚܝܠܗ. ܘܕܫܡܐ
ܗܘܐ ܗ̇, ܕܠܘܬ ܒܟܠܐ[3] ܐܠܝܨܐ ܡܕܡ ܡܢ ܡܟܐ ܕܡܟܐ ܠܫܒܘܬܐ ܠܐ
ܢܣܐ. ܘܗܠܝܢ ܡܢ ܒܒܥܝܐ ܕܐܝܬܘܗܝ, ܫܠܝܐ ܕܡܥܒܕ ܠܐܚܪܢܐ ܐܝܟ
ܕܢܦܠܐ. ܒܪ ܢܦܪ ܐܘ ܕܢܠܐ ܐܘ ܬܠܬܐ ܐܘ ܚܠܝ ܐܘ ܫܚܝ.

[5*] om. RVLl [6] ܠܡܬܢܝ̈ܚܝܢ RVLl

5 [0] ܕܐܪܒܥ l (cf. supra 3-4[5*]) [1*] ܘܡܐܝܩܪܬܐ RVLl [2] ܗܕܪ̈ܐ RVLl [3] ܕܗܘܢ RVLl [4] om. RVL [5] ܠܡܥܒܕܗ RVL [6] ܙܒܘܬ RVLl [7] ܡܠܦ̈ܢܬܐ RVLl

6 [0] ܕܚܡܫ l (cf. supra 3-4[5*]) [1] om. RVLl [2] ܪܘܚܐ RLl; ܪܘܚܢܐ V [3] om. F

THREE.[11] Good birth is to be from the race native to the city and its ancient (members), or from wise men or famous leaders, many free men admired for (their) abundant good deeds. It is derived from the branches of both paternal and maternal uncles. Prosperity in children consists in (their) abundance, stature, beauty, strength, prowess, temperance, and courage. Everyone has a specific desire for his offspring, because its beauty should be appropriate for it, masculine for one and feminine for another. There is an excellence specific to the female: for the body, beauty and stature; for the mind, temperance, concord (with her) husband, and industry. (As for) people like the Lacedaemonians, their women were only necessary for decoration. It is said that Phriton, author of books of cosmetics, is one of them.

FOUR.[12] The parts of wealth are abundance of darics, lands, properties, possessions, and all things which are valuable, striking, securely held, and useful for enjoyment according to desire. (As for) lands whose fruits are gathered without toil and harvests whose revenues are abundant, they are pleasant to their owners, especially when their master may live in them without fear and without vexatious partners (and is able), when he wishes, to own or to alienate, whether by gift or sale. To sum up, being rich (lies) in using, not in concealing and guarding.

FIVE.[13] Reputation is the renown of a man for prudence of thought and good conduct, for the latter is a virtue according to the populace and many desire it. Honour, also, is linked to good conduct, and it comes about either justly, as to those who do good, or not justly, as to those who are able to do good but do not do so, like kings, rich men, and warriors who are served because they are able to bestow rank, riches, or salvation from harm. The parts of honour are: a good memorial, a perfect sacrifice, a consecrated offering, a front seat, gifts—which the rich desire for possession, but the honourable because a gift is a sign of honour—burials after death, statues which are erected, (and) public maintenance according to the law and manner of the time.

[11] **2.2.3** AR 1.5 60b31-61a12; IS 2.2 (66.2-67.1).
[12] **2.2.4** AR 1.5 61a12-25; IS 2.2 (67.2-67.8).
[13] **2.2.5** AR 1.5 61a25-61b2; IS 2.2 (67.9-68.7).

ܕܫܒܥ.⁰ ܡܫܝܢܘܬ ܬܪܥܝܬܐ ܗ̇ܝ، ܗܝ، ܕܢܦܫܐ ܚ̈ܒܪ ܫܠܝܢ ܒܐܘܪܚܐ ܘܡܗܝܡܢܐ ܘܦܬܝܐ ܕܠܐ ܡܫܘܚܬܐ[1] ܫܠܝܢܐ. *ܒܪ ܗܠܝܢ[2] ܗܦ̈ܟܝ ܡܫܘܚܬܐ ܐܘ ܡܬܝܢ ܘܕܚܝܠܘܗܝ ܐܘ ܠܐ ܡܬܬܙܝܥܝܢ. ܘܐܝܟܢܐ ܕܟܠܗ ܘܕܟܐ ܕܡܕܒ̈ܪܢܘܗܝ، ܠܟܠܝܢ ܡܕܒ̈ܪܐ ܕܟܬ̈ܐ. ܒܟ̈ܢܐ ܡܒܝܢ ܗܠܝܢ ܘܡܣܬܝܡܐ ܠܐ ܒܥ̈ܝܢ[3] ܘܒܟܐ ܐܝܟ ܠܐ ܡܢܬ ܗܘܕ̈ܝܐ ܐܘܢ. ܘܗܦܟ ܡܢ ܠܒܢܐ ܕܐܬܕܡܝ ܒܗ ܘܥܢ̈ܝܐ ܕܠܚܫܝ ܒܗܝܢ. ܘܫܠ ܬܫܬܡܫܐ ܡܢ ܙܒܘܬܐ ܘܙܕܝܩܘܬܐ ܘܩܠܝܠܘܬܐ ܡܙܒܢ. ܒܪ ܐܝܟܢ ܥܩܐ ܘܕܚܝܠܐ ܠܕܘܫܐ *ܚ̈ܒܪ ܒܪܗܛܗ.[4] ܘܗ̇ܘ ܕܒܪ ܡܐܟܠ ܚ̈ܠܒ ܕܪܘܪܐ[5] ܗܘ. ܘܡܢ ܕܠܬ̈ܬܘܗܝ ܚܡܝ ܦܐܪܣܛܣܛܝܩܐ ܗܘ. ܘܐܝܟܢܐ ܕܒܡ ܗܠܝܢ *ܥܦܪ ܚ̈ܪܦ[6] ܘܒܫܘܦܐ ܐܪܒ[7] ܘܒܠ ܙܒܥܐ[8] ܦܪܩ ܣܡܝܟ ܐܝܟܘܬܐ ܗܘ.

ܕܬܡܢܝܐ.⁰ ܘܫܝܢܘܬܐ ܠܒܗܬܐ ܐܝܬܝܗ̇ ܕܡܫܬܘܕܝܢܘܬ ܒܡ ܠܐ ܒܡܬܘܬܬܐ[1] ܢܫܐܒ ܐܝܟ. ܒܪ[2] ܡܢ ܕܡܫܬܪܗܒ ܦܐܒ ܘܐܦܢ ܠܗ ܒܡܬܐܬ ܐܘ ܡܢ ܕܡܫܬܪ ܦܐܒ ܒܢܩ ܒܡܬܐܬ ܥܦܪ ܗܡܒܬܐ ܠܐ ܐܬܬܘܗܝ، ܘܒܫܦܝܢܘܬ ܫܠܝܘܬܐ ܘܪܘܚܐ ܒܠ ܐܦ̈ܝ ܠܒ̈ܬܐ ܕܗܘܝܢ ܠܒܪܝܐ ܗܦ̈ܟܐ ܡܬܗܦܟܝܢ.

ܕܬܫܥ.⁰ ܠܒܗܬ ܠܒܝܐ ܕܝܢ ܐܝܬܝܗ̇ ܒܪ ܡܢ ܠܒܝܐ ܠܒ̈ܬܐ ܙܘܪ̈ܬܐ ܢܗܘܝܢ ܠܐܚܪ. ܠܐ ܡܢ ܐܘܡܢܘܬܐ ܐܦܠܐ ܡܢ ܒܒܝܐ ܕܒܢܝܐ. ܘܐܦܢ ܐܝܬ ܠܒ̈ܬܐ ܕܒܐܘܡܢܘܬܐ ܗܘ̈ܝ. ܐܝܟ ܫܘܠܡܢܐ ܒܐܫܘܬܐ. ܥܘܦܪܐ ܕܝܢ ܘܪܒܘܬ ܠܘܫܡܐ ܒܝܢܐ ܗܘ ܒܠܬܗܘܢ.[1] ܘܠܒ̈ܬܐ[2] ܠܒ̈ܝܢܬܐ ܗܠܝܢ ܐܚܝܢ ܕܠܗܝܢ ܢܘܦ ܫܘܡܐ. ܐܝܬܘܗܝ، ܕܝܢ[3] ܠܒܝܐ ܡܢ ܬܠܠܬܐ ܕ̈ܟܠܬܐ ܕܠܐ ܒܠܒ̈ܬܐ[4] ܐܘܦܠܐ ܒܒܢܫܬܐ[4] ܡܬܝ̈ܪܦܝܢ. ܒܥܘܪܒܐ ܒܝ̈ܢܝܐ ܡܢ ܐܡܒܠܐ ܕܗ̇ܘ ܡܢ ܒܪ ܐܝܣܗ̈ܘ، ܥܦܪܢܝܢ ܗ̇ܘ ܡܥܒܪ. ܗܢܐ ܒܝܢ̈ ܐܝ̈ܠܐ[5] ܡܥܒܪܐ ܥܦܪܐ. ܡܬܒܝܢܐ[6] ܕܝܢ ܐܡܒܠܐ ܕܗ̇ܘ ܡܢ ܒܠܒ. ܗܘܘ ܕܒܡܗ ܢܟܝܢ ܫܡܬܐ. ܗܢܐ ܕܝܢ ܘܐܝܢܐ ܒܪ ܐܒܝܢܐ ܣܢܝܢ ܗܘܘ. ܒܐܝܟܘܬܐ *ܒܣܒܪܗ ܠܐ[7] ܒܗ ܐܬܡܠܠ ܒܐܘܪܚܐ. ܘܡܛܠ ܡܫܝܢܘܬܐ ܕܡܫܬܘܕܝܢܐ ܒܪ ܒܠ ܡܘܠܟܢܐ ܡܒܠܠܝܢ ܐܡܪܝܢ.

---

7 ⁰ ܕܫܒܝܥܝܬ l (cf. supra 3-4⁵*) ²* ܒܗܠܝܢ RVLl ³ ܒܥܝܢ F ⁴* ܚ̈ܒܪ ܕܪܗܛܗ RVLl ⁵ ܕܪܘܪܐ RVLl ⁶* ܢܓܪ̈ܦ RVL; ܚܪܦ l ⁷ ܐܪܒ RVL ⁸ pl. RLl

8 ⁰ ܕܬܡܢܐ l (cf. supra 3-4⁵*) ¹ ܒܡܬܘܬܬ RVL ² ܒܪ RVL

9 ⁰ ܕܬܫܝܥܝܐ l (cf. supra 3-4⁵*) ¹ ܬ̈ܠܬܗܘܢ RVLl ² i. om. RVL ³ om. RVL ⁴ sg. RVLl ⁵ om. RVLl ⁶ ܡܬܒܝܢܐ RVL; ܡܬܒ̈ܝܢܬܐ l ⁷ ܒܣܒܪܗ ܗܢܐ F

SIX.[14] Excellences of body (are) innate health, because as Perodiqus said, there is no one who takes no happiness in his wealth because in his health he resembles a sick man. Health differs according to the stages of life, because a youth in good health is not fit for running or force, but a young man should be fit for speed and fighting, and an old man should not notice (his) old age in any necessary toil after that point. They (are linked) with strength, which is the ability to move another as one wills, pulling, pushing, lifting, squeezing, or pressing.

SEVEN.[15] Excellence of stature (is) surpassing (others) in height, depth, and breadth without excessive fatness, because those who are very fat either have slow movements or do not move (at all). When the movement of anyone's limbs ceases, he is like someone deprived of limbs. Therefore those who are gross and pampered are not fitted for movement, like those who possess no limbs apart from a tongue by which they can whisper or teeth by which they can chew. Competitive strength is compounded of size, swiftness, and speed, because he who has lengthy swift strides covers a distance in his running, he who fights standing up is a wrestler, he who is fitted for both of them an (athlete) of the pancratium, and he who in addition to these shoots well, attacks with the sword, and is first on horse is an (athlete) of the pentathlon.

EIGHT.[16] A good old age is when someone ages slowly with no pain; for (neither) he who ages rapidly, even if not painfully, nor he who ages slowly but painfully, is well in old age. By 'a multitude of companies and friends' (he means that) many exert themselves in order to provide benefits for the person (in question).

NINE.[17] Good fortune is when mighty good things come to someone by luck, not by art or by the working of nature. Although there are goods which come about by art, such as health by medicine, nature is the cause of beauty and bodily stature. Goods due to fortune are those to which envy adheres, but fortune is among the false causes

[14] **2.2.6** AR 1.5 61b3-18; IS 2.2 (68.8-68.10).
[15] **2.2.7** AR 1.5 61b18-26; IS 2.2 (68.10-68.14).
[16] **2.2.8** AR 1.5 61b26-28; 35-39; IS 2.2 (69.1-69.2).
[17] **2.2.9** AR 1.5 61b39-62a14; IS 2.2 (69.3-69.13).

ܦܘܫܩܐ ܬܠܝܬܝܐ
ܡܛܠ ܗܠܝܢ ܕܦܫܝܛܝܢ
ܬܐܘܪ̈ܝܐܘܣ ܬܡ̈ܢܝܐ

ܡܕܡܚܝܬܐ. ܡܛܠ ܓܒܪ ܕܗ̇ܘ[1] ܕܫܠܝܛ ܗ̇ܝ ܕܦܫܝܛܐ ܫܠܝܛ ܠܟܠ ܗܠܝܢ ܕܦܫܝܛܝܢ. ܐܠܝܨܐ ܠܡܐܡܪ ܒܗ. ܐܡܪܝܢ ܕܦܪܝܫܐ[2] ܗ̇ܝ ܥܠܬܐ ܡܢ ܗ̇ܝ ܕܦܫܝܛܐ. ܒܗ̇ܝ ܕܥܠܬܐ ܗ̇ܝ ܗ̣ܝ ܡܛܠܬܗ̇[3] ܡܬܟܢܝܐ. ܐܘ ܐܚܪܢܐ ܡܛܠܬܗ̇.[3] ܗ̇ܝ ܕܦܫܝܛܐ ܕܐܝܬ ܗ̣ܝ ܡܛܠ ܐܚܪܢܐ ܡܬܟܢܝܐ ܘܡܬܩܪܝܐ ܕܦܫܝܛܬܐ ܐܝܬܝܗ̇. ܘܥܠܬܐ ܗ̇ܝ ܐܝܬܝܗ̇ ܗ̇ܝ ܕܠܗ̇ ܡܬܝܐܒ ܟܠܗܝܢ ܕܐܝܬ ܒܡܢܝܢܐ ܘܡܫܘܚܬܐ. ܠܦܘܬ ܕܐܝܟܢ ܒܥܒܕܬܐ. ܒܗ̇ܝ ܕܠܗ̇ܘ ܡܢ[4] ܕܓܒܝܐ ܒܗܘܢܐ ܠܗ ܠܥܠܬܐ ܫܪܫܝܢ ܐܝ̈ܠܝܢ.[5] ܘܗ̇ܘ ܕܒܪ̈ܢܫܐ ܓܒܝܐ ܗܘܘ ܠܥܠܬܐ. ܘܒܠܚܘܕܝܗ̇ ܕܒܬ ܢܫܐ ܪܘܚܢܐ. ܒܗ ܓܒܝܐ ܕܢܛܪ ܠܥܠܬܐ ܡܕܡ. ܒܗ̇ܝ ܕܦܠ ܢܘܗܪܐ ܒܚܘܒܗ̇.

ܕܬܪ̈ܬܝܢ. ܡܫܬܘܕܥܐ ܕܝܢ ܥܠܬܐ ܕܗ̇ܝ ܗ̣ܝ، ܢܝܫܐ. ܘܡܛܠܗ̇ ܗܘ ܦܫܝܛܘܬܐ ܠܗ̇ܝ ܕܦܫܝܛܐ ܕܐܝܬܝܗ̇[1] ܒܡܢܝܢܐ ܘܦܠܓܘܬܐ[2] ܕܥܠܬܐ. ܒܗ̇ܝ ܕܬܪ̈ܬܝܗܝܢ[3] ܫܠܝܛ ܦܫܝܛܐ. ܗ̇ܝ، ܡܢ ܡܛܠܬܗ̇ ܕܠܝܬܗ̇. ܗܕܐ ܕܝܢ ܡܛܠ ܐܚܪܢܝܬܐ. ܘܐܝܟ ܐܝܟܢܐ ܕܠܡܠܦܘܬܐ ܕܗ̇ܝ[4] ܕܦܫܝܛܐ. ܘܐܦ ܡܫܡܠܝܐ ܫܠܝܛ ܘܐܡܝܪ[5] ܠܗ̇، ܕܬܗܘܐ ܚܠܝܦ. ܘܡܠܟܐ ܕܠܐ ܠܐܝܬܘܬܗ ܗ̇ܘ، ܒܠܚܘܕ[6] ܫܘܠܡܢܐ. ܐܠܐ ܕܪܘܚܢܐ ܕܠܗ ܢܦܫܐ ܠܐܝܬܘܬܐ. ܒܗ ܒܗܢܐ ܫܠܝܛ ܠܡܕܒܪܘ ܡܢ ܬܠ̈ܬܐ ܒܡܫܚܬܐ ܘܢܩ̈ܦܝܗ̇. ܘܗ̣ܘ ܢܦܫܐ ܐܘ ܐܚܪܢܝܬ ܗ̇ܘܐ. ܐܝܟ ܢܕܥܬܐ ܕܒܬܪ ܡܠܦܢܐ ܗܘܝܐ. ܐܘ ܒܢܕܐ. ܐܝܟ ܫܘܢܝܬ ܡܫܠܡܢܐ ܕܒܗ ܗ̇ܝ، ܕܠܡܚܝܐ ܫܦܝܪ ܗܘܝܐ. ܘܥܠܬܐ ܒܡܕܒܪܢܘܬܐ ܐܘ ܡܢ ܡܕܒܪܢܘܬܐ ܗܘ ܫܘܡܠܝܗ̇. ܐܝܟ ܡܫܠܡܢܐ ܘܫܘܠܡܢܐ.[7] ܐܘ ܗ̣ܘ ܒܚܝܠܗ̇[8] ܐܝܬܘܗܝ، ܥܠܬܐ ܒܐܘܣܝܘܬܗ̇[8] *ܐܝܟ ܡܫܪܪܬܐ ܠܫܘܠܡܢܐ. ܐܘ ܠܗ ܒܐܘܣܝܘܬܗ̇[9] ܐܠܐ ܒܡܕܒܪܢܘܬܗ̇ ܐܝܟ ܕܪܘܚܢܐ ܠܫܘܠܡܢܐ.

1 [1] i. om. RVLl [2] pl. RL [3] f ܗ RVLl [4] om. R [5] sg. RVLl
2 [1] i. ܘ RVL [2] ܐܘ ܦܠܓܘܬܐ RVLl [3] ܕܬܪ̈ܬܝܢ RVL [4] i. om. F [5] ܒܗ ܐܡܝܪ RVLl [6] ܒܠ RVL [7] om. F [8] f. ܗ F [9*] om. F

which care neither for good nor for evil. With natural things, for instance when one whose brothers are beautiful is himself ugly, it (determines) the ugly and the beautiful between the brothers. But with the voluntary, for instance, one person may find a treasure without those who are with him, although the one and the other were looking together; (or) at an (archery) contest an arrow fell on someone's companion, not on him. We shall speak about virtue based on opinion when we discuss praise.

## SECTION THREE
## On Things which are Expedient
## Eight Theories

ONE.[18] Because he who advises what is expedient advises on the kinds of things which are expedient, it is necessary when we speak (on this matter) to deal with what distinguishes the good from the expedient, because the good is desired for itself, or something else (is desired) for its sake, but the expedient is desired for the sake of something else and could be evil. The good is that which everyone who has perception and intelligence desires, in accordance with his degree of knowledge, because people regard that which the unlearned (man) chooses (as) not good, and that which the prudent (man) chooses is the good. Therefore an orator is greatly advantaged, when wishing to establish something (to be) a benefit, by the fact that some learned person has chosen it.

TWO.[19] The good shares (with the expedient) that it is an aim (of the deliberative orator), and for the sake of it there is a need for the expedient, which is the producer and preserver of the good. Because an orator may advise both of them, the former for its own sake, the latter for the sake of something else, there are also times when he may advise (both) that which follows upon the expedient and (the expedient) even if it is opposite (to the good) and say (for example), 'Be wearied, in order that you may be healthy!' It is obvious that weariness is not the cause of health, but the exercise upon which weariness follows. In the same way he may advise to stay away from

[18] **2.3.1** AR 1.6 62a17-27; IS 2.2 (69.14-70.3).
[19] **2.3.2** AR 1.6 62a27-34; cf. 63a5; IS 2.2 (70.4 -71.4).

ܕܬܠܬ. ܗܠܝܢ ܕܦܫܝܛܝܢ ܐܘ ܠܦܬܝܐ ܐܝܟ ܐܘ ܒܥܘܡܩܐ ܕܡܬܠ[1] ܦܫܝܛܐ ܕܡܢ ܒܥܘܡܩܐ ܕܢܘܪ̈ܝܢ ܦܫܝܛܝܢ. ܦܘܫܟܐ ܠܒܪ ܕܡܢ ܒܥܘܡܩܐ ܥܒܕ ܠܦܬܝܐ ܡܢ ܡܘܠܟܐ ܡܬܬܘܕܝܐ. ܦܫܝܛܐ ܕܝܢ ܠܗ ܒܠܚܘܕ ܒܒܕܝܬ[2] ܠܦܬܝܐ ܕܠܐ ܐܬܝܬܝܗ ܐܠܐ ܘܐܝܕܐ ܕܚܠܦܘܗܝ ܕܐܬܝܬܝܗ ܡܬܩܦܐ. ܐܦܠܐ ܬܘܒ ܦܘܪܫܬ ܡܢ ܒܥܘܡܩܐ ܠܒܪ ܒܠܚܘܕ. ܐܠܐ ܘܐܝܕܐ ܕܡܢ ܗܕܐ ܡܬܚܙܝܐ. ܘܒܒܕܝܬ ܠܦܬܝܐ ܕܝܢ ܦܫܝܛܐ ܡܬܝܕܥܐ. ܡܬܦܪܫܐ ܒܥܘܡܩܐ ܕܝܢ ܐܫܬܟܚܬ. ܘܡܬܚܫܒܬܐ ܕܗܢܝܢ ܠܦܬܝܐ ܡܬܝܕܥܬܐ ܡܛܠ ܠܦܬܝܐ ܕܠܚܘܕܝܗܝܢ ܦܫܝܛܝܢ. ܐܦ ܠܒܪ ܡܢ ܗܝܕܐܘܬܐ ܠܦܬܝܐ ܗܝ ܠܗܘܝܐ. ܒܕܠܗ̇ ܘܒܗܝܢܐ[3] ܣܘܟܠܐ *ܕܠܐ ܡܬܚܠܠܝܢ ܡܬܐܡܪܝܢ.[4] ܘܒܪ[5] ܟܠ ܕܝܠܗܐ ܐܘ[6] ܥܘܒܪ ܐܘ ܗܘ ܐܘ ܦܘܫ. ܐܝܟܢܐ ܕܗܝܕܝܢܐ ܠܦܬܝܐ[7] ܫܒܝܠ. ܗܟܢܐ ܬܬܝܬܝܬ ܗܝܕܝܢܐ ܕܥܘܒܪ ܐܘ ܦܘܫ.

ܕܐܪܒܥ. ܘܡܢ ܠܦܬܝܐ ܕܦܫܝܛܝܢ ܚܕ. ܡܘܠܟܐ ܐܬܬܣܝܡ ܡܠܘܫܘܬ ܒܗܘܢܐ. ܢܗܝܪܘܬ ܡܕܥܐ. ܥܘܒܪܘܬ ܡܘܟܠܐ. ܒܗܘܕܝܐ. ܡܠܦܢܐ. ܣܪܝܩܘܬ ܘܦܬܝܐ ܒܝܕܥܬܐ ܘܐܘܡܢܘܬܐ. ܗܠܝܢ ܠܒܪ ܡܢܗܝܢ ܘܠܗܝܢ ܡܬܝܠܕܢ ܘܠܢܬܗܝܢ ܡܬܝܠܕܢ. ܘܡܫܡܠܝܢ ܒܢܝܢ ܘܡܫܟܚܝܢ. ܘܦܫܝܛܐ ܕܒܝܢܐ ܡܬܦܫܛܝܢܐ ܠܕܐܝܟ ܗܠܝܢ ܠܦܬܝܐ ܒܥܘܡܩܐ ܢܚܬ. ܘܠܡܫܡܠܝܘܬܗܝܢ ܠܦܬܝܐ ܕܦܫܝܛܝܢ. ܐܝܟ ܠܒܪܘܬܐ ܕܒܥܘܬܐ ܒܪ[1] ܠܡܠܬܒܒܝܢ[2] ܗܘܝܐ. ܘܕܝܠܝܘܬܗ ܠܦܬܝܐ ܕܦܫܝܛܐ ܠܝ ܐܬܝܬܗ. ܒܕܠܝܗ̇ ܡܢܐ ܕܦܫܝܛܘܬ ܡܬܐܡܪܐ ܕܡܫܠܡܐ ܡܠܦܢܘܬܐ ܒܒܕܐ.

ܕܚܡܫ. ܐܝܬ ܐܡܪܐ ܕܒܟܕܐ ܗܝܟܢܐ[1] ܡܬܚܙܝܢܐ ܢܗܘܐ ܗܘܐ ܒܢܝܢܐ. ܐܝܟ ܣܕܪܘܬܐ[2] ܕܦܪܐܘܡܦ ܡܠܟܐ ܕܐܬܠܝܢ ܗܘ ܕܒܪ ܐܬܦܠܠ ܗܦܟܪ ܒܗ̇ ܡܢ ܐܚܠܦ ܒܦܘܪܢܣܐ[3] ܥܡܠ ܡܢܗ ܐܡܪܢܐ ܕܬܠܬ ܠܗ ܡܠܬܗ ܡܠܦܢܐ. ܘܡܢܐ ܕܢܗܘܐ ܘܒܝܬܐ ܢܦܫ ܦܬܘܪܗ ܐܝܟ ܢܗܘܐ ܕܝܘܢ ܘܒܬܘܪܘܬܐ ܗܘ ܡܘܢܝܗ. ܠܒܝܢ ܒܢܝܫܐ ܡܢܝܚ ܗܘܐ ܠܬܘܪܬܐ ܘܡܠܦܬܐ ܡܬܪܢܝ ܗܘܐ ܠܡܠܬܒܗ ܒܪ ܡܘܕܐ ܕܠܦܬܘܬܐ ܐܢܬܐ ܐܚܪܢ ܒܗ. ܘܡܢܟܐ ܢܗܝܪܘܬ ܠܕܐ ܡܠܦܢܐ. ܒܪ ܠܗ ܡܢ ܗܠܝܢ ܕܡܬܚܙܝܢ ܗܝ ܦܫܝܛܐܝܬ. ܒܢܝܢܐ ܗܢܐ ܡܬܚܙܝܢܐ ܗܘܐ.

3 [1] ܕܡܢ F [2] ܚܒܪ RVLl [3] ܘܒܫܝܢܐ R [4*] ܕܠܗ̇ ܡܬܚܠܠܝܢ RVLl [5] ܘܒܪ RVLl [6] om. RVL [7] ܠܦܬܝܐ RVLl
4 [1] ܡܢ RVLl [2] ܠܡܠܬܒܒܝܢ F
5 [1] om. RVLl [2] f ܗ RVLl [3] pl. F

the causes of evil and the things which follow upon it. That which follows may come about subsequently, like knowledge which comes about after learning, or simultaneously, like being worthy of praise, which comes about (simultaneously) with living well. A cause is a producer either because its name is from the activity, like being healthy and health; or its very nature is a cause in its essence, like food for health; or (it is so) not in its essence but in its quantity, like exercise for health.

THREE.[20] Things which are expedient are either goods, or evils which are expedient for deliverance from greater evils, for he who delivers from evil is acknowledged a benefactor by the populace. Not only is producing a good which did not (previously) exist expedient, but also adding to that which does exist; and neither is only complete delivery from evil (expedient), but also subtracting from it; but producing a good is properly expedient, reducing an evil secondarily (so). The virtues, which are proper goods, are expedient for the common goods. Pleasure, indeed, is a common good, because even irrational animal natures desire it. And since everything which is chosen is either fine or pleasant or expedient, if the pleasant is reckoned a good, how much more (is) the pleasant which is fine or expedient.

FOUR.[21] Among the goods which are expedient among the populace are subtlety of understanding, splendour of intellect, comeliness of appearance, memory, learning, (and) acuteness of ability in sciences and arts, for they are chosen for their own sake and desired for themselves. Their opposites are evil and harmful. It is possible in a sophistical way to make such goods evils, and their opposites expedient goods. For example, courage is evil when it is our enemy's, and his cowardice is a good expedient for us; therefore when it is simply assumed that it is harmful, it makes a fallacy.

FIVE.[22] Sometimes a hateful deed becomes in a way a cause for rejoicing, like the joy of Priam, king of Ilium, who, when his son Hector was slain by Achilles, submissively asked of him how he might

[20] **2.3.3** AR 1.6 62a34-62b9; IS 2.2 (71.5-72.3).
[21] **2.3.4** AR 1.6 62b23-33; IS 2.2 (72.3-72.9).
[22] **2.3.5** AR 1.6 62b33-63a10; IS 2.2 (72.9-72.16).

ܕܫܬ. ܐܝܟܢܐ ܕܠܠܚܡܬܐ ܡܬܝܗܒܐ ܒܠܒܒܐ ܗܘܐ ܡܗܝܡܢ ܘܠܐ ܡܣܝܟ
ܡܫܠܡ ܠܗ. ܗܟܢܐ ܘܠܫܝܫܬܐ. ܐܝܟ ܦܘܪܫܢܐ ܕܒܝ[1] ܐܘܣܒܝܘ ܕܐܡܝܣܐ
ܡܢ ܡܫܡܫܢܘܬܗ ܒܢ̈ܫܬܐ ܐܫܬܠܡܘܗܝ. ܦܘܪܫ ܫܘܚ̈ܠܦܐ ܐܝܟ ܡܢ ܦܬ̈ܓܡܐ
ܕܦܫܝ̈ܩ ܐܢܘܢ، ܡܠܘܫܐܠܐ ܠܡܫܐܠܬܐ[2] ܡܢ ܦܬܓܡܐ ܘܫ̈ܢܐ ܒܡܫܡܫܢܘܬܗܘܢ ܒܠ
ܫܒܠܐ ܘܫ̈ܢܝܐ ܒܕܘܟܝܬܐ ܘܒܙܒܢܐ. ܐܝܟ ܕܐܡܪ ܐܘܣܒܝܘܣ ܒܝ ܓܒܐ
*ܬܪܝܢ ܡܫܠܬܐ.[3] ܐܘܕܥܘܗܝ ܡܠܟܐ ܓܒܪܐ ܕܐܬܘܡ، ܘܐܟܠܘܗܝ ܓܒܪܐ.
ܘܫܡ ܐܝܟ ܢܫܐ ܠܒܝܬܐ ܘܫܘܠܛܢܐ. ܘܐܡܪ ܠܡܫܠܡܘ ܓ̈ܒܪܐ ܬܪܝܢ.
ܐܠܒܫܝܢܘܗܝ ܓܒܪܐ ܐܢܫܘ، ܕܡܬܓܪ ܘܡܠܟܐ ܓܒܪܬܐ ܐܢܬܬ
ܡܫܝܚܠܝܗܘܢ ܡܠܟܐ ܕܡܠܟܐ. ܘܫܡ ܐܝܟ ܢܫܐ ܠܓܒܪܐ ܘܓܒܪܬܐ.
ܘܗܟܢܐ ܓܒ̈ܪܐ ܠܡܫܐܠܬܐ ܘܒܢ̈ܫܬܐ ܠܓ̈ܒܪܐ ܐܝܟ ܡܬܡܪܝܢܘܬ ܚܠܗ ܦܪܝ.

ܕܫܒܥ. ܦܘܪܩܢܐ ܡܫܬܟܚܢܐ ܒܚܝܠܐ ܡܬܚܡܨ. ܒܕܝܠܗ ܐܢܫܐ
ܕܦܘܪܩܢܐ ܒܡܪܢܐ ܡܪܝܐ ܘܒܡܪܢܐ ܦܪܥ ܠܟ ܡܒܝܢ. ܘܐܢܫܐ ܕܬܒܪ ܫܠܡ
ܡܪܝܐ ܘܫܠܡ ܦܪܥ ܡܒܝܢ. ܒܪ ܡܢ ܬܒܪ ܫܠܡܢܐ ܒܡܪܢ ܗܘ ܫܠܡܢܐ.
ܘܗܟܢܐ[1] ܐܦ ܡܫܬܠܡܢܘܬ ܢܦܫܐ[2] ܒܐܢܫܐ ܒܪ ܕܟܝܢܐ ܕܦܘܪܩܢܐ[3] ܗܘܐ ܠܐ
ܡܚܝܠܐ. ܘܡܢܐ ܕܝܢܐ[4] ܘܠܬܚܝܡ ܐܢܫܐ ܒܒܪܐ ܠܐ ܡܫܬܡܒܪܐ
ܘܠܡܬܦܘܪܩܢܐ ܠܐ ܡܫܟܚܐ. ܒܢܐܫܬ ܕܝܢ ܦܪܥ ܐܢܫܐ ܕܚܠܦ ܓܒܪܬܐ
ܠܡܪܬܐ ܕܢܦܫ ܫܩܝܪܬܐ ܢܗܠ. ܘܚܠܦ ܠܡܬܪܐ ܓܒܪܐ ܘܐܠܗܝܐ ܕܚܠܝܐ
ܘܫܪܝܐ. ܘܦܘܪܩܢܐ ܕܒܪܢܫܐ ܒܟܗ ܡܢܐ ܕܦܪܥ ܗܘ ܒܦܫܛܐ ܘܒܡܫܝܚܘܬܐ
ܗܘܐ. ܘܦܘܪܩܢܐ ܗܘ ܕܝܢ ܡܬܠܡܠ ܡܢܐ ܕܒܪܝܫܬܐ ܠܐ ܢܦܪܘܥ ܐܢܫܐ
ܕܦܪ̈ܥܬܐ ܡܪܝܐ ܠܡܦܪܥ.

ܕܬܡܢܐ. ܡܢ ܦܘܪ̈ܩܢܐ ܐܢܬ ܐܢܫܐ ܕܠܘ[1] ܢܒܝܫܢܐ ܗܘ. ܐܝܟ ܡܪܘܪܘܬ
ܪܘܓܙܐ ܘܡܚܫܒܘܬ ܚܫܝܐ. ܘܡܫܬܪ̈ܘܬܐ ܒܒܕܝܬ ܚܫܝܘܬܐ ܘܡܬܕܒܪܢܘܬܐ
ܒܢܬܗܘܢ.[2] ܚܠܦ ܠܫܘܬ ܗ̇ܘ ܡܢܐ ܕܐܬܘܗܝ، ܡܛܠܒܐ ܒܚܝܠܗ ܘܡܚܫܒܐ
ܒܒܝܫ̈ܗ. ܐܦ ܗܘܕܝܐ ܗܘܐ ܘܡܠܟܐ ܡܬܘܬܪܐ ܦܘܪ̈ܩܢܐ ܐܝܟܢ. ܡܬܪ
ܕܝܢ ܡܬܠܡܠ ܦܘܪܩܢܐ. ܐܢ ܒܝܢ ܫܘܝܫܐ ܘܙܕܩܬܐ ܗ̇ܘܐ. ܗܘܐ ܓܒܪ ܠܗ
ܒܠܫܘܢ ܗܢܝܐܐ. ܐܠܐ ܘܡܬܝܪܐ ܡܬܝܚܐ. ܒܪ ܓܒ ܒܠܫ ܡܕܡ ܕܫܠܝܐ
ܐܝܟ. ܗܢܐ ܕܝܢ ܫܠܦܝܐ. ܗܢܐ ܕܝܢ ܘܒܫܝܬܐ. ܘܗܢܐ ܗܘܐ ܐܝܟܢܐ.
ܘܐܢܫܝܢܐ ܒܚܘܪܐ. ܘܐܢܫܝܢܐ ܐܢܫܝܢܝܬܐ. ܡܢ ܗܠܝܢ ܓܒܪ ܐܬܪ̈ܘܬܐ
ܠܡܫܟ̈ܢܬܐ ܘܠܓ̈ܒܪܬܐ ܢܡܫܝܢ.

6 [1] i. om. RVL [2] om. RVL [3*] trp. RVLl
7 [1] i. om. l; ܗܟܢܐ F [2] pl. R [3] ܕܦܘܪܩܢܐ RVLl [4] ܕܒܝܢܐ RVLl
8 [1] ܕܠܐ RVL [2] sg. F

give him his slain offspring; and after he had taken him and given honour to his body by cremation according to the law of his generation and placed his ashes in an urn, before the eyes of the crowds he raised the urn and offered a prayer to his enemy, acknowledging that he had conferred a great favour on him. And so the receipt of the slain offspring, while not simply among those things which give cause for rejoicing, in this way became a cause for rejoicing.

SIX.[23] Just as even enemies acknowledge a personal good and cannot reject it, so also an evil, like the Corinthians who, when they thought that they had been slandered by Simonides, inflicted evil upon him. Therefore the repayment by expedient goods to virtuous men and women is chiefly by supporting them against the foolish and dissolute in word and deed; as Homer did when he chose two virtuous people, Odysseus the good king of Ithaca, and the brave Achilles, making them an object of glory and praise, and set up opposite them two dissolute people, the adulterer Alexander, brother of Hector, and the adulteress Helen, wife of Menelaus, king of Hellas, making them an object of shame and blame. In this way he repaid goods to the virtuous and evils to the dissolute according to his capability.

SEVEN.[24] The expected repayment is to be measured by (one's) ability. Therefore he who can (make) a small repayment and repays a small (amount) does not do little, but he who can (repay) very much but repays much does do little, because much is less than very much. Similarly the stupidity of a friend in distress is not grievous when the period is short, but when it drags on and overruns the time of the distress it is unbearable and cannot be excused. But he repays badly who, in return for a greater good which he has received gives a lesser, and for a general and necessary profit (gives) a particular and worthless (one). A similar repayment consists in that which is close in kind and quantity, and then a repayment is praised when he who is able to make the repayments big does not make them small.

[23] **2.3.6** AR 1.6 63a10-19; IS 2.2 (72.16-73.13).
[24] **2.3.7** AR 1.6 63a19-33; IS 2.2 (73.14-75.4).

ܦܘܫܩܐ ܕܒܢܝܐ

ܡܛܠ ܗ̇ܝ ܕܝܬܝܪܐ ܗ̇ܘ ܕܒܨܝܪܐ

ܬܐܘܪ̈ܝܐܣ ܬܫܥ

ܘܡܕܡܝܬܐ. ܡܫܬܘܬܦ ܕܝܢ ܪܘܠܦܐ ܠܡܟܬܒܘ ܦܪ̈ܘܛܘܣ ܡܢܙܪ̈ܪܝܬ ܗ̇ܝ ܕܗܕܐ
ܠܟܠܐ ܝܬܝܪ ܡܝܬܪܐ. ܘܗܕܐ ܕܦܫܝܩܐ ܝܬܝܪ ܡܟܬܒܢܐ. ܘܠܒܢܬܐ ܕܝܬܝܪ
ܡܝܬܪܐ[1] ܐܝܬܝܗ̇ ܗ̇ܝ ܕܝܬܝܪ ܠܒܨܝܪܐ ܘܝܬܝܪ ܐܚܪܢܐ. ܘܗ̇ܝ ܡܛܠܬܗ̇ ܘܠܘ[2]
ܡܛܠ ܐܚܪܢܬܐ ܠܒܨܝܪܐ.[3] ܘܠܒܢܬܐ ܕܝܬܝܪ ܡܢ ܠܒܢܬܐ ܐܚܪܢܬܐ ܡܝܬܪܐ
ܪܒܬܗ̇ ܝܬܝܪ ܡܢ ܪܒܬܐ ܕܗ̇ܝ ܡܝܬܪܐ. ܒܐܡܬ ܒܕ ܠܒܨܝܪܐ ܝܬܝܪ[4] ܡܢ ܢܫ̈ܐ
ܡܝܬܪܝܢ. ܠܒܨܝܪܐ[5] ܪܒܐ ܝܬܝܪ ܡܢ ܐܚܪܢܬܐ ܪܒܬܐ ܡܝܬܪ. ܘܒܗܦܟܐ.
ܒܐܡܬ ܒܕ[6] ܢܒܥܬܗ ܕܐܠܗܐ ܕܫܒܥܬܐ ܗ, ܪܒܬܐ. ܝܬܝܪ ܡܢ ܬܠܬܐ
ܐܚܪܢܬܐ ܕܒܢܘܬܐ ܗ, ܪܒܬܐ ܡܝܬܪܐ. ܫܒܥܬܐ ܝܬܝܪ ܡܢ ܒܢܘܬܐ[7]
ܡܝܬܪܐ. ܘܠܒܢܬܐ ܕܠܗ̇ ܠܒܢܬܐ ܐܚܪܢܬܐ ܢܦܩܐ. ܘܗ̇ܝ ܠܗ̇ ܠܐ ܢܦܩܐ.
ܝܬܝܪ ܡܝܬܪܐ. ܐܡܝܕܐ ܗ̇ܘ ܠܥܘܠܛܢܐ[8] ܐܝܬܪܐ. ܒܗܬ ܕܝܢ ܠܥܘܠܛܢܐ
ܒܗܬܪܐ. ܘܡܣܝܟܐ ܠܗ̇ ܕܢܣܒܝܗ̇ ܕܢܦܠܘ. ܘܡܠܝܐ ܕܠܐ ܠܟܠ ܐܝܬܪܐ ܐܘ
ܒܗܬܪܐ ܥܘܠܛܢܐ ܢܦܩ. ܐܦܠܐ ܒܠ ܐܝܟܐ ܕܟܠ ܡܢܝܢ.

ܕܬܪ̈ܬܝܢ. ܦܫܝܩܐ ܬܘܒ ܚܒܒ ܐܘܠܦܢ ܕܠܐ ܡܝܬܪܐ ܕܦܠܓܘܬܐ ܚܒܒ ܙܘܓܬܐ
ܝܬܝܪ ܐܠܦܐ ܡܢ ܡܝܬܪܐ. ܐܝܟ ܫܘܡܠܝܐ ܗ̇ܘ ܕܠܗ ܦܠܓܘܬܐ ܗܘ ܐܝܟ
ܥܘܦܪܐ ܘܒܗ ܗ̇ܘ ܡܟܐ ܕܡܝܬܪ ܡܢ ܥܘܦܪܐ ܦܩܐ ܒܙܥܐ. ܘܡܫܬܠܡܢܘܬܐ
ܒܕ ܠܐ ܡܝܬܪܐ ܡܢ ܗܝܐܘܬܐ ܒܠܚܘܕ ܗ̇ܘ ܡܟܐ ܕܡܝܬܪ ܡܢ ܗܝܐܘܬܐ
ܗܘܝܐ. ܐܠܦܐ ܐܪܐ ܫܘܡܠܝܐ ܡܢ ܥܘܦܪܐ ܘܡܫܬܠܡܢܘܬܐ ܡܢ
ܗܝܐܘܬܐ. ܘܗ̇ܘ ܕܗܘ ܡܛܠܬܗ ܐܝܬܘܗܝ ܒܒܢܐ. ܐܝܟ ܠܐ ܢܦܩ ܠܗ ܗ̇ܘ
ܐܚܪܢܐ ܝܬܝܪ ܐܠܦܐ. ܐܠܦܐ ܒܪ ܫܘܡܠܝܐ ܕܠܐ ܥܘܦܪܐ ܘܫܒܝܐ ܥܘܦܪܐ
ܕܠܐ ܫܘܡܠܝܐ. ܘܗ̇ܘ ܕܐܝܬܘܗܝ ܘܠܪܬܗ ܡܬܟܒܐ. ܐܝܟ ܫܘܡܠܝܐ. ܝܬܝܪ
ܐܠܦܐ ܡܢ ܐܚܪܢܐ ܕܡܥܪܐ ܠܡܗܘܐ. ܘܐܦ ܠܪܬܗ ܡܬܟܒܐ. ܐܝܟ
ܗܝܐܘܬܐ. ܐܘ ܡܥܪܐ ܠܡܗܘܐ ܘܡܛܠ ܐܚܪܢܐ ܡܬܟܒܐ. ܐܝܟ ܕܪܘܥܐ.
ܘܐܚܪܢܐ ܡܛܠܬܗ ܐܚܪܢܐ. ܐܝܟ ܬܠܓܪܬܐ ܕܡܛܠܬܗ ܡܛܠ ܡܝܬܪܐ. ܝܬܝܪ
ܐܠܦܐ ܡܢ ܐܚܪܢܐ ܕܡܛܠ ܐܚܪܢܐ. ܐܝܟ ܬܠܓܪܬܐ ܕܡܛܠ ܒܡܝܬܪܐ.

1 [1] ܡܘܬܪܐ RVL [2] ܘܠܐ RVL [3] ܒܨܐ RVL [4] om. RVL [5] i. add. ܘ RVLL [6] i. add. ܕ F [7] scripsi; ܒܢܘܬܐ codd. [8] i. add. ܘ RVLl

EIGHT.[25] Among repayments there is that which is not financial, like giving delight to a friend, annoyance to an enemy, and actions (each) productive of pleasure or astonishment when they are seen. According to what it is, everyone is ready (for it) by his nature or experienced (in it) by his habit. Direction and useful advice are also repayments, but above all being praised is a repayment, if it comes at a time of need and desire, for this will not only be pleasant, but he will also be seen as virtuous, although indeed each man desires something particular—this one learning, that one victory, this one honour, another one wealth, and others other things. From these *topoi*, then, we derive the rhetorical *pisteis*.

## SECTION FOUR
### On the Greater and the Lesser
### Nine Theories

ONE.[26] An orator needs to prepare premisses proving that 'This good is better' or 'This expedient is more advantageous'. The good which is better is that which is more general and more lasting, and is chosen for its own sake and not for the sake of another. (When one) good is better than another good, a large one of it is better than a large one of the other. For example, as men are better than women, a large man is better than a large woman; and conversely, for example, as the knowledge of God is the greatest (part) of wisdom (and) better than continual prayer, the greatest (part) of asceticism, wisdom is better than aceticism. The good on which another good follows, without the former following on the latter, is the better. Honour (follows) simultaneously on power, but wealth subsequently on power, and theft potentially (follows) on sacrilege, but it is evident that power does not follow on every honour or wealth, nor does everyone who steals commit sacrilege.

TWO.[27] An orator may effect persuasion that (among two things, the one which) is not better (but) which produces a great good is more desirable than the better. For example, perseverance is not a good

---

[25] **2.3.8** AR 1.6 63a33-63b4; IS 2.2 (75.4-75.15).
[26] **2.4.1** AR 1.7 63b5-33; cf. 64b26; IS 2.3 (76.3-77.2).
[27] **2.4.2** AR 1.7 63b33-64a9; IS 2.3 (77.3-77.16).

ܕܬܠܬ. ܡܫܬܘܕܝܢܐ[1] ܕܟܠ ܥܘܪܐ ܘܟܠܬܐ ܕܡܕܡ ܝܕܥ ܗܘ ܡܢܗ. ܠܘ ܕܝܢ
ܫܘܬܐܝܬ. ܠܟܠܗ ܟܝܢ ܗܘܐ ܡܬܝܕܥܐ ܡܢ ܟܝܢܘܬܗ ܕܐܠܗܘܬܗ ܝܬܝܪܬܗ.
ܘܡܛܠ ܕܟܠ ܠܟܠܗ ܡܠܟܘܬܐ ܝܚܝܕܝܘܬܐ ܗܝ. ܦܠܓܝ ܐܕܫܐ ܡܠܟܝܐ. ܟܕ
ܕܐܝܬܘܗܝ ܕܟܠܗ ܐܝܬ ܐܝܬ ܟܠ *ܐܝܬ ܝܕܥ. ܘܟܠܗ ܟܠܬܐ ܕܐܝܬ ܝܕܥ ܐܝܬ
ܝܕܥܐ. ܘܡܢܟܐ ܕܢܦܫܗ ܐܝܠܦܢ ܕܗܝ ܝܕܝܥܬܗ ܟܢܬܗ ܐܝܬ ܝܕܥܐ[2]. ܐܝܟ
ܠܕܐܡܪܗܘܢ ܗܘ ܗܘ ܕܟܘܟܒ ܗܘ ܠܦܠܝܣܛܪܐܛܝܣ ܗܘ ܕܡܠܟ ܠܟܬܒܘܗܝ
ܕܢܟܘܠ ܡܦܠܓܝ ܘܐܡܪ. *ܕܝܠܗ ܡܠܘܟܐ[3] ܐܝܬ ܝܕܥ ܡܢ ܗܘ ܗܘ ܕܐܟܘܠ.
ܟܕ ܐܠܘ ܠܐ ܡܠܟ ܡܠܘܟܐ ܠܐ ܗܘܐ ܡܫܘܪܐ. ܟܕܘܢ ܕܝܢ ܠܟܬܒܘܗܝ
ܡܟܢܫܐ ܘܐܡܪ ܕܝܠܗ ܫܘܪܝܐ ܐܝܬ ܝܕܥ ܡܢ ܗܘ ܕܡܠܟ. ܟܕ ܐܠܘ ܠܐ
ܐܬܦܠܣ ܫܘܪܝܐ ܠܐ ܗܘܐ ܡܠܟܐ ܕܡܠܘܟܐ.

ܕܐܒܘܗܝ. ܗܘ ܗܘ ܕܟܝܢܐ ܥܡܗ ܐܝܟ ܕܗܘܐ ܐܝܬ ܡܬܝܕܥ ܐܝܟ ܕܐܒܐ
ܐܦܠܘ. ܘܟܝܢܐ ܐܒܗܝܐ ܗܘ ܕܐܝܬܘܗܝ ܢܚܝܬ ܐܝܟ ܦܪܨܘܦܐ ܐܝܬ ܡܬܝܕܥ.
ܡܟܝܢܐ ܐܦ ܡܟܝܢܐ. ܘܐܦ ܡܥܡܐ ܕܟܠܗܘܢ ܟܝܢܐ ܥܡܗ. ܘܟܝܢܐ ܗܘ
ܗܘ ܕܐܝܬ ܒܗܘܢ ܥܡܗܘܬܗ ܐܝܬ ܡܬܝܕܥ ܡܛܠ ܕܟܠ ܒܐܝܬܘܬܗ. ܟܝܢܐ
ܕܝܢ ܗܘ ܕܦܪܨܘܦܐ ܥܡܗܘܬܗ ܐܝܬ ܡܬܝܕܥ ܡܛܠ ܕܢܚܝܬ ܠܝ ܒܟܝܢܬܗ. ܘܐܝܟܢܐ
ܕܡܫܡܠܝܐ ܐܝܬ ܗܘ ܡܫܠܡ. ܝܕܥ ܗܘ ܢܗܝܪܗ. ܘܐܝܟܢܐ ܕܟܠܝܠܘܬܗ ܐܝܬ
ܡܫܠܡܐ. ܥܡܗܘܬܗ ܐܝܬ ܡܬܝܕܥܐ. ܘܟܕܕܐ ܕܫܘܠܡܗ ܐܝܬ ܠܟܠ ܐܦ
ܗܘ ܠܟܠ. ܘܕܫܘܠܡܗ ܐܝܬ ܟܕ ܐܦ ܗܘ ܟܕ. ܘܟܝܢܐ ܕܐܝܬ ܡܫܠܡܐ
ܐܝܬ ܡܟܠ. ܐܝܟ ܫܘܠܡ ܚܝܘܬܐ ܕܐܝܬ ܡܢ ܫܘܠܡ ܡܕܝܢܘܬܐ ܡܟܠ. ܟܕ
ܗܝ ܕܚܝܐ ܐܝܬ ܡܢ ܗܝ ܕܝܕܥ ܡܟܠܝܐ. ܘܝܕܥܬ ܚܟܡܐ[1] ܐܝܬ ܡܢ ܝܕܥܬ
ܢܦܫܐ ܡܬܝܕܥܐ. ܟܕ ܚܟܡܐ ܐܝܬ ܡܢ ܒܝܕܥܐ ܡܬܝܕܥ. ܘܡܬܝܕܥܢܘܬܐ[2] ܟܕ ܗܝ
ܕܫܠܝܡܬܐ ܐܝܟ ܕܟܕܕܐ ܡܬܝܕܥܐ ܐܝܬ ܡܫܠܡܝܢ ܡܬܝܕܥܝܢ. ܘܐܝܟܢܐ ܕܫܠܡܘܬܗ
ܐܝܬ ܡܬܝܕܥܐ ܐܝܬ ܡܬܝܕܥ.

3 [1] om. F [2*] om. F [3*] ܕܐܝܬܘܗܝ ܠܘܬܗ F

4 [1] sg. RVLl [2] sg. F

like beauty, but by it a man may acquire that which is greater than beauty; and although health is not greater than pleasure, it is the cause of that which is greater than pleasure. Therefore perseverance is more desirable than beauty, and health more than pleasure. And that which exists for its own sake is preferable, even if the other more desirable does not follow on it. So health without beauty is desirable, and beauty without health is detestable. And that which exists and is sought for itself, like health, is more desirable than that which is introduced to bring into being (something else), even if it is sought for itself, like pleasure, or is introduced to bring into being (another) and is sought for the sake of the other, like exercise. And that for which another (exists), like wealth for which trade (exists), is more desirable than that which (exists) for the other, like trade which (exists) for wealth.

THREE.[28] It is supposed that every beginning and cause of something is greater than the (thing itself), but (this is) not truly (so), for a good may be better than its choice, which is its beginning. And because every deliberative good is voluntary, the deliberative species are multiple, because that is greater of which the cause is greater, and the cause of a greater effect is greater (than the cause of a lesser effect). An orator *can* also argue that the origin of (something) is in its essence greater (than the thing itself). For example, at one time Leodamas was prosecuting Callistratus—who had advised Chabrias to do wrong—and saying that the fault of the adviser was greater than (that of) him who did the wrong, because if the adviser had not advised, the doer would not have acted. However, at another time he was vituperating Chabrias and saying that the fault of the doer was greater than (that of) the adviser, because if the doer had not been persuaded, the advice of the adviser would not have done harm.

FOUR.[29] What is scarcer, like gold, is better, as Aphunus said, but in another way what is more useful, like iron, is better. So also water, even if ointment of balsam is scarcer. In one way that which is more difficult to find is better, because it is exalted in its essence, but in another way that which is easier to find is better, because it gives us pleasure to search for it. (If) the opposite of (something) is more

[28] **2.4.3** AR 1.7 64a10-23; IS 2.3 (77.16-78.8).
[29] **2.4.4** AR 1.7 64a23-64b7; IS 2.3 (78.9-79.5).

ܕܚܡܫ. ܢܒܬܐ ܕܒܬܪ ܡܛܪܐ ܡܣܕܘܪܘܬܗ ܒܬܪ ܡܛܪܐ. ܐܣܛܘܬܐ ܐܪܐ
ܒܬܪ ܡܢ ܝܘܠܦܢܐ ܟܢܘܬܐ ܕܡܛܪܐ. ܘܝܘܠܦܢܐ ܗܘ ܕܡܫܝܢܘܬܗ ܒܬܪ
ܥܣܪ̈ܝܢ ܒܬܪ ܡܛܪܐ. ܟܐܘܡܣܦܝܪܐ ܐܪܐ ܕܟܠ ܐܠܝܚܬ ܘܡܟܠܐ ܡܫܪܪܐ
ܒܬܪ ܡܛܪܐ ܡܢ ܐܬܢܘܟܐ ܕܟܠ ܡܬܩܢܘܬܐ ܒܢܝܐ.[1] ܘܗܘ ܕܙܝܪܟܐ
ܘܡܫܝ̈ܢܐ[2] ܐܘ ܦܪ̈ܘܫܐ ܠܡܛܪܘܬܗ ܡܫܪܝܢ ܒܬܪ ܡܛܪܐ ܦܫܝܛܐܝܬ. ܒܗ̇
ܕܡܦܪ ܡܢ ܫܡܝܐ ܕܢܚܬܝܢ.[3] ܘܐܝܢܐ ܕܒܬܪ ܗܘܝܐ ܒܬܪ ܠܒܢܝܐ. ܒܗ
ܗܘܝܘܬܐ ܡܢ ܟܠܗ ܡܦܪܫܐ[4] ܠܝܬܗ̇ ܡܬܚܒܢܐ.[5] ܡܠܘ ܕܝܢ ܗ̇ܝ ܕܒܬܪ ܠܐ
ܡܢܝܢܐ ܘܒܬܪ[6] ܒܪܢܫܐ ܘܒܬܪ ܡܫܬܘܬܐ ܘܒܬܪ ܥܦܪܐ. ܘܡܫܬܦܠܬܐ ܬܘܒ.
ܐܢ ܗ̇ܝ ܕܒܪܢܫܐܬ ܒܬܪ ܡܢ ܗ̇ܝ ܕܡܬܦܫܬ ܡܛܪܐ. ܒܪܢܫܘܬܐ[7] ܒܬܪ ܡܢ
ܢܦܫܘܬܐ ܡܛܪܐ. ܘܗ̇ܝ ܕܡܫܝ̈ܢܐ ܐܘ ܡܪ̈ܝܐ ܐܘ ܡܕ̈ܡܟܐ ܒܟܠܝܢ ܠܗ̇
ܒܬܪ[8] ܡܛܪܐ. ܫܦܝܠܬܐ ܗܝ ܒܢܝ ܗ̇ ܕܠܐ ܢܗܘܐ ܡܢ ܐܠܝܢ ܕܐܝܟ
ܐܘܪ̈ܝܘܢ ܘܡܬܚܫܒܝܢ ܬܘܒ ܙܘܪ̈ܝܢ. ܐܢܫܐ ܒܢܝ ܐܪ̈ܙܐ ܐܟܡܢܐ ܡܛܠ
ܐܘܟܝܬ ܫܦܘܬ ܘܡܟܠܐ ܐܬܘܗܝ.

ܕܫܬ. ܫܪܟܐ ܪܟܐ ܒܗ ܠܒܢ̈ܝܬܗ ܡܬܦܠܓ ܒܬܪ ܡܬܘܪܒ. ܐܝܟ ܕܐܡܪ
ܐܦܠܛܘܢ. ܕܡܫܝܚܬܐ ܗ̇ܝ ܗܘܕܐ ܐܢ ܒܦܘܪܫܐ ܡܢ ܡܠܟܘܬܗ ܡܬܚܒܢܐ.
ܒܢܫܬܐ ܡܫ̈ܝܚܬܐ ܡܢܗ ܡܫܟܢܐ. ܠܒܢ̈ܝܫܐ ܡܢ ܦܠܓ ܘܡܢܝܢ. ܠܗ̇ ܕܝܢ ܒܠܗ̇[1]
ܡܡܫ ܒܢܘܪܐ. ܘܬܠܕܐ[2] ܡܬܬܘܕܝܢ. ܒܐܡܬ ܒܠܝܫ ܒܥܡܟܐ ܕܝܠܕܗ[3] ܦܪܐ ܒܗ
ܫܢܐ ܠܗ ܕܐܟܒ. ܘܐܝܬ ܐܡܟܐ ܕܒܡܫ ܡܒܢ̈ܝܬܐ ܘܪܘܒܒܗܝܢ ܒܬܪ ܡܢ
ܦܘܪܫܗܝܢ ܙܒܢܬ ܒܢ̈ܝܬܐ[4] ܡܫܝܚܐ. ܐܝܟ ܕܐܦܝܩܘܪܘܣ ܣܒܪ. ܘܐܝܢܐ
ܕܒܬܪ ܒܫܡܐܝܬ ܘܫܪܐ ܠܒܥܡܐ ܢܗܘܐ[5] ܒܬܪ ܪܒ. ܠܦܘܬ ܕܝܢܐ ܘܡܘܬܒܬܐ
ܘܕܘܟܝܬܐ[6] ܘܡܟܢ̈ܫܬܐ ܘܫܝܢܐ.

ܕܫܒܥ. ܗܘܪܐ ܡܢ ܬܫܥܝܬܐ ܕܠܐ ܢܕܢܚ ܠܢ ܘܠܗܠܝܢ ܕܟ̈ܬܒܝܢ[1] ܐܝܟ ܕܟܝܢ
ܘܐܡܪ. ܡܢ ܗܘܪܐ ܠܢ ܐܦ ܒܬܘܟܬܐ[2] ܥܠ ܐܘܠܘܡܦܝܐܕܘܣ[3] ܒܡܫܦܛܝܢ
ܕܐܝܬ ܠܗ ܥܠ ܒܬܘ̈ܬܗ ܙܪܝܕܐ ܘܦܬܝܢ ܡܬܒܐ ܡܢ ܐܦܢܘܗܝ ܢܚܝܐ ܘܥܠ
ܐܪܟܐ ܥܕܡܗ. ܗܫܐ ܕܝܢ ܒܣܘܦܐ ܘܟܐ ܒܐܦܢܘܬܐ. ܒܗ ܒܦܣܩܝܢ ܗܘܘ
ܡܢ ܘܟܢܐ. ܘܡܒܝܢܐ ܡܬܠܝܬܐ ܙܒܢܐ[4] ܗܘܐ ܥܠ ܐܪܟܐ ܐܘܦܘܪܛܝܣ ܒܗ
ܗ̣ܘ ܡܠܟܐ ܗܘܐ ܘܐܡܪ ܠܗܠܝܢ ܕܡܢܗܘܢ ܗܢ̈ܘ. ܗܠܝܢ ܒܡ ܥܒܝܕܘܬܐ
ܕܡܫܝܚܝ ܕܐܦܝܦܢܝܘܣ[5] ܗ̇ܝ ܕܒܬܪ ܒܫܡܐ. ܘܡܢܝܢ ܕܗܕܐ ܐܡܪ
ܘܐܦܝܠܐ ܕܠܝܦ ܡܢ ܢܬܗ ܐܝܬ.

5 [1] ܒܢܝܐ RVLl [2] ܐܘ ܡܫܝ̈ܢܐ RVLl [3] om. F [4] om. RVLl [5] ܡܬܚܒܢܐ RL [6] i. om. RVLl [7] i. add. ܘ RVLl [8] om. RVLl
6 [1] ܒܗ ܠܗ̇ RVLl [2] sg. F [3] ܕܝܠܕܗ F [4] pl. RVLl [5] ܗ̇ܘܐ RVLl [6] trp. ante ܕܐܦܝܩܘܪܘܣ RVL
7 [1] ܟ̈ܬܒܝܢ RVLl [2] pl. RVL [3] ܐܘܠܘܡܦܝܐܕܘܣ RVLl [4] scripsi; ܐܢܪ F; ܐܢܪ̈ RVLl
[5] ܕܐܦܝܦܢܝܘܣ R

harmful, its usefulness is greater; and (if) its absence is more harmful, its presence is more advantageous. (If) the end of an action is better, it itself is good; but (if) the end is worse, it itself is bad. The property of a superior is superior; for example, healthy sight is superior to healthy smell, because seeing is superior to smelling. Love of comrades is better than love of riches, because a comrade is better than wealth. Because virtues are the causes of virtuous actions, they are better than them, and that is better for which the desire is better.

FIVE.[30] A science is better, the action of which is better, therefore medicine is better than cosmetics. The discipline whose demonstrations are surer is better, therefore geometry, which is sure because of necessary acceptance, is better than ethics, which is built upon reputable (premisses). That to the virtue of which the prudent or the majority or the best testify is simply better, because they judge without passion. That which is more pleasant is preferred, because pleasure is sought for itself by the whole populace, but even more that which is less grievous, and longer lasting, and more secure, and finer. Furthermore, with (grammatical) inflexions, if *courageously* is better than *temperately*, *courage* is better than *temperance*. That which many, or authorities, or the learned choose is better. It is a disgrace not to accept (the word) of those whose losses like their honours are great, for honour is some (sort of) esteem or worthiness of acceptance.

SIX.[31] A great matter, when divided into its parts, may be magnified. As Homer says: 'If this city is violently subjugated by Meleager, it will suffer many evils from him; the people he will slay and ravage, the (city) he will totally burn with fire, and the children will be acknowledged'—that is, everyone will call on the name of his child when he sees him perishing. Sometimes a combination of parts and their building up shows the magnitude of an evil better than their division, as Epicharmus did. That which comes about with more difficulty and more rarely is greater, according to the occasions, ages, places, times, and powers.

---

[30] **2.4.5** AR 1.7 64b7-65a9; IS 2.3 (79.5-80.9).
[31] **2.4.6** AR 1.7 65a10-24; IS 2.3 (80.9-81.5).

ܕܐܬܚܙܝܐ. ܡܛܠܬܐ ܕܢܛܝܪܬܐ ܕܗܘ̇ ܕܡܟܠܠ ܠܘܬܢ ܡܫܝܚܐ. ܐܝܟ ܕܐܡܪ ܦܘܠܘܣ
ܕܦܘܪܢܣܐ ܕܛܠܠܐ ܡܢ ܡܪܢܝܬܐ ܠܚܡܘܢ ܕܐܬܐܐ ܡܢ ܫܡܝܐ ܕܝܢܐ. ܘܐܝܟܢܐ
ܕܟܠܗܝܢ ܫܘܠܡܐ ܠܬܪܬܐ[1] ܗܘܐ. ܐܝܟ ܕܥܘܬܪܐ ܒܫܘܒܚܘܬܐ ܘܒܡܪܡܘܬܐ.
ܬܪܬܝܢ ܡܢܬܐ. ܘܦܠܓܘܬܐ ܕܒܫܘܠܡ ܫܢܝܐ ܗܘܝ ܬܪܬܝܢ ܡܢ ܗܠܝܢ ܕܟܠܝܠܘܬܐ
ܡܢܬܐ̈. ܗܘ̇ ܕܠܢܬܬܗ[2] ܡܬܠܒܫܐ ܬܪܬܝܢ ܡܢ ܐܝܕܐ ܕܡܟܠܠ ܥܘܒܕܐ
ܡܢܬܐ.[3] ܒܐܡܬܝ ܗ̇. ܕܐܝܬܝܗ ܬܪܬܝܢ ܡܢ ܗ̇. ܕܢܬܘܬܐ. ܘܗ̇ܘ ܕܠܘܬ[4] ܗ̇
ܕܠܡܫܝܚܐ ܘܡܥܡܝܪ[5] ܠܡܫܝܚܐ ܟܕܢ. ܐܝܟ ܫܘܠܡܝܐ ܘܡܬܬܐ ܬܪܬܝܢ ܡܢܬܐ.
ܠܡܢܬܐ ܓܢܙ ܡܟܠܝܢ ܘܠܗܝܡܢܘܬܐ ܒܢܒܝܐ ܘܕܠܐ ܒܢܒܝܐ ܡܫܟܠܝܢ.
ܗ̇ܘ ܕܠܡܢܬܐ ܝܗܒ. ܐܢܫܝܢ ܕܝܢ ܦܠܓܘܬܐ ܕܬܪܬܝܢ ܪܟܐ ܘܡܢܒܝܐ ܐܬܬܗ̇. ܝܗܒ
ܐܢܫܝܢ ܕܝܢ[6] ܒܗ ܥܙܝܙܐ ܐܣܝܪܐ. ܗܟܢܐ ܐܦ ܡܢ ܦܘܠܚܢܐ ܐܝܬ ܐܝܟܢܐ
ܕܬܪܬܝܢ ܪܒ. ܐܝܟ ܗ̇. ܕܢܫܡܥܐ ܒܝܢܐ ܕܒܢܝܢܐ ܡܢ ܗ̇. ܕܢܫܡܥܐ ܒܝܢܐ
ܕܬܪܬܝܢ ܒܢܝܐ.

ܕܐܬܒܥܐ. ܗܝܡܢܘܬ ܐܕܢܐ ܦܩܝܚܐ ܒܡܠܟܘܬ ܫܡܝܐ ܘܦܪܘܩܐ ܘܥܡܡܐ
ܕܥܝܢܐ ܡܕܝܢܝܐ ܘܐܣܝܪܐ ܬܪܬܝܢ ܗܘܝܐ. ܘܒܢܒܝܘܬܐ ܬܘܒ ܕܦܘܠܘܦܐܘ
ܐܘܟܝܬ ܡܕܝܢܝܘܬܐ ܥܠ ܕܠܘܬ ܐܚܝܢ. ܘܡܛܠ[1] ܐܢܝ ܐܡܪ ܐܚܝܢ.
ܕܡܫܘܦܪܝܬܐ ܕܒܫܡܝܐ[2] ܡܬܦܠܓܐ ܘܒܐܣܘܪܬܐ ܡܬܦܠܓܐ.
ܘܐܪܥܦܠܘܦܪܝܬܐ ܐܘܟܝܬ ܦܪܘܬ ܐܣܝܪܘܬܐ ܕܒܫܡܝܐ ܡܫܡܫܝܢ ܢܡܘܣܐ
ܗܘܐ ܘܒܦܪܘܦܬܗ ܡܬܦܠܓܐ. ܘܠܣܝܪܘܬ ܪܥܝܢܘܬܐ ܕܒܡܫܒܚܐ ܗܘܐ
ܘܒܐܣܘܪܐ ܡܬܦܠܓܐ. ܘܠܟܠܣܘܪܐ ܡܢܗܘܢ[3] ܚܪܝܐ ܐܝܬ ܕܬܠܝܢܐ ܘܐܠܝܟ
ܕܢܕܒ ܐܢܘܢ ܡܠܟܐ. ܘܗܠܝܢ ܕܝܢ ܡܛܠ ܐܕܥܘܗܝ ܡܠܟܝܢܐ ܕܪܘܦܪܘܬܐ
ܡܡܫܝܢܘܬ ܐܬܐܡܪ[4].

8 [1] f. om. F [2] om. RVLl [3] ܡܘܬܪܐ RVLl [4] ܕܠܘܗ F [5] ܘܡܬܪ RVLl [6] ܡܢ RVLl
9 [1] i. om. RVL [2] ܕܒܫܘܫܡܐ RVLl [3] ܡܢ ܗܠܝܢ RVLl [4] f. om. l; ܐܬܐܡܪܘ RVL

SEVEN.[32] At this point our master quoted paradigms incomprehensible to us or our teachers and said: 'Hence, too, we may add what is written on the Olympian victor, who had on his shoulders a patchwork and carried fish from Argos, and threw it on the ground. But now he was victorious in the race, (that is,) in the contest, as they were bent down by revelling. And the third armed man, Iphicrates, was lying on the ground when praising and describing these by which these came, with the sudden growth of Epictetus, which was harder. On this account the poet said, "Self-taught am I".'

EIGHT.[33] The top part of that which is exalted is better; as Pericles said that the expulsion of the youths from the city was like the departure of spring from the year. That which comes at a time of greater need is better, like wealth (which comes) in old age or illness, and goods which come at the end of life are better than those (which come) in youth. That which is sought for itself is better than that which (is sought) for glory—that is, gaining (an advantage) is greater than conferring (an advantage). What is helpful for living and living well, like health and wealth, is better, for they drive away pain and increase pleasure, knowingly and unknowingly. Being wealthy is a greater good and more cherished by some, by others (when accompanied) by other things. So also with damage there is a greater, like putting out the eye of a one-eyed man over putting out an eye of a two-eyed man.

NINE.[34] The *pistis* of the expedient species (of rhetoric) has now been well covered by the extensive paradigms, reading, and attention (I have given) to primary and subsequent matters, and also by the knowledge of the six constitutions or civic (governments) which I have taught. According to our master there were four: democracy, which is distributed by lot and preserved for freedom; aristocracy or pre-eminence of rule, which comes about by legislation and is preserved for the observance of the (law); and sole authority, which comes about by force and is preserved for honour. Each of them has its specific customs, and the deliberative (orator) must know them. Enough has now been said on the deliberative species of rhetoric.

---

[32] **2.4.7** AR 1.7 65a24-30; IS 2.3 (81.5).
[33] **2.4.8** AR 1.7 65a30-65b19; IS 2.3 (81.5-82.10).
[34] **2.4.9** AR 1.7 65b19-8 66a2; 12; 17-22; IS 2.3 (82.11-83.10).

## ܩܦܠܐܘܢ ܬܠܝܬܝܐ
## ܥܠ *ܐܕܫܐ ܚܡܫܐ¹ ܕܪܘܚܢܘܬܐ
## ܘܒܗ ܐܝܬ ܦܘ̈ܫܩܐ ܐܪܒܥܐ

## ܦܘܫܩܐ ܩܕܡܝܐ
## ܥܠ ܐܕ̈ܫܐ ܕܡܫܝܚܘܬܐ ܘܒܝܫܘܬܐ
## ܬܘܪ̈ܐܢܗ ܬܪ̈ܬܝܢ

ܩܕܡܝܬܐ. ܡܛܠ ܓܝܪ ܕܒܗܠܝܢ ܕܡܫܝܚܝ̈ܢ ܘܫܦܝ̈ܪܢ ܠܘ ܒܠܚܘܕ ܠܒܢܝ̈ܢܫܐ ܘܡ̈ܠܐܟܐ ܐܠܐ ܐܦ ܘܠܟܠ ܩ̈ܠܝܠܐ ܘܠܐ ܡܬܦ̈ܫܩܐ ܡܠܗܝܢ. ܐܝܟܢܐ ܕܠܡܫܝܚܘܬܐ ܘܐܕ̈ܫܝܗ̇ ܥܡ ܩܘܠܣ̈ܝܗܘܢ ܒܡܫܟܚܬ ܚܘܘܝܐ ܢܫܟܚ. ܘܐܡܪܝܢ ܕܫܦܝܪܘܬܐ ܗ̇ܝ ܐܝܬܝܗ̇ ܗ̇ܝ *ܕܗ̇ܝ ܡܛܠܬܗ̇¹ ܓܒܝܐ ܘܡܫܒܚܐ. ܘܐܡܪܐ ܕܡܛܠ ܓܒܝܘܬܗ̇ ܚܙܝܐ ܗܘܬ ܫܦܝܪܐ. ܘܡܫܝܚܘܬܐ ܒܗ̇ܝ ܕܐܒܣܘܣ ܗ̣ܘ ܕܒܗ̇ ܫܦܝܪ ܡܬܚܙܝܐ² ܓܒܐ. ܐܘ ܗ̇ܘ ܡܢܐ ܕܡܫܬܟܚ ܓܒܐ. ܐܕܫܐ ܕܫܦܝܪܘܬܐ ܐܝܬܝܗ̇ ܕܠܘܬ ܒܠܚܘܕ ܪܘ̈ܚܢܝܬܐ ܗܢܝܐ ܐܘ ܢܛܪܐ. ܡܢ̈ܘܬܗ̇ ܕܝܢ ܐܝܬܝܗܝܢ ܕܡܫܝܚܘܬܐ. ܓܒܝܘܬܐ. ܦܘܫܩܘܬܐ. ܢܟܦܘܬܐ. ܪܚܡܘܬ ܢܦܫܐ. ܫܦܝܪܘܬܐ. ܚܣܝܘܬܐ. ܒܪܝܟܘܬܐ. ܘܡܕܡ ܕܗܠܝܢ ܐܟܘܬ ܐܡܪܐ³ ܕܠܘܬ ܐܚܪܢܐ ܗܘܐ ܒܪܢܫܐ. ܐܝܟ ܕܕܡܫܝܚܘܬܐ. ܓܒܝܘܬܐ. ܘܫܦܝܪܘܬܐ. ܘܒܠܚܘܕ ܠܐܢ̈ܫܐ ܘܓܒܝܐ ܘܫܦܝ̈ܪܐ ܡܫܡܗܝܢ. ܒܗ̇ܝ ܕܠܡܠܐܟ̈ܐ⁴ ܡܢ ܟܠ ܡܫܡܠܝ ܐܡܝܪܐ.

ܕܬܪ̈ܝܢ. ܕܕܡܘܬܐ ܗ̇ܝ ܡܫܝܚܘܬܐ ܒܟܝܢܐ ܕܠܡܠܐܟ¹ ܕܕܡܘ̈ܗܝ، ܒܡܫܡ̈ܫܢܐ ܡܦܠܓܐ. ܒܟܠܗܘܬܐ ܕܝܢ ܒܗ̇ ܢܘܟܪ̈ܝܬܐ ܕܠܐ ܕܠܗ ܢܫܟ ܒܢܝܐ. ܘܓܒܝܘܬܐ ܗ̇ܝ ܐܝܬܝܗ̇ *ܡܫܝܚܘܬ ܩܘܪܒܬܐ² ܕܒܢ̈ܝܐ ܓܒ̈ܝܐ ܒܡܐܪ̈ܫܐ³ ܘܦܠܓܘܬܐ ܕܝܠܗܘܢ ܘܡܫܡܫܢܝܬܗ. ܘܕܫܠܛܘܬܐ ܕܝܢ ܒܗܘܦܟܐ. ܘܦܪܘܫܘܬܐ ܗ̇ܝ ܐܝܬܝܗ̇ ܡܫܝܚܘܬܐ ܒܒܪܬ ܓܒܝܘܬܐ ܒܡܫܬܪܚܘܬ ܡܐܟ̈ܠܬܐ. ܦܠܓܘܬܐ ܕܝܢ ܒܗܘܦܟܐ. ܘܢܟܦܘܬܐ ܗ̇ܝ ܐܝܬܝܗ̇ ܡܫܝܚܘܬܐ ܕܒܗ̇ ܡܫܬܘܬܦ⁴ ܐܢܫ ܠܪ̈ܓܓܬܐ ܦܓܪ̈ܢܝܬܐ ܒܡܫܡܫܢܘܬܐ ܕܦܓܪ ܢܦܫܐ. ܙܪܝܙܘܬܐ ܕܝܢ ܒܗܘܦܟܐ. ܘܪܚܡܘܬ ܢܦܫܐ ܗ̇ܝ ܐܝܬܝܗ̇ ܡܫܝܚܘܬܐ ܕܒܗ̇

Titulus [1*] pl. RVLl

1 [1*] ܗ̇ܝ ܕܡܛܠܬܗ̇ RVLl [2] ܡܬܚܙܝܐ RVLl [3] ܐܡܪܐ RVL [4] sg. l; ܕܡܠܐܟ̈ܐ RL; ܕܡܠܐܟܐ V

2 [1] i. ܘ RVLl [2*] ܡܫܝܚܘܬܐ ܩܘܪܒܬܐ RVLl [3] sg. RL [4] ܡܫܬܘܬܦ RVLl

## CHAPTER THREE
## ON THE DEMONSTRATIVE SPECIES OF RHETORIC
## FOUR SECTIONS

### SECTION ONE
### On the Species of Virtue and Vice
### Two Theories

ONE.[1] Because for things which are virtuous and noble we may praise not only men and angels but also irrational and inanimate (beings), it is necessary to examine virtue and its species along with their opposites in sufficient (detail) for demonstration. Let us say (then) that the noble is that which is chosen for itself and praised, and that which because of its goodness is pleasant is likewise noble. Because virtue is a habit by which the good or that which seems good is nobly preserved, it is the species of the noble which with respect to anything may produce or preserve great things. Its parts are justice, courage, superiority, temperance, magnanimity, liberality, gentleness, prudence, and wisdom. Among these some surpass others, such as justice, courage, and liberality. Therefore we honour just, courageous, and liberal (men), because on those who do good, honour is bestowed by everyone.

TWO.[2] Justice is an equitable virtue which distributes to everyone his lawful dues; injustice (is that) by which a man takes alien things which are not his. Courage is the virtue of performing good actions in wars and (in) keeping with the law and obedience to it; cowardice is the opposite. Superiority is a virtue producing benefit by making foods abundant; worthlessness is the opposite. Temperance is a virtue by which someone participates in bodily desires in the measure which the law prescribes; wantonness is the opposite. Magnanimity is a virtue by which a man effects great and praiseworthy things; small-mindedness is the opposite. Liberality is a virtue producing

[1] **3.1.1** AR 1.9 66a23-24; 28- 66b9; IS 2.4 (84.3-84.11).
[2] **3.1.2** AR 1.9 66b9-22; IS 2.4 (84.12-85.6).

ܪܘܪ̈ܒܘܬܐ ܘܡܫܒ̈ܚܢܘܬܐ[5] ܥܒܕ ܒܪܢܫܐ. ܙܥܘܪܘܬ ܢܦܫܐ ܕܝܢ ܒܗܦܟܐ. ܘܫܦܝܥܘܬܐ ܕܝܢ ܐܝܬܝܗ̇ ܡܝܬܪܘܬܐ ܒܥܒܕܬ ܫܦܝܪ̈ܬܐ[6] ܒܡܣܟܢܘܬܐ. ܘܠܘܛܬܐ ܕܝܢ ܒܗܦܟܐ. ܘܚܣܝܢܘܬܐ ܕܝܢ ܐܝܬܝܗ̇ ܡܝܬܪܘܬܐ ܕܒܗ̇ ܠܡܬܩܢܢܘܬܐ ܠܐ ܒܡܘܬܪܐܝܬ ܦܓܠ ܒܪܢܫܐ. ܬܒܝܪܘܬܐ ܕܝܢ ܒܗܦܟܐ. ܘܒܪܝܟܘܬܐ ܕܝܢ ܐܝܬܝܗ̇ ܡܝܬܪܘܬܐ ܬܡܝܡܬܐ ܕܒܗ̇ ܥܦܝܪ[7] ܡܬܪܢܐ ܘܡܬܡܠܟ ܒܪܢܫܐ ܠܘܬ ܒܥܝܘܬ ܦܬ̈ܓܡܐ. ܒܨܝܪܘܬܐ ܕܝܢ ܒܗܦܟܐ. ܘܫܒܝܩܘܬܐ ܕܝܢ ܐܝܬܝܗ̇ ܢܒܥܐ ܕܪ̈ܙܐ ܘܡܝܬܪܘܬ ܦܬ̈ܓܡܐ. ܫܦܠܘܬܐ ܕܝܢ ܒܗܦܟܐ.

ܦܘܫܩܐ ܬܪܝܢܐ
ܡܛܠ ܬ̈ܠܠܬܐ ܘܫܘܕ̈ܥܐ ܕܡܝܬܪܘܬܐ
ܬܐܘܪ̈ܝܣ ܐܪܒܥ

ܩܕܡܝܬܐ. ܘܗܠܝܢ ܕܝܢ ܡܝܬܪ̈ܬܐ ܡܬܠܡܕ̈ܢܝܬܐ. ܕܥܒܪܐ ܕܝܢ ܒܥܕ̈ܕܬܐ ܐܝܟ ܕܡܝܬܪ̈ܘܬܐ ܘܫܘܕ̈ܥܐ[1] ܕܒܟܠܗܘܢ. ܐܝܟ ܐܩ̈ܠܝܬܐ ܕܥܠ ܓܒܪ̈ܐ. ܘܢܫ̈ܐ ܕܟܠܠܘܡܢܐ ܒܕܝܢ ܒܠ ܒܥ̈ܝܢܐ. ܘܒܗܘܢ ܡܬܬܠܡܕܝܢ ܒܗ ܣܐܥܝܢ. ܐܝܟ ܐܢܫܐ ܕܦܓܠ ܥܬ̈ܕܐ ܠܡܥܠܡܘ ܒܥܠܡܐ ܘܐܟܠܐ ܠܡܪܗ ܠܐ ܡܥܠܡ. ܘܡܢܐ ܕܠܢܫܐ ܒܐܢܐܝܬ ܢܣܒܘܢ ܡܫܩ̈ܠܝܢ. ܡܬܛܟܣܝܢ[2] ܒܗ ܣܐܥܝܢ. ܘܡܢ ܫܘܕ̈ܥܐ ܕܡܝܬܪ̈ܬܐ ܐܝܟ[3] ܐܢܫܐ ܕܐܬܪ ܡܬܥܒܕ ܐܒܗ̈ܬܐ ܕܐܬܬܠܡܕܐ. ܦܘܪܥܢ ܐܦܪܐ ܐܬܪ ܡܢ ܦܘܪܥܢ ܢܦܩܐ ܡܐܢܐ. ܘܫܡܘܪܬܐ ܕܠܘ ܡܛܠ ܦܘܪܥܢܐ ܫܘܕ̈ܥܐ ܗܘ. ܣܘܟܠܗ ܕܫܘܐ ܠܡܘܠܫܐ ܒܗ[4] ܒܗ̇[5] ܠܒܢ̈ܬܐ ܗ̇ܝ. ܡܛܠܬܗ̇ ܡܬܒܥܝܢܐ. ܘܟܠܗܘܢ ܕܗܘܢ ܒܒܢ̈ܝܐ ܒܕܘܟ̈ܬܐ ܡܬܠܘܫ. ܟܝܢܐ ܕܝܢ ܡܢܗ ܒܗܘܢ ܫܢܝܐ. ܒܗ ܥܬ̈ܐ ܒܠܒܗ ܫܘܒܚ ܦܘܪܥܢܐ. ܘܐܬܪ ܟܝܢܐ ܡܢ ܗܘܝܐ ܟܝܢܐ ܦܘܪܥܢ ܥܦܝܪ̈ܬܐ ܠܫܡܘܪܝܗܘܢ ܘܟܠܬܐ ܗܠܝܢ ܙܟܝܐ. ܩܕܡܝܬܐ ܕܝܢ ܠܒܢܘܬܐ ܙܒܢܐ. ܬܪܝܢܐ ܕܝܢ ܙܒܘܪܬܐ. ܘܬܠܝܬܝܐ ܠܐ ܠܒܢܘܬܐ.

ܕܬܪ̈ܬܝܢ. ܘܡܢ ܫܘܕ̈ܥܐ ܕܡܝܬܪܘܬܐ ܡܒܗܬܢܘܬ ܐܢܫܐ ܕܡܬܕܠܡܒ ܠܡܝܬܪܘܬܐ. ܒܗ ܦܘܫܩܐ ܡܬܒܥܝܢ ܠܡܐܡܪ ܘܠܡܦܫܩ ܥܦܝܪ̈ܬܐ. ܘܒܗ ܓܒܢ ܕܢܓܒܪܘܢ ܠܡܝܬܪܐ. ܡܓܠܒܝܢ ܡܒܗܢ. ܐܒܗܬܐ ܕܫܒܝܚܘܬܐ[1] ܗܐܦܐ ܒܓܘܪܢܐ ܐܠܦܐܗܘ ܒܝܫܬ ܒܗ ܡܛܠ ܗܘܒܢܐ ܥܒܝܪܐ ܪܓܙ ܠܗ ܘܐܓܙ. *ܕܒܢܝܐ ܐܢܫܐ ܠܡ ܕܐܡܪ[2]ܡܕܡ ܕܒܠܒܝ ܐܟܠܐ ܠܝ ܒܠܝܬܐ ܒܗܬܬܐ. ܗܕܐ ܕܝܢ ܢܣܐܝܬ ܘܡܢܝܕܐܝܬ ܒܗ ܠܡܝܬܪܘܬܐ ܡܗܝܡܢܐ ܒܐܓܒܪܐ ܘܠܐ ܚܕܐ ܡܠܐ ܕܢܓܘܫܬܐ ܙܕܩܬ. ܐܠܐ ܐܝܟ ܠܐ ܡܫܬܐܠܐ ܢܗܘ ܒܝܫܐ ܘܠܐ ܡܒܝܢܐ ܠܡܚܙܐ ܗܘ ܡܢܐ ܕܐܚܪܢܝܬܐ ܒܪܦܘܬܗ، ܢܝ̈ܫ ܗ،

5 i. om. RVLl 6 ܫܦܪ̈ܬܐ RVL 7 f. add. ܐ RVLl
1 1 sg. RVLl 2 ܡܬܛܟܣܝܢ RVLl 3 om. RVL 4 ܒܗ RVLl 5 f. ܗ F
2 1 ܕܫܒܝܚܘܬܐ R 2* rep. R

noble (things) by donations; avarice is the opposite. Gentleness is a virtue by which a man bears afflictions without distress; indignation is the opposite. Prudence is an intellectual virtue by which a man may consider well and take good counsel in relation to the abundance of goods; naivety is the opposite. Wisdom is knowledge of the truth and the doing of good (deeds); madness is the opposite.

## SECTION TWO
## On the Causes and Signs of Virtue
## Four Theories

ONE.[3] These are praiseworthy virtues, while the rest are doings of virtues and signs of them, like lamentations on behalf of courageous men, and sufferings which unjustly afflict just men for which, when they suffer, they may be praised. For example, he who endures tortures (designed) to make (him) hand over a deposit, but (who) nevertheless does not betray its owner, (is praiseworthy); but when offenders justly deserve the sufferings, they may be rebuked when they suffer. Among the signs of virtues there is that which is more praiseworthy, such as what (is given) to a champion. A reward of honour is more noble than a reward of money, and a deed which is not (done) for a reward is a true sign that (someone) is worthy of praise, as in it the good is sought for its own sake. Therefore the remembrance of the departed by alms(-giving) is praised, while the commemoration of the living is inferior to it, because (an offering for) the departed is without expectation of reward. Greater or lesser (resulting) from this inferior one is the reward of noble deeds to their perpetrators, and in these three ways: first, (for) a great kindness; second, (for) a small one; and third, (for what is) no kindness.

TWO.[4] Among the signs of virtue (is) the shaming of him who acts contrary to virtue, because many intend to speak and do disgraceful things, but although they may wish to dishonour virtuous (people), they are shamed by them. For instance, the wise Sappho scoffed at the tyrant Alcaeus when he beckoned to her for a disgraceful act and

---

[3] **3.2.1** AR 1.9 66b22-67a6; IS 2.4 (85.7-86.15).
[4] **3.2.2** AR 1.9 67a6-18; IS 2.4 (86.16-87.14).

ܠܗ̇ ܚܘܒܬ. ܐܦ ܬ̈ܢܢܐ ܚܒܪ̈ܬܐ ܕܒܟܝܗ̇ ܟܕ[3] ܥܠ ܢܦܩܘܬܗ̇ ܪܓܫܬ ܡܢ ܥܠ
ܘܠܠܐ ܬܒܟܝܢ ܗܘ̈ܝ ܠܐ ܐܫܬܪܪ̈ܝ. ܗܕܐ ܕܝܢ ܥܠܗ̇ ܕܗܘܬ ܥܠ ܐܒܫܥܢ[4]
ܕܒܪܘܢܐ ܘܐܓܘܢܐ ܒܢܦܫܐ ܐܬܥܒܕܬ ܫܪܒܬ. ܗܘܠܠܐ ܓܝܪ ܕܡܫܒܚܬ̈ܐ
ܠܓܠܬܐ ܕܒܚܝܢܐ ܚܝ̈ܢ ܘܒܗ ܢܒܥܐ ܡܛܠ ܫܘܒܚܐ ܘܐܝܩܪܐ ܠܝ̈ܢ.

ܕܬܠܬ. ܟܕ ܬܬܪ̈ܝܢ ܬܠܠܝ̈ܢ ܗܘ̇ܐ ܒܚܘܕܐ. ܚܕܐ ܡ̣ܢ ܡܢܬܐ ܢܦܫܐ ܡܛܠ
*ܫܘܒܗܪ̈ܐ ܝܚܝܕܝ̈ܐ.[1] ܐܚܪܬܐ ܕܝܢ ܟܕ ܡܬܕܒܪܐ ܠܡܬܒܥܐ ܒܚܕܝܬܐ
ܒܫܠܝܘܬܐ ܕܐܘܝܐ. ܐܝܟ ܗܘ̇ ܕܣܒܪ ܒܢ̈ܝܐ ܡܬܝܚܐ. ܘܠܫܒܪܗ̇[2] ܡܒܣܡܬܐ.

ܕܐܪܟܒ. ܡܬܬܠܩܝܢ ܕܝܢ[1] ܘܡܬܒܪ̈ܐ ܕܡܛܠ[2] ܒܫܘܡܠܝܐ ܕܐܚܪ̈ܢܐ ܡܫܬܟܠܠܝܢ.
ܘܟܠܗܕܐ ܒܐܝܢܘܬܐ ܘܙܗܝܪܘܬܐ ܓܒ̈ܝܢ. ܗܒܝܢܐ ܘܡܫܡܠܝܘܬܐ[3] ܕܡܢ ܒܟܠܕܒܪܐ
ܘܠܐ ܬܒܝܢܘܬܐ ܕܒܝܬܗܘܢ. *ܘܦܘܪܫܢ ܓܒܝܬܐ ܘܡܫܝܚܘܬܐ[4] ܒܐܝܢܘܬܐ ܗܘ.
ܘܒܐܝܢܘܬܐ ܫܦܝܪܐ. ܘܗ̇ܝ ܕܓܒܝܢܐ ܝܕܥܐ ܘܠܐ ܢܕܥܐ. ܟܕ ܐܒܝܘܬܐ
ܘܐܝܣܪܐ ܡܢ ܫܦܝܪ̈ܬܐ ܕܓܒܝܢܐ ܐܝܟ. ܘܗ̇ܝ ܕܒܟܪ̈ܐ ܢܟܒܕ ܐܝܟ
ܬܫܒ̈ܘܚܬܐ ܕܡܬܓܠܓܠܝܢ ܘܠܕܪܐ ܐܚܪ̈ܢܐ[5] ܡܬܟܬܫܝܢ. ܡܬܬܠܩܝܢ ܕܝܢ ܐܦ
ܫܘܕܪ̈ܐ ܕܐܚܪ̈ܢܝܬܐ. ܐܝܟ ܡܬܦܪܢܣܢܘܬ[6] ܠܡܕܒܪܢܘܬܐ ܘܡܫܝ̈ܢܬܐ *ܕܡܫܪܝܗܘܢ.
ܐܝܟܐ ܗ̣ܝ ܓܝܪ ܗܕܐ ܕܡܬܠܒܬ ܠܗܘܢܝܐ. ܘܟܠܗܕܐ ܡܢܝ̈ ܘܡܫܝ̈ܢܬܐ[7] ܒܟܪ̈ܐ
ܕܐܓܢܪܐ ܠܐ ܒܕܝܢ ܗܘܘ ܐܦܠܐ ܐܡܬܝܢܘܬܐ ܐܝܕܐ ܦܠܚܝܢ ܗܘܘ. ܟܕ
ܠܐ ܫܘܝܘܬܐ ܕܥܠ ܐܚܪ̈ܢܐ ܗܝ̣ ܗܝ ܚܐܪܘܬܐ.

---

[3] ܒܕ RVL [4] ܐܘܫܥܢ RVL

3 [1*] sg. RVLl [2] pl. RVLl

4 [1] add. ܕܝܢ RVLl [2] i. om. R [3] pl. RVLl [4*] pl. RVLl [5] ܐܚܪ̈ܢܐ RVLl [6] ܡܦܪܢܣܢܘܬ RVLl [7*] om. RVL

said, ‘I wish to say something which is in my heart, but shame hinders me.’ Serenely and modestly, upholding (her) virtue by (her) discipline, she uttered not a single word of condemnation, but behaved outwardly as if his evil intention were inoffensive and incapable of causing the suffering which other (women) suffer by their weakness. Also the women companions who were with her were not alarmed, because they trusted in her temperance being superior to any ignominy. But this whole happening pointed to the habit which by exercise and discipline had been fastened into (her) soul, for the majority of virtues resist natural desire and with the will fight for glory and honour.

THREE.[5] Shame arises through two causes. One is when the soul (itself) recoils on account of despicable actions. The other is when the reprehensible deed of a person is mentioned to those present, as if displayed before the eyes, and shames its perpetrator.

FOUR.[6] Actions may also be praised which are done for the delight of others, and justice and righteousness are therefore good. The same also (applies to) vengeance on enemies and not being reconciled with them. The rewarding of good and evil is justice, and justice is noble; as is the fact that a courageous man is victorious and not defeated, because victory and honour are among the noble (attributes) of courageous men; as is the fact that the deeds which someone may do are (sufficiently) remarkable to be spread abroad and written down for later generations. The signs of being free-born may also be praised, like the Lacedaemonians’ enlargement of the curls of their hair, for this was an index of high birth. Those who had curls therefore did not do the work of hired servants or cultivate any craft, because independence of others is what being free-born is.

[5] **3.2.3** IS 2.4 (87.14-88.6).
[6] **3.2.4** AR 1.9 67a18-32; IS 2.4 (88.6-88.12).

ܦܣܘܩܐ ܬܠܝܬܝܐ
ܥܠ ܦܘ̈ܠܚܢܐ ܫܡܝ̈ܢܝܐ
ܬܐܘܪ̈ܝܐ ܚܕܐ

ܡܕܒܪܢܘܬܐ. ܠܦܘ̈ܠܚܢܐ ܫܡܝ̈ܢܝܐ ܬܪ̈ܝܢ ܐܢܘܢ ܠܦܘ̈ܩܕܢܐ. ܚܕ ܡ̣ܢ ܒܕ ܠܒܪܐ ܠܐ ܡܬܚܙܝܐ ܒܐܣܟܡܐ ܡܬܚܙܝܐ ܢܣܒܘܗܝ,[1] ܪܫܛܘܪ ܘܟܕ ܢܬܠܒܟ ܠܚܘܠܫܐ ܠܣܘ̈ܟܕܐ. ܐܣܪܝܐ ܕܝܢ ܡܢܐ ܕܠܐ ܡܬܚܙܝܐ ܒܡܬܚܙܝ̈ܢܘܬܐ ܕܠܐ ܕܝܠܗܘܢ ܢܬܦܪܫ ܕܢܦܠܘ. ܘܟܝܢܐ ܕܝܢ ܡܕܒܪܢܐ ܐܠܗܝܐ ܕܒܣܘܟܠܐ[2] ܡܕܡ ܢܗܘܐ *ܡܫܬܘܬܦܐ. ܐܠܐ ܠܐ ܡܬܚܙܝܐ[4] ܠܒܪܐ ܡܬܚܙܝܐ ܕܒܠܦܣܘܗ[3] ܡܫܬܟܚܢ. ܒܬܪܝܢܐ ܕܝܢ ܐܠܗܝܐ ܕܒܝܬܝܘܬܐ ܡܕܡ ܬܗܘܐ ܡܬܝܕܥܐ ܒܗܘܢܗ̇ ܕܡܬܪܘܬܐ ܠܢܦܫܗ̇. ܐܝܟܢܐ ܕܐܝ̈ܬܝܗ̇ ܡܢ ܗ̇ܘ ܠܗܢܐ ܢܒܥ ܦܘܠܚܢܐ ܐܟܚܕܐ ܕܡܬܚܙܝܢܐ.

ܕܬܪ̈ܬܝܢ. ܟܝܢܐ ܕܝܢ ܡܕܒܪܢܐ ܠܣܘܦܣܝܛܐ[1] ܡܬܕܒܪܐ ܪܗܛܪܐ ܡܫܠܡܢܐ ܡܢ ܠܕܐܬܗܘܣܝܣ ܠܐ ܡܫܡܫܢܘܬܐ ܒܟܘܢܝܐ ܡܫܡܫܢܐ ܢܟܝܠ. ܐܟܚܕܐ ܕܠܡܕܒܪܢܐ ܡ̣ܢ ܒܐܝܕܐ ܫܦܝܪ ܡܠܟܐ ܢܟܝܠ. ܠܪܘܚܢܐ ܕܝܢ ܦܓܪܢܐ ܣܠܩ ܒܣܝܐ. ܘܠܡܢܐ ܪܘܚ ܒܗܝܢܘܬܐ. ܘܠܘܠܦܐ ܫܦܝܪ ܦܘܪܫܢܐ. ܘܠܬܪܘܝܬܐ ܕܒܝܓܠ ܡܬܒܒܪ ܦܫܝܛܐ. ܘܠܡܪܘܐ[2] ܚܒܪܐ. ܘܠܡܫܠܡܗ, ܪܓܬܐ ܘܦܓܥܗܐ ܢܦܩܐ. ܘܠܐܣܘܦܐ ܕܡܦܪܫ ܢܦܫܗ̇, ܒܪ̈ܓܝܓܬܐ ܩܢܝܬܐ[3] ܫܦܝܪܐ.

ܕܬܠܬ. ܘܡܢ ܪܫܝܐ ܠܐ[1] ܡܬܚܙܝܐ ܕܒܐܣܟܡܐ ܡܬܚܙܝܐ ܡܬܦܠܣܝܢ ܡܫܬܕܠܢܘܬ ܒܪܢܫܐ ܠܦܘܕܐ. ܒܪܡ ܠܒܘܪܐ. ܗܕܐ ܓܝܪ ܫܘܕܥܐ ܗ̄ܝ ܕܬܪܝܢܘܬ ܡܠܬܐ[2] ܡܢ ܗ̇ܘ ܡܢܐ ܕܐܣܪܝܐ ܡܣܬܪܗܒܐܝܬ[3] ܣܐܒ. ܡܛܘܠ ܕܝܢ ܘܐܝܢܐ ܕܠܐ ܫܘܝ ܡܫܬܕܠ ܡܛܠ ܗܘܢܐ ܬܡܝܗܐ ܘܗܝܡܢܘܬܐ ܕܠܐ ܦܕܐ. ܡܬܘܠܫ ܕܝܢ ܘܗ̇, ܕܠܪ̈ܚܡܐ ܘܩ̈ܢܝܐܐ[4] ܠܡܡܒܥ ܫܦܝܪ. ܡܬܚܙܝܢܘܬܗ̇ ܓܝܪ ܕܡܬܚܙܝܢܘܬܐ ܗ̇ܝ, ܗ̄, ܕܠܟܠ ܢܦܐܒ. ܐܦ ܒܐܝܢܘܬܐ ܠܪ̈ܚܡܐ ܠܡܦܐܒܘ ܘܠܩ̈ܢܝܐܐ ܠܡܒܐܫܘ ܡܕܘܡܐ. ܘܒܚܕܐ ܠܡܐܡܪ. ܠܟܠ ܐܕܫܐ ܡܫܡܫܢܐ ܕܠܟܠ ܦܪ̈ܨܘܦܐ ܕܠܒܐܝܬ ܠܢܦܫ ܦ̇ܠܐ ܠܡܒܕ ܪܘܦܠ ܐܝܟܢܐ ܕܒܗ̇ܘ ܡܢܐ ܕܐܢܐ ܠܗ ܢܠܒܫܘܗܝ, ܠܦܘܬ ܐܬܪ̈ܘܬܐ ܘܐܡܘ̈ܬܐ ܘܐܡܬ̈ܢܐ. ܒܕ ܡܚܕܐ ܕܝܡܘܬܐ ܡܕܡ ܟܠ ܐܬܠܬܐ[5] ܡ̣ܢ ܡܢܘܪܐ. ܟܠ ܦܘܪ̈ܣܢܐ[6] ܕܝܢ ܡܒܝܢܐ. ܘܒܝܬ ܡܡ̈ܬܠܐ ܫܦܝܪܐ. ܘܒܝܬ ܠܡܕ̈ܚܘܠܐ ܫܒܝܪܐ. ܘܡܢ ܦܝܠܣ̈ܘܦܐ ܪܫܝܡܐ. ܘܡܢ ܚܒ̈ܝܒܐ ܣܘܝܐܐ.

---

1 [1] ܢܣܒܢܘܗܝ RVLl [2] ܕܒܣܘܟܠܐ RVLl [3*] om. RVLl [4] scripsi; i. add. ܠ F
2 [1] ܠܣܘܦܣܝܣܛܐ RL; ܠܣܘܦܣܝܛܘܬܐ l [2] ܘܠܡܪܘܪܢܐ RVLl [3] om. RVL
3 [1] om. RVLl [2] ܡܠܬܐ RVLl [3] ܡܣܪܗ ܘܡܬܐܒܬ RVLl [4] i. om. RVLl [5] ܐܬܠܬܐ RVL
[6] scripsi; ܦܘܪ̈ܣܢܐ FVLl; ܦܘܪܣܢܐ R

## SECTION THREE
## On Tropical Praises
## Five Theories

ONE.[7] With tropical praises there are two types. One (is) when in some way an orator gives someone who is not virtuous a virtuous semblance and by it artfully contrives to praise deficient people. The other (is) when he contrives to praise those who are not virtuous with virtues which are not theirs (but belong to others). In the first way it is necessary that there should be some shared common ground, but nevertheless someone who is not virtuous is presented in some way in the form of someone who is. In the second it is necessary that there be some relationship between the donor of the virtue and its recipient, so that by its means praise may apparently pass from one to the other.

TWO.[8] In the first way, an orator who praises is like a sophist when he adorns an inglorious condition with a glorious appellation. For instance, he may call a crafty man 'prudent, excellent in counsel', a lascivious one 'merry, sweet of acquaintance', a greedy one 'fond of abundance', an avaricious one 'excellent in guardianship', an irascible one who quickly becomes angry 'open', a headstrong one 'courageous', a world-weary and faded one 'temperate', and a profligate one who squanders his riches on foul desires 'lavish'.

THREE.[9] Among the ways (in which) people who are not virtuous may be presented in a virtuous semblance is a man's being enticed into errors— small ones, that is—for this (can be made) a sign of lack of the fear with which others are afflicted (in the presence) of danger. However, one who is in no way enticed may also be praised for not erring on account of sound mind and caution. Acting well towards friends and enemies may also be praised, for the height of virtue is that we do good to all, even if justice declares it right to do good to friends and evil to enemies. In a word, for every laudatory species the orator must know what is particularly appropriate for

[7] **3.3.1** AR 1.9 67a32-36; IS 2.4 (88.13-89.1).
[8] **3.3.2** AR 1.9 67a37-b3; IS 2.4 (89.1-89.4)
[9] **3.3.3** AR 1.9 67b3-12; IS 2.4 (89.5-89.12).

ܕܐܪܒܥ. ܒܝܘܡܐ ܕܝܢ ܬܪܝܢܐ ܡܢ ܐܒܫܒܐ ܕܕ̈ܪܥ ܐܒܗ̈ܬܐ ܘܐܬܡܗ̈ܬܐ ܕܦܪܕܒܐ ܡܣܪܘ ܢܦܩ ܐܪܬܪܘ ܘܩܠܝܡܐ ܠܡܫܪܐ ܘܩܠܝܡܐ ܕܢܫܐܒ ܡܢ ܕܡܕܒܪܐ ܕܐܒܗ̈ܘܗܝ. ܒܕ ܬܠܒ ܪܒ ܢܦܫܐ ܕܢܘܡܘ ܥܠ ܥܦܪ̈ܬܐ ܕܐܝܟܝܢܗ ܢܦܩ ܘܡܢ ܐܒܗ̈ܐ ܠܡܐܪܬ ܘܩܠܝܡܐ ܠܗ ܡܢܥ. ܐܠܐ ܕܒܡܫܝ̈ܚܘܬܐ ܬܠܒ ܡܢ ܗܘܢ ܢܝܠܚ ܘܢܬܪܘ ܡܢܗܘܢ ܢܬܠܝܬܐ ܐܒܘ. ܐܝܟ ܕܐܡܪ ܐܦܝܣܩܘܦܘܣ.[1] ܘܐܠܡܦܝܐܢܘܣ ܘܪܬܘܪܐ[2] ܒܡ̈ܢܝܢ ܫܢܝܢܘܣ. ܕܗܢܐ ܠܗ ܬܒܥܐ ܡܢ ܐܡܢܘܬܐ ܡܢܝܢ̈ܬܐ ܕܐܦܬܪܘܢ[3] ܡܢ ܒܝܬ ܒܬ̈ܘܠܬܐ ܥܠ ܐܒܐ ܐܒܐ ܘܐܡ̈ܬܐ ܐܬܬܘܣܦ. ܒܐܝܕܐ ܐܒܢܐ ܕܕܝܪܐ ܪܡ ܡܢ ܒܬ̈ܘܠܬܐ ܗܢܐ ܒܢܝܐ ܕܡܢܬܗ ܡܢ ܪ̈ܒܝ ܬܠܗܝܡܗ.

ܕܚܡܫ. ܡܒܘܪܬܐ ܝܒܝܫܬܐ ܠܩܘܠܣܐ ܥܩܝܢ. ܘܠܐ ܗܘܝܢ ܦܬ̈ܓܡܐ ܕܒ̈ܕܩܝ. ܐܠܐ ܒܒܪ ܢܬܒܥܘܢ ܒܗܝܢܢ. ܘܗܘܝܢ ܡܬܩ̈ܠܝܢ ܒܐܝܕܐ ܕܒܢ̈ܬܐ ܡܬܒܥܦܐ. ܐܝܟ ܗ̇ܝ ܕܝܒܝܫ ܡܒܘܪܐ ܘܠܐ ܡܢ ܒܕܐ ܗܘܐ ܡܫܬܒܪܐ. ܡܬܩܘܝܢܬܐ ܒܕܝܢ ܫܬ̈ܝܬܐ ܗܠܝܢ ܕܝܒܝܫܐ[1] ܐܝܟ. ܡܫܬܒܪܢܝܬܐ ܕܝܢ ܘܐܫܬܝܬܐ ܗܘܝܢ ܕܡܫܦܪܘܬ ܬܘܗܡܐ. ܠܐ ܓܝܪ ܐܪܥܐ ܡܬܠ ܕܐܪܥܐ ܢܠܐ. ܡܬܩܠܐ. ܐܦܠܐ ܝܘܡܐ ܒܪ[2] ܝܘܡܐ *ܢܠܐ ܡܬܓܒܠܐ.[3] ܗܒܢܐ ܘܡܫܬܪ̈ܝܬܐ ܕܡܢ ܒܪ̈ܕܘܬܐ ܘܬܘܪܓܐ ܡܫܬܩܝܢ. ܘܠܐ ܗܘܝܢ ܕܒܢܝܐ. ܘܒܠܗܕܐ ܠܦܚܪ[4] ܥܦܪ̈ܬܐ ܕܒܗܝܢ ܐܬܪܒ ܡܩܠܣܝܢ. ܒܕ ܢܒܥܝܢ ܕܡܫܬܪܝܬܐ ܐܒܣܩܣܝܬܐ ܕܒܗ ܐܬܡܒܒܬ ܐܝܠܝܢܐ ܒܠܬ ܡܒܘܪܬܗ. ܡܒܘܪܬܐ ܐܪܥܐ ܡܬܠܠ ܡܫܬܪܝܬܐ ܡܬܩܠܣܐ. ܘܡܫܬܪܝܬܐ ܗ̇ܝ ܡܬܠܠܬܗ̇. ܒܕܓܒܝ ܠܐܝܢܐ ܕܡܫܬܪܝܬܗ ܗܘܝܢ ܡܩܠܣܝܢ. ܘܐܦ ܠܗ ܢܝܫܐ ܕܗܦܟ ܥܦܪ̈ܬܐ. ܢܬܪ ܕܝܢ ܥܦܪܐ ܠܩܘܠܣܐ ܗ̇ܘ ܒܒܕܐ. ܒܕ ܒܗ ܗܘܐ ܠܒܡܘܬܐ. ܠܒܡܘܬܐ ܕܝܢ ܠܒܡܬܐ ܡܢ ܒܕܐ. ܘܐܒܡܐ ܕܒܗܝܡܘܬܐ ܓܒܫܐ[5] ܗ̇ܝ ܕܡܫܬܪܝܬܐ. ܓܕܐ ܓܒܫܐ ܗܘ ܕܠܒܡܘܬܐ.

4 [1] ܐܦܣܩܘܦܘܣ RVLl [2] pl. RLl [3] ܕܐܦܬܪܘܢ F

5 [1] ܕܝܒܝܫܐ RVLl [2] ܒܪ RVLl [3]* ܠܕܡܬܓܒܠܐ RVL [4] i. om. RVLl [5] ܠܒܡܘܬܐ RVL; om. l

each person, so that he may praise him with that which is suitable for him according to places, peoples, and professions, because it is possible that something might be honourable to the Athenians but despicable to the Persians, noble among the Scythians but disgraceful among the Lacedaemonians, beloved by the philosophers but hated by the masses.

FOUR.[10] In the second kind, an orator borrows praise from the worth of the ancestors and the remarkable deeds which they did in the past (to give it) to him who is in need of praise (and) who is inferior to the mould of his forebears, although a magnanimous (man) is anxious to add to the noble deeds of his people and does not agree to inherit praise from (his) ancestors, but endeavours by praiseworthy deeds to be more successful than they and to surpass them, as Iphicrates said. And the Olympian victory orator in the praises of Simonides (said), 'This man from the virtuous nation of the Saturannoi was from the shoulders up more than father and brothers'; for indeed as the head rises above the shoulders, so did his virtues (rise) above the elders of his family.

FIVE.[11] Voluntary actions are worthy of praise, not those coincidences which happen by chance, unless maybe their occurrence is repeated. Then they may be praised on account of their being repeated many times, as that would be opined to occur by the will of the doer and not by fortune. Therefore those of the will are true praiseworthy (acts), but those which (come) through noble birth are based on opinion and tropical. Thus a lion is not praised because it begets a lion, nor a snake blamed when it begets a snake. In the same way also virtues which (come) from discipline and correction are praised, not those of nature. Therefore we may praise him who does the noble things in which he was brought up, because we know that the habitual virtue which has been fixed into him is the cause of his action. Now action is praiseworthy for the sake of virtue, virtue for its own sake. Therefore we may praise him whose virtue we have believed, even if we do not see that he has done noble things, but the

---

[10] **3.3.4** AR 1.9 67b12-20; IS 2.4 (89.12-90.5).
[11] **3.3.5** AR 1.9 67b21-36; IS 2.4 (90.6-91.6).

## ܦܣܘܩܐ ܪܒܝܥܝܐ
## ܡܛܠ ܫܘܬܦܘܬ ܩܘܠܣܐ ܠܡܠܟܐ
## ܬܐܘܪ̈ܝܐܣ ܬܠܬ

ܩܕܡܝܬܐ. ܐܝܬ ܠܗ̇ ܕܝܢ ܐܕܫܐ ܡܕܡ ܚܕܬܐ ܠܡܠܬܐ ܕܩܘܠܣܐ ܘܕܡܠܟܐ. ܐܡܪ ܕܝܢ. *ܒܐܡܬ ܡܡܠܠܐ[1] ܒܟܝܢܐ ܕܬܪ̈ܝܗܘܢ. ܐܝܟ ܗܘ ܡܢ ܕܠܝܢܐ ܕܠܒܫ ܡܢܗܘܢ ܗ̇ܘ ܕܡܫܒܚܘ[2] ܦܪ̈ܨܘܦܘܗܝ.[3] ܟܕ ܐܝܬ ܗܘ ܫܪ̈ܒܐ ܐܠܝܢ ܕܡܠܐܐ *ܕܩܘܠܣܐ ܐܢܘܢ ܘܒܣܘܠܦ ܠܒܣܡ ܡܠܐܐ[4] ܕܡܠܟܐ[5] ܗܘܝ. ܘܒܗܦܟܐ. ܐܝܟ ܕܐܡܪ ܡܠܘܟܐ. ܠܐ ܙܕܩ ܠܟ ܐܘ ܡܫܬܪܝܐ ܕܡܕܡ ܪܒܐ ܬܬܪܒܐ ܥܠ ܦܘܩܕܢܘܬܐ ܗ̇ܝ ܕܒܓܕܐ ܡܢܟ. ܐܠܐ ܡܠܘܢ ܥܠ ܐܢܫܐ ܕܓܒܝܢܐ ܒܢܬ ܐܢܫ̈ܝܢ ܦܠܐ ܐܝܬ. ܗܟܢܐ[6] ܓܝܪ ܡܡܠܠܐ ܟܕ ܡܠܟܐ ܗܘ ܣܓܘܪܐ ܘܡܠܟܢܐ. ܒܗ ܒܙܢܐ ܡܛܠ ܡܬܩܠܣܢܐ ܐܡܪ[7]. ܗܘ ܕܝܢ ܡܢܝܗ̇[8] ܛܒܐ ܕܫܦܝܪܬܐ. ܠܘ ܡܢ ܓܒܪܐ ܒܓܕܫܐ. ܐܠܐ ܒܣܦܝܩܘܬܗ ܓܒܝܢܬܐ ܘܐܪܘܬܗ ܢܦܘܫܬܐ. ܒܕܓܘܢ ܟܕ ܢܓܕܒܬ ܕܬܘܠܣ ܐܘ ܪܓܝܓ. ܟܕ ܫܪ̈ܒܐ ܬ̈ܠܒܝܫܐ ܡܬܕܠܩܝܢ ܠܫܪ̈ܕܐ ܘܥܠ ܗܕܐ[9] ܬܗ ܡܠܟܘܬ ܐܝܬ. ܡܢ ܗܢܐ ܕܝܢ ܢܓܪ ܐܝܬ. ܒܗܘ ܡܟܐ ܕܡܓܕܓܠ ܐܝܬ ܦܠܐ ܘܒܗܘ ܡܟܐ ܕܢܓܪ ܐܝܬ ܓܒܢܐ. ܘܗܟܢܐ ܡܢ ܓܘܪܓܐ ܘܣܓܝܪܐ. ܠܗܬ ܩܘܠܣܐ ܘܓܒܝܢܐ[10] ܫܢܐ.

ܕܬܪ̈ܬܝܢ. ܙܕܩ ܕܝܢ ܠܗܓܡܘܢܐ ܕܒܟܠܗ ܩ̈ܠܐ ܡܙܘܪ̈ܙܝܬܐ ܠܩܘܠܣܐ ܘܡܠܟܐ ܢܙܪ. ܟܕ ܐܡܪ ܗܘܘ ܣܕܝܢܐ ܕܝܒܘܗ. ܘܠܣܘܕܝܐ ܒܕܝܪܗ. ܘܗ̇ܘ ܠܣܘܕ ܫܦܝܪ. *ܘܗ̇ܘ ܩܕܡܝܐ ܫܦܝܪ. ܘܗܠܟ ܡܠܝܠܐܝܬ ܫܦܝܪ.[1] ܘܬܪܝܨܐܝܬ ܫܦܝܪ. ܘܒܥܒܕܐ ܘܒܥܒܕܐ ܕܐܣܝܪܐ ܠܐ ܡܣܝܡ ܗܘܘ ܠܡܫܟܚܘ ܗ̣ܘ[2] ܫܦܝܪ. ܘܗ̣ܘ ܕܕܫ ܐܘܪܚ[3] ܥܒܝ̈ܕܬܐ ܠܦ̈ܓܥܐ ܕܒܗ ܢܬܒܥܘܢ. ܘܡܬܕܒܪܢܐ ܬ̇ܡܢ ܒܪܡ ܠܘ ܒܡܬܝܬܐ ܥܘܩ̈ܝܐ[4] ܐܝܟ ܐܣܦܘܠܛܘܣ[5] ܘܟܪܘܡܕܘܣ. ܐܠܐ ܒܡ̈ܬܠܝܐ ܘܪ̈ܗܛܐ ܐܝܟ ܐܪܣܛܘܛܠܝܣ. ܘܠܘ ܒܠܒܕ *ܦܣܩ ܕܢܦܫܗ[6] ܢܦܫܗ ܒܐܣܝܪܐ. ܟܕ ܣܓܝ̈ܐܐ ܠܒܘܪ̈ܟܬܐ ܡܬܪ̈ܬܚܘܬܗܘܢ[7] ܡܘܕܝܢ ܘܠܬܘܕ̈ܝܬܐ ܫܒܝ̈ܚܘܬܗܘܢ[8] ܡܒܪܟܝܢ ܘܠܐܣܝܪ̈ܐ ܒܗܦܟܐ ܡܒܪܟܝܢ. ܘܐܝܟ[9] ܕܐܡܝܢܐ ܠܓܠܐ ܕܒܟܝܢ ܐܣܘܗܘܢ ܣܝܡ ܘܠܦܘܪܫܬܐ ܕܟܝ̈ܢܬܗܘܢ[10] ܠܐ ܣܝܡ. ܘܠܘ ܒܠܒܕ[11] ܐܝܟ ܐܣܩܘܪܛܦܣ[12] ܗ̇ܘ ܕܠܒܢ̈ܘܗܝ, ܒܒܝ̈ܬܐ ܕܐܢܫܐ ܡܣܟ̈ܢܐ ܡܦܣܩ ܗܘܐ. ܘܗܟܐ ܕܠܐܣܝܪ[13] ܡܢ ܫܪ̈ܒܐ ܡܫܡܫ ܗܘܐ. ܕܗ̇ܢ ܗܘܐ ܢܦܫ ܘܡܣܝܒ.

---

1 1* ܠܐ ܡܡܠܠܬܐ RVLl 2 ܕܡܫܒܚܝܢ RVLl 3 i. add. ܘ RVLl 4* trp. ante ܦܪ̈ܨܘܦܘܗܝ F 5 pl. F 6 ܗܢܐ RVLl 7 ܡܩܠܣܢܐ ܗܘ RL; ܡܬܩܠܣܢܐ ܗܘ V; ܡܩܠܣܢܐ ܐܡܪ l 8 ܡܢܝܗ̇ F 9 ܗܢܐ RVLl 10 i. om. RVL

2 1* om. F 2 om. Fl 3 ܐܘܪܚܬܐ RVLl 4 ܥܘܩ̈ܐ RVL; ܥܘܒܩ̈ܐ l 5 ܐܣܦܘܠܛܘܣ RVLl 6* ܦܣܩ̈ RVLl 7 ܡܬܪ̈ܬܚܘܬܗܘܢ RVLl 8 ܫܒܝ̈ܚܘܬܗܘܢ RVLl 9 i. om. RVL 10 sg. RLl 11 i. add. ܠ RVLl 12 ܐܣܩܘܪܛܦܣ F; ܐܣܩܘܦܛܣ V 13 ܕܐܣܝܪ F

deed itself is more worthy of praise, because blessing comes by it. Remarkable blessedness, however, (comes) from fortune, and as abundance is a kind of virtue, fortune is a kind of blessedness.

## SECTION FOUR
### On the Partnership of Praise with Advice
### Three Theories

ONE.[12] There is a certain new species to speech of praise and of advice, says our master, inasmuch as the discourse is common to both. That which we have already laid out is different from what is particular to each of them, because it is (to do with) matters which are material of praise and by a change of expression become material of advice, and vice-versa. For example, an adviser may say, 'It is not right or virtuous for you to think highly of blessedness which you acquire by chance, but rather of that which you acquire voluntarily by yourself,' for the discourse is thus when it is restraining or hortatory advice. For (making someone) praiseworthy he will say it this way: 'He is a good possessor of merit, not from fortune by chance, but by his voluntary diligence and his attentive freedom.' Therefore, O orator, when you wish to praise, since deliberative matters are opposed to one another and you encourage one but restrain the other, praise with that which you exhort and blame with that which you restrain. Similarly for exhortation or restraint, change (what you do) with praise and blame.

TWO.[13] The orator should strengthen praise and advice by amplifying expressions, saying (for example) he is the only one of his time, or unique in his generation, or he acted alone, or he acted first, or he acted very quickly, or he especially acted, or he acted at a time and occasion when others were unable to act, or he trod the path of noble deeds for many who emulate him. He may be compared, not with virtuous traders like Hippolochos and Barmodes, but with exalted and proud (people) like Aristogiton. Not everyone is able to compare himself with others, because many amplify small things (pointing to) their virtue, diminish great things (pointing to) their

---

[12] **3.4.1** AR 1.9 67b36-68a10; IS 2.4 (91.7-91.17).
[13] **3.4.2** AR 1.9 68a10-22; IS 2.4 (92.1-92.14).

ܕܬܠܬ. ܒܕܐܝܟ ܗܠܝܢ ܚܢܢ ܕܐܬܐܡܪ̈ܝ[1] ܗܘܐ ܪܘܪܒ ܘܩܘܠܣܐ ܕܟܠ
ܬܘܫܒܘܚܬܐ ܕܡܫܠܡܘܬܐ ܡܥܘܕܕ. ܒܠܐܝܬ ܕܝܢ ܪܘܪܒܐ[2] ܗ̇ܝ ܠܩܘܠܣܐ
ܒܥܬ، ܬܫܡܫܬܐ ܕܝܢ ܠܡܠܟܐ. ܒܗ̇ ܩܘܠܣܐ ܗ̇ܝ ܒܡܠܟܘܬܐ ܕܡܬܬܘܕ̈ܝܢ
ܗܘܐ. ܡܠܟܐ ܕܝܢ ܒܡܬܕ̈ܢܚܬܐ ܕܡܬܩܪܝܢ. ܘܥܠܡܐ ܕܠܘ ܡܬܬܘܕܝܢܐ ܐܠܐ
ܡܫܬܒܪܢܐ ܡܛܠ ܒܫܘܪܝܗ ܫܝܢܐ ܥܠ ܥܘܕܪ̈ܐ[3] ܬܫܡܫܬܢܐ ܠܗܠܝܢ
ܕܒܬܪ̈ܝ ܠܡܫܡܫܘ ܡܢ ܗܠܝܢ ܕܩܕܡ ܗܘ̈. ܘܐܝܟ ܐܝܟܐ ܕܒܫܡܫܘܬ
ܡܡܘܫ̈ܠܝܢܐ ܡܢ ܣܦܪ̈ܐ ܘܟܗ̈ܢܐ ܗ̇ܝ ܩܘܠ̈ܣܐ[4] ܡܬܚܫܠܝܢ. ܡܢ ܬ̈ܠܬܐ
ܒܬܪ̈ܐ ܕܝܢ ܬ̈ܠܬܐ ܬܪ̈ܝܢܐ ܡܬܦܠܓܝܢ.

3 [1] f. ܘ RVL [2] ܗܘ ܪܒܐ RVLl [3] ܥܘܕ̈ܪ RVLl [4] sg. RVLl

deficiency, and do the reverse with those of others. As is said, they see the chip in their brother's eye but do not see the plank in their (own) eyes. And not everyone (is) like Isocrates, who would compare his behaviour with the behaviour of honoured people, and when he was like one of the foolish, he would judge himself and be found guilty.

THREE.[14] By such things as have been mentioned, there is amplification of praise pointing to superiority. In general, however, amplification is suitable for praise and paradigm for advice, because praise is for present things which are agreed, but advice for future things which are presaged, and evidently, being not agreed but opined, on account of its obscurity needs paradigmatic confirmation of things to come in the future from those which have happened in the past. Sometimes praises are invented from insults and invectives by the adoption of opposites, and correct counsels formed from perverse counsels.

[14] **3.4.3** AR 1.9 68a22-24;26-37; IS 2.4 (92.15-93.1).

ܩܦܠܐܘܢ ܪܒܝܥܝܐ
ܡܛܠ ܐܕܫܐ ܕܦܘܐܣܝܐ ܕܪܗܛܪܘܬܐ
*ܘܗܘ ܐܝܬ[1] ܦܣܘ̈ܩܐ ܐܚܪܬܐ[2]

ܦܣܘܩܐ ܩܕܡܝܐ
ܡܛܠ ܬܚܘܡ ܒܡܠܐ ܟܠܬ ܡܡܠܠܐ ܘܡܦܩ ܒܝܘܢܝܐ
ܬܐܘܪ̈ܝܣ ܬܪ̈ܬܝܢ[3]

ܡܫܘܚܬܐ. ܕܐܝܟ ܕܝ ܗܘܝ ܣܘܠܘܓܣܡܘ[1] ܕܡܘ̈ܣܝܩܝܐ ܘܡܢ ܐܝܠܝܢ ܫܪ̈ܒܐ ܡܬܢܣܒܝܢ[2] ܦܪ̈ܘܛܐܣܝܣ ܕܢܝܗܘܢ ܡܢܝܢܐ ܠܡܐܡܪ ܗܟܢܐ. ܘܠܚܘܕ ܠܒܡܠܐ ܦܠܐ ܕܬܚܘܡ. ܒܪ ܟܠܗ، ܗܘܐ ܡܡܠܠܐ ܘܫܩܠܗ، ܡܦܩ ܒܝܘܢܝܐ. ܘܐܡܪܝܢ ܕܒܡܠܐ[3] ܐܝܬܘܗ، ܡܫܝܢܘܬܐ[4] ܠܐ ܢܣܡܣܡܬܐ ܕܡܢ ܡܫܝܢܐ ܗܘܝܐ. ܘܗܘ ܢܣܡܣܡܐ ܐܘ ܕܠܝܢܐ ܗܘ ܒܬܝܒܘܬܐ ܠܦܘܬ ܣܘ̈ܡܟܐ ܘܐܬܬܪ̈ܘܬܐ ܘܕܝ̈ܢܐ. ܐܘ ܠܡܘܢܐ ܠܗ ܒܬܝܒܘܬܐ ܕܡܢ ܦ̈ܠܓܐܐ ܡܬܬܘܕܝܐ. ܒܡܠܐ ܡܕܝܢ ܗ̇ܘ ܗܘ ܕܡܢܝܢܐ ܡܠܬܐ. ܒܪ ܐܝܟܐ ܕܡܢܝܢܐ ܡܫܘܚܐ ܐܘ ܡܣܟܦ ܠܗ ܡܬܘܠܣ ܐܦܠܐ ܡܬܢܝܐ.

ܕܬܪ̈ܬܝܢ. ܐܝܟܐ ܕܡܢܝܢܐ ܡܣܟܦ ܐܘ ܒܡ ܒܗܘܝܐ ܦܬܪ. ܘܗܘܘ ܒܬܪܐ ܒܠܐ. ܐܘ ܒܡܢܝܢܘܬ ܬܪ̈ܬܝܢܐ. ܘܗܘܘ ܒܬܪܐ ܠܬܪܬܐ ܕܡܬܦܠܓ ܡܢ ܫܘܪܝܐ ܕܚܘܝܐ ܐܡܪ ܦܠܓܐ *ܐܘ ܫܡܥܬܐ[1] ܐܘ ܕܢܝܠܐ ܡܕܝܕܐ ܘܠܫܘܪܬܐ ܡܬܬܘܬܐ. ܐܡܡܐ ܦܪ̈ܫܐ ܠܐܝܢܐ ܕܠܐ ܢܚܝ ܦܠܓܬܐ ܒܪ ܚܕܐ. ܘܠܬܪ̈ܝܢܐ ܒܪ ܡܡܠܠ ܚܝܘܢܐ ܦܪ̈ܘܢܐ. ܘܠܫܝܢܐ ܒܐܬܪܐ ܕܝܢܐ. ܘܠܬܫܝܒܘܬܐ ܠܗܘ ܡܐܪ̈ܐ[2] ܒܪ[3] ܠܟ̈ܠ ܦܘܬ ܐܝܬܘܬܐ ܘܬܠܕܐ ܒܐܬܪܐ، ܫܩܠܐ[4] ܡܫܠܡ. ܘܠܬܪܝܢ ܐܡܘܪܐ ܠܗܘܢ ܫܘܚܠܦܐ. ܘܠܬܚܘܬܐ[5] ܠܗܘܢ ܒܡܪܘܬ ܫܡܥܬܐ. ܘܠܬܪܝܢ ܕܗܘܐ ܠܗܘܢ ܕܕܘܩܐ ܕܒܬܪ ܦܘܫܩܐ. ܘܠܫܬܝܬܐ ܒܪ ܡܬܦܠܓܐ. ܘܠܦܠܓܐ ܕܡܫܬܘܠ ܒܪ ܠܗ ܦܘܪ ܒܢ̈ܝܐ ܗ، ܕܒܐܝܢܐ ܠܗ، ܕܒܡܠܐ. ܘܠܦܘܡܒܕܢܐ ܢܚܝܐ ܦܝܪ. ܢܬܦܠܓ ܒܪܝܐ ܕܒܪܐ ܘܡܬܦܠܓܬܐ ܫܩܠܬܐ ܕܡܬܠܬܗ، ܡܫܘܦ ܘܠܬܝ ܒܡܢܝܢܐ ܡܢ ܐܦܩܘܗ، ܦܬܦ. ܗܠܝܢ[6] ܫܪ̈ܒܐ ܠܡܡܠܠܘ ܡܬܦܪܫ ܒܣܝܡܐ ܠܚܣܢܐ. ܒܐܡܬ ܚܝܘܬܐ ܠܬܪܝܢܐ ܘܦܪܐ ܠܬܪܬܐ ܘܪܒܐ. ܘܡܢܝܢܘܬܗܘܢ[7] ܐܝܟ ܡܬܝܪܝ ܪܦܬܪ.

Titulus [1*] om. F [2] ܣܡܘܟܐ F [3] ܬܪܝܢ F
1 [1] ܣܘܠܘܓܣܡܘܣ RVL [2] ܡܬܢܣܒܢ̈ RVLl [3] add. ܡܢ RVLl [4] ܡܫܝܢܘܬܐ RVLl
2 [1*] ܘܫܡܥܬܐ RVLl [2] sg. F [3] ܒܪ F [4] sg. F [5] ܘܠܬܚܘܬܐ RV; ܘܠܬܚܘ̈ܬܐ Ll [6] add. ܕܝܢ RVLl [7] pl. RVL

## CHAPTER FOUR
## ON THE JUDICIAL SPECIES OF RHETORIC
## SIX SECTIONS

### SECTION ONE
### On the Definition of Injustice, the Cause of Accusation and Defence
### Two Theories

ONE.[1] It is now time to say how adversarial syllogisms come about and from what things their premisses are derived, but first it is necessary to define injustice, because accusation arises against it and defence on account of it. Let us say that injustice is unlawful harm which comes about voluntarily. The law is either the specific written (law) corresponding to the legislators, places and times, or the common unwritten (law) which is recognised by many. Injustice is that which harms voluntarily, because he who produces benefit or damage naturally is neither praised nor blamed.

TWO.[2] He who does damage willingly acts either with understanding, and (then) he is an unjust evil (man), or through deficient intelligence, and (then) he is an agitated evil (man) who is easily overcome by passions of the soul like lust, anger, or fear, and may afterwards feel remorse. It may happen, for example, to the despicable, when he is rich; to the lascivious, when he discovers bodily pleasure; to the slothful, when at ease; to the cowardly, in battles, when he surrenders the members of his battle line, wife, and children into the hands of the captors; to the ambitious, with glory; to the irascible, with angry desire; to him who loves victory, with pursuing the genus (of victory); to the proud, when he is brought down; to the foolish, who is beguiled because he does not distinguish between the just and the unjust; and to the impudent (who, when) occupied with a small profit, persists in a contemptible trade for the sake of it and wipes the

[1] **4.1.1** AR 1.10 68b1-10; IS 2.5 (93.14-94.14).
[2] **4.1.2** AR 1.10 68b10-26; IS 2.5 (94.14-96.1).

ܦܘܫܩܐ ܬܪܝܢܐ
ܥܠ ܦܘܠܓ ܫܘܪܝܬܐ ܕܠܗܘܢ ܢܦܩ ܟܠܗ
ܬܐܘܪܝܐ ܐܪܒܥ

ܡܕܡܟܝܬܐ. ܥܕܟܐ ܗܟܢ ܕܟܝܢܗܘܢ ܗ̇ܘܐ *ܡܬܡܠܝܐ ܟܠܗ̇. ܗܠܝܢ ܕܝܠܦܢܗܘܢ ܗ̇ܘܐ[1] ܡܣܡ ܒܪܘܚܐ ܡܬܬܚܡܝܢ. ܕܡܢܐ ܘܡܟܡܐ[2] ܘܐܝܠܝܢ ܐܝܟܢ. ܟܕ ܠܐ ܡܨܐ ܠܡܗܘܐ ܡܣܡ ܒܪܘܚܐ ܐܠܐ ܠܡܣܒ ܡܘܦܠܓܐ ܦܪܘܫܐ ܐܘ ܙܕܩܝܐ ܐܘ ܡܫܬܟܚܢܐ. ܟܕܝܢ ܐܡܪܝܢ ܕܟܠ ܫܘܪܝܬܐ[3] ܕܦܬܟܪ ܒܙܢܝܐ ܐܘ ܡܫܟܚܢܘܬܐ ܗ̇، ܐܘ ܠܐ ܡܫܟܚܢܘܬܐ. ܐܘܟܝ، ܗܕܐ ܐܘ ܠܕܝܢܘܬܐ[4] ܗ̇، ܐܘ ܐܢܫܘܬܐ. ܐܘܟܝ، ܗܕܐ ܐܘ ܒܝܫܘܬܐ ܗ̇، ܐܘ ܡܛܝܒܘܬܐ. ܘܫܘܪܝܘܬܐ ܡܫܟܚܢܘܬܐ ܐܘ ܠܒܪܐ ܢܦܩܐ ܐܘ ܠܓܘܐܝܐ ܫܘܬܦܢܐ. ܡܛܠ ܗܢܝܘܬܐ ܡܢ ܒܪܝܬܐ. ܡܛܠ ܕܒܗܘܬܐ ܕܝܢ ܒܫܡܝܬܐ. ܐܘ ܠܓܘܐܝܐ ܫܘܬܦܢܐ ܐܘ ܠܓܘܐܝܐ ܡܠܠܝܐ. ܘܗܠܝܢ ܡܢ ܥܒܕܐ ܦܘܠܓܐ. ܟܝܢܝܐ. ܓܢܣܐ. ܡܦܪܫܐ. ܓܫܡܢܝܐ. ܢܦܫܢܝܐ. ܪܓܫܢܝܐ. ܗܘܢܐ ܐܢܫܐ ܐܢܫ. ܟܕ ܠܐܘܪܫܐ. ܢܦܫܢܝܐ. ܘܐܘܪܫܐ. ܣܝ ܦܘܠܐ. ܘܐܡܪܝܢ ܐܡܪܝܢ ܕܢܦܫܢܝܐ[5] ܡܢ ܠܡܬܚܫܒܢܐ ܦܠܐ. ܒܡܠܠܝܐ ܕܝܢ ܠܡܘܬܢܐ.[6]

ܕܬܬܝܢ. ܦܘܠܓ ܫܘܪܝܬܐ ܠܦܘܬ ܡܘܫܚܬܐ ܘܬܪܒܝܬܐ.[1] ܐܝܟ ܗ̇، ܕܛܠܠܐ ܡܢ ܒܢܝ̈ܐ ܘܐܫܬܘܕܥܬ ܕܒܐ ܡܟܘܠ. ܗܟܢܐ ܕܝܢ ܒܟܘܫܐ. ܘܟܬܪܐ ܬܘܒ ܒܪ̈ܓܝܓܬܐ. ܠܐ ܦܘܠܓܐ ܗ̇ܘ ܐܘܫܢܐ. ܟܕ ܛܠܠܐ ܡܢ[2] ܠܐ ܒܗ̇، *ܕܛܠܠ ܛܠܠܐ[3] ܡܕܢܐ. ܐܠܐ ܒܗ̇، ܕܒܪܓܬܐ ܢܦܩ. ܐܦܠܐ ܒܗ̇، ܕܛܠܠ ܦܠܠ. ܐܠܐ ܒܗ̇، ܕܪܓܘܬܢ. ܘܫܒܩܐ ܠܗ ܒܗ̇، ܕܡܫܚ ܡܫܘܚܠ[4] ܘܦܬܪ ܒܡܬܪܐ. ܐܠܐ ܒܗ̇، ܕܡܕܝܢ. ܘܟܬܪܐ ܠܐ ܒܗ̇، ܕܒܗܘܢ ܡܬܦܫܡ. ܐܠܐ ܒܗ̇، ܕܡܟܝܐ. ܘܙܕܩܐ[5] ܠܐ ܒܗ̇، ܕܒܘܗ̇، ܠܐ ܢܦܠ. ܐܠܐ ܒܗ̇، ܕܡܫܘܪ. ܘܕܐܝܟ ܗܠܝܢ ܡܢ ܐܘ ܪܫܝܡܝܢ ܡܢ ܚܫܟܐ ܐܘ ܡܪܟܢܝܢ ܠܗ. ܪܫܝܡܐ ܡܢ ܐܝܟ ܦܘܠܓ ܒܪܢܫܐ ܠܚܘܪܐ ܘܐܘܟܡܐ. ܘܠܫܚܡܬܐ ܘܠܓܢܪܐ.[6] ܠܗܠܝܢ ܓܒܪ ܠܚܬ ܒܬܘܬܬܐ *ܓܠܝܬܐ ܠܘܬ ܒܢܕܪܐ. ܡܪ̈ܟܐ ܕܝܢ ܐܝܟ ܦܘܠܓ ܒܪܢܫܐ[7] ܠܛܠܠܐ ܘܫܟܠܐ. ܘܙܕܩܐ ܘܡܟܠܐ. ܘܟܬܪܐ *ܐܘ ܡܫܟܢܐ.[8] ܠܚܠܝܫ ܡܢ ܗܠܝܢ ܓܒܪ ܒܢܕܪܐ ܐܝܟ ܕܬܠܝܐ ܕܡܬܚܠܦܝܢ ܡܢ ܢܕܪܐ.

1 [1]* om. F [2] ܘܐܡܟܡܐ RV [3] pl. RL [4] ܠܕܝܢܘܬܐ RVL [5]* om. F [5] scripsi; ܕܒܢܦܫܢܝܐ RVLl [6] ܠܡܘܬܢܐ F

2 [1] sg. RVLl [2] om. F [3]* ܕܛܠܠܐ RVLl [4] ܡܫܘܚܠܐ RVLl [5] i. om. RVLl [6] ܘܓܢܪܐ RVLl [7]* om. F [8]* ܘܡܫܟܢܐ RVLl

sweat from his face. These things bring about wrongdoing through the readiness of the agreeable; that is, pleasure with the lascivious, shame with the proud, and so on. The orator is greatly assisted by knowledge of them.

## SECTION TWO
### On the Division of Actions to which Injustice Adheres
### Four Theories

ONE.[3] The things by which accusation comes about may be defined without those for which defence comes about, counting both how many and what they are, because it is not possible for defence to come about except against a specified, indicated, or expected charge. Therefore let us say that every action which someone does is either voluntary or involuntary, (of which) the latter is either accidental or necessary, and (of which) that latter is either natural or compelled. A voluntary action follows either habit, or animal longing—for pleasure because of desire, for victory because of anger— or calculating longing, or rational longing. These are the seven divisions: accidental, natural, compelled, habitual, calculating, irascible, and appetitive. Our master put it down thus, counting two longings, calculating and rational, as one. Some say that by 'calculating' (longing) he seeks (to indicate) the imaginative, by 'rational' the intellectual.

TWO.[4] A division of acts according to ages and minds (would be), for example, that a young man does wrong on account of women and shedding of blood, an old man on account of money, and a rich man on account of desires. But that division is not substantial, because a young man does not fornicate because he is young, but because he is burning with desire, nor kills because he is young, but because he is irascible. An old man hordes and hangs on to wealth not because he is old, but because he is greedy. A rich man enjoys himself not because he is wealthy, but because he wants to. And a just man does not seize (things) not because he is ascetic, but because he is self-

[3] **4.2.1** AR 1.10 68b26-69a7; IS 2.5 (96.2-97.3).
[4] **4.2.2** AR 1.10 69a7-31; IS 2.5 (97.3-97.16).

ܕܬܠܬ[1]. ܡܟܪܙܘܬܐ ܠܒܪ̈ܝܬܐ ܠܐ ܡܬܚܙܝܢ. ܘܒܢܝܢܬܐ ܐܚܪ̈ܢܝܢ ܘܡܟܢܫܢ
ܘܐܡܝܢ ܕܒܫܘܠܡܐ ܗܘܝܢ. ܘܡܠ̈ܝܘܬܐ ܒܟܠܢ ܕܠܒܪ[2] ܡܢ ܚܝܐ ܡ̈ܢܝܢ.
ܘܒܝܢܬܐ ܒܚܝܘܬܐ ܘܫܟܝܚܐ ܕܟܠܢ[3] ܕܒܦܫܐ ܢܦ̈ܫܐ ܐܢܫ̈ܝܢ ܡܬܠܒ̈ܟܢ.
ܘܡܫܡ̈ܫܢܘܬܐ ܒܟܠܗ ܫܘܠܛܢܐ ܕܡܪܝܐ ܡܬܗܘܝܢ ܠܒܢܝ̈ܐܢܫ ܡܫܬܡ̈ܠܝܢ.
ܘܡܠܐܟܐ ܫܡܝܢܐ ܗܘܘ[4] ܡܕܒܪܢܐ ܡܛܠ ܗ̇ܝ ܕܦܩܝܕܐ ܘܠܐ ܡܛܠ ܙܒܢܬܐ
ܐܘ ܠܒܗܬܐ ܡܟܠ. ܫܪܝܪܐ ܕܝܢ ܪ̈ܘܚܢܝܬܐ[5] ܠܐ ܡܛܠ ܗ̇ܝ ܕܦܩܝܕܐ ܐܠܐ
*ܡܛܠ ܗܝܡܢܘܬܐ[6] ܒܗܝܡܢܘܬܐ ܡܫܡ̈ܠܝܢ. ܘܫܡ̈ܫܬܐ ܪ̈ܘܚܢܝܬܐ ܡܛܠ
ܠܒܗܬܐ ܕܠܟܒܢ ܒܢܬܐ ܘܠܐ ܡܛܠܬܗ̇,[7] ܕܢܛܪܐ ܗܘ ܕܐܫܟܠ. ܦܢܫ ܕܝܢ
ܬܫܡܫܐ ܡܕܒܪܢܝܬܐ ܡܢ ܒܢܬܐ. ܒܗ̇ ܕܡܕܒܪܢܘܬܐ ܗ̇ܝ[8] ܬܘܪ̈ܝܢ ܡܫܡܠܝܐ
ܡܬܟܒܐ. ܒܢܬܐ ܕܝܢ ܠܐ ܗܘܐ ܒܫܡܫܐ ܒܠܚܘܕ ܗܘܐ ܕܬܬܗܫܫ.
ܐܠܐ ܒܒܘܕܐ ܬܘܒ. ܒܐܡܬ ܚܝܐ ܘܪܘܪܐ ܕܒܘܣܡܬܐ.

ܕܐܪܒܥ. ܠܟܠ ܐܢܫܐ ܕܢܦܩ ܠܫܘܡܠܝܐ ܐܘ ܠܚܒܝܒܐ ܐܘ ܠܝܠܝܐ ܐܘ ܠܚܫܐ ܢܦܫܢܝܐ.[1]
ܗܝܡܢܘܬܐ ܐܝܬ ܒܗ̇ ܗܘ ܡܐ ܕܒܥܐ ܘܦܩܕ. ܘܠܟܠ ܗܝܡܢܘܬܐ ܒܠܬܐ ܐܝܬ ܐܝܬ
ܒܢܝܢܬܐ ܐܘ ܒܢܝܢܘܬܐ.[2] ܒܕ ܩܠܝܠܬܐ ܡܢ ܡܟܪܙܘܬܐ[3] ܕܠܐ ܗܝܡܢܐ
ܒܚܝܠܐ ܗܝܡܢܘܬܐ ܗܘܝܢ ܒܒܢܝܐ. ܐܘ ܒܢܝܫܘܬܐ ܠܡܐܡܪ. ܒܠܚܡܐ
ܕܒܢܝܫܘܬܐ ܡܫܬܡܪ[4] ܡܛܠ ܠܚܡܬܐ ܘܗܝܡܢܘܬܐ ܫܠܝܛܬܐ ܘܡܫܬܠܛܢܝܬܐ
ܡܬܟܒܐ. ܒܕܠܗ̇ ܦܐܐ ܠܝ ܕܢܐܡܪ ܗ̇ܝ ܕܦܩܝܕܐ ܗܘ̇ܝ ܕܗܝܡܢܐ. ܒܪܡ[5]
ܗ̇ܝ ܕܦܩܝܕܐ ܒܟܠܢ ܫܠܝܚܐ ܠܡܘܕܝܢ ܐܬܐܡܪܬ. ܡܕܡ ܗ̇ܝ ܕܗܝܡܢܐ
ܫܪܒܐ[6] ܕܬܬܐܡܪ.

3 [1] f. add. ܐ F [2] i. ܘ RVL [3] i. om. F [4] i. add. ܕ RVLl [5] ܪ̈ܘܚܢܝܬܐ RVLl [6*] ܡܛܠܬܗ̇ ܕܗܝܡܢܘܬܐ RVLl [7] ܡܛܠ RVL [8] om. RVL

4 [1] ܢܦܫܢܐ RVL [2] add. ܐܘ ܒܢܝܫܘܬܐ RVL [3] sg. R [4] ܡܫܬܡܪ̈ܝܢ RVL [5] ܒܗ̇, RVL [6] ܫܪܒܐ RVLl

denying. Such things are either far from the point, or near it. Far from it, for example, is the classification of a man as white or black, fat or emaciated, for these have no evident connection with habits. Near it, for example, is the classification of a man as young or old, just or unjust, rich or poor, for each of these has specific habits different from the others.

THREE.[5] Accidental acts are undefined, natural ones regular and established and come about generally, compelled ones come to pass through those things which are reckoned outside of nature, habitual ones through the sight and sound of those things which spread in the soul, and calculating ones are accomplished by art through a wish for the preconceived end. A calculating or crafty wrongdoer does wrong for the sake of the expedient, not on account of desire or victory, but the lustful intemperate do wrong with pleasure not for the sake of the expedient, but on account of pleasure, while the angry irascible seek revenge on account of victory, not in order to punish the offender. Corrective punishment is different from revenge, because by correction the reformation of the offender is sought, but by revenge not for the sufferer only does a condition come about, but also for the doer, (who gains), namely, satisfaction and exultation through the vengeance.

FOUR.[6] For everyone who follows calculation, habit, or emotion, there is pleasure in that which he seeks and does, and for every pleasure, there is a natural or habitual cause, because many of the acts which are not pleasurable by nature become pleasurable by habit. Or to put it succinctly, everything which is done voluntarily is sought for good or pleasure, true or opined. Therefore it is right for us to say what is expedient and what is pleasurable. But the expedient was discussed earlier in the deliberative (sections), so now the pleasurable remains to be discussed.

[5] **4.2.3** AR 1.10 69a32-b14; IS 2.5 (98.1-99.3).
[6] **4.2.4** AR 1.10 69b14-32; IS 2.5 (99.3-99.11).

ܦܘܫܩܐ ܬܠܝܬܝܐ
ܡܛܠ ܛ̈ܠܠܬܐ ܕܗܝܡܢܘܬܐ ܒܠܬ ܒܠܐ
ܬܐܘܪ̈ܝܐ ܥܒܕ

ܘܕܡܘܬܐ. ܗܝܡܢܘܬܐ ܡ̣ܢ ܐܝܬܝܗ̇ ܡܬܬܝܕܥܢܘܬ ܢܦܫܐ ܡܫܠ ܒܡܪ̈ܓܢܝܬ ܙ̈ܓܓܝܬܐ[1] ܕܚܒܝܫ ܠܙܓܓܝܬܐ. ܠܗܕܐ[2] ܕܝܢ ܗܘܝܐ ܒܡܪ̈ܓܢܝܬ ܗ̇ܘ ܡܐ ܕܡܣܟܠ ܠܗܝܢ ܡܙ̈ܓܓܝܬܐ. ܙܘ̈ܓܐ ܐܘܪܐ ܒ̈ܢܝܐ ܟܠܗܘܢ ܗܘܝܢ. ܗܘܝܐ ܘܡܬܕܢܝܐ ܒܗ ܚܕܐ ܐܢܫܐ ܠܚܝܐ ܡܬܚܙܝܢܐ[3] ܡܬܕܡܐ. *ܘܡܣܬܒܠܢܐ ܘܠܐ ܒ̈ܢܝܐ[4] ܘܗܘܘ̣ ܠܐ ܡܬܕܢܝܐ ܬ̈ܠܝܐ ܐܝܟ ܘܡܬܚܙܝܢܐ. ܘܟܕ ܗܘܐ ܐܬܦܩܘܬܐ ܡ̣ܢ ܘܣܦܝܩܘܬܐ ܘܐܬܚܙܝܢܘܬܐ ܡܢ ܡܬܚܙܝܢܘܬܐ[5] ܐܝܢ. ܢܚܙܝܢܘܬܐ ܕܝܢ ܘܠܐ ܒܡܬܠܬܘܬܐ ܘܡܬܗܦܟܢܘܬܐ ܘܡܪܕܘܬܐ ܘܚܣܝܢܘܬܐ ܘܥܒܝܘܬܐ ܡ̣ܢ ܗܝܢܐܝܬ. ܘܙ̈ܓܓܝܬܐ ܐܝܟ ܕܗ̇ܘ ܗܘ. ܡܬܠܬܠܬܐ ܗܘܬ ܗ̇ܝ ܙܓܓܝܬܐ ܐܘ ܠܐ ܡܬܠܬܠܬܐ. ܕܒܝܬܐ ܠܚܝܐ ܘܙܓܓܝܬܐ. ܐܝܟ ܙܓܓܬ ܘܗܘܓܐ[6] ܘܠܒܘ̈ܫܐ ܘܙ̈ܪܝܚܐ ܘܒܫܒ̈ܝܚܐ[7] ܘܡܢ ܙ̈ܓܓܐ[8] ܥܡܒܪܐ ܘܚܙܝܬܐ ܕܠܐܝܬ ܗܝܢܐܝܬܐ ܘܗܝܢܝܘܬܐ ܠܢܦܫܐ ܡܬܚܠܝܢ. ܐܝܟ ܐܢܫܐ ܕܒܗ ܥܒܕ ܡܛܠ ܡܬܚܘܪܬܐ ܡܕܡ ܢܪ̈ܓܢܝܗ̇.[9] ܘܒܗ ܚܙܐ ܒܚܕܐ ܡܕܡ ܥܦܪܐ ܥ̈ܒܕ ܐܒܗܬܗ.

ܕܬܪ̈ܬܝܢ. ܦܠܦܣܐ ܡ̣ܢ ܡܪ̈ܓܢܝܬܐ ܗ̣ܝ ܡܚܠܬܐ. ܕܒܡܗܕܢܐ[1] ܘܣܘܒܐ ܗܝܡܢܘܬܐ ܙܓܓܝܬܐ ܡܢܐ. ܒܗ ܠܗ̇ܘ ܡܐ ܕܡܕܡ ܚܙܐ ܒܙܪܥܐ ܡܬܒܗܪ. ܐܝܟ ܡܣܒܐ. ܘܙܓܓܝܬܐ ܡ̣ܢ ܒܗ̇ܘ ܕܡܐܟ ܗ̣ܝ. ܒܡܗܕܢܐ ܕܝܢ ܠܒܝܬܐ. ܘܣܘܒܐ ܠܗ̇ܘ[2] ܕܒܠܥ. ܘܐܝܬ ܐܢܬ، ܕܒܡܗܕܢܐ ܘܣܘܒܐ[3] ܕܙܓܓܝܬܐ[4] ܕܡܬܠܬܥ ܡܬܪ ܡܢ ܙܓܓܝܬܐ ܕܡܬܒܥܐ ܒܒܕܝܢ ܗܝܡܢܘܬܐ. ܒܗ ܒܡ ܡܬܦܠܦܠܘܬܐ ܦܛܠ ܡܐܟܐ ܘܢܦܩ ܡܟܒܐ ܐܟܐ ܕܡܐܬܐ. ܘܡܢ ܒܡܗ̈ܕܢܐ ܗܘܝܐܐ ܒܡܗܕ ܒܟ̈ܠܐ ܡܟ̈ܝܢܐ ܕܦܟܠ[5] ܒܙܪܥܐ ܘܪܝܢܐ ܘܠܕܐ[6] ܡܢܕܘܒܣ[7] ܐܫܬܘܒ ܡܗܘܢ ܗܘܘ̣ *ܘܡܬܬܒܠ ܡܢܝܗܘܢ ܐܝܟܢ.[8] ܐܦ ܪܘܓܙܐ ܒܡܬܠܓܠܓܘܬ ܘܒܗܬܐ[9] ܕܗܝܡܢܐ ܒܟܪ̈[10] ܗܝܡܢܘܬܐ. ܐܝܟ ܕܐܡܪ ܐܡܬܪܝܘܣ. ܕܪܘܓܙܐ ܠܡ ܡܬܪ ܡܢ ܢܦ̈ܠܦ ܕܒܥܐ ܚܠܐ.[11] ܘܐܠܠܐ ܘܒܗܬܐ ܠܐ ܐܗܘܐ ܪܘܓܙܐ. *ܒܠ ܗܕܐ ܒܠ ܡ̣ܢ ܕܡܚܝܠ ܒܡܪܢ ܗܘ ܪܘܓܙܐ.[12] ܒܗ ܒܡܪܢ ܗܝܡܢܐ ܒܒܗܬܗ. ܘܗܕܐ ܒܠ ܡ̣ܢ ܕܦܣܩ ܡܒܪܐ ܕܒܗܬܐ ܡܢܗ ܡܛܠ ܒܥܘܡܗ.

1 [1] ܕܚܠܐ RVLl [2] ܠܗܕܐ R [3] ܡܬܚܙܝܢܐ RVLl [4*] ܘܡܣܬܒܠܢܐ ܕܒ̈ܢܝܐ R; ܘܡܣܬܒ̈ܠܢܐ ܕܒܢܝܐ V; ܘܡܣܬܒ̈ܠܢܐ ܕܒ̈ܢܝܐ Ll [5] sg. R [6] pl. RVLl [7] i. om. RVLl [8] sg. RVL [9] ܒܐܪ̈ܓܢܝܗ̇ RVL

2 [1] i. ܘ RVL [2] om. RVLl [3] i. ܒ RVLl [4] i. om. RVLl [5] ܕܦܟܠ R [6] ܘܠܐ R [7] ܡܢܕܘܒܣ RVL [8*] om. RVL [9] add. ܠܐ ܐܗܘܐ RVL; add. ܠܐ ܗܘܐ l [10] om. RVLl [11] ܚܠܐ R [12*] om. F

## SECTION THREE
### On the Causes of the Pleasure (which is) the Cause of Injustice
### Seven Theories

ONE.[7] Pleasure, then, is movement of the soul, suddenly, by the sensing of the desirable which is natural to sensation, while pain comes about by the sensing of that which is contrary to the nature of sensing. Therefore all natural things are pleasurable, and similarly the habitual, because habit is similar to acquired nature; the contraries, both the unnatural and the non-habitual, are painful and troublesome. For a similar reason diligence and care and persistence are among the painful things, but slothfulness, absence of toil, carelessness, disobedience, leisure, and sleep are among the pleasurable, as the desirable is pleasurable. Desire may be rational or irrational, which (latter) is proper to nature and sensation, like desire for sex, taste, smell, and incense. But among the senses, hearing and sight specifically transmit to the soul intellectual pleasures, as when someone hears about some virtue he may desire it, or when seeing some fine deed may do something like it.

TWO.[8] *Phantasia* is a weak sensing, which by memory and hope obtains sensual pleasure, because someone remembering what he has previously seen may afterwards hope (for it). Sensation is in the present, memory (belongs) to the past, hope to the future. Sometimes memory and the hope that the desirable which is yet to be produced (will be) greater than the desirable already produced create pleasure, because with attainment longing ceases and fulfilment follows, a source of enmity. Among pleasurable memories is the memory of hard toils which a man endures and from which he has escaped without peril and prospered through the fulfilments of his wish. Even anger produces pleasure through the pleasurable image-evocation of victory. As Homer said, 'Anger is far sweeter than drops of honey'. But unless victory does not bring pleasure to anger, on this account anger is less pleasurable against him who is weak, because it is less pleasurable (evoking an image of such a) victory, and similarly against him from whom the hope of vengeance is cut off on account of the power (of him who is angry).

---

[7] **4.3.1** AR 1.11 69b33-70a27; IS 2.6 (99.14-100.10).

[8] **4.3.2** AR 1.11 70a27-b14; IS 2.6 (100.10-101.6).

ܕܬܠܬ. ܪ̈ܓܝܓܬܐ[1] ܓܝܪ ܦ̈ܓܪܢܝܬܐ ܕܐ̈ܪܓܝܓܐ ܒܡܫܟܢܗ ܒܬ̈ܪܝܢ ܗܢܝܐܘܬܐ. ܐܝܟ ܐܡܝܪ̈ܝ، ܒܐܫܬܘܬܐ ܕܒܝܢܝܗܐ[2] ܡܫܬܠܡܢܝܢ ܘܒܗ ܡܬܬܒܪܝܢ ܐܟܚܕ، ܕܐܫܬܘܝܘ[3] ܘܡܬܡܨܝܢ ܠܡܚܫܬܐ ܣܓܝ. ܘܦ̈ܓܪܢܝܐ ܒܗܘܢ̈ ܗܢܝܐܘܬܐ ܕܒܗܝܢ ܐܬܟܫܦܘ ܘܫܡܫܢܐ ܕܗܢܝܢ ܕܒܬ̈ܪܝܢ ܠܪ̈ܓܝܓܬܐ ܕܡܬܓܪ̈ܝܢ ܠܗ ܦܘܪܢܝܢ. ܐܦ ܓܝܪ ܘܒܢܫܐ[4] ܠܕܟܝܐ ܐܝܟ ܒܗܘܢ̈ ܣܓܝܒܐ ܗܢܝܐܘܬܐ ܘܒܡܘܬܐ ܐܒܢܝܐ[5] ܡܬܒܪ̈ܝܢ.[6] ܗܢܝܐܘܬܐ ܗ̇ܝ ܒܒܗܘܢ̈ ܗ̇ܘ ܡܟܐ ܕܦܓܪ ܗܘܐ ܘܕܐܝܟ ܐܝܠܝܢ ܐܬܬܗ، ܗܘܐ. ܒܡܬܐ ܕܝܢ ܒܡܓܠܝܘܬܐ ܕܒܗܘܢ. ܐܝܟ ܕܐܡ̈ܪ[7] ܐܒܪܗܡ ܡܛܠ ܐܒܝܠܐ. ܗ̇ܘ ܕܒܪ ܐܟܠܐ[8] ܗܘܐ ܠܡܚܬ ܗܘܐ ܠܒܢܝܬܐ ܠܒܝܬܐ ܘܗܢܝܐܘܬܐ ܠܐ̈ܒܝܠܐ[9] ܐܡܝܪܬ.

ܕܐܪܒܥ. ܡܢ ܗܢܝܐܘܬܐ ܬܘܒ ܗ̇ܝ، ܕܠܡܬܒܥܘ ܒܢܬܐ ܗܘ̇، ܕܠܐ ܢܬܠܒܫ ܒܠܒܒܐ. ܐܒܝܠܐ ܕܝܢ ܡܚܝܠܘܬܗ ܕܠܒܝܒܐ ܗ̇، ܕܠܐ ܢܬܡܟܟ ܠܡܬܢܚܡܘ. ܘܐܝܟ ܗܘ ܕܡܬܒܥܐ ܕܢܬܠܓ[1] ܒܠܒܐ. ܫܪܐ ܒܡܒܪܐ. ܐܦ ܗ̇، ܕܠܡܒܥܐ ܗܢܝܐܐ. ܠܘ ܒܠܚܘܕ ܠܒ̈ܢܝܢܫܐ ܪ̈ܚܡܝ ܕܟܠܗܘܢ. ܐܠܐ ܘܠܦܓܪܐ ܕܢܦܫܗ. ܘܒܠܗܘܕܐ ܗܘ ܐܬܬܚܢܢܐ ܕܢܦܫܐ ܢܐܡܦܪܐ[2] ܘܡܦ̈ܣܩܐ ܘܡܗܦܟܢ ܘܦܩ̈ܣܩܐ ܘܬܒܪܐ ܐܬܒܪ. ܘܡܒܕܩ ܡܢ ܗܘܠܝܢ. ܐܠܐ ܒܬܪ ܦܠܘܣܘܦܘܬܐ. ܠܐ ܗܘܐ ܗܢܝܐܘܬܐ. ܐܝܟ ܡܗܦܟܝܢ ܘܦܣ̈ܩܐ. ܠܡܕܡ ܕܝܢ ܒܪ ܥܡܗ ܢܦܩ ܗܢܝܐܘܬܐ. ܐܝܟ *ܝܕܥܐ ܘܟܠ ܢܣܝܢܘܬܐ.[3] ܘܝܕܥ ܐܢܫ ܗ̇ܝ ܕܟܘܬܐ ܒܐܝܢܐ ܗܢܝܐܐ. ܝܕܥ[4] ܐܢܫܝܐ ܕܝܢ ܗ̇،[5] ܦܝܠܘܣܘܦܘܬܐ ܐܘܟܝܬ ܫܪܝܪܬܐ. ܐܝܟ ܕܡܬܕܒܪܢܐ ܗܘܐ ܠܦܘܬ ܬܪ̈ܥܝܬܐ.

ܕܚܡܫ. ܐܝܟ ܕܡܫܠܡܢܐ ܕܒ̈ܬܐ ܘܫܦܪ ܡܛܠ ܦܘܠܚܢܐ ܕܡܫܒܚܐ ܘܐܡܪܐ ܡܬܩ̈ܒܠܝܢ. ܐܝܟ ܗ̇ܘ ܕܢܦܩ ܒܡܬܘܪܬܐ ܕܡܛܠ[1] ܬܫܒܘܚܬܐ ܕܐܡܪܐ ܠܡܫܡܫܘ[2] ܒܠܚܘܕ ܡܬܦܪܫ. ܘܐܡܪܐ ܡܢ ܦ̈ܪܒܐ ܘܡܕܒ̈ܪܢܐ ܘܐܝܠܝܢ ܕܡܬܚܝܢ ܘܒܪ̈ܟܐ ܘܦܓܪ̈ܐ[3] ܢܬܪ ܡܢ ܙ̈ܢܝܐ ܘܐܒܕ̈ܢܐ ܘܐܝܠܝܢ ܕܒܬܕܝܢ ܘܫ̈ܦܝܪܐ ܘܒܗܘܢ، ܡܢܝܢܐ ܙܒܝܢ. ܘܡܢ ܦܛܪ ܒܡܢܝܢܐ ܐܝܟ ܠܠܘܩܒܠ ܘܒܢܝܢܐ ܠܐ ܐܢܫ ܚܕܐ ܐܡܪܐ. ܘܙܒܢܐ ܒܗ̇ܘ ܡܟܐ ܕܙܒܢ ܡܬܒܫܡ. ܡܬܒܫܡ ܕܝܢ ܡܛܠ ܦܘܠܚܢܐ ܕܠܒܬܐ ܕܗܘܝܐ[4] ܠܗ ܡܢܗ. ܗܢܝܐܘܬ ܒܙܒܢܐ ܕܝܢ ܒܗ̇، ܕܢܬܙܒܢ ܘܢܬܩܒܠ[5] ܡܛܠ ܢܦܫܗ ܗ̇،[6] ܠܚܘܕ. ܘܗܒܢܐ[7] ܗ̇، ܕܢܬܬܕܪ.[8] ܘܒܠܗܘܕܐ ܐܬܠܝܠܐ ܠܟ̈ܘܪ، ܢܫܝܢ̈ܐ[9] ܘܦ̈ܠܓܐ[10] ܫܠܘܬܐ ܙ̈ܕܐ[11] ܘܡܫܘܢܝܐ ܚܒܪ ܕܕܒܪܐ ܢܬܝܠܐ. ܘܡܦܪܕܝܣܐ *ܬܘܒ ܗܢܝܐ. ܘܡܦܪܕܝܣܐ[12] ܒܗ̇ܘ ܡܟܐ[13] ܕܡܬܝܚܘܪܐ ܡܢ ܙܝܢܘܬܐ ܡܬܬܕܪܝܢ.[14]

---

3 [1] ܪ̈ܓܝܓܬܐ RVL [2] ܕܒܝܬܝܐ RL [3] ܕܐܫܬܘܝܘ R; ܐܫܬܘܝܘ V; ܕܐܫܬܘܝܘ L; ܕܐܫܬܘܝܘ l [4] i. om. RVLl [5] f. om. RLT [6] ܡܬܒܪܝܢ R [7] om. F [8] ܐܟܠ V [9] sg. F
4 [1] om. RVLL [2] sg. RVLl [3*] ܐܘ ܟܠ ܢܣܝܢܘܬܐ RL; ܟܠ ܢܣܝܢܘܬܐ V; ܟܠ ܢܣܝܢܘܬܘܬܐ l [4] om. F [5] om. RVLl
5 [1] i. ܘ R [2] ܫܡܫܘ RVL; ܕܐܫܬܡܫܘ l [3] i. add. ܘ RVLl [4] i. om. RVL [5] ܡܬܩܒܠ F [6] om. F [7] i. om. RVL [8] ܕܢܬܬܕܪ RVLl [9] ܢܫܝܢܬܐ RVL [10] ܘܦܠܓ̈ܐ VLl [11] om. RVL [12*] om. R [12] ܒܡܦܪܕܝܣܐ VLl [13] om. F [14] ܡܬܬܕܪ RVLl

THREE.[9] Many desires produce pleasure by the hope of the desired, as those gripped by fever who are burning with thirst are glad both remembering when they drank and hoping to drink. And many do not come close to desirables which are present on account of recollection of pleasures which they have enjoyed and hope of those to come. Even by some chance, like the recollection of a beloved, pleasure and pain may be gathered together: pleasure by the recollection of what he used to do and what he was like, pain by being bereaved of him; as Homer said about a mourner, that while he was lamenting his dead (one), a grief-stricken and pleasurable cry seized the audience.

FOUR.[10] Among pleasures is also the exaction of revenge and the failure of an enemy to prosper, just as among the afflictions of an oppressed man is his inability to take vengeance. If, however, he may hope that the oppressor will be punished, he rejoices in the hope. And winning is pleasurable, not only to people, who love victory, but also to all other creatures, and therefore a game with ankle-bones, balls, dice, chess, counters, or other kinds is pleasurable. With some of these there is no pleasure except after (achieving) excellence (at them), such as chess and counters. With others, however, pleasure follows on immediately, such as hunting and all chasing. To some people a just victory is pleasurable, but to others an eristic or contentious one, as it comes by cajolings corresponding to (their) intentions.

FIVE.[11] Victories and so on are usually sought for the *phantasia* of reputation and honour, as he who is diligent in virtue for the sake of increase of honour will contrive to add to it. Honour is more lovely (coming) from neighbours, fellow-citizens, contemporaries, the prudent, and the many, than from those at a distance, strangers, posterity, the foolish, and the few in number. From those greatly despised, like little children and cattle, no one seeks honour. A lover takes delight in that which he loves, taking delight because of the *phantasia* of the good which he gets from it, but the pleasure of a person in being loved and cherished is solely because of himself. Being ad-

---

[9] **4.3.3** AR 1.11 70b14-29; IS 2.6 (101.6-101.12).
[10] **4.3.4** AR 1.11 70b29-71a8; IS 2.6 (101.12-102.5).
[11] **4.3.5** AR 1.11 71a8-24; IS 2.6 (102.5-103.2).

ܕܫܬ. ܒܗܦܦ ܚܘܝܐ ܗܘ. ܘܡܚܒܪܐ ܗܘ. ܘܫܘܠܦ ܓ̈ܒܘܬܐ[1] ܡܛܠ
ܣܗܕܬ ܡܓܒܝܢܘܬܐ ܒܗܡܝ ܗܘ. ܒܕ ܗܘ ܡܢܐ ܕܦܪܥ ܠܗ ܡܥܒܕ ܒܓܒܝܢܘܬܐ
ܒܗܬܪܗ. ܗܘ̇ ܕܠܡܐܠܦ ܚܘܝܐ. ܡܛܠ ܗܓܓܐ ܕܕܡܚܝܪܘܬܐ[2] ܒܫܡܠܝܐ
ܘܡܛܠ ܡܬܓܠܝܢܘܬ ܗܘ ܡܢܐ ܕܓܠܝܪ ܒܚܝܠܐ. ܘܒܒܥܘܬܐ ܫܦܝܪܬܐ ܒܕ
ܡܗܬܒܪܐ ܘܫܦܝܫܘܬܐ[3] ܫܦܝܪܬܐ ܒܣܘܡܗܐ ܚܘܝܐ. ܗ̇ܝ ܕܝܢ ܡܛܠ
ܫܦܝܪܘܬܐ ܘܡܬܡܚܝܢܘܬ ܚܝܠܐ. ܗܕܐ ܕܝܢ ܡܛܠ ܡܬܡܚܝܢܘܬ ܚܝܠܐ
ܒܠܝܚܕ. ܗ̇ܝ ܕܢܗܕܐ ܘܢܬܪܝ ܚܘܝܐ ܗܘ̇ ܕܢܒܠܐ ܣܦܝܪܬܐ ܠܗܦܝܟܐ
ܚܘܝܐ. ܘܡܕܡܝܢܘܬܐ ܒܠܗܝܢ ܐܝܟ ܝܪܘܬܐ ܘܓܠܦܘܬܐ ܘܫܦܪ
ܗܘܝܢ. ܒܕܡܐ ܕܐܦ ܝܠܕܐ ܠܒܐ ܫܒܝܪܐ[4] ܕܝܢ[5] ܒܐܫܬܐ ܗܘ ܡܛܠ
ܫܦܝܪܘܬ ܕܘܡܝܗ ܕܒܪܫ ܬܦܢܒܐ ܚܘܝܐ. ܐܦ ܦܐܪܐ ܕܒܗܘܢ ܗܘܐ
ܫܘܪܒܐ ܡܢ ܦܪܕܝܣܐ[6] ܒܗ̇ ܕܕܡܝܢ ܗܘܝܢ.[7]

ܕܫܒܥ. ܟܠܗܘܢ ܗܠܝܢ ܒܗ̇ ܕܒܢܝܐ ܐܣܬܟܠܘܗܝ ܗܘܝܢ. ܒܕܡܘܬ
ܗܘ ܡܢܐ ܕܕܡܐ ܠܚܘܝܐ ܗܘ. ܘܡܛܠ[1] ܕܠܝܬܗ ܪܘܚ ܟܠ[2] ܡܕܡ. ܐܦ
ܘܠܗܘ ܡܢܐ ܕܕܚܠ ܠܗ ܪܘܚ. ܠܠܒܐ ܠܠܒܐ ܘܓܒܪܐ ܠܓܒܪܐ ܘܓܘܫܡܐ
ܠܓܘܫܡܐ. ܘܐܝܣܘܬܐ ܒܢܝܢܐ ܗܒܗܬ[3] ܗܘܝܢ. ܐܦ ܗ̇ܝ ܕܫܬܠܛ
ܘܣܒܝܒܐ[4] ܢܫܬܪ ܘܠܡܬܪܒܐ ܒܐܪ ܠܟܠܫ ܗܘܝܢ. ܡܠܝܫܛܐ ܠܪܫܒ
ܐܝܦܪܐ. ܒܢ ܗ̇ܝ ܕܢܕܪܫ ܗܘ ܠܗ ܒܪܫܐ ܒܡܚܝܠܬ̈ܐ. ܐܝܟ ܕܐܡܪ
ܦܘܐܠܛܐ ܕܡܦܠܛ ܠܗ ܢܡܗ ܘܠܡܚܝܠܬ̈ܐ ܢܠܘ ܫܘܠܛܢܗ. ܘܓܢܣܒ̈ܘܬܐ
ܘܦܢܣܝܘܬܐ ܒܬܘܢܝܐ ܘܒܥ̈ܒܕܐ ܗܘܝܢ. ܗܠܝܢ ܐܝܟ ܗܘܝܢܐܬܐ
ܘܩܘܡ̈ܠܬܗܝܢ[5] ܡܫܡܫܢܘܬܐ.

6 [1] ܠܓ̈ܒܘܬܐ F [2] ܕܡܚܝܪܘܬܐ RVL [3] f. om. RVLl [4] ܫܒܝܪܐ RVLl [5] i. om. RVL; ܝܪܐ l [6] ܦܘܪܕܝܣܐ RLl; ܦܪܕܝܣܐ V [7] ܗܘܝܢ F
7 [1] i. om. RVL [2] ܟܠ R [3] om. RVLl [4] i. om. RVLl [5] i. om. R

mired is similar, and therefore a warrior breaks through ranks of fighters and arrays of companies and creates perils in order that he may appear marvellous. A flatterer is also pleasurable, but a flatterer is a cause of amazement on account of the ostentatious show of love.

SIX.[12] The repetition of the pleasurable is pleasurable, and the habitual is pleasurable. And the change of things is pleasurable, on account of the renewal of sensing through them, because (with) that which is present, its continuance is not effective in sensation. Learning is pleasurable, on account of the image-evocation of wonder at the completion, and on account of the uncovering of that which is hidden in nature. Fine doing when acting and fine suffering in endurance are pleasurable, the former on account of fineness and sufficiency of strength, the latter on account of sufficiency of strength alone. Directing and setting right is pleasurable, and supplying the wants of the needy is pleasurable. All works of imitation, such as painting, sculpture, and the rest, are pleasurable, to the extent that even a vile image which is painted on a wall is pleasurable on account of the fineness of its likeness to the odious prototype. Ways by which deliverance from dangers comes about are also pleasurable, because they are admired.

SEVEN.[13] All resemblances, in that their relationship is natural, are pleasurable, therefore that which is similar to the pleasurable is pleasurable. And because everything loves itself, it also loves that which is like it: youth to youth, man to man, bird to bird. Habitual relationships are likewise pleasurable, and being in charge, being supposed wise, and criticising the neighbours are pleasurable to everyone, especially the ambitious. Thus the fact that someone trains himself in virtues (means), as the poet said, that 'he divides his day and allots the greater part of it to virtues'. Laughing and merrymaking with stories and deeds are pleasurable. These are the pleasures, their opposites the painful.

[12] **4.3.6** AR 1.11 71a24-b12; IS 2.6 (103.2-104.3).
[13] **4.3.7** AR 1.11 71b12-72a3; IS 2.6 (104.3-104.9).

ܦܘܫܩܐ ܪܒܝܥܝܐ

ܡܛܠ ܬ̈ܠܠܝܬܐ ܕܒܝܕܗܝܢ ܡܚܘܐ ܒܪܝܐ ܦܫܝܩܐܝܬ

ܬܐܘܪ̈ܐܡ ܥܣܪ

ܡܕܡܝܢܬܐ. ܬ̈ܠܠܝܬܐ ܕܒܗ̈ܝܢ ܐܡܪܐ ܠܗ̇، ܕܐܬܚܒܠܐܝܬ ܢܚܘܐ ܒܪܝܐ ܗܠܝܢ ܐܝܢ. ܗ̇ܝ ܕܡܬܚܫܒܐ ܕܢܚܘܐ ܘܠܐ ܡܬܦܪܫܐ. *ܘܐܦ ܡܬܦܪܫܐ[1] ܡܬܚܫܒ ܟܝܢܐ ܡܢ ܡܕܡ ܕܢܦܠ ܢܣܒܪ. ܠܐ ܕܝܢ ܦܢܝܬ ܡܢ ܬܠܝܬܝܘܬܐ ܐܝܟܢܐ ܕܟܬܒ ܠܗܘܢܐ ܦܓܪܢܝܐ ܐܘ ܪܘܚܢܝܐ ܚܬ̈ܝܬܐ ܘܡܬܢܪܐ ܢܗܘܘܢ ܠܗ. ܘܒܪܘܚܐ ܒܗ̇، ܕܡܫܟܚ ܘܡܕܡ ܠܦܓܪܐ ܡܬܪܟܐ ܒܠܒܝܠܐ ܡܚܕܐ ܐܚܕ. ܘܪܘܚܐ ܕܕܢܚܐ ܒܦܓܪܢܐ ܡܚܕܐ. ܘܒܪܝܘܬܐ ܘܡܫܝܚܐ ܘܒܥܘܬܐ ܠܬܓܪܐ ܒܥܕ. ܓܘܪܐ ܘܥܡܪ ܦ̈ܓܪܢܝܐ ܡܚܘܝܢ. ܘܒܢܝܢܐ ܘܡܦܩܢܐ ܟܕ ܠܐ ܡܫܬܟܚܝܢ ܠܠܘܚ̈ܐ ܐܬܚܒܠܐܝܬ ܡܚܘܝܢ. ܘܗ̇ܝ ܕܐܠܒ[2] ܚܝܢ ܒܓܠܐ ܢܗܘܐ ܒܗܠܐ ܒܕܢܐ[3] ܠܒܗܠܐ. ܒܗ̇، ܕܐܡܪܝܢ. ܐܠܠܐ ܡܢܐ ܗܘܐ ܕܕܡܐ. ܠܐ ܓܠܝܐܝܬ ܐܚܘܐ. ܘܕܡܢ ܕܐܝܟ ܗܢܐ ܒܗܠܐ ܠܐ ܡܬܝܕܥܐ ܠܡܕܪܘܗܝ. ܟܕ ܟܠܝܫ ܡܢ ܗܠܝܢ ܕܡܬܒܪܝܢ ܡܕܪܘܗܝ. ܘܡܢ ܠܐ ܡܬܒܪܝܬܐ ܠܐ ܦܢܝܬ. ܘܟܠܗܕܐ ܠܐ ܐܚܕ ܢܦܠ ܢܣܒܗ ܡܢ ܪܘܚܗ.

ܕܬܪ̈ܬܝܢ. ܐܝܟܢܐ ܕܢܦܫ ܕܒܠܒܒܐ ܠܝܬ ܠܗ ܘܠܟܠܝܫ ܪܘܚܐ ܢܦܫ ܠܗ ܒܓܠ ܡܬܬܒܪ. ܟܕ ܠܐ ܡܬܕܪܟ. ܘܐܝܬ ܐܝܟܢܐ ܕܠܐ ܡܬܕܪܟܝܢ ܐܝܟܢܐ ܕܐܘܪ̈ܝܐ ܡܬܗܘܢ ܠܐ ܢܬܕܪܟܘܢ. ܘܗܟܢܐ ܡܬܟܣܝܢ ܐܦܢ ܠܡܚܙܝܘ. ܘܟܕ ܢܦܩ ܙܘܥܐ ܒܐܣܩܘܦܐ ܦܬܝܠܐ ܕܒܠܝܦܝܢ ܐܦ̈ܐ ܡܫܬܒܚܝܢ. ܡܚܕܐ ܕܝܢ ܪܘܚܐ ܐܝܟܢܐ ܕܢܦܩܐ ܠܡܦܠܚܗ ܒܗܘܢ ܒܕܘܟܝܬܐ ܓܒܝܢܬܐ. ܐܘ ܒܪܢܫܐ ܕܒܗܘܢ[1] ܡܕܪܕܪ. ܐܘ ܒܡܒܪܝܬܘܬܐ ܕܒܗ̇ ܡܬܚܫܒܐ[2] ܒܟܠܗ. ܗܟܢܐ[3] ܘܐܝܟܢܐ ܕܡܐܠܐ[4] ܠܕܢܚܐ ܐܘ ܠܟܠܕܢܚܐ ܒܡܫܝܚܘܬܗ̇، ܦܓܪܢܝܐ. ܘܐܝܟܢܐ[5] ܕܟܕ ܢܦܩ ܡܬܠܘܝܐ ܕܢܗܘ ܡܛܠ ܕܡܫܡܫܐ ܠܕܘܟܬܗ. ܕܐܬܝܠܕܗ̇، ܕܡܬܦܠܓܐ ܕܢܚܐ ܐܘ ܡܬܚܫܒ ܒܡܛܠܠ[6] ܢܗܘܫܐ. ܘܐܝܟܢܐ ܕܢܗܘܫܐ ܕܡܪܝܡ ܘܠܝܬ[7] ܠܗ ܚܝܠܐ ܠܡܫܡܫܘ.

1 1* ܘܐܦ ܡܬܚܫܒ ܘܠܐ RVLl 2 add. ܠܒ RVLl 3 f. om. F

2 1 ܕܒܗܘܢ RVL 2 ܡܬܚܫܒܬܐ RVL 3 i. add. ܘ RLl 4 ܕܡܐܠܐ RVL; ܕܡܠܐ l 5 ܐܘ ܐܝܟܢܐ RVLl 6 ܡܛܠܠ RVLl 7 ܐܘ ܠܝܬ RVL

## SECTION FOUR
### On the Reasons why Someone Does Wrong Readily
### Seven Theories

ONE.[14] The reasons which lead someone confidently to do wrong are that it is possible to do wrong and not be detected, or if detected be punished (but) lose less than the gain. He who has many kinsmen or powerful and rich friends is not afraid of punishment. Someone may with confidence do wrong among friends, because (a friend) will hold back and seek reconciliation before a dispute, and a friend of a judge among many may do wrong. In (the case of) the weak, the feeble, him who deserves lashes on account of adultery, and so on, many do wrong, and shameful and poor men confidently do wrong because they do not seem (to be) wrongdoers. The fact that wrong-doing may happen quite publicly is advantageous to the wrongdoer, because (people) say, 'If he had not had justification, he would not have done wrong openly'. It is not possible to guard against such wrongdoing, for everyone guards against accustomed things, but does not fear the unaccustomed. Therefore no one guards himself against his friend.

TWO.[15] He who thinks he has no enemy and considers everyone his friend is easily hurt because he does not take precaution. There are also people who do not take precaution in order that others will not take precaution against them. In this way they find an opportunity to do wrong and, because they defend themselves by (this) simple pretence which they put on, they seem innocent. He does very much wrong who is able to conceal his wrongdoing in hidden places, or in ways by which it may be justified, or by an abundance in which his wrongdoing may be concealed. Likewise he who wearies the judge or the adversary with his many objections; he who, because he will lose, defers his sentence because he hopes for avoidance, which is the judge turning aside or being corrupt in annulling the law; and he who pretends that he is poor and has no wealth to lose.

---

[14] **4.4.1** AR 1.12 72a4-28; IS 2.7 (104.14-105.15).
[15] **4.4.2** AR 1.12 72a28-36; IS 2.7 (105.15-106.11).

ܕܬܠܬ. ܐܢܬ ܐܢܐ ܕܫܠܦ ܡܬܘܪܐ ܙܒܢܐ ܘܓܠܝܢܐ ܘܡܓܠܝܢܐ ܣܘܥܪܢܐ
ܐܒܘܪܐ ܘܒܣܝܡܐ ܘܪܚܝܡܐ ܦܠܓ.[1] ܡܚܕܐ ܕܬܚܒܫܬܐ ܕܝܢ ܒܟܘܬܝܐ ܣܘܥܪܢܐ ܐܒܘܪܐ
ܒܟܝܢܐ ܡܓܠܝܢܐ ܘܥܠ ܣܘܥܪܢܐ ܙܒܢܐ ܠܡܫܝܚܐ ܡܟܣܐ. ܘܐܢܬ ܗܪܟܐ
ܐܢܫܐ ܕܡܣܬܟܠܝܢ ܠܗܢܐ. ܒܐܝܟܢ ܡܛܠ ܗܝܡܢܘܬܐ ܠܡܫܝܚܘܬܐ ܒܡܠܬܐ
ܒܟܝܢܘܬܐ ܡܫܠܝܢ. ܘܕܗܠܝܢ ܚܠܬܝܐ ܕܬܚܒܫܬܗܘܢ ܘܡܢܝܢܝܢ. ܘܦܠܘܓܐ
ܕܠܐ[2] ܡܬܬܟܒ ܕܠܐ ܕܫܠܐ ܡܡܠܠ. ܘܡܟܝܠ ܘܐܝܟܐ ܕܦܠܓܝܢܐ ܠܘܬ
ܘܠܡܫܐ ܚܕܐ ܠܗ. ܐܝܟܢܐ ܕܫܠܦ ܐܒܐ ܦܠܝܠܐ ܐܘ ܐܝܟܢܐ ܐܒܗ̈ܬܐ
ܦܠܚܐ ܐܘ ܐܡܗ̈ܬܐ ܢܦܠܘܠ ܐܚܪ. ܐܝܟ ܕܐܡܪ ܐܫܥܝܐ. ܡܡܠܠ ܕܝܢ
ܘܐܢܫܐ ܕܦܫܝܩ ܒܠܥܘܗܝ ܣܗܘܪܐ ܘܡܢܝܢܐ. ܘܐܢܬ ܐܢܫܐ ܕܦܫܝܩ ܠܗ
ܒܠܝܐ ܕܢܦܩ ܠܗ ܡܢ ܦܪܘܩ *ܐܘ ܥܢܝܕܐ.[3] ܡܢܐ ܕܠܐ ܢܣܒ ܡܡܘܢܐ. ܕܠܒܠܝܬ
ܬܘܒ ܡܡܠܠ ܡܢ ܕܒܢܝܢܐ ܐܬܪܐ ܘܠܥܒܕܐ ܐܬܚܙܝ.. ܘܒܠܗܕܐ ܦܪܘܬܐ[4]
ܕܢܗܘ ܦܪܝܐ[5] ܠܒܢܝܐܬ[6] ܗܘܐ ܒܐܓܘܢܐ.

ܕܐܘܪܚܐ. ܦܫܝܩܐܝܬ ܕܝܢ ܡܡܠܠ ܐܢܐ ܕܡܬܓܠܝܢ ܠܟܘܢ ܐܘܪܚܐ ܕܟܝܢ.
ܒܪܐ ܘܓܒܝܐ ܘܒܡܓܠܝܢܐ[1] ܐܡܠܠ. ܐܘ ܒܪ ܐܘܪܚ ܡܢ ܒܢܝܐ ܐܘ ܒܢܝܐ
ܦܪ.. ܐܘ ܡܬܠܒܢܐ ܡܢ ܒܡܠܐ ܒܪ[2] ܐܡܪ. ܠܒܢܝܐ ܒܗ ܡܡܠܠ ܗܘܝܬ ܒܪ ܠܐ
ܚܫܘ ܐܢܐ ܕܐܡܠܠ. ܘܗܝ ܚܫܝܫܘܬܐ ܐܘ ܒܐܝܫܘܬܐ ܗܘܝܐ ܠܡܣܟܢܐ ܐܘ
ܒܝܫܘܬܐ ܠܚܬܝܪܐ. ܘܡܬܝܪܐ ܕܒܡܠܐ ܡܓܠܝܢ ܠܐ ܡܬܒܥܝܢ ܐܠܐ
ܡܬܓܢܝܐ. ܡܬܬܡܠܠ ܕܝܢ ܙܒܢ[3] ܒܝܫܐ ܕܠܝܬ ܠܗ ܐܪܥܐ. ܘܐܢܫܐ ܕܪܫܐ ܗܘ ܘܗ̇
ܡܢ ܕܠܒܡܠܐ ܡܬܒܥܝܢ ܠܘܬ ܫܪܘܬܐ ܐܘ ܦܘܫܩܐ. ܘܐܢܫܐ ܕܪܚܡ
ܘܡܣܪܐܝܬ ܡܬܦܪܥ. ܘܠܦܪܥܗ ܠܐ ܡܚܝܡ. ܐܘ ܐܝܬܘܗܝ ܡܢ ܡܫܟܚܐ
ܕܒܠ ܡܬܪܐ ܠܐ ܡܬܚܪܝܢ. ܐܝܟ ܦܪܒܘܢܝܐ[4] ܕܒܢܘܪܗܘܢ ܡܬܠܚܡܝܢ.
ܐܦ ܓܒܪ ܘܡܗܝܡܢܐ[5] ܒܝܢܐ ܘܡܫܝܕܐ ܠܐ ܢܐܬܐ ܡܬܓܠܓܠ. ܐܝܟ ܕܐܡܪ
ܡܬܠܐ ܕܐܒܢܐ[6] ܠܟܝ *ܕܠܗܘܢ ܠܐ[7] ܓܠܓܠ[8] ܓܠܓܠܝܢ. *ܡܗܝܡܢܐ ܘܐܢܫܐ[9]
ܕܣܓܝ[10] ܐܬܓܠܓܠ ܘܐܬܬܕܝܫ ܐܘ ܢܫܦܪ ܘܡܪܦܝ ܘܫܦܝܪ. ܐܘ ܐܫܟܚ ܗܘ
*ܐܘ ܐܡܗ̈ܘܗܝ, ܐܘ ܐܚܘ̈ܗܝ,[11] ܘܪܚܡܘܗܝ.. ܗܠܝܢ ܓܒܪ ܡܢ ܕܒܢ̈ܝܐ[12] ܒܪܫܝܢ
ܘܡܢ ܒܪ̈ܝܬܐ ܬܘܒ[13] ܡܠܝܢ.

---

3 [1] ܓܒܠ RVLl [2] i. om. RVL [3*] ܘܥܢ̈ܝܕܐ RVLl [4] ܦܪܘܬܐ F [5] pl. RVL [6] ܠܒܢܝܐ RL; ܠܒ̈ܢܝܐ Vl

4 [1] ܐܘ ܒܡܓܠܝܢܐ RVLl [2] ܒܪ RVLl [3] om. RVLl [4] sg. RVL [5] om. RVLl [6] sg. RVLl [7*] ܕܠܐ RVL [8] add. ܠܗܘܢ RVL [9*] ܗܘܐ ܐܘ ܐܢܫܐ RVLl [10] add. ܕܠܐ RVL [11*] ܘܐܡܗ̈ܘܗܝ, ܘܐܚܘ̈ܗܝ, RVLl [12] sg. RVL [13] om. RVL

THREE.[16] Someone may for a large, evident, and present profit endure a small, unclear, and remote penalty, while he who is weak of mind is pleased with an early small profit and scorns a later large penalty. There are also people here who act contrary to this, namely, endure early pain for later pleasure; such (are) strong of mind and prudent. A tyrant, who is not punished, does wrong without fear, and similarly he for whom injustice leads as far as praise, as when a man kills many fathers and mothers (in revenge) for (his own) slain father or mother, as Zeno said. He for whom the penalty is easy does wrong, and he who escapes, and there are people for whom wrongdoing is easy to whom (only) disgrace attaches or torments, when money is not lost. He who is brought up with torments and is accustomed to lashes commits wrong readily, and therefore a warrior with experience of battle boldly sticks to the fight.

FOUR.[17] He readily does wrong who is prepared to make the defence that he did wrong by accident or chance, or by necessity, or when overcome strayed on account of nature or habit, or distances himself from wrongdoing by saying, 'Why would I have done wrong when I have no need to do wrong?' Need arises through necessity for the poor or through greed for the rich. A rich man who becomes prosperous through wrongdoing is not praised but vituperated, while a shameful man who has no defender suffers much wrong. He who possesses that which is desired by a wrongdoer for surfeit or pleasure (may also suffer wrong), and he who is sedate and later on is punished, and (he who) does not distress his neighbour, or is from peaceable people who do not strive for advantages, like the Carthaginians, who were financially successful. For the modest trusting (person), and the gentle uncontentious (one), is cheated; as the proverb said, 'Men cheat whoever does not cheat them'. Similarly he (suffers wrong) who has been greatly cheated and rejected, or envied, scorned, or disdained, or caused suffering—he or his ancestors, brothers, or friends; for these men shun the judges and are fearful of (being declared) blameworthy.

---

[16] **4.4.3** AR 1.12 72a36-b16; IS 2.7 (106.9-107.6).
[17] **4.4.4** AR 1.12 72b16-73a4; IS 2.7 (107.6-108.15).

ܕܢܣܒ. ܪܕܝܐ ܕܡܗܝܡܢܐ ܒܢܝܫܗ ܫܦܝܐ ܠܡܬܬܒܥܘ. ܘܗܝ ܡܗܝܡܢܘܬܐ ܐܢ ܒܚܝܪܐ ܒܚܝܪ ܡܟܝܠܐ. ܘܐܢ ܪܒܐ ܪܒܬ ܡܟܐܟܐ. ܡܢ ܒܠܐܒ̈ܟܐ ܕܝܢ ܐܦ ܪܒܐ ܠܐ ܡܚܝܡܐ. ܘܡܐܡܢܘܬܐ ܘܦܬܟܐ ܘܒܢܝ̈ܢܐ. *ܡܒܠܝܢ ܐܢܫܐ[1] ܒܢ̈ܫܐ ܠܘ ܡܛܠ ܡܘܬܪܐ ܐܠܐ ܡܛܠ[2] ܚܝܐܘܬܐ. ܒܗ̇ ܕܦܝܣܐܘܬ ܡܬܪܥܝܢ[3] ܘܒܚܘܪ̈ܬܐ ܡܬܬܦܩܝܢ. ܚܝܐܐ ܓܒܪ[4] ܡܬܓܒܪܢܘܬ ܡܢ ܕܒܓܠ ܙܟܐ. ܘܒܠܗܕܐ ܫ̈ܠܝܐ ܒܕܘܒܐ[5] ܡܬܓܪܝܢ. ܘܐܝܟܢܐ ܕܡܫܝܒ ܒܗܠܝܢ ܘܒܟܐ ܕܡܛܝ ܡܬܟܒܪ. ܡܛܝ ܥܬܝܕ. ܚܝܐܐ ܕܝܢ ܘܗ̇ܝ ܕܒܫܒܪ̈ ܒܢ̈ܫܬܐ ܢܒܘܠ ܐܝܟ. ܘܒܗܘܢ ܕܡܒܕܪܝܢ ܠܗܘܢ ܘܢܕܝܢ ܒܗܘܢ ܘܡܬܕܒܪܝܢ ܒܒܕ̈ܝܠܐ ܒܒܕ̈ܝܢܗܘܢ. ܚܝܐܐ ܗܘܐ ܘܠܠܗܒܘܬ ܢܚܝܫ̈ܬܐ. ܒܪ ܒܫܘܡܫܗܘܢ ܡܬܕܒܪܝܢ ܠܠܗܝ̈ܒܘܢ ܘܡܬܒܠܝܢ ܒܠ ܢܫܘܬܗܘܢ ܘܠܐ ܡܛܠܝܢ ܡܢ ܡܬܢܘܡܢܘܬܗܘܢ. ܘܠܐܝܠܝܢ[6] ܕܦܪܩ ܡܒܠ ܕܠܐ ܙܘܥܪ ܓܠܠ ܓܠܡܟܐ. ܐܡܟܢܐ ܕܠܕܝܘܢ[7] ܒܒܪ ܡܐܠܝܦܘܣ[8] ܒܪ ܐܡܪ. ܕܠܐ ܡܢ ܡܛܠܐ ܕܡܒܠܝܐ ܟܠܐ ܗܘܐ. ܘܗܘܐ ܗ̇ܘܐ ܘܒܒܪ.

ܕܢܬܠ. ܠܡܒܠܘ ܒܗܘܢ ܕܡܬܕܝܢ ܕܢܒܠܘܢ ܠܗ ܒܡܠܐ ܗܘ.[1] ܐܝܟ ܕܐܡܪ ܐܢܫܘܢ ܬܗܓܓܝܐ ܕܙܕܩ ܕܢܓܠܘܢ ܒܗܢ ܐܝܟ ܐܡܒܢܐ ܕܢܬܡܟܐ ܠܡܫܒ ܙܕܩܐ ܘܬܪܢܝܬܐ ܩܕܝܫܘܬܐ ܠܡܒܒܪ. ܘܐܝܠܝܢ ܬܘܒ ܕܡܬܕܝܢ ܠܡܬܓܠܓܠܘ ܕܠܟܐܢܘܬ ܡܬܓܠܓܠܝܢ. ܐܝܟ ܗܢܘܢ ܕܒܓܕܪ̈ܬܐ ܕܕܡܓܠܘܝܐ ܒܪ ܐܕܪܒ ܕܒܠܕܒܒܐ ܪܢܫܐ ܒܠܛܝ ܕܢܐܘܠ ܒܠܝܗܘܢ ܐܓܠܒܗ[2] ܠܡܬܠ ܠܗ ܡܒܐܬܐ. ܘܒܪ ܓܒ ܡܚܝܢ ܗܘܘ ܕܢܬܚܪܘܢ. ܠܗ̇ ܕܦܝܣܐܘܬ ܡܬܝܣܬܐ ܓܒܗ. ܐܠܐ ܡܟܐ ܕܒܗܕܐ ܥܒܕ̈ܝܗܘܢ ܐܓܪܒܘ. ܡܢܩ ܕܐܣܢܐ ܢܒܘܠ ܢܒܦܪ ܐܢܘܢ. ܗܢܘܢ ܒܠܗ ܘܥܒܕ ܐܢܘܢ[3] ܒܪ ܐܡܪܝܢ. ܕܠܐ ܡܛܝ ܡܢ ܕܠܝܘܒ̈ܢܐ ܙܕܩܐ ܒܬܟܘܢ.

ܕܢܥܒܕ. ܗ̇ܘܐ[1] ܕܝܢ ܦܝܣܐ ܒܡܠܐ ܒܥܪ̈ܒܝܢܐ[2] ܕܡܬܓܥܝܢ ܘܒܗܠܝܢ ܕܡܫܒܪܐ ܕܥܒܒܝܢܐ ܐܝܬ ܒܗܘܢ ܡܛܠ ܕܒܘܪܬܗܘܢ ܐܘ ܓܠܝܠܘܬܗܘܢ ܒܒܓܠ. ܐܝܟ ܦܠܓ̈ܐ. ܐܘ ܥܓܠܝܢܗܘܢ[3] ܒܐܣܡܒܐ ܘܓܒܘܢܐ. ܐܝܟ ܦܐܪܐ ܙ̈ܢܝܐ. ܐܘ ܒܒܪܓܠܐ. *ܐܝܟ ܩܛܒܪܢܐ. ܘܕܐܝܠܝܢ ܕܡܢܐ ܗܘܐ ܒܒܠܐ ܐܒܪܬܗܘܢ.[4] ܐܡܒܢܐ ܕܒܪ ܢܬܒܫܘܢ ܐܢܕܪܗܘܢ. ܠܐ ܢܬܦܪܥܘܢ ܡܢ ܗܠܝܢ ܕܠܗ ܘܐܝܟ[5] ܠܐ ܗܢܝܣܐ ܡܚܝܢ ܠܗ. ܘܒܐܝܠܝܢ ܕܒܗܬܝܢ ܗܢܘܢ[6] ܕܡܬܓܠܓܠܝܢ ܡܢ ܗ̇ܘ ܕܠܒܢ̈ܝܐ ܝܒܠܘܢ ܐܢܘܢ ܒܪ[7] ܩܪܬܗܘܢ ܢܐܪܐ ܠܗܘܢ ܫܐܪܝܢ. ܐܝܟ ܗܢܘܢ ܕܒܥܝܢܗܘܢ ܘܒܝܬܗܘܢ ܘܐܣܝܘܬܗܘܢ ܗ̇ܘܐ ܒܒܠܐ.

---

5 [1*] ܘܐܦ̈ܪܐ F [2] om. RVL [3] ܡܬܪܥܝܢ RVLl [4] ܕܝܢ RVL [5] ܒܕܘܒܐ RVLl [6] ܘܠܐ RVL [7] scripsi; ܕܠܕܝܘܢ codd. [8] ܡܐܠܝܦܘܣ RVL

6 [1] ܗ̱ܘ RVLl [2] ܐܓܠܒܗ F [3] ܗܢܘܢ RVLl

7 [1] ܗܘܝܐ RVL [2] ܒܥܪ̈ܒܝܐ F [3] pl. RVLl [4*] om. F [5] i. om. F [6] i. add. ܕ RVLl [7] ܒܪ RVLl

FIVE.[18] A friend who neglects his friend deserves to suffer wrong; if the neglect is minor, the offence is minor, if greater, it causes greater pain. (Neglect) by enemies, on the other hand, and by strangers, labourers, and rustics, even if great, is not painful. Evil men do wrong not for profit but for pleasure. Because they are easily blamed and are agitated by small things, the provocation of him who angers quickly is pleasurable. Children therefore provoke a madman, and if he endures them and rages all the more, the more boisterous they become. It is also pleasurable for someone to do wrong on evildoers, and on those who assist them and rejoice through them and look with admiration on their blameworthy deeds. Also pleasurable is doing injustice to the wise, because those being unjust to them look with wonder on their constancy, depend upon their gentleness, and do not fear their vengeance. One may also commit injustice without warning on him whom one has formerly accused, as Callippus did to Dion, saying, 'The fear of impeachment restrained me, but behold, it has come and gone'.

SIX.[19] To do wrong against those who are going to do wrong is not a wrongdoing. As Jason the Thessalian said, sometimes it is right to do what is unjust in order to be able to grasp the right and do many upright things. And those who are prepared to suffer injustice do easily suffer injustice, like those on the islands of Demogelone who, realising that a distant enemy was going to invade them, got ready to pay tribute to it. Although they were able to resist, they opted for that which could easily be remedied, but when their neighbours realised this, before anyone else could wrongly plunder them they came in and seized them, saying, 'Your booty should be ours rather than foreigners'.'

SEVEN.[20] Easy wrongdoing occurs with trifles which may be concealed and with those for which there is a supposition of pardon on account of their triviality or quick consumption, such as confectionery, or their variation in form and colour, like fresh fruit, or by mixing, like drugs. Also (with) such which are similar to what the wrongdoer (already) possesses, so that when they are discovered on

---

[18] **4.4.5** AR 1.12 73a4-21; IS 2.7 (108.15-109.16).
[19] **4.4.6** AR 1.12 73a21-27; IS 2.7 (109.16-110.8).
[20] **4.4.7** AR 1.12 73a27-37; IS 2.7 (110.8-14).

ܦܣܘܩܐ ܚܕܥܣܪܐ

ܡܛܠ ܪܒܘܬ ܣܟܠܘܬܐ[1] ܘܝܩܝܪܘܬܗ̇[2] ܠܘܬ ܢܡܘܣܐ[3]

ܬܐܘܪܐܡ ܬܡܝܢܝܐ

ܡܕܡܝܢܘܬܐ. ܛܠܘܡܝܐ ܡܢ ܓܝܪ ܐܘ ܥܒܪ ܢܡܘܣܐ ܠܐ ܟܬܝܒܐ ܗ̇ܘܐ ܐܘ ܥܒܪ ܢܡܘܣܐ ܟܬܝܒܐ. ܘܢܡܘܣܐ ܠܐ ܟܬܝܒܐ ܓܘܢܐ ܗܘ. ܒܗ̇، ܕܟܝܢܐ ܗܘ ܫܘܡܗܘ ܘܕܠܐ ܛܘܒ، ܒܠܒܝ ܦܩܡ ܠܗ. ܐܝܟ ܕܐܡܪܬ ܐܢܛܝܓܘܢ ܠܦܘܠܘܢܝܩܣ[1] ܕܢܡܘܣܐ ܟܝܢܐ ܘܠܐ ܡܬܟܬܒܢܐ ܚܒܝܫ ܠܦܘܠܘܢܝܩܣ. ܗ̇ܘ ܕܠܘ ܒܠܚܘܕ ܐܬܡܠܝ[2] ܐܠܐ ܐܦ ܗܫܐ ܘܒܐܡܝܢܘ ܡܬܘܡܐܝܬ ܐܝܬܘܗܝ، ܘܢܡܘܣܐ ܟܬܝܒܐ ܕܝܠܝܐ ܗܘ ܘܒܐܢܫܝ̈ܢܝܐ ܠܘܬ ܟܠܚܕ ܚܕ ܡܬܝܕܥ. ܐܝܟ ܕܐܡܦܕܘܩܠܝܣ ܐܡܪ. ܠܐ ܠܡ ܢܩܛܘܠ ܠܡܢܦܫ̈ܐ. ܗܐ ܓܝܪ ܠܐܢ̈ܫܝܢ ܡܢ ܙܕܩܐ ܗܘ. ܠܐܢ̈ܫܝܢ ܕܝܢ ܠܘ ܙܕܩܐ. ܘܗܪܟܐ ܬܘܒ ܬܫܥܝܬܐ ܒܬܫܥܝܬܐ ܕܠܐ ܡܬܒܝ̈ܢ ܒܐܘܟܠܝܢ ܡܢܝܬܐ ܙܒܢ. ܐܝܟ ܢܡܘܣܐ ܗܘ ܕܟܠ ܒܢ: ܐܘܕܘܗܡܘܕܘܢ ܡܛܠ ܐܬܪܐ. ܐܡܝܢܐ ܕܗܠܝܢ ܒܘܬ ܡܛܠ ܕܪܝܫܗ̇[3] ܕܐܘܠܨ. ܘܐܝܟ ܕܒܡܟܬܒܢܘܬܐ ܕܡܣܢܝܣ ܐܡܪ ܐܠܩܝܕܡܐܘܣ[4] ܠܘܬ ܐܝܠܝܢ ܕܐܬܚܪܪ.

ܕܬܪ̈ܬܝܢ. ܟܠ ܛܠܘܡܝܐ ܐܘ ܠܘܬ ܚܕ ܗܘ. ܐܝܟ ܐܢܫܐ ܕܡܚܝܐ ܠܚܕ: ܘܓܐܪ ܒܚܕܐ. ܐܘ ܠܘܬ ܓܘܐ. ܐܝܟ ܐܢܫܐ ܕܥܪܩ ܡܢ ܦܠܚܐ ܕܦܘܠܚܢܐ[1] ܘܠܐ ܡܫܬܘܬܦ ܒܐܣܛܪܛܝܐ. ܘܛܠܘܡܝܘܬܐ[2] ܐܝܬܝܗ̇ ܕܬܫܘܗܣ ܕܗܘܝܐ ܠܛܠܘܡܝܐ ܡܢ ܨܒܝܢ ܛܠܘܡܝܐ. ܘܐܢܫܐ ܕܢܦܩ ܪܘܚܐ ܐܘ ܠܐ ܡܗܕܪܐ ܒܗܠܝܢ ܕܠܒܢܐ ܐܬܟܬܒ ܡܛܠܠܬܗ. ܐܘ ܡܗܕܪܐ ܕܗܦܟ ܒܢܘܩ ܠܗ ܒܝܢܐ ܕܛܠܘܡܝܘܬܐ.[3] ܐܝܟܢܐ ܕܡܘܕܐ ܕܢܣܒ ܐܠܐ ܠܐ ܓܢܒ. ܐܘ[4] ܓܢܒ ܐܠܐ ܠܐ ܚܛܝ *ܒܝܬ ܡܩܕܫܐ ܒܪ. ܠܐ ܓܢܒ ܐܢ ܡܢ[5] ܗܝܟܠܗ ܕܐܠܗܐ ܢܣܒ. ܘܐܬܚܒܝ[6] ܐܠܐ ܠܐ ܙܢܝ. ܘܙܢܝ ܐܠܐ ܒܫܬܪܐ ܘܠܐ ܒܣܢܝܩܘܬܐ. ܘܐܫܬܘܕܝ: ܠܡܠܕܟܢܐ ܒܪܡ[7] ܠܐ ܠܡܩܠܝܘ ܠܗ ܣܡܟܐ ܐܠܐ ܠܡܬܒܠܘܬܗ. ܘܠܝܬ ܓܝܪ ܡܕܝ̈ܢ[8] *ܠܡܠܟܐ. ܒܪ[9] ܙܟ ܡܠܟܐ ܐܝܟ ܓܢܒܘܬܐ ܘܡܓܒܪܢܘܬܐ ܘܙܢܘܬܐ ܘܣܦܪ ܠܗ ܒܫܬܗܘܢ ܒܥܢܝܢ.[10] ܐܠܐ ܒܗ̇، ܕܒܣܦܣܝܪܐ ܘܡܪܘܛܘܢܘܬܐ[11] ܘܡܕܒܪܢܘܬܐ ܘܒܠܐ ܡܫܬܪܝܢ ܡܬܛܠܡܝܢ.

Titulus [1] ܣܘܟܠܘܬܐ RVLl [2] f. ܗ RVLl [3] pl. RVLl

1 [1] scripsi; ܠܦܘܠܘܢܝܩܘܣ F; ܠܦܘܠܘܢܝܩܣ RVLl [2] i. add. ܕ RVL [3] f. ܗ RVLl [4] ܠܩܝܕܡܐܘܣ F

2 [1] om. RVL [2] ܘܛܠܘܡܝܘܬܐ F [3] pl. RVLl [4] om. RVLl [5*] om. RVL [6] ܘܐܬܚܒܝ R [7] ܐܠܐ RVLl [8] sg. RVL [9*] ܒܪ ܐܠܗܐ F [10] om. RVLl [11] scripsi (?); ܘܡܪܘܛܢܘܬܐ codd.

him, they are not separable from his own things and appear (to belong) to him as if he (had had) no need (to steal them); and with things which those who are wronged are ashamed to reveal to judges, because their concealment is preferable to them, like those (who are) free on whose wives, daughters, or sisters a wrongdoing occurs.

## SECTION FIVE
## On the Magnitude of Wrongdoing and its Triviality According to the Law
## Eight Theories

ONE.[21] Injustice occurs either through transgression of the unwritten law, or through transgression of the written law. The unwritten law is common, because nature is its author, and without contract everyone divines it. As Antigone said to Sophocles, 'The natural and unspoken law buried Polyneices, which not only has been fulfilled, but also now and for eternity exists perpetually.' The written law is particular and specifically defined with every individual. As Empedocles said, 'Let us not kill living beings, for behold, for some it is just, but for others not just'. Here again our master produces old paradigms which are not understood in our time, like the universal law by Eudumedon about the ether, that is, about the propagation of light, and as Alcidamas said in the book of Messene about the things which he defined.

TWO.[22] Every injustice is either to an individual, as when one strikes an individual or commits adultery against an individual (woman), or to the community, as when one flees from the line of battle and does not participate in military service. Being wronged is a state which applies to him who is wronged by the will of a wrongdoer. A defendant may either not confess to what is written about him in the indictment, or confess that he did (it) but not in the manner of a wrongdoing. For example, he may confess that he took (something) but did not steal ; or stole (something) but did not commit sacrilege against a sanctuary, because he did not know if he took

[21] **4.5.1** AR 1.13 73b1-18; IS 2.8 (111.4-6).
[22] **4.5.2** AR 1.13 73b18-29; 39-74a18; IS 2.8 (111.6-112.5).

ܕܬܠܬ. ܒܐܝܢܘܬܐ ܘܒܡܠܐ ܒܢܡܘܣܐ ܠܐ ܥܠܡܝܐ ܠܦܘܬ ܦܘܪܥܢܐ ܕܡܬܘܪܬܘܬܐ ܘܒܫܝܚܘܬܐ ܬܪܝܢܝܬ ܡܬܦܪܫܝܢ. ܒܗ̇، ܕܐܘ ܡܢ ܒܢܝܢܫܐ ܥ̈ܒܕܐ ܠܡܘܠܫܢܐ ܐܘ ܠܫܡܘܕܐ ܐܬܡܠܗܘܢ. ܐܝܟ ܐܡܬܐ ܕܐܡܪ ܦܘܠܐ ܠܡܒܕܒܕ: ܥܦܝܪ ܠܟܝ ܕܟܬܒ: ܥܦܝܪ. ܐܢ ܟܬܒ: ܡܚܝܐ ܡܬܩܠܐ. ܘܐܠܐ ܡܬܚܫܒ.. ܐܘ[1] ܡܢ ܒܢܝܢܫܐ ܥ̈ܒܕܐ ܠܬܘܪܬܐ ܐܘ ܠܫܝܛܘܬܐ. ܐܝܟ ܐܡܬܐ ܕܐܡܪ ܦܘܠܐ ܠܡܒܕܒܕܘ ܠܐܢܫܐ ܒܠܗܘܢ. ܐܢ ܟܬܒ: ܡܚܝܐ ܡܬܬܥܝܩ.[2] ܘܐܠܐ[3] ܡܬܬܥܝܩ. ܘܐܦ ܒܐܝܢܘܬܐ ܩ̈ܕܡܝܬܐ ܒܢܡܘܣܐ ܥܠܡܝܐ ܠܐ ܡܬܦܪܫܝܢ. ܐܝܟ ܒܡܫܝܚܘܬܐ ܕܒܢܡܘܣܐ ܥܠܡܝܐ ܦܫܝܛܐܝܬ ܒܐܝܢܘܬܐ ܡܬܚܫܒܐ. ܘܒܢܡܘܣܐ ܠܐ[4] ܥܠܡܝܐ ܡܬܦܠܓܐ ܡܦܪܫܐܝܬ. ܗܘ̣ ܠܐ ܡܬܚܫܒܢܘܬܐ ܒܢܡܘܣܐ ܥܠܡܝܐ ܒܝܕ ܬܪ̈ܬܝܢ ܓܒ̈ܐ. ܚܕܐ ܡܢ ܠܐ ܫܩܘܠܬ ܫܘܩܠܐ ܠܗ̇، ܕܐܝܟ ܕܕܝܢܐ ܢܦܪܥ ܘܢܬܚܝܒ.[5] ܐܚܪܬܐ ܕܝܢ ܠܐ ܡܫܡܠܝܘܬܐ ܕܥ̈ܒܕܐ ܡܬܠܐ ܕܠܐ ܗܘܦ ܡܫܬܪܒܝܢ[6] ܘܠܡܬܚܫܒܘ ܠܐ ܡܚܝܒܝܢ. ܘܒܠܗܕܐ ܡܢܝܢܐ ܒܠܝܢܐ ܒܠܝܫܘ: ܡܥܠܡ ܗܐܟ ܕܢܡܘܣܐ ܥܠܡܝܐ. ܘܕܝ̈ܢܐ ܠܦܘܬ *ܒܢܡܘܣܐ ܠܐ ܥܠܡܝܐ[7] ܡܦܪܫܝܢ ܐܢܘܢ. ܐܝܟܢܐ ܕܐܡܪ. ܡܢ ܕܒܦܘܪܥܢܐ ܦܠܠ ܒܦܘܪܥܢܐ ܡܬܦܠܠ. ܘܠܐ ܢܬܚܫܒ ܕܢܦܪܥ[8] ܒܠܗܘܢ *ܐܦ ܡܠܠܐ[9] ܐܕ̈ܢܐ ܐܘܪ̈ܚܢܝܬܐ[10] ܦܬܓܡܐ ܐܝܟܐ ܠܟܠܗܘܢ ܐܫܟܚܢܘܬ ܡܠܠܐ ܘܐܬܝܢܐ ܐܚܪ̈ܢܐ. ܕܟܬܒ ܒܠܒܐ ܘܠܐ ܡܬܚܫܒ.

ܕܐܪܒܥ. ܐܝܬ ܐܚܪܢ، ܕܠܢܡܘܣܐ ܥܠܡܝܐ *ܒܢܡܘܣܐ ܠܐ ܥܠܡܝܐ ܥܒܪ. ܐܒܕܐ ܕܢܡܘܣܐ ܥܠܡܝܐ[1] ܕܐܪ̈ܥܝܢ ܒܠܬ̈ܘܡܐ ܦܦܪ: ܗܘܐ ܕܟܝ ܕܒܠܝܦ ܒܐܘܬܐ ܒܡܥܒܕܗ. ܐܝܟܢܐ ܕܢܦܩ ܐܢܫ ܘܠܐ ܢܦܩܝܢ ܣܝܡܗ̇[2] ܠܥܠܡܗ.[3] ܢܬܚܝܒ ܘܢܬܕܪܐ. *ܘܐܝܟ ܒܢܡܘܣܐ ܠܐ ܥܠܡܝܐ ܠܐ ܡܬܚܝܒ.[4] ܘܐܝܬ ܐܚܪܢܐ ܕܢܡܘܣܐ ܠܐ ܥܠܡܝܐ ܒܢܡܘܣܐ ܥܠܡܝܐ ܥܒܪ. ܐܝܟ ܗ̇، ܕܠܦܘ̈ܕܐ ܘܒܘܪܐ ܘܣܘܪܚܢܐ ܒܝ̈ܕܪܐ. ܘܫܘܠܛܢܐ ܕܡܢ ܛܠܒܝܢ ܘܠܐ ܡܢ ܥܘܕܠܐ[5] ܘܒܡܬܚܝܒܘܬܐ ܘܒܝܫܘܬܐ ܒܪܝܢ ܥܘܒܕܢܐ ܢܒܚ. ܘܒܗ ܠܠܘ̈ܕܐ ܕܒܡܐܟܠܬܐ[6] ܡܫܟܚܝܢ ܒܡܫܡܫܢܘܬܐ ܢܬܚܝܒ ܒܢܡܘܣܐ ܒܝܢܝܐ ܦܦܪ.. ܘܒܠܒܘܬܐ ܚܕ ܕܕܝܢܐ ܟܝܢ: ܐܬܝܢ ܘܕܘܒܪܐ ܕܕܝܢܐ ܟܝܢ: ܐܚܪ̈ܢܐ[7] ܠܟܘܫܡ ܐܡܪܐ ܕܒܠܒܐ ܒܢܡܘܣܐ ܥܠܡܝܐ ܡܠܝܠ.

3 [1] ܐܢ RVLl [2] ܡܬܬܥܝܩ F [3] add. ܠܐ F [4] om. F [5] ܡܬܚܝܒ RVL [6] ܡܫܬܪܒܝܢ RVL [7*] pl. F [8] ܦܪܥ RVL [9*] om. F [10] ܐܘܪ̈ܚܢܝܢ RVL; ܐܘܪ̈ܚܢܢ l

4 [1*] om. RVL [2] f. ܗ RVLl [3] ܠܥܠܡܗ̇ F [4*] om. RVLl [5] ܕܠܐ RVLl [6] ܕܒܡܐܟ̈ܠܬܐ F [7] sg. RVLl

(it) from the temple of God; or had a sexual relation but did not commit adultery; or committed adultery but in secret and not openly; or talked with an enemy, however not to deliver to him the fortress, but to entice him (into a trap). These things diminish the wrongdoing, because the sorts of wrongdoing like theft, outrage, adultery, and the like are not evil by themselves, but do harm because they are done in cheating, plucking, extorting, and deceiving (others).

THREE.[23] In the unwritten law justice and wrongdoing, corresponding to the distinction of virtue and vice, are distinguished in two ways, because they are either from the genus deserving praise or dishonour—like that which says one ought to act well to him who acts well; if one so acts one should be praised, if not, reviled—or from the genus deserving honour or contempt—like that which says one ought to help all friends; if one so acts one should be honoured, if not, despised. The many kinds of justice are not distinguished in the written law, like leniency, which in the written law is simply reckoned justice, but in the unwritten law is separate. That lack of definition in the written law occurs through two (circumstances): either the inability of the legislator properly to separate and distinguish it, or the limitlessness of the particular matters which branch out endlessly and cannot be defined. The legislator of the written law therefore only hands down universal rules, and judges articulate them in accordance with the unwritten law. As it says, he who kills by iron should be put to death by iron, but it is not possible to articulate all ways of killing, (all) species of iron instruments, the manner of killing (to be used) with all of them, and other diverse matters, for the world would end while they were still being enumerated.

FOUR.[24] There are times when the unwritten law dismisses the written law, such as the written law which ordered some ancient people that if anyone who wore a ring on his finger raised his hand without turning its back towards himself, he was guilty and should be punished, but according to the unwritten law he is not guilty. Sometimes the written law dismisses the unwritten law, as with small

[23] **4.5.3** AR 1.13 74a18-33; IS 2.8 (112.5-113.10).
[24] **4.5.4** AR 1.13 74a33-b9; IS 2.8 (113.10-114.12).

ܕܢܚܪ. ܠܡܫܠ ܐܝܟܐ ܕܫܒܠ ܬܪܝܢ ܦܪ̈ܘܫܝܢ[1] ܡܢܗܝܢ. ܐܝܟܐ ܕܢܦܩ ܙܘܥܐ
ܘܐܝܟܐ ܕܫܐܠ ܫܘܒܩܢܐ. ܘܠܡܦܩ ܒܪܘܚܐ ܒܗ: ܐܝܟ ܚܝܠܐ ܗܒܪܝܢ.
ܠܫܘܒܩܢܐ[2] ܢܫܒܘܪ. ܒܗ: ܐܡܪܝܢ ܕܐܝܟܐ ܕܬܒܥ ܫܘܒܩܢܐ ܒܡܫܡܫܢܘܬܐ ܬܒܥ
*ܐܘ ܠܡܫܡܫܢܘܬܐ.[3] ܒܡܫܡܫܢܘܬܐ ܗ̇ܝ ܕܠܐ ܢܬܓܠܐ. ܕܢܬܬܢܚܘܢ[4] ܡܛܠ ܚܘܠܗ.
ܠܡܫܡܫܢܘܬܐ ܕܝܢ ܕܠܐ ܐܝܟ ܕܐܢܫܐ ܢܬܬܚܣܪ. ܘܒܬܫܡܫܬ ܫܘܒܩܢܐ
ܕܐܝܟ ܗܠܝܢ ܦܐܐ ܠܡܐܡܪ. ܕܒܫܡܫܘܬܐ ܗ̇ܝ ܗ̇ܝ, ܗ̇ܝ, ܫܘܒܩܢܐ. ܘܦܠ̈ܓܐ
ܗ̈ܝ ܠܐ ܗܘܐ[5] ܒܢܝܚܘܬܐ ܕܫܐܩ ܢܚܘܬܐ ܣܢܝܢ ܐܠܐ ܒܟܒܪ̈ܘܗܝ,
ܘܒܫܡܫܘܬܗ ܘܡܪܚܡܢܘܬܗ. ܘܠܐ ܠܦܘܬ ܚܒܪܐ ܕܡܫܡܠܝܐ ܐܠܐ ܠܦܘܬ
ܬܪܒܝܬܗ ܕܝܠܝ ܠܗ. ܘܠܐ ܒܫܡܠܝܘܬܗ ܐܠܐ ܒܡܬܬܢܝܚܘܬܗ ܡܢܗܝܢ.

ܕܢܚܬ. ܢܬܚܫܚ ܕܝܢ ܘܒܕܐܝܟ ܗܠܝܢ ܦܬܓ̈ܡܐ ܡܫܡܠܝܐ ܕܫܐܠ ܟܠ
ܫܘܒܩܢܐ ܘܐܡܪ. ܠܐ ܬܬܚܫܒ ܕܐܝܟܐ ܐܚܪ ܐܝܬ, ܗܫܐ ܐܠܐ ܕܐܝܟܐ
ܐܝܬ, ܗܘܝܬ ܡܢ ܩܕܡ ܘܒܪ ܡܢܗ. ܘܐܬܬܕܒܪ ܠܦܬܓ̈ܡܐ ܘܒܗܘܢ ܬܫܥܐ
ܠܒܢ̈ܝܬܐ. ܘܐܟܚܕ ܙܘܓܐ ܘܠܐ ܬܫܘܪܒ ܠܡܫܡ ܒܪܢܫܐ ܕܠܒܐ ܒܫܘܪܗܝܢ
ܬܬܘܚ. ܘܗ̇ܝ[1] ܕܒܚܠܬܐ ܠܗ ܒܒܪܐ ܬܪܘܢ ܬܫܦܪ ܠܟ. ܘܒܗ̇ܝ[2] ܕܠܬܪܘܬܐ
ܬܬܕܒܪ[3] ܠܗ ܠܡܫܘܚܬܐ ܚܕ: ܒܗ ܡܫܝܚܐ ܘܢܝܫܐ ܠܢܝܫܐ ܢ̈ܟܬ[4] ܘܬܢܝܢܐ
ܘܢܝܒܐ ܠܢܝܢܐ. ܘܐܝܟ ܠܡܚܒܝܢܐ ܠܡܬܚܡܘ ܡܬܪ̈ܚܩܢ. ܐܝܬ ܒܫܡܫܐ
ܠܡܫܡܫܘܬܝܢ ܡܛܠ ܫܡܠܝܘܬܗ[5] ܠܐ ܬܘܟܒ..

ܕܫܒܒ. ܐܟܚܕܐ ܕܠܐܝܠܢܐ ܕܢܦܩ ܙܘܓܐ ܐܬܝܢܐ ܐܝܬ ܡܒܢ̈ܝܢܐ[1] ܕܫܡܠܝܘܬܐ
ܙܘܟܝܬܐ. ܗ̣ܘ ܗܟܘܬ ܠܐܝܠܢܐ ܕܦܫܠ ܐܬܝܢܐ ܐܝܬ ܡܬܒܢ̈ܝܢܐ ܕܫܡܠܝܘܬܐ
ܘܒܙܘܟܝܬܐ. ܙܒܢܐ ܕܝܢ ܗ̇ܘܐ ܠܠܡܚܒܝܢܐ ܐܘ ܡܢ ܟܠܗܐ ܕܠܠܡܚܒܝܢܐ ܐܘ ܡܢ
ܟܠܗܐ ܕܠܠܡܚܒܝܢܐ ܐܘ ܡܢ ܟܠܗܐ ܕܠܠܡܚܒܝܢܐ. ܡܕܡܢܐ ܗܝ ܐܟܚܕܐ[2] ܕܐܝܟ
ܙܒܢܐ ܠܗ ܫܘܡܐ ܢܚܠܦ. ܘܒܐܬܪܗ ܟܕ ܕܘܟܐ ܙܘܬܝܢ *ܒܗ ܟܠ[3] ܙܒܢܬ

5 [1] ܦܪ̈ܘܫܐ RVLl [2] i. om. RVLl [3*] ܘܠܡܫܡܫܢܘܬܐ RVLl [4] i. ܘ RVLl [5] om. RVL
6 [1] ܘܒܗ̇ܝ RVL; ܘܠܗ̇ܝ l [2] ܘܗ̇ܝ RVL; ܘܠܗ̇ܝ l [3] ܬܬܕܒܪܝܢ RVL; ܬܬܕܒܪܝܢ l [4] ܢ̈ܟܠܐ RVLl
7 [1] ܡܬܒܢ̈ܝܢܐ RVLl [2] ܐܟܚܕܐ RVLl [3*] ܘܕܟܠܐ RVL

errors and minor faults, and we may grant forgiveness (to) failings which happen by mistake and not because of allurement, excitement, or evil. On wrongdoers who cause harm for victuals the natural law requires us to use leniency, yet for the theft of a dinar with some, or of a quarter dinar with others, the written law justifies cutting off the hand of a thief.

FIVE.[25] Two approaches may be taken against an accuser: that of the defendant, and that of the pleader for forgiveness. Having dealt with defence according to the (best of our) ability, let us deal with forgiveness, declaring that he who requests forgiveness requests leniency or graciousness—leniency so as not to be lashed as punishment for his wrongdoing, graciousness so as not to be penalised as he penalised (his victim). In requesting forgiveness he must say things such as these: leniency is forgiveness; good men give heed not to the law of the legislator but to his deeds, leniency, and compassion; they judge an offender not according to his action but according to his intention; and they consider not his offence but his remorse.

SIX.[26] An offender who seeks forgiveness may also use statements such as these and say: 'Do not look at the person I am now, but at what I was previously and whose son I am'; 'Remember the good things, and on their account forget the bad things'; 'Be patient and do not hasten to punish, lest by your haste you feel remorse'; 'It is right that you should judge by word, not by deed'; 'Because you are invited to a banquet, do not take pleasure in confrontation, because he who is peaceable and quiet gives heed to quiet, and he who is fervid and knavish to controversy'; and, 'If a shameless person longs to find peace, you who are lenient should not do away with your leniency on account of his offence'.

SEVEN.[27] Just as a defendant has methods of diminishing major offences, so also an accuser has methods of amplifying minor offences. A wrongdoing may be great either from the side of the wrongdoer, or from the side of the wronged, or from the side of the wrongdoing. The first, for example, is a great man who has no need

[25] **4.5.5** AR 1.13 74b10-15; IS 2.8 (114.13-115.4).
[26] **4.5.6** AR 1.13 74b15-23; IS 2.8 (115.4-11).
[27] **4.5.7** AR 1.14 74b24-30; IS 2.8 (115.12-116.15).

ܒܢܘܬܗ ܡܥܒܕܢ. ܬܪܝܢܐ ܕܝܢ ܐܚܪܢܐ ܕܡܢ ܗܢܟܠ ܦܘܕܫܐ ܢܬܠܘܢ ܐܝܟ.[4] ܐܝܟ ܡܗܠܟܢܘܬܗܘܢ ܕܡܫܬܪܐ ܠܗ ܘܠܡܫܬܪܐܬܘܢ ܘܐܡܪ ܕܬܠܬܐ ܥܒܕ̈ܝܢܐ ܠܒܒ ܡܢ ܐܘܟ̈ܝܢܐ ܒܒ̈ܪ؛[5] ܢܦܫܐ ܒܫ̈ܝܢܐ. ܒܠ ܠܒܪ ܗܘܕܐ ܒܡܢܘܬܐ ܒܝܬܪܐ ܐܦ ܢܡܢܘܢܐ ܠܒܪ ܕܢܝܐ ܦܠܝܐ ܠܐ ܡܦܘܡ. ܐܠܐ ܡܬܠ ܦܫܘܬܗ̇[6] ܡܠܝܟܘܬܐ ܕܒܢܝܢܬܐ ܢܪܒܐ ܦܠܘܬܐ. ܘܬܠܝܬܝܐ ܬܘܒ ܒܪ ܗ̇ܘ ܠܠܡܕܢܐ ܕܒܘܪܐ ܗܦܟܦܢܐ[7] ܟܒܪ ܪܟܐ. ܐܝܟ ܡܫܡܗܢܐ ܕܢܕܪܐ ܦܢܐ ܦܪܬܐ ܘܢܦܫܗ̇ ܒܬܪܐ ܘܒܢܒܝܗ̇ ܠܐܪܥܗ.

ܕܬܡܢܝܐ. ܠܠܡܕܢܐ ܕܒܘܪܐ ܕܠܐ ܦܫܩ ܒܠ ܐܦܘܬܐ ܒܬܪܒܘܬܐ ܐܘ ܒܠ ܕܢܐ ܒܡܦܘܩ ܒܪܢܫܐ ܠܐ ܥܦܐ ܠܡܐܟܠ ܥܘܒܢܐ. ܘܡܢ ܡܘܪ̈ܒܝܢܘܬܗ ܕܠܠܡܕܢܐ ܗ̇ܝ ܕܠܒܪ ܠܒ̈ܪܬܐ ܢܦܩ. ܘܗ̇ܝ ܕܗܘ ܡܕܡܢܐ ܡܕܡ ܡܢ ܐܕܫ̈ ܣܠܝܬܐ ܢܦܪܘܢ. ܘܗ̇ܝ ܕܒܡܢܐ ܕܒܬܝܢ ܗ̱ܝ ܒܪ ܗ̱ܝ ܢܣܠܐ. ܘܠܐܢܫܐ ܕܡܦܡܢܐ ܠܒܠܬܗ ܢܒܐܫ. ܘܒܐܢܫܐ ܒܪܢܝܐ ܠܒܢ̈ܝ ܡܢ ܪ̈ܫܒܐ ܢܦܦܩ. ܘܒܒܝܫ ܐܦܪܐ ܒܦܦܐ ܠܠܡܕܢܐ[1] ܢܡܒܐ. ܐܝܟ ܗ̇ܘ ܕܒܐܪܥܦ. ܕܒܗ ܢܦܪ̈ܘܗܝ ܒܟܫ ܡܢ ܣܘܬܐ ܥܢܐ ܠܐܦܪܐ ܡܬܦܫܝܢ. ܘܗ̇ܝ ܕܪ̈ܥܡܘܗܝ ܬܬܪ ܢܕܠܦܘܢ ܡܢܗ. ܘܗ̇ܝ ܕܠܐ ܢܥܪ ܥܦܘܕܝܗ ܘܢܡܪ ܒܠ ܡܡܡܬܗ ܘܢܦܠ ܠܒܠܒܝܐ ܕܠܘܬܗ ܘܠܐܢܬܬܐ ܒܦܘܩܐ ܥܡܢܪܐ ܢܡܪ. ܠܗܠܝܢ ܠܒܪ ܠܗ ܒܠܘܫ. ܠܡܥܢܘܦ ܦܠܐ. ܐܠܐ ܘܠܡܒܢܘܬܗ ܒܒܘܦܫܬܐ. ܐܚܪܢܐ ܕܒܦܕ̈ܪܐ ܕܥܦܘܪܐ ܡܦܬܠܪܐ. ܘܚܒܪ ܢܡܘܦܐ ܠܐ ܒܬܘܒܐ ܬܬܪ ܪܒ. ܒܗ̇ܝ ܕܬܠܪܘܬܗ ܬܬܪ ܐܠܝܢ ܚܢܒ ܒܠܗ ܠܒܐ. ܒܕ ܠܪܘܒܐ ܒܫܝܢܐ ܕܒ̈ܐ. ܘܕܢܡܘܦܐ ܒܬܘܒܐ ܬܘܒ ܪܒ. ܒܪܡ ܚܢܒ ܗܢܘܢ ܕܠܗܘܢ ܦܫܩ.

---

[4] om. RVL [5] ܒܒܝܢ RVL [6] f. ܗ RL [7] i. add. ܘ RVLl

8 [1] ܠܠܡܕܢܐ RVLl

(of something) seizing (it), for his minor (offences) are great because they reveal the magnitude of his avarice. The second, for example, is someone doing wrong against a holy temple, like Melanopus whom Callistratus accused, saying that he stole three obols from the priestly craftsmen builders of temples. For although the law did not decree a heavy sentence for this trivial amount, nevertheless the offence was great because of the great hideousness of the deed. The third is when a wrongdoing small (in) itself creates great damage, like (that done to) the poor man who had one ewe lamb which the rich man seized and killed for his guest.

EIGHT.[28] It is not appropriate to ask forgiveness (for) a small wrongdoing which does not need remedy by reconciliation or sentence by punishment. Among the amplifications of a wrongdoing (are the following): it harms him who does good; (the wrongdoer is) the first to commit a few species of failing; he makes the same mistake many times; he does evil to him who hopes for his kindness; (it is done) by men (whom) we typify as brutes devoid of mercy; it puts him who is wronged into a rough prison, like that at Argos, where the guards mangle the prisoners worse than a wild animal; (the man's) relatives are especially afraid of him; (the wrongdoer) does not keep his promise, breaks his oath, squanders the trust (placed) in him, and dishonours ladies by shameful unions. For it is not only necessary to punish these (wrongdoings), but also to disgrace (their perpetrators) in the assembly, as is done with false witnesses. Transgression of the unwritten law is greater (than of the written), inasmuch as its observance is more necessary for the whole community, because it is similar to natural matters. (Transgression) of the written is also great, but with those on whom it is laid.

[28] **4.5.8** AR 1.14 74b30-75a21; IS 2.8 (116.16-117.7).

## ܦܘܫܩܐ ܬܠܝܬܝܐ
## ܡܛܠ ܗܝ̈ܡܢܘܬܐ ܕܠܘ ܒܐܘܡܢܘ[1] ܗܘ̈ܝ
## ܬܐܘܪ̈ܝܐܣ ܬܥܒ

ܩܕܡܝܬܐ. ܢܚܙܐ ܐܝܟ ܗܝ̈ܡܢܘܬܐ ܕܠܘ ܡܢ ܐܘܡܢܘܬܐ ܗܘ̈ܝ ܘܟܫܝ̈ܪܬܐ ܕܐܘܡܢ̈ܘܬܐ ܕܬ̈ܠܝܢ. ܢܓ̈ܪܬܐ. ܣܝ̈ܕܪܐ. ܛܝܘ̈ܝ. ܥܬ̈ܝܕܐ. ܡܣ̈ܝܡܬܐ.[1] ܘܒܢܡܘ̈ܣܐ ܐܝܟ[2] ܡܢ ܕܟܬܒܐ ܣܘܩܒܠܐ ܠܢܩܫܗ ܕܗܦܟܐ ܢܗܐ. ܒܠܐ ܟܬܒܐ ܢܬܚܙܐ ܘܠܟܬܒܐ ܢܕܠܘܩ. ܟܕ ܐܢܫ ܕܗܦܟܪ, ܘܡܫܐ ܘܒܠܗܕܐ ܠܦܘܬ ܐܢܫܐ ܡܬܚܠܦ ܘܡܬܠܠ. ܘܠܐ ܟܬܒܐ ܒܢܝ ܘܒܫܡܝܢ ܘܐܡܝܢܐܝܬ ܡܟܬܪ ܘܠܐ ܡܬܚܠܦ ܡܫܬܠܦ. ܐܡܢܐ ܕܦܝܠܘܣܘܦܘܣ[3] ܠܐܢܛܝܠܝܩܘܣ ܢܦܩ ܪܘܚܐ ܕܠܒܪ ܡܢ ܢܡܘܣܐ ܒܟܬܒܐ ܕܦܘܪܐܘܢ[4] ܠܦܠܘܣܘܦܘܣ ܦܟܪ ܘܐܡܪ. ܕܠܐ ܒܢܡܘܣܐ ܕܗܫܐ *ܘܐܬܬܚܠܝ ܐܝܬܘܗܝ.[5] ܐܠܐ ܒܗܘ ܕܐܡܝܢܐܝܬ ܡܬܬܩ ܗܘ ܒܚܝܘܗܝ. ܘܡܛܠ ܕܫܟܝܚ ܗܘ ܢܡܘܣ ܠܟܠ. ܕܐܝܢܐ ܐܝܢܐ ܒܗܘܢܗ ܢܬܗܕܐ ܘܐܝܟ ܢܘܪܐ ܡܕܒܢܝܬ ܘܐܡܬܐ ܡܢ ܘܠܐܝܠܐ ܠܒܝܢܐ ܡܢ ܠܐܦܝܐ ܢܦܪܫ.

ܕܬܪ̈ܬܝܢ. ܐܘ ܢܡܘܣܐ ܠܐ ܟܬܒܐ ܣܘܩܒܠܐ ܗܘ ܠܢܩܫܗ ܕܗܦܟܪܐ. ܒܟܬܒܐ ܢܬܚܙܐ ܘܠܠܐ ܟܬܒܐ ܢܕܠܘܩ. ܟܕ ܐܢܫ ܕܒܢܡܘܣܐ ܚܝܠܐ ܫܪ̈ܟܐ ܕܬܠܝܢ ܠܗ[1] ܡܬܚܫܒ. ܟܕ ܗܘ ܚܟܡܬܐ ܦܝܠܘܣܘܦܘܬܐ ܡܬܚܟܡܢܐ. ܘܠܐ ܐܝܟ ܡܛܠ ܚܟܡܬܐ ܒܠܚܘܕ ܫܐܠ ܕܐܝܢܐ. ܐܠܐ ܡܛܠ ܚܟܡܬܐ ܡܕܡ. ܒܚܟܡܢ ܐܢ[2] ܕܐܝܢܐ ܒܡܕܡ ܡܢ ܫܪ̈ܟܐ ܠܢܡܘܣܐ ܟܬܒܐ ܠܡܚܙܝܐ ܠܐ ܢܕܒ. ܠܚܟܝܪ ܕܐܝܢܐ ܠܐ ܢܣܪܗܒ ܐܠܐ ܢܬܬܗܐ ܒܕܡܐ ܕܗܘ ܫܪܪܐ ܠܗ ܢܬܝܠܐ. ܟܕ, ܕܟܝܢܘܬ ܡܕܒܪܐ ܕܕܐܝܢܐ ܒܒܘܣܝܐ ܕܐܘܢܬܐ ܡܠܬ ܡܢ ܟܝܢܘܬ ܡܕܒܪܐ ܕܐܘܣܝܐ ܒܕܒܪܐ ܕܪܢܝܐ ܡܣܬܒܪܐ. ܕܐܝܢܐ ܐܪܐ ܢܚܬܐ ܘܡܗܢܪܐ ܘܠܐ ܠܡܗܘܐ.

ܕܬܠܬ. ܣܦܪܐ ܐܘ ܒܬܪ̈ܝܬܐ ܐܝܟ ܐܘ ܢܛܪܬܐ. ܘܒܬܪ̈ܝܬܐ ܠܝ ܐܢܫܐ ܐܝܟ ܒܬ̈ܝܐ ܘܒܝܢܪܐ ܕܒܣܗܕܘ̈ܬܗܘܢ[1] ܫܪ̈ܟܐ ܕܒܟܪ ܐܘ ܕܒܬܕܝܢ ܠܡܗܘܐ ܡܬܬܪܝܢ ܐܘ ܠܐ ܗܘܘ ܐܘ ܠܐ ܗܘܝܢ. ܒܐܝܢܬ[2] ܐܘ ܒܠܐܝܬ. ܗܘ ܕܗܘܘ ܠܝ ܐܝܟ ܐܬܚܝܢܐ ܕܡܛܠ ܣܠܡܐ ܒܣܗܕܘܬ ܐܘܡܢܘܣ

Titulus [1] ܒܐܘܡܢܐ RVL
1 [1] sg. RVLl [2] ܘܗܘ RVLl [3] scripsi; ܦܝܠܘܣܘܦܣ codd. [4] om. RVL [5*] ܘܐܝܬܘܗܝ, RVL
2 [1] om. RVLl [2] om. F
3 [1] sg. RVLl [2] ܒܝܐܝܬ RVL

## SECTION SIX
### On the *Pisteis* which Do not Come by Art
### Nine Theories

ONE.[29] The *pisteis* which do not come from art are five and are specific to judicial matters: laws, witnesses, contracts, tortures, oaths. With laws, when the written is contrary to the aim of the orator, he may use the unwritten and contradict the written, saying that it is violent and harsh and therefore in accordance with the times changes and passes away, while the unwritten is natural, lenient, remains for ever and never changes. Accordingly Sophocles defends to Antigone (his) burying of Polyneices outwith the written law of Creon, and says that he buried him 'not by the law which is now and complete, but by that which is perpetually everlasting'. Because the common law is general, a righteous judge should follow his understanding and, like fire purifying silver of dross, distinguish the pure from the counterfeit.

TWO.[30] If the unwritten law is contrary to the aim of the orator, he may use the written and contradict the unwritten, saying that particular matters are not tried by the common law, because by it the good is chosen generally, but no one seeks a judgement concerning the universal good, but concerning some good. Therefore if a judge does not know how to apply the written law in some cases, he should not rush to make a judgement, but hold back until the truth becomes clear to him. Because lack of knowledge on the part of a judge in a judicial trial is more harmful than lack of knowledge on the part of a physician in the management of a sick man, a judge must therefore be wise and practised.

THREE.[31] Witnesses are either ancient or recent. The ancient are just and renowned men by whose testimonies things are established to have happened in the past or not, or to have been about to happen or not, justly or unjustly. Examples concerning the past are the testimony of Homer (which) the Athenians used, the testimony of Peri-

---

[29] **4.6.1** AR 1.15 75a22-b8; IS 2.9 (117.10-118.13).
[30] **4.6.2** AR 1.15 75b8-26; IS 2.9 (119.1-15).
[31] **4.6.3** AR 1.15 75b26-76a11; IS 2.9 (120.1-9).

ܐܬܚܫܒܘ. ܘܦܓܪ̈ܝܐ ܒܣܗܕܘܬ ܦܘܪܫܢܘܗܝ ܘܪܚܫܬܐ. ܘܡܠܐܟܘܗܝ ܥܠ
ܡܘܪܓܫܘ[3] ܒܟܠܗܘܢ، ܕܗܐܠܝܢ ܒܗ ܐܡܪ. ܠܐ ܓܝܪ ܡܬܘܡ ܒܒܪ ܗܘܐ
ܗܐܠܝܢ ܕܐܡܪܬ ܠܝ. ܐܘ ܡܘܪܓܝܐ[4] ܕܒܫܡܪܐ ܫܘܡܡܐ ܐܫܬܡܥܬ
ܕܡܬܝܕܥ ܗܘܝܬ. ܫܪܝܪܐ ܕܝܢ ܕܒܬܕܝܪ ܐܝܟ ܗܢܘܢ ܕܡܬܚܠܠܝܢ ܡܢܟܪܐ
ܡܕܡ ܡܬܕܟܝܢ ܒܠܒܗܘܢ. ܐܝܟ ܕܐܡܪ ܬܗܡܣܛܘܦܘܠܘܣ[5] ܕܒܣܪܐ ܗܘܐ
ܕܡܫܐ ܡܢ ܟ̈ܠܦܐ ܒܠܒܐ ܕܢܬܬܦܪ. ܘܐܝܟ ܐܢܫܐ ܕܐܟܠܝܢ ܕܠܐ ܢܒܒ.
ܙܥܪܐ ܗܒܐ ܒܗ ܗܒ̈ܠܐ ܩܛܝܥܐ ܠܥܕܬܐ ܒܢܝ̈ܗܘܢ ܡܠܠܘ. ܒܙܒܢ
ܐܒܗ̈ܐ ܦܠܐ ܠܡܦܠܠ ܘܒܢ̈ܝܐ ܠܡܒܥܡ. ܗܘ̈ܕܐ ܕܝܢ ܣ̈ܒܪܬܐ ܐܬܝܗܘܢ
ܗܘܝ ܕܠܥܪ̈ܒܐ[6] ܘܒܢ̈ܝܐ ܕܡܐܡ ܡܙܪܢ. ܘܡܕ̈ܒܚܝܗܘܢ ܒܣܢܝܢ[7] ܒܐܝܬܘܬܗܘܢ
ܘܡܐ ܕܠܐ ܡܬܦܠܓܐ ܒܫܘܬܦܘܬ ܦܠܓܘܬܐ ܘܡܬܒܢܝܢܘܬܐ ܕܡܢ ܡܢܕܝܢܘ
ܢܗܘܘܢ. ܐܝܟ ܕܐܡܠܘ ܦܐܘܠܘܣ ܡܠܦܢ ܠܪܘܡܝܐ ܕܢܝܐ ܡܕܡ ܦܠܓܘܢ.

ܕܐܡܪܬ. ܐܝܬ ܕܝܢ ܗܘ̈ܕܐ ܕܠܘ ܐܢ̈ܫܐ ܐܢܘܢ. ܐܠܐ ܐܬܬܘ̈ܬܐ ܘܡܣܘܪ̈ܒܐ
ܠܫܐ̈ܕܐ. ܘܒܗܘܢ ܡ̇ܢ ܠܗ ܒܠܫܢܗ ܒܗ ܠܐ ܢܗܘܘܢ ܗܘ̈ܕܐ ܐܠܐ ܘܒܗ[1]
ܐܬܬܝܗܘܢ ܡܫܬܡܥ ܕܢܫܐ ܒܡܘܒܠ[2] ܫܘܘܕܝܗܘܢ ܘܡܫܪܝܬܗܘܢ. ܘܥܠ
ܫܘܘܕܝܬܐ ܐܘ ܥܠ ܒܥܠܕܒܒܐ ܗܘܐ ܕܢܫܠܡ ܐܘ ܕܓܠ. ܐܘ ܥܠ ܫܘܒܪܐ
ܕܐܝܬܘܗܝ، ܐܘ ܠܐ ܐܝܬܘܗܝ. ܘܗܝ، ܗ، ܐܠܝܨܘܬܐ ܕܠܐ ܡܬܘܡ ܐܝܬ
ܠܡܣܠܩ ܡܢܗ. ܐܘ ܥܠ ܙܢܐ. ܐܚܪܢܐ ܕܢܫܘܕ ܥܠ ܐܢܫ ܕܐܝܬܘܗܝ، ܦܠܓܐ
ܐܘ ܒܫܡܝܐ. ܘܠܒܠܝܕܝܗ ܕܐܝܬܘܗܝ، ܒܝܫܐ ܘܛܐܒܐ. ܘܒܡܦܠܠ ܫܘܘܕܝܬܐ
ܡܢ ܗܘܐ[3] ܒܗ ܫܘܕܐ ܙܒܢܐ[4] ܢܫܐ ܕܡܢ ܠܗ ܦܪܘܕ. ܐܘ ܫܘܢܝܐ[5] ܕܗܢܘ
ܕܒܠܗܘܢ، ܦܘܕܪ. ܐܢܫ ܢܒܥܐ ܡܢ ܬܐܪ̈ܗܘܢ ܢܗܘܐ. ܫܘܘܕܝܬܗ ܥܒܕܐ
ܠܡܦܩܠܐ. ܐܝܟ ܒܟܝܢ.

ܕܢܫܒܥ. ܡܢ ܕܠܒܝܬܗ ܥܒܕܐ[1] ܗܘܐ، ܡܦܘܪܐ ܘܡܫܘܪܐ ܠܒܝܬܗ ܗ، ܗܘܐ،
ܘܥܒܛܐ ܘܡܥܒܪܐ ܠܗ،[2] ܕܒܠܕܝܢܗ. ܒܗ ܗܘܐ، ܒܒܕܐ ܦܢܩܐ ܠܕܢܝܐ
ܘܠܥ̈ܬܒܒܐ.[3] ܘܒܠܗܘܕܐ ܠܐ ܦܠܐ ܠܡܥܢܝܐ ܡܢܗ.[4] ܘܗܘܐ، ܡܢ ܢܡܘܣܐ
ܡܕܡ ܗ، ܕܗܬܝܢ ܦܪ̈ܘܣܝܢ ܐܢܘܢ ܫܘܚܠܦܘܗܝ،. ܘܐܝܟ ܐܝܟܢܐ ܕܠܒܪ ܡܢ
ܙܘܡܐ ܕܢܡܘܣܐ ܗܘܐ. ܐܚܪܢܐ ܕܡܢܟܪܐ ܢܡܘܣܘܗܝ[5] ܠܫܪܕܐ ܕܠܐ
ܒܬܠܬܐ ܐܦܠܐ ܒܒܝܫܬܐ ܢܬܦܪܥܘܢ.[6] ܘܗܢܝܢ ܡܢ ܕܠܬܗܘܢ، ܥܠܡܐ
ܒܒܝܬܗ ܐܡܪ ܠܒܝܬܗ ܕܐܢܫܐ ܕܬܓܠܐ ܠܬܘܢ، ܠܢܡܘܣܐ ܬܓܠܐ. ܒܗ
ܩܛܝܥܘܬܐ ܒܫܘܠܦ ܪ̈ܓܝܐ ܠܦܘܬ ܬܘܢ، ܡܫܬܘܪ̈ܐ. ܘܐܢ ܡܫܬܪ̈ܪܐ[7] ܬܘܢ،

[3] ܦܘܪܓܫܘ F [4] ܡܘܪܓ RVLl [5] scripsi; ܬܗܡܣܛܘܦܠܘܣ F; ܬܗܡܣܛܘܦܘܠܘܣ RLl; ܬܗܡܣܛܘܦܘܠܘܣ V [6] f. ܐ RVL [7] ܒܣܢܝܢ F

4 [1] add. ܠܐ RVLl [2] ܒܡܘܒܠ ܫܘܘܕܐ F [3] scripsi; ܗܘܐ codd. [4] ܙܒܢܐ RVLl [5] ܫܘܢܝܐ RVLl

5 [1] ܥܠܡܐ RVLl [2] ܐܝܟ RVLl [3] ܠܥܘܡܐ RVL [4] f. ܗ F [5] ܢܡܘܣܘ̈ܗܝ RVL [6] ܠܐ ܒܒܝܫܬܐ RVLl [7] ܡܫܬܪܪܐ RVLl

ander of Corinth (which) the Tenedians (used), and the words of Solon (used by) Cleophon against Critias, saying, 'For never had Solon made (it) that he should say to me, "O Critias, who by the red hair it has been heard that you have been becoming known".' Examples concerning the future are events which the utterances of oracles reveal in advance. For example, Themistocles said, 'This wooden wall (signifies) we shall be attacked by ships'; and he who advises that we should not befriend an old man because many old men have for causes killed their children (can say), 'Therefore it is necessary to kill the fathers and leave the children'. Recent witnesses are those who establish contemporary things. Their acquaintances test their justice, and when no accusation is made against it, there will be (witnesses) with a share of the benefit and exclusion from the risks (of perjury), as Eubulus prosecuted a lawsuit against Chares before Plato.

FOUR.[32] There are witnesses which are not people, but suitable indexes and signs, and by them, not only when there are not (other) witnesses but also when there are, a judge will benefit by acceptance of their testimonies or their deceptiveness. Every testimony is either about an adversary that he is unjust or false, or about a fact that it is or is not, and what is necessary is never to be unable (to do) that. Now concerning the method, one may for example testify about someone that he is good or lenient, or against one's adversary that he is evil or false. The rejection of testimony happens when the witness is a friend of him for whom he testifies, or an enemy of him against whom he testifies. However, if he is a stranger to both, his testimony is fit for acceptance, if he is just.

FIVE.[33] (As for) him whose case is tantamount to a contract, the contract itself may amplify or harm his case, and bring contempt and disgrace on that of his adversary, because a contract effects persuasion on a judge and audience, and it is therefore not right to depart from it. A contract is a sort of law, of which two people are the authors, and sometimes (departure) happens unlawfully. For example, they may make a covenant with each other that neither for good nor for evil will they be parted, and then he whose activity adheres to

[32] **4.6.4** AR 1.15 76a12-33; IS 2.9 (120.9-121.11).
[33] **4.6.5** AR 1.15 76a33-b19; IS 2.9 (121.12-122.14).

ܡܬܬܦܝܣܐ ܚܫܝܫܘܬܐ ܕܒܢܝ̈ܢܫܐ. ܘܡܢ ܕܠܬܗܘܢ ܠܐ ܥܠܡ ܥܪܒܗ ܐܡܪ̈. ܒܠ ܗܘܘ, ܕܒܢܡܘܣܐ ܠܐ ܐܬܬܢܝܚ ܦܘܠܚܢܗ̇. ܘܡܢ ܕܠܬܗܘܢ, ܢܬܢܪ ܡܢ ܕܠܢܡܘܣܐ ܡܬܦܠܣܘܢ ܠܥܠܡ ܢܡܘܣܐ ܥܐܦ ܘܡܢ ܠܐ ܢܡܘܩܝܐ ܡܢܐ.

ܕܥܬ. ܠܕܝܢܐ ܕܝܢ ܢܐܡܪ ܐܝܢܐ ܕܥܕܪܐ ܠܗܘܢ.. ܕܕܝܢܐ ܡܢ ܣܘܢܩܬܐ ܗܘ ܕܗܘܝܐ ܘܡܣܝܒܪܢܐ[1] ܕܢܡܘܣܐ. ܒܕܝܠܗܘܢ ܚܙܐ ܕܠܒܠ ܗܘܘ, ܕܣܘܡܒܠܝܐ ܠܢܡܘܣܐ ܢܦܠܠ. ܟܕ ܢܡܘܣܐ ܒܥܠܝܡܘܬ ܣܒܝܬܐ ܥܠܝܗ ܫܢܐ ܐܬܬܣܝܡ. ܘܬܘܒ, ܐܝܟ ܐܡܪܬ, ܕܒܡܕܒܪܐ ܘܒܥܘܡܪܐ[2] ܗܘܝܐ. ܘܐܝܟܢܐ ܕܒܢܡܘܣܐ ܒܬܒܟܐ ܕܡܕܝܢܬܐ ܗ̇, ܐܦ ܕܐܘܡܬܐ ܐܚܪܬܐ ܐܦ[3] ܒܢܡܘܣܐ ܠܐ ܒܬܒܟܐ ܦܘܩܕܢܐ ܫܬܘܪܐ[4] ܕܬܗܘܢ, ܢܚܡܣ ܙܝܦܘܪ. ܗܢܝܢ ܐܝܟ ܢܫܡܗ ܡܫܬܡܠܐ ܗܒܪܗ. ܘܗܟܢܐ ܐܦ ܢܚܡܣ ܗܘܘ, ܐܘܪܚܬܐ ܕܡܕܝܢܬܐ ܘܠܐܘܪܚܬܐ[5] ܥܪܒܐ. ܢܐܡܪ ܕܗ̇,[6] ܡܕܡܝܢܬܐ ܡܪܝܢܐ. ܟܕ ܐܠܐ ܒܐܝܢ ܒܦܠܠ ܒܬܘܡܬܐ. ܐܦ ܒܦܠܠܗ̇ ܕܝܚܕܬܐ ܒܐܝܢ. ܘܐܦ ܢܚܡܣ ܗܘܘ, ܣܘܣܒܠܝܬܐ ܕܐܘܪܚܐ[7] ܡܢ ܐܚܪܐ ܕܡܪܟܐ ܕܒܦܠܠܗ̇. ܢܐܡܪ ܕܐܘܪܚܬܐ ܡܪܝܢܐ. ܟܕ ܐܠܐ ܫܬܬܬܐ ܗܘܬ ܒܬܘܡܬܐ. ܠܐ ܐܬܬܣܝܡܬ[8] ܒܚܕܬܐ. ܙܕܩ ܕܝܢ ܕܒܚܝܢ ܒܦܠܠܐܝܬ[9] ܘܠܬܘܒܚܬܐ ܗܘܘ, ܘܐܫܦܪܐ[10] ܕܡܬܒܬܒܝܢ. ܐܦ ܗܘܐ ܒܗܘܢ ܒܪܬ ܩܠܐ ܕܡܘܪܐ ܥܡܗ̇. ܘܗܟܢܐ ܡܟܝܠ ܕܢܐܡ ܩܠܐ ܠܒܦܠܠ ܠܗܘܢ.

ܕܥܒܕ. ܡܕܝܢ̈ܝܬܐ ܕܝܢ ܘܒܡܘܫܐ ܕܒܝܬܪܘܐ ܘܠܡܘܫܐ ܘܥܒܕ̈ܐ ܘܥܘ̈ܠܐ ܗܘܘ. ܒܗܘܢ ܗܘܒ ܡܚܝ̈ܢܘܬܐ ܗܘ̈ܝ. ܒܕܝܠܗܘܢ ܐܦ[1] ܡܕܝܢܝܬܐ[2] ܠܒܠܬ ܗܘܢܝܐ ܥܠܡܐ. *ܗܘܕܘܬܐ ܐܘܪܚܬܐ ܠܐ ܡܬܒܥܝܐ. ܘܐܦ ܠܐ ܥܠܡܐ.[3] ܘܠܐ ܡܬܚܫܒܢܐ. ܐܝܟ ܕܒܣܘܟܠܐ ܡܢ ܐܘܠܝܢܐ ܡܕܒܪ ܐܢܫ ܐܡܢܐ ܕܢܣܒ ܒܡܕܒܪ ܡܢ ܥܒܕܐ. ܘܗܢܐ ܕܡܕܒܪܐ ܘܠܝܠ ܡܢ ܥܘܢܩܐ ܢܣܬ ܬܫܩܘܬܐ ܕܗܘܐ; ܡܢ ܒܪܐ ܘܠܕܝܢܐ ܢܒܝܢ ܡܢ ܕܒܠܘܬܐ ܕܐܘܪܚܐ ܒܐܘ̈ܠܝܢܐ. ܘܕܚܠܬܐ ܦܪܙܐ ܘܡܟܝܢ ܢܦܫܐ ܚܠܝܐܝܬ ܡܚܡܣܝܢ ܒܐܘ̈ܠܝܢܐ. ܘܕܚܠܬܐ ܘܡܝܬܠܐ ܡܕܡ ܕܢܣܒܘܢ ܐܘ̈ܠܝܢܐ ܡܬܬܕܝܢ.[4] ܘܡܠܗܕܐ ܠܗܬ ܡܕܡ ܕܡܗܝܡܢ ܒܥܒ̈ܕܐ.

6 [1] ܘܣܝܒܪܢܐ RVLl [2] ܘܒܥܘܡܪܐ RVLl [3] om. F [4] om. F [5] pl. R [6] i. ܕ RVLl [7] ܕܐܘܪܚܐ RVLl [8] ܐܬܬܠܝܦܬ RVLl [9] ܦܠܝܠܐܝܬ RVLl [10] ܘܕܐܫܦܪܐ R; ܘܐܕܫܦܪܐ V; ܘܕܐܫܦܪܐ Ll

7 [1] ܐܝܬ RVL [2] ܡܕܝܢܝܬܐ RVLl [3*] om. RVL [4] ܡܬܬܕܝܢ RVLl

the contract can say to his partner that whoever wipes out the contract wipes out the law, because most things are done by voluntary exchange according to contract, and if a contract is dissolved, the needful (business) of men is wiped out. He whose cause does not conform to the contract can say (that) any contract which is not according to the law is an error, and he who obeys a contract in preference to the law treats the legislator with contempt and is counted among the lawless.

SIX.[34] He who dissolves a contract may say to a judge that a judge is an attendant upon reason and a defender of law. Therefore he ought to invalidate every contract which is contrary to the law, because the law is sanctioned by the agreement of the wise without passion, and a contract sometimes comes about by seduction or compulsion. If an orator finds in the written law of that city or another people, or in the unwritten law, an ordinance nullifying the contract, then according to its intention his hope can be fulfilled. Similarly if he finds another contract which is earlier and dissolves the later one, he can say that the earlier is authoritative, because if the abolition of the old were just, the abolition of the new would also be just. Also if he finds a contrary contract which is later than that which he wishes to abolish, he can say that the later is authoritative, because if the old had been proper, it would not have been replaced by the new. We should also examine carefully both the clauses of the contract and the written deeds, if there is an expression in them which may point to its dissolution, and similarly a judge may find an opportunity to nullify the contract.

SEVEN.[35] (As for) confessions and investigations which take place with assaults, threats, tortures, and torments, *pisteis* may also come about by them. Therefore if the confession agrees with the statement of the avenger, another testimony is not required, but if it does not agree, neither is it credible, as usually someone will lie under compulsion in order to gain speedy relief from the tortures, and after being quickly released from torment produce paradigms which have just recently happened and are known to the judges of lying by others under compulsion, of the healthy of body and strong of soul

[34] **4.6.6** AR 1.15 76b19-31; IS 2.9 (122.14-123.16).
[35] **4.6.7** AR 1.15 76b31-77a7; IS 2.9 (124.1-13).

ܕܬܡ̈ܢܝܐ. ܘܡܘܡܬܐ ܐܪܒܥܐܝܬ ܡܬܦܠܓ. ܟܕ ܡܝܡܐ ܐܘ ܠܡܥܒܕ ܢܦ̈ܩܐ ܐܘ ܐܣܘܪܐ ܘܩܛܪ ܢܕܪܐ. ܠܐ ܠܡܐܟܠ. ܐܘ ܠܡܐܟܠ ܠܐ ܠܡܥܒܕ. ܐܝܟ ܐܝܟܐ ܕܢܕܪܐ ܡܛܠ ܡܠܕܐ ܕܠܐ ܕܝܠܗ ܗܘ ܕܠܐ ܢܣܒܪ ܢܦ̈ܩܬܗ. ܘܡܢܗܘܢ ܠܐܚܪܢ ܢܗܒ ܠܗ. ܐܘ ܠܡܥܒܕ ܘܠܡܐܟܠ. ܐܘ ܠܐ ܠܡܥܒܕ ܐܦܠܐ ܠܡܐܟܠ. ܐܠܐ ܡܫܬܘܕ ܒܠܚܘܕ. ܘܗܘ ܡܢܐ ܕܦܩܕ ܦܓܠ. ܘܒܗܠܝܢ ܕܝܢ ܐܘ[1] ܠܬܒܥܐ ܡܢܕܪܘܣܐ ܡܘܡܬܐ ܐܘ ܠܡܬܬܒܥܢܐ. ܘܐܦ[2] ܕܢܘܡܘܣܐ ܡܦܩܕ ܘܐܡܪ[3] ܕܦܫܝܛܐܝܬ ܐܡܪ ܥܠ ܡܘܡܬܐ. ܠܡܘܡܬܗ ܡܫܡܠܝܘܬܗ ܠܐ ܢܦܩܐ. ܘܐܦ ܕܡܣܬܒܪܐ ܠܓܒܪ. ܟܕ ܢܕܪܐ ܡܓܢܗܐ ܡܢ ܬܟܒܬܐ. ܘܐܢ ܠܐ ܢܕܪܐ ܢܛܪ ܒܪܡ ܡܬܬܒܥ.

ܕܬܫܥ. ܡܢܐ ܕܠܡܘܡܬܐ ܡܢܝܦ ܐܣܛܘܪ ܐܡܪ. ܕܗܢܐ ܠܟ ܠܐ[1] ܦܘܪܫܐ ܡܣܝܒܬܐ ܬܘܕܝܬܗ ܘܠܐ ܬܚܝܒܬܐ ܡܘܡܬܗ. ܘܟܕ ܟܘܠ ܡܛܠ ܝܬܝܪܐ ܦܓܪܝܐ ܒܒܢܝܐ. ܥܠ ܚܘܣܪܢܐ ܢܦܫܝܐ ܠܦܫܝܐ ܡܒܥܘܪ. ܘܙܕܝܩܐ ܢܛܪ ܘܠܐ ܢܕܪܐ. ܡܛܘܠ ܓܒܪ ܠܢܕܪܐ ܡܓܢܝܐ ܕܐܠܗܐ ܘܠܡܬܦܪܥ ܠܡܠ̈ܘܗܝ، ܣܢ̈ܝܬܐ ܘܐܚܪ. ܘܡܢܗܝܢ ܕܢܐܡܐ[2] ܒܪܡ ܚܝܒ ܒܡܘܡܬܐ ܘܒܐܝܕܝܐ ܕܢܕܪ ܘܡܫܬܐ[3] ܘܩܒܪܐ ܒܝܫܐ ܢܣܒ ܡܢܗ. ܘܐܦ ܕܡܡܘܡܬܐ ܕܓܠܝܬܐ ܡܬܦܪܥܐ ܡܬܓܒܐ ܠܐܘܦܪܐ ܡܢܗ ܟܕ ܐܡܪ. ܕܡܦܢܝܐ ܕܒܪܘܢ *ܘܡܢ̈ܠܝܢܗܘܢ ܫܩܠܘܗܝ[4] ܕܐܡܪܐ. ܘܡܫܬܩܠܬ[5] ܟܕ ܠܐ ܢܕܪ *ܐܝܟܐ ܡܝܬ.[6] ܘܡܦܘܡܐ ܠܐ ܒܬܪܝܢܬܐ ܡܝܬ.

---

8 [1] ܠܐ RVL [2] ܘܗܘ RVLl [3] ܘܝܗܒ RVLl

9 [1] om. RVLl [2] ܕܢܐܡܪ F [3] f. ܗ RVLl [4*] om. F; ܘܫܩܠܘܗܝ RVL [5] f. ܝ RVL [6*] ܗܘܬ RVLl

bravely holding out under compulsion, and of the timid and cowardly confessing before they see the compulsion. Therefore nothing credible (is achieved) by tortures.

EIGHT.[36] An oath may be divided four ways, because he who swears swears either (1) to take wealth, honour, or the rest, not to give, or (2) to give, not to take. For example, he may swear that a child is not his to avoid paying his expenses, or similarly he may give him to another. Or (3) to take and give, or (4) neither to take nor give. But he may only talk and accept that which he inflicts, and in these cases, either for the avenger or for the culprit, an oath is justified. (As for) him who is renowned for impiety and knows that he may easily violate the oath, his credibility does not accompany his oath; but he who is renowned for truth is delivered from punishment when he swears. If he does not swear he will lose but still be praised.

NINE.[37] When an orator declares an oath to be false he may say, 'The confession of this undiscerning man is weak and his oath unreliable, and because he has done wrong for the sake of early profit of the body, he scorns later deprivation of the soul.' A righteous man may suffer loss and not swear, for he magnifies the adorable name of God and trembles to touch his living words, but it is possible for him to swear, with great difficulty, however, and by necessity, that he affirms the truth and puts an evil opinion far from him. And he who is maligned by a false oath may reject the reproach, saying, 'By force they led me and by their words seduced me into swearing, and in my simplicity being ignorant I swore, but I swore with the mouth not the mind.'

---

[36] **4.6.8** AR 1.15 77a7-20; IS 2.9 (124.14-125.8).
[37] **4.6.9** AR 1.15 77a20-b11; IS 2.9 (125.9-126.13).

## ܩܦܠܐܘܢ ܚܡܝܫܝܐ
### ܡܛܠ ܒܢ̈ܝܐ ܘܫ̈ܒܝܐ ܢܦܫ̈ܢܝܐ
### *ܘܒܗ ܐܝܬ[1] ܦܣܘ̈ܩܐ ܚܡ̈ܫܐ

### ܦܣܘܩܐ ܩܕܡܝܐ
### ܡܛܠ ܢܓܝܪܘܬ ܪܘܚܐ ܘܐܝܟ ܫܘܬܦܘܬ[2] ܥܠܬ[3] ܪܘܓܙܐ ܬܐܘܪ̈ܝܐ ܬܪ̈ܝܢܐ

ܩܕܡܝܬܐ. ܟ̈ܠܐ[1] ܢܓܝܪܬ ܕܪܘܚܐ ܒܡܫ̈ܠܡܐ ܕܕܪ̈ܓ ܕܪ̈ܘܚܐ ܒܢܗܝܪܘܬ ܡܕܒܪܐ ܘܠܐ ܢܗܝܪܘܬܗ ܫ̈ܠܦ. ܡܠܝܫܛܐ ܒܡܬܡܠܟܢܘܬܐ. ܒܪ ܡܬܕܝܢܘܬܐ ܢܡܘܣܐ ܛܒ ܡܢ ܪܚܝܩܐ ܡܚܝܠ. ܪܗܛܐ ܡܕܝܢ ܒܪ ܢܕܒ ܕܕܐܝܟ ܐܝܠܢܐ ܐܝܬܘܗܝ, ܕܢܝܐ. ܪܒܬ ܡܬܒܪܪ. ܒܪ ܕܢ̈ܝܐ ܠܘ ܫܘܐܝܬ ܡܬܛܠܠ ܠܐܝܠܢܐ ܕܐܣܟܡ ܘܠܐܝܠܢܐ[2] ܕܗܢܝ. ܒܓܠܘܢ ܒܪ ܐܢܫ ܕܢܝܐ ܠܗܛܪܐ ܐܘ ܥܦܪ ܒܗ ܡܒܪܗ ܡܛܠ ܡܒܬܪܘܬܗ. ܗܢܐܝܬ ܥܒܕ ܠܗ. ܘܒܥܦܐܝܬ ܐܪܒ ܠܒܟܠ ܕܢܩܗ. ܡܬܗܢܝܢ ܕܝܢ[3] ܗܘ ܕܡܒܠܠ ܒܪ ܢܗܘܐ ܒܪܝܡ ܐܘ ܡܬܛܪ ܐܘ ܐܘܐ ܒܪܚܡܬܐ.[4] ܘܡܬܕܓܠ ܗܘ ܕܒܪܝܪ ܘܥܛܠ ܘܫܘܐ. ܐܟܡܐ ܕܡܬܕܓܠ ܡܠܘܒܐ ܗܒܠܐ ܘܒܠܥܐ. ܘܕܠܐ ܥܡܠ ܦܘܬܐ[5] ܕܡܬܡܠܟܢܐ ܘܠܗܕܪܐ ܡܠܟܐ ܦܠܝܪܐ ܢܠܝܟ ܠܗ. ܘܫܢܝܐ ܕܒܪܚܡܬܐ ܘܫܦܝܛܘܬܐ ܡܢ ܗܠܝܢ ܕܡܣܬܠܦܐ ܘܓܘܢܐ ܐܡܪܝܢ ܡܬܢܫܒ. ܘܕܐܘܘܬܐ ܘܪܚܡܬܐ[6] ܡܢ ܗܠܝܢ ܕܒܢ̈ܫܐ ܢܦܫ̈ܢܝܐ ܐܡܪܝܢ. ܡܡܕܡܐ[7] ܡܢ ܪܘܓܙܐ ܘܪܓܙܢܘܬܐ ܡܬܪܓܙܢܐ ܢܚܪܐ.

ܕܬܪ̈ܬܝܢ. ܪܘܓܙܐ ܐܝܬܘܗܝ, ܣܘܓܦܐ ܢܦܫܢܝܐ ܒܐܝܡܡܘܬ ܒܢܝܫܐ ܠܥܘܠ ܐܢܫܐ ܕܡܬܦ ܠܗ. ܘܒܠܗܕܐ ܪܘܓܙܐ ܠܘ ܒܠ ܥܘܕܐ ܒܠܢܫܐ ܗܘܐ. ܒܪ ܥܘܒܕܬܐ ܡܢ ܒܠܢܫܐ ܠܐ ܗܘܝܐ. ܡܬܪܓܙܢܐ ܡܕܝܢ ܐܘܡܢܬ ܗܘ ܕܒܠܗܘܢ, ܗܘܐ ܪܘܓܙܐ. ܫܢ ܗܘ ܡܘܡܝܐ ܐܘ ܢܛܪ ܡܢ ܫܢ. ܘܡܢ ܒܪܘ ܢܒܡܬܗ ܠܡܢܝܢܘܬܐ ܕܢܡܘܣܐ ܠܪܘܓܙܐ ܘܠܡܣܬܦܩܘܬܗ[1] ܒܒܝܫܐ. ܘܥܦܪ ܐܡܪܝܢܐ ܡܛܠ ܫܡܬܐ ܕܐܝܬܪ ܡܢ ܕܒܥܐ ܘܒܒܪܢܝܬܐ[2] ܒܓܘ ܫܢܝܐ ܕܓܒܪܐ[3] ܫܢܝܐ ܘܐܝܟ ܬܢܝܐ ܒܒܪܐ. ܘܗܢܝܐܘܬܐ ܕܡܢ ܗܓܝܐ ܘܗܓܓܝܐ ܕܢܡܘܣܬܐ

Titulus [1*] om. F [2] ܫܘܬܦܘܬܐ RVLl [3] ܥܠ RVLl

1 [1] ܟ̈ܠܝܐ RVLl [2] ܘܐܠܐܠܝܢ RVLl [3] om. RVL [4] ܒܪܚܡܘܬܐ RVLl [5] ܦܘܬܐ RVLl [6] ܘܪܚܡܬܐ RVL [7] ܘܡܕܡܐ RVLl

2 [1] f. ܗ RVLl [2] ܘܒܒܪܢܝܬܐ F [3] sg. RVLl

## CHAPTER FIVE
## ON CHARACTER AND PASSIONS OF THE SOUL
## FIVE SECTIONS

### SECTION ONE
### On the Inducement of a Judge and the Kinds of Scorning, the Cause of Anger
### Eight Theories

ONE.[1] The words which will induce a judge differ according to differences in the conditions of the judges in regard to clarity of mind or lack of it, especially in deliberation, because (in) judicial proceedings (it is) law rather than intellect (which) produces the result. Therefore when an orator knows that a judge is of a certain sort, he is greatly advantaged, because judges do not incline evenly to whom they like and whom they hate. Thus when the judge likes the orator, or has a good opinion of him because of his virtue, he listens to him with pleasure. He may angrily refute his adversary, but the speaker may be believed when he is prudent, virtuous, or well disposed in friendship, but considered false when he is foolish, vile, and hateful. Similarly an adviser (who is) a fool and a wrongdoer will be thought false, as will one who has no concern for the advisee and therefore gives him raw advice. The test of prudence and care is taken from those things which we said about praise and blame, and (that) of concord and friendship from those which we are going to say about the passions of the soul. Let us begin first with anger, the angry subject, and the object of anger.

TWO.[2] Anger is damage to the soul by the desire of a man for the punishment of him who scorns him. Therefore anger does not come about against a universal object, because scorn does not come from a universal. Thus the object of anger, that is to say, he against whom

---

[1] **5.1.1** AR 2.1 77b16-78a30; IS 3.1 (129.3-130.8).
[2] **5.1.2** AR 2.2 78a31-b13; IS 3.1 (130.9-16).

ܒܬܪܥܝܬܐ ܗܘܐ ܠܗܝܡܢܘܬܐ ܕܐܝܟ ܣܠܩܐ ܕܡܛܝܐ. ܘܡܫܝܚܘܬܐ ܗܝ
ܗܘܐ ܗܘܐ ܕܒܡܠܬܐ ܘܒܥܒܕܐ[4] *ܠܐ ܢܫܬܐܠܐ[5] ܡܕܡ ܠܐܘܪܚܐ
ܘܠܡܫܝܚܐ. ܒܗ̇ ܠܐ ܝܗܒܬܗ ܡܬܠܡܢܝܐ ܐܦܠܐ ܒܫܬܗ ܡܬܪܥܝܐ.

ܕܬܠܬ. ܠܡܫܝܚܘܬܐ ܕܒܪܘܪܬ ܢܦܫܐ ܦܪܐ ܕܐܝܟ ܘܐܡܪ ܕܒܬܠܬ[1] ܗܘܐ.
ܒܡܫܝܚܘܬܐ ܒܡܦܪܫܘܬܐ ܒܡܨܝܕܘܬܐ. ܘܡܫܝܚܘܬܐ ܗܝ ܐܬܝܗ̇،
ܡܒܪܝܐܬ ܢܦܫܐ ܕܡܬܡܫܚܐ. ܒܗ̇ ܐܝܟܐ ܕܣܒܪܗ ܡܫܡܫܐ ܒܗ ܘܒܪܐ ܢܦܫܗ.
ܡܦܪܫܘܬܐ ܕܝܢ ܐܬܝܗ̇، ܡܫܡܠܝܘܬ[2] ܥܘܒܕܐ ܠܡܬܥܒܕܢܘܬܐ ܡܢ ܗܘ ܡܢܐ
ܕܢܦܩܐ ܠܡܫܡܫ. ܒܗ̇ ܕܬܪ ܡܢ ܦܘܪܢܣܐ ܘܗܝܡܢܘܬܐ ܕܗܘܐ ܠܡܫܡܫܢܐ
ܒܬܘܪܬ ܡܬܡܫܚܢܐ ܘܫܘܠܡܗ ܢܦܫܐ ܐܝܢܐ ܠܐ[3] ܢܗܘܐ ܠܗ. ܠܐ ܕܝܢ
ܡܬܬܪܦ ܐܠܐ ܠܡܢܐ[4] ܕܠܐ ܐܝ ܙܪܝ ܡܫܝܡ. ܐܦܠܐ ܐܝ ܡܬܪܥܐ
ܡܣܝܪܐ. ܐܝܟ ܕܐܡܪ ܐܘܡܪܝܢܘܣ ܕܠܐܟܣܢܕܪܘܣ[5] ܒܗ̇ ܕܙܒܢܐ ܐܡܫܦ
ܐܠܟܣܡܢܘܣ.[6] ܐܡܪ، ܕܡܪ ܘܢܦܩ ܕܪܘܚܘܬܗ ܘܐܡܪ[7] ܕܠܡܘܢ ܠܗܘܢܐ ܫܦܝܪܐ
ܫܡܫܐ.[8] ܘܡܡܝܢܘܬܐ ܗܘܬ ܡܫܝܚܘܬܐ ܗܘܐ ܠܡܝܢܪܐ ܒܗܠܝܢ
ܕܒܢܝܐ. ܘܡܡܫܡܫܢܘܬܐ[9] ܗ̇ܝ، ܕܡܬܬܪ ܡܢ ܗܘ ܕܡܠܝܪ ܘܡܫܬܪ ܡܢ ܡܢܐ
ܕܠܗܘ ܒܗ ܡܝܬܪ. ܘܒܗܕܐ ܓܠܬ ܬܠܬܐ ܘܡܬܪܐ ܡܝܬܪܝܢ. ܒܗ̇ ܡܬܪ،
ܡܢ ܐܝܬܐ ܗܘܘ ܠܗܘܢ ܡܪܝܡ.

ܕܐܪܒܥ. ܡܬܪ ܕܝܢ ܠܐ ܡܫܝܒܪ ܝܬܝܪܐ ܗܝ ܕܡܬܝܪܐ ܗܘ ܠܗ ܫܪܐ
ܒܠܗܘܢܐ ܐܘ ܒܚܝܠܐ ܐܘ ܒܡܠܦܢܘܬܐ ܐܘ ܒܡܠܟܘܬܐ ܐܘ ܒܥܘܬܪܐ.
ܘܗܝ ܕܣܠܩ ܐܡܪܐ ܕܡܫܒܚܐ ܡܝܬܪ. ܗܘ ܐܘ ܐܢܫ ܡܢ ܕܠܗ. ܘܗܟܢܐ
ܗܝ ܕܡܟܐ ܒܢܫܝܐ ܒܪܘܚܐ ܐܘ ܡܫܡܫܢܘܬܐ ܐܘ ܒܟܠܗܘܢ ܝܬܝܪܘܬܐ ܡܢ
ܟܠܗܘܢ[1] ܡܝܬܪ. ܡܛܠ ܕܝܢ ܡܬܪ ܒܢܦܫܐ ܟܠ ܐܢܫܐ ܕܠܐ ܡܫܒܚܐ
ܠܗ ܒܟܠ ܒܪܘܚܗ ܐܘ ܒܝܬܪܘܬܗ ܐܘ ܒܡܪ̈ܘܗܝ. ܐܘ ܠܐ ܦܪܥ ܠܗ
ܕܙܕܩ ܕܢܫܒܚܘܬܗ. ܐܘ ܟܠܐ ܠܗ ܡܢ ܗ̇ܝ، ܕܡܫܬܟܚܐ ܝܬܝܪܗ ܘܡܠܬܐ ܝܬܝܪܬܗ.
ܘܡܢ ܟܠܗܘܢ ܕܡܝܬܪܘܬܐ ܐܬܝܗ̇ ܫܘܦܪܐ ܗ̇ܘ ܡܢܐ ܕܡܫܬܠܛܐ[2] ܠܗ
ܝܬܝܪܝܢ[3] ܘܡܫܘܬܦܝܢ. ܐܝܟ ܕܠܘܬ ܦܝܠܣܘܦܘܬܐ[4] ܒܡܠܦܢܐ ܒܪ[5] ܐܝܟ
ܕܡܫܬܟܚܐ ܒܢܦܫܐ ܫܦܝܪܬܐ ܡܬܬܐܠܝܢ. ܘܠܡܫܬܠܛܐ ܡܬܠܒܝܢ. ܘܒܗܘܢ
ܐܝܟ ܕܒܗܘܢ ܕܠܗܘܢ ܒܟܠܝܢ ܘܒܫܪܝܪܘܬܐ ܫܪܝܪܝܢ ܡܬܬܠܝܢ
ܡܬܚܫܒܝܢ.[6] ܗܠܝܢ ܕܝܢ ܒܟܠܝܢ[7] ܡܛܠ ܕܠܝܘܬܪ ܢܟܣܐ ܠܐ ܢܟܝܢ. ܐܝܟܐ
ܒܗ̇ ܫܐܝܢ ܛܘܒܢܘܬܗܘܢ ܘܐܫܟܚܬܗܘܢ ܠܥܬܝܪܐ ܘܟܠܒܘܬܐ ܘܡܫܝܢܘܬܗܘܢ
ܠܓܠܘܬܐ ܘܒܙܬܐ. ܡܪܝܒܝܢ ܘܡܝܬܪܝܢ ܠܗܘܢ.

---

4 ܐܘ ܒܥܒܕܐ RVLl 5* om. RVL

3 1 ܕܒܬܠܬ ܙܒܢܝܢ RVLl 2 ܡܫܡܠܝܘܬ RVL 3 i. add. ܕ F 4 i. om. F 5 ܕܠܐܟܣܢܕܪܘܣ RVLl 6 ܐܠܐ ܡܫܡܫܢ RVLl 7 i. om. F 8 ܒܪܝܫܗ RVLl 9 f. om. RVLl

4 1 ܡܠܬܐ RVLl 2 ܕܡܫܬܠܛܐ RVL 3 ܝܬܝܪ RVLl 4 ܦܝܠܣܘܦܘܬܐ RVLl 5 om. RVL 6 ܡܬܚܫܒܝܢ F 7 ܒܟܠܝܢ RVLl

anger arises, is a single person or more than one. Now you (can) understand the pleasure which accompanies anger and seeks its increase, and (why) it was appropriately said about rage that 'it is sweeter than honey and the honeycomb within the breast of men and works like smoke'. The pleasure which comes from the dwelling on, and imagination of, vengeance in the mind is like the pleasure from a dream. Scorning happens when by word or deed something is not thought worthy of honour or praise, because neither the good (in) it is sought nor the bad (in) it shunned.

THREE.[3] Our master calls scorning 'smallness of soul' and says that it comes about in three ways: by disdain, by domination (?), and by insult. Disdain is the diminution of the soul of the disdained, because the soul is reduced of him whose companion disdains him. Domination is the hindering by the scorner of him who is scorned from that which he wishes to do, although the hinderer has no other aim above the enjoyment and pleasure which comes to him by the confounding and humiliation of him who is hindered. But (someone) only becomes domineering against one who if angry will not cause (him) distress, nor if reconciled (with him) make (him) glad; for example, Homer said that Agamemnon scorned Achilles when he was angered, for he laid hold of and took his concubine and left him as a scorned exile. In insult also there arises pleasure for the insulter by the imagination of victory, and by the sneer that he is superior to him who is insulted and free from that for which he insults him. For this reason the young and the rich are insulting, because they suppose themselves superior to others.

FOUR.[4] Especially intolerant of insult is the person who considers himself superior in birth, power, learning, authority, or wealth, and the person who instead of (receiving) the honour he was expecting receives an insult (directed at) himself or one of his. And similarly whoever is subjected to a trial of illness, poverty, or deprivation of desire will be angry on account of a small cause. Someone immediately becomes angry against one who does not comfort him when he is ill, in poverty, or in battles, or does not return to him the dues of

---

[3] **5.1.3** AR 2.2 78b13-34; IS 3.1 (130.16-131.9).

[4] **5.1.4** AR 2.2 78b34-79b4; IS 3.1 (131.10-132.12).

ܕܫܡܝܐ. ܘܡܢ ܗܠܝܢ ܕܡܒܝܢܝܢ ܢܘܗܪܐ ܐܝܬܘܗܝ، ܦܫܩܐ ܕܒܝܬܐ ܒܟܒܘܕܘܬ
ܥܒܝܕܘܬܐ. ܘܐܝܟ ܗܿܝ، ܕܣܠܩ ܠܥܠܡܐ ܠܐ ܢܦܘܩ ܠܥܠܡܐ ܥܡܗܘܬܐ ܒܢܘܪܐ ܠܐ
ܦܘܪܫܢܐ ܡܢܘܗܪܐ. ܒܡܐ ܡܬܐܡܪܐ ܗܿܝ، ܕܣܠܩ ܠܥܠܡܐ ܒܢܗܝܪܬܐ ܢܦܘܩ
ܒܢܘܪܐ.[1] ܘܫܟܢܘܪܘܬ ܡܪܟܒܬܐ ܡܢ ܫܡܝܐ. ܡܬܝܚܝܕܬܐ ܕܝܢ ܡܠܬܐ ܫܡܝܐ.
ܘܬܠܬܝܬܐ ܠܝܬ ܡܠܟܘܬܐ ܠܫܡܝܘܬܗܿ. ܢܘܗܪܐ ܕܝܢ ܐܚܝܕ ܟܠ ܢܘܗܪܗ ܒܗ. ܥܠܐ
ܘܠܐ ܐܫܪ ܫܦܝܪ ܡܠܠܬܗ. ܡܠܫܡܠܐ ܡܢܐ ܕܒܫܡܝܐ[2] ܢܦܠ ܘܒܫܡܫܗ ܠܐ
ܢܫܝ ܒܡܗܘ. ܐܝܟܢܐ ܕܦܠܓܡܘܣܘܣ[3] ܗܿܘ ܕܐܬܠܝܦܘ ܒܡܗܠܡܐܢܘܣ.
ܠܐ ܡܥܒܕܬܘܬ ܝܘܡܐ ܚܙܝ ܥܘܕܪܢܐ ܗ، ܕܥܒܘܕܘܬܐ.[4] ܘܥܒܘܕܘܬܐ
ܒܕܘܟܬܐ ܐܝܬܝܗܝܢ ܥܒܘܕܘܬܐ ܕܢܘܪܐ ܒܢܘܪܐ. ܘܕܗܘ ܕܒܠܗܘܢ، ܢܗܝܪ
ܘܡܫܝܢ. ܘܕܗܘ ܕܒܗ ܡܬܕܒܪ[5] ܡܢ ܕܕܒܪܐ ܢܗܝܪ ܠܒܗܝܪܐ. ܘܕܒܪ، ܪܕܝܐ.
ܘܒܠܗܘܪܐ ܢܘܗܪܐ ܗܦܟ[6] ܐܝܟܢܐ ܒܠ ܒܢܝܢܗܘܢ، ܘܢܗܝܐ ܡ̈ܫܠܡܢܘܬܐ ܒܠ
ܒܬܠܝܬܝܢ. ܥܒܘܕܘܬܐ[7] ܕܝܢ ܗܿܘ، ܕܡܕܘܪܐ ܠܫܘܦܘܬܐ ܕܐܝܬܪܐ ܢܦܘܩ.[8]
ܗܿܘ، ܕܡܢ ܡܢܟܬ ܫܒܝܐ[9] ܗ̇ܘ ܠܗ[10] *ܠܫܘܕܐܝܬ ܟܠ.[11] ܗܿܘ، ܕܐܬܝܚܝܕܐ ܡܢ
ܢܘܗܪܐ[12] ܒܕܡܐ ܠܗܿ، ܕܐܦ ܠܒܗܝܪܐ ܢܦܫܐ ܡܢ[13] ܒܗܘܕܝܗ. ܘܗܠܝܢ ܡܢ
ܗܠܝܢ ܕܢܘܗܪܐ. ܡܟܝܠ ܝܕܥ. ܗܠܝܢ ܕܒܗܝܢ ܡܬܚܘܐ ܢܘܗܪܐ ܢܗܝܪ.

ܕܫܒܬ. ܡܥܝܬܗܐ ܕܝܢ ܢܘܗܪܐ ܒܠ ܐܝܢܐ ܐܝܟ[1] ܕܠܐ ܡܢܒܝܢܐ ܐܠܐ
ܒܠܒܝܢ ܘܟܦܘܪܐ ܫܠܝܐ. ܘܒܠ ܐܝܢܐ ܕܡܢ ܡܬܢܗܪܢܘܬܐ ܠܝܬ ܠܗܿ، ܕܢܣܝܡ
ܢܦܩ. ܒܕܝܠܗܿ ܡܢ ܢܘܗܪܐ ܓܠܝܐ ܥܘܡܩܐ. ܘܒܠ ܐܝܢܐ ܕܗ̇ܘ[2] ܠܗ ܐܝܟܢܐ
ܕܐܬܝܚܕܐ ܥܐܦ. ܘܒܠ ܐܝܢܐ ܕܡܘܕܐ ܕܐܬܡܠܐ ܘܒܠܬܒܘܬܐ ܥܐܠ
ܥܘܡܩܐ. ܐܝܟܢܐ ܕܒܠ ܦܢܝܐ ܕܒܦܪ ܘܡܬܒܐ ܗ̇ܘ ܠܗ ܚܙܐ ܢܘܗܪܐ.

5 [1] ܒܢܗܪܐ RVLl [2] pl. RVL [3] ܕܦܠܓܡܘܣܘܣ RVLl [4] ܕܥܒܘܕܘܬܐ RVL [5] ܡܬܕܒܪ R [6] om. RVLl [7] ܥܒܘܕܘܬܐ RVL [8] ܢܦܘܩ RVLl [9] ܫܒܝܐ RVLl [10] om. RV [11*] ܠܫܘܕ ܡܬܟܠ RVLl [12] pl. RVLl [13] om. RVL

6 [1] om. RVLl [2] ܕܗ̇ܘ، RVL

his love, or prevents him accomplishing his will and fulfilling his desire. To the genus of insult belongs the scorning of that which worthy people desire and honour, like the study of philosophy, for the populace for the most part deride those who love wisdom, belittle the worthy, and ridicule them as those who labour for nothing and use up their life in vanity. They do this because they do not know the profit of knowledge, (but) then when they see the integrity of the (wise), their love of truth and good, and their hatred of falsehood and evil, they magnify and honour them.

FIVE.[5] Among things which arouse anger is stopping the habit of doing what is noble; and if it causes anger that an undiscerning person does not for a good repay an equal good, how much more does someone's repayment of good with evil. Doing the first is detestable, the second more detestable, and there is no word for the vileness of the third. A man will be angry with his friend if he keeps quiet or does not speak well of him, especially when (the man) falls into difficulty and in his suffering (the friend) does not suffer with him, as Antiphon's Plexippus in *Meleager*; for not sharing in suffering is a sign of scorning. Reprehensible scornings are: scorn of a man's person; (scorn) of him by whom one is loved and honoured; of him whom one admires, when one would love to be admired; and of those with rights—and on this (last) ground parents may be very angry with their children, and masterful wives with their husbands. Scorn also (includes) meeting with irony the earnestness of others; seizing on someone by himself from among colleagues; and being forgetful of a friend to the extent of wiping out his name from one's memory. These things (are all to do) with anger, so now let us go on to those by which anger is calmed.

SIX.[6] Anger is calmed against him, for example, who sins not by intention but by mistake or error; against him with whom one goes from being angry to punishing—therefore one is occupied with punishment rather than anger; against him who scorns himself just as he does others; and against him who confesses that he has done wrong

[5] **5.1.5** AR 2.2 79b4 - 3 80a7; IS 3.1 (132.13-133.11).
[6] **5.1.6** AR 2.3 80a7-33; IS 3.1 (133.11-134.9).

ܘܥܠ ܐܝܠܝܢ ܕܡܬܬܥܝܢ ܘܥܠܐ. ܘܗܠܟ ܡܗܘܕܝܢܘܬܐ ܡܚܡܬܢܘܬܐ ܒܪܘܡܐ
ܡܫܠܡܐ ܡܬܦܠܓܘܢ. ܐܦ ܩܠܝܠܐ ܚܙܪ ܠܐܝܠܐ ܕܢܦܩ ܠܐ ܡܕܥܝܢ.
ܘܠܕܡܬܦܠܓܐ ܒܗܘܢ ܢܬܠܝܢ. ܘܥܠ ܐܝܠܝܢ ܕܢܦܩܝ ܚܕ ܘܦܪܝܫ. ܒܕ[3]
ܦܪܝܫܘܬܐ[4] ܠܚܒܪܘܬܐ ܦܠܓܘܬܐ ܕܦܘܪܫܢܐ ܒܝܢܐ ܕܡܝܢܐ. ܘܥܠ ܐܝܠܝܢ
*ܕܚܝܝܢ ܘܦܪܝܫ.[5] ܘܥܠ ܕܝܢܝܢ ܘܡܥܡܝܢ ܘܡܫܝܢ ܘܡܥܝܢ ܘܠܐ ܡܦܪܚܝܢ.
ܐܝܟ[6] ܓܒܪ ܘܣܒܪܐ ܠܚܒܝܐ ܢܦܫ. ܘܥܠ ܐܝܠܝܢ ܕܕܚܝܠ ܐܝܟ ܫܠܝܛܐ
ܘܚܣܝܪܐ ܐܝܟ ܚܝܠܬܐ. *ܒܕ ܪܘܓܙܐ[7] ܘܕܚܠܬܐ ܘܚܘܣܪܐ ܠܐ ܡܬܟܢܫܝܢ
ܐܚܝܕܐ.

ܕܫܒܒ. ܫܘܦܛܬ ܪܒܐ ܠܥܘܪܐ ܠܐ ܡܪܓܫܐ. ܒܕ ܒܝܢܐ ܕܡܪܕܘܬܐ ܠܐ
ܕܢܥܒܕ ܡܬܘܒܠ. ܡܫܬܥܗܝ ܚܙܪ ܕܥܘܪܐ ܒܕ ܪܒܐ ܠܗ، ܕܢܫܘܦܛܘܗܝ
ܡܢܘܐ ܠܗ. ܘܡܢ ܕܓܘܫܡܐ ܘܦܘܪܓܝܐ ܦܐܫܘܫܬܐ ܚܒܕ ܠܐ ܡܨܝܘ.
ܒܕܠ ܒܝܢܐ ܕܒܗܝܠܐ ܐܠܐ ܕܪܫܝܡܬ ܚܫܝܐ ܗܝܠܐ ܦܓܪ. ܘܐܝܠܐ
ܕܒܐܫܬܐ[1] ܡܬܦܪܓܝܢ ܒܪܗ ܒܢ ܗܒܪܐ ܦܠܓܐ ܕܡܢܐ ܠܐ ܪܓܙ. ܡܫܬܝܘ[2]
ܕܝܢ ܪܘܓܙܐ. ܘܒܝܢܐ ܕܡܫܘܐ[3] ܠܫܠܝܛܘܬܐ ܘܠܢܫܐ ܡܢ ܠܗܘܢ[4] ܒܗܘܢܝܐ
ܪܘܫܡܗ.[5] ܐܦ ܚܙܪ ܘܢܫܡܬܐ ܘܢܫܝܡܬ[6] ܒܝܪܬܐ ܐܦ[7] ܡܢ ܫܡܝܐ[8]
ܡܫܘܚܐ ܠܪܘܓܙܐ. ܐܝܟ ܕܐܡܪ ܦܠܘܛܪܘܦܘܣ.[9] ܒܕ ܪܓܙ ܗܘܐ ܒܠ
ܡܘܦܠܐ. ܕܠܐ ܠܡ ܢܐܚ ܐܝܟ ܐܠܐ ܡܟܐ ܕܢܝܚܬ ܡܢܘܗܝ ܐܝܟ ܕܦܠܝܦ
ܘܫܒܪܐ. ܘܗܟܢܐ ܐܪܣܛܘܛܠܝܣ ܡܬܒܣܡ ܗܘܐ ܒܡܠܫܬܐܝܣ ܒܪܒܐ
ܕܒܫܬܐ ܪܒܬܐ ܣܒܐ ܕܫܒܠ ܘܒܪܝܡ.

ܕܬܬܒܪܐ. ܐܝܠܝܢ ܕܪܕܒ ܕܩܘܪܐ ܠܡܬܬܫܝܠܘ ܒܕ ܡܬܬܫܝܠ ܠܐ ܪܓܙ.[1]
ܘܠܗܕܪܐ ܒܝܪܐܘܬ[2] ܡܬܦܠܓܝܢ ܒܒܕܪܐ ܒܕ ܡܬܕܪܝܢ. ܗܟܢܐ ܘܐܝܟܢܐ ܕܪܕܒ
ܡܚܠܘܬܗ. ܡܚܠܝܢ ܕܝܢ ܒܕ ܡܬܒܣܡ ܠܗܘܕܝ ܒܚܠܝܬܐ ܕܒܣܘܡܐ ܫܘܪܒܬܗ.
ܡܬܪ ܕܝܢ ܪܓܙ ܡܢ ܕܒܫܠܝܬܗ ܠܐ ܡܬܪܓܙ ܘܠܐ ܒܪܝܟܐ ܫܪܐ ܗܘ ܠܗ.
ܡܬܪ ܪܓܙ ܬܘܒ ܘܐܝܠܐ ܕܡܬܪܓܙ ܒܝܪܐ ܕܗܘܝܐ ܠܗ. ܘܐܝܠܐ ܕܠܐ ܡܬܪܓܙ

[3] ܒܕ: RVL [4] i. add. ܒ RVL [5*] trp. RVLl [6] i. add. ܘ RVL [7*] ܒܪܘܓܙܐ RV
7 [1] [?]ܕܒܐܫܬ F; ܕܒܐܫܬܝܢܐ l [2] ܡܫܬܝܘ F [3] ܕܡܫܐ F [4] ܠܢܘܚܐ RVLl [5] f. ܗ RVL [6] f. add. ܐ R [7] ܐܦ RVLl [8] ܫܡܝܐ F [9] ܦܠܘܛܪܘܦܘܣ RVL
8 [1] ܪܓܙ RVLl [2] ܒܝܪܐܘܬ RL

and in repentance asks for forgiveness, just as (on the contrary) anger flares up against the insolent man who denies (his wrongdoing) and justifies himself. (Anger is also calmed) against him who humbles himself and keeps silent, and instead of a shaming confession takes refuge in praiseworthy silence, for even dogs do not attack someone who is sitting down, yet they bite someone who picks a quarrel with them. (Anger is also calmed) against him who is very joyous and cheerful, because cheerfulness is like making good the required recompense; against him who is needy and lacking; against him who is gentle, humble, mild, peaceful, and not insulting, if perchance sometimes he may fail; and against him who is feared, like a ruler, or revered, like a wise man, because anger and fear or reverence do not go together.

SEVEN.[7] The scorn of a greater for an inferior does not incite anger, because it is received in the manner of instruction, not vengeance, for the inferior can boast because the greater considers him worth scorning. Whoever effects a dishonouring (?) with laughing and pleasure does not cause distress, because he does it not in the manner of despising, but of love of pleasant company. One with whom (people) amuse themselves because of (his) misfortune may not be angry on account of the good hope which he possesses. Anger may abate, and through the manner in which (someone) is recompensed for an offence, he may even blot out its mark from his memory. Also vengeance and the taking of revenge, even by heaven, calms anger; as Philocrates said when angered by the mob, 'I shall only be at peace when I have seen one of them smitten and thrown down.' Similarly Ergophilus was indignant with Callisthenes, until he saw the great evil which he was suffering and let (him) go.

EIGHT.[8] He who knows that he deserves to be scorned is not angry when he is scorned, and therefore slaves scarcely complain when chastised. The same applies to him who understands his offence, especially when he has previously been reproved by a word which shows up his fault, but whoever does not perceive his offence and

[7] **5.1.7** AR 2.3 80a34-b16; IS 3.1 (134.9-135.2).
[8] **5.1.8** AR 2.3 80b16-29; IS 3.1 (135.2-8).

ܠܐ ܢܓܠܐ. ܬܪܝܨܐܝܬ ܡܕܡ ܐܬܐܡܪܬ ܠܐܕܘܣܘܣ. ܕܠܐ ܠܡ ܟܒܫ ܡܕܝܢܬܐ ܐܢܛܝܟ. ܒܕܠܐ ܡܙܠܓ ܐܢܬ ܒܨܪܒܐ ܗܠܝܢ ܕܒܢܝܗ̇ ܥܕܡ ܟܝ. ܒܬܪ ܕܝܢ ܪܘܓܙܐ ܘܒܣܡܘܬܐ ܕܢܦܫܐ. ܒܕܓܠܘ ܥܦܪ ܐܒܢ ܦܘܐܬܐ ܒܕ ܢܨܒܐ ܗܘܐ ܕܢܚܫ ܠܟܠܗܘܢ ܡܢ ܪܘܓܙܗ ܥܠ ܗܘܦܠܪ ܒܕ ܡܚܫܬ. ܕܡܟܠ ܠܐܪܒܐ ܫܦܝܪܬܐ ܡܒܣܡ ܐܢܬ ܐܡܝܢܐܝܬ. ܒܐܡܬ ܐܣܘܐ ܢܓܠܐ ܐܢܬ ܥܠ ܡܢ ܕܒܢܝ. ܒܕܠܐ ܡܙܠܓ ܒܪܘܓܙܟ ܕܢܦܫܟ. ܐܝܟ ܕܐܦ ܐܪܒܐ[3] ܠܐ ܡܙܠܓܐ ܐܦܠܐ ܡܦܫܐ.

ܦܣܘܩܐ ܬܪܝܢܐ
ܡܛܠ ܐܕܫ̈ ܪܚܡܬܐ ܘܕܚܠܬܐ ܘܠܒܝܒܘܬܐ
ܬܐܘܪ̈ܝܐܣ ܚܕ

ܡܕܡܝܬܐ. ܪܚܡܬܐ ܡܢ ܐܠܗܘܬܗ ܕܐܬܗܘܦܟ ܕܒܗ̇ ܢܨܒܐ ܒܪܢܫܐ ܠܒܠܬܐ ܠܒܪܢܫܐ ܐܚܪܢܐ ܡܛܠܬܗ ܕܗ̇ܘ ܐܚܪܢܐ ܘܠܘ ܡܛܠܬܗ ܕܝܠܗ. ܘܪܚܡܐ ܐܠܗܘܬ, ܗ̇ܘ ܕܪܚܡ ܘܡܬܪܚܡ ܐܚܝܕܐ. ܘܡܫܬܘܬܦ ܒܡܚܫܒ̈ܢܝܬܐ *ܕܪܚܡܗ ܘܒܡܚܫܒܬܗ[1] ܡܛܠ ܪܚܡܗ ܘܠܘ ܡܛܠܬܗ. ܒܕ ܪܚܡܐ ܫܪܝܪܐ ܒܡܚܫܒ̈ܢܝܬܐ ܕܪܚܡܗ ܫܪܝܪܐ ܘܒܡܚܫܒܬܗ ܡܬܬܚܝܡ. ܗܢܐ ܕܝܢ ܒܗܦܟܐ. ܒܐܡܬ ܒܡܚܫܒܬܐ ܕܗܢܐܗ ܫܪܝܪܐ ܘܒܡܚܫܒ̈ܢܝܬܗ ܡܬܬܚܝܡ. ܡܬܪܚܡ ܕܝܢ ܡܢܟ ܐܝܠܝܢ ܕܥܦܪ ܒܕܡ ܠܟ ܐܘ ܠܗܠܝܢ ܕܝܠܟ. ܡܛܠ ܕܝܢ ܒܕ ܪܘܟܒܬܐ ܚܘܫܚܐܝܬ ܗܕܝܢ. ܡܬܪܚܡ *ܕܝܢ ܐܦ[2] ܪܚܡܐ ܕܪܚܡܐ. ܘܒܠܕܒܒܐ ܕܒܠܕܒܒܐ. *ܘܐܝܢܐ ܕܫܢܝܐ ܠܒܠܕܒܒܐ ܐܘ ܠܗ ܗܘ ܫܢܝܐ[3] ܒܠܕܒܒܐ. ܘܐܝܠܝܢ ܕܥܦܪ ܗܕܝܢ ܘܠܐ ܡܬܦܪܚܝܢ. ܐܝܟ ܥܦܪ̈ܒܐ ܘܒܢܒܪܐ. ܘܐܝܠܝܢ ܕܒܡܠܐ ܕܐܢ̈ܫܘܗܝ ܐܒܠܝܢ. ܐܝܟ ܦܬ̈ܟܐ ܘܐܒܪܐ. ܘܐܝܠܝܢ ܕܦܫܝܛܝܢ ܘܠܐ ܢܕܡܝܢ ܠܡܛܠܡ.

[3] i. add. ܠ RVLl

1 [1] ܘܡܚܫܒ̈ܢܝܬܐ ܕܪܚܡܗ RVLl [2*] om. RVL; ܕܝܢ l [3*] ܐܘ ܠܗ RVL [3] om. l

considers himself not blameworthy is more angry. Also more angry is he who perceives an insult directed at him, while he who does not perceive (it) is not angry. Rightly, therefore, it was said to Odysseus, 'You are not the sacker of the city, because you do not perceive the insults which its children hurl against you.' Anger also ceases at the death of the scorner. Therefore the poet well said, when wishing to calm Achilles' anger against the dead Hector, 'From henceforth you will embrace the silent earth forever'; that is to say, 'In vain you are angry against him who has departed, because he perceives not your anger that he may answer you, as the earth neither perceives nor answers.'

## SECTION TWO
### On the Species of Friendship, Fear, and Confidence
### Seven Theories

ONE.[9] Friendship is a condition in which someone wishes good for someone else for the sake of the other and not for his own sake. A friend is one who both loves and is loved, and shares in the joys and sorrows of his friend for his friend's sake and not his own, because a true friend rejoices in the joys of his friend and grieves in his sorrows. An enemy, by contrast, rejoices in the sorrows of his enemy and is grieved by his joys. Those who do well to you or yours are loved by you, the more so when they do big things gladly. A friend of a friend is also loved; and an enemy of an enemy; and he who hates an enemy, or whom an enemy hates; and those who act nobly and do not receive recompense, like the generous and the brave; and those who eat the labour of their own hands, like labourers and husbandmen; and those who are simple and do not know (how) to commit injustice.

TWO.[10] Those respected for virtues on whom, unless they allow (it), no one dares to confer anything, heap up great kindness on anyone who does confer (it), if they accept (it), and therefore they are espe-

[9] **5.2.1** AR 2.4 80b34-81a25; IS 3.2 (135.11-136.9).
[10] **5.2.2** AR 2.4 81a25-b33; IS 3.2 (136.9-137.12).

ܕܬܪܬܝܢ. ܡܩܒܠܝܢ ܒܬܪܬܝܢܘܬܐ¹ ܗܢܘܢ ܕܐܠܐ² ܡܩܘܡܝܢ ܠܐ ܡܡܪܚܝܢ³ ܐܝܟ
ܠܡܫܡܥܘ ܠܗܘܢ ܡܛܠ ܕܒܩܘܫܬܐ ܙܕܩܬܐ ܥܠ *ܚܕ. ܕܡܫܡܫ ܒܫܡ⁴ ܐܝܟܘ
ܕܡܫܡܠܝܢ. ܘܒܠܗܕܐ ܡܛܠ ܡܬܪܚܡܝܢ. ܡܬܬܪܚܡܝܢ ܕܝܢ ܘܡܬܡܪܡܪܐ ܗܢܝܐ،
ܒܚܝܠܐ. ܕܠܡܫܘܐ ܒܡܫܘܢ ܒܠܗ ܢܫܡܬܐ ܐܝܟ ܐܝܟ. ܒܗ̇، ܕܦܫܝܩܝܢ
ܘܠܒܘܫܪ، ܙܢܚܐ ܠܐ ܡܫܡܫܝܢ ܘܠܐ ܡܬܬܟܠܝܢ ܐܦܠܐ ܗܪܪܝܢ.
ܘܫܘܫܛܠܐ ܕܗܠܝܢ ܢܝܚܝܢ ܘܡܫܡܫܝܢ ܘܡܫܡܫܪܐ ܕܡܘܪܐ⁵ ܠܦܠܓܐ ܙܘܪܐ
ܡܫܪܚܝܢ. ܡܬܪܚܡܝܢ ܬܘܒ ܥܡܦܪܝܡܐ. ܢܩܕ، ܠܒܡܥܐ. ܘܐܡܠܝܢ ܕܠܫܦܠܐ
ܠܐ ܡܫܡܫܝܢ ܘܐܡܬܐ ܠܐ ܢܦܪܝܢ ܘܠܐ ܒܕܠܝܢ. ܘܕܠܠܐܬܐ ܡܬܪܚܡܝܢ.
ܘܠܒܫܘܗܝ ܢܦܪܝܢ ܘܕܐܡܪܘ، ܒܫܡܬܐ ܠܐ ܡܕܡܝܢ. ܙܒܢ ܕܝܢ ܒܙܒܢܐ
ܠܕܘܟܐ ܠܗ ܒܐܡܪܐ ܘܙܢܐ. ܘܠܐܢܫܐ ܕܦܠܓܐ ܒܗ ܘܙܟܝ ܕܢܗܘܐ
ܐܡܬܗ. ܘܠܡܢ *ܕܡܫܘܪ ܠܗ⁶ ܘܒܥܬ ܡܢܗ. ܘܠܡܢ ܕܡܫܬܪ ܡܫܡܥܐ⁷
ܘܒܥܬ ܕܢܦܪܫܐ ܐܚܪܐ. ܘܒܠܗܕܐ ܐܦ ܒܢܫܐ ܠܒܡܫܬܬܐ⁸ ܙܢܝܢ.

ܕܬܠܬ. ܐܕܫܐ ܕܙܢܝܘܬܐ ܬܠܬܐ ܐܝܬܝܗܘܢ. ܚܒܪܘܬܐ ܕܐܝܬܝܗ̇
ܕܬܗܘܦܐ ܕܒܦܠܓܘܬ ܚܝܠܐ ܡܬܪܪܐ. ܘܚܝܬܘܬܐ ܕܐܝܬܝܗ̇ ܗܝܐܘܬ
ܦܠܓܐ.¹ ܘܐܢܫܝܘܬܐ ܕܐܝܬܝܗ̇ ܥܡܦܬܘܬ ܠܒܗܡܐ ܐܘ ܐܡܝܢܐ² ܐܘ
ܚܝܕܐ ܐܘ ܗܡܘܪܬ ܠܦܠܓܐ. ܘܡܢ ܬܠܬܐ ܒܡܕܪ̈ܬܐ ܕܙܢܝܘܬܐ ܗ̇، ܕܒܗ
ܠܐ ܗܢܝܢ ܐܝܟ ܢܫܐ ܒܐܝܟ³ ܠܒܡܘܬܐ. ܘܒܗ ܒ̈ܢܝ ܠܐ ܢܛܪܢ.
ܒܠܒܒܘܬܐ ܕܝܢ ܡܢ ܗܫܘܠܝܬܐ ܕܙܢܝܘܬܐ ܡܬܕܝܢܐ. ܘܡܢ ܬܠܬܐ
ܒܡ̈ܕܝܬܐ ܕܒܠܒܒܘܬܐ ܗܝܐܬܐ⁴ ܘܦܠܓܐ. ܒܬܪ ܙܘܠܓܐ ܥܠ ܡܘܡܐ
ܗ̇ܘܐ. ܗܝܐܬܐ ܕܝܢ ܐܦ ܥܠ ܐܕܫܐ ܗܘܝܐ ܘܠܗ̇ ܡܢܐ ܕܕܘܟܐ ܠܐܕܫܐ.
ܠܒܗܡܐ ܒܪ ܒܠܥ ܦܝܠܐ ܦܫܦܠܐܝܬ. ܘܡܢ ܗܠܝܢ ܐܕܫܐ ܡܬܬܡܝܐ
ܙܗܦܠܐ ܕܫܪܪ ܒܢܦܫ ܕܢܝܐ ܘܡܫܡ̈ܥܐ ܒܠܒܒܘܬܐ ܕܒܠܒܝܗ
ܕܫܦܪܝܗ، ܘܙܢܝܬܗ ܕܠܗ ܕܫܦܪܝܗ،⁵

ܕܐܪܒܥ. ܕܢܠܬܐ ܕܝܢ ܐܝܬܝܗ̇ ܒܡܬܐ ܘܡܠܝܫܘܬ ܢܦܫܐ ܒܡܬܗܦܠܝܫܘܬ
ܒܥܬܐ ܕܒܬܪܐ ܠܡܫܒܠܘ ܐܘ ܠܡܥܡܘ. ܒܕܠܘ ܥܠ¹ ܒܥܬܐ ܕܢܠܬܐ. ܐܝܟ
ܫܡܥܐ ܘܫܒܝܚܘܬܐ. ܕܢܠܬܐ ܕܝܢ ܒܥܬܐ ܕܪܘܒܐ ܘܒܬܪܐ ܠܡܫܒܠܘ ܐܘ
ܠܡܥܡܘ. ܒܕ ܐܬܪܐ ܕܡܢ ܡܟܘܠ ܗ، ܐܘ ܒܚܙܬ ܠܐ ܕܢܠܬܐ. ܘܒܠܗܕܐ
ܠܐ ܕܢܠ ܒܠܒܝ ܡܢ ܡܢܬܐ. ܘܐܝܟ ܢܕܒ ܒܠܒܝ ܕܡܒܬ ܡܐܬܐ. ܐܠܐ ܒܕ
ܙܢܫܐ ܗܦܪܝܢ ܠܗ ܠܐ ܙܢܝ. ܕܢܠ ܕܝܢ ܡܢܗ ܙܒܠ ܐܝܬܐ ܕܒܐܝܫܐ ܙܒܢܐ.

2 ¹ sg. RVLl ² ܕܐܠܐ RVLl ³ ܡܡܪܚ. F ⁴ ܗ̇ܘ ܕܡܫܡܫ ܙܥܡ RVLl ⁵ i. add. ܕ RVLl ⁶* ܕܡܫܪܬܢ ܡܫܡ̈ܥܐ RVLl ⁷ sg. RVLl ⁸ ܠܒܡܫܬܬܐ RVL
3 ¹ ܦܠܓܐ RL; ܦܠܓܐ V; ܦܠܓܐ l ² pl. RVL ³ ܒܐܝܟܢ RVLl ⁴ i. add. ܘ RVLl ⁵ ܕܫܦܪܝܗ، RVLl
4 ¹ om. RVLl

cially loved. The admired who are pleasant company are also loved, those with whom one may desire to be all day, because they are easy-going, neither condone nor are harsh to the failings of friends, and are not quarrelsome. The opposites of these are contentious and obstinate and send forth major rebukes for minor failings. Also loved are flatterers; the well-dressed; those who neither condone sinners nor harbour a grudge and find fault; those who are easily appeased; and those who guard their tongue and do not know (how) to speak evil. Someone loves one who is similar to himself in craft and manner; one whom he emulates and desires to be like; whomsoever he honours and by whomsoever he is ashamed; and whoever conceals blemishes and is ashamed to expose mysteries. Therefore even evil men like modest people.

THREE.[11] The species of friendship are three: companionship, which is a condition which is established by length of acquaintance; intimacy, which is pleasure in (the other's) presence; and kinship, which is a sharing of descent, profession, custom, or doing good. Among the causes productive of friendship is doing a kindness to someone when one is not bound (to do so), and not revealing it when doing it. Enmity is revealed by the opposites of friendship, and among the causes productive of enmity are hatred and anger. Anger is (directed) at an individual, but hatred is also (directed) against a species and at that which is like a species, for generally everyone hates a thief. By these species an orator is able to establish in the soul of the judge and the audience the enmity of his adversary, in order that they may regard him unfavourably, and his own friendship, in order that they may honour him.

FOUR.[12] Fear is distress or agitation of the soul (caused) by the imagination of an evil which is going to be destructive or distressing; for not every evil is feared, like envy and slothfulness, but evil is feared which is near and going to be destructive or distressing, because that which is far off or past is not feared. Therefore no one fears death, and although everyone knows that he will certainly die,

---

[11] **5.2.3** AR 2.4 81b33-82a7; 16-19; IS 3.2 (137.13-138.4).

[12] **5.2.4** AR 2.5 82a21-b3; 10-12; IS 3.2 (138.5-139.2).

ܕܣܢܝܩܐ ܡܕܝܢ ܗܠܝܢ ܐܝܟ ܕܡܨܝܢ ܣܢܝܩܐ ܠܡܣܒܠܘ ܐܘ ܠܡܫܡܥܘ ܠܦܘܩܕܢܐ ܕܡܬܝܗܒ ܠܡܠܝܠܘܬܐ ܟܝܢܐ. ܘܠܦܘܩܕܢܗ[2] ܕܐܝܬܘܗܝ ܡܬܦܪܢܣܢܘܬ ܗܝ ܕܕܣܢܝܩܐ. ܕܣܢܝܩܐ ܕܝܢ ܘܐܝܠܢܐ ܕܡܨܝܐ ܠܡܦܪܢܣܘ ܟܠܗܝܢ. ܘܐܝܠܢܐ ܕܡܨܝܐ ܠܡܫܠܛܘ ܘܐܦ ܠܐ ܫܠܛ. ܘܐܝܠܢܐ ܕܢܕܒܪ ܕܡܬܠܐ ܠܡܬܕܒܪܘ ܝܬܝܪ ܡܢ ܐܝܠܢܐ ܕܦܩܕ ܕܢܕܒܪ.

ܕܫܡܥ. ܐܝܠܢܐ ܕܠܝܬ ܒܗ ܫܘܬܦܐ ܒܦܘܪܫܢܐ. ܐܝܟ ܡܠܟܐ. ܝܬܝܪ ܕܣܢܝܩ. ܘܐܝܠܢܐ ܕܟܠ ܦܬܓܡܐ ܐܘ ܡܬܠܐ ܕܣܢܝܩ ܟܠ ܫ̈ܐܠܬܐ ܘܡܦܫ̈ܩܢܐ ܝܬܝܪ ܕܣܢܝܩ. ܘܫ̈ܪܟܐ ܕܢܣܒܝܢ ܘܒܗܠܝܢ ܝܬܝܪ ܡܢ ܫ̈ܪܟܐ ܣܟܠܬܐ ܕܒܡܨܥܬܐ ܐ̈ܦܐ ܡܚܝܡܝܢ ܕܣܠܝܢ. ܒܕܠܐ ܦܫܝܩܐܝܬ ܡܬܬܡܨܝܢܐ ܕܬܪܝܨܘܬܗܘܢ ܐܦܠܐ ܒܠܕܒܒܘܬܐ[1] ܢܨܝܪܬܐ ܡܐܢܐ ܠܗܘܢ. ܘܡܢ ܥܪܒܐ ܗܟܢ ܕܣܢܝܩܐ[2] ܗܠܝܢ ܕܠܐ ܡܨܝܐ ܠܡܬܕܪܫܘ ܦܘܕܢܝܗܘܢ. ܘܗܠܝܢ ܕܠܝܬ ܐܝܟܐ ܘܡܕܒܪܢܐ ܒܕܝܠܗܘܢ. ܠܐ[3] ܕܝܢ ܕܫܠܝܛ ܒܐܝܪܐ ܕܒܡܗܝܡܢܘܬܐ ܪܒܬܐ ܐܝܬܝܗܘܢ ܘܒܠܗܕܐ ܡܟܣܝܢ ܘܦܫܝܩܝܢ ܘܣܬܝܪܝܢ. ܘܠܥܒܪܐ ܕܐܥܒܪܐ[4] ܥܢܝܢ ܘܡܬܦܪܫܝܢ. ܡܠܘ ܕܝܢ ܒܡܘܡܬܐ ܕܚܠܝܡܘܬܐ ܘܫܠܝܡܘܬ ܦܓܪܐ ܘܬܩܝܦܘܬ ܚܝܠܐ ܘܫܦܝܪܐܝܬ ܙܪܝܙܐ. ܘܗܝ ܕܒܡܬܡܠܟܢܘܬܐ ܢܬܩܘܦ ܥܘܕܪܐ ܗܘ ܕܕܣܢܝܩܘܬܐ. ܡܢ ܗܠܝܢ ܡܕܝܢ ܡܢ ܕܡܬܝܬܐ ܗܝ ܕܠܡܕܒܪ ܢܦܫܐ ܕܢܙܪ ܒܗܦܟ ܒܝܬܐ ܐܝܟ ܐܬܘܪ̈ܬܐ ܢܩܒ ܘܒܬܠܐ..

ܕܢܬܐ. ܠܥܒܕܘܬܐ ܕܝܢ ܐܝܬܝܗ ܐܟܡܐ ܕܗܘ ܥܒܕ ܗܒܪܐ ܕܦܘܪܫܢܐ ܗܘܐ ܒܪܥܝܐ ܘܠܕܣܢܝܩܘܬܐ ܗܝ ܐܘ ܕܠܐ ܐܝܬܝܗܝܢ ܐܘ ܠܢܘܡܘܣܐ ܐܝܬܝܗܝܢ ܫܪܐ ܠܗܝܢ. ܒܗܝ ܕܠܫܠܛܬܐ ܕܦܘܪܫܢܐ ܠܦܘܪܫܢܐ ܫܪܐ. ܐܝܟ ܡܬܬܚܡܢܘܬ ܣܢܝܩܐ ܕܬܘܪܝ ܒܥܒܕܐ ܕܡܫܬܥܒܕܐ. ܘܡܨܝܐܘܬܐ ܕܡܕܒܪܢܐ ܘܣܢܝܩܘܬܗܘܢ[1]. ܘܗܝ ܕܠܐ ܢܗܘܐ ܡܫܠܡܢܐ ܘܠܐ ܡܫܠܡܢܐ ܐܚܪܢܐ ܠܥܒܕܐ ܡܠܟܬܐ. ܒܪ ܗܝ ܕܠܐ ܡܫܠܡܢ ܥܒܕ ܗܒܪܗ. ܘܒܗܝ ܕܠܐ ܡܫܬܕܪ ܕܢܫܠܡ ܚܠܝܦܐܝܬ ܡܫܬܥܒܕ. ܠܐ ܓܝܪ ܡܨܝܐ ܕܢܫܬܥܒܕ ܐܝܠܢܐ ܕܣܢܝܩܐ ܠܝܬ ܠܗ. ܐܚܝܕ ܣܢܝܩܐ ܐܝܬ ܠܗ ܘܣܠܩ ܙܪܥܐ ܕܠܐ ܢܚܠܘ ܗܦܝ. ܐܠܐ ܥܒܕ ܚܒܝܒ ܠܗ ܒܪ ܒܝܬܗ ܐܘ ܚܕ ܡܛܠܬܗ ܒܪ ܗܢܘܢ ܐܟܣܢܝܐ ܫܠܝܘܗܝ ܐܝܬܘܗܝ ܕܡܫܬܥܒܕ. ܗܕܝܢ ܐܝܟ ܦܪܘܫܐ ܠܥܒܕܐܝܬ ܡܕܡ ܒܟܝܢܐ. ܡܬܠܒܒ ܝܬܝܪ ܥܒܕܐ ܦܠܚܐ ܘܠܐ ܡܬܠܬܐ ܒܡܘܡܬܐ. ܒܪ ܡܟܝܦ ܥܐܟܦ ܠܟܝ ܕܒܩܪܐ ܡܚܘ. ܘܥܒܕܐ ܕܒܠܝܗܘܢ ܡܬܠܒܒ ܓܝܪܐ ܗܘܢ ܕܠܐ ܥܒܕܘ ܠܣܒܠܐ. ܘܡܫܡܠܝܢ ܛܘܟܣܘܬܐ ܐܝܬܝܗܘܢ.

---

[2] ܘܠܦܘܩܕܢܗ RVL; ܘܠܦܘܩܕܢܗ l

5 [1] i. add. ܒ F [2] i. om. RVLl [3] ܠܐܠܝܢ RVLl [4] sg. RVLl

6 [1] ܘܕܣܢܝܩܘܬܗܘܢ RVLl

nevertheless because it is remote, (all) suppose they should not think about it, but (everyone) fears that which necessarily concerns (him) much more than it. Feared, therefore, are those things which have the ability to destroy or to produce harmful injuries which tend to (produce) great vexation, and danger, which is the approach of that which is feared. Feared also is he who can always hurt, and he who can be unjust even though he is not unjust. He who knows that he is going to be hurt is more fearful than he who supposes (it).

FIVE.[13] He who has no associate in government, like a king, is more feared, and he who is feared by brave or virtuous men is more feared by weak and feeble ones. Cunning men who are mild and tranquil are more feared than quick-tempered, who are annoying by (their) outspokenness, because the mind (of the cunning) is not easily fathomed and lengthy enmity does not irk them. Among things greatly feared are those, the errors of which it is impossible to correct, and those for the repulsion of which there is no help or helper. The rich who live in great abundance are not afraid and are therefore insolent, headstrong, and haughty. They despise the rest of mankind and glorify themselves, especially in youth, bodily health, force of power, and multitude of friends. Taking refuge in deliberation is a sign of fear. Therefore from these things, when it is better to create fear, someone (who) wishes to establish (it) in a man's soul may select and prepare *topoi*.

SIX.[14] Confidence is a habit in which a person is hopeful of salvation and perceives fearful things either not to exist or to be far away, because he perceives the causes of salvation as at hand, like the possibility of correcting an approaching evil, or a multitude of helpers together with their strength. Not being a wrongdoer and not being wronged together give confidence to a person, because his hope is not to be unjust, and because he does not suffer being wronged, he strives valiantly. He who has no power cannot strive, but if he has power his striving (can) also be on behalf of a friend who has never cheated him, but (on the contrary) acted well towards him by helping

---

[13] **5.2.5** AR 2.5 82b13-26; 35-83a14; IS 3.2 (139.2-14).

[14] **5.2.6** AR 2.5 83a14-25; IS 3.2 (139.15-140.3).

ܕܥܒܕ. ܥܠ ܕܫܬܠܡܬܐ ܡܬܠܒܒ ܒܢܫܐ ܐܘ ܒܗ̇، ܕܠܐ ܢܗܒ ܢܣܝܒܘܗܝ ܐܘ
ܒܗ̇، ܕܡܥܒܕ ܠܗ ܐܢܫܐ ܒܡܘܗܒ. ܐܝܟܢܐ ܕܥܠ ܦܘܪܫܢܗ ܕܐܡܪܐ ܡܒܣܪ
ܐܡܪܐ ܕܒܡܣܒܢܐ ܒܡܣܒܢܘܬܗ، ܠܐ ܡܣܒܪ. ܐܘ ܡܣܒܪ ܐܠܐ[1] ܥܠ ܡܩܒܘܠܐ[2]
ܫܡܥܐ ܡܬܬܟܠ. ܡܬܠܒܒ ܗܘܐ ܥܠ[3] ܗ̇ܘ ܕܕܚܠ ܐܢܫܐ ܕܢܕܥ ܕܐܫܪܪܐ
ܕܐܒܘܬܗ ܐܫܬܘܕܥܘ ܡܢܗ. *ܐܘ ܒܙ[4] ܗ̇ܘ ܕܬܫܝܬ ܐܢܫܐ ܡܫܬܪ ܡܢ ܪܫܐ
ܐܘ ܫܘܐ ܠܗ ܚܢܐ ܗ̣ܘ ܠܗ. ܡܬܠܒܒ ܒܠܒܗ، ܕܢܚܠ[5] ܕܝܢ ܪܫܐ ܕܫܬܪ
ܕܒܪ ܒܡܫܪܬܘܬܗ ܒܫܠܡܘܬܗ ܢܒܩܐ ܦܓܪܐ ܘܡܫܟܢܘܬܗ ܡܒܕܪܐ ܒܢ̈ܝ
ܐܬܪܗ.[6] ܕܢܚܠ ܕܝܢ ܐܦ ܕܢܫܐ[7] ܒܐܢܫܐ ܡܕܡ ܐܠܗܐ ܘܡܕܡ ܒܒܢ̈ܝܫܐ
ܘܗܘܡܝܕܐ[8] ܡܢ ܣܟܠܘܬܐ ܘܫܦܝܪܐ[9] ܘܡܗܘܪܐ. ܘܡܢ ܗܠܝܢ ܕܡܠܒܒܝܢ
ܠܦܪ̈ܝܠܐ[10] ܘܦܪ̈ܝܠܐ. ܒܕܡ ܠܒܐ ܒܙ ܪܗܛ ܐܦ ܠܢܫܐ[11] ܡܠܒܒ. ܘܦܪ̈ܝܠܐ
ܕܐܝܟ ܗܢܐ ܒܠܐ ܡܣܒܐ ܒܙ ܡܬܛܠܡ ܛܒܪ ܡܬܬܒܪ. ܡܫܬܒܪܐ ܠܒܪ
ܐܠܗܘܬܐ ܕܠܛܠܝ̈ܐ ܡܒܕܪܐ. ܡܬܠܒܒ ܕܝܢ ܘܐܢܫܐ ܕܡܕܡ ܡܒܪ[12] ܕܠܐ
ܚܐܒ. ܐܘ ܛܒܪ ܢܬܪ. ܐܘ ܠܬܘܪܒܬܐ ܢܣܒܟ ܕܠܐ[13] ܬܘܒ ܢܣܒܪ.

ܦܣܘܩܐ ܬܠܝܬܝܐ
ܡܛܠ ܒܗܬܬܘܬܐ[1] ܘܟܒܝܫܘܬܐ ܘܦܠܚܘܬܐ
ܦܘܪ̈ܩܐ ܬܫܥ

ܡܕܡܝܬܐ. ܐܝܬܝܗ̇ ܕܝܢ ܒܗܬܬܐ ܓܢܚܘܬܐ ܘܟܒܝܫܘܬܐ ܒܡܬܚܫܕܢܘܬ[1]
ܓܒܪܐ ܒܒܥܝܬܐ ܕܗܘܬ ܐܘ ܕܗܘܝܐ ܐܘ ܕܥܬܝܕܐ. ܘܟܒܝܫܘܬܐ ܐܝܬܝܗ̇
ܕܡܬܗܦܟ ܕܒܗ̇ ܓܒܪܐ ܠܐ ܒܠܐ ܡܬܚܫܒܢܘܬܐ ܢܟܐ ܐܦܠܐ
ܒܡܬܚܫܕܢܘܬܐ[2] ܡܬܒܥܐ. ܡܬܦܫܛܐ ܕܝܢ ܐܝܬܝܗܝܢ ܒܬܫܥܐ ܕܐܝܟ
ܗܠܝܢ. ܠܡܒܗܬ ܡܢ ܗܕܪܐ ܕܡܪܟܐ. ܠܡܕܪܐ ܐܢܫܐ ܘܫܒܪܐ ܒܝܕ ܕܚܠܬܐ.
ܠܡܛܠ ܒܡܠܬܐ. ܠܡܛܠܠ ܠܒܢ̈ܝܐ. ܠܡܬܟܝܫ ܒܡ ܒܢ̈ܝܐ. ܠܡܚܠ ܐܡܬܐ
ܕܠܐ ܙܕܩ ܒܥܕܢܗ. ܠܡܚܒܐ *ܘܡܬܪܐ ܥܝܫܠܐ[3] ܒܥܕܢܗ. ܐܝܟ ܬܘܠܡܢ
ܡܩܒܠܐ ܐܘ ܡܬܦܠܬܐ. ܘܡܢ ܗܘܟܐ ܐܡܪ ܡܠܠܐ ܕܐܦ ܡܢ ܡܒܗܬܐ ܡܐܬܐ
ܡܩܘܬܗ ܢܗܘܐ. ܠܡܦܩܕܘ ܒܙ ܚܛܝܪ. ܠܡܫܐܠ ܡܢ ܗ̇ܘ ܕܐܦܪܢ ܡܢܗ.
ܠܡܐܦ ܒܙ ܠܐ ܦܣܝܩ. ܠܡܦܩ ܒܙ ܡܬܠܒܒܐ ܕܢܬܠ. ܠܡܬܠ ܒܙ ܠܐ[4] ܦܣܝܩ
ܕܢܗܘܐ.

7 [1] ܒܪܡ RVLl [2] ܡܩܒܘܠܐ RL [3] om. RVLl [4*] ܘܒܙ RVLl [5] ܕܢܚܠ RVLl [6] f. ܐ RVLl [7] ܪܫܐ RVLl [8] pl. RVLl [9] ܘܫܦܪܐ RVLl [10] ܠܦܪ̈ܝܠܐ RVLl [11] ܘܠܢܫܐ RVLl [12] i. add. ܘ RVL [13] i. ܘ RVLl

Titulus [1] ܒܗܬܬܘܬܐ RVLl

1 [1] ܒܡܬܚܫܕܢܘܬ RLl; ܒܡܬܚܫܪܢܘܬ V [2] ܒܡܬܚܫܕܢܘܬܐ RVLl [3*] pl. RVLl [4] om. RVLl

him, or suffered on his behalf by bearing afflictions for him. Then as a brave man he may confidently rise up to the challenge. He who is of noble birth and unblemished by defect is especially confident, because he utterly despises whoever is inferior to him. The things on account of which a man may be confident are those which are not reduced to corruption, but have lasting (value).

SEVEN.[15] A person may be confident about fearful things either because he has not been tested by them, or because help is available to him in them. For example, someone may scorn the dangers of the sea who has not experienced its violent storms, or has experienced (them) but has confidence in a wise helmsman. About that which is fearful he is confident who knows that others like him have been saved from it. And when he who is under a ruler perceives himself better than the ruler or equal to him, he is confident in relation to him, but a ruler is feared who has a greater advantage through copious wealth, bodily strength, and numerous helpers among the people of his territory. Feared is also a judge (who is) righteous before God and men and recognised by wise, learned, and rational men. Among the things which give confidence is the seething of anger, because a seething heart may even give confidence to a frail man. Such anger is especially aroused in (someone who is) not guilty (of wrongdoing) when he has been wronged, for divinity is supposed to aid those who are wronged. He also is confident who is sure in advance that he will not suffer, or is especially successful, or repairs a breach so that he no longer suffers loss.

## SECTION THREE
### On Shame, Shamelessness, and Kindness
### Six Theories

ONE.[16] Shame is the distress or disturbance (suffered by) a person through being blamed for an evil which is past, present, or future, and shamelessness is a condition in which a person neither suffers for not being honoured nor is vexed for being blamed. Things caus-

---

[15] **5.2.7** AR 2.5 83a25-b11; IS 3.2 (140.15-141.13).

[16] **5.3.1** AR 2.6 83b12-30; IS 3.3 (142.3-12).

ܕܬܪ̈ܬܝܢ. ܡܛܡܘܬܐ[1] ܕܝܢ ܗܘ̇ܝ ܕܢܦܠܘ ܡܛܠ ܡܘܬܪܐ ܡܫܬܟܚܢܐ ܘܝܕܝܥܐ
ܒܦܘܡ ܩܢܪܐ. ܗܢܘ ܕܝܢ ܥܘܦܪܕܘܬܐ ܕܕܠܐ[2] ܒܪܘܡܐ ܡܟܪܝܟ ܘܡܣܝܟ. ܘܗ̇ܝ
ܕܢܣܒ ܥܠ ܟܐܒܐ *ܘܦܘܫܩܢܐ ܕܚܘܪܐ[3] ܐܚܪܢܐ ܕܢܐܟܝܢ ܩܘ̈ܠܐ ܘܡܦܘ̈ܬܐ
ܘܡܬܠܠܬܐ ܘܗܘܢ[4] ܕܢܗܘܐ ܡܣܬܟܠܐ ܘܣܟ̈ܝܠܐ. ܒܠܗܘܢ ܓܝܪ ܐܬܬ̈ܐ ܐܝܟ
ܕܪܦܘܬܐ. ܘܗ̇ܝ ܕܢܬܠܒܫܪ ܐܝܟ ܒܪ ܥܦܪ ܚܒܪ ܐܘ ܣܐܒܐ. ܐܬܬܐ ܗܝ ܓܝܪ
ܗܕܐ ܕܡܒܘܪܬ ܢܦܫܐ. ܗܟܢܐ *ܘܗ̇ܝ ܕܫܘ ܠܗ ܢܥܒܕ ܘܗ̇ܝ ܕܥܦܪ̈ܢܝܬܐ
ܕܐܣܪ̈ܢܐ ܕܠܗ ܢܐܡܪ.[5] ܗܠܝܢ ܓܝܪ ܐܬܬ̈ܐ ܐܝܟܝܢ[6] ܕܣܘܬܪܐ.[7] ܘܡܢ
ܡܟܬܒܢܘܬܐ ܒܢ̈ܫܐ ܗ̇ܝ ܕܠܫܒܐ ܩܢܝܐ ܢܩܒܠ ܐܝܟ ܒܡܘܒܠܗ. ܒܪ ܐܝܟ
ܕܒܡܟܠܘܬܐ ܠܩܢܝܬܐ ܕܐܣܪ̈ܢܐ ܒܐܘܟܡ̈ܝܗܘܢ ܘܒܘܪ̈ܟܝܗܘܢ[8] ܢܬܕܒܪ.
ܘܠܟܒܪܐ[9] ܥܒܝܪܐ ܗܪ̈ܟܝܗܘܢ ܢܬܠܝ. ܘܢܣܒܪ ܒܢ̈ܫܬܐ ܕܡܫܬܒܪ̈ܢ ܒܗ. ܐܢ
ܢܒܐ ܘܐܢ ܠܐ ܢܒܐ. ܡܛܠ ܗ̇ܝ ܕܐܣܪ̈ܢܐ ܒܗ ܢܬܡܫܡܫܘܢ. ܐܝܬ ܓܝܪ
ܡܫܒܪܢܘܬܐ ܕܕܝܠܢܝܘܬܐ ܗ̇ܝ ܘܠܘ ܒܒܪܢܘܬܐ. ܐܝܟ ܗ̇ܝ ܕܠܐ ܢܬܒܥ
ܒܪܬܐ.

ܕܬܠܬ. ܒܪ ܒܠܬ ܒܗܬܬܐ ܡܬܗܦܟܢܘܬ[1] ܠܐ ܡܫܬܒܚܢܘܬܐ ܐܡܬܝ.
ܗܢܘܢ ܕܡܢܗܘܢ ܦܠܐ ܠܡܒܥܬ ܗܠܝܢ ܐܝܟ. ܠܗܘܦܟ ܡܢ ܡܫܬܒܚܢܐ. ܒܪ
ܡܢ ܕܡܘܬܐ ܘܡܒܥ̈ܘܬܐ ܠܐ ܐܝܟ ܒܥܬ. ܒܥܬ ܕܝܢ ܐܦ ܡܢ ܗܢܘܢ ܕܒܗܘܢ
ܡܬܕܒܪܝܢ. ܐܘ ܗܢܘܢ ܕܒܗ[2] ܡܬܕܒܪܝܢ ܐܘ ܢܒܐ ܕܡܬܕܒܪܢܘ ܒܗ
ܘܡܘܪܘܡܘܗܝ. ܒܪ[3] ܢܣܒ ܕܢܬܟܒܪ ܡܢܗܘܢ ܒܗ̇ܝ ܕܗܢܘܢ ܒܠܚܘܕ. ܐܘ ܫܘܐ
ܠܡܘܪܐ ܠܗܘܢ. ܐܘ ܐܬܠܝܗܘܢ ܒܪ̈ܝܐ ܐܘ ܡܫܝܚܐ ܐܘ ܕܪܐ.
ܘܒܡܬܘܬܐ ܕܡܢܥ ܒܪ̈ܝܐ ܘܡܢ ܒܪܬ ܢܛܪ ܒܥܒܕܐ ܡܢ ܗ̇ܝ ܕܒܚܝܠܐ
ܘܗܬܐ. ܐܝܟ ܗ̇ܝ[4] ܕܐܬܛܝܒܐ ܒܪ ܐܣܦܪ. ܡܒܠܝܢ ܗܘܘ ܓܝܪ ܕܡܢ̈ܝܐ
ܘܡܢ ܠܡܕܝܢܬܗܘܢ ܘܢܣܒ. ܘܡܢ ܕܡܘܬܐ ܕܡܢ ܦܪ̈ܘܫܐ ܘܡܢ̈ܝܢܐ ܢܛܪ ܐܬܪܐ
ܡܢ ܐܬܪܐ *ܕܡܢ ܪ̈ܘܚܐ[5] ܘܡܒܪ̈ܝܐ. ܢܛܪ ܕܝܢ ܒܥܬ ܒܢܝ̈ܐ ܡܢ ܗܢܘܢ
ܕܡܘܫܐ ܘܪ̈ܘܚܐ ܣܓܝ ܠܗ ܘܠܐ ܚܙܐ ܠܗܘܢ ܐܚܪ̈ܝ ܠܒܗ. ܘܠܘ ܥܠ
ܪ̈ܘܚܐ ܥܠ ܐܪ̈ܥܐ[6] ܡܫܡܫܝܢ. ܒܪ ܢܒܚܐ[7] ܠܦܪ̈ܚܬܐ ܕܪܘܚܗ. ܐܝܟ ܕܒܡܘܪܐ
ܦܐܪܐ. ܘܡܢ ܕܐܝܟ ܗܠܝܢ ܡܬܠܬܐ ܒܢܘܚܡܬܐ ܘܒܪ̈ܘܚܐ ܘܡܒܪ̈ܟܬܐ. ܠܐ
ܡܬܬܠܘܢ ܒܥܬ ܐܝܟ. ܐܠܐ ܡܛܠ ܗ̇ܝ ܕܠܗܘܢ ܕܦܠܐ ܠܡܒܥܬ
ܗܢܘܢ ܒܡܪܝܐ[8] ܡܒܠܝܢ.

2 [1] pl. RVLl [2] i. om. RVLl [3*] ܘܚܠ ܦܘܫܩܢܐ ܐܚܪܐ RVLl [4] i. om. RVLl [5*] ܗ̇ܝ ܕܗܘ RVLl [6] om. RVLl [7] ܕܣܘܬܪܐ F [8] i. ܕ RVL [9] ܘܐܢ RVLl

3 [1] f. add. ܐ R [2] i. om. F [3] ܒܪ R [4] om. RVLl [5*] ܕܪ̈ܘܚܐ RVLl [6] pl. RVLl [7] ܢܒܚܐ RVLl [8] sg. RVL

ing shame are evil deeds such as these: fleeing from the line of battle; throwing away armour and shield for fear; seizing a deposit; being unjust to evil persons; having intercourse with evil persons; licentiously entering where it is not proper; disgracefully gaining a contemptible profit, like plundering the poor or the dead—therefore a proverb says, 'Even from a dead man he will take the grave clothes'—; keeping (money) in reserve when one is rich; asking from him who is more needy than oneself; borrowing when one has no need to; taking when there is a need to give; (and) giving when there is no need to take.

TWO.[17] It is shameful to praise (someone) for the sake of an anticipated advantage or to blame (him) for the dashing of a hope, for a flatterer is he who wrongly honours or reviles; to suffer on account of a minor pain or injury as do the old, the pampered, those in authority, and those who are very weak and lazy, for all of these are indices of softness; to boast when doing or experiencing good, for this is an index of smallness of soul; and similarly to honour oneself or claim as one's own the admirable deeds of others, for these are indices of pride. Also among the evil things causing shame are someone's acceptance in his own person of foul passions when, for example, in mockery he imitates the foul things of others by his gestures and his movements; or gives his members over to shameful acts; or endures evil things perpetrated upon him, whether he wishes it or not, so that others may have pleasure by him, for that (sort of) endurance is (one) of cowardliness, not courage, like not demanding vengeance.

THREE.[18] Since the cause of shame is the imagination of not being honoured, those before whom it is necessary to feel shame are the following. First, the honoured, because no one feels shame before madmen or children, but (someone) may feel shame before those whom he admires, or those who admire him or whom he wishes to admire and honour him, because he is anxious to be praised by them because he needs them, or (to be) equal in honour to them, or (because) they are prudent or older or educated. The shame which is

---

[17] **5.3.2** AR 2.6 83b30-84a23; IS 3.3 (142.12-143.10).

[18] **5.3.3** AR 2.6 84a23-b1;5-11;19-36; IS 3.3 (143.10-144.15).

ܕܐܘܪܚ. ܟܕ ܕܝܢ ܒܪܢܫܐ ܐܦ ܡܢ ܐܠܗܐ ܕܡܚܣܢ ܠܗ ܒܐܡܚܣܢܘ ܘܡܢ ܐܠܗܐ ܕܢܓܕܐ ܠܡܗܘܐ ܠܗܘܢ ܙܘܟܐ. ܐܝܟ ܗܘܦܪܕܝܣܘܣ ܡܢ ܒܢ̈ܝ ܗܪܐܩܘܣܐ.[1] ܘܐܝܟ[2] ܕܐܡܪ ܐܪܟܝܠܘܟܘ ܦܘܐܪܟܝܠܐ. ܟܕ ܟܠܗ ܬܕܝܪ ܗܘܐ ܠܡܬܦܠܠܘ ܡܢ ܡܠܟܐ ܕܡܩܕܘܢܝܘܣ[3] ܡܛܠ ܕܚܣܡ. ܟܕ ܚܙܐ ܠܐܠܗܐ ܕܒܬܪܝܢ ܗܘܐ[4] ܠܡܚܙܐ ܒܚܠܡܐ ܕܡܣܦܩܝܢ ܐܦܝܗܘܢ. ܘܢܦܩܝܢ[5] ܒܩܪܒܐ ܕܡܕܝܢܬܐ. ܕܕܩ ܬܬܝܗܘܢ ܡܚܙܐ ܠܐܠܗܝܢ ܕܗܫܐ ܚܝܝܢ ܐܝܬܝܗܘܢ ܘܬܬܒܗܘܢ ܡܢܗܘܢ ܡܚܣܝܢ ܐܝܬܝܗܘܢ ܐܦܝܗܘܢ. ܟܕ ܬܘܒ ܬܒܥ ܐܝܟ ܡܢ[6] ܐܠܗܐ ܕܡܢܨܚܢܘܬܐ ܢܨܚܝܢ ܗܘܘ ܠܗ ܘܡܢܗܐ ܠܐ ܚܙܐ ܒܗ. ܟܕ ܕܝܢ ܠܐ ܒܠܚܘܕ ܡܢ ܒܒܕܐ ܡܒܗܘܬܐ ܐܠܐ ܐܦ ܡܢ ܥܘܒܕܝܗܘܢ، ܘܐܬܩ̈ܢܬܗ. ܘܡܢ ܗܿܝ، ܕܢܬܠܠܘܗܝ. ܠܐ ܕܝܢ ܟܕ ܡܢ ܡܢܝܢܐ ܘܙܘܟܐ ܕܠܡܣܥܬܝܢ. ܘܡܢ ܠܐ ܥܒܝܕܐ ܕܕܡܝܢ ܠܚܙܝܐ ܘܒܒܗ̈ܬܐ. ܐܒܕܐ ܕܡܫܕܐܘܣ[7] ܡܛܠ ܢܬܪܬܐ ܕܟܣܐܘܡܣ ܬܪܥܡ. ܬܫܒܘܚܬܐ ܠܒܪ ܡܢ ܐܠܗܐ ܕܢܕܡܝܢ ܥܙܝܙܐ. ܘܡܢ ܠܐ ܢܩ̈ܒܐ ܗܒܝܪܐ.[8]

ܕܢܚܫܐ. ܘܡܠܝܢ ܗ̈ܠܝܢ[1] ܡܛܠ ܒܗܬܬܐ. ܠܡܡܚܝܘܬܐ ܕܝܢ ܐܘܚܕܢܬ ܠܐ ܡܬܚܝܢܘܬܐ ܡܢ ܗܘܦܩܠܝܬܘܣ[2] ܗܘܐ. ܡܚܝܠ ܡܛܠ ܘܟܠ ܠܦܘܠܚܢܬܐ ܘܒܦܘܪܢܗ̇ ܢܐܡܪ.[3] ܘܦܘܠܚܢܬܐ ܗ̈ܢܝ ܐܬܬܝܗ̇ ܡܟܘܬܐ ܡܬܚܪܢܝܬܐ ܕܟܕ[4] ܗܘܐ ܡܢ ܒܪܢܫܐ *ܠܐܚܪܢܐ ܦܠܐ ܕܢܘܕܐ ܡܛܠܗ ܗܿܘ[5] ܐܚܪܢܐ ܐܘ ܢܫܬܥܒܕ ܠܗ ܘܢܫܥܒܕܘܗܝ، ܘܟܠ ܦܘܠܚܢܬܐ *ܐܘ ܒܫܬܥܒܕܘܬܐ[6] ܐܘܚܕܢܬ ܡܟܒܕܢܘܬܐ ܦܘܪܢܣܬܐ ܕܡܬܪܬܐ ܗܘܐ. ܐܘ ܒܡܗܡܢܘܬܐ ܕܐܘܣܝܐ ܡܬܪܬܢܘܬܐ. ܘܪܒܘܬ ܠܦܘܠܚܢܬܐ ܒܦܓܥܐܘܬ ܫܘܡܢܐ. ܐܘ ܒܫܘܫܬ ܕܒܢܐ ܗܘܐ. ܐܘ ܕܒܗ ܠܫܘܕܘܗܝ، ܗܒܪܗ̇. ܐܘ ܗܿܘ ܡܕܡܐ ܐܝܟ ܒܗ. *ܐܘ ܡܛܠ ܐܝܟ ܒܗ.[7] ܘܗܘܦܟܐ ܗ̈ܢ ܠܡܟܘܬ ܗܿܘ ܡܛܐ ܕܡܫܕܐ ܟܕ ܡܪܒ ܐܘ ܡܚܫܘ ܟܕ ܐܫܘ ܐܬܬܗܘܢ، ܐܝܟ ܙܘܟܐ. ܡܬܠ ܕܝܢ ܗܫܘ ܒܪܢܫܐ ܟܠ ܗܿܘ ܡܟܐ ܕܟܠܦܘܦ ܦܓܪܐ ܘܒܪ̈ ܡܐܪܫܐ ܠܗ ܡܬܠܐܟ. ܟܕ ܢܓܪܝܢ ܐܘ ܚܪܫ ܐܘ ܡܛܠܥ. ܐܝܟ ܗܿܘ[8] ܕܒܠܘܡܝܘ ܡܟܒ ܗܘܐ ܠܦܘܪܣܘܣ. ܡܬܠ ܕܝܢ ܙܒܢܐ ܠܦܘܠܚܢܬܐ ܕܡܬܢܘܣܝܐ ܐܦ[9] ܚܠܝܐ. ܐܒܕܐ ܕܗܿ، ܕܒܓܠܝܢܐ ܘܡܦܠܚܢܘܬܐ[10] ܡܫܬܒܪܐ ܒܪܝܪܐ.[11]

4 [1] ܗܪܩܘܣܐ RVL [2] i. om. RVL [3] ܕܡܩܕܘܢܘܣ RVLl [4] om. RVLl [5] ܘܢܦܩܝܢ RVLl [6] i. add. ܘ RVLl [7] ܕܡܫܕܪܝܐܘܣ F [8] ܗܒܝܪܐ F

5 [1] om. F [2] ܗܘܦܩܠܝܬܘܗܝ F [3] ܕܐܡܪ R [4] i. om. RVL [5*] ܠܚܪܢܐ R [6*] om. RVL [7*] om. F [8] om. F [9] om. RVLl [10] scripsi; ܡܦܠܚܢܘܬܐ F; ܡܦܠܚܢܘܬܐ RVLl [11] ܒܪܝܪܐ RVLl

before the eyes and in the open is greater than that which is in hiding and secret, like that of the Athenians when they were put to shame, for they were supposing that the Greeks were standing around them and looking. And the shame which is before those who are near and known is greater than that before those who are distant and strange. A person feels more shame before those who perceive him as honourable and educated, and he will not reveal to them the secrets of his heart. Not every friend is trustworthy with a secret, because (he can be) perfidious with the failings of his friend, trumpeting (them). One feels shame before such mockers of friendship and scoffers and deriders, not because of them, but because they publish faults of which it is necessary to be ashamed.

FOUR.[19] A person also feels shame before those who continually praise him and before those with whom he wishes to become a friend, like Euripedes before the Syracusans. And as the poet Antiphon said, when he was about to be put to death by King Dionysius because he had rebuked him, when he saw that those who were going to die with him were covering their faces and going through the gate of the city: 'Will you be seen tomorrow by those whom you see now and before whom you feel shame, covering your faces?' A person also feels shame before those who knew him long ago and saw no fault in him, and feels shame not only at a shaming deed, but also at its signs and indices, and also in speaking of it. However, one does not feel shame before servants and friends who are true, or before those who are not praiseworthy who resemble animals and children, as Cydias held forth on the allotment in Samos, for reverence before those who know is true, but before the ignorant supposed.

FIVE.[20] So much for shame; shamelessness or immodesty arises from their opposites. Let us therefore now speak about the acceptance and denial of kindness. Kindness is an advantageous matter which, when it comes about from one person to another, requires the other to give thanks on account of him, or submit to him, or serve him. Every kindness is either through a service or bodily action which is advantageous, or through an advantageous gift of substance.

---

[19] **5.3.4** AR 2.6 84b11-27;32-33;85a9-13; IS 3.3 (144.15-145.6).
[20] **5.3.5** AR 2.6 85a13 - 7 85a34; IS 3.3 (145.7-146.5).

ܫܬ. ܡܬܒܥܝܐ ܕܝܢ ܠܡܠܟܘܬܐ ܘܡܬܒܣܪܐ ܟܕ ܢܐܡܪ ܪܓܓ ܠܡܠܟܘܬܐ
ܠܫܡܥܘܗܝ. ܕܡܠܠ ܘܬܪܥܝܢ ܫܡܥܬܘܢ ܐܘ ܫܡܥܬ ܠܝ. ܘܠܐ ܫܡܠܝܬܗ̇
ܠܡܠܟܘܬܐ. ܘܡܙܪܬ ܡܢ ܡܐ ܕܚܙܐ ܗܘܬ ܠܡܣܒܪ. *ܘܠܐ ܟܕ[1] ܡܛܝܐ ܐܝܬ
ܐܘ ܢܕܥ ܐܝܬ ܐܬܓܠܝܬ ܐܠܐ ܐܝܟ ܕܡܓܕܫܐ ܘܡܢ[2] ܓܒܐ ܐܘ ܐܢܫܐ.
ܐܘ ܕܬܬܦܪܥ ܐܟܦܐ. ܒܟܠܗܝܢ ܓܝܪ ܗܠܝܢ ܕܒܪܐ ܠܡܠܟܘܬܐ ܘܡܫܬܠܛܐ.
ܘܡܢܝܢܐ ܕܢܦܩ ܠܐܢܫܐ[3] ܡܦܪܫܐ ܗܘ. ܒܐܝܡܬ ܟܕ ܡܬܦܠܓܐ ܒܪܢܫܐ
ܒܡܠܟܘܬܐ[4] ܕܡܢ ܐܢܫܐ. ܡܢܗ ܡܫܬܟܚܐ. ܘܐܝܟܐ ܐܝܬ ܐܡܟܐ ܕܠܐ ܢܦܩ
ܡܢܝܢܐ ܠܐܢܫܐ. ܒܐܝܡܬ ܟܕ ܡܬܬܘܚ ܘܡܬܚܠܦܝܢ ܥܠ ܡܠܟܘܬܐ ܕܡܢܗ
ܗܘܝܐ ܠܐܢܫܝܢ. ܗܠܝܢ ܓܝܪ ܟܠܗܝܢ ܠܘܬ ܡܫܝܚܘܬܐ ܘܡܟܘܠܢܐ ܘܡܟܫܦ
ܒܪܘܚܐ ܦܩܝܢ. ܘܐܬܘܬܐ ܡܫܪ̈ܪܢܬ ܠܡܠܟܘܬܐ ܗܠܝܢ ܐܝܟ. ܗ̇ܝ ܕܡ̈ܢܝܢܐ
ܘܣܟܐ ܬܫܬܥܪ. ܘܕܠܐ[5] ܒܡܪ[6] ܬܫܬܥܪ. ܘܡܢ ܒܡܠܕܒܒܐ ܐܟܘܬܗ̇[7,8]
ܬܫܬܥܪ. ܟܕ ܐܠܐ ܙܒܢܘܬܗ ܐܬܟܢܫܬ ܥܡ ܗܢܐܗ. ܐܟܡܐ ܕܒܡܗ ܠܐ
ܐܬܫܬܥܪܬ. ܘܡܢܝܢܐ ܐܝ ܒܡ[9] ܡܠܟܘܬܐ ܬܬܚܙܐ ܒܢܫܬܐ. ܠܐ ܗܘܐ
ܡܠܟܘܬܐ. ܟܕ ܠܡܠܟܘܬܐ ܡܫܘܕܥܬܐ ܕܒܠܗ ܦܘܢܝܐ ܢܦܩܐ. ܘܠܐ ܐܠܐ ܐܝܟ
ܡܕܪܐ ܕܗܘܐ ܥܠ ܒܢܫܬܐ.

6 [1*] ܘܟܕ ܠܐ RVL [2] i. om. RVLl [3] ܠܐ ܐܢܫܐ RVL [4] i. om. RVLl [5] ܕܠܘ RVL [6] f. add. ܐ RVL [7] f. ܗ RVL [8] add. ܠܐ RVLl [9] om. RVLl

The magnitude of the kindness corresponds to the amount of the need, or the difficulty of the time, or (the fact) that he alone did it for him, or was the first to confer (it) upon him, or especially conferred (it) on him. A need is a desire for that (over) which one rejoices when near or grieves when far, like a friend, but a person especially needs that which he desires in bodily sufferings and time of calamity, when he is poor, or shunned, or in hiding, like that which (someone) gave to Phormos in (the) Lyceum. The kindness which is veiled is specially great and sweet, as that which is done in the open and proclaimed is bitter.

SIX.[21] A kindness is dismissed and denied when he who unjustly denies it to him who does it says: 'You served me for your own advantage rather than conferring it on me, and (so) you did not perform a kindness'; or, 'You did less than what you were obliged to do'; or, 'You did good neither willingly nor knowingly, but by chance and from luck or necessity, or to get double recompense'. For by all of these the kindness is diminished or rejected. (Or he may say:) 'The will, adhering to necessity, is under compulsion'; that is, when someone wills a kindness which (derives) from necessity, it is done by that (necessity). Sometimes the will does not follow the necessity, namely, when (someone) sighs and regrets the good which was done by him for another. All these (devices) are expedient for prosecution, accusation, and defence. The indices establishing a kindness are the following: (a deed) is done with will and love; it is done without omission (of anything); it is done in like manner as with an enemy, because if friendship with his adversary is not sought, so also it is not done with him. Similarly, if evil is mixed with good, there is no kindness, because an acknowledgement of the fulfilment of a need follows a kindness, and no one acknowledges that he has need of evil.

---

[21] **5.3.6** AR 2.7 85a34-b11; IS 3.3 (146.6-147.7).

ܦܘܫܩܐ ܕܒܪܝܬܐ

ܡܛܠ ܒܪܝܬܐ ܘܫܡܝܐ ܘܦܠܓܘܬܐ ܘܦܠܚܐ ܘܡܬܩܢܘܬܐ[1]

ܬܐܘܪܝܐ ܚܕ: ܚܫܝܪܐ

ܩܕܡܝܬܐ. ܒܪܝܬܐ ܐܝܬܝܗ̇ ܥܠܬܐ ܕܗܘܝܐ ܠܒܪܝܬܐ ܥܠ ܒܥܬܐ ܕܡܣܟܠܐ
ܐܘ ܡܣܝܡܐ ܠܒܪܝܬܐ ܐܚܪܝܬܐ ܕܠܐ ܓܘܐ ܐܘ ܠܐ ܡܫܟܚܐ ܠܗ̇. ܘܟܠ
ܐܝܠܝܢ ܕܠܒܪ ܐܟܘܬ ܠܐ ܒܪܝܐ ܠܐܚܪ. ܒܕܠܐ ܡܫܬܟܚܐ ܠܗܘܢ ܚܝܠܐ
ܐܚܪܢܐ. ܐܦܠܐ ܥܠ ܓ̈ܒܝܐ. ܒܕ ܐܦܠܐ ܠܗܘܢ ܡܫܬܟܚܐ ܚܝܠܐ. ܠܐ ܕܝܢ
ܒܪܝܐ ܠܡܦܢܩ ܒܡܣܬܢܩܢܘܬܐ. ܒܕ ܡܚܝܠܘܬ ܡܘܡܬܐ ܐܘ ܫܘܠܛܢܐ
ܕܢܩܘܦܐ. ܘܠܐ ܠܬܡܢ ܘܪ̈ܕܝܐ ܘܡܦܩܢ ܗܟܢܐ ܕܐܝܬ ܠܗܘܢ ܐܟܡܐ ܐܘ
ܒܝܫܐ ܐܘ ܛܒܐ. ܐܦܠܐ ܠܓܒܪܐ ܘܬ̈ܓܡܘܬܐ ܘܡܛܠ ܡܕܡ ܘܡܢ̈ܒܝܢܐ.
ܠܐ ܓܝܪ ܗܠܝܢ ܒܪܝܐ ܠܗܘܢ. ܐܦܠܐ ܠܗܘܢ ܡܒܪܝ ܣ̈ܓܝܐܐ ܘܕ̈ܘܟܝܐ
ܘܟܪ̈ܝܗܐ. ܒܕ ܣܟܠܘܢ ܡܢ ܗ̇ܝ ܕܟܠ ܐܝܪܢܐ ܕܟܢܐ ܠܗܘܢ ܚܠܦ ܠܗܘܢ.
ܒܡܬ̈ܓܪܢܘܬܐ[1] ܕܝܢ[2] ܐܪܐ ܕܐܠܝܨܐ ܒܪܝܬܐ. ܟܠ ܕܝܢ ܥܬܝܕܐ[3] ܘܡܟܬܒܢܐ ܠܐ
ܠܐܚܪ ܒܪܝܐ. ܒܕ ܐܝܟ ܠܐ ܐܬܚܗܘܢ ܣܓܝܐܝܢ. ܘܟܠܗܕܐ ܡܬܒܥܝܐ ܠܐ
ܒܪܝܐ ܠܗܘܢ ܥܠ ܐܚܪ. ܡܟܝܠ ܓܝܪ[4] ܕܠܝܬ ܐܚܪܢܐ ܐܚܪܝܢܐ[5] ܡܦܪܢ[6]
ܡܒܪܝܢ.

ܕܬܪܬܝܢ. ܬܠܬܐ ܕܡܬܬܠܬܝܢ ܒܪܝܐ ܠܐܚܪ ܥܠ ܐܚܪܝܢ ܗܠܝܢ ܐܝܟ.[1]
ܫܘܒܩܢܐ[2] ܡܘܬܒ̈ܢܐ. ܒܥܕܢܐ. ܠܦܘܪܫܐ.[3] ܫܒܝܚܘܬܐ. ܡܘܬܪܢܐ. ܦܪܘܫܘܬܐ.
ܡܦܠܚܢܘܬܐ. ܒܫܒܬ ܡܢܐ ܗ̇ܝ ܕܠܡܬܬܠܝܘ ܡܢ ܐܢܫܐ. ܗ̇ܝ ܕܡܢ ܐܡܟܐ[4]
ܕܡܫܬܟܚܐ ܠܟܠܗ ܬܠܝܐ ܒܫܒܬܐ. ܗ̇ܝ ܕܡܢ ܚܘܠܛܢ ܠܟܠܗ ܬܫܘܪܘ
ܒܫܒܬܐ. ܗ̇ܝ ܕܒܬܪ ܕܒܢܐ ܕܡܢ ܠܡܬܟܫܦܘ ܢܬܠܛܝܢ ܒܫܘܒܚܐ. ܒܪܝܐ ܕܝܢ
ܠܐܚܪ ܥܠ ܚܒܪܐ ܘܚܘܫܬܐ ܘܐܪ̈ܚܝܢ ܘܢܕ̈ܒܢܐ. ܘܠܘ ܥܠ ܗ̇ܘ[5] ܕܕܡܘܬ ܢܬܠܗ
ܐܬܬܘܗܝ ܠܗ ܐܝܟ ܛܒܐ. ܘܟܠܗܕܐ ܠܐ ܡܫܬܡܥ ܕܒܪܝܐ ܠܐܚܪ ܥܠ
ܩܢܘܡܗ. ܐܦܠܐ ܕܢܣܒ ܗܘ ܟܠܗܘܢ. ܐܠܐ[6] ܕܕܢܝܠ ܗܘ ܟܠܗܘܢ ܕܐܝܠܝܢ
ܕܒܒܪܐ ܠܒܪܝܬܐ ܘܠܣܘܥܪܢܘܬܐ. ܐܝܟ ܕܐܡܪܐܦܣܘܩ ܐܚܪ ܗ̇ܘ ܕܒܕ
ܡܬܒܥܐ ܗܘܐ ܒܪܗ ܘܡܢܟ ܕܢܦܩܬ ܠܗ ܕܒܕ. ܟܠ ܐܪܚܩܗ ܕܝܢ ܒܕ
ܐܦܬܪܝܢ ܘܣܓܪ ܗܘܐ ܘܥܐܠ ܘܬܘܒܐ ܒܪܬ ܠܗ ܘܒܓܢܐ.

ܕܬܠܬ. ܒܪܝܐ ܬܘܒ ܠܐܚܪ ܥܠ ܗܘܢ ܕܕܡܝܢ ܠܗ ܒܡܘܡܬܐ ܘܣܝܡܘܬܐ
ܕܟܝܢܐ ܘܬܪܒܝܬܐ ܘܙܪ̈ܥܐ. ܘܟܠܡܐ ܕܢܦܩ ܐܚܪ ܕܠܐ ܢܓܕܒܗܘܢ. ܒܕ ܓܒܪ

Titulus [1] ܘܡܬܩܢܘܬܐ RLl; ܘܡܬܩܢܘܬܐ V
1 [1] ܒܡܬ̈ܓܪܢܘܬܐ RVL [2] om. RVLl [3] ܥܬܝܕܐ R [4] om. F [5] ܐܚܪܝܢܐ F [6] om. RVLl
2 [1] ܐܝܟ RLl; om. V [2] ܥ̈ܘܕܪܐ RVLl [3] ܠܦܘ̈ܪܫܐ RVLl [4] om. RVL [5] ܗ̇ܝ F [6] ܘܠܐ F

## SECTION FOUR
### On Pity, Envy, Indignation, Emulation, and Contempt
### Eleven Theories

ONE.[22] Pity is a pain which comes upon a person on account of an evil which destroys or grieves another person who neither deserves nor expects it. No one has pity on those who are utterly ruined, because further suffering is not expected for them, nor on the fortunate, because suffering is also not expected for them. Pitiless are those who take pleasure in distress because of old age or long experience, as well as those laid low, the educated, those happily trusting that they have parents, children, or wives, the courageous, the angry, the stubborn, and the insolent. These (people) do not have pity, neither (do) the morose, the wretched, and the sick, because their (own) suffering prevents them feeling pity for others. Pity, therefore, is particular to those in the middle, but no one has pity on the contemptible and the humiliated, because they are treated as non-existent. The warlike, therefore, do not have pity on anyone, for they suppose that there is no one else apart from them.

TWO.[23] The causes for which someone may have pity on another are as follows: ruinous torments, pains, anxieties, old age, diseases, poverty, mutilation, the ill fortune to be torn away from friends, for evil to strike from where good was expected, for evil to be deprived of contact with good, (and) for a delight to be present (only) after the time in which it is possible to enjoy (it). One has pity on neighbours, equals, friends, and acquaintances, but not on one who is as like oneself as is a son. Therefore it should not be said that someone has pity on himself, nor that he feels for him (who is like him), but that he fears for him the fear which surpasses pity and compassion. (Take) Amasis, for example, who did not break into tears when his son was being led away and was near to dying, but, when his friend was reduced to begging and asking for alms, had pity on him and wept.

THREE.[24] A person, furthermore, may have pity on those who are like him in age, manner of character, thoughts, and ranks, and when

---

[22] **5.4.1** AR 2.8 85b11-86a4; IS 3.4 (147.11-148.13).

[23] **5.4.2** AR 2.8 86a4-24; IS 3.4 (148.14-149.7).

[24] **5.4.3** AR 2.8 86a24 - 9 86b16; IS 3.4 (149.7-150.8).

ܠܢܦܫܗ ܒܪܐ ܠܗ ܟܠܗܘܢ. ܘܟܠܗܕܐ ܠܐ ܒܪܐ ܠܐܢܫ ܥܠ ܒܢ̈ܝܫܬܐ ܕܡܢ
ܐ̈ܟܘ ܫܢ̈ܝܐ ܗܘ̈ܝ. ܒܪܐ ܕܝܢ ܠܐܢܫ ܐܦ ܥܠ ܗ̇ܝ ܕܐܣܬܟܠܬܐ ܕܠܠܗܟܘܬܐ
ܘܒܢ̈ܝܫܐ ܒܟܠܗ ܘܣܝܡܬܐ ܒܟܘܠܦ. ܕܗܢܐ ܓܝܪ ܐܦܢ ܠܐ ܡܬܢܣܝܢ ܒܢ̈ܝܫܬܐ
ܕܗܒܠ. ܐܠܐ ܗ̤ܘ ܕܒܗܘܬܗ ܐܝܟ ܕܗܘܐ ܒܢ̈ܝܫܐ ܡܣܒܪܐ[1] ܢܦܫܗ̇. ܡܒܪܝܢ
ܕܝܢ ܐܦ ܫܘܗ̈ܕܢ ܒܢ̈ܝܫܐ ܒܬ̈ܪܐ ܘܢܦܫܘܐ ܕܗܕܐ ܥܠ ܐܢܫܐ ܕܠܐ ܥܘܐ.
ܘܐܝܟ[2] ܗ̇ܝ ܕܡܫܡܠܝܐ ܗܘܐ[3] ܒܡܠܬܐ ܠܒܡܠܬܐ ܕܗܘܝܐ ܒܡܬܠܚܡܘܬ ܐܢܫܐ
ܕܠܐ ܥܘܐ. ܡܫܡܠܝܘܬܐ ܒܪܡ ܠܗ ܫܘܬܬܐ ܒܗ ܬ̈ܪܬܝܗܝܢ ܗܠܝܢ ܒܩ̈ܝ.
ܒܪܕܐ ܗܘ ܦܓܪܐ ܒܠܚܘܕܝܗܝܢ. ܒܗ̇[4] ܕܒܪ ܒܟܠܗ ܗ̤ܘ، ܗ̇ܝ ܕܠܒܪ ܡܢ ܐܒܗܝܐ[5]
ܗܘܝܐ. ܠܡܬܒܣܣܘ ܙܕܩ ܒܐܝܠܝܢ ܕܕܠܐ ܒܪܕܘܐ ܗܘ̈ܝܢ. ܐܝܕܝܢ ܒܠܒܪ
ܫܘܪܝ ܒܪܢܫܐ ܘܕܠܐ ܒܠܬܐ ܡܕܡܬܐ. ܐܠܐ ܐܝܟ ܕܒܫܠܡܐ[6] ܗܘ̈ܝ ܦܓ̈ܪܬܐ
ܘܒܢ̈ܝܫܬܐ ܠܠܐ ܥ̈ܘܐ. ܡܬܒܝܢܐ ܒܡܠܬܐ ܕܒܗܝܢ. ܐܡܪ ܓܝܪ ܐܝܟ ܕܡܪܐ
ܫܠܡܐ ܚܒܝܒ. ܘܐܝܟ ܕܪܕܐ ܡܦܪܫ. ܘܗܒܢܐ ܒܪܙܐ[7] ܒܡܠܬܐ.[8]

ܕܐܪܟܒ. ܒܪ ܒܪܝܘܬܐ ܒܡܠܬܐ ܕܗܘܝܐ ܠܐܢܫ ܥܠ ܒܢ̈ܝܫܬܐ ܕܒܕܝܐ ܥܠ
ܐܢܫܐ ܕܠܐ ܥܘܐ ܠܗ̇ ܐܝܬܘܗ̇. ܘܫܡܫܐ[1] ܒܡܠܬܐ ܕܗܘܝܐ ܠܐܢܫ ܥܠ
ܦܓܪܬܐ ܕܡܬܠܚܡ[2] ܒܗ̇ ܐܢܫܐ ܕܥܘܐ ܠܗ̇[3] ܐܝܬܘܗܝ. ܘܡܫܬܒܪܢܘܬܐ[4] ܕܡܫܡܠ
ܗܘ ܫܡܫܐ ܠܒܪܝܘܬܐ. ܡܛܠ[5] ܕܫܡܫܐ ܒܡܠܬܐ ܕܗܘܝܐ ܒܡܬܠܚܡܢܘܬ
ܐܚܪܢܐ ܐܝܬܘܗܝ. ܒܪ ܒܪܢܫܐ ܠܐ ܒܪ ܗܘ ܐܠܐ ܒܠܐ ܡܬܠܚܡܢܘܬܗ ܕܠܗ
ܡܬܬܒܝܢ. ܠܐ ܡܬܐܡܪ ܕܢܦܫܗ. ܒܪ ܗܘܐ ܚܫܐ ܐܠܝܨ، ܘܒܟܠ ܒܗ ܢܦܫ.
ܒܠܚܘܕ ܓܝܪ ܚܫܐ ܡܐ ܕܐܚܪܢܐ ܠܦܓܪܬܐ ܡܕܡ ܢܦܫܘ̈ ܘܗ̇ܘ ܢܬܟܠ. ܬܬܪ
ܕܝܢ ܡܬܬܒܝܢ ܒܪܢܫܐ ܒܡܬܠܚܡܢܘܬ ܒܠܒܪܒܗ. ܒܪ ܗܘܝܢ ܬܬܪ ܡܥܒܕ
ܕܢܦܪܘܗܝ.

ܕܫܡܫ. ܐܝܬ ܗܪܟܐ ܚܕܘܬܐ ܒܐܢܫܬܐ ܕܗܘܝܐ ܠܒܪܢܫܐ ܒܒܫܝܬܐ[1] ܕܦܓܪܐ
ܒܥܘ̈ܠܐ. ܐܝܟ ܗܢܘ̈ ܕܠܐܒܫܝܬܗܘ̈ ܡܫܚܝܢ. ܘܠܒܗܘܢ̈ ܦܓ̈ܪܐ[2] ܠܫܝܢ.
ܘܒܦܓܠܐ ܡܫܬܒܝܢ. ܘܒܫܘܒܠܐ ܡܫܬܒܝܢ. ܐܝܬ ܕܝܢ ܘܐܚܪܢܝܬܐ ܚܕܘܬܐ

3 [1] ܡܣܒܪܝܢ RVLl [2] i. om. RLl; deest V [3] ܗ̤ܝ ܗܘܐ RLl; deest V [4] ܒܪܢܩ RVL [5] ܐܘܣܝܐ RVLl [6] ܕܒܫܠܡܬܐ F [7] i. om. RL [8] ܒܫܝܬܐ RVLl
4 [1] i. om. RVLl [2] i. ܘ F [3] ܗܠ R [4] i. om. F [5] i. add. ܘ Fl
5 [1] ܒܒܫܝܬܐ RVLl [2] sg. R

there happens to someone's friend whatever he (himself) fears should not happen to him, he has pity on him. Thus a person does not have pity on account of evil things which happened ten thousand years ago, but he does have pity on whoever puts on an act (consisting) of oppressed (men) and evil (men) by sound and sight, for even if the evils which this (person) bears are not visible, nevertheless his play-acting makes his sufferings visible as (if they were) before (our) eyes. Signs of damages to come and a trial which falls upon one who does not deserve (it) also excite pity, as does the opposite—the (opposite) pain to that pain—which comes from success (falling upon) one who does not deserve (it), although the opposition is not real because both of them are pains. The cause of (both of) them is a good character, because when that which occurs outside of (anyone's) desert is unjust, it is right to be indignant at what wrongly occurs. But if without human determination and without known cause, but rather as if by fate, good or evil things happen to the undeserving, the pain which (is felt) at them is middling, for one may say that the Lord of fate is wise, and as he knows (how) to rule, so also (he knows) about going through pain.

FOUR.[25] While pity is a pain which comes upon someone on account of evil falling on one who does not deserve it, envy also is a pain which comes upon someone (but) on account of good by which one who deserves it prospers, and (thus) it would seem that envy is opposed to pity. Because envy is a pain which comes about at the success of another, when a person is pained not by this but by his own lack of success, he is not said to be envious, because this (latter) emotion is necessary and implanted in every nature. For every person suffers when others deserve some good and he is destitute (of it), but a person is specially pained by the success of his enemy, because (his enemy) is then all the more able to molest him.

FIVE.[26] Here there is a just joy which a person has at evil which batters those who deserve (it), such as those who strike their parents, efface the remembrance of good (men), are defiled by murder, or are in need of destruction. But there is also a different, unjust joy which

---

[25] **5.4.4** AR 2.9 86b16-25; IS 3.4 (150.13-151.8).

[26] **5.4.5** AR 2.9 86b25-87a5; IS 3.4 (151.8-14).

ܒܥܠܬܐ ܕܗܘܐ ܠܒܪܢܫܐ ܒܒܝܫܘܬܐ ܕܗܘܐ ܠܗ̈ܠܟܐ. ܘܡܛܠ ܗܢܝܢ ܬܪ̈ܬܝܢ ܣܕ̈ܩܢ ܫܘܫ̈ܠܝܢ. ܘܐܝܟ ܬܘܒ ܬܪ̈ܬܝܢ ܒܢ̈ܝ ܫܘܫ̈ܠܝܢ. ܣܒܪܐ ܗܢܘ ܗ̇ܝ ܕܒܡܬܠܒܫܘܬ ܥܘܠܐ. ܘܫܡܫܐ ܡܫܬܡܗ ܘܒܥܠܬܐ ܗ̇ܝ ܕܝܠܗ̇. ܐܚܪܬܐ ܕܐܝܟ ܗ̇ܝ ܕܒܡܬܠܒܫܘܬ ܠܐ ܥܘܠܐ. ܘܦܓܪܐ ܡܬܩܪܐ ܘܒܐܒܘܬܐ ܗ̇ܝ ܕܝܠܗ̇. ܘܡܛܠ ܗܢܐ ܙ̈ܘܓܐ ܡܫܬܠܦܐ ܡܢ ܚܘܒܬܐ ܘܚܕܘܬܐ. ܘܦܓܥܬܐ ܘܒܝܫܬܐ. ܘܫܘܝܘܬܐ ܘܠܐ ܫܘܝܘܬܐ.

ܕܫܬ. ܫܒܥܐ ܒܟܠ ܦܓܥܬܐ ܢܦܫ. ܕܒܗ̇ ܕܐܦ ܒܥܘܦܪܐ. ܡܬܦܓܪܢܐ ܕܝܢ ܒܡܫܬܪ̈ܝܬܐ ܠܐ ܡܬܦܓܪ. ܒܕ ܐܝܢܐ ܕܠܐ ܫܘܐ ܠܡܫܬܪܘܬܐ ܡܫܬܪܐ ܠܐ ܗ̇ܘܐ. ܡܬܦܓܪ ܕܝܢ ܒܦܓ̈ܥܬܐ ܒܪ̈ܝܬܐ ܕܠܐ ܡܫܬܪܐ ܕܠܐ ܫܘܐ ܦܢܐ ܠܗܝܢ. ܘܦܓ̈ܥܐ ܕܥܠܝܢ ܡܬܦܓܪܝܢ ܡܢܗܝܢ. ܘܒܠܚܘܕܐ ܒܦܓ̈ܥܬܐ ܒܬܝܩܬܐ[1] ܠܐ ܡܬܦܓܪ. ܒܕ ܡܘܪܟܐ[2] ܕܗ̇ܝ ܕܒܒܝܫܐ ܡܬܚܫܝܢ. ܐܝܟ ܦܓܥܬ ܦܓܗܡܐ ܘܥܘܦܪܐ. ܐܦܠܐ ܒܦܓ̈ܥܬܐ ܕܪ̈ܝܫܬ. ܒܕ ܐܝܟ ܕܪܩܐ ܐܠܩܝܐ[3] ܡܫܬܒ̈ܪܢ. ܒܪܓܠܗ̇ ܥܠܝܠܐ ܠܐ ܡܬܝܪܐ ܕܡܬܕܪܟܐ ܒܗ̇ܘ. ܒܕ ܡܢ ܒܪܘ ܥܘܠܠܢܐ ܡܢܐ ܗܘܐ. ܠܐ ܐܝܟ ܡܬܦܓܪ ܒܗ. ܘܗ̇ܝ ܥܘܝܘܬܐ[4] ܠܐ ܥܘܝܐ ܒܚܠܝܨ. ܒܕ ܠܚܠܝܨ[5] ܦܓܥܬܐ ܐܝܟ ܕܠܝܫܬܐ ܒܦܫܚܗ. ܘܒܠܚܘܕܐ ܐܝܢܐ ܘܥܘܦܪܐ ܠܐ ܠܒܘܫܐ ܐܠܐ ܠܐܬܠܝܠܐ ܠܫܒܚܝܢ. ܘܙܘܥ̈ܪܐ ܕܙܝܢܐ ܘܕܪ̈ܘܒܬܐ ܦܬܝ̈ܚܬܐ ܠܗ ܠܐܝܢܐ ܕܡܕܒܪܢܘܬ ܒܬܪ ܐܠܐ ܠܕܒܪ ܦܓܥܬܐ ܒܬܪ ܐܝܢ. ܒܕ ܒܬܪ ܐܬܪܐ ܣܕܬܐ ܠܗܘܕܡ ܕܕ̈ܩܝ ܒܬܪܐ ܢܣܒܐ *ܡܢ ܐܝܩܪܐ ܘܫܦܝܪ.[6] ܐܝܟܐ ܕܠܐ ܢܬܓܠܐ ܒܥܘܬܪܗ.

ܕܫܒܥ. ܠܐ ܦܠܐ ܠܗܘ ܕܒܚ̈ܝܪ ܕܒܠ ܗ̇ܘ ܕܡܒܠܝ ܫܒܥܐ ܘܦܘܬܪܟܐ ܒܒܗܘ ܢܒܒ. ܡܠܘܢ ܕܝܢ ܡܢܐ ܕܒܢ̈ܝ ܚܕ ܒܢܫܐ ܢܗܘܘܢ. ܘܒܠܗܕܐ ܒܕ[1] ܡܕܡ ܕܐܝܟ ܗܢܐ ܗ̇ܘܐ. ܒܒܢ̈ܝ ܣܠܩܐ ܡܬܒܪܢܐ. ܐܒܒܐ ܕܠܐܘܦ ܒܪ ܦܠܗܒܘܢ ܐܬܐܡܪܬ ܕܠܗ[2] ܘܐܘܦ ܒܠܗ ܗܘܐ ܕܒܡ ܒܪܐ ܕܠܒ ܡܢܗ ܢܦܪܒ. ܘܐܠܐ ܐܡܝܢܐ ܘܒܪܐ ܒܪܒܐ ܢܬܠܛ. ܐܝܟ ܘܒܪܐ ܒܕܪܡܐ. ܘܫܪ̈ܟܐ ܗܘܢ ܕܬܚܫܬ[3] ܣܠܩܐ ܐܬܬܚܝܗܘܢ ܬܪܝܢ ܐܝܟܘܢ. ܣܒ ܗܢܐ ܒܕ ܠܐ ܥܘܐ[4] ܠܦܓܥܬܐ ܦܓ̈ܥܬܐ ܙܘܒ̈ܬܐ ܦܢܐ. ܐܚܪܢܐ ܕܝܢ ܒܕ ܥܘܐ[5] ܠܦܓ̈ܥܬܐ ܙܘܒ̈ܬܐ ܦܓܥܬܐ ܘܒܙܘܬܐ ܠܐ ܦܢܐ. ܒܡܛܠܝܢ ܒܪܢ ܙܢܡ ܐܡܝܪܐ ܡܬܦܪ ܡܬܦܓܪ. ܒܗ̇ ܕܒܫܘܝܘܬܐ ܘܠܐ ܫܘܝܘܬܐ ܣܒܪ. ܘܡܢ ܕܙܘܒ̈ܘܬܐ[6] ܕܥܠ̈ܬܝܦ ܫܘܩ̈ܝ ܠܗ. ܘܐܦܢܐ ܕܠܒܬܪ̈ ܣܒܪܐ ܒܢܪ ܘܒܫܘܕܐ ܠܐ ܣܒܥ. ܠܐ ܡܬܦܓܪ. ܒܕ ܟܠ ܫܘܝܘܬܐ ܠܐ ܒܦܝܠ ܠܗ.

6 [1] ܒܬܝܩܬܐ RVLl [2] i. add. ܒ RVLl [3] ܢܝ̈ܩܐ RVLl [4] ܥܘܢܪܬܐ F [5] ܠܚܠܝܨ RVL [6]* om. F

7 [1] ܒܕ RVLl [2] ܕܠܗ RVLl [3] add. ܣܕ RVLl [4] ܥܘܐ RVLl [5] om. RVL; ܥܘܐ l [6] i. om. F

a person has at evil which comes to good (men), and these two joys are opposed. There are also two opposed pains. One is at the success of him who deserves it; it is called envy and its cause is injustice. The other is at the success of him who does not deserve it; it is called indignation and its cause is justice. These are the various combinations of pain and joy, good and evil, worthiness and unworthiness.

SIX.[27] An envious person is envious at every good, even at beauty, but an indignant person is not indignant at virtuous things, because he who does not deserve virtue is not virtuous. However, one may be indignant at external goods which an undeserving non-virtuous person possesses and of which deserving good men are deprived. Therefore one is not indignant at old (established) goods, because they seem close to that which is natural, like good birth and beauty, nor at those which are inherited, because they seem like necessary rights. Therefore no one is indignant at a non-virtuous ruler who has recently become rich, because he already possessed power. What is deserved is not the same for everyone, because everyone has a particular good appropriate to him. Therefore armour and beauty are not appropriate to the hermit but to the warrior, and marriages of many sorts and diverse concubines are suitable not for one who has recently become rich, but for one who is rich from birth, because the newly rich man should first gain the due respect (given to) the rich by donations and so forth, then be open with his wealth.

SEVEN.[28] It is not right for one who is lesser to contend with one who is superior and to cause a split with him, especially when they are of the one kind. Therefore when something such as this occurs, it is reckoned among the works of fate, as was decreed for Ajax, son of Telamon, that Zeus had fated him to fight with a better man. And if (they are) not (of the one kind), how can the inferior be a match for the greater, like a musician for a just person? The matters which are subject to fate are two. One is when (a person) who does not deserve good possesses great goods; the other when, deserving great goods, he does not posses (even) an inferior good. The ambitious person is

[27] **5.4.6** AR 2.9 87a5-32; IS 3.4 (151.15-152.12).
[28] **5.4.7** AR 2.9 87a32-b20; IS 3.4 (152.12-153.5).

ܕܬܡܢܝܐ. ܫܡܫܬܐ ܕܝܢ ܐܝܬܝܗܘܢ ܗܠܝܢ ܕܒܗ̇ ܗ̇ܝ ܕܒܦܠܓܘܬܐ ܡܦܠܓܝܢ
ܠܗܠܝܢ ܕܒܗܘܢ ܫܡܫܝܢ ܕܝܢ. ܕܡܢܝܢܘܬܐ ܐܚܪܢܝܐ ܒܦܘܠܓܐ ܒܡܘܡܬܐ
ܒܐܘܡܢܘܬܐ ܒܥܘܒܕܐ ܒܒܘܬܪܐ. ܒܪܘܫܡ[1] ܕܕܪ̈ܓܐ ܫܡܫܬܐ ܘܫܡܫܝܬܐ
ܡܬܬܗܐ ܫܡܫܬܐ. ܘܒܡܘܪܒ ܕܕܪ̈ܓܝܗܘܢ ܚܙܝ. ܘܫܡܫܬܐ ܗ̇ܘ ܗܘ ܕܡܠܠ
ܢܫܦܪ[2] ܡܢ ܡܘܠܐ ܠܒܘܬܐ. ܘܐܦܢ ܦܪܚ ܠܗ. ܘܒܠܗܕܐ ܒܫܡ̈ܫܬܐ[3] ܟܠ
ܐܢܫܐ ܕܒܝ̈ܫܐ ܫܒܩ *ܬܘܒ ܡܢ ܐܢܫܐ ܕܠܐ ܗܘܝܢ ܫܒܩ[4] ܢܦܫܗ. ܘܒܐܢܫܐ
ܕܦܠ̈ܓܘܬܐ ܘܪܘ̈ܒܬܐ ܦܩܕ ܐܢܫܐ ܕܦܠܓܘܬܐ ܡܕܡ ܦܩܕ ܬܘܒ ܡܢ ܐܢܫܐ ܕܠܐ
ܗܘܝܢ ܦܩܕ ܢܦܫܗ. ܠܝܬ ܓܝܪ ܦܘܪܣ ܡܢ ܕܡܢܘܬܐ. ܐܝܟ ܕܐܡܪ ܡܬܠܐ
ܕܐܢܫܘܬܐ *ܚܠܬܐ ܗ̱ܝ ܠܡܠܦ[5] ܘܠܡܫܡܫ. ܫܡ̈ܫܬܐ[6] ܙ̈ܢܝܢ ܐܝܬܝܗܝܢ *ܬܘܒ
ܕܝܢ[7] ܫܡܫܝܢ. ܗܟܢܐ ܘܐܝܠܝܢ ܕܒܒܢ̈ܝܐ ܘܢܒ̈ܫܐ ܡܬܟܫܝܢ. ܒܟܠܡܕܡ ܓܝܪ
ܥܒܕܐ ܫܡܫܬܐ ܐܝܬ. ܡܠܘ ܕܝܢ ܒܗ̇ܘ ܡܢܐ ܕܐܪܟ ܫܡܫܬܐ.

ܕܬܫܥܐ. ܠܐ ܕܝܢ ܡܫܬܡܫܝܢ ܐܝܠܝܢ ܕܕܪ̈ܓܐ ܥܒ̈ܝܕܐ ܐܝܬ ܠܗܘܢ ܕܒܝܕܘ.
ܘܗܠܝܢ ܙܕ̈ܝܩܐ ܐܚܪ̈ܢܐ ܕܡܣܒܪ ܗܘ[1] ܥܒܝܠܐ ܠܘܬ ܡܕܒܪܢܘܬܗܘܢ. ܐܝܟ
ܐܝܠܝܢ ܕܙܕܩܝܢ ܚܕ. ܦܬ̈ܓܡܗ ܕܗܪܘܦܠܝܢ. ܒܐܡܬ ܒܓܙ̈ܪܬܐ ܕܦܠܘ̈ܓܬܐ[2]
ܕܒܦ̈ܩܕ ܡܒܪܟܐ. ܘܗܠܝܢ ܦܩܕ ܒܝܢܝܐ[3] ܘܒܫܝܢܐ. ܘܗܠܝܢ ܦܩܕ
ܗܕܝܪܐ ܘܡܕܒܪܢܐ[4] ܕܒܦܠܚܘܬܐ ܠܐ ܡܬܦܪܢܣܢܘܬܐ ܡܦܠܓܝܢ. ܡܬܚܫܒܝܢ
ܕܝܢ ܐܢܫܐ ܕܠܝܫܢ ܠܡܬܬܡܨܘ ܠܡܘܒܠܗ ܘܠܝܫܢ ܠܡܫܬܡܫܘ ܒܬܠܝܬܗ
ܘܡܓܢܐ ܠܡܡܠܠܘ ܫܡܫܬܐ ܐܝܟ ܦܠܓܘܬܗ *ܐܘ ܐܝܬ ܗܘܐ[5] ܒܝܢ ܐܒܘܬܗ.[6]
ܘܪܒܐ ܘܥܡܝܩܐ ܒܒܢ̈ܝܐ ܒܗ̇ܘ ܕܕܒܪ ܘܦܠܓܐ ܢܦܫܗ ܒܗ ܡܦܠܓܝܢ. ܘܗ̇ܘ
ܕܗܘܐ ܦܪܝܫ ܒܡܫܟܐ ܒܗ̇ܘ ܕܡܠܠ ܒܪܐ. ܘܟܢ ܕܠܡܫܡܫ ܡܫܡܫ ܠܒܘܬܐ ܒܟܠ
ܕܟܠ ܡܫܡܫ. ܒܕܐܝܟ ܗܠܝܢ ܐܕ̈ܢܐ ܡܓܝܐ ܙܘܦܪܐ ܠܡܒܢܘ ܘܠܡܒܢܝܐ.
ܘܠܡܫܡܫܘ ܘܠܡܬܦܠܓܘ.[7]

8 [1] i. add. ܘ RVLl [2] ܢܫܦܪ RVLl [3] sg. RVL [4*] om. R [5*] om. RVLl [6] sg. RVL; ܫܡܫܬܐ l [7*] ܟܠ ܬܘܒ RVLl

9 [1] ܗܘܐ RVLl [2] ܕܦܠܓ ܦܠܓ ܙܘ̈ܓܘܬܐ RVL [3] sg. R [4] ܘܡܕܒ̈ܪܢܐ R [5*] ܘܐܝܬ ܠܗ RVLl [6] f. ܗ̇ RVL [7] ܘܠܡܬܦܠܓܘ F

especially indignant at these things, because he pays attention to worthiness and unworthiness. (Someone) for whom worthless inferior things are sufficient does not become indignant, nor does the cheat who deceives free men and is not pained by a shameful act, because he is not concerned about worthiness.

EIGHT.[29] The envied are those who, while prospering with goods, are like those who envy them. The likeness, I mean, is in (terms of) birth, age, craft, honour, and wealth. When the conditions of the envious and the envied are far apart, envy is weak, but when they are close, it is strong. The envious (person) is the one who is slightly short of the complete good, though close to it. Therefore he who is a little wise is more envious of the wise than he who is not wise at all, and he who does some good is more envious of him who does great goods than he who does not do (good) at all. For (envy) is impossible without likeness; as the proverb said, 'Kinship is the cause of emulation and envy.' The ambitious wise are especially envious, and similarly also those who are honoured for deeds and possessions, for with every fine thing there is envy, above all for that which the envious desires.

NINE.[30] Those who departed ten thousand years ago are not envied; nor those of a distant place, the way to whose abode is stopped up, like those who are scattered around the pillars of Hercules—that is, on the islands of the blessed at the limits of the west; nor those very low and scorned; nor those greatly honoured and advantaged who prosper in unapproachable blessedness. But envied is he against whom it is appropriate to strive, whose desires it is appropriate to share, goods similar to whose it is possible for the envious person to acquire, or like whom he sometimes was. A man of high rank and an old man with wealth envies one of low rank and a youth when he prospers, he who spends much money (envies) him who spends little, and he who attains the good with difficulty (envies) him who attains (it) easily. With such kinds (of arguments) a rhetor is able to create pity, consolation, envy, and indignation.

---

[29] **5.4.8** AR 2.10 87b21-88a9; IS 3.4 (153.5-16).

[30] **5.4.9** AR 2.10 88a9-28; IS 3.4 (154.1-11).

ܕܒܫܪ. ܘܗܪܟܐ ܐܝܬ ܡܕܡ ܕܕܡܐ ܠܛܒܬܐ ܘܡܬܐܡܪܐ ܛܒܐ.
ܘܐܝܬܘܗܝ, ܒܥܬܐ ܕܗܘܝܐ ܠܐܢܫܐ ܕܓܒܪܐ ܠܡܚܝܠܘ ܘܠܐ ܡܚܝܠ. ܡܟܐ
ܕܐܢܫܝܐ ܕܗܘܒܬ ܓܒܪܐ ܠܡܚܝܠܘ ܡܚܝܠ. ܘܡܬܘܚܡܐ ܡܢ ܡܕܡܝܐ ܦܪܫ
ܡܢ ܢܫܡܬܐ ܛܒܐ. ܟܕ ܢܫܡܬܐ ܟܕ ܠܐ ܓܒܪܐ ܠܡܚܝܠܘ ܢܫܡ. ܘܛܒܐ ܟܕ
ܓܒܪܐ ܠܡܚܝܠܘ ܛܠܠ. ܟܬܫܘܡܐ ܕܝܢ ܬܢܝܢܐ ܦܪܫ ܡܢ ܛܒܬܐ ܛܒܐ.
ܟܕ ܡܬܛܒܬܐ ܟܠܗ ܥܡܐ ܕܡܚܝܠ *ܡܬܛܒܪ. ܘܛܒܐ ܟܥܡܐ ܕܡܚܝܠ[1]
ܛܠܠ. ܠܐ ܕܝܢ ܛܠܠ ܐܠܐ ܐܢܫ ܛܒܥܬܐ ܕܡܬܬܘܚ ܥܠ ܛܝܒܘܬܗ.
ܟܕܛܝܢ ܐܝܟ ܢܦܫܐ ܗܘܝܢ ܐܘܝܢ ܛܒܐ. ܡܠܘܝܢ ܕܝܢ ܗܘܝܢ ܕܠܐܬܝܢ
ܐܬܥܗܘܝܢ ܘܟܬܝ ܛܘܗܡܗܘܢ ܐܘ ܐܘܟܡܬܗܘܢ ܐܘ ܡܕܝܢܬܗܘܢ
ܕܐܝܟ ܗܢܝܢ ܛܒ̈ܥܬܐ ܗܘ̈. ܛܝܢܬܐ ܕܝܢ ܐܝܬܝܗܝܢ ܓܒ̈ܠܬܐ ܡܬܚ̈ܝܠܬ[2]
ܐܝܬܐ ܘܥܒܕܝܐ ܕܠܐܢܫܝܐ ܡܘܬܪ̈. ܐܝܟ ܒܘܬܪܐ ܘܥܘܦܪܐ. ܠܐ
ܐܝܟ ܢܘܠܡܝܐ ܕܠܐ ܡܕܡ ܐܝܬܪܐ ܟܕ ܠܗ ܠܐܢܫܐ ܡܘܬܪ.

ܕܟ̈ܐ. ܛܒܐ ܕܝܢ ܐܦ ܒܒܪܝܬܐ ܘܥܒܕܬܐ ܘܪܥܝܢܬܐ. ܟܕ ܪ̈ܥܝܢܐ
ܘܗܕܪܐ ܐܝܬ ܐܘܒܕܢܐ ܘܡܫܬܥܝܢܘܬܐ ܕܟܠܗ ܐܝܟ ܪ̈ܘܚܢܝܬܐ ܘܦܓܪܢܝܬܐ
ܠܦܓܪܢܝܐ ܡܬܝܢ ܠܡܒܕܒ ܥܡܪ. ܛܒܐ ܕܝܢ ܒܗܢܐ ܒܗܘܢ ܘܒܐܢܫܐ
ܕܡܬܕܒܪܐ ܒܗܘܢ. ܘܢܦܫܐ ܕܡܬܕܒܪܐ ܒܗܘܢ. ܘܡܫܡܫ ܥܠ ܗܢܝܢ
ܕܡܬܢܝܢ ܡܢܗܘܢ ܘܡܫܡܫܝܢ[1] ܠܗܘܢ. ܟܕ ܡܫܡܫܢܘܬܐ ܡܫܡܫܢܐ
ܠܛܒܐ. ܒܗ̇ ܕܛܒܐ ܗ̇ܝ ܒܡܫܡܫܢܘܬ ܡܬܛܒܢܐ ܗ̇ܘܐ. ܡܫܡܫܢܘܬܐ ܕܝܢ
ܒܥܒܕܬ ܡܬܬܡܫܢܢܐ.[2] ܘܟܕ ܡܫܡܫܢܐ ܡܫܡܫܢܘܬܐ ܠܛܒܐ. ܡܢܟܐ
ܠܗ ܘܡܫܡܫܐ ܒܗ. ܟܕ ܐܝܬܐ ܕܥܠ ܛܒܐܐ ܡܫܡܫ ܢܘܪܐ ܕܛܒܘܬܗ ܓܒܪ.
ܘܛܒܐ ܗ̇ܝ ܓܠܝܐ ܡܢ ܛܒܬܐ ܕܒܗ̇ ܛܠܠ. ܡܬܬܡܫܢܢܐ ܕܝܢ ܟܕ ܠܐ
ܓܒܪܐ ܡܢ ܓܒܪܐ ܗܘܬ ܠܗ ܛܒܬܐ ܕܠܐ ܒܥܠܬܐ. ܘܥܠ ܕܐܝܟ ܗܢܐ
ܡܫܡܫܢ ܐܢܫܐ. ܒܗ̇ ܕܦܫܝܛܘܬ ܡܢܟܝܢ ܡܐܕܘܗܝ ܢܫܐ. ܘܛܒܬܗ ܠܐ
ܡܬܬܡܫܐ ܥܕܝܢ ܘܡܬܛܠܠ.

---

10 1* om. F 2 ܡܬܚ̈ܝܠܬ RVLl
11 1 ܘܡܫܡ̈ܫܢܐ RVLl 2 ܡܬܬܡܫܢܢܐ RVLl

TEN.[31] There is something here which is similar to indignation and is called emulation. (This) is a pain which comes on someone who deserves to succeed but does not succeed, when another person who likewise deserves to succeed does succeed. With the first (part of the) definition emulation is distinguished from envy, because the envious person is envious when he does not deserve to succeed, but the emulous person is emulous when he does deserve to succeed. With the second (part of the) definition emulation is distinguished from indignation, because the indignant person is indignant at the undeserving who succeeds, but the emulous is emulous at the deserving who succeeds. He does not emulate, but rather does he love, the good whose absence he regrets. Therefore the high-minded are emulous, especially those whose ancestors, kinsmen, nation, or city had such goods. Objects of emulation are things bringing honour and praise which are advantageous to others, like wealth and beauty, not like health, which does not attract honour because it is not advantageous to others.

ELEVEN.[32] Courage, wisdom, and authority are also emulated, because rulers, generals—that is, heads of armies—and virtuous people such as rhetors and poets are able to benefit many. One emulates them and anyone like them, and one wishes to be like them, but one despises those who are inferior to them and opposite to them, because contempt is the opposite of emulation, for emulation arises in the honouring of him who is emulated, but contempt in the scorning of him who is despised. Although contempt is the opposite of emulation, it sets it in motion and causes increase in it, because he who despises an impure person kindles the fire of his emulation. The emulous man lacks the good of which he is emulous, but the undeserving despised one gets the good by luck without labour. People despise someone such as this, because emotions easily go against him and dissolve and make void his unfounded good.

---

[31] **5.4.10** AR 2.11 88a29-b14; IS 3.4 (154.12-155.4).

[32] **5.4.11** AR 2.11 88b14-30; IS 3.4 (155.4-14).

ܦܣܘܩܐ ܫܪܝܪܐ
ܥܠ ܡܫܠܡܢܘܬ ܒܒܢ̈ܝܢܫܐ ܒܒܪ̈ܐ
ܬܐܘܪ̈ܝܐ ܗ ܬܠܬ ܡܫܪܐ

ܩܕܡܝܬܐ. ܡܛܠ ܟܠ ܫܪ̈ܟܐ ܕܡܬܐܡܪܝܢ ܠܘܬ ܒܪ̈ܢܫܐ ܪܕܘ ܕܡܫܘܕܥ ܠܘܬ ܢܫ̈ܐ ܘܬܪ̈ܒܝܬܐ ܘܩܘܫ̈ܬܐ ܘܓܒܪ̈ܐ[1] ܘܢܦ̈ܩܬܐ. ܫܪ̈ܟܐ[2] ܕܝܢ ܐܝܟ ܙܘܥܪܐ ܘܫܡܫܬܐ. ܬܪ̈ܒܝܬܐ ܕܝܢ ܐܝܟ ܗ̇ܝ ܕܢܣܒܐ ܐܝܬ ܫܘܠܛܢܐ ܐܘ ܕܡܕܒܪܐ ܐܘ ܟܗܢܘܬܐ ܐܘ ܡܕܡ ܡܢ ܐܘܡܢ̈ܘܬܐ. ܘܩܘܫ̈ܬܐ ܐܝܟ ܫܠܝܛܘܬܐ ܘܡܪܘܬܐ ܕܒܥܠܕܒܒܘܬܐ ܘܫܝܒܘܬܐ. ܘܓܒܪ̈ܐ ܐܝܟ ܛܒܘܬ ܛܘܗܡܐ ܘܒܘܬܪܐ ܘܫܠܝܚܘܬܐ. ܘܢܦ̈ܩܬܐ ܐܝܟ ܢܦܩܐ ܒܥܒܕܬܐ ܘܢܦܩܐ ܒܡܫܬܘܬܐ ܘܢܦܩܐ ܪܒܬܐ ܘܢܦܩܐ ܠܟܘܪܬܐ. ܘܟܕ ܡܢ ܩܘܫ̈ܬܐ ܡܫܪܝܢ ܐܡܪܝܢ ܕܟܗ̈ܢܐ ܗ̇ܢܝܢ ܕܟܗܢܝܢ ܗܦܟ ܪ̈ܓܫܐ. ܘܡܢܝܢ ܠܡܕܡ. ܗ̇ܘ ܡܐ ܕܪ̈ܓܫܝܢ. ܘܠܪ̈ܓܝܓܬܐ ܐܦܪܘܕܝܛܝܣܛܘܬܐ[3] ܕܚܕ ܦܓܪܐ. ܐܝܟ ܡܕܪ̈ܘܓܬܐ ܘܡܬܠܒܒ̈ܢܐ[4] ܘܡܬܬܦ̈ܝܣܢܐ ܢܦܫܝܢ. ܘܕܠܝܠܝܐܬ[5] ܡܫܬܠܦܝܢ ܘܡܢ ܪ̈ܓܫܐ ܒܟܠ ܫܥܝܢ. ܪ̈ܓܝܫܝܢ ܡܬܬܪܐܝܬ ܘܡܒܟܝܢ ܪܗܝܒܐܝܬ. ܟܕ ܚܙܩܘܦܬ ܒ̈ܢܝܗܘܢ ܘܠܐ ܡܣܝܒܘܬ ܪ̈ܚܡܝܗܘܢ. ܐܝܟ ܪ̈ܚܡܝܗܘܢ ܕܟܠܐ ܘܟܪ̈ܝܗܐ ܕܒܢܝܢܫܐ[6] ܦܓܪܐ ܡܬܦܠܓܝܢ.

ܕܬܪ̈ܬܝܢ. ܬ̈ܠܬܐ ܗܠܝܢ ܪ̈ܓܫܘܬܝܢ.[1] ܟܠܗ̇ ܕܐܡܪܢܐ ܗܠܝܢ ܐܢܫܝܢ. ܒܪܓܘ ܡܬܬܦܝܢ ܘܠܐ ܡܫܬܒܩܝܢ ܟܕ ܡܬܚܠܠܝܢ.[2] ܡܛܠ[3] ܕܠܝܬܘܗܝ ܪܓܬܐ ܫܠܝܛܘܬܐ. ܘܥܒܘܬܐ ܪܓܬܐ[4] ܡܕܡ ܗܘ. ܠܗ̇ ܡܢ ܢܦܫܐ ܬ̈ܠܬܐ ܪ̈ܓܫܝܢ. ܠܢܦܫܐ ܕܝܢ ܒܪܓܙ ܡܬܚܠܠܝܢ. ܟܕ ܠܐ ܡܬܚܡܣ ܐܬܢܦܫܘ ܒܪ̈ܓܘܬܐ. ܐܝܟ ܕܐܡܪ ܦܠܐܛܘܢ ܒܦܐܝܕܪܘܣ. ܕܠܝܬ ܡܢ ܕܐܡܪ ܠܗ ܒܪ̈ܢܫܐ ܢܦܫܐ ܐܠܐ ܒܪ̈ܢܫܐ ܦܠܓܐ. ܟܕ ܠܐ ܚܙܐ ܒܪ̈ܢܫܐ ܐܦܠܐ ܒܢܦܫܬܐ.[5] ܘܕܠܝܠܝܢ ܠܡܗܡܢܘ. ܟܕ ܥܦܝܪ ܡܟܪܐ ܐܢܘܢ ܡܛܠ ܡܬܘܡܢܘܬܗܘܢ ܫܡܝܢܝܐ. ܕܕܒܪܐ ܠܡܬܘܡ ܪܘܚܐ ܕܡܬܠܒܒܐ ܢܦܫܗܘܢ. ܘܠܐ ܡܫܬܠܝܢ ܘܠܐ ܒܛܠܝܢ. ܘܡܬܠܐܐ[6] ܕܘܪܐ ܠܗܘܢ ܦܩܩ. ܟܕ ܡܒܪܐ ܕܪܘܚܐ ܕܚܬܝܪ ܐܝܬ ܠܗܘܢ. ܡܬܚܡܕܝܢ ܕܝܢ[7] ܩܠܝܠ ܘܡܫܡܝܢ ܗܟܢ. ܐܟܚܕܐ ܕܫܦ̈ܝܪܐ ܡܬܚܡܕܝܢ ܗܟܢ ܘܡܫܡܝܢ ܩܠܝܠ.

1 [1] sg. RVL [2] sg. RVL [3] ܦܪܘܕܝܛܝܣܛܘܬܐ [4] ܡܬܠܒܒ̈ܢܐ R; ܡܬܬܠܒ̈ܒܢܐ l [5] ܡܠܝܠܝܐܬ RVLl [6] i. ܕ RVLl

2 [1] ܪ̈ܓܫܝܢ RVLl [2] ܡܫܬܒܩܝܢ ܕܡܬܚܠܠܝܢ RVLl [3] i. om. R [4] ܪܓܘܬܐ RVL [5] sg. F [6] ܘܡܬܠܐ F [7] ܒܪ RVLl

## SECTION FIVE
### On the Diversity of People in Character
### Thirteen Theories

ONE.[33] We ought therefore now to indicate the things which affect character in relation to emotions, intentions, ages, fortunes, and souls. Emotions, for example, are anger and rage; intentions, for example, are that one chooses power, government, asceticism, or one of the arts; ages, for example, are youth, prime of vigour, and old age; fortunes, for example, noble birth, wealth, and strength; and souls, for example, an Ethiopian soul, a Scythian soul, a big soul, and a small soul. Beginning with the ages, we may say that with the young the impulses of desire are pressing, and they are able to do what they desire. They follow the sensual desires surrounding the body, like those of copulation, dress, and smell. They are fickle and quickly satisfied of a desire. Greatly do they desire and rapidly are they satisfied, on account of the sharpness of their wishes and the instability of their opinions, like their vain and weak thirsts which are quenched by a cool breeze.

TWO.[34] The young are especially irascible, because they love special honour. Therefore they become enraged and cannot endure being rejected. And because youth desires greatness, and victory is a certain greatness, the young love it more than riches. They reach out less for riches, because they have never been afflicted by poverty. As Pittacus said in Maphiarnus, 'There is none among us with an evil character, but (only) good characters, because they have not seen evil (men) or evil (things).' They are ready to trust, because they are of good hope on account of their hot constitution, which resembles the constitution of the drunken whose soul is encouraged. They neither give way nor flee, and little gain is adequate for them. Because they have hope for the future, they remember little and look forward much, as the old remember much and look forward little.

THREE.[35] Because the hope of the young is noble, they are easily led astray. Similarly, they are also courageous, and therefore are

---

[33] **5.5.1** AR 2.12 88b31-89a9; IS 3.5 (156.1-157.1).

[34] **5.5.2** AR 2.12 89a9-25; IS 3.5 (157.1-9).

[35] **5.5.3** AR 2.12 89a25-36; IS 3.5 (157.9-158.6).

ܕܬܠܬ. ܛܠܝܐ ܒܪ ܥܣܪ ܫܒܪܝܗܘܢ. ܦܫܝܩܐܝܬ ܡܫܬܕܠܝܢ. ܗܟܢܐ ܐܦ
ܠܓܒܪܐ. ܘܒܠܚܘܕܐ ܒܫܘܪܗܒ ܪܘܓܙܐ ܡܫܬܟܚܝܢ. ܫܦܝܪܘܬ ܗܟܢܐ
ܠܕܚܠܬܐ ܕܐܢܫܐ ܘܬܫܡܫܬ ܪܘܓܙܐ ܠܒܥܒܕܬܐ ܡܒܥܝܐ. ܘܒܠܗܘܕܐ ܕܐܢܫܐ ܕܚܠܬܐ
ܘܪܘܓܙܐ ܠܐ ܡܬܟܢܫܝܢ ܐܚܝܕܐ. ܠܐ ܓܝܪ ܒܪ ܙܟܐ ܐܝܟ ܕܢܬܠ. ܟܠܒ ܕܝܢ
ܒܘܚܕܐ ܥܠ ܛܠܝܐ. ܒܪ ܠܐ ܒܥܕܢܐ ܐܬܝܗܒ ܒܥܒܕ̈ܬܐ ܡܥܕܪܢܝܬܐ
ܘܡܥܪ̈ܩܢ، ܘܠܝܬܝܬܐ. ܘܢܫܝܪ، ܝܕܥܬܐ ܗܘܐ ܠܗܘܢ ܡܟܠܝܢ. ܘܠܫܦܝܪܘܬ
ܫܒܪܝܗܘܢ ܐܝܬ ܕܢܫܡܥܘܢ ܢܦܫܐ. ܘܒܠܗܘܕܐ ܠܐ ܫܒܝܠܝܢ ܕܡܬܒܥܝܢ[1]
ܡܬܡܛܠܝܢ. ܒܗ̇، ܕܒܥܘܕܪܢܬܐ[2] ܠܐ ܡܫܬܟܚܐ ܐܢܘܢ. ܒܨܠܘܢ ܙܘܪ̈ܬܐ
ܡܬܪܒܝܢ. ܘܠܦܘܫܩܐ ܐܘܪܚܬ ܡܬܪܬܐ ܕܢܡܘܣܗܘܢ، ܢܛܪ ܡܢ ܓܠܝܐ
ܕܒܪܘܫ[3] ܠܐ ܢܦܘܩ ܡܬܓܠܝܢ. ܒܠܗ ܓܝܪ ܫܘܒܚܗܘܢ ܒܟܢܐ ܕܚܒܪܬ[4]
ܡܬܓܠܝܐ. ܡܘܬܪܐ ܕܝܢ ܕܐܪܝܗܘܢ ܗܘܘ ܗܢܝܐܐ. ܘܫܘܒܚܗܘܢ
ܢܛܘܦܐ ܕܗܢܝܐܐ ܠܒܢܝܐ ܡܫܬܒܚ.. ܘܫܘܒܚܐ ܢܛܘܦܐ ܕܓܠܝܐ ܠܗ ܠܒܢܝܐ
ܐܠܐ ܠܚܐܪܘܬܐ ܡܫܬܒܚ.. ܗܢܝܐ ܦ̇ܠܐ ܠܡܫܬܒܠܘ ܡܠܬ[5] ܐܢ ܗܘܝܐ.

ܕܐܪܒܥ. ܛܠܝܐ ܠܫܒܪ̈ܝܗܘܢ ܘܠܐܣܝܚܗܘܢ ܘܒܢ̈ܝ ܩܘܡܬܗܘܢ ܢܛܪ
ܢܡܘܣܝܢ. ܒܗ̇، ܕܠܡܫܒܕܐ ܢܛܪ ܢܓܒܝܢ[1] ܘܫܒܘܬܐ ܒܒܢܝܢܐ ܘܫܒܪܘܬܐ[2]
ܡܬܓܒܪܐ. ܒܗܝܢ ܕܝܢ ܠܐ ܗܘܐ ܠܦܘܫܩܐ ܫܠܝܛܬܐ ܐܠܐ ܠܦܘܫܩܐ ܕܠܘܬ
ܗܢܝܐܘܬܐ ܡܬܒܠܐ. ܠܢܫܒܐ ܡܢ ܡܛܠ ܢܛܪܐ ܗܢܝܢܐ ܘܠܐ ܗܘܢܝܢܐ
ܢܫܒܝܢ. ܘܒܠܗܘܕܐ ܡܢ ܗܢܝܐܘܬܗܘܢ ܢܛܪ ܐܝܟܐ ܘܒܢܝܢܐ ܢܛܠܬܗܘܢ. ܒܪ
ܠܐ ܡܥܡܢܝܐܝܬ ܢܫܒܝܢ ܘܫܠܝܢ. ܘܒܪ ܠܐ ܡܥܡܢܝܢ. ܫܒܪܝܢ[3] ܒܢܝܫܗܘܢ
ܕܒܠ ܡܒܪ ܥܣܪ ܫܢܝܢ. ܘܓܠܝܐܝܬ ܓܠܝܢ. ܘܐܦ ܒܪ ܡܬܒܕܠܝܢ
ܡܢܓܠܝܢ. ܒܪ ܒܒܢܝܐ ܠܒܥܒܕܬ ܫܒܘܪܘܬܐ ܢܩܝܢ. ܒܪ ܫܒܥ ܓܒܝܢ ܘܡܠܝܠ
ܒܘܪܝܢ. ܘܒܡ ܗܠܝܢ ܐܦ ܡܪܚܡܝܢ. ܒܪ ܠܒܠ ܐܢܫܐ ܕܐܫܡܥܬܐ ܓܠܝܐ
ܓܠܝܦ ܒܓܠܠ ܡܬܗܝܢ. ܘܒܠܐ ܡܪܕܝܬܗܘܢ ܠܡܪ̈ܕܝܐ ܫܬܝܢ. ܢܠܐ
ܠܗܘܢ ܕܝܢ ܓܘܢܐ. ܡܛܠ ܢܫܒܬ ܚܕܘܬܐ ܘܪܘܪܐ ܘܡܢܝܠܘܬ ܡܫܒܚܬܐ
ܕܒܥܒܕܘܗܝ ܬܢܝܐ ܦܝܫܘܬܐ ܘܒܢܝܬܘܬܗ̇[4] ܡܢܪܐ.

3 [1] ܕܡܬܒܥܘܢ RVL [2] ܕܒܥܘܕܪ̈ܢܬܐ RVL [3] scripsi; ܕܒܪܘܫ codd. (cf. 9[2]) [4] om. RVL [5] i. add. ܠ RVL
4 [1] ܢܓܒܝܢ RVLl [2] om. RVLl [3] ܫܒܪܝܗܘܢ RVL [4] f. ܗ R

quick to anger. Noble hope drives away fear, and force of anger strengthens confidence. Therefore fear and anger do not come together, for a man is not afraid when he is angry. But shame weighs heavily on the young, because they have not yet been tried by rash misdeeds or brought low by necessities, and being deficient in knowledge they restrain themselves. Their magnanimity of soul accords with their nobility of hope, and therefore they do not suppose that they will ever be impoverished, because they are unacquainted with misery. Therefore they think great things, and tend towards the expedient or advantageous which they have experienced more than the good which until now they have not experienced. For all their calculation chooses that which is advantageous, but with them the advantageous is the pleasurable. Their calculation inducing the pleasurable is subject to nature, but the calculation inducing the good is subject not to nature but to virtue. In this way it is necessary to understand the word of our master here.

FOUR.[36] The young especially love their companions, friends, and contemporaries, because they particularly desire to rejoice, and rejoicing is accomplished through company and companionship. They seek not the true expedient, but the expedient which leads to pleasure. Therefore they love friends for the sake of the advantage (which is) pleasurable, not mental, and therefore with their pleasure their failing is very great and vehement, because they love and hate immoderately. And because they are not moderate, they suppose themselves to know everything well. They openly do wrong, and even being found guilty are disgraced, because by nature they are inclined to mischief, because they are very angry but have little shame. But along with these they are also compassionate, for they easily believe everyone who wears an appearance of being wronged, and because of their lack of cunning reject the cunning. Laughter is sweet to them, on account of love of rejoicing, merrymaking, and weakness of thought, for when (thought) strengthens cheerfulness weakens, and when (thought) is abundant (cheerfulness) is scarce.

---

[36] **5.5.4** AR 2.12 89a36-b12; IS 3.5 (158.7-18).

ܕܢܣܒ. ܫܟܝܚܐ ܕܝܢ ܫܘܠܛܢܐ ܕܒܝܬܝܗܘܢ ܫܩܝܠܝܢ ܠܒܢܝܐ ܕܛ̈ܠܝܐ. ܐܚܪܝܢ
ܓܒܪ ܘܢܫܝܢ ܒܒܝܬܗܘܢ. ܘܡܕܒܪ ܚܝܠܗܘܢ. ܘܠܐܢܫ ܠܐ ܫܠܛܝܢ. ܒܪ ܡܢ
ܢܫܐ ܘܡܢ ܐܬܬܢܝܚܘ. ܘܡܢ ܒܢܝܬܐ ܫܘܠܛܢܐܝܬ ܕܡܕܒܪܝܢ ܒܗܘܢ ܠܦܘ[1]
ܕܠܐ ܢܦܩܘܢ. ܘܟܕ ܡܬܦܠܓܝܢ ܒܠ ܥܘܒܕܐ. ܠܢܫܐܝܬ ܡܕܡ ܠܐ ܦܣܩܝܢ.
ܘܟܕ ܦܘܩܕܢܗܘܢ ܢܛܪܐ ܒܠ ܗܘ ܡܢܐ ܕܠܐ ܢܫܘ. ܒܪ ܫܒܩܝܢ ܕܒܠܚܘܕ
ܚܕ ܠܡܕܡ ܠܐ ܢܕܝܢ. ܘܠܦܘܠܚܢܐ ܘܒܢܝܐ ܐܝܟ ܠܐ ܡܕܡ ܣܓܝܢ. ܘܟܕ
ܒܠ ܗܘ ܕܒܝܬܐ ܡܫܬܘܕܝܢ ܒܐܘܪܚܐ ܦܘܫܩܢܐ ܐܝܟ ܒܒܪ ܘܕܡ ܘܕܠܒܐ
ܡܕܡ ܕܐܡܪܝܢ ܐܚܪܝܢ. ܘܡܛܠ ܒܢܘܬ ܡܫܠܡܢܘܬܗܘܢ ܒܢܝܢ ܒܝܬܝܗܘܢ.
ܘܡܛܠ ܡܢܗܝܢܘܬܗܘܢ ܟܠܗ ܠܐ ܡܗܝܡܢܝܢ. ܒܟܠܗܘܢ ܠܐ ܢܣܒܝܢ ܫܘܚܕ
ܘܠܐ ܚܢܝܢ ܫܘܚܕ. ܐܠܐ ܠܦܘܬ ܗܠܝܢ ܐܠܝܬܝܐ. ܘܟܕ ܢܣܒܝܢ ܐܝܟ ܗܢܘܢ
ܕܗܢܝܢ ܐܢܘܢ. ܘܟܕ ܗܢܝܢ ܐܝܟ ܗܢܘܢ ܕܢܣܒܝܢ.

ܕܢܫܬ. ܫܟܝܚܐ ܐܦܘܪ ܢܦܫܐ ܐܝܬܝܗܘܢ. ܐܝܟ ܗܢܘܢ ܕܦܣܝܩ ܫܪܝܗܘܢ.
ܘܒܠܗܕܐ ܠܡܫܠܪ ܡܢ ܗܘ ܕܠܦܘܩ ܚܢܐ ܡܬܒܥܐ ܠܐ ܢܓܝܢ. ܠܗܢܐ ܕܝܢ
ܢܛܪ ܐܚܪܢ. ܒܪ ܡܢ ܫܘܡܠܝܐ ܘܚܠܦܬ[1] ܬܫܒܘܚܬܐ ܡܠܠܝܢ. ܘܒܠܗܕܐ
ܠܐ ܥܒܕܝܢ ܐܠܐ ܡܠܘܠܝܢ. ܒܪ ܡܢ ܢܦܫܐ ܠܒܣܝܡܘܬ ܡܢܝܚܐ ܘܦܪܝܩܘܬ
ܐܒܕܢܐ ܡܠܦܘ. ܒܠܒܐ ܕܝܢ ܒܠܒܗܘܢ ܕܢܠܬܐ. ܘܒܠ ܐܝܠܝܢ ܕܒܬܪܝܢ ܥܦܪ
ܡܕܡ ܐܚܪܝܢ. ܐܒܒܒܐ ܕܫܘܒܚܬܐ ܡܕܡܬ ܗܕܐ ܐܢܘܢ. ܘܒܢܝܢܐ
ܡܢܒܢܐ ܫܩܝܠܝܢ ܠܛ̈ܠܝܐ. ܘܦܣܩܬ ܡܢܪܘܬ ܡܘܠܕܗܘܢ ܠܥܠܡܐ ܢܛܪܐ
ܚܠܝܢ ܘܒܠܗܕܐ ܕܢܠܬܝܢ. ܘܡܛܠ ܕܢܠܬܗܘܢ ܡܢܝܢ.[2] ܘܡܛܠ ܕܫܦܪ
ܢܣܒ ܚܢܐ ܐܢܘܢ. ܡܠܘܢ ܕܝܢ ܠܟܦܪ̈ ܢܡܘܣܐ ܐܚܪܢܐ[3] ܒܛܠܐ[4] ܢܛܪܬܗܘܢ
ܕܠܘܩܒܐ. ܘܡܬܚܪܝܢܐ ܚܪܝܓܐ ܘܪ̈ܓܝܓܐ. ܒܪ ܠܐ ܦܣܝܩܝܢ ܒܠܒܗܘܢ.
ܘܟܕ[5] ܛܒ ܢܛܪܝܢ ܒܢܘܡ ܦܠܓ̈ܬܐ.

5 [1] ܒܦܘ RVLI
6 [1] i. om. RVLI [2] ܡܬܡܡܝܢ RVLI [3] ܐܚܪ̈ܢܐ RVLI [4] ܒܛܠܐ RVL [5] ܟܕ ܛܒ RVLI

FIVE.[37] The character of the old is for the most part opposite to the character of the young, for their character is pliable and feeble, and their disposition bitter. They do not assent to anyone because they have experienced much and often been deceived, and because of the many evils which have come upon them they have learnt not to go astray. When in doubt about an opinion they do not decide something definitely and, through their excessive uncertainty about what they have not experienced, while they *suppose* they know everything they do not *know* anything. They reckon praise and blame as nothing, and when talking about the future they qualify anything they say with particles of hesitation such as 'perhaps', 'maybe', or 'perchance'. Because of their pessimistic supposition their character is evil, and because of their experience they do not readily trust. Therefore they neither love nor hate strongly, but according to what is necessary. When they love they are like those who hate, and when they hate like those who love.

SIX.[38] The old are small of soul, as those whose hope is cut, and therefore desire nothing beyond what is required for the support of life. However, they are very careful over this, because they shy away from poverty and hard trading. Therefore they are not lavish but stingy, because they have learnt by experience the difficulty of gaining and the ease of losing. Fear holds sway over them, and they devoutly predict the future as old age has formerly directed them. In impulsive manners they are opposite to the young, and because of the coldness of their constitution they tend towards excessive stillness and therefore are cowardly. They are greedy because of their fear and because they greatly love life, but especially towards the last day their desire for copulation ceases, and (for) elegant and desirable visible (things), because they have no need of them, but yet they greatly desire delicate foods.

SEVEN.[39] The old love justice on account of their frailty and cherish righteous judges, as the cause of the love of justice is either virtue of soul, or smallness of soul and fear of injustice, and in the case of the old the latter is manifestly evident. Because they love them-

---

[37] **5.5.5** AR 2.13 89b13-24; IS 3.5 (159.1-10).

[38] **5.5.6** AR 2.13 89b24-35; IS 3.5 (159.11-160.2).

[39] **5.5.7** AR 2.13 89b35-90a16; IS 3.5 (160.2-15).

ܕܥܒܕ. ܗܟܢܐ ܡܛܠ ܫܠܡܘܬܗܘܢ ܒܟܐܢܘܬܐ ܐܣܝܪܝܢ ܘܠܕ̈ܝܢܐ ܒܟ̈ܐܢܐ
ܡܣܬܟܝܢ. ܟܕ ܟܠܗܬ[1] ܕܐܣܝܪܬ ܒܟܐܢܘܬܐ ܐܘ ܡܬܚܪܪܘܬ ܢܦܫܐ ܐܬܚܝܠܬ. ܐܘ
ܘܥܘܪܘܬ ܢܦܫܐ ܘܕܫܠܝܘܬܐ ܕܡܢ ܛܠܘܡܘܬܐ. ܘܟܠܗܝܢ ܕܒܫ̈ܡܝܐ ܗܕܐ ܐܚܪܢܝܬܐ
ܟܠܗܝܢ. ܘܒܗ̇ ܕܐܣܝܪ ܢܦܫܗܘܢ ܐܝܢܘܢ. ܠܗ̇ ܕܦܩܕܐ ܠܐ ܠܗ̇ ܕܥܒܕܐ
ܐܚܝܢ. ܟܕ ܠܗ̇ ܕܦܩܕܐ ܗ̣ܘ ܡܛܠܬܗ ܥܒܕܐ ܒܪܝܐ. ܘܠܗ̇ ܕܥܒܕܐ ܡܛܠ
ܐܚܪܢܐ. ܒܐܝܕܐ ܡܛܠ ܗ̇ ܕܢܚܡܘܢܘܗܝ. ܒܕܝܢ ܠܐ ܒܗܬܝܢ ܐܦܠܐ
ܡܬܚܣܕܝܢ. ܟܝܢܐ ܕܝܢ ܗܟܢܘܗܝ. ܟܕ ܢܦܩ ܕܟ̈ܝܢܬܐ ܒܟܠܗܐ ܣܬܪ ܗ̈ܠܝܢ
ܡܢ ܛܒ̈ܥܬܐ. ܘܫܠܦ ܗܢܝܐܘܬܐ ܕܒܡܕܒܪܐ ܒܗܘܢ ܗܢܝܢ ܕܒܒ̈ܢܝ
ܡܬܒܣܡܝܢ. ܘܡܬܚܙܘܢ ܡܢ ܚܪܦܐ. ܟܝܢ ܕܝܢ ܡܚܝܠܐ. ܚܪܝܦܘܬܐ ܡܢ
ܒܗ̇ ܕܦܝܣܐܝܬ ܢܐܟܝܢ. ܡܚܝܠܘܬܐ ܕܝܢ ܒܗ̇ ܕܠܐ ܚܒܠܐ ܫܠܡܘܢ. ܐܦ
ܓ̈ܠܬܐ ܡܬܚܡܝܢ ܡܢ ܟܪ ܒܗܘܢ. ܡܬܚܡܝܢ ܕܝܢ ܐܡܬܝ̈ܠܐ. ܘܟܠܗܕܐ ܠܡܬܒܪܝܐ
ܠܐ ܠܗܘܝܐ ܡܬܐܡܪܝܢ. ܘܒܕܝܢ ܢܦܩܐ ܡܣܬܒܪܝܢ. ܢܦܩܐ ܟܝܢ
ܕܐܝܟܐ ܠܐ ܕܡܬܚܙܝܐ ܡܬܒܪܐ.

ܕܬܪ̈ܝܢܐ. ܗܟܢܐ ܒܡܫܝܚ[1] ܡܬܒܪܝܐ ܠܡܠ̈ܟܐ ܛܠܡܝܢ. ܒܪܝܬܐ ܕܡܬܚܫܒܐ[2]
ܟܝܢ. ܠܐ ܒܟܠܗ̇ ܡܒܪܝܢܐ. ܘܡܬܐܡܪܝܢ ܬܘܒ ܟܝܢ ܠܗ ܡܛܠ ܐܣܝܪܬ
ܐܢܫܘܬܐ. ܐܝܟ ܛܠ̈ܠܐ. ܐܠܐ ܡܛܠ ܫܠܡܘܬܐ ܘܡܬܬܓܡܪܘܬ ܒܢܫܬܐ
ܐܝܟ ܗ̇ ܕܠܗܘܢ ܦܪܝܟܐ[3]. ܒܕܝܢ ܡܟܝܢ ܒܢ̈ܫܐ ܐܢܘܢ ܘܠܐ ܕܠܒܠ
ܠܡܫܬܐܠܘ. ܐܦܠܐ ܦ̈ܓܪܢܝܐ[4] ܠܢܘܣܒܐ. ܟܕ ܡܚܝܢܘܬܐ ܕܒܢ̈ܫܐ
ܫܘܫܟܠܐ[5] ܠܢܘܣܒܐ. ܘܗܢܘܢ ܕܒܥܒܘܪܐ ܕܫܝܒܘܬܐ ܡܬܒܝܢܝܢ
ܒܕ̈ܪܝܗܘܢ[6] ܟܕ ܠܡܟܘܬܐ ܡܪܝܫܐ ܘܕܫܠܝܘܬܐ ܢܦܫܐ. ܘܒܡܬܚܡܘܬ
ܠܒܪܡ ܘܠܐ ܗܡܝܢܘܬ ܠܒܪܡ. ܒܬܪ̈ܬܝܗܘܢ ܐܝܟ ܕܗܕܐ ܐܢܘܢ. ܠܗ̇
ܓܝܪ ܕܡܘܬܐ ܒܗ̇ ܕܦܫܝܛܐ ܡܬܓܠܝܢ. ܘܠܗ̇ ܕܒܪܝܬܐ ܒܗ̇ ܕܓܘܫܡܐ.
ܘܠܓܘܪܬܐ ܒܦܘܩܕܬܐ. ܘܛܠܠܐ ܡܢ ܓܒܪ̈ܝܢ ܘܪܫܝܢ. ܐܟܚܕܐ ܕܗܟܢܐ
ܕܫܘܠܛܢܝܢ ܘܒܝܫܝܢ. ܐܝܬܝܗܘܢ ܕܝܢ ܒܗܘܢ ܕܦܓܪܐ ܡܢ ܬܠܬܝܢ ܒܕܡܘܬܐ
ܠܬܠܬܝܢ ܘܫܬܐ. ܘܡܫܬܟܚ ܒܗܘܐ[7] ܒܕܡܘܬܐ ܠܫܒܥܝܢ.

ܕܬܫܥܐ. ܫܦܝܪ ܠܗܘܢܐ ܕܝܢ ܗܟܢ ܐܣܝܪܝܢ ܐܝܟܢܐ ܘܡܬܕܒܪ̈ܢܝܬܐ
ܒܡܟܠܠܘܬܐ ܕܕ̈ܝܢ ܐܟܬܝܒܘܢ ܐܢܘܢ.[1] ܗܒܝܢ ܓܝܪ ܕܟܠܗܐ ܕܐܬܪ ܩܕܝܡ
ܐܬܪ ܐܦ ܘܡܟܠܐ. ܘܟܠܗܘܢ ܫܘܬܦܝܢ ܘܡܣܒܪܝܢ ܘܠܝܠܝܢ ܘܡܚܫܒܝܢ
ܘܫܠܝܛܝܢ. ܘܟܕ ܐܦ ܛܒܝܢ ܘܟܐܢܝܢ. ܒܕܟܐ ܕܐܬܪܐ ܢܛܪ ܒܗܘܢ
ܒܗܘܢ[2] ܘܟܓܪܐ ܕܒܟܢܐ ܠܒܢ̈ܝܗܘܢ ܕܐܬܪ ܡܢ ܐܟܬܝܒܘܢ ܠܐ ܒܕܒܠ
*ܢܫܠܦ ܐܘ ܠܢܟܐ.[3] ܐܠܐ ܠܢܪܬܐ ܡܢ ܓܒܘܬ ܠܗܘܢܐ ܠܥܒܪ[4] ܢܫܠܘܬܐ

---

7 [1] pl. RVL [2] om. F

8 [1] add. ܟܠܗܐ RVLl [2] ܕܡܬܚܫܒܐ RVLl [3] ܦܪܝܟܝܢ RVLl [4] ܦܓܪܢܝܐ F [5] ܫܘܫܟܠܝܢ RVLl [6] ܒܕ̈ܪܝܗܘܢ RVLl [7] add. ܕܦܓܪܐ RVL

9 [1] om. RVLl [2] scripsi; ܒܗܘܢ codd. (cf. 3[3]) [3*] pl. F [4] ܠܥܒܪ RVLl

selves they desire the expedient, not the noble, because a person seeks the expedient for himself, and the noble for others—that is, in order that they may praise him. Therefore (the old) have neither shame nor modesty, but their hope is low because they have experienced (the fact) that evils are more numerous in the world than goods. Instead of pleasure in hope they take delight in the memory of what is past. Their rage is sharp but weak. The sharpness is because they easily suffer, the weakness because their faculty does not respond. (As for) desires, some of them have ceased in (the old), others have become weak, and therefore they long for the advantageous, not the pleasurable. Thus they seem temperate, but temperate by necessity, not by virtuous intention.

EIGHT.[40] The old commit wrongs to gain what is advantageous, but by veiled cunning, not shameful exposure. They are also compassionate, but not for love of mankind, like the young, but on account of weakness and imagining evil as being near to them. Therefore they are constantly suffering and are not easily diverted (from this conviction). Neither are they much (given) to laughter, for constant suffering is opposite to laughter. Those in the prime of old age are midway in their character between headstrong fortitude and feeble cowardice, trust in everything and lack of trust in everything. With both of them they are as is right, for they blend the advantageous with the noble, the true with the laughable, and courage with temperance. The young are courageous and unrestrained, as the old are cowardly and temperate. The body's prime is from thirty to thirty-five, the completion of the prime up to fifty.

NINE.[41] Those of noble birth greatly love honour and imitate the exalted rank of their ancestors, for they suppose that whatever is anterior is more elevated and exalted. Therefore they are haughty, arrogant, worthless, scornful, and aggressive. Sometimes (however) they are good and righteous, as long as honour is preserved in them until the present and the lengthy (passage) of time has not yet altered or effaced the character which they have inherited from their forefathers. Then finally (those) of noble birth turn into demented mani-

---

[40] **5.5.8** AR 2.13 90a16 - 14 90b13; IS 3.5 (160.16-161.16).

[41] **5.5.9** AR 2.15 90b14-31; IS 3.5 (162.1-8).

ܥܒܝܕܝܢ. ܡܛܠ ܗ̇ܝ ܕܠܘܩܒܠ ܡܪܕܘܬܐ ܠܐ ܡܫܬܡܥܝܢ. ܐܝܟ ܗܢܘܢ ܕܡܢ ܐܠܘܡܦܝܐܕܝܣ[5] ܘܡܢ ܕܝܘܣܩܘܪܘܣ ܗ̇ܘ ܡܕܡܝܢܐ ܡܬܬܠܝܢ.[6] ܐܚܪ̈ܢܐ ܕܝܢ ܡܢܗܘܢ ܠܘܬ ܠܐ ܫܡܫܘܬܐ ܘܩܫܝܫܘܬܐ ܪܕܦܝܢ. ܡܛܠ ܗ̇ܝ ܕܠܡܐܠܦ ܐܘܡܢܘܬܐ ܘܡܬܠܡܕܘܬܐ[7] ܠܐ ܡܬܕܪܝܢ. ܐܝܟ ܗܢܘܢ ܕܡܢ ܩܘܠܘܢ ܘܦܪܘܠܝܣ ܘܣܩܘܪܛܝܣ ܢܣܛܝܪ.

ܕܚܡܫ. ܚܢܢ܆ ܟܬܒܢܐ ܕܝܢ ܡܥܠܠܘܬܐ ܘܥܒܗܪܘܬܐ ܘܡܬܟܪܝܢܘܬܐ ܐܝܬܝܢ. ܗ̇ܝ ܕܡܕܡ ܙܒܢܐ ܢܣܒܪܘܢ ܗܢܘܢ ܠܗܘܢ. ܐܝܟܢ ܕܐܝܬ ܠܗܘܢ *ܒܠܗܝܢ ܦܬ̈ܓܡܐ.[1] ܕܒܐܝܕܝܗܘܢ ܡܬܚܙܝܐ ܠܗܘܢ ܕܒܠܚܘܕ ܕܒܢܝܐ ܗܘ ܠܗܘܢ. ܐܦ ܡܕܒ̈ܪܢܐ ܐܦ ܣܛܘܝܩܘܣ ܘܣܛܘܠܝܩܘ[2] ܐܘܟܝܬ ܥܒܗܪ̈ܐ ܐܢܫܝܢ ܘܥܠܡܐ[3] ܐܝܬܝܢ. ܡܕܒ̈ܪܢܐ ܓܝܪ ܡܛܠ ܒܡܝܢܘܬܗܘܢ ܕܒܟܐܢܘܬܐ. ܥܒܗܪ̈ܐ ܕܝܢ ܐܟܡܐ ܕܐܬܡܢܝܘ ܡܢ ܦܝܠܘܣܘܦܐ ܕܠܘܬܗܘܢ ܕܪܥܝܢ ܐܘܪ̈ܚܬܗܘܢ. ܘܕܡܢ ܠܒܪ ܕܗܝܡܢܘܬ ܡܬܚܫܒܝܢ ܗܟܢܐ ܟܕ ܦܘܠܓܝܐ ܥܠ ܐܝܠܝܢ ܕܗܢܝܢ ܦܣܩܝܢ. ܘܡܢܗ̇ ܕܗܕܐ ܐܝܬܝܗ ܕܐܝܢܘܢ ܟܕ ܥܠܬܗ ܠܦܝܠܘܣܘܦܘܣ ܕܐܝܕܐ ܡܬܕܪܐ. ܕܢܗܘܐ ܐܝܟ ܟܬܒܢܐ ܐܘ ܢܝܫܐ. ܦܝ ܠܗ̇. ܕܢܝܫܐ ܡܢ ܕܕܥ ܐܣܟܡܘܬܐ ܕܟܬܒܢܐ.[4] ܟܕ ܢܕܥ ܕܗܝܢܘ ܗܘ ܒܡܘܢܝܩ *ܦܓܪܗ ܥܠ ܡܕܡ ܕܐܝܬ ܠܗ̇. ܟܬܒܢܐ ܕܝܢ ܓܝܪ. ܢܝܫܐ ܠܐ ܓܐܒ. ܟܕ ܠܐ ܢܕܥ ܕܗܝܢܘ ܗܘ ܒܡܘܢܝܩ[5] ܢܦܫܗ ܥܠ ܡܕܡ ܕܐܝܬ ܠܗ̇. ܟܬܒܢܐ ܐܘܪܐ ܣܦܪ ܡܕܒܪܐ ܗܘ.

ܕܫܬ. ܕܟܬܒܢܐ[1] ܟܬܡܝܐ ܬܪܝܢ ܪܒܐ[2] ܢܦܫܐ. ܘܕܟܬܒܢܐ ܚܕܬܐ ܕܒܪܝܐ. ܟܕ ܕܒܘܪܬ ܢܦܫܐ ܢܘܟܪܝܐ ܐܚܪܬ ܒܗ̇. ܘܟܬܒܢܐ ܒܠܠܒܘܬܗܘܢ ܒܠܒܘܬܐ ܠܬܠܬܐ ܕܡܢܝܢ. ܐܟܡܐ ܕܐܝܬ ܠܗܘܢ ܒܪ ܠܐ ܒܝܢܬܐ ܐܦܠܐ ܒܗܘܢܐ ܒܝܢܝܢ ܘܡܬܕܪܫܝܢ. ܟܕ ܒܟܬܒܐ ܐܝܟ ܒܡܒܪܐ ܕܡܢ ܗܘܠܝܐ[3] ܢܦܫܐ ܐܚܪܢܝ. ܚܠܦ ܕܝܢ ܒܗܘܢ ܚܢܢ ܕܠܚܝܠܐ ܓܠܝܢ ܥܒܕܝܢ. ܐܝܟ ܗܢܘܢ ܕܒܬܘܩܦܐ ܕܚܝܠܗܘܢ ܡܬܚܦܝܢ ܒܬܘܩܦܗܘܢ. ܐܘ ܡܬܚܝܠܢܐ ܐܝܟ ܗܢܘܢ ܕܒܚܝܠܗ ܚܝܠܗܘܢ ܠܡܬܢܨܚܢܘܬܐ ܗܘܝܐ ܒܬܪܗܘܢ.[4] ܘܗܠܝܢ ܐܚܪ̈ܢܐ ܐܘܟܝܬ ܐܢܫܐ ܬܪܝܢ ܒܒܪ̈ܢܫܐ ܘܡܦܠܓܝܢ ܕܒܝܢܬܗܘܢ. ܘܬܪܝܢ ܡܢ ܡܬܦܫܛ ܒܗܘܬܐ ܡܢܝܢ ܚܝܠܐ. ܟܕ ܒܬ̈ܪܝ ܚܝܠܐ ܡܢ ܕܒܗܘܬܐ ܘܐܝܟܢܐ ܐܝܬܝܗܘܢ. ܕܡܚܝܠܘܬܐ ܕܝܢ ܡܬܓܘܪܐ ܘܬܘܩܦܬܐ ܕܒܠܐܐ. ܘܗܢܘܢ ܗܠܝܢ ܒܚܝܠ ܢܦܫܗܘܢ ܒܪܘܚܬܐ ܕܬܪܝܢ ܩܢܝܢ ܘܕܒܚܝܠܐ ܢܬܪܕܘܢ ܠܐ ܡܫܬܡܥܝܢ. ܒܙܒܢ ܡܬܢܨܚܝܢ ܘܒܥܘܕܪܢܘܬܐ ܪܕܝܬܐ ܥܒܗܪܬ[5] ܐܣܟܝܡܐ ܡܬܟܢܫܝܢ. ܘܐܦ ܠܬܠܬܝܢ. ܠܐ ܠܬܠܬ ܟܕܘܢܝܬܐ ܐܝܬܝܢ ܐܠܐ ܠܬܠܬ ܪ̈ܘܪܒܬܐ.

---

[5] ܐܠܘܡܦܝܐܕܝܣ RLl; ܐܠܘܡܦܝܕܝܣ V [6] ܡܬܬܠܝܢ F; ܡܬܠܝܢ V [7] ܘܠܐ ܕܡܬܠܡܕܘܬܐ RVLl
10 [1*] ܦܬܓܡܐ F [2] scripsi; ܕܣܛܘܠܝܩܘ F; ܘܣܛܘܠܝܩܘ RVLl [3] pl. F [4] pl. R [5*] om. F
11 [1] i. ܘ F [2] ܪܒ RVLl [3] pl. RVLl [4] i. add. ܒ RVLl [5] ܥܒܗܪܬܐ RVLl

acs because they pay no regard to education, like those descended from Alcibiades and the elder Dionysius. Some others, however, are reduced to insufficiency and want because they do not apply themselves to learning a craft or business, like those descended from Conon, Pericles, and Socrates.

TEN.[42] The character of the rich is domination, arrogance, and insolence, and they suppose anything great (to be) theirs, as if they had all the good things. Therefore it appears to them that everything can be bought by them. They are both luxurious and swaggering and offensive, that is, they are vainglorious lovers of praise. They are luxurious because of their abundance in luxuries, vainglorious as long as they are accustomed (to requests) from the needy who tread their way to them, and they suppose that they are rightly envied by everyone because many need what they possess. For this reason when the wife of Hieron asked Simonides which was better, to be rich or wise, he answered her, 'The wise man treads the thresholds of the rich man'—because (the wise man) knows that for the sustenance of his body he needs anything which (the rich man) has, but the rich man does not visit the wise man, because he does not know that for the sustenance of his soul he needs anything which (the wise man) has. Therefore the rich man is lacking in understanding.

ELEVEN.[43] A person of old (established) wealth has a bigger soul than one who is newly rich, because smallness of soul spreads through him. By their open wrongdoing the rich are like the young, for like them they are adulterous and headstrong without cunning or caution, because they are protected by wealth as by a shield which keeps (them) from harm. Among them character inclined to power exceeds noble (character)—for example, those who by the force of their power increase their wealth, more than the honourable whose desire with their power is for virtue. Those who love honour are more courageous in their character, and their opinions are more worthy, and they are more capable than those who accumulate wealth, because victory, greatness, and honour are deeds of power, but business and accumulation of wealth (deeds) of weakness. With

---

[42] **5.5.10** AR 2.16 90b32-91a12; IS 3.5 (162.9-16).

[43] **5.5.11** AR 2.16 91a14 - 17 91a30; IS 3.5 (162.17-163.11).

ܕܝ̈ܢ. ܒܢ̈ܝܐ ܕܝܢ ܠܦܘܬ ܦܘܬܟܐ ܕܒܗܝܡܝܐܝܬܐ ܘܦܘܪܥܢܐ ܕܒܛ̈ܠܝܬܐ
ܦܓܪ̈ܢܝܬܐ ܡܛܠ ܢܚܝܢ ܘܡܬܡܨܝܢ. ܘܗܕܡܐ ܠܐ ܐܝܟ ܐܘ ܚܪܝܦܝܢ. ܚܕ ܒܢܝ
ܐܢܐ ܠܒܢܐ ܢܦܩ ܠܒܢܝܘܬܐ. ܕܐܬܝܠܕܘܢ[1] ܗܟܢ ܐܝܟ ܐܠܗܐ. ܘܐܒ̈ܝܠ
ܥܠ ܐܠܗܘܬܐ ܕܒܠܥܕ ܠܒܘܬܐ ܡܠܒܒܐ ܠܗܘܢ ܠܒܢܐ. ܘܐܦ ܣܘܣܟ̈ܠܐ
ܕܗܠܝܢ ܡܢ ܣܘܣܟ̈ܠܐ[2] ܕܐ̈ܢܫܘܗܝ ܡܬܬܕܒܪܝܢ.

ܕܝܟ̈. ܡܛܠ ܠܒܢܝ ܕܡܬܘܪܝ[1] ܩܕ̈ܠܐ[2] ܡܦܢܣܢܝܬܐ ܗ̇ܝ ܕܦܢܣܐ ܦܢܣܝܐ ܬܗܘܐ
ܐܝܬܘܗܝ. ܘܦܢܣܐ ܠܐ ܗܘܐ ܐܠܐ ܒܪ ܠܐ ܦܪܫܐ ܫܢܝܘܬܐ ܥܠ ܡܠܬܐ.
ܘܠܫܪ̈ܟܐ ܡܬܦܪ̈ܢܣܐ ܠܡܬܦܘ ܠܐ ܦܢܣܐ. ܡܢ ܐܠܦ̈ܬܐ[3] ܡܬܡܪܐ ܕܢܝܐ
ܕܠܠܐ ܡܬܦܢܣܢܐ[4] ܢܒܗ ܒܪ ܡܦܢܣ[5] ܕܢܬܠ ܒܠܚܘܕ. ܡܢ ܡܬܬܕ̈ܝܢܐ ܗ̇ܘ
ܡܢܐ ܕܢܒܪ[6] ܠܗ. ܘܒܠ ܡܠܬܐ ܒܠܚܘܕ ܡܢܗܘܢ ܗܕܪܐ ܢܦܩ. ܕܠܐ
ܒܡܫܒ[7] ܢܦܫܐ ܢܬܚܫܒ. ܡܢ ܐܢܫܐ ܐܪܐ ܠܡܗܘܐ ܗܪܟܐ[8] ܡܬܬܕ̈ܝܢܐ
ܘܕܝܢܐ ܘܫܪܟܐ[9] ܘܡܫܪ̈ܐ.[10] ܘܡܢܗܘܢ ܕܒܢ̈ܝܐ ܗܠܝܢ ܦܬܓܡܐ[11] ܡܬܪܬܝܢ[12]
ܪܘܦܪ ܒܦܪܘܦܣܝܣ ܡܫܬܒܪܢܘܬܐ ܕܒܢܝܢ ܗܢܝܢ̈ܘܬܐ ܡܡܠ̈ܠܬܐ ܒܡܠܐ
ܡܠ̈ܝܬܐ ܘܡܫܢܝܬܐ[13] ܘܡܬܬܕ̈ܝܢܬܐ ܡܬܪ̈ܒܢ.

12 [1] i. ܘ RVL [2] ܗ̇ܝ RVL; ܘܐܦ ܣܘܣ̈ܟܠܐ l

13 [1] i. om. RVL [2] om. F [3] sg. RL [4] pl. RVL [5] ܡܦܢܣ RVLl [6] ܕܢܒܪ RVLl [7] i. om. RVL [8] ܗܘܐ RVLl [9] i. ܕ R [10] i. om. F [11] sg. F [12] ܡܬܪܬ (?) F [13] ܡܫܢܝ̈ܘܬܐ RVLl

their own power these people acquire great prudence and refuse to exalt themselves forcibly. Therefore they are self-effacing, and their dignified bearing (is characterised) by mild severity and well-mannered humility. Even if they do wrong, they are not small wrongdoers but great ones.

TWELVE.[44] (Those) fortunate in relation to indulgence in pleasures and excess in bodily goods are specially greedy and vainglorious and are not mindful or careful of anything. One good condition follows on good fortune, namely, that (such people) are great lovers of God. Those to whom good is presented without labour are confident in the divine. The conditions of the opposites of these are evident from the opposites of their conditions.

THIRTEEN.[45] Because the use of persuasive speeches is that persuasion come about, and persuasion does not come about except when the need for speech ceases; and for individuals in controversy it is not easy to keep silent—of necessity (therefore) a judge must be sought who will admonish a disobedient (person) while persuading each of the accused to say what is helpful to him. In addition to a speech, each of them should produce witnesses, so as not to be blamed for dissimulation, so of necessity there must be here an accused, a judge, spectators, and witnesses. From the different characters an orator has an abundance of opined premisses from which acceptable *pisteis* may be composed for deliberative, demonstrative, and judicial speeches.

[44] **5.5.12** AR 2.17 91a30-b7; IS 3.5 (163.12-15).
[45] **5.5.13** AR 2.18 91b8-27; IS 3.5 (163.16-164.8).

## ܩܦܠܐܘܢ ܫܬܝܬܝܐ

## ܡܛܠ ܫܪ̈ܟܐ ܕܓܢ̈ܝܢ ܠܬܠܝܬܝܘܬ ܐܕ̈ܫܐ ܕܦܝܠܘܣܘܦܘܬܐ

## ܘܒܗ ܐܝܬ ܦܣ̈ܘܩܐ ܫܒܥܐ

### ܦܣܘܩܐ ܩܕܡܝܐ

### ܡܛܠ ܡܬܡܨܝܢܐ ܘܠܐ ܡܬܡܨܝܢܐ ܘܗ̇ܘ ܕܗ̣ܘܐ ܘܗ̇ܘܐ ܘܪܘܪܒܐ[1]

### ܘܙܥܘܪܐ

### ܬܐܘܪܝܐ ܬܠܬ

ܡܬܡܨܝܢܘܬܐ. ܗܠܝܢ ܓܝܪ ܐܝܟ ܕܓܢ̈ܝܢ ܠܬܠܝܬܝܘܬܐ ܐܕ̈ܫܐ ܐܠܐ[1] ܡܬܡܨܝܢܐ[2] ܘܠܐ ܡܬܡܨܝܢܐ ܠܡܠܘ̈ܟܐ[3] ܦܬܪ ܥܠܬ܉ ܘܗ̇ܘ ܕܗ̣ܘܐ ܘܗ̇ܘܐ ܠܕܡܝܘ̈ܬܐ. ܘܪܘܪܒܐ[4] ܘܙܥܘܪܐ ܒܡܫܘܚ̈ܬܐ. ܒܕܝܠܗ̇ ܐܡܪܝܢ. ܐܢ ܗܡܡܠܝܐ ܕܡܕܡ ܡܨܐ ܐܦ ܗ̣ܘ ܡܨܐ. ܒܐܡܬ ܐܢ ܡܨܐ ܕܢܬܦܠܓ ܒܬܪܝܢ ܡܨܐ ܕܢܬܒܢܐ. ܘܐܢ ܗ̇ܘ ܕܕܢܚܐ ܠܡܕܡ ܡܨܐ ܐܦ ܗ̣ܘ ܡܨܐ. ܘܐܢ ܗ̇ܘ ܕܢܬܪ ܒܣܡ ܡܨܐ ܗ̣ܘ ܕܦܣܝܩ ܡܨܐ. ܘܐܢ ܥܘܩܪܐ ܕܡܕܡ[5] ܡܨܐ ܐܦ ܗ̣ܘ ܡܨܐ. ܒܐܡܬ ܐܢ ܥܦܝܪܘܬ ܒܝܫܐ ܡܨܝܐ ܐܦ ܒܝܫܐ ܡܨܐ. ܘܗ̇ܘ ܡܢܐ ܕܥܒܘܪܗ ܡܨܐ ܐܦ ܥܒܘܕܗ ܡܨܝܐ ܒܕܐܝܬܝܐ ܕܠܐ ܡܥܠܡ ܠܐ ܥܒܪ܉ ܘܗ̇ܘ ܡܢܐ ܕܥܒܘܕܗ ܡܨܐ ܐܦ ܥܒܘܪܗ ܡܨܝܐ ܒܕܐܝܬܝܐ ܕܠܐ ܥܒܪ܆ ܠܐ ܡܥܠܡ. ܘܐܝܟܢܐ ܕܐܢܫܐ ܒܚܝܠܐ ܡܨܐ ܗ̇ܘ ܡܕܡ ܡܨܐ. ܒܐܡܬ ܐܢ ܡܨܐ ܒܝܫܐ ܠܡܗܘܐ ܛܒܐ ܡܨܐ ܠܡܗܘܐ ܐܦ ܛܠܝܐ. ܘܡܗܦܟܐ.

ܕܬܪܝܢ. ܫܪ̈ܟܐ ܕܒܡܠܝܐ ܪܓܠ ܒܝܫܐ ܡܬܡܨܝ̈ܢܐ ܐܝܟܢ. ܠܡܢ ܓܝܪ ܐܝܟ ܕܠܐ ܡܬܡܨܝܢܘܬܐ ܡܬܝܪ̈ܢܐ. ܘܫܪ̈ܟܐ ܕܒܡܫܡܫܢܘܬܐ[1] ܘܐܡܪܫܘܬܐ[2] ܐܝܟ ܐܣܘܬܐ ܘܐܒܗܒܘܬܐ ܗܠܝܢ ܡܬܡܨܝ̈ܢܐ ܐܝܟܢ. ܗܟܢܐ ܘܗܠܝܢ ܕܕܠܐ ܗ̣ܘ ܦܘܪܫܢܗܘܢ ܘܐܠܝܨܝܢ ܠܗܘܢ ܘܫܡܫܝܢ ܒܠܗܘܢ. ܗܢ ܒܢܝܐ ܗܠܝܢ ܕܒܫܘܡܠܐ ܕܡܠܬܐ ܘܫܪܟܐ ܗܘܝܢ. ܘܐܝܟܢܐ[3] ܕܡܠܟܐ ܡܢܬܐ ܡܨܝܐ ܒܗܠܝܢ ܡܨܐ. ܘܐܢ ܒܗܠܝܢ ܡܨܐ ܐܦ ܠܒܪܐ ܡܢ ܡܢܘܬܐ ܡܨܝܐ.

---

Titulus [1] ܘܪܘܪܒܐ RVL

1 [1] ܠܐ F [2] pl. F [3] sg. F [4] i. om. F [5] i. om. F

2 [1] i. ܘ RVL [2] sg. F [3] ܘܐܢ RVL

## CHAPTER SIX
## ON SUBJECTS WHICH ARE COMMON TO ALL THREE RHETORICAL SPECIES
## SEVEN SECTIONS

### SECTION ONE
### On the Possible and Impossible, Past and Future, and Amplification and Diminution
### Three Theories

ONE.[1] Although these (subjects) are common to the three species, nevertheless the possible and impossible is most appropriate to the deliberative, past and future to the judicial, and amplification and diminution to the demonstrative. Therefore we may say, if the opposite of something is possible, it (itself) is also possible. For example, if it is possible for a man to be cured, it is possible for him to fall ill. And if what is similar to something is possible, it also is possible. And if the harder is possible, the easier is possible. And if beauty of something is possible, it too is possible. For example, if the beauty of a building is possible, also the building is possible. And that of which the beginning is possible, so too is its end possible, because that which does not end has not begun. And that of which the end is possible, so too is its beginning possible, because that which has not begun does not end. And if the later by nature is possible, the prior is possible. For example, if it is possible for a human being to become a man, it is also possible to become a youth, and vice versa.

TWO.[2] Things which one naturally desires are possible, for no one desires those which are impossible. And things which come about through sciences and arts like medicine and agriculture are possible. Similarly also those of which control is ours, or by which we are constrained, or of which we have need. In the same manner also

---

[1] **6.1.1** AR 2.18 91b28 - 19 92a23; IS 3.6 (164.11-165.10).

[2] **6.1.2** AR 2.19 92a23-b14; IS 3.6 (165.10-166.3).

ܘܐܢܘܢ ܕܒܢܝ ܐܕܫܐ ܡܟܝܟܐ ܒܢܝ ܠܒܘܫܐ ܡܟܝܟܐ. ܒܐܝܡܬ ܐܝܟ ܐܠܦܐ ܗܟܢܐܝܬ ܠܩܕܡ ܡܥܡܘܕܝܬܐ ܠܡܗܘܐ ܐܦ ܐܠܦܐ ܕܬܠܬ ܠܩܕܡ ܡܥܡܘܕܝܬܐ. ܘܒܗܦܟܐ. ܘܐܢ ܚܕ ܡܢ ܗܠܝܢ ܕܠܘܬ ܡܕܡ ܡܟܝܟܐ ܐܦ ܚܒܪܗ ܡܟܝܟܐ. ܘܗܘ ܕܠܗܕܝܘܛܐ ܘܒܘܪܐ ܘܡܣܟܢܐ ܡܟܝܟܐ ܠܢܕܘܒܐ[4] ܘܐܘܡܢܐ ܘܡܟܝܠܢܐ ܬܘܒ ܡܟܝܟܐ. ܐܝܟ ܕܐܡܪ ܐܦܘܣܛܘܠܘܣ. ܕܚܫܒܐ ܐܬܬܝܗ̇ ܐܢ ܗܘ ܡܢܐ ܕܗܟܠܐ ܡܠܦ. *ܐܢܐ ܠܐ ܐܬܡܟܟܐ[5] ܕܐܠܦ. ܘܠܠܐ ܡܬܡܟܟܢܐ ܡܢ ܗܠܝܢ[6] ܫܩ̈ܒܠܢܐ ܕܗܠܝܢ *ܡܬܡܟܝܢ ܐܕܫܐ.[7]

ܕܬܠܬ. ܘܐܕܫ̈ܐ ܗ̇ܝ[1] ܕܐܝܟ ܐܝܪܐ ܗܘܐ ܡܕܡ ܐܘ ܠܐ ܗܘܐ ܡܢ ܗܠܝܢ ܡܬܬܕܝܢ. ܠܚܘܕ ܗܝ ܐܝܟ ܗܘ ܕܒܝܢܝ ܟܢܝ ܠܗܘܢܐ ܗܘܐ[2] ܗܘ ܕܬܬܪ ܟܢܝ ܗܘܐ. ܘܐܝܟ ܢܦܫܐ ܡܬܢܦܫܐ ܗܘܐ. ܒܐܝܡܬ ܐܝܟ ܐܬܬܥܝܪ ܐܝܟ ܡܕܡ ܠܦ ܗܘܐ. ܘܐܝܟ ܬܠܡ̈ܝܕܐ ܗ̇ܘ̣ܝ ܒܠܬܘܕܐ ܗܘܘ. ܒܐܝܡܬ ܐܝܟ ܡܟܝܟܐ ܚܝܠܐ ܘܡܟܝܠܐ ܦܫܪ ܐܝܟ[3] ܡܕܡ ܡܢ ܠܒܪ ܠܐ ܒܟܠ. ܐܝܟ ܕܒܫܘܬܦܐܐ ܒܪ ܗܠܝܢ ܕܪܒܢ ܐܝܟ ܡܢܟ ܒܟܕܝܢ. ܘܐܝܟ ܠܦܘܬܐ ܕܡܕܡ ܡܕܡ ܗܘܘ ܐܦ ܗܘ ܗܘܐ. ܐܝܟ ܗ̇ܝ ܕܐܝܟ ܐܡܪ ܒܢܝ ܐܬܡܠܝ. ܘܐܝܟ ܐܟܘܬ ܪܒܡ. ܘܐܝܟ ܐܬܒܠܥ ܠܬܪܝܢܐ ܗܘܐ ܡܕܡܝܢܐ. ܐܝܟ ܗ̇ܝ ܕܐܝܟ ܐܐܪ ܪܒܡ ܐܟܕܡ. ܘܐܝܟ ܐܬܠܒܫ ܒܢܝܫܐ ܠܡܪܒܐ ܡܕܡ ܗܘܐ ܒܟܠܐ.[4] ܘܐܕ̈ܫܐ ܗ̇ܘ ܡܢܐ ܕܠܐ ܗ̇ܘܐ[5] ܡܢ ܐܕ̈ܫܐ ܗ̇ܘ ܡܢܐ ܕܗ̇ܘܐ ܡܬܠܦܝܢ. ܘܠܦܘܬ ܪܘܪܒ ܥܘܒܐ ܘܘܒܪܐ ܦ̈ܩܕܝ ܗܢܝܢ ܕܒܥܘܪܢܐ ܦ̈ܠܚܢܝܐ ܕܐܬܟ̈ܗܕܝ.[6]

ܦܘܣܩܐ ܬܪܝܢܐ
ܡܛܠ ܬܫܒ̈ܘܚܬܐ ܪܘܚ̈ܢܝܬܐ
ܬܐܘܪ̈ܝܐ ܐܪܒܥ

ܡܕܡܝܢܘܬܐ. ܬܪܝܢ ܐܢܘܢ ܠܒܢ̈ܝ ܗܝܡܢ̈ܘܬܐ ܠܒܢ̈ܝܢܐ. ܬܫܒܘܚܬܐ ܘܡܬܪ̈ܥܝܢܘܬܐ. ܠܒܢ̈ܝܢ ܕܝܢ ܐܘܡܢܘܬ ܪܒܢܝܐ ܡܥܡܕܢܐ ܒܗܘ̈ܠܦ ܕܡܬܪܥܝܢܘܬܐ ܒܟܠܐ. ܘܠܩܘܕܡ ܗ̇ܝ ܡܛܠ ܬܫܒܘܚܬܐ ܕܡܫܘܚܬܘܬܐ

[4] pl. RVLl [5]* ܐܢ ܠܐ ܡܟܝܟܐ ܐܢܐ RVLl [6] om. RVLl [7]* ܡܬܡܟܝܢ ܐܕ̈ܫܐ RVL

3 [1] ܗ̇ܢܘܢ RVLl [2] ܗ̇ܘܐ RVLl [3] i. add. ܘ RVLl [4] ܕܟܠܐ RVL [5] ܗܘܐ RVL [6] ܐܬܗܘܝ R; ܐܬܟܗ̈ܕܝ L; ܐܬܟܗ̈ܕܝܢ l

those which come about through the support of virtuous people and friends. If the part is possible, the whole is possible, and if the whole is possible, each one of the parts is possible. If the nature of the species is possible, the nature of the genus is possible. For example, if a multi-oared ship can exist, so can a ship with three oars, and vice versa. If one thing which (belongs) with something (else) is possible, its companion is also possible. That which is possible for an unlearned, simple, or inferior person is more possible for a learned, skilled, or superior person. As Isocrates said, 'It would be perverse if I were unable to learn what a fool has learned.' As for the impossible, the species is found from the things opposite to these.

THREE.[3] The species of 'whether something has happened or not' will be evident from the (following). First, if that which is less opportune to happen has happened, then that which is more opportune has happened. And if the following has happened, the preceding has happened. For example, if someone has forgotten something, he had learnt it. And if the causes have happened, the effects have happened. For example, if (someone) was able and wished (to do something), he did (it), if nothing external hindered him, because for the most part (people) do what they desire if they are able. And if preparations for something previously happened, it also happened. For instance, if the air was cloudy, it rained, and if there was lightening, there was thunder. And if there was preparation for the second, the first had happened. For instance, if the air was thunderous, there had been lightening, and if someone has prepared for war, an offence has previously occurred. The species of 'that which does not happen' are learnt from the species of 'that which does happen'. On the amplification or diminution of a thing, what was mentioned on deliberative subjects is sufficient.

[3] **6.1.3** AR 2.19 92b14-93a21; IS 3.6 (166.4-167.6).

ܡܬܘܪܓܡܢܐ ܗܘܪܐ ܐܡܪܝܢ ܕܬܪܝܢ ܐܢܘܢ ܐܪ̈ܥܬܗ. ܚܕ[1] ܡܢ ܐܪܥܐ ܕܬܫܡܫܬܐ ܕܡܫܬܡܫܐ ܡܢ ܥܒ̈ܕܐ *ܕܗܘܘ ܘܐܣܝܪܐ ܕܝܢ ܐܪܥܐ ܕܬܫܡܫܬܐ ܕܡܫܬܡܫܐ ܡܢ ܥܒ̈ܕܐ[2] *ܒܗ̇ ܗ̇ܘ[3] ܒܪܢܫܐ ܒܪܐ ܠܗ. ܘܗ̇ܘ ܗܢܐ ܐܘ[4] ܡܬܡܟܝܢܐ ܗܘ ܘܦܩܐܪܒܘܠ ܐܡܒܝܬ[5] ܡܛܠ ܣܓܝܐܬܐ ܡܬܘܪܐ ܐܪܥܐ ܐܘ ܡܛܠܠܬܐ ܗܘ ܕܟܠܐ ܐܝܟ ܗܘܢ ܕܡܣܡܣܘܢ ܘܠܒܫܘܢ ܕܡܢ[6] ܦܪܘܦ ܠܐ ܬܠܝܬܐ *ܥܒ̈ܕܐ ܬܠܝܬܝܐ[7] ܙܒܢܘ. ܘܗܠܝܢ ܡܢ[8] ܬܠܬܐ ܦܘܣܩܢܐ ܕܬܫܡܫܬܐ[9] ܘܡܢ[10] ܥܒ̈ܕܐ ܕܗܘܘ ܘܡܢ ܥܒ̈ܕܐ ܕܠܐ ܗܘܘ ܡܬܡܟ̈ܝܢܐ ܒܝܬ ܘܠܐ ܡܬܡܟ̈ܝܢܐ.

ܕܬܪ̈ܬܝܢ. ܛܘܦܣܐ ܡܢ ܡܕܡܝܐ ܐܝܟ ܕܐܡܪ ܙܘܛܪ ܠܡܠܟܐ ܕܡܢ̈ܝܐ ܕܠܐ ܬܫܒܘܩ ܠܛܘܪܐ ܕܠܡܪܝܡ ܢܦܘܠ ܒܗ ܕܪܘܫ ܒܗܬ ܕܠܡܪܝܡ ܐܝܟ. ܠܐܬܪ̈ܘܬܐ ܕܡܢ̈ܝܐ ܒܒܪ. ܘܡܕܡܝܘܗܝ ܬܘܒ ܐܫܟܚܢ ܐܠܐ ܠܐ ܢܦܩ ܠܡܪܝܡ ܠܒܝܬ ܢܘܢ ܠܐ ܒܠ. ܘܛܘܦܣܐ ܕܝܢ[1] ܬܘܠܢܐ ܐܝܟ ܕܐܡܪ ܣܘܪܛܝܣ ܕܠܐ ܦ̈ܠܐ ܕܡܢ ܦܩ̈ܐ ܢܗܘܘܢ ܐܢ̈ܫܐ *ܥܠ̈ܬܝܐ. ܐܡܟܢܐ ܕܠܐ ܦ̈ܠܐ ܕܡܢ ܦܩ̈ܐ ܢܗܘܘܢ ܐܢ̈ܫܝܢ[2] ܐܬܠܬܝܐ. ܐܠܐ ܐܠܝܢ ܕܠܡܒܒܒ. ܐܝܟܢܐ ܡܕܒܝܢ. ܘܛܘܦܣܐ ܬܠܝܬܝܐ ܬܘܒ ܐܝܟ ܕܐܡܪ ܐܣܛܘܟܝܣܪܘܣ[3] ܕܗܘܛܪܐ ܒܡܬܪܓܡ ܠܒܢ̈ܝ ܒܝܬܗ ܕܣܘܟܐ ܚܕ ܐܝܟ. ܗܘܐ ܡܙܝܓܐ ܒܠܚܘܕܘܗܝ. ܘܒܗ ܒܠܬ ܐܠܗܐ ܘܣܒܠܬ ܠܢܒܝܗ ܐܬܙܓܘ ܒܒܪܝܬܐ ܕܢܬܝܗܡ ܡܢܗ. ܘܗ̇ܘ ܐܡܪ ܠܗ ܕܟܒܪ ܐܢܐ ܗܕܐ ܐܢ̱ ܡܟܦ ܐܢܬ ܠܡܡܠܠܘ ܦܘܠܓܕܬܐ ܐܦ ܠܐ ܬܫܟܚ ܒܠ ܣܢܝܩ ܒܗ ܐܝܟ. ܐܢܐ ܥܠܬܝܐ.[4] ܘܒܗ ܐܫܦ ܣܘܣܝܐ ܘܟܒܒ[5] ܒܠܘܗܝ ܒܪܝܐ. ܣܠܩ ܗ̇ ܕܢܬܝܗܡ ܡܢ ܐܠܗܘܬܐ ܠܒܪܝܐ ܐܫܬܟܚ. ܡܟܝܠ ܐܦ ܐܢܘܢ ܗܢܘܢ ܕܬܫܡܫܬ ܐܘܣܝܢ ܢܣܘܪܐ ܐܣܛܘܟܣܝܘܢ[6] ܐܡܒܝܬ *ܐܣܝܪ ܦܘܬܗ[7] ܐܬܒܛܠܘܢ. ܐܢ ܬܬܠܘܢ ܐܝܟ ܠܛܘܪܐ ܦܠܐܪܝܘܣ ܗܟܝܠ ܕܗ̇ܘ ܣܘܣܝܐ ܬܫܒܘܢ.

ܕܬܠܬ. ܗܘܣܦܘܣ *ܪܘܛܪܐ ܬܘܒ[1] ܒܡܐܡܪܘܣ[2] ܒܗ ܒܟܒܪ ܣܘܐܓܪܘܬܐ ܠܕܡܟܓܓܘܣ ܥܠܬܝܐ ܒܗ ܡܬܬܕܝܢ ܗܘܐ ܠܡܚܒܬ ܐܡܪ. ܬܠܬܐ ܒܗ ܟܒܪ ܗܘܐ ܒܢܗܪܐ ܐܬܕܚܝ ܠܗܘܬ ܓܒܪ̈ܬܐ ܘܒܪܒܢܐ ܣܓܝܐܐ ܠܡܣܝܡ ܐܬܡܢܝ ܕܢܩܘܡ ܠܣܦܪܐ. ܘܬܡܢ ܕܟ̈ܒܝ ܒܠܒܐ ܣܓ̈ܝܐܐ ܣܒܒܘ ܒܗ. ܡܦܪܐ ܕܝܢ ܒܗ ܣܓܝܗ ܕܡܬܬܠܝܢ ܘܦܗܝܐ ܡܬܬܟܒܠ[3] ܣܡܟ ܒܠܘܗܝ ܘܐܡܪܬ ܠܗ ܕܐܢ̱ ܢܦܠܐ ܠܡܦܘܩ ܡܢܗ ܕܟ̈ܒܐ. ܗ̇ܘ ܕܝܢ ܐܡܪ ܠܗ ܠܐ ܘܐܬܠܬܗ

1 [1] ܚܕܐ F [2*] om. F [3*] ܗܘܘ RVLl [4] ܕܐܘ RVLl [5*] ܐܡܪ F [6] i. om. FRVL [7*] om. F [8] om. F [9] pl. F [10] om. Fl

2 [1] om. RVLl [2*] om. F [3] ܐܣܛܘܟܣܝܘܣ RVLl; ܐܣܛܘܟܣܝܘܣ l [4] scripsi; ܣܠܝܩܬܐ codd. [5] i. om. RVLl [6] ܐܣܛܘܪܦܘܣܪ RL; ܐܣܛܘܪܦܘܣ V [7*] ܐܣܝܪ̈ܬܗ RVLl

3 [1*] trp. RVLl [2] ܒܡܐܡܪܘܣ RVL [3] ܘܡܬܬܟܒܠ RVLl

## SECTION TWO
### On Rhetorical Paradigms
### Four Theories

ONE.[4] The genera of common *pisteis* are two: paradigm and enthymeme. The *gnome* or reputable maxim, however, is included among the materials of the enthymeme. First, then, let us say about the paradigm, which here is called a demonstration, that its species are two: one species of paradigm is derived from things which have happened, the other species of paradigm is derived from things when a person himself creates it. The latter is either possible and is called a *parabole* or true proverb, or is an untrue discourse like those of Aesop and Libuqu, who by personification of irrational subjects constructed rational (ones). Thus there are three types of paradigm, and (they are derived) from things which have happened, and from things which have not happened, (the latter divided into) the possible or impossible.

TWO.[5] An example of the first type is an orator saying to the king of the Greeks, 'Do not allow the tyrant to enter Egypt, because after Darius seized Egypt, he crossed over to the territories of the Greeks. And before him, furthermore, if Xerxes had not taken Egypt, he would not have entered the homeland of Greece.' An example of the second type is Socrates saying that it is not right that men should become rulers by lots, just as it is not right that men should become athletes by lots, but (athletes should be) those who know (how) to contend. An example of the third type is the orator Stesichorus saying when haranguing his people, 'A lone horse had a meadow to himself, and when a stag came in and damaged his pasture, he turned for help to a man to take vengeance on her. The (man) said to him, "I will do this, if you agree to take the bridle and you take me up on your back while I hold a rod (?)." When the horse agreed and the man mounted him, instead of being avenged on the stag, he became enslaved to the man. So also if you who are under the control of a general (as) *autocrat*, that is, one who controls himself, lift a hand against the tyrant Phaladirios, you will suffer the (fate) of that horse.'

---

[4] **6.2.1** AR 2.20 93a22-30; IS 3.6 (167.7-14).

[5] **6.2.2** AR 2.20 93a30-b23; IS 3.6 (167.15-168.10).

ܕܡܛܠ ܡܢܐ ܘܗܘ ܦܢܐ. ܕܗܠܝܢ ܕܝܢ ܡܢ ܒܗܘ ܫܒܒܐ. ܡܢ ܕܒܪ ܘܗܘܝܐ ܡܢܐ ܡܠܝܠ
ܡܕܡ ܡܬܠܝܢ[4]. ܘܐܝܟܢܐ ܕܠܗܠܝܢ ܛܦܣܝܢ ܐܚܪܢܐ ܡܬܪ ܢܦ̈ܫܗ ܠܒܪܢܫܐ ܐܬܠܝܢ
ܘܠܕܡܝܐ ܒܝܘܢܐ ܕܥܪܩ ܒܗ ܥܠܬܝܢ. ܗܟܢܐ ܐܦ ܐܢܬܘܢ ܡܫܝ̈ܚܝܐ[5] ܗܢܐ
ܡܢ ܥܠܝܠܘܬܗܘܢ ܡܠܝܠ ܡܕܡܐ. ܒܬܪܐ ܗܘ ܟܢ. ܐܝܟܢܐ ܕܝܢ[6] ܕܠܗܝܢܐ
ܬܘܠܠܝܗܘܢ ܐܚܪܢܐ ܐܢ̈ܬ ܕܪ̈ܥܝܢ ܘܗܠܝܢ ܕܠܡܬܠܘܢ[7] ܘܕܡܘܬܐ ܡܬܠܝܢ.

ܕܐܒ̈ܪܗ. ܬܫܡܫܬܐ ܕܝܢ ܗܠܝܢ ܠܗܘܬ ܗ̇ܝ، ܕܒܡܠܟܘܬܢ ܡܬܪ ܡܠܟܘ̈ܬܐ ܒܗ.
ܗܘܒ̈ܪܐ ܡܬܠܬ̈ܐ ܕܡܬܢ̈ܝܐ ܠܐ ܗܘܘܢ. ܒܗ ܠܡܒܥܐ ܥܒ̈ܪܐ ܬܫܡܫܬܐ ܕܠܐ
ܐܢܬܘܢ. ܐܝܟ ܦܫܝܛܐ. ܐܠܐ ܗܘܒ̈ܪܐ ܕܗܘܘ ܡܠܬ ܡܬܟܫܝܢ. ܘܐܝܟܢܐ
ܕܡܬܠܬ̈ܐ ܐܢܬܢܐ ܡܢ ܥܒܕܐ ܕܦܝܠܘܣܘܦܐ[1] ܐܝܟܢ. ܘܡܕܒ̈ܪܢܐ ܒܗܠܝܢ
ܢܫ̈ܐ. ܒܡܐ[2] ܡܬܐܪܐܬ ܒܒܘܫ̈ܢܐ[3] ܗܠܝܢ ܡܫܬܠܐ. ܙܕܩ ܕܝܢ ܠܡܬܚܫܒܘ
ܒܬܫ̈ܡܫܬܐ ܐܡܟܐ ܕܠܝܬ ܡܬܪܚܫܢܘܬܐ. *ܒܗ ܗܝܡܢܘܬܐ ܒܡܬܪܚܫܢܘܬܐ[4]
ܗܘܝܐ ܘܬܫܡܫܬܐ ܕܥܒܕ ܗܘ̈ܕܐ[5] ܡܬܟܠܢܐ. ܘܡܥܕܪ ܒܠܒܝܐ ܠܗܘܦܟܢܐ
*ܕܡܫܢܐ. ܘܐܝܟ ܠܗܘܦܟܐ ܗܘܦܟܢܐ[6] ܠܐ ܒܥܬܐ ܐܠܐ ܚܕܐ ܠܡܒܥܐ.
ܘܡܬܪܚܫܢܘܬܐ ܕܝܢ ܒܗ ܟܠ ܥܘܪ̈ܪܐ ܒܬܫܡܫܬܐ ܚܫܝܡܐ. ܠܗܘܕܩ ܬܫܡܫܬܐ
ܦܠܐ ܠܡܫܠܡܘ. ܒܗ̇[7] ܟܢ ܢܦܫܐ ܠܗܘܟܠ ܡܬܪܚܫܢܘܬܐ ܡܬܒܠܒܬܐ. ܘܒܗ
ܡܬܪܚܫܢܘܬܐ ܡܕܡܐ ܘܠܐ ܡܦܫܩܐ. ܟܠ ܬܫ̈ܡܫܬܐ ܡܦܪ̈ܫܬܐ ܡܡܫܡܫܢܐ
ܕܬܦܫܩ. *ܗܡܕܐ ܟܢ[8] ܒܟܠ ܕܗܘܝܢ ܡܦܫܩܢܐ ܗܘ. ܘܐܝܬ ܐܚܪܬ، ܕܚܙܐ
ܬܫܡܫܬܐ ܡܬܡܬܠܐ ܐܝܟܢܐ ܕܚܙ ܗܡܕܐ ܐ̱ ܠܦܪܘܐ ܗܘ ܡܬܡܬܠ.

ܦܫܘܩܐ ܬܠܝܬܝܐ
ܡܛܠ *ܪ̈ܒܢܐ ܪ̈ܗܒܢܐ[1]
ܬܐܘܪ̈ܝܐ ܫܒܥ

ܘܕܡܝܬܐ. ܪܒܢܐ ܕܝܢ ܐܝܬܘܗܝ، ܦܪܘܛܘܣ[1] ܒܠܫܢܐ ܘܠܘ ܡܬܡܬܠܐ ܒܪ̈ܚܝܐ
ܗܒܘܪ̈ܐ. ܒܗ̇، ܕܡܬܟܒܝܢ ܐܘ ܡܬܟܘܝܢ. ܘܡܬܪܚܫܢܘܬܐ ܪܒܢܘܬܐ[2] ܦܪܝܫܐ
ܠܫܘܠܛܢܐ ܦܣܝܢܘܬܐ ܒܡܫܠܡܢܘܬܐ ܘܡܫܘܕܥܢܘܬܐ ܕܪ̈ܒܢܐ[3] ܡܢ
ܕܠܗܘܕܝܗܘܢ ܡܬܗܫܟܝܢ ܐܦ ܗܘܝܢ ܪܒ̈ܢܐ ܐܝܟ *ܐܝܟܢܐ ܕܦܪܘܛܘܣ
ܕܠܗܘܢ ܪܒ̈ܢܐ ܐܝܟ[4]. ܘܒܗ̇ ܡܬܪܚܫܢܘܬܐ ܒܗ ܒܠܫܬܐ *ܡܬܬܘܣܦܐ ܗܘܬ[5]

---

[4] ܡܢܬ ܥܡ F [5] ܡܫܝ̈ܚܝܐ RVL [6] om. RVLl [7] om. RVLl

4 [1] ܕܦܝܠܘܣܘܦܐ RVLl [2] ܒܡܐܪܬ RVLl [3] i. ܕ RVL [4*] om. RVL [5] sg. RVLl [6*] om. F [7] ܒܗ FRVL [8*] ܘܗܡܕܐ F

Titulus [1] pl. RLl

1 [1] pl. R [2] ܪܒܢܘܬܐ RL; ܪ̈ܒܢܘܬܐ V [3] ܘܡܫܘܕܥܢܫܡܛܐ RVL; ܘܡܫܘܕܥܢܡܛܐ l [4*] om. R [5*] ܡܬܬܘܣܦܐ RL [5] om. Vl

THREE.[6] When the orator Aesop in Samos was making a plea for a ruling demagogue who was being indicted for the death (penalty), he said (as follows): 'When a fox was crossing a river, he was carried into a whirlpool, and (only) over a long period with great difficulty was he able to get out to the bank. There many dog-fleas set upon him, but seeing him suffering and wandering and tottering, a hedgehog took pity on him and asked him if he wished (her) to remove the fleas from him. He told (her) not (to do so), and (when) she asked (the reason) why, he replied, "They are already filled with my blood and now draw little, but if you remove them, others more thirsty for blood will come and drink the meagre blood that remains in me." Similarly also you Samians, this ruler of yours will do little damage, for he is a rich man; but if you put him to death, another will come who is poor, and he will seize what is yours and public.'

FOUR.[7] These paradigms are more advantageous for deliberating (than are those from things which have happened), because similar particular things do not happen (and) because it is easy to create non-existent paradigmatic events. Nevertheless, things which have happened are more persuasive. And if existent particulars are part of the foundation of philosophy, and (past) experiences are helpful in (establishing) these, how much more (helpful) are they in these flimsy disputations! It is right to use paradigms (in those cases) where there is no enthymeme, because *pistis* comes about through the enthymeme and a paradigm (associated with an enthymeme merely) serves instead of witnesses. In establishing a universal it resembles induction, and although induction is not appropriate for an orator, nevertheless (he may use it) sometimes. When an enthymeme needs a paradigm to establish it, it is necessary to present the paradigm first, for by it the soul is prepared towards the enthymeme. When the enthymeme comes first and does not persuade, it needs many paradigms in order to persuade. Everywhere a witness is persuasive, and sometimes a single paradigm may be accepted as long as a single witness, if expert, is accepted.

[6] **6.2.3** AR 2.20 93b23-94a2; IS 3.6 (168.11-169.6).
[7] **6.2.4** AR 2.20 94a2-18; IS 3.6 (169.7-170.5).

ܒܗ̇ ܗܘܝܢ[6] ܡܦܝܣܐ. ܐܟܡܐ ܕܢܐܡܪ. ܠܡܠܦܘ ܠܛܠܝܐ ܚܟܡܬܐ ܡܢ ܬܘܪܐ ܐܠܗܝܐ. ܗܢܐ ܓܝܪ ܪܘܚܢܐ ܗܘ ܘܦܝܠܣܘܦܘܬܐ ܕܪܘܚܢܐ. ܐܦ ܡܠܬܐ ܕܝܗ̇، ܟܕ ܗ̇ܘ ܡܐ ܕܠܐ ܢܛܪ ܒܗ[7] ܡܢܝܢ ܠܐ ܬܬܘܣܦ ܒܗ. ܠܐ ܡܦܘܬ. ܒܕܠܐ ܡܬܡܠܠ ܐܠܐ ܒܬܪ ܡܘܟܠܐ *ܦܪܘܛܘܦܣ ܕܐܝܬܘܗܝ ܒܠܬ ܡܘܟܠܐ.[8] ܐܠܝܓܐ ܐܝܟ ܕܒܠܬܐ ܬܬܟܡܪ، ܡܢ ܦܝܠܣܘܦܘܬܐ ܘܗܢܝܢ ܡܬܪܓܡܢܘܬܐ ܕܡܦܝܣܢܐ ܗܘܝܐ ܗ̇ܝ، ܒܫܥܒܘܬܐ.

ܕܬܪܬܝܢ. ܡܢ ܗܠܝܢ ܕܐܬܐܡܪ، ܐܠܝܓܐ ܕܐܪܒܥܐ ܢܗܘܘܢ ܐܕ̈ܫܐ ܪ̈ܚܡܐ.[1] ܡܕܡܝܐ ܠܗ̇ ܪ̈ܚܡܐ ܕܠܐ ܚܘܣ ܥܠ ܡܥܠܬܐ ܐܚܪܢܐ ܕܢܦܩ[2] ܠܗ ܡܛܠ ܕܓܠܐ ܒܝܬܗ. ܐܝܟ ܗ̇ܝ، ܕܠܓܒܪܐ ܠܡܬܝܠܕܘ ܠܗ ܡܢ ܣܛܪ ܠܒܪܬܐ ܗ̇ܘ. ܬܘܒܐ ܕܡܢ ܪ̈ܚܡܐ ܕܠܐ ܚܘܣ ܥܠ ܡܥܠܬܐ ܐܚܪܢܐ ܒܗ̇ܝ، ܕܓܠܐ ܠܗ̇ܘ ܕܠܘܬܗ ܡܠܬܐ ܐܘ ܠܕܟܝܪܘ ܡܬܟܬܒ. ܐܝܟ ܗ̇ܝ، ܕܠܒܬ ܪܫܡܐ ܙܒܢܐ ܕܐܡܝܢܐܝܬ ܠܐ ܢܦܩ. ܬܠܝܬܝܐ ܬܘܒ ܪ̈ܚܡܐ ܕܚܘܣ ܥܠ ܡܥܠܬܐ ܐܚܪܢܐ ܕܢܬܗܘܐ ܚܝܐ ܘܠܐ ܚܘܒܐ ܒܗ ܗ̇ܘ ܡܚܘܝܢܐ. ܐܝܟ ܗ̇ܝ، *ܕܠܐ ܙܕܩ ܠܡܓܙܪ ܐܡܝܢܐܝܬ ܙܘܓܐ. ܘܪܒܝܥܝܐ ܪ̈ܚܡܐ ܕܚܘܣ ܥܠ ܡܥܠܬܐ ܐܚܪܢܐ ܕܢܬܗܘܐ ܚܝܐ ܘܚܘܒܐ ܒܗ ܗ̇ܘ ܡܚܘܝܢܐ. ܐܝܟ ܗ̇ܝ،[3] ܕܙܘܓܐ ܠܐ ܡܥܘܬܐ ܠܐ ܬܓܙܪ ܐܢܬ ܕܐܡܝܢܐܝܬ ܡܥܘܬܐ. ܒܐܡܪܬ ܒܗ̇ܝ، ܕܡܥܘܬܐ ܐܢܬ ܐܝܟ ܡܥܘܬܐ ܐܬܪܒܐ ܘܠܐ ܐܝܟ ܠܐ ܡܥܘܬܐ. ܘܗܢܐ ܪ̈ܚܡܐ ܒܗ̇ܝ، ܕܡܚܝܐ ܠܡܠܬܐ ܡܬܪܓܡܢܘܬܐ ܗ̄ܘ[4] ܡܫܡܠܝܬܐ. ܘܬܠܝܬܝܐ ܕܠܐ ܡܚܝܐ ܠܡܠܬܐ[5] ܠܐ ܡܬܪܓܡܢܘܬܐ ܗ̄ܘ ܐܠܐ ܡܢܬ ܡܬܪܓܡܢܘܬܐ.

ܕܬܠܬ. ܡܢ[1] ܪ̈ܚܡܐ ܗܢܘܢ، ܥܠ ܡܥܠܬܐ ܐܚܪܢܐ ܕܢܬܡܠܠܘܢ ܐܝܬܝܗܘܢ، ܪܚܡܐ ܐܚܝܐ ܕܒܕ ܒܠܚܘܕܘܗܝ، ܡܬܐܡܪ ܠܗ ܒܠܚܘܕ ܠܦܐܝܬ ܠܐ ܡܬܡܠܠ. ܐܠܐ ܒܚܪܢܐ ܡܬܡܦܪ. ܘܐܦ ܡܥܠܬܐ ܐܚܪܢܐ ܠܐ ܢܦܩ ܠܗ ܠܐ ܡܦܝܣ. ܘܒܕܐܝܟ ܗܢܐ ܐܠܝܓܐ[2] ܕܢܬܡܠܠ ܗܘ ܗ̇ܘ ܡܥܠܬܐ. ܐܝܟ ܐܢܫܐ ܢܫܐ ܕܐܡ̇ܪ ܐܢܐ ܡܢ ܗܘܝܠ ܙܕܩ ܠܝ ܕܠܐ ܐܬܕܪܐ ܒܟܕܘܡ ܡܢ ܡܢܬܪܬܐ. ܘܓܠܝܐ ܕܗܢܐ ܡܐܡܪܐ ܒܕ ܒܠܚܘܕܘܗܝ، ܡܬܐܡܪ ܦܓܪ ܥܒܕܪ ܘܡܦܪ. ܘܡܐ ܕܡܕܡܝܢ، ܢܐܡܪ ܐܢܐ ܡܢ ܗܘܝܠ ܡܛܠ ܗ̇ܝ، ܕܠܐ ܐܬܚܫܡ ܘܦܓܘ̈ܡܝܐ ܕܡܬܚܫܒܝܢ ܘܡܬܬܠܬܠܝܢ[3] ܠܚܫ̈ܡܝܐ ܠܐ ܐܦܠ. *ܙܕܩ ܠܝ ܕܠܐ ܐܬܕܪܐ ܒܟܪ ܢܬܗܡܝܢ ܘܢܥܡܚ ܕܢܦܫܗ.[4] ܘܐܦܢ ܐܡܝܢܐ ܕܒܠܬܐ ܠܘ ܪ̈ܚܡܐ ܗܘ، ܐܠܐ ܪܚܢܐ ܦܘܐܛܪܘܦܝܢܐ[5] ܘܡܡܠܠܬܐ ܡܬܗܓܓܝܢܐ.[6] ܐܝܟ ܕܐܡܪ ܗܦܠܣܛܪܘܣ[7] ܒܠܡܘܪܐܣ.[8] ܣܘ ܠܐ ܬܗܘܘܢ ܡܦܓܪ̈ܢܝܢ ܐܡܝܢܐ ܕܠܐ ܦܠܓܡܗܘܢ ܐܡܝܢܬ ܗܦܝܣܘܬܐ ܡܢ ܐܪܒܥܐ ܣܝ̈ܓܐ. ܗܪܟܐ ܒܦܝܣܘܬܐ[9] *ܠܐܪ̈ܒܥܐ ܢܠܚܐ[10] ܚܕܐ ܕܡܢ ܢܣܒܬܐ ܕܢܦܪܐ ܪ̈ܘܟܒܐ[11] ܒܒܝܬ ܪ̈ܘܟܒܐ.

[6] ܗ̇ܝ، RVLl [7] ܒܗ̇ RVL [8]* om. RVL

2 [1] sg. RVL [2] ܢܦܩ F [3]* om. RVL [4] ܗ̄ܘ، RVLl [5] i. om. RVLl

3 [1] i. add. ܘ RVLl [2] i. add. ܕ RVLl [3] i. om. RVLl [4]* om. RVLl [5] ܦܘܐܛܪܦܝܐ RVLl [6] ܡܗܓܓܝܢܐ Fl [7] ܗܦܠܣܛܪܘܣ F [8] scripsi; ܒܠܡܘܪܐܣ F; ܒܠܡܐܪܘܣ RLl; ܒܠܡܘܪܣ V [9] i. om. F [10]* sg. R [11] ܪ̈ܘܟܒܐ F

## SECTION THREE
## On the Rhetorical Maxim
## Seven Theories

ONE.[8] A maxim is a premiss, universal and not particular, on practical matters, with regard to their being sought or avoided. A gnomic enthymeme is close to a full syllogism, and gnomic conclusions, when taken by themselves, are also maxims, just as their premisses are maxims. The enthymeme, when the cause has been added to the (premiss), is then persuasive, just as one may say, 'To teach a young person wisdom is superfluous'. This (example) is a maxim and a gnomic conclusion. If the cause is not added to it, namely, 'because they would gain that from which they have no advantage', (the maxim) is not useful, because it will not be admitted unless after the admission also the premiss which would be the cause of the admission (is stated). It is therefore necessary that the cause is mentioned with the conclusion, and then the conjunction (of conclusion and cause) becomes a persuasive enthymeme.

TWO.[9] From what has been said, there are necessarily four species of maxims. First, the maxim which does not need other discourse adhering to it because it is clear by itself; for example, 'The very best thing for a man is to recover health.' Second, the maxim which does not need other discourse because it is clear to him who has reason, or to him who considers (it) well; for example, 'There is no true lover who does not love always.' Third, the maxim which needs other discourse in order for the meaning to become evident and in which the pointer is not mentioned; for example, 'It is not right to harbour anger for ever.' Fourth, the maxim which needs other discourse for the meaning to become evident and in which the pointer is mentioned; for example, 'Do not harbour immortal anger, you who are mortal.' This means, 'Because you are mortal, think like a mortal, not like an immortal!' This fourth (species), because it points out the cause, is a complete enthymeme, while the third (species), which does not point out the cause, is not an enthymeme, but part of an enthymeme.

---

[8] **6.3.1** AR 2.21 94a21-b6; IS 3.6 (170.9-171.1).
[9] **6.3.2** AR 2.21 94b7-25; IS 3.6 (171.1-9).

ܕܐܪܥܐ. ܒܗܘܡܠܘܓܝܐ ܐܘܕܝܬ ܡܠܬܐ ܪܚܝܡܬܐ ܠܗ ܠܒܠܥ ܠܝܡܐ
ܠܡܚܒܕ. ܐܠܐ ܠܗܘܢܐ ܕܡܬܦܫܩܐ ܐܝܟ ܘܡܦܝܣ؛ ܦܘܪܥܢܐ. ܒܠܗܕܐ
ܠܡܟܠܠܘ ܒܡܬܠܘܓܝܐܘ ܐܘܕܝܬ ܩܠܐܬܐ ܠܗܝ ܕܒܗܝ ܠܗ ܡܗܝܡ
ܕܦܠܓܘܬܐ[1] ܗ̇ܝ ܘܠܐ ܐܪܗܘܛܐ. ܘܟܠ ܐܢܫܐ ܒܠܐܝܬ ܡܬܚܫܒ ܘܠܐ
ܡܬܚܫܒܐܝܬ ܐܘ ܐܝܟ ܕܒܦܘܠܓܐ ܡܬܬܦܪܫ. *ܒܕܠܓܘܢ ܒܗܝ[2] ܗ̇ܝ[3]
ܗܟܢܐ ܗ̣ܘ ܡܬܐܡܪ. ܒܗܝ ܕܝܢ ܦܘܠܓܐ ܕܗܘ ܗܟܢܐ ܗܘ. ܘܒܠܝܫܘܬܐ[4]
ܡܬܒܥܝܐ ܒܗܘܢ. ܘܗܘܢ ܗܠܝܢ ܒܡܫܝܚܘܬܐ ܘܒܩܕܫܘܬܐ ܡܦܫܩܝܢ.
ܗܟܢܐ ܐܬܘ̈ܬܐ ܘܥܘ̈ܕܪܢܐ. ܙܕܩ ܕܝܢ ܡܬܚܫܒܐ ܒܪܫܝܬܐ[5] ܗ̇ܘ ܡܐ
ܕܠܦܘܠܓܐ ܡܬܬܕܪܐ ܠܗܘܬ ܒܗܘܢܐ *ܐܘ ܚܒܪܐ.[6] ܘܐܦ ܡܢ ܦܬܓܡܐ
ܦܪ̈ܫܐ ܠܐ ܢܗܘܐ. ܐܝܟ ܐܘܢܘܡܝܐ[7] ܦܪܘܣܐ ܘܚܒܪܘܬܐ[8] ܕܡܬܚܒܪܬܗ
ܬܟܒ ܘܠܡܬܒܪܟܐ ܕܐܝܟ ܘܚܕ. ܡܢ ܒܪܢܫܐ ܠܥܒܕܐ ܦܠܓ ܠܗ ܠܐ ܠܦܠܓܐ ܡܢ
ܚܕܗ ܐܬܬܘܕܝ.

ܕܡܫܝܚܐ. ܒܡܬ̈ܠܐ ܡܫ̈ܠܡܐ ܐܝܟ ܕܒܟܠܢܫܐ ܦܠܐ ܠܡܬܚܫܒܘ. ܘܗܠܝܢ ܗ̇ܝ
ܐܦ ܡܢ ܡܘܠܕܐ ܡܫܠܡ. ܐܠܐ[1] ܒܫܘܬܦܘ ܠܐ ܡܫܡܫܝܢ. ܐܝܟ ܗ̇ܝ
ܕܐܦܝ̈ܡܐ ܒܠܘܬܐ ܐܝܟ ܘܡܬܦܠܓܐ ܕܚܠܐ. ܘܐܦ ܬܘܒ ܠܡܬܚܫܒܘ
ܒܬܚܘܝܐ ܕܠܒܠ ܡܕܡܝܢ. ܐܝܟ ܗ̇ܝ ܕܐܡܪܝܢ ܕܒ ܢܬܝܢ. ܘܗܕܐ[2] ܠܦܘܠܓܐ
ܘܚܘܝܢܐ ܠܡܫܝܚܐ.[3] ܐܝܟ[4] ܗ̇ܝ ܕܐܠܗܐ ܡܕܒܪܬ ܒܝܕܝܢ ܠܐ ܐܬܕܪܬ
ܒܒܝܕܝܢ.[5] ܘܗܢܐ ܠܦܘܠܓܐ ܘܡܦܢܝܐ ܠܢܦܫ. ܘܫܒܩ ܡܢ ܗܠܝܢ ܫܘ̈ܐ
ܡܥܒܕܝܢ ܒܦܪܨܐ. ܐܝܟܢܐ ܕܐܡܪ ܐܝܬ ܠܐܝܢܐ ܕܐܟܝܢ ܒܝܕ ܡܫܘܕ ܕܫܡܥܬ.
ܕܡܐܒܠܘܪܓܐ ܗ̇ܝ ܗܢܐ ܐܝܟܢܐ ܕܐܝܢܐ ܢܕܒ ܕܒܠܐ ܗܘ. ܘܐܝܟ ܗܢܐ
ܡܐܡܪܐ[6] ܡܟܝܢ ܫܡܝܐ. ܘܐܝܟܢܐ ܕܢܬܐܡܪ. ܐܠܐ ܦܠܓ ܢܕܒ ܗ̣ܘ ܠܗ ܠܐ
ܡܬܘܦ ܢܦܫ ܗܘܐ[7] ܢܦܫܗ ܠܡܕܒܪܘ ܫܠܘܬܐ. ܘܕܐܝܟ ܗܢܐ ܡܐܡܪܐ
ܡܢ[8] ܫܡܥܬܐ ܕܪܒ ܫܠܐ.

4 [1] i. om. RVLl [2*] ܒܗܝ R; ܒܕܠܓܘܢ V [3] add. ܗܘ RVLl [4] ܘܒܠܝܫܘܬܐ RVLl [5] pl. RVLl [6*] ܘܚܒܪܐ RVLl [7] scripsi; ܐܘܢܘܡܝܐ F; ܐܘܢܐܠܝܘܣ RLl; ܐܘܢܠܝܘܣ V [8] i. ܕ RVLl
5 [1] ܠܐ F [2] ܘܗܕܐ RVLl [3] ܠܢܫܐ RVLl [4] i. add. ܘ RVLl [5] pl. R [6] add. ܡܢ RVLl [7] om. RVL [8] ܡܢܗ RVLl

THREE.[10] Among the maxims needing other discourse to be admitted is the maxim which, when stated by itself, is not only directly inadmissable, but is (also) disallowed in a dispute. If other discourse is not attached to it, it will not be persuasive, and in (a case) like this it may be necessary for that discourse to come first. For example, one may say, 'As for me, then, it is right that I not be trained in any one of the virtues.' It is clear that when this saying is stated by itself it is highly disgraceful and repugnant. But when one prefaces it, 'As for me, then, in order not to be envied nor to fall into the pits which are dug out and excavated for the envied,' (then), 'It is right that I not be trained' may be accorded *pistis* and be able to persuade. Sometimes the cause is not a maxim, but a poetic riddle and imaginative discourse, as Stesichorus said among the Locrians, 'Watch, do not be insolent, lest the *tettiges*, namely the swallows, chirp from the ground.' Here by 'swallows' he seeks (to show) feeble men that they make great noises on account of minor injuries.

FOUR.[11] It is not appropriate for everyone to make a gnomology or enigmatic word, but for the old who are experienced and discriminating. Therefore to speak in tales or allegories is foolish for him who is not experienced in them and (shows) lack of education. Every maxim is (either) accepted universally and without limitation, or put forward (as valid) for the most part. Therefore sometimes it is said, 'It is this way', but sometimes, 'Mostly it is this way'. The universal is lacking in the (latter), and they persuade by harshness and roughness in like manner as indices and signs. That which is acknowledged by the populace according to law or custom ought to be assumed in a maxim, even if it is not among the (widely) disseminated well known ones; for example, 'Enualios is the bravest, seeks satisfaction for his city, conquers enemies, and having killed the children with the men is acknowledged by his people as no wrongdoer.'

FIVE.[12] One may rightly use (generally) accepted proverbs as universals. (While) accepted by the populace, they should nevertheless not be credited with truth. For example, 'Athenians are foreigners',

[10] **6.3.3** AR 2.21 94b25-95a2; IS 3.6 (172.11-173.4).
[11] **6.3.4** AR 2.21 95a2-17; IS 3.6 (173.5-174.1).
[12] **6.3.5** AR 2.21 95a17-24; IS 3.6 (174.1-13).

ܕܫܢܬܐ. ܐܝܬ ܕܝܢ ܡܐܡܪܐ ܙ̈ܒܢܐ ܕܒܢ̈ܝܢܐ ܐܝܠܝܢ. ܐܝܟ ܗ̇ܘ ܕܐܡܪܝܢ. ܠܐ ܦܠܐ ܠܒܪܢܫ ܐܝܟ ܗ̇ܘ ܕܠܡܫܝܚܐ ܐܠܐ ܙܢܝܐ ܙܢܝܬ ܝܬܝܪ ܡܢ ܗܢܐܬ ܗܢܐܐ ܦܠܐ ܕܬܗܘܐ. ܠܡܬܚܫܒܘ ܕܝܢ ܐܠܝܟܐ ܕܝܗ̇ ܠܚܫܘܫܘ[1] ܠܡܬܬܬ ܫܘܟܠܐ ܡܬܪ̈ܝܢܐ ܬܫܘܕܒ. ܘܐܦ ܠܐ ܒܦܘܫܘܐ ܢܬܚܫܚ. ܒܐܡܪܬ ܠܐ ܢܐܡܪ. ܦܠܐ ܠܒܪܢܫ ܝܬܝܪ ܡܢ ܕܠܡܫܝܚܐ. *ܒܡܘܦܩ ܒܪ ܗܘܟܠܐ. ܐܠܐ ܢܦܫ ܘܢܐܡܪ ܦܠܐ ܠܒܪܢܫ ܠܙܕܘܩܐ ܝܬܝܪ ܡܢ ܕܠܡܫܝܚܐ[2] ܠܗܢܐܐ. ܘܒܐܡܝܢܘ ܦܠܐ ܠܒܪܢܫ ܙܢܝܐ ܕܠܡܫܬܝܢ. ܐܝܟܢܐ ܢܗܘܐ ܠܚܠܬܐ ܘܢܐܡܪ. ܒܕ[3] ܙܢܝܬܐ ܕܫܘܒܐ ܠܗܢܐܬܐ ܐܦ ܠܢܒܠܐ[4] ܕܠܐ ܝܬܝܪ ܫܘܒܗ ܐܦܠܐ ܡܘܫܐ ܒܫܘܕܝܗ ܘܡܓܠ ܦܢܐ ܫܘܠܛܢܐ ܫܡܫܢܐ[5] ܐܘ ܢܐܡܪ ܒܥܒܕܐ ܐܚܪܢܐ. ܦܠܐ ܕܬܗܒܝܢ *ܙܢܝܬ ܙܢܝܐ ܐܚܪܢܐ ܕܦܠܐ ܕܬܗܒܝܢ[6] ܗܢܐܬ ܗܢܐܐ. ܘܗܕܐ ܬܘܒ ܢܫܝܒܘܬ ܒܠܬܐ ܗ̇ܝ ܒܐܒܢܐ ܕܕܠܡܘܒܠܘܬܐ.

ܕܥܒܕ. ܒܡܒܠܠ ܙܢܝܐ ܡܬܝܢ ܫܒ̈ܘܥܐ ܒܕ ܢܗܘܐ ܗܦܟ ܫܘܒܚܗܘܢ ܘܒܬܪ ܫܘܒܠܗܘܢ. ܗܠܝܢ ܒܪ ܒܕ ܫܒ̈ܘܥܐ ܡܬܝ̈ܢܐ ܢܗܘܘܢ ܠܗܘܢ ܗܘܢ ܘܠܐ ܡܥܒܕܝܢ ܕܠܘܬ ܫܘܒܠܐ ܒܠܒܢܐ ܢܒܠܘܢ ܐܝܠܝܢ. ܒܕ ܠܫܘܝܐ ܒܠܒܢܐ ܥܒܕܝܢ ܒܗ ܠܡܬܝ̈ܢܐ ܗܘܢ ܒܫܢܐ ܫܢܝܢ. ܘܗܕܝܢ ܐܝܟ ܗܘܢ ܕܠܬܘ ܡܢ ܕܒܝܢ ܗܘܘ ܐܫܒܘܚ. ܘܡܛܠ ܕܝܗ̇ ܡܐܡܪܐ ܒܠܒܢܐ ܠܐ ܡܫܒܚܐ ܢܗܘܐ. ܘܡܢܐ ܕܫܢܝܢ[1] ܫܒ̈ܘܥܐ ܕܠܫܒ̈ܘܥܐ ܡܬܝ̈ܢܐ ܕܢܫܘ ܥܠܡ. ܡܫܕܪܐ ܡܡܠܠ ܠܗ ܘܡܫܒܚܝܢ. ܐܝܟ ܐܢܫܐ ܕܡܢ ܐܠܬܐ ܫܒ̈ܘܥܘܗܝ، ܘܐܠܬܐ ܘܐܣܦ̈ܓܐ ܒܢ̈ܘܗܝ. ܐܬܬܒܪ ܒܕ ܫܒܥ ܠܐܡܘܪܐ[2] ܕܐܡܪ ܠܗ ܡܕܡ ܕܝܬܝܪ ܒܢܫ ܡܢ ܫܒ̈ܥܐ. ܘܐܚܪܢܐ[3] ܕܐܡܪ ܠܗ ܠܓܠܬܐ ܐܦܠܐ ܚܕܐ ܒܒܢܝܢܘܬ[4] ܒܢܝܐ. ܪܒܬ ܡܬܒܢܝܐ[5] ܘܚܕܐ ܘܡܗܘܡܢ. ܐܠܝܐ ܐܪܐ ܕܠܗܦܪܐ ܕܠܒܫ ܫܒ̈ܥܐ ܘܕܢܝܐ ܢܣܒܐ[6] ܘܠܝܠܘܡܠܘܠܝܢܫܐ[7] ܢܒܢܐ. ܡܗܦܪ ܕܝܢ ܙܒܢܝܐ ܘܡܢܕܪܐ ܡܬܪܐ[8] ܒܡܐܡܪܐ ܐܣܘܦܝܛܝܩܐ. ܘܒܗܘܢ ܡܬܪܬܐ ܡܡܠܠܐ ܘܐܝܟ ܗܐܡ ܢܒܗܫܐ ܡܬܫܪ ܐܡܘܪܐ ܘܒܡ ܫܒ̈ܥܐ ܡܬܒܥܐ.

6 [1] ܠܡܚܫܘܫܘ RVLl [2*] om. FRVL [3] ܒܕ ܕ RVLl [4] ܠܢܒܝܐ RVLl [5] ܫܡܫܢܐ RVLl [6*] om. F

7 [1] ܕܫܐܢܝܢ F [2] pl. RL [3] ܘܐܠܐܚܪ̈ܢܐ RLl; ܘܐܠܐܚܪܢܐ V [4] ܒܒܢܝܢܘܬ RVLl [5] ܡܬܒܢܝܐ RLl; ܡܬܒܢܝܐ V [6] ܢܣܒܐ RVLl [7] ܘܠܝܠܘܡܠܘܠܝܢܫܐ RVLl [8] i. add. ܘ RVLl

and 'Cretans are liars'. It is also right to use maxims known to all. For example, they say, 'Know yourself'; this is appropriate for praise and blame. (Another) example: 'If I had known your custom, I would not have been astonished at your action'; this is appropriate for accusing and releasing. Some of them affect passions in the soul. For instance, someone may say to another who is angered by something which he has heard, 'This is a calumny, as I know it is false'; such a word calms wrath. And as is said, 'If so and so had known himself, he would never have permitted himself to be in command of armies'; such a word establishes the wrath of a commander.

SIX.[13] There are gnomic sayings which are ethical, which say, for example, that it is not right to love as to hate, but the love of him who loves should be greater than the hate of him who hates. It is necessary to take care that the language makes clear the exactitude of the enthymematic thought, but if it does not, one should use an explanation. For example, one should not (merely) say, 'It is right to love more than hate[,' for the thought is obscure, but one should explain (it) and say, 'It is right to love a friend more than hate] an enemy, and it is right to love a true friend for ever.' Then one should show the cause and say, 'Because the love which is equal to hate (is that) of the traitor, whose love does not abide, and who does not keep to his promise but quickly finds a possible variation.' Or one might say in another manner, 'It is right that love of a friend should be great, just as it is right that hatred of an enemy should be great.' This is taking up the cause in the manner of opposition.

SEVEN.[14] Listeners derive benefit from gnomic discourse when their attention is dull and their intelligence crass, for when they have particular opinions and themselves are not able to enter into a universal thought, on hearing a universal precept they see in it the particulars, and then (they are) like those who have found that which they were seeking. It may also be that a universal proposition is not possible, but when the listeners see that (a maxim) accords with the particular opinions which they know by experience, they will immediately accept it and hold (these) opinions. For example, someone who has been hurt by his debauched neighbours, or his vile and

---

[13] **6.3.6** AR 2.21 95a24-32; IS 3.6 (174.13-175.7).
[14] **6.3.7** AR 2.21 95b1-19; IS 3.6 (175.8-17).

## ܦܘܫܩܐ ܕܪܒܝܥܐ
## ܡܛܠ ܦܘܪܫܢܐ ܕܒܝܢ ܦܪ̈ܘܛܣܝܣ ܕܐܦܘܕܝܩܛܝܩܝܬܐ ܘܕܕܝܐܠܩܛܝܩܝܬܐ
## ܬܐܘܪ̈ܐܣ ܬܠܬ

ܩܕܡܝܬܐ. ܦܪ̈ܫܢ ܕܝܢ ܦܪ̈ܘܛܣܝܣ ܕܡܬܚܘܝܢܘܬܐ[1] ܡܢ ܗܝ ܕܕܝܐܠܩܛܝܩܝܬܐ.[2] ܒܗ̇، ܕܒܕܝܐܠܩܛܝܩܐ ܗ̇ܝ ܦܪ̈ܘܛܣܝܣ ܗܝ ܕܫ̈ܐܠܝܢ ܡܢ ܒܥܬܐ ܡܬܢܣܒܝܢ ܘܡܢܗܘܢ ܠܗ̇ܬ ܕܒܥܬܐ ܒܝܕ ܡܫܐ̈ܠܬܐ[3] ܗ̇ܘܐ ܕܐܘܪܟܐ. ܘܡܬܢܣܒܝܢ ܬܘܒ ܒܗ̇[4] ܦܪ̈ܘܛܣܝܣ ܬܪ̈ܬܝܢ ܠܣܛܪ̈ܐ ܘܣܘܩܒܠܬܐ *ܬܘܒ ܒܝܕ[5] ܡܢ ܗܝ ܕܠܬܪ̈ܬܝܢ ܡܬܚܫ̈ܒܢ. ܒܡܬܚܘܝܢܘܬܐ ܕܝܢ ܦܪ̈ܘܛܣܝܣ ܡܢܣܒܬ[6] ܠܚܕܐ ܡܬܢܣܒܝܢ. ܘܗܘܡܘܣ̈ܝܬܐ ܕܠܐ ܗܘܝ ܓܠܝܢ ܘܠܡܬܚܘܝܢܘܬܗܘܢ ܠܐ ܗܢ̈ܝܢ ܐܦܠܐ ܗܘܐ ܒܗܢ̈ܝܢ ܘܡܢ ܡܕܡ ܕܒܥܬܐ ܠܐ ܡܬܕܪ̈ܟܢ ܐܠܐ ܗܝ ܡܫܐ̈ܠܬܐ ܕܒܕ ܡܬܒܥ̈ܝܢ ܡܬܡܟ̈ܠܝܢ. ܡܢ[7] ܓܒܪ ܕܚܫܒܐ ܠܐ ܕܕܪ̈ܫܐ ܘܠܐ ܡܕܒ̈ܪܢܐ ܢܦܪ ܫܡܥܐ ܕܩܘܦܠܝܐ. ܘܟܠܗܝܢ ܐܟܚܕ ܦܘܐܬܠܝܐ ܕܓܒܪܐ ܠܐ ܕܕܪܫܐ ܒܢ̈ܢܫܐ ܬܪ̈ܝܢ ܡܢ ܕܕܪܫܐ ܡܦܝܣ.[8] ܒܕ ܠܕܕܪܫܐ ܕܡܬܬܚܝܬܐ ܡܛܠܠ ܠܗ ܗܫܐܝܬ ܫܡܥܝܢ ܒܚܬܝܬܐ. ܘܠܐ ܕܕܪܫܐ ܕܫܟܝܚܬܐ[9] ܡܫܬܘܕܥ ܕܠܝܠܝܬ ܡܬܗܡܢ ܘܫܪܝܪܐܝܬ ܡܬܩܒܠ.

ܕܬܪ̈ܬܝܢ. ܪܗܛܪܐ ܗ̇ܝ ܒܕ ܫܪܒܐ[1] ܕܠܒܘܬܐ ܘܟܠ ܡܕܡ ܐܡܪ. ܒܝܫܐ ܕܬܫܥܝܬܐ ܡܘ̈ܬܐ ܦܠܐ ܕܢܫܬܪܝ ܐܢܘܢ. ܘܐܠܝܐ ܕܫܡܥܢܐ ܚܡܫܠ ܡܢ ܕܬܢܐ ܢܗܘܘܢ. ܘܠܐ ܡܢ ܟܠ ܦܘܪܣ ܒܐܠܝܬܐ ܢܬܚܫܒ ܐܠܐ ܘܒܗܠܝܢ ܕܐܝܟ ܕܒܗܘܓܠܐ. ܘܐܝܢܘ ܕܒܚܝܪܐ[2] ܠܐ ܢܗܐ ܒܓܠܝܢ ܫܪܒܐ ܕܒܗ[3] ܗ̇ܝܕܝܢ. ܘܒܝܢ̈ܬܗܘܢ، ܕܡܬܠܬܐ ܕܦܬܪ. ܠܐ ܢܦܠܠ ܒܗ. ܐܝܟܢܐ ܓܒܪ ܡܫܟܚܢ[4] ܕܢܦܠܠ ܠܬܠܝܬܐ ܕܢܦܪܩܘܢ. ܒܕ ܠܐ ܡܦܩܚܝܢ[5] ܒܡܫܘܚܬܐ ܕܢܠܗܘܢ ܘܒܡܟܘܢܘܬܐ ܪܫܡܐ ܡܕܪ̈ܫܝܗܘܢ ܘܕܒܠܕܒܒ̈ܐ ܚܘܦܝܗܘܢ ܘܒܐܡܝܢܘܬܐ[6] ܡܕܢ̈ܚܐ ܦܪ̈ܝܫܝܗܘܢ. ܐܝܟܢܐ ܕܢܕܒ ܐܢܫܐ ܦܪܘܫܐ ܠܗܘܢ ܦܩܕ. ܗ̇ܘ ܒܥܝܢܐ ܕܬܓܠܝܬܐ[7] ܐܘ ܗ̇ܘ ܢܡܟܢܐ ܕܬ̈ܠܦܐ. ܘܐܝܟܢܐ ܬܘܒ ܠܦܪܘܫܐ ܕܬ̈ܠܦܐ ܢܦܠܘ. ܒܕ ܠܐ ܡܕܒܝܢ ܢܟ̈ܢܐ ܡܟܢܝܢܐ ܕܒܡܠܟܢܝܢܐ ܘܬܟܬܫܐ[8] ܕܒܟܐܪܐܬܐ ܘܐܠܝܢ ܕܝܠܦ ܗ̈ܘܠܢܕܐ[9] ܐܣܬܒܪ ܘܦܫܪ. ܐܦܠܐ ܬܘܒ ܠܦܘܪܫܐ[10] ܡܥܝܢܐ[11] ܡܦܝܢ[12] ܕܢܓܪܐ. ܒܕ ܠܐ ܡܕܒܝܢ ܐܝܟܢܐ ܐܦܝ̈ܢܐ *ܘܦܘܪܬܠܝܐ ܒܪܒܪܐ[13] ܐܬܪܘܬ ܒܝܥܐ ܘܠܝܘܢܝܐ ܒܒܢ̈ܝ ܫܐܪܐ ܒܟܠܘ.[14] ܗܘ ܒܝܬܐ ܘܒܝܕܝܥܬܐ ܡܢܗܘܢ ܕܡܬܠܬܐ ܐܠܝܐ ܠܡܣܒܐ ܡܠܐܐ.

---

Titulus [1] add. ܕ RVL

1 [1] pl. RVLl [2] i. add. ܕ RVL [3] sg. RVLl [4] om. F [5*] om. F [6] sg. RL [7] i. add. ܘ RVL [8] ܡܦܝܣ RVL [9] i. om. RVL; ܒܕ ܫܟܝ̈ܚܬܐ l

2 [1] sg. RVL [2] sg. RVLl [3] i. om. RLl [4] ܡܫܟܚܢ R [5] ܡܦܩܚܝܢ RVL; ܡܦܩܚܢ l [6] ܘܒܡܟܘܢܘܬ RVL [7] om. RVLl [8] pl. RVLl [9] ܗ̇، ܕܩܠܢܕܐ RVLl [10] ܠܦܘܪܫܐ F [11] pl. RL [12] ܡܦܝܢ RVLl [13*] ܘܦܘܪܬܠܝܒܪܒܪ RVL; ܘܦܘܪܬܠܝܒ ܒܪܒܪܐ l [14] f. om. RVLl

prodigal children, will be greatly comforted and rejoice and give assent on hearing a speaker say there is nothing worse than neighbours, or another saying there is not a single good thing about begetting children. Therefore it is necessary for an orator to take note of the disposition of listeners and judges and make gnomic utterances (accordingly). In declarative speeches he (can) express (both) maxims and virtuous character, and in them discourse may be elevated, and the speaker honoured like a legislator and find favour with listeners.

## SECTION FOUR
### On the Difference between Rhetorical and Dialectical Premisses
### Three Theories

ONE.[15] The premisses of an enthymeme differ from dialectical (premisses), because in dialectic premisses are assumed which are distant from the desired conclusion, and step-by-step progress from the (premisses) to the conclusion is achieved by middle terms. Furthermore, in (dialectic) better known premisses are assumed, and also obscure (premisses) when they follow from well known (ones). In rhetoric, however, premisses are assumed which are close to the desired conclusion, and conditions which are neither very evident and do not need to be mentioned, nor very mysterious and beyond the knowledge of the masses, but ones in the middle which, when mentioned, are accepted; for the attention of the populace turns away from untrodden and unfamiliar thoughts. Therefore the poets say that an unlearned man creates greater enjoyment in gatherings than a learned, because the masses do not listen with pleasure to a learned one expounding scholarly thoughts, while an unlearned one propounding banalities is readily given credence and gladly received.

TWO.[16] When an orator says things which are known (in) common and to everyone, he should put them forward in the manner of canonical definitions. It is necessary that they be reputable (premisses) accepted by judges; but he should not use necessaries as (his) entire resource, but also (use) those (things which are true) for the most

[15] **6.4.1** AR 2.22 95b22-31; IS 3.7 (176.4-177.8).
[16] **6.4.2** AR 2.22 95b29-96a23; IS 3.7 (177.8-178.13).

ܕܬܠܬ. ܐܝܟܢܐ ܕܒܚܠܝܦܘܬܐ ܐܦ ܗܪܟܐ ܙܕܩ[1] ܠܡܬܦܠܓܘ ܐܬܪ̈ܘܬܐ ܠܟܠ
ܫܘܪ̈ܪܐ[2] ܘܒܥܠܡܐ. ܘܐܝܟܢܐ ܕܗܘܬܪܝܢ ܐܬܪܐ ܕܬܚܬ ܩܪܝܒ ܘܬܚܬ ܕܟ̈ܐ
ܠܬܪܥܐ ܬܚܬ ܡܟܝܢ. ܗܕܟܐ ܐܕܫܐ ܕܬܚܬ ܩܪܝܒ ܘܠܡܫܟܐ *ܬܚܬ ܟܬܚܬ,[3] ܬܚܬ
ܡܟܝܢ. ܒܗ̇، ܕܒܚܠܝܬܘܬܐ ܠܐ ܟܘܢܝ̈ܬܐ ܡܬܚܪܪ ܗܘܟܢܐ. ܐܟܠܗܘܢ ܓܝܪ
ܠܗ ܒܗ̇، ܕܒܘܢܫܐ ܗܘ ܘܡܢ ܐܝܬܝܬܐ[4] ܘܐܬܪܐ ܘܟܫܝܠܘܬܗ ܕܠܗ ܓܢܣ
ܓܢܣܐ ܡܬܠܝܘ. ܒܗ̇، ܕܐܦ ܘܠܡܬܝܕܥܢܘܬܗ[5] ܘܠܦܢܝ̈ܢܐ ܐܚܪ̈ܢܐ
ܐܬܠܝܗܘܢ. ܡܫܬܟܚ ܕܝܢ ܒܟܠܝܢܘܬܗ[6] ܗܝܢ ܕܠܐܝܬ ܐܚܪܝܢ ܠܐ ܓܒ̈ܝܢ.
ܐܝܟ ܗ̇، ܕܦܠܓ ܠܗܘܦܠܘܪ[7] ܦܘܪܐ ܕܦܪ̈ܘܐܣ. ܘܠܗܘܢܘܢ ܐܬ̣ ܗ̇ܝ، ܒܕܡܐ
*ܕܒܡܬܐ ܣܒܪ̈ܘܗܝ،[8] ܘܠܐ ܐܘܕܥ. ܘܒܦܠܠܘܬܗ ܒܪ ܠܐ ܢܩܒ[9] ܗܘܐ ܢܣܝܒܐ
ܓܝܣ.[10] ܒܗܠܝܢ ܓܝܪ ܒܫܟܝܚܬ ܡܬܐܬܝܢ. ܘܗܘܝܢ ܗܠܝܢ ܐܬܪ̈ܘܬܐ
ܐܦܘܕܝܩܛܝܩܝ ܡܬܚܘܝܢܘܬܐ[11] ܐܝܟܢ.

ܦܣܘܩܐ ܫܒܝܥܝܐ
ܡܛܠ ܐܕ̈ܫܐ[1] ܕܡܬܚܘܝܢܘܬܐ
ܬܘܪ̈ܝܐܦ ܐܪܟܣܪܐ

ܡܕܡܝܢܘܬܐ. ܟܠ ܡܬܚܘܝܢܘܬܐ ܐܘ ܡܫܪܪܢܘܬܐ ܗ̇ܝ، ܘܡܢ ܦܪ̈ܘܛܣܝܣ
ܡܬܬܘܕܝܢܘܬܐ ܡܬܝܕܥܢܐ. ܐܘ ܡܦܝܣܢܘܬܐ ܗ̇ܝ، ܘܡܢ ܦܪ̈ܘܛܣܝܣ ܩܒܝ̈ܠܬܐ
ܡܬܚܙܝܢܝܬܐ. ܒܟܠ ܥܘܪܟܐ ܐܝܟܢܐ ܕܗܘ̣ ܡܠܟܐ ܢܗܘܐ ܐܘ ܡܣܬܒܪܐ ܕܢܗܘܐ ܐܘ
ܕܢܗܘܐ[1] ܐܘ ܫܪܝܪܐ ܘܡܬܚܙܐ. ܐܕ̈ܫܐ ܕܝܢ ܕܒܗܘܢ ܗܘܬܐ ܡܬܚܘܝܢܘܬܐ ܗܠܝܢ
ܐܢܘܢ. ܚܕ ܕܝܢ ܐܕܫܐ ܕܫܘܝܐ ܡܢ ܣܘܦܠܝܢܐ ܠܐܚܪܝܐ. ܐܝܟ ܗ̇ܝ،
ܕܐܢ *ܗ̇ܝ، ܕܬܬܒܥܘ[2] ܠܦܬܐ ܗܘ، ܗ̇ܝ، ܕܫܬܪܝܚ[3] ܒܫܬܐ ܗܘ، ܘܐܝܢܗܘ ܕܗܘܝܐ
ܒܠܬܐ ܗܘܐ ܕܫܒ̈ܬܐ ܣܦ̈ܝܢܬܐ[4] ܐܝܟܢܐ ܕܒܟܐܣܝܣ.[5] ܫܒܝܠܐ ܒܠܬܐ
ܗܘܐ[6] ܕܦ̈ܠܛܐ ܙܘܪ̈ܝܬܐ. ܒܡ ܫܒܝܠܐ ܐܘܪܚܐ ܙܕܩ ܠܡܬܦܪܣܘ. ܘܐܕܫܐ[7]
ܐܚܪܢܐ ܡܢ ܡܦܩܬܐ ܕܣܬܝܪܬܐ. ܐܝܟ ܗ̇ܝ، ܕܐܢ ܒܐܝܬܘܗ ܠܗ ܒܠܗ̇ ܦܠܓܬܐ
ܗܘ، ܐܦ ܗ̇ܝ، ܕܒܐܝܬܝܐ. ܠܐ ܓܝܪ ܓܒܝܢܐ ܠܡܬܒܠ ܒܐܝܬܝܬ. ܘܐܕܫܐ
ܐܚܪܢܐ ܡܢ ܗܠܝܢ ܕܠܘܬ[8] ܡܕܡ. ܐܝܟ *ܐܢ ܗ̇ܝ، ܕܠܡܟܒܫ ܫܦܝܪܐ. ܐܦ
ܗ̇ܝ، ܕܠܡܟܣܢ ܫܦܝܪܐ. ܘܐܝܟ ܐܢ[9] ܗ̇ܝ، ܕܠܡܟܝܠܘ ܦ̈ܠܓܐ ܕܡܣܬܒܪܢܘܬܐ
ܡܣܬܟܐ ܫܦܝܪܐ. ܐܦ ܠܝ ܗ̇ܝ، ܕܠܡܟܠܝܢ ܦ̈ܠܓܐ[10] ܫܦܝܪܐ.

3 [1] ܙܕܩ̈ܝܢ RVL [2] scripsi; ܒܬܚܘܡܐ codd. [3*] ܕܬܚܬ ܟܬܚܬ RVLl [4] ܐܝܬܝܬܐ RVLl [5] ܘܠܡܬܝܕܥܢܘܬܗܘܢ RVL; ܘܠܡܬܝܕܥܢܘܬܗ l [6] ܒܟܠܝܢܘܬܗ RVL [7] ܠܗ ܦܠܘܪ RVL [8*] ܕܒܡܬ ܗܘ ܘܣܒܪ̈ܘܗܝ RVLl [9] om. RVL [10] ܓܝܣ RVLl [11] sg. RVLl

Titulus [1] sg. RL

1 [1] ܕܢܗܘܐ RVLl [2*] ܢܬܒܥܘ RVLl [3] ܕܠܐ ܢܬܒܥܘ RVLl [4] om. RVL [5] ܕܒܟܐ ܣܝܣ RVLl [6] ܗܘ RVLl [7] i. om. RVLl [8] ܠܘܬ RVLl [9*] om. F [10] sg. RVL

part. If he is not an expert on the kind of thing which he is addressing, or on the ways of the particular (matter) which he treats, let him not speak on it. How can we say to the Athenians that they may go to war, when we do not know the measure of their strength, the number of friends who help them and enemies who trouble them, and the nature of their previous wars? How can we know what war is expedient for them, a land one of foot-soldiers or a sea one of galleys? And how, again, can we praise a war of galleys when we do not know (about) the naval triumphs at Salamis, the conflict at Marathon, what was done for the Heraclidae, and so forth? Neither are we able to put blame on a land war when we do not know how the barbarian Aphenians and Poritaeans were the best on land and enslaved the free Greeks. In this way also in judicial (speeches) it is necessary to obtain the material from the particulars (of the case).

THREE.[17] As in dialectic, so also here it is right to provide *topoi* for every establishment or refutation; and just as there the *topos* which is nearer and more similar to the matter produces the better result, so here the species which is nearer and more suitable to the aim is more successful, because a thing is established by specifics, not common things. For Achilles is not praised because he is a man, or from demigods or (some) place, or (because) with his own wealth (?) he went on the expedition; because these are also (applicable) to Diomedes and many others. He is praised for his specifics, which applied to no other man. For example, he killed Hector, the best of the Trojans; and he held back Cynus until his companions had crossed and was not overpowered; and in his youth he went on the expedition although he had not taken an oath. For these he is properly admired, and these *topoi* are the elements of enthymemes.

## SECTION FIVE
### On the Species of Enthymeme
### Fourteen Theories

ONE.[18] Every enthymeme is either a confirmation, and composed from agreed premisses, or a refutation, and put together from dis-

[17] **6.4.3** AR 2.22 96a33-b22; IS 3.7 (178.14-179.4).
[18] **6.5.1** AR 2.22 96b22 - 2.23 97a29; IS 3.7 (179.5-12).

ܕܬܬܪܝܡ. ܐܝܬ ܐܕܫܐ ܕܟܠܐ ܬܘܣܟܐ ܕܦܘܫܩܐ ܠܦܘܬ ܒܚܝܢ ܒܡܠܬܐ. ܐܝܟܢܐ
ܕܐܠܗܘܬܗܘܢ[1] ܠܬܐܘܕܝܩܘܣ[2] ܐܡ̣ܪ. ܕܠܐܠܗܐ ܓܝܪ ܕܠܝܬ ܐܠܟܣܢܕܪܝܢܐ[3]
ܠܐ ܐܝܬ ܒܪ̈ܢܫܝܬܐ[4] ܦ̇ܣܝܩܐ ܗܘܐ. ܘܗܪܟܐ ܦ̇ܠܐ ܠܡܬܚܫܒܘ ܒܡܠܬܐ
ܕܡܬܠܠܬܗ̇ ܡܬܚܫܒܐ ܗܘܬ ܗܕܐ. ܘܐܝܟܢ ܗ̇ܝ، ܬܘܒ ܕܐܡ̣ܪ
ܕܡܬܚܫܒܢܘܬܗ[5] ܕܐܢ ܒܐܕܫܐ ܠܡܡܠܠܐ ܠܡܬܡܠܠ ܐܝܟ ܗ̇ܘ ܕܒܬܗܘܒܐܝܣ
ܡܡܠܠ. ܐܦ ܠܝ ܒܐܕܫܐ ܕܐܡܠܠ ܘܗܪܟܐ ܬܘܒ ܠܡܬܡܠܠ ܠܐܕܫܐ ܕܡܡܠܠ.
ܦ̇ܠܐ ܠܡܦܩܘ ܒܪ̣ ܒܬܗܘܒܐܝܣ ܗ̇ܘ ܕܡܡܠܠ ܐܬܡܠܠ ܒܐܕܫܐܝܬ. ܘܐܕܫܐ
ܐܚܪܢܐ ܡܢ ܗ̇ܝ، ܕܡܬܬܪܐܝܬ ܘܡܬܒܪܢܝܬ. ܐܝܟ ܗ̇ܝ، ܕܐܢ ܐܠܗܐ ܒܠܒܘܫ
ܠܐ ܢܕܒܝܢ ܒܒ̈ܢܝܢܐ ܗܘܝܢ ܠܐ ܡܕܡ ܢܕܒܝܢ. ܘܐܢ ܗܢܐ ܠܐܒܗ̈ܘܗܝ، ܬܫܝܐ
ܠܐ ܕܡܢܐ ܕܠܡܪ̈ܒܢܘܗܝ،[6] ܢܦܩܝܢ. ܘܣܡܣܡܘܦܪܝܘܣ[7] ܗ̇ܘ ܕܠܠܝܕܗ ܫܪܕܬܐ
ܥܡ ܥܪܒܐ[8] ܕܒܢ̈ܘܗܝ، ܐܘܒܕ ܠܐ ܬܗܘܐ ܐܢ ܠܐܒܘܗܝ، ܗܘܘ ܦܘܩ ܢܦܠܠ.

ܕܬܠܬ. ܘܐܕܫܐ ܐܚܪܢܐ ܕܡܢ ܦܪ̈ܨܘܦܐ ܡܕܡ̈ܝܢܐ ܡܬܝܕܥ. ܐܝܟ ܗ̇ܝ،
ܕܐܢ ܬܫܡܫܘܢ[1] ܠܐ ܡܕܡ ܠܟܠ ܐܦܠܐ ܐܠܟܣܢܕܪܘܣ ܠܟܠ ܗܘܐ.
ܘܐܠܗܐ ܗܢܝܐ ܒܪܬ ܠܦܘܪܢܝܘܣ[2] ܥܒܕܗ ܕܐܠܟܣܢܕܪܘܣ ܠܐ ܐܫܬܡܥ.
ܘܐܠܗܐ ܦܛܘܠܡܐܘܣ ܗܦܟܪ ܠܐ ܐܬܡܠܠ. ܘܐܠܗܐ ܐܠܟܣܢܕܪܘܣ
ܐܟܝܠܗܘܣ ܠܐ ܐܬܚܙܝ. ܘܐܠܗܐ ܐܘܩ̈ܝܢܐ ܘܐܦ̈ܪܝܢܐ[3] ܦܝܠܘܣ̈ܘܦܐ[4] ܠܐ
ܐܬܝܠܕܘ. ܘܐܢ ܦ̇ܠܐ ܠܡܕ̈ܝܢܬܐ[5] ܕܒܫܝܢܘܢ[6] ܐܦ ܐܝܬܘܢ ܠܫܢ̈ܝܐ
ܥܒܪܝܐ. ܘܗܠܝܢ ܬܫܥ̈ܝܬܐ ܐܚܪ̈ܢܝܬܐ ܕܠܡܫܝܚܘܬܐ ܐܝܬ، ܙܟܝ. ܐܝܟ ܗ̇ܝ،
ܕܐܠܘ ܠܐ[7] ܐܝܬ ܣܒܪܬ ܘܦܠܝ ܐܦܠܐ[8] ܐܝܟܐ ܣܒܪܬ *ܘܦܠܝ. ܘܡܛܠ ܕܐܝܬ
ܠܐ ܣܒܪܬ ܐܦܠܐ ܐܝܟܐ ܣܒܪܬ.[9] ܘܐܕܫܐ ܐܚܪܢܐ ܕܡܢ ܬܫܥܝܬܐ ܣܒܪ̈ܢܝܐ
ܢܦܩ. ܐܝܟ ܗ̇ܝ، ܕܐܢ ܥܒܕܐ ܐܢܫܐ ܐܘܒܕܬ ܡܠܟܐ ܐܠܗܐ[10] ܐܬܘܗܝ، ܐܘ
ܒܒܪܐ ܕܐܠܗܐ. ܐܠܝܨܐ ܠܡܒܪܒ ܕܐܝܬ ܐܠܗܐ. ܘܐܝܟ[11] ܕܐܡ̇ܪ
ܐܘܣܛܘܦܣ.[12] ܕܐܪܝܣܛܘܢܝܘܣ ܘܐܪܝܣܛܘܛܠܝܣ[13] ܠܐ ܐܫܬܥܝܘ ܦܪ̈ܘܬܐ
ܒܕܒܐ ܕܐܝܠܝܢܘܬܐ ܣܘܣܐ. ܦܪܘܬܐ ܐܝܟ ܗ̣ܝ، ܗ̇،[14] ܐܝܠܝܢܘܬܐ. ܘܒܡܕܒܪܢܐ
ܦ̇ܡ ܦܣܩܐ ܢܦܩ ܡܢ ܬܫܥܝܬܐ. ܒܬܪܢܐ ܕܝܢ *ܬܫܥܝܬܐ ܡܢ[15] ܦܣܩܐ.

---

2 [1] ܕܐܠܗܘܬܗܘܢ RVLl [2] ܠܬܐܘܕܝܩܘܣ RVLl [3] ܐܠܟܣܢܕܪܝܐ RVLl [4] ܒܪ̈ܢܫܝܬܐ RVLl [5] ܕܡܬܚܫܒܢܘܬܗ F [6] ܐܢ ܠܡܪ̈ܒܢܘܗܝ RVLl [7] scripsi; ܘܦܪܝܘܣ ܘܡܣܡܣܡܘܗ F; ܘܦܪܝܘܣܡܣܡܣܘ RVLl [8] ܥܪܒܐ RVLl

3 [1] ܐܫܡܫܘܢ F [2] ܠܦܘܪܢܝܘܣ RVL [3] ܦܪ̈ܢܐ RL [4] ܦܝܠܘܣ̈ܘܦܐ RVLl [5] sg. RL [6] ܕܒܫܝܢܘܢ RVL; ܕܒܫܝܢܘܢ l [7] om. RVLl [8] om. RVLl [9*] om. R [10] ܐܠܗܐ ܡܕܡ RVLl [11] i. om. RVLl [12] ܐܣܛܘܦܪܣ RLl [13] ܘܐܪܝܣܛܘܛܠܝܣ RVL [14] om. RVLl [15*] trp. RVLl

puted premisses, on any matter which may be advice, or shaming (?), or contention, or emotions and habits. The species by which an enthymeme is produced are as follows. One species is that of transition from the opposite to the other. For example, if being temperate is good, being intemperate is bad; and if war has been the cause of many evils, as at Mesene, peace is the cause of great blessings, therefore it is right to correct (them) with peace. Another species is from similar inflexions. For example, if justice is not entirely good, also (the same applies to) that which (happens) justly, for it is not desirable to die justly. Another species is from correlatives. For example, if to do well (is predicated of one), also to suffer well (is predicated of the other); and if Diomedon scorned the selling of youths as shameful, the buying of youths is also shameful to us.

TWO.[19] Sometimes error may intrude through the indetermination of a statement, as when Alcmaeon said to Theodectes, 'For no one among mortals (?) hated Alphesiboia your mother'; here the cause on account of which she was loved ought to have been defined. Also Demosthenes said, 'If it is just to kill the killer, like him who killed at Thebes, it is also just for me to kill, and here again to kill the killer'; he ought to have added, 'Because at Thebes the killer was justly killed'. Another species is from the more and less. For example, 'If the gods do not know everything, men do not know anything'; and, 'If he beats his parents, it is no wonder that he beats his neighbours'; and, 'Sosmenoiktros, who slew his new offspring with the rest of his children, is no marvel if Hunus kills his father'.

THREE.[20] Another species is that taken from earlier persons. For example, if Theseus did not do wrong previously, neither was Alexander doing wrong; had it not been for Helen the daughter of Tyndareus, the affair of Alexander would not have happened; had it not been for Patroclus, Hector would not have been killed; had it not been for Alexander, Achilles would not have been famous; had artists not been false, philosophers would not have been honoured; and if simple people should praise you, so you in turn should praise the Greeks. In the same way our master adduced other examples for refutation. For example, 'If you had not done such and such, I would

[19] **6.5.2** AR 2.23 97a29-b20; IS 3.7 (179.12-180.4).
[20] **6.5.3** AR 2.23 97b20-98a28; IS 3.7 (180.5-181.4).

ܕܐܬܟܒ. ܘܐܕܫܐ ܐܚܪܢܐ ܢܦܝܫ ܡܢ ܦܘܠܓܐ. ܒܙܒܢܐ ܕܡܦܩܬܢܘܬܐ ܒܥܕܢܐ ܩܝܛܝܢܐ. ܐܝܟ ܗ̇ܝ ܕܒܢ̈ܝܢܫܐ ܡܛܠ ܬܠܬ ܬ̈ܠܝܢ ܛܠܡܝܢ. ܘܦܠܓ ܡܛܠ ܬܐ̈ܡܝܢ ܡܬܝܠܕܝܢ ܠܐ ܦܠܓܝ. ܡܕܝܢ ܡܛܠ ܗ̇ܝ ܬܠܝܬܝܬܐ ܦܠܓܝ. ܘܐܕܫܐ ܐܚܪܢܐ ܢܦܝܫ ܡܢ ܣܘܓܐܐ ܕܬܘ̈ܠܕܬܐ ܕܚܝ̈ܘܬܐ. ܐܝܟ ܐܝܢܐ ܕܒܬܘ̈ܠܕܬܐ ܡܥܙ̈ܐ[1] ܗܡܝܢܘܬ ܣܘܓܐܐ ܒܗ ܩ̇ܠܝܢ. ܐܟܡܐ ܕܠܗܘܦܪܐ ܕܡܬܝܠܕܐ ܗܘܐ ܐܡܪܐ ܡܢܝܢܐ ܒܐܬܢܣ ܕܡܢ ܡܥܒܕܬܘܬ ܣܓܝ̈ܐ ܐܡ̈ܗܬܐ ܒܠܚܘܕ ܒܥܕܪܐ ܡܠܟ̈ܐ ܠܒܢ̈ܝܗܘܢ. ܘܐܝܟ ܐܪܝܣܛܘܛܠܝܣ[2] ܗ̇ܘ ܕܡܛܠ ܗ̇ܝ ܕܗܝܟܠܘܬܐ ܒܒܝ ܠܐܘܡܝܢܣܝܘܣ ܒܝ ܡܬܦܠܛܪ ܗܘܐ ܒܡ ܗܦܠܝܒܘ ܒܠܒܘܗܝ ܕܒܪܗ ܗ̇ܘܐ ܐܣܛܒܪ. ܘܬܗܘܕܝܦܘܣ ܒܝ ܠܪ̈ܒܒܐ ܢܒܪܢܐ ܕܒܝܬܐ ܠܐ ܐܫܠܡ ܠܒܢ̈ܝܗܘܢ ܐܬܗܡܝܢ ܠܡܛܪ ܬ̈ܠܦܐ ܢܒܪ̈ܢܝܬܐ ܣܛܪ̈ܦܬܐ.

ܕܚܡܪ̈ܐ. ܘܐܕܫܐ ܐܚܪܢܐ ܢܦܝܫ ܡܢ ܕܒܝܚܐ *ܘܦܣܘܩܝܐ ܕܚܝ̈ܘܬܐ.[1] ܒܗ̇ܝ ܕܐܝܟ[2] ܕܐܡܪ ܐܪܣܛܘܛܠܝܣ. ܕܟܠ ܠܚܝ̈ܘܬܐ ܡܣܩܪܝܢ. ܦܐܪ̈ܘ *ܠܐܪܣܛܘܛܠܝܣ ܢܩܘܪ[3] ܘܐܦ ܠܓܪܦ. ܘܒܢ̈ܝ ܒܗܘ ܠܐܘܩܝܢܘܣ ܘܐܦ ܠܗ ܒܪ ܡܕܝܢܬܗܘܢ ܗ̇ܘܐ. ܘܒܢ̈ܝ ܡܛܠܩܝܢܐ ܠܣܐܦܐ ܣܡܝܟܬܐ ܘܐܦ ܐܢܬܬܐ. ܘܠܡܕܡ̈ܝܢܐ ܠܡܫܚܘܢ *ܒܝ ܛܠܐ ܗܘܐ[4] ܒܡ ܗܦ̈ܟܐ ܛܒܡܘ[5] ܒܕܪ̈ܫܡ ܩ̈ܠܐ ܗܘܘ. ܘܒܢ̈ܝ ܐܛܠܠܝܐ ܠܦܛܪܘܣ[6] ܘܠܡܩܝܡܘܢ ܒܒܥܝܐ ܚܙܒܘ ܘܠܐܢܒܘܣܐ ܛܢܘܪܘܣ ܒܝ ܐܣܩܝܢܐ ܗܘܐ ܒܐܩܘܪܐ ܒܩܝܘܡܝ، ܘܐܬܝܢ̈ܐ[7] ܒܢܡܘܣ̈ ܣܘܠܝ ܐܬܚܫܒܘ ܘܠܡܕܡ̈ܝܢܐ ܒܢܡܘܣ̈ ܠܡܦܪܓܘܣ ܐܝܠܝܢ. ܘܪ̈ܫܐ ܬܡܒܗܣ[8] ܦܠܩܘܣܐ[9] ܗܘܘ ܒܠܗܘܢ. ܘܡܢ ܬ̈ܠܝ ܣܚ̈ܬܪܐ ܒܬܪ ܡܢ ܕܡܢܝܐ ܡܬܢܣܒܝܢ. ܐܝܟ ܗ̇ܝ ܕܐ̇ܢ ܣܚܝܢ ܕܢܦܪ ܠܐܠܗܐ ܐܦ ܠܐܒܗ̈ܬܐ ܘܬ̈ܠܦܢܐ ܣܚܝܢ ܕܢܦܪ. ܘܐܝܟ ܕܐܡܪ ܡܚܣܢܢܝܢܢܘܣ[10] ܠܐܘܛܘܠܘܩܘܣ[11] ܐ̱ ܐܠܗܝ̈ܬܐ ܒܢ̈ܝܢ ܐܦ ܬܪ̈ܬܝܢ ܕܐܪܘܡܩܠܝܣܘܣ[12] ܒܢ̈ܝܢ. ܒܬܪ ܕܝܢ ܕܠܡܩܒܠܢܐ. ܐܝܟ ܕܐܡܪܬ ܣܐܦܐ ܕܗ̇ܝ[13] ܕܢܝܚܘܬ ܒܢܫܬܐ ܗ, ܒܗ̇ܝ ܕܐ̈ܠܗܐ ܕܛܠܝܢ ܠܐ ܡܢܬܝܢ.

4 [1] ܡܥܙܐ RVL [2] ܣܘܩܘܣܛܠܛܗܬ F

5 [1*] trp. RVL [2] om. RV [3*] ܢܩܘܪ ܠܐܪܣܛܘܛܠܝܣ F [4*] ܗܘܐ ܛܠܐ F [5] add. ܗܘܘ RVL [6] ܠܦܛܪܘܣ RVL [7] ܘܐܬܝܢ̈ܐ RVLl [8] ܬܡܒܗܣ F [9] ܦܠܩܘܣܐ RVLl [10] ܡܚܣܢܢܝܢܢܘܣ RVLl [11] ܠܐܘܛܘܠܘܩܘܣ RLl; ܠܐܘܛܘܠܘܩܘܣ V [12] ܕܐܪܘܡܩܠܝܣܘܣ RVL [13] i. ܘ R

not have done such and such'; and, 'Because you have not done (it), I have not done (it)'. Another species is that derived from a definition based on opinion. For example, if a demon or angel is divine or the work of God, one must know that there is a God. And as Iphicrates said, 'Harmodius and Aristogiton were not designated excellent until they had demonstrated valour'; therefore excellence is valour. In the first (case) a decision is derived from a definition, but in the second a definition from a decision.

FOUR.[21] Another species is derived from division with a kind of induction in questions of motive. For example: 'Men do wrong on account of three causes. So and so does not do wrong on account of two of them, therefore he does wrong on account of the third.' Another species is derived from a multitude of similar examples, such as establishing by examples the reliability of a person of compassion when advising. For instance: 'A soothsayer at Athens said to an orator in dispute (with him), that because of the sharing of emotion, mothers advise their sons (on) everything with the truth; and Thettaliscus, because he made a plea for Ismenias when he was struggling with Stilichon at Thebes, was assumed to be his son; and when Theodectes did not hand over the foreign horsemen of spoil to their masters, he was trusted to keep the violent foreign ships.'

FIVE.[22] Another species is derived from the judgement and decree of the wise, because as Arcidamas said: 'All honour the wise; the Parians honoured Archilochus, even though he reviled (them); the Chians Homer, even though he was not a native of their city; the Mitylenaeans the wise Sappho, even though she was a woman; the Lacedaemonians ranked Chimon among the elders although he was young, because they were lovers of words; the Italiotes considered Pythagoras and Masecus among the prophets, and buried Anaxagoras with honour although he was a foreigner; the Athenians employed the laws of Solon and the Lacedaemonians prospered under the laws of Lycurgus; and the rulers of Thebes were all philosophers.' And among the words of the wise (judgements) are sometimes derived from similar (matters). For example, 'If we ought to honour God, we ought also to honour parents and teachers.' And as Mixidemidelus

[21] **6.5.4** AR 2.23 98a29-b9; IS 3.7 (181.4-7).

[22] **6.5.5** AR 2.23 98b9-29; IS 3.7 (181.8-9).

ܕܫܡܥܬ. ܘܐܝܕܐ ܐܘܪܚܐ ܢܗܝܪ ܡܢ ܒܟܠ ܗܘ ܕܡܬܡܛܝܪܟ ܡܢܐ ܕܠܗܘ
ܕܗܝܡ ܠܐ ܢܬܠܒܟ. ܐܝܟ ܕܐܡܪ̈ ܡܬܕܒܪܢܘܬܗܘܢ[1] ܠܐܬܠܒܟܢܐ. ܐܝ̈ ܗܘܦܟܝܗܘܢ
ܒܦܘܪܫܐ ܗܘ ܐܝܟ ܕܐܡܪܢܘܬܗ̈.[2] ܒܐܝܢܐ ܐܘܪܚܗ̈ ܐܡܠܟ ܐܘ ܠܐܝܢܐ
ܐܠܗܐ ܡܢ ܗܠܝܢ ܕܒܢ̈ܝ ܡܕܝܢܬܗ̈ ܡܫܡܫܝܢ ܒܗܘܢ̈ ܠܐ ܢܦܪ. ܘܐܝܕܐ
ܐܘܪܚܐ ܢܗܝܪ ܡܢ ܢܦܩܬܐ ܕܚܘܫܒܐ. ܐܝܟ ܕܐܡܪܝܢ ܠܐ ܬܗܘܐ ܡܕܒܪܢܘܬܐ
*ܕܠܐ ܬܬܚܫܒ. ܐܘ ܐܡܪܝܢ ܡܢ ܡܕܒܪܢܘܬܐ[3] ܕܬܬܚܫܒ. ܘܐܝܕܐ ܐܘܪܚܐ
ܕܡܩܪܒ ܗܘ ܠܗܝܢܐ ܒܗ. ܐܦ ܗܘ ܡܢ ܢܦܩܬܐ ܕܚܘܫܒܐ. ܦܠܝ ܕܝܢ ܡܢܗ
ܒܗ̇ ܕܚܙܐ ܢܦܩܬܐ ܘܡܬܚܠܦܢܘܬܐ ܠܬܪ̈ܝܗܘܢ ܒܗ ܢܦܫ. ܕܐܝܟ ܐܢܫܝܢ
ܐܢܐܘܪܐ ܒܡܕܒܪܢܘܬܐ ܠܐ ܥܒܝܕܐ ܗܘܬ ܠܒܪܗ ܕܐܠܗܐ. ܐܡܪܬ ܠܟ ܕܐܝ̈
ܥܢܝܬܐ ܐܡܪ ܐܢܬ ܒܢ̈ܝܢܫܐ ܗܢܝܢ ܠܟ. ܘܐܝ̈ ܕܛܠܝܬܐ ܛܠܝܐ. ܬܘܪܓܡܐ
ܐܪܐ ܠܐ ܦܠܛ. ܐܘܪܚܐ ܕܝܢ ܠܬܘܪܓܡܗ ܡܠܟܬ ܠܒܪܗ. ܐܡܪܬ ܠܟ ܕܐܝ̈
ܥܢܝܬܐ ܐܡܪ ܐܢܬ ܛܠܝܐ ܙܕܩܝܢ ܠܟ. ܘܐܝ̈ ܕܛܠܝܬܐ ܒܒܢ̈ܝܢܫܐ.
ܬܘܪܓܡܐ ܐܪܐ ܦܠܛ.

ܕܥܒܕ. ܙܟܝ ܕܝܢ ܬܫܘܒܚܬܐ ܐܘܪܚܬܐ ܠܗܕܐ ܐܝܟ ܕܐܬܬܗ̇ ܗ̇ܝ ܕܐܡܪܝܢ.
ܫܠܝܐ ܡܢ ܒܗ̇ ܕܐܝ̈ ܒܥܪ̈ܐ ܬܠܠܬܗ̇ ܐܬܬܪ. ܘܐܝ̈ ܠܐ ܒܥܪ̈ܐ ܠܐ ܬܫܡܪ
ܒܕܠܐ ܡܬܚܫܠܐ ܫܠܝܐ. ܦܘܫܐ ܕܝܢ ܗܕܐ ܡܢ ܗ̇ܝ ܕܡܕܒܚܗ̇ ܒܗ̇ ܕܗܪܟܐ
ܛܒ ܚܙ ܢܦܘܫܐ ܠܒܪܐ ܠܬܪܝܢ ܕܠܡܫܟܠܢܐ.[1] ܐܝܟ ܒܥܪܘܬ ܫܠܝܐ ܘܠܐ
ܒܥܪܘܬܗ̇ ܢܦܫ. ܗ̇ܝ ܬܘܒ ܕܝܢ ܬܪܝܢ ܕܠܡܫܟܠܢܐ ܐܝܟ ܗܝܡܢܘܬܐ ܘܪܚܡܬܐ
ܠܚܕ ܡܬܚܫܒܐ ܐܝܟ ܬܘܪܓܡܐ ܢܦܫܐ. ܘܒܗܕܐ ܐܘܪܚܐ ܒܗ ܐܝܟ ܥܪܒܐ
ܡܕܡ ܕܢܚܡ ܡܟܠ ܒܠܗ̇ ܒܫܒܬܐ ܕܒܗ ܘܡܟܠܝܐ ܒܠܗ̇ ܐܘܪܚܬܐ ܢܗܝܬܐ.
ܐܝܟ ܐܢܫܐ ܕܡܟܠ ܗܝܐܬܐ ܡܬܦܪܫ ܒܬܠܡܝܕܘܬܐ ܘܒܗ ܢܟܝܐ[2] ܕܢܝܚ
ܡܢܗ ܫܦܝܪܐ ܐܡܪ. ܕܐܝܟܐ ܛܒ ܗܒܠ ܡܬܚܫܒ ܐܝܟܐ[3] ܒܡܕܡ ܡܢ
ܗܝ̈ܐܬܐ ܡܟܠ ܢܦܪ ܡܢܘܟܝ ܘܡܫܟܚ ܣܠ.[4] ܕܕܠܒܐ ܒܗ ܢܫܘܒ ܠܗ
ܦܬܪ. ܬܬܚܒ ܒܒܗ ܐܦ ܢܦܫ ܘܡܢ ܦܘܠܚ ܘܕܘܟܬܐ ܠܟܬܪ ܐܟܠ.[5]
ܘܗܝܐ ܛܒ ܐܬܪܐ ܬܡܢ ܘܦܠܛ ܡܟܫܐ.

6 [1] ܘܡܬܕܒܪܢܘܬܐ RVLl [2] ܕܐܡܪܝܢܘܬܗ̈ RVL; ܐܝܟ ܕܐܡܪܝܢ l [3*] om. R
7 [1] i. om. RVLl [2] om. RVL [3] om. R [4] ܣܠ R [5] ܟܠܠ RVLl

said to Autocles, 'If divine things are venerable, the right things of Areospagus are also venerable.' Sometimes, however, (they are derived from) opposites. For example, Sappho said, 'That we die is evil, because the gods who are good do not die.'

SIX.[23] Another species is derived from the refutation of what is affirmed when it is not discovered in the subject. For example, Theodectes said to the Athenians, 'If Socrates is an unbeliever as you say, against what holy place has he done evil, or which god of those to which the people of your city make supplication has he not honoured?' Another species is derived from the consequences of a precept, as (when people) say, 'You should not acquire education lest you be envied', or say, 'Acquire education that you may be honoured!' Another species is close to this one because it too is derived from consequences, but differs from it because in it one consequence follows on two contrasting (statements). For example, Anareia the priestess did not allow her son to speak in public, for she said, 'If you speak the truth, men will hate you, but if lies, the gods (will); public speech is therefore improper.' The other (way of arguing is that) she advised her son to speak in public, for she said, 'If you speak the truth, the gods will love you, but if lies, men (will); public speech is therefore proper.'

SEVEN.[24] Our master added another example to this, which is (as follows). (People) say, 'Buy a field, because if its produce is good, you will gain, but if it is not good, you will not lose, because the field is not destroyed.' This differs from its predecessor because in this one one good consequence follows on two opposites, like the excellence of a field or its uselessness, while in the previous one two opposites, like hate and love, followed on one thing which could have a consequence, namely public speaking. Someone (uses) another method when he loves some thing on account of a secret cause in it and openly alleges a different cause. For example, when someone for the sake of pleasure is excessive in (his) desires and wishes to remove ignominy from himself, he may say, 'I employ some of the pleasures to preserve my constitution and maintain my strength, lest my body being weak, my soul also is brought down with it and I de-

[23] **6.5.6** AR 2.23 99a6-25; IS 3.7 (181.9-182.2).
[24] **6.5.7** AR 2.23 99a25-32; IS 3.7 (182.3-12).

ܕܬܘܒܐ. ܘܒܬܪ ܐܘܪܚܐ ܕܫܘܡܠܝܬ ܕܠܡܫܡ̈ܠܝܐ. ܐܝܟ ܗܒܐ
ܐܦܝܣܩܘܦܘܣ ܗ̣ܘ[1] ܕܠܛܠܝܐ ܒܪܗ ܡܫܡܫ ܗܘܐ. ܘܟܕ ܐܬܚܫܒ ܐܡܪ
ܠܡܫܡ̈ܫܢܘܗܝ. ܐ̱ܢ ܗ̣ܘ *ܕܠܛܠܝܐ ܐܘܪܚܐ ܒܥܝܐ[2] ܫܒܩܬܘܢ.[3] *ܠܒܥܝܐ
ܒܪܝܐ ܛܠܝܐ[4] ܫܒܩܘ. ܒܐܡܬ ܠܝ ܠܒܥܝܐ ܒܪܝܐ ܐܝܟ ܛܠܝܐ ܡܫܡ̈ܫܢܐ
ܕܒܢ ܐܘܪܚܐ ܫܘܒܩܢܐ. ܘܐܝܟ ܕܐܡܪܢ ܐ̱ܢ ܠܐܘܪ̈ܚܬܐ ܘܐܦ
ܠܒܢ̈ܝܬܐ ܡܫܚܝܢ ܠܗ ܦܘܡ ܢܡܘܣܐ ܠܡܦܩ. ܠܐܘܪ̈ܚܬܐ ܗܠܝܢ ܕܡܫܚ̈ܬܐ
ܡܫܪܝܢ ܐܝܟ ܐܣܦܪܛܒܘܣ ܘܒܪܝܫܐܝܬܘܣ[5] ܐܘܪܚܐ ܬܪܬܝܢ ܫܒܩܬܘܢ
ܠܡܦܩܕ. ܘܒܬܪ ܐܘܪܚܐ[6] ܕܢܘܦܩܬ ܦܘܡܐ ܠܕܠܡܫܡ̈ܠܝܐ. ܐܝܟ
ܕܡܫܡܘܦܐܝܣ ܐܡܪ ܗܘܐ. ܗ̇ܘ ܕܐܡܪ ܕܐܠܗܐ ܒܒܢ̈ܝܢܐ ܐܝܬܘܗܝ ܘܠܐ
ܒܡܕܡ ܦܘܫ ܡܢ ܐܢܫܐ ܕܐܡܪ ܕܐܠܗܐ ܡܫܡܠܝܐ ܐܝܬܘܗܝ. ܬܘܒܘܗܝ ܒܪ ܗ̇ܘ،
ܕܠܐ ܬܠܗܐ[7] ܐܝܬܘܗܝ ܐܡܪܝܢ. ܘܗܟܢܐ ܒܪ ܠܐܢܫܐ ܕܠܝܬ ܢܟܝܬܐ ܡܫܬܐܠܝܢ
ܕܐܢ ܐܘܪܐ ܦܠܐ ܠܡܚܒܪ ܦܝܠܘܣܘܦܘܬܐ[8] ܐܘ ܠܐ ܦܠܐ. ܐ̱ܢ ܐܡܪ ܐܢܐ
ܐܡܪ ܕܐܡܠܬ ܡܚܕܬܐ. ܘܐ̱ܢ ܐܡܪ ܕܠܐ ܗܘܝܬ ܐܡܪ ܕܐܡܠܬ ܡܚܕܬܐ.
ܒܡܚܕܬܐ ܒܪ ܐܡܪ ܕܠܐ. ܗܟܢܐ ܗ̇ܘ ܕܢܬܠ ܐܘܪܚܐ ܐܘ ܡܢܐ ܠܐܢܫܝܢ.
ܬܐܡܪܘܢ ܒܪ ܐܝܬܐ ܕܡܥܒܕܢܐ ܐܝܬܘܗܝ.

ܕܬܫܒܘ. ܘܒܬܪ ܐܘܪܚܐ ܢܗܝܒ[1] ܡܢ ܬܪܝܢ ܡܫܡ̈ܠܝܐ ܒܬܪܝܢ ܒܕܪ̈ܐ.
ܠܡܕܒܪܝܢ ܘܠܫܪ̈ܒܬܐ ܘܒܫܘܡܠܝܐ. ܐܝܟ ܐܢܫܐ ܕܐܡܪ ܒܪ ܐܠܗܝܢ ܗܘܝܬ[2]
ܡܢܪ ܗܘܝܬ ܕܢܫܐ ܐܡܫܐ. ܘܡܫܐ ܕܢܫܐ ܗ̣ܘܐ ܠܝ ܡܟܝܠ ܐܢܐ ܕܠܐ
ܐܢܪ. ܘܡܟܝܠܐ ܕܡܫܘܡܠܝܐ ܢܬܡܪ. ܕܠܐ ܡܢܪ ܗܘܝܬ ܡܟܠ ܕܐܠܗܝܢ
ܗܘܝܬ. ܘܡܫܐ ܕܐܬܬܚܫܒܬ[3] ܡܢܪ ܐܢܐ. ܘܒܬܪ ܐܘܪܚܐ ܒܪ ܡܕܡ ܠܐܬ
ܡܕܡ ܢܗܘܐ. ܫܘܡܠܝܘ ܠܐܬ ܫܘܡܠܝܐ ܕܗ̇ܘ ܡܕܡ ܐܠܝܐ ܕܢܗܘܐ.
ܐܝܟ ܗ̇ܘ ܕܐ̱ܢ ܒܪ ܢܚܒܠ ܠܒܠܒܟ[4] ܫܒܩܬܗ. ܒܪ ܢܗܒ ܐܢܫܬ[5] ܡܢܗ
ܐܒܝܘܣܗ. ܘܟܕ ܥܒܕܐ ܡܕܡ ܠܐܬ ܗܝܢ ܫܘܡܠܝܐ ܢܗܘܐ. ܠܐ ܦܠܐ
ܠܡܬܕܠܠܘ ܒܡܪܢ[6] ܡܢܗܘܢ. ܐܝܟ ܗ̇ܘ ܕܒܥܐ ܗ̇ܝ ܢܗܒ ܡܬܠܫܝܢܘܬܐ
ܠܒ̈ܢܝܐ. ܠܐ ܒܪ ܢܕܒ ܘܡܦܩܕܬܐ[7] ܡܬܪܒܐ ܠܗܘܢ. ܐܠܐ ܕܡܢ ܒܢ̈ܝܐ
ܢܬܫܡܫܘܢ ܘܠܒܪ̈ܬܗܘܢ[8] ܢܦܘܩܘܢ. ܘܐܝܟ[9] ܕܐܡܪ ܐܬܦܘܩܘܢ[10]
ܕܗܢܘܢ ܕܢܦܩܘ ܡܢ ܡܫܬܐܠܢܘܬܗ ܒܪ ܦܠܛ ܠܢܫܐ ܥܒܕܐ ܠܗ ܕܬܕܘܪܝܢܘܗܝ،
ܢܦܩܘ. ܐܠܐ ܕܠܗܬ ܡܫܝܚܐ ܫܡܪܬ ܢܗܝܪܘܬܐ ܢܦܩܘܢ ܠܗ. ܘܐܝܟ
ܕܐܡܪ ܐܦ ܗܘ ܠܡܬܐܠܠܦܘ[11] ܕܕܡܒܝܢܘ ܡܢ ܠܫܪ̈ܬܐ ܕܐܬܦܪܫܘܗܝ ܐܘܠ
ܠܗ ܒܪ ܡܠܦܪ ܠܗ. ܐܠܐ ܡܣܬܝܪܐ ܕܢܝܫܐ ܡܦܘ̈ܩܘܗܝ ܘܢܦܘܩܘܗܝ.

8 [1] ܗܘ R [2*] pl. RVLl [3] ܫܒܩܝܢ R; ܫܒܩܬܘܢ V [4*] pl. RVLl [5] ܘܒܪܝܫܐܝܬܘܣ RVLl [6] om. F [7] add. ܡܬܪ̈ܬܐ R [8] ܦܝܠܘܣܘܦܘܬܐ RL; ܦܝܠܘܣܘܦܝܐ Vl

9 [1] add. ܕ RVLl [2] om. RVL [3] om. F [4] f. , RVLl [5] ܐܢܐ RVLl [6] i. om. RVLl [7] sg. RLl [8] ܘܠܒܪ̈ܬܗܘܢ RVL [9] i. om. RVL [10] ܐܬܦܘܩܘܢ F [11] ܠܡܬܐܠܠܦܘ RVLl

sist entirely from the labour of righteousness.' This *topos* is striking and very persuasive.

EIGHT.[25] (Another is) by another way, namely the proportion of opposites. An example is the old man Iphicrates who was serving his son, a boy, and when he was ridiculed he said to those ridiculing him, 'If you consider a tall boy a man, consider a short man a boy!' In other words, 'Consider me, a short man, as a boy serving my tall son!' And as (people) say, 'If your law does not command (you) to keep your guests even if they do dreadful things, you ought to reserve a special honour to your guests like Strabax and Charidemus who do praiseworthy things.' (Another is) by another way, namely the affinity of outcome of (two apparent) opposites. Thus Xenophanes used to say, 'He who says that gods are manufactured is in no way different from him who says gods are mortal, for both of them are saying that there are no gods.' And similarly when we ask someone who (claims) there is no knowledge whether or not it is right to philosophise, if he says 'Yes' he is saying that there is knowledge, and if he says 'No' he is likewise says that there is knowledge, for by knowledge he says 'No'. The same (applies to) giving earth or water to another, for both of them are an index of submission.

NINE.[26] Another way is taken from two opposites at two times, before and after, and with a reversal. For example, one may say, 'When I was compelled I fought, that I might find peace; but now that I have peace, I pray that I may not fight.' And it can be said in reverse: 'I did not fight because I was compelled; but now that I am at peace I may fight.' Another way, when something is the cause of something (else), (is to say that) it is necessary that its opposite is the cause of the opposite of that something (else). For example, if when you give (something) to your colleague you make him glad, when you take it away from him he is distressed. And when something may be the cause of two opposites, it is not proper (for it) to be indicated by (only) one of them. For example, 'Fortune gives success to many, not knowing and purposing fine things for them, but in order for them to be envied by evil men and unmask their reproaches.' And as Antiphon said, 'Those who went out with Meleager when he

[25] **6.5.8** AR 2.23 99a32-b13; IS 3.7 (182.12-183.15).

[26] **6.5.9** AR 2.23 99b13-30; IS 3.7 (183.15-184.9).

ܕܒܫܡܝܐ. ܐܬܬܘܪ̈ܬܐ ܡܢ ܗܠܝܢ ܕܐܬܐܡܪܘ ܠܡܠܘܫܐ ܘܒܘܝܢܐ[1] ܘܡܕܒܠܢܐ ܘܡܫܡ ܒܢܘܗܪܐ ܠܒܢ̈ܝ. ܘܗܢܐ ܐܣܝܪܐ ܒܡ̈ܠܟܐ[2] ܘܕܝ̈ܢܐ ܕܬܠܝ.[3] ܐܝܟ ܡܐ ܕܐܡܪ ܪܡܘܬ ܗܢܐ ܠܡ ܥܪܒܐ ܡܢܐ ܘܦܓܥܘ ܘܡܬܘܪ ܠܝ ܘܠܬ̈ܢܝܢ. ܒܗ ܥܠܝܟ ܡܢ ܥܠ ܗܕܐ ܦܠܐ ܠܝ ܕܐܬܡܣܪܝܢܘܗܝ. ܒܗ ܢܦܩ ܪܘܚܐ ܕܝܢ ܒܠܗܕܐ ܐܢܐ ܐܢܬܗ ܡܣܒܪܬ ܐܡܪ. ܘܡܫܡܫܢ̈ܝܢܘܗܝ ܒܗ ܚܠܐ ܡܢ ܠܐ ܠܡܣܒܪ. ܒܗ ܡܫܠܡܢ ܕܝܢ ܐܢܬ ܡܣܒܪܬܝܗ، ܐܡܪ. ܒܕܐܝܟ ܗܢܐ ܠܒܪ[4] ܐܬܬܐ ܡܐܠܦܘܗܝ[5] ܘܡܒܢܝܢܘܗܝ ܪ̈ܗܛܝܐ ܡܢ ܐܬܚܫܒܘ. ܘܐܬܬܐ ܐܣܝܪܐ ܢܡܘܣ[6] ܡܢ ܒܥܠ ܡܠܘܬܐ ܕܠܐ ܡܬܬܘܕܝܐ ܘܠܐ ܡܦܫܩܐ. ܐܝܟܢܐ ܕܦܓܥܘܗܝ ܒܗ ܡܫܠܡܢ ܠܢܩܫܬܐ ܒܠ ܕܐܡܝܪܐ ܠܗܘܢ، ܪܘܚܐ ܐܡܪ. ܕܢܩܫܬܐ ܒܠ ܢܦܫܬܐ ܡܬܝܪܬܐ ܚܫܝܢ. ܘܠܗܕܐ ܒܦܐ ܕܢܘܠܫ ܘܐܡܪ. ܡܕܝܢ ܐܦ ܢܩܫܐ ܡܢ[7] ܢܩܫܐ ܒܢܒܪܐ ܡܬܬܙܝܥܝܢ. ܒܠ ܡܠܫܐ ܚܫܝܢ. ܘܒܥܒܠ ܘܠܐ ܕܒܢܝܗܘܢ ܗܘܐ ܡܫܝܐ ܒܠ ܡܫܝܐ ܚܫܝܢ.

ܕܢܚܒܪ. ܘܐܬܬܐ ܐܣܝܪܐ ܢܡܘܣ ܡܢ ܣܡܟܬܗ ܕܒܥܠܕܢܐ ܕܘܒܢܐ ܘܚܒܪܐ ܒܒܕܘ ܠܗ ܐܘ ܒܝܒܝܢܗ ܗܘ̈ܢ ܠܗ. ܘܡܢ ܡܬܬܬܒܪܬܐ ܕܐܠܗ ܕܐܡܘܪܐ. ܐܒܒܐ ܕܐܡܪ ܗܘ ܡܢ ܒܥܒܐ ܗܘ ܠܒܘܢ ܪܘܚܐ. ܐܢܐ ܕܝܢ ܒܡܘܒܪܢܐ. ܘܗܘ ܡܢ ܘܠܐ ܡܒܕܡ ܐܘܦ ܠܒܘܢ. ܐܢܐ ܕܝܢ ܠܗܝܟܢܐܐ ܡܒܒܘܢ ܡܟܝܢ ܡܗܒܠܬ. ܘܐܬܬܐ ܐܣܝܪܐ ܕܠܡܦܠ ܗܘ ܕܡܒܒܘܢ ܡܬܬܙܝܥ. ܐܝܟܢ ܐܢܬܬܐ ܗܝ، ܕܒܕ ܐܬܚܫܒܬ[1] ܒܠ ܕܠܓܠܓܠܐ ܢܦܩܬ ܐܡܪܬ. ܐܠܐ ܕܚܫܒܐ ܗܘܬ ܠܢܦܫܬܗ.[2] ܐܡܪܐ ܠܒܪܗ ܠܐ ܢܦܩܬ. ܘܐܝܟܢ ܕܐܡܪ ܬܐܘܕܘܦܘܣ. ܐܒܒܪܐ ܒܗ ܒܡ ܐܢܫܐ ܕܢܦܩ ܡܢܗ ܠܗ ܡܦܪܥ ܡܬܚܫܒ. ܐܐܘܣ ܒܗ ܒܡ ܐܕܘܡܘܗܝ ܠܐ ܐܘܦܒ ܠܒܢܐ ܐܬܬܒܫ. ܘܗܢܐ ܐܣܝܪܐ ܡܢ ܢܡܘܣܬ ܒܒܬܐ ܕܡܢ ܥܘܕܢܐ. ܐܝܟܢܐ ܕܐܬܐܡܘܟܠܘܗܝ[3] ܒܗ ܡܫܠܡܢ[4] ܠܠܐܘܕܐܡܘܗܝ[5] ܘܐܡܪ. ܕܡܠܠܒܢܐ ܐܝܟ ܗܘ ܕܡܦܠܓܠܓܠܢܝܐ[6] ܐܬܬܝܟ ܒܒܢܝܟ ܡܒܠܠ ܐܢܬ. ܦܪ ܠܗ. ܕܡܠܠ[7] ܗܘ، ܕܡܦܠܓܠܓܠܢܝܐ[8] ܐܢܐ ܒܒܢܝܟ. ܘܗܘܝܐ ܗܘ ܕܐܡܪ ܐܢܬܘܢ، ܡܠܠ ܕܐܢܬܘܢ، ܘܠܐ ܐܢܬܘܢ، ܡܠܠ ܕܠܐ ܐܢܬܘܢ،.

ܕܬܪܥܘܢ. ܘܗܢܐ ܐܣܝܪܐ ܕܒܘܝܢܐ ܐܝܟ ܐܢܐ ܕܐܡܪ ܠܒܢܬܗ. ܡܠܠܒܢܐ ܒܒܕܬ ܗܒܢܐ. ܘܡܢ ܗܘܝܬ ܠܡܒܒܕ ܒܒܕܐ ܡܬܬܪܐ. ܘܐܬܬܒ ܢܐܡܪ ܐܘܗܝ ܕܗܘ ܡܐ ܕܥܠܝܟ ܐܢܬ ܡܒܘܪ. ܠܒܘܢ ܐܝܟ ܐܡܪ ܐܢܬ ܠܐ ܦܩܪ ܐܢܬ. ܘܗܢܐ ܐܣܝܪܐ ܕܒܘܝܢܐ ܢܡܘܣ ܡܢ ܡܫܒܠܢܐ ܡܒܠܠ ܠܢܪܕܐ.

10 [1] ܘܠܒܘܝܢܐ RVLl [2] sg. R [3] ܕܬ̈ܠܝܢ F [4] ܕܝܢ RVL [5] ܒܐܠܦܘܗܝ F [6] i. add. ܕ RVLl [7] i. add. ܕ RVLl

11 [1] ܐܬܚܫܒܬ RVLl [2] f. ܐ RVLl [3] scripsi; ܕܐܬܐܡܘܟܠܘܗܝ F; ܕܐܬܐܡܘܟܠܘܗܝ RVLl [4] ܡܫܠܡܢ RVLl [5] ܠܠܐܘܕܐܡܘܗܝ RVLl [6] ܕܡܦܠܓܠܓܠܢܝܐ RVLl [7] i. ܘ RVL [8] ܕܡܦܠܓܠܓܠܢܝܐ RVL

killed the wild beast did not go out to help him, but to be witnesses of his virtue to the Greeks.' And as Ajax said to Theolectes, 'Diomedes went to see Odysseus not honouring him, but to see his blemishes and unmask him.'

TEN.[27] These *topoi* which have been mentioned are common to praise and blame and prosecution and defence. Another way is specific to deliberations and lawsuits. For example, an orator may say, 'This thing is possible and easy and advantageous to you and your friends.' When advising (he will then say), 'Therefore it is right for you to do it;' and when defending (himself) he will say, 'Therefore I did it.' With their opposites, when dissuading (he will say), 'Do not do (it);' but when prosecuting he will say, 'You did it.' The rhetors Callipus and Pamphilus made much use of such a *topos*. Another *topos* is taken from the refutation of a statement which is not acknowledged and not persuasive. Thus when Pitteus was speaking against the laws, because they raised an uproar against him he said, 'The laws need a correcting law.' Diocles also did this refuting and said, 'So also fish feed on fish in the sea. They need salt, and the residues of the olive-tree, from which oil comes, need oil.'

ELEVEN.[28] Another *topos* is taken from the deficiencies of the adversary, which time and fortune have made for him or (which) have happened to him by his own free will, and (from) the virtues of the speaker himself. He may say, for example: 'He loves you in name, but I (do so) in deed'; or, 'He has not lent you anything, but I have given freely to many of you.' Another *topos* is that of opposing what is (wrongly) supposed of you, like the woman who, when reproached because she kissed a youth, said, 'If his kiss were shameful, a mother would not kiss her son.' And as Theodectes said, 'If a man is reproached when he does not go to war with one who is weaker than himself, why was Ajax praised when he did not go to war with Odysseus?' Another way of taking on the dispute (is to make it) one of origin. For example, when Thrasybulus was prosecuting Leodames and said, 'Why are you speaking as if you were a Stilitiqean by your origin?' he answered him, 'Because I am a Stilitiqean by my origin.'

---

[27] **6.5.10** AR 2.23 99b30-00a14; IS 3.7 (184.9-16).
[28] **6.5.11** AR 2.23 00a14-35; IS 3.7 (184.16-185.10).

ܐܝܟ ܕܐܡ̣ܪ ܒܣܗܘܦܢܝܣ ܠܒ̈ܢܝܐ ܕܬ̈ܠܝܢ ܗܘܘ؛ ܠܡܬܝܬܗܝܢ[1] ܘܡܬܒ̈ܩܝܢ
ܣܠܩܘܗܝ. ܕܐܢ ܐܝܟ ܕܐܡܪ̈ܢ ܐܝܬܝܗ ܠܒ̈ܢܝܐ ܠܦܘ̈ܩܕܢܐ ܐܚܝܕܘ. ܠܡܠܟܐ
ܒܒ̈ܢܝ ܐܝܬܝܗ ܒܠܘܗܝ. ܘܐܢ ܠܒܣܪܐ ܣܪܝܟ. ܠܡܠܟܐ ܕܒ̈ܢܝܐ ܕܬܘܕܝܬܐ
ܡܦܪ̈ܫܢ ܐܝܬܝܗ ܡܛܠܬܗ. ܘܐܬܪܐ ܐܚܪܢܐ ܕܒܗܘܢ ܐܝܟܐ ܕܦܐܪ ܒܣܝܣܗ.
ܐܒܗܬܐ ܕܒܦܪܘܣܘܦ ܡܛܪܝܢ ܐܪ̈ܒܥ ܠܡܠܟܐ ܐܒܗ̈ܝܢ[2] ܕܡܛܠܬ ܠܒܪܗ.[3] ܘܗ̣ܝ
ܕܒ ܡܟܝܢܐ ܠܡܠܟܘ ܢܦܫܗ ܐܡܪܬ. ܕܠܐ ܡܬܬܘܡ ܡܛܠܬ ܠܛܠܝܘܬܐ ܒܪ،
ܐܦܠܐ ܠܐܢܫܘܢ ܒܒܠܢ. ܘܡܒܢܐ ܗܘ[4] ܐܬܪܐ ܠܡܛܠ̈ܝܢܘܗܝ[5] ܕܒܡܛܠܬܐ[6]
ܕܠܒܢ̈ܘܗܝ[7] ܬܘܒ ܢܛܠܝܢܘܗܝ.[7] ܘܕܐܝܟ ܗܢܐ ܐܕܫܐ ܕܡܬܝܢܝܢܘܬܐ
ܐܝܬܝܗ ܗܘܬ ܐܒܗܘܬܗ ܡܕܡܝܐ ܕܐܬܩܘܪܘܦܘ ܪܛܠܐ.

ܕܐܬܬܠܒܫܪ. ܘܗܢܐ ܐܚܪܢܐ ܢܗܝܒ ܡܢ ܦܐܘܡܒܐ ܘܒܐܝܠܘܬܐ ܘܡܘܒܠ
ܒܡܗܡܐ.[1] ܒܡܘܠܗܒܐ ܗ̇ܢ ܐܝܟ ܗ̇ܝ، ܕܚܒ̈ܝܒܐ ܒܚܪ̈ܪܐ ܐ̈ܠܗܐ ܐܝܢܘܢ
ܐܒܗܬܐ ܕܡܬܠܦܢ. ܒܟܠܗܘܢܐ ܕܝܢ ܐܝܟ ܗ̇ܝ، ܕܐܬܦܘܡܒܠܘܢ[2] ܒܚܪ̈ܪ[3]
ܠܛܠܡܒܐ[4] ܗܘܐ ܒܒܢܐ ܕܡܬܠܒܝܢܐ. ܘܐܝܟ ܕܐܡܪ ܦܪܘܕܘܡܘܣ
ܠܐܬܦܘܡܒܘܣ ܕܢܝܛܢܝܘܣ. ܕܒܚܪ̈ܪܐ ܐܬܦܘܡܒܘܣ[5] ܐܝܬܝܗ ܐܝܟ
ܕܐܬܪܘܢ ܢܝܟܐ ܘܡܪܝܐ. ܘܐܝܟ ܕܐܡܪܝܢ ܢܒܣܘܗ ܕܕܪܐܘܢ ܐܝܟ
ܕܪܐܘܢ[6] ܗܘ. ܐܘܟܝܢ ܐܝܬܢܐ[7] ܒܣܘܐ. ܘܢܒܗܘ ܐܘܡܐܒܝ ܕܒܐܘܦܪܝܣ
ܡܠܟܐ ܕܐܦܘܪܕܛܐ ܐܒܘܬܗ[8] ܕܐܦܘܪܕܛܐ ܣܒܘܬܐ ܘܪܘܪܐ ܡܠܟܐ.

ܕܐܬܒܠܬܒܪ. ܡܒܘܝܢܘܬܐ ܠܬܪ ܡܢ ܡܬܪܝܢܘܬܐ ܡܬܠܒܫܐ ܒܗ،
ܕܠܣܘܒ̈ܠܝܐ ܐܝܟ ܕܡܩܕ ܒܢ̈ܝܐ[1] ܣܘܒܐ. ܘܫܒܪܝܗ ܫܪܪܐ ܠܫܘܠܡܗ
ܢܗܘܐ ܒܦܪܝܒܘ. ܐܝܟ ܗ̇ܝ، ܕܐܠܘ ܣܒܪܬ ܐܢܬ[2] ܘܦܠܝ. ܐܢܐ ܣܒܪܬ ܘܦܠܝ.
ܘܡܒܘܝܢܐ ܠܬܒܘܝܢܐ ܒܪ ܣܘܠܦܢܘܦܐܬ ܫܦܝܪ ܘܡܒܝܢ ܪܟܫ ܚܝܐ[3]
ܒܗ، ܕܦܫܝܛܘܬܗ ܐܒܗܬܗ ܕܡܣܬܠܒܘܬܐ ܕܦܫܝܛܘܬ ܡܣܬܠܒܘܬܐ ܡܚܝܐ.

12 [1] ܠܡ̈ܬܝܬܗܝܢ RVL [2] ܐܒܗܬܐ R [3] f. ܗ R [4] ܗܘܐ RVLl [5] sg. R [6] ܕܡܛܠܬܗ RVLl [7] f. ܗ R

13 [1] ܐܡܗ̈ܬܐ RVL [2] scripsi; ܕܐܬܦܘܡܒܠܘܢ F; ܕܐܬܦܘܡܒܠܘܢ RVLl [3] om. RVL [4] ܠܛܠܡܒܐ RVL [5] ܐܬܦܘܡܒܘܣ RVLl [6] i. add. ܕ RVLl [7] ܐܬܪܢܐ RVLl [8] f ܗ RL; om. Vl

14 [1] sg. RVLl [2] om. F [3] add. ܚܝܐ F

And thus what he is saying (is), 'It is because it is, and is not because it is not.'

TWELVE.[29] Another way of refutation is when someone says to his colleague, 'Why did you act in this way? Were you not able to do a better deed?' And again, he may say, 'If what you advise is advantageous, why do you not do as you say?' Another way of refutation is taken from contraries cancelling each other. For example, Xenophanes said to the women lamenting their dead (one) and making sacrifices for him, 'If as you say he is worthy of blessed life, why do you weep for him? And if he is reduced to destruction, why do you offer sacrifices of praise for him?' Another *topos* is that of the refutation of him whose negligence produces failure. For example, in Carcinus some people accused Medea of having killed her son, and when she wanted to vindicate herself she said, 'I would never have killed my little boy nor my husband Jason.' And so the same *topos* (applies) also to her accusers who accuse her of the murder of her husband. The first *Art* of the rhetor Theodorus was such a species of enthymeme.

THIRTEEN.[30] Another way is taken from a paronym, metaphor, or transference of name. In praise, for example, heavenly (people) are truly 'gods' as they are called; while in blame, Thrasybulus was truly 'an oppressor' as he is named. Prodicus said to Thrasymachus the dialectician, 'Truly, Thrasymachus, you are as you are called, contentious and bold'; and (people) say that the law of Dracon is like a *dracon*, i.e. a fierce dragon. The law of Hecuba, in Euripedes the temple of Aphrodite, like Aphrodite herself is filled with gladness and merrymaking.

FOURTEEN.[31] Refutation is more successful than enthymeme because it places opposites as if before the eyes, and its beginning provides confirmation of its conclusion by proximity. For example, 'If you had done such and such, I would have done such and such.' The refuter greatly rejoices on account of the refuted when he stirs and

[29] **6.5.12** AR 2.23 00a35-b16; IS 3.7 (185.10-186.15).
[30] **6.5.13** AR 2.23 00b16-25; IS 3.7 (186.15-187.2).
[31] **6.5.14** AR 2.23 00b25-33; IS 3.7 (187.2-7).

ܦܣܘܩܐ ܫܬܝܬܐ

ܡܛܠ ܡܬܪ̈ܥܝܢܘܬܐ ܠܒ̈ܝܫܬܐ ܕܡܬܟ̈ܬܫܢ ܘܕܡܫܬ̈ܠܛܢ ܒܗܘܢܬܐ[1]

ܬܐܘܪ̈ܝܡܐ ܐܪܒܥ

ܘܕܡܝܢܬܐ. ܡܬܪ̈ܥܝܢܘܬܐ ܠܒ̈ܝܫܬܐ ܠܚܝܢ ܠܐ ܣܬܪ̈ܬܐ[1] ܦܘܐ ܪܒܝ. ܘܗܝ ܕܡܬܟܬܫܐ ܐܘ ܒܒܪܬ ܩܠܐ ܗܘܝܐ ܒܥܘܠܬ ܥܒܕܐ. ܐܘ ܒܡܫܡܥܐ ܒܗ. ܐܦܠܐ ܡܫܬܪܐ ܕܡܚܒܝܢ ܐܠܐ ܗܝ ܐܡܘܪܐ ܐܝܟ ܒܡܚܒܝܢܐ ܡܬܚܫܚ ܒܗ. ܒܥܘܠܬ ܥܒܕܐ ܡܢ ܐܡܪܐ ܕܦܫܪܘܗ ܒܗ ܠܟܠܒܐ ܡܚܠܨ ܐܡܪ. ܗܘ ܠܡܒܬܢܐ ܕܡܢ ܡܠܬ̈ܐܐ ܡܬܚܫܒ ܘܡܢ[2] ܥܪܒܐ ܕܒܗܪܐ ܥܡ̈ܝܢܐ ܢܗܪ ܟܠܒܐ ܕܓܢܒܪܐ ܡܬܟܢܫܐ. ܡܕܝܢ ܘܠܐ ܚܙ ܟܠܒܐ ܐܝܬ ܠܗ ܡܚܘܪܐ. ܒܐܡܫܡܥܐ ܕܝܢ ܐܝܟ ܕܐܡܪ ܐܘܕܘܬܡܚܘܣ ܕܦܠܛ ܠܗ ܢܒܚ ܐܬܬܐ[3] ܘܡܢܟܝܢܐ. ܡܕܝܢ ܐܦ ܐܦܘܣ ܐܘܚܕܬ ܡܐܡܪܐ ܡܫܬܚܠܦܐ ܢܒܚ ܕܐܡܪ. ܘܦܠܓ ܐܚܪܢܐ ܐܬܡܠܝ. ܘܗܘܐ ܡܢܕܥ ܐܬܦܠܓ. ܘܡܢ ܒܥܘܐ ܐܚܪܢܐ ܗܘܐ ܠܟܠܒܐ. ܘܗܝ[4] ܗܘܐ ܒܬܪ ܡܢ ܐܝܟ ܕܒܥܘܠܐ ܡܬܐܡܪ. ܒܬܪ ܕܝܢ ܐܝܟ ܕܒܥܘܠܐ. ܘܐܝܟܢܐ ܕܒܒܪ ܫܘܚܪܐ ܒܪܟܐ ܒܗ ܠܐ ܡܢܟܐ ܕܢܥܘܠ ܕܠܐ ܒܒܪܗ. ܒܫܠܝ̈ܐܬܐ ܡܦܪܫܐ ܥܒ̈ܪܘܬܗ. **ܒܪܓܘ̈ܢ ܒܚܫܐܬ ܡܥܒܕ ܕܢܟܐ ܠܥܒܕ ܐܢ̈ ܒܒܪܗ ܐܘ ܠܐ. ܒܪܐܢ̈ ܒܒܪܗ ܐܢܒܐ *ܡܚܘܫܐ ܠܗ ܥܒܪ̈ܘܬܗ.[5] ܐܘ ܐܢ̈ ܠܐ ܒܒܪܗ ܐܢܒܐ[6] ܡܚܘܫܐ[7] ܕܠܐ ܒܒܪܗ.

ܕܐܬܪ̈ܐ. ܘܒܢܒܐ ܐܚܪܢܐ ܕܢܫܒܘܬ ܐܬܐ. ܐܝܟ ܗ̇ܝ[1] ܕܠܟܠܗܘܢ ܡܕܒ̈ܪܢܐ ܦܘܢܝ̈ܢ[2] ܐܪ̈ܓܘܢܣ ܐܘܚܕܬ ܬܘܫ̈ܒܐ. ܒܗ̇ܝ ܕܐܪ̈ܘܣ ܕܐܪܓܘܪܘܣ ܘܐܪܓܘܠܛܢ ܗܫܘܗ ܗܘܐ ܠܛܪ̈ܘܢܐ ܡܦܪ̈ܢܘܣ[3] ܡܢ ܐܬܬܚܬ. ܘܐܝܟ ܗ̇ܝ ܕܕܘܒܘܣܘܣ[4] ܠܢܒܐ ܗܘ ܒܗ̇ܝ ܕܒܢܫܐ ܗܘ. ܘܡܠܝܢ ܡܢ ܙܘܒܒܐ ܐܚܘ̈ܢ ܠܒ̈ܝܫܬܐ. ܒܕܠܐ ܒܠ ܐܢܫܐ ܕܠܐܬܚܝܘܣ[5] ܦܫܛ ܠܡܕ̈ܝܢܬܐ ܒܠܗܝܢ ܦܫܛ ܐܠܐ ܒܗܦܟܐ. ܐܦܠܐ ܬܘܒ ܒܠ ܒܢܫܐ ܠܢܒܐ ܐܠܐ ܒܗܦܟܐ. ܘܢܒܐ ܡܕܡܝܢܐ ܡܢ ܒܐܡܫܡܥܐ ܬܪܝܢܐ. ܐܝܟ ܐܪܘܣ ܦܫܛ ܠܐܬܚܝܘܣ[6] *ܘܒܠ ܕܦܫܛ ܠܡܕ̈ܝܢܬܐ ܒܠܗܝܢ ܦܫܛ ܠܐܬܚܝܘܣ.[7] ܢܒܐ ܬܪܝܢܐ ܕܝܢ ܒܐܡܫܡܥܐ ܬܠܝܬܝܐ. ܐܝܟ ܕܕܘܒܘܣܘܣ[8] ܒܢܫܐ ܗܘ ܕܕܘܒܘܣܘܣ[8] ܠܢܒܐ ܗܘ. ܘܢܒܐ ܐܚܪܢܐ ܢܫܒ ܡܢ ܒܕܫܐ ܐܝܟ ܕܐܡܪ[9] ܦܠܘܛܪܓܘܣ[10] ܡܛܠ ܐܪܓܢܐ. ܕܒܪܘܢ̈ ܒܗ ܦܫܘܛ ܘܐܒܠܘ ܡܕܪ ܡܬ̈ܬܐ ܕܒܠܒܒܬܝܢ. ܘܬܘܒ ܐܢ̈ ܗ̇ܝ ܕܒܫܡܫܬܐ ܢܛܘܪܐ ܐܚܪ ܡܚܘܪܐ. ܐܒܠܘܗܝ[11] ܠܦܘܠܘܛܘܣ[12] ܒܗ̇ܝ ܕܠܐ ܐܬܡܪ ܢܓܪ ܒܠ ܒܢܬܐ. ܘܦܓܪ ܐܚܪܬܐ ܘܐܠܦ ܐܚܪܢ ܕܐܬܬܥܝܦ. ܒܪܫܬ ܕܝܢ ܗܘܐ ܒܗ̇ܝ ܕܠܐ ܐܬܡܪ.

Titulus [1] i. ܠ RVLl

1 [1] ܣܬܪ̈ܬܐ RVL [2] i. om. RVL [3] ܐܬܪ̈ܘܬܐ RVL [4] i. om. RVLl [5**] om. V [6*] om. R [7] ܠܐ ܡܚܘܫܐ RLl

2 [1] om. RVLl [2] ܦܘܢܝ̈ܢ RVLl [3] ܦܪ̈ܢܘܣ F [4] ܕܕܘܒܘܣܘܣ RVLl [5] ܕܠܐܬܚܝܘܣ RVLl [6] ܠܐܬܚܝܘܣ RVLl [7*] om. Fl [8] ܕܘܒܘܣܘܣ RVLl [9] om. F [10] ܦܠܘܛܪܓܘܣ RVL [11] ܐܒܠܘܗܝ RVLl [12] ܒܦܘܠܘܛܘܣ RVLl

agitates (him) by a syllogism, because facility in explanation gives pleasure like facility in understanding.

## SECTION SIX
## On Slanted Enthymemes Accepted or Rejected in Rhetoric
## Four Theories

ONE.[32] Our master calls 'slanted' enthymemes those which are not true. The slant either comes about verbally by homonymy, or by the form when not even (on the basis) of opinion has he who asserts it reached a (syllogistic) conclusion, but he uses it as if he had done so. For homonymy (let us take) as an example: 'Pindar said when praising the Dog (Sirius), "That blessed one, who is honoured more than many and is brighter than the rest of the heavenly luminaries, is called the dog of Orion." There is therefore not a single unhonoured dog.' For figure, for example, that Eudythemus said, 'So and so knows letters and reading, therefore he also knows how to recite *epos*, that is, verse.' Or, 'How can so and so have been made healthy? Look, he must have been ill again.' Or, 'How can good come from evil?' This is sometimes said for refutation, sometimes for demonstration. When he who has done a culpable deed is not able to show that he has not done it, by many things may his wickedness be veiled. Therefore with difficulty is a judge able to know whether he has done it or not, because if he did it, how does he demonstrate to him his misdeeds, and if he did not do it, how does he demonstrate that he did not do it?

TWO.[33] In another way (slanted enthymemes happen) by acceptance of an index. For example, '*Orutes*, that is, regulations, are expedient for all cities, because the *orus* (regulation) of Harmoris and Armogiton deposed the tyrant Hipparchus from Athens'; or, 'Dionysius is a thief because he is an evil man.' These are slanted compositions, because not everything which is expedient for Athens is expedient for all cities, although (it is true) in reverse, and neither is every evil man a thief, although (that is true)in reverse. The first way is in the Second Figure, as *eros* is expedient for Athens and whatever is ex-

[32] **6.6.1** AR 2.24 00b34-01b9; IS 3.8 (187.11-188.16).
[33] **6.6.2** AR 2.24 01b9-20; IS 3.8 (189.1-11).

ܕܬܠܬ. ܘܒܚܝܠܐ ܐܚܪܢܐ ܕܢܨܝܚܘܬ ܕܡܕܝܢܬܐ. ܐܝܟ ܐܝܠܐ ܕܐܡܪ.
ܐܠܟܣܢܕܪܘܣ[1] ܥܒܕ ܒܚܝܠܐ ܕܦܪܫܐ ܘܒܐܢܕܝܘܣ ܠܦܘܪܐ ܡܕܝܢ ܗܘܐ
ܒܥܠܝܐ ܕܢܦܫܗ. ܡܕܝܢ ܐܦ ܢܦܫܐ ܗܘܐ ܒܕ̈ܪܐ ܢܦܫܐ ܥܠܝܐ ܠܟܠܗܝܢ.
ܘܡܐܠܝܦܘܣ[2] ܒܠܠܝܐ ܦܫܐ ܗܘܐ. ܡܕܝܢ ܠܒܪܐ ܗܘ ܒܪ[3] ܠܒܪܐ ܗܘܐ ܗܒܝܢܐ
ܒܒܪ̈ܝܢ. ܘܬܘܒ ܡܫܒܚܬܐ ܕܠܐ ܡܢܝܢ ܬܐܢ̈ܐ ܒܡܬܒܠܐ ܒܒܪ̈ܝܢ ܘܐܟܠܝܢ
ܘܡܢܘܡܝܢ. ܘܠܡܪ̈ܘܡܐ ܥܠܝܟ ܗܘ ܠܡܣܒܪ ܟܠ ܐܡܬܐ ܕܢܨܒܝܢ. ܡܛܠ[4]
ܕܐܘܟܠܐ ܘܡܫܬܝܐ ܗ̇ܝ[5] ܕܐܡܬܐ[6] ܕܢܨܒܐ[7] ܢܛܪܐ ܐܝܟ ܠܡܛܪܬܐ ܐܬܝܗܘܢ.
ܡܕܝܢ ܡܫܒܚܬܐ ܘܡܪ̈ܘܡܐ ܒܠܚܘܕ. ܘܡܢ ܗܠܝܢ ܬܘܒ ܢܫܬܒܩ ܠܐ ܒܠܚܘܕ
ܐܝܟ ܒܠܚܘܕ. ܐܝܟ ܕܐܡܪ *ܕܡܬܐܡܪܝܢ ܦܘܠܝܛܝܩܐ[8] ܕܐܠܘ ܠܐ ܐܬܐ
ܠܡܕܝܢܬܐ ܕܡܬܦܬܚܝܢ.[9] ܠܐ ܠܒܪ ܠܝ ܗܠܝܢ ܒܢ̈ܬܐ. ܡܣܒܪܐ ܠܒܪ ܕܐܬܐ
ܒܪܝ ܦܪܟܐ ܘܒܦܢܝܐ ܘܡܬܢܝܬܐ.

ܕܐܡܪܢ. ܟܠܗ ܡܬܚܫܒܢܘܬܐ ܕܦܫܩܐ ܬܘܒ ܡܕܝܠܝܢ ܡܬܬܪܝܨܘܬܐ. ܐܝܟ
ܗ̇ܝ ܕܒܐܢܝܬ ܢܩܒ ܐܠܟܣܢܕܪܘܣ ܠܡܠܟܐ. ܠܘ ܕܝܢ ܦܢܛܐܣܝܐܝܬ. ܐܠܐ *ܒܗ̇ܝ
ܕܐܟܡܗ̇[1] ܡܕܡ[2] ܒܟܗ̇[3] ܠܗ. ܘܠܐ ܦܐܝܐ ܠܡܚܫܒܐ ܠܒܢ̈ܝ ܚܐܪܐ. ܒܪܡ
ܟܕ ܠܐ ܢܫܬܠܡ.[4] ܕܐܠܝܦܛܝܩܐ[5] ܠܒܪ[6] ܟܠܐ ܠܬܘܫܒܐ. ܘܗܘܦܪܒܘܠܝܩܐ[7]
ܐܘܟܝܬ ܗܘܦܪܒܘܠܐ ܡܟܠܐ ܠܗ ܘܡܫܘܚܬܐ ܕܠܐ ܬܬܦܪܫ. ܘܗܟܢܐ ܠܗ̇ ܗܘ̇
ܡܐ ܕܠܘ ܦܢܛܐܣܝܐܝܬ ܡܬܐܡܪ[8]. ܦܢܛܐܣܝܐܝܬ ܡܬܐܡܪ. ܘܒܕܐܝܟ ܗܠܝܢ
ܡܬܪܝܨܘܬܐ ܗܘܝܢ[9] ܕܠܗܘܦܪܒܘܠܐ ܡܦܩܝܢ ܪ̈ܗܛܘܪܝܢ ܘܐܡܪܝܢ ܕܠܐ ܡܦܩܝܢ
ܠܒ̈ܝܬܐ. ܐܝܟ ܗ̇ܘ ܕܐܡܪܝܢ.[10] ܐܢܫܘ ܕܪܗܛܘܪܐ ܒܪ ܡܫܡܠ ܠܐ ܡܬܚܫܒܐ.
ܒܪ ܡܬܚܫܒ ܬܘܒ ܠܗ ܦܠܐ ܕܬܬܚܫܒ. ܒܕܠܐ ܒܪ ܫܠܝܡ ܐܫܟܚ. ܕܓܠܝܬܐ[11]
ܠܒܪ ܗܕܐ ܘܠܐ ܡܫܬܡܥܝܢ. ܘܒܠܗܕܐ ܒܐܢܝܬ ܡܬܚܫܒܝܢ ܗܘܘ ܡܕܡ̈ܝܢܐ
ܒܐܘܡܢܘܬ ܦܘܪܐܘܣ[12] ܘܡܘܣܦܐܝܠܛܐ[13] ܐܘܡܢܘܬ ܪ̈ܘܡܝܐ ܫܦܝܪܐ
ܕܦܪܘܛܓܘܪܘܣ.

3 [1] i. add. ܕ RVL [2] ܢܝܠܘܦܘܣ RVL [3] ܒܪ RVLl [4] i. add. ܘ RVLl [5] ܗ̇ܝ ,ܗܝ RVLl [6] ܕܐܡܬܐ RVLl [7] ܕܢܨܒܐ RLl; ܢܨܒܐ V [8*] ܕܡܬܐ ܕܡܫܬܘܕܥܐ RVL [9] ܕܡܬܦܬܚܝܢ RVLl

4 [1*] trp. RVLl [2] i. add. ܕ RVLl [3] ܒܟܗ̇ RV [4] ܢܫܬܠܡ RVLl [5] ܕܐܠܝܦܛܝܩܐ RVLl [6] om. RVLl [7] ܘܗܘܦܪܒܘܠܝܩܐ RVLl [8] ܡܬܐܡܪ F [9] add. ܐܝܠܝܢ RVLl [10] ܕܐܡܪܝܢ RVL; ܕܐܡܪ l [11] add. ܗܝ RVLl [12] scripsi; ܦܘܠ ܐܢܫ F; ܦܘܠܐܢܫ RVLl [13] ܘܡܘܦܐܝܠܛܐ RVLl

pedient for all cities is expedient for Athens; the second way is in the Third Figure, as Dionysius is an evil man (and) Dionysius is a thief. Another way is derived from accident, as Polycrates said about mice, 'They assisted when they cut and consumed the bowstrings of our enemies.' Or, 'If someone being invited to dinner is (thereby) honoured, at Tenedos Achilles was angry with the Greeks because he was not invited.' He nursed (his) anger as one who had been insulted, but this happened by accident because he was not invited.

THREE.[34] (There are slanted enthymemes) in another way by the acceptance of resemblances, like saying: Alexander abandoned the company of the many and dwelt by himself in solitude on Mount Ida; therefore he was high-minded, because the high-minded choose solitude. Or Callipus wanders about at night; therefore he is an adulterer, because adulterers act like this. Or again, poor people who do not have houses live in temples and eat and dance, and fugitives are allowed to live anywhere they wish. Because eating and drinking and living where one wishes are for the rich, therefore poor people and fugitives are rich. Among these (slanted enthymemes) is also the acceptance of a non-cause as a cause. For example, Demades the politician (?) said, 'If Demosthenes had not come to our city, these evils would not have happened to us, for as soon as he came, war occurred, and famine and plague.'

FOUR.[35] Enthymemes are also slanted by non-limitation of a precept. For example, 'Justly did Alexander take Helen'—not generally, however, but because his father had previously chosen her for him. Or, 'It is not right to beat free men'—but (only) when they are not offensive. For dialectic reveals the limitation, but an eristic (disputant), that is, a sophist, reveals or conceals it so that it is not detected. Similarly when (someone) is not being accused generally, (a sophist may insinuate that) he is being accused generally. With such enthymemes, those which persuade the populace are rhetorical, and those which do not persuade (it) are slanted. For example, (take) the saying, 'If when a sick man is offensive he should not be beaten, neither should he be beaten when he is cured, because he was not offensive when he was healthy.' This is a lie and is not persuasive,

[34] **6.6.3** AR 2.24 01b20-34; IS 3.8 (189.11-190.5).
[35] **6.6.4** AR 2.24 01b34-02a8;17-29; IS 3.8 (190.5-191.1).

ܦܘܫܩܐ ܕܡܐܡܪܐ
ܡܛܠ ܗܝܡܢܘܬܐ
ܬܐܘܪ̈ܝܐܣ ܬܠܬ

ܡܕܡܝܢܬܐ. ܒܪܢܫܐ ܕܝܢ ܘܫܘܬܦܘܬܐ ܕܡ̈ܠܐ ܐܘ ܒܫܡܗܐ ܕܡܚܝܢ ܐܝܦܣܛܣܝܣ ܕܒܘܚܢܗ ܕܒܟܠܕܝܐ ܗ̄ܘܐ. ܐܘ ܒܗܝܡܢܘܬܐ ܐܘܟܝܬ ܫܘܬܦܘܬ ܦܘܠܡܐ ܘܒܦܘܪܣܐ ܕܦܪܘܣܘܦܘܢ[1] ܕܗܟܝܢ. ܘܐܢܐ ܕܝܢ ܡܕܡܝܢܐ ܠܐܕ̈ܕܐ ܗܠܝܢ ܕܗܟܢܝܐ[2] ܕܠܬܪ̈ܝܗܘܢ ܐܝܦܘܩܪܝܣܝܐ ܠܚܕܐ ܗ̄ܘܐ. ܐܕܫܐ ܕܝܢ ܬܪܝܢܐ ܒܗܠܝܢ ܕܗܫܐ ܡܫܡܠܝܢ. ܘܗܝ ܗܝܡܢܘܬܐ ܐܪܬܘܕܘܟܣܝܬܐ ܡܫܬܘܕܥܐ ܠܕܐܠܝܦܠܝܘܢܐ[3] ܒܗ̇، ܕܐܦ ܗ̣ܝ ܙܒܢܐܝܬ ܗܘܬ. ܡܛܠ ܕܐܢܫܐ ܕܩܕܡ ܐܘ ܠܗ̇ ܠܦܪܘܣܘܦܘܢ[4] ܡܕܡܝܢ. ܐܘ ܒܕܡܝܢܗ ܗ̇ܘ ܡܢܐ ܕܫܘܡܠܝ ܠܦܘܫܩܗ ܡܬܝܪ. ܐܝܟܢܐ ܕܒܗ ܢܐܡܪ ܐܚܕ ܐܡܝܢܐܝܬ ܐܢܫܐ ܕܒܪ ܒܪ ܫܡܠ ܗܢܐ. ܢܐܡܪ ܫܬܘܪܐ ܐܦ[5] ܡܢ̈ܝܢܐ ܡܢ ܐܝܠܝܢ ܕܒܪ ܒܪ ܫܡܠܝ ܙܒܢܝܢ. ܐܘ ܒܫܘܡܠܝܗ[6] ܗ̇ܘ ܡܢܐ ܕܕܝܢܐ ܠܗ ܡܣܘܝܐ. ܐܝܟܢܐ ܕܒܗ ܢܐܡܪ ܐܚܕ ܒܪܢܫܐ ܠܒܪܐ ܠܙܒܢܘܗܝ، ܡܛܠܐ ܕ. ܢܐܡܪ ܫܬܘܪܐ ܐܦ ܒܢ̈ܝܐ ܒܫܢ̈ܝܐ ܠܙܒܢܘܗܝ ܥܠܡܐ ܒܙܒܢܝ. ܐܘ ܡܕܡ[7] ܡܢ ܡ̈ܠܐ ܘܡܠ̈ܟܐ ܢܡܘܣ̈ܝܐ[8] ܡܫܬܐ. ܐܝܟܢܐ ܕܒܗ ܢܐܡܪ ܐܚܕ ܠܙܘܥܐ ܕܡܬܒܥܐ ܠܗ ܦܠܓܐ ܠܡܒܪܕܐ[9] ܒܗ ܒܠܐ ܢܕܒܘܬܐ ܡܢܝܫܐ. ܢܐܡܪ ܫܬܘܪܐ ܦܝܠܐܣܘܦܘܣ[10] ܕܢܫܐ ܠܒܪܗ ܗ̇ܘ ܕܙܘܪ ܘܐܫܒܠ ܒܪ̈ܐ.[11]

ܕܬܪ̈ܬܝܢ. ܐܦ ܓܒܪ ܘܡܬܬܪ̈ܝܨܘܬܐ ܙܒܢܐܝܬ ܗܘܬܝܢ. ܡܢ ܕܩ̈ܢܘܡܐ ܕܐܬܝܠܕܗܝܢ ܙ̈ܒܢܐ ܡܫܬ̈ܚܠܦܐ. ܘܡܢ ܡܫܘ̈ܚܠܦܘܬܐ ܗ̇ܝ ܕܡܬܝܠܕܢ ܠܘܬ ܦܘܫܩܐ ܒܠܒܝܐ ܡܫܒܚܐ ܐܚܕ. ܒܗ ܡܢܗ ܡܬܬܪ̈ܝܨܘܬܐ ܡ̈ܢܐ.. *ܘܡܢ ܫܘܬܐܡܐ ܒܐܣܟܡܐ ܡܕܡܝܢܐ.[1] ܘܡܢ ܙܘܫܡܐ ܘܐܬܬܐ ܒܠܒܐܝܬ ܕܝܢ ܒܐܣܟܡܐ ܬܪ̈ܝܢܐ. ܡܬܐܡܬ ܕܝܢ ܒܐܣܟܡܐ ܬܠܝܬܝܐ. ܒܫܘܡܡܘܬܐ ܘܡܪܒܥܘܬܐ. ܘܠܐ ܢܫܒܪ ܐܚܕ ܕܙܘܝܬܐ ܒܐܣܟܡܐ ܡܫܪ. *ܒܕ ܗ̇ܘ ܕܐܝܟ ܕܒܫܘܡܠܝܐ ܡܫܪ[2] ܙܘܝܬܐ ܗܘ ܗܘܪܐ. ܘܡܬܩܠܠܐ ܡܪܒܥ ܡܢ ܬ̈ܪܝܢܐ ܒܪܬܐ ܕܦܪܘܣܘܦܘܢ ܒܠܝܫܕ[3] ܡܬܕܠܡܒ ܒܠܒܕ ܡܫܠܝܡܘܬ ܐܣܟܡܐ. ܘܗܝ ܦܪܘܣܘܦܘܢ ܡܬܬܪܝܐ ܒܕ ܠܘ ܒܐܡܝܢܘ ܡܫܪܐ ܘܒܕ ܠܐ ܐܠܝܨܐ ܘܐܦ ܙܘܝܐ ܘܒܕ ܦܫܝܛܐܝܬ ܘܠܘ ܡܬܬܡܝܢܐܝܬ ܦܘܠܘܓܝܬܐ ܗܘܬ[4] ܡܢ ܢܡܘܣܐ. ܒܕܝܠܗ̇ *ܡܢ ܕܒܬܪ̈ܝܨܘܬܐ[5] ܫܦܝܪܬܐ ܡܬܬܪܝܨܐ ܘܒܪܒܝܐ ܡܕܡ ܐܘ ܡܘܒܪܐ ܬܪܝܨܬܐ ܡܬܬܪܝܨܐ ܡܬܕܠܠܐ. ܠܢܦܫܗ[6] ܕܒܠܒܝܐ ܫܬܪܐ ܘܡܬܕܠܠܐ.

1 [1] pl. RVLl [2] i. om. RVLl [3] ܠܕܐܠܝܦܠܝܘܢܐ F [4] pl. RV [5] ܐܦ RVLl [6] scripsi; ܒܫܘܡܠܝܗ̇ F; ܒܫܘܡܠܝܗ RVLl [7] om. RVL [8] ܢܡܘܣ̈ܝܬܐ RVL [9] ܠܡܒܪܕܐ (?) F [10] ܦܝܠܘܣܘܦܘܣ RVL; ܦܝܠܐܣܘܦܘܣ l [11] ܙܒܢ F
2 [1*] om. R [2*] om. RVL [3] om. RVLl [4] ܗܘ RVLl [5*] om. RVL [6] ܠܢܦܫܗ F

and therefore justly were the ancients indignant at the *Art* of Corax and at the announcement, that is, the false compositions, of Protagoras.

## SECTION SEVEN
## On *Enstasis*
## Three Theories

ONE.[36] The dissolution and destruction of statements occurs either by an argument which produces a conclusion opposite to that of an adversary, or by *enstasis*, that is, objection and rejection of a premiss of his argument. The first way happens with those types based on opinion which suit two opposites, while the second type (happens) through what we will now present. Rhetorical *enstasis* is associated with the dialectical (variety) because it too comes about in four ways, since he who destroys (a statement) either (1) opposes the premiss itself; or (2) with one which is similar to it establishes what is contrary to its consequence—for example, when someone says, 'Truly he who suffers nothing but evil hates,' the destroyer may say, 'Yet many of those who suffer nothing but evil love'; or (3) with one which is contrary to it demonstrates (a consequence) which is similar to it—for example, when someone says, 'A good man does good to his friends,' the destroyer may say, 'Excited evil men also do well to their friends'; or (4) adduces something from legal statements or actions—for example, when someone says, 'It is not right to chastise an abusive drunkard, because he reviles (people) in ignorance,' the destroyer may say, 'Pittacus the judge beat his son who was drunk and offensive.'

TWO.[37] Enthymemes too arise in four ways: from obligatories, which are reputable thoughts; from the paradigms from which one moves to a general precept and so makes from it an enthymeme; from a sign in the First Figure; and from an indication or index, generally in the Second Figure but partly in the Third Figure, in affirmation or negation. No-one supposes that the obligatory is always true, because here the obligatory is that which for the most part is

[36] **6.7.1** AR 2.25 02a30-37; b4-12; IS 3.8 (191.2-16).
[37] **6.7.2** AR 2.25 02b12-03a2; IS 3.8 (191.17-192.17).

ܕܬܬܠ. ܪ̈ܘܫܡܐ ܕܝܢ ܒܬܪܝܢ ܐܢ̈ܫܝ ܡܬܬܠܡܕܝܢ. ܚܕ ܕܝܢ ܒܪ ܗܘ ܡܬܐܡܪܐ ܠܐ ܡܬܦܠܓܢܐ ܗܘܐ. ܐܝܟܢܐ ܕܐܦ ܒܪ ܗܘ ܦܪܨܘܦܐ ܠܐ ܫܪܝܪܬܐ ܗܘܬ. ܘܡܬܠܡܕܢܘܬܗ ܕܦܪܨܘܦܐ ܕܝܢ[1] ܠܒ ܚܠܠܐ. ܒܕܐܝܟ ܕܒܫܘܠܡܐ ܡܬܬܘܕܝܢܝܬܐ ܗܘܐ ܒܪܘܚܢܝܬܐ. ܘܬܫܡ̈ܫܬܐ ܒܬܫܡ̈ܫܬܐ ܕܐܠܗܘܬ ܡܬܬܠܡܕܝܢ. ܘܐܦ ܠܐ ܡܬܟܦܠܐ ܬܫܡܫܬܐ ܒܬܫܡܫܬܐ ܕܠܐ ܐܠܗܝܐ ܘܐܦ ܫܟܝܢܐ. ܐܘ ܕܠܝܬܝܢܐ ܕܝܗܒ ܠܐ ܕܒܝܢܐ ܦܠܐ ܠܡܐܡܪ[2]. ܘܫܘܕ̈ܥܐ ܒܡܫܡܫܢܘܬ[3] ܪܘܚܢܐ ܠܐ ܡܬܬܝܢ ܒܕܡܝܢ ܐܫܡܥܐ ܐܝܟ ܡܕܡܐ. ܒܕܡܝܢ ܐܝܟ ܡܫܪܝܢ ܦܪܨܘܦܐ ܕܠܗܘܢ. ܠܐ ܡܬܟܦܠܝܢ ܐܠܐ ܠܡܥܠܡ ܐܝܟ ܐܠܗܐ. ܘܪܘܪܒܐ ܘܡܕܒܪܢܐ ܠܗ ܡܢ ܐܣܛܘ̈ܟܣܐ ܡܬܚܘܝܢܘܬܐ[4] ܡܫܪܪܝܢܬ[5] ܐܕ̈ܫܐ ܪܗܛܪ̈ܝܐ ܐܝܟ ܐܠܐ* ܡܢ[6] ܢܦ̈ܫܐ. ܒܦܠܠܗܘܢ ܐܝܟ ܠܗ[7] ܐܣܛܘܟܣܝܢܐ ܗܘ. ܘܥܠ ܫܘܪܝܐ ܐܘ ܕܠܡܥܠܐ ܕܪܝܫܐ ܕܡܠܟܘܬܗ ܡܪܝܪ ܐܘ ܗܘܦܘܣܛܣܝܣ[8] ܡܢܝܢ. ܘܗܝ ܗܘܦܘܣܛܣܝܣ ܠܗ ܡܬܚܘܝܢܘܬܐ ܗܝ ܒܡܕܡܠܠ ܐܚܪܢܘܗ[9] ܕܡܠܟܘܬܐ ܠܐ ܦܩܚ ܕܢܪܪ ܐܚܪܢ ܫܘܪܝܐ. ܐܠܐ[10] ܫܦܝܪ ܗܘ ܕܢܣܒܐ ܪܘܚܗ ܒܫܡܝܐ.

3 [1] om. RVL [2] add. ... ܐܘ? [3] ܒܡܫܡܫܢܘܬ RVLl [4] pl. RVLl [5] ܡܫܪ̈ܝܢܬܐ RVL; ܡܫܪ̈ܝܢܬܐ et trp. post ܐܕ̈ܫܐ l [6*] ܡܢ RVL; ܘܡܢ l [7] om. RVL [8] ܗܘܦܘܣܛܣܝܣ RL [9] f. ܐ RVL [10] ܠܐ RVLl

true, and discourse composed of (such) conceptions may only be opposed by dissolution of the premisses, without rejection of the Figure. The premiss may be dissolved when it is not always true, when it is not necessary even if it is obligatory, and when generally, and not (merely in some) particular, it has been falsely inferred (?) from a law. Therefore when it is judged by fine understanding and specified of some time or particular fact, (that) will destroy and make void the aim of an adversary.

THREE.[38] Indications may be opposed in two ways: one when the statement does not yield a conclusion, the other when the premiss is not true. Contradicting a premiss is very hard, because in rhetoric it is usually accepted. Paradigms may be opposed in an 'obligatory' way by paradigms; and if a paradigm is not made void by (another) paradigm which (shows that the first one) is not necessary, even if frequent, it is necessary to say either that it is not similar to the present point (or ...). Signs may not be dissolved by faulting the composition, because they are from the First Figure. Therefore if their premisses are true, they cannot be made void but must be accepted. Amplification and diminution are not among the elements of an enthymeme establishing the rhetorical species, but among the addenda; therefore their annulling is not elemental. Every destroyer either establishes the contrary of the thought of his adversary, or brings an *enstasis*, and an *enstasis* too is not an enthymeme, because annulling an adversary's thought is not sufficient to establish the thought of the destroyer. On the contrary, it is inadequate to demonstrate the truth of his argument.

---

[38] **6.7.3** AR 2.25 03a2 - 26 03a33; IS 3.8 (192.18-193.16).

### ܩܦܠܐܘܢ ܫܒܝܥܝܐ

### ܡܛܠ ܒܢ̈ܬ ܩܠܐ ܪܗܛ̈ܘܪܝܬܐ ܘܡܛܟܣ̈ܬܗܝܢ[1]

### ܘܒܗ ܐܝܬ ܦܣܘ̈ܩܐ ܥܣܪܐ

### ܦܣܘܩܐ ܩܕܡܝܐ

### ܡܛܠ ܡܫܡܫ ܒܡ̈ܦܩܐ

### ܬܐܘܪ̈ܝܐ ܐܪܒܥ

ܩܕܡܝܬܐ. ܡܛܠ ܕܐܬܠܝ ܐܝܟ ܗܠܝܢ ܕܦܪ̈ܓܡܛܝܘܬܐ[1] ܩ̇ܠܐ ܠܡܡܠܠܐ. ܗܪܟܐ. ܚܫ̈ܚܘܬܐ. ܒܢ̈ܬ ܩܠܐ. ܡܛܟܣ̈ܘܬܐ. ܒܗ ܠܚܫ̈ܚܘܬܐ ܡܢ ܒܕܘ ܡܢܝܢ. ܠܬܪ̈ܬܝܗܝܢ ܐܫܝ̈ܢܬܐ ܫܪܒܐ ܠܡܡܠܠ. ܘܐܝܬ ܗܪܟܐ ܕܠܐ ܐܫܝܢܐ ܠܒܪ ܡܢ ܩܠܐ ܘܩܘܒܠܗ̇. ܟܝܬ، ܕܝܢ ܠܐܝܢܘܬܗ ܕܐܡܘܪܐ ܘܕܡܘܬܗ. ܗ̇، ܕܒܝܠܐ ܪܒܐ ܫܘܚܠܦܐ ܕܢܝܫܐ ܡܩܒܠܢܐ. ܘܠܫܘܡܠܝܐ ܠܘܬ ܗ̇، ܕܢܒܥܐ. ܐܘ ܚܝܐ ܡܟܠܕܐ. ܘܗܘ ܗܢܐ ܕܐ ܡܫܡܫ ܒܡ̈ܦܩܐ ܡܫܬܡܗ. ܘܐܟܒܪܐ ܕܠܦܐܝܛܝܩܐ[2] ܒܗ ܒܢܝܐ ܘܠܪܐܛܘܪܝܩܐ ܠܣܡ. ܒܗ̇، ܕܡܬܓܠܝܢܘܬܐ ܛܒ ܡܦܝܣܢܐ ܘܠܘܬ ܗܡܟܝܢܘܬܐ ܢܓܕܐ. ܡܠܝܫܛܐ ܒܫܘܠܦ ܢܟ̈ܡܬܗ ܕܐܡܘܪܐ. ܒܐܘܒܕܢܐ ܘܐܪܝܐ.[3] ܒܐܡܪܬ ܢܦܪܘܬ ܩܠܐ ܘܫܪܝܦܘܬܗ. ܘܡܬܡܟܢܘܬ ܙܬܡܬܐ. ܒܗ ܡܢ ܚܡܬܐ ܢܡܟܬܐ ܡܕܡ ܙܠܝܠܐ ܡܬܬܡܪܐ. ܘܡܢ ܕܠܬܐ ܢܡܟܬܐ ܡܬܡܟܟܬܐ. ܘܡܢ ܚ̈ܝܠܐ ܐܫܝ̈ܢܐ ܢܡܟ̈ܬܐ ܐܫܝܢܘܬܐ. ܘܒܕܐܝܟ ܗܠܝܢ ܡܬܚܫܚ ܪܗܛܘܪ. ܐܟܢܐ ܕܠܗ ܠܝܢܐ ܡܫܝܢܐ ܘܢܒܥܐ. ܐܘ ܢܚܝܐ ܘܡܬܢܚܐ. ܐܘ ܪܓܝܓܐ ܘܣܢܝܩܐ ܬܐܪܡܐ[4] ܫܡܥܘܢܐ.

ܕܬܬܒܝܢ. ܐܬܠܩܫܐ ܕܪ̈ܗܛܘܪܐ ܠܐܡܫܝܫ ܗܕܐ ܕܡܫܡܫ ܒܡ̈ܦܩܐ ܡܢ ܦܘ̈ܝܛܐ ܢܫ̈ܐ[1] ܒܡ̈ܦܩܐ ܘܡܢ ܕܡ̈ܛܘܬܐ ܕܡܕܒܪܢܐ ܦܘܠܝܛܝܩܐ ܡܬܬܓܪܝܢ. ܘܟܠ ܫܪܒܐ ܕܒܗܘ̈ܢ ܗ̇ܘܐ ܡܫܡܫ ܒܡ̈ܦܩܐ. ܒܕܡܘܬܐ ܠܒܢ ܪܟܢ ܠܐ ܐܚܕ ܡܠܠ. ܘܗܘ̈ܝܢ ܗܠܝܢ. ܐܦ ܒܟܝܢ ܡܬܝܚܕܘܬܐ ܠܐ ܒܐܠܝܢ. ܐܠܐ ܛܒ̈ܢܐ[2] ܐܝܟ̈ܢ ܗܘ̈ܝܢ̈ܐ، ܢܘܬ̈ܪܐ. ܒܢܩ̈ܠܘܬܐ ܓܢܒ ܚܬ̈ܝܬܐ ܠ ܒܢ̈ܬ ܩܠܐ ܡܥܕܒܢܝܬ[3] ܗܘܟܠܐ ܫܠܡܐ ܗܡܟܝܢܘܬܐ ܡܫܝܢܐ.[4] ܘܒܪܐܝܛܘܩܐ ܦܢܣܐ. ܘܒܦܐܝܛܝܩܐ ܡܡܓܠܝܢܘܬܐ. ܒܫܘܠܦܬ ܡܡܠܠܐ ܘܡܫܬܚܠܦܘܬܗ ܢܬܪܘܬܐ ܘܡܬܝܪܘܬܐ ܚ̈ܝܐ.[5] ܘܠܗܕܢܐ ܠܐܟܡܦܝܪܐ ܒܡ ܫܪܒܐ ܕܗܪ̈ܐ، ܢܕ̈ܟܬܐ ܡܬܚܫ̈ܬܐ ܕܝܩܘܒ ܡܡܠܠܐ ܠܗ ܢܦܩܝܢ. ܫܪ، ܕܝܢ ܕܒܗܠܝܢ ܥܠܠ ܒܠ ܡܫܡܫ

---

Titulus [1] sg. RVLl

1 [1] ܕܦܪ̈ܓܡܛܝܘܬܐ RVLl [2] ܕܠܦܐܝܛܝܩܐ RVLl [3] ܘܐܪܝܐ R [4] ܬܐܪܡܐ RVLl

2 [1] ܢܫ̈ܐ RVLl [2] sg. RVL; ܛܒ̈ܢܐ l [3] ܡܥܕܒܢܝܬ RVL [4] ܡܫܝܢܐ RVL [5] ܚܝܐ R

## CHAPTER SEVEN
## ON RHETORICAL WORDS AND THEIR ARRANGEMENTS
## TEN SECTIONS

### SECTION ONE
### On Delivery
### Four Theories

ONE.[1] Because the things which the treatise must deal with here are three—*pisteis*, words, arrangements—as we have already treated *pisteis*, it remains to treat the other two. Apart from an utterance and its meaning, there is another way here, particular to the manner and bearing of the speaker, which evokes images of various meanings with great power and prepares the hearer to act or be affected. This way is called delivery, and just as it is suitable for poetry (to use) this way, so also for rhetoric, because image-evocation is very persuasive and induces *pistis*. Especially (is this achieved) by the various tones of the speaker, with *oxeia* or *areia*, i.e. heavy or sharp voice, or with intermediate whisper, because out of anger some fearful tone is let loose, out of fear a humble tone, and out of other emotions other tones. A rhetor may employ such things, so that the listener may yield to a hard and indignant, or gentle and meek, or desiring and sighing manner.

TWO.[2] The champions of the rhetors acquire this style of delivery from declaiming poets and from the bearings of political leaders. Concerning the matters by which delivery comes about, no one had spoken until the time of our master, yet these things, although they do not enter into the nature of an enthymeme, are very advantageous arts. For in true sciences every word indicative of a complete meaning bestows *pistis*, but in rhetoric persuasion, and in poetry image-evocation, may be subject to exaggeration or diminution by polishing or shrivelling the speech. Therefore a geometer and other

[1] **7.1.1** AR 3.1 03b6-32 (cf. 04a10-12; 17-19); IS 4.1 (197.3-198.4).
[2] **7.1.2** AR 3.1 03b32-04a18; IS 4.1 (199.2-200.12).

ܒܐܘܪܚܐ ܕܟܠܠ ܬܐܘܣܒܝܘܣ ܪܘܡܝܐ ܕܠܝܘܦܠܝܡܘܣ.[6] ܘܡܫܡܫ ܒܐܘܪܚܐ ܡܢ
ܠܥܕܬܐ ܒܝܬܝܐ ܢܦܩ. ܠܒܪܝܐ ܕܝܢ ܒܬܪ ܩܠܝܠ[7] ܠܐܘܪܫܠܡ.[8] ܒܕܝܠܗ ܢܫܡ
ܒܐܘܪܚܐ ܡܫܡܫ ܟܠ ܗܘ ܡܢܐ ܕܢܣܒܐ ܠܗ ܡܫܡܫܢܐ. *ܘܟܕ ܕܒܪܐ[9] ܠܡܫܡܫ
ܡܡܠܠܗ ܗܘܐ ܡܢ ܐܢܫܐ ܕܠܐ ܡܪܐ ܐܝܟ ܐܝܟܢܐ ܥܒܕܐ.

ܕܬܠܬ. ܐܟ̈ܪܙܬܐ ܪܘܚܢܝܬܐ ܕܡܬܚܬܝܢ ܫܠܝܚܐܝܬ ܡܬܒ̈ܥܢ. ܒܬܪ ܠܐ
ܒܡܫܡܫ ܒܐܘܪܚܐ. ܐܠܐ ܒܝܬܝܐ ܠܡܣܩܢܝܐ. ܡܫܡܫ ܒܐܘܪܚܐ ܗܘܐ ܠܐ
ܡܬܒܠܒܠ.[1] ܘܐܝܬ[2] ܘܒܬܪܐ[3] ܕܗܫܐ ܥܒܕ ܗܘܒܠܐ ܘܒܬܪ ܗܠܝܢ ܗܕܝܪܬܐ
ܡܚܠܝܐ ܣܦܝܪܘܬܗ.[4] ܘܐܦ ܡܫܡܫ ܒܐܘܪܚܐ ܠܗ ܡܫܡܫ ܠܗ. ܐܬܗܕܝܘ ܕܝܢ
ܥܘܬܪܝ[5] ܦܘܐܪܐ ܠܡܬܥܣܩܘ ܒܥܕܬܐ ܠܗ ܐܘܦܠܘܩܝܐ. ܒܕ ܒܢܝܫܘܢ
ܠܗ[6] ܥܠ ܫܬܐܣܬܐ ܫܪܝܪܬܐ ܗܝܡ. ܐܠܐ ܥܠ ܗܝܟܠܐ ܒܠܝܫܘܕ.. ܒܕܒܪܗ
ܠܡܫܡܫܘ ܦܬܠܐ ܚܝܦܘ[7] ܘܠܡܫܬܚܬܐ ܒܒܠ ܡܕܝ̈ܢ ܘܒܒܠ ܕܡܕ̈ܝ ܕܒܢܝܐ
ܦܬܟܪܐ ܕܒܢܝܐ. ܘܡܢ ܗܪܟܐ ܐܘܡܢܘܬܐ ܕܦܠܘܪܣܬܐ ܕܦܘܣܕܘܢܝܐ[8]
ܘܐܘܦܘܪܛܝܩܐ[9] ܐܘܡܢܬ ܕܕܘܒܪܐ[10] ܡܕܝ̈ܢܝܐ ܘܡܬܒܩܠܝܬ[11] ܬܘܒܢܐ
ܐܬܦܢܝܬ.[12] ܘܒܠܗܕܐ ܦܘܐܬܐ ܒܕ ܡܫܡܫ ܠܡܫܡܫܘ ܒܒܪܬ ܩܠܐ
ܦܫܝܛܬܐ ܒܠܒܕ ܪܒܝܐ ܡܣܬܝܢܐ. ܐܝܟ ܠܒܪܢܫܐ. ܥܡܣܢܐ ܫܬܪܐ ܦܢܐ
ܘܡܬܬܒܡܗ.

ܕܐܪܒܥ. ܥܡܣܒܬ ܒܬܪ ܩܠܐ ܘܦܫܝܛܘܬܗ ܠܗ ܠܒܠ ܡܡܠܠܐ ܦܘܐܪܐܝܬܐ
ܦܐܝܐ. ܐܠܐ ܠܗܠܝܢ ܩ̈ܠܠܐ ܘܚܒܪܐ ܕܡܘܒ̈ܠܐ ܡܬܡܫܟܢܐ ܕܦܪܘܫܘܬܐ ܡܢܗ.
ܐܝܟ ܗܘܝܢ ܙ̈ܒܢܝܢ ܡܒ̈ܥܝܢܬܐ ܘܥܬܬܝܬܗܝܢ. ܘܒܠܗܕܐ ܒܕ ܫܬܪ
ܐܪܒܬܐ ܒܒܕܝܢ ܠܡܥܣܩܘܬܐ. ܐܚܒܪܐ ܕܒܦܪܐܟܣܘܕܘܣ[1] ܠܒܬܪ ܩܠܐ ܫܬܪ
ܡܗܕܝܢ. ܠܐ ܕܝܢ ܩܠܐ ܠܗܦܪܐ ܕܢܒܪܐ ܒܦܘܐܪܐ ܚܝܘܒܬ ܡܡܠܠܐ.
ܐܚܒܪܐ[2] ܘܗܐ ܐܦܠܐ ܦܘܐܪܐ ܒܐܡܝܢܘ ܡܬܥܣܩܝܢ ܒܗ. ܠܐ[3] ܪܕܡ
ܕܒܕܘܟ ܕܘܟ. ܐܠܐ ܒܒܠ ܕܘܟ ܫܬܐܬܬ ܡܠܬܐ ܢܒܒܕ ܘܡܡܠܠܝܢܬ
ܗܘܒܠܐ ܘܦܫܝܛܘܬܗ ܠܒܬܪ ܩܠܐ ܢܦܩܡ. ܘܒܕ ܡܡܠܠܐ ܪܘܥܡܐ ܡܕܡ
ܠܡܘܥ ܗܘܒܠܐ ܐܬܬܘܗܝ. ܐܢ ܠܐ ܡܥܘܕܒ ܠܗ ܡܘܬܪ. ܘܐܢ ܡܥܘܕܒ
ܘܠܐ ܡܬܗܠܟ ܒܝܪ ܡܘܬܪ. ܒܕܒܪܗ ܐܠܝܟܐ *ܕܡܥܘܕܒܢܐ ܘܡܬܗܠܟܢܐ[4]
ܐܚܝܕܐ ܢܗܘܐ. ܘܠܐ ܒܗܝܢܪܐ[5] ܐܦܠܐ ܗܠܟ ܗܕܝܪܐ. ܐܦ ܠܒܪ
ܘܦܐܪܘܩܝܬܐ ܕܡܡܠܠܐ ܒܒܢܝܐ. ܒܬܪ ܥܡܪܝ[6] ܡܣܬܘܕܐ ܒܡܒܕ̈ܐ
ܘܡܐܡܪܐ ܦܪ̈ܝܫܐ ܡܢ̈ܬܝܐ ܒܥܣܡܘܬܐ ܘܐܡܣܘܡܐ.[7] ܠܐ ܗܕܝ̈ܪܬܐ
ܐܦܠܐ ܡܠܦ̈ܢܝܐ ܥܠ̈ܠܐ ܗܘܒܠܐ ܡܬܥܣܩܐ.

[6] ܕܠܝܘܦܠܝܦܠܝܡܘܣ RVL [7] ܗܝ RVL [8] sg. F [9*] ܟܕ ܕܒܪܟܐ RVLl

3 [1] f. add. ܐ RVLl [2] i. ܕ RVLl [3] ܘܚܠܐ RVLl [4] f. ܗ RVLl [5] ܥܘܬܪܐ RVL [6] om., et ins. ܠܐ ante ܗܝܡ F [7] ܚܝܦܘ RVL [8] scripsi; ܕܦܘܣܕܘܢܝܐ codd. [9] ܘܐܘܦܘܪܛܝܩܐ RVL; ܘܐܘܦܘܪ̈ܛܝܩܐ l [10] i. om. RVLl [11] sg. RVLl [12] ܐܬܦܢܝ RVLl [13] ܘܡܬܬܒܡܗ RVLl

4 [1] ܕܒܦܪܐܟܣܘܕܘܣ RVLl [2] i. add. ܘ RVLl [3] ܐܠܐ RVLl [4*] trp. RVL [5] ܒܗܝܢܪܐ RVL; ܒܗܝܢܪ l [6] ܥܡܪܝܐ RVLl [7] ܐܡܣܘܡܐ F

masters of proper sciences are not concerned about the ornamentation of speech, but the dialectical rhetor Thrasymachus made a start in briefly speaking about delivery. Delivery depends on natural things, but verbal art on artistic. Therefore one (capable of) declaiming may scorn that which an ordinary (man) will not scorn, and he who is able to polish his speech desires a contest with words more than him who is not able (to do so).

THREE.[3] Rhetorical letters which are written have a powerful effect, not by delivery, however, but by stylistic methods. For delivery is not written, and sometimes the thought is very ordinary, but an adorned word may compensate for its deficiency even though delivery does not assist the (word). The poets were first led to use non-primary things, because their edifice is based not on a true foundation, but solely on image-evocation. They therefore took care to beautify words and imitated the manifold and various tones of diverse modes. Hence the rhetorical arts of rhapsody, *hypocrity*—that is, (the art) of civic government—and the arrangements of narratives were established. Therefore when a poet is able to evoke an image by a simple word without musical inflection, like Gorgias, he gains special glory and is admired.

FOUR.[4] Verbal plainness and simplicity is not appropriate for all poetic discourse, but for those light and short ones which have thoughts miming cheerfulness, like tetrameters and hexameters. Therefore when (poets) compose a more lengthy metre, as they adorn words more in tragedies, it is not necessary for an orator to imitate a poet in the embellishment of speech, as indeed even the poets do not employ it constantly. It is not correct that here and there, but rather everywhere, we should produce verbal accuracy and put the words on a level with the loftiness or baseness of the thought. And as speech is some indication spying out meaning, if it does not make (it) known, it is not of use, and if it makes (it) known but does not evoke an image, it is of little use. Therefore it is necessary that signifying and image-evoking should be together, and (speech) neither abject nor greatly adorned. For the poetic (style) of speech is indeed popular, but it communicates correctly using clear nouns and verbs,

[3] **7.1.3** AR 3.1 04a18-27; IS 4.1 (200.12-201.5).
[4] **7.1.4** AR 3.1 04a27 - 3.2 04b8; IS 4.1 (201.9-202.17).

ܦܘܫܩܐ ܬܪܝܢܐ
ܕܥܠ ܐܝܬܘܬܐ ܘܩܢܘܡ ܡܠܬܐ
ܘܐܪ̈ܘܬܗ ܬܫ

ܘܕܡܘܬܐ. ܡܬܒܢܝܢܘܬ ܡܠܬܐ ܒܐܝܬܘܬܐ ܘܫܘܠܡܐ ܠܗ̇ ܕܒܢ̈ܝܢܫܐ
ܐܦ̈ܝܢܐ ܡܦܩܗܐ. ܒܡܠ̈ܬܐ[1] ܠܒܪ ܬܦܩܗ ܒܪܢܫܐ. ܘܒܗܝܢ ܙܘܘܕܐ ܡܢ܆
ܗܘ ܘܗܘ ܡܢ ܦܓܪܗ. ܘܐܝܟܢܐ ܕܠܒܢ̈ܝܐ ܠܐ ܦܪܫ[2] ܠܗ. ܐܦ ܡܘܠܕܐ
ܠܘܬ ܡܠܒܫܐ ܗ̇ܝ، ܒܕ ܗ̇ܝ ܚܠܫ. ܒܠܒܢ ܙܕܩ ܠܡܠܦܢܘܬܐ ܕܐܝܟܢܐ ܢܒܥ܆
ܡܠܠܗ. ܐܝܟܢܐ ܕܥܠ ܕܡܟܪܐ ܘܕܘܫܠܐ ܗ̇ܘܐ ܫܘܡܐ. ܘܠܡܫܘܚܬܐ
ܡܒܪܢܘܬܐ ܐܝܬ ܕܪܬܐ ܒܗܘܢ. ܘܚܫܘܫܬܐ ܕܒ̈ܠܐ ܐܝܬ̈ܠܐ ܘܡܫ̈ܝܚܬܐ
ܠܡܐܡܪܐ ܡܫܘܫܚ̈ܠܢܐ ܡܬܪ ܡܢ ܠܬܘܪ̈ܓܡܐ ܦܬ̈ܓܡܐ ܡܢܐ.
ܘܡܬܘܪ̈ܓܡܐ ܬܘܒ ܠܐ ܫܘܐ ܗܘܐ. ܒܕ ܗ̇، ܕܠܓܒܪܐ ܕܠܐ ܢܕܒ ܐܝܬ
ܫܡܗ. ܒܕ ܬܐܡܪ ܐܘ ܠܒܪܐ. ܠܘ ܐܝܟܢܐ ܕܬܐܡܪ ܐܘ ܠܠܘܩܒܠ ܐܬܬܗ̇.
ܗܘܐ ܠܒܪ ܡܛܠ ܠܗ[3] ܦܐܝܐ. ܘܐܦ ܐܝܬ ܠܗ̇ ܕܘܟܬܐ ܕܠܫܡܐ ܠܗ̇.

ܕܬܪ̈ܬܝܢ. ܐܝܬܘܬܐ ܒܬܘܪܓܡܐ ܠܘ ܐܝܟ ܐܝܬܘܬܐ ܡܬܒܥܝܢܐ. ܐܠܐ
ܐܝܟ ܕܠܡܬܓܠܝܘ ܓܝܢܘܬܐ[1] ܕܡܘܬܪܐ. ܘܠܡܓܕ. ܐܝܟ ܕܒܡܕܠܐ ܠܘܬ
ܗܝܡܢܘܬܐ. ܐܝܟܢܐ ܕܡܬܬܒܠܝܢ ܡܫܬܡ̈ܠܢܐ ܘܡܬܚ̈ܠܠܢܐ[2] ܒܡܥ̈ܒܕܢܐ
ܡܒܣܪ̈ܢܝܢܗܘܢ. ܘܐܝܬ ܗܘ ܐܝܢܐ ܡܢ ܗܢܐ ܕܣܓܝ ܗܝܢܐ. ܐܝܟܢܐ
ܕܬܘܕܝܘܬܗ[3] ܦܬܪ ܗܘܐ. ܡܛܠ ܗܘܐ ܠܒܪ ܐܫܬܡܥ ܗܘܐ ܘܒܕ[4] ܡܬܕܪܟܐ
ܒܡܠ̈ܬܐ ܒܠܒܢܐ ܕܡܫܬܡܠܝ ܡܢ ܗ̇ܘ ܕܐܬܬܗ ܡܬܪ̈ܓܡ ܗܘܐ. ܘܒܕ
ܠܡܬ̈ܠܐ[5] ܠܐ ܫܦܪܐ ܗܘܬ ܗܘܐ ܒܡܕܬܗ. ܒܕ ܡܢ ܕܐܬܠܡܠܡܘܣ[6] ܐܘܒܕܬ
ܡܫܒܕܒܢܘܬܐ[7] ܡܚܒܕܬܐ ܥܒܕܐ ܗܘܐ. ܡܢ ܠܐ ܪ̈ܕܝܐ[8] ܡܬܬܡܝܗ ܗܘܐ.
ܘܐܝܬ ܐܝܟܢܐ ܕܘܗܡܐ ܒܦܘܐܠܝܡܐ[9] ܡܬܚܫܒ. ܐܝܟܢܐ ܕܦܘܐܠܐ[10]
ܒܬܘܪܓܡܐ ܗܘ ܕܠܡܐܡܪܐ[11] ܠܐ ܡܫܬ̈ܠܡܢܐ ܕܙܕܩܝܢ ܒܡܫܘܚܬܐ
ܡܪܒܒ. ܐܝܟܢܐ ܕܐܘܪܦܣܝܣ[12] ܒܒܕ ܘܕܡܝܐ. ܘܠܕܐܡܘܬܗ ܠܒܪܐ ܦܪܐ
ܪܡ.

ܕܬܠܬ. ܒܬܠ ܩܠܐ ܕܡܢܗܘܢ ܪܘܓܙܐ ܡܬܪܒܒܐ ܐܣܦܩܘܠܝܬܐ[1] ܕܒܬܠܝܢ
ܘܦܪ̈ܝܫܝܢ ܒܗܘܢ. ܘܒ̈ܠܐ ܐܝܬ̈ܠܐ *ܘܠܡܫܘܚ ܒܘܕܝܐܬܐ[2] ܐܝܟ ܡܥ̈ܕܒܐ
ܒܗܘܢ ܒܠܝ. ܘܐܝܬ ܗܘܒܐ[3] ܒܬܠ ܩܠܐ ܕܠܦܐܠܝܡܐ ܠܢܩ ܡܐܡܪ̈ܝܢ.[4]

1 [1] sg. RVLl [2] add. ܦܪܫ RVLl [3] om. F

2 [1] ܠܓܢܘܬܐ RVLl [2] ܡܬܬ̈ܚܠܢܐ R [3] add. ܐܝܟ RVLl [4] i. om. RVL [5] sg. RVLl [6] ܕܐܠܡܠܡܘܣ RVL [7] ܡܫܒܕܢܘܬܐ RL [8] sg. RVL [9] ܕܦܘܐܠܝܡܐ RLl ; ܕܦܘܐܠܝܡܐ V [10] ܕܦܘܐܠܐ RVL; ܕܦܘܐܠܐ l [11] ܕܠܡܐܡܪ RVLl [12] ܕܐܘܪܦܣܝܣ RVL

3 [1] ܐܣܦܩܘܠܝܬܐ F [2*] pl. RVLl [3] ܗܘ RVLl [4] pl. RVL

intermediate between plainness and dignity, neither unlearned, nor studied (and) difficult of comprehension.

## SECTION TWO
## On Metaphor and Transference of Speech
## Six Theories

ONE.[5] Solemnity of speech through metaphor and substitution may be compared to what (one feels about) foreign men, for a person will revere aliens. In front of a nobleman (someone) will gaze upon him and shrink from his presence, and will not ascribe to him the (same) honour which (he gives) to acquaintances, as a villager feels the very same towards a citizen. Therefore it is right for an orator to make his speech foreign, just as it may need wonder and terror. Metre has a great influence on this, and the employment of metaphorical words and follies is more suitable for metrical compositions than for prosaic discourses. In discourses, furthermore, this (solemnity of speech) is not proper, because saying to a man whose name you do not know, 'Hey man', is not the same as saying, 'Hey kid'. The latter is more inappropriate (here), even if there is (another) occasion for which it may be suitable.

TWO.[6] Metaphor is not needed in rhetoric as a foundation, but to lead (someone) into an error which is advantageous and to induce *pistis* by seduction, just as things which are drunk and eaten may be disguised by seasonings sweetening them. There is a way of (doing) this which is extremely odious, as Theodorus did; for he would change his manner, and when imitating aliens would declaim in a voice which differed from that of his (own) locality. Although his action did not please the well informed, because he was departing from the customary *dialektos*, i.e. denotation, he was admired by the ignorant. Sometimes an orator employs poetry, just as a poet (employs) rhetoric when he composes in metre speeches (which are) not image-evoking (and) which are true, as Euripedes first did. Our master calls someone like him a 'thief'.

---

[5] **7.2.1** AR 3.2 04b8-18; IS 4.1 (203.1-10).
[6] **7.2.2** AR 3.2 04b18-26; IS 4.1 (203.10-204.6).

ܘܒܦܪܨܘܦܐ ܦ̇ܠܐ ܕܢܣܬܠܩ ܡܛܠ ܕܠܫܡܝܐ[5] ܡܬܠܝܢ. ܘܡܬܠܒܫܢܘܬܐ[6] ܠܦܪܨܘܦܐ ܣܛܪ ܡܢ ܕܠܦܪܨܘܦܐ ܒܠܚܘܕ. ܘܡܪܒܘܬܐ ܗܝ ܕܫܘܝܘܬ ܫܡܐ ܗܘܐ ܠܗܘܦܘܣܛܐܣܝܣ[7] ܝܚܝܕܐ. ܘܡܬܩܪܝܐ ܫܡܐ ܬܘܒ ܐܝܟ ܗܝ ܕܠܡܪܕܐ ܚܕܐ ܘܠܡܫܠܡܘ ܒܦܪܨܘܦܐ ܡܫܘܕܐ. ܒܪ ܒܡܦܩܢܐ ܡܫܬܪܪܐ ܡܫܬܡܠܝܢܘܬܐ. ܘܐܚܪܢܐ ܕܡܫܘܚܢܘܬܐ ܒܦܪܨܘܦܐ ܠܐ ܡܬܕܪܐ.[8] ܐܘ ܒܥܕܢܐ ܒܪܢܐ ܡܬܕܪܐ. ܒܗ ܒܗܢܐ ܘܒܬܪ ܩܠܐ ܦܘܐܝܛܝܩܘܬܐ.[9]

ܕܐܘܒܕ. ܡܫܬܡܠܝܢܘܬܐ ܘܐܦܝܣܩܘܦܐ ܐܘܒܕܬ ܫܐܠܘܬܐ ܐܘ ܒܥܕܬ ܥܠܐ ܠܡܝܬܘܬܐ ܗܘܝܢ ܐܘ ܒܥܕܬ ܥܠܐ ܒܕܝܢܘܬܐ ܐܘ ܒܥܕܬ ܥܠܐ ܕܠܐ ܡܛܠ ܠܡܝܬܐ ܐܦܠܐ ܡܛܠ ܒܕܝܢܐ. ܒܪܡ ܕܝܢ ܦܐܝܐ ܘܗܘܝܐ. ܘܒܕܝܢܐ ܠܡܐܡܪ ܡܢ ܗܠܝܢ ܒܠܗܝܢ. ܒܗ̇ ܕܦܐܝܐ ܘܒܥܠܬܐ ܠܡܫܐ ܦܠܐ ܠܡܬܝܕܥܘ. ܠܐ ܐܝܟ ܕܐܬܝܐ. ܐܠܐ ܒܩܘܫ ܫܘܩܠܐ ܒܢܕܪܐ. ܕܢܬܕܪܟ ܐܢܕܐ ܠܡܢܐ ܠܫܡܐ. ܠܗܡܐ ܓܝܪ ܡܢ ܬܘܓܡܬܐ ܕܥܠܝܐ ܕܠܡܫܐ. ܗܘ ܕܠܛܠܠܐ ܠܐ ܠܢܫ ܠܢܫ. ܘܡܡܢܐ ܠܛܠܠܐ ܠܢܫ ܗܘ ܕܠܗܡܐ ܠܐ ܠܢܫ. ܘܐܡܝܢ ܕܗܘܐ[1] ܙܕܩ ܠܗܘܦܪܐ ܕܡܢ ܓܝܫܐ ܒܥܠܬܐ ܕܩܘܝܒ ܢܬܝܚ ܠܐܫܬܠܡܘܬܐ ܘܡܫܬܡܠܝܢܘܬܐ. ܒܐܡܬܝ ܒܪ ܢܓܒܐ ܕܢܓܒܐ ܠܐܢܫܐ ܕܫܐܠ ܘܫܠܝܛܘܗܝ. ܕܦܠܛܐ ܘܫܪܪ ܢܐܡܪ. ܘܒܪ ܢܓܒܐ ܕܢܘܕ ܠܡܒܪܝܐ ܘܢܠܒܫܘܗܝ[2] ܒܪܝܬܐ ܘܚܝܐ[3] ܢܛܘܗܝ. ܐܝܟ ܕܐܦ ܠܫܦܠܐ ܘܓܒܝܫܐ ܘܥܬܝܪܐ ܫܦܝܪ ܦܘܪܫܐ ܠܢܕܪܐ ܡܫܡܗܝܢ.

ܕܣܡܟ. ܐܝܬ ܐܢܫܐ ܕܫܐܠܘܬܐ ܘܡܫܬܡܠܝܢܘܬܐ ܠܘܬ ܣܘܩܒܠܐ ܠܐ ܡܦܩܝܢ. ܐܠܐ ܒܠܚܘܕ ܡܒܪܝܢ ܐܘ ܡܩܪܒܝܢ ܠܝܩܪܐ. ܒܘܟܪܐ ܗ̇ܟ ܐܚܪܢܐ ܕܠܐܢܫܐ ܕܛܠܡ ܘܚܛܐ ܕܢܣܒ ܐܘ ܐܫܡܠ ܢܐܡܪ. ܘܠܡܢ ܕܓܢܒ ܐܘ ܓܢܒ ܕܢܫܒ ܐܘ ܐܬܚܒܫ. ܒܘܥܪܢܐ ܕܝܢ ܐܚܪܢܐ ܕܠܐܢܫܐ ܕܢܣܒ ܐܘ ܐܫܡܠ ܕܐܬܢܒ[1] ܐܘ ܐܬܚܒܫ ܢܐܡܪ. ܘܠܡܢ ܕܢܫܒ ܐܘ ܐܬܚܒܫ ܕܓܢܒ ܐܘ ܠܗܠܝܢ. ܢܩܦ ܕܝܢ ܦܘܕܐ ܒܥܘܕܪܢܐ ܐܦ[2] ܡܢ ܫܩܠܐ ܘܡܬܪܫܬܐ ܘܐܡܫܢ[3] ܕܒܡܐ ܘܦܘܪܩܢܐ. ܘܒܪ ܠܐ ܢܗܘܐ ܠܚܫܐ ܫܡܝܐ. ܡܢ ܫܘܬܦ ܒܐܕܫ̈ܐ ܘܐܫܝܢܐ ܙܕܩ ܠܗܘܦܪܐ ܕܒܪܐ ܫܡܝܐ. ܦܪܝܫܐ ܒܪܡ ܘܠܐ ܒܡܛܠܐ.

[5] pl. RVLl [6] pl. F [7] ܠܗܘܦܘܣܛܐܣܝܣ RVLl [8] ܡܬܕܪܐ RVL [9] ܦܘܐܝܛܝܩܐ RVL

4 [1] om. F [2] ܐܘ ܢܠܒܫܘܗܝ RVLl [3] ܐܘ ܚܝܐ RVLl

5 [1] i. ܘ RVLl [2] ܐܦ RVL [3] sg. F

THREE.[7] The words from which rhetoric is composed (are) the primary (ones) which are proper and clear, and metaphors and a foreign style come in with them as seasonings. Here there are words whose diction is suitable for poetry, but they must be rejected in rhetoric, because they mislead the hearer, and deception is more proper to poetry than to rhetoric. Chicanery achieved by homonymy is useful in sophistry; synonymity is advantageous in poetry—for example, 'to go' and 'to walk'—because image-evocation is established by repetition. And as metre is not helpful in rhetoric, or provides (only) a little help, in the same way poetic words (are of little or no help).

FOUR.[8] Transference and *epitheta* or metaphor happen either with a well known word, or a foreign word, or a word which is neither very well known nor very foreign, but comely and pleasant. In all of these (cases) it is necessary to use what is comely and suitable to the subject, not (merely) as it comes, but in a comparison of opposites one with another, so that it may be evident what is suitable for whom. For in the matter of characteristic elegance of dress, that which is not suitable for a young man is suitable for an old man, and similarly that which is not suitable for an old man is suitable for a young man. The orator should in some way bring the metaphor and transference from a suitable neighbouring genus. Thus when he wants to vituperate someone who is asking (for something) and to treat him with contempt, he may say, 'He goes around begging'; but when he wants to extol and praise a crafty (fellow), he may call him 'prudent and expert', as robbers, brigands, and thieves call each other 'resourceful'.

FIVE.[9] Sometimes metaphor and transference do not come out to the opposite, but only belittle or exaggerate the thing (itself). In belittling, for example, one may say of one who has done wrong and made a false accusation that he 'has made a mistake' or 'been foolish', and of him who has stolen or plundered that he has 'taken' or 'acquired'; while in exaggeration, for example, one may say of one who has made a mistake or been foolish that he has been 'wicked' or 'shameless', and of him who has taken or acquired that he has

[7] **7.2.3** AR 3.2 04b26-05a8; IS 4.1 (204.7-205.5).
[8] **7.2.4** AR 3.2 05a8-26; IS 4.1 (205.6-206.3).
[9] **7.2.5** AR 3.2 05a26-b19; IS 4.1 (206.3-208.5).

ܘܪܗܛܐ ܒܫܢܬܐ ܠܡܒܘܬܐ ܥܒܝܪܬܐ ܠܗ ܒܥܒܪܗ̇ ܡܢܘܪ. ܐܠܐ ܒܒܘܫܐ ܠܐ ܡܫܢܝܐ ܡܚܫܒܢ ܠܗ̇. ܘܒܗܡܢ ܐܦ ܡܙܓܠ. ܥܒܪ ܡܙܓܠ. ܘܐܝܬ ܐܝܟܐ ܕܐܡܝܢ ܕܢܗܪܐ ܠܥܠܡܐ ܗܢܐ ܡܬܐܙܠ. ܘܗܘ ܗܢܐ ܐܬܪܐ ܠܗ ܗܘ ܡܠܐܘ. ܒܕ ܪܗܛܐ ܒܡܒܠܠܐ ܣܓܝ ܕܢܦܩ. ܠܐ ܒܥܬܝܩܐ. ܘܒܣܕܪܐ ܠܡܐܡܪ ܒܠ ܫܐܠܬܐ ܐܘ ܡܢ ܥܙܝܙܐ ܥܘܕܪ ܫܒܩܐ ܗܘܐ. ܐܘ ܡܢ ܕܡܬܢܐ ܒܫܠܐ. ܒܐܡܪܬ ܡܢ ܒܒܘܕܬܐ ܐܘ ܫܥܘܫܬܐ. ܐܘ ܒܐܫܝܘܬܐ ܡܬܪܥܝܢܬܐ ܡܬܚܫܚܬܐ ܘܗܦܪ.

ܕܝܠܬ. ܡܒܒܕܒܘܬ ܡܐܡܪܐ ܫܐܠܬܐ ܒܢܦܩܬܐ ܠܐ ܫܘܝܐ. ܒܕ ܐܝܟܐ ܕܠܝܫܡܥܬܐ[1] ܗ̇ܡܫ[2] ܕܢܠܗܘ ܒܕ ܘܕܝܕܝܫܬ ܦܣܩܬܐ ܐܡܪ ܐܠܦܪ ܡܢ ܒܕ. ܗܡܒܡܬ ܦܣܩܬܐ ܢܐܡܪ ܡܚܝܪ. ܒܕ ܘܕܝܕܫܘܬܐ ܒܡ ܗܡܒܡܘܬܐ ܕܝܐ ܐܚܪܢܐ ܕܐܠܦܪ[3] ܢܢ ܒܡܘܦ ܣܒܒܬܐ ܡܗܓܓܐ. ܐܠܦܪ ܕܝܢ ܥܒܝܪܐ ܡܢ ܕܡܘܕܪܬܐ[4] ܦܣܩܬܐ ܢܐܡܪ. ܒܕ ܗ̇ܝ ܗܕܐ ܒܡ ܗܡܒܡܘܬܐ ܡܗܓܓܢܘܬ ܬܘܠܒܐ ܢܕܝܕܬܐ ܡܒܠܐ. ܒܗ ܒܕܢܐ ܐܦ ܒܒܢܬ ܩܠܐ ܗܡܝܬܐ ܕܠܐ ܫܐܠܝܢ ܐܢܬ ܐܢܕܐ ܕܡܫܘܪܐ ܘܐܫܪܬܐ ܕܡܫܢܝܐ. ܠܡܕܝܢܐ ܓܒܪ ܒܕ ܒܪ ܗܡܗܬܐ ܠܐ ܡܢ ܗܡܗܢܐ ܐܡܪ ܐܢܬ. ܐܠܦܪ ܡܢ ܡܐ ܕܒܪܐ ܕܡܒܪܐ ܠܐ ܡܢ ܐܬܠܐ ܬܐܡܪܪ[5] ܡܘܪܒ ܐܢܬ. ܐܦ[6] ܣܝ ܗܘ ܢܫܐ ܒܬܪܡܘ̱ ܒܘܬܐ. ܡܒܠܐ ܐܦ ܢܡܪܐ ܒܐܡܫܠܐ ܒܡܪܬܐ ܒܒܪ ܠܡܒܘܬܐ. ܠܢܫܬܐ ܓܒܪ ܒܕ ܢܫܬܘܐ ܬܐܡܪ ܡܫܡܪ ܐܢܬ. ܘܒܕ ܐܗܦܟܬܐ ܬܐܡܪ ܓܡܪܐ ܐܢܬ. ܘܡܒܠܐ[7] ܠܕܡܒܐ ܕܡܒܘܢܐ ܡܒܪ ܘܗܫܢܐ ܡܘܪܒ. ܒܗܦܟܐܬ ܕܘܟܝܬܐ ܕܝܢ ܡܢ ܬܐܪܗܝܢ ܠܐ ܡܡܫܚܬܐ[8] ܦܠܐ ܠܡܒܕܪܘ.

ܦܘܣܩܐ ܬܠܝܬܝܐ

ܡܛܠ ܒܢܬ ܩܠܐ ܠܐ ܦܫܝܛܬܐ ܕܡܪܕܝܬܐ ܡܬܐܡܪܝܢ

ܬܐܘܪܝܐ ܚܕܐ

ܘܕܡܝܬܐ. ܒܢܬ ܩܠܐ ܗܟܝܠ ܕܠܗܝܢ ܘܡܪܕܝܬܐ ܦܘܐ ܪܝܢ ܐܒܝܫܬ ܐܕܫܐ ܐܚܝܢ. ܐܕܫܐ ܘܕܡܝܐ. ܗ̇ܝ ܕܐܝܬ ܫܡܥܐ ܡܐܡܪܐ ܡܪ̈ܒܒܐ ܕܒܫܝܢ ܡܢ ܢܫܐ ܪ̈ܫܡܐ ܕܠܐ ܕܐܠܝܢ ܡܬܚܫܒܢ. ܐܝܟܢܐ ܕܠܗܘܦܪܘ̱ ܠܫܡܥܐ ܗ̇ܢ ܗܟܢ ܦܪ̈ܘܦܐ[1] ܦܘܐ. ܠܐܘܒܐ ܕܝܢ ܫܘܪܝܬ[2] ܘܦܘܣܬܐ. ܘܡܢܪܓܫܘ[3] ܠܫܦܪܘܕܘܐ ܪܫܡܐ ܕܒܢ̱ ܗܘܝܘܐ ܫܡܗ. ܐܠܡܕܐܡܪܐܘ[4] ܠܢܦܫܬܐ[5] ܠܡܒܡܬܐ ܡܢ ܐܪܥܐ ܒܢ. ܠܐܫܬܗ ܕܡܒܐ ܕܝܢ ܦܘܠ ܠܓܘܐ. ܒܢܬ ܩܠܐ ܕܝܢ[6] ܕܐܝܟ

6 [1] ܕܠܝܫܡܥܬܐ RVLl [2] ܡܢܗ̇ RVL [3] i. om. R [4] ܕܠܝܫܢܕܝܬ RVLl [5] om. RVLl [6] i. add. ܘ RVLl [7] i. om. RVLl [8] pl. F

1 [1] sg. RVLl [2] ܫܘܦܬ RVLl [3] ܘܡܢܪܓܫܘ R [4] ܐܠܡܕܐܡܪܐ F; ܠܡܕܐܡܪܐܘ RVL [5] ܠܢܦܫܬܐ R [6] ܠܒܪ Rl

'stolen' or 'robbed'. A fault may also adhere to the sign in respect of syllables, expressions, and particles of connection or division. When an object has no name, it is right for an orator to create a name from things equivalent in species and akin (to it), but (it must be) clear and not obscure. An expert orator does not disclose a disgraceful thing by its name, but dignifies it with an appellation (that is) not vile, and thereby, even if he is being untruthful, is being nobly untruthful. Sometimes he may allude to an odious matter as in a riddle, but this practice is not greatly admired, because an orator has a duty to persuade by speech, not by silence. In a word, every metaphor comes either from homonymous things, or from (things) similar in import, that is to say, in action or usage, or in a quality (which is) perceptible, visible, and so on.

SIX.[10] The effect of metaphorical expressions on souls is not uniform, because he who seeks to praise (his ) beloved sings (her praises) more when he says 'rosy-fingered' than when he says 'red-fingered', as 'rosiness' with redness evokes (an image of) another kind which is more attractive for the person of the beloved, but more unattractive when he says 'scarlet fingers', because with redness this introduces the image-evocation of an abominable worm. In the same way also with epithets which are not metaphorical there is that which is honoured and that which is despised. For when you say of a mule 'son of a mare, not of a stallion', you magnify (him) more than when you say 'son of an ass, not of a she-ass', even though the same meaning is (inherent) in both designations. Similarly a diminutive always demeans a thing, for when you call a cloak 'a cloaklet' you pour contempt (on it), and when you call (it) 'a robe' you honour it. And in the same way 'goldlet' belittles gold and 'refined' magnifies (it). However in most places one must guard against immoderate (use) of both of them.

[10] **7.2.6** AR 3.2 05b19-33; IS 4.1 (208.5-209.9).

ܗܠܝܢ ܕܝܢ ܡ̈ܬܕܒܪܢ. ܕܘܒܠ ܬܫܡܫܬܐ ܐܘ ܙܘܥܙܥܐ ܐܘ ܕܠܚܘܕܘܬܐ ܠܐ ܡ̈ܫܟܚܢ. ܐܦܠܐ ܠܚܕ ܐܡܘܪܐ ܡܫܟܚܝܢ. ܠܦܘܐܛܝܩܐ ܕܝܢ ܢ̈ܟܝܢ. ܒܪܡ ܠܐ ܒܗ̇ ܕܡܫܬܕܪܝܢ. ܐܠܐ ܒܗ̇ ܕܠܝܬܐ ܕܗܘܝܢ ܒܐܝܕܐ ܡ̈ܕܡܝܢ.

ܕܬܪ̈ܬܝܢ. ܐܕܫܐ ܬܪܝܢܐ ܗ̇ܘ ܕܠܡܬܬܣܝܡܘ ܒܠܚܘܕܘܗܝ ܠܐ ܡܫܟܚܬܐ ܡܢܗ ܕܠܥܠܐ ܐܘ ܡܢ ܠܥܠܐ ܒܕܘܟܐ. ܗ̇ܘ ܕܝܢ ܐܚܪܢܐ ܕܝܠܗ ܦܘܪܫܢܐ ܕܐܟܠ ܬܪ̈ܝܢܐ ܐܠܗܝܐܝܬ ܠܐܣܝܪܐ ܦܘܫܩܐ ܦܪܐ. ܘܠܗܡܝܬ ܦܪܝܫܐ ܗܘܢܪܐ̈ ܐܡܝܢܬ ܓܢܒܐ. ܗܢܐ ܕܝܢ ܐܚܕܐ ܕܐܝܟ ܗܘܝܢܐ ܒܝܕ ܒܒܢ̈ܝܬ ܩ̈ܠܐ ܕܐܪ̈ܡܝ[1] ܐܬܬܣܝܡ ܡܡ̈ܠܠ ܒܢܪܐ[2] ܐܡܝܢܬ ܡܛܐ ܐܙܠ. ܘܡܕܝܢܬܐ ܩܘܦܐܢܬ ܗܘܐ ܐܡܝܢܬ ܪ̈ܘܝܐ.[3]

ܕܬܠܬ. ܐܕܫܐ ܬܠܝܬܝܐ ܗ̇ܘ ܕܒܢ̈ܬ ܩ̈ܠܐ ܕܡܬܒܢܝܢ ܡܢ ܥܒܪܐ ܠܡܫܘ̈ܬܐ ܡܢ ܡ̈ܬܢ. *ܠܡܣܒܣܘ ܣܟܠܘܬ[1] ܕܡ̈ܫܘܬܐ ܢܫܡܝܢ[2] ܘܡܣܬܟܠܢܘܬ ܠܐ ܡܬܡܨ̈ܝܢ ܒܗ̇ ܕܐܪ̈ܡܝܢ ܣܓܝܐ̈. ܐܝܟ ܢܒܘܟܕܢܨܪ.[3] ܐܘ ܒܗ̇ ܕܐܠܝܨ ܥܣܩ ܕܘܒܪܗܘܢ[4] ܘܒܢܝܐ. ܐܝܟ ܗ̇ ܕܐܟܠ ܐܢ ܐܘܠܝ ܘܒܢܝܢ. ܗܠܝܢ ܓܝܪ ܒܐܣܟܡ ܘܒܢܐ ܕܒܬܪ ܘܒܢܐ ܕܒܠܗܝ ܒܒܢ̈ܝ. ܐܘ ܒܗ̇ ܕܣܒܝܣ ܣܘܟܠܗܝܢ ܒܐܣܪܢܐ. ܐܒܟܢܐ ܕܠܒ̈ܢܐ ܘܫܠܒܐ ܬܪܝܢ ܣܘܪܐ ܦܘܡ ܩܛܝܢܐ. ܕܐܝܟ ܗܠܝܢ ܗ̇ܢ ܒܡܒܠܠܐ ܙܘܓܪܐ ܠܐ ܥܒܝܕ̈ܢ. ܘܐܦ ܢܣܩܝܢ ܕܓܒܒ̈ܝܢ. ܐܦܠܐ ܗܠܝܢ[5] ܕܡܢ ܦܐܓܪܡܐ[6] ܡܬܢܩܦܝܢ. ܒܗ̇ ܕܐܡܣܝܣܬܐ ܒ̈ܢܬ[7] ܠܠܡܣܝܣ[8] ܘܠܗܘܕܐ[9] ܠܗܬ ܡܣܒܘܬܐ ܠܦܓܪܐ ܠܐ ܝܗ̇ܒ̈.

ܕܐܪܒܥ. ܠܗܠܝܢ ܥܐܠ̈ܬܐ ܦܘܐܓܝܡܐ[1] ܠܡܒܟܕ ܠܐ ܦܐܫܐ. ܡܛܠ ܒܡܦܓܓܘܬܗܘܢ ܘܒܓܠܠܬ ܣܘܟܠܗܘܢ. ܘܡܢ ܗܠܝܢ ܐܡܬ ܐܡܕܐ ܕܣܓܝ ܕܡܕܪܐ ܘܡܣܝܐܐ. ܐܒܟܢܐ ܕܠܒܢܐ ܓܒܪܐ ܕܓܒܪ̈ܬܐ[2] ܕܦܠܡ ܡܢ ܡܣܩܘܬܐ. ܒܝܕ ܣܘܪܘܬܗܘܢ ܢܩܢܐ.[3] ܘܠܬܪ̈ܬܐ ܬܪܝܢ ܒܘܪܟܠܐ ܬܐܪ̈ܬܐ. ܒܗ̇ ܕܐܒܘܬܗܘܢ ܟܠܗ ܘܐܪܘܒܗ ܙ̈ܥܝܪܘܗܝ. ܘܡܢ ܒܩܦܓܬܐ ܬܘܒ ܐܡܬ ܐܡܕܐ ܕܒܥܘܪܐ ܦܘܪܐ ܘܡܢ ܘܒܠܐ ܒܝܕ ܡܬܒܕܪܐ ܡܬܟܠܐ. ܘܒܢ̈ܬ ܩ̈ܠܐ

2 [1] ܐܪ̈ܡܝܬܐ RVLl [2] ܒܢܪܐ RVLl [3] ܒܢ̈ܘܝܐ RVLl
3 [1*] ܠܡܣܒܣܘ ܣܟܠܘܬ R; ܠܡܣܒ̈ܣܘ ܣܟܠܘܬ VL [2] ܢܫܡ̈ܝܢ RVL [3] ܢܒܘܟܕܢܨܪ F [4] ܥܣܩ ܕܘܒܪܗܘܢ RVLl [5] ܗܠܝܢ RVLl [6] sg. RVLl [7] om. RVL [8] ܠܠܡܣܝ̈ܣ RVL [9] i. om. RVLl
4 [1] ܦܘܐܓܝܡܐ RLl; ܦܘܐܓܝܡܐ V [2] ܓܒܪ̈ܬܐ F [3] ܢܩܢܐ F

## SECTION THREE
### On the Inelegant Words called Frigidities
### Five Theories

ONE.[11] The words which our master calls frigidities (fall into) four species. The first species is when, instead of names, compound expressions which are not specific are adopted, which are gathered from remote subjects. For example, Lycrophon called heaven 'many-faced' and earth 'black-topped', and Gorgias named a flatterer 'a friend in the moment of need'. Alcidamas designated the soul 'bolder than a lion', and the bottom of the sea 'blue-coloured'. When words like these are mentioned, they do not fulfil the task of definition, indication, or specification, nor do they make comprehensible the subject of the speaker. They are useful in poetry, but not because they are indicative, but because they liken the subject under consideration to another.

TWO.[12] The second species (of frigidity) is the use of an uncustomary expression, from the language itself or from a foreign language. For example, Alcidamas calls Xerxes the Persian 'wolfish of mind' rather than 'warlike', and (says) 'the ploughshare Sciron' rather than flint. This is the same as a Syrian, when using words which we (Syrians) have blown up, saying 'torrents of the barren' for the sea, and 'a city (with) a multitude of depths' for winds.

THREE.[13] The third species is when words laid down originally for things by masters of style are foul of form and cannot be accepted with pleasure because they are very long, like 'Nebuchadnezzar'; or because their temporal sign is slanted, like, 'If we went and bought', for in the form of the past tense these are pointing to the future; or because their meaning is crowded with others, as many call water and milk 'two whites'. Such are not pleasing in rhetorical speech, and even though those which are well known may be, those which are used by poets are not, because they make the style foreign and therefore do not lead the populace to *pistis*.

---

[11] **7.3.1** AR 3.3 05b34-06a6; IS 4.1 (209.10-17).
[12] **7.3.2** AR 3.3 06a6-10; IS 4.1 (210.1-4).
[13] **7.3.3** AR 3.3 06a10-14; IS 4.1 (210.5-211.5).

ܒܦܬ̈ܝܘܬܐ ܠܡܥܡܘܕܝܬܐ ܗ̇ܝ܂ ܕܐܬܐܘܪܡܘܢ ܡܬܩܪܝܐ ܠܫܡܝܢ܂ ܟܕ ܒܗ̇ *ܫܪ̈ܒܐ ܡܫܪ̈ܝܢܐ ܘܡܫܬܚܠܦܢܐ[4] ܡܬܢܣܒܝܢ܂ ܗ̇ܝ ܕܝܢ ܗܕܐ ܒܟܦܝܦܘܬܗ̇[5] ܐܪܝܡܬܐ ܕܪܘܚܐ ܡܬܓܠܝܐ[6] ܘܠܡܗܘܡܐ ܒܡܦܪܢܐ ܢܬܦܐ܂ ܘܗܘܝܢ *ܕܒܠ̈ܬܝܐ ܢܒܪ̈ܝܐ[7] ܡܬܠ̈ܒܢܝܢ ܠܡܥܡܘܕܝܬܐ ܗ̇ܝ܂ ܕܐܡܦܝ[8] ܣܝ̈ܡܝܢ܂ ܟܕ ܒܗ̇ ܫܪ̈ܒܐ ܢܡܘ̈ܣܐ ܡܫܡ̈ܠܝܐ[9] ܘܡܓܠ̈ܝܢܐ ܕܟܒܪ̈[10] ܥܠ ܢܡܘܣܐ ܡܬܬܬܝܢ܂ ܢܒܪ̈ܝܐ ܕܝܢ ܐܝܟ ܕܐܡܪܝܢ ܐܚܕ ܘܕܚܠ܂ ܘܗܘܝܢ ܫܡ̈ܠܝܬܐ ܒܡܥܡܘܕܝܬܐ ܕܐܬܡܪܡܘ[11] ܒܫ̈ܠܝ܂ ܐܝܟܢܐ ܕܡܬܚܫܒܐ܂

ܕܢܣܒܐ܂ ܐܘܕܥܐ ܪܒܝܥܝܐ ܕܒܢ̈ܝܬ ܩܠܐ ܦܘܪ̈ܫܬܐ ܗ̇ܘܐ ܒܫܐܠ̈ܬܐ ܠܐ ܡܬܚܫ̈ܒܬܐ[1] ܠܗܝܦܘܟܬܐ܂ ܡܛܠ ܒܢܒܝܘܬܗܘܢ ܐܦܘܓܪܝܣܝܩܘܬܐ ܐܘܡܢܘܬ ܡܠܝܠܘܬܐ܂ ܐܘ ܡܛܠ ܥܛܦܘܬܗܝܢ ܘܡܟܣܕܢܘܬܐ ܕܡܠܬܐ ܘܡܓܠܝܢܐ܂ ܘܐܦ[2] ܗ̇ܝ ܡܗܠܝܢܘܬܐ ܠܡܘܓܠܐܐ ܕܐܕ̈ܫܐ ܦܐܓܦܝܩܝܐ ܕܒܗܘܢ *ܓܢܝܐ ܘܡܠܠܐ[3] ܡܬܬܬܝܢ ܠܢܣܒܐ܂ ܘܡܢܘܝܢܐ ܕܡܢܝܢܐ ܠܡܬܓܢܝܢܐ ܫܐܠܬܐ ܒܢܬ܆ ܒܢܝܐ܂ ܦܢܫ ܕܝܢ ܡܢܗ ܒܗ̇܂ ܕܫܐܠܬܐ ܐܣܢܝܐ ܒܒܕܐ ܠܒܕܩ܂ ܕܡܢܝܘܬܐ ܕܝܢ ܠܗ ܐܣܢܝܐ ܐܠܐ ܐܝܟ ܐܣܢܝܐ܂ ܐܝܟ ܕܐܬܐܡܪܬ ܡܛܠ ܐܚܝܠܘܣ[4]܂ ܕܐܝܟ ܐܪܝܐ ܫܘܪ܂ ܘܦܛܪܘܩܠܘܣ ܡܛܠ ܒܢ̈ܝ ܣܐܡܘܣ ܐܡܪ܂ ܕܕܡܝܢ ܠܚܙܝܐ ܕܠܫܡܝܐ ܐܚܠܝܢ ܘܫܥܘܬܗ ܠܐ ܢܓܚܢ܂ ܘܕܡܝܘܬܐ ܟܕ ܡܢ ܥܬܐܦܫ ܦܐܓܦܝܩܝܐ ܐܬܝܬܗ̇܂ ܐܚܡܝܐ ܕܫܐܠܬܐ ܒܦܓܘܪܝܩܝܐ ܡܘܬܪܐ܂ ܘܟܕ ܟܬܪܝܢ ܫܪ̈ܒܝܢ ܗܘܝܐ ܣܥܝܘܬܐ ܕܡܝܢܝܘܬܐ ܘܫܐܠܬܐ܂ ܫܘܪ[5] ܓܢܝܐ ܦܠܐ ܕܢܗܘܘܢ܂ ܒܐܡܟܬ ܟܕ ܠܦܘܪܦܘܪܐ *ܐܣܢܝܬ ܒܗܝܐ[6] ܐܡܪ[7] ܐܝܟ܂ ܠܦܪܘܣ ܐܣܝܪ ܗܒܪܐ ܦܠܐ ܕܢܐܡܪ܂

ܦܣܘܩܐ ܪܒܝܥܝܐ

ܥܠ ܗܕܪܐ ܕܡܠܟܐ ܪܘܦܝܢܐ

ܬܐܘܪ̈ܝܐܣ ܐܪܒܥ

ܡܕܡܝܢܘܬܐ܂ ܣܡܟ ܦܠܐ ܠܚܦܪ ܒܡܕܪܘܬ ܡܡܠܠܐ܂ ܚܕܐ ܡܢ ܕܠܐ ܬܗܐ ܕܡܢܬ ܠܡܣܡܟܘ[1] ܒܡܝܡܘܬܐ ܡܥܡܝܢܘܬܐ ܐܠܐ ܗܦܝܟܘܬܐ ܘܬܐܪܡܬܐ܂ ܒܕ ܒܡܝܡܘܬܐ ܡܥܝܦܬܐ[2] ܠܗܘܡܠܐ܂ ܕܬܐܪܝܢ[3] ܕܝܢ ܦܘܪܡܝܢ ܐܗܘܪܐ ܕܡܠܝܠܘܬܐ ܟܠܒ ܒܡܫܐ ܒܡܢܝܢܐ[4] ܘܥܘܓܢܐ ܕܡܬܝܢܐ܂ ܐܡܡܐ ܕܒ ܢܐܡܪ ܐܢܐ ܡܢ ܐܡܪܬ܂ ܒܕܓܘܢ ܐܠܝܓܐ ܕܢܡܠܐ ܠܦܬܓܡܐ ܒܕ ܐܡܪ ܐܢܬ ܕܝܢ ܠܐ ܗܡܢܬ܂ ܦܠܐ ܢܐܣܘ ܐܗܘܪܐ ܡܢ ܐܗܘܪܐ ܒܡܬܘܪܬܐ ܕܡܦܪܘܡܐ ܡܗܡܝܡܘܬܗܘܢ܂ ܘܢܦܪ ܬܗܘܒ ܕܘܝܐ ܕܡܕܡܝܢܘܬܐ ܘܐܪܘܪܬܐ ܒܕ ܐܡܪ܂

4* sg. F 5 f. ܗ F 6 ܡܓܠܝܐ RVLl 7* sg. RVLl 8 ܕܐܡܦܝ RL; ܕܐܡܦܪ V; ܕܐܡܦܝ ܡܬܦܪܫܐ l 9 ܡܫܡܠܝܐ RVL; ܡܫܠܡܢܐ l 10 ܕܟܒܪ̈ RVL 11 ܕܐܬܡܪܡܘ RVLl

5 1 ܡܬܚܫܒܬ RL; ܡܬܚܫܒܬ V; ܡܬܚܫ̈ܒܬ l 2 ܘܐܦ RVLl 3* pl. RVLl 4 ܐܚܝܠܘܣ RVLl 5 ܫܘܪ RVL; ܫܘܪ̈ l 6* ܐܣܝܪ ܬܗܝܐ RVLl 7 om. RVL; ܢܐܡܪ l

1 1 ܠܡܣܡܟܘ RVL 2 ܡܥܝܦܬܐ RVLl 3 ܕܬܐܪܝܢ RVLl 4 ܕܡܢܝܢܐ RVL

FOUR.[14] To make poetry with an abundance of metaphors is not seemly, on account of their obscurity and the difficulty of their comprehension. Yet some of them can be highly admirable and pleasing; for example, on account of their whiteness one may call teeth 'a flock of shorn sheep which comes up from the dipping', or two breasts 'twin fawns' because like them they have raised and lifted up their heads. Among obscurities there is also that which initially was frigid but becoming familiar with time becomes sweet. Double words are appropriate to the metre called dithyrambic, because joyous and festal subjects are used in it; for with its lengthy doubling it ridicules what is frigid and draws out gladness by force. Those which are sounded in alien tongues use epic metre, because frightening and threatening legal issues of transgressions against the law may be brought into it; for as we have said, the alien is terrible and fearful. Metaphors enter into the metre of iambics, as it appears.

FIVE.[15] The fourth species of frigid words occurs in metaphors (which do) not enliven rhetoric, (either) because of their tragic or lofty dignity, or because of their comic contempt which mocks and ridicules. Yet derision is appropriate to the majority of poetic species in which blame and slighting result. Coining a simile is in a way akin to metaphorical transference, but differs from it in that metaphor makes something another, but similarity is not (being) another but (being) like another. As was said of Achilles, 'He leapt like a lion'; and Pericles said of the Samians, 'They are like children who eat bread and do not understand its use'. While similarity is among the foundations of poetry, like metaphor it is useful in rhetoric. When with two things the use of simile or metaphor arises, they must be of the same genus; so when someone says 'holder of a cup' for Aphrodite, he must also say 'holder of a shield' for Ares.

---

[14] **7.3.4** AR 3.3 06a14-b4; IS 4.1 (211.5-212.3).
[15] **7.3.5** AR3.3 06b4 - 4 06b26;07a1-3;14-17; IS 4.1 (212.4-16).

ܗ̇ܘܐ ܘܦܠ ܡܛܠ ܕܡܒܥܐ ܗ̇ܘܐ ܗܘ܂ ܟܡܕܡܐ ܡܢ ܠܥܪܒܐ ܦܠܐ ܕܢܕܒܪ܂ ܐܝܠܐ ܢܣܒܐ ܥܠܬܗ܂ ܘܐܡܪܬ ܐܡܬܐ ܕܥܠܬ ܥܪܒܐ ܡܢܟܝܐ[5] ܒܪܬܡܐ ܠܥܪܒܐ܂[6] ܐܝܟ ܐܡܝܢܐ ܕܐܡܪ܂ ܐܝܢܐ ܗܘ ܡܛܠ ܕܢܣܒܬܟ ܝܘܪܒܐܝܬ ܥܒܘܬ ܐܝܟ ܘܐܢܫܝܢ ܘܢܦܩܬܟ܂ ܗܘ ܕܝܢ ܒܪ ܐܥܬܘܕ܃[7] ܡܢ ܦܪܝܫܐ[8] ܒܐܢܫܐ ܕܡܬܝܠܘܬܐ ܢܦܩ ܠܗ܂

ܕܬܪܬܝܢ܂ ܕܬܠܬ[1] ܗ̇ܝ ܕܟܬܒܐ ܩܠܐ ܗܢܝ ܕܐܬܝܠܘܬܐ ܠܐ ܡܬܟܒܝܢܐ ܒܗܝܢ ܕܠܒܬܗܘܬܐ ܠܐ ܢܛܝܢܘܬܐ ܢܗܘܝ܂ ܐܦܠܐ ܡܢ ܗܢܝ ܕܟܫܘܒܠܗܝܢ[2] ܢܣܒܢܐ ܒܪ܂ ܥܪܒܐ ܫܘܩܠܐ ܡܥܒܕܢ ܡܠܦܢ܂ ܐܟܡܐ ܕܡܫܬܘܕܥܝܢ ܐܬܢܣܒ ܒܐܣܦܪܐ ܗ̇ܝ܂ ܕܐܡܪ ܕܠܗ̇ ܗ̇ܦܟ ܠܡܠܐ ܘܒܢܐ ܡܕܡ ܐܟܡܐ ܕܡܢܗ̇ ܥܪ܂ ܘܒܢܐ ܡܕܡ܂ ܘܐܟܡܐ ܕܒܫܢܝܐ ܒܡܕܪܐ ܐܝܟ ܐܡܪ܂ ܕܦܘܣܩܘܣ ܡܠܟܐ ܕܡܩܝܢܐ ܒܪ܂ ܐܠܘܦ ܢܗܪܐ ܢܟܪܝ܂ ܡܠܟܘܬܐ ܪܒܬܐ ܢܣܬܪ ܘܢܒܛܠ܂ ܘܒܪ ܒܪܗ ܠܢܗܪܐ ܦܬܟ ܒܗ ܒܡܪܙ ܡܠܟܐ ܕܦܪ̈ܣܝܐ ܘܐܬܪܘܗ ܘܒܛܠ ܡܠܟܘܬܗ܂ ܘܗ̇ܘ ܦܘܣܩܘܣ ܠܐ ܐܫܟܚ ܠܡܬܦܠܓܘ ܠܒܡܪܐ܂ ܒܪ[3] ܠܐ ܗ̇ܘ ܕܐܢܫܐ ܡܢ ܬܪ̈ܬܝܗܝܢ ܡܠܟ̈ܘܬܐ ܒܥܠܠ ܒܡܥܒܪܬܗ ܕܠܢܗܪܐ܂ ܘܗܟܢܐ ܥܠܘܗܝ *ܒܡܥܪܐ ܡܦܩ[4] ܡܢ̈ܪܐ ܘܒܠܝܢܐ ܘܐܣܛܪ̈ܛܠܛܐ ܡܠܟ̈ܐ ܒܥܒܕ̈ܐ ܦܫܘܩܐ ܠܘܬܢ ܠܐ ܡܬܝܕܥܐ ܕܟܘܣܝ ܘܠܥܪܒܐ ܦܬܓܡܐ ܠܬܚܝܢ܂

---

5 ܡܢܕܝܐ RVLl 6 ܠܥܪܒܝܐ RVLl 7 ܐܥܬܘܕܝ RVL; ܐܘܕܝ l 8 pl. RVLl
2 1 om. F 2 ܕܫܘܒܠܗܝܢ RVL 3 ܒܪ RVLl 4* om. RVLl

## SECTION FOUR
### On the Beauty of Rhetorical Speech
### Four Theories

ONE.[16] It is necessary to observe five (things) for beautiful speech. First (is) that the form of the language should not be absurdly obscure, but polished and correct, because obscurity renders the thought contemptible. The second (is) a logical connecting response free of quantitative error or displacement. For example, when one says, 'I on the one hand (ܡܢ) said', it is necessary on that account to complete the sentence saying, 'you on the other hand (ܕܝܢ) did not act', and not distance the connecting particles from each other so excessively as to split apart their closeness. One should also observe the right (order) of priority and posteriority, saying, 'Such and such happened, because similarly this happened.' For first it is necessary to mention the thing, then show the cause of it. Sometimes the cause of a thing is present when one utters the thing; as for example when one says, 'Because I loved you greatly, I left my brothers and kinsmen and followed you, but when he was abandoned by (his) neighbour, he followed you by necessity (born) of penury.'

TWO.[17] Third is that words in which a metaphor is not intended should be specific, not general, and should not be among those which, pointing to (two) opposite things, may lead (one) astray in their singular understanding. For example, Empedocles used a sphere, (about) which he said, 'The world will return to it some time, just as it began from it some time'; and in an oracle a certain priest said, 'When Croesus king of the Greeks crosses the river Alus, he will destroy and bring to ruin a great kingdom.' When he crossed the river, Cyrus king of the Persians met him and put him to flight, destroying his kingdom. Croesus could not blame the priest, because (the priest) had not declared which of the two kingdoms would perish by his crossing of the river. Similarly all priests putting forth oracles and revelations, and astrologers reasoning by the stars, make undefined statements which are general and fit diverse things.

---

[16] **7.4.1** AR 3.5 07a19-30; IS 4.2 (213.5-214.7).
[17] **7.4.2** AR 3.5 07a30-b6; IS 4.2 (214.9-215.5).

ܕܬܬܠܬ. ܕܐܡܪܢ ܗ̇ܝ ܕܠܒܪܘܬܐ ܕܫܟ̈ܝܚܐ ܘܟ̈ܠܐ ܘܠܒܘܣܡܬܗܘܢ ܒܐܬܘ̈ܬܗܘܢ ܘܒܥܘܗܕ̈ܢܝܗܘܢ[1] ܢܛܪ ܒܟܬܝܒܬܐ ܘܒܡܪܢܝܐ. ܐܝܟܢܐ ܕܠܐ ܢܓܕܫ ܦܘܕܐ. ܘܕܢܣܒ ܗ̇ܝ ܕܠܒܘܫܢܝܐ ܘܣܕܝܪܘܬܐ ܒܕܡܘ̈ܬܗܘܢ ܢܛܪ. ܗܟܢܐ ܘܠܐܕ̈ܡܝܐ ܕ̈ܚܝܠܐ ܕܡܢ ܠܐܣ̈ܛܘܟܣܘ[2] ܢܦ̈ܩ ܦܘܫ̈ܩܐ ܡܫܬܡܗܝܢ. ܟܕ ܡܢ ܫܡܝܐ ܕܝܢ ܦܬܓܡܐ ܒܡܘܠܦ ܐܪܝܐ ܗܘܟܠܐ ܡܫܬܠܦܐ ܡܬܕܪܝܢ. ܐܝܟ ܐܝܠܝܢ ܕܐܡܪ ܠܚܒܪܗ. *ܐܝܬ ܕܐܬܝܬ ܐܝܢܐ ܠܐ ܫܬܐ. ܐܝܢܐ ܐܝܢܘ ܕܒܣܘܣܝܐ ܡܬܠܩ ܕܠܐ ܫܬܐ ܚܡܪ. ܘܐܝܢܘ ܕܒܝܫܐ ܛܥܝܬܐ ܡܬܠܩ ܕܫܬܐ ܡܫܬܪܝܐ. ܗܟܢܐ ܘܠܬܪ̈ܝܢܘܬܐ ܕܦܠ̈ܓܘܬܐ ܐܠܗܐ ܕܐܚܝܢ. ܐܝܟ ܕܐܡܪ ܗܪܩܠܝܛܘܣ ܒܡܐܡܪܐ ܕܬܠܬܗ. ܕܬܠܬܐ ܗܕܐ ܟܕ ܐܝܬܝܗ̇ ܐܡܝܢܐܝܬ ܠܚ̈ܕܐ ܣܢܝܩܐ ܗܘܐ. ܒܕܠܟܢ ܐܢ ܥܘܕܝܐ ܚܝ. ܐܝܬܝܗ̇ ܡܬܬܦܝܣܐ. ܗܘܐ ܐܡܝܢܐ ܕܒܠܬܐ ܠܣܢܝܩܐ ܢܗܘܐ. ܘܐܢ ܚܝ. ܐܡܝܢܐܝܬ ܡܬܬܦܠܣܐ. ܗܘܐ ܐܡܝܢܐ ܠܒܠܬܐ ܡܕܘܡܐ. ܘܗܘܝܢ ܗܠܝܢ ܢܬ̈ܐ ܒܡܪܝܐ ܘܪܘܫܡܐ ܠܬܪ̈ܝܗܘܢ ܗܦܟܐ. ܢܘܢܐ ܘܗܘܪܝܐ ܕܐܠܝܐܝܬ ܥܒܝܫܝܢ. ܘܡܢ ܦܪ̈ܫܐ ܘܡܦܪܐ ܐܚܪ̈ܢܐ ܕܠܐ ܢܗܝܢ ܘܠܐ[4] ܢܗܝܢ.

ܕܐܡܪܢ. ܗܟܢܐ ܕܠܡܕܡ ܒܠܚܘܕܘܗܝ، ܡܕܒܪ ܐܝܬ. ܒܕܪܬ ܘܠܐ ܕܐܠܝܐܝܬ ܥܒܕܝܢܘܗ، ܒܐܡܬ ܕܟܠ ܚܝܢܐ ܕܣܘܬ ܐܡܪ. ܠܐ ܐܬܓܫܬ. ܟܕ ܐܬܓܫܬܐ ܠܡܫܬܘ̈ܬܗܘܢ ܐܬ̈ܓܫܬܐ ܠܣܡܟܐ. ܘܟܕ ܠܡܕܡ ܡܢ ܐܚܪܢܐ ܬܕܒܪ. ܒܕܪܬ ܘܠܐ ܠܚܘܫܬܐ ܐܬܚܫܒ. ܒܐܡܬ ܕܟܠ ܚܝܢܐ ܘܐܕܪܢܐ ܐܚܫܒܐ ܕܐܬܓܫ ܐܡܪ. ܘܠܐ ܗܘܝܘ ܐܝܬ ܕܐܬܡܪ ܚܝܢܐ ܣܘܬ ܘܐܕܪܢܐ ܥܒܕܬ. ܐܠܐ ܟܕ ܡܬܐܡܪܬ ܦܫܝܛܐ ܬܡܝܡܐ ܠܡܕܡ. ܘܠܡܕܡܬܐ ܡܢ ܕܒܪܐ ܕܐܬܐܡܪܬ ܥܒܕܝܢ. ܐܝܟ ܐܬܘ ܐܚܪ̈ܢܐ ܘܐܣܩܘ̈ܬܐ. ܘܡܡܠܠܐ ܒܡܡܠܠܐ ܠܡܡܠܠܘ ܫܦܝܪܐ. ܐܝܟ ܐܝܠܝܢ ܕܐܡܪ ܠܚܒܪܗ[3]. ܝܕܥܐ ܐܝܬ[5] ܕܫܬܐ ܠܘܬܟ ܒܢܘܡܐ. ܒܡܕܒܪܐ ܕܝܘܡܢ ܐܬܪ̈ܐ ܠܚܝܠܬܗܘܢ ܘܠܡܫܡܫܘ ܡܬܒܬܕܝܢ. ܡܛܠ ܕܡܫܡܫܐ ܚܪܒ ܘܠܠܝܐ ܦܪܒ. ܘܡܟܐ[6] ܕܠܝܠܝܐ ܒܟܪ̈ܝܘܬܐ ܕܝܕܥܐ ܕܐܬܡܫܠ. ܕܫܡܫܐ ܠܐ ܒܠܘܢܡܫܐ ܐܬܚܫܒ. ܘܟܕ ܦܫܛܐ ܚܕܐ ܐܝܬ[7] ܠܫܡܫܐ ܒܠܘܢܡܫܐ ܢܠܦ. ܘܡܟܐ ܕܫܡܫܐ ܦܪܣܐ ܝܕܥܐ ܢܡܐ. ܒܠܐ ܝܕܥܐ ܢܠܦܝܘܗ، ܒܐܡܬ ܢܠܦ ܡܕܒܪܐ ܕܐܬܝܬܐ ܦܘܪܫܢܐ ܐܡܪ. ܘܢܠܦ ܒܦܫܛܐ ܐܦܘܪܫܢܐ ܕܬܚ̈ܐ. ܘܢܠܦ ܙܘܘܓܐ ܣܡܡܢܐ.

3-4 [1] ܘܒܥܘܗܕܢܗܘܢ RVLl [2] ܠܐ̈ܣܛܘܟܣܘ RVL [3]* om. F [4] scripsi; ܠܐ RVLl [5] ܐܝܬ RVLl [6] ܒܡܕܐ RVLl [7] ܐܝܢ RVLl

THREE.[18] Fourth is that one should observe the masculine and feminine gender of nouns and verbs with their indices and signs in writing and reading, so that a fault does not occur. Fifth is observing plural and singular with their forms. The same also applies to the sorts of modulation which by grammarians are called 'accent signs', because from the sound of one phrase with a difference in modulation various meanings may be derived. For example, (suppose) someone says to his companion, '(It is) you who have come; I am not coming./I am not coming?' If it ends with a 'stop', he is asserting that he will not come, but if it ends with a 'lower sign', he is agreeing to come. Similarly, it is necessary to point out the joints of sentences. For example, Heraclitus said at the beginning of his book, 'This Word which exists eternally belongs to wise men.' Therefore if the joint is placed at 'exists', what is eternal is that the Word belongs to the wise, but if it is set at 'eternally', 'eternal' is attributed to the Word. These signs for reading and writing are present in their particular way in both languages, Greek and Syriac, and among the Persians and other languages known or unknown to us.

FOUR.[19] When you mention something by itself, indicate it specifically by word; for example, about the eye say that it saw, not that it sensed, because sensation is appropriate to the five senses. But when you mention something together with something else, use the common word; for example, about the eye and the ear together say that they sensed. You do not need to say (that) the eye saw and the ear heard, except when you especially wish to effect persuasion. Indicate the feminine and masculine (together) by the masculine; for example, 'brothers and sisters came (*masc.*)'. It is stupid to pile speech on speech, like someone who says to his companion, 'I wish to come to you in the evening, at the time when people resort to their houses and prepare to dine, because the sun has set and the night is nigh.' When you wish to make a point concisely, use the name not the definition, but when you (wish to) effect persuasion, replace the name with the definition. When the explicit name is rude, replace it with one that is not rude. For example, instead of 'a woman's womb', say 'a woman's private parts'; instead of 'menstruation', 'women's flow', and instead of 'copulation', 'knowledge'.

---

[18] **7.4.3** AR 3.5 07b6-19; IS 4.2 (215.5-216.1).
[19] **7.4.4** AR 3.5 07b19 - 6 07b31; IS 4.2 (216.1-217.6).

## ܦܘܣܩܐ ܫܒܝܥܝܐ
## ܡܛܠ ܗܝܢ ܕܠܦܘܐܛܝܩܐ ܠܐܬܝ̈ ܘܠܪܝܛܘܪܝܩܐ ܠܐ ܠܐܬܝ̈
## ܬܐܘܪ̈ܝܐ ܫܬ

ܡܕܒܪܢܘܬܐ. ܦܘ̈ܐܛܝܩܐ[1] ܗܝ ܒܡ̈ܠܐ ܡܬܬܦܣܩܢܐ ܕܫܬܐܣܝܢ ܠܐ ܡܬܚܫܒܢ. ܘܠܐܝܠܘܬܐ ܒܡܠܝܠܘܬܐ ܪܘܚܐ ܣܓܝܐܝܢ. ܐܝܟܢܐ ܕܐܠܨ ܡܕܡ ܚܕ ܒܢܘܬܐ ܘܡܦܠܓܐ ܦܐܐ ܠܬܘܪܐ. ܘܫܡܗ ܒܢܘܬܐ ܬܪܬܝܢ ܒܢܬ، ܠܗ ܒܪ ܒܢܬ ܡܬܩܪܐ ܗܘ ܕܓܒܪܐ ܘܒܢܬ[2] ܒܗܬܗ. ܗܘ̇ ܠܘ ܒܢܬܐ ܐܠܐ ܡܦܠܓܐ ܩܢܝ. ܒܗ̇، ܕܢܣܒܐ ܬܪܬܝܢ ܡܬܕܡܟ. ܘܠܡܥܒܕ[3] ܡܢ ܕܪ̈ܫܐ ܐܦܕܝܐ[4] ܗܟܢ ܬܪ̈ܟܐ. ܘܕܐܦܠܓܐ ܐܘܟܝܬ ܬܪ̈ܝܢ ܐܦ̈ܐ ܘܐܬܚܙ̈ܝܬܐ ܩܢܝ. ܘܥܒܘܕܘܬ ܐܘܣܝܐ ܒܦܘ̈ܫܩܐ ܚܒܪܐ ܠܡܠܠܐ. ܘܡܬܚܫܒܢܘܬܐ ܐܡܟܐ ܕܒܬܪ ܩܠܐ ܡܬܚܫܒܢܘܬܐ ܡܣܡܟܐ ܠܢܝܫܐ ܥܦܝܪܐ. ܚܕܪܐ ܕܝܢ ܒܪ[5] ܕܡܬܚܫܒܢܘܬ ܥܡܘܕܐ ܥܒܝܪܐ. ܘܒܓܪ̈ܣܐ ܕܒܗܘܢ ܡܬܕܡܟܢܘܬܐ ܘܬܗܘܬܐ ܡܬܟܒܢܐ. ܘܒܡܘܠܡܠܐ ܘܒܓܘ̈ܢܐ ܕܒܗܘܢ ܠܟ̈ܠܬܐ ܘܒܢ̈ܬܐ ܡܬܩܠܝܢ. ܘܒܥܩܡ[6] ܒܪܘܚܐ. ܐܝܟ ܕܐܡܪܝܢ ܦܘ̈ܐܛܝܩܐ ܕܡܠܠܐ ܡܚܫܚܬܢܐ ܩܢܝܐ ܠܐ ܡܬܬܪܪܢܘܬܐ ܘܠܐ ܦܫܝܩܘܬܐ ܐܬܝܗ̇. ܐܝܟܢܐ ܕܡܦܫܩܢܘܬܐ ܕܒܢܘܪܐ ܢܥܒܕܗ ܠܐ ܬܬܪܝܬܐ ܐܬܝܗ̇. ܒܪ ܡܢ ܠܓܘ̈ܬܐ[7] ܡܬܝܡ ܥܡܘܕܐ.

ܕܬܬܝܡ. ܒܬܪ ܩܠܐ ܫܘܠܬܐ ܡܫܠܡܢܘܬܐ ܡܫܒܠܢܘܬܐ ܢܗܘܐ. ܘܡܗܦܟܢܘܬܐ ܡܦܠܓܢ ܬܘܒ ܡܦܠܓܢܐ. ܒܐܡܬ ܒܡ ܗ̇، ܕܡܫܡܠܐ ܡܗܕܪܐ ܐܘ ܡܥܕܪܐ.[1] ܐܝܟܢܐ ܕܠܓܒܪܐ ܢܒܠܐ ܕܐܦܢܐ ܢܥܡܗ. ܗܘܝܐ ܓܪ ܒܡ ܢܒܠܐ ܢܗܝܪܘܬܐ ܕܝܬܝܪ ܡܬܒܪܘܟܐ ܡܕܡ. ܘܐܠܦܐ ܕܗ̇، ܕܡܗܦܟܢܐ ܡܣܡܡܝܬܐ[2] ܬܗܘܐ. ܘܐܝܬܝܗ̇ ܗ̇، ܕܠܐ ܕܓܠܘܬܗ̇ ܡܢܝܚܐ ܐܦܠܐ ܒܢܝܪܘܬܗ̇[3] ܡܢ ܗ̇، ܕܬܬܗܦܟ ܣܒܪܐ. ܘܒܠ ܙܘܪ̈ܒܬܐ ܝܬܝܪ ܡܒܐܝܬ ܠܐ ܐܡܪܐ ܐܦܠܐ ܡܛܠ ܒܝܢܬܐ[4] ܗܟܢ ܒܢܒܐܝܬ. ܘܠܒܬܪ ܩܠܐ ܥܒܝܪ̈ܬܐ ܢܦܠ ܪܝܦܐ. ܐܠܐ ܡܢ ܕܠܥܝܪܐ ܓܒܪܐ ܠܡܫܡܥܘ[5] ܢܓܕܐ. ܒܗܠܝܢ ܓܪ ܢܥܫܐ ܡܬܓܢܝܐ ܘܠܡܗܡܢܘ ܡܬܓܒܪܐ ܘܠܡܬܦܠܣܘ ܡܬܪܥܝܐ. ܘܡܕܡܘܬ[6] ܢܦܫܗ ܕܐܡܘܪܐ ܡܬܦܣܩܐ. ܒܗ̇، *ܕܠܒܪܬ ܩܠܐ[7] ܥܠܦܓܐ ܐܝܬ ܕܒܝܐ. ܒܕܓܠܘ ܩܦܠܝܢܐ ܒܪ ܥܓܝܢ ܠܥܒܕ̈ܐ ܡܬܗܘܝܢ. ܘܡܢ[8] ܡܡܠܠܐ ܡܫܝܚܐ ܡܣܒܪܐ ܡܬܬܒܪ[9] ܥܡܘܕܐ. ܐܝܟܢܐ ܕܒܪ ܢܐܡܪ ܐܝܟ ܒܠ ܡܪܐ ܗܘܝܐ ܢܪܒ ܕܗܘܡ ܗܘ ܗܘܝܐ. ܒܗ̇ ܬܘܒ ܥܡܘܕܐ ܕܢܐܡܪ ܠܗ ܗܘܡ ܗܘ.

---

1 [1] ܦܘܐܛܝܩܐ RVLl [2] ܐܘܡܢܬ F [3] ܠܡܥܒܕ F [4] ܐܦܕܝܐ F [5] ܒܪ F [6] ܘܒܥܩܡ RVLl [7] sg. RVLl

2 [1] ܡܥܕܪܐ RVLl [2] ܡܣܡܡܝܬܐ RVLl [3] i. ܕ RVLl [4] ܡܙܪܬܐ RVL [5] ܠܡܫܡܥܘ RVL [6] f. om. F [7*] pl. RVLl [8] i. ܕ RVLl [9] ܡܬܬܒܪ RVLl.

## SECTION FIVE
## On What is Appropriate for Poetry and Inappropriate for Rhetoric
## Six Theories

ONE.[20] Poets do not use epithets which are exact, and with great diligence they look for a metaphor. For example, when it would be proper to call something a 'house' or a 'chamber', but the name 'house' would be more suitable for it because it is the habitation of a man and his night abode, they do not call it 'house', but 'chamber', because (the latter) evokes an image of greater calm. Some courtyards they call 'a palace of many gates and *diaptuke*', i.e. two and twinned faces. The omission of connecting particles makes speechconcise. Transference is fine where a proportional word makes clear the meaning, and useful where the open expression of the name would be vile, in threats in which astonishment and alarm is sought, in laudations and vituperations in which good and evil are sought out, and in defence. For example, poets say that metrical speech is 'lyreless and non-dancing melody', just as blowing a trumpet is 'stringless music', thus producing a sign by privations.

TWO.[21] A polished word gives perfect understanding, while an image-evoking one also misleads; that is, together with giving understanding, it adorns or disfigures. For example, one may call a guileful man false, for together with guile this brings in (the image of) an abomination which is specially to be avoided. That which evokes an image must be proportioned: a thing, the falsehood of which is not made explicit, must (still) not be evoked in an image as if it were true. Great things must not be spoken of in a very lowly way, nor a lesser thing very solemnly. An orator should reject vile words, except when he wants to pour hatred on despicable things. By these (representations) the soul is led astray, induced to believe, and inclined to be persuaded. It is persuaded by the appearance of the soul of the speaker, because the word (appears) to have justifiable right. Therefore many, when stirring listeners, entrance (them), and a listener is immediately affected by a speech arousing pathos; just as when someone says, 'Everyone with a mind knows that this is so', the listener is ashamed to say, 'It is not so'.

---

[20] **7.5.1** AR 3.6 07b31-08a9; IS 4.2 (217.7-218.16).
[21] **7.5.2** AR 3.7 08a10-25; 32-36; IS 4.2 (219.1-220.13).

ܕܬܬܠܬ. ܕܐܝܟܢܐ ܒܗܘܢ ܠܟܠ ܢܦܩ ܡܢ ܗܠܝܢ ܢܦܩܐ ܠܟܠ ܡܕܡ ܒܗܘܢ ܘܥܒܘܕܐ ܕܥܪܪܐ ܠܟܠ ܡܕܡ ܟܕܪ. ܒܐܘܪܚܐ ܕܠܟܠ ܗܟܐ ܕܐܡܪ ܐܡܘܪܐ ܗ̇ܝ[1] ܕܠܝܬ ܦܘܠܓܐ ܥܠ ܗܠܝܢ ܕܐܡܪ ܐܢܐ ܘܓܠܝܢܐ ܕܗܠܝܢ ܗܟܢܐ ܐܝܢ ܢܦܩ. ܒܗܘܢ ܓܝܪ ܡܕܡ ܙܟܪ ܡܢ ܣܘܟܐ ܠܥܘܒܕܐ. ܘܠܐ ܙܕܩ ܠܗܘܦܟܐ ܕܐܡܘܢܐܝܬ ܒܡܫܩܠܐܝܬ[2] ܢܬܚܫܒ. ܒܗ̇ܝ ܕܐܝܟ ܕܒܫܘܠܡܐ ܒܠܐ ܡܬܓܫܡܐ ܡܬܠܓܒ ܥܡܘܕܐ. ܒܬܪ ܗ̇ܢ ܗܟܐ ܕܠܬܒܢܝܬܐ ܡܥܝܢܐܝܬ[3] ܢܦܪܘܫ ܪܘܚܢܐ. ܒܬܪ ܕܝܢ ܗܟܐ ܕܠܡܥܒܕܢܘܬܐ ܪܒܝܥܐܝܬ ܢܥܬܕܘܢ[4]. ܘܥܒܕܗܐ ܡܬܬܦܫܛܢܐ ܘܡܦܫܛܐ ܘܐܡܦܫܛܢܐ ܠܒܐܡܪܐ *ܒܡܫܟܢܐ ܢܬܪ[5] ܠܢܣܒܝܢ. ܒܡܬܠܫܐ ܘܓܘܢܐ. ܘܦܘܓܪܐ ܘܢܦܫܗܘܬܐ. ܐܒܝܒܐ ܕܐܣܛܘܟܣܐܘܪܓܘܣ ܒܣܝܓܬܗ ܐܡܪ ܗܘܐ. ܕܦܘܪܫ ܗܘ ܕܢܬܬܟܠ ܓܒܝܠ. ܒܗ̇ܝ ܐܬܬܟܠ ܫܘܒܗܪ. ܘܐܢܐ ܕܒܪܪܐ ܡܫܒܗ ܦܓܠܐ ܠܓܒܗ. ܒܕܐܝܟ ܗܠܝܢ ܓܝܪ[6] ܦܐܓܠܐ ܒܬܘܦܐ ܡܬܚܫܒ ܗܘܘ ܘܒܢܝܢܐ ܡܬܡܢܝܢ. ܘܡܐܡܪܢܘܗܝ ܡܬܬܘܕܝܢ ܘܡܣܬܒܪܝܢ ܡܬܗܡܢܝܢ.

ܕܐܪܒܥ. ܐܣܛܘܟܣܐ ܗ̇ܢܘܢ ܐܦ ܡܬܚܫܒܐ ܒܡܕܡ ܡܢ ܗܠܝܢ ܫܪܟܐ. ܕܠܐ ܡܥܘܫܬܐ ܒܢܘܢ ܘܕܠܐ ܡܢܝܢܐ ܐܪܡܘܢܝܩܐ ܦ̇ܠܐ ܠܡܗܘܐ ܡܐܡܪܗ. ܘܐܠܐ ܓܒܝܠܐ ܗ̇ܢ ܘܡܗܘܓܠܢܐ ܘܡܬܗܡܢܐ ܒܐܣܟܝܡܗ. ܠܐ ܡܦܫܩܐ ܕܝܢ ܘܠܐ ܡܬܗܡܢܢܐ ܒܫܘܟܠܗ ܡܬܚܫܐ. ܘܗܟܢܐ ܥܡܘܕܐ ܒܒܪܬ ܡܠܐ ܬܗܘܝܢ ܘܠܢܫܐ ܥܡܘܝܢ. ܐܝܟ ܗܢܘܢ ܕܒܥܘܡܩܐ. ܒܕ ܡܢ ܦܠܘܩܐ ܕܗܘܦܟܝܢ ܡܕܡ ܒܢܘܪܐ ܠܗܠܝܢ ܕܐܡܪ ܡܫܬܟܠܝܢ. *ܗܟܐ ܕܦ̇ܠܓܐ[1] ܠܗܬܘܢ ܠܗ ܡܬܦܫܬ ܢܬܠܝܢ ܠܗ. ܘܡܬܠܠܐ ܐܪܘܡܘܢ ܐܡܪܝܢܬ ܦܫܝܫܐ ܗ̇ܘ ܗܘ ܕܡܦܫܩܐ ܒܗ ܥܠ ܒܪܬ ܡܠܐ ܡܢ ܣܒܪܬܗ̇ ܘܠܐ ܒܡܦܫܩܘܬܐ ܐܦܠܐ ܒܡܦܪܫܘܬܐ ܡܫܬܟܚܝܢ ܦܬܓܡܘܗܝ. ܗ̇ܘ ܓܝܪ ܕܐܝܟ ܗܢܐ ܓܠܝܢ ܡܢ ܗܝܡܢܘܬܐ ܐܬܬܘܗܝ.

ܕܚܡܫ. ܕܗܒܡܐ ܘܦܘܪܩܐ ܒܡܡܠܠܐ ܙܗܘܪܐ ܡܥܘܫܬܐ ܡܕܡ ܗܘ. ܒܢܘܢ ܠܗ ܡܢܝܢܘܬܐ ܕܣܬܬܐ. ܦܐܓܠܘܬܐ ܗܝ، ܓܝܪ ܗܕܐ. ܘܐܢܘܢ ܕܡܥܘܫܬܐ ܡܢܝܢܬܐ ܡܢܬܐܝܬ ܬܘܩܦܘܗܝ. ܢܬܪ ܡܢܝܢܐ ܠܗ. ܐܒܝܒܐ ܕܒܡܐܡܪܐ ܗܐܪܘܩܢܐ ܢܘܐܝܬ ܘܒܡܫܪܘܩܢܐ ܦܪܝܐܝܬ ܘܒܗܠܝܢ ܕܐܢܐ[1] ܒܡܕܡ ܡܢ ܐܓܪܬܗ ܡܬܚܫܒ ܐܢܐ ܫܘܪܝܐܝܬ. ܘܡܢ ܗܠܝܢ ܡܥܘܫܬܐ ܐܝܬ ܐܢܕܐ ܕܠܥܘܠܡ ܥܠ ܦܐܓܠܐ ܙܬܟܐ ܐܘܒܢܬ ܒܠܟ ܘܠܐ ܢܦܩ. ܒܕ ܒܢܝܐ ܢܗܐ ܡܡܠܠܐ ܐܒܝܒܐ ܕܒܡܐܡܪܐ ܗܘܢ ܕܐܝܡܒܘ[2] ܘܐܢܐܡܒܝܢܐ ܡܢ ܢܬܝܢܐ ܡܬܬܡܗܝܢ. ܐܦ ܓܝܪ ܘܬܟܐ ܙ̈ܒܢܐ ܡܥܘܫܬܐ ܕܦܪܘܐܘܣ ܡܬܒܢܐ ܒܦܫܝܢܐ ܗܘ ܠܒ. ܘܬܪܐܘܣܡܒܐܘܣ[3] ܘܕܡܐܢܐ ܣܪ، ܕܢܬܚܫܒ ܒܗ.

3 [1] i. add. ܒ RVL [2] sg. F [3] ܒܥܝܢܐܝܬ RVLl [4] ܢܥܬܕܪ F [5*] ܒܡܫܟܢܐܝܬ RLl; ܒܡܫܟܢܐܐܝܬ V [6] om. RVLl

4 [1*] ܒܕ ܦ̇ܠܓܐ RVLl

5 [1] ܕܐܪܐ RVLl [2] ܕܐܢܐܡܒܝܢܐ RVLl [3] ܘܬܪܐܘܣܡܒܘܣ RVLl

THREE.[22] Choosing a suitable time for each of these things is common to everything, and a declaration of truth is helpful to everything. For example, to everything a speaker says he may add, 'There is no doubt about the things that I say, and it is evident that they are so', for thereby he restrains in advance the listener from contention. An orator should not always use proportioned (words), because a listener will usually be seduced by unbalanced (ones), sometimes when an orator tears harshly into gentle things, sometimes when he speaks gently of harsh things. Epithets, doubled words, and foreign words are more appropriate to speeches arousing pathos, in laudations and vituperations, and (speeches expressing) anger or love. For example, Isocrates used to say in his laments, 'My wish is close to being fulfilled, because my perseverance has been fulfilled, and he who perseveres in truth attains his desire.' The old poets used to employ such things and were numbered among the prophets; their words were approved and their oracles believed.

FOUR.[23] Although rhetoric does indeed use some of these things, its speech must nevertheless be without metre and without musical number. Although (by them it may) be shaped, image-evoking, and admirable in its form, it will not be persuasive nor seem credible in its content. In this way listeners would be fascinated by the wording but miss the point, like those in the square who, although perceiving the things a herald is saying from little boys running in advance of him, do not give careful attention to him when he reaches them. '*Arhymic*' or loose speech is that in which every word is detached from its neighbour, and its phrases are not limited by joining together or setting apart. (Speech) such as this is deprived of pleasure.

FIVE.[24] The binding and sundering in rhetorical discourse is some (sort of) metre, but not an exact numerical (one), for that is poetic. (However), if a numerical metre adheres to it in part, it makes it more solemn, as in heroic speeches in Greek and *khusrawāniyyāt* in Persian, as also in those which I myself use in some of my letters in Syriac. Among these metres is that (in) which an accent (*rethmā*) or rising of the voice accompanies the end of every phrase, when the

[22] **7.5.3** AR 3.7 08a36-b20; IS 4.2 (220.14-221.14).
[23] **7.5.4** AR 3.8 08b21-28; IS 4.2 (221.15-222.12).
[24] **7.5.5** AR 3.8 08b28-09a13; IS 4.2 (222.12-224.8).

ܘܐܝܬ ܐܕܫܐ ܡܕܡ ܕܬܡܝܗܐ ܕܐܝܟ. ܣܘܬܩ ܦܣܘ̈ܩܐ ܕܡܬܬܡܠܬܐ ܘܡܢ
ܘܬ̈ܢܝܐ ܦܘܗܝ̱ ܡܬܘܪܐ. ܘܗܘ ܡܬܦܪܫ ܡܢ ܫܘܪܝܐ ܫܘܠܡܐ.

ܕܫܠܬ. ܒܡܘ̈ܫܠܦ ܠܫ̈ܢܐ ܡܫܚܠܦܝܢ ܬܪ̈ܬܡܐ. ܘܠܟܠ ܠܚܕܐ ܐܕܫܐ ܡܕܡ
ܕܬܡܝܗܐ ܒܝܬ. ܘܠܫ̈ܢܝܐ ܢܫ̈ܝܟܬܐ ܐܝܬ ܦܘܠ̈ܚܢܝܬܐ ܕܠܝ ܠܐ ܢܕܥܝܢ ܐܦܠܐ
ܒܫܦܝܪ̱ ܗܢܐ ܡܘܬܪ̱. ܗܪܟܐ ܕܝܢ ܐܬ̈ܘܬܐ ܢܘܟ̈ܪܝܬܐ ܕܐܪ̈ܡܝܐ ܘܡܬܠܚܢܝܢ
ܘܐܚܪ̈ܝܬܐ ܕܒܢ̈ܝܢ ܘܡܦܩ̈ܢܝܢ ܐܝܟ ܪܒܢ. ܘܐܡܪ ܕܫܦܝܪܬ ܬܪܬܡܐ ܪܕܡ
ܕܬܗܘܐ ܠܒܣܝܣ ܘܠܐ ܡܫܝܚܘܬܐ ܒܐܡܬ ܡܥܡܘܫܬܐ ܡܕܡ. ܘܐܝܟ ܠܗ
ܚܬܝܬܬܐ ܬܗܘܐ ܠܗ̇. ܘܐܘܟܘܬܐ ܬܘܒ ܐܬܬܘܬܢܝܬܐ ܬܗܘܐ ܒܢܝܢ
ܦܬܓ̈ܡܐ ܪܗܛܘ̈ܪܝܩܐ ܘܐܝܠܠܓܢܐ ܒܐܪܒܥܘܬܐ ܘܒܪܘܚܬܐ ܐܝܟ ܐܡܪ ܐܢܐ.
ܐܟܡܐ ܕܒܗ ܗܘܪܝܢܐ ܢܗܘܐ ܪܗܛܘܪܐ ܘܫܡܥܘ ܗܕܐ ܗܟ̈ܢܐ ܕܗ̈ܢܐ ܐܡܪ.
ܒܬܪܗ̇[1] ܘܦܬ̈ܓܡܐ ܕܗ̈ܢܐ[2] ܢܐܡܪ. ܘܠܐ ܢܐܡܪ ܒܠܫ̈ܢܐ ܫܒܝܚܐ. ܘܒܬܪ
ܡܫܡܥܬܐ ܒܐܝܟܢܘܬܐ ܦܬܓܡܢܘܬܐ ܦܫܝܛܬܐ ܢܐܡܪ. ܠܐ ܚܘܪ̈ܬܐ ܗܕܝ̈ܪܬܐ. ܘܒܬܪ
ܐܟܐ ܕܠܒܐ ܒܡܟܐ ܕܫܡܥܐ ܢܐܡܪ. ܠܐ ܦܫܪܐ ܕܪܫܡܘܬܐ.[3] ܕܐܝܟ ܗܠܝܢ
ܓܝܪ ܫܦܝܪܬ ܠܒܪܐ ܘܚܝܠܬ ܫܡܥܐ ܠܡܡܠܠܐ ܒܒ̈ܢܝ̱.

ܦܘܣܩܐ ܫܬܝܬܝܐ
ܥܠ ܡܫܘܚܬܐ ܕܡܡܠܠܐ ܪܗܛܘܪܝܐ
ܬܐܘܪ̈ܐܣ ܬܠܬ

ܡܕܡܝܢܘܬܐ. ܐܡܪ ܓܝܪ ܪܒܢ ܕܡܡܠܠܐ ܡܢ ܪܗܛܘܪ̈ܝܩܐ ܡܦܘܪܫܐ[1] ܦ̇ܠܓܐ
ܠܬܠܬܐ. ܒܐܝܕܐ ܕܐܬ̈ܘܬܐ ܐܝܟ ܕܠܡܡܠܠܐ ܦܘܐܠܓܝܐ ܢܗܘܘܢ ܠܗ.
ܘܠܫܪܪܐ ܡܢ ܐܬ̈ܘܬܗ ܠܐ ܬܗܘܐ ܠܡܦܪܢܣܘ ܒܝܬܗ̇. ܐܠܐ ܒܪ ܒܐܢܫܐ
ܕܒܬܪܗ̇ ܬܬܐܡܪ ܢܬܡܠܠ ܫܘܟܠܗ̇. ܐܟܡܐ ܕܢܐܡܪ ܕܠܐ ܬܗܘܐ ܒܒ̈ܢ.
ܗܘܒܪ̱[2] ܪܘܚܐ. ܘܐܝܟ ܬܫܒܘܚ ܬܘܒ ܪܘܚܐ. ܕܠܡܐ ܢܗܘܝܢ ܡܢ ܕܢܦܠܐ[3]
ܘܠܬ̈ܠܬܝܢ ܒܠܒܗܘܢ ܢܦܠܐ. ܒܟܠܝܢ ܓܝܪ ܐܬ̈ܘܬܐ ܡܕܡܝܢܘܬܐ ܒܬܪܝܢܘܬܐ
ܐܫܘܪܐ. ܘܬܠܬܝܬܐ ܒܪ̈ܒܝܥܬܐ. ܘܒܠܗܝܢ ܒܝܕ ܬܘܗܡܐ ܘܪ̈ܬܡܐ ܡܦܪ̈ܫܢܐ
ܘܡܠܬ̈ܚܡܐ ܥܒܝܪ ܡܬܬܫܪ̈ܝܢ. ܘܐܡܪ ܬܘܒ ܕܠܡܡܠܠܐ ܪܗܛܘܪܝܐ
ܒܦ̈ܠܓܐ ܦܠܓ ܠܬܠܬܐ. ܒܐܝܕܐ ܕܒܪܬ ܡܠܐ ܕܡܕܪܐ ܒܗ̇ ܢܬܠܡ. ܒܡܘܒܬ
ܫܘܒܠܐ ܐܘ ܒܐܚܪܝܢܘܬܗ.[4] ܡܒܢܐ ܓܝܪ ܡܫܘܚܬܐ ܘܗܘܝܢܐ ܘܕܠܠ[5]
ܠܬܘܢܝܐ[6] ܗ̇ܘܐ. ܒܪ ܡܡܠܠܐ ܕܡܢܝܐ ܘܡܦܠܓܐ ܘܡܫܘܚܬܢܝܬܐ ܢܬܪ ܦܪ̈ܫܝܢ
ܒܡܘܕܝܐ.

6 [1] om. RVLl [2] ܕܗ̈ܢܐ RVLl [3] i. ܘ RVLl
1 [1] ܡܒܘܪܚܐ F [2] ܗܘܒܪ̱ RVLl [3] ܕܡܦܠܐ RVLl [4] ܒܐܚܪܝܢܘܬܗ RVL [5] ܘܕܠܠ F [6] ܠܬܘܢܝܐ RVLl

speech is sorrowful as in those speeches which are called iambics or iambic by the Greeks. Also the tetrametric accent called trochaios is very skipping, and Thrasymachus first began to use it. And there is some accented species which falls at the end of sections and is called 'paean' by the Greeks. In it the end is distinguished from the beginning.

SIX.[25] Accents differ among various languages, and some accented species is peculiar to every tongue. There were many things necessary to the Greeks which are not understood by us nor useful in our language. Here our master cited Greek letters which are long or lengthened and others which are short or contracted, and said that style should be well accented and not loose, that is, it should have some metre, but not an exact (one). I say there should also be concord of letters between rhetorical phrases and proportion in the length or brevity (of them). For example, when a Syrian is an orator and says *shma' hādhē sābhē zhayyā* ('hear this, noble elders'), after it he will say, *wa-ṭlāyē zhayyā* ('and noble youths'), and not *'laymē shbhīḥē* ('praiseworthy lads'); or after *saybūthā gīthā* ('pleasant old age') he will say *ṭaybūthā pīthā* ('comely kindness'), not *ḥewwārāthā hdhīrāthā* ('adorned age'); or after *'ebbā d-lebbā* ('produce of the heart') he will say *'ūbhā d-ḥubbā* ('womb of love'), not *pērā d-reḥmthā* ('fruit of friendship'). For such things make speech good-sounding and pleasant-of-hearing.

## SECTION SIX
## On the Metre of Rhetorical Speech
## Three Theories

ONE.[26] Our master said that rhetorical speech must be distinct, that is, it should have 'twins' like poetic speech. Each one of its 'twins' should not be complete in itself, but when bound with that which is after it, its meaning should be completed. As long as what one says does not produce gibberish even if breath happens to run out, (can) anyone who examines (it) condemn you and reject all your arguments? With these 'twins' the first is bound to the second, and the

---

[25] **7.5.6** AR 3.8 09a13-23; 08b30-32; IS 4.2 (224.11-225.12).
[26] **7.6.1** AR 3.9 09a24-b9 (cf. 10a22-28); IS 4.3 (226.6-227.3).

ܕܬܪ̈ܬܝܢ. ܐܘܪܒܐ ܕܬܐܘ̈ܡܬܐ ܡܣܡܝܢܐ ܦܠܐ ܠܡܗܘܐ. ܕܡ ܠܐ ܢܬܠܝܐ
ܗܠܝܢܐ ܕܬܐܡܘܬܐ ܘܕܡܝܢܬܐ ܒܗܘܢ. ܐܦܠܐ ܬܘܒ ܒܪܢܐ ܕܒܗܘܢܒܘ
ܡܬܦܣܩ ܢܗܘܐ. ܘܒܝ̈ܢܬ[1] ܫܪ̈ܝܬܐ ܕܬܐܘ̈ܡܬܐ ܦܘܪܫܐ ܠܝܬܐ ܠܐ ܢܗܘܐ.
ܘܡܛܠܠ ܕܫܪ̈ܝܬܐ ܗ̇ܝ ܗܘ ܕܬܐܘ̈ܡܬܐ ܡܢܐ ܘܕܠܝܠ ܠܡܬܦܩܐ ܒܦ̈ܠܓܘܗܝ.
ܘܡܛܠܠ ܕܠܐ ܫܪ̈ܝܬܐ ܗ̇ܝ، ܬܐܡܘܬܐ ܚܣܝܪܬܐ ܐܝܬܝܗ̇. ܘܒܚܝܪܐ ܠܡܐܡܪ.
ܡܣܡܝܢܝܬ ܒܪܝܘܬܐ ܘܐܪܒܥܘܬܐ. ܦܠܐ ܕܢܗܘ̈ܘܢ ܬܐܘ̈ܡܬܐ. ܒܪ ܒܪ̈ܝܬܐ ܗܠܝܢ
ܠܡܒܪܕܘ ܒܢܘܫܐ ܠܐ ܣܦܩ. ܘܐܪ̈ܒܥܬܐ[2] ܗܠܝܢ ܡܠܐܟ̈ܐ ܘܠܥܘܪܗܘܢ ܡܫܐ[3]
ܥܠܡܗܘܢ. ܐܝܟ ܕܐܦ ܡܒܕܪܬܐ ܕܠܘܬ ܠܡܐܡܪܐ ܗ̇ܝ، ܐܚܪܐ ܕܗܠܝܢ ܒܪܐ
ܡܢ ܠܒܪܐ ܕܡܫܠ ܒܡܫܐ ܠܐ ܡܚܕܪܐ. ܘܐܚܪܐ ܕܗܠܝܢ ܐܘܪܒܐ ܠܡܫܘܪ
ܚܠܦ ܠܐ ܚܝܠܐ. ܘܐܝܟ ܐܘܪܚܐ ܡܚܪܬܐ ܕܒܗ̇ ܫܘ̈ܦܐ ܫܬܠܬܐ ܠܠܐܬܐ
ܕܡܢܗܘܢ ܡܗܠܟܝܢ ܥܡܡܝܢ. ܐܘܪܚܐ ܡܢܝܢ ܠܡܗܘܪܐ ܘܡܥܡܪܐ ܡܠܟܐ.
ܘܒܪܢܐ ܠܥܡܘܪܐ ܡܠܦ ܒܪ ܠܝܬ ܠܗ ܣܘܓܐܐ ܐܘܪܚܬ ܡܦ̈ܩܬܐ ܕܟܠ ܫ̈ܕܢܐ
ܬܚܠܦ ܘܠܫܕ̈ܢܐ ܡܟ̈ܕܢܝܢ.

ܕܬܠܬ. ܡܛܠܠ ܕܒܢܘܐ ܒܝܬܐ ܕܒܝܢ ܡܦܠܓܢܐ ܗܘ. ܐܝܟܢܐ ܕܢܐܡܪ ܐܢܫ.
ܡܬܕܪܝ ܐܢܐ ܒܦܠܓ. ܐܝܟܢܐ ܐܡܪ ܐܘ ܣܒܪ ܕܦܠܓ ܘܦܠܓ. ܘܐܝܬ ܐܝܟܢܐ
ܕܕܠܡܩ̈ܒܠܐ[1] ܣܡܝܢ ܦܠ̈ܓܐ. ܐܝܟ ܗ̇ܝ ܕܐܡܪܢܐ ܠܟ. ܡܢܗܘܢ ܗܟܝܠ ܠܒܪ̈ܩܐ
ܡܬܐܡܪܝܢ. ܡܢܗܘܢ ܕܝܢ ܠܦܘܪ̈ܓܝܐ. ܘܐܝܟ ܗ̇ܝ ܕܒܪ̈ܝܬܐ ܡܢ ܐܣܦܪ.
ܓ̈ܠܝܐ ܕܝܢ ܐܒܟܪܘ. ܘܐܝܟܢܐ ܕܐܠܘܣܩܘܦܘܢ ܒܢܝܬ ܕܐܝܟܐ ܐܡܪ ܒܠ[2]
ܦܠܘܬܘܣ[3] ܐܝܟ. ܕܗܠܝܢ ܡܢ ܒܪ ܒܬ̈ܠܝܢ ܐܝܠܝܢ ܡܬܒܝܢ ܗܘܘ. ܒܪ ܕܝܢ
ܐܬܘ ܠܘܬܢ ܐܙܕܒܢܘ. ܘܕܠܡܩ̈ܒܠܐ ܒܪ ܥܠܡܝܢ ܡܬܠܝܣܝܢ. ܒܗ̇ܝ ܕܒܫ̈ܕܪܐ
ܡܬܕܪܝܢ. ܡܐܡܪܐ ܡܕܝܢ ܕܒܢܘܐ ܐܘ ܡܦܠܓܢܐ ܐܝܬܘܗܝ. ܐܘ ܕܠܡܩ̈ܒܠܐ.
ܐܘ ܠܐ ܥܩܒ ܒܐܘܪܒܘܬܐ ܘܒܪܝܘܬܐ ܒܬܪ ܕܐܣܬܟܠܬܐ ܡܕܡ ܬܗܘܐ
ܠܗܘܢ. ܐܘ[4] ܬܐܡܪ̈ܬܢܐ ܘܐܝܬܝܗܘܢ ܡܢܝܢ ܥܘܪܢܐ ܘܥܘܠܡܢܐ ܕܬ̈ܚܝܢܐ[5].
ܐܝܟ ܗ̇ܝ ܕܐܣܛܪܘܢܐ ܠܒܪ ܢܣܒܬ. ܐܣܛܪܘܢܐ ܠܒܪ ܕܠܗ ܒܐܝܪܐ ܗܘܐ
ܠܗ. ܘܐܝܟ ܗ̇ܝ ܕܒܪܐ ܡܢ ܡܬܠܠ ܠܗ ܐܒܠܬ. ܘܗܘܐ ܗ̇ܘܐ ܠܗ ܐܒܟܪܐ
ܕܐܒܠܬ. ܘܗܠܝܢ ܡܢ ܥܒ̈ܕܝ ܣܘܒܠܐ ܡܥܫܠܦܘܗܝ ܕܝܢ. ܐܝܟ ܥܠܬܬܐ ܠܒܪ
ܒܐܪ̈ܝܢ ܚܪܒܐ. *ܘܥܠܬܐ[7] ܬܘܒ ܒܐܪ̈ܝܢ[8] ܚܪܒܐ.[6] ܐܦ ܠܒܪ ܘܐܣܬܪܚܬܐ
ܬܫܥܝܬܐ ܐܝܬ ܗ̇ܪܝ. ܘܒܗ̇ܝ ܕܣܘܪܚܢܐ ܠܢܫܐ[9] ܠܐ ܥܠ̈ܬܐ ܥܡܡ ܐܝܟ.

2 [1] ܘܒܝ̈ܢܬ F [2] ܘܐܪܒܥܬܐ F [3] ܡܫܟܐ RVLl
3 [1] i. om. F [2] om. RVLl [3] ܦܝܠܘܐܘܣ F; ܦܝܠܘܬܐܘܣ RVL [4] ܐܝܟ RVL [5] ܕܬ̈ܚܝܢܐ RVLl [6*] om. R [7] i. add. ܬ l [8] f. ܐ VLl [9] f. ܢ RVLl

third to the fourth, and all of them are properly made clear by means of separating and connecting pauses and accents. He also said that rhetorical speech should have 'returns', that is, it should end with the word with which it began, with the same meaning or a different one, for in this way it is limited, pleasant, and easy to learn, because rhymed, recurring, and metrical speech sticks better in the memory.

TWO.[27] The length of the 'twins' should be moderate, so that the image-evocation of the first 'twin' is not erased with it. Neither should it be (so) short that it breaks off in haste, and there should not be excessive looseness among the joints of the 'twins'. Speech (constructed) of joints is (speech) which possesses 'twins' and with its divisions is easy to breathe, but speech without a joint is a solitary 'twin' and to be uttered in one. 'Twins' should be spoken in the mean between brevity and length, because very short ones are not able to last for a breath, and very long ones are too full and their end makes one forget their beginning. Similarly a crossing to a haven which is very short does not provide safety from an unexpected knock against the earth, and the response (to) that which is very long is not to jump over it. Like a long road on which strong travellers leave behind the weary who walk with them, (what is) long for the speaker also wearies the listener, but (what is) short will deceive the listener because it does not have circularity, that is, parts which return to each other and explain each other.

THREE.[28] Conjoined speech is often dividing, as when someone says, 'I admire so and so, how he said or did such and such.' Sometimes the divisions are contraries, as when someone says, 'Some long for wealth, others for pleasure'; or, 'The prudent were put to shame, but the foolish prospered'; or as Lycophron said in court against a certain Peilothaus, 'When we were at home, these men were selling, but when they came to us, they were bought.' When contraries follow (one another) they are successful, because they are clarified by each other. Therefore conjoined speeches are either dividing, or contrary, or unequal in length or brevity after they have some arrangement, or doubling and possessing a similar beginning or end. For example, '*For the field* I took, *for the field* (which was) his came

[27] **7.6.2** AR 3.9 09b13-32; IS 4.3 (227.3-228.1).
[28] **7.6.3** AR 3.9 09b32-10b5; IS 4.3 (228.1-10).

# ܦܘܣܩܐ ܥܣܝܪܝܐ
## ܡܛܠ ܗܝܡܢܘܬܐ ܠܝܫܘܥ
## ܬܐܘܪ̈ܝܐ ܚܕܐ

ܘܕܡܘܬܐ. ܠܝܫܘܥ ܕܡܫܡܠܝܐ ܗܝ ܗܝܡܢܘܬܐ. ܘܗ̇ܝ ܕܡܫܡܠܝܐ ܘܓܠܝܐ ܒܒܪܐ
ܠܫܘܡܠܝܐ ܡܠܝܐ. ܘܫܘܡܠܝܐ ܫܐܠܬܐ ܗܘܝܢ ܗ̇ܘܐ ܗܝܡܢܘܬܐ ܒܪ ܫܪܒܐ
ܠܡܘܡܝܘ[1] ܒܒܪܐ. ܠܐ ܠܒܒܪܐ ܢܬܒܥܐ. ܐܒܒܐ ܕܠܐ ܢܬܐܡܪ ܫܡ̈ܐ
ܫܒܪ̈ ܠܚ̈ܬܐ ܐܢܘܢ. ܐܠܐ ܢܬܐܡܪ ܫܡܘܬܐ ܫܒܝܪܬ ܠܒܬܐ ܐܬܝܬܗ̇.
ܘܗܝܐ ܫܘܡܗܐ ܒܗܢ ܐܝܟ ܒܫܡܐ. ܘܠܐ ܫܒܩ ܦܠܐ ܠܡܬܚܫܚܘ
ܒܡܐܢ̈ܐ. ܐܘܠܐ ܒܐܡܩ̈ܝܢܘܬܐ. ܒܪ ܫܢܝܐ ܒܡܝܢܘܬ ܡܟܠܠܐ ܕܡܢ
ܩܠܝܐ ܒܫܡܐ. ܐܝܟ ܕܐܦ ܠܝܫܘܬܗ̇[2] ܗ̇ܝ ܕܠܒܠ ܠܒܐ ܒܫܡܐ. ܡܫܘܪܐ
ܕܝܢ ܠܝܫܘܥ ܗ̇ܝ ܕܡܠܬܐܠܐ ܠܠܒܐ ܦܬܓܡܐ ܣܡܟܝܢ ܠܗ̇. ܒܒܘܫܐ ܒܢܘܪ
ܦܫܘܩܐ. ܠܐ ܒܫܘܫܒܐ ܒܡܘܩܐ. ܗܘ ܕܐܝܟ ܗܕܐ ܒܗ̇ ܕܡܫܡܠܝܐ
ܗܝܡܢܐ. ܡܠܘܢ ܕܝܢ ܒܪ ܡܢ ܕܠܡܩܠܝܐ ܘܐܡ̈ܠܬܐ ܕܠܘ ܫܒܩ ܙ̈ܒܢܝܢ
ܡܬܢܫܒܐ. ܘܪܘܡ ܕܐܝܟ ܕܡܘܡ ܒܒ̈ܢܐ ܢܫܝܡܝܢ ܠܝܒܘܬܐ ܫܘܠܝܐ.

ܕܬܪ̈ܬܝܢ. ܒܠ ܠܝܫܘܥ ܗܝܡܢܬܐ[1] ܬܠܬܐܝܬ ܗܘܐ. ܒܫܘܠ̈ܝܐ.
ܒܐܠܬܗ̈ܘܬܐ ܐܘܒܢ ܠܡܩܠܝܬܐ. ܒܡܒܒܕ̈ܢܘܬܐ.[2] ܘܫܘܠ̈ܝܐ ܐܪ̈ܒܐ
ܐܢܘܢ. ܘܕܡܝܐ ܗ̇ܝ ܕܡܫܝܐ.[3] ܐܝܟ ܕܐܡܪ̈ ܦܪܘܠܘܣ[4] ܡܛܠ ܛܠܬܐ
ܕܐܒܒܐ ܒܦܪܘܐ ܕܡܬܠܬܐ ܡܢ ܒܒܢ̈ܝܬܐ[5] ܐܝܟ ܬܪܐܐ ܡܢ ܗܘܪܝܐ
ܕܝܢܐ. ܬܠܝܐ ܕܝܢ ܫܐܠܬܐ ܕܡܢ *ܕܠܡܘܠܐ. ܐܒܒܐ ܕܒܡܫܝܐ ܫܒܩ
ܘܗܪܐ ܢܦܪܐ. ܬܠܬܐ ܗܘܐ ܫܐܠܬܐ ܕܡܢ ܕܡܫܝܐ.[6] ܐܒܒܐ ܕܠܒܠܐ
ܡܠܝܐ ܕܐܬܪܐ ܢܒܒܐ. ܘܪܒܝܒܐ ܫܐܠܬܐ ܕܡܢ ܫܒܩ ܒܪܛܠ̈ܝܐ.
ܐܒܒܐ ܕܠܫܪܝܘܢ ܢܒܘܫܐ ܫܒܝܐ ܢܒܒܘܗ. ܘܠܡܘܠܒܘܢܬܐ ܐܝܟ
ܡܬܪܓܢܐ ܕܡܬܝܐ. ܒܒܕܐ ܠܪܒܐ. ܘܡܒܒܕ̈ܢܘܬܐ ܠܗܘ ܕܡܘܡ ܒܒ̈ܢܐ
ܡܫܩ̈ܠܝ. ܘܐܬ ܐܝܟܐ ܕܫܐܠܬܐ ܒܡ ܦܘܫܩ ܡܒܒܕ̈ܢܘܬܐ ܡܬܪܒܒܢܐ
ܘܫܘܪܐ. ܐܒܒܐ ܕܠܒܪܐ ܡܠܒܘܫܐ ܠܠܛܪ̈ܝܘܢ[7] ܢܦܪܐ. ܒܐܡܬ
ܡܡܫܢܐ ܕܠܐ ܢܬܪ ܒܗ ܒܒܐ ܡܢ ܒܒܐ.

1 [1] f. ܗ̇ R [2] ܠܝܫܘܬܗ̇ RVLl

2 [1] ܗܝܡܢܬܐ RVLl [2] i. add. ܕ F [3] ܕܡܫܝܐ RVLl [4] scripsi; ܦܪܘܠܘܣ F; ܦܪܘܠܘܣ RVL; ܦܪܘܪܘܠܘܣ (?) l [5] sg. RVLl [6*] ܕܡܫܝܐ F; ܕܠܡܘܠܐ RVL [7] ܠܠܛܪ̈ܝܘܢ RVL; ܠܠܛܪ̈ܝܘܢ l

to me in a gift'; or, 'That a son is born to me *I thought*, and behold he is mine as *I thought*.' Synonymous ones, but (with) its differences, (are) like, 'For there ruled (*fem.*) in our land desolation, and still there ruled (*masc.*) in our land desolation.' Our master cited yet other paradigms, but because they do not yield sense in Syriac we have omitted them.

## SECTION SEVEN
### On Pleasantness of Style
### Five Theories

ONE.[29] Style which gives understanding is pleasant, and that which is obscure and hidden makes understanding difficult. Metaphorical transference is therefore pleasant when a thing is attributed to an attribute of the agent, not the agent (himself). For example, it should not be said (that) old men are doers of good (things), but it may be said (that) old age is a doer of good, and this attribute is common, like a genus. It is not right to make extensive use of metaphors, nor of foreign words, because extreme speech which is hidden from the many is detestable, just as superficial (speech) which is evident to everyone is despicable; but the style is held in honour which competent people understand without rustics (doing so), (which) however is clear on examination (and does) not (require) profound thought. A (style) such as this is pleasant because it is temperate, especially when it takes on contraries and metaphors that are not very remote, and the transference is right that puts the thing as it were 'before the eyes'.

TWO.[30] Every pleasant style comes about in three ways: by transferences, by antitheses or opposites, by actualizations. Transferences are (of) four (kinds). The first is simile; thus Pericles said about the youth which perished in the war that it was effaced from the cities like spring from the course of the year. The second is metaphor from the opposite; thus one calls a blind man 'great of sight'. The third is metaphorical from the similar; thus one calls a king 'the pilot of the

---

[29] **7.7.1** AR 3.10 10b10-35; IS 4.3 (228.10-229.10).

[30] **7.7.2** AR 3.10 10b35-11a4; 31-b23; 11 11b23-28; (cf. 10b17-18;) IS 4.3 (229.10-230.5).

ܕܬܠܬ. ܘܡܢ ܫܐܠܬܐ ܠܡܫܩܠܢܝܬܐ[1] ܗ̇ܝ ܕܠܡܥܒܕܢܘܬܗ ܠܐ ܡܫܬܦܩܐ
ܒܡܥܒܕܢܘܬܐ ܕܡܫܬܦܩܐ ܡܕܒܪܢܐ. ܘܒܗ̇[2] ܗܟܢ ܡܬܚܫܚ ܐܘܡܢܘܬܗ ܐܝܟ
ܐܢܫܐ ܕܐܡܪ̈ܢ. ܫܡܗܬܐ ܐܟܚܕܐ. ܘܦܠܓܘܬܐ ܡܫܬܠܚܢܐ. ܘܚܡܫܬܐ ܡܢܘܬܐ
ܡܢܝܢܬܐ. ܥܬܝܪ ܐܝܟܐ ܗ̇ܝ، ܕܠܘ ܗܟܢ ܐܣܝܩܐ. ܐܠܐ ܦܫܝܛܐ ܘܡܫܝܚܐ.
ܐܦܠܐ ܬܘܒ ܗܟܢ ܓܠܝܐ ܘܦܫܝܩܐ. ܟܕ ܕܡܫܘܚܬܐ ܦܫܝܛܬܐ ܠܐ ܗܘܐ
ܒܡܓܢܝܐ ܒܠܫܢܐ ܕܡܬܗܪܐ ܐܠܐ ܒܣܘ̈ܟܠܐ[3] ܬܘܒ ܡܬܓܠܝܐ. ܘܡܢ
ܒܡܓܢܝܐ ܫܦܝܪܐ ܕܢܬܠܒܐ ܐܝܟ ܗ̇ܘ ܡܐ ܕܡܕܪܐ ܘܠܐ ܢܫܘܐ ܕܢܒܥܐ
ܡܕܪܐ. ܐܘ ܢܫܘܐ ܕܡܒܥܐ ܡܕܪܐ. ܘܟܕ ܡܬܒܥܪ ܡܬܠܠܗ ܡܬܚܒܫ[4] ܕܠܘ
ܡܒܥܐ ܡܕܪܐ. ܘܗܠܝܢ ܗ̇ܢܝܢ ܒܐܘܡܘܡܢܐ ܗܟܢ ܗܘܝ̈[5].

ܕܐܡܪܢ. ܗ̇ܘܐ ܕܝܢ ܒܢܝܢܐ ܗܘܝܢܐ ܟܕ ܗܘ ܠܗ ܗܘܬ ܡܡܠܠܐ ܘܫܬܐܣܬ
ܕܝܗܘ ܠܗ ܒ̇ܢܝܐ. ܘܗܝܡܢܘܬ ܡܬܩܒܠ[1]. ܐܝܟ ܐܝܠܝܢ ܕܐܡܪܢ. ܦܬ̈ܐ ܠܝ
ܠܡܒܥܬ *ܩܕܡ ܗ̇ܝ،[3] ܕܢܫܘܐ ܠܡܒܥܬܐ.[2] *ܡܢܐ ܓܝܪ ܒܗ̇، ܕܐܡܒܥ ܦܬ̈ܐ ܠܝ
ܠܡܒܥܬ ܠܫܘܘܬ ܡܒܥܬܐ ܫܘܕܥ. ܒܕܓܘܢ ܐܝܟ ܗ̇ܘ ܗܘ ܕܐܡܒܥ. ܫܘܝܢ
ܠܡܒܥܬܐ ܩܕܡ ܗ̇ܝ، ܕܢܒܥܐ ܗ̇ܘ ܡܐ ܕܒܗ ܢܫܘܐ ܠܡܒܥܬܐ.[4] ܘܕܐܝܟ ܗܠܝܢ
ܡܐܡܪܐ ܒܥܐ ܕܡܬܦܫܩܝܢ ܡܬܦܪܫܝܢ. ܘܡܒܥܐ ܕܡܫܬܠܚܝܢ ܡܬܒܥܝܢ.
ܘܢܐ ܡܕܡ ܫܪܪܐ ܦܠܐ ܕܢܗܘܐ ܠܗܘܢ. ܗܟܢ ܡܢܗ ܕܫܐܠܐ ܕܠܐ[5] ܡܕܪ.
ܒܢܩ ܗ̇ܘ ܗܢܐ ܫܪܪܐ[6] ܟܕ ܡܬܬܦܪܫ ܡܫܬܠܡ ܒܗ ܒܡܡܠܠܐ. ܐܡܒܥܐ
ܕܐܢ ܢܐܡܪ ܐܢܫ. ܙܕܩ ܠܝ ܠܡܒܥܬ ܡܘܬܐ ܠܐ ܒܕܝܠܐ ܩܕܡ ܕܢܫܟܠ
ܘܠܡܒܥܬܐ ܒܥܐ ܢܬܠܡ[7].

ܕܢܫܕܐ. ܫܐܠܬܐ ܕܗܝܢܐ ܐܦ ܒܡܟܗ̈ܢܐ ܗ̇ܘܝܐ. ܐܝܟ ܐܝܠܝܢ ܕܠܫܟܪܐ
ܐܣܩܦܐ ܕܐܪܝܘܣ ܦܢܐ. ܘܠܡܫܬܐ ܕܠܐ ܬܠܬܐ ܩܢܘܡܐ ܕܠܐ ܡܫܚܬܐ. ܘܗܠܝܢ
ܗ̇ܢܝܢ ܐܝܟ ܕܒܪܘܒܒܐ. ܦܫܝܩܐܝܬ ܕܝܢ ܐܢ ܗܟܢ ܡܒܪܐ ܐܣܩܦܐ ܬܬܬܘܪܐ.
ܘܫܟܬܐ ܦܫܬܪܐ. ܠܐ ܡܬܩܒܠܐ ܫܐܠܬܐ. ܘܐܝܬ ܐܝܟܐ ܕܫܟܢܐ
ܘܫܘܡܗܐ ܘܡܥܒܕܢܘܬܐ ܗܘܝܐ ܫܐܠܬܐ ܗܢܝܬܐ. ܐܝܟ *ܗ̇ܝ، ܕܦܠܓ[1]
ܕܟܢܐ ܠܡܘܦܐ ܕܐܪܫ ܒܐܒܗܒܐ. ܓܠܝܢ ܕܝܢ ܦܘܐܓܠܐ ܘܠܐ ܡܬܓܠܝܢ ܡܟܐ
ܕܒܪܝܬܐ ܒܒܢܝܢ ܢܘܩܠܐ ܘܕܘܟܝܐ. ܐܡܒܥܐ ܕܐܡܪܝܢ. ܦܠܓ ܠܗ ܒܡܩܩܡܢ[2]
ܫܩܘܗ̇، ܐܝܟ ܒܦܩܘܬܐ. ܕܘܟܝܐ ܓܝܪ ܫܘܓܢܝܐ ܐܝܬܘܢ. ܘܫܘܓܢܝܐ ܐܘ
ܕܘܟܝܐ ܐܝܬܘܢ ܦܬܓܡܐ ܐܘ ܫܐܠܬܐ ܦܬܓܡܬܐ ܐܝܟ[3] ܬ̈ܠܬܐ. ܘܒܢ̈ܝܢܐ
ܐܡܩܢܝܐ. ܕܒܫܘܓܠܐ ܙܥܒܕܐ ܗܘܝܢ. ܡܐܡܪܐ ܐܝܬܘܢ ܠܐ ܒܢܬ ܩ̈ܠܐ
ܦܬܓܡܬܐ.

3 [1] ܠܡܫܩܠܢܘܬܐ RVL [2] f. ܗ RVLl [3] sg. RVLl [4] ܡܬܚܒܫ. RVLl [5] ܗܘܝܢ RVL
4 [1] f. add. ܐ RVLl [2*] trp. post ܕܒܗ ܢܫܘܐ ܠܡܒܥܬܐ infra F [3] om. RVLl [4*] om. RVLl [5] i. om. RVL [6] ܫܪܐ RVLl [7] ܢܬܬܠܡ RVL
5 [1*] ܕܗܘܐ ܦܠܓ RVL [2] scripsi; ܒܡܩܩܡܗ̇ F; ܒܡܩܩܡܢ RVLl [3] ܐܘ RVLl

country'. The fourth is metaphor from the bare name; thus one calls Sirius 'the heavenly barker'. Opposition (is) like 'perceptible which is visible', 'action to thing'. Actualizations make clear that which is before the eyes. Sometimes metaphor is combined with the clarification (provided by) actualization and is appropriate; for example, calling a self-controlled man 'four-square', that is, balanced so that no side is no greater than (any other) side.

THREE.[31] Among stylistic metaphors is that which likens actualization of the inanimate to actualization of the animate. Homer made great use of it, saying heat is wrathful, desire enticing, and distress bitter gall. It is more comely not to be very remote, but close and related, and not very obvious or superficial, because close similarity is not only useful in transferences, but is also valuable in the sciences. Among appropriate transferences is what someone may say when he believes but does not openly (say) that he believes thus, or (the opposite, that) he openly (says) that he believes thus, but when his speech is subjected to examination it emerges that he does not believe thus. These things often happen by a homonym.

FOUR.[32] A pleasing retort occurs when the speech tears itself down and it was supposed that it would build itself up. (This) is received with pleasure. For example, (take) him who said, 'Good it is for us to die before we are worthy of death.' Because he said, 'Good it is for us to die', he showed the worth of death. Therefore it is as if he had said, 'We are worthy of death before we do that for which we are worthy of death.' Such words are appropriate as long as they are brief, but are marred when they are diffuse. They must have some true aspect, apart from the metaphorical (one), which is not true, but this true one, when it is made explicit, will be fully expressed in speech, for example, if someone says, 'We ought to die a blameless death before we go wrong and are delivered to an evil death.'

FIVE.[33] Metaphor which is pleasing may also come about by names, like calling a shield 'a round plane of Ares', and an archer without a bowstring 'a stringless lyre'. These are as in a construction, but if a

[31] **7.7.3** AR 3.11 11b31-12a12; 17-23; 12b10-11; IS 4.3 (230.6-231.1).
[32] **7.7.4** AR 3.11 12b1-32; IS 4.3 (231.1-9).
[33] **7.7.5** AR 3.11 12b32-13a28; IS 4.3 (231.10-232.2).

ܦܘܣܩܐ ܬܡܝܢܝܐ

ܡܛܠ ܒܢ̈ܝܐ ܕܦܐܫܝܢ ܒܡܣܟܢܘܬܐ ܘܒܢ̈ܝܐ ܕܦܐܫܝܢ ܒܐܝܬܝܪ̈ܘܬܐ

ܬܐܘܪ̈ܐܡܐ ܚܕ

ܘܕܡܣܟܢܘܬܐ. ܘܡܢ ܥܘܬܪܐ ܐܝܠܝܢ ܕܠܙܘܘܪܢܐ ܡܬܡܣܟܝܢ. ܒܡ ܝܕܥܬܐ ܕܕܓܠܘܬܗܘܢ. ܐܝܬܘܗܝ܆ ܡܐܡܪܐ ܕܝܢ ܕܐܡܪܝ. ܐܦܠܐ ܐܢ ܐܝܟ ܗܘܐ ܥܠܐ ܢܬܝܗܒ ܕܗܘܐ ܠܝ[1] ܠܗܕܐ ܠܝܠܕܘܬܐ ܟܠ ܐܢܫ. ܘܐܝܟ ܕܐܡܪ ܐܓܡܡܢܘܢ[2] ܒܪ ܐܛܪܝܘܣ[3] ܕܐܦܠܐ ܐܦܘܪܕܝܛܐ[4] ܕܡܛܬ ܠܗܕܐ ܦܣܩܐ ܒܗܕܐ ܥܦܪܘܬܐ. ܗܠܝܢ ܓܝܪ[5] ܠܐ ܬܬܠܐ ܐܢܘܢ *ܘܠܐ ܕܘܒܪ̈ܐ. ܘܕܐܦܠܐ ܥܬܝܪ̈ܘܬܐ ܐܢܘܢ[6] ܢܕܥܐ ܡܢ ܗܝ ܕܠܐ ܡܣܟܢܐ[7] ܡܕܡ ܡܬܠܟܐ ܒܗܘܢ ܘܒܥܒܪܬ ܡܠܐ[8] ܕܠܐ ܕܠܗ ܡܬܬܘܕܐ. ܐܠܐ ܥܘܬܪܐ ܐܢܘܢ ܕܛ̈ܠܐ ܛ̈ܠܝܐ. ܘܠܡܣܟܢܘܬܐ ܡܬܬܗܦܟܢܘܬܐ[9] ܠܐ ܠܡܣܟܢܘܬܐ ܡܬܬܪܝܨܘܬܐ[10] ܠܫܡܝܢ. ܒܗ̇ ܕܒܡܣܟܢܘܬܐ ܡܢ ܡܬܓܒܝܢ ܡܐܡܪܝܢ. ܒܐܝܬܝܪ̈ܘܬܐ[11] ܕܝܢ ܠܐ ܡܬܠܚܡܐ ܙܘܥܡܗܘܢ ܘܕܠܠܝܢ ܒܗܘܢ ܕܓܠܘܬܐ ܢܒܬܪ ܥܒܝܪܐ. ܐܦܠܐ ܬܘܒ ܬܘܪܓܡܐ ܒܡܠܝܢܐ ܘܡܠܘܟܐ ܕܟܠ ܙܒܢ ܒܡܟܐ ܡܬܬܪܝܪ ܠܡܠܘܟܐ ܕܝܗܒ ܠܐܢܫܝܐ ܕܒܫܐ. ܬܘܪܓܡܐ ܓܝܪ ܙܘܘܪܢܐ ܢܬܪ ܒܟܠܐ. ܘܐܡܝܢ[12] ܕܗܘ ܠܢܝܐ ܕܦܫܐ ܘܢܝܐ[13] ܠܣܘܦܝܘܬܐ ܕܦܫܐ[14] ܠܣܘܓܦܐ ܘܠܐ ܕܢܕܒ. ܘܠܟܠ ܡܘܡܐ ܦܠܝܬܗ ܢܬܠ. ܘܠܐ ܢܬܠܝܢ ܠܡܥܠܐ ܐܝܟ ܠܐ ܒܬܘܒܐ.

ܕܬܪ̈ܬܝܢ. ܒܪܬ ܩܠܐ ܡܬܬܒܣܝܡܘܬܐ ܢܛܪܬ[1] ܫܠܝܬܐ ܕܒܙ ܕܬܗܘܐ. ܘܡܬܬܡܪܝܢܘܬܐ ܢܛܪܬ ܢܗܒܠ ܐ̈ܦܐ ܒܕܝܢܘܬܐ ܕܬܗܘܐ ܐܘ ܫܟܝܚܘܬܐ. ܘܢܗܒ̈ܠ ܐ̈ܦܐ ܠܦܪܢܣܐ ܕܒܬ̈ܐ ܕܢܗܘܘܢ ܡܗܒ ܒܐ̈ܦܐ ܢܦܫܢ ܢܛܪܬ ܐܟܡܝܢ. ܘܒܬ̈ܐ ܠܦܪܢܣܐ ܕܒܬ̈ܐ ܕܢܗܘܘܢ ܢܦܫܢ ܦܐܝܬ ܡܟܠܠܐ ܢܛܪܬ ܚܪܦܝܢ. ܗܢܝܐ ܐܦ ܦܘܐܓܠܐ. ܘܒܪܬ ܩܠܐ ܕܡܫܬܡܫܐ[2] ܘܠܐ ܡܬܬܡܬܐ *ܓܢܠ ܡܬܥܢܝܐ[3] *ܘܠܐ ܡܬܒܣܝܐ.[4] ܘܟܠܗܕܐ ܦ̈ܓܥܐ ܡܢ ܝܕ̈ܥܐ ܫܦܪܐ[5] ܒܬ̈ܐ ܡܗܘܪܐ ܡܢ ܗܝ ܕܒܡܒܠܠܐ ܢܦܫܗܘܢ ܥܦܪ ܝܕܥܝܢ ܘܡܠܝܛܝܢ. ܘܡܬܬܒܬܬ ܐܓܪ̈ܬܐ[6] ܗܕܘܓܝܢ ܒܗ̇ ܕܡܫܒ ܒܐ̈ܦܐ ܒܐܓܘܢܐ ܫܘܕܝܐ ܢܛܪ ܠܫܡ. ܒܗ ܕܝܢܐ ܐܦ ܥܡܘܡܬ ܐܡܪܐ[7] ܘܡܘܦܦ ܡܐܡܪܐ ܡܫܕܝܐ ܒܐܓܘܣܛܘܡܘܬܐ ܚܠܝܢ. ܘܡܬܬܒܬܘܬܐ ܗܠܝܢ.[8]

---

1 [1] om. RVLl [2] ܐܓܡܡܢܘܢ F [3] ܐܛܪܝܘܣ RLl; ܐܛܪܝܘܣ V [4] ܦܘܪܕܝܛܐ F [5] om. RL; ܟܝ V [6]* om. R [7] ܡܣܟܢܘܬܐ RVLl [8] om. F [9] scripsi; ܡܬܬܗܦܟܬܐ F; ܡܬܬܗܦܟܬܐ RVLl [10] scripsi; ܡܬܬܪܝܨܬܐ codd. [11] sg. RVL [12] ܘܐܡܝܢ F [13] sg. RVL [14] ܕܦܫ̈ܐ F

2 [1] om. RVL [2] ܕܡܫܬܡܫܢܐ F [3]* ܒܐܦܝ̈ܗܘܢ ܡܬܢܟܦܢܐ F [4]* ܘܡܬܢܟܦܢܐ F [5] pl. RVLl [6] sg. RVLl [7] sg. F [8] ܡܫܠܡ RVLl

shield is simply called 'a round plane', or an archer 'a lyre', the metaphor will not be accepted. Sometimes a pleasing metaphor comes about by name, attribute, and actualization; for example, 'So and so is like an ape playing on a flute.' Poets err and are not successful when they make similes with remote (things), saying, for example, 'So and so's legs are curly like parsley.' For similes are transferences, and transferences are either simple similes or simple metaphors, like proverbs. Strange retorts, which are mostly constructions, are statements, not single words.

## SECTION EIGHT
### On Retorts which are Comely in Utterances and Retorts which are Comely in Letters
### Five Theories

ONE.[34] Among those things which are said for exaggeration, in the knowledge of their falsity, is the statement of him who says, 'Not even if gold were given to me as this sand would I marry this girl.' And Agamemnon son of Atreides said, 'Not even gold-like Aphrodite is comparable to this beautiful one.' These are not proverbs or similes, and that they are also not metaphors is evident from the fact that no meaning is intended through them or communicable in a different wording, but the things are manifest falsehoods. They are suitable for an evanescent utterance, not a permanent record, because the statement of them terminates with the (vocal) utterance, but in letters their (visual) indication is not blotted out and the monument of falsity remains shameful for ever. Furthermore, neither an encomiastic nor deliberative address which is proclaimed in front of the people is like the advice of one (person) to another, for an address makes more effort at exaggeration. It is necessary to know how (to create) the manner proper to the evanescent and the manner proper to the written, to give to each category its due, and not to be forced to keep silent as a non-writer.

TWO.[35] It is right that the written word should be more exact, and the spoken, (being) more for delivery, should be ethical or emotional.

---

[34] **7.8.1** AR 3.11 13a28 - 12 13b8; IS 4.3 (232.2-16).
[35] **7.8.2** AR 3.12 13b8-21; IS 4.3 (233.1-10).

ܕܬܠܬ. ܫܘܠܛ ܡܫܝܚ ܒܐܦܐ[1] ܒܥܕ̈ܢܝܐ ܗܟܢ ܡܦܝܣ. ܒܗ̇ ܕܠܡܛܠܒܘ
ܠܬܪܥܝܬܐ ܠܫܪ̈ܪܐ ܡܩܒܠܝܢ. ܘܒܢ̈ܬ ܩ̈ܠܐ ܠܐ ܐܫܬܪܝܬܐ. ܐܝܟ ܐܢܬܬܐ
ܒܚܢܬ. ܟܠܗ̇ ܐܘܪܚܐ. ܕܝܠܝܐܝܬ ܘܠܐ ܒܦܘܪܫܢܐ ܠܫܪܪܐ ܡܥܒ̈ܕܝܢ. ܗܟܢܐ
ܐܦ ܙ̈ܒܢܐ ܦܫܝܛܐ. ܘܗ̇ܝ ܕܫܒܩܘܬ ܐܘܪܐ ܘܦܫܝܛܘܬܐ[2] ܗ̇ ܒܪܬ ܩܠܝܬܐ.
ܘܠܐ ܡܦܫܘܬܐ ܘܫܠܝܘܬܐ. ܒܗ̇ ܕܐܘܪܚܐ ܠܡܫܠܡܘܬܐ ܗܟܢܐ ܒܫܝܢ ܡܫܒܚ.
ܘܫܒܩܘܬܗ ܠܡܫܠܡܘܬܐ ܡܫܝܚܐ ܡܫܪܐ ܘܡܫܪܐ ܘܕܡܩܒܠܝܢ ܡܫܠܡܐ ܡܫܠ.
ܐܝܟ ܐܝܢܐ ܕܠܐ ܐܟܪ. ܐܬܬܐ ܘܦܓܥܬ[3] ܘܡܠܠܬ ܘܐܬܟܫܦܬ. ܐܠܐ ܐܟܪ.
ܐܬܬܐ ܦܓܥܬ ܡܠܠܬ ܐܬܟܫܦܬ. ܗܢܐ[4] ܓܝܪ ܙܕܩܐ ܦܓܥܬܐ ܡܠܠ ܕܒܪ.[5]

ܕܐܪܒܥ. ܡܢ ܦܘܠܛܝܩܘܣܡܘܣ ܡܫܘܕܥܢܘܬܐ ܕܢܝܫܐ ܦܐܝܐ ܠܡܫܪܝܘ
ܒܬܘܕܝܬܐ. ܐܚܪܢܐ ܕܝܢ ܠܡܫܠܡܘ ܠܗܕܐ ܢ̈ܟܣܐ ܪܗܛܐ. ܡܢ
ܬܫܒܘܚܬܐ ܠܐܠܗܐ ܡܫܠܠܐ ܕܐܦܝܣܩܘܦܐ ܢܛܪܐ. ܘܒܕܘܒܪܢ ܒܢ̈ܝܐ
ܠܗܘ ܕܬܘܩ ܠܒܪܢܫܐ ܫܘܝܐ ܠܒܢ̈ܝܐ[1] ܢܐܡܪ. ܘܒܐܚܪܢܐ ܐܚܪܝܬܐ ܗܘܝܢ
ܕܐܝܟ ܙܘܥܐ ܩܕܡ ܝܘܬܪܐ ܡܠܦܘ. ܒܗ̇ ܕܐܝܟܢܐ ܕܗܟܢ *ܢܗܘܐ ܒܢܝܐ.
ܗܟܢ ܙܕܩ[2] ܕܢܗܘܐ. ܘܡܟܠ ܢܦܫܗ. ܒܕ ܗܘܐ ܒܪܐ ܘܗܕܝܩܐ ܒܗܘܢ.
ܘܡܫܒܚܘܬܗܘܢ ܦܫܝܛܐ. ܘܡܫܒܚܘܬܐ ܕܡܠܦ̈ܢܐ ܘܪܕ̈ܝܐ ܒܫܘܝܐ.
ܘܫܘܠܡܗܘܢ ܦܫܝܛ. ܘܡܫܠܠܐ ܕܒܡ ܦܢ̈ܝܬܐ ܗܢܐ ܫܒܝܬܐ ܘܠܐ ܡܫܘܚܐ
ܦܠܐ ܕܢܗܘܐ. ܟܠܗܘܢ ܕܝܢ ܡܟܐ ܕܩܕܡ ܣܝ ܕܢܗܐ ܗܘܐ. ܒܕܝܢܐ ܡܕܝܢ
ܢܗܪܘܬ ܡܫܠܠܐ ܦܪܝܫܐ ܟܠܝܫܐ ܡܬܟܫܝܐ. ܘܟܬܘܪ̈ܓܡܐ[3] ܕܟܠ ܒܫܬܟܠܐ[4]
ܐܫܠܘܬܐ ܡܬܟܫ̈ܝܢ ܦܓܥܬܐ ܘܕܘܩ̈ܝܐ ܡܬܗܘܝܐ. ܘܟܠܗܕܐ ܗܘܝܢ
ܕܠܬܘܪ̈ܓܡܐ ܡܫܝܢ ܩܕܡ ܕܝ̈ܢܐ ܒܕܝܢܐ ܠܐ ܡܫܥܝܢ. ܒܕ ܡܫܝܚ ܒܐܦܐ
ܒܬܘܪ̈ܓܡܐ. ܕܠܐ[5] ܫܬܝܬ ܗܟܢ ܒܗܘܢ ܡܫܠܠܐ. ܫܬܪ ܡܫܠܛ. ܒܕ
ܡܫܠܡܘܬ ܒܢܝܐ ܠܗܘܬ ܗܘܠ ܒܕܘܪܐ ܕܒܗܘܢ ܦܠܐ ܕܬܗܘܐ.

3 [1] i. om. F [2] ܘܦܫܝܛܘܬܐ RVLl [3] i. om. F [4] ܗܘܐ RVL [5] i. om. RVLl
4 [1] ܠܒܢ̈ܝܐ RVLl [2*] om. F [3] sg. RVLl [4] ܡܬܟܫܝܐ RVL [5] i. om. RVLl

Actors are more anxious to read books from which they may learn delivery, writers more concerned to read books from which they may learn elegant discourse. Similarly also poets. A word which is heard but not written is quickly forgotten and not subject to examination. Therefore many of those familiar with a book (on delivery) are skilled writers inasmuch as they well know and understand (how) to persuade in speech, but are incompetent in letter-writing, because delivery is especially appropriate in verbal struggle. In the same way asyndeta and the repetition of a single word are sweet-sounding in debate, but dreadful in writing.

THREE.[36] The mingling of delivery with transferences is very persuasive, because they pave the way for each other to lead the mind astray. And asyndeta—like, 'I came, I sought', without a conjunction—indicate meaning by suggestion, not in a clear way. Similarly (with) modulations in reading. Asyndeton is verbal contraction, not contraction of meaning, because a conjunction gathers multiple speech into one, but its omission separates and sunders single speech, and its multiplication of meanings is deceptive. (Take,) for example, him who does not say, 'I came and arrived and spoke and made supplication,' but says instead, 'I came, I arrived, I spoke, I made supplication.' He may deceive (us into thinking) that he is doing many things.

FOUR.[37] It is comely to begin addresses with a prologue indicative of the aim. For example, when an orator wishes to praise the martyrs, he may begin with a glorification of God who crowns the runners and in the commemoration of the departed say of him that he has fixed for man the limit of his temporal life. With others he may outline other things, like a sketch preceding a picture; because the bigger the crowd, the more he ought to explain and the less to persuade, because the understanding of the unlearned and ignorant is slow, but their credulity (*pistis*) quick, while the credulity (*pistis*) of the educated and well-informed is slow, but their understanding quick. Speech with the able must (therefore) be more exact and not devious, the more so when it is before a single judge. For judgement only the lucidity of clear speech is required, but in addresses on ros-

[36] **7.8.3** AR 3.12 13b21-14a1; IS 4.3 (233.10-234.5).
[37] **7.8.4** AR 3.12 14a1-17; IS 4.3 (234.6-235.11).

ܕܢܣܒܝ. ܡܛܠܠ ܡܬܩܢܝܢܐ ܕܗܘܘ¹ ܒܥܕܢܐ ܠܐ ܡܫܬܟܚܢܐ ܐܘ ܠܐܓܪ̈ܬܐ
ܒܥܬܝ، ܐܘ ܠܐܓܪ̈ܬܐ² ܕܕܪ̈ܐ ܘܪ̈ܗܛܐ ܡܥܪ̈ܪܝܢ. ܘܒܗܘܢ³ ܕܐܓܪ̈ܬܐ ܠܐ ܒܠ
ܦܘܠܐ ܒܠܚܘܕ. ܗܘܐ ܫܘܒܚܐ. ܘܒܗܘܢ ܕܐܓܪ̈ܬܐ⁴ ܦܐܝܘܬܐ ܡܬܚܫܚܬܐ ܒܠܒ.
ܙܘܘܓ ܡܛܠܠ ܗܬܢܐ ܡܬܟܒܢܐ. ܘܐܝܟܢܐ ܕܗܟܢ ܬܘܪܝܐ. *ܘܪܝܫ ܡܢ
ܒܠ ܒܡܘܫܐ ܢܗܐ. ܘܠܐ ܒܝܕܥܐ⁵ ܐܦܠܐ ܒܡܢܝܢܐ. ܒܗ، ܕܐܓܪ̈ܬܐ⁶ ܗܬܢ ܡܢ
ܐܓܪ̈ܬܐ ܡܢܬܝ. ܘܗܬܢ ܡܢܬܝ. ܘܗܬܢ ܐܚܝܢ. ܘܒܠܗܕܐ ܐܝܟܢܐ ܕܦܪ̈ܝܫܐ
ܠܐ ܐܬܩܢܝܐ ܐܝܟܢܐ ܗܘܐ ܡܦܫܩܢܐ ܢܦܫܗܘܢ ܦܬܓܡ̈ܝܗܘܢ، ܒܗ̇ ܡܦܫܩܢܘܬܐ
ܡܬܬܪܓܡܐ ܠܥܘܡܠ ܐܟܘܬܗܘܢ. ܢܬܠܘܢ ܐܢ ܒܗܘܢ *ܬܪܓܡ̈ܢܐ ܡܕܡ
ܡܬܕ̈ܪܐ.⁷ ܘܡܠܠ ܡܢ ܢܒܝܘܬܐ ܐܬܚܙܝܬܐ. ܘܡܕܡ ܡܢ ܡܬܚܫܚܬܐ ܪܘܚܢܝܬܐ
ܒܢ̈ܝܢܐ ܡܫܟܚܐ ܕܐܬܚܝܢ.

ܦܘܫܩܐ ܬܢܝܢܐ
ܡܛܠ ܡܠܬܐ ܕܡܐܡܪܐ ܕܪܗܛܐ ܘܠܡܫܡܗܝܢ ܒܬܠܝܬܝܘܬ ܐܕܫ̈ܐ
ܬܐܘܪ̈ܝܐ ܦ ܚܕܡܫܪܐ

ܡܕܡܥܬܐ. ܪܗܛܘܬܐ ܗ̇ܝ ܓܒܪ ܠܗܬܝܪ ܥܒܕܝܢ ܒܥܬܐ. ܠܦܘܪܥܢܘܬܐ
ܐܘܒܕܬ ܥܒܕܐ ܡܬܟܒܢܐ ܕܡܛܠܠܬܗ ܒܠܬܐ. ܘܠܥܒܕܐ ܡܥܪ̈ܪܢܐ ܕܠܗ
ܕܥܒܕܐ. ܘܠܡܐܡܪܐ ܕܪܗܛܐ ܗܠܝܢ ܐܝܟ ܡܢ̈ܐ. ܦܘܪܥܢܐ ܐܘܒܕܬ
ܡܕܡܘܬ ܡܛܠܠܐ. ܘܐܦܛܪܘܦܘܬܐ ܐܘܒܕܬ ܗܘܝܐ ܕܠܗ ܕܥܒܕܐ.
ܘܐܦܟܕܘܣ ܐܘܒܕܬ ܫܒܝܬܐ. ܘܦܘܪܥܢܐ ܐܝܟ ܪܥܒܕܐ ܗܘ ܠܥܒܕܐ.
ܘܬܒܥܐ ܐܝܟ ܪܥܒܕܐ ܗܘ¹ ܠܡܥܒܕܢܘܬܐ. ܘܫܬܡܥܐ ܒܥܒܕܐ ܗܘ ܕܗܘ
ܡܢ ܕܐܬܥܪܪ. ܘܡܥܒܕܢܘܬܗ ܒܦܘܫܩܐ.

---

5 ¹ ܕܗܘܝܘ RVLl ² ܠܐܓܪܬܐ RVLl ³ ܘܒܗܝ، RVL ⁴ ܕܐܓܪܬܐ RVLl ⁵* om. F ⁶ ܕܐܓܪܬܐ RVLl ⁷* sg. RVLl

1 ¹ om. RVLl

trums numerous metaphors and stunning similes are required. Therefore those who are used to (giving) addresses may be unsuccessful before judges in lawsuits, because delivery produces more success in addresses, in which speech is not very exact, as the intelligence of the crowd is of necessity in proportion to the understanding of the unlearned among them.

FIVE.[38] Visible discourse, which is written, not for hearing, is appropriate either for letters or for the deeds which judges and orators authenticate. For that of letters the requirement is only for reading, for deeds a middling comeliness without excessive magnification of discourse is needed. It must be quite correct, free of all deviousness, and neither lowly nor trivial, because a deed is more excellent than a letter, more lasting, and more necessary. Its words must therefore be clear, not strange, and also not abridged, because abridgement reduces the meaning of these sorts of things. However, some customary transferences may be mixed in with them, and a sprinkling of strange uses, and a bit of rhetorical metre, in the persuasive ways which have been mentioned.

## SECTION NINE
### On the Parts of a Rhetorical Speech and their Arrangement in the Three Species
### Eleven Theories

ONE.[39] Rhetoric is associated with two things: the *problema* or matter to be investigated, which (is what) the speech is about; and the argument establishing the matter. A rhetorical speech has three parts: proemium or preface; *antiparabole* or narration of the matter; and *epanodos* or conclusion. The proemium is like a sketch of the aim; the narration like a sketch of the proof (*pistis*); and the conclusion is a recapitulation of that which has been established, and its recollection in abridged form.

---

[38] **7.8.5** AR 3.12 14a17-29; IS 4.3 (235.11-236.6).
[39] **7.9.1** AR 3.13 14a30-36; IS 4.4 (236.11-237.2).

ܕܬܪ̈ܬܝܢ. ܡܠܟܐ ܓܝܪ[1] ܠܐ ܚܝܣ ܥܠ ܬܝܒܘܬܐ. ܟܕ ܬܝܒܘܬܐ ܬܝܒܘܬܐ ܗܘ ܕܗܘ̇ ܡܐ ܕܗܘ̣ܐ.[2] ܫܦܝܪ ܐܘ ܥܒܝܪ ܐܡܡܐ ܕܟܘܠܗܘܢ ܘܠܡܠܘܟܐ. ܘܒܐܝܢ *ܐܘ ܟܠܗ̇[3] ܐܡܡܐ ܕܟܘܠܗܘܢ. ܘܡܡܠܟܐ ܠܝܬ ܗܘ̇ ܡܐ[4] ܕܡܬܬܥܒܕܐ ܕܢܬܠܘܫ ܐܘ ܢܬܒܥܐ ܐܘ ܢܬܒܥ. ܐܠܐ ܥܘܕܪܢܐ ܒܠܚܘܕ ܐܝܬ ܒܗ. ܟܠ ܗܘ̇ ܡܐ ܕܦܩܕ ܐܘ ܠܐ ܦܩܕ. ܚܝܣ ܕܝܢ ܡܠܟܐ ܒܢܬܢܘ ܥܠ ܦܘܩܕܢܘܗܝ. ܐܝܟܢܐ ܕܢܦܪܘܩ ܢܕܒ ܥܡܘܕܐ ܠܝܢܩܐ. ܘܥܠ ܣܘܬܦܐ ܬܘܒ ܚܝܣ. ܐܝܟܢܐ ܕܢܐܡܪ ܐܠܝܫܪ ܡܠܘܟܐ. ܗܐ ܐܢܐ ܗܘ̇ ܡܐ ܕܐܡܪܬ ܠܗܘܢ[5] ܐܡܪܬ. ܘܗܝ̇ ܕܬܡܢܥܘܢ ܐܘ ܬܗܦܟܘܢ ܕܠܒܘܢ ܗܝ. ܘܠܡܕܪܩ ܡܢ ܡܚ̈ܠܝܐ ܠܐ ܦܠܐ ܠܡܘܪܒ ܒܬܝܒܘܬܐ. ܘܗܕܐ ܓܝܪ ܡܐ ܕܦܩܝܣܘܬ ܡܚܠܠܐ ܡܬܟܒܝܐ.

ܕܬܠܬ. ܦܘܩܕܢܘܗܝ ܘܬܝܒܘܬܐ ܘܣܘܬܦܐ ܡܐܡܪ̈ܐ ܐܝܟܢ ܕܠܘ ܠܐܦ̈ܐ ܒܒܠܕܝܢܐ. ܐܠܐ ܠܐܦ̈ܐ ܥܡ̈ܡܐ ܡܬܬܦܝܣܝܢ.[1] ܘܠܐܦ̈ܐ ܒܒܠܕܝܢܐ ܗܝܡܢܘܬܐ ܡܬܬܦܝܢܐ ܘܠܡܗܕܪܐ ܡܬܚܦܦܐ ܠܡܒܗܪܘ ܐܦ ܠܡܫܡܠܘ. ܘܦܘܩܕܢܘܗܝ ܠܗܘܢ ܡܐܡܪ̈ܐ[2] ܦܣܩܐ ܩܠܐ ܕܢܘܣܚܝܐ ܠܗܘܢ ܩܝܢܬܐ ܘܕܠܡܠܟܐ ܠܗܘܢ ܘܡܐܪܐ ܕܒܐܝܒܐ. ܒܠܗܘܢ ܓܝܪ ܥܘܪ̈ܢܐ ܘܥܡ̈ܠܐ ܠܗܘܢ ܗܘ̇ ܡܐ ܕܒܠܬܗܘܢ ܐܝܬܝܗܘܢ. ܘܠܟܘܠܗܘܢ ܘܠܓܘܢܐ ܢܐܐ ܦܘܩܕܢܘܗܝ. ܐܝܟ ܕܐܡܪ[3] ܠܦܪܓܝܢܐ ܒܡܐܡܪ̈ܐ[4] ܐܠܡܦܝܣܘܗܝ[5] ܕܥܘܠܐ ܠܡܬܕܪܟܘ ܒܡܢܬܘܬ ܡܘ̈ܢܐ. ܡܢ ܥܙ، ܠܡܒܥܐ ܚܕܐ ܚܕܐ ܡܢ ܣܥܪ̈ܢܘܗܝ. ܘܗܟܢܐ ܒܡܠܟܐ.[6] ܐܡܡܐ ܕܐܡܪ ܐܝܠܦܪ ܙܕܩ ܠܡܫܘܪ ܠܦܬ̈ܐ. ܐܠܐ ܠܗܘܢ ܒܘܣܐ ܕܢܝܟܐ ܕܢܦܘܫܗ، ܢܬܡܠܐ ܒܬܘܪܓܡܗ. ܘܒܗ ܒܢܝܐ ܘܒܦܘܩܕܢܐ[7] ܐܡܡܐ ܕܐܡܪ. ܕܗܐ ܡܠܠ ܦ̈ܬܐ ܚܕܐ ܒܕܡܐ ܠܢܦܫܐ ܘܠܢܪ ܠܦܘܪ ܒܗܘ ܠܦܘܫܐ. ܘܠܡܒܠܝܐ ܢܬܢ ܢܐܐ ܠܡܘܪܒܘ ܦܘܩܕܢܘܗܝ. ܡܬܚܣܢ ܕܝܢ ܒܦܘܩܕܢܘܗܝ ܠܐ ܗܘܐ ܙܠܝܠܐ ܒܠܚܘܕ. ܐܠܐ ܐܦ ܦ̈ܐܬܝܐ ܠܦ̈ܐ. ܒܥܪ̈ܒܐ ܡܟ̈ܠܝܐ ܒܢܩ ܘܬܡܢܗܘܢ. ܠܐ ܒܒܣ̈ܝܐ ܘܒܣܦܝܪܐ.[8]

2 [1] om. RVLl [2] ܕܗ̇ܘܐ R [3*] ܘܒܟܠܗ̇ RVLl [4] om. RVLl [5] f. ܝ RVL

3 [1] sg. RVLl [2] sg. RVLl [3] i. om. F [4] pl. F [5] ܐܠܡܦܝܣܐ RVLl [6] pl. RVL [7] pl. RVLl [8] ܘܒܣܦܝܪܐ F; ܘܒܣܝܓܪܐ V

TWO.[40] Deliberation has no need of narration, because narration is a narration of that which is, good or bad as in praise and blame, just or unjust as in prosecution. But that which is related in order that it may (then) be praised, blamed, or prosecuted is not (present) in deliberation; only a sign is (present) in it. For that which is expedient or not expedient, deliberation has need, rather, of a proemium, so that the listener may know beforehand the aim, and it also has need of a conclusion, as for example a deliberative orator may say, 'Behold, what I have (to say) I have said; to accept or reject is your (decision).' For some prosecutions it is not right to make the narration lengthy; this is the case when abridgement of the discourse is required.

THREE.[41] Proemium, narration, and conclusion are statements delivered not before an adversary at law, but before listeners, while proof (*pistis*) is delivered before an adversary at law and may therefore be repeated to aid memory and understanding. A proemium in relation to speeches is comparable to clearing the throat in singing and spitting in playing the flute, for all these are beginnings and directions for what comes after them. A proemium is suitable for praise and blame, as Gorgias said in the *Olympic Speech* that it was worthy to admire the virtue of the Greeks, and then began to recount each one of their sciences. And similarly in deliberation; for example, an orator may say it is right to honour good men, then in his address proceed to a man whom he wishes them to honour. And in the same way in prosecution he may say, for example, 'Behold, the waters have reached the soul, and the flood has covered the top of the mountain.' A proemium is especially suitable for lengthening a prosecution, but not only orators make use of a proemium. Good poets (do so) also, but on exalted and wonderful subjects, not on despised and worthless ones.

FOUR.[42] As for devices which are outside the matter under discussion, some of them are helpful to the speaker when he is praising himself, some evoke an image of the matter itself, and some are dis-

[40] **7.9.2** AR 3.13 14a36-b7; cf. 14 15a23; IS 4.4 (237.2-10).

[41] **7.9.3** AR 3.13 14b7-12; 14 14b19-21; 29 - 15a10; 23-24; IS 4.4 (237.10-238.8).

[42] **7.9.4** AR 3.14 15a24-b10; cf. 15b37-38; IS 4.4 (238.9-239.6).

ܕܐܪܒܥ. ܦܘܪܫܢܐ ܕܠܒܪ ܡܢ ܥܘܠܡܐ ܡܬܚܙܝܐ.[1] ܡܢܗܘܢ ܕܝܢ ܠܐܡܘܪܐ
ܒܕܪܝܢ ܡܢܐ ܕܡܬܒܥܐ ܗܘ ܠܗ. ܡܢܗܘܢ ܕܝܢ ܠܗ[2] ܠܥܘܠܐ ܡܬܓܠܝܢ.
ܘܡܢܗܘܢ ܬܘܒ ܠܒܥܠܕܒܒܐ ܡܡܘܠܝܐ ܡܫܠܝܢ. ܘܐܟܠܡܪܝܐ ܕܩܒܠ ܡܢ
ܥܘܪܢܐ ܙܪܥ ܠܗ ܕܢܫܡܐ ܡܬܪܒܝܬܗ ܘܫܡܝܪܘܬ ܒܠܕܒܗ. ܘܡܦܫܝܢܐ ܕܢܦܩ
ܙܘܥܐ ܠܦܘܫܐ ܡܬܓܠܠܐ ܕܡܐܟܠܡܪܝܐ ܢܦܘܫ ܠܡܦܪܩ. ܐܝܟܢܐ ܢܟܠ
ܦܘܪܫܢܐ. ܘܟܕ ܕܡܥܠܐ ܐܘ ܡܓܠܢܐ ܠܡܫܡܫܘܬܐ ܢܦܪܩ ܒܪܗܡܐ ܠܡܥܪܘ
*ܠܥܒܝܕܬܐ ܐܘ ܥܒܝܕܬܐ.[3] ܟܕ ܢܗܘܐ ܦܘܪܫܢܐ. ܘܐܟܠܡܪܝܐ ܐܝܟܢܐ
ܕܦܘܪܫܢܗܘܢ ܢܗܘܐ ܐܦ[4] ܢܘܪܐ. ܘܕܠܐܘܪܚܬ ܥܡܘܕܐ[5] ܒܐܒܢ ܕܝܢ
ܒܡܦܪܫܢܘܬܐ[6] ܘܐܘܣܘܬܐ *ܗܘܝܐ. ܒܗܝܢ ܕܝܢ ܕܡܪܫܡܢܘܬܐ ܘܡܬܓܒܝܢܘܬܐ.
ܘܐܘܣܘܬܐ[7] ܕܦܪܗܣܝܐ ܘܥܡܘܕܬ ܡܬܬܠܐ ܘܦܫܝܛܘܬ ܐܝܟ ܗܘܝܐ. *ܘܟܕ
ܐܘܣܘܬܐ[8] ܠܐ ܒܕܪܐ ܒܡܫܡܫܘܬܐ ܐܠܐ ܠܡܓܠܝܘ. ܘܥܡܘܕܐ ܦܫܝܛܐ
ܦܫܝܛܘܬ ܡܬܓܠܝܐ.. ܘܒܠܘܕܐ ܐܠܐ ܠܡܬܬܠܘ ܒܗܘܢ ܠܦܘܪܫܢܗܘܢ ܢܓܕܐ
ܕܬܒܥܝܬܐ. ܘܡܬܒܠܬܐ ܘܡܬܚܪܒܐ.

ܕܚܡܫ. ܠܡܪܢܘ ܡܢ ܗܟܢ ܒܫܪܝܬܐ ܒܡܘܠܕܐ ܓܫܡܢܐ. ܐܝܟ ܡܘܠܕܐ[1]
ܕܒܪ ܡܪܝܐ ܐܡܪ[2] ܠܒܥܠܕܒܒܘܗܝ. ܦܩܕ ܐܢܬ ܗܘ ܠܡܓܫܡܘ ܡܢܟ ܒܡܘܬܟ.
ܘܐܝܟ ܡܠܘܟܐ ܕܢܦܪܐ[3] ܠܡܐܡܪ. ܟܕ ܒܡܫܢܩ ܬܪܝܗܘܢ ܢܬܬܪܝܡ. ܘܐܦ ܠܐ
ܬܫܬܠܡ ܠܗ ܒܠܒܗ[4]. ܒܦܫܐ ܕܢܦܠܐ ܢܦܠܘܢ ܒܠܒܗܘܢ. ܘܦܘܪܫܢܗܘܢ ܕܝܢ
ܡܛܠ ܥܡܘܕܐ ܡܬܒܥܐ. ܘܒܠܘܕܐ ܩܛܝܢܐ ܒܐܪܝܟܘܬܗ ܡܬܦܫܝܢ.
ܒܪܡ ܐܪܝܟܘܬܗ ܦܫܝܛܬܐ ܡܢ ܕܫܠܝܐ ܘܬܘܫܠܝܬܐ ܕܡܢ ܒܗܕܡ ܢܦܫܐ
ܐܬܝܐ. ܐܝܟ ܒܬܕܪܐ ܗܘܢ ܕܠܘ ܗܘ ܡܢܐ ܕܐܝܠܝܢ ܥܐܠܝܢ. ܐܠܐ ܗܠܝܢ
ܕܠܫܘܕܪܐ ܕܪܓܠܬܗܘܢ ܦܪܘܣܘܦܐܣܛܐ[5] ܒܒܕܝܢ. ܒܪ ܠܡܦܪܫܘ ܒܬܠܬܗܘܢ
ܡܠܝܢ. ܘܥܡܘܕܐ ܒܪ ܡܬܠܦܫܝܢ ܡܬܓܒܝܢ. ܘܒܪ ܕܢܒܐ ܐܘ[6] ܒܠܒܢܐ ܐܘ
ܥܡܘܕܐ ܠܡܚܫܒܬܐ ܕܡܠܦܬ ܡܩܒܠܢܐ[7] ܠܐ ܡܕܒܝܢ. ܗܢܝܢ ܐܟܠܡܪܝܐ
ܕܩܒܠ ܘܡܦܬܪܟ ܠܡܪܒܐ[8] ܦܘܪܫܢܗܘܢ ܡܬܠܝܢ.

ܕܫܬ. ܐܝܟܢܐ[1] ܕܢܦܩ ܙܘܥܐ ܒܐܒܢ ܕܝܢ ܕܠܐ ܐܬܒܝܬܗܘܢ ܗܠܝܢ ܕܒܗܝܢ
ܡܬܦܪܫܢ ܐܘ ܡܕܡ ܡܢܗܝܢ ܐܡܪ. ܒܗܝܢ ܕܝܢ ܕܗܘ̈ܐ، ܒܪܡ ܠܐ *ܡܫܬܟܚܝܢ
ܗܟܢ. ܐܘ ܠܐ ܡܫܬܟܚܝܢ ܗܟܢ. ܘܒܗܝܢ ܬܘܒ ܐܡܪ ܕܗܘ̈ܐ، ܒܪܡ ܠܐ[2]
ܥܒ̈ܝܕܢ ܗܟܢ. ܐܘ ܒܪܝܬ ܥܒ̈ܝܕܢ. ܐܘ ܢܘܕܐ ܕܐܝܟܢܐ ܘܐܡܬܝ. ܐܘ ܢܐܡܪ
ܡܕܡ ܐܢܬ ܗܘ[3] ܠܡܡܠܠ ܗܟܢ ܟܠ ܘܟܠ ܐܝܢܐ ܐܝܟܢܐ. ܐܘ ܢܐܡܪ

4 [1] ܡܬܚܙܝܢܐ RLl [2] om. RVLl [3*] sg. RVLl [4] ܐܘ RVL [5] sg. RLl [6] ܒܡܦܪܫܘܬܐ F [7*] om. F [8*] ܘܒܪ ܕܐܘܣܘܬܐ RVLl

5 [1] ܡܘܠܕܐ RVLl [2] om. F [3] ܕܢܘܚܐ RVL [4] ܒܠܒܗܘܢ RVLl [5] ܦܪܘܣܘܦܐܣܛܐ RVLl [6] ܠܗ RVLl [7] sg. RVL [8] i. add. ܕ F

6 [1] ܐܝܟܐ F [2*] om. RV [3] om. RVL

missive of an opposing adversary at law. An impeaching accuser should show his (own) virtue and his adversary's deficiency at the beginning, and a responding defendant first disclose the reply confuting the accusation, then introduce the devices. Whoever praises or blames will speedily put the proof (*pistis*) first to establish the noble or despicable, then produce the devices, but an accuser must arrange a proemium at length. The inducement of listeners sometimes occurs by coming together and concord, sometimes by distancing and provocation. Concord occurs with familiarity, sitting together, and cheerful countenance, but when concord does not help, it is necessary to take shelter in proof (*pistis*). The simple listener is easily led, and therefore with him it is right to make (as) a guide for (his) mind a lengthy proemium (which is) both ornamental and amplifying.

FIVE.[43] To begin a prosecution with extremely base things is ridiculous—like a prosecutor who on beginning says to his adversary, 'You are close to being delivered from me by your death'; or like a deliberative (orator) who begins by saying, 'After my departure you will understand my usefulness, and if all of you do not give heed to me, you will all fall into the trap which is laid.' A proemium is intended for listeners, and for this reason many take delight in making it lengthy, but extreme length is the result of fear and weakness in the exposition of the case; like servants who ask not for what they desire, but things all around their desire, making a *proemi-ization* because they are afraid to disclose their request. Listeners may be seduced when praised, and when a judge, adversary, or listeners do not understand the magnitude of the offenders' offence, then the prosecuting and impeaching accuser is compelled to produce a lengthy proemium.

SIX.[44] A defendant may sometimes say that the things of which he is accused, or some of them, are not (true), but sometimes that they happened but are in no way harmful, or not very harmful. Sometimes he may say that they happened but are in no way disgraceful, or (only) slightly disgraceful; or confess that he has made a mistake and committed an offence; or say, 'You are in the habit of frequently

[43] **7.9.5** AR 3.14 15b10-16a3; IS 4.4 (239.7-240.2).
[44] **7.9.6** AR 3.15 16a4-b15; IS 4.4 (240.3-241.2).

ܒܬܪܥܘܬܐ ܠܥܠܡܐ ܫܠܝܛܝܢ ܘܗܘܝܐ ܫܠܝܛܢܐ ܕܡܬܬܙܝܥܝܢ ܗܘܐ. ܐܝܟ[4]
ܐܝܟܢܐ ܕܢܗܘܐ ܒܫܠܝܛܘܬܐ ܘܐܡܪ ܕܫܠܝܛ ܡܫܝܚܐ *ܘܡܒܣܪܝܢ ܠܗ ܡܫܝܚܐ.[5] ܐܘ
ܢܦܫ ܫܠܝܛܘܬܗ ܡܣܝܒܪܐ *ܒܡܘܬܪܘܬܗ، ܫ̈ܠܝܛܐ.[6] ܘܠܡܕܪܐ ܒܪ̈ܢܫܐ ܒܝ.
ܠܫܘܠܛܢܗ ܠܐܝܬ ܙܒܢ ܒܫܘܠܛܢܘܬܐ ܠܥܠܡܝܢ ܠܗ ܐܡܪܝܢܢ ܕܠܐ ܢܥܒܪ ܒܥܠܡܐ.
ܐܘ ܢܐܡܪ ܐܦܢ[7] ܐܝܟܐ ܡܛܠ ܐܡܪܬܝܢ ܐܠܐ ܐܝܬ ܫܠܝܛ ܡܢ ܗܪܟܐ[8]
ܕܐܬܬܥܝܪܬ ܒܫܘܠܛܢܗ. ܘܐܦܢ ܡܢ ܗܘ ܕܠܐܠܗܐ ܐܝܟܐ ܐܝܬ ܦܘܪܫܢ، ܡܛܠ ܐܬܦܥܠܬ
ܐܠܐ[9] ܡܢ ܟܠܗ ܒܗܢܐ ܦܘܢ[10] ܐܫܬܠܡܬ. ܘܐܝܟܢܐ ܕܢܦܩ ܙܘܗܪܐ ܡܢܗܪ ܡܢ
ܐܟܠܡܘܣܐ. ܒܝ ܗܘ ܟܝܢ ܠܫܘܠܛܢܗ ܘܐܝܬܘܬܗ ܡܫܪܪ. ܗܢܐ ܕܝܢ ܒܥܠܡܐ
ܘܫܠܡܐ.

ܕܢܣܒ. ܬܘܒܝܢܐ ܠܥܒܕܐ ܛܠܝܐ ܘܡܫܒܕܐ. ܘܦܠܐ[1] ܠܐ ܠܡܦܠ ܒܗ ܕܕܩ
ܫܪܝܪܐ. ܐܠܐ ܡܛܠܬܐ ܡܢܬܐ ܠܡܫܪܪܘ.[2] ܒܗ، ܕܐܝܟ ܘܡܫܡܫܐ ܠܡܫܒܚܘܬܐ
ܒܫܘܪܥܐ ܪܒܐ. ܒܗܕܐ ܕܒܬܪܟܢ[3] ܡܫܬܡܠܝܐ. ܐܦ ܠܒܪ ܫܪ̈ܟܐ ܐܝܬ
ܫ̈ܠܝܛܐ ܕܠܠܝܢ ܘܒܠ ܬܘܒܝܢܐ[4] ܠܗ ܫܘܫܛܝܢ. ܐܠܐ ܥܠ ܡܫܒܚܘܬܐ. ܕܗܘܝܐ
ܒܫܘܪܥܐ. ܒܐܝܕܬ ܒܝ ܢܟܝܐ ܕܢܦܠܘܢ ܠܐܝܢܐ ܕܒܠܗܘܢ ܐܝܬ̈ܐ[5] ܠܗ[6] ܗܘ
ܡܫܒܚܝܢ ܘܡܫܬܪܝܐܝܬ ܠܡܫܬܪܪܘܬܗ *ܠܐ ܡܫܒܚܝܢ. ܠܬܘܒܝܢܐ ܠܐ ܢܘܪܝܢ. ܐܠܐ
ܠܡܫܬܪܪܘܬܗ[7] ܠܚܘܒܫܬܐ[8] ܕܕܠܝܠܝܢ ܒܗ[9] ܢܦܘܩ ܘܠܫܡ̈ܥܐ[10] ܢܫܒܩ ܐܝܟ ܒܝ.
ܐܡܪ. ܕܠܒܪ ܘܒܒ ܘܫܡܝܢ ܘܒܐܝܢ. ܒܗܘܢ ܠܒܪ ܢܟܝܐ[11] ܡܫܬܪܪܘܬܐ.
ܘܠܫܪ̈ܟܐ ܒܪ̈ܝܐ ܕܒܫܘܪܪܐ ܘܠܒܢܝܢܐ ܠܫܘܪܪ ܡܫܒܚܘܬܐ ܢܨܚܐ. ܐܝܟ
ܫܘܪܪܬ ܠܒܫܐ ܘܠܒܘܫ ܬܪܝܨܘܬܐ ܘܐܡܪ. ܕܕܡܐܬ ܠܒܪ ܡܢ ܠܒ̈ܢܐ ܠܒܢܐ.
ܘܡܢ ܕܒܫܪܪܘܬܐ ܐܬܪܒܝ ܪܒܐ. ܘܡܫܬܒܠܝܢܐ ܒܝܘܡܐ ܕܠܫܒܝܩ ܡܫܬܠܒܢܐ
ܘܦܠܛܐ ܠܫܠܒܐ. ܐܝܟ ܕܠܦܩܬ. ܐܡܪܗܐ ܕܒܝ ܬܐܡܪ ܡܫܪܪܐ ܗܘ ܦܠܝ
ܒܗ، ܕܦܠܝ ܘܦܠܝ ܦܐܪ. ܡܦܠܛ ܐܝܬ. ܘܐܦ ܬܐܡܪ ܦܐܪ ܕܦܠܝ ܘܦܠܝ
ܕܡܫܬܪܝܐ ܬܗܘܐ. ܦܠܝܢ ܐܝܬ. ܘܡܦܠܛܢܐ ܡܫܒ̈ܚܢܐ[12] ܬܐܡܪ ܦܠܝ ܠܐ
ܬܦܠ ܥܠ ܠܒܗ ܐܠܐ ܥܠ ܒܥܠܗ. ܘܡܫܠܡܐ ܠܗ ܬܬܦܠ ܥܠ ܠܒܝܢ ܐܠܐ
ܐܬܬܦܠ ܥܠ ܒܥܠܝܢ ܐܡܪ ܐܝܬ.

---

[4] i. add. ܘ RVL [5*] om. RV [6*] ܒܡܘܬܪܘܬܗ، RVL; ܒܡܘܬܪܘܬܐ ܗܘ l [7] ܐܦ RVLl [8] om. RVLl [9] ܐܝܬ RVL [10] om. RVL

7 [1] i. om. RVLl [2] ܠܡܫܪܪܘܬܐ (?) F [3] ܕܒܬܪܟܢ RVL [4] pl. RVLl [5] sg. RVLl [6] rep. RVL [7*] om. F [8] ܠܚܘܒܫܬܐ RVLl [9] om. RVLl [10] sg. RVL [11] ܢܟܝܐ RVLl [12] ܡܫܒ̈ܚܢܐ RVLl

making accusations against me and others at random'; or say, 'With a good intention I did you harm, and this harm is of advantage to you', like him who swears falsely and says, 'With my tongue I have sworn, but with my mind I have not sworn'; or compare his solitary harm with his many advantages—and therefore when the prudent wish to harm someone, they cover him with favours, so that he does not suppose evil—; or say, 'Although I have harmed you slightly, nevertheless your complaint is greater than your injury'; or, 'Although I have been lightly prosecuted for that of which you accused me, nevertheless you have been greatly rejected by the whole people.' A defendant is more virtuous than an accuser, because he (seeks to) establish good and justice, while the latter (seeks to establish) evil and wrongdoing.

SEVEN.[45] The narration lays bare and exposes the matter. It is not necessary to keep the right order in it, but to indicate part by part, because like a sketch it depicts the proof (*pistis*) in the soul (of the listener), until it is subsequently filled in. Now there are many matters which are evident and have no need of narration, but (do have need) of proof (*pistis*), which comes about by detailed explication. Thus when one wishes to praise someone whom all men glorify, but whose virtuous (deeds) they do not know in detail, one does not make a lengthy narration, but one details the common virtuous (deeds) which are proper to him and explains them to the listeners, saying, 'He is courageous and temperate and wise and just,' for by these virtue is magnified. Surrounding external and common matters one may cite as confirmation of the proof (*pistis*), like noble birth and good upbringing, and say, 'Rightly he is a good man from good men, and he who has been brought up with discipline is an educated man.' With a slight transference of expression praise may be changed to advice, as I have (already) explained. For example, when you say, 'So-and-so is a virtuous man because he does such-and-such,' you are praising (him); but if you say, 'Do such-and-such that you may become virtuous,' you are advising. In searching encomia you may say, 'So-and-so trusts not in his fortune, but in his labour,' and in advice you may say, 'Trust not in your fortune, but trust in your labour.'

---

[45] **7.9.7** AR 3.16 16b16-29; 1.9 67b26-68a10; IS 4.4 (241.3-242.8).

ܕܬܡܢܝܐ. ܦܘܪܡܝܢ ܘܬܘܢܝܐ¹ ܡܡ̈ܫܚܢܐ ܙܪܡ ܕܒܢܝܗܘܢ܂ ܘܠܐ ܫ̈ܠܝܛܐ
ܒܡܫܡܘܬܐ ܕܠܐ ܢܬܓܠܒ ܠܚܡܐ. ܐܠܐ ܒܒܪ ܒܐܝܕܐ ܕܠܕܢܐ ܗܘܝܐ
ܠܡܥܒܕ. ܘܠܡܦܫܝܢܐ ܒܡܪܝ ܢܗܘܐ ܬܘܝܢܐ ܒܦܓܪܐ. ܡܠܘܢ ܡܢ
ܕܟܢܪܐ ܒܠܗ *ܐܘ ܒܡܦܫܚܝܢ² ܚܦܪ. ܘܢܐܐ ܠܗ ܕܢܙܪ ܒܦ̈ܚܡܐ ܒܦܘܪܢܘ.
ܘܒܡܗܘܕܢܐ ܕܒܢ̈ܕܐ ܡܢܬܪܐ ܦܐܐ ܕܒܢܝܢ ܐܡܗܪܐ ܡܡܠܠܗ. ܐܡܒܢܐ
ܕܡܢ ܠܒ̈ܐ ܢܬܬܒܪ. ܒܢܐܐ ܠܒܪ ܡܒܢܝܢܐ ܗܘ. ܘܟܠܗܕܐ ܒܡܬܬ̈ܠܛܐ
ܡܡܠܠ ܒܢܝܢܐ ܕܥܦܪܐ ܘܥܡܪܐ ܘܡܬܘܪܬܐ ܘܡܗܘܪܢܐ ܠܐ ܐܝܬ. ܐܠܐ
ܡܚܢ. ܐܢܫܝܢ ܡܢ ܕܒܝܬ ܩܘܦܠܝܣ ܘܡܡܐܡܪܐ ܒܢ̈ܝܢܐ ܕܩ̈ܕܘܗܝ ܕܡܠܢ̈ܝܢܐ
ܡܬܕܢܝܢ. ܐܝܟ ܗ̇ܝ ܕܦܠܓ ܡܡܠܠ ܘܡܬܠܛ ܐܡܢܕܐ. ܗܕܐ ܓܒܪ ܒܠ
ܒܬܥܒܘܬܗ ܡܥܡܕܐ³ ܘܕܥܝܢܐܝܬ ܘܡܥܒܕܢܐ ܡܡܠܠ. ܘܒܪ ܗܡܒܢܘܬܐ
ܒܡܡܠܠܐ ܠܗ ܗܘܝܐ ܠܒܠܬܗ ܢܣܘܐ. ܐܡܒܢܐ ܕܗܦܦܠܝܣܘ⁴ ܡܦܠܓ
ܐܬܦܠܓܘ ܐܦܪ ܕܢܦܩܐ ܗܘܬ ܕܐܢܫܘ̇ܗ. ܠܐ ܕܒܢܝ̈ܗ ܘܕܒܠܗ̇. ܒܪ ܗܠܝܢ
ܐܦ ܐܒܢܝܢ⁵ ܗܘܝܢ. *ܐܢܫܐ ܕܝܢ ܠܐ⁶ ܗܘܐ *ܒܪ ܐܡܒܐ⁷ ܘܐܡܒܐ ܠܬܪ̈ܝܗ̇
ܕܥܡܠ ܢܣܬܘ.

ܕܬܫܥܐ. ܙܪܡ ܕܝܢ ܠܡܦܫܝܐ ܕܢܗܠܐ ܠܡܫܚ ܒܫ̈ܦܐ ܕܒܗ ܡܬܢܥܫ ܗ̇ܘ
ܕܡܦܠܓܐ. ܐܡܒܢܐ ܕܢܐܡܪ ܠܗ. ܗܘܝܐ ܒܒܢܝܢ ܒܒܢܝܐ ܗܘ¹ ܕܡܒܕܪܒܐ.
ܘܒܪ̈ܡܒܐ ܠܦܢ ܣܡܡܝܢ ܠܒܪ̈ܢܝܢ. ܘܥܪܒܐ ܕܠܗܠܝܢ ܕܡܢ. ܘܬܘܢܝܐ ܒܡ̈ܠܒܐ
ܐܝܟ ܕܒܦܠܓܐ ܒܐܠ. ܒܪ ܒܗܘܕ ܥܪܒܐ ܕܗ̣ܘܐ ܘܦܠܓܬܐ ܕܢܦܩܬ ܠܗ
ܐܘ ܒܫܡܬܐ ܢܦܠܐ ܕܢܫܬܐ. ܐܬܦܠܐ ܠܗܬ ܡܠܒܐ ܢܒܝܐ ܡܒܗ. ܘܗܡܒܢܐ ܡܢ
ܕܡܥܪܐ ܠܡܫܬܠܛ ܬܫܘܫܬܐ ܐܘ ܠܡܫܠܡܘ. ܡܢ ܢܒܪ ܓܒܪ ܡܠܒܐ. ܘܟܠܗܕܐ
ܦܫܩ ܕܢܙܪ ܬܘܦܫܗ ܐ̱ ܡܬܕܓܠ. ܡܠܫܛܠܐ ܡܦܠܓܢܐ ܡܢܐ² ܕܒܠܕܢܗ
ܠܡܗܘܪܐ³ ܕܐܫܒܠ. ܒܗ̇ܝ ܕܐ̱ ܢܘܕܐ ܘܢܐܡܪ ܐܡܪܬܝܢ. *ܒܪܡ ܕܐܢܬ
ܗܘܝܬ ܒܠܬ ܗ̇ܝ ܕܐܡܪܬܝܢ⁴ ܘܐܢܬ ܥܪܝܬ ܠܡܗܘܪ. ܗܕܝܢ ܗܘܝܐ ܕܢܦܩ
ܪܘܢܝܐ ܒܠ ܦ̈ܠܓܢܐ⁵ ܡܥܪ̈ܪܐ ܫܒܫ. ܘܚܪܝܢ ܐܢܫܐ ܕܢܦܩ ܪܘܢܝܐ
ܕܒܟܒܐܝܬ ܗܘ̇ܐ. ܕܠܐ ܦܟܪ ܦܢ. ܐܘ ܦܟܪ ܐܠܐ ܠܗ ܠܐ ܦܠܓ. ܐܘ
ܠܡܬܪܘ ܦܠܓ. ܐܘ ܠܡܦܠܓܘ ܒܪܡ ܒܐܢܫܬ.

8 ¹ pl. RVLl ²* ܘܡܦܫܚܝܢ RVLl ³ f. om. F ⁴ ܕܗܦܦܠܝܣܘ F ⁵ ܐܒܢܝܢ F ⁶* ܐܢܫܐ ܕܝܢ ܕܠܐ F ⁷* ܒܪ ܐܡܒܐ RVLl
9 ¹ om. RVL ² ܒܗ̇ܝ RVLl ³ ܠܐ ܡܗܘܕܐ RVLl ⁴* om. F ⁵ ܦ̈ܠܓܢܐ RVL; om. l

EIGHT.[46] Proemium and narration should be moderate, and not mixed with proof (*pistis*) lest the arrangement be confused, unless by (that) means it is pleasant for the judge to hear (it). For the respondent the narration may be short in rebuke, especially when one totally denies the matter or its harmfulness, and it is proper for him to establish his denial by counter arguments. A speaker should dignify his speech by the mention of virtuous character, so that he may be supposed (to be) among the good. For character is voluntary, and therefore in mathematics there is no ethical talk of noble and disgraceful, or useful and injurious. However, among some of the Socratics and in ethical discourses the manners of an adversary may be revealed; for example, 'So-and-so talks and walks at the same time,' for this indicates his excitability and that he speaks rashly and indiscriminately. When a proof (*pistis*) does not occur in the speech, one may show the cause; for example, Sophocles said of Antigone that she cared for her brother, not her children or her husband, for the latter, even if lost, may be (re-)produced, but not a brother when father and mother have gone down to the depths of Sheol.

NINE.[47] A respondent should refute the delivery utilised by him who makes the accusation; for example, he may say to him, 'This weeping lamentation of yours is that of the cunning, and prudent people soon get wise to your arts,' and so on in similar vein. In deliberations narration comes in as by chance, when one wishes to bring to mind a thing which is past and the good or evil which followed it, then move from it to the advice; and similarly when one begins by producing a paradigm or praising, and then crosses over to advice. Therefore (a speaker) needs to establish his narrative if he is suspected of being false, especially when his adversary is making an accusation against the speaker of having done wrong, because if he agrees and says, 'I harmed you, but you were the cause of my harming you, and you started the harming,' then the defendant needs many counter arguments establishing (his narrative). The contention of a defendant may be in four ways: he did not do it at all; or he did it but caused no harm; or caused harm in order to be useful; or (did it) in order to cause harm, but justly.

---

[46] **7.9.8** AR 3.16 16b32-17a36; IS 4.4 (242.8-243.5).
[47] **7.9.9** AR 3.16 17a36 - 17 17b38; IS 4.4 (243.5-244.3).

ܕܟܐܒ. ܬܫܒܘܚܬܐ ܗܝ ܒܥ̈ܠܬܐ[1] ܫܦܝܪ ܡܗܕܪ̈ܢ. ܒܗ ܒܗܘܢ ܗܠܝܢ ܕܫܦܝܪ̈ܢ
ܠܡܗܘܐ ܒܗܠܝܢ ܕܗܘ̈ܐ ܡܬܦܫܩ̈ܢ. ܡܬܬܪ̈ܝܨܘܬܐ ܕܝܢ ܒܡܫܒ̈ܠܢܐ. ܒܗ
ܡܦܪ̈ܓܢܐ ܒܗܘ ܗܝܐ ܕܗܘܐ ܗܘܐ. ܒܟܠܗܘܢ ܥܠ ܫܘܪ̈ܝܐ ܚܝܘܬ. ܘܠܐ
ܙܪܘ ܕܠܡܬܪ̈ܝܨܘܬܐ[2] ܒܫܪܪܐ ܢܟܣܝܢ. ܐܝܟܢܐ ܕܒܝܠܘܦܣܝܐ ܐܬܝܗܘ. ܐܠܐ
ܐܝܟܢܐ ܕܫܠܝܛܝܢ ܡܠܬܐ ܘܫܪܪܘܬܐ ܡܬܟܪܙܐ. ܘܒܗ ܫܒ̈ܝܐ[3] ܬܫܒܘܚܐ
ܠܡܒܥܒܥ. ܠܐ ܬܬܡܪ ܡܬܪ̈ܝܨܘܬܐ ܗܝ. ܒܗ ܕܫܒܝ ܠܫܕ̈ܪܐ ܐܝܟ ܫܒ̈ܝܐ[3]
ܘܡܫܒܚܘܬܐ. ܐܝܟܢܐ ܕܝܢ ܕܒܪܐ ܠܐܘܪܚܐ ܕܡܫܬܝܘ. ܐܢ ܒܐܒ ܠܗ
ܚܠܦܘܗܝ، ܠܐ ܡܗܝܡܢ ܕܢܦܩܐ ܠܥܘܠܐ. ܘܐܢ ܡܗܝܡܢ ܕܢܦܩܐ ܠܡܬܝܘܬ ܠܐ
ܒܐܒ ܠܗ ܚܠܦܘܗܝ. ܘܡܠܟܐ ܒܗܘ ܡܢ ܦܘܪܢܣܐ. ܒܗ ܫܘܪܪ ܗܘ ܕܒܫܝܪ.
ܫܦܝܪ ܡܢ ܫܘܪܪ ܗܘ ܕܗܘܐ ܚܠܦܝ. ܘܐܝܬܝܗܘܬ ܕܢܗܘܐ ܒܦܘܪܢܣܘܬܐ
ܫܘܪܪܐ[4] ܗܘ، ܢܨܝܚܐ. ܒܗ ܠܐ ܐܝܟ ܦܓܥܐ[5] ܕܫܪ̈ܝܘܗܝ، ܐܝܟ ܕܠܫܪܒܐ
ܕܦܘܪ̈ܢܣܘܗ. ܐܠܐ ܒܗܢ ܦܓܥܐ ܠܦܘܡ ܕܢܗܘܐ ܢܦܩ.

ܕܟ̄ܐ. ܡܫܒ̈ܚܢܘܬܐ ܠܐ ܫܬܝ̈ܬܐ ܠܡܘܠܕܐ ܠܐܚܪ̈ܢ. ܘܡܒܣܡܢܘܬܐ ܒܗ̇،
ܕܡܫܝܚܝܐ[1] ܘܠܟܠܕܝܐ[2] ܡܫܝܚܐ ܘܡܒܣܡܢܐ ܫܦܝܪ ܡܢ ܡܫܝܚܘܬܐ ܕܠܐ[3]
ܡܫܝܚܐ *ܐܘ ܡܫܠܝܐ[4] ܡܢܠܝܐ. ܘܡܫܠܠܗ ܕܟܠܕܝܐ ܡܢܗ ܗ̇ܝ
ܒܗܘܦܛܝܩܐ ܡܬܩܪܐ. ܡܢܗ ܕܝܢ ܒܗܘܠܦܝܣܡܘܣ. ܘܡܫܠܚܐ
ܘܡܦܪ̈ܓܢܐ[5] ܠܡܐܡܪܗ ܕܟܠܕܝܐ ܦܠܐ ܠܡܪܐ ܠܗܘܢ. ܡܢ ܠܡܪܘ
ܕܠܗܘܠܐ ܕܗܡܢܗ. ܒܗ ܡܠܘܐ ܡܢܐ ܕܡܫܠܠ ܡܠܡܗ ܕܐܫܪܝܐ ܫܦܝܪ ܡܢ
ܗ̇، ܕܫܪܝܐ ܠܡܫܠܝܢ ܡܬܬܝܟܝܢ.[6] ܡܬܒܪ ܕܝܢ ܬܘܒ ܐܝܟܢܐ ܕܢܦܩ ܙܘܥܐ ܒܗ
ܐܡܪ ܠܦܝܠܣܘܦܐ.[7] ܕܐܝܟܢܐ ܕܗܘܐ ܒܦܘܡܗ ܕܠܐ ܬܬܦܫܘ[8] ܠܐ[9] ܡܬܦܫܘ.
ܘܡܫܬܡܫܬܐ[10] ܒܟܝܢܟ *ܕܬܫܘܝܐ ܠܫܪܪܐ[11] ܚܝܢܐ ܠܟ. ܘܢܕܒܪ ܐܝܟܢܐ
ܕܠܦܘܩܬܐ ܠܟܝܢܟ ܘܡܫܬܠܛܢܟ ܪܚܡ ܐܢܬ. ܐܠܐ ܦܘܩ ܐܠܗܐ ܠܐ
ܬܦܩܝܢ ܝܬܝܪܐ. ܐܘ ܦܘܩ ܒܟܢܫܐ ܬܦܩܝܢ. ܐܘ ܢܟܣܝܢ. ܐܢܬ ܒܢܝܪܐ[12] ܐܢܬ
ܘܠܐ ܢܕܒܪ ܐܢܬ ܡܢܐ ܐܡܪ ܐܢܬ. ܘܡܬܕܒܪ ܐܝܟܢܐ ܒܗ ܐܝܟܢܐ
ܐܝܟܢܘܬܟ[13] ܕܐܡܠܠ ܒܟܝܢ.

10 [1] sg. RVLl [2] sg. F [3] sg. RVLl [4] ܫܘܪܪܐ RVLl [5] ܦܠܐ RVLl
11 [1] ܕܡܫܝܚܘܬܐ RVL; om. l [2] i. om. RVL; i. ܕ l [3] ܕܠܐ RVLl [4*] ܘܡܫܠܝܐ RVLl [5] scripsi; ܘܦܪܓܐ F; ܘܦܪܓܐ RVLl [6] ܡܬܬܝܟܝܢ RVLl [7] ܠܦܝܠܣܘܦܐ RVLl [8] add. ܐܠܐ ܠܗ̇، ܕܠܐ ܬܬܦܫܘ RLl [9] om. RVLl [10] ܘܡܫܬܡܫ RVL [11*] om. F [12] f. om. RVLl [13] ܐܝܟܢܘܬܟ RVLl

TEN.[48] Paradigms are specially useful in deliberations, because in them things of the future may be compared to things of the past, enthymemes (specially useful) in prosecutions, because an indictment occurs for what is past, (and) therefore needs establishment. One should not pronounce enthymemes in order, as has (also) been shown in dialectic, except where the argument is strong and is made evident by setting (them) in order. When you wish to create emotion, do not use an enthymeme at all, because emotion and proof (*pistis*) are mutually repellent. For if he who sees another person suffering feels pain for him, he does not believe that he deserves the suffering, but if he believes that he deserves to suffer, he feels no pain for him. Advice is more difficult than rebuke, because establishment of the future is harder than establishment of the past. Taking hold of the law is powerful establishment in accusations, because no one presumes to repudiate it as (one does) other premisses, unless perhaps doubt adheres to the interpretation of the law.

ELEVEN.[49] Untrue reputable (things) are suitable for praise, while refutation, because it arouses emotion and humbles and humiliates an adversary, is more successful than demonstration, which neither praises nor refutes. The speech of an adversary may be demolished partly by *enstasis* and partly by syllogism. In deliberation and prosecution one should first demolish the word of an adversary, then establish the opposite of his thinking, because when a deliberative (orator) brings to nought the advice of another, he gets a better hearing than if he were to begin by giving (his own) advice. Furthermore, a defendant may also be helped by saying to an accuser, 'He who has set his soul on not being persuaded will not be persuaded, and your stubborn will forces you to reject the truth. I know that you justify yourself by your sharp tongue and your powerful speech, but your stratagems are not effective before God, even if they are effective before men.' Or he may say, 'You are an idiot and do not know what you are saying. I am amazed at myself in having agreed to talk with you.'

---

[48] **7.9.10** AR 3.17 17b38-18a32; IS 4.4 (244.4-15).
[49] **7.9.11** AR 3.17 18a39-b33; cf. 18a27-28, 32-33; IS 4.4 (244.15-245.10).

ܦܘܫܩܐ ܡܐܡܪܐ

ܡܛܠ ܫܘܐܠܐ ܕܗܪܛܝܩܐ ܘܕܐܡܢܐ ܙܕܩ. ܘܡܛܠ ܦܘܫܩܐ

ܬܐܘܪܝܐ ܬܠܬ

ܡܕܡܝܢܘܬܐ. ܒܪܗܛܘܪܘܬܐ ܕܝܢ ܠܘ ܡܛܠ ܦܪܘܛܣܝܩܘܢ ܐܠܐ ܡܛܠ ܕܢܚܐ
ܐܣܝܪܐ ܐܪܒܥܝܢܐ[1] ܗܘܐ ܫܘܐܠܐ. ܚܕ ܕܝܢ ܒܗ ܢܫܐܠ ܪܗܛܘܪ ܡܛܠ
ܥܒܕܐ ܐܝܟܢܐ ܕܐܝܟ ܒܐܝܢ ܗܘܐ ܦܘܫܩܗ ܕܫܡܠܝܘܗܝ ܢܬܠܝܢ ܐܡܪܘܗܝ.
ܘܐܝܟܢܘ ܕܟܠܐ ܢܦܫܐ ܡܢ ܥܒܘܕܐ ܢܬܚܡܘ. ܕܬܘܒ ܕܝܢ ܒܡܦܩܐ ܕܗܘܝܢ.
ܒܐܡܬܝ ܐܝܟܢܘ ܕܟܠܐ ܢܦܫܐ ܕܠܐ ܢܫܡܪܘܗܝ ܢܬܠܝܢ. ܘܐܝܟ ܒܐܝܢ ܢܦܫܐ
ܢܬܒܥܘܢ. ܕܬܠܬܐ ܒܗ ܢܗܘܐ ܬܒܥܠ ܗܘ ܕܡܫܐܠ ܕܒܡܬܪܥܝܢܘܬܐ
ܡܬܒܥܝܢܘܬܐ[2] ܕܒܡܬܗ ܗܘܐ ܦܘܫܩܗ. ܐܡܟܢܐ ܕܢܐܡܪ. ܠܡܢܐ ܠܘ ܡܢ
ܡܛܠܬܟ ܕܠܒܫܬ ܐܝܟ ܕܬܒܥܬ ܒܪܦܬ. ܘܡܢܐ ܕܢܦܫܐ ܐܝܟ ܢܐܡܪ. ܡܕܝܢ ܐܝܬ
ܥܠܬܗ̇.[3] ܘܗܢܐ ܫܘܐܠܐ ܐܝܟܢܐ ܕܟܠܗ ܥܠܡܘܬܐ ܠܐ ܗܘܐ ܫܪܝܪܐ
ܡܘܬܪ. ܘܐܡܟܢܐ[4] ܕܦܘܫܩܐ ܡܬܕܠܡܟܢܐ ܒܠܬܗ ܗܘ ܡܦܫܩܐ ܕܢܫܪܘ. ܐܝܟܢܐ
ܕܒܒܪܘܬܗ ܢܬܚܡܘ. ܕܐܪܒܥܐ ܒܗ ܫܘܐܠܐ ܗܟܢ ܕܬܢܐ[5] ܢܗܘܐ. ܒܝܬܝܢ
ܐܝܟܢܘ ܕܦܪܫ ܒܐܪܒܥ ܡܦܫܩܐ ܕܢܦܩܘ ܡܬܐܒܪ. ܒܗ ܒܡܬܚܬܐ ܦܘܫܩܐ
ܚܪܝܢ ܘܦܫܩ ܒܗܝܢ. ܘܐܝܟ ܒܠܒܗ ܦܘܪܫܐ[6] ܢܦܫܐ ܡܬܝܚܕ.

ܕܬܪܬܝܢ. ܫܘܐܠܐ ܕܗܪܛܝܩܐ ܠܐ ܡܬܬܚܡܐ ܐܝܟܢ. ܘܒܠܗܘܢܐ[1] ܐܠܝܐ
ܕܒܬܪ ܒܡܘܬܐ ܘܠܘ ܡܣܒܪܐ ܢܗܘܐ ܦܘܫܩܗܘܢ. ܘܡܫܐܠܢܐ ܕܝܢ ܠܘ ܗܘ
ܡܢܐ ܕܒܝܬܐ *ܐܠܐ ܗܘ ܡܢܐ ܕܡܒܥܐ ܗܘ ܡܢܐ ܕܒܝܬܐ[2] ܢܫܐܠ. ܡܦܫܩܢܐ ܕܝܢ
ܠܕܠܘܩܒܠܐ ܕܢܫܘܗ ܕܡܫܐܠܢܐ ܢܦܫܐ. ܘܠܐ ܙܕܩ ܬܘܒ ܕܠܣܘܦܣܛܝܩܘܬܐ
ܢܫܐܠ ܗܘ[3] ܕܡܫܐܠ. ܐܠܐ[4] ܠܗܘ ܡܢܐ ܕܢܦܩ ܠܗ. ܘܠܗܠܝܢ ܒܠܗܝܢ ܡܢ
ܒܕܘ ܒܛܘܦܣܐ ܠܦܬ. ܘܐܝܟܢܐ ܕܐܠܗܐ ܒܬܗܠܠܬܐ. ܘܠܐ ܠܡܬܒܕܪܘ
ܒܐܦܘܬܐ. ܘܠܒܪ ܣܐܪܐ ܡܢ ܐܕܫܐ ܕܘܒܐ ܗܘ ܡܢܐ ܕܪܡܙܘܢ ܠܢܫܡ.
ܒܐܡܬܝ ܕܠܣܘܟܠܐ ܢܒܘܢ ܘܠܐ ܢܦܪܘܢ[5] ܘܦܪܘܫܐ. ܘܠܡܘܡܝܗ ܕܠܗ ܢܟܝܢ
ܘܠܟܠܕܝܢܐ[6] ܢܟܗ.[7]

1 ¹ ܐܪܒܥܝܢܐ RVLl ² ܡܬܒܥܝܢܘܬܐ F ³ ܥܠܬܗܝ RVL ⁴ ܘܐܝܟܢܐ RVL ⁵ ܕܬܢܝܢܐ F ⁶ ܦܘܫܩܐ F

2 ¹ i. om. RVLl ²* om. R ³ i. add. ܠ RVL ⁴ ܐܦܠܐ RVLl ⁵ ܢܦܪܘܢ F ⁶ i. ܘܒܕ F ⁷ ܢܟܗ RVLl

## SECTION TEN
## On Rhetorical Interrogation and its Correct Manner, and on Response
## Three Theories

ONE.[50] In rhetoric, not about premisses but about other points, interrogation may occur in four ways. One is when an orator puts a question about a matter to which, if the response is yes, he who makes the assertion is forced to follow it through, but if he answers with a no, he is rejected by the listeners. The second is the reverse of this, namely, if he answers with a no, he is forced not to do it, but if he answers with a yes, he is rejected. Third is when the interrogator is confident that the response will be an enthymeme which implies what he wants. For example, (suppose) he says, 'At the time of your entry into my house did not my chattels go missing?' and (the opponent) answers 'Yes', he can say, 'Then you took it.' This interrogation is useful where without unanimity there (can) be no establishment, and where the respondent is preparing to put forward an opposing response, in order that he may be (left) speechless in his stupidity. Fourth is when the interrogation is manifold. Therefore if the respondent separates (the various parts) at (great) length, he is assumed to be babbling, because the populace seek a response (which) is short and sharp; but if he answers without distinguishing (the various parts), he is condemned.

TWO.[51] Rhetorical interrogations are undefined, and therefore their answer should emerge after examination, not immediately. An interrogator asks not for what he wants, but that which brings the conclusion which he wants, while a respondent may give an answer opposite to the interrogator's intention. Furthermore, it is not right for the interrogator to interrogate the conclusion, but that from which it follows. All these things I have already explained in the *Topics*. Where it is necessary (to employ) mockery, it must be to advantage in contests. Among the species of irony, that which is allusive is appropriate for a free man; that is, he will put the point in a wily manner, not openly and nakedly, keeping his own dignity and putting down the adversary.

---

[50] **7.10.1** AR 3.18 18b39-19a19; IS 4.5 (245.15-246.15).
[51] **7.10.2** AR 3.18 19a19-b9; IS 4.5 (246.15-247.9).

ܕܬܠܬ. ܠܐܬܘ̈ܬܐ ܪܗܛܘܪ̈ܝܐ ܘܐܕ̈ܫܐ. ܗܘ̇ ܕܠܡܠܘܐ ܘ*ܠܡܫܡܪ.
ܘܠܫܡ̈ܘܥܐ[1] ܠܡܫܝܚܘ. ܘܡܢ ܗܠܝܢ ܕܡܬܩ̈ܢܐ ܡܫܬܪܪܐ ܢܫܠܠ. ܘܠܡܬܩ̈ܢܘܬ
ܪܗܛܘܪܝܩܐ. ܘܡܦܝܣܢܘܬܐ. ܕܗܪܟܐ ܐܝܬ ܒܡܕ̈ܥܘܗܝ ܐܝܟ ܡܢ ܗܘ̇ ܡܟܐ[2]
ܕܐܬܬܘܕܥ ܒܬܠܬܐ ܗܢܐ ܐܫܬܘܕܥܬ. ܘܠܝܬ ܡܬܘܪ̈ܬܐ[3] ܒܡܦܩܦܩܘܗܝ.
ܘܫܠܡ ܬܘܪ̈ܓܡܐ ܐܘܣܦܬ ܫܘܬܦ ܡܐܡܪܐ ܡܦܪ̈ܫܐ ܠܐ ܐܝܟ ܐܘܣܝܐ ܐܦܠܐ
ܣܒܝܒܐ ܒܗ̇ܘ ܡܢ ܕܗܕܒܝܢ. ܦ̇ܠܐ ܠܡܗܘܐ. ܡܠܝܫܬܐ ܠܡ̈ܠܬܐ.
ܐܡܡܐ ܕܐܡ̈ܪܝ. ܗܝܟܘ ܡܢ ܕܐܡܪܝܬ. ܘܡܫܬܡܥܝܢ.[4] *ܗܡܢ ܐܢܫܘܢ[5]
ܒܫ̈ܢܝܗܘܢ[6] ܘܠܗܘܢ ܕܘܝܘ.

ܫܠܡ ܟܬܒܐ ܕܪܗܛܘܪܝܩܐ ܡܢ ܟܬܒܐ ܕܚܐܘܬ ܚܟܡܬܐ[1]

3 1* lect. incert. (--ܠܡ ܪܘ--) F 2 om. RVLl 3 pl. F 4 i. ܕ R 5* trp. l 6 ܒܫ̈ܢܝܗܘܢ V; lege? ܕܫ̈ܢܝܗܘܢ

Subscriptio 1 pl. RVLl; add. ܘܠܐܠܗܐ ܫܘܒܚܐ ܕܝܗܒ ܠܫܘܠܡܐ ܐܡܝܢ R; add. ܘܠܐܠܗܐ ܫܘܒܚܐ ܐܡܝܢ VL; add. ܘܠܐܠܗܐ ܫܘܒܚܐ ܐܡܝܢܐ ܠܥܠܡܝܢ ܐܡܝܢ l

THREE.[52] I recognise that at this point our master reminds (us) of what has been previously presented in this book—the rhetorical *topoi* and species; amplification and depreciation; arousing the emotion of listeners; speaking out of virtuous character; the parts of rhetoric; *enstasis*—but there is no advantage (to be gained) by their repetition (here). The conclusion of the address, that is, the epilogue of the discourse, must be separate, not bound or mixed with what is before it. Especially in deliberations, for example, one may say: 'This is what I have said, and you have listened, therefore you (have the judgement?) in your midst, so you judge!'

The End of the Book of Rhetoric from the Book of the Cream of Wisdom

[52] **7.10.3** AR 3.19 19b10-20b3; IS 4.5 (247.10-15).

# COMMENTARY

# COMMENTARY

On the general structure of Bar Hebraeus' *Cream of Wisdom* and the place of the *Book of Rhetoric* within it, see the Introduction, pp. 17-18, 20.

The three books of Aristotle's *Rhetoric* (AR) are treated in four chapters by Ibn Sina (IS) and seven chapters by Bar Hebraeus (BH). Ibn Sina deals with AR 1.1-2 in his first chapter, with AR 1.3 (the three kinds of rhetoric) and the rest of AR 1 (4-8 deliberative rhetoric, 9 epideictic rhetoric, and 10-15 judicial rhetoric) in his second chapter, and AR 2 and 3 in his third and fourth chapters. Bar Hebraeus carries his first chapter (his ܦܪܘܬܐܘܪܝܐ, προθεωρία, 'introduction') through to the tripartition of rhetoric in AR 1.3, gives a separate chapter to each of deliberative, epideictic, and judicial rhetoric, and splits AR 2 into two chapters, dividing *pathos* and *ethos* (AR 2.1-17, BH 5) from the logical topics of AR 2.18-26 (BH 6).

## CHAPTER ONE

BH 1.8 deals with the tripartition of rhetoric (AR 1.3; IS 2.1[53-57]), while the preceding seven sections are closely aligned with the seven sections of IS 1 (AR 1.1-2). Only at the transition from section 6 to section 7 do the divisions slightly diverge, and the titles of the first six sections are nearly identical in the two authors. These seven sections of BH may therefore fairly be characterised as a paraphrase of IS rather than AR, although here as elsewhere BH clearly kept his eye on the Syriac version of Aristotle (ARsyr). While considerably shorter than the account in IS, and foregoing some of its details and subtleties, BH nevertheless gives a clear and generally coherent exposition of the main points in IS 1. There is a German translation and commentary of IS 1 in Würsch, *Avicennas Bearbeitungen* 140-174 and 175-212. The logical background to the treatment of AR 1.1-2 in the Arabic philosophers is discussed at length by Würsch 14-108, and by Black, *Logic and Aristotle's Rhetoric*, 52-179.

**1.1.** BH 1.1 is unconnected to the text of AR, but presents a summary of IS 1.1. The title, 'the usefulenss of rhetoric', is that of IS's first section. The 'usefulness' of a book is one of the preliminaries (*prolegomena*) which, according to the Greek commentators on Aristotle, ought to be discussed at the outset of a commentary on it. Cf. E. Riad, *Studies in the Syriac Preface*, 41-72.

**1.1.1.** The idea that apodeixis, dialectic, and rhetoric are concerned, in decreasing order of rigour and certainty, with logical argument leading to conviction, sophistic with protection from error, and poetics with something quite other than truth or conviction, goes back at least as far as the Neoplatonic commentators on the *Organon*. In a Syriac author, although not preserved in Syriac itself, it appears as early as Paul the Persian; cf. Gutas, 'Paul the Persian', 231-267. On poetics, see below on 1.4.2 and 4.3.6. While the distinction between the wise and the populace, with the function of rhetoric being to persuade the populace, is here drawn directly from IS, these conceptions go back to classical antiquity, both Plato and Aristotle. In Syriac literature before BH they are present in the treatise on rhetoric by Antony of Tagrit; cf. Watt, 'The Syriac Reception of Platonic and Aristotelian Rhetoric', 579-601. *Pistis* translates the Syriac ܗܝܡܢܘܬܐ, which in this section, as elsewhere in BH, corresponds to تصديق in IS (rendered by Würsch 'Glaubhaftmachung', 'making credible').

When BH, from 1.2 onwards, links up with the text of AR, ܗܝܡܢܘܬܐ corresponds to the Greek πίστις. ܗܝܡܢܘܬܐ is the regular rendering in Syriac translation literature of πίστις, in the sense of 'faith'. Following the example of Kennedy's translation, *Aristotle 'On Rhetoric'*, I have in some passages kept *pistis* (plural *pisteis*) as a technical term rendering ܗܝܡܢܘܬܐ (or plural), rather than adopt the various English terms appropriate to its different contexts in Aristotle ('proof', 'means of persuasion', 'belief', etc., cf. Glossary, s.v.). It can be assumed that ARsyr translated πίστις by ܗܝܡܢܘܬܐ, just as تصديق stands for it in ARar, and that Syriac Aristotelians did not take it in the usual religious sense of 'faith'.

**1.1.2.** The superiority of the apodeictic syllogism to the rhetorical goes back to the Neoplatonic commentators and is maintained throughout the Syro-Arabic Aristotelian tradition; cf. Gutas, 'Paul the Persian', 238-255. IS 2.15-16 distinguishes between تصديق الخواص (assent of the distinguished, by apodeixis) and تصديق العوام (assent of the populace, by rhetoric). On victory in debate as the goal of dialectic, cf. Hadot, 'Philosophie, dialectique, rhétorique', 139-166.

**1.1.3.** A tripartition of humanity, with a group intermediate between the wise and the populace and particularly able to make use of dialectic, is attested before IS in al-Farabi; cf. Würsch 33-34 and 175-176. In Syriac before BH it is found in Antony of Tagrit; cf. Watt, 'The Syriac Reception of Platonic and Aristotelian Rhetoric', 585-586. 'Reputable arguments' (ܦ̈ܚܡܐ ܡܫܒ̈ܚܐ) is BH's shorthand for arguments based on reputable premisses (Aristotle's ἔνδοξα, Ibn Sina's محمودات or مشهورات) ; BH more often uses for 'reputable' forms of ܫܒܚ (cf. below on 1.3.7). For the difference between dialectical and rhetorical premisses, see 1.2.1 below.

**1.2.** At this point Ibn Sina and, following him, Bar Hebraeus start to paraphrase the text of Aristotle. BH 1.2 and IS 1.2 correspond to AR 1.1-5. The 'inner pillar' is derived from Aristotle's 'body of *pistis*' (54a15); cf. below on 1.2.3.

**1.2.1.** The idea that rhetoric shares with dialectic the aim of victory in verbal parley (ܚܒܝܫܐ, مفاوضة) goes back to al-Farabi; cf. Würsch 180. BH's 'complaisance (of the speaker)' (ܦܣܘܪܐ, contrasted with ܩܛܝܪܐ, 'compulsion') is probably his way of paraphrasing the idea in IS that the common person will accept a rhetorical argument when his soul has an affection (ميل) for it; cf. Würsch 34. The phrase 'anything to which they take a desire' (ܟܠ ܡܕܡ ܕܪܓܬܗ ܢܣܒܐ ܢܦܫܗܝܢ) is reminiscent of Antony of Tagrit's definition of rhetoric: 'a faculty of persuasive speech ... on any matter to which it takes a desire (ܟܠ ܡܕܡ ܕܪܓܬܗ ܢܣܒܐ ܢܦܫܐ) ...', on which cf. Watt, 'The Syriac Reception of Platonic and Aristotelian Rhetoric', 585-586. While Antony's definition is in general closer to Dionysius of Halicarnassus than to Aristotle, the phrase in question may come from the Syro-Arabic translation of Aristotle's definition of rhetoric; cf. below on 1.5.1. The contrast between true (ܫܪܝܪܬܐ) premisses and those based on opinion (ܡܣܬܒܪܢܝܬܐ) follows IS 7.11-12 حقيقية and ظنية. BH's succint formulation paraphrases the idea of IS that while in rhetoric the speaker need not use true premisses but merely those in accord with the opinion (ظن) of the multiude, in dialectic that is insufficient and the premisses must be reputed (محمود, esteemed) to be true by each party to the parley. Only apodeixis, however, need employ premisses which are unconditionally and necessarily true, not merely reputed. For the background in al-Farabi and Ibn Sina on the distinction between dialectical and rhetorical premisses, on which there is no clear statement in Aristotle himself, cf. Würsch 28-36 and 182, Black, *Logic and Aristotle's Rhetoric*, 138-152, and Aouad, 'Les fondements de la Rhétorique', *passim*.

**1.2.2.** BH follows IS quite closely. However, in place of IS's 'faculty' (ملكة), BH uses 'habit' (ܐܟܣܝܣ); cf. on 1.5.1 below. It may be assumed that he took it from ARsyr (AR 54a7 ἕξις) where ARar has قنية راسخة, 'embedded possession'.

**1.2.3.** BH largely follows IS's exposition of AR 54a11-18, but radically truncates it. Where IS writes 'The First Teacher' (Aristotle), BH says 'Our Master'. 'Pillar' (ܥܡܘܕܐ, عمود) comes from the 'body (σῶμα) of *pistis*' of AR 54a15, rendered عمود التصديق in ARar (presumably ܥܡܘܕܐ ܕܗܝܡܢܘܬܐ in ARsyr?); 'outer aids' (ܡܥܕܪܢܐ ܒܪܝܐ, IS 8.11-12 and 13 الأمور الخارجة عن عمود and اعوان) are the προσθῆκαι ... τῶν ἔξω τοῦ πράματος of 54a14-15. BH links IS 8.14 to 12.5, cutting out all in between, his 'opined' (ܡܣܬܒܪ) picking up IS يظن (8.13). The rather tortuous 'dressing up of an orator in an acceptable outward appearance' (ܡܣܬܟܡܘܬܗ ܕܪܗܛܪܐ ܒܐܣܟܡܐ ܡܩܒܠܐ) corresponds to IS 12.6 ايهام بخلق. With reference to AR 54b16-22, IS and BH put *taxis* in the category of aids and add in *pathos* and *ethos*. 'Slander, compassion, and anger', not in IS, are taken by BH from AR 54a16-17: διαβολή, ἔλεος, ὀργή.

**1.2.4.** IS 13.1-6 speaks of two schools of thought, one allowing the outer aids, the other forbidding them. This is an elaboration of ARar (and ARsyr?) 54a21-23, which speaks of two factions (Lyons 2.6; cf. Würsch 187). IS does not mention any specific place, but identifies the first of the two schools as the right one. BH follows this and additionally specifies 'the court of the Areopagus at Athens' (from AR 54a23) as a place where the right school held sway. Through this sequence of elaborations, BH thus says the opposite of Aristotle, according to whom in the court of the Areopagus one was rightly forbidden to speak outside the subject.

**1.3.** Paraphrase of IS 1.3, AR 1.1.6-11. In the title 'points' (ܢܩܥܐ) renders IS اغراض, 'nature' (ܐܝܟܢܝܘܬܐ) كيفية.

**1.3.1.** BH's introduction here of 'particular matters' as the province of rhetoric follows IS. See below on 1.4.1 and 1.5.1. Similarly following IS is the mention by BH of the three time references and the three pairs of goals of the three kinds of rhetoric. BH stays close to AR when speaking of the lawmaker, but follows IS in attributing the outcome to the victor of the dispute between two contenders (ܡܬܕܝ̈ܢܢܐ ... ܢܙܟܘܢ), IS 14.7 الخصمين يتشاجرا..., rather than the decision of the dicast (AR 54a30).

**1.3.2.** In separating the evaluation of the just and the expedient, BH follows IS. His 'climes' ܩܠܝ̈ܡܐ renders IS 14.10 اقاليم. Also taken from IS is the distinction of 'evident/hidden' advantage or harm (in IS evident to the populace/known only to the learned) and evident/hidden effectuation (BH ܡܫܡܠܝܘܬܐ, IS 15.1 تأدية) of advantage or harm. The latter may have been suggested by ARar (and ARsyr?) at 54b13, which speaks of judges' difficulty in the discernment (النظر) of the just and the useful, rather than their proper judgement of it. Cf. Lyons, 229 who suggests the possibility of ARar/syr reading καὶ ὡς for καλῶς.

**1.3.3.** BH abbreviates but largely follows IS, who here employs the terminology of Islamic jurisprudence. BH 'decisions' (ܦܣܩ̈ܐ) are IS 16.9 احكام, his 'customs' (ܥܝܕ̈ܐ) IS 16.14 تفريعات ('secondary things'). BH 'lawmaker, prophet, or wise man' corresponds to IS 16.14 'the lawmaker and the imams'.

**1.3.4.** BH follows IS in the main, but adds in points from AR, notably the references to proemium and narrations. BH's 'custom' in this instance renders IS's 17.13 نتيجة ('inference', contrast 1.3.3 above), his 'devices' (ܦܘܪ̈ܣܐ) IS's 17.10 حيل ('stratagems). BH's ܟܢܘܫܗ ܕܠܒܪܝܘܬܐ ܒܡ̈ܠܐ ܡܬܚܫܒܝܢ (bringing together in words the outside of the subject) may be the rendering in ARsyr of τὰ ἔξω τοῦ πράγματος τεχνολογοῦσιν (54b17). In BH as in AR it is the judge (κριτής, ܕܝܢܐ), in IS the hearer (سامع) to whom the devices outside the subject are directed. The explicit reference to the *Analytics* comes from BH

(IS 18.5-6: 'you already know what the enthymeme is'). He will have been referring to *An. Pr.* 2.27(70a10).

**1.3.5.** BH 'exposition/contention' (ܬܘܪܓܡܐ/ܕܝܢܐ) follows IS 18.7-8 تفسير or مشاجرة/تبيين, as does the limitation of the devices to a commercial (lit. 'of taking and giving', IS 18.11 اخذ وعطاء, BH ܡܣܒܐ ܘܡܬܠܐ) conflict. BH's ܡܬܘܕܘܣ presumably follows ARsyr (AR 54b23 μέθοδος); ARar has حيلة او صناعة here, and IS 18.14-15 صناعة. BH follows IS in likening disputes to do with the state to expositions and the outer devices to adornment (IS 19.2-3 'in part equipment and in part adornment'). 'Matter of the sign' (ܨܒܘܬܐ ܕܫܘܕܥܐ) renders IS 19.3 شأن الدليل.

**1.3.6.** Abbreviates but closely follows IS. BH's 'action' (ܣܘܥܪܢܐ) supports the emendation of العلة to الفعلة in IS 19.7; cf. Würsch, 190. BH 'belief' (ܬܘܕܝܬܐ) renders IS 19.8 رأى. IS 20.13-14 contends that in deliberative decisions rules are rarely prescribed *except for resistance and war*; this last phrase shows Islamic influence (cf. Würsch, 190) and is not taken over by BH. In place of IS 20.11 'to the lawgivers there is a duty ... to forbid the judges ... overstepping what is in their book', BH has 'the law itself forbids him to speak outside the book', closer to AR 55a2 ὁ νόμος κωλύει λέγειν ἔξω τοῦ πράγματος. ܟܬܒܐ probably stood here for πράγματος in ARsyr, rather than ܣܦܪܐ (suggested as a possibilty by Lyons, 230, whose other suggestion is γράμματος); ARar has الكتاب. The Syriac translator may have been stimulated to write 'outside the book' (from which presumably comes the infrequent 'prescription' of rules in deliberative matters in IS [20.13 يفترض] and BH [ܡܣܬܝܡ]) by the κοινότερον of AR 54b29, taken in the sense of 'more commonly understood'; cf. ARar اكثر واعم. 'Judicial matters' ܕܐܓܘܢܐܣܘܐ corresponds here to δικανικά AR 54b31, التشاجر in ARar and تشاجرية in IS 20.12.

**1.3.7.** The understanding of an enthymeme as a truncated syllogism in which the major premiss is usually suppressed is standard in the Syro-Arabic tradition; cf. Würsch 26-27 and Black, *Logic and Aristotle's Rhetoric*, 156-163. 'Reputable' renders ܡܫܒܚܢܐ, Greek ἔνδοξα, Arabic محمودات. Like the Greek δοξάζειν the Syriac ܫܒܚ means both 'to opine' and 'to praise'. 'Praiseworthies', by which محمودات is often rendered, might be thought to come closer to representing BH's intention, but 'reputable' may better suit the Aristotelian context. (Würsch uses 'anerkannt' in IS, Aouad 'loué' in IR.) The distinction between the dialectical and rhetorical syllogism as resting on the difference between true reputable (premisses) ܡܫܒܚܢܝܬܐ ܕܫܪܝܪܬܐ and opined reputable (premisses) ܡܫܒܚܢܝܬܐ ܡܣܬܒܪܢܝܬܐ follows IS 21.7-11 محمودات حقيقية and those of opinion ظن; cf. above on 1.1.3 and 1.2.1.

The last sentence combines AR 55a15-17 with *Matthew* 7, 13-14. BH was no doubt reminded of the gospel passage by the concluding clause of IS (21.15): 'but the way to it is hard; some attain to it, and some attain to what is similar to it'. Biblical reminiscence may also be behind BH's 'shadow'; cf.

*Colossians* 2,17; *Hebrews* 8,5; 10,1.

**1.4.** Paraphrase of IS 1.4 (AR 1.1.12-15)

**1.4.1.** The explicit linking of rhetoric to communal or political life here abbreviates the longer account of this in IS. On the view that rhetoric, unlike dialectic, is primarily concerned with particulars rather than universals, see below on 1.5.1. The assertion that dialectic 'replaces' apodeixis for unlearned souls in dealing with universals, and rhetoric exact wisdom (ܚܟܝܡܘܬܐ ܫܪܝܪܬܐ, IS 22.12 تعقل صحيح, 'proper insight') in treating particulars, follows IS. The reading ܡܬܕܒܪܐ, 'he who is governed', against the MSS. (cf. apparatus) is based on IS 23.3 المدبر. The 'scholarly word of wisdom' (ܡܠܬ ܚܟܝܡܘܬܐ ܡܠܦܢܝܬܐ) corresponds to AR 55a26 διδασκαλία γάρ ἐστιν ὁ κατὰ τὴν ἐπιστήμην λόγος, ARar الكلام الذي يحمل على العلم المستقصي, IS 23.4 البيان العلمي; BH may be citing ARsyr.

**1.4.2.** The expansion of AR 55a31 (οὐ γὰρ δεῖ τὰ φαῦλα πείθειν, 'one should not persuade what is debased') into 'just, proper, or praiseworthy' (ܟܐܢܐ ܘܦܐܝܐ ܘܡܫܒܚܐ) follows IS 23.12 عدل صواب محمود. Similarly sophistic misleading (ܛܥܝܐ) and poetic production of imagination (ܡܚܝܠܢܘܬܐ) render IS 24.7-8 تغليط and تخييل. On poetics and 'image-evocation', see below on 4.3.6. The clause 'produces a syllogistic opposite' paraphrases IS 24.5 نقيس فيها على المتقابلين, 'by which we syllogise from opposites'. Cf. AR 55a34-36.

**1.4.3.** With 'strength, health, wealth, and military strategy' (AR 55b5-6) BH clearly follows ARsyr rather than IS or ARar. IS 24.15 has 'health, wealth, and courage (بسالة), ARar 'strength, health, wealth, and power (سلطان), BH and AR 'strength, health,wealth, and ܐܣܛܪܛܝܓܘܬܐ/στρατηγία'. In place of IS 25.1 'the need for the good is pressing', BH alludes to AR 62a21-22 ἀγαθὸν ὃ ἂν αὐτὸ ἑαυτοῦ ἕνεκα ᾖ αἱρετόν ('a good is whatever is chosen for itself'). BH omits the Arabic proverb cited by IS ('iron is cleft with iron'; cf. Würsch, 196) but follows him in contrasting man with animals and designating 'the organ of speech' (ܐܪܓܢܘܢ ܕܡܠܬܐ, IS 25.4 اللسان والبيان 'speech and eloquence') as special to him (ܕܝܠܗ ܠܚܘܕܝܗ, IS 25.4 يخصه, AR 55b1 μᾶλλον ἴδιον ... ἀνθρώπου).

**1.4.4.** Both Ibn Sina and Bar Hebraeus were medical doctors, but neither elaborated on Aristotle's comparison of rhetoric with medicine. In this paragraph BH again closely follows IS, although the 'difficult persuasion' (ܡܬܛܦܝܣܝܢ) rather than 'installation' (تقرير IS 25.12) of matters in some souls may be influenced by AR 55b10-11 πεῖσαι ... πιθανά.

**1.4.5.** 'Resemblance' (ܕܡܘܬܐ) may be taken as a parahrase of Aristotle's 'apparent' (AR 55b16-17 φαινόμενος, ARar and IS 26.5 يرى), but BH may be alluding to 55a14 τὸ ὅμοιον τῷ ἀληθεῖ; cf. BH 1.3.7. 'Immediately' (ܡܚܕܐ) renders IS 26.6 فى بادئ الرأى 'at first glance', a concept important in al-Farabi's differentiation of dialectic and rhetoric. Cf. Würsch 28-36; Black,

*Logic and Aristotle's Rhetoric*, 148-152; Aouad, 'Les fondements de la Rhétorique', *passim*. BH is closer in this paragraph to IS than to AR, although he radically abbreviates him. However his choice of ܠܘܬ ܚܟܡܬܐ 'in accordance with wisdom' rather than IS 26.14f. عن بصيرة ومعرفة 'out of insight and knowledge' for the 'good part' of rhetoric may draw from ARsyr at 55b19 κατὰ τὴν ἐπιστήμην (ARar من جهة العلم).

**1.5.** Paraphrase of IS 1.5 and AR 1.2.1-7. The title in IS includes 'definition of rhetoric', but 'the kinds of *pisteis*' is BH's own formulation, perhaps picking up the end of IS's first sentence (28.10 'how through [the parts of rhetoric] one attains the aims which are special to it').

**1.5.1.** In the definition of rhetoric in BH, the 'striving for the possible persuasion' of IS and ARar (تتكلف الاقناع الممكن) appears as 'persuasive as far as possible' (ܡܦܝܣܢܝܬܐ ܟܡܐ ܕܡܫܟܚܐ) which may be the rendering in ARsyr of 55b27 τὸ ἐνδεχόμενον πιθανόν. If this is so, ARsyr may have translated περὶ ἕκαστον by 'on every one of the particular matters' (ܒܟܠܚܕ ܡܢ ܨܒ̈ܘܬܐ ܡܬܝܚܕ̈ܝܬܐ), possibly taking a clue from AR 55b34 οὐ περί τι γένος ἴδιον ('not about a particular genus'). ARsyr may also have omitted τοῦ θεωρῆσαι, or alternatively translated it by ܕܠܘܬܗ ܢܣܒ ܚܐܦܐ, 'to which it may take a desire', as it appears here before the mention of 'category' and in 1.2.1. This rather puzzling phrase, literally 'to which it may take a rushing', found also in Antony of Tagrit (see above on 1.2.1) could be behind the تكلف ('striving') of ARar and IS, but the reason for such a translation of θεωρῆσαι would be obscure.

In subsequently explaining some individual words or phrases in the definition, BH is following IS. The same procedure was already followed by al-Farabi (cf. Würsch 197-198) and in Syriac literature by Antony of Tagrit (cf. Watt, 'Syriac Rhetorical Theory', 249-250; idem, 'The Syriac Reception of Platonic and Aristotelian Rhetoric', 585-586). In the rest of the paragraph BH is considerably shorter than IS, but generally follows him. For IS 28.12 'ability (ملكة) of the soul' BH has 'habit (ܐܡܘܢܘܬܐ) of the soul'; cf. on 1.2.2 above. While IS 29.6-8 speaks both of the individual (مفرد) and particular (جزئى), BH speaks only of the particular (ܡܬܝܚܕܬܐ), but follows IS in interpreting this as any category (ܡܩܛܐܓܘܪܝܐ, مقولة). On the introduction of 'particulars' and 'categories' into the Arabic discussion of rhetoric, cf. Würsch 25-26, 181, 198; Black, *Logic and Aristotle's Rhetoric*, 114-115. AR 55b30-31 συμβεβηκότα πάθη was presumably rendered in ARsyr ܓܕ̈ܫܐ ܟܝܢܝ̈ܐ ('natural accidents', ܓܕܫ from συμβαίνειν 'to happen by chance'). ARar has 'forms which happen' (الاشكال التي يحدث), and IS does not allude to it (except in posing the question whether medicine is natural or accidental [30.4 بالعرض]).

**1.5.2.** The introduction here of *topoi* and species stems from IS (cf. AR 58a26-32 and 03b14-15), as does the additional division (over and above Aristotle's non-artistic and artistic) into those forming the premisses of syllogisms and those elements and rules (ܐܣܛܘܟ̈ܣܐ and ܩܢܘ̈ܢܐ, IS 32.15 أصول and قوانين) from which rhetorical premisses may be derived during a 'parley'. (For this last term see on 1.2.1 and 1.8.1). The example given by IS of moving from an opposite (ضد) has Zayd and 'Amr where BH has ܩܪܣܩܘܣ (Crescus?) and Socrates, and states that it is derived 'from a rule with us' (33.5) without specifying it. BH's specification of that 'rule', 'it is right to do good to your friends and do evil to your enemies', is probably taken from AR 63a20-21, but cf. below on 3.3.3.

**1.5.3.** Paraphrase of AR 1.2.3-7 and IS 1.5(33.6-34.5), with the divergences from AR stemming from IS. Both IS and BH substitute 'pillar' for 'logos' and name it first. The enumeration of a speaker's desirable character-traits is from IS, but the expression '*pistis*-worthy' ܫܘܐ ܠܡܗܝܡܢܘ is the ἀξιόπιστις of AR 56a5, no doubt from ARsyr. ܒܐܝܩܘܬ ܐܣܟܡܐ 'fair manner' will be the rendering in ARsyr of ἐπιειχεῖς 56a6 (ARar and IS صالح and صلاح). 'Verification' (ܫܘܪܪܐ) is IS's تثبيت (cf. AR 56a19 ἀληθὲς ἢ φαινόμενον δείξωμεν), and the restriction of the efficacy of ethos to the past is also taken from IS. The Arabic (and possibly Syriac) translation of AR 56a7 περὶ πάντων μὲν ἁπλῶς by 'in all evident matters' may have led to this restriction; cf. Würsch 203.

**1.5.4.** The description of rhetoric's common ground with politics follows IS (who however expressly mentions ethics), but that of the common ground of dialectic and rhetoric is BH's own paraphrase of AR 56a32-34 (cf. IS 34.11: '... dialectic in view of what we have mentioned'). I read 'supposed to be some compound (ܪܘܟܒܐ) of dialectic and politics'; the ܕܘܒܒܐ of the MSS. is incomprehensible, and ܪܘܟܒܐ ܡܕܡ looks like the Syriac version of AR 56a25 παραφυές τι (ARar بمنزلة التركيب). 'Sharing subject matter' and 'as shown with apodeixis' are drawn from IS 34.13-15, where the connection is between the demonstration that no art is compounded from parts of another art and his treatise on apodeixis; cf. Würsch 164 and 203 (n. 107).

**1.5.5.** Paraphrase of IS 35.6-9 ('The First Teacher says ...'), an elaboration of AR 56a28-30.

**1.6.** Paraphrase of IS 1.6 (35-43) and AR 1.2.8-15.

**1.6.1.** A brief summary of a lengthy section in IS (35.12-37.14), the paraphrase of AR 1.2.8-10. The list of terms with which it begins is taken from IS: *verification* (ܫܘܪܪܐ) corresponds to IS تثبيت, *enthymeme* (ܡܬܪܥܝܢܘܬܐ) to IS ضمير, *thought* (ܡܬܚܫܒܢܘܬܐ) to IS تفكير, *demonstration* (ܡܚܘܝܢܘܬܐ) to IS اعتبار/برهان. BH's explanation of the difference between enthymeme and thought, however, is different from that of IS, according to whom in a تفكير the middle term requires thought; cf. Würsch 51 and Black, *Logic and Aristotle's Rhetoric*, 159, n. 57. ARar renders παράδειγμα by برهان, normally for IS the equivalent of apodeixis (cf. Lyons II 110; Würsch 204); ARsyr appears to have rendered it by ܦܪ̈ܕܝܓܡܐ or ܬܚܘܝܬܐ (cf. below at BH 6.2.1). While *verification*, [*enthymeme*,] *thought*, and *demonstration* (and most of what follows) is in the main BH's rendering of IS, the terms used for *syllogism*, *induction* (ܡܦܩܠܝܐ, IS استقراء), *enthymeme*, and *paradigm* (ܦܪ̈ܕܝܓܡܐ, IS تمثيل) (cf. AR 56b1-3) will have been taken from the wording of ARsyr. On the term ܡܦܩܠܝܐ (*induction*, ἐπαγωγή, استقراء), see below on 6.5.4. The statement about the differing relative benefits of syllogism and induction in dialectic and rhetoric, as well as the subsequent remarks about what the populace will or will not accept, is derived from IS 37.6-14. It stands in contrast to AR 56b22-24 (' ... speeches with enthymemes receive more applause'), but is comprehensible in the light of ARar, according to which such speeches produce more controversy (شغب, Lyons 10.20). ARar and IS may have been influenced by *Topics* 105a16-19, 'Induction is more convincing ... and familiar to the multitude, syllogism more cogent and effective against opponents'. Cf. Würsch 73-75.

**1.6.2.** Brief paraphrase of IS 38.15-40.4 (cf. also 40.12-13), itself an interpretation of AR 1.2.11. BH modifies IS 39.3 'the reputable is what is persuasive in itself', into 'the reputable is that which is persuasive immediately it is heard'. Cf. AR 56b27 'the persuasive ... is immediately persuasive and convincing in itself' and ARar '... immediately produces conviction for the hearer' (Lyons 10.24). The immediacy of the reputable emerges again at IS 40.3 with the re-appearance of the phrase فى بادئ الرأى ('at first glance'; cf. above on 1.4.5): 'The true reputable (premisses) are reputable at first glance'. The contrast between individuals and 'the whole populace' (cf. AR 56b33 τοιοῖσδε, 'certain kinds of people') comes from IS 39.10, 'reputable according to the thinking of the populace or groups within it'.

**1.6.3.** Paraphrase of IS 41.7-42.14, interpreting AR 1.2 (57a1-13). The passage is the clearest account in this book of BH of the difference between 'reputation' and truth. Premisses are reputable because they are widely esteemed, not because they are true. Their truth or untruth can only be discerned by the studious (ܡܠܝ̈ܠܐ), who alone will cease to consider them reputable if they are found by investigation to be untrue. Premisses which the populace considers reputable on the basis of opinion, however, will lose their reputation with the populace if it renounces them (for reasons other than their scientifically established untruth). 'Renunciation' (ܟܦܘܪܘܬܐ) in BH corresponds to IS 42.2-3, 'Opined reputable premisses may also lose their reputation on account of repulsiveness' (شنعة). IS thus gives a moral slant to the opposite of 'reputable' which is absent from Aristotle himself (cf. Würsch 38 and 206 n. 120) and not necessarily implied in BH's term. The remainder of the paragraph is closely based on IS. The passage in Aristotle to which their comments on the Second Figure refer is *Anal. Pr.* 1.5.

**1.6.4.** Paraphrase of IS 42.14-43.7, a free interpretation of AR 57a13-57b1. IS considers that orators deal with necessary things either when they stray into things like physics and metaphysics where oratory does not properly belong - this case not being mentioned by BH - or when they employ necessary premisses - the case of interest to BH. IS's examples, from which BH's are taken, read as follows: 'So and so does not unite in himself love of cravings and the virtue of temperance'; 'So and so does not fear God as long as he believes the resurrection to be inconceivable and affirms the destruction of the soul'; and (for that concerning possible things) 'So and so slandered so and so, for the ruler was taking advice from him when he gave the order to hold him'. BH's concluding 'If he openly expresses a universal major (premiss) ...' is his adaptation of IS 43.7, ' If he is explicit about a statement (applying) to the whole ...'. IS meant that whatever is said of the subject is said of the predicate; cf. Würsch 207 n. 123.

**1.7.** Paraphrase of IS 1.6 (43.10)-1.7, a free interpretation of AR 1.2.14-22.

**1.7.1.** The statement that enthymemes may be generated from necessary premisses or those which are 'even possibles' (ܡܬܡܨܝ̈ܢܐ ܫܘ̈ܝܐ) is taken from IS 43.10. 'Even possibles' (ممكنات بالتساوى) are premisses of which the opposite is equally possible. Their special association with rhetoric goes back to the Alexandrian discussion on the classification of the sciences, according to which that which could be equally true or false was the province of rhetoric; cf. Black, *Logic and Aristotle's Rhetoric*, 152-154. From ARar of 57a32-33 the reader would not discover that enthymemes can be made from probabilities (εἰκότα) and signs, but from truths (صادقات) and signs (Lyons 12.26). IS immediately (43.12) identifies 'the true' (صادقات) and 'the true reputable' (محمودات حقيقية), from which comes BH's 'true reputable' (ܡܫܬܒܚ̈ܢܐ ܫܪܝܪ̈ܬܐ). Unlike BH, IS keeps the separate category of 'mostly true premisses' (AR 57a31-32; cf. Würsch 207 n. 124). 'Socrates is wise ...' in BH replaces 'Zayd is learned ...' in IS (cf. AR 57b12); the example of a necessary sign ('this girl is a married woman') is identical in each. BH's first two examples of possibles are taken from IS's (45.1-4) of 'the mostly true' (اكثريات), with 'Zayd' again being replaced by 'Socrates'. The last example ('Dorieus ... crown') is added by BH from AR 57a19-21.

**1.7.2.** 'Index' (ܐܬܐ) in BH corresponds to IS علامة, 'sign' (ܫܘܕܥܐ) to دليل. ARar in this chapter uses دلالة for sign and necessary sign (AR σημεῖον and τεκμήριον) and علامة for a not necessary sign (σημεῖον), but the usage fluctuates. For that of ARar, cf. Lyons II 129 and 138 (Greek-Arabic), 202 and 247 (Arabic-Greek), and on the general issue Würsch 56-57. For BH's usage of the two terms, cf. the Glossary to this volume. The example of a pregnant woman, taken by BH from IS, comes ultimately from

*Anal. Pr.* 2.27 (70a20-24); in the other examples 'Socrates' once again replaces IS's 'Zayd', and 'the noble and modest Joseph' is the replacement for the 'brave and ungreedy Ali', the last two examples in BH again belonging to IS's 'mostly true premisses'.

**1.7.3.** Abbreviated paraphrase of IS 45.11-47.9, with reference to AR 1.2.19. The explanation of 'even possibles' is abbreviated from IS 45.11-46.3, but the example is taken from AR 57b30-35. IS himself speaks of 'the freshly killed Zayd' and subsequently says that 'the First Teacher did not go into the even possible (الممكن المتساوى) at this point' (47.5-6).

**1.7.4.** Brief paraphrase of IS 47.10-49.4 and AR 1.2.20-22. 'Species' and *topoi* are examined at length in BH 6 (AR 2.18-26). 'The five' to which BH refers are, in addition to rhetoric and dialectic, 'ethical, physical, and political questions', in accord with IS 48.8-9, although he also mentions, with Aristotle, the judicial (cf. AR 58a12-13 and 18-20).

**1.8.** Paraphrase of AR 1.3, the division of the three kinds of rhetoric. On the whole it is closer to IS (53.1-57.6) than to AR himself, although at this point, the beginning of IS's chapter two, IS starts to adhere much more closely to AR than heretofore.

**1.8.1.** In describing a rhetorical situation as a dispute (ܚܪܝܢܐ) or parley (ܥܢܝܢܐ), BH picks up both from 1.2.1 (on which see above) and the opening statement of IS (53.5): 'Dispute (منازعة) whether something is or is not is common to all rhetorical species'. Cf. also IS's use of 'parley' (مفاوضة) at 54.2 and 5. The specific distinction of a popular (ܥܡܡܝܐ) parley as that between good and evil is also from IS (53.6-7): 'Most kinds (اصناف) of popular disputes (حاورات عامية) are on matters being good or evil'. BH also follows IS, briefly paraphrasing 53.7-55.1, in here differentiating the three kinds of rhetoric according to time before speaking in 1.8.2 of the different kinds of hearers, i.e. reversing the order of AR 58a36-b8 and 58b13-20.

**1.8.2.** BH's three hearers, namely an adversary, judge, and spectators (ܒܥܠܕܒܒܐ, ܕܝܢܐ, and ܚܙܝܐ), are taken from IS 55.2 خصم, حاكم, and سامعون نظار, not AR 58b2-3 ἢ θεωρὸν εἶναι ἢ κριτήν. The third kind of hearer, the adversary, was introduced into the Arabic tradition by al-Farabi; it may be the case, however, notwithstanding the text of AR 58b2-3, that in a long tradition going back to the Greek commentators there was an assumption that Aristotle intended to speak of three kinds of hearer. Cf. Würsch 185 n.39. 'Governing ruler of the assembly' (ܪܫܢܐ ܡܕܒܪܢܐ ܕܟܢܫܐ) may be a conflation of ἐκκλησιαστής (58b5) in ARsyr (ܪܫܢܐ ܕܟܢܫܐ, cf. ARar رئيس الجمع, Lyons 16.8) and IS 55.3 الرئيس المدبر لأمر الجماعة 'governing ruler for the proceedings of the assembly'. 'Examining arbitrator' (?, literally 'examining intermediary') (ܡܨܥܝܐ ܡܒܨܝܢܐ) may be ARsyr's version of δικαστής (ܡܒܨܝܢܐ?; cf. ARar فاحص) joined to IS 55.4 المتوسط الموثوق بفحصه 'the arbitrator (intermediary) trustworthy in his examination'. IS may have introduced 'arbitrator' (intermediary) here on account of ARar 86b14, 'those who arrive at that without (having made a prior) judgement or decision should be set in the middle' (appointed arbitrators?) (يوسطوا); cf. Lyons 112.7 and 323.

**1.8.3.** The reformulation of AR 58b30 ('... sometimes one does not dispute about the others') into the positive statement that a deliberative orator may advise the honourable follows IS 56.1-3. The 'similarly' (ܗܟܢܐ) of BH, and كذلك of IS 56.3, thus have a different point than that at AR 58b38 (ὁμοίως). BH presumably considered his expression 'the slaughter of martyrs for piety, persecution for true confession' to be more suitable for his Christian readers than what stood in his Muslim *Vorlage* (IS 56.5-6): 'those fighting in the cause of God may be killed, thrown out, and stripped'. IS 56.6 makes no mention of Achilles and Patroclus (AR 59a3-4), merely saying that 'often a discerning man (عقل) is praised for preferring death to life'. 'Because of him he would die' (ܡܛܠܬܗ ܡܐܬ) is doubtless the rendering in ARsyr of 59a4, 'it was necessary for him to die'. Cf. ARar يموت بسببه, Lyons 17.20 and 242: δεῖ αὐτὸν taken as δι' αὐτοῦ.

**1.8.4.** Paraphrase of AR 1.3.7-9, but rather closer to IS 56.6-57.6. As in AR 57a32 (cf. above on 1.7.1), ARar renders εἰκότα 59a8 by 'truth' (صدق, Lyons 17.23-24). The sequence in BH ('reputable premisses, sign, index') is not that of AR 59a7-8 (τεκμήρια, εἰκότα, σημεῖα), but that of IS 56.8. As in 1.7.2 BH renders دليل by ܥܘܗܕܢܐ ('sign') and علامة by ܐܬܐ ('index').

## CHAPTER TWO

BH chapter 2 is devoted to deliberative rhetoric, AR 1.4-8. Its four sections correspond to each of AR 1.4-7; the substance of AR 1.8, on constitutions, is treated in connection with AR 1.4.12 (BH 2.1.8), and then briefly mentioned again at the end (BH 2.4.9). The procedure is the same in IS. IS 2.2 covers AR 1.5-6 (BH 2.2-3), but otherwise the divisions (IS 2.1-3) are the same.

**2.1.** AR 1.4, IS 2.1 (57.7 and following). The terminology 'great (i.e public) subjects' (ܨܒ̈ܘܬܐ ܪ̈ܘܪܒܬܐ, as contrasted with the 'private subjects' of BH 2.2) is taken from the الأمور العظام in the title of IS 2.1 at 53.4. That in turn is probably derived from ARar (from ARsyr?) 60b1 الأمر العظمى (Lyons 22.12) rendering τὰ μέγιστα ('the most important subjects).

**2.1.1.** BH's 'definition' of deliberation ('speech causing motion of the will towards the attainment of good and warning of bad') - a paraphrase of AR 59a37-39 (which in [ARsyr? and] ARar reads, 'it is clear and plain in how much deliberation occurs, and that is in all the things that can be done through us and the occurrence of which comes about by our accord', cf. Lyons 19.2-4 and 243) - is taken from IS 57.10-11. The examples of involuntary possibles are also taken from IS (57.14-16). The initial statement ('deliberation aims towards some good goal [ܢܝܫܐ ܡܕܡ]') appears to be an echo of AR 60b4-5, 'there is some goal (σκοπός τις) at which they aim', in IS 57.7 'deliberation is a means to a good goal (غرض)'. BH does not paraphrase AR 60b4 (at 2.2.1), but his use of ܢܝܫܐ here suggests that was the rendering of σκοπός in ARsyr at 60b4. At that point, however, ARar has ألم (suffering), emended by the editor to ارب (goal, cf. Lyons 22.16 and note). The suggestion by Panoussi that ARar misread ܚܫܐ for ܢܝܫܐ is attractive (cf. Lyons 247 and Panoussi, 'The Unique Arabic Manuscript', 234), but it requires us to assume that IS ignored the senseless Arabic and correctly perceived (from AR 62a18, where غرض renders σκοπός?) that 'goal' was the true sense.

**2.1.2.** The paraphrase of AR59b4-11 makes use of IS 58.5-6, 'we restrict ourselves to what is sufficient on the basis of opinion, because rhetoric is not intended for truth, but is an art in which the syllogistic art is conducted with materials from politics'.

**2.1.3.** BH's recasting of AR 59b27-28 ('if any [of the expenses of the city] is superfluous it may be eliminated, and if any too great reduced') as '... expel the idle man who does not put his hand to an art which is useful to the city, and establish a moderate level for him who is brought down from (his) wealth' is similar to IS 58.13-59.1, but will have been consistent with ARsyr and may have been based upon it. Cf. ARar (Lyons 20.5 and 244): 'if there is anyone unemployed or out of work, he should be removed, and if there is anyone of great manliness (? IS and IR give 'expenditure'), he should be brought down from that rank.'

**2.1.4.** For AR 59b33-34 'the strength of the city' ARar has 'the strength and power of the affair (قوة الأمر وقدره) and the condition of the city' (cf. Lyons 20.12-13 and 245), IS 59.5-6 'the strength of the matter (قوة الخطب) provoking strife'. BH is thus following IS, but presumably also a reading something like ܚܝܠ ܣܘܥܪܢܐ in ARsyr. The attention given to the relative danger of war, and that of changing numbers and strength over time, is taken from IS. The latter point comes from the (Syro-?)Arabic translation of 60a3 πλεονεκτεῖν ἢ ἐλαττοῦσθαι ('to be superior or inferior') as 'perhaps they breed and multiply' (Lyons 20.19-20 and 245); cf. IS 60.4, 'they may have increased in numbers from small to large and from weakness to strength'.

**2.1.5.** Abbreviated paraphrase of IS 60.7-14 rather than AR 60a6-11. Points not in AR ('lowland and mountainous, inland and coastal setting ... surprises and ambushes ... the treacherous with the trustworthy') are all in IS. That it is possible (according to IS and BH) for the orator to advise on defensive locations even when he does *not* know the city by sight (contrast AR 60a9 ἀδύνατον) comes from the reading of (ARsyr? and) ARar, 'this is possible even if he does not have experience of the country' (Lyons 21.5-6 and 245).

**2.1.6.** 'How much expenditure is adequate for the city' (ܟܡܐ ܕܐܦܐܢ ܡܣܦܩܐ ܠܡܕܝܢܬܐ) will be ARsyr of 60a12 πόση δαπάνη ἱκανὴ τῇ πόλει. ARar differs: وبكم من النزل يكتفى المدينة (? cf. Lyons 21.9 with n. 6 and 246); and IS 60.14 paraphrases الحاصل من القوت ('the total requirement of food'?). The rare ܕܐܦܐܢ must be derived from ARsyr (δαπάνη > ܕܐܦܐܢ). (For δαπανήματα at 59b30 BH 2.1.3 has ܢܦܩܬܐ, as also at 59b26 for δαπάναι in 2.1.3 above. ARar has نفقة at 59b26 and 30, as does IS 58.12 and 59.2.) The second half of the paragraph ('since when food ...') is a paraphrase of IS 61.2-7 rather than AR 60a14-17.

**2.1.7.** The paragraph as a whole is a paraphrase of IS rather than AR (60a17-37). BH first adheres to IS's (61.8-15) paraphrase of AR 60a18-25, and then adds from AR 60a27-30 the comparison with noses (not in IS). 'Anarchy', ܠܐ ܢܡܘܣܘܬܐ, not in AR, probably comes from IS 63.16 لم قانون. The final sentence on 'legal matters in written stories' is derived from AR 60a34-37 and IS 64.4. Cf. ARar (and syr?) 60a35-37, 'as for the types of deliberation on enemies, written stories about matters provide information on that'; and IS 64.4, 'examination of stories from the past is helpful in deliberation on legislative affairs.'

**2.1.8.** Having said above that a rhetor engaging in legislation needs to know the forms of government, IS and BH here go on to discuss just that, antiçipating the attention Aristotle pays to it in 1.8 (65b22-66a22). BH's six forms are, much abbreviated, those expounded in IS 62.1-63.10, IS however explaining (unlike BH) at the start of his account that the four types of government (i.e. of AR 65b29-30: democracy, oligarchy, aristocracy, and monarchy) branch out into six. On the basis of the six (twice three) forms of government of *Nicomachean Ethics* 1160a31-b22, he will have divided monarchy into 'kingdom' and 'tyranny' - this also from ARar 65b37-66a2 (Lyons 41.5-8 and 226) - and added 'government of honour' (كرامة, τιμοκρατία); cf. Würsch 191-193. BH's 'tyranny' ܛܘܪܢܐ renders IS's سياسة تغلبية (AR 66a2, 6 τυραννίς, ARar فتنة); BH 'government of graciousness' ܕܘܒܪ ܛܝܒܘܬܐ IS سياسة الكرامة; BH 'government of vileness and minority ܕܘܒܪ ܥܛܠܘܬܐ ܘܒܨܝܪܘܬܐ' IS سياسة الخسة and سياسة القلة; BH 'government of unanimity' ܕܘܒܪ ܫܠܡܘܬܐ and 'democracy' ܕܝܡܘܩܪܛܝܐ IS سياسة الاجماعية and الديمقراطية; BH 'government of pre-eminence' ܕܘܒܪ ܝܬܝܪܘܬܐ IS سياسة الخير; and 'royal government' ܕܘܒܪܐ ܡܠܟܝܐ IS سياسة الملك. BH's meaningless classification of 'royal' under 'aristocratic' comes from the fact that IS 63.10 classified them both as 'Socratic' (السقراطية), which BH 'corrected' to 'aristocratic' (ܐܪܝܣܛܘܩܪܛܝܩܐ) - that of course being correct only for 'the government of pre-eminence'. In IS 63.4-5 it is said that royal government will be successful if the ruler adds theoretical to political (مدنية) virtue. The subject of the kinds of government appears again briefly in 2.4.9, on AR 65b22-66a2.

**2.2.** AR 1.5, deliberations on private (ܡܬܚܬܝܬܐ, IS جزؤية) subjects, the counterpart to the previous section on great (ܪ̈ܘܪܒܐ, عظام), i.e. public, subjects.

**2.2.1.** ܡܗܢܝܢܘܬܐ, 'prosperity', presumably stood in ARsyr for εὐδαιμονία; the Arabic, both in ARar and here in IS, is صلاح الحال, 'good state'. From IS (64.13) comes the remark on the unbounded number of *topoi* on personal subjects (cf. above at 1.6.2 and IS 1.6 the contrast between 'persuasive to the individual' and 'persuasive to the whole populace'). Also from IS is the contrast 'true or opined' (for which cf. also AR 65b1), and the transformation of Aristotle's remarks on happiness and its amplification or diminution (60b9-14) into a discussion of persuasion (IS 65.4-7: 'The First Teacher ...'). This change will have been occasioned by the translator of ARsyr/ar taking the four appearances of 'this' in 60b9-11 as all referring to persuasive amplification or diminution, not happiness, and by his translation of 65b11-12 ('one should do things that provide this or one of its parts or make it greater rather than less') by 'those who lay down some part for that (the basis of the 'orators' of IS 65.4 and 'predecessors' of BH?) think that the speaker should make the thing small in place of great or great in place of small' (Lyons 22.20-23.1 and 247).

**2.2.2.** BH's definition of 'prosperity' paraphrases AR 60b14-18, but with (ARsyr? and) ARar omitting 'bodies', and adding 'with love and honour from men' from IS 65.9. (For some further remarks on the translation, cf. Introduction, pp. 40-41.) In the list of its component parts in AR 60b19-24, BH like (ARsyr and) ARar omits χρηστοφιλία ('worthy friendships') and εὐτεκνία ('good children'), but adds 'kindness to others' (ARar حسن الفعال) before 'a good old age'; his list is fuller than ARar (Lyons 23.6-10 and 248) or IS (65.12-16). BH takes his last sentence from IS (66.1 'he who lives such a life, and whose destiny after death is favourable, is fortunate according to the populace'), but in conformity with AR 60b29-30 ('life would be most secure') replaces the comment about destiny after death with 'up to the end' (i.e. of life).

**2.2.3.** The paraphrase of AR 1.5.5-6 is close to that of IS 66.2-67.1. However (ܕܒܢܝܬܐ) ܒܘܟܢܝܗ̇ 'native (to the city)', AR 60b31 αὐτόχθονες, will no doubt have been taken from ARsyr, as ARar reads بنكا (?), emended by Lyons (23.20 and n. 7) to بكناء, and IS 66.2 إما بنكاء. The inversion of *bkn* to *bnk* is likely to have been an Arabic corruption, as the transliteration from Syriac was incomprehensible. Cf. Lyons 248 and Würsch 123. The appearance here and in IS 66.4 of 'free men' comes from the rendering of 60b33 in (ARsyr and) ARar (Lyons 23.21 and 248). The final remarks about the Lacedaemonians are from IS 66.12-67.1, who follows a false reading of ARar 61a11 (زينة 'decoration' for ريبة 'suspicion', Lyons 24.14-15 [with 249] 'they look on the women with suspicion) and then adds a remark about

Chriton (اقريطن), an author on cosmetics from the first century (cf. Pauly-Wissowa, *Realencyclopädie*, Bd. 11, 1935-1938), who will have been known to him from the Arabic translations of Galen; cf. Würsch 125, Ibn al-Nadim, *Fihrist*, 293 Flügel/690 Dodge. Chriton has become Phriton (ܐܦܪܝܛܘܢ) in BH by error of *f* (ف) for *q* (ق).

**2.2.4.** Based on IS 67.2-8, but with variations, sometimes from the underlying AR 1.5.7. For 'cash' (νόμισμα) BH has 'darics', ARar 'dinars' (Lyons 24.16), while IS omits. The rendering of 61a18-19 ('by *enjoyable* that from which there is no gain beyond the use of it') in (ARsyr? and) ARar by 'those revenues are enjoyable which their possessor gathers without toil' (Lyons 24.21-22 and 250) has influenced the paraphrases of IS (67.4-5) and BH.

**2.2.5.** Close to IS 67.9-68.7, but briefer. BH ܡ̈ܠܟܐ ܘܥܬܝܪܐ ܘܓܢܒܪ̈ܐ 'kings, rich men, and warriors' corresponds to IS 68.1 السلطان والغنى والنجد القوى. In 'the 'parts of honour' in ARar 61a35 'memorials in verse and prose' is rendered 'memorials in offerings' (Lyons 25.14 and 250). ARsyr presumably had something similar, for that is close to BH but omitted by IS.

**2.2.6.** BH conflates here the (Syro-)Arabic text of Aristotle with IS. 61b4-5 reads in ARar, 'as Perudiqus (corruption in ARsyr from ܕܗܪܘܕܝܩܘܣ to ܕܦܪܘܕܝܩܘܣ ?) said, no one takes happiness in himself ...' (Lyons 25.23-26.1), and IS simply writes that 'many of the healthy are like the sick' (68.9). BH's substitution of *wealth* (for ARsyr? *himself*, or AR *health*?) appears to be his own interpretation, as does his repeated mention of *health* differing according to the stages of life (against AR 61b7 and following, κάλλος, *beauty*, ARar حسن).

**2.2.7.** BH's first and last sentences are his paraphrase of AR 61b18-26. The middle two sentences ('When the movement of anyone's limbs ceases ... teeth by which they can chew') are taken from IS 68.10-14, a lengthy excursus on self-inflicted causes of bad health; cf. Würsch 131.

**2.2.8.** 'A good old age' is omitted by IS. 'A multitude of friends', ܣܘܓܐܐ ܕܪ̈ܚܡܐ, renders πολυφιλία (AR 61b35). The 'companies' are BH's addition corresponding to the 'many ' who 'exert themselves' on behalf of the person in question.

**2.2.9.** AR 62a7-8, 'the other brothers are ugly but he is handsome', is rendered in ARar, 'a man may be uglier in appearance than others ... and a man may be more handsome in appearance than another' (cf. Lyons 28.3-4 and 252-253). To judge from BH, the shift from 'many ugly' to 'one ugly' occurred in ARsyr. ARsyr certainly preserved the reading 'brothers', as it appears in BH, while IS 69.9 follows ARar 'others'. ARar (and presumably ARsyr), IS, and BH all invert the order of AR 62a8-9, 'others did not see the treasure, but he found it' (cf. Lyons 28.4-5 and IS 69.10-11). 'Virtue based on opinion' (ܡܝܬܪܘܬܐ ܕܡܣܬܒܪܐ) rather than bare 'virtue' (AR 62a12) follows IS 69.13 بحسب الظن ... الفضيلة.

**2.3.** Paraphrase of AR 1.6 and IS 2.2 (69.14-75.15).

**2.3.1.** Much closer to IS 69.15-70.3 than to AR 62a17-27. The remarks on the distinction between the expedient and the good, as also the shift to 'everyone who has perception and intelligence' and 'that which the prudent man chooses is the good' from AR 62a23-26, 'everything which has perception and intelligence' and 'what intelligence would give ... is the good', follow IS. The omission of ἢ πάντα at 62a23 in (ARsyr? and) ARar (Lyons 28.18 and 253) will have opened the way to this shift.

**2.3.2.** The expansion over AR 62a27-34 is based on IS 70.4-71.4, notably in the example, 'Be wearied, in order that you may be healthy' (cf. IS 70.7-8), and the paraphrase of 62a31-34 ('Things are productive in three ways ...') which summarises IS 70.12-71.4, 'As for productive causes (العلل الفاعلة) ...'. BH omits, however, IS's excursus (71.3-4) on the dangers of too much or too little exercise; cf. Würsch 131-132. The rendering of AR 62a31 as 'being worthy of *praise* is (simultaneous) with living well', rather than 'being *healthy* is simultaneous with living', accords with ARar المدح (emended by Lyons to المصح [health], see Lyons 29.5 and 254) and IS 70.11 المديح. Was ܚܘܠܡܢܐ (health) misread as ܩܘܠܣܐ (praise) within the transmission of ARsyr?

**2.3.3.** The introduction of 'proper' (ܚܬܝܬܬܐ) goods and the contrasted 'secondarily' (ܫܐܠܐܝܬ) follows IS (71.14 حقيقية and لا حقيقية), as does the introduction of 'the populace' (ܩܗܠܐ, الجمهور) and 'common' (ܒܓܘܢܐ, عامية), stemming no doubt from (ARsyr? and) ARar 62b5, 'it is necessary to say with each of them what it is and how it is classified' (Lyons 29.17-18 and 254), and picking up the 'common expediency' and 'advantage to the citizens' of 62b28 and 33. 'Increasing a good or decreasing an evil', rather than 'acquiring a greater good or lesser evil' (AR 62a37-62b2), also follows IS (71.7-9), while the final sentence follows IS 72.1-3. For the triad in that final sentence 'fine-pleasant-expedient', cf. *Nicomachean Ethics* 1104b36-38.

**2.3.4.** IS (72.3) omits AR 1.6.8-14 (62b9-23), and then (72.3-9) paraphrases AR 62b23-33. BH follows him. The list here ('subtlety of understanding ...') is taken from IS 72.3-5 rather than AR 62b23-29. That the members of this list are 'chosen for their own sake' (as in IS 72.4) and are not 'productive of goods' (as in AR 62b25) arises from the rendering in (ARsyr? and) ARar, 'they belong to what is good' (Lyons 30.13 and 255). BH's 'sophistical' (ܣܘܦܣܛܝܩܝܐ) and 'fallacy' (ܕܛܥܝܘܬܐ) render IS's مغالطة (72.6 and 9).

**2.3.5-6.** These paragraphs are somewhat remote from AR 1.6.20-25 (62b33-63a19) and closer, but by no means identical, to IS 72.9-73.13. *Iliad* 1.255, cited at AR 62b35 and said by Nestor of the quarrel of Achilles and Agamemnon, is expanded in (ARsyr? and) ARar, 'Priam, that he said when he turned from the enemies and was very joyful at having turned away from his enemy' (Lyons 30.23 and 255). This evidently caused IS to connect it with the death of Hector (in *Iliad* 22 and 24) and to paraphrase (72.10ff.), 'like the joy of the greatest of the besieged kings when his enemy slew his son ...'. BH paraphrases IS (72.10-16), adding 'Priam' from AR 62b36 and other names from his knowledge of the *Iliad*. (Bar Hebraeus knew a Syriac translation or epitome of the *Iliad* from the hand of Theophilus of Edessa; cf. Baumstark, *Geschichte*, 341). The 'submissive request' of Priam comes from ARar (and ARsyr?) 63a5-6, 'Priam humbly implored' (Lyons 31.10 and 255; IS 72.11).

In 2.3.6 BH largely follows IS 73.7-13, but also tries to stay closer to AR 63a11-19 than does IS. ARar (and ARsyr?) 63a11-14 is rather different from the Greek and reads, 'Friends and enemies and the evil acknowledge what is good. But those to whom great harm has been done acknowledge the good because it can be seen obviously, and the enemies also are not able to reject and deny it' (Lyons 31.13-16 and 256). Neither ARar nor IS makes mention of Simonides and the Corinthians (AR 63a14-16), which BH has evidently taken from ARsyr, but it is impossible to say whether or not ARsyr asserted that the Corinthians 'inflicted evil upon' Simonides. ARar 63a17-19 reads, 'Homer chose Odysseus the Athenian, Helen, Alexander, and Achilles' (Lyons 31.18-19 and 256), while IS 73.9-11 reads, 'Homer ... chose Theodore (ثاوذروس) king of Athens and Helen his daughter and he chose the brave Achilles ... and put them opposite Alexander the son of a Berber king'.

**2.3.7-8.** These paragraphs are remote from AR 63a19-b4, but much closer to IS 73.14-75.15. The thrust of the passage appears quite different in IS and BH from that in AR, since they write about 'repayment' while AR is about 'things that are chosen' (63a19 τὰ προαιρετά). The change will have been made possible by (ARsyr? and) ARar 63a19-20, 'he chooses to do what he prefers to friends and enemies' (Lyons 31.20-21 and 256, thus eliminating 'things that are chosen' as the subject of it all), but more particularly (ARsyr? and) ARar 63a26-27, 'when a mistake is made in the repayment (τιμωρία > ܦܘܪܥܢܐ > المكافأة) either through what is small or through what is particular' (Lyons 32.5-6 and 257). IS does not in fact use the word 'repayment' until 74.14, but in the whole passage 73.14-75.15 he has in mind a reaction rather than action. BH however uses 'repayment' not only at the start of 2.3.7, but already in 2.3.6 with reference to 'the acknowledgement of good and evil'. Presumably IS and BH took AR 63a19 and following as a continuation of the exposition of 'the acknowledgement of good and evil' of 63a11 and following (see above on 2.3.6).

**2.4.** Paraphrase of AR 1.7 and IS 2.3.

**2.4.1.** Abbreviated paraphrase of IS 76.3-77.2 with elements of AR 63b5-33. 'More general and more lasting' comes from IS 76.6, but is consistent with (ARsyr? and) ARar 63b8-9 ('The better is that which is good in everything ... then that which lasts longer', Lyons 33.1-2 and 257; cf. AR, 'Let *exceeding* be as great and more ... and let *greater* and *more* always be ...'). While the example of men and women (AR 63b23-26) is omitted by IS, BH's 'converse example' (the knowledge of God and asceticism) is taken from IS 76.9-10, his 'asceticism' ܚܒܝܫܘܬܐ rendering IS's 'worship' عبادة (similarly at 4.2.2 below). IS adds another example concerning the Quran and the Prophet, which is omitted by BH. (On IS's two examples, cf. Würsch 128). The rendering here of Aristotle's 'greater' (ὑπερέχω, μείζων) in ARar by افضل or اعظم will be from ARsyr ܡܝܬܪ, as in BH, 'better' or 'greater'.

**2.4.2.** AR 63b33-37 is garbled in (ARsyr? and) ARar (Lyons 34.1-3 and 258-259); BH follows IS both here (77.3-5) and also through the remainder of the paragraph. The examples of perseverance and beauty (IS 77.5 جلد and جمال), health and beauty (IS 77.10 صحة and جمال), and wealth and trade (IS 77.14-16 يسار and تجارة) are all taken from IS.

**2.4.3.** Paraphrase of AR 1.7.12-13 and IS 77.16-78.8, being closer on the whole to the latter. The introduction of 'choice' (ܠܓܒܝܬܐ) in connection with 'beginning' comes from IS (77.17 اختيار), as does the addition (presumably by deduction from Aristotle's argument, rather than knowledge from elsewhere of the events and personalities to which it refers) that Callistratus advised Chabrias to do wrong (IS 78.4-5).

**2.4.4.** The explicit mention of iron as better, not simply as more abundant, accords with IS (78.9), although he makes no mention of 'Aphunus', a misconstrual in (ARsyr and) ARar of 64a24 τοῦ ἀφθόνου ('than the abundant') as '(a word) of ܐܦܢܘܣ' (from ܐܦܬܢܘܣ?; ARar افنوس, Lyons 35.7 and 260). 'Ointment of balsam' is from IS 78.12, 'the property of a superior is superior' follows IS 79.1 ما هو خاص بالاعظم اعظم (from AR 64a37, cf. ARar Lyons 35.22-23 and 260). BH's 'because virtues (ܡܝܬܪܘܬܐ) are the causes of virtuous (ܡܝܬܪܐ) actions, they are better (ܡܝܬܪ̈ܢ) than them' is derived from IS 79.3-4, 'the virtues (الفضائل) themselves as beginnings are better (افضل) than virtuous (الفاضلة) actions'; cf. ARar, 'the virtues themselves are better and much more beautiful than beautiful virtuous things (الفاضلات) (Lyons 36.2-3 and 261), against AR 64b3-4, 'and correspondingly, excesses of better things are better and of beautiful things more beautiful'.

**2.4.5.** A considerably abbreviated paraphrase of AR 1.7.20-30 and IS 79.5-80.9, but in content generally closer to the latter. BH takes his first two sentences from IS 79.5-7. He then cuts out a long comment of IS on the sciences, including a remark on the superiority of (Islamic) theology to physiognomy, picks him up (at 79.14) where he rejoins AR (64b11) on the judgement of the prudent, and paraphrases 79.14-80.9, itself an abbreviated paraphrase with some additions of AR 64b19-65a9. The final sentence blends IS 80.6-7, 'It is a sort of disgrace not to accept the word (قول) of a man, both those who are greater in honour and those having more weight on account of loss (ضر) or gain', with AR 65a7-8, [literally] 'for honour is a sort of esteem, and of which the punishments are greater'.

**2.4.6.** The construal and wording of the free citation of *Iliad* 9.592-594 from AR 65a11-15 is close to that in IS 80.11-14. IS's version clearly depends upon ARar (Lyons 38.6-8 and 263), but ARsyr will presumably have been similar. It is IS who identifies 'the poet' as Homer. IS 80.13, 'everyone will acknowledge his son', ويعترف كل بولده, presupposes the reading 'the children will be acknowledged' in ARar, واعترف بالاولاد (Lyons 38.8 n. 5); and BH will have taken this from ARsyr. The explanation of it as 'everyone will call on the name of his child' comes from IS 80.13-14. IS omits the mention of Epicharmus (65a16); BH 'as Epicharmus did' will depend upon ARsyr, rather than ARar 'as is told in the story of Epicharamus' (Lyons 38.9 and 263).

**2.4.7.** For AR 65a24-30, IS merely states (81.5) that he does not understand the examples (امثلة) in the First Teaching. BH evidently cites or alludes to ARsyr, from which the incomprehensible ARar was no doubt derived. For a comparison of all four extant texts - AR, ARar, IS, and BH - see the Introduction, p. 23. The first example, the epigram on the Olympic victor, is clear enough: Argos is correctly taken as a place name (ARar takes it as the name of a fish; cf. Lyons 38.19 and 263), but εἰς Τέγέαν has become '(threw it) on the ground' (εἰς τὴν γῆν, as in ARar, cf. Lyons, ibid.). The second ('But now he was victorious in the race ...') has no counterpart in our Greek MSS. but appears in a slightly different but equally incomprehensible form in ARar (Lyons 38.19-21 and 264). The third is a scarcely comprehensible rendering with additions of 65a28-29, similar to ARar (Lyons 38.21-39.2 and 264). The emendation 'the third armed man was *lying*' (ܪܡܐ) for the obscure ,ܐܪܝ or ܐܪܝܢ of the MSS. is based on ARar ملقى (Lyons 38.21), but this, together with the translation of these two whole sentences, is quite uncertain. Even the spelling of 'Iphicrates' is puzzling; did BH think of Hippocrates?

**2.4.8.** Abbreviated paraphrase of AR 1.7.34-41 and IS 81.5-82.10. IS omits the name of Pericles (he has only 'as is said'). 'That which is sought for itself is better than that which is sought for glory' relies on IS's expansion of 65b1 ('things related to truth than things related to δόξα ['opinion']', rendered in ARsyr and ARar not 'opinion' but 'glory' [ܫܘܒܚܐ] and 'praise' [حمد]; in ARar also the comparison is rendered as a sequence, Lyons 39.12 and 264) as, 'what is sought for itself and found in truth is preferable to what is sought for praise' (81.16-82.1). So also the following 'gaining is greater than conferring' depends on IS 82.2, استفادة of goods is preferable to their افادة; cf. AR 65b2-3.

**2.4.9.** A brief account (shorter than but parallel to IS 82.11-83.10) of AR 1.7.8, on the forms of government, previously treated in 2.1.8, where there were said to be six (cf. the commentary on 2.1.8 above). Perhaps for that reason BH writes here that '*our master*' (to be differentiated from the implied Ibn Sina in 2.1.8?) said they were four (AR 65b29-30), but in fact BH mentions only three, omitting oligarchy (by oversight?). 'Democracy' corresponds to number four in the previous list, 'aristocracy' to number five ('pre-eminent rule', the genuine aristocracy) and possibly number six (if 'royal government' here, as in 2.1.8, is taken as 'aristocratic'), and 'sole authority' to numbers one and two (although of course Aristotle's monarchy fits with numbers one [tyranny] and six [royal government]). 'Oligarchy' would have corresponded to number three ('vileness and minority'). The characterisation of the 'end' of sole authority is taken from IS 83.2-3; for its origin in force, cf. 2.1.8 above.

## CHAPTER THREE

Epideictic ('demonstrative', ܚܘܝܝܐ) rhetoric, AR 1.9, IS 2.4, the 'end' of the epideictic orator being the noble (ܫܦܝܪܘܬܐ, τὸ καλόν) or disgraceful (ܫܟܝܪܘܬܐ, τὸ αἰσχρόν).

**3.1.1.** Aristotle's extension of praise to 'a man and a god' (66a30) appears both in IS (84.3) and BH as 'men and angels'; ARar has 'man or a spiritual being' (Lyons 42.17). In describing virtue as a 'habit' (ܐܟܣܝܣ), BH follows neither AR 66a37-38 (δύναμις 'faculty'), ARar (قوة), nor IS (84.7 قوة أى ملكة). He may well have intentionally substituted this term on the basis of *Nicomachean Ethics* 2.5-6: virtue is neither an emotion nor a faculty but a habit. Cf. also 1.2.2 (AR 54a7). That it is a habit which preserves the good *or that which seems good* is a result of the connection of ὡς δοκεῖ to ἀγαθῶν in (ARsyr? and) ARar 66a37 (Lyons 43.3 and 267), as also in IS 84.7 . That it is 'a species of the noble (ܫܦܝܪܘܬܐ)' comes from IS 84.6-7, but BH has 'clarified' that by inserting '*nobly* (ܫܦܝܪ, 'well') preserved'. The list of the parts of virtue accords with AR 66b1-3 except for the transfer of σωφροσύνη to follow μεγαλοπρέπεια. In ARar it is transferred to follow μεγαλοψυχία (Lyons 43.5 and 267), but IS 84.9 has the same order as the Greek Aristotle. The final sentence, a paraphrase of AR 66b4-6, is taken directly from IS 84.11, 'each and every one of these is honoured, because honour is bestowed by everyone on those who act beneficially (للنافعين)'.

**3.1.2.** The addition of *equitable* to 'justice is a virtue ...' (66b9) follows (ARsyr? and) ARar 66b9 (Lyons 43.12 and 267) and IS 84.13 فضيلة عادلة. That 'superiority' (ܦܪܘܫܘܬܐ, μεγαλοπρέπεια) creates abundance of 'foods' rather than 'expenditures' conforms to (ARsyr? and) ARar 66b18 (Lyons 43.23 and 267: δείπνοις for δαπανήμασι) and IS 85.2-3. The remarks about 'gentleness' and 'wisdom' have no counterpart here in AR or IS and stem from BH himself. IS however adds (85.5-6) that the foregoing sketches (رسوم) are acceptable in terms of 'appearance' (ظاهر), but are not scientific (علمي), possibly intending a comment on AR 66b22-24.

**3.2.1.** Generally closer to IS 85.7-86.15 than to AR 1.9.14-19, although considerably shorter than either. The remarks about lamentations, torture, handing over a deposit, and commemoration of the departed are derived from IS (85.9-12; 86.7-8). 'Among the signs of virtues there is that which is more praiseworthy, such as what (is given) to a champion [ܐܬܠܝܛܐ]', however, differs in IS (86.4) and will have been taken from ARsyr of 66b34 (in Greek, 'things of which the prizes [τὰ ἆθλα] are an honour are noble'), in ARar 'the things of which the rewards of the struggle [جزاء الجهاد] are an honour are good' (Lyons 44.11-12).

**3.2.2.** The transformation of AR 67a6-8 from 'the opposites of those of which people are ashamed ...' into 'the shaming of him who acts oppositely' will be due to ARsyr, as ARar reads, 'the things in which there is disgrace and shame for opponents' (Lyons 44.22-23 and 268). The following remarks on Sappho represent a free paraphrase by BH out of both ARsyr (cf. ARar, Lyons 44.24-45.5 and 268-269, changing Sappho's direct speech of 67a11-14 into a narrative about her and linking up 67a15-18 so as to make a comment about those with her and the struggle of virtues against nature for glory and honour) and IS's elaboration of ARar (IS 87.2-14; cf. thereto Würsch, 110-111). See also Introduction, p. 43, n. 152.

**3.2.3-4.** The brief statement on shame is a summary of IS 88.1-6, with no counterpart in AR at this point. IS presumably introduced it here to guard against a reader assuming that shame would only arise when a perpetrator (such as Alcaeus) was publicly shamed by another (such as Sappho); cf. the discussion of shame in AR 2.6. In the following paragraph BH is generally closer to IS 88.6-12 than to AR 1.9.23-27, but while IS 88.10-11 merely mentions 'signs of gentility like long hair' without reference to Lacedaemon, from ARsyr 67a29 BH will have taken 'the enlargement of the Lacedaemonians of (the curls of) their hair' (ARar Lyons 45.16-17).

**3.3.** 'Tropical praises' (ܫܘܒܚܐ ܫܐܝܠܐ) appears to be BH's own terminology for dealing with qualities close or attendant to real ones, the subject of AR 1.9.28-34. ܫܐܝܠܐ/ܫܐܝܠܘܬܐ are the terms for metaphorical/metaphor in BH Chapter 7 (AR Book 3).

**3.3.1.** BH's first type of 'tropical praises' are those of AR 67a32-b12, his second those of 67b12-20 (BH 3.3.4), but the explicit formalisation of two 'types' comes from BH himself. The rather contorted exposition of the first type (corresponding to AR 67a32-34 and 36) has been influenced by the equally tortuous explanation of IS 88.13-89.1 (e.g. ܐܣܒܒܐ < معرض, ܡܫܘܬܦܘܬܐ < تشارك).

**3.3.2.** BH draws the comparison with sophistry from IS (88.13), or possibly from ARsyr of 67b4 (παραλογιστικόν), and composes his own list of examples from ARsyr (over against AR67a34-b3 ARar has 'excellent in counsel' and 'sweet of acquaintance', Lyons 45.23 and 270), or from the similar list in IS (89.1-4).

**3.3.3.** BH weaves together ARsyr and IS. The opening statement on enticement or non-enticement in essence comes from IS (89.5-7), but 'danger' (ܩܝܢܕܘܢܘܣܐܝܬ, κινδυνευτικός, omitted by IS) must come from ARsyr (cf. ARar, 'the reason is that where there is not violent compulsion to fear or danger [خطر]', Lyons, 46.6-7 and 270). IS (89.8) introduces 'enemy' alongside 'friend', but 'even if justice declares it right to do good to friends and evil to enemies' is BH's own addition here. As above at 1.5.2, this will probably be derived from AR 63a20-21, but an echo of Plato's *Republic* 332D ('he says justice is to do good to friends and evil to enemies'), taken perhaps from a collection of Platonic or Wisdom sayings, is not impossbible; there is an echo of this text of Plato (combined with 335A and *Laws* 801E) in Antony of Tagrit ('justice is to praise friends only when they have gone before and toiled and brought in something praiseworthy', cf. Watt, 'The Syriac Reception', 593). The second part of the paragraph is BH's paraphrase of AR 67b7-11 ('Consider also in whose presence the praise [is given] ...'), but with an eye on IS 89.9-12. IS does not specify any peoples, but declares that the orator must adopt the appropriate praise according to countries, peoples, and confessions (الملل). BH seems to have intentionally 'secularised' the (Islamic) ملل as professions (ܐܘ̈ܡܢܐ), taking note of AR 67b10 'philosophers'.

**3.3.4.** On the two kinds of tropical praise, cf. 3.3.1 above. This whole paragraph (paraphrase of 67b12-20) is taken both by IS and BH to be about praise derived from ancestors, on account of (ARsyr and) ARar 67b12-13, 'the status of ancestors and past heritage is part of honour' (Lyons 46.16-17 and 270; cf. AR, 'if they are worthy of the ancestors and earlier actions'). IS omits 'the saying of Iphicrates' (on the spelling of whom see on 2.4.7 above), and paraphrases the following lines, differently from BH, thus: 'As someone said in the praise of *Swsds* as he addressed his father and brothers, today it is among the Saturannoi, as if the Saturannoi were a nobler tribe than the Greeks' (cf. Würsch 124). The 'Saturannoi' come from misreading (or rather, mis-dividing in uncial Greek script) τ' οὖσα τυράννων (67b20) as τοῦ σατυράννων (cf. Lyons 271), BH ܣܐܛܘܪܢܘܣ, ARar الساطورانون. On the basis of ARar and BH, it might be supposed that BH construed the conflated citation of 67b18-20 ('In the past, having on the shoulders a rough ...' and of Simonides, 'She whose father and husband and brothers were tyrants') in ARsyr along the lines of the following: 'That which is on (your) shoulders, O Simonides, is more in its quality than what can be said for the father and brothers of the man of the Saturannoi'. πρόσθε μέν was read as προσθετεόν, while τραχεῖαν and ἀνδρός were omitted; cf. Lyons 46.24-47.2 and 270-271.

**3.3.5.** While generally close to AR 1.9.32-34, this is even closer to IS 90.6-91.6. From IS 90.10-11 comes 'lion begets lion, and snake begets snake'. Signs of ARsyr, however, may be detected in the 'habitual' (virtue), ܐܡܥܝܕܘܬܐ, AR 67b32 τῆς ἕξεως (ARar على الفعال, Lyons 47.14 and 271), and the 'we have believed', ܗܝܡܢܢ, AR 67b33 πιστεύοιμεν (ARar, Lyons 47.15 and IS 91.2 تيقنا, 'we were sure').

**3.4.1.** Aristotle's 'common species' (67b36 κοινὸν εἶδος) of praise and deliberations appears in (ARsyr? and) ARar as a 'new (καινόν) species' (Lyons 47.19 and 271). The wording of the paragraph is closer on the whole to IS 91.7-17 than to AR 1.9.35-37.

**3.4.2.** Most of the paragraph depends on IS 92.1-14, but the sentence concerning Hippolochos, Barmodes (AR 68a18 Harmodius), and Aristogiton is BH's own and the passage is ignored by IS. Either BH considerably modified ARsyr here, or the latter differed both from AR and ARar, which reads, 'That is like what was done with Hippolochos, Harmodius, and Aristogiton, where they stood in the market and were praised there' (Lyons 48.18-20 and 272). The allusion to *Matthew* 7.3-5 par. *Luke* 6.41-42 ('They see the chip in their brother's eye but not the plank in their own eyes') comes from IS 92.10-11; the Gospel passage was well known among Muslim writers, cf. Würsch 128. 'Not everyone is able to compare himself with others' (AR, 'If you do not have enough with the man himself, compare him with others') is consistent with (ARsyr? and) ARar 68a19-21 (Lyons 48.21-22 and 272), as is the assertion that Isocrates spoke about 'behaviour' (AR, 'inexperience of forensic speaking', cf. Lyons 48.22-23 and 272). BH corrects IS 92.11 'Socrates' (سقراط) to Isocrates (68a20, ARar اسوقراطيس).

**3.4.3.** Brief paraphrase of AR 1.9.39-41 and IS 92.15-93.11.

## CHAPTER FOUR

Judicial rhetoric, AR 1.10-15, IS 2.5-9. BH's first two sections correspond to IS 2.5, the other four to IS 2.6-9.

**4.1.** IS's title for his section 2.5 is 'On the accusation of injustice and the defence of non-injustice'.

**4.1.1.** Abbreviated paraphrase of AR 68b1-10 and IS 93.14-94.14. The last sentence ('Injustice ... blamed') is a paraphrase of IS 94.12-13 ('The unjust person is he who harms voluntarily, and if a deed emanates from someone by nature or compulsion, he is not counted as good or evil'), rather than AR 68b9-10 ('People act voluntarily when they know what they are doing, and are not under compulsion').

**4.1.2.** BH weaves together ARsyr 68b10-26 and IS 94.14-96.1. 'Understanding' (ܒܘܝܢܐ) for 68b11 προαιρούμενοι ('deliberately choosing') may be his rendering of IS 94.15 روية rather than ARsyr (ARar reads تقدم فاختار), his 'deficient intelligence' (ܒܨܝܪܘܬ ܬܪܥܝܬܐ) for ἀκρασία (68b14) corresponds to ARar (from ARsyr?) ضعف رأى, as in IS 94.16. The description of the 'agitated evil man' overcome by 'lust, anger, or fear', who 'may afterwards feel remorse', comes from IS 95.1-4. The list of examples blends AR 68b16-23 with IS 95.4-13. 'Despicable' is literally 'he who has not known the good', AR 68b16 ἀνελεύθερος, ARar and IS 95.4 النذل. The final application of this to oratory comes from IS 96.1.

**4.2.1.** The opening statement on the 'defining' of accusation is derived from IS 96.2-4, but will have been consistent with ARsyr if that read with ARar, 'As for the accuser, it is known that he must be known and defined in regard to what and how much he makes his accusation and what is that which is his opponent's accusation' (Lyons 51.4-6 and 274, cf. AR 68b29-30, 'it is clear that the accuser should examine the number and nature of the things to be found in the opponent'). The change from the 'twofold longing' (rational, irrational) of AR 69a2-3 into the 'threefold longing' (animal, calculating, rational) of BH is due to IS 96.9-10, 'some follow animal longing ... some follow calculating (فكرى) longing or rational (منطقى) longing'. It will go back, however, to a 'threefold longing' in (ARsyr? and) ARar 69a2-4, 'calculating ... rational' (ARar 69a2-3, Lyons 51.18 and 275) and 'irrational' (غير منطقى, ARar 69a4, Lyons 51.20). Hence BH has to affirm that 'calculating' (فكرى, ܚܘܫܒܢܐ, 69a7 διὰ λογισμόν) includes 'rational' in Aristotle's count of seven. The 'some' who equate this with 'imaginative and intellectual' will be IS (96.12-13 'imaginative فكرى' and 'rational فكرى in truth'); on IS, cf. Würsch 116 and 118.

**4.2.2.** IS 97.3-16 is a free paraphrase of AR 1.10.9-11, and BH adheres closely to IS. BH's 'ascetic' (ܚܒܝܫ) renders IS 97.10 عابد 'worshipper', as in 2.4.1 above; cf. Würsch 118.

**4.2.3.** BH weaves elements from IS 98.1-99.3 into his selective paraphrase of AR 69a32-b14. Thus the cause of habitual acts as 'the sight and sound of those things which spread in the soul' is derived from IS's remark (98.9-10) that 'he who experiences a stimulation in soul or habit is he who has confronted something and having seen it been moved by it'. 'Speculative' (ܚܘܫܒܢܝܐ) here corresponds to AR 69b7 διὰ λογισμόν, as at 69a6 in 4.2.1 (also λογιστικὴ 69a1); again this will be the terminology of ARsyr, in ARar بالفكر (Lyons 53.14).

**4.2.4.** Brief paraphrase of AR 69b14-32. The opening clauses ('For everyone ... cause'), differing from 69b16-17 ('The familiar and habitual are among the pleasurable'), are virtually a translation of IS 99.3-4.

**4.3.** Paraphrase of AR 1.11, IS 2.6. The title, linking pleasure to injustice (cf. AR 72a4), exactly matches that of IS (99.13).

**4.3.1.** Aristotle's definition of pleasure at 69b33-35 gave the translator of (ARsyr? and) ARar some difficulty. ARar reads, 'Pleasure is a movement of the soul, and a state comes about suddenly by sensation in the very nature of the thing' (فى طبية الشيء نفسها, Lyons 54.15-16). If this was similar to the reading of ARsyr, BH may have read the last phrase (ܒܟܝܢ ܪܓܫܐ ܢܦܫܗ?) as 'into the nature of the thing itself', i.e. 'sensation into the nature of sensation', and thus got to 'sensing of [that] which is natural to sensation', then limiting it to 'the desirable'; for his later 'the desirable is pleasurable', cf. AR 70a16-18. He will have been led in the direction of this 'reflexive' interpretation by IS 99.14-15, 'Pleasure is movement of the soul towards a state which with an impression produces sensation suddenly, and that impression is natural to that sensation'. In general, BH weaves together ARsyr and IS, although the overall outline is much closer to the latter. The references, however, to 'sex, taste, smell, and incense' (ܙܘܘܓܐ ܘܛܥܡܬܐ ܘܡܪܝܚܐ ܘܒܣܡܐ), not present in IS, are no doubt taken from ARsyr 70a23-24 (AR γευστὰ καὶ ἀφροδίσια ... και περὶ ὀσμὴν εὐωδίας, ARar المطاعم والباه ... والشم مثل ... والطيوب, Lyons 55.20-21 and 277), but the mention of *virtue* ('when someone hears about some virtue', cf. AR 70a26 'many things ... after hearing about them') comes from IS (100.8-9). 'Disobedience' (ܡܪܘܕܘܬܐ, ARar 70a15 معصية, IS 100.3 العصيان) may come from misreading αἱ παιδιαί ('games') as ἀπείθεια; cf. Lyons 55.12 and 277.

**4.3.2.** BH's definition of *phantasia* comes from IS (100.10-11), but will also have been close to ARsyr (contrast AR 70a28-30), as ARar reads, 'Imagination (التخيل) is a weak sensing imagined (يتوهم) always by memory and hope' (Lyons 56.1 and 278). In the remainder of the paragraph BH continues to adhere more closely to IS than to AR, for instance in the comment that 'with attainment longing ceases and fulfilment follows, a source of enmity' (cf. IS 100.15-16). That anger produces pleasure (AR 70b10-11) *through the pleasurable image-evocation of victory* comes from IS (101.2). For φαντασία at AR 70a28, BH uses ܦܢܛܣܝܐ (while ARar and IS have التخيل), but where further on IS has تخيل independently of AR, BH translates it ܡܬܗܠܠܢܘܬܐ ('image-evocation'); cf. Introduction, pp. 44-45 and below on 4.3.6. The wording of AR (70b12) can be detected in BH's version of the citation from Homer (*Iliad* 18.109, 'sweeter than dripping honey') against IS's simple 'honey' (101.3, ARar 'drops of honey', Lyons 56.20-21).

**4.3.3.** Here BH depends mainly on ARsyr, while IS omits the examples of the fevered and the lovesick. The curious statement that 'many do not come close to desirables which are present ...' will have arisen from the rendering in (ARsyr and) ARar of 70b22-24 ('The beginning of love ... not only present ... but also absent ...') as 'the true of love ...' (Lyons 57.8 and 279, suggesting a confusion between ܫܘܪܝܐ and ܫܪܝܪܐ). That the recollection of a beloved may be 'by some chance' (ܚܕ ܠܦܓܥܐ) will be either from IS 101.9 (فى عارضة) or from the wording of ARsyr and ARar 70b24, 'And they want when a misfortune happens that he should not be present at the funeral meeting and the lamentations. Similarly a type of desire may be sorrow and pleasure' (Lyons 57.10-12 and 279). From ARsyr also may come the mention in BH of mourning and lamentation, the identification of 'the sayer' (AR 70b28, quoting *Iliad* 23.108, *Odyssey* 4.183) as Homer, and the 'grief-stricken and pleasurable cry' (cf. Lyons 57.14-16 and 279). The same points, however, occur in IS (101.10-12, cf. Würsch 110).

**4.3.4.** Generally close to (ARsyr and) ARar, with occasional distinctive elements evident from IS. The failure of an *enemy* to succeed is consistent with (ARsyr and) ARar 70b3 (cf. Lyons 57.17 and 279), but the extension of the pleasure of winning to *all other creatures* (ܫܪܟܐ ܕܒܪܝܬܐ) comes from IS 101.15 سائر الحيوان. AR 71a2-3, ARar, and IS all list four games, BH five. 'Hunting and all chasing' must come from ARsyr (AR 71a5 κυνηγία καὶ πᾶσα θηρευτική); ARar has 'all varieties of chasing' (الصيد, cf. Lyons 57.27 and 280), IS 102.3 simply 'chasing' (الصيد). The final sentence is close to IS 102.3-5, although the 'just victory' corresponds to (ARsyr? and) ARar 71a7 الغلبة بالعدل (cf. Lyons 58.2 and 280: δικαία νίκη for δικανική) rather than IS's paraphrase الغلبه بالواجب والقسط. BH's ܗܪܝܣܛܝܩܘܬܐ 'eristic' is no doubt from ARsyr (71a7 ἐριστική); ARar and IS 101.4 have مشاغبة.

**4.3.5.** Most divergences from AR are explicable from (ARsyr and) ARar, but BH has also been influenced by IS. Thus at the outset 'victories' are an addition of IS (102.5), but 'diligence in virtue' is already present in (ARsyr and) ARar (Lyons 58.5-6 and 280). 'A person is loved and favoured because of himself' is (ARsyr's and) ARar's rendering of 72a21 (cf. Lyons 58.19-20 and 280); but the 'warrior (ܐܬܠܝܛܐ) breaking through ranks of fighters and arrays (ܣܕܪ̈ܐ) of companies' is taken from IS 102.16, 'the proud man

(المعجب) fights by himself among the ranks and bands (مجمع) of the crowd', although the basis for it lies in (ARsyr and) ARar 71a22, 'the man who is haughty (?) and before whom the ranks are arranged' (cf. Lyons 58.21-22 and 281, suggesting τάξασθαι for τιμᾶσθαι). The rare ܡܬܟܠܐ ('arrays'?), v. l. ܡܬܚܠܐ (neither form is listed in *ThesSyr* or *BrLex)*, is glossed in the margin of the Florence manuscript (fol. 233rb) as ܣܕܪܐ. The final sentence paraphrases IS 103.2, 'the flatterer causes astonishment towards himself in making a show of his friendship'. As in 4.3.2 above, ܦܢܛܣܝܐ (*phantasia*) appears in BH where φαντασία is present in AR (71a9 and 19).

**4.3.6.** Here BH followed in the main IS, but nevertheless sometimes will have been closer to ARsyr than the Greek would suggest. 'The repetition of the pleasurable is pleasurable' reproduces IS 103.2 وتكرير اللذيذ لذيذ, (cf. ARar 71a24-25, 'to do the same thing is often pleasurable', Lyons 59.1-2). 'Learning is pleasurable on account of the image-evocation of wonder at the completion (ܗܓܓܐ ܕܬܕܡܘܪܬܐ ܒܫܘܠܡܐ) and ... uncovering of that which is hidden in nature', rather different from AR 71a26-27 and 31-34, depends on IS 103.6-7, 'Learning is pleasurable ... according to the image-evocation of wonder from it when completed (تخيل من التعجب منه إذا استكمل), because learning reveals things hidden in the power of nature'. IS is paraphrasing ARar, which at 71a27 (Lyons 59.4) reads الوهم ('imagination') for ἕξις, paraphrased as تخيل by IS and appearing as ܗܓܓܐ in BH. The suggestion of Lyons 281 that ARsyr/ar read δόξας for ἕξεως is not very convincing, although hardly less so than my alternative proposal that ܗܓܓܐ was misread for ܗܟܣܝܣ within the Syriac tradition. If, however, ܗܓܓܐ, 'image-evocation', was indeed present at some stage in ARsyr, here in this passage in this version 'image-evocation' and 'imitation' will have stood in close proximity. The linkage of these two is central in al-Farabi's interpretation of the *Poetics* and his theory of religion; cf. on this Heinrichs, 'Die antike Verknüpfung', esp. 252-273. Al-Farabi's interpretation of the *Poetics* may go back to the circle of Syro-Arabic Aristotelians at Baghdad around Abu Bishr Matta, the first translator of the *Poetics* from Syriac into Arabic; cf. my 'The Strategy of the Baghdad Philosophers: the Aristotelian Tradition as a Common Motif in Christian and Islamic Thought'. BH's term for 'works of imitation', ܡܕܡܝܢܘܬܐ, will be from ARsyr (71b6 μεμιμημένον); cf. ܡܬܕܡܝܢܘܬܐ for μίμησις in the Syriac translation of *Poetics* 1449b-1450a cited by Jacob Bar Shakko (ed. Margoliouth, *Analecta orientalia*, 77-79 [Arabic pagination]).

**4.3.7.** Follows the general outline of IS 104.3-10, incorporating features of ARsyr. The initial sentence combines IS 104.3, 'These correlations (مناسبات) are things in nature and what is similar to the pleasurable is pleasurable', with (ARsyr and) ARar 71b12, 'and this is pleasurable, in that it is in nature' (Lyons 60.1 and 282). 'Bird to bird' is BH (AR 'horse to horse', IS 'thief to thief'). 'Habitual relationships' are from IS (104.5), but BH's 'criticising the neighbours' is from AR 71b29-30 (Lyons 60.21, contrast IS 104.6). That 'someone should train himself in virtues' comes from (ARsyr and) ARar 71b30-31 (Lyons 60.22-23 and 283, IS 104.7-8), and IS leaves out all mention of 'the poet'. BH's citation is a free rendering of AR 71b32-33, and markedly different from ARar (Lyons 60.23-25 and 283) .

**4.4.** AR 1.12, IS 2.7. BH's title is an adaptation of the first part of IS's, 'On the causes (الاسباب) facilitating (المسهلة) wrongdoing'. Presumably the intention was to differentiate it as much as possible from the title of IS 2.6, BH 4.3.

**4.4.1.** Abbreviated paraphrase of AR 1.12.1-6 and IS 104.14-105.15. BH is generally quite close to AR, although he selects and abbreviates, but the final remark that 'no one guards himself against his friend' is taken from IS 105.15. 'Kinsmen' (ܒ̈ܢܝ ܛܘܗܡܐ), in addition to 'powerful and rich friends', comes from IS 105.3 العشيرة ('the clan').

**4.4.2.** The additive interpretation of AR 72a28-29 to the effect that he who has no enemy *is easily hurt* comes from IS 105.15-106.1. 'Abundance in which his wrongdoing may be concealed' may be BH's interpretation of ARsyr of 72a33 διαθέσει εὔπορος, ARar 'there is scope by this possession' (Lyons 62.11 and 284), or of IS 106.6 'hiding in a crowd'. ܕܝܘܣܝܣ 'avoidance' is evidently from ARsyr (δίωσις 72a33, 35); ARar and IS have جنف and/or حيف (Lyons 62.12, 14; IS 106.8).

**4.4.3.** IS's paraphrase of AR 72a36-b16 is quite free, and for the most part BH is dependent upon it. IS, however, makes no mention of Zeno and talks of 'killing soul for soul' (106.13); (ARsyr and) ARar have 'as Zeno did' and (with AR 72b5) 'avenging father and mother' (Lyons 63.1-2). That wrongdoing is easy for some if money is *not* lost (contrast AR 72b5-6) is from IS (107.1), as is the mention of someone 'brought up with torments and accustomed to lashes' (cf. IS 107.1-2). 'The warrior who boldly sticks to the fight', however, is not mentioned by IS and is clearly taken from AR 72b10-11.

**4.4.4.** The paragraph displays noticeable divergences from both AR 1.12.14-23 and IS 107.6-108.15 and is considerably shorter than either of them. BH appears to have made his own paraphrase, while drawing on both of them. 'Why would I have done wrong when I have no need to do wrong?' is taken directly from IS 107.10, but the formulation of much of the remainder seems to be due to BH himself. IS does not mention the Carthaginians by name, but refers (108.6) to 'a strong, careful people disdainful of argument'; (ARsyr and) ARar are faithful to the Greek of 72b28 ('those robbing the Carthaginians'). 'He will be harmed who harms not men' is IS's paraphrase (108.7, cf. Würsch 117) of the proverb (قيل, BH ܡܬܠܐ) 'Mysian spoil' (72b33); ARar has مسحون ابدا ('Mysian always', Lyons 64.13 and 285).

**4.4.5.** As in the previous paragraph, BH offers a paraphrase noticeably differing from both AR 1.12.24-29 and IS 108.15-109.16, while adopting some points from each. Much of it is clearly influenced by IS, in particular the part commencing 'evil men do wrong' and running to 'do not fear their vengeance' (cf. IS 109.4-13). The strange 'endurance' (ܚܡܣܢܘܬܐ) of a madman comes in the context of IS's statement to the same effect (109.8 يحتملون), but appears to have its source in (ARsyr? and) ARar الصابرون ('those that endure, Lyons 65.16) rendering 73a17 ἐρωμένοις ('to those they love'); Lyons 287 suggests it may have been understood as a form of ῥώννυμι. The final sentence, with the example of Callippus and Dion, is BH's paraphrase of AR 73a18-20, passed over or rendered very freely (with no mention of any names) in IS 109.13-16.

**4.4.6.** IS renders this pericope rather differently, in particular omitting all names, and BH depends for the most part on ARsyr. However the inversion in the order of the two cases, putting that of 'those who are going to be attacked by others' (AR 73a21-24) after 'doing wrong afterwards to do right' (AR 73a24-27), is taken from IS. 'The islands of Demogelone' (73a22 'Aenesidemus to Gelon', Αἰνεσίδημος Γέλωνι read as as ἐν νήσῳ δημογέλωνι, 'in the island Demogeloni'), these islanders' suffering of *injustice* (AR 73a23 'having sent the kottabus after the enslavement of the city'), and their opting for *that which could easily be remedied* (AR 73a25 'easily remedying') all depend on the rendering of the passage in (ARsyr? and) ARar: 'In the island of Dimaghiluni by those who trouble them with hostility or contemptible persons. They had enslaved them by force and injustice because they met them on the point of departure, the point being that they were able to take vengeance on the one who wronged them, but, as they were able to do that, if they did it, justly, they had recourse to what could easily be remedied' (Lyons 65.22-66.4 and 287).

**4.4.7.** Paraphrase of AR 1.12.32-33 and IS 110.8-14. 'Trifles which may be concealed' corresponds to the rendering in (ARsyr and) ARar of 73a28-29 ῥᾴδια κρύψαι ('things easy to conceal') as 'they think they can conceal small trifling matters' (Lyons 66.8-9 and 287); IS 110.8-9 is similar. 'Confectionery' and 'fresh fruit' are BH's own wording, but 'mixing, like drugs' is from IS 110.10. 'Revealing to judges' as a paraphrase of 'a litigious complainant' (73a35-36) comes from IS 110.12, but the restriction to 'those (who are) free' is particular to BH.

**4.5.** AR 1.13, IS 2.8. For the title of this section BH takes the idea of 'magnitude and triviality' from that of IS (111.2-3: تعظيم and تصغير).

**4.5.1.** Paraphrase of AR 1.13.1-3. The opening sentence is taken from that of IS (111.4-5), except that BH inverts IS's order of 'written' and 'unwritten'. However, after adding a brief remark to the effect that all this refers to property, honour, or well-being, IS passes over the remainder of the section and jumps to 73b18 (BH 4.5.2). The rest of BH's paragraph is his own paraphrase of AR 73b4-18, and clearly points to his having had before him a text of Aristotle which was neither the Greek nor the Arabic known to us, but in all probability the lost Syriac version, ARsyr. The differences between BH's paraphrase and the Greek text of AR 73b4-18 are plain to see, but two of them are significantly shared with ARar: 'Antigone said to Sophocles' - the natural, if not the only possible, rendering of the Syriac and Arabic - for 73b9 ἡ Σοφοκλέους Ἀντιγόνη φαίνεται λέγουσα (cf. Lyons 67.8 and 288, noting that 'Sophocles' Antigone said' is also possible); and the omission of the negative ('*not* just for some and unjust for others') in 73b15 which turns Empedocles' remark (73b14) into a statement about a particular rather than the universal law (cf. Lyons 67.11-14 and 288). For BH's 'The natural and unspoken law buried Polyneices, which not only has been fulfilled ...', ARar 73b10-11 has, 'The obligatory about which there is no discussion buried Polyneices, as that was obligatory for him by nature' (Lyons 67.8-9 and 288). BH could not have read about 'the universal law of Eudumedon' from our text of ARar, for it omits 73b16-17, two lines of the citation of Empedocles, which BH has as 'the universal law through Eudumedon', clearly a misunderstanding of πάντων νόμιμον διά τ' εὐρυμέδοντος αἰθέρος ('the universal law through the wide-ruling ether'), with εὐρυμέδων (then ܐܘܪܘܡܗܕܘܢ to ܐܘܕܘܡܗܕܘܢ) misconstrued as the name of the inventor of a law concerning the propagation of light. The Syriac contains two loan-words from the Greek text, ܐܛܝܪ (αἰθήρ, ether) and ܐܘܓܝ (αὐγή, light), which must have stood in ARsyr The former is rare in Syriac but known (cf. *ThesSyr* 422, *BrLex* 56b), the latter apparently unknown; the same applies in Arabic (cf. Endress and Gutas, *A Greek and Arabic Lexicon*, I, 46-47). It is of course possible that the omission of 73b16-17 was an error of the scribe of the Paris manuscript and not of ARar as a whole, but it is noticeable that IR (Aouad II, 113 and III, 189) makes no allusion to the passage. The final remark concerning Alcidamas is consistent with (ARsyr and) ARar 73b18-19, 'and Alcidamas said that in the book of Messin where he defined it in two ways' (Lyons 67.14-15 and 288). Cf. on 4.6.1 below, where *Antigone* is cited again (AR 75b1-2).

**4.5.2.** IS summarises AR 73b29-38 in a couple of lines (111.8-9), BH passes over it altogether. BH's 'one flees from the line of battle and does not participate in military service (ܐܣܛܪܛܝܐ)' blends IS's 'flees from the army and does not participate in the allegiance (البيعة, 111.7)' with AR(syr) 73b24, ὁ δὲ μὴ στρατευόμενος, 'he who does not serve in the army', ARar الدخول فى الشرطة. The designation of being wronged as a 'state' (ܕܝܐܬܗܣܝܣ) comes from IS (111.8 حال). 'Committed adultery but in secret and not openly' comes from the rendering in (ARsyr and) ARar of 74a5 ('he trespassed but not on state property') as 'he acted and abused but not openly' (Lyons 68.23); 'not to deliver to him the fortress' from (ARsyr and) ARar 74a6 'not to deliver the city' (Lyons 68.24 and 289; cf. AR 'not to have committed treason', and IS 111.14 simply 'against him [the enemy] not for him').

**4.5.3.** Paraphrase of AR 1.13.11-13, but much closer to IS 112.5-113.10. The reformulation of the two kinds of justice and wrongdoing in the unwritten law (praise/dishonour, honour/contempt) comes from IS 112.6-7 (هوان/كرامة, ذم /مدح). This interpretation arose from the mistranslation (omitting 'omitted', ἔλλειμμα) of 74a25-26 ('and on the other hand things omitted by the specific and written law', appearing in ARar as 'as for what there is of the specific, written law', Lyons 70.1-2 and 290), forcing the interpreter to find 'two kinds' in 'praise/honour'. The remainder of BH renders IS quite faithfully, but he does not reproduce in full IS's assertion (112.16-113.1) that 'the legislator is not supported from heaven but is imposed artificially and therefore' unable to define the details of the written law. ܒܣܝܡܘܬܐ ('leniency') was presumably the rendering of τὸ ἐπιεικές in ARsyr, ARar and IS الحلم. The paraphrasing of 'a lifetime would be insufficient' (AR 74a33) as 'the world would end' comes from (ARsyr and) ARar (Lyons 70.9-10 and 290; IS 113.8).

**4.5.4.** Paraphrase of IS 113.10-114.12, considerably elaborating and expanding AR 1.13.14-16. The section is considerably longer in IS than in BH, but the content of BH is all taken from IS (especially 113.10-114.6), including the juxtaposition of written and unwritten law (in AR 'general terms' or 'fairness'), the 'reversing' of the ring (AR 74a35 'or struck', ARar 'did not lower it', Lyons 70.13 and 291), and the penalty for 'the theft of a dinar with some, or of a quarter dinar with others' (on which cf. Würsch 128). AR 74b5 ἁμαρτήματα and ἀτυχήματα ('failings and mishaps') is, however, glimpsed in BH ('failings which happen by mistake'; cf. ARar الاساءة and الخطا, Lyons, 70.19-20) but passed over in IS. BH 'causing harm for victuals (ܡܐܟ̈ܠܬܐ)' paraphrases IS 114.5 'stealing trivia (الطفيف)'.

**4.5.5.** Paraphrase of IS 114.13-115.4. AR 1.13.17 is the basis, but IS, and BH in his train, considerably modify, elaborate, and expand it. The 'remorse' (ܡܬܬܘܝܒܘܬܐ) of the final clause (modifying AR 74b14-15 'not the part but the whole') is BH's paraphrase of IS's 'not rare sin but continuous submissiveness' (115.4 طاعة).

**4.5.6.** Again BH paraphrases IS (115.4-11), who differs from AR (1.13.18-19). BH's 'whose son I am' (ܒܪ ܡܢܘ) may be his own interpretation of AR 74b16 αἰεί, 'always' (omitted in ARar, Lyons 71.3). The 'invitation to a banquet (ܫܪܘܬܐ)', which is opposed to 'confrontation' or 'controversy' (ܡܨܘܬܐ, ܚܪܝܢܐ, AR 74b20 δίκη, ARar خصومة), is consistent with (ARsyr and) ARar 74b20-21 الولائم ('banquets') and المؤلم ('banqueted', Lyons 71.7-8, similarly IS 115.8-9, Würsch 124-125), and no doubt comes (thus Lyons 291) from a misreading by the translator of δίαιταν and διαιτητής ('arbitration' and 'arbitrator') as δεῖπνον and δειπνήτης ('food' and 'meal-guest').

**4.5.7.** The opening sentence is taken (with inversion of the order) from IS 115.12-13, and the triple attribution (wrongdoer, wronged, wrongdoing) builds on the double attribution (wrongdoer, wronged) of IS 116.1. In much of the remainder BH prefers ARsyr 74b24-30, and also introduces elements of his own. ARar (and syr?) 74b24-25 reads: 'Great wrongdoing is what comes from a great man, and for that reason small things may be found to be great, either because of the greatness of the evil, or because of the greatness of the injury' (Lyons 71.11-13 and 291). BH's first example is drawn from IS 115.13-14. For the second he turns to AR 74b25-26, in which 'priestly craftsmen builders of temples' rather than 'consecrated (obols from) the temple-builders' corresponds to (ARsyr and) ARar. ܒܢ̈ܝ ܢܘܣܐ ('builders of temples') will be ARsyr 74b27 ναοποιοί, 'priestly craftsmen builders of temples' will be the reading of ARsyr, ARar الصناع المقربين صانعى المحاريب. IS 116.3 does not mention Melanopus or Callistratus and has 'stealing a *dirham* from a mosque (المسجد). 'Like the poor man who had one ewe lamb' alludes to *2 Samuel* 12,1-4. BH substitutes this biblical allusion in place of IS's (116.10) 'like the hermit did to the weasel'; on the latter, cf. Würsch 118.

**4.5.8.** BH's first sentence is a paraphrase of (ARsyr and) ARar 74b30-33: 'When consideration is based on the damage, judgement concerning revenge is indifferent to it, but it quickly disappears and there is no reconciliation (صلح), sentence (حكم), or suffering (احتمال) for it' (Lyons 71.18-20 and 292). The remainder, a paraphrase of AR 74b34-75a21, abbreviates the whole passage in a manner somewhat similar, but not identical, to IS 116.16-117.5. While BH modelled the summary on IS, the wording is sometimes closer to AR. IS, for example, does not mention the prison at Argos. 'Brutes devoid of mercy' will have come from ARsyr of 75a6 θηριωδέστερον ('the more brutal [a wrongdoing]', ARar 'the wrongdoing of those thrown to the wild beasts', Lyons, 72.10 and 292). Similarly the references to 'relatives' and 'the assembly' will have come from (ARsyr and) ARar 75a7 and 12 (Lyons 72.12 and 19 and 293).

**4.6.** AR 1.15, IS 2.9, the 'non-artistic' or 'atechnic' means of persuasion (*pisteis*, ܡܦܝ̈ܣܢܘܬܐ, تصديقات). On the term *pisteis*, cf. above on 1.1.1. BH's title for the section mirrors that of IS.

**4.6.1.** Paraphrase of AR 1.15.1-5. BH makes some use of the paraphrase in IS 117.10-118.6, but he leaves aside IS's lengthy elaboration (118.6-13) of the judge as an assayer of silver (AR 75b5). The emendation (by Grignaschi and Lyons) of the unexpected 'artistic' at ARar 75a22 to 'non-artistic' (بلا صناعة) is supported by BH's '*pisteis* which do not come from art (ܠܐ ܡܢ ܐܘܡܢܘܬܐ) and IS 117.10 (تصديقات which are not from art [ليست عن صناعة]').' IS passes over the citation from *Antigone* (75b1-2). BH's version of it ('Sophocles defends to Antogone', cf. AR 74a33-34 'what is said in Sophocles' *Antigone*') accords with ARar ('what is said by Sophocles to

Antigone where she defends herself and says that he was buried ...', Lyons 73.15-16 and 293), except for the feminine gender and the omission of 'Polyneices'. Cf. the citation from *Antigone* in 4.5.1 above. The strange 'desire' for γνώμη in ARar 75a29 (Lyons 73.11 and 293) may, as Lyons suggests, have arisen by the misreading ܣܘܚܐ for ܗܘܢܐ in ARsyr, as BH writes that 'the righteous judge should follow his ܗܘܢܐ (understanding)'; the parallel passage in IS 118.5, however, has عقل (understanding).

**4.6.2.** A summary of IS 119.1-15, rather than AR 1.15.9-12. BH follows the sense of IS quite faithfully, although his account is much shorter. The opening sentence is a paraphrase of IS 119.1-4, itself a free interpretation of ARar 75b8-18 (Lyons 74.2-11 and 294). The reference to 'a judge not knowing how to apply the written law in some cases' comes directly from IS 119.4-5, but stems ultimately from (ARsyr and) ARar 75b18, 'If one does not know what the law says, it is necessary that he should not pass beyond it' (Lyons 74.11-12 and 294). The same applies to the necessity for 'a wise and practised judge' (IS 119.13; ARsyr/ar 75b23-25 'he must be very wise and skilled with regard to the law and its actions', Lyons, 74.18-19 and 295). This will be why BH attributes harm to 'lack of knowledge' on the part of a judge rather than to 'being accustomed to disobey one who is in charge' (AR 75b23). However, in the comparison between a judge and a physician, BH otherwise stays closer to ARsyr than to IS (119.10-12, cf. Würsch 131). 'Lack of knowledge' (of a physician/judge) rather than 'a mistake' (AR 75b22) corresponds to (ARsyr and) ARar (Lyons 74.16 and 294, ἀμαθία read for ἁμαρτία).

**4.6.3.** IS 120.1-9 abbreviates AR 1.15.13-15, omitting all the examples, and this paragraph of BH is based primarily on AR. BH paraphrases quite freely, but many striking divergences from the Greek text of Aristotle are also reflected in ARar and will be derived from ARsyr. This applies to the 'just and renowned men' (Lyons 75.3-4 and 295, cf. AR 75b28-29), the 'words' of Solon (Lyons 75.8 and 295, cf. AR 75b32 ἐλεγείοις), the quotation of Solon (Lyons 75.9-10 and 295, cf. AR 75b33-35), the remark about old men, fathers, and children (Lyons 75.15-18 and 295, cf. AR 76a3-7), the 'testing of recent witnesses by their acquaintances' (Lyons 75.19-21 and 295-296, cf. AR 76a7-9), and the prosecution 'before Plato' (Lyons 75.22 and 296, cf. AR 76a10).

**4.6.4.** In contrast to the previous paragraph, IS here freely paraphrases AR 76a12-33 at length, and BH bases his expostion on IS, closely reproducing IS 120.9-121.11, but eliminating the section 121.1-8 (on which see Würsch 129). The differences over against AR stem mainly from IS's free paraphrase. The assertion that 'every testimony is either about an adversary ... or about a fact' is identical to IS 120.12-13; cf. ARar 76a23-25, 'testimonies about something in part concern the adversary, in part the fact, and in part the method or manner' (Lyons 76.17-18 and 296). The awkward clauses following this - 'and what is necessary is never to be unable (to do) that. Now concerning the method' - are BH's paraphrase of IS 120.14: وهو الأصل الذى لا محيص عنه. فأما الشهادة على النحو والكيفية, 'and is the foundation from which there is no escape. As for testimony, concerning the method and the manner ...'.

**4.6.5.** Free paraphrase of AR 1.15.20-23 and IS 121.12-122.14. BH's exposition is shorter than that of IS but for the most part makes use of it in preference to AR, as in the example of two people 'making a covenant with each other that neither for good nor for evil will they be parted' (cf. IS 122.4-5 and Würsch 118). BH's ܣܢܝܩܘܬܐ, 'the needful (of men is wiped out)', will be from ARsyr of 76b13 χρεία ('needful business'), ARar معاملة (in the plural at IS 122.8). BH's final sentence depends on IS 122.10-11, 'He who finds the contract to be contrary to his intention must say, "Any contract not in the Book (i.e. the Qur'an) is a fabrication and every fabrication is an error"' (cf. Würsch 128-129), but BH removes the reference to 'the Book' and returns to AR's 'law(s)' (76b15-19).

**4.6.6.** Paraphrase of AR 76b19-31 and IS 122.14-123.16. Divergences from AR frequently depend upon IS, such as the change at the beginning from the judge as 'an umpire of justice' to 'an attendant upon reason and a defender of law' (cf. IS 122.15 'an official of reason and law'). However, while BH follows IS in asserting that 'the law is sanctioned by the agreement of the wise' (cf. IS 123.3-4), he leaves out the statement that 'there is no contract in disobedience to God' (IS 123.2). As in 4.5.4 above, BH juxtaposes written and unwritten law, but on this occasion he is in accord with (ARsyr and) ARar 76b25 (Lyons 78.6 and 298), whereas AR and IS (123.5-7) have 'written' and 'common'.

**4.6.7.** Paraphrase of AR 1.15.26, selectively employing IS 124.1-13 (but omitting, e.g., the passage [124.5-8] discussed by Würsch 119). 'Healthy of body and strong of soul' is taken from (ARsyr and) ARar 77a7 (AR 'slow-witted and thick-skinned and strong of soul'; cf. Lyons 78.23 and 299). That 'the timid and cowardly *confess* (ܡܫܬܘܕܝܢ) before they see the compulsion' has its parallel in IS 124.12, 'the imminence of a threat forces a weak person to confess (يقرره )', but also in the reading of (ARsyr and) ARar 77a7c يقرون (Lyons 79.2, Greek καταθαρροῦσιν or καταγορεύουσιν or κατεροῦσιν; cf. Lyons 299).

**4.6.8.** The interpretation of 'give and take' (AR 77a8-10, give and take [of oaths]) as 'give and take of wealth, honour, or the rest' is that of IS (124.14-15); it no doubt stems from the mention of 'money' at 77a15. The example of the child comes from IS 125.2-3. The latter part of the paragraph, contrasting 'him who is renowned for impiety' with 'him who is renowned for truth', is apparently a paraphrase of the maxim that it is easier for an impious man to take an oath than a pious (AR 77a19-20). IS 125.4-8 is very obscure in its wording, but appears to be rather similar and to have served as a source for BH's paraphrase.

**4.6.9.** Brief and free paraphrase of AR 77a20-b11. IS 125.9-126.13 is much longer, but it also is a free rendering. The mention of 'a righteous man suffering loss and not swearing, for he magnifies the adorable name of God and trembles to touch his living words' arises from (ARsyr and) ARar of 77a25-27 (Lyons 80.5-7 and 300: 'if the reliable and trustworthy man wishes to give and he honours God, he should not need anything better than this'). Cf. IS 126.2-3: 'the reliable and trustworthy man may prefer the penalty, for God is too great for his invocation (يجل لله عن ذكره)'.

## CHAPTER FIVE

Paraphrase of AR 2.1-18, on *pathos* and *ethos* (emotion and character), corresponding to IS 3.1-5. While IS's Chapter Three covers the whole of Book Two of Aristotle's *Rhetoric*, Bar Hebraeus puts *pathos* and *ethos* in one chapter, and the dialectical topics of AR 2.18-26 in a subsequent one. The division at 2.18 (91b27/28) corresponds to that of IS 3.5/6.

**5.1.** Paraphrase of AR 2.1-3, on anger and calmness, corresponding to IS 3.1.

**5.1.1.** Paraphrase of AR 2.1, the introduction to *pathos* and *ethos*. The highly condensed paraphrase in IS 129.3-130.8 is further shortened by BH, who nevertheless follows the general line of IS while reducing yet further the content of the exposition. The initial remarks are closely based on IS, but some significant differences from AR will probably also have been present in ARsyr. Thus ARsyr 77b24 will probably have read like ARar (Lyons 82.1-2 and 301) 'but also (the speech) which brings the judge to weakness and partiality' (AR 'but also [for the speaker] to show himself as a certain kind of character and to prepare the judge'), and ARsyr 77b31-32 will like ARar (Lyons 82.9-10 and 301) have attributed love, hate, and anger to the *judge*. The remarks concerning the intellects of the judges, the greater importance of the law in judicial proceedings, the adviser who gives 'raw advice', and the reference to what was said about praise and blame in the 'test of prudence and care' are all derived from IS (129.4-6, 130.2-6), as is the concluding triad of 'anger, the angry subject, and the object of anger' (130. 9 الغضب والمغضب والمغضوب عليه). BH, however, also keeps his eye on ARsyr; cf. 77b25 μάλιστα μὲν ἐν ταῖς συμβουλαῖς, BH ܡܠܝܣܛܐ ܒܡܬܡܠܟܢܘܬܐ; ARar لا سيما في المشورات (Lyons 82.3) and IS خصوصا في المشوريات (129.4).

**5.1.2.** Paraphrase of AR 78a31-b13 with close attention to IS 130.9-16. 'Damage by desire' (AR 78a31 'desire with distress') corresponds to IS 130.10 but also to (ARsyr? and) ARar (Lyons 83.22 and 302). IS omits the comment on rage and vengeance and the citation of *Iliad* 18.109-110 (AR 78b5-7); BH's 'and (works) like smoke' will be from ARsyr which had a version of the end of the line omitted by Aristotle (ἠύτε καπνός, ARar وانّ له مثل الدخان Lyons 84.8 and 302). By contrast, the final sentence on scorning is derived from IS 130.14-16 rather than AR 78b10-13.

**5.1.3.** Paraphrase of AR 78b13-34. For the most part BH is guided by the condensed paraphrase of this section in IS 130.16-131.8, but he adds material from ARsyr and expansions of his own. The identification of 'scorning' and 'smallness of soul' will be due to the blending of IS's 'scorning' (استحقار, from the previous paragraph) with 'smallness of soul' (not in IS), the rendering of AR 78b10 and 14 ὀλιγωρία ('belittling') in (ARsyr and) ARar (صغر النفس). Cf. at 80a9 ARar 'smallness of soul and contempt' (صغر النفس والتهاون Lyons 89.14 and 307) for ὀλιγωρία. The form ܡܫܥܒܕܘܬܐ, here rendered 'domination (?)', is unknown to *ThesSyr* or *BrLex*, but other forms from the same root are attested with the connotation of servility (cf. *ThesSyr* 3755, *BrLex* 699). The example of Achilles and Agamemnon (78b31-34) is omitted by IS and was evidently taken by BH from ARsyr. Like ARar (Lyons 85.14-16 and 303) ARsyr will have expanded Aristotle's citation (from *Iliad* 1.356 and 9.648) by 'Homer said', the mention of Agamemnon, the explanation 'his concubine', and the addition of the verb 'he left him'.

**5.1.4.** The paragraph is closely based on IS 131.10-132.12, itself a fairly free paraphrase of the longer section AR 78b34-79b4. AR 79a36-b2 ('these things much more if they suspect they do not have them, either not at all or not strongly, or not apparently, for whenever they confidently think they excel in the matters in which they are scoffed at, they do not care') makes its appearance in BH as, 'The populace for the most part deride those who love wisdom, belittle the worthy, and ridicule them as those who labour for nothing ... but when they see the integrity of the wise ... they magnify and honour them'. This is adapted from IS 132.3-10, but to some extent it is consistent with the rendering of the passage in (ARsyr? and) ARar, 'How much more do these people think that there is no benefit in that for them at all, or else they think without force or they do not think; but if they think there is a great benefit in it for them, for the most part they think of mercy or sympathy' (Lyons 87.8-11 and 305).

**5.1.5.** Again based very closely on IS (132.13-133.10), reformulating and substantially abbreviating AR 79b4-80a7. The recasting in (ARsyr? and) ARar of 79b14-15 (Aristotle: 'if they are insensitive to those in need') as, 'if they do not perceive or suffer' (Lyons 87.24 and 306), might conceivably have been influenced by a Christian translator's reminiscence of *Romans* 12,15 ('weep with them that weep'). This mention of suffering appears in both IS 133.1-2 and BH ('in his suffering does not suffer with him'). Only BH, however, records the reference to the *Meleager*; in that, ARar makes

Plexippus the companion (صاحب) of Antiphon (Lyons 88.1 and 306), but BH (and ARsyr) may have been aware that Antiphon was the author ('Plexippus, that of Antiphon'). The first three 'reprehensible scornings' accord with those of IS (133.5-6). The fourth, however, is quite different (in IS: 'scorning something which brings shame on a friend'), and for IS the anger of a parent or a masterful wife (متسلطة) is not legitimate, but one of the types of anger requiring censure (133.5-7).

**5.1.6.** The section for the most part reproduces the thought of IS's short paraphrase (133.11-134.9) of AR 80a7-33. BH occasionally adds a touch from ARsyr - e.g., the one who is 'not insulting' (cf. AR 80a29 μὴ ὑβρισταῖς, cf. IS 134.7 'holding the tongue') - or adds a touch of his own - e.g., at the end not only replacing IS's 'embarrassment' (خجل) by 'fear' (ܕܚܠܬܐ, cf. AR80a32 'fear or reverence'), but also adding the explanatory 'wise man' (for the 'reverence') and 'ruler' (for the 'fear'). The calming of anger against 'him who is very joyous and cheerful' (similarly IS 134.4-5) comes from the translation in (ARsyr? and) ARar of 80a27 τοῖς μείζω κεχαρισμένοις ('those who have done greater favour') as 'those who are very joyous' (Lyons 90.9 and 308).

**5.1.7.** A loose paraphrase of AR 80a34-b16 and IS 134.9-135.2. The examples of Philocrates and Ergophilus are omitted by IS and clearly have been taken by BH from AR. 'Revenge *from heaven*' is derived from IS 135.2, and in general BH's remarks in this section, with the exception of the Greek examples, are closer to IS than to AR, but he has nevertheless paraphrased both quite freely. This freedom includes the use of the rare ܦܪܐܣܝܘܬܐ, 'dishonouring (?)' (cf. *ThesSyr* 3282), for which there seems to be no basis in either AR or IS, and the free adaptation of the examples of Philocrates and Ergophilus. The opening remarks concerning 'the greater and the inferior' have no exact equivalent in IS, but the mention of 'instruction' (ܡܪܕܘܬܐ, IS 134.10 تأديب) derives from the rendering of AR 80b3 παιδιᾷ ('play') as παιδείᾳ in (ARsyr? and) ARar (أدب Lyons 91.1 and 308).

**5.1.8.** Paraphrase of AR 80b16-29 (IS 135.2-8 is shorter and quite different, and again omits the Greek examples; cf. Würsch 129). BH will have taken the citations of *Odyssey* 9.504 and *Iliad* 24.54 from ARsyr. On the basis of ARar it may be assumed that in the former ARsyr read, 'Rightly it was said of Odysseus, "You are *not* the sacker of cities/the city",' (Lyons 91.20-21 and 309, contrast AR 80b23, 'Say it was Odysseus, sacker of cities') and in the latter, 'From henceforth you will embrace the silent earth forever' (Lyons 92.4-5 and 309, contrast AR 80b29, 'It is unseemly to rage at silent earth'). The explanatory additions to the citations are from BH himself.

**5.2.** AR 2.4-5, IS 3.2. The title abbreviates that of IS 135.10, 'On the species of friendship, reliability, fear, confidence, and cowardice'.

**5.2.1.** Closer on the whole to IS 135.11-136.9 than to AR 80b34-81a25. The description of friendship as a 'condition' (ܕܝܬܗܣܝܣ) derives from IS 135.11 (الصداقة حالة) or from the expansion in ARar (and ARsyr?) of 81a3 οἱ οὕτως ἔχειν as 'those who are in this condition' (cf. Lyons 92.16-17 and 309), the reference to 'a true friend' from IS 136.1 صدق الصداقة 'the veracity of friendship'. BH's final 'those who are simple (ܕܦܫܝܛܝܢ) and do not know (how) to commit injustice' is marginally closer to AR 81a25 τοὺς σώφρονας, ὅτι οὐκ ἄδικοι ('the temperate, because not unjust') and ARar 'these are thought to be particularly chaste (اعفاء) and are not wrongdoers' (Lyons 93.15-16 and 310), and presumably to ARsyr, than to IS 136.8-9 'the peaceful in heart ... for they are harmless'.

**5.2.2.** Paraphrase of IS 136.9-137.12 rather than AR 81a25-b33. The cumbersome initial sentence is apparently BH's rendering of IS 136.9-11, itself a paraphrase of AR 81a26-28 ('to those with whom we wish to be friends, if they seem to wish it; such are those who are good by virtue and the respected, either among all or among the best'). BH slightly abbreviates the remainder of IS's exposition, but is otherwise close to him. However, BH's 'easily appeased' (ܕܠܝܠܐܝܬ ܡܬܪܥܝܢ, AR 81b5 εὐκατάλλακτοι) has no parallel in IS and will have come from ARsyr (ARar يرض سريعا). The recasting of AR 81b14-16 ('those similar to themselves and having similar interests, provided they do not become annoying or get their livelihood from the same source, for then it becomes a case of "potter against potter"') as 'someone loves one who is similar to himself in craft and manner' accords with IS 137.5-6, 'there is no resentment ... (against) an associate in profession or custom'.

**5.2.3.** Both BH and IS jump from AR 82a7 to 82a16, thus omitting some of the discussion of anger and hate in AR. BH mostly keeps close to IS, particularly in the expansion of 81b34 to define companionship, intimacy, and kinship. However the paraphrase of 81b35-37 ('Among the causes productive of friendship is doing a kindess when one is not bound to do so, and not revealing it when doing it') is lacking in IS. AR 82a6-7 'thief and sycophant' is in IS and BH merely 'thief'.

**5.2.4.** BH goes from AR 82b3 to b10-12, omitting what AR has to say on the fear of accomplices in wrongdoing; IS is similar. In general BH is closer here to AR than to IS. That he draws on ARsyr seems likely on account of his use of ܩܝܢܕܘܢܘܣ ('danger', AR 82a32 κίνδυνος, ARar and IS خطر); cf. also ܒܐܢܢܩܐ ('necessarily', AR 82a28 ἀνάγκη, ARar لا محالة, IS 138.12 يوجب), and BH ܫܓܘܫܬܐ 'agitation', a clearer rendering of AR 82a21 ταραχή than ARar and IS 138.5 اختلاط ('disorder' but also 'mixing').

**5.2.5.** Both IS and BH abbreviate and paraphrase AR 2.5.9-15, omitting 82b26-35. BH in general follows IS's abbreviated paraphrase, but in small details goes his own way, notably his rendering of 82b13 ἀνταγωνισταί by 'he who has no associate in *government* [ܦܘܪܢܣ], like a king' (cf. ARar المنازعون, IS 139.2 'one who can enter a *dispute* [منازعة] having no associates, like a king') and his reference at the end to a *better* (course), ܡܝܬܪܐ, AR 83a8 βέλτιον, ARar انتفع, which IS omits in 139.13-14. On the wording of the sentence, 'Among things greatly feared ... to correct', cf. Introduction, pp. 28-29

**5.2.6.** BH follows quite closely on IS 139.15-140.13, who paraphrases and considerably expands AR 83a14-25. The additions in BH over against AR all stem from IS.

**5.2.7.** BH blends ARsyr (2.5.18-22) with IS 140.15-141.13. The '*dangers* (ܣܘܟ̈ܢܐ) of the sea and its violent *storms*' (ܥܠ̈ܥܠܘܗܝ) are derived from AR 83a30 (κινδύνοις and χειμῶνος, ARar هول and هيج الامواج, IS omits both terms), while the 'wise helmsman' is from IS 141.1 الربان الحصيف. The mention of a 'ruler' (ܪܝܫܐ) and the formulation of the possibility that a subject could think himself better than or equal to the ruler come from IS (141.2-3); cf. AR 82a32 'nor to those inferior and whose superiors they think themselves to be', ARar '... and people who think that they are better than those who are in their power or under their authority' (Lyons 101.4-6 and 315). The 'judge righteous before God and men and recognised by wise, learned, and rational men' is from IS 141.6-78, 'If the one above (المستعلى) him is of good reputation and standing with God, he will not be preoccupied by anyone trying to overcome him, and similarly when intellectuals, legal experts, and orators (الخطباء) have a high opinion of him'. Cf. AR 83b5 'if it is well with them before the gods, from other things and signs and oracles (λόγια)'; and (ARsyr and) ARar 'if they are in good standing with God, and similarly everything else, and then the things marked by signs, and then with logicians or intellectuals' (Lyons 101.15 and 315). The '*seething* of anger' comes from IS 141.9 '*burning* (اشتعال) of anger'.

**5.3.** Paraphrase of AR 2.6 (Shame and Shamelessness) and 2.7 (Kindness); IS 3.3. The title is taken from IS (142.2).

**5.3.1.** IS 142.3-12 is generally quite close to AR 83b12-30; where they diverge, BH may be closer to one or the other. The opening definition of shame follows IS, as does the definition of shamelessness as a condition (ܕܝܐܬܗܣܝܣ, cf. IS 142.5, shamelessness is a خلق; and 5.2.1, 'friendship is a condition', IS حالة). IS, however, fails to note that '(taking) the grave clothes from the dead' is a proverb (AR 83b25 ἡ παροιμία, BH ܡܬܠܐ, ARar المثل), unlike the preceding 'plundering of the poor'; IS 142.9-10 reads, 'such as (مثل) plundering of the poor and ransacking the grave clothes of the dead'. BH's paraphrase of the proverb (AR 83b25 'even taking from a dead man') appears in ARar ('even the grave clothes from the dead'; cf. Lyons 102.13 and 316) and will no doubt have been taken from ARsyr.

**5.3.2.** Paraphrase of IS 142.12-143.15, rather than AR 83b30-84a23. IS omits AR 84a9-16 and paraphrasing 84a16-18 adds the comments about mockery (استهزاء), gestures (تعريض), and imitation (محاكات) followed by BH (ܡܗܠܘܬܐ, ܐܣܟܡ̈ܐ, ܢܬܕܡܐ). IS's introduction of 'imitation' may have been motivated by the rendering of AR 84a7-9 ('the actions and signs and the like that result from other vices of character, for these are disgraceful and things to be ashamed of') in (ARsyr? and) ARar as 'each of the evils and faults of character have actions and indices, and those who resemble these people are also foul and reprehensible' (Lyons 103.7-9 and 316-317). The final remark in BH, adding to 'cowardliness' 'the absence of vengeance', also comes from IS (143.10 القعود عن الثأر).

**5.3.3-4.** In these two pericopes, covering AR 2.6.14-27 (84a23-85a13), some sections of AR are transposed and some omitted. In this BH is largely following IS (143.10-145.6), although he frequently mentions points from AR that IS omits. The first part of section 5.3.3 is close to AR 84a23-35, and even more so to IS 143.10-144.4, but then from 'shame which is before the eyes and in the open is greater than that which is in hiding and secret' BH jumps to 'the shame of the Athenians' (AR 84b33-34), absent from IS. The remainder of BH 5.3.3 abbreviates IS 144.4-15, itself an abbreviated paraphrase of AR 84b5-27. In 5.3.4 BH basically follows IS 144.15-145.6, essentially a paraphrase of AR 84b11-27, but the various Greek examples cited throughout this section by Aristotle are lacking in IS. 'Euripedes before the Syracusans' is taken by BH from AR 84b16, the incident of Antiphon and Dionysius from AR 85a9-13, and 'Cydias on the allotment in Samos' from AR 84b32-33.

**5.3.5.** Closer in most respects to IS 145.7-146.5 than to AR 2.7.1-4. The definition of kindness as 'an advantageous matter ...' comes from IS (145.8-13: الأمر النافع ...); for BH's 'advantageous gift of substance' (ܡܘܗܒܬܐ ܕܐܘܣܝܐ ܡܘܬܪܢܝܬܐ) cf. IS 145.11 (اعطاء جوهر ينتفع به). After 'poor, shunned, or in hiding', IS 146.2-3 goes on to list 'those who are despised by enemies and opponents, he who is in a similar position to them, and he who is in a worse condition than them', while BH instead gives the example from AR (85a28), again absent from IS, 'like that which (someone) gave (ܝܗܒ ܗܘܐ) to Phormos in the Lyceum'. Emendation to the passive participle (ܝܗܝܒ ܗܘܐ) would give the smoother reading, 'like that which was given to Phormos in the Lyceum'. ARar reads (Lyons 107.21-22 and 320) 'like he who gave Firamis (فيراميس) what he gave in the Lyceum'. It seems likely that ARsyr (and BH) as well as ARar took τὸν φορμὸν as a proper name, but if the Syriac treated ܦܘܪܡܘܣ as a loan-word, it could be translated, 'as (someone) [*or* like he who] gave the mat in the Lyceum'. There appears, however, to be no other evidence for its appearance in Syriac as a loan-word. The final contrast between veiled and trumpeted kindness comes from IS (146.3-4).

**5.3.6.** Although BH slightly abbreviates IS 146.6-147.7, he follows in the main his thought and departs markedly from AR 2.7.5-6. The increased emphasis over against AR on the will (ܨܒܝܢܐ) comes from IS 146.9-14 (قصد or ارادة). The misunderstanding of AR 85b5 κατηγορίας ('categories') as 'prosecution' (ܡܩܛܪܓܢܘܬܐ, BH also adds ܡܚܘܠܢܐ) will have come initially from ARsyr, from whence it was transmitted to ARar (جميع الشكايات) and IS (شكاية). As a result both IS and BH omit 'substance, quality, quantity, time, or place' and talk instead of 'expediency for prosecution and defence'. The rather cryptic remark on 'done in like manner as with an enemy' is BH's brief paraphrase of IS's difficult argument in 146.17-147.5; its ultimate basis lies in the intrusion of a negative in (ARsyr? and) ARar 85b7-8 ('and if they have *not* done that to the enemies', Lyons 108.19-20 and 320). The rendering of φαῦλος ('trifling', AR 85b9-10 'if [the service] was knowingly trifling, for no one admits needing the trifling') by شر ('evil') is quite frequent in ARar (cf. Lyons II 148) and may also derive from ARsyr (ܒܝܫܘܬܐ, BH 'if evil ... no one acknowledges that he has need of evil').

**5.4.** Commentary on AR 2.8-11, IS 3.4. IS's title (147.9-10) differs slightly from that of BH, BH having no equivalent of IS's 'vengeance' (النقمة).

**5.4.1.** The paraphrase is considerably closer to IS 147.12-148.13 than to AR 85b11-86a4. Like BH, IS has 'the ruined' as the object rather than the subject of 'non-pity' (BH ܘܡܚܠ ܐܡܠܝ ... ܠܐ ܚܢܢܐ ܠܟܐܒ; IS فلا يهتم ملا وقع لهم, contrast AR 85b19-20 'those who are utterly ruined do not feel pity'). The remainder of the section, while shorter than IS, is largely dependent upon it. The negative intrusion at 85b24 (AR 'the kind of people who think they might suffer', ARar Lyons 109.14-15 and 321 'amongst these are those who think they will not suffer', IS 148.5 'those who do not pity and do not care are those who are accustomed to endure evils ...', BH 'pitiless are those who take pleasure in distress ...') was presumably present in ARsyr. The remarks about the 'non-existence of the contemptible and the humiliated' and about the 'warlike' (ܡܩܪܒܬܢܐ, IS الجبابرة, 'oppressors') are taken directly from IS 148.11-13; cf. 85b35-86a1 'for he who thinks no one is', ARar 'whoever thinks there is no one in the world' (Lyons 110.3-4 and 321).

**5.4.2.** Paraphrase of AR 86a4-24, IS 148.14-149.7, drawing from both. IS abbreviates this section of AR, and in general BH is closer to IS's abbreviation than to the text of AR. However, the lists of both the causes of pity and the people pitied are slightly different in each of the three writers; 'mutilation' (ܦܘܫܚܢܘܬܐ) must be taken from AR (86a11 ἀναπηρία) as it is omitted by IS (148.15-16, cf. ARar زمانة). Similarly 'Amasis' must be taken from AR, as IS merely has 'someone' (149.5 واحد). BH's 'his son was being led away and was near to dying' (ܡܬܕܒܪ݂ ܗܘܐ ܒܪܗ ܘܩܪܒ ܕܢܡܘܬ) will be the reading in ARsyr of 86a19-20 τῷ υἱεῖ ἀγομένῳ ἐπὶ τὸ ἀποθανεῖν. ARar جلد ('was being beaten', Lyons 111.4) could be a corruption of جلب, but is more likely to be the translation of the ambiguous ܡܬܢܓܕ ('led' or 'beaten', thus Lyons 322, whose conjecture as to the Syriac root is supported by the reading of BH). IS 149.6 omits the 'leading/beating' and simply has 'on the brink of destruction'.

**5.4.3.** In outline BH follows IS's abbreviated paraphrase of AR 86a24-b16, but he does not do so slavishly, and his exposition is more clear and concise. Whereas IS 150.7-8 paraphrases AR 86b14-16 ('what takes place contrary to [anyone's] desert is unjust, therefore we attribute being indignant to the gods') as, 'Neither determination nor decree (القضاء والقدر) are limited to what is deserved ... (but are) entrusted to Allah', BH has, 'The Lord of fate (ܡܪܐ ܫܠܡܐ; presumably ARsyr simply read ܐܠܗܐ for 86b15 θεοί, ARar and IS لله) is wise, and as he knows (how) to rule, so also (he knows) about going through pain'. The description of the pain resulting from the results of 'divine decree' (BH 'without human determination and without known cause, but rather as if by fate') as 'middling' comes from IS (150.3-4). While following in general the structure of IS's paraphrase, BH's use of ARsyr can nevertheless be seen in this section, for example, in his phrase 'outside of (anyone's) desert' (ܠܒܪ ܡܢ ܐܟܣܝܐ, AR 86b15 παρὰ τὴν ἀξίαν); ARar has خارجا من الطبيعة ('outside of nature', Lyons 112.8 and 323), while IS 150.2 has غير مستحقه ('undeserving of it'), rightly restoring the sense of 'desert'. ARar 'nature' can be most convincingly explained by supposing that the translator or Ibn al-Samh read the familiar ܐܘܣܝܐ in place of the rare ܐܟܣܝܐ in his copy of ARsyr.

**5.4.4.** Generally closer to IS 150.13-151.8 than to AR 86b16-25, although BH is more concise than IS. The 'emotion (which) is necessary and implanted in every nature' - i.e. the pain 'when a person is pained not by (the success of another) but by his own lack of success' - an elaboration absent from AR, is taken from IS, who describes it as 'almost necessary (قريب من واجب), and no nature is devoid of it' (151.4-5). IS's interpretation is derived from (ARsyr? and) ARar of 86b20-22: 'as for what happens not because another man has obtained what is exactly like that, but because of himself, this is near to or incumbent on all' (Lyons 112.14-15 and 323; cf. AR 'what must similarly be present in all not because the other may happen to himself, but on account of the neighbour ...'). From IS also (151.6-8) BH derives the mention of 'the success of an *enemy*'.

**5.4.5.** BH closely follows IS 151.8-14, a rather free paraphrase of AR 86b25-87a5. However his mention of 'those who strike their parents' and his reference to 'just/justice and unjust/injustice' are drawn from Aristotle. IS has no equivalent to AR 86b28 'parricides' and refers not to 'justice and injustice' but to 'virtue and vice' (فضيلة, رذيلة); cf. AR 86b31 δίκαια, ARar عدل, BH ܟܐܢܘܬܐ/ܟܐܝܢܘܬܐ.

**5.4.6.** In general a paraphrase of IS 151.15-152.12 rather than of AR 87a5-32, although some individual differences over AR are reflected in ARar and presumably were present in ARsyr, from where they passed to BH. Thus AR 87a29 ὅπλων κάλλος ('beauty of armour') becomes 'armour and appearance' in ARar, BH 'armour and beauty', but IS 152.10 'ornamental clothing and armour'. 'Hermit' (ناسك) is the rendering of ARar (and IS 152.9) of δίκαιος in this passage of Aristotle, BH and presumably ARsyr ܚܣܝܐ. IS omits AR 87a30 'distinguished (διαφέροντες) marriages', for which ARar (Lyons 114.21 and 325) has 'inter-marriage', BH (and presumably ARsyr) the rendering 'marriages of many sorts' (ܙܘ̈ܘܓܐ ܫܢ̈ܝܐ), taking διαφέροντες as 'differing'. BH's 'concubines' may be his own addition to 'marriages', or a misreading or misinterpretation of IS 152.15, who considers as inappropriate for the newly rich an abundance of 'troops', سرايا ; cf. Arabic سراری, 'concubines'. The reference to 'donations' (ܐܦܪܐ) at the end of BH, not present in IS, comes from the rendering in (ARsyr and) ARar of 87a31-32 ('If a man being good does not obtain what is fitting, it is a cause of indignation') as, 'If ... , (he may get) this from gifts or allowances' (Lyons 114.22-24 and 325).

**5.4.7.** BH has here freely paraphrased AR 87a32-b20 with some reference to IS 152.12-153.5. While IS omits the example of Ajax (*Iliad* 11.542), the reference in BH to the fateful ordination of his battle comes from the rendering in (ARsyr and) ARar of νεμέσασχ' ('was indignant') in 87a35 (*Iliad* 11.543 not in the MSS. of Homer but in Aristotle and Plutarch) as 'fated'. ARar reads (Lyons 115.2-4 and 325): 'Thus was said what was ordained for the battle of Ajax, son of Telamon, that he was a man fated (مقدور) by Jupiter (المشترى) when he fought against a better man'. Cf. BH, who doubtless here cites ARsyr 87a34-35: 'As was decreed for Ajax, son of Telamon, that Zeus had fated him (ܕܠܗ ܙܐܘܣ ܦܠܓ ܗܘܐ) to fight with a better man'. ARar and IS continue rendering (as in the previous section) δίκαιος by ناسك at AR 87b2, but BH, presumably following ARsyr, reverts to the normal ܙܕܝܩܐ. The remainder of the section paraphrases AR 87b2-20 in much the same way as does IS 152.14-153.5. That both of them speak of 'matters subject to fate' (ܨܒ̈ܘܬܐ ... ܕܬܚܝܬ ܦܠܓܐ) rather than 'people prone to indignation' derives from the translation of AR 87b4 αὐτοὶ νεμεστικοί ('people prone to indignation) in (ARsyr and) ARar as 'matters subject to fate' (الأمور ... تحت القدر, Lyons 115.7-8); cf. IS 152.15-153.1 الأمور المنسوبة ... الى القدر ('the matters linked ... to fate').

**5.4.8.** A free paraphrase of AR 87b21-88a9. While in overall shape and length it adheres more closely to IS 153.5-16 than to the original, the component parts are often closer to AR. Thus, for example, the first sentence paraphrases AR 87b21-25 more closely than does IS 153.5-8. IS omits the proverb 'kinship knows also to envy' (AR 88a7-8, attributed by a Greek scholiast to Aeschylus); BH is probably paraphrasing but might be citing ARsyr (cf. ARar المضارعة قد تحسن ان تحسد, 'kinship is proficient at envying'). However the reading in BH is uncertain: ܥܠܬܐ ܗܝ ܠܚܣܡܐ ('is the cause of emulation') is found only in F and may be from a second hand. IS 153.14 speaks of honour 'through slaves (بالرقيق) and possessions', rather than 'deeds (88a1 ἔργοις, BH ܥܒ̈ܕܐ) and possessions'; ARar reads بالعبيد ('through slaves'), doubtless mistranslating ARsyr ܥܒ̈ܕܐ (cf. Lyons 327), which in BH is here translated 'deeds', although the translation 'slaves' is also possible.

**5.4.9.** Free paraphrase blending AR 88a9-28 with IS 154.1-11. 'Those of a distant place ... who are scattered (ܕܒܕܝܪܝܢ) around the pillars of Hercules' (AR 88a10-11 'those around the pillars of Hercules') may be assumed to reflect ARsyr in this passage, which by a misreading of ܕܒܕܝܪܝܢ as ܕܙܕܝܩܝܢ, 'those who are just', has become in ARar 'those at a distance among the just men (الابرار), like those by the pillars of Hercules' (Lyons 117.13-14 and 327). IS 154.2 has 'those in a distant place ... like those living by the lighthouse (منار) of Hercules'. 'Islands of the blessed at the limits of the west' is due to BH; it is possible that the correct reading may be that of RVL, 'islands which are very distant at ...'. As in the previous paragraph, 'an old man with wealth (ܥܒ̈ܕܐ)' could be taken as 'an old man with slaves'. The final sentence is taken from IS 154.10-11.

**5.4.10.** A free paraphrase of AR 88a29-b14, with some borrowing from IS 154.12-155.4. The definition of emulation is largely BH's own paraphrase of 88a30-33 ('emulation is a pain ... not that the other has them but that the emulator does not'). IS's paraphrase of the same section (154.12-15) is rather different, but in what follows BH takes one item from him, that the emulous person loves (ܪܚܡ, يحب) the good whose absence (ܒܚܣܝܪܘܬܗ, فوته) he regrets (ܡܬܬܘܝ, يأسف) The remainder is BH's own paraphrase of AR 88b2-14, with occasional reference to IS 155.1-4: both IS and BH leave out 'the young' beside the 'high-minded' (AR 88b2), and both add 'praise' (الحمد, ܬܫܒܘܚܬܐ) to 'honour' at 88b10.

**5.4.11.** BH adheres more closely to AR 88b14-30 than does IS 155.4-14. The rare ܦܗܕܪܐ, 'general', is a loanword from Persian نه دار; cf. *ThesSyr* 2310 and especially the *Supplement* 207a. ܦܗܕܪ̈ܐ ܐܘܚܕܢܬ ܪ̈ܫܝ ܚܝ̈ܠܘܬܐ, 'generals or heads of armies', may have been the reading (or reading with gloss) of στρατηγοί in ARsyr at 88b18; cf. 93b21 στρατηγὸς αὐτοκράτωρ appearing in BH 6.2.2 as ܦܗܕܪܐ ܐܘܛܘܩܪܛܘܪ ܐܘܚܕܢܬ ܐܚܝܕ ܢܦܫܗ ('general, *autokrator* or controller of himself'). At 88b18 ARar merely has قواد الجيوش ('heads of armies', Lyons 119.18-19 and 328), at 93b21 سلطان اوطقراطور وهو الممسك بنفسه (Lyons 135.12-13 and 339). In neither case is there an equivalent passage in IS. That contempt 'sets emulation in motion and causes increase in it ...' comes from IS 155.9-11, but is consistent with (ARsyr and) ARar 88b24-25, 'It is necessarily like this when a man shows self-emulation when people are contemptuous ...' (Lyons 120.2-3 and 329, cf. AR, 'Necessarily those in a situation to emulate or be emulated by others are contemptuous of those who have the bad attributes which are opposites of the emulated good ones'). BH's 'undeserving despised one (who) gets the good by luck *without labour*' may stem from ARsyr of 88b28 ('without valued goods', ARar 'without the virtues which deserve that' [Lyons 120.7-8 and 329]) or from IS 155.13-14, 'without being deserving, its beginning not being from suffering and hardship'. BH understood the creation and dissolution of emotions in AR 88b29-30 to refer to the issue of 'the undeserving despised man', not as a summary of the whole of AR 2.2-11; IS appears to have done the same, as he continues with a remark about the 'fragility' (وهى) of his situation (أمر), without, however, making any mention of emotions (πάθη).

**5.5.** AR 2.12-18, IS 3.5, on ethos ('character', ἤθη, BH ܥܝ̈ܕܐ, IS اخلاق). The title is from IS (156.2).

**5.5.1.** The opening list, with 'intentions' (ܬܪ̈ܥܝܬܐ, ARar همم) rendering ἕξεις ('habits') and 'fortunes and souls' (ARar 'souls and fortunes') in place of 'fortunes' will reflect ARsyr (cf. Lyons 120.11). For 'emotions' and 'fortunes', IS 156.3-4 has 'contingencies' and 'borders'; read ألم for اعاض and جدود for حدود (Würsch 119 and 127)? 'Power, government, asceticism, or one of the arts' comes from IS (156.6), as do the various souls, IS's (156.8) 'Arab and non-Arab (عجمية)' being replaced in BH by 'Ethiopian and Scythian'. The wording of 'instability of youthful opinions' and 'the quenching of thirsts by a cool breeze' is taken from IS 157.1 (cf. AR 89a6-8), but the term ܐܦܪܘܕܝܛܝܩܝܬܐ ('sensual', 'of Aphrodite', 89a5 ἀφροδίσια) doubtless comes from ARsyr (cf. ARar and IS الزهرة, 'Venus').

**5.5.2.** IS omits the example of Pittacus and Amphiaraus (AR 89a16-17, 'as the saying of Pittacus on Amphiaraus has it'), which in ARar (and doubtless similarly in ARsyr, on which BH depends) is expanded: 'like what is indicated by the saying of Pittacus, where he says of the people of Amphiaraus (فى اهل امفياروس) that there is no evil-natured man among them, but (only) those of good character, because they have not seen evil or boorish men' (Lyons 121.7-10 and 329-330). Probably 'of the people of Amphiaraus' has been deformed to BH's 'in Maphiarnus' (ܒܥܡ ܐܡܦܝܐܪܐܘܣ > ܒܥܡܐ ܡܦܝܐܪܐܘܣ > ܒܡܦܝܐܪܢܘܣ?). 'They neither give way nor flee' will have come from the rendering in ARsyr of 89a20-21, 'they have not yet experienced many failures', which in ARar appears as 'they do not weaken or shrink quickly' (Lyons 121.12-13 and 330).

**5.5.3.** While in the first part of the section BH departs little from the sense of AR 89a25-33, even though following more closely IS 157.9-158.1, in the second he paraphrases IS's expansion and transformation of AR 89a34-36. This transformation (from AR's 'the young choose to do fine things rather than advantageous things' to [IS 158.12 and] BH 'the young tend towards the expedient and advantageous which they have experienced more than the good which until now they have not experienced') results from the rendering in (ARsyr and) ARar 89a34-35, 'they choose to do good things more with regard to expedient things, for they are more accustomed to these things' (Lyons 122.5-6 and 330). As a consequence, IS 158.2-4 introduces a 'calculation (فكر) (i.e. of the young) founded on nature (فطرة) towards the expedient and pleasurable', against AR's assertion that the young live by nature (ἦθος) rather than calculation (λογισμός). BH follows IS here, as also in his closing remark that 'in this way it is necessary to understand this passage' (158.6). On IS's interpretation, cf. further Würsch 116-117.

**5.5.4.** BH mostly follows IS (158.7-18) more closely than AR 89a36-b12. The contrast of the 'true expedient' and the 'expedient which leads to pleasure' (AR 89b1 'they do not judge anything by the expedient') follows IS 158.9, but the change over against AR is necessitated by the 'tendency (of the young) towards the expedient' in the previous paragraph. The omission of 'contrary to the maxim of Chilon' (158.11) follows ARar (Lyons 122.11 and 330) and presumably also reflects ARsyr. Similarly, 'weakness of thought' (ܡܚܝܠܘܬ ܡܚܫܒܬܐ) was presumably the rendering in ARsyr of 89b11 πεπαιδευμένη ὕβρις ('cultured insolence', cf. ARar and IS ضعف الروية, Lyons 122.20-21 and 330, IS 158.17). BH's 'wears an appearance of being wronged' (ܠܒܝܫ ܠܥܠܝܒܐ ܐܣܟܡܐ) renders IS 158.16 'presented (as) wronged' (المتظلم المتعرف, cf. AR 89b10 'they suppose them to be suffering undeservedly'). IS's apparent statement (158.8) that joy is accomplished through *health* (صحة) and companionship (معاشرة معا) is probably a scribal or editorial error for *company* (صحبة) and companionship, as in ARar 89b1 (صحبة and عيش معا, Lyons 122.9) and BH (ܚܒܝܫܐ and ܣܚܪܘܬܐ).

**5.5.5.** Paraphrase drawing on both ARsyr (89b13-24) and IS (159.1-10). The first two sentences are close to IS, though the 'pliable and feeble character' of the old appears in (ARsyr and) ARar (Lyons 123.1 and 331, cf. AR 89b14 merely 'character'). BH, however, will definitely have drawn on ARsyr in the paraphrase of 89b17-18, for ARar and IS do not reproduce Aristotle's, 'They *suppose*, but they *know* nothing', but paraphrase it, 'They have experienced (جربوا) everything and it is as if they do not know anything' (ARar, Lyons 123.5 and 331), and, 'Despite the amount of their experience they have not experienced (لم يجربوا) anything' (IS 159.6). The appearance of 'praise and blame' may come from IS (159.7) or, as with the preceding 'suppose', may derive from the mention of 'praise' in ARsyr (ARar 'they have doubts about praise and what is praiseworthy', Lyons 123.6 and 331, AR 89b18 'and being doubtful'). That they love or hate 'according to what is necessary' rather than 'according to the advice of Bias' (AR 89b23) accords with (ARsyr and) ARar (Lyons 123.12 and 331) and IS 159.10 (Würsch 125-126).

**5.5.6.** The paraphrase blends IS 159.11-160.2 with AR 89b24-35. That the old *predict* (AR 89b29 *fear*), that their desire *ceases* (AR 89b33-34 'because desire is present for what is absent'), and that they have *no* need for desirable things (AR 89b34-35 'people most desire what they lack') all come from (ARsyr and) ARar (Lyons 123.18, 23-24 and 331). That 'they shy away from poverty and hard trading' paraphrases IS's 'from fear of breaching a deadline (?) (159.13 خوفا من ادراك الأجل), and the mention of copulation, desirable *visible* things, and foods is also taken from IS (160.1-2).

**5.5.7.** BH abbreviates but generally follows quite closely IS (160.2-15). The expansions over AR 89b35-90a16 (such as the remarks at the beginning about justice and 'smallness of soul') and modifications (such as the contrast between necessity and virtue at the end) mostly stem from IS. 'Righteous judges' (ܕ̈ܝܢܐ) in BH renders IS's 'righteous *imams*'. However BH's '(the old) have neither shame nor modesty' (ܠܐ ܒܗܬܝܢ ܐܦܠܐ ܡܬܚܡܣܢܝܢ) may be taken from the rendering in ARsyr of 90a2 ἀναίσχυντοι μᾶλλον ἢ αἰσχυντηλοί ('shameless more than modest'); ARar simply has 'have no shame' (لا يستحيون, Lyons 124.4 and 331), IS 'they are scandalmongers having no shame' (هم اوقاع لا يستحيون, 160.8).

**5.5.8.** BH is again generally closer to IS (160.16-161.16) than to AR (90a16-b13). The opening sentence, however, is consistent with (ARsyr and) ARar, 'They do wrong by cunning and artifice, not by means of the shameful and exposures' (Lyons 124.20, AR 90a18-19 'They commit wrongs for vice, not for insolence'); IS paraphrases, 'They greatly seek to gain the expedient by skill, swindling, and deception, not by frankness' (161.4-5). The curious 'prime of old age' (ܥܠܡܐ ܕܣܝܒܘܬܐ, AR 90a29 οἱ ἀκμάζοντες, 'those in their prime') is from IS 161.11 عنفوان التشييخ (ARar عنفوان العمر). Likewise the closing remark about 'completion of the prime' (AR 90b10-11 'the soul about forty-nine') is from IS (161.16 'its completion up to fifty').

**5.5.9.** BH's opening may be influenced by IS, but is consistent with (ARsyr and) ARar 90b18-20: 'Noble birth is an exaltation on account of ancestors. They suppose that they resemble their ancestors, and because this is something distant and anterior and not near, it is more exalted and noble than what is near' (Lyons 126.7-10 and 333). IS 162.1-2 has: 'The noble born, possessing lineage, greatly crave honour, imitating their ancestors, and suppose that whatever is anterior is more exalted and glorious'. Lyons 333 suggests that ARar 'suppose' (يتوهمون, IS يظن, BH [from ARsyr?] ܣܒܪܝܢ) may have come from misreading 90b19 καταφρονητικόν ('contemptuous') as a form of φρονεῖν ('suppose'). In much of the sequel BH follows IS rather than AR, but the examples towards the end are drawn from AR. The elimination of the difference between 'good birth' and 'noble (birth)' (AR 90b22) is due to IS, as is the introduction of 'education' and 'learning a craft' (162.6). However IS makes no mention of the descendants of Alcibiades, Dionysius, Cimon (Conon), Pericles, and Socrates, and blends AR's two classes (the 'degenerate' and the 'stupid') more than does BH. The corruption Conon (ARar قونون) for Cimon (Κίμων) probably occurred within ARsyr (ܩܝܡܘܢ > ܩܘܢܘܢ ?).

**5.5.10.** BH makes use of both ARsyr and IS. At the beginning he adheres more closely to IS, but IS omits the names of Hieron and Simonides and paraphrases (162.13-16) this passage of AR (91a8-12) very freely. BH, however, while taking the final sentence about the rich man's deficiency in 'understanding' (ܡܕܥܐ) from IS (162.14 'the wise man will have understanding' [بصير]), cites the example of Hieron and Simonides from AR and elaborates it independently, though the point of his elaboration is the same as that of the response of Aristippus (Diogenes Laertius 2.69), 'Philosophers know what they need, the rich do not' (cf. Grimaldi, *Aristotle, Rhetoric II*, 219). Conceivably this might have been quoted in a scholion here in ARsyr; cf. Introduction, pp. 30-31. 'Treading the threasholds' is the rendering in (ARsyr and) ARar (Lyons 127.15 and 333-334) of 91a12 'spending time at the doors'; IS does not have the expression. ܣܠܐܩܘܢܘܣ ('swaggering', σαλάκωνες 91a3-4) and ܣܘܠܘܩܘ ('offensive', σόλοικοι 91a4-5) will have come from ARsyr. The terms in ARar are ذوى فخر and صلف (Lyons 127.8-9); IS has the latter (162.11).

**5.5.11.** BH differs quite markedly from the Greek of AR 91a14-30, but mostly conforms in substance, though not always in wording, to IS 162.17-163.11. ARar also differs markedly from the Greek in this section, so much of BH's exposition is likely to have been consistent with ARsyr. The most important difference - which turns 91a20-30 into a contrast between the wealthy powerful (who in truth are 'weak') and the honour-loving powerful - is the translation of 91a21-26: 'Among them are those who employ power to acquire wealth, and others direct that (wealth) to virtue, like those more desirous of honour and worthy in character. These have greater power than the wealthy ... and the actions of power urge them and drive them on to virtue' (Lyons 128.4-9 and 334). The opening substitution of the converse of AR 91a14-17 ('the newly rich have greater vices than those of old wealth') follows (ARsyr and) ARar (Lyons 127.19-22), the comparison with the young IS 163.1.

**5.5.12.** BH's recasting of AR 91a31-b1 ('... tend towards these, and also good fortune offers advantages in good children and bodily goods. Although people are more arrogant and unreasonable because of good fortune ...') is in accord with (ARsyr and) ARar, '... tend towards these things of good children and bodily goods and produce for those who have them greed with regard to delight and pleasures. They are more insolent and less mindful of their prosperity and good condition' (Lyons 128.15-18 and 334-335). That the fortunate receive their good *without labour* comes from IS (163.14).

**5.5.13.** Both BH and IS take the opening remarks of Aristotle chapter 18 (91b8-27), as far as 'speeches appropriate to character (ἠθικοὺς τοὺς λόγους) and we have delineated the teaching on this' (ARar, Lyons 129.19), as the final part of the teaching on ethos ('diversity of people in character'). BH is close to IS in this section and rather far removed from AR, and ARar (and presumably ARsyr) differs markedly from the Greek. 'The use of persuasive speeches is persuasion' is from IS alone (163.16, AR 'the use of persuasive speeches is towards judgement' [κρίσις, فحص]), but 'of necessity a judge must be sought who will ...', while directly dependent on IS (164.2-4), is consistent with (ARsyr? and) ARar, 'there must be one single judge with regard to whoever must undertake the persuasion' (Lyons 129.4-5 and 335, AR 91b11-12 'a single individual is no less a judge, for [he is] one who must be persuaded'). The introduction of 'witnesses' is due to BH. 'Opined premisses' (ܦܪ̈ܘܛܐܣܝܣ ܡܣܬܒܪܢܝܬܐ) is BH's modification of 'opinions and premisses' (91b24 δόξαι καὶ προτάσεις, ARar الظنون والقضايا); on the terminology, cf. 1.2.1, 1.4.5, 1.6.3, and Glossary s.v. ܣܒܪ.

## CHAPTER SIX

Commentary on AR 2.18-26, the *koina* (subjects for argument common to all three species of rhetoric), corresponding to IS 3.6-8. BH 6 and IS 3.6 start not at the beginning of AR 2.18 (cf. above on 5.5.13) but at 91b28 (ARar Lyons 129.19-20), 'It remains for us to deal with the *koina*'. The title is BH's adaptation of IS, 'On the species (انواع) common to rhetorical subjects (أمور).

**6.1.** Commentary on AR 2.18 (91b28) -19. IS 3.6 covers the ground of BH 6.1-3.

**6.1.1.** Both IS 164.11-165.10 and BH briefly paraphrase the introductory section AR 91b28-92a7 (effectively reducing it to 92a4-7, the most appropriate species for each 'subject'), but cover more fully the beginning of the exposition of 'the possible and impossible' in 92a8-23. The transformation of AR from 'past to judicial and possibility and future to deliberative' to 'past and future to judicial and possible and impossible to deliberative' is due to BH himself; ARar (and presumably ARsyr) and IS 165.2-3 are in accord with AR 92a6-7. 'That which does not end has not begun', and 'that which has not begun does not end' are also from BH himself (AR 'for no impossible thing comes into being nor begins to come into being', and 'for all things come from a beginning'). 'Later by *nature*' (ܐܚܪܝܐ ܒܟܝܢܐ) may be ARsyr of 92a20 τὸ ὕστερον τῇ οὐσίᾳ ('later in being') as in ARar (Lyons 130.20-21 and 336). *Human being* becoming youth or man is from IS (165.10).

**6.1.2.** A blend of ARsyr and IS. Like IS, BH omits some of AR's examples (the sole and the shoe, double and half, the saying of Agathon);

however, while IS omits those of the ship and the saying of Isocrates, BH includes them. '(The things) by which we are constrained or of which we have need' may be BH's adaptation of ARsyr; cf. AR 92a27 'things we can compel or persuade', ARar 'things to which we compel people and for which we plead' (Lyons 131.3-4). Possibly BH's 'we are constrained' (ܐܠܝܨܝܢ) is a misreading of ARsyr 'we compel' (ܐܠܨܝܢ). 'The support of virtuous people and friends' (AR 92a28-29 'over which we are stronger or have authority or friends') will be consistent with (ARsyr and) ARar, 'in the possession of virtuous people and friends' (Lyons 131.5 and 336). The reduction of AR 92a33-b2, 'If the genus ... also the species, and if the species, also the genus', to, 'If the species is possible, so also the genus', comes from (ARsyr and) ARar (Lyons 131.9 and 336), the addition *nature* from IS 165.16. The changes from AR's 'ship' (92b2) to 'multi-oared ship' and from the proper name Euthynus (92b12) to 'a fool' correspond to (ARsyr and) ARar (Lyons 131.10-11, 21 and 336-337).

**6.1.3.** IS 166.4-167.6 considerably abbreviates AR 92b14-93a21; BH follows IS's general outline, with variations. Where IS (166.7) refers to 'causes' and 'the thing (itself)' (الاسباب and الشيء), BH speaks of 'causes' and 'effects' (ܥܠܬܐ and ܥܠܝܠܬܐ, cf. AR 92b26-29, ὅσα ... ἕνεκα and ὅσα ... οὗ ἕνεκα). The addition of the example on the preparation for war and offence is from IS 166.13-14. The reference on amplification and diminution back to the treatment of deliberative rhetoric follows AR 93a8-13; see AR 1.7 and BH 2.4. The same back reference appears in IS 167.4.

**6.2.** Paraphrase of AR 2.20, on the paradigm.

**6.2.1.** ܬܚܘܝܬܐ ('paradigm') was evidently the normal rendering in ARsyr of παράδειγμα. When BH says that 'paradigm is here called demonstration (ܡܚܘܝܢܘܬܐ)', he is following IS 167.9, 'مثل we will here call برهانات', who is setting his preferred term (مثل) beside that of ARar (برهان); cf. Würsch 75. Cf. the terminological discussion in 1.6.1, '*Demonstration* is used for every paradigm which shows forth the aim quickly'. 'The reputable maxim is included among the materials of the enthymeme' is likewise derived from IS (167.8, AR 'the *gnome* is a part of the enthymeme'), as is also the wording of the contrast '(true) proverb' against 'untrue discourse' (IS مثل and كلام كاذب). (Explicit mention of 'truth' appears in ARar 'induction is truer' [Lyons 134.5 and 338], AR 93a27 'induction is a beginning'.) 'Aesop and Libuqu (ܠܝܒܘܩܘ)' corresponds to (ARsyr and) ARar (Lyons 134.9 and 338), cf. AR 93a30 'the Aesopic and Libyan (Λιβυκοί)'; IS substitutes 'The Book of Kalilah and Dimnah' (167.14). On 'paradigm' in IS, cf. also Würsch 78-82.

**6.2.2-3.** While BH's versions of the four examples depart markedly from the text of AR, they are much closer to it than are those of IS. The latter's account is quite radically different, and omits, for example, the introductions and concluding applications of the latter two examples. Furthermore, there is no mention in IS of Darius, Xerxes, Stesichorus, Phaladirios (Phalaris, Φαλάριδι 93b23 to ܦܐܠܐܕܝܪܝܘܣ, ARar has the correct Phalaris), Aesop, or 'a demagogue'. BH was clearly paraphrasing ARsyr and took little or no notice here of IS. Some variations of (ARsyr and) ARar over against the Greek appear in BH's paraphrase, notably: the placing of Xerxes 'before' Darius (93b1 πάλιν 'again', cf. Lyons 134.13-14 and his suggestion 338 of πάλαι, but cf. also the inversion of Darius and 'Xerxes' in the Bible [Ezra 4,7-24]); 'Stesichorus said to his people' (Lyons 135.1 and 338, BH 'Stesichorus saying when haranguing his people', AR 93b9-11 'what Stesichorus said ... the people of Himera'); the addition to the transliteration of 93b21 αὐτοκράτωρ of the explanation 'one who controls himself' (Lyons 135.12-13 and 339); the addition of 'meagre' to 'the blood I have left' of 93b31-32 (Lyons 135.25 and 339); and the separation of 'yours' and 'public' at 94a1-2 (Lyons 136.3 and 339). ARsyr can be seen in ܐܬܠܝܛܐ, 93b5 ἀθληταί (ARar صراع Lyons 134.18, in II 5 [Glossary] the conjecture صارع) and ܡܚܒܪ ܐܓܘܢܐ, 93b6 ἀγωνίζεσθαι (ARar يصطرعو Lyons 134.19). On the rare ܗܘܪܕܐ, 'general', see above on 5.4.11, and on the combination ܗܘܪܕܐ ܐܘܛܘܩܪܐܛܘܪ ('general [as] *autocrat*') cf. AR 93b21 στρατηγὸς αὐτοκράτωρ (the passage is not present in IS). The ܣܥܠܬܐ of the manuscripts (Apparatus, n. 4; 'and you take me up on your back while I hold a ܣܥܠܬܐ') is incomprehensible. The correction offered in the Text is ܫܒܛܐ, 'rod', on the basis of AR 93b17 ἀκόντια, 'javelins', and ARar and IS قضيب, 'rod'.

**6.2.4.** The change from AR 94a5-6 ('if one can see the likeness, which is easy from philosophy', and possibly also 94a8-9, 'for the most part the future is similar to the past') to BH's 'if existent particulars ... flimsy disputations' depends on IS 169.9-10, 'As consideration of existent particulars is part of the foundations of philosophy, since experience (تجربة), as you know, is among the most important of its principles, how much more so (is it important) in flimsy discussion!' For the remainder, BH's account is a paraphrase of AR, adhering to it more closely than does IS. On the form ܗܦܩܠܘܣܐ (induction), cf. below on 6.5.4.

**6.3.** Paraphrase of AR 2.21, the maxim ('gnome', AR γνώμη, BH ܚܘܫܒ or ܪܢܝܐ, ARar غنومى or رأى and IS رأى).

**6.3.1.** BH's exposition diverges somewhat from AR 94a21-34 (the examples of 94b1-6 being omitted), but paraphrases fairly closely IS 170.9-16. The example, 'To teach a young person wisdom is superfluous ... because they would gain that from which they have no advantage', is taken from IS 170.12-14. AR 94a29-34 is rather different, as is also the damaged ARar (Lyons 137.9-14 and 340). The expression (in IS and BH) 'gnomic enthymeme' will be derived from the rendering of 94a26 ('enthymemes are the syllogism about such things') in (ARsyr and) ARar, 'enthymemes of this species are analogous to a syllogism' (Lyons 137.6-7).

**6.3.2.** AR's 'supplement' (ἐπίλογος) is تقديم كلام in ARar, in IS and BH simply كلام and ܡܡܠܠܐ ('discourse'). In IS the third and fourth species of maxim are linked to 'discourse which points to the aim, either resulting from it or producing it' (171.3-4). BH's differentiation of these two species (the pointer is not mentioned, the pointer is mentioned) may be his interpretation of (ARsyr and) ARar 94b20, 'the reason for what is said is finished' (Lyons 138.14 and 340, AR 'the reason for what is said is clear'). BH's distinction between an enthymeme and part of an enthymeme will be from (ARsyr and) ARar 94b17-19, 'Some are parts of enthymemes ... others enthymemes' (Lyons 138.11-14, AR, 'Some are part of an enthymeme ... others enthymematic').

**6.3.3.** BH's paraphrase is a blend of AR and IS. IS omits the allusion to 'dispute' (94b27 ἀμφισβητουμένων, BH ܚܪܝܢܐ) and does not name Stesichorus or the Locrians (he simply has 'someone who said'), but BH's 'poetic riddle and imaginative discourse' is taken from IS 173.2 رمز شعرى وكلام تخيل rather than ARar (and presumably ARsyr) 94b33-34 'laconic apothegms/كلمات and enigmas/ارماز' (Lyons 139.7-8). The reading 'that *I* may not be envied' for 'one ought not to be envied' at 94b30 (Lyons 139.3 and 341) appears in ARar (and presumably ARsyr); this is the reason for the form of the maxim in IS and BH, '*I* need not be educated'. '*Tettiges* (in Greek 'grasshoppers') or swallows chirp (نسيق) from the ground' will be the reading of ARsyr 95a2, ܛܛܝܓܝܣ being glossed ܨܨܪܝܬܐ. Both ARar and IS differ: ARar (Lyons 139.10 and 341) has 'swallows waddle on the ground'; IS 173.3 'you insolent annoy the swallows of the ground'. The concluding sentence freely adapts IS 173.3-4, 'By *swallows of the ground* he meant the week, the annoyed, and those who slander and howl when something is imposed upon them'.

**6.3.4.** Damage to ARar at this point obscures the sources of BH's paraphrase, but while the major part of the paragraph is closer to IS than to AR, the concluding example (absent from IS) is clearly taken from ARsyr. That a maxim may be universally true or mostly true corresponds to IS 173.10-12, but is also consistent with IR (Aouad II 232 and III 303-304); ARar is damaged, but the 'harshness and roughness' by which mostly true maxims effect persuasion can nevertheless be observed there (Lyons 139.18-140.2 and 341, IS 173.13 has for the last phrase 'dissimulation and compulsion'). Compare AR95a8-9, 'To speak universally of what is not universal is especially suitable in complaint and exaggeration'. IS substitutes for 95a13-17 (exhortation of the troops) an example of his own (173.15-174.1, the wrongfulness of متعة [temporary marriage] and unjust defamation of women; cf. Würsch 129-130). BH, however, follows ARsyr, but damage to ARar makes it impossible to say how closely. Like IS, IR offers his own examples here, thus also giving no assistance in the reconstruction of ARar (cf. Aouad, ibid.) However from what can be salvaged of ARar (see Lyons

140.6-9 and 341-342), common to BH/ARsyr and ARar against AR are 'seeks satisfaction for his city', 'conquers enemies', and 'killing the children of the enemy is not wrong'. 'Enualios is the bravest' must be derived from ARsyr at 95a15 (Greek 'Enualios ['The Warlike'] is impartial'), for ARar simply has 'and to people' (ولناس, cf. Lyons 342 ܐܢܘܐܠܝܘܣ to [انواليوس to] ولناس?).

**6.3.5.** Generally close to IS 174.1-13, which diverges quite markedly from AR 95a17-24. The first two sentences render IS 174.1-3, but for 'an Attic neighbour' (AR 95a18) IS 174.3 has 'dogs to cattle' (cf. Würsch 119-120). The proverb is lost in ARar on account of damage to the Paris *unicum*, and IR does not cite it. Evidently ARsyr took πάροικος not as 'neighbour' but as 'foreigner' (ܒܠܘܢܐ); BH 'Athenians are foreigners'. 'Cretans are liars' is from BH himself. This proverb (of Epimenides) was widely quoted in the ancient world; its appearance in the New Testamant (*Epistle to Titus* 1,12) guaranteed its long-term survival. The disappearance from IS and BH of AR's 'maxims *contrary* to popular wisdom' (95a19 παρὰ τὰ δεδημοσιευμένα) is due to the translation in (ARsyr and) ARar 'maxims (based) on what is known to all' (Lyons 140.11-12 and 342). The example, 'If I had known your custom ...', is BH's own, but the addition of 'blame, accusing, and releasing' to AR's 'praise' follows IS, as do the closing remarks on the calming of wrath and the wrath of a commander. The word in BH to an angry man, 'This is ... false', comes from (ARsyr and) ARar 95a23-24, 'as one says to an angry man, "This is false, as far as I know"' (Lyons 140.15-16 and 342, AR, 'if someone in anger were to say that it is false that one should know oneself').

**6.3.6** Closer to IS 174.13-175.7 than to AR 95a24-32. 'There are gnomic sayings which are ethical ...' renders IS 174.13-15 (AR 95a24-26, 'And character would be better ...', ARar, 'The ethical is what befits virtue ...' [Lyons 140.18 and 342]). AR 95a26-27, 'It is necessary for the *lexis* to make clear the purpose (*prohairesis*)', appears in ARar as, 'It is necessary that what comes from the enthymeme (عن الضمير) is clear in the language (Lyons 141.1). IS 174.16 has, 'The language should correspond to the essence (كنه) of what is in the enthymeme (لما في الضمير)', BH, 'The language (*lexis*) should make clear the exactitude of the enthymematic thought'. Probably, therefore, *enthymeme* as the translation of *prohairesis* here is due to ARsyr. The bracketed section is present in only one manuscript (manuscript l), and may therefore be an addition; however, it is roughly parallel to IS 175.2-3.

**6.3.7.** The bulk of the paragraph is close in substance to AR 95b1-12, though often closer in wording to IS 175.8-15. AR 95b13-16 ('for it makes speech ethical; speeches have character, inasmuch as choice is clear, and all maxims accomplish this because he who speaks a maxim makes a universal declaration [ἀποφαίνεσθαι] about preferences') is mutilated in ARar (Lyons 142.1-3) and appears in IS (175.16) as, 'it makes speech ethical, that is, wise in ethics'. The 'elevation' of discourse and the comparison of a speaker to a legislator follow IS (175.16-17).

**6.4.** Paraphrase of AR 2.22, on enthymemes. IS 3.7 covers AR 2.22-23, BH 6.4-5. The title of BH 6.4, 'On the difference between rhetorical and dialectical premisses', is taken from the title of IS 3.7 (176.2).

**6.4.1.** BH's exposition of the difference between rhetorical and dialectical premisses paraphrases IS 176.4-11 more closely than AR 95b22-26. His unusual ܗܘܦܘܬܩܝܬܐ (conditions?) appears to be his rendering of IS 176.9 شرط (conditions?). ܝܬܝܪ ܡܒܣܡ ('creates greater enjoyment') may have been based on the rendering in ARsyr of 95b29 μουσικωτέρος ('more inspired by the Muses'), ARar افكه ('merrier', Lyons 142.18 and 20 and 343). IS does not mention 'the poets' (AR 95b28), and the formulation concerning the response of 'the masses' to a learned or unlearned man is BH's own.

**6.4.2.** The remarks at the outset, as also the closing sentence, are closer to IS 177.8-11, 178.1-7 and 178.12-13 than to AR 95b29-96a7 and 21-23. The examples, however, are drawn from AR, as IS ignores all those in AR and for praise or blame offers one of his own (Hassan ibn Thabit first ascertained the relevant facts from Abu Bakr al-Siddiq before composing a poem on the misdeeds of Abu Sufyan, cf. Würsch 129). Most of the Greek proper names are rendered fairly accurately in (ARsyr and) BH, but 96a19-20 'Aeginetans and Potidaeans' appears in BH as 'Aphenians (ܐܦܝܢܝܐ) and Poritaeans (BH ܦܘܪܝܛܝܐ < ARsyr ܦܘܕܝܛܝܐ < ܦܘܛܝܕܝܐ ?)', and in ARar (Lyons 144.8) as 'Athenians (الأثينيين < ܐܬܝܢܝܐ < ܐܦܝܢܝܐ ?) and Foditaeans (الفوديطيين < ܦܘܕܝܛܝܐ ?). Syriac grammar does not distinguish between the third masculine singular and first person plural of the verb in the imperfect tense. In agreement with AR, ARar reads 'how can we ... we ...' etc, but IS 178.9-10 has 'he' (namely, 'the orator'). BH can be read either way. AR 96a23-33 is passed over.

**6.4.3.** As in the previous section, in making the general point BH adheres closely to IS (178.14-179.3), but takes the subsequent examples from AR (96b12-19, and 21-22). 'As in dialectic, so also here it is right to provide *topoi* for every establishment (in the manuscripts 'purpose') or refutation' is taken from IS 178.14-15; contrast AR 96a33-96b6, 'Since everyone seems to make demonstations this way ... and since it is impossible through speech to make demonstations in another way, it is evidently necessary, as in the *Topics*, to have selected statements ...'). '(Achilles) with his own wealth' is apparently the rendering in ARar (بماله Lyons 145.18) of ARsyr/BH ܒܚܝܠܗ; 'with his own army' is also a possible rendering of the Syriac (Lyons 345 suggests 96b13 ἴλιον may have been read/corrupted ἴδιον - perhaps ARsyr ܒܕܝܠܗ than corrupted to ܒܚܝܠܗ?). The statement about 'Cynus' (ܩܘܩܢ, ARar قنوس, for Κύκνος/ν) may be a misrendering in ARsyr of 96b17-18 'and Cycnus, who prevented all from disembarking, being invulnerable'; ARar is damaged and cannot be construed (Lyons 146.2-3 and 345, and IR, like IS, omits the examples), but 'his companions' (اصحابه, BH ܚܒܪ̈ܘܗܝ) is discernible.

**6.5.** Most of the twenty-eight *topoi* of AR 2.23 receive a mention in one way or another in BH 6.5.1-13, as also in IS 179.10-187.2, although quite frequently they have undergone a considerable reformulation. From the numerous examples from Greek history and literature cited by Aristotle in this chapter, only Thrasymachus (AR 00b19, BH 6.5.13) is mentioned by name in IS, although he does paraphrase the substance of a few others. A great many more, however, are cited in BH, along with the Greek proper names, a pattern already evident in 6.4.2-3. From 6.4.2 to 6.5.13, therefore, Bar Hebraeus' use of the Syriac text of Aristotle alongside the Arabic of Ibn Sina is particularly in evidence.

**6.5.1.** BH begins by closely paraphrasing IS 179.5-8 (demonstrative and refutative enthymemes, contrast AR 96b23-97a6). '(Advice or) *shaming*' is an attempt to render the puzzling ܚܘܝܢܐ ܕܙܢܐ (literally, 'demonstration that he committed whoredom'?), which appears to correspond to IS 179.7 'advice or منافرة ('avoiding'?); cf. AR 96b32 'honourable or shameful'. 'Species' as a synonym for *topos* in IS and BH comes from (ARsyr and) ARar of 96b28-30, 'We are now near to having a knowledge of each one of the useful and necessary species in which are the *topoi* (Lyons 146.13-15 and 345, contrast AR, 'The *topoi* about each of the species of the useful and necessary species [of rhetoric] are more or less known to us'). From the mention of the first *topos* ('opposites') BH follows the examples of ARsyr, most of which were omitted by IS. In the examples, the readings '*if* being temperate ...', 'war ... *at Mesene (Masini*?)', and Diomedon's statement on *youths* will all be from ARsyr and make their appearance in ARar (Lyons 147.6-7; 148.1 and 345-346; cf. AR 'being temperate ...', 'in the *Messeniacus* ... war ...', and Diomedon on *taxes*).

**6.5.2.** The paraphrase seems to link 97a29 ('but there may be in this *topos* fallacious reasoning') to 97b5 ἀλλὰ διαλαβόντα, the last presumably being interpreted in ARsyr not as 'dividing' but 'defining' (ܬܚܡ). However ARar is damaged here (and cannot be restored from IR), and there is no trace in it of διαλαβόντα (Lyons 148.12-15 and 346). BH's 'Alcmaeon said to Theodectes' appears in ARar (Lyons 148.10-11) as 'Theodectes said to Alcmaeon' (AR 97b3 'in the *Alcmaeon* of Theodectes'). The quotation itself is badly corrupted in (the damaged) ARar, but appears comparatively unscathed in (ARsyr and) BH, especially if τις ... βροτῶν, which can hardly be identified in ARar, manifests itself in ARsyr as ܐܢܫ ܒܪ̈ܡܝܘܬܐ ('one of the mortals'?), taking the strange ܒܪ̈ܡܝܘܬܐ as some compound of 'son' and 'mortals' ( read ܒܪ̈ ܡܝ̈ܘܬܐ?). The examples of Demosthenes and Thebes are as radically transformed in ARar (AR 97b7-11, ARar Lyons 148.15-20 and 346-347) as they are in BH, but differently. The disappearance of the name Nicanor is common to both, but the combination of the two examples is a feature of BH alone. In BH as in ARar (Lyons 149.11-13 and 347) σὸς μὲν οἰκτρός (97b18-19, 'pitiable is your ..') appears as a proper name ('Sosmenoiktros') and Οἰνεὺς (Oeneus) as 'Hunus' (AR 97b18-20), although the citation is differently construed. IS 179.12-180.4 deals with the issue of error quite differently; he mentions no Greek names and focuses on 'if it is just that the killer should be killed, it is just for me to kill him' (179.13). On the topic of 'the more and less', he merely mentions the species (نوع) and leaves it at that (180.4).

**6.5.3.** A much abbreviated paraphrase of AR 97b20-98a28. The examples of Theseus, Helen, Patroclus, Alexander, artists, and 'simple people', which in AR (97b20-27) belong to the *topos* of 'neither more nor less', are classed by BH as belonging to that of 'earlier persons' (AR 97b27 'looking at the time'). While that topic is indeed closely related to the 'more and less', its 'relocation' to head rather than follow these examples seems to be BH's doing. IS omits these examples and begins 'a very partial species "from earlier times"' (180.5) with, 'If you had done such and such, I must do the same'. In the examples themselves, many of the changes in BH over against AR are present in (ARsyr and) ARar, which reads: 'If Theseus did no wrong, neither did Alexander; had it not been for the action of Helen, daughter of Tyndareus, Alexander would not have acted; had it not been for the killing of Patroclus, Hector would not have been killed; had it not been for the mischief-making (?) of Alexander, there would not have been the story of Achilles; had artists not been fraudulent, neither would philosophers; ... and if it is proper that the crowds should care about your praise, so you should care about the praise of the Greeks' (Lyons 149.13-21 and 347-348). The section from AR 97b27 to 98a12 is omitted, but those examples (or those from 98a3 onwards) may be the examples to which BH refers when he says, 'In the same way our master adduced other examples for refutation ...' (cf. AR 98a12-15, ARar 'this method is one of those used for reproach ...', Lyons 150.17-20 and 348-349). BH no doubt speaks of 'from definition *based on opinion*' (AR 'from definition') because he read in IS (180.16-181.1) 'from induction from the definition, even if it is not a true definition, but based on opinion'. ARar omits 'or the work of a god' (AR 98a16, which, from the evidence of BH, will have been present in ARsyr), but the appearance of 'valour' (ܫܠܝܛܘܬܐ, AR 98b19-20 'something noble') is common to ARsyr/BH and ARar (شجاعة); cf. Lyons 150.21-151.3. As before, IS omits all the Greek references and only adds some generalised examples (such as 'if you had done such and such ...', as above) to the basic description of the *topoi*.

**6.5.4.** The *topos* of 'various meanings' (AR 98a28) is not mentioned by IS or BH. BH links *division* (98a29) and *induction* (98a32); 'men do wrong on account of three causes' is Aristotle's example of division, the others are of induction. IS designates the first species 'from division and refutation of various motives by argument or by capitulation' (181.4-5), the second 'from induction (اعتبار) and the citation of many examples from particulars' (181.5). The addition of 'examples from particulars' was doubtless suggested to IS by Aristotle's *Topics* 108b10-12 ('by induction of particulars on the basis of similarities we infer the universal'). From the same passage of the *Topics* BH may have drawn the mention of 'similarities' and the substitution of ܗܦܩܛܝܩܐ (ἐπακτικός, not attested in *ThesSyr* or *BrLex*) for the expected ܗܦܓܘܓܐ (AR 98a32 ἐπαγωγή, ARar الايفاغوغى اى الاعتبار). The only example adduced by IS is 'confirming the reliability of the person of compassion (الشفيق) in advising' (181.6). BH will therefore have taken this phrase from IS, although the rendering in ARsyr of 98a32 Πεπαρηθίας ('of Peparethus', read as συμπαθείας as suggested by Lyons 349?) will have been the source of his 'sharing of emotion', ARar الاشتراك فى الألم (Lyons 151.18). The paraphrase of AR 98b1-9 in BH is lacking in IS. 'Soothsayer ... to an orator' will be from the rendering of 98b1 Μαντίᾳ τῷ ῥήτορι ('Mantias the orator') in ARsyr as in ARar (تكهنت ... للريطورى Lyons 151.19-20 and 349) as 'foretelling to the orator', while 'Stilichon' (ܣܛܝܠܝܟܘܢ) will be from a misreading by BH or a scribe of ARsyr of 'Stilbon' (ܣܛܝܠܒܘܢ?, ARar سطيلبون). How closely or otherwise in other respects ARsyr accounts for the differences between BH's examples and those of the Greek is impossible to tell; ARar differs markedly from both of them (Lyons 151.19-152.6 and 349-350).

**6.5.5.** The remaining examples in Aristotle of induction, from Alcidamas' 'all honour the wise' (98b9) to the philosopher-rulers of Thebes (98b19) are considered by BH to belong to a species (*topos*) 'from the judgement and decree of the wise'. 'Judgements from similars' and 'judgements from opposites', Aristotle's *topos* 'judgement about (the same) or a similar or opposite' (98b19-20), are in BH two sub-species of 'judgement of the wise'. The examples are all derived from AR, IS giving none at all. Divergences from AR can mostly be accounted for from (ARsyr and) ARar (Lyons 152.6-153.8 and 350). This applies to the names Arcidamas (AR Alcidamas), Chimon (AR Chilon), and Areospagus (AR Areopagus), and also to 'and Masecus' ([ܘܠ]ܡܣܩܘܩܘܣ, AR 'Lampsacenes' Λαμψακηνόι, ARar ومساقيس); to 'Mixidemidelus (the final ܠܘܣ being an error for ܐܘܣ in BH, easily made in Jacobite script? ARar final ياوس) said to Autocles' (AR 'Autocles said to Mixidemides'); and to Sappho's 'the gods do not die' (AR 'otherwise they would die'). ARsyr evidently took 98b14 ἥκιστα (not covered in ARar) with Chilon (Chimon), 'although he was young'; contrast AR, 'the Lacedaemonians, least lovers of words ...'. 'If divine things are venerable, the right things of Areospagus (the Areopagus) are venerable' is obviously a paraphrase of AR 98b26-27, but ARar is damaged here and it is impossible to guess what might have stood in ARsyr. In BH's paraphrase, therefore, only the *reckoning* of Pythagoras and 'Masecus' *among the prophets* appears to have no basis whatsoever in what can plausibly be reconstructed of ARsyr from AR and ARar.

**6.5.6.** The first *topos* here is Aristotle's 'from the parts' (99a6-7), but ARar and presumably ARsyr omitted ἐκ τῶν μερῶν leaving only, 'Another species is as discussed in the *Topics*, namely, what kind of motion applies to the soul' (Lyons 153.19-20). From the allusion to 'the motion of the soul' IS evidently picked up the reference to *Topics* 111a33-b12 and formulated the *topos* as 'looking at the particulars of what is affirmed (المحمولات) and not discovering them in the subject' (181.9-10), and this will have been the source of BH's similar formulation. BH, however, may also have turned to the *Topics* passage, as evidenced by his use of 'refutation' (ܣܘܬܠܠ, ἀνασκευάζειν 111b22; cf. also ܡܬܩܛܪܓ 'affirmed', κατηγορεῖσθαι 111a33f.). 'Theodectes said to the Athenians, "If Socrates ..."' is neither AR ('from the *Socrates* of Theodectes') nor ARar ('in that saying of Socrates on Theodectes', Lyons 153.20-21 and 351); IS gives an example of his own, but takes (181.12) that concerning education from AR, and BH's wording in the latter case is closer to IS than to AR. 'Anareia (ܐܢܐܪܝܐ, for ܐܝܐܪܝܐ ?) the priestess' may be a transcription with gloss in ARsyr of 99a21 ἱέρεια (ARar simply ايارية Lyons 154.12 and 351). Neither IS (182.1-2) nor BH transpose the order of 'speak what is just and the gods will love you' and 'speak what is unjust and people will' of 99a23-25, as does ARar (Lyons 154.15-16 and 351). BH follows IS in replacing 'just' with 'truth' and 'unjust' with 'lies', but follows AR (also ARar and presumably ARsyr) with 'gods', IS 'God' (لله). BH comes back to this example in the next section.

**6.5.7.** 'To buy the land with its contents' is the rendering in (ARsyr? and) ARar (Lyons 154.16) of 99a25 'to buy the swamp with the salt'. BH's paraphrase is dependent upon IS (182.3-4, cf. Würsch 126), as is the following comment on the difference from the previous example, although BH expands on what is said by IS. AR 99a26-28, 'This βλαίωσις (retort to a dilemma) occurs when good and evil, each opposite the other, follow either of two opposites', appears in (ARsyr? and) ARar as: 'The former occurs when in one thing there are two opposites, good and evil; while the latter with opposites is when both things are in each' (Lyons 154.17-19 and 351-352). IS 182.4-5 paraphrases, 'This differs from the first one because one condition, which is only good, follows on two opposites (طرفين)'. The point of Aristotle's open/secret contrast, namely, to draw the other conclusion from what the opponent says (99a31), is lost in (ARsyr and) ARar (Lyons 154.23-155.1). The intrusion of 'pleasures' (AR 99a30 'privately', cf. Lyons 352 ἡδέα read for ἰδίᾳ?) will be from (ARsyr and) ARar ('pleasures are advantageous', Lyons 154.22-23). From this IS (182.7-9) elaborates a statement about a lover of pleasures wishing to remove ignominy from himself, and BH further embroiders it.

**6.5.8.** 'Another way is from what is imposed by measure and proportion' is the rendering in ARar (Lyons 155.3) of 99a32-33 'from consequences by analogy'. IS 182.13 expands this with 'the measure imposes a collation of opposites', from which evidently comes BH's 'proportion of opposites'. The 'affinity of outcome of (two apparent) opposites' is BH's paraphrase of AR 99b5, 'if the result is the same, the things from which it resulted are the same'. In ARar this appears as, 'from what necessarily follows, and that is if what follows from what follows is one (and the same) thing (Lyons 155.11-12 and 352), in IS 'this (one) origin necessitated by two ends' (183.3-4). IS deals freely with the examples, including eliminating the Greek names, and for most of them BH reverts to AR. From the evidence of ARar, we may assume that 'serving' and 'ridiculing' in the example of Iphicrates will be derived from ARsyr (cf. Lyons 155.4-5 and 352), as will 'your law' and the treatment of 'guests' in that of Strabax and Charidemus (Lyons 155.7-10 and 352). The rendering of Xenophanes' saying, however, differs from AR (99b6 'those who say that the gods are born') and is closer to IS (183.5 '[he who says] God is created [مكون]', cf. Würsch 130); and the example of knowledge and philosophy, while consistent with (ARsyr and) ARar in the elimination of Isocrates (Lyons 155.17-19 and 352), is closer to IS 183.7-8. That of earth and water, which IS omits, will have come from ARsyr, and BH's 'index of submission' (ܐܬܐ ܕܫܘܥܒܕܐ) will have been its rendering of 99b11 δουλεύειν 'to be a slave'. This last phrase appears in ARar as السبي الاذعان; the first word is uncertain (see Lyons 155.19 where الذل is given as an alternative), and from BH one may propose دليل or علامة.

**6.5.9.** BH's paraphrase of the topic and example 'not always choosing the same before and after but the reverse' is closer in substance to IS 183.15-184.2 ('another way is from two opposites at two times, in which the matter can be reversed'), whom he evidently followed here, than to AR 99b13-19. The next topic, 'the possible purpose for which something might exist is the cause for which it does exist' (99b19-20), of which the text in ARar is doubtful (cf. Lyons 156.10-11 and 353), is reformulated by IS (184.2-4) and following him BH into 'the opposite of the cause (if it exists) is necessarily the cause of the opposite effect'. The wording of this example in BH also follows IS (184.4-5), as does the introduction of a 'cause of two opposites' (IS 184.5-6). BH's paraphrase of the remaining examples is apparently quite free. That of 'Fortune' (ὁ δαίμων, ܓܕܐ, الجد) shows the influence of IS 184.6-7 in its second half, but is marginally closer to AR 99b22-23 in its first. The other two examples are lacking in IS. BH has embellished that of Meleager (AR 99b25-27, ARar Lyons 156.15-18). 'Ajax said to Theolectes' (clearly an error for Theodectes) preserves 'Ajax' (AR 99b28) as against ARar's 'Odysseus' (Lyons 156.18 and 353), but ARar ('Theodectes said in *Odysseus*') does not garble Aristotle's 'from the *Ajax* of Theodectes' as does BH's 'Ajax said to Theolectes'.

**6.5.10.** While BH is dependent on IS for his reformulation of the general staements about the *topoi*, the Greek examples come from AR and are omitted by IS. The opening sentences are derived from IS (184.9-10): 'These *topoi* are useful (*sic.*) in blame, infidelity (كفر الملة), advice, praise, and defence. Another way is specific to litigation and counsel'. BH observes AR 99b30 κοινός 'common' (against IS's 'useful'), and his modification of IS's enumeration includes dropping the Islamic كفر الملة ('infidelity'). His reformulation of the second *topos*, Aristotle's 'from the implausible ... (which) would not seem true unless they were facts or close to being facts' (00a5-9), into a 'refutation of the unacknowledged and unpersuasive' may owe something to IS 184.15-16 ('A way refutes [(يتبخ)] this in dealing with the well-known and the close to the well-known, like the reiterated') but also to the recasting in (ARsyr and) ARar: 'Another way is necessary if the statement is among those which are opined and thought. As for (what comes?) from those things which are not believed, it cannot be confirmed at all unless it happens close at hand' (Lyons 157.13-15 and 353). In ARar 'Androcles the Pitthean' has become 'Androcles son of Fithaos' (Lyons 157.18-20), while in BH one of his statements is attributed to 'Pitteus' ('the laws need a correcting law') and the other to 'Diocles' ('fish ...'). 'Diocles' (ܕܝܘܩܠܣ) could be an inner-Syriac error for 'Androcles' (ܐܢܕܪܘܩܠܣ, ARar is correct), but the possibility that it was the reading of ARsyr's Greek exemplar (but not ARar's), or alternatively came from a Greek scholion taken over by ARsyr and subsequently substituted for its text, is raised by the attribution of the statement to 'Diocles' (Διοκλῆς) in the commentary on Hermogenes by John the Deacon (ed. H. Rabe, 'Aus Rhetoren Handschriften: 5. Des Diakonen und Logotheten Johannes Kommentar zu Hermogenes Περὶ μεθόδου δεινότητος', *Rheinisches Museum* 63 (1908), 137; cf. K. Jander, *Oratorum et rhetorum graecorum fragmenta nuper reperta*, p. 40). Like BH, ARar (and presumably ARsyr) refers to fish *in the sea* (Lyons 157.20-21), although it has nothing about 'fish feeding on fish'.

**6.5.11.** BH's 'deficiences' (ܚܣܝܪܘܬܐ) is probably his paraphrase of IS 184.16, 'what is not attributed since it is (merely) imitated'; AR's 'looking at contradictions (ἀνομολογούμενα)' is paraphrased in AR, 'looking at what they agree upon in mention and praise' (Lyons 158.4-5 and 354). 'Time, fortune, or free will', and 'the virtues of the speaker himself' also come from IS (185.1-2). For the rest, however, BH in the main freely paraphrases AR, while IS omits or modifies the examples and mentions no Greek names. 'I have given freely to many of you' (AR 'I have ransomed many of you') is similar to ARar (Lyons 158.14-15 and 354) and will be from ARsyr. BH's *topos* 'making the dispute one of origin (ܫܘܪܝܐ, 'beginning')' will be his paraphrase of AR 00a29 'from the cause'. (ARsyr and) ARar 00a29-30 continues: 'that is that he says that it is because it is, and is not because it is not' (Lyons 159.3-4 and 355), which is BH's concluding sentence.

'Stilitiqean' (ܣܛܝܠܝܛܝܩܝܐ) is the transcription of 00a32 στηλίτης ,'inscribed on a pillar', but BH appears to have understood it as an ethnic designation. ARar also transcribed it, but continued, 'because it was written down at the head of the city on a cell there' (Lyons 159.7-8 and 355).

**6.5.12.** Both IS and BH freely modify the examples concerning Xenophanes and Medea, but unlike IS, BH keeps most of the Greek names. While Leucothea (00b6) appears once in ARar (Lyons 159.20 and 355) as 'the goddess' (الالهة), in IS (186.7 ميت [cf. BH ܡܝܬܗܘܢ, 'their dead one'] and الله) and BH the masculine prevails throughout. BH's 'refutation of him whose negligence produces failure' is his paraphrase of the topic 'to accuse or defend on the basis of mistakes' (00b8-9). 'In Carcinus' (taken as a place name? AR 009b9-10 'in the *Medea* of Carcinus') and the intrusive negative and gloss '*nor* my *husband* Jason' (AR 009b13 'not the children but Jason') will both have come from ARsyr (ARar Lyons 160.4, 7 and 355). IS proceeds independently and also omits the remark about the *Art* of Theodorus; cf. Würsch 112 on his rendering of the two examples.

**6.5.13.** 'Paronym, metaphor, or transference of name' (AR 'from the name') is based on ARsyr, to judge from ARar (Lyons 160.10-12 and 356): 'from the name itself - as Sophocles employs the name *iron* in truth - metaphor, or transference of name'. 'Paronym' (ܦܪܐܘܢܘܡܐ), rather than 'from the name itself', may be BH's own terminology, taken from *Topics* 109b5 and *Cat.* 1a12; cf. the citation from the *Cream* (*On Categories* 1.2) in *ThesSyr, Supplement* 272: ܦܪܐܘܢܘܡܐ ܐܘܟܝܬ ܕܡܢ ܫܡܐ. It may also have been influenced by IS 186.15-16, 'another way is by derivation of the name (اشتقاق الاسم)'. BH's 'heavenly (people) are truly gods' will also be from the ARsyr reflected in ARar 'as was customary to call people gods' (Lyons 160.12 and 356, cf. AR 00b18, 'as people are accustomed to speak in praises of the gods'). In IS (186.17) 'so and so' is an 'oppressor' and Thrasymachus a 'dialectician'. 'Prodicus' (ܦܪܘܕܝܩܘܣ) for 00b19 'Herodicus' (ܗܪܘܕܝܩܘܣ or ܗܐܪܘܕܝܩܘܣ) is probably an inner-Syriac corruption, as ARar has the correct name and, as in BH, speaks *to* Thrasymachus (Lyons 160.14 and 356). For Aristotle's 'law of Dracon ... of a *drakon*' and 'Aphrodite ... *aphrosyne*', IS 187.1-2 has 'the law of *mūsā* (Moses) is like a *mūsā* (razor)' and 'the religion of Muḥammad is *muḥammada* (praiseworthy)'. Any guess as to what may have been in BH's text of ARsyr at 00b22-24 is highly speculative, as his paraphrase differs so markedly both from the Greek ('As Hecuba in Euripedes says of Aphrodite, "And rightly the name of the goddess begins like *aphrosyne*"') and the Arabic ('And as Hecuba in Euripedes said to Aphrodite, "The name rightly has sole control over the goddess of confusion"', Lyons 160.18-161.1 and 356). With this caveat, however, the suggestion may be offered that ARsyr was based on a Greek text which compared both the *Aphrodision* (the temple of Aphrodite) and *aphrosyne* (folly) to Aphrodite, that these went into Syriac or reached BH as 'the temple of Aphrodite' and 'gladness and merrymaking', and that 'law' was added to Hecuba as a counterpart to 'the law of Dracon'. None of this, however, has any direct support from ARar, and it is impossible to say how much may have been due to BH himself, or indeed to translate the passage with any degree of certainty.

**6.5.14.** 'Refutation is more successful than *enthymeme* ... its beginning provides *confirmation* of its conclusion by proximity' may be a careless error or misunderstanding of IS (187.2-5), 'refutation is more successful than *confirmation* (تثبيت) ... its beginning points (ينبه) to its conclusion by proximity'. The section as a whole is based on IS 187.2-7 rather than AR 00b25-33, but the appearance of *enthymeme* here may be because BH had his eye on ARsyr. Cf. (ARsyr? and) ARar 00b25-26, 'refutations among (*mn*) enthymemes are more successful ...' (Lyons 161.4), misunderstood by BH as, 'refutations are more successful than (*mn*) enthymemes ...'? The example, 'If you had done such and such ...' is from IS (187.4), but it has its negative counterpart in 6.5.3.

**6.6.** Paraphrase of AR 2.24, fallacious enthymemes, IS 3.8 (187.11-191.1). The title is from IS (187.9). The terminology 'slanted' (ܡܨܠܝܐ, محرف) comes from (ARsyr? and) ARar at 01a3-5: 'it is not this that is inclined (and) slanted (المنحرف), for the inclined (and) slanted must be in the enthymemes' (Lyons 162.1-2 and 357, AR 'therefore neither this nor that, necessarily therefore this or that, and in the case of enthymemes ...'). Lyons suggests that the double τὸ καὶ τό of 01a4 was misread/misunderstood as κάμπτον/καμπτόμενον (bent, bending). BH uses the same term again in 7.3.3, but in a different context.

**6.6.1.** Short paraphrase of AR 00b34-01b9, following the general line of IS 187.11-188.16 but drawing some particulars from ARsyr (such as the mention of Pindar and Eudythemus [from Euthydemus, omitting 01a27-28 'the trireme in the Piraeus'] and 'the dog of Orion'). The limitation of 'verbally' to homonymy and its separation from 'form' (contrast in AR the apparent enthymeme παρὰ τὴν λέξιν [verbal] is either παρὰ τὸ σχῆμα τῆς λέξεως [form of the expression]or παρὰ τὴν ὁμωνυμίαν [homonymy]) comes from IS 187.12-13 (some by لفظ [verbal] such as لفظ مشترك [mixed expression] and some by شكل [form]). The refashioning at the end of this section of 'exaggeration which occurs when one amplifies the action without demonstrating it was performed ...' (AR 01b3-9) depends upon IS 188.10-13, which in turn depends upon an intrusive negative in (ARsyr? and) ARar at 01b6 ('there is *no* reason', Lyons 163.21 and 358, IS 188.10-11 'there is *no* proof to show that he did not do it'). The *topos* is introduced in (ARsyr? and) ARar as, 'It is difficult to know whether that took place' (Lyons 163.18 and 358, cf. AR 01b3-4, 'constructing or demolishing by exaggeration').

**6.6.2.** The references to the Second and Third Figures are taken from IS, but otherwise IS proceeds differently, omitting the examples (but introducing one of his own from Persian history, cf. Würsch 120), while BH reverts to AR. The surprising 'regulations' (ܬܘܩܢ̈ܐ) for AR 01b11 ἔρωτες ('lovers) and 'regulation' (presumably) for ἔρως arises from BH's reading of ܐܪܘܣ and ܐܪ̈ܘܛܠܗܘܣ as the Syriac transliteration of ὅρος. The cause of the misunderstanding can be illustrated from Antony of Tagrit's discussion of foreign words derived from Greek translations (*Rhetoric* Book 1, chapter 26 [MS Harvard, Houghton Syr. 25, fol. 48r]) where his first mention of ܐܘܪܘܣ is rendered ܚܘܒܐ ('love') and his second ܬܘܩܢܐ ('regulation'). BH presumably thought that 'regulations' was more likely to be the meaning than 'love'. ܐܪ̈ܓܠܐ ('mice') is rare in Syriac, but corresponds to 01b16 μῦς ('mice') and ARar (lost by damage to the Paris codex, but preserved in IR, Aouad II 255) جرذان ('rats').

**6.6.3.** A blending of ARsyr 01b20-34 and IS 189.11-190.5. 'Acceptance of resemblances' is from IS (189.12 اعتبار المعادلة); ARar renders the underlying AR 01b20 τὸ παρὰ τὸ ἑπόμενον, 'the (fallacious) consequence', by الاعتزال او المباينة, 'isolation or separation' (Lyons 164.16 and 358). (ARsyr and) ARar speak only of 'Alexander' (not *The Alexander*) and expand 'Ida' to 'Mount Ida' (Lyons 164.17-18 and 359), and take 01b24 καλλωπιστής ('dressed up') as a proper name (Lyons 165.1 قالوافسطى, BH ܩܐܠܦܘܣ, did ARsyr read καλλωπις τῆς and ARar καλλωπιστής?). IS names 'Alexander', but not 'Qalufisti' (cf. Würsch 112), Demades, or Demosthenes. '*Eat* in temples' (AR '*sing*') will be from ARsyr having read 01b25 ᾄδουσι as ἔδουσι (ARar Lyons 165.3 and 359), while ARar's 'palaces' (قصور, IS رباطات, 'hospices') will have come from the ambiguous Syriac ܗܝܟ̈ܠܐ ('temples' or 'palaces', cf. Lyons ibid.). BH's 'eating and drinking' following his 'eat and dance' will no doubt be an oversight, while ܐܡܪ ܕܡܐܕܝܣ ܦܘܠܝܛܝܩܐ means either 'Demades the politician said' through misunderstanding of πολιτεία, or 'Demades said (about) the policy'; cf. ARar 'Demades said that the policy (تدبير) of Demosthenes ...', Lyons 165.11, and IS 190.5 'If the sinister so-and-so had not come, so-and-so would not have died'.

**6.6.4.** Selective paraphrase of AR 01b34-02a29, omitting in particular the section 02a9-16. The selection is similar, but not identical, to IS 190.5-191.1, and BH takes individual particulars both from ARsyr and IS. His 'non-limitation' (ܠܐ ܡܬܚܡܢܘܬܐ) appears to be his adaptation of IS's 'rejection of conditions' (اطراح الشرائط), since ARar (and presumably ARsyr) render 01b34 'the omission of when and how' quite literally (Lyons 165.13). IS omits the example of Alexander and Helen, in which the surprising '*his* father ... for *him*' (AR 01b36 'the father ... for *her*') will be from ARsyr, as in ARar (Lyons 165.14 and 359). The example of the beating of an offensive sick man is taken from IS 190.12-191.1 (cf. AR 02a18-24, 'If a weak man were charged with assault ... to make the weaker seem the better cause'), but IS omits the references to the *Art* of Corax and the ἐπάγγελμα (BH from ARsyr ܡܘܠܟܢܐ, ARar سنة) of Protagoras (AR 02a17 and 25).

**6.7.** Paraphrase of AR 2.25-26, refutation and a note on amplification and diminution, corresponding to IS 3.8 (191.2-193.16). *Enstasis* ('bringing an objection') as the heading of this section will have been taken from the last phrase of the title of IS 3.8 (which covers BH 6.6-7) at 187.10 (وفى اصناف المقاومات, 'and on the types of objections'). BH will, however, have known the term *enstasis* (ἔνστασις, ܐܢܣܛܣܝܣ) only from ARsyr (ARar uses مقاومة).

**6.7.1.** Paraphrase of AR 02a30-b12, omitting 02a37-b4, making use of IS 191.2-16, and also adding some variations of his own. The wording of the four sorts of objections uses (with adaptations) the expansion in IS 191.10-13 of AR 02a36-37 ('from itself, or from the similar, or from the opposite, or from the judgements'), but IS omits the examples illustrating similar and contrary premisses. BH's adaptation of the former ('many of those who suffer nothing but evil love', cf. AR 02b8 'those who have been well treated do not always love') is his own, while that of the latter ('excited evil men also do well to their friends') is more closely tied to (ARsyr and) ARar 02b6 'but the evil man is not the one who acts badly towards his friends' (Lyons 167.14 and 360). IS gives his own examples about drunkenness, while BH's paraphrase of that concerning Pittacus (AR 02b11-12) depends on the reformulation in (ARsyr and) ARar, 'If Pittacus had held this view, he would not in his law (سنته, cf. IS 191.13 اقاويل الشرائع والحكام, AR ἐνομοθέτησεν) have imposed heavy fines on drunkards when they committed that offence with his son' (Lyons 167.21-23 and 360, with confirmation of his conjecture [n.8] بابنه).

**6.7.2.** Paraphrase of AR 02b12-03a2, but mostly following IS 191.17-192.17, in the first part especially with very similar wording. The four-membered sequence (AR 02b14) εἰκὸς παράδειγμα τεκμήριον σημεῖον ('probability, paradigm, *tekmerion*, *semeion*) appears in ARar (Lyons 167.24-25) واجب برهان علامة رسم ('obligatory, paradigm, *'alāma, rasm*') but in IS (191.17-192.3) واجبات برهانات دليل رسوم وعلامة ('obligatories, paradigms, *dalîl*, *rusûm* or *'alâma*'). BH's ܙܕܩܘ̈ܬܐ ܡܬܚܘܝܢܘ̈ܬܐ ܫܘܘܕܥ̈ܐ ܪܘܫܡܐ ܘܐܬܐ follows IS. 'Obligatory' (واجب, ܙܕܩܘܬܐ) is the rendering of 'probability' (εἰκός); on 'sign' and 'index', see above on 1.7.2 and Glossary s.v. ܫܘܘܕܥܐ and ܐܬܐ. Towards the end of the paragraph BH uses IS more freely and also reverts for a detail or two to ARsyr. The translation of ܦܪܘܠܘܓܝܙܬܝܢܐ (from παραλογίθηναι?), rendered here 'falsely inferred', is uncertain. ARar translates 02b26 παραλογισμός and 02b31 παραλογιζόμενος ('fallacy', 'reasoning falsely') by تقديم الكلام ('preceding the *logos*', Lyons 168.14 and 21 and 361), thus taking Greek *para-* or Syriac ܦܪܘ as *pro-*. The rendering in 7.8.4 of 14a6 παραλογισμός by ܦܪܘܠܘܓܝܣܡܘܣ, 'prologue', might be considered an argument in favour of this interpretation here, but a convincing translation of BH along these lines can hardly be made: '... it has been preceded by a law'? Judgement 'by *fine* understanding (ܒܬܪܥܝܬܐ ܫܦܝܪܬܐ)' follows AR 02b33-34 γνώμῃ τῇ ἀρίστῃ (ARar Lyons 169.1 بحسن النية) rather than IS 192.14 بحكم العقل ('by judgement of the intellect').

**6.7.3.** Paraphrase of AR 03a2-33, in the first part especially adhering more closely to IS 192.18-193.16. On the refutation of frequent paradigms, the ܐܘ ('either') of BH ('either that it is not similar to the present point') seems to indicate that the author himself or an (early) copyist has omitted by oversight a passage giving the remainder of AR 03a9-10 ('either that the present case is not similar or not in the same way or has some difference'); here IS 193.1-3 paraphrases more freely. 'Amplification and diminution are not among the elements of an enthymeme establishing the rhetorical species' depends on the omission of 'to amplify and diminish' at 03a20 in (ARsyr and) ARar, '... the element or *topos* in which fall many enthymemes for establishing that this thing is great or small' (Lyons 170.2-3 and 362). BH, however, is directly dependent on IS 193.10-11, 'Amplification and diminution are not elements of the enthymeme by which one achieves success in disputes, deliberations, and (epideictic) demonstrations, but are among its addenda'.

## CHAPTER SEVEN

The commentary on Aristotle Book 3, Ibn Sina Chapter 4, on style and arrangement (λέξις and τάξις). In BH and presumably ARsyr λέξις is usually rendered by the singular or plural of ܡܠܬܐ ܡ̈ܠܐ, 'word(s)', sometimes by ܠܟܣܝܣ; ARar uses لفظ or مقالة. While BH divides this chapter into ten sections, IS only has five.

**7.1.** On 'delivery' (ܡܣܒ ܒܐ̈ܦܐ), AR 3.1, but also including the introductory remarks in 3.2 (04b1-8) on the virtue of style. IS's first section includes BH's first three.

**7.1.1.** BH interweaves AR 03b6-32 and IS 197.3-199.2, abbreviating and cutting out much from both of them. I take BH to have understood ܦܪ̈ܓܡܐܛܘܬܐ from ARsyr (03b6 πραγματευθῆναι) as 'treatise' (πραγματεία); ARar (cf. Lyons 171.2 and 363) took it in the sense of 'the art'. ܡܣܒ ܒܐ̈ܦܐ, 'taking faces', renders ὑπόκρισις; I have consistently translated it here by 'delivery', rather than oscillating between 'delivery' and 'acting', ܢܣܒ ܒܐ̈ܦܐ by 'declaim'. The introduction to the subject of delivery by the remark about the 'other way' is derived from IS (197.5-7), who writes of the 'modes' (هيئات) of speakers, BH's 'manner and bearing' (ܐܣܟܡܗ ... ܘܕܘܒܪܗ) of a speaker. The mention of 'image-evocation' in this section (cf. AR 04a11 φαντασία) also follows IS (197.9-10); in the Syriac and Arabic tradition of the *Poetics* 'image-evocation' is of course the aim of poetry (cf. above on 4.3.2 and 4.3.6). 'With *oxeia* or *areia*' (ܒܐܘܟܣܝܐ ܘܐܪܝܐ) may have stood in BH's copy of ARsyr, rendering 03b29 ὀξείᾳ καὶ βαρείᾳ ('with rising or falling accent'). We may suppose that a scribe of ARsyr (or BH himself) mistook ܘܒܐܪܝܐ 'or *bareia*' for 'or with *areia*' and omitted what he took as an unnecessary repetition of the preposition 'with' (ܒ). ARar has only the Arabic terms for 'sharp' and 'heavy' (الحادّة الثقيلة, Lyons 172.12). IS has similar terms (197.10) but transposes them; since IS's order is that in BH, it is more likely that BH translated the Syriac terms for 'heavy and sharp' from IS's Arabic than that they stood either in the text or in a scholion of ARsyr. BH's closing remarks on emotions (anger and fear) and manner of delivery are derived, with modifications, from IS 197.12-198.4.

**7.1.2.** The section as a whole is an abbreviated paraphrase of IS 199.2-200.12 rather than AR 03b32-04a18. An echo of ARsyr is present in BH's ܐܬܠ̈ܝܣܐ ('champions' or 'contests'). Presumably 03b32 ἆθλα was rendered ܐܬܠ̈ܝܣܐ (as if from ἆθλος, 'contest'?); Syriac ܐܬܠܝܣܐ can be taken as a variant of ܐܬܠܝܛܐ (ἀθλητής), and this sense of 'champion', 'contestant', appears in ARar (ذوو المنازعة, Lyons 172.14 and 363) and IS (منازعون, 199.2). BH seems to have taken it this way. There is also an echo of ARsyr in his 'declaiming poets' (AR 03b34-35 τῶν ποιητῶν οἱ ὑποκριταί connected, as in ARar, to give ܦܘܐ̈ܛܐ ܢܩܫ̈ܐ ܕܩܪ̈ܝܐ, ARar الأخذ بالوجوه من الفيوئطيّين (Lyons 172.16-17 and 363), IS 199.3 المنازعين من الشعراء), and no doubt in his use of ܐܓܘܢܐ (AR 03b32 and 34 ἀγῶνες). The statement that 'one (capable of) declaiming may *scorn* (ܡܒܣܪ) ...' is rather strange; probably BH misread يبسر ('will frown') in IS 200.11, 'one capable of declamation will dare (يجسر) to do what the naive person will not dare to do'. The structure and tenor of BH's paragraph is otherwise close to that of IS, although shorter. It is, for example, from IS, who frequently eliminates Greek proper names, that BH takes the mention of 'the dialectical rhetor Thrasymachus'.

**7.1.3.** Paraphrase of IS 200.12-201.5 rather than AR 04a18-26. 'Rhetorical letters which are written' is from IS 200.12 الرسائل الخطبية المكتوبة; ARar of 04a18 οἱ γραφόμενοι λόγοι ('written speeches') is الكلام الذى يكتب ('speech which is written', Lyons 173.18). Similarly the substitution of 'image-evocation' for 'imitation' in the paraphrase of 04a20-21 ('the poets were naturally the first to set in motion, for words are imitations') derives from IS, making use of the other prong of the Arabic (or Syro-Arabic) theory of poetics. From IS also (201.3) comes the reference to the rhetorical arts of 'civic government' and narrative. On the other hand 'rhapsody (and) hypocrity' comes from AR 04a23, and the example of Gorgias from 04a26. That a poet like Gorgias 'gains special glory and is admired' will be from

(ARsyr and) ARar 04a26-27, 'The majority of the uneducated think that they achieve their aim when they use this type of speech, ornamented and adorned' (Lyons 174.6-8 and 365). BH's references to the beautifying (ܩܘܣܡܘܣ) of words and the imitation (ܕܡܝܐ) of diverse modes (ܙܢܝܐ) have no counterpart in IS and may have been taken from this passage of ARsyr or from 04a34-36 ('... with which they had at first ornamented their diction, as the writers of hexameter poetry still do. As a result it is absurd to imitate ...').

**7.1.4.** The thrust of AR04a27-39, namely the movement from an ornamental to a more conversational style even on the part of the poets, is lost in IS and BH, whose exposition here is effectively a paraphrase of IS. Instead, they differentiate between different styles of poetry for different situations (although only BH mentions tragedies, IS speaking of 'grandeur', تفخيم). The cause will have been the garbling of 04a28-29 ('The *lexis* of prose differs from that of poetry. This is clear from what has happened') in (ARsyr and) ARar, 'This is not permissible except for other kinds of speech apart from poetry, I mean that a description should be given in whatever words occur' (Lyons 174.8-10 and 365). Only BH mentions 'hexameters' here (AR 04a31 'iambic', ARar 'other metres', Lyons 174.12 and 365). 'Light and short (poetic discourses) which have thoughts miming cheerfulness' renders a similar phrase in IS 202.12-13. Neither IS nor BH break the sequence of thought at the end of AR 3.1. The addition of 'image-evocation' (ܡܚܝܠܢܘܬܐ, تخييل) to 'signifying' (ܡܫܘܕܥܢܘܬܐ, دلالة) in the paraphrase of AR 04b2-3 ('speech is a kind of sign, so if it does not make clear, it will not perform its function') comes from IS (202.9-13), as does the mention of the popular (ܥܡܡܝܐ, عامى) character of an intermediate *poetic* style (IS 202.13-17). The rendering of ταπεινή ('mean' of style) by 'abject' (ܡܣܝܪܐ) accords with (ARsyr and) ARar (حقير).

**7.2.** Commentary on AR 3.2, metaphor (in BH ܫܐܝܠܘܬܐ 'metaphor' and ܡܫܬܚܠܦܢܘܬܐ 'transference') and the virtues of a good prose style. In most of this section, however, as in the previous one, BH adheres more closely to IS, whose paraphrase often differs quite markedly from AR.

**7.2.1.** The mention of 'nobleman', 'villager', and 'citizen' is unique to BH, but otherwise the paragraph may be taken as an abbreviated paraphrase of IS (203.1-10), markedly divergent in places from AR 04b8-18. IS of course depends on ARar, which, in 04b13-20 (and similarly in ARsyr?) is quite corrupt (cf. Lyons 175-176 and 366). This corruption (Lyons 175.15-16 and 366) lies at the basis of IS's (203.7-8) and BH's transformation of Aristotle's remarks about the inappropriate use of fine language by a young man (04b15) into the inappropriate address to a young man 'Hey kid' (BH ܛܠܝܘܣܐ, ARar غليم). ܬܘܪܓܡܐ ܦܫܝܛܐ, 'prosaic discourses', presumably stood in ARsyr for 04b17 ψιλοὶ λόγοι, and ARsyr can also be glimpsed in BH's ܐܟܣܢܝܐ, singular and plural, rendering 04b9 and 11 ξένοι and ξένη,

ARar and IS using the forms of root غرب.

**7.2.2.** Paraphrase of IS 203.10-204.6, again quite remote from the text of AR (04b18-26). The opening statement (derived from IS 203.10-11) depends on an intrusive negative in ARar (and ARsyr?) at 04b18 ('it is necessary that they do *not* conceal', Lyons 175.18 and 366), and the reference to 'error' and 'seduction' (cf. IS 203.11-12) on the rendering in (ARsyr and) ARar, 'they put that in their speech like fraudulent cheating' (Lyons 176.1-2 and 366), for 04b20, 'for men become resentful at someone plotting against them'. The comparison of the seasoning of *food* and drink (cf. 04b21 'mixed wines'), and the action of Theodorus (IS 'Idrus', but ARar 'Theodorus') in speaking in a manner different from his *locality* (IS بلد, BH ܐܬܪܐ) closely follow IS (203.12-16), as does the closing remark about rhetoric and poetry (IS 204.1-5). The latter two, however, have their roots in (ARsyr and) ARar, in the rendering of 04b23 ἀλλότριαι ([the voice of] 'the others') by غريب ('foreigner', Lyons 176.5) and the addition of يخيل ('causes to imagine') to κλέπτεται ('it is concealed') at 04b24 ('deceives and causes to imagine', Lyons 176.6 and 366). Because BH abbreviates IS, it is not clear in BH, as it is in IS, that the 'theft' to which they refer is the poet's 'theft' from the orator of 'true and not image-evoking' words, which the poet then puts into metrical form, attempting thereby to make the listener think that he is writing poetry. The phrase 'departing from the customary *dialektos* (ܕܝܐܠܩܛܘܣ), i.e. denotation' will have been taken from ARsyr of 04b24 ἐκ τῆς εἰωθυίας διαλέκτου; ARar has من الكلام الجارى المتعود (Lyons 176.6), IS عن العادة (203.16).

**7.2.3.** Paraphrase of IS 204.7-11 and 204.16-205.5, again radically different from AR (04b26-05a8). From (ARsyr and) ARar come the readings 'to cause errors or conceal' (Lyons 176.18 and 367) for 04b36 λανθάνειν ('to escape notice', cf. above on 04b18), and 'metrical speech is amongst the petty advantages' (Lyons 177.8-9 and 367) for 04a7 'since speech (λόγος) has fewer resources than metres'. These readings lie behind BH's mention of 'misleading and deception' (from IS 204.17-18), and the 'little help' of metre and poetic words in rhetoric (from IS 205.3-5). IS omits the example of synonymity ('go' and 'walk', AR 05a1), and ARsyr is glimpsed in BH's ܠܐܣܟܡܐ ܒܪܝܬܐ, 'foreign style' (AR 04b33 λέξις, 36 ξενικόν); ARar has كلام and غريب (Lyons 176.13, 17-18), IS 'foreign languages' (204.9 اللغات الغريبة).

**7.2.4.** The paraphrase is close to that of IS (205.6-206.3). The opening statement that transference and metaphor (ܡܫܚܠܦܘܬܐ and ܫܐܝܠܘܬܐ ) may occur with a well known (ܝܕܝܥܐ), foreign (ܒܪܝܬܐ), or comely word is taken from IS 205.6-7, 'Metaphor (استعارة) and transference (تغيير) may occur with a well known (مشهور) word used with a different meaning, or with a foreign word, or with a word that is neither very well known, nor foreign, but pleasant'. *Epitheta* (ܐܦܝܬܗܛܐ) presumably stood in ARsyr for 05a10 ἐπιίθετα ('epithets') and appears to have been understood by BH as a (singular) synonym for 'metaphor'; ARar reads الموضوعات والتغييرات (Lyons 177.11-12) for AR τὰ ἐπίθετα καὶ τὰς μεταφοράς. ARar consistently uses تغيير for μεταφορά; it is hardly possible to say whether ARsyr used both ܫܘܚܠܦܬܐ and ܡܬܚܠܦܢܘܬܐ or whether the use of the two terms in BH is modelled on the two terms in IS. From ARsyr, however, will have come BH's ܥܬܝܪ̈, ܦܘܪܣܐ ('resourceful') for 05a26 πορισταί ('purveyors', ARar and similarly IS 206.3 محتالون, cf. Lyons 178.10 and Würsch 126) and ܠܦܛܝܐ ('robbers') for 05a25 λῃσταί.

**7.2.5.** IS 206.3-208.5 is a free paraphrase of AR 05a26-b19. BH's exposition is lightly adapted from IS 206.3-13; 207.3-9; 208.3-5. While the main themes of the paragraph (belittling and exaggeration with the examples, faults in syllables, expressions, and particles, 'good manners' [أدب, BH ܚܣܝܪܐ 'expert'] in rhetoric, riddles and silence, and the summary) are all taken principally from IS, from ARsyr BH will have drawn the terms ܟܘܢܝܐ 'appellation' (cf. ARar ذو اسم [Lyons 179.6], AR05b3 πρόσθεσίς ('application')/πρόθεσίς? [Lyons 368], IS 207.6 بدل?) and ܫܘܐ ܒܐܕܫܐ 'equivalent in species' (AR 05a36 ὁμοειδῆ, ARar منقارب فى الصورة [Lyons 179.2], IS 206.11 مناسبة). The unusual ܡܠܬ̈ܐ in the sense of 'expressions' ('a fault ... of syllables, expressions, and particles of connection or division') seems to be BH's rendering of IS 206.8 اعراب ('expression').

**7.2.6.** IS 208.5-209.9 is a free paraphrase of AR 05b19-33, omitting some material (such as Simonides and the mule race) and adding some of his own. All BH's material comes from IS, but he considerably abbreviates him. In (ARsyr? and) ARar 'rosy-fingered dawn (Eos)' has become simply 'rosy-fingered' (Lyons 180.2-3), which IS expands with 'the beloved' and the contrast of redness and 'an abominable worm' (IS 208.5-10, cf. Würsch 111). BH also takes the formulation of 'son of a mare' from IS (208.14-209.2, cf. Würsch ibid.), but omits IS's citation from Abu al-Tayyib (209.4, cf. Würsch 121).

**7.3.** Paraphrase of AR 3.3, 'frigidities', and AR 3.4, similes, the latter treated in 7.3.5 together with inappropriate metaphors, the fourth species of 'frigidity'. AR's ψυχρά (frigidities) are ܩܪ̈ܝܪܬܐ in BH and presumably ARsyr, باردة in ARar and IS.

**7.3.1.** Almost the entire passage is derived from IS 209.10-17, differing from and adding to AR 05b34-06a6. How much of the difference can be attributed to ARsyr is hard to tell, for ARar is damaged here (cf. Lyons 180.18-181.4 and 369), and IR (Aouad II 284) here as elsewhere eliminates the examples. However, BH takes 'Lycrophon' and 'Gorgias' from ARsyr, as IS does not mention them. 'Black-topped' (ܫܘܝܪܬ ܡܩܦܪܬܐ F) presumably stood in BH's copy of ARsyr, reflecting μελανοκορύφου at 05b36; IS 209.12 has 'great topped' (جماء الهامة) reflecting μεγαλοκορύφου. ARar is unreadable here (IR omits the examples), and BH also has the variant reading 'level-topped' (ܫܘܝܘܬ ܪܘܫܦܬܐ RVLl).

**7.3.2.** BH takes the opening sentence from IS 210.1-2 (cf. Würsch 120); his 'uncustomary expression' renders IS لغة غريبة, while ARar has 'languages and tongues' (الالس واللغات, Lyons 181.6, AR 06a7 γλῶτται, 'glosses', literally 'tongues'). In place of IS's Arabic example - 'Renown raised up in us so *irfana'a'ā* (?)' (cf. Würsch ibid.) - BH brings his own examples of elaborate expressions which Syrians have 'blown up' (ܐܪܒܝ). IS (and IR) omitted the examples of AR 06a7-10, much of which is largely 'unrecognizable' in ARar (Lyons 181.6-8 and 369). BH, however, seems to have done his best with what he found in ARsyr. With its 'Alcidamas' instead of 'Lycrophon' and its 'warlike' instead of 'monster' (ARar, 'Alcidamas with art called Xerxes in place of war "base of mind", and in place of [...] war Sciron'), it was evidently in some respects quite similar to ARar. The Syriac expressions 'torrents of the barren' and 'a city with a multitude of depths' are taken (or rather adapted) from Antony of Tagrit in his model for the vituperation of a city (*Rhetoric* Book 1, chapter 11, MS. Harvard Syriac 25, fol. 22r, transl. Eskenasy 174). What Antony wrote is that his vituperated city was 'barren, waterless, (with) a multitude of depths and a scarcity of thickets' (ܒܝܪܬܐ ܘܕܠܐ ܡܝ̈ܐ. ܣܓܝܐܘܬ ܬܗܘ̈ܡܐ ܘܒܨܝܪܘܬ ܚܠ̈ܬܐ). Cf. Bar Hebraeus, *Splendours* 30, 20 (Moberg, *Splendeurs*, p. 32, *Strahlen* I, p. 68): 'Antony the Rhetor calls the winds 'depths' and says in his vituperations 'a city (with) a multitude of depths and a scarcity of thickets'.

**7.3.3.** Paraphrase of AR 06a10-16, on 'epithets that are long or untimely or crowded', but much closer to IS 210.5-211.5, though briefer. '(Words) laid down (ܒܢ̈ܬ ܩ̈ܠܐ ܕܣܝ̈ܡܢ) ...' may be the translation in ARsyr of ἐπίθετα, cf. ARar موضوعات (Lyons 181.9), IS 210.5 الفاظ موضوعة. 'Masters of style' is probably BH's rendering of IS's 'experts' (211.5 بصير), 'Nebuchadnezzar' is BH's own example of an unduly long word (IS's is *al-'ashannaq* - from the root عشق?). IS 211.2-3 distinguishes between 'eloquence (بلاغة) aiming at admiration (تعجيب)' and 'rhetoric (خطابة) aiming at *pistis* (تصديق) for the populace'. BH's 'slanted temporal sign' (AR 06a11 ἄκαιρος, ARar لا زمنى) is his adaptation of IS 210.7-8 مبهمة لا يدل على زمانها, '(when a word) is ambiguous not indicating its time'. BH presumably adopted the term 'slanted' for IS's 'ambiguous' from 6.6 (on which see the Commentary above).

**7.3.4.** The paraphrase of AR 06a14-b4 is very free, as is that of IS (211.5-212.3). In effect, IS and BH begin by paraphrasing AR 06a14-17 - in (ARsyr and) ARar, 'And thus there is use of this (understood by IS and BH as *poetry,* from 06a14?) ... but it is necessary to aim for economy in that, for the use of what is connected and abundant is said in vain' (Lyons 181.14-17 and 370). In place of AR's examples from Alcidamas (06a18-32), IS produces his own from Arabic, while BH brings some from the biblical *Song of Songs*: 'a flock of shorn sheep ...' is from 4,2 and 6,6, 'twin fawns' from 4,5 and 7,3. However, 'among obscurities there is also that which initially was frigid but becoming familiar with time becomes sweet', BH takes from IS 211.11-12. The interpretation stems from (ARsyr and) ARar 06a34-35, 'when something is added or subtracted, with one who can see what was obscure becomes clear' (Lyons 182.14-15 and 371, AR, 'for when a speaker throws more words at someone who already understands, he destroys the clarity by the darkness'). The remainder of BH follows the outline of IS 211.13-212.3, with Syriac terminology derived from ARsyr (06a36-b3). The back reference to the 'terrible and fearful alien' is to 7.2.1; the same back reference is made by IS.

**7.3.5.** Paraphrase of AR 06b4-8 on frigidity in metaphor (omitting the examples of 06b8-18, but alluding to the 'rebuke' [in IS and BH 'derision'] of 06b18), then 06b20-26 on simile and the example of Achilles, 07a1-3 on Pericles and the Samians, and 07a14-17 on two species of the same genus. The selection is similar to that of IS, but IS does not mention the example of Pericles. The version of this example in BH, which reads 'who eat bread and do not understand its use', corresponds to (ARsyr and) ARar (Lyons 184.18 and 372, AR 'accept the morsel and wail'). IS 212.13-15 has the juxtaposition as in BH of Aphrodite (الزهرة) and Ares (المريخ), as against ARar (Lyons 185.12-14 and 373) Zeus and Ares and AR 07a16-17 Dionysus and Ares. However IS juxtaposes 'holder of a cup' with 'holder of a spear (حربة)'. ܣܟܪܐ 'shield' as in BH is presumably the reading of ARsyr for 07a16 ἀσπίδα. IR (Aouad II 286) also has مجن 'shield'; the *unicum* of ARar is damaged but appears to have been different, cf. Lyons 185.14 and n.13 and 373, and Aouad III 375.

**7.4.** On the 'beauty of rhetorical speech', paraphrasing AR 3.5, *to hellenizein* ('to speak good Greek'), for which ARar has تعلم اليونانية ('the study of Greek'). Neither IS nor BH mentions 'Greek'. 'Beauty' may be assumed to be BH's term, IS (213.2) has 'gratification by speech' (اشباع الكلام). IS's chapter 4.2 corresponds to BH 7.4-5, AR 3.5-8.

**7.4.1.** ARar (Lyons 185.16 and 173) and IS (213.5-6), as also IR (Aouad II 287-288) omit the mention of 'five' (ways of speaking good Greek), which will therefore have come from ARsyr. BH makes 'connection' the second (not, as in AR, the first) rule, following IS who writes that 'it is first necessary that style should be clear and correct without barbarism in language' (cf. ARar 07b18-19, 'that so-and-so has committed a barbarism', Lyons 188.2 and 374, AR, 'the lack of correspondence creates a solecism'). The '*logical* connecting response' (ܦܘܪܥܢ ܐܣܪܐ ܕܡܠܝܠܘܬܐ) will be close to ARsyr of 07a20-21 συνδέσμοις, ἄν ἄποδιδῷ τις ὡς πεφύκασι, as ARar has *logical* (Lyons 185.17 المنطقية, paraphrasing 'natural'?); IS differs here. The addition over above AR of 'mentioning the thing and showing the *cause*' is due to IS, and from IS BH has adapted the three examples of direct speech (IS 213.10-11, 213.14-214.1, and 214.3-7).

**7.4.2.** Having introduced in the previous paragraph the additional requirement that 'the form of the language should not be absurdly obscure, but polished and correct', BH has to conflate AR's second and third requirements (avoidance of circumlocutions and amphibolies) in order to keep to the number five. (ARsyr and) ARar, by contrast, faithfully represent AR's second and third requirements (07a30-32, ARar Lyons 186.11-14). The example of Empedocles follows the paraphrase of IS (214.11-12, cf. Würsch 113); the idea that 'Empedocles used a sphere to deceive' (contrast AR 07a35 ... 'Εμπεδοκλῆς· φενακίζει γὰρ τὸ κύκλῳ πολὺ ... , 'such as Empedocles. When there is much going around in a circle, it deceives ...') is already present in ARar (Lyons 186.18 and 373), and will be from ARsyr (κύκλῳ > ܒܐܣܦܝܪܐ > بالكرة). BH's 'when Croesus king of the Greeks crosses the river Alus' will be a conflation of ARsyr 07a38 'Croesus crosses the river Alus' (cf. ARar 'Croesus crossing the river Alras [Als?]', Lyons 186.21) and IS 214.14 'when the Greek king crosses the river'. That Cyrus met him and destroyed his kingdom comes from IS 214.15.

**7.4.3.** BH begins by lightly paraphrasing IS 215.5-7. Both of them omit AR's equivalent of 'neuter' (which does not exist in Syriac or Arabic grammar, cf. Würsch 113), but BH then inserts his own comment on 'the sorts of modulation which by grammarians are called accent signs'. These 'accent signs' (ܢܝ̈ܫܝ ܦܘܚ̈ܡܐ) are treated at length by Bar Hebraeus in his *Book of Splendours* 246, 15- 252, 15 (Moberg, *Splendeurs*, pp. 243-248, *Strahlen* II, pp. 108-116. ܦܣܘܩܐ (*pāsōqā*, usually ܦܘܣܘܩܐ), 'stop', one point on the line, indicates a level tone, 'the lower sign' (*tachtâyâ*), a point on the line with another below it, a falling tone. Bar Hebraeus outlines at the beginning of this section of his *Book of Splendours*, with reference to *John* 7, 42 and *1 Corinthians* 11, 13, how the meaning of a sentence depends on these accent signs, which can indicate a statement (*pāsōqā*) or its reverse (other signs). See the translation of this passage from the *Book of Splendours* and the discussion of the whole question in Segal, *The Diacritical Point and the Accents in Syriac*, 58-64, 73-74, 148-150. BH gets the name of Heraclitus from AR, as IS does not mention it. 'The Word which exists eternally *belongs to wise men* (ܠܚܟܝ̈ܡܐ ܡܫܬܟܚܐ ܗܘܐ)' will also be from ARsyr, as ARar reads the same (Lyons 187.22-23), although followed by IS 215.12-13, against AR 07b17 ('Of the Logos ... ignorant are men'). Interestingly, in mentioning 'Greek and Syriac' BH is only following IS, who writes about accentual signs: 'This (feature, i.e. of different 'weighting', تثقيل) occurs often in the Syriac and Greek languages (لغة)' (215.10-11). He also adds that explanatory signs are present in Arabic writing, but do not appear in the speech of the Arabs. BH's mention of Persians may have been prompted by, if not actually a misunderstanding of, IS 215.16 الاعجام (either 'providing with a diacritical point' or 'non-Arab, Persian').

**7.4.4.** Paraphrase of AR 07b19-31, but much closer to IS 216.1-217.6. The addition to AR (inserted at the point of 07b21), 'Indicate the feminine and masculine together by the masculine', is taken from IS 216.7 (cf. Würsch 121). The same rule is presented by Bar Hebraeus in the *Book of Splendours* 15, 15 - 16, 1 (Moberg, *Splendeurs*, pp. 17-18, *Strahlen* I, pp. 36-37). Older Syriac usage is more flexible, and allows the writer to adopt one or the other according to position or assumed importance (cf. Nöldeke, *Syriac Grammar*, par. 322); Bar Hebraeus (ibid.) was aware that combinations involving masculines had feminine verbs in *1 Corinthians* 13, 13 and *Proverbs* 30, 29f. but attributed this to an implied (feminine) ܨܒܘܬܐ ('thing'). In IS there is no break of section between AR 3.5 and 3.6, while BH has a break (7.4 to 7.5) not at the beginning of AR 3.6 (07b26), on expansiveness and conciseness, but at a few lines into it (07b31). (ARsyr and) ARar failed to produce a recognizable rendering of 07b26 'expansiveness of style (ὄγκος τῆς λέξεως)' (cf. Lyons 188.10-11 and 375: 'it is appropriate that this should be used in aiding the words, from what it is possible to seek help in respect of the words'). Hence IS and BH have 'persuasion' rather than 'expansiveness' as the reason for using a definition in preference to a name.

**7.5.** Paraphrase of AR 3.6-8 (with the exception of the beginning in 7.4.4 above), IS 4.2 (217.7-218.16), on metaphor, stylistic propriety, and prose rhythm. BH's title for this section is derived from IS's title for his section 4.2 (covering BH 7.4-5), which includes, in addition to 'gratification by speech' (cf. above on 7.4) also 'what is appropriate for poetry and inappropriate for rhetoric, and what is appropriate for both' (IS 213.3-4).

**7.5.1.** The paraphrase is fairly remote from AR 07b31-08a9, but close to IS 217.7-218.16, with omissions. ARsyr can be glimpsed in 07b35 διαπτυχαί ('folds'), BH ܕܝܐܦܛܘܟܐ *diaptuke*; cf. ARar (Lyons 188.21 and 375) 'and among them those of many gates and possessors of two faces (ذوات وجهين)' and IS 217.12-13 'many gates ... two faces (لها وجهان)'. ARsyr probably both transcribed διαπτυχαί and glossed it as 'two faces', and took πολύθυροι ('with many folds') in its literal sense of 'many gates'. IS 218.11 has 'poetry is lyreless melodies', but BH follows (ARsyr and) ARar 08a6-7 'lyreless and non-dancing melody' (Lyons 189.9 and 375, AR 'stringless and lyreless melody').

**7.5.2.** The exposition is loosely related to AR 08a10-25; 32-36, and much more closely to IS 219.1-10; 219.14-220.1; 220.7-10. BH omits much of what AR and IS have to say here about 'proportioned' ethos and pathos, and concentrates instead on the 'image-evocation' (ܡܗܠܠܐ, تخييل) brought in here by IS, in particular its tendency to mislead and the need for it (in rhetoric) to be proportioned. When he writes that 'by these (*sc.* representations?) the soul is led astray, induced to believe (ܡܗܝܡܢܘ), and inclined to be persuaded (ܡܬܛܦܣܘ)', he is not so much following AR 08a19-

23 ('... the mind of the listener draws a false conclusion concerning the truth of what the speaker says ...') as IS 219.14-15: 'If words are linked to these states [cf. ARar 08a21, Lyons 190.1 and 376: 'he who is in a state like this'], they lead souls astray, induce them to belief (جناب التصديق), and force them to persuasion (قناعة).

**7.5.3.** Essentially a paraphrase of IS 220.14-221.14, although not as remote from (ARsyr and) ARar as from AR 08a36-b20. Whereas in the previous paragraph BH maintained that (in rhetoric) image-evocation must be proportioned, here he asserts that 'an orator should not always use proportioned (words)', permitting the seduction of the listener. The assertion is taken from IS (221.3-8), not AR 08b4-5 ('Do not use analogous effects together, for thus the hearer is tricked'). The transformation will have been occasioned by the reading *persuasive* in (ARsyr and) ARar 08b10 (Lyons 191.13 and 377), against AR, 'if gentle things are said harshly and harsh things gently, the result is *unpersuasive*'. Paraphrasing AR 08b15, IS 221.10-11 substitutes 'shyness' (احتشام) and 'intimacy' (تقرب) for 'anger' and 'love'; however (ARsyr and) ARar (Lyons 191.18) and BH agree with AR. BH's remarks about Isocrates (IS 'Socrates' but ARar 'Isocrates') and the old poets depend primarily on IS 221.11-14, although the idea of a 'successful wish' originates in (ARsyr and) ARar 08b16 (Lyons 192.1 and 377, AR 'fame and name') and the appearance of 'prophets' stems from (ARsyr? and) ARar 08b14 'let him act and let him prophesy' (Lyons 191.17 and 377, AR 'causes them to be stirred'; IS's interpretation is cited by Würsch 121, who takes the appearance of 'prophets' here as a 'misreading' by IS, reading root *nby* for *nb'*). BH's comment that Isocrates said this in his *laments* (for the departed), ܣܘܦܝܬܗ (AR 08b15-16 'in the *Panegyricus*, at the end'), can be connected to some degree with (ARsyr and) ARar if the reading الاخريات (Lyons 191.18) is taken in the sense of 'the things of the hereafter'. IS 221.11 has simply 'what Socrates used to say'.

**7.5.4.** Paraphrase of AR 08b21-28, both IS and BH correctly conveying the central point that metrical speech is unpersuasive and obscures the content. BH's wording, while dependent in places on IS, is generally quite close to (ARsyr and) ARar. This applies to 'without metre and without number' (Lyons 192.7 and 378, AR 08b21-22 'neither metrical nor unrhythmical'), not only the 'shaping' (08b22) but also the 'admiration' evoked by metrical sppech (Lyons 192.9 and 378, AR 08b23 'diverts attention', 'image-evocation' being from IS), and the transformation of 08b24-25 to imply that the children preceding the herald somehow announce his message in advance ('as the children precede the herald when he declares something noble or ignoble, it is in a way as though the proclamation had been made by their companions', Lyons 192.10-12 and 378). The meaningless '*arhymic* [ܐܪܘܡܐܣ] or loose speech' will depend partly on ARsyr, inaccurately transcribing and then glossing 08b26 ἄρρυθμον ('unrhythmical'), ARar الاوراموں or 'weak' (سخيف, Lyons 192.13 and 378). The gloss reading 'loose' (ܡܫܝܣܐ), however, is likely to have been taken from IS 222.8 اللفظ المتخلخل, 'loose speech'.

**7.5.5.** The opening two sentences, while a paraphrase of AR 08b28-33, are based on IS 222.12-223.4, although here and in what follows IS makes some remarks about Arabic metres which are passed over by BH. '*Khusrawāniyyāt* in Persian' BH takes from IS 223.3-4: 'Prose can be made metrical by lengthened vowels (مدات), like *khusrawāniyyāt* (الخسروانيات), for they are made metrical by lengthened vowels adhering to them'. IS does not explain what he means by *khusrawāniyyāt*, but *khusrawāni* was the name of a melody composed at the court of the Sasanid Shah Khusraw II. Cf. thereto Würsch 121-122. BH's remark about the metres in his own letters is evidently in place of IS's discussion of Arabic metre. One of his own metrical letters is extant, that to the Catholicus Mar Denha, in heptasyllabic metre, ed. and tr. Chabot, 'Une lettre de Bar Hébréus au Catholicos Denha Ier'. ܪܛܢܐ ('accent') will have been the rendering in ARsyr of ῥυθμός ('rhythm') in this section (AR 08b29-09a23), ARar نبرة or نغمة. The normal meaning of the Syriac term is 'whisper' or 'utterance', but in addition it has according to Bar Hebraeus a technical meaning among East Syrian grammarians indicating an emphatic accent (written with a point above the line), the equivalent of West Syrian ܙܘܥܐ ('movement'). Cf. the *Book of Splendours* 258, 5 (Moberg, *Splendeurs*, p. 253, *Strahlen* II, 126); and in general Segal, *The Diacritical Point and the Accents in Syriac*, 84-85, 122-123. The brief remarks on iambic and trochaic metres and the paean are taken from ARsyr 08b33-09a2, 09a9-11 and IS 224.1-8. Neither IS nor BH could have had much understanding of Aristotle's meaning here; IS admits his ignorance and makes the Muslim confession 'God knows best' (224.2, cf. Würsch 115).

**7.5.6.** BH could make little of Aristotle's remarks on scansion in 09a13-21. However, that 'style should be well accented and not loose' corresponds to (ARsyr and) ARar 09a21-22 'well accented and not weak' (Lyons 194.11-12, AR 'well rhythmed and not unrhythmical'), with 'loose' for 'weak' as above in 7.5.4 (AR 08b26). IS also observed that 'the Greeks had things in this regard which did not reach us ... (and) which we do not find useful today' (224.12-13). He went on (225.1-11) to mention (and provide examples of) five kinds of 'balance' (معادلة) in Arabic which make prose close to poetry - section length, number of words, words and letters, length of syllables, and similarity of syllables - and the 'similarity of letters of the component (sections)' (225.10 تشابة حروف الاجزاء) which applies to rhymed prose (سجع). BH simplified this to 'concord of letters (ܐܬܘܬܐ ܐܫܬܘܝܘܬܐ) between rhetorical phrases and proportion (ܐܢܠܘܓܝܐ) in the length or brevity (of them)', although in practice the Syriac examples he provided obey most of IS's rules for Arabic. There is an elaborate account of Syriac assonant letters

(ܐܘܢ̈ܝܬܐ ܐܬܘ̈ܬܐ) in Jacob Bar Shakko's *Dialogues* (ed./tr. Martin, *De la métrique chez les Syriens,* 37-67). Most of this will be derived from Antony of Tagrit, the manuscripts of whose treatise break off shortly after the beginning of this section (ed./tr. Watt, *The Fifth Book of the Rhetoric of Antony of Tagrit,* 84-87/72-74). The model speeches of Antony in his *Rhetoric*, Book 1, provide many examples of his use of assonant phrases; an example is the set of phrases vituperating the city cited above in the Commentary on 7.3.2.

**7.6.** Paraphrase of AR 3.9, the periodic style, and IS 226.6-228.10. BH's title is drawn from that of IS 4.3 (226-236), which covers AR 3.9-12, BH 7.6-8.

**7.6.1.** IS 226.6-227.3 is a free and condensed paraphrase of AR 09a24-b12. With a few allusions to AR (notably the running out of breath, cf. 09a32-33), BH's exposition is based on that of IS, which disregards the continuous style and concentrates exclusively on the periodic. ܬܐܡ̈ܬܐ 'twins (like poetic speech)' may have been the rendering in ARsyr of 09a26 ἀντίστροφοι 'antistrophes (of the old poets)'; ARar has كرور 'recurrences', IS مصاريع 'hemistichs'. ܚܘܠܦ̈ܐ, 'returns' or 'connections', may have been the rendering in ARsyr of περίοδοι ('periods', literally 'circuits', 09a35); ARar has تعاطف(م), IS عطوف. In Syriac and Arabic, words from this root (ܚܠܦ, عطف) could have been taken in the 'circular' or the 'copulative' sense. That a 'return' has the same word (BH ܒܪܬ ܩܠܐ, ARar مقال, IS لفظ) at its beginning and end is from the reading of (ARsyr and) ARar (Lyons 195.6) at 09a35-36 (AR 'a period is an expression (*lexis*) having a beginning and end in itself'). 'Rhymed (ܕܡܝܐ, literally 'similar') speech' is BH's rendering of IS's مسجع. Although BH was following IS (226.7-11) in the wording about the complete sense of a couplet, the idea was familiar to him from Syriac verse (*madrashe*) and rhythmical prose (*memre*) works.

**7.6.2.** The paraphrase of AR 09b13-32 is guided for the most part by IS 227.3-228.1; neither BH nor IS makes any reference to 09b24-30 (on long periods and the parody by Democritus of Chios). ARsyr presumably translated κῶλον by ܗܕܡܐ, 'member' or 'joint'; ARar took it as the latter (وصل), as also, we may assume, did BH, taking his cue from IS (توصل). Neither BH nor IS knew that 'a colon is one of the two parts of a period' (AR 09b16), for ARar, and presumably ARsyr, garbled 09b16 ('the other part of this is not opened') and translated 09b13 (AR 'a period is either in cola or simple') as 'the joint must not be wide-open (منفرج)' (Lyons 195.16-19 and 380), from which comes BH's 'there should not be excessive looseness among the joints of the twins'; cf. IS 227.5-6 'the joint between the hemistichs should not be variable (متباين)'. The disappearance of the *image-evocation* is an expression from IS (227.4), but the *haven* will be from ARsyr, misconstruing 09b20 ὁρμῶν ('rushing') as from ὅρμος ('haven'; cf. ARar مرسى, Lyons 195.22 and 380); IS has 'the river and the crossing' and 'crossing to the shore' (227.11 and 13) and elaborates at greater length (cf. Würsch 122). IS is the source of the remark that in long (hemistichs/twins) 'the end makes one forget the beginning' (cf. IS 227.12), and also the proximate source (although presumably consistent with ARsyr) of the final comment that very short ones do not have 'circularity (ܡܣܘܚܪܐ, استدارة), that is, parts which return (ܬܗܦܟܢ, يعود) to each other' (cf. AR 09b31 'those too short do not constitute a period', ARar 'are not circular and do not return', Lyons 196.12-13).

**7.6.3.** BH mainly follows IS's (228.1-10) highly condensed paraphrase of AR 09b32-10b5, like him omitting the examples but including from ARsyr those of Peitholaus (BH Peilothaus) and Lycrophon and two/three of those of paromoiosis (10a28-31), none of which is mentioned by IS. 'Conjoined speech is often dividing (ܡܦܠܓܢܐ)' is taken from IS (228.1-2), 'conjoined speech ... may be in divisions and called divided (مقسم)', as are the examples of 'longing for wealth' and 'the prudent are put to shame' (228.4-5). ARar has 'Peitholaus said to Lycrophon' (10a17, Lyons 197.13), as well as 'when *you* were at home', 'have come to *us*', and 'they *were bought*' for Aristotle's 'when *they* were at home', 'have come to *you*', and 'they *bought you*' (10a18-19, Lyons 197.14-15). 'Unequal (in length or brevity ...') has its basis in (ARsyr? and) ARar (AR 10a23 'equal', ARar 'not equal' Lyons 197.21-198.1 and 382, fully in IS 228.7-8: 'their divisions vary in length or brevity'). The examples of 'a field/gift' and 'a son' (AR 10a28-31 citing Aristophanes/*Iliad* 9.526), passed over by IS, will have come from ARsyr. ARar is damaged at this point, but features of BH are discernible in it (' ... the tax (?) I took and the field which belonged to him came through honour [كرامة from ܐܝܩܪܐ 'honour' or 'gift' from δωρητοί] ... I thought that a child was born to me', Lyons 198.5-8 and 382). The final example is BH's own; 'desolation' (ܚܘܪܒܐ) is in Syriac a noun of common gender, allowing either masculine or feminine forms of the verb to be used with it.

**7.7.** Paraphrase of AR 3.10-11, style and actualization (putting before the eyes). Throughout this section BH adheres closely to the structure and argument of IS 228.10-232.2, for the most part taking only words and phrases from ARsyr. The number of examples given by Aristotle is radically curtailed in IS, especially those involving Greek names. BH generally follows IS in this respect, but does on occasion include an example from AR which IS has omitted

**7.7.1.** The paraphrase conforms closely in content and wording to IS 228.10-229.10, itself only loosely related to, and much shorter than, AR 3.10.2-6. BH's use of ܠܟܣܝܣ ('style') will not be unconnected to AR's use of λέξις 10b20 (ARar المقالات, IS عبارة), but its appearance as the subject of this section (contrast AR 10b10, 'To learn easily is naturally pleasant to all') comes from IS (228.10-11), 'You must grasp that style (عبارة) which gives understanding is pleasant by what is understood'. BH's ܫܘܡܗ ('attribute') is his rendering of IS's صفة (228.13-15). 'Old men/age ... doer(s) of good ...' appears as in IS (228.14-15), but ARar's rendering of 10b14, 'When he calls old age stubble (καλάμην), he gives (ἐποίησε) [understanding] ...', as 'Old age did good things' (καλὰ μὲν ἐποίησε? Lyons 199.5 and 383) was presumably that of ARsyr.

**7.7.2.** IS eliminates the long list of examples of metaphors in AR 3.10.7 and transforms the section by his interpretation - taken over by BH - of Aristotle's four kinds of metaphor (cf. *Poetics* 21.7-14: genus to species, species to genus, species to species, and analogy) as simile (تشبيه), 'from the opposite', 'from the similar', and 'from the name alone' (229.14-16). BH's (and presumably ARsyr's) ܡܫܡܠܝܘܬܐ is closer in meaning to AR's ἐνέργεια, 'actualization', than is IS's and IR's فعل, 'act' (ARar has فعال). BH includes the example of Pericles on the loss of the youth (AR 11a1-4), omitted by IS, but otherwise, apart from some terminology (ܐܢܛܝܬܝܣܝܣ [antitheses], ܛܛܪܓܘܢܘܣ [four-square]), he is completely dependent upon IS (229.14-230.5). BH's 'blind man great of sight' as an example of 'metaphor from the opposite' is his adaptation of IS's 'father of white for black' (229.15), but 'the pilot of the country' and 'Sirius the heavenly barker' are directly from IS (229.16). (German translation of IS 229.10-17 in Würsch 122.) BH does not appear to know a technical term for ἀστεῖα ('urbanities', 'smart sayings') and seems to render it by ܫܦܝܪܐ ('is appropriate', AR 11b21 'that urbanities come from metaphor by analogy and by putting before the eyes has been explained'; IS 'the metaphor may be combined with the clarification of act and be good [تحسن]'; BH 'sometimes metaphor is combined with the clarification provided by actualization and is appropriate'), and ܫܦܝܪܐ (AR 12a18, BH 7.7.3 'appropriate transferences', IS حسنة). Cf. however ARar 11b21 اسطيون حسنا (Lyons 202.18 and 386, *asteion* is well [said to be among the most metaphorical usages]); ARar is lacking at 12a18 (see below).

**7.7.3.** BH's account is again derived almost in entirety from IS (230.6-231.1), apart from the mention of Homer (IS 230.7 'he who says' - in fact the examples are not from Homer [as are those of AR 11b31-12a8] but are adapted from IS 230.7-8) and some terminology (ܐܘܡܘܢܘܡܝܐ, yet following IS's علوم he has ܝܘܠܦܢܐ at 12a11 φιλοσοφία, ARar فلسفة). IS's account is a radical curtailment of AR 3.11.1-8 (12b11), eliminating almost all AR's examples while adding a few of his own. BH's 'stylistic metaphors' (ܫܐܝܠܬܐ ܠܚܬܡܝܬܐ) is his rendering of IS (230.6) الاستعارة اللفظية, his 'appropriate transferences' (ܫܘܚܠܦܐ ܫܦܝܪܐ) of IS (230.12) التغييرات الحسنة (cf. AR 12a18 'urbanities are mostly through metaphor', and the commentary on 7.7.2 above). BH's 'what someone may say when he believes ... it emerges that he does not believe thus' is his reformulation of IS 230.12-16, itself an interpretative summary of AR 12a18-b11. ARar breaks off at 12a16 through loss of a folio in the Paris manuscript, resuming at 15a5 (BH 7.9.3); cf. Lyons 204 and 387. The passage in the missing folio was known, however, to IS and IR.

**7.7.4.** Follows, as before, the structure and argument of IS. IS 231.1-9 is a paraphrase of AR 12b11-32, leaving out all examples save that of 'Good it is to die before doing anything worthy of death' (12b16-17). That BH describes this as a 'retort' (ܚܢܝܢܐ) will presumably be on account of the rendering in ARsyr of 12b27 ἀντικειμένως ('[spoken] with a contrast'); IS (231.5) and IR (Aouad II 316) both have مقابلة ('opposition').

**7.7.5.** The exposition, a radically curtailed paraphrase of AR 12b32-13a28, depends on IS 231.10-232.2. 'Metaphor ... by names' will no doubt be related in some way to ARsyr (12b32-13a1); IS (231.10) has, 'Not all metaphors are in acts and attributes, but they may be in named things (مسميات)', and IR (Aouad II 317), 'As transference may occur in acts, so also it may occur in names'. BH's 'metaphor by name, attribute, and actualization' comes from IS (231.14) 'metaphor by name and metaphor by attribute and act'. Both IS and IR only use افراطات, 'hyperboles', later at a point corresponding to 13a29, and for AR's 'hyperboles' (13a19) use at this point اغرابات, 'strange things', corresponding to BH's 'strange retorts' (ܚܢ̈ܝܢܐ ܐܟܣܢ̈ܝܐ)' (cf. IS 232.1-2, IR Aouad II 318). BH might have taken ܐܟܣܢ̈ܝܐ from IS's اغرابات, but ܐܟܣܢ̈ܝܐ could possibly have been the reading of ARsyr for ὑπερβολαί, rather than ܪܘܪܒܐ, which in BH 7.8.1 corresponds to تعظيم in IS 232.2 افراطات الاشياء اتى تقال للتعظيم, 'hyperboles of things which are said for exaggeration' (AR 13a28-29, 'Hyperboles are adolescent, for they exhibit vehemence'). BH's ܦܘܚ̈ܡܐ ܘܡܬ̈ܠܐ, '(Poets err and are not successful when they make) similes', may also have been the reading of ARsyr at 12b32 εἰκόνες, IS and IR تشبيه.

**7.8.** Paraphrase of AR 3.12 (preceded by 3.11 13a28-34), on oral and written style, and deliberative, judicial, and epideictic style. The title in BH picks up the last part of the title of IS 4.3 (226.5, 'what is good in rhetoric [يحسن مخاطبة] and what is good in writing [كتابة]'). 'Retorts', however, may be there simply to establish continuity with the 'retorts' of 7.7; there is no further mention of them in the body of the section.

**7.8.1.** The passage is evidently a paraphrase of AR 13a28-b8, but it differs radically from it. It is, however, close to IS 232.2-16. BH cuts out a little from IS, but in the example of AR 13a31-34 ('Not even if he gave me as much as the sand ... Athene in workmanship') he gives more of the Greek names than does IS, albeit construed differently from the Greek and, as in IS, separated into two citations (cf. Würsch 113-114). With the lacuna in the manuscript of ARar it is impossible to determine how much of the difference between IS and BH on the one hand and AR on the other is due to (ARsyr and) ARar. However, the fact that IR (Aouad II 319) as well as IS (232.8-10) and BH speak of the temporary character of the spoken word as against the permanence of the written indicates that this point, not found in the Greek of 13b3-8, was probably present in the oriental versions. The same applies to the surprising appearance of 'letters' (ܐܓܪ̈ܬܐ, رسائل, 'epistles'), where one would rather have expected from the text of AR something closer to 'written style' (λέξις γραφιxή), as in 7.8.2 below. However, the notion of the falsehood (as against adolescent vehemence or passion) of hyperbole seems to have been introduced by IS (232.2, 5-6; contrast AR 13a28-29 [cited on 7.7.5 above] and similarly IR Aouad II 318-319), as does the distinction between 'encomiastic and deliberative address proclaimed in front of the people' (على رأس الملأ, BH ܥܠ ܪܝܫ ܥܡܐ) and 'the advice of one (person) to another' (cf. IS 232.10-12).

**7.8.2.** Paraphrase of AR 3.12.2, but much closer to IS 232.2-16. Again the lacuna in ARar makes it impossible to see from where BH has drawn all his assertions. From the beginning of the paragraph as far as 'a word heard but not written is quickly forgotten and not subject to examination', the paraphrase is close to IS (233.1-6) and, being similar also to IR (Aouad II 319-320), may be assumed to reflect to some degree ARsyr and ARar of 13b8-14 (13b14 παραβαλλόμενοι οἱ λόγοι taken as 'words [heard] are forgotten'?). BH then apparently goes his own way in contrasting skill in the writing of speeches with that in the writing of letters. IS (233.6-8) and IR (Aouad II 320), on the other hand, both make the different point that many skilled writers are *not* persuasive in speech, while many skilled orators are incompetent in persuasion (effected by delivery) through the use of their hands (cf. AR 13b14-16). That BH made use of the terminology of ARsyr here, even though it is likely that his exposition diverges from it, is clear from the transliteration of ἰδιωτιxοί (13b16) and ἀγών and ἀγωνιστιxή (13b4, 9, 12, 15, 17), none of which is transliterated in IS or IR (cf. Introduction, p. 26).

**7.8.3.** Paraphrase of AR 13b21-23 and 29-14a1, but closer to IS 233.10-234.5. IR (Aouad II 320-321) also exhibits some similarities to IS and BH over against AR, and these will be from (ARsyr and) ARar. See especially the opening remark, 'The mingling of delivery with transferences is very persuasive' (as in IS and IR, against AR 13b21-23, 'It is necessary to change when speaking the same thing; this, as it were, paves the way for the delivery').

**7.8.4.** Paraphrase of IS 234.6-235.11, rather than AR 14a1-17. 'Prologue' evidently comes from the transliteration in ARsyr of παραλογισμός ('fallacy', 14a5-6, 'he amplified with a single mention by the fallacy') as (ܦܪܘܠܘܓܝܣܡܘܣ then?) ܦܪܘܠܘܓܘܣ (πρόλογος). IS (234.6) and IR (Aouad II

321) have forms of صدر, doubtless from ARar. Compare the apparent rendering in 6.7.2 above of 02b26/02b31 παραλογισμός/παραλογιζόμενος by ܦܪܘܠܘܓܝܣܬܝܢܐ (παραλογίθηναι/προλογίθηναι?), ARar تقديم الكلام, 'preceding the *logos*'. That the prologue should be 'indicative of the aim' and 'like a sketch preceding a picture' will have been the interpretation of ARsyr and ARar (cf. AR 14a1-2 and 8, 'This is Homer's intention' and 'the demegoric style seems like an outline painting'), to judge from the common interpretation of BH, IS (234.6-7) and IR (Aouad ibid.). While IS 234.9 transmuted *Iliad* 2.671-674 (AR 14a2-3) into 'the praise of God who gives strength to his friends and destroys his enemies', BH makes it into a laudation of the martyrs for whom, as 'runners' (ܐܓܘܢܣܛ̈ܐ), God may be praised (cf. *Epistle to the Hebrews* 12, 1, especially ἀγῶνα/ܐܓܘܢܐ and AR14a13 ἀγών) and in the commemoration of whom (cf. AR 14a6) he may be praised for fixing the limit of man's temporal life (cf. *Job* 14,5; 13-14). The remainder of BH's exposition is close to IS (234.9-235.11, considerably abbreviated). 'The bigger the crowd, the more the orator ought to explain ...', and 'speech with the able must be more exact ... the more so before a single judge ... (but) in addresses on rostrums numerous metaphors and cunning similes are required ...' are consistent with the thrust of IR (Aouad II 321-322) and will therefore reflect to some degree the rendering in (ARsyr and) ARar of 14a8-17.

**7.8.5.** 'Visible discourse (ܡܡܠܠܐ ܡܬܚܙܝܢܐ), which is written ...' corresponds to IS (235.11-12) اللفظ المرئى and IR (Aouad II 322) الخطب المرئية. It may have been the rendering in ARsyr of 14a17 ἡ ἐπιδεικτικὴ λέξις, 'the epideictic style', although ARsyr normally appears to have rendered 'epideictic' by ܡܚܘܝܢܐ, 'demonstrative'. (Was ܡܚܘܝܢܐ corrupted to ܡܬܚܙܝܢܐ in ARsyr?) The content of the paragraph differs radically from AR 14a17-29, but is close to IS 235.11-236.6 and similar to IR (Aouad II 322-323). The major differences from AR will therefore be due to (ARsyr and) ARar. Most notably, the 'letters' and 'deeds which judges and orators authenticate' will probably stem from an interpretation and expansion of 14a17-18, γραφικωτάτη ('most suited for writing') ... ἀνάγνωσις ('reading') ... δευτέρα δὲ ἡ δικανική ('the judicial second') ... .

**7.9.** Paraphrase of AR 3.13-17, *taxis*, the arrangement of the parts of a speech (exclusive of interrogation and epilogue, the subjects of 7.10), corresponding to IS 4.4. BH's title is derived from that of IS (236.8-10), 'On the parts of rhetorical speech, their arrangement, their characteristic in each of the three branches (of rhetoric) [and what the respondent should do about them' - this last corresponding to BH 7.10]. For 'arrangement' IS has ترتيب or نظم, IR نظام (Aouad II 323), while BH has ܠܛܘܟܣܐ (cf. AR 14a29 τάξις, 03b8 τάξαι τὰ μέρη τοῦ λόγου, 'to arrange the parts of the speech'). The sequence of ideas in the 'theories' of this section is often markedly different from AR, but generally adheres to that of IS. The lacuna in the Paris codex of ARar ends at 15a5 (BH 7.9.3).

**7.9.1.** The structure of BH's paragraph is that of IS 236.11-237.2, paraphrasing AR 14a30-36. That a rhetorical speech has *three* parts, with 'the proemium like a drawing (ܪܘܫܡܐ, IS رسم) of the aim, the narration like a drawing of the proof, and the conclusion a recapitualtion ...' is from IS 236.12-237.2, an expansion over AR not to be found in IR (Aouad II 323). The Greek terms (*problema, [prooimion,] antiparabole, epanodos*) are found neither in IS nor IR (Aouad II 323-324) and have evidently been added by BH from ARsyr (cf. 14a35, 14b1-2 [فروميون occurs in ARar at 15b39]). From its position between *prooimion* and *epanados* at 14b1-2, BH (or the translator or glossator of ARsyr) apparently misunderstood *antiparabole* ('refutation by comparison') as a synonym of 'narration' (ܬܘܢܝܐ, διήγησις).

**7.9.2.** Paraphrase of AR 14a36-b7, but following the sequence and argumentation of IS 237.2-10. That narration belongs in judicial *and* epideictic speeches, being inappropriate only in deliberative rhetoric, is an interpretation taken from IS (237.2-5); since IR (Aouad II 324) goes along with AR 14a36-38 in limiting narration to the judicial, the transformation will be due to IS, and not derived from ARsyr and ARar. The 'sign' (ܫܘܕܥܐ) present in deliberative speeches is in IS 237.5 a 'sign (دلالة) to a coming benefit'; it may stem from the translation of AR14b4 ἀλλ' οὐχ ᾗ συμβουλή ('but not insofar as there is deliberation') as 'but only a sign (σύμβολον?)'. That proemium and conclusion are especially appropriate in deliberation is taken from IS 237.6-10, but is in accord with IR (Aouad ibid.). ARar may therefore have omitted *antiparabole* from the sequence in 14b1-2 ('proemium, *antiparabole*, and conclusion occur in public speeches'), while ARsyr transcribed it (see above on 7.9.1). IS explained this usefulness of proemium and conclusion by drawing on 15a23 (the proemium should make clear the *telos* ['end', 'aim'] of the speech) and the model epilogue at the very end of Aristotle's treatise (20b3, 'I have spoken ... you decide!').

**7.9.3.** From the four parts of AR 14b8-9 (proemium, *prothesis*, *pistis*, conclusion), IR (Aouad II 325) has five: proemium (صدر), aim (غرض), narration (اقتصاص), *pistis* (تصديق), conclusion (خاتمة). IS has four, as in IR but without 'aim', and BH is in accord with IS, like him asserting that three are delivered before listeners, but *pistis* before an adversary 'to aid memory and understanding' (cf. IS 237. 10-12). This last point is presumably derived from AR 14b11-12 ('One who does this [*antiparabole*] demonstrates something, but the proemium does not, nor the conclusion, but it serves as a reminder'); IR (and thus ARsyr and ARar) is closer to AR in stating that 'the conclusion ... is in the mode of recollection'. The remainder of the paragraph paraphrases a few portions of AR 14b19-15a24, following the pattern of IS 237.12 - 238.8. 'Clearing the throat (ܢܘܚܬܢܐ) in singing and spitting

(ܠܦܬܓܡܐ) in playing the flute' corresponds to IS 237.13 'clearing the throat (تنحنح) in calling to prayer (أذان) and chanting (ترنم) in playing the flute'; cf. AR 14b19-20, ' a *prologos* in poetry and *proaulion* in playing the flute'. *Chanting* was probably the reading of ARar, as it also appears in IR (Aouad II 325 يترنمون); *spitting* is perhaps more likely to have been BH's formulation in parallel to IS's 'clearing the throat'. 'Gorgias in the *Olympic Speech*' (14b31) is specified only by BH; cf. IS 238.1 'the saying' (قول القائل) and IR (Aouad II 326) 'the saying of so and so' (قول فلان). Perhaps ARsyr and ARar abbreviated 14b32-35 and had Gorgias praising the Greeks for their wisdom (cf. 14b34-35, ['Isocrates blames them ...] for they offered no prize to men of wisdom', IR [Aouad II 326] '... the Greeks who are wise', BH '... to admire the virtue of the Greeks, and then began to recount each one of their sciences', IS [238.2] '... recount their virtues'). The lacuna in the Paris codex of ARar ends at 15a5. IS 238.4-5 eliminates the Greek citations of 15a15-18 and substitutes two Arabic proverbs: 'The torrent has reached the brim' (see on this Aouad III 297), and 'Fatten your dog and he will eat you' (see Würsch 120). IR (Aouad II 327-328) keeps the first of these proverbs (and adds another), but also preserves *Odyssey* 1.1 (cited in AR15a16) and its continuation as cited in ARar (Lyons 204.16-18 and 388). BH keeps the general structure of IS's exposition but replaces his proverbs with two biblical passages: 'The waters have reached the soul' (*Psalm* 69,1[2]), and 'The flood has covered the top of the mountain' (*Genesis* 7,19-20).

**7.9.4.** The paragraph is a slightly abbreviated rendering of the content of IS 238.9-239.6, a paraphrase of AR 15a24-b10 but only quite loosely related to it. 'Devices' stems from (ARsyr? and) ARar of 15a24-25, 'As for these other matters, they are employed as types of devices and cures' (Lyons 205.1-2 and 388); 'outside the matter' from AR 15b5 (Lyons 205.25). The remark concerning 'the speaker ... the matter ... the adversary at law' is taken from IS's (238.10-12) adaptation of AR 15a25-27 (Lyons 205.3-4). In (ARsyr and) ARar the prosecution's attack should come at the *beginning* of the speech (Lyons 205.8-13 and 388), not in the epilogue (AR 15a28-34), from which come IS's (238.12-14) and BH's comments on the accuser exhibiting his own virtue and the adversary's deficiency at the beginning. 'Familiarity, sitting together, and cheerful countenance' is BH's rendering of IS 239.3 'closeness, position, and pleasant appearance' (cf. ARar of 15b2, 'those whose appearance is remarkable', Lyons 205.20-21 and 389, AR 'marvels and pleasures', and 15b27 'friendship'). 'Ornamental and amplifying' (from IS 239.6) comes from Aristotle's discussion of deliberative proemia (15b37-38).

**7.9.5.** BH continues to base his exposition on IS (239.7-240.2), a free paraphrase of AR 15b10-16a3. However, individual phrases and words drawn from ARsyr become more noticeable in BH here, replacing those used by IS. 'Beginning a prosecution with extremely base things is *ridiculous* (ܠܓܚܟܐ)' is such an example; cf. AR 15b10 γελοῖον, ARar [Lyons 206.5-6 and 389] 'to begin with everything weak is laughable', IS 'beginning a prosecution with extremely base things ... is bad'). BH's examples are his own, but more similar to those of IS 239.8-10 than to those of AR 15b12-15; there is a play on words in 'if you do not *give heed* (ܬܪܡܘܢ), you will fall into the trap which *is laid* (ܪܡܝܐ)'. 'A proemium is intended for listeners', as in IS 239.10-11, depends on (ARsyr? and) ARar of 15b17, 'what is intended to be towards the listener or not towards the listener ...' (Lyons 206.11-12 and 389, AR 'it is clear that this is not to the listener as listener'); similarly, 'all around (their desire) making a *proemi-ization*' (ܚܕܪܝܢ ܦܪܘܐܘܡܝܐܣܣܬܐ, AR 15b24 'go round in a circle and *proemi-ize*', ARar [Lyons 206.18] حول الشيء ويفعلون تقديم الكلام) evidently depends on ARsyr (the equivalent passage in IS 239.14 has يطيف, 'go around'). That (as in IS 239.14-15) 'listeners may be seduced when praised' relates to (ARsyr? and) ARar (Lyons 206.23-24) of 15b28-29, 'one must praise the listener' (AR, 'make the listener believe he shares the praise'), but the remainder of the sentence depends only on IS's (240.1-2) paraphrase of 15b35-38: 'when the listener or adversary does not understand the magnitude of the matter, its magnitude needs indicating in the proemium' (ARar 15b35-38 is garbled, cf. Lyons 207.7-12 and 390).

**7.9.6.** Paraphrase of AR 3.15 (16a4-b15), a defendant's means of repulsing an attack, following the pattern of that of IS (240.3-241.2). 'Your complaint is greater than your injury' belongs in the same context as IS 240.15 ('If I did wrong by acting, you did wrong by complaining'), but is more closely based on the intrusive negative and expansion in (ARsyr and) ARar at 16a34, 'one should not make a complaint to that very same extent' (Lyons 209.12-13 and 392). The following contrast between a 'light prosecution' and a 'great rejection by the whole people' is an adaptation of IS 240.16-17, 'The slanderer is lightly praised by the slandered, but censured by many people'; cf. (ARsyr and) ARar 16b4-5, 'he is praised little but vituperated much' (Lyons 209.19-20 and 392). The final sentence depends on IS's paraphrase (240.17-241.2) of AR 16b10-11 ('the accuser should attribute the evil motive ... the defendant the better').

**7.9.7.** Paraphrase of AR 16b16-29 followed by the repetition, as in the Greek, Arabic, and no doubt Syriac manuscript tradition, of 67b26-68a10 from Book 1.9, on praise. BH's paraphrase runs along the same lines as IS 241.3-242.4. The presentation of the narration as a sketch (ܪܘܫܡܐ, رسم) of what is later explicated in detail (ܒܦܘܪܫܐܝܬ, بالتفصيل) in the proof follows IS 241.3-7 (cf. AR 17a36 'will make the thing clear'). That 'right order' (BH ܢܩܝܦܘܬ ܣܕܪܐ, IS عقوق الترتيب) is not necessary (AR 16b16 not ἐφεξῆς ['not continuous']) is in accord with IS 241.5-6. The exposition of the repeated section AR 67b26-68a10 is similar to IS 241.16-242.4. BH's 'as I have (already) explained' [cf. IS 242.1 'as you have (already) learnt] refers to the change of praise to advice in 3.4.1 (AR 67b26 68a10). BH's 'searching encomia' is a misreading of IS (242.3) 'encomia (to do with) fortune' (بختية misread as بحثية, 'searching'), and his 'labour' from the sequel in IS, 'Trust not in fortune (*jadd*) but in labour (*kadd*)'.

**7.9.8.** The exposition is based mainly on IS 242.8-243.5, but BH concludes with the example of Sophocles from AR 17a28-33, omitted by IS. The remark that 'proof should not be mixed with proemium or narration', while drawn directly from IS, is consistent with (ARsyr? and) ARar of 16b34, 'one should not mention the proofs in (the proemium)' (Lyons 212.16-17 and 394, AR 'one should not narrate at length ... nor speak proemia at length, nor proofs'). The subsequent comment on arrangement and 'what is pleasant for the judge to hear' is from IS, although the latter also appears at AR 17a7. (ARsyr and) ARar translated 17a19 οἱ μαθηματικοὶ λόγοι ἤθη ('mathematical treatises [have no] moral character') as 'in mathematics [there is no] moral talk', and hence failed to appreciate Σωκρατικοί as 'Socratic λόγοι'. Thus ARar and IS refer to 'the followers of Socrates' (اصحاب سقراطيس) (Lyons 213.19-214.3 and 395, IS 243.1), BH (and ARsyr?) 'some of those of the house of Socrates' (ܐܢܫܝܢ ܡܢ ܕܒܝܬ ܣܘܩܪܛܝܣ). 'When a proof (ܗܝܡܢܘܬܐ) does not occur in the speech' is BH's paraphrase of 17a27-28 'if it is incredible (ἄπιστον)', IS 243.4 'if proof (تصديق) does not occur in that'. *Antigone* was not recognised as the title of a drama; BH (and ARsyr?) saw therein the name of 'the wife', ARar by contrast apparently that of 'the husband' (Lyons 214.11 and 395).

**7.9.9.** BH follows IS 243.5-6 in replacing AR 17a36-b11 (on 'speaking from the emotions' and the supporting examples) with the advice to a respondent to refute the accuser's delivery (أخذ بالوجوه, ܢܣܒ ܒܦܪ̈ܨܘܦܐ). The comment depends on the mistranslation in (ARsyr? and) ARar of 17b8 ('... and the adversary, but do it inconspicuously') as 'when the adversary is seen in this state [of weeping, 17b6], he leads astray' (Lyons 215.7-8 and 396; cf. IS, 'It may be necessary for the respondent to refute the delivery, saying, "This is a trick, and the weeping of scoundrels"'). BH's paraphrase of 17b11-20 (narration in deliberative oratory) follows IS 243.7-15; from IS (243.7 and 9) come the modifications that in deliberation narration only appears *by chance* (AR 17b12 'least', ARar 'most reluctantly'), and a speaker may *begin by producing a paradigm* or praising (AR 17b15 'criticising or praising'). The closing remarks on the four means of defence interweave IS 244.1-3 (who substitutes 'is not useful' for 'caused harm', 17b25 ἔβλαψεν) and AR 17b21-26; (ARsyr? and) ARar (Lyons 216.4 and 397) omit 17b25 οὐ τοσόνδε, 'not so important', and BH's 'caused harm in order to be useful' is evidently inspired by the 'not useful' of IS.

**7.9.10.** The structure of the exposition mirrors that of IS 244.4-15, a selective paraphrase of AR 17b38-18a32, although BH draws details not present in IS from ARsyr. The analogy with dialectic is taken from IS 244.6, who will have had in mind *Topics* 156a23, propositions should not be established in order (συνεχῆ). The modification over against Aristotle of 18a5-6 ('enthymemes should not be pronounced ἐφεξῆς but mixed up, otherwise they damage one another') is derived from IS 244.6-8; by contrast, the example of suffering (in effect commenting on 18a12-15) is BH's own. 'Taking hold of the law ... premisses' is BH's rendering of IS 244.13-14, paraphrasing 18a25-26 ('the law is a hypothesis in judicial cases: having a starting point, it is easier for one to find proof'). For IS (244.15), however, the exceptional provision for repudiation of the law is 'doubt about the matter of the law (*sharî'a*) itself'. BH's statement that the exception is doubt about the law's *interpretation* (ܦܘܫܩܐ) agrees with that of IR (Aouad II 345 and III 435, تأويل). The source of both is evidently related to the reading of ARar 18a29, 'The doubter or the challenger (طاعن, from Syriac ܛܥܘܢܐ?) on the law (*sunna*) should do what the orators at Athens and Isocrates do' (Lyons 218.4-5 and 399). It would seem that BH's remark reflects the reading of ARsyr, and IR's an earlier reading of ARar closer to ARsyr than is that of the Paris codex.

**7.9.11.** The exposition is quite remote from its basis in AR 18a39-b33, but in general quite close to IS 244.15-245.10. The initial sentence, close to IS 244.15-17 (who has 'reputable things on the external' rather than BH's 'untrue reputable things'), is evidently a paraphrase of 18a39-b4 ('to seem virtuous ... opposites are clearer when side-by-side'), but rather different, even from the inaccurate rendering of ARar (Lyons 218.15-21 and 399). What follows conveys the substance of 18b6 and 9-13, omitting 7-9 (the case of the opening speaker stating his own premisses first). In concluding by giving examples of what a defendant may say, BH follows IS 245.6-10, slightly modifying his wording. These examples, however, are founded on the wording of (ARsyr and) ARar. The 'stubborn will of an accuser' is taken from their rendering of 18b14-16 (Lyons 219.10-12 and 400, 'the man with whom some false accusation has already been lodged, his soul will not accept a word, and that is if he wishes to say what is opposite or contrary'), the contrast between 'before God' and 'before man' from the translation of 18b24 εἰς δὲ τὸ ἦθος ('in regard to *ethos*') as 'before God' (εἰς δὲ τὸν θεόν? cf. ARar بينه وبين الله, Lyons 219.16 and 400).

**7.10.** Paraphrase of AR 3.18-19 (Interrogation and Epilogue), IS 4.5.

**7.10.1.** Paraphrase of AR 18b39-19a19, but differing markedly from it while adhering more closely to IS 245.15-246.15. The 'first way' of IS (245.16-246.2) and BH is evidently an interpretation of AR 19a1-5 (Pericles' question on the sacred rites). The second and third (IS 246.2-9) are only loosely connected to Aristotle's (19a12-13, the opponent drawn into contradiction or paradox; 19a5-12, the response to the initial question leads to the desired conclusion); the example of theft from a house is taken from IS 246.4-6 (cf. Würsch 122-123). The 'fourth way' in IS and BH is clearly an interpretative paraphrase of AR's fourth (19a13-16, the sophistic answer, 'yes and no').

**7.10.2.** BH in general follows IS 246.15-247.9, but with individual variations and with an eye on AR 19a19-b9. 'Rhetorical interrogations are undefined (ܠܐ ܡܬܬܚܡܢܐ)' is his rendering of IS 246.15 'rhetorical interrogations are مهملات (lacking?)', but cf. AR 19a19-20, 'amphibolies need to be answered by defining them logically' (διαιροῦντα λόγῳ, [ARsyr and] ARar '[amphibolies are] not with the word which defines' [يفصل, Lyons 221.9 and 402]) The reference to the *Topics* (Book 8) is from Aristotle himself (19a24, cf. IS 247.3, 5). The closing remarks, with their contrast between subtle and open irony, depend on IS 247.7-9. That contrast (AR 19b7-9, 'irony is more gentlemanly than buffoonery') in turn depends on the translation of 'than buffoonery' (βωμολοχία) in (ARsyr and) ARar as 'with a concealed reason' (Lyons 222.13-14 and 403).

**7.10.3.** ARar (and presumably ARsyr) did not recognise 19b10-20b2 as pertaining to the epilogue of a speech; cf. the translation of ἐπίλογος at 19b10 by تقديم الكلام (Lyons 222.15) as against that at 20b2 منتهى المقالة (Lyons 224.13). As a result, IS (247.10-11), IR (Aouad II 350-351 and III 442), and BH consider 19b10-20b2 as a summary of the principles of rhetoric treated in the whole book. For all of them the discussion of the epilogue proper only begins at 20b2 (AR, 'Asyndeton is appropriate for the end of the discourse, since this is an *epilogos*, not a *logos*'). For BH's terminology ܫܘܠܡ ܬܘܪܓܡܐ ܐܘܟܝܬ ܣܘܟܡ ܡܐܡܪܐ, cf. IS 247.12 آخر الخطبة وهو خاتمة; IR (Aouad II 352) has خواتم الخطب. BH's 'separate, not bound or mixed with what is before it' is from IS; cf. ARar, 'not bound or connected like the prologue' (Lyons 224.14 and 404), and IS, 'separate, not mixed with what is before it, like the prologue' (247.12-13). 'Especially in deliberations' comes from IS (247.13). From the celebrated four-word peroration (AR 20b3, εἴρηκα, ἀκηκόατε, ἔχετε, κρίνατε), 'This is what I have said (ܗܢܘ ܡܐ ܕܐܡܪܬ)', 'and you have listened (ܘܫܡܥܬܘܢ)', and 'so you judge! (ܘܠܟܘܢ ܕܘܢܘ)' (the last omitted by IS) probably appeared in ARsyr much as they do in BH; cf. ARar هذا قولي, سمعتموه, and فاحكموا. In the third element the manuscripts indicate that BH wrote ܒܝܢܬܟܘܢ ('in your midst'), but the translation is difficult: 'therefore you (have the judgement) in your midst'? Or taking it together with what follows: 'therefore between and for yourselves, you judge!'? والحكم اليكم is the reading of ARar, IS, and IR, 'and the judgement is up to you'. An emendation of one letter, ܒܝܢܬܟܘܢ to ܕܝܢܬܟܘܢ ('your judgements') would bring BH, or possibly the original ARsyr, closer to ARar: 'therefore (it is now up to) you, your judgements'? Whereas IS replaced 'you judge!' with an Islamic conclusion ('As is said with us, I give this my speech and pray to God the Exalted One for forgiveness for myself and for you, for he is forgiving and merciful'), BH left the last word with Aristotle.

# SELECT GLOSSARIES

# SYRIAC - GREEK - ARABIC
## BAR HEBRAEUS - ARISTOTLE - IBN SĪNĀ
(Cf. Introduction, pp. 42-43)

ܐܒܒܐ produce 1.5.4
 παραφυές 1.5.4

ܐܓܘܢܐ challenge, discipline, contest, struggle 3.2.2, 5.2.6, 7.1.2, 7.8.2, 7.10.2. ܥܒܕ ܐܓܘܢܐ contend 6.2.2. ܐܓܘܢܣܛܐ runners 7.8.4.
ܐܓܘܢܣܛܝܩܘܬܐ debate 7.8.2
 ἀγών, ἀγωνιᾶν, ἀγωνίζεσθαι, ἀγωνιστική 3.2.2, 5.2.6, 6.2.2, 7.1.2, 7.8.2, 7.8.4, 7.10.2
 اجتهاد 3.2.2 — مصارعة 6.2.2 – منازعة 7.1.2, 7.8.2 — أولياء 7.8.4

ܐܓܪܘܣܐ field 7.6.3
 ἀγρός 7.6.3

ܐܓܪ̈ܬܐ letters 7.8.title, 7.8.1, 7.8.5. ܐܓܪ̈ܬܐ ܟܬܒܘܬܐ letter-writing 7.8.2
 كتابة 7.8.title — رسائل 7.8.1, 7.8.5

ܐܕܫܐ species, type, sort, kind *passim*. ܫܘܐ ܒܐܕܫܐ equivalent in species 7.2.5
 εἶδος 1.7.4, 1.8.1, 2.1.2, 2.1.5, 2.1.7, 3.4.1, 5.2.3, 6.1.2, 6.2.1, 6.3.2, 6.5.1, 6.5.12, 7.5.5. ὁμοειδῆ 7.2.5 — γένη 5.2.3 — μέρη 2.2.2
 نوع *passim* — ضرب 7.3.5. ضربون 6.2.1 — مناسبة 7.2.5 — وجوه 7.3.1

ܐܘܐ ܒܪܚܡܘܬܐ well disposed in friendship 5.1.1. ܐܘܝܘܬܐ concord 5.1.1, 7.9.4
 εὔνοια, εὔνους 5.1.1, 7.9.4
 ثقة بمؤالفته وصداقته 5.1.1. ألفة 5.1.1 — استئناس/تحبب 7.9.4

ܐܘܓܐ light 4.5.1
 αὐγή 4.5.1

ܐܘܛܘܩܪܛܘܪ autocrat 6.2.2
 αὐτοκράτωρ 6.2.2

ܐܘܟܣܝܐ oxeia 7.1.1
 ὀξείᾳ 7.1.1

ܐܘܠܘܡܦܝܘܢܝܩܘܣ Olympic victor 2.4.7. Cf. ܐܠܘܡܦܝܐܢܝܩܘܣ
 ὀλυμπιονίκῃ 2.4.7

ܐܘܡܘܢܘܡܝܐ homonym 7.7.3
 ὁμωνυμία 7.7.3
 اتفاق الإسم 7.7.3

ܐܘܣܝܐ substantial 4.2.2. ܐܘܣܝܘܬܐ essence 2.3.2

ذاتية 4.2.2 — كيفية 2.3.2

ܐܘܦܘܩܪܝܛܝܩܐ *hypocrity* 7.1.3
ὑποκριτική 7.1.3

ܐܘܪܓܢܘܢ ܕܡܠܬܐ organ of speech 1.4.3
δύναμις τῶν λόγων 1.4.3
اللسان والبيان 1.4.3

ܐܚܝܢܐ kindred 7.2.5. ܐܚܝܢܘܬܐ kinship, relationship 4.3.7, 5.2.3
συγγενές 4.3.7, 7.2.5. συγγένεια 5.2.3
مشاكلة 7.2.5 — وصلة/قرابة 5.2.3 — مناسب 4.3.7

ܐܛܪܓܘܕܝܩܘܬܐ tragic 7.3.5
τραγικόν 7.3.5
اطراغودية 7.3.5

ܐܝܐܡܒܘ iambics 7.3.4, 7.5.5. ܐܝܐܡܒܝܩܐ iambic 7.5.5
ἴαμβος, ἰαμβεῖα 7.3.4, 7.5.5
أيامبيقى 7.5.5

ܐܝܗܪܘܢ holiness 6.5.6
ἱερός 6.5.6

ܐܝܟܢܝܘܬܐ character, nature 1.3 title, 1.5.3
ἦθος 1.5.3
كيفية 1.3.title, 1.5.3

ܐܝܠܐ defender 4.4.4
ناصر 4.4.4

ܐܝܡܝܬܐ demigods 6.4.3
ἡμίθεοι 6.4.3

ܐܝܦܣ epic 7.3.4
ἐποποιοί 7.3.4
افي 7.3.4

ܐܝܣܪ randomly 7.9.6
بالجزاف 7.9.6

ܐܝܬܝܐ real 6.2.4
موجودات 6.2.4

ܐܝܬܝܩܐ ethics 2.4.5. ܐܝܬܝܩܝܐ moral, ethical 1.5.3, 1.7.4
ἠθικά 1.7.4
أخلاق 2.4.5. خلقيات, خلقية 1.5.3, 1.7.4

ܐܟܠ ܩܪ̈ܨܐ, ܐܟܠ ܩܪ̈ܨܐ, ܐܟܠܩܪ̈ܨܘܬܐ accuse, accuser, accusation 7.9.4-6
διαβάλλειν, διαβολή 7.9.4-6
شكا, شاكي, شكاية 7.9.4-6

ܐܟܣܝܐ worth, estimation, desert 2.4.5, 3.3.4, 5.4.3. ܐܟܣܝܘܡܐ dignity 7.1.4
ἀξία 2.4.5, 3.3.4, 5.4.3. ἀξίωμα 7.1.4
شهادة 2.4.5 — صالح 3.3.4 — مستحق 5.4.3 — درجة 7.1.4

التصديق .6.3.7 تلقى تصديق .5.5.2 سرعة التصديق .5.1.1 يقع التصديق 7.2.2 أكد — 6.5.4 إصابة — 3.3.5 يقن — 5.3.3 قائمون — 7.5.2 جانب — قنع 1.6.3.

ܐܡܢܐ craft, profession, practice 3.3.3, 5.2.2, 5.2.3, 7.2.5. ܐܘܡܢܐ skilled, craftsman, artist 4.5.7, 6.1.2, 6.5.3. ܐܘܡܢܐܝܬ by art 1.2.2. ܐܘܡܢܘܬܐ art, craft 1.1.2, 1.2.2, 1.3.7, 1.4.title, 1.4.2, 1.5.1, 1.5.2, 1.5.4, 1.7.4, 2.1.2, 2.1.3, 2.2.9, 2.3.4, 3.2.4, 4.6.title, 4.6.1, 5.4.8, 5.5.1, 5.5.9, 6.1.2, 6.5.12, 6.6.4, 7.1.3. ܐܘܡܢ ܡ̈ܠܐ art of speeches 1.2.3. ܐܘܡܢܝܐ technical, artistic 1.1.1, 1.2.2, 1.2.3, 1.3.7, 1.5.2, 1.5.3, 7.1.2

τέχνη 1.2.2, 1.4.2, 1.5.1, 1.7.4, 2.1.2, 2.2.9, 2.3.4, 6.1.2, 6.5.12, 6.6.4, 7.1.3. τέχναι τῶν λογῶν 1.2.3. τεχνῖται 6.5.3. ἔντεχνος 1.2.3, 1.3.7, 1.5.2, 7.1.2. ἄτεχνοι 1.5.2, 4.6.1 — βίος 5.2.2 — ἕξις? 5.4.8

صناعة 1.1.2, 1.2.2, 1.3.7, 1.4.title, 1.4.2, 1.5.1, 1.5.2, 1.5.4, 1.7.4, 2.1.2, 2.2.9, 2.3.4, 4.6.title, 4.6.1, 5.5.1, 5.5.9, 6.1.2, 7.1.2, 7.1.3. صناعية 1.2.2, 1.2.3, 1.3.7, 1.5.2, 1.5.3, 2.2.9 — خطابة 1.2.3 — حرفة 2.1.3, 5.2.2, 5.4.8 — مذهب 7.2.5

ܐܢܠܘܓܝܐ proportion 7.5.6

معادلة 7.5.6

ܐܢܐܪܐܝܐ ܟܘܡܪܬܐ Anareia the priestess 6.5.6 (cf. Commentary on 6.5.6)

ἱέρεια 6.5.6

ܐܢܛܝܛܘܣܝܐ opposites 1.1.2, 1.7.3, 6.7.1

ἐναντία 6.7.1

مقابلة 1.7.3. متقابلات 1.1.2, 6.7.1 — نقيض 1.7.3, 6.7.1

ܐܢܛܝܣܝܣ opposite 6.7.1

ἀντισυλλογίζεσθαι 6.7.1

نقيض 6.7.1

ܐܢܛܝܦܪܐܒܘܠ *antiparabole* 7.9.1

ἀντιπαραβολή 7.9.1

ܐܢܛܝܬ̈ܐܣܝܣ antitheses 7.7.2

ἀντίθεσις 7.7.2

المتقابلات 7.7.2

ܐܢܢܩܐ necessity, emergency 1.7.title, 2.3.7, 4.4.4, 4.6.9, 5.2.4, 5.3.6, 5.5.7, 5.5.13, 7.4.1. ܐܢܢܩܐܝܬ necessarily 2.1.1. ܐܢܢܩܝܐ necessary 1.6.4, 1.7.1, 1.7.2, 1.8.4, 2.1.1, 4.2.1

ἀναγκαῖον 1.6.4, 1.7.1, 1.7.2, 4.4.4, 7.4.1. ἀνάγκη 4.2.1, 5.2.4, 5.5.13. ἐξ ἀνάγκης 2.1.1, 4.2.1. συναναγκάζεσθαι 5.3.6 — βία 4.6.9

ضرورى 1.7.1, 1.7.2, 1.8.4, 2.1.1. ضرورة 2.3.7, 5.3.6, 5.5.7. بالضرورة 2.1.1. بالاضطرار 4.2.1 — استصعب 4.6.9 — وجب 5.2.4. واجبات 1.6.4

ܪܚܡܬ ܐܢܫܘܬܐ love of mankind 5.5.8

φιλανθρωπία 5.5.8

محبة للناس 5.5.8

ܐܣܝܘܬܐ medicine 1.5.1, 2.2.9, 2.4.5, 6.1.2
ܐܣܛܘܟܣ̈ܐ elements 1.5.2, 6.4.3, 6.7.3. ܐܣܛܘܟܣܝܐ (ܠܐ) elemental, primary, non-primary 6.7.3, 7.1.3, 7.2.3
  στοιχεῖον 6.4.3, 6.7.3 — κύρια 7.2.3
  اسطقس 6.7.3 — أصل 1.5.2, 7.1.3 — أول 7.2.3
ܐܣܛܪܛܝܓܘܬܐ military strategy 1.4.3
  στρατηγία 1.4.3
  بسالة 1.4.3
ܐܣܛܪܛܝܐ military service 4.5.2
  στρατευόμενος 4.5.2
  بيعة ? زحف ? 4.5.2
ܐܣܟܡܐ figure, form, appearance, manner, semblance 1.5.3, 1.6.3, 1.7.1, 1.7.2, 1.7.3, 3.3.1, 3.3.3, 4.4.7, 5.5.4, 6.6.1, 6.6.2, 6.7.2, 6.7.3, 7.2.2, 7.3.3, 7.5.4 — (outward) act, pretence 4.4.2, 5.4.3 — gesture 5.3.2 — character 1.2.3 — ܫܦܝܪܬ ܐܣܟܡܐ fair manner 1.5.3. ܬܪܝܨܬ ܐܣܟܡܐ well mannered 5.5.11 — ܡܣܬܟܡ presented 3.3.1. ܡܣܬܟܡܢܘܬܐ impression 1.2.3
  σχῆμα 4.4.7, 5.4.3, 6.6.1, 7.5.4. εὐσχήμων 5.5.11 — ἀπολογία ? 4.4.2 — δοκεῖν 3.3.3 — ἐπιεικεῖς 1.5.3
  شكل 1.6.3, 1.7.1, 1.7.2, 4.4.7, 5.4.3, 6.6.1, 6.6.2, 6.7.2. حسن الأشكال 5.5.11 — حجة 4.4.2 — خلق 1.2.3 — سمت 1.5.3 — صلاح 1.5.3 — تعريضه 5.3.2. معرض 3.3.1 — متعرف 5.5.4 — إيهام 1.2.3
ܐܣܦܝܪܐ ball 7.4.2
  κύκλος 7.4.2
  كرة 7.4.2
ܐܣܪ bind 7.6.1, 7.10.3. ܐܣܪܐ connection, connecting particle, conjunction 7.4.1, 7.5.1, 7.8.3. ܒ̈ܢܬ ܩܠܐ ܠܐ ܐܣܝܪ̈ܬܐ asyndeta 7.8.3. ܫܒܘܩܬ ܐܣܪܐ asyndeton 7.8.2, 7.8.3
  σύνδεσμος 7.4.1, 7.5.1, 7.6.1, 7.8.3. ἀσύνδετος 7.8.2, 7.8.3, 7.10.3
  رباطات 7.4.1, 7.8.2, 7.8.3. روابط 7.5.1, 7.8.3. لا رباطات 7.8.2. عن رباطات 7.8.2. ترك الرباطات 7.8.3 — يصل 7.6.1
ܐܦܢܘܕܘܣ epanodos [recapitulation] 7.9.1
  ἐπάνοδος 7.9.1
ܐܦܘܕܝܩܛܝܩܐ apodeixis 1.1.1, 1.1.2, 1.1.3, 1.3.7, 1.4.1, 1.4.2, 1.5.4. ܐܦܘܕܝܩܛܝܩܝܐ apodeictical 1.3.7
  ἀπόδειξις 1.3.7
  برهان 1.1.1, 1.1.2, 1.1.3, 1.3.7, 1.4.1, 1.5.4. برهانية 1.4.2
ܐܦܝܬܛܐ epitheta 7.2.4
  ἐπίθετα 7.2.4
ܐܦܪܘܕܝܣܝܩܬܐ sensual 5.5.1
  ἀφροδίσια 5.5.1
  إلى الزهرة 5.5.1

ܐܪܘܐܡܘܣ arhymic 7.5.4
ἄρρυθμον 7.5.4
ܐܪܘܣ, ܐܪ̈ܘܛܝܣ *orus, orutes* (regulation), cf. ὅρος 6.6.2
ἔρως, ἔρωτες 6.6.2
ܐܪܝܐ areia 7.7.1 (cf. Commentary on 7.7.1)
βαρείᾳ 7.7.1
ܐܪܝܣܛܘܩܪܛܝܐ aristocracy 2.1.8, 2.4.9
ἀριστοκρατία 2.1.8, 2.4.9
سياسة سقراطية 2.1.8
ܐܪܝܟܐ tall, long 6.5.8, 7.3.3, 7.5.6, 7.6.2. ܐܘܪܟܐ length 1.6.3 — height 2.2.7
ἡλικία 6.5.8. μακρά 7.3.3, 7.5.6, 7.6.2. μῆκος 1.6.3, 2.2.7
طول 6.5.8, 7.3.3, 7.5.6. طويل 7.6.2
ܐܪܡܘܢܝܩܝܐ musical 7.5.4
ἁρμονία (AR 08b33) 7.5.4
ايقاعي 7.5.4
ܐܬܐ index 1.7.2, 1.7.3, 1.8.4, 3.2.4, 4.6.4, 5.3.2, 5.3.4, 5.3.6, 6.3.4, 6.5.8, 6.6.2, 6.7.2, 7.4.3
σημεῖον 1.7.2, 1.8.4, 3.2.4, 5.3.2, 5.3.4, 5.3.6, 6.3.4, 6.6.2, 6.7.2
علامة 1.7.2, 1.7.3, 1.8.4, 5.3.2, 5.3.4, 5.3.6, 6.3.4, 6.7.2 — دليل 3.2.4, 4.6.4, 7.4.3
ܐܬ̈ܘܬܐ letters 6.6.1
στοιχεῖα 6.6.1
حروف 6.6.1
ܐܬܝܪ ether 4.5.1
αἰθήρ 4.5.1
ܐܬ̈ܠܝܛܐ athletes 6.2.2. ܐܬܠܝܣܐ champion 3.2.1, 7.1.2
ἀθληταί 6.2.2. ἆθλα 3.2.1, 7.1.2
منازعون 7.1.2
ܐܬܪܐ *topos* 1.5.2, 1.7.4, 2.2.1, 2.3.8, 5.2.5, 6.4.3, 6.5.7, 6.5.10, 6.5.11, 6.5.12, 7.10.3. locality 7.2.2
τόπος 1.7.4, 6.4.3, 6.5.7, 6.5.10, 6.5.12, 7.10.3
موضع 1.5.2, 1.7.4, 2.2.1, 2.3.8, 5.2.5, 6.4.3, 6.5.7, 6.5.10, 6.5.11, 7.10.3 — بلد 7.2.2

ܒܐܫ does evil 4.5.8. cf. ܒܝܫ
κακῶς ποιεῖν 4.5.8
جار 4.5.8
ܡܬܒܗܪ boast 5.3.2
ἐπαγγέλλεσθαι 5.3.2
زهو 5.3.2

ܒܗܬ is ashamed, feels shame, shames 3.2.3, 5.2.2, 5.3.2, 5.3.3, 5.3.4. ܡܒܗܬܢܐ, ܡܒܗܬܢܘܬܐ shaming 3.2.3, 5.3.4. ܡܒܗ̈ܬܢܝܬܐ things causing shame 5.3.1, 5.3.2. ܠܐ ܒܗܬܝܢ not ashamed 5.5.7. ܒܗܬܬܐ shame 3.2.2, 5.3.1, 5.3.3, 5.3.5. ܒܗܬܬܘܬܐ shame 5.3.title. ܒܗܬܬܢܐ modest 5.2.2
αἰσχύνεσθαι 3.2.2, 5.2.2, 5.3.2, 5.3.4. αἰσχυντηλά 5.3.4. αἰσχρά/αἰσχυντικά 5.3.1, 5.3.2, 5.3.3. αἰσχύνη 5.3.1, 5.3.3, 5.3.5. ἀναίσχυντοι 5.5.7 — αἰδώς 3.2.2
خجل 3.2.2, 5.3.1 — استحياء, استحى, حيى, حي 3.2.2, 5.2.2, 5.3.title, 5.3.1, 5.3.3, 5.3.4, 5.3.5, 5.5.7 — مخازى 5.3.2 — فضيحة, فضائح, فاضحات, افتضاح 3.2.2, 5.3.1, 5.3.2, 5.3.3

ܒܘܢܐ perception 2.3.1. understanding 2.3.4, 4.1.2
αἴσθησις 2.3.1 — προαιρούμενοι 4.1.2
بصيرة 2.3.1 — تمكن 2.3.4 — روية 4.1.2

ܒܘܪܐ unlearned 7.8.4
جمهور 7.8.4

ܒܘܣܪܐ shame 2.3.6
ذم 2.3.6

ܒܚܝܪܐ expert 6.4.2
بصير 6.4.2

ܒܘܛܠܐ refutation 1.4.5, 6.4.3, 6.5.6
ἀνασκευάζειν 6.5.6
إبطال 1.4.5, 6.4.3

ܒܝܐܘ console 5.4.9
تسلية 5.4.9

ܒܝܫ bad, evil 1.8.1, 2.3.1, 2.3.6, 4.5.6, 4.6.4, 4.6.5, 5.1.2, 5.1.4, 5.1.5, 5.1.7, 5.2.2, 5.2.4, 5.3.1, 5.3.2, 5.3.6, 5.4.1, 5.4.2, 5.4.3, 5.4.4, 5.4.5, 5.5.2, 5.5.5, 5.5.7, 5.5.8, 6.3.7, 6.5.1, 6.5.5, 6.5.9, 6.6.1, 6.6.2, 6.6.3, 6.7.1, 7.5.1, 7.9.6, 7.9.9. shameful 4.4.1. ܥܒ̈ܕܝ ܒܝܫܬܐ evildoers 4.4.5. ܒܝܫܘܬܐ evil, vice 3.1.title, 4.5.3, 4.5.4
ἀδοξεῖν 4.6.4 — αἰσχρός 4.4.1 — βλαβερόν 6.5.1. κακός 4.5.6, 5.1.2, 5.1.7, 5.2.2, 5.2.4, 5.3.1, 5.3.2, 5.4.1, 5.4.2, 6.5.1, 6.5.5, 6.6.1, 6.6.3, 7.5.1, 7.9.6. κακία 4.5.3. κακοπραγεῖν 5.4.5. κακοπραγίαι 5.4.3 — μοχθηρία 4.5.4. μοχθηρός 6.7.1 — πονηρία 4.5.4, 5.5.2. πονηρός 6.6.2 — φαῦλον 5.3.6, 5.4.4, 5.5.5, 5.5.7
خسيسة 5.3.2, 7.9.6 — إخفاق 5.5.7 — رذيلة 3.1.title — سوء, مسيئون 2.3.6, 4.4.5, 5.1.5, 5.4.1 — شر 1.8.1, 2.3.1, 4.5.3, 5.1.2, 5.2.2, 5.2.4, 5.3.1, 5.3.6, 5.4.1, 5.4.2, 5.4.3, 5.4.4, 5.4.5, 5.5.5, 5.5.8, 6.3.7, 6.5.9, 6.6.2, 7.5.1, 7.9.9 — قبيح 4.5.4, 4.5.6 — منكر 4.6.5

ܒܝܬܝ personal, suitable, appropriate, proper 2.4.4, 6.1.1, 7.2.3, 7.2.4, 7.8.5. ܒܝܬܝܘܬܐ relationship, intimacy 3.3.1, 5.2.3. ܡܬܒܝܬܝܐ attributed 7.7.1
οἰκεῖον 6.1.1, 7.2.3. οἰκειότης 5.2.3 — πρέπουσα/ἁρμόττειν 7.8.5

أخوي/أولى 7.2.3 — خاص 2.4.4, 6.1.1 — مناسب 7.2.4 — ينسب 7.7.1 —
أنس 5.2.3

ܒܘܒܢܝܐ native 2.2.3
αὐτόχθονες 2.2.3
إم بنك 2.2.3

ܡܒܣܪ, ܡܬܒܣܪܢܐ, ܡܬܒܣܪܢܘܬܐ disdains, disdained, disdain 5.1.3
καταφρονεῖν, καταφρόνησις 5.1.3
استهانة, مستهان 5.1.3

ܒܣܝܡܐ lenient 4.5.6, 4.6.1, 4.6.4. ܒܣܝܡܘܬܐ leniency 4.5.3, 4.5.4, 4.5.5, 4.5.6
ἐπιεικές 4.5.3, 4.5.4, 4.5.5, 4.5.6, 4.6.1. ἐπιείκεια 4.6.4
حلم 4.5.3, 4.5.4, 4.5.5. تحلام 4.5.6. حليم 4.6.4

ܒܣܝܐ neglect 6.5.12
ἐκ τῶν ἁμαρτηθέντων 6.5.12

ܡܬܒܥܝܐ desired, lacking 6.3.1, 6.3.4. ܒܥܬܐ desired conclusion 1.6.1, 6.4.1
αἱρετά 6.3.1
يؤثر 6.3.1 — مطلوب 1.6.1, 6.4.1

ܒܥܠܕܒܒܐ enemy 5.2.1, 5.3.6, 5.4.4, 6.3.4. ܒܥܠܕܒܒܘܬܐ enmity 5.2.3, 5.2.5.
ܒܥܠܕܝܢܐ enemy, adversary, adversary at law 1.8.2, 4.4.2, 4.6.4, 4.6.5, 5.1.1, 5.2.3, 6.5.11, 6.7.1, 6.7.2, 6.7.3, 7.9.3, 7.9.4, 7.9.5, 7.9.8, 7.9.9, 7.9.11, 7.10.2
ἀμφισβητῶν 4.6.4, 4.6.5, 6.5.11. ἀμφισβητεῖν 5.2.3 — ἀντίδικος 7.9.3, 7.9.4, 7.9.9, 7.9.11 — ἀντιλέγοντες 7.9.5 — ἐναντίοι 7.10.2 — ἐχθρός 4.4.2, 5.2.1, 5.3.6, 6.3.4. ἔχθρα 5.2.3
خصم 1.8.2, 4.6.4, 5.1.1, 5.2.3, 6.7.1, 6.7.3, 7.9.3, 7.9.4, 7.9.8, 7.9.9, 7.9.11, 7.10.2 — مشاجر 4.6.5 — عدو 4.4.2, 5.2.1, 5.3.6, 5.4.4. عداوة 5.2.3, 5.2.5 — موبخ 6.5.11

ܒܨܝܪܐ lowly 7.8.5. ܡܒܨܪ depreciation 7.10.3. ܒܘܨܪܐ faults 5.3.3. ܒܨܝܪܘܬ ܬܪܥܝܬܐ deficient in intelligence 4.1.2. ܝܬܝܪܐ ܘܒܨܝܪܐ the more and the less 1.7.4. ܡܢ ܗܝ ܕܝܬܝܪܐܝܬ ܘܒܨܝܪܐܝܬ from the more and the less 6.5.2
ταπεινή 7.8.5. ταπεινοῦν 7.10.3 — ἁμαρτίαι 5.3.3 — ἀκρασία 4.1.2 — μᾶλλον καὶ ἧττον 1.7.4. ἐκ τοῦ μᾶλλον καὶ ἧττον 6.5.2
تصغير 7.10.3 — مساوي 5.3.3 — ضعف رأي 4.1.2 — الأقل والأكثر 1.7.4. من الأقل والأكثر 6.5.2

ܒܪܝܐ outer, external 1.2.title, 2.2.2, 5.4.6, 7.9.7. ܡܬܒܪܝܢܘܬܐ outside 4.6.3. ܒܪܝܪܐ idiot 7.9.11. ܒܪܝܪܘܬܐ stupidity 7.10.1
ἐκτός 4.6.3. τὰ ἐκτὸς/ἔξω 2.2.2 — ἀγροικία 7.9.11
خارجة 2.2.2, 5.4.6. خارجية 7.9.7 — بله 7.10.1. أبله 7.9.11

ܣܓܝܘܬ ܒܢܝܐ abundance of children 2.2.3. ܣܓܝܐܘܬ ܕܒܢ̈ܝܐ numerous children 2.2.3

εὐτεκνία 2.2.3. πολυτεκνία 2.2.3
حال الأولاد 2.2.3— كثرة 2.2.3

ܓܐܘܡܛܪܝܐ geometry 1.5.1, 2.4.5. ܓܐܘܡܛܪܐ geometer 7.1.2
γεωμετρία 1.5.1. γεωμετρεῖν 7.1.2
هندسة 1.5.1, 2.4.5. مهندس 7.1.2

ܓܒܝܐ chosen 3.1.1. ܓܒܝܘܬܐ choice 2.4.3
αἱρετόν 3.1.1
اختيار 2.4.3. مختار 3.1.1

ܓܒܝܠܐ shaped 7.5.4
πεπλάσθαι 7.5.4

ܓܢܒܪܐ courageous, mighty 2.3.6, 3.2.1, 3.2.4, 3.3.2, 5.4.1, 5.5.3, 5.5.8, 5.5.11. 7.9.7. ܓܢܒܪܐܝܬ 2.4.5. ܓܢܒܪܘܬܐ courage 2.2.2, 2.2.3, 2.2.4, 2.4.5, 3.1.1, 3.1.2, 5.4.11, 5.5.8. ܠܐ ܓܢܒܪܘܬܐ not courage 5.3.2
ἀνδρεῖος 3.2.4, 3.3.2, 5.5.8, 7.9.7. ἀνδρειότεροι 5.5.3. ἀνδρωδέστεροι 5.5.11. ἀνδρεία 2.2.2, 2.2.3, 2.2.4, 2.4.5, 3.1.1, 3.1.2, 3.2.1, 5.4.1, 5.4.11, 5.5.8. ἀνανδρία 5.3.2
شجع 5.5.3, 5.5.8. شجاع 2.3.6, 3.2.1, 3.2.4, 3.3.2. شجاعة 2.2.4, 2.4.5, 3.1.1, 3.1.2, 5.4.1, 5.4.11, 5.5.8. شجاعية 2.4.5. لا شجاعة 5.3.2 — بسالة 2.2.2, 2.2.3 — أفحل 5.5.11

ܓܕܐ fortune, luck, accident 2.2.9, 3.3.5, 3.4.1, 4.4.4, 5.3.6, 5.4.11, 5.5.1, 6.5.9, 6.5.11, 7.9.7. ܛܒܘܬ ܓܕܐ good fortune 2.2.9 — ܒܝܫܘܬ ܓܕܐ ill fortune 5.4.2. ܓܕܢܐ fortunate 2.2.2, 5.4.1, 5.5.12. ܓܕܝܐ due to fortune, accidental 2.2.9, 4.2.1, 4.2.3. ܓܕܝܘܬܐ good fortune, good luck 2.2.2, 5.5.12
τύχη 2.2.2, 2.2.9, 5.3.6, 5.4.11, 5.5.1, 7.9.7. τύχη κακῶν 5.4.2. διὰ τύχην 3.4.1, 4.2.1, 4.4.4. ἀπὸ τύχης 2.2.9, 3.3.5, 4.2.3. εὐτυχία 2.2.2, 2.2.9, 5.5.12 — δαίμων 6.5.9. ὑπερευδαιμονεῖν 5.4.1
بخت 2.2.2, 2.2.9, 3.3.5, 5.4.1, 5.4.2 — جد, جدية, مجدودون 5.4.11, 5.5.1, 5.5.12, 6.5.9, 7.9.7 — سعيد, سعادة 2.2.2, 2.2.9 — اتفاق, انفاقي 3.3.5, 3.4.1, 4.2.1, 4.2.3, 4.4.4, 5.3.6

ܓܕܫ happen, happen by chance, happen by accident 3.3.5, 6.6.2, 6.6.3, 7.4.3. ܓܕܫܐ chance, accident 3.4.1, 4.3.3, 4.4.4, 5.3.6, 6.4.3, 6.6.2, 7.9.9. ܓܕ̈ܫܐ ܟܝ̈ܢܝܐ natural contingencies 1.5.1
τύχη, διὰ τύχην, ἀπὸ τύχης 3.4.1, 3.3.5, 4.4.4, 5.3.6 — συμβαίνειν, διὰ τὸ συμβεβηκός 6.4.3, 6.6.2, 6.6.3. συμβεβηκότα πάθη 1.5.1
ذات 1.5.1 — عرض, عرضية 3.3.5, 4.3.3, 6.6.2, 7.9.9 — اتفاق, انفاقي 3.4.1, 4.4.4, 5.3.6 — وقع 7.4.3

ܓܘܐ common, community 2.2.2, 4.5.2, 4.5.8, 4.6.1. inner 1.2.title. ܕܓܘܐ common, public 6.2.3, 6.4.2. ܓܘܢ common, general 1.1.3, 1.7.4, 1.8.1, 2.1.1, 2.3.3, 2.4.1, 3.4.1, 4.1.1, 4.5.1, 4.6.2, 6.title, 6.1.1, 6.2.1, 6.4.3,

6.5.10, 7.4.2, 7.4.4, 7.5.3, 7.7.1, 7.9.7. public 2.2.5. ܓܘܢܐܝܬ commonly 2.1.1

34

δημόσιαι 2.2.5 — διὰ τῶν γενῶν 7.4.2 — κοινός 1.7.4, 3.4.1, 4.1.1, 4.5.1, 4.5.2, 4.6.1, 6.1.1, 6.2.1, 6.2.3, 6.4.2, 6.4.3, 6.5.10, 7.4.4. κοινῇ 2.1.1 — περιέχοντα 7.4.2

مشتركة 1.7.4, 4.6.1, 4.6.2, 6.title, 6.1.1, 6.2.1, 7.4.2 — مطلق 1.1.3 — عام 1.8.1, 2.1.1, 2.2.2, 2.2.5, 2.3.3, 2.4.1, 3.4.1, 4.1.1, 7.4.4, 7.5.3, 7.7.1 — عند الناس 7.9.7 — مدينة 4.5.2 — كلية 7.4.2 —

ܓܚܝܟܐ laughable 5.5.8. ܓܘܚܟܐ laughing, laughter 5.1.7, 5.5.4, 5.5.8

γέλως 5.1.7. φιλόγελως 5.5.4, 5.5.8

مزاح 5.1.7 — هزل 5.5.4, 5.5.8

ܓܠܝܙܘ̈ܬܐ privations 7.5.1

στέρησεις 7.5.1

سلب 7.5.1

ܓܘܡܕܢܘܬܐ shamelessness 5.3.title, 5.3.1, 5.3.5

ἀναισχυντία 5.3.1, 5.3.5

غير استحياء 5.3.title — وقاحة 5.3.1, 5.3.5

ܓܢܐ blame, rebuke, vituperate 1.2.2, 1.8.1, 1.8.2, 1.8.3, 2.4.3, 3.3.5, 3.4.1, 4.1.1, 4.4.4, 5.3.2, 5.3.4, 6.4.2, 7.2.4, 7.9.2, 7.9.4. ܡܓܢܝܢܐ of blame 1.8.1.

ܓܘܢܝܐ blame, invective, vituperation 1.5.3, 2.3.6, 3.4.1, 3.4.3, 5.1.1, 5.5.5, 6.3.5, 6.5.10, 6.5.13, 7.3.5, 7.5.1, 7.5.3, 7.9.2, 7.9.3

ἀδοξεῖν 4.4.4 — ψέγειν 1.8.1, 1.8.2, 1.8.3, 2.3.6, 6.4.2, 7.2.4. ψόγος 1.8.1, 3.4.3, 7.5.3, 7.9.3

ذم 1.2.2, 1.5.3, 1.8.1, 1.8.2, 1.8.3, 2.4.3, 3.4.3, 4.4.4, 5.1.1, 5.3.2, 6.3.5, 6.4.2, 6.5.10, 7.5.3, 7.9.2, 7.9.3. مذمة 5.5.5 — مؤذيات 7.3.5 — قبح 7.2.4 — هجاء, هجائية 2.3.6, 7.5.1

ܓܢܘܡܝ, ܓܢܘܡܘܠܘܓܝܐ, ܓܢܘܡܘܠܘܓܝܩܐ gnome, gnomology, gnomic utterances 6.2.1, 6.3.4, 6.3.7

γνώμη, γνωμολογεῖν 6.3.4, 6.3.7

كلام رأيي, رأي 6.3.4, 6.3.7

ܓܢܣܐ genus, kind, race, birth, origin 2.2.3, 2.3.7, 3.3.5, 4.1.2, 4.5.3, 5.1.4, 5.4.8, 6.1.2, 6.2.1, 6.4.2, 6.5.11, 7.2.4, 7.7.1. ܥܬܝܪܘܬ ܓܢܣܐ noble birth 7.9.7

ἔθνος 2.2.3 — εὐγένεια 7.9.7 — γένος 2.3.7, 5.4.8, 6.1.2, 6.2.1, 7.2.4, 7.7.1

جنس 2.3.7, 3.3.5, 4.5.3, 5.1.4, 6.1.2, 6.2.1, 6.4.2, 7.2.4, 7.7.1 — قبيلة 2.2.3 — نسب 5.4.8

ܓܪܓ, ܓܘܪܓܐ excite, exhortation 1.3.5, 3.4.1

ܪܘܡܬ ܓܘܫܡܐ bodily stature 2.2.2

μέγεθος 2.2.2

جسامة 2.2.2

5.5.13 — قدر 2.4.5 — قاضي 1.3.1, 5.1.title, 5.1.1, 7.8.5. قضاء 7.8.4 — سياسات 2.1.8 — مدنيات, مدنية 2.1.7, 2.1.8, 2.4.9, 7.1.3

ܕܚܝܠ feared, fearful 5.2.6, 5.2.7. ܕܚܠܬܐ fear 4.1.2, 5.2.title, 5.2.4, 5.2.5, 5.3.1, 5.4.2, 5.5.3, 5.5.6, 5.5.7, 7.1.1. ܕܚܝܠܘܬܐ, ܕܚܘܠܬܢܘܬܐ cowardice, cowardliness 3.1.2, 5.3.2, 5.5.8. ܕܚܘܠܬܢܝ cowardly 5.5.6

δειλία 3.1.2, 5.3.1, 5.3.2, 5.5.7. δειλοί 5.5.6 — δεινόν 5.4.2 — φοβεῖσθαι 5.5.3, 5.5.8. φοβερόν 5.2.6, 5.2.7. φόβος 5.2.4, 5.2.5, 5.5.6

جبن 3.1.2, 5.3.1, 5.3.2, 5.5.6, 5.5.7, 5.5.8. يجبنون 5.5.6 — خوف 4.1.2, 5.2.title. 5.2.4, 5.2.5, 5.4.2, 5.5.3, 5.5.6, 7.1.1. مخوف 5.2.7 — مكروه 5.2.6

ܕܝܐܠܩܛܘܣ dialektos 7.2.2

διάλεκτος 7.2.2

ܕܝܐܦܛܘ̈ܟܐ diaptuke 7.5.1

διαπτυχαί 7.5.1

لها وجهان 7.5.1

ܕܝܐܘܣܝܣ see ܕܝܘܣܝܣ

ܕܝܘܣܝܣ avoidance 4.4.2

δίωσις 4.4.2

ܕܝܠܝܬܐ characteristic 7.3.1. ܕܝܠܝܘܬܐ specifity 1.8.1. ܕܝܠܢܐܝܬ specifically 2.1.1, 2.1.2, 7.4.4. ܕܝܠܗ specific, particular, special, own, proper 1.3.title, 1.4.3, 1.7.4, 1.8.2, 2.2.3, 4.1.1, 4.5.1, 4.6.1, 4.6.2, 5.4.6, 6.4.3, 6.5.10, 7.4.2, 7.9.7

ἴδιος 1.4.3, 1.7.4, 2.1.1, 2.2.3, 4.1.1, 4.5.1, 4.6.1, 6.4.3, 7.4.2

خص, خاص, خاصة, مخصصة, تخصيص 1.3.title, 1.4.3, 1.7.4, 1.8.1, 1.8.2, 2.1.2, 2.2.3, 4.1.1, 4.6.2, 6.4.3, 6.5.10, 7.3.1, 7.4.2, 7.4.4

ܕܝܠܩܛܝܩܐ dialectic 1.1.1, 1.1.2, 1.1.3, 1.2.1, 1.3.7, 1.4.1, 1.4.2, 1.4.5, 1.5.4, 1.6.1, 1.6.2, 1.7.4, 6.4.1, 6.4.3, 6.6.4, 7.9.10. ܕܝܠܩܛܝܩܘܣ dialectical, dialectician 1.4.2, 6.5.13, 7.1.2. ܕܝܠܩܛܝܩܝܐ dialectical 1.3.7, 6.4.title, 6.4.1, 6.7.1

διαλεκτική 1.2.1, 1.3.7, 1.4.2, 1.4.5, 1.5.4, 1.6.1, 1.6.2. διαλεκτικός 1.7.4, 6.4.1, 6.6.4

جدل 1.1.2, 1.1.3, 1.2.1, 1.3.7, 1.4.1, 1.4.2, 1.4.5, 1.5.4, 1.6.1, 1.6.2, 1.7.4, 6.4.1, 6.4.3, 7.9.10. جدلي 1.1.1, 1.3.7, 6.4.title, 6.4.1, 6.5.13, 6.6.4, 6.7.1, 7.1.2

ܕܝܡܐܓܘܓܘܣ demagogue 6.2.3

δημαγωγός 6.2.3

ܕܝܡܘܩܪܛܝܐ democracy 2.1.8. ܕܝܡܘܩܪܛܝܘܬܐ democracy 2.4.9

δημοκρατία 2.1.8, 2.4.9

ديمقراطية 2.1.8 — اجماعية 2.4.9

ܕܝܩܐܣܛܝܩܐ, ܕܝܩܣܛܝܩ̈ܐ, ܕܝܩܐܣܛܝܩ̈ܐ, ܕܝܩܣܛܝܩܐ judicial, judicial matters 1.3.6, 1.8.1, 1.8.4, 4.title, 4.6.1, 6.1.1, 6.4.2

δικαζόμενος 1.8.4. δικανικός, δικανικά 1.3.6, 1.8.1, 4.6.1, 6.1.1
تشاجرية 1.3.6. مشاجر 1.8.4. مشاجرات 4.6.1, 6.4.2. متشاجرون 6.1.1

ܕܝܐܬܣܝܣ, ܕܝܐܬܐܣܝܣ state, condition 3.3.2, 4.2.3, 4.5.2, 5.2.1, 5.2.3, 5.3.1
δiάθεσις 4.2.3 (AR 70a2)
حال 4.2.3. حالة 5.2.1, 5.2.3 — خلق 5.3.1

ܕܡܐ be like, liken, imitate 5.3.2, 7.1.3, 7.2.2, 7.3.1, 7.3.5. ܡܕܡܝܢܐ ܕܡܘܝܐ coining a simile 7.3.5. ܕܡܘܬܐ play-acting 5.4.3. ܕܡܝܘܬܐ similarity 7.3.5, 7.7.3. ܕܡܝܐ similar, rhymed, appropriate 2.3.7, 7.6.1, 7.7.2. ܩܒܘܠܬ ܕܡܝܢܐ acceptance of resemblances 6.6.3. ܕܘܡܝܐ likeness, simile 4.3.6, 7.7.2, 7.7.5, 7.8.1, 7.8.4. ܫܘܝܐ ܘܕܡܝܐ similar 7.7.5. ܡܕܡܝܢܘܬܐ works of imitation 4.3.6
ἁρμόττοντα 2.3.7 — μεμιμημένον 4.3.6. μιμήματα, μιμητικώτατον 7.1.3 — ἐοικέναι 7.3.5 — τὸ παρὰ τὸ ἑπόμενον 6.6.3 — οἱ ὅμοιοι 5.3.2. τὸ ὅμοιον 7.7.3 — ὑπόκρισις 5.4.3
محاكاة, محاكيات 4.3.6, 5.3.2. تحاكي 7.3.1 — شبيه 7.7.2. تشبه 7.2.2. تشبيه 7.3.5, 7.7.2, 7.7.5, 7.8.1, 7.8.4. تشبيه تجري 7.3.5 — اعتبار المعادلة 6.6.3 — بالمثل 2.3.7 — هيئة 5.4.3

ܐܬܕܡܪ admire 5.3.3
θαυμάζειν 5.3.3
تعجب 5.3.3

ܕܪܩܘܢ dracon (dragon) 6.5.13
δράκων 6.5.13

ܕܘܪܓܐ step-by-step progress 6.4.1
تدرج 6.4.1

ܕܪܝܟܘܢܐ darics 2.2.4
νόμισμα 2.2.4

ܕܘܪܫܐ exercise 2.3.2
γυμνάζεσθαι 2.3.2
حركة/ارتياض 2.3.2

ܡܚܝܠ evoke an image 7.1.3, 7.1.4, 7.2.6, 7.5.1, 7.5.2, 7.9.4. ܐܬܚܝܠ is evoked as an image 7.5.2. ܚܝܠܐ imagination, image-evocation 4.3.6, 5.1.2, 5.1.3, 7.1.3, 7.6.2. ܚܝܠܢܐ imaginative 4.2.1. ܡܚܝܠܐ evocation of images 7.1.1. ܡܚܝܠܢܐ imaginative, image-evoking 6.3.3, 7.1.4, 7.2.2, 7.5.4. ܡܚܝܠܘܬܐ image-evocation 7.1.1, 7.1.2, 7.2.3, 7.2.6. ܡܚܝܠܢܘܬܐ productive of imagination, image-evoking 1.4.2, 7.5.2. ܡܬܚܝܠܢܘܬܐ imagination, image-evocation 4.3.2, 5.2.4, 5.3.3, 5.5.8
φαντασία 5.1.2, 5.2.4, 5.3.3, 7.1.1, 7.1.2
خيل 7.1.3. تخيل, تخييل 1.4.2, 4.2.1, 4.3.6, 5.1.3, 5.2.4, 5.5.8, 6.3.3, 7.1.1, 7.1.2, 7.1.3, 7.1.4, 7.2.2, 7.2.3, 7.2.6, 7.5.1, 7.5.2, 7.5.4, 7.6.2, 7.9.4 — وهم 5.3.3

ܗܓ̈ܡܘܢܐ leaders 2.2.3
 ἡγεμόνες 2.2.3
 رؤساء 2.2.3
ܗܕܝܘܛܐ, ܗܕܝ̈ܘܛܐ unlearned, simple, incompetent, ignorant 1.1.2, 1.4.1, 6.1.2, 6.5.3, 7.1.4, 7.8.2, 7.8.4
 ἰδιώτης, ἰδιωτικοί 6.5.3, 7.8.2
 لا يجيدون 7.8.2 — جاهل 6.1.2 — عامي 1.1.2, 7.1.4
ܗܕܪܐ, ܗܕܝܪܘܬܐ beauty 7.4.title, 7.4.1
 ἑλληνίζειν 7.4.1
 إشباع 7.4.1
ܗ̈ܘܠܣ materials 6.2.1
 مواد 6.2.1
ܗܘܢܐ reason, understanding 4.6.1, 4.6.6. ܗܘܢܢܝܐ intellectual, mental 4.2.1, 4.3.1, 5.5.4. ܡܗ̈ܘܢܐ rational 5.2.7. ܩܕܡ ܡܬܗܘܢ pre-conceived 4.2.3
 γνώμη 4.6.1 — μετὰ λόγου 4.3.1
 خطباء 5.2.7 — عقل 4.6.1, 4.6.6. عقلية 4.3.1, 5.5.4 — قدم برؤية 4.2.3
ܗܐܪ̈ܘܐܐ heroic 7.5.5
 ἡρῷος 7.5.5
ܡܗܠܠܘܬܐ, ܡܗܠܝܢܬܐ, ܬܗܠܠܬܐ mockery, derision 5.3.2, 7.3.5, 7.10.2
 γέλως/γελοῖος 7.10.2
 استهزاء 5.3.2, 7.3.5 — هزل 7.10.2
ܗ̈ܡܘܣܬܐ conditions 6.4.1
 شرط 6.4.1
ܗܢܝ pleasurable, pleasant, pleasing 2.2.2, 2.3.3, 2.3.7, 2.3.8, 2.4.5, 3.1.1, 4.2.4, 4.3.1, 4.3.2, 4.3.3, 4.3.4, 4.3.5, 4.3.6, 4.3.7, 4.4.5, 5.1.7, 5.5.3, 5.5.7, 5.5.12, 7.2.4, 7.3.4, 7.6.1, 7.7.1, 7.7.2, 7.7.4, 7.7.5, 7.9.8. ܗܢܝܢܐ pleasurable 5.5.4. ܗ̈ܢܝܐ, ܚܒܝܒܐ pleasant company 5.2.2. ܗܢܝܐܝܬ with pleasure 5.1.1, 6.4.1, 7.3.3, 7.7.4. ܗܢܝܐܘܬܐ pleasure, pleasantness 2.4.8, 4.3.title, 4.2.3, 4.2.4, 4.3.2, 4.3.3, 4.3.4, 4.3.5, 4.4.3, 4.4.5, 5.1.2, 5.1.3, 5.2.3, 5.5.4, 5.5.7, 6.5.7, 7.7.title. ܚܠܝܠ ܡܢ ܗܢܝܐܘܬܐ deprived of pleasure 7.5.4. ܐܗܢܝ bring pleasure 4.3.2. ܡܗܢܝܐ produce benefit 1.3.3, 4.1.1
 ἥδεσθαι 5.5.7. ἡδύς 2.2.2, 2.3.3, 2.3.8, 3.1.1, 4.2.4, 4.3.1, 4.3.2, 4.3.4, 4.3.5, 4.3.6, 4.3.7, 4.4.3, 4.4.5, 5.1.1, 6.5.7, 7.2.4, 7.6.1, 7.7.1, 7.9.8. ἡδεῖς συνδιαγαγεῖν καὶ συνδιημερεῦσαι 5.2.2. ἡδεώς 4.2.3. ἡδονή 2.4.5, 2.4.8, 4.2.3, 4.3.1, 4.3.3, 5.1.2, 5.1.3, 5.1.7. ἀηδές 7.5.4 — εὐδοκιμεῖν 7.7.4, 7.7.5 — εὐφραίνειν 4.3.2
 لذ 4.3.2, 4.3.4. لذيذ 2.3.3, 2.3.8, 3.1.1, 4.2.4, 4.3.1, 4.3.2, 4.3.3, 4.3.4, 4.3.5, 4.3.6, 4.3.7, 4.4.5, 5.5.7, 5.5.12, 7.2.4, 7.3.3, 7.3.4, 7.6.1, 7.7.1. ألذيذ 2.4.5. لذة 2.4.5, 2.4.8, 4.2.3, 4.2.4, 4.3.title, 4.3.1, 4.3.3, 4.4.3, 4.4.5, 5.1.2, 5.5.3, 5.5.4, 6.5.7. يلتذ 5.1.3, 7.9.8. لم يلتذ 7.5.4. التذاذ 4.3.5, 5.2.3, 5.5.7 — ملح 7.7.4 — هوى 2.3.7

μειοῦν 6.1.1, 6.7.3 — μικρότης 6.1.3 — ἐλάχιστα 4.5.7
تحقير 6.1.1, 6.1.3 — تصغير 6.7.3 — هون 4.5.7

ܙܪܝܙܘܬܐ swiftness 2.2.7
τάχος 2.2.7

ܚܒܪܘܬܐ companionship 5.2.3
ἑταιρεία 5.2.3
صحبة 5.2.3

ܣܟܪ dissuade, restrain 1.2.2, 3.4.1. ܣܘܟܪܐ dissuasion, restraining 1.3.5, 1.5.3, 3.4.1. ܣܟܘܪܐ dissuasion, restraining 1.8.1, 3.4.1
ἀποτροπή 1.8.1
اجتناب 1.8.1 — منع 3.4.1

ܕܘܒܪܐ ܠܚܘܕܝܐ sole government 2.1.8. ܚܘܕܝܘܬ ܪܫܢܘܬܐ sole supremacy 2.4.9 — ܡܚܕܐ immediately 1.4.5, 1.6.2, 7.10.2
μοναρχία 2.1.8, 2.4.9 — εἷς κύριος 2.4.9 — εὐθύς 1.6.2, 7.10.2
سياسة وحدانية 2.1.8. وحدانية الرياسة 2.4.9 — في بادئ الرأي 1.4.5, 1.6.2

ܚܘܐ show 2.2.1. ܡܚܘܐ demonstrate 6.6.1, 6.7.1. ܚܘܝܐ demonstration 3.1.1, 6.6.1. ܬܚܘܝܬܐ paradigm 1.6.1, 1.6.2, 2.4.7, 2.4.9, 3.4.3, 4.5.1, 4.6.7, 6.2.title, 6.2.1, 6.2.4, 6.5.3, 6.5.4, 6.5.7, 6.7.3, 7.6.3, 7.9.9, 7.9.10. ܬܚܘܝܬܢܝܐ paradigmatic 3.4.3, 6.2.4. ܡܚܘܝܢܐ, ܡܚܘܝܢܝܐ demonstrative 1.8.1, 1.8.2, 1.8.4, 3.title, 5.5.13, 6.1.1, 6.5.1. ܡܚܘܝܢܘܬܐ paradigm, demonstration 1.6.1, 2.4.5, 6.2.1, 6.7.2, 7.9.11. ܢܬܚܘܐ appear, seem 4.3.5, 7.5.4
ἀπόδειξις 3.4.3. δεικτικόν 6.6.1, 7.9.11 — ἐπιδεικνύναι, ἐπιδεικτικός 1.8.1, 1.8.4, 5.5.13, 6.1.1 — παράδειγμα 1.6.1, 2.2.1, 3.4.3, 4.6.7, 6.2.1, 6.2.4, 6.7.2, 6.7.3, 7.9.10 — δοκεῖν 7.5.4
برهانات 3.4.3, 6.2.1, 6.7.2 — إثبات, تثبيت 2.4.9, 6.6.1, 7.9.11 — يجعل 6.7.1 — دلالات 3.4.3 — مشهود 6.2.4 — اعتبار 1.6.1 — مثال 1.6.1, 1.6.2, 2.4.7, 4.6.7, 6.2.1, 6.2.4, 6.5.4, 6.7.3, 7.9.9, 7.9.10 — منافر, منافرية 1.8.1, 1.8.2, 1.8.4, 3.title, 6.5.1

ܚ̈ܙܝܐ spectators 1.8.2, 5.5.13. ܡܬܚܙܝܐ is visible, appears 1.6.3, 5.5.10. ܡܬܚܙܝܢܘܪܐ ostentatious show 4.3.5. ܡܬܚܙܝܢܐ visible 7.8.5. ܡܬܚܙܝܢܢܘܬܐ visualizable 7.2.5
θεωρός 1.8.2, 5.5.13 — φαίνεσθαι, φαινόμενος 5.5.10, 4.3.5 — ἐπιδεικτική 7.8.5 — ὄψις 7.2.5
نظار 1.8.2, 5.5.13 — ظهر, ظاهر 4.3.5, 1.6.3 — لاحظ 5.5.10 — مرئى 7.8.5 — مبصرة 7.2.5

ܣܟܠ make a mistake 4.5.8, 7.2.5, 7.9.6. ܣܟܠܘܬܐ, ܣ̈ܟܠܘܬܐ failing, failings 4.5.4, 4.5.8, 5.5.4
ἁμαρτάνειν 4.5.8, 5.5.4, 7.2.5, 7.9.6. ἁμάρτημα, ἁμαρτήματα 4.5.4, 7.9.6

خطأ 5.5.4, 7.2.5, 7.9.6

ܚܝܠܐ strength 1.4.3, 2.2.7 — power, faculty, ability, potential 1.4.3, 1.4.5, 1.5.1, 2.1.7, 2.3.7, 2.4.1, 4.3.6, 5.1.4, 5.5.7, 5.5.11, 7.1.1
  ἰσχύς 1.4.3 — ἀρετή 2.2.7 — δύναμις 1.4.5, 1.5.1, 2.3.7, 2.4.1, 5.1.4, 5.5.11, 7.1.1. δύνασθαι 1.4.3
  قدير 1.4.3. الاقتدار 4.3.6 — قوة 1.4.3, 1.4.5, 1.5.1, 2.1.7, 2.3.7, 2.4.1, 5.1.4, 5.5.11 — نحيزة 5.5.7

ܚܟܝܡ wise 1.1.1, 1.1.3, 1.3.3, 4.3.7, 4.4.5, 4.6.2, 4.6.6, 5.1.6, 5.2.7, 5.4.3, 5.4.8, 5.5.10, 6.5.5, 7.4.3, 7.9.7. ܚܟܡܬܐ wisdom 3.1.1, 3.1.2, 5.4.11, 6.3.1. ܚܟܡ̈ܬܐ sciences 7.9.3. ܪ̈ܚܡܝ ܚܟܡܬܐ lovers of wisdom 5.1.4. ܚܟܡܘܬܐ wisdom 2.1.2. ܚܟܝܡܘܬܐ wisdom 1.4.1, 1.4.5. ܚ̈ܟܝܡܘܬܐ sciences 6.1.2
  σοφός 4.3.7, 5.5.10, 6.3.1, 6.5.5, 7.9.7. δοξόσοφοι 5.4.8. σοφώτερον/παρασοφίζεσθαι 4.6.2. σοφία 3.1.1, 5.4.8, 5.4.11 — ἐπιστήμη 1.4.1, 1.4.5, 2.1.2. ἐπιστῆμαι 6.1.2 — εὖ φρονεῖν 7.9.3
  أمام 1.3.3 — بصيرة ومعرفة 1.4.5. مستبصر 4.6.2 — حكيم 1.1.1, 1.1.3, 4.4.5, 5.5.10, 7.4.3. حكمة 3.1.1, 4.3.7, 5.4.11, 6.3.1. أهل الاجتهاد الحكمة 5.1.4 — حصيف 5.2.7 — عقلية 2.1.2. تعقل 1.4.1. عقلاء 5.2.7 — علمي 1.4.1. علوم 6.1.2. علماء 4.6.6 — فضائل 7.9.3

ܚ̈ܘܠܛܢܐ mixed (constitutions) 2.1.7
  خلطية 2.1.7

ܚܘܠܡܢܐ health 1.4.3, 1.5.1, 2.2.2, 2.2.6, 2.2.9, 2.3.2, 2.4.8, 5.2.5, 5.4.10. ܡܚܠܡܢܐ being healthy 2.3.2. ܐܬܚܠܡ recover health, be cured 6.1.1, 6.3.2, 6.6.1
  ὑγίεια 1.4.3, 2.2.2, 2.2.6, 2.2.9, 2.3.2, 2.4.8, 5.4.10. ὑγιεινόν 1.5.1, 6.6.1. ὑγιαίνειν 2.3.2, 6.3.2. ὑγιασθῆναι 6.1.1
  صح 1.5.1, 6.6.1. صحة 1.4.3, 2.2.2, 2.2.6, 2.2.9, 2.3.2, 2.4.8, 5.2.5, 5.4.10. مصحح 2.3.2

ܚܘܠܦܐ substitution 7.2.1
  ἐξαλλάττειν 7.2.1
  تبديل 7.2.1

ܚܠܝܨܘܬܐ strength 5.5.1
  δυνάμεις 5.5.1
  جلد 5.5.1

ܚܠܩ fated 5.4.7. ܚܠܩܐ fate 5.4.3, 5.4.7
  νεμεσᾶν 5.4.3. νεμέσασχ' 5.4.7
  قدر 5.4.3, 5.4.7

ܚܘܣܢܐ strength 2.2.2
  ἰσχύς 2.2.2
  جلد 2.2.2

ܚܡܫ ܐܬܠܘܢܐ of the pentathlon 2.2.7
  πένταθλος 2.2.7

ܚܡܬܐ anger, rage, wrath 4.1.2, 4.2.1, 5.1.2, 5.5.1, 5.5.7, 6.3.5, 7.1.1. ܚܡܬܢܐ, ܚ̈ܡܬܢܐ irascible 4.2.1, 4.2.3
θυμός 4.2.1, 5.1.2, 5.5.7 — ὀργή 4.2.1, 4.2.3, 5.5.1
غضب 4.1.2, 4.2.1, 5.5.7, 7.1.1. غضبي 4.2.1 — غيظ 6.3.5

ܚܣܕ revile 4.5.3, 5.3.2. ܚܣܕܐ dishonour 4.5.3. ܡܬܚܣܕܢܘܬܐ being blamed 5.3.1
ἀτιμία 4.5.3
ذم 4.5.3, 5.3.1. مذموم 5.3.1

ܚܣܡ envy, be envious 5.4.4, 5.4.6, 5.4.8, 5.4.9, 5.4.10. ܚܣܝܡ envied 5.4.8, 6.3.3. ܡܚܣܡܘ excite envy 5.4.9. ܐܬܚܣܡ be envied 5.4.9, 5.5.10, 6.3.3, 6.5.6, 6.5.9. ܚܣܡܢܐ envious 5.4.6, 5.4.8, 5.4.9, 5.4.10. ܚܣܡܐ envy 2.2.9, 5.2.4, 5.4.title, 5.4.4, 5.4.5, 5.4.8, 5.4.10
ἄδικος? 5.2.4 — ζηλοῦν 5.5.10 — φθονεῖν 5.4.8, 5.4.9, 5.4.10. φθονεῖσθαι 6.3.3, 6.5.6. φθονερός 5.4.5, 5.4.8. φθόνος 2.2.9, 5.4.4, 5.4.8, 5.4.10
حسد, يحسد, محسود 5.4.6, 5.4.8, 5.4.9, 6.5.6, 6.5.9. استحسد 5.5.10. حاسد 2.2.9, 5.4.6, 5.4.8, 5.4.9, 6.3.3. حسد 5.2.4, 5.4.title, 5.4.4, 5.4.5, 5.4.8. تحسيد 5.4.9

ܚܣܝܪܐ deficient 1.8.2. ܚܣܝܪ̈ܬܐ deficiencies 6.5.11. ܚܘܣܪܢܐ penalty 4.4.3.
αἰσχρόν 1.8.2 — ἀνομολογούμενα 6.5.11 — ζημία/τιμωρία 4.4.3
نقيصة 1.8.2 — عقوبة 4.4.3

ܚܪܝܢܐ dispute, contention 6.3.3, 7.5.3, 7.9.9. ܡܬܚܪܝܢܐ in dispute 6.5.4. ܡܬܚܪ̈ܝܢܐ in debate 5.5.13
ἀγῶνες 5.5.13 — ἀμφισβητεῖν 6.3.3, 6.5.4. ἀμφισβήτησις 7.9.9 — προεπιπλήττειν 7.5.3
ممارة 7.9.9 — محاورات 5.5.13

ܚܫ suffer 5.1.5, 5.2.6, 5.2.7, 5.4.4, 5.5.7, 6.2.2. ܡܚܫܘ arouse emotion 7.10.3 ܚܫܐ, ܚ̈ܫܐ passion(s), emotion(s), suffering(s) 1.2.3, 1.3.3, 1.5.3, 1.5.4, 4.1.2, 4.2.4, 5.title, 5.1.1, 5.1.5, 5.4.1, 5.4.3, 5.4.4, 5.4.11, 5.5.1, 5.5.8, 6.3.5, 6.5.1, 6.5.4, 7.1.1, 7.9.10. ܣܛܪ ܡܢ ܚܫܐ without passion 2.4.5. ܕܠܐ ܚ̈ܫܐ without passion 4.6.6. ܚܫܘܫܬܐ emotional 7.8.2. ܡܚܫܫܢܐ arousing pathos 7.5.2, 7.5.3. ܡܚܫܫܢܐ creating emotion 7.9.11
πάσχειν 5.2.7, 5.4.1, 5.5.8, 6.2.2. πάθος, πάθη 1.2.3, 1.5.3, 1.5.4, 4.2.4, 5.1.1, 5.4.3, 5.4.11, 5.5.1, 7.1.1, 7.9.10. παθήματα 6.5.1. παθητική 6.3.5, 7.5.2, 7.8.2. παθητικῶς 6.3.5, 7.5.3. παθητικὸν ποιεῖν 7.9.11. πάθη καταστῆσαι/ ἄγειν 7.10.3 — κατὰ τὴν φρόνησιν 2.4.5
انفعال, انفعالات 1.2.3, 1.3.3, 1.5.4, 4.1.2, 4.2.4, 5.1.1, 5.5.7, 7.9.10. انفعالى 1.5.3, 6.5.1, 7.5.2, 7.5.3, 7.8.2 — أذيات 5.5.8 — إحداث الألم 7.9.11. ألميات 7.10.3 — مضرة 5.2.7. — اغتم 5.4.4 — قاسا 5.2.6 — عن أهواء 2.4.5 — عن رضى 4.6.6

شكاية 1.3.5, 1.5.3 — نقم 5.4.6, 5.4.10. ناقم 5.4.6, 5.4.7. مناقمة 5.4.5. تنقيم 5.4.9 — حمية 5.4.title — مشاجرة 7.9.10

ܛܘܗܡܐ birth, descent, family 2.2.2, 3.3.4, 5.1.4, 5.2.3, 5.2.6. ܛܒܘܬ ܛܘܗܡܐ good birth, noble birth 5.4.6, 5.5.1, 5.5.9. ܛܘܗܡܐ ܫܦܝܪܘܬ good birth, noble birth 2.2.2, 3.3.5. ܛܘܗܡܐ ܫܦܝܪ of good birth, of noble birth 2.2.3, 5.5.9. ܛܘܗܡܐ ܡܥܠܝܘܬ high birth 3.2.4

γένος 5.1.4 — εὐγένεια 2.2.2, 2.2.3, 3.3.5, 5.4.6, 5.5.1, 5.5.9. εὐγενεῖς 5.4.6, 5.5.9 — ἐξ οἵων 3.3.4

حسب 5.1.4, 5.5.1 — ذوو الأبوة 5.5.9 — زكاء المحتد ,زكاء المحتد 2.2.2, 2.2.3 — شرف 3.2.4 — قبيلة 3.3.4 — نسب 3.3.5, 5.2.6. الأنسباء 5.5.9

ܛܒܐ good *passim*. ܛܒ̈ܬܐ ܦܓܪ̈ܢܝܬܐ goods of the body 5.5.12. ܛܝܒܘܬܐ goodness, graciousness, kindness, favour, blessing 3.1.1, 3.2.1, 3.3.5, 5.3.title, 5.3.5, 5.3.6. ܛܒܘܬܐ preference 2.3.1 — ܛܘܒܬܢܘܬܐ blessedness 3.3.5

ἀγαθός *passim*. κατὰ τὸ σῶμα ἀγαθά 5.5.12 — εὐεργετήματα 3.2.1 — εὐδαιμονισμός 3.3.5 — εὐδοκιμεῖν 4.6.4. εὐπραγίαι 5.4.3 — καλόν 5.5.3, 7.9.6 — μακαρισμός 3.3.5 — χάρις 5.3.5, 5.3.6

خير *passim*. خيرية 3.1.1 — أولى 4.5.5 — جميل 4.5.6, 5.1.5, 5.5.3, 7.9.6 — حسن 2.3.7, 3.2.1, 3.2.4, 5.1.4, 5.1.6, 5.3.6. حسن السيرة 4.6.4 — سعادة 3.3.5 — مصلحة 4.5.8 — تفضل 4.5.5. فضيلة 7.9.6. فضائل 7.9.3. فاضلون 7.9.7 — منافع 7.9.6

ܛܘܪܢܐ see ܛܪܘܢܐ

ܛܛܪܓܘܢܘܣ four-square 7.7.2

τετράγωνον 7.7.2

مربع الجوانب 7.7.2

ܛܟܢܐ art, technique 1.3.3, 1.5.2, 1.5.4, 7.1.2, 7.9.9. ܛܟܢܐܝܬ by art 4.2.3. ܐܬܛܟܢ artfully manage 3.3.1

τέχνη 7.1.2

حيلة 1.3.3, 4.2.3, 7.1.2, 7.9.9 — صنع 1.5.2. صناعة 7.1.2 — تلطف 3.3.1

ܛܟܣܐ arrangement, order 2.2.1, 7.9.8. ܛܘܟܣܐ arrangement 7.9.title. ܡܛܟܣܢܘܬܐ arrangement, order 2.2.1, 7.title, 7.1.1, 7.1.3, 7.6.3. ܡܛܟܣܐ self-controlled 7.7.2

τάξις 7.9.title (AR 14a29). τάττειν/τάξαι 7.1.1

ترتيب 7.1.1, 7.9.title — نظام 2.2.1, 7.6.3, 7.9.title, 7.9.8

ܛܠܝܐ young man, boy, youth 2.2.6, 6.1.1, 6.3.1, 6.5.1, 6.5.8, 7.2.4. ܛܠܝܘܬܐ youth 5.5.1, 5.5.2, 6.4.3, 7.7.2

νέος 2.2.6, 6.5.1, 7.2.4. νεώτατος 6.4.3, 6.5.8. νεότης 5.5.1, 5.5.2, 7.7.2 — παῖς 6.1.1, 6.3.1, 6.5.8

حداثة 5.5.1. أحداث 6.3.1 — صبى ,صبا 6.5.8, 7.2.4 — غلام 6.1.1, 6.5.8

ܛܠܡ do wrong, be unjust, commit injustice 4.4.5, 4.4.6, 4.5.7, 5.2.1, 5.2.4, 5.3.1, 5.5.4, 5.5.8, 5.5.11, 6.5.3, 6.5.4, 7.2.5 — unjustly deny 5.3.6. ܛܠܝܡܐ wronged 4.5.2, 4.5.7, 4.5.8, 5.2.6, 5.2.7, 5.5.4 — oppressed 5.4.3.

ܡܬܛܠܡܢܘܬܐ being wronged 4.5.2. ܐܬܛܠܡ suffer injustice, be wronged 4.4.6, 4.4.7, 5.2.6, 5.2.7. ܛܠܘܡ̈ܐ wrongdoers 5.5.11. ܛܠܘܡ unjust 4.6.4, 5.2.6. ܛܠܘܡܐ wrongdoer, oppressor 4.5.2, 4.5.4, 4.5.7, 5.2.6, 6.3.4, 6.5.13. ܛܠܘܡܘܬܐ wrongdoing, doing injustice 4.4.5, 4.5.2, 5.5.11. ܛܠܘܡܝܐ unjust, injustice, wrongdoing 3.2.1, 4.4.3, 4.4.5, 4.5.1, 4.5.7, 4.5.8, 5.5.7, 5.5.8, 7.9.6

ἀδικεῖν 4.4.5, 4.4.6, 4.5.2, 4.5.7, 5.2.6, 5.5.4, 5.5.8, 5.5.11, 6.3.4, 6.5.3, 6.5.4, 7.2.5, 7.9.6. ἀδικεῖσθαι 4.4.7, 4.5.2, 5.2.6, 5.2.7. ἀδικουμένοι 5.2.7. ἀδίκημα 4.4.3, 4.5.2, 4.5.7, 4.5.8, 5.5.8, 5.5.11. ἀδικία 5.2.4, 5.3.1. ἄδικος 4.5.1, 4.5.2, 5.2.1, 5.2.4. ἀδίκως 3.2.1 — ἀφαιρεῖσθαι 5.3.6

جار 4.4.5. جور 3.2.1, 4.4.3, 4.4.5, 4.5.7, 7.9.6. مجور 4.5.7. جائر 4.5.7 — ظلم 4.4.7, 4.5.2, 5.2.6, 5.2.7, 5.3.1, 5.5.4, 5.5.11, 6.3.4. مظلوم 4.5.2, 5.4.3. متظلم 5.5.4. ظالم 4.6.4, 5.2.4, 6.5.13, 7.2.5. ظلم 4.4.5, 4.5.1, 4.5.2, 4.5.8, 5.2.6, 5.5.11. ظلامة 4.5.2 — أذى 5.2.1 — مغافص ? 5.2.4 — بريء 5.2.7 — يحتج في إبطال 5.3.6

ܛܢ emulate 5.2.2, 5.4.8, 5.4.10, 5.4.11. ܛܢܝܐ emulated 5.4.11. ܛܢ̈ܝܬܐ objects of emulation 5.4.10. ܡܬܛܢܝܢܐ emulated 5.4.11. ܛܢܢܐ emulous 5.4.10, 5.4.11. ܛܢܢܐ emulation 5.4.title, 5.4.10, 5.4.11

ζῆλος 5.4.10, 5.4.11. ζηλοῦν 5.4.10, 5.4.11. ζηλοῦσθαι 5.2.2, 5.4.11. ζηλωτικοί 5.4.10. ζηλωτοί 5.4.11. ζηλωτά 5.4.10

حمى 5.4.11. حمية 5.4.10, 5.4.11 — عجب 5.2.2 — غير 5.4.11. غيرة 5.4.title, 5.4.11

ܛܪܐܓܘܕܝܣ tragedies 7.1.4

τραγῳδίαι 7.1.4

ܛܪܘܟܐܘܣ trochaios 7.5.5

τροχαῖος 7.5.5

ܛܘܪܢܐ, ܛܪܘܢܐ tyrant 1.7.3, 4.4.3, 6.2.2, 6.6.2. ܛܪܘܢܝܐ tyranny 2.1.8

τυραννίς 2.1.8, 4.4.3. τύραννος 6.6.2

سياسة تغلبية 2.1.8 — فتنة أو وقوع هرج 4.4.3

ܐܬܝܪܘ were the best 6.4.2. ܕܘܒܪ ܝܬܝܪܘܬܐ pre-eminent government 2.1.8. ܐܚܝܕܘܬܐ ܝܬܝܪܘܬ pre-eminent rule 2.4.9

ἀριστεύειν 6.4.2

سياسة الأخيار 2.1.8 — رياسة شريفة 2.4.9

ܡܬܐܒ desires 5.3.5. ܐܒܝܘܬܐ desire 5.1.2, 5.3.5. ܘܐܒܐ longing 4.2.1, 4.3.2

ἐπιθυμεῖν 5.3.5 — ὄρεξις 4.2.1, 5.1.2, 5.3.5

شوق 4.2.1, 4.3.2, 5.1.2 — مشتهى 5.3.5

ܡܘܕܝܢ acknowledge 2.3.6. ܡܫܬܘܕܝܢ agreed 3.4.3. ܡܫܬܘܕܝܢܐ agreed, accepted 1.6.3, 3.4.3, 6.5.1, 6.7.3

ὁμολογεῖν 2.3.6, 3.4.3. ὁμολογούμενα 1.6.3, 6.5.1
حمد/شكر 2.3.6 — مسلمة 6.7.3 — ضبط 1.6.3 — يقر بها 6.5.1

ܝܕܥܬܐ knowledge, science 1.1.1, 1.2.2, 2.3.4, 2.4.5, 5.5.3. ܝܕ̈ܘܥܐ learned 2.4.5, 6.1.2. ܝܕܘܥܬܢ learned 1.1.2, 1.1.3. ܡܕܥܐ mind, understanding 5.1.1, 5.5.10, 7.9.6. ܡܘܕܥ make known 7.1.4. ܫܘܕܥܐ sign 1.3.5, 1.7.1, 1.7.2, 1.8.4, 2.2.5, 3.2.title, 3.2.1, 3.2.2, 3.2.4, 3.3.3, 4.6.4, 5.1.5, 5.2.5, 5.3.4, 5.4.3, 6.3.4, 6.7.2, 6.7.3, 7.2.5, 7.3.3, 7.4.3, 7.5.1, 7.9.2. ܫܘܕܥܐ ܫܪܝܪܐ certain sign 1.7.1. ܡܘܕܥܢܐ signifying 7.1.4. ܡܘܕܥܢܘܬܐ denotation 7.2.2
εἰδότες 2.4.5 — ἐπιστῆμαι 2.3.4, 2.4.5 — φρήν 7.9.6 — σημεῖον 1.7.1, 1.7.2, (1.8.4?), 2.2.5, 3.2.1, 3.2.4, 5.1.5, 5.2.5, 5.3.4, 5.4.3, 7.2.5 — τεκμήριον 1.7.1?, 1.8.4?, 6.7.2, 6.7.3 — συμβουλή/ σύμβολον 7.9.2 — δηλοῦν 7.1.4
بصير 5.5.10 — خاصي 1.1.2. خاصية 1.1.3 — صنائع 1.1.1 — معرفة 5.5.3 — علم 1.2.2, 2.3.4, 2.4.5. عالم 2.4.5, 6.1.2 — نية 7.9.6 — أمارات 4.6.4 — دل 3.3.3, 7.1.4, 7.3.3, 7.5.1. دليل 1.3.5, 1.7.1, 1.7.2, 1.8.4, 2.2.5, 5.1.5, 5.3.4, 6.7.2, 6.7.3. دلالة 2.2.5, 7.1.4, 7.2.5, 7.9.2 — علامة 3.2.1, 3.2.2, 3.2.4, 5.2.5, 5.4.3, 6.3.4, 7.4.3

ܝܘܠܦܢܐ learning 2.3.4, 2.3.8, 5.1.4. ܝܠܦ ܡܢ ܗܘ̇ self-taught 2.4.7
εὐμάθεια 2.3.4. αὐτοδίδακτος 2.4.7
تعلم 2.3.4

ܝܡܐ swear 4.6.8, 4.6.9. ܝܡܝܐ he who swears 4.6.8. ܡܘܡܬܐ oath 4.6.1, 4.6.8, 4.6.9
ὀμνύναι 4.6.8, 4.6.9. ὀμόσας 4.6.8 — ὅρκος 4.6.1, 4.6.8
حلف 4.6.8, 4.6.9 — قسم 4.6.8 — يمين 4.6.1, 4.6.8, 4.6.9

ܡܚܘܝܢܐ ܕܕܡܝܢܐ coining a simile 7.3.5. ܡܬ̈ܠܐ ܘܕܡܘ̈ܬܐ similes 7.7.5
εἰκών 7.3.5. εἰκόνες 7.7.5
تجري تشبيه 7.3.5. تشبيه 7.7.5

ܝܩܪ honoured 6.5.6. ܝܩܝܪܐ honourable 2.2.5. ܝܩܪ (pa''el) honour 3.1.1, 5.1.4, 5.2.2, 5.2.3, 5.3.3, 6.5.9, 7.2.6, 7.9.3. ܡܝܩܪܐ honourable 3.3.3, 5.3.3, 5.5.11, 7.2.6. ܡܝܩܪ honoured, held in honour 5.1.5, 6.6.2, 7.7.1. ܠܐ ܡܝܩܪܐ unhonoured 6.6.1. ܡܝܩܪܢܘܬܐ honouring 5.4.11. ܐܬܝܩܪ honoured 4.5.3, 6.5.3, 6.5.6, 6.6.1. ܐܝܩܪܐ honour 2.2.2, 2.2.5, 2.3.8, 3.1.1, 3.2.1, 3.2.2, 3.2.4, 4.3.5, 4.5.3, 4.6.8, 5.1.2, 5.1.4, 5.3.3, 5.4.10, 5.5.9, 5.5.11, 6.5.5, 6.5.8, 7.2.1 — reward, gift, donation, value 2.4.5, 2.4.9, 5.4.6, 7.6.3. ܪܚܡ ܐܝܩܪܐ ambitious, lover of honour 4.1.2, 4.3.7, 5.4.7, 5.4.8, 5.5.2, 5.5.9, 5.5.11
βελτίων 7.2.6 — δωρητοί 7.6.3 — πρὸς δόξαν 5.2.2 — εὐδοκιμεῖν 7.7.1 — θαυμάζειν 5.4.11 — πολυωρεῖσθαι 5.1.4 — τιμᾶν 3.1.1, 5.1.5, 5.4.10, 6.5.5, 6.5.6, 6.5.9, 7.9.3. τιμή 2.2.2, 2.2.5, 2.3.8, 2.4.5, 3.2.1, 3.2.4, 4.3.5, 4.5.3. τιμήματα 2.4.9. τίμιον 3.3.3, 5.3.3, 6.6.1. τιμιώτατος 6.6.2. ἀτιμότατον 6.6.1. ἐντιμότης/ἐντιμότερα 5.5.9.

ἀγαθόν 6.2.4 — βοήθεια 6.3.7 — κέρδος 4.4.3, 5.5.7 — λῆψις 4.4.4 — λυσιτελεῖν 4.4.5 — συμφέρον 1.3.2, 1.8.3, 5.5.3, 5.5.8 — ὑπουργεῖν 5.3.5 — χρήσιμος 1.4.1. χρῆσις 5.5.13 — ὠφέλεια 4.4.3, 6.3.7. ὠφέλιμον 6.5.10, 7.9.6, 7.9.8, 7.9.9

فحائل 6.5.12 — حقوق 4.4.4 — مصالح 5.5.4. مصلحة 7.9.6 — نفع 6.3.1, 7.9.9. نفع 1.4.1, 1.8.4, 2.1.3. نافع 1.3.1, 1.3.2, 1.8.3, 5.3.5, 5.5.3, 5.5.7, 5.5.8, 6.5.10, 7.9.8. أنفع 5.5.3. منفعة 1.1.title, 4.4.3, 4.4.5, 5.1.4. منافع 5.5.8, 5.5.13, 6.3.7. انتفع 6.2.4, 6.3.1. استنفع 5.3.6

ܠܐ ܡܬܝܪܬܐ stringless 7.5.1

ἄχορδον 7.5.1

غير عودى 7.5.1

ܟܐܢ, ܟܐܢܐ just, righteous 1.3.1, 1.3.6, 1.4.1, 1.4.2, 1.8.4, 3.2.1, 4.1.2, 4.3.4, 4.6.1, 4.6.3, 4.6.4, 4.6.6, 5.2.7, 5.4.5, 6.5.2, 7.9.2, 7.9.7. ܟܐܢܐܝܬ justly 2.2.5, 3.2.1, 4.6.3, 6.5.1, 6.5.2, 6.6.4, 7.9.9. ܟܐܢܘܬܐ justice 1.3.1, 1.3.2, 3.2.4, 3.3.3, 4.5.3, 4.6.2, 4.6.3, 5.4.5, 5.5.7, 6.5.1, 7.9.6

ἀδιάφθοροι 4.6.4 — βελτίων 4.6.1 — δίκαιος 1.3.1, 1.3.2, 1.4.1, 1.8.4, 3.2.1, 4.1.2, 4.3.4, 4.5.3, 4.6.1, 4.6.3, 4.6.6, 5.4.5, 6.5.1, 6.5.2, 7.9.7. δικαιοσύνη 3.2.4. δικαίως 2.2.5, 3.2.1, 6.5.1, 6.5.2, 6.6.4, 7.9.9. δικανική 4.3.4 — καλῶς ἔχειν 5.2.7

براء 3.3.3 — حسن السيرة 5.2.7 — ترافع 4.6.2 — صواب 4.1.2. صائب 4.6.3 — عدل 1.3.1, 1.3.2, 1.3.6, 1.4.1, 1.4.2, 1.8.4, 2.2.5, 3.2.1, 4.5.3, 4.6.6, 5.5.7, 6.5.2, 7.9.2, 7.9.6, 7.9.9. عدلاء 3.2.4. عادلون 3.2.1 — فاضل 4.6.1. فضيلة 5.4.5 — لا ميل 4.6.4 — بالواجب والقسط 4.3.4

ܟܗܝܢܘܬܐ abundance, prosperity 2.2.1, 2.2.2, 3.1.2, 3.3.2, 3.3.5, 5.2.5, 5.5.10. ܟܗܝܢܘܬ ܒܢܝܐ abundance of children 2.2.3.

εὐδαιμονία 2.2.1, 2.2.2, 3.1.2, 3.3.5, 5.5.10 — εὐτυχίαι 5.2.5 — εὐτεκνία 2.2.3.

حسن الحال 5.5.10 — صلاح الحال 2.2.1, 2.2.2, 3.3.5 — حال الأولاد 2.2.3

ܟܝܢܐ (ܟܗ 1) nature 2.2.9, 2.3.2, 3.3.5, 4.1.1, 4.2.4, 4.3.1, 4.4.4, 5.4.6, 5.5.3, 5.5.4, 6.1.1, 6.1.2. ܟܝܢܝܐ natural 2.2.9, 4.2.1, 4.2.3, 4.2.4, 4.3.1, 4.5.4, 4.5.8, 4.6.1, 7.1.2 — physical 1.7.4

ἀναγκαζόμενοι 4.1.1 — οὐσίᾳ 6.1.1 — πεφυκός 4.3.1 — φυσικά 1.7.4. φύσις, φύσει, διὰ φύσιν, κατὰ φύσιν 2.2.9, 4.2.1, 4.2.3, 4.2.4, 4.3.1, 4.4.4, 4.6.1, 5.4.6, 6.1.2, 7.1.2 — ἦθος 5.5.3

مشتركة 4.5.4 — طبع 2.2.9, 5.4.6, 6.1.1, 6.1.2. طبيعة 4.1.1, 4.2.1, 4.2.3, 4.2.4, 6.1.2, 7.1.2 — غريزي 3.3.5 — فطرة 5.5.3

(ܟܣ 2) ܟܣ refute 6.5.10. ܟܘܣܝܐ refutation 6.5.10, 6.5.12, 6.6.1. ܡܟܣܢܐ refuter 6.5.14. ܡܟܣܢܘܬܐ refutation 6.5.1, 6.5.3, 6.5.14. ܡܬܟܣܢܐ refuted 6.5.14

ἐλεγτικός 6.5.12 (AR 00a14), 6.5.14, 6.6.1. ἔλεγχος 6.5.1 — ἐξελέγχειν ? 6.5.3

وبخ 6.5.10. موبخ 6.5.14. توبيخ 6.5.1, 6.5.12, 6.5.14, 6.6.1

ܒܗܬܬܐ shame 3.2.3, 5.5.3. ܡܬܒܗܬܝܢ modest 5.5.7

αἰσχυντηλοί 5.5.3, 5.5.7

حياء 5.5.3. استحياء 3.2.3

ܟ̈ܡܘܢܘܗܝ storms 5.2.7

χειμών 5.2.7

ܟܘܠܐ whole 6.1.2. ܒܟܠ universally 1.7.2. ܕܟܠ universal 4.5.1. ܠܟܠ everyone 6.4.2. ܟܠܢܐܝܬ universally, generally, in general 3.4.3, 6.3.4, 6.7.2. ܟܠܢܝܐ universal, general 1.2.2, 1.3.3, 1.3.4, 1.4.1, 1.6.4, 4.5.3, 4.6.2, 5.1.2, 6.2.4, 6.3.1, 6.3.4, 6.3.5, 6.3.7, 6.7.2.

καθόλου 1.3.3, 1.6.4, 1.7.2, 4.5.3, 6.3.1, 6.3.4, 6.3.7, 6.4.2, 6.7.2 — τὸ ὅλον 6.1.2. ὅλως 3.4.3 — πάντων 4.5.1

بالجملة 3.4.3 — مطلق 4.6.2 — عامي 6.3.7 — كل 1.6.4, 6.1.2, 6.4.2. في الكل 1.7.2. كلى 1.3.4, 5.1.2, 6.3.7, 6.7.2. كليا 6.3.4. كلية 1.2.2, 1.3.3, 1.4.1, 1.6.4, 4.5.3, 6.3.1, 6.3.4, 6.3.5, 6.7.2

ܟܠܐ dissuade 1.8.2, 6.5.10

ἀποτρέπειν 1.8.2, 6.5.10

مشورة 6.5.10 — لا فعل 1.8.2

ܟܠܒܐ ܕܓܢܒܪܐ dog of Orion 6.6.1

μεγάλας θεοῦ κύων 6.6.1

ܟܡܝܘܬܐ quantity 2.3.2

كمية 2.3.2

ܟܘܢܝܐ appellation, designation 3.3.2, 7.2.5, 7.2.6

πρόσθεσις? 7.2.5

عبارة 3.3.2 — بدل 7.2.5

ܟܢܝ dignify 7.9.8, 7.10.2. ܟܢܝܘܬܐ dignity 7.3.5. ܡܟܢܝܐ makes solemn 7.5.5. ܡܬܟܢܝܢܘܬܐ solemnity 7.2.1.

σεμνός 7.3.5, 7.5.5. σεμνοτέρα 7.2.1 — σπουδή 7.10.2

بعد 7.3.5 — رنق/روعة 7.2.1— يفيد سمتا 7.9.8 — تفضيل 7.10.2

ܡܟܢܫ bring a conclusion 7.10.2. ܡܟܢܫܐ yields a conclusion 6.7.3. ܡܟܢܫܢܘܬܐ implying 7.10.1. ܢܬܟܢܫܘܢ follow 6.4.1. ܟ̈ܢܫܐ gatherings 6.4.1. ܟܘܢܫܬܐ assembly 4.5.8. ܟܢܘܫܘܬܐ conjunction 6.3.1. ܟܘܢܫܐ combination 2.4.6 — recapitulation 7.9.1

ἀσυλλόγιστον 6.7.3 — δικαστήριον 4.5.8 — ἐπάνοδος 7.9.1 — ὄχλος 6.4.1— συλλογίζεσθαι/ συμπεραινόμενον 7.10.2. συμπέρασμα 7.10.1 — συνάγειν 6.4.1 — συντιθέναι 2.4.6

مجلس القضاء 4.5.8. مجالس 6.4.1 — جمع 7.9.1 — إجمال 2.4.6 — يقرن 6.3.1 — ينتج 7.10.1. منتج 6.7.3. منتجة 6.4.1

ܡܟܣܢܘܬܐ refutation 7.9.11. ܡܬܟܣܣ rejected 7.10.1
 ἔλεγχος 7.9.11
 توبيخ 7.9.11

ܟܣܪܘܢܝܐ *khusruwaniyyat* 7.5.5
 خسروانيات 7.5.5

ܟܦܝܪܘܬܐ renunciation 1.6.3. ܟܦܝܪܬܐ disputed 6.5.1
 ἀνομολογούμενα 6.5.1
 شنعة 1.6.3. مستشنعة 6.5.1

(ܟܪܐ 1) ܟܪܝܐ short 7.5.6, 7.6.2. ܟܪܝܐܝܬ concisely 7.4.4
 βραχεῖαι 7.5.6. βραχύκωλοι 7.6.2 — μικρόν 7.6.2 — συντομία 7.4.4
 قصر 7.5.6. قصير 7.6.2 — إيجاز 7.4.4

(ܟܪܐ 2) ܟܪܐ to pity 5.4.1, 5.4.2, 5.4.3. ܡܟܪܝ excite pity 5.4.1, 5.4.2.
ܟܪܝܘܬܐ pity 5.4.1, 5.4.2
 ἐλεεῖν 5.4.1, 5.4.2, 5.4.3. ἐλεεινόν 5.4.2. ἔλεος 5.4.1
 شفقة 5.4.2 — عناية 5.4.2 — هم 5.4.3. اهتم 5.4.1, 5.4.2. مهتم 5.4.1.
 اهتمام 5.4.1, 5.4.2

ܟܬܝܒܐ written, ܠܐ ܟܬܝܒܐ unwritten 4.1.1, 4.5.1, 4.5.3, 4.5.4, 4.5.8, 4.6.1, 4.6.2, 4.6.6, 7.8.5. ܟܬܝܒܬܐ epigram 2.4.7. ܟܬܘܒܐ writers 7.8.2. ܟܬܘܒܘܬܐ writing 7.8.2. ܡܟܬܒܢܘܬܐ record 7.8.1. ܡܬܟܬܒܢܝܬܐ written 7.8.2
 γεγραμμένος, ἄγραφος 4.1.1, 4.5.1, 4.5.3, 4.5.4, 4.5.8, 4.6.1, 4.6.2, 4.6.6. γραφική 7.8.1, 7.8.2. γραφικοί 7.8.2. γραφικωτάτη 7.8.5 — ἐπίγραμμα 2.4.7
 مكتوبة, غير مكتوبة 4.1.1, 4.5.1, 4.5.3, 4.5.4, 4.5.8, 4.6.1, 4.6.2, 4.6.6, 7.8.1. مكتوب 7.8.2, 7.8.5. كتابة 7.8.2. كتاب 7.8.2

ܟܬܝܫܐ agitated 4.1.2. ܬܟܬܘܫܐ strife, competitive 2.2.6, 2.2.7. ܬܟܬܘܫܢܝܐ prowess 2.2.3
 ἀγωνιστική 2.2.7. δύναμις ἀγωνιστική 2.2.3 — βία 2.2.6
 انفعال 4.1.2 — قوة 2.2.3

ܠܐܟܣܝܣ see ܠܟܣܝܣ

ܡܠܒܒ give confidence 5.2.6, 5.2.7. ܡܬܠܒܒ be confident 5.2.6, 5.2.7. ܠܒܝܒܐܝܬ confidently 1.2.3, 5.2.6. ܠܒܝܒܘܬܐ confidence, fortitude 5.2.title, 5.2.6, 5.5.8
 θαρραλέοι 5.2.6, 5.2.7. θαρραλέον 5.2.6, 5.2.7. θαρρεῖν 5.5.8. θάρσος 5.2.6
 جريء 5.2.6 — شجع 5.2.6, 5.2.7. شجاعة 5.2.title, 5.2.6, 5.5.8. مشجعات 5.2.7

ܠܒܒ exhort, encourage, persuade 1.2.2, 1.8.2, 3.4.1. ܠܘܒܒܐ inciting 1.5.3. ܡܠܒܒܢܐ hortatory, of exhortation 1.8.1, 3.4.1
  προτρέπειν 1.8.2. προτροπή 1.8.1
  راد 1.8.2. إرادة 1.8.1 — مشورة 1.2.2 — يطلق, إطلاق 3.4.1

ܠܗܟܣܝܣ see ܠܟܣܝܣ

ܠܘܓܝܩܐ logic 1.2.2
  منطق 1.2.2

ܡܢ ܗܠܝܢ ܕܠܘܬ ܚܕܕ̈ (ܠܘܬ) (species of) from correlatives 6.5.1
  ἐκ τῶν πρὸς ἄλληλα 6.5.1
  من المتضايفات 6.5.1

ܡܠܒܟܢܐ connecting 7.6.1
  σύνδεσμος/εἰρομένη? 7.6.1
  تصل 7.6.1

ܠܟܣܝܣ (ܐܠܟܣܝܣ, ܠܗܟܣܝܣ) style, language, expression 3.4.1, 6.3.6, 7.1.2, 7.2.3, 7.3.3, 7.4.1, 7.5.6, 7.7.title, 7.7.1, 7.7.2, 7.9.7. ܠܟܣܝܣ ܠܐ ܡܥܝܕܢܝܬܐ uncustomary expression 7.3.2. ܠܟܣܝܣܝܐ stylistic 7.1.3. ܠܟܣܝܣܝܬ stylistic 7.7.3
  λέξις 3.4.1, 6.3.6, 7.1.2, 7.1.3, 7.2.3, 7.3.3, 7.4.1, 7.5.6, 7.7.1, 7.9.7 — γλῶτται 7.3.2
  لفظ — 7.3.2 لغة غريبة 7.2.3. لغات 7.7.1 — عبارة 3.4.1 — أمور خطابية 6.3.6, 7.1.3, 7.3.3, 7.4.1. لفظى 7.7.3, 7.9.7

ܠܣܛܝܐ robbers 7.2.4. ܠܣܛ robbed 7.2.5
  λῃσταί 7.2.4
  لص 7.2.4 — انتهب 7.2.5

ܠܚܢܐ voice 7.2.2. ܥܢܝܢܘܬ ܠܚܢܐ good sounding 7.5.6
  φωνή 7.2.2
  صوت 7.2.2 — غناء كثير في اللفظ 7.5.6

ܠܫܢܐ ܢܘܟܪܝܐ alien tongues 7.3.4
  γλῶτται 7.3.4
  غريب 7.3.4

ܠܐܝܩ appropriate, suitable 7.5.title, 7.9.11
  ἁρμόττειν 7.9.11
  حسن 7.5.title — تصلح 7.9.11

ܡܐܬܘܕܘܣ, ܡܐܬܘܕܘܣ method 1.3.5, 1.3.7, 1.5.2
  μέθοδος 1.3.5, 1.3.7, 1.5.2
  آلة 1.3.7 — حيث/فكرة 1.5.2

ܡܘܬܘܠܘܓܝܐܣ tales 6.3.4
  μυθολογεῖν 6.3.4
  أمثال 6.3.4

ܡܝܡܣܐ miming 7.1.4
μιμεῖσθαι 7.1.4
ܡܠܝܠܬܐ logical 1.3.7. ܡܠܝܠܐ rational 4.2.1, 4.3.1 ܡܠܝܠܘܬܐ logic title, 1.3.7, 7.4.1. ܡܡܠܠܐ discourse 7.8.5. ܪ̈ܚܡܝ ܡ̈ܠܐ lovers of words 6.5.5
λογικοί 1.3.7. λογιστική 4.2.1 — λέξις 7.8.5 — φιλόλογοι 6.5.5
منطق 1.3.7. منطقي 1.3.7, 4.2.1 — لفظ 7.8.5
ܡ̈ܠܝܦܐ studious, scholarly, well informed, competent, educated 1.6.3, 6.4.1, 7.2.2, 7.71, 7.8.4. ܡܬ̈ܠܝܦܐ studied 7.1.4
خواص 7.8.4 — محنكون 7.2.2 — متكلفة مجاوز 7.1.4 — اماثل 7.7.1
ܡܠܝܫܦܐ especially 5.1.1, 5.1.5
μάλιστα 5.1.1. ἔτι μᾶλλον 5.1.5
خصوصا 5.1.1, 5.1.5
(ܡܠܟ 1) ܡܠܟܐ king 5.2.5. ܕܘܒܪܐ ܡܠܟܝܐ royal government 2.1.8
βασιλεία 2.1.8
ملك 5.2.5. سياسة الملك 2.1.8
(ܡܠܟ 2) ܡܠܟ advise, give advice, deliberate 1.3.6, 1.8.3, 2.1.3, 2.1.4, 2.1.6, 2.3.1, 2.4.3, 4.6.3, 5.1.1, 6.2.4, 6.5.4, 6.5.6, 6.5.10, 6.5.12, 7.9.7, 7.9.11. ܡܠܟܐ advice, deliberation, counsel 1.8.4, 2.1.title, 2.1.1, 2.1.2, 2.1.7, 2.2.title, 2.2.1, 2.3.8, 2.4.3, 3.4.title, 3.4.1, 3.4.2, 3.4.3, 5.1.1, 6.5.1, 6.5.10, 7.8.1, 7.9.2, 7.9.3, 7.9.7, 7.9.9, 7.9.10, 7.9.11, 7.10.3. ܡܠܘܟܐ deliberative, deliberative (orator), adviser 1.8.2, 1.8.3, 1.8.4, 2.1.1, 2.1.3, 2.1.4, 2.2.1, 2.4.3, 2.4.9, 3.4.1, 5.1.1, 5.5.13, 6.1.1, 7.8.1, 7.9.2, 7.9.5, 7.9.11. ܡܠܘܟܘܬܐ advising 2.4.3. ܡܠܟܢܝܐ deliberative 1.3.5, 1.3.6, 1.6.4, 1.8.1, 2.title, 2.2.1, 2.4.3, 2.4.9, 3.4.1, 4.2.4, 6.1.3. ܡܠܟܢܝܬܐ deliberated 2.1.1. ܡܬܡܠܟܢܐ advisee 5.1.1. ܡܬܡܠܟܢܘܬܐ deliberation 5.1.1, 5.2.5
βουλεύειν 2.4.3. βουλεύεσθαι 2.1.1, 2.1.2, 2.3.1, 5.2.5, 6.2.4, 7.9.9 — δημηγορεῖν 7.9.10. δημηγορία 7.9.2, 7.9.9. δημηγορικός 1.3.5, 6.2.4, 7.8.1, 7.9.2, 7.9.5. δημηγορικώτατα 7.9.10 — συμβουλεύειν 1.8.2, 1.8.3, 1.8.4, 2.1.1, 2.1.3, 4.6.3, 5.1.1, 5.5.13, 6.5.10, 6.5.12, 7.9.10. συμβουλευτικόν 1.8.1, 3.4.3, 4.2.4, 6.1.1, 6.1.3. συμβουλή 2.1.1, 2.1.7, 3.4.1, 5.1.1, 7.9.3, 7.9.7, 7.9.11 — προτρέπειν 2.4.9, 6.5.6, 6.5.10 — ὑποθήκη 3.4.1. ὑποτίθεσθαι 7.9.7
أشار 1.3.6, 2.1.6, 2.3.1, 2.4.3, 5.1.1. مشير 1.8.3, 1.8.4, 2.1.1, 2.1.3, 2.1.4, 2.2.1, 2.3.1, 2.4.9, 3.4.1, 5.1.1, 7.9.11. مشورة 1.3.5, 1.8.2, 1.8.4, 2.1.1, 2.1.7, 2.2.1, 2.4.3, 3.4.1, 3.4.2, 3.4.3, 4.2.4, 5.2.5, 6.2.4, 6.5.4, 6.5.10, 7.8.1, 7.9.2, 7.9.3, 7.9.5, 7.9.7, 7.9.9, 7.9.10, 7.9.11. مشورى 1.6.4, 1.8.3, 2.title, 2.1.title, 2.1.1, 2.1.2, 2.2.title, 2.2.1, 2.4.3, 2.4.9, 3.4.1, 5.1.1, 6.1.1, 6.1.3, 7.8.1, 7.10.3. مشاورية 1.3.6, 1.8.1. مشاورة 6.5.1, 6.5.10. مشاورون 7.9.2 — نصيحة 2.3.8
ܕܠܐ ܡܢܝܢܐ ܐܪܝܬܡܘܣܝܐ without musical number 7.5.4. ܡܢܝܢܝܬܐ numerical 7.5.5
μήτε ἄρρυθμον 7.5.4. ἀριθμός 7.5.5

ἀνάλογον 7.5.1 — μέσον 7.8.5. μετρίως 7.9.8 — μετρεῖται 7.6.1. μέτρον 7.5.5, 7.5.6. μήτε ἔμμετρον 7.5.4 — ῥυθμός 7.8.5
أشعار 7.5.1 — معتدل 7.5.1, 7.6.2, 7.7.1, 7.9.8 — وزن 7.5.5, 7.6.title, 7.8.5. موزون 7.6.1. لا وزن 7.5.4

ܡ̈ܬܬܚܝܢ lengthened 7.5.6
μακρά 7.5.6
طول 7.5.6

ܡܬܠܐ proverb 4.4.4, 5.3.1, 5.4.8, 6.2.1, 6.3.5, 7.7.5, 7.8.1
παροιμία 4.4.4, 5.3.1, 6.3.5, 7.7.5
حكاية 6.2.1 — قيل 4.4.4 — مثل 5.3.1, 6.3.5, 7.7.5, 7.8.1

ܡܬ̈ܡܛܝܩܐ mathematics 7.9.8
μαθηματικοί 7.9.8
تعاليم 7.9.8

ܢܒܝܐ prophet 1.3.3, 7.5.3
ἔνθεον 7.5.3
إمام 1.3.3 — نبي 7.5.3

ܕܒܪ lead, induce, seduce 1.1.1, 5.1.1, 5.4.2, 7.1.1, 7.2.2, 7.3.3, 7.5.2, 7.9.4, 7.9.5. ܕܘܒܪܐ guiding, inducing 1.3.5, 7.9.4. ܕܘܒܪܘܬܐ inducement 1.2.3, 1.3.3, 1.5.3, 5.1.title, 7.9.4
ἄγεσθαι 5.4.2 — διατιθέναι 1.5.3 — διαφέρειν 5.1.1 — προάγειν/ἀνάγειν 7.9.4
أكد 7.5.2 — جذب 7.5.2 — خالب 7.9.4 — يستدرج 5.1.1. استدراج 1.2.3, 1.3.3, 1.5.3, 7.9.4, 7.9.5. استدراجية 1.3.5, 5.1.title — عون 7.1.1

ܗܓܡܘܢܐ general 5.4.11, 6.2.2
στρατηγός 5.4.11, 6.2.2

ܢܝܚܘܬܐ gentleness 3.1.1, 3.1.2
πραότης 3.1.1
حلم 3.1.1

ܒ̈ܢܝ ܢܘ̈ܣܐ building temples 4.5.7
ναοποιοί 4.5.7

ܨܒܐ end, goal, aim, intention, object, meaning, subject, case, disposition *passim* — domains 1.8.4 — mode 7.1.3— sign 7.4.3
πρᾶγμα 7.9.5 — σκοπός 2.1.1, 2.2.1. σκοπεῖν 7.2.4 — τέλος 1.8.1, 1.8.2, 7.9.2 — τρόπος 7.1.3 (AR 04a30; 36)
أبواب 1.8.4 — حول 6.3.7 — شيء 1.3.4, 7.2.4, 7.2.5 — مطلوب 6.3.2 — معنى 7.2.6, 7.5.1 — غرض 1.3.title, 1.8.2, 2.1.1, 2.2.1, 4.2.2, 6.4.3, 7.3.1, 7.5.4, 7.8.4, 7.9.1, 7.9.2, 7.10.2 — قصدي 1.8.1. مقصود 1.6.1, 2.3.2 — هدف 2.3.6 — وجه 6.7.3 — وفق 4.6.2

μικροψυχία 3.1.2, 5.3.2, 5.5.7. μικρόψυχοι 5.5.6 — ὀλιγωρία 5.1.3
صغر النفس 3.1.2, 5.3.2, 5.5.7, 5.5.11. صغار الأنفس 5.5.6

ܪܒܘܬ ܢܦܫܐ magnanimity 3.1.1, 3.1.2, 5.5.3. ܪܒ ܢܦܫܐ magnanimous, high-minded 3.3.4, 6.6.3
μεγαλοψυχία 3.1.1, 3.1.2, 5.5.3. μεγαλόψυχος 3.3.4, 6.6.3
كبر نفس 5.5.3 — كبر الهمة 3.1.1, 3.1.2. كبير الهمة 3.3.4 — عز 6.6.3

ܢܨܝܐ contentious, adversarial 1.3.5, 1.8.2, 5.2.2. ܡܨܘܬܐ conflict 1.3.5, 1.3.6. ܡܨܘܬܢܝܐ adversarial 1.8.1, 4.1.1
δικανικά 1.3.5. δικαζόμενος 1.8.2 — δυσέριδες 5.2.2
مشاجرة 1.3.5, 1.3.6, 1.8.2. مشاجرية 1.8.1, 4.1.1 — صخابون 5.2.2

ܒܘܨܪܐ diminutive 7.2.6
ὑποκορισμός 7.2.6
تصغير 7.2.6

ܢܩܡܬܐ vengeance 5.1.2, 5.1.7. ܐܬܢܩܡ take vengeance 6.2.2
τιμωρία 5.1.7. τιμωρεῖσθαι 5.1.2. τιμωρήσασθαι 6.2.2
إدراك الثأر 5.1.7

ܢܩܘܦܐ consequence 6.5.7. ܡܢ ܢܩܘܦܐ from consequences 6.5.6. ܢܩܝܦܘܬܐ ܕܠܩܘܒܠܝܐ affinity of outcome of opposites 6.5.8
ἕπεσθαι 6.5.7 ἐκ τοῦ ἀκολουθοῦντος 6.5.6. ἐκ τοῦ τὸ συμβαῖνον … ἐξ ὧν συμβαίνει 6.5.8
خصلة 6.5.7 — لوازم 6.5.6 — وضع حكم بأزاء 6.5.8

ܣܒܐ old man, elder 2.2.6, 6.3.4, 6.5.5, 6.5.8, 7.2.4, 7.7.1. ܣܝܒܘܬܐ old age 2.2.6, 5.4.2, 5.5.1, 5.5.6, 7.7.1. ܣܝܒܘܬܐ ܛܒܬܐ good old age 2.2.2, 2.2.8. ܫܦܝܪ ܣܝܒܘܬܐ well in old age 2.2.8
γέρων 2.2.6, 6.5.5, 7.2.4. γῆρας 2.2.6, 5.4.2, 5.5.6, 7.7.1. εὐγηρία 2.2.2, 2.2.8. εὔγηρως 2.2.8 — πρεσβύτεροι 6.3.4
شيبة 5.5.1. شيبة حسنة 2.2.2 — شيخ 7.2.4. مشايخ 6.3.4, 7.7.1. شيخوخة 7.7.1 — كبر 5.4.2, 6.5.8

ܣܒܪ opine, suppose, assume, think; *passive* opined, according to opinion, based on opinion, seem 1.2.3, 1.3.7, 1.4.1, 1.4.5, 1.5.4, 1.6.2, 2.2.9, 2.3.6, 2.4.3, 3.1.1, 3.3.5, 4.3.7, 4.4.2, 5.1.3, 5.2.4, 5.2.7, 5.3.4, 5.4.1, 5.4.4, 5.4.6, 5.5.3, 5.5.4, 5.5.5, 5.5.7, 5.5.9, 5.5.10, 6.5.3, 6.5.4, 6.6.1, 6.7.1, 6.7.2, 7.7.4, 7.9.6, 7.9.8, 7.10.1 ܣܒܪܐ opinion, supposition 1.4.5, 4.4.7, 4.6.9, 5.1.1 — hope 4.3.4, 5.5.6, 5.5.7. ܫܦܝܪ ܣܒܪܐ happily trusting, of good hope 5.4.1, 5.5.2. ܫܦܝܪܘܬ ܣܒܪܐ noble hope 5.5.3 — ܡܣܒܪܢܘܬܐ opinion 2.2.2. ܡܣܬܒܪܢܐ opinion, opined, based on opinion 1.2.1, 3.4.3. ܡܣܬܒܪܢܐܝܬ in manner of opinion 1.2.3. ܡܣܬܒܪܢܘܬܐ manner of opinion 2.1.2. ܡܣܬܒܪܢܝܬܐ opined, supposed 1.6.3, 2.2.1, 3.3.5, 4.2.4, 5.5.13 — ܣܝܒܪ endure 4.4.5

ἐλπίζειν 5.5.3, 5.4.1. ἐλπίς 5.5.2, 5.5.7. εὔελπις 5.5.3. εὔελπιδες 5.5.2. εὐλόγιστοι 5.4.1 — ἐρώμενοι 4.4.5 — διακεῖσθαι 5.5.10 — δοκεῖν 2.4.3, 3.1.1, 3.3.5, 4.3.7, 4.4.2, 5.4.4, 5.4.6, 7.10.1. δόξα 5.3.4, 5.5.13. ἔνδοξα 6.7.1 — νομίζειν 5.2.4, 6.5.4 — οἴεσθαι 4.4.7, 5.1.3, 5.5.4, 5.5.5, 5.5.10, 7.7.4 — ὁμολογεῖν 2.2.2 — ὑπολαμβάνειν 2.3.6, 5.2.7, 7.9.6, 7.9.8 — φαίνεσθαι 5.1.1, 5.5.7, 6.6.1. φαινόμενος 1.4.5, 4.2.4

أمل 5.5.2. تأميل 5.5.7 — محمود 1.4.5 — حمل 4.4.5 — رأي 1.4.5, 3.1.1, 4.3.7, 5.4.6. مرآيه 4.4.2 — رجاء 4.3.4 — شبهة 4.6.9 — ظن 1.2.3, 1.3.7, 1.6.3, 2.1.2, 2.2.9, 2.3.6, 3.3.5, 4.2.4, 5.2.4, 5.2.7, 5.3.4, 5.4.4, 5.5.7, 5.5.9, 6.5.3, 6.6.1, 6.7.1, 6.7.2. ظن 1.3.7, 1.4.1, 1.4.5, 1.6.2, 2.2.1, 2.2.2, 5.1.1, 5.5.3, 5.5.4. حسن الظن 5.4.1, 5.5.2, 5.5.3. ظنية 1.2.1 — قدر 5.4.1, 5.5.3 — وهم 2.4.3, 5.1.3, 7.9.8, 7.10.1

ܡܣܓܐܐ multiplication 7.8.3 — ܫܘܝܘܬ ܫܡܐ synonymity 7.2.3

αὔξησις 7.8.3 — συνώνυμα 7.2.3

يوهم كثيرة 7.8.3 — ترادف 7.2.3

ܣܓܦ do harm, be harmful, do damage 1.8.2, 1.8.3, 4.1.1, 4.1.2, 5.2.4, 7.9.6, 7.9.9. ܡܣܓܦܢ harmful 1.3.1, 7.9.6. ܣܘܓܦܢܐ harm, harmfulness, damage, injury 1.3.2, 1.8.4, 2.4.8, 5.1.2, 5.2.4, 7.9.6, 7.9.8. ܣܘܓܦܢܘܬܐ mutilation 5.4.2

ἀναπηρία 5.4.2 — βλαβερόν 1.8.2, 1.8.3, 7.9.6, 7.9.8. βλάβαι 5.2.4. βλάπτειν 4.1.2, 5.2.4, 7.9.6, 7.9.9 — ζημία 2.4.8 — λύπη 5.1.2. λυπηρόν 7.9.6

أذي 7.9.6. أذى 5.1.2 — ضر 7.9.6. ضرر 2.4.8, 5.2.4, 7.9.8. ضار 1.3.1, 1.3.2, 1.8.2, 1.8.3, 1.8.4

ܬܪܝܨ ܛܟܣܐ right order 7.9.7. ܒܛܟܣܐ in order 7.9.10. ܛܟܣܢܘܬܐ setting in order 7.9.10

ἐφεξῆς 7.9.7, 7.9.10

على النسق والترتيب 7.9.7. على الترتيب 7.9.10. ترتيب 7.9.10

ܣܗܕܐ witness 1.5.2, 4.6.1, 4.6.3, 4.6.4, 5.5.13, 6.2.4, 6.5.9. ܣܗ̈ܕܐ ܕܫܘܩܪܐ false witnesses 4.5.8. ܣܗܕܘܬܐ testimony 4.6.3, 4.6.4, 4.6.7

μαρτυρία 4.6.3, 4.6.4, 4.6.7, 6.2.4. μάρτυς 1.5.2, 4.6.1, 4.6.3, 4.6.4, 6.2.4, 6.5.9. ψευδομαρτυροῦντες 4.5.8

شاهد 1.5.2, 4.6.1, 4.6.3, 4.6.4, 6.2.4. شهود الزور 4.5.8. شهادة 4.6.3, 4.6.4, 4.6.7, 5.5.13

ܡܬܚܡܐ limited 7.6.1. ܠܐ ܡܬܚܡܢܝܬ not limited 7.5.4. ܠܐ ܡܬܚܡܢܘܬܐ limitlessness 4.5.3

(οὐκ) ἄπειρον 7.6.1. ἄπειρον 7.5.4. ἀπειρία 4.5.3

محصور 7.6.1 — لا حدود 7.5.4 — لا نهاية 4.5.3

ܣܘܠܘܓܝܣܡܘܣ syllogism 1.3.7, 1.4.5, 1.5.2, 1.6.1, 1.7.4, 1.8.4, 4.1.1, 7.9.11. ܣܘܠܘܓܝܣܡܘܬܐ syllogism 1.6.2. ܣܘܠܘܓܝܣܡܛܝܩܝܐ syllogistic 1.6.2. ܣܘܠܘܓܝܣܛܝܩܘܬܐ syllogistic 1.4.2. ܣܘܠܘܓܝܣܛܝܩܘܬܐ syllogism, syllogistic

2.1.2, 6.3.1. ܣܘܠܘܓܝܣܛܝܩܐܝܬ by syllogism 6.5.14. ܡܣܠܓܣ argue syllogistically 1.4.2

σuλλογίζεσθαι 1.4.2, 1.6.2. συλλογισμός 1.3.7, 1.4.5, 1.6.1, 1.7.4, 1.8.4, 4.1.1, 6.3.1, 6.5.14, 7.9.11

قاس 1.4.2. قياس 1.3.7, 1.4.5, 1.5.2, 1.6.1, 1.6.2, 1.7.4, 1.8.4, 4.1.1, 7.9.11. قياسية 2.1.2 — مستنتجة 6.3.1

ܣܘܠܘܩܘܣ offensive 5.5.10

σόλοικοι 5.5.10

ܒܢܬ ܩܠܐ ܣܝܡܬܐ epithets 7.2.6. ܒܢܬ ܩܠܐ ܕܣܝܡܢ words adopted 7.3.3. ܫܡܗܐ ܡܬܬܣܝܡܢܐ epithets 7.5.1. ܡܬܬܣܝܡܢܐ epithets 7.5.3

ἐπίθετα 7.2.6, 7.3.3, 7.5.1, 7.5.3

أسماء موضوعة 7.2.6, 7.5.3. أالفاظ موضوعة 7.3.3. إسم/لفظ موضوع 7.5.1

ܣܘܡܦܪܣܡܐ conclusion 6.3.1, 7.10.2

συμπέρασμα 6.3.1, 7.10.2

نتيجة 6.3.1, 7.10.2

ܣܘܢܘܠܐ attendant 4.6.6

خليفة 4.6.6

ܣܘܦܣܛܐ sophist 3.3.2, 6.6.4. ܣܘܦܣܛܝܐ sophistry, sophistic 1.1.1, 1.4.2, 1.4.5, 7.2.3. ܣܘܦܣܛܝܩܐ sophistical 2.3.4

σοφιστής 1.4.5, 7.2.3. παραλογιστικόν 3.3.2

سوفسطيقي 6.6.4. سوفسطائية 1.4.2, 1.4.5 — مغالطة 2.3.4, 3.3.2. مغالطية 1.1.1, 7.2.3

ܣܚܝܚܐ fluid 7.5.4, 7.5.6

ἄρρυθμος 7.5.6

متخلخل 7.5.4

ܣܛܝܘܬܐ see ܥܘܛܠܘܬܐ

ܣܝܪܝܘܣ Sirius 7.7.2

الشعري 7.7.2

ܣܟܝܐ hopes 4.3.2, 4.3.3, 4.3.4. ܣܘܟܝܐ hope 4.3.2, 4.3.3

ἐλπίζειν 4.3.2, 4.3.3

أمل 4.3.2, 4.3.3. تأميل 4.3.2. مؤمل 4.3.3 — رجا 4.3.4

ܣܟܠ give understanding 7.7.1, 7.9.3. ܣܘܟܠܐ thought, meaning, intelligence 2.3.1, 7.1.1, 7.1.2, 7.1.3, 7.1.4, 7.6.1 — ܣܟܠܘܬܐ offence 4.5.5, 4.5.6, 4.5.7. ܣܘܟܠܠܘܬܐ wrongdoing 4.5.title. ܡܣܟܠܢܐ offender 4.5.5, 4.5.6

διάνοια 7.1.1, 7.1.3, 7.6.1 — νοῦς 2.3.1 — ποιεῖν μάθησιν 7.7.1 — ἀποδεικνύναι 7.9.3 — ἀδικεῖσθαι 4.5.6

معنى 7.1.1, 7.1.2, 7.1.3, 7.1.4, 7.6.1 — معرفة 2.3.1 — مفهمة 7.7.1. تفهيم 7.9.3 — جناية 4.5.title — خطيئة 4.5.5 — ظلم 4.5.7 — فعل 4.5.7 — عامل 4.5.5

ܣܠܩܘܢܘܣ swaggering 5.5.10

σαλάκωνες 5.5.10

صلفون 5.5.10

فائدتها 7.9.4 — نفع 5.1.1, 7.9.4 — اعوان 1.2.3 — نصرة 1.2.4

ܡܬܥܗܕ remember 4.3.2. ܡܥܗܕܘ to aid memory 7.9.3. ܥܘܗܕܢܐ memory, recollection, reminder 4.3.2, 4.3.3, 7.10.3. ܡܥܗܕܢܘܬܐ recollection 7.9.1

ἀναμιμνήσκειν 7.9.3, 7.10.3. ἀνάμνησις 7.10.3. εὐμνημόνευτον 7.9.1. μνημονεύειν 4.3.2, 4.3.3. μνημονευτά 4.3.2

ذكر 4.3.2. ذكر 4.3.2, 4.3.3. تذكير 4.3.2, 7.9.1, 7.9.3

ܥܝܕܐ custom, habit, familiarity 1.2.2, 1.3.2, 2.3.8, 4.2.1, 4.2.4, 4.3.1, 4.4.4, 5.1.5, 5.2.3, 6.3.4, 6.3.5. character 5.4.3, 7.9.8. ܥܝ̈ܕܐ habits, character, behaviour 1.5.4, 2.4.9, 4.2.2, 5.title, 5.4.3, 5.5.title, 5.5.1, 5.5.5, 5.5.8, 5.5.9, 5.5.10, 5.5.11, 5.5.13, 6.3.7, 6.5.1, 7.9.8, 7.10.3. ܥܝ̈ܕܐ ܛܒ̈ܐ good character 5.5.2. ܥܝ̈ܕܐ ܒܝ̈ܫܐ evil character 5.5.2, 5.5.5. ܥܝܕܝܐ habitual, familiar 1.2.2, 1.2.3, 4.2.1, 4.2.3, 4.2.4, 4.3.1, 4.3.7. ethical 6.3.6, 7.8.2, 7.9.8. ܡܥܝܕܐ habitual, customary, accustomed 4.3.6, 4.4.1, 7.2.2. ܠܐ ܡܥܝ̈ܕܐ unaccustomed, non-habitual 4.3.1, 4.4.1. ܠܚܫܘܫܐ ܠܐ ܡܥܝܕܬܐ uncustomary expression 7.3.2. ܡܬܥܝܕܐ familiar 7.3.4

ἐθίζεσθαι 4.2.4, 4.3.1, 5.1.5. εἰθισμένον 4.3.1. ἐθιστόν 4.2.4. ἔθος 4.2.1, 4.2.3, 4.3.1, 4.4.4 — εἰωθότα 4.4.1. εἰωθυῖα 7.2.2 — ἕξεις 4.2.2, 5.4.3, 6.5.1 — ἦθος 5.4.3, 5.5.8, 6.3.6, 6.3.7, 7.9.8. ἤθη 1.5.4, 2.4.9, 5.4.3, 5.5.1, 5.5.5, 5.5.9, 5.5.10, 5.5.11, 5.5.13, 6.5.1, 7.9.8. εὐήθεις 5.5.2. κακοήθεις 5.5.2, 5.5.5. ἠθική 7.8.2, 7.9.8. συνήθεια 1.2.2. τὸ σύνηθες 4.3.6 — γλῶτται 7.3.2

عادة 4.2.1, 4.2.4, 4.3.1, 4.3.7, 4.4.4, 5.1.5, 6.3.4, 7.2.2. عادات 5.5.9. عادي 4.2.1. اعتياد 1.2.2, 2.3.8, 4.2.4, 7.3.4. اعتيادية 1.2.2, 1.2.3. معتاد 4.3.1, 4.3.6, 4.4.1 — خلق 4.2.1, 4.2.4, 5.4.3, 5.5.1. أخلاق 1.5.4, 2.4.9, 4.2.2, 4.2.3, 5.4.3, 5.5.title, 5.5.5, 5.5.8, 5.5.10, 5.5.11, 5.5.13, 6.3.7. سيئة أخلاقهم 5.5.5. خلقي 4.2.1, 6.3.6, 6.5.1, 7.8.2, 7.9.8, 7.10.3. متخلق 4.3.1 — لغة غريبة 7.3.2 — نوادر 4.4.1

ܐܥܘܠ do wrong, do evil 1.8.2, 2.4.3, 4.1.2, 4.4.title, 4.4.1-6, 4.6.9, 6.5.6. ܡܬܥܘܠ suffer wrong 4.4.4, 4.4.5. ܥܘܠ unjust 1.3.1, 1.3.6, 1.8.4, 4.1.2, 4.2.2, 5.4.3, 5.4.5, 7.9.2. ܥܘܠܐ wrongdoer 4.2.3, 4.4.1, 4.4.4, 4.4.7, 5.1.1. ܥܘܠܐ injustice, wrongdoing 4.1.title, 4.1.1, 4.2.title, 4.3.title, 4.4.1, 4.4.2, 4.4.4, 4.4.6, 4.4.7, 4.5.2, 4.5.3, 4.5.5. ܥܘܠܐܝܬ unjustly 4.6.3. ܥܘܠܘܬܐ injustice 1.3.1, 1.3.6, 3.1.2, 5.4.5

ἀδικεῖν 2.4.3, 4.1.1, 4.4.1, 4.4.3, 4.4.4, 4.4.5, 4.4.7, 4.6.9, 5.1.1. ἀδικεῖσθαι 4.4.4, 4.4.5. ἀδικήματα 4.4.1. ἀδικία 3.1.2. ἄδικος 1.3.1, 1.8.4, 4.1.2, 4.2.2, 4.5.3, 4.6.3, 5.4.3 — ἀσεβεῖν 6.5.6 — κακία 4.1.2 — φαῦλα ποιεῖν 4.1.2 — ὕβρεις 4.4.7

جار 2.4.3, 4.4.title, 4.4.1-6. جور 1.3.1, 1.3.6, 1.8.4, 3.1.2, 4.1.1, 4.1.2, 4.2.title, 4.2.2, 4.2.3, 4.3.title, 4.4.1, 4.4.2, 4.4.4, 4.4.6, 4.4.7, 4.5.3, 4.5.5, 7.9.2. جائر 4.4.1, 4.4.4, 4.4.7 — خطأ 4.1.2, 4.6.3 — رذيلة 5.4.5 — شرارة 5.1.1 — ظلم 1.8.2, 4.1.title, 4.5.2

ܥܩܬܐ pain, distress 4.4.3, 5.2.4. ܡܥܝܩ annoy 5.2.5. ܡܥܝܩܘܬܐ vexation 5.2.4
λύπη 5.2.4. λυπηρόν 4.4.3
حزن 5.2.4 — مضرة 4.4.3

ܥܘܪܬܐ vengeance, satisfaction 5.3.2, 6.3.4
ثأر 5.3.2

ܥܘܪܐ prime 5.5.8. ܥܘܪܐ ܕܚܠܝܡܘܬܐ prime of vigour 5.5.1. ܥܘܪܐ ܕܣܝܒܘܬܐ prime of old age 5.5.8
ἀκμή 5.5.1, 5.5.8. ἀκμάζοντες 5.5.8
شباب 5.5.1 — عنفوان التشييخ 5.5.8

ܥܛ̈ܦ return 7.6.2. ܥܛ̈ܘܦܐ returns 7.6.1. ܥܛܘܦܐ recurring 7.6.1
περίοδοι 7.6.1. ἐν περιόδοις 7.6.1
يعود 7.6.2 — عطوف 7.6.1. معطف 7.6.1

ܩܕܡ ܥܝ̈ܢܐ before the eyes 7.7.1, 7.7.2
πρὸ ὀμμάτων 7.7.1, 7.7.2
نصب العين 7.7.1. بحذاء العين 7.7.2

ܥܠܬܐ cause 2.2.9, 2.4.2, 2.4.3, 2.4.4, 3.2.title, 3.2.3, 3.3.5, 4.1.title, 4.2.4, 4.3.title, 4.4.title, 4.4.1, 5.1.title, 5.1.4, 5.2.3, 5.2.6, 5.3.3, 5.4.2, 5.4.3, 5.4.5, 5.4.8, 5.5.7, 6.1.3, 6.3.1, 6.3.2, 6.3.3, 6.3.6, 6.5.1, 6.5.2, 6.5.4, 6.5.7, 6.5.9, 7.4.1, 7.6.1, 7.9.8. ܢܣܒܘܬ ܠܐ ܥܠܬܐ ܐܝܟ ܥܠܬܐ acceptance of a non-cause as cause 6.6.3. ܥܠܘ̈ܠܐ effects 6.1.3
αἰτία 2.2.9, 5.4.2, 5.4.5, 6.3.1, 6.3.6, 7.9.8. αἴτιον 2.4.3, 2.4.4, 5.5.7, 6.3.2. αἴτιος 6.5.1 — ποιητικόν 2.4.2 — πράττειν 4.2.4 — παρὰ τὸ ἀναίτιον ὡς αἴτιον 6.6.3
آثر 2.4.2 — حجة 6.5.7 — دعوى 7.4.1. داعية 4.3.title — مبدأ 2.4.3. مبادئ 2.4.4 — سبب 4.3.title, 4.4.title, 5.2.6, 5.4.2, 5.4.3, 6.1.3, 6.5.9 — علة 2.2.9, 4.2.4, 6.3.1, 6.3.3, 6.3.6, 7.9.8 — أخذ ما ليس علة بعلة 6.6.3

ܡܥܠܝ honourable 1.3.1. ܡܥܠܝܘܬܐ loftiness 3.4.3
καλόν 3.4.3
فضيلة 1.3.1 — شرف 3.4.3

ܥܠܝܡܐ young man 2.2.6
ἀκμάζοντος 2.2.6

ܥܡܐ populace 1.6.3. ܥܡ̈ܡܐ populace, masses 1.1.1, 1.1.3, 1.6.1, 3.3.3, 5.1.4, 6.4.1, 7.10.1. ܥܡܡܝܐ popular 1.8.1, 7.1.4
ὄχλοι 6.4.1
جمهور 1.1.1, 1.6.1, 5.1.4, 7.10.1 — عامة 1.1.1, 1.1.3, 1.6.1. عامي 1.8.1, 6.4.1, 7.1.4 — قوم 1.6.3

ܥܡܘܕܐ pillar (of rhetoric) 1.2.title, 1.2.3, 1.2.4, 1.3.4, 1.3.5, 1.4.4, 1.5.3, 1.6.title
σῶμα 1.2.3
عمود 1.2.title, 1.2.3, 1.2.4, 1.3.4, 1.4.4, 1.5.3, 1.6.title

ܥܡܝܩܬܐ obscure 7.4.1. ܥܡܝܩܘܬܐ obscurity 7.4.1. ܥܘܡܩܐ depth 2.2.7

ἀσαφές 7.4.1 — βάθος 2.2.7
ܥܢܝܢܐ address, parley, converse 1.1.1, 1.2.1, 1.5.2, 1.6.3, 1.8.1, 1.8.2 — retort 7.7.4, 7.7.5, 7.8.title — acquaintance, company 5.2.3, 5.5.4, 6.6.3 — ܒܪ ܥܢܝܢܐ addressee 1.1.2 — ܗܢܝܐ, ܥܢ̈ܝܢܐ pleasant company 5.2.2
ἀντικεῖσθαι 7.7.4 — ἀποδιδῶσιν? 7.7.5 — ὁμιλία 6.6.3 — συζῆν 5.5.4 — ἡδεῖς συνδιαγαγεῖν καὶ συνδιημερεῦσαι 5.2.2
أجاب ? 7.8.title — محاورة 1.5.2 — مخاطب 1.1.2. مخاطبة 1.1.1 — مقابلة 1.2.1, 1.8.1, 1.8.2 — تشاهد 5.2.3 — مفاوضة 5.5.4 شحة/شحبة 7.7.4 — موقع ? 1.6.3 — في عشرتهم الألذاء 5.2.2
ܡܬܥܡܡܘ to be indignant 5.4.3
νεμεσᾶν 5.4.3
ܥܦ̈ܝܦܐ doubled 7.5.3. ܥܦ̈ܝܦܬܐ double 7.3.4
διπλᾶ 7.5.3. διπλῆ 7.3.4
مضاعفة 7.5.3. مضعفات 7.3.4
ܥܪ̈ܝܡܐ prudent 2.4.5, 3.3.2, 4.3.5, 5.1.1, 5.3.3, 7.6.3, 7.9.6, 7.9.9. ܥܪ̈ܝܡܬܢ prudent 4.4.3. ܥܪܝܡܘܬܐ prudence 2.2.2, 3.1.1, 3.1.2, 5.1.1, 5.5.11. ܥܪܝܡܘܬ ܪܥܝܢܐ prudence of thought 2.2.5
ἐπιμέλεια? 5.5.11 — φρόνησις 2.2.2, 3.1.1, 3.1.2, 5.1.1. φρόνιμοι 2.2.5, 2.4.5, 4.3.5, 5.1.1, 5.3.3, 7.6.3. φρονιμώτεροι 4.4.3 — τεχνικώτατοι 7.9.6
أجل 4.4.3 — أصالة العقل 2.2.2. أصالة الرأي 2.2.5 — محصلون 4.3.5 — دهاة 7.9.6 — عصيف 5.3.3 — عقلاء 2.4.5, 7.6.3 — لب 3.1.1, 3.1.2. ثقة بلبه 5.1.1. أصالة لبه 5.1.1. فضيل لب 5.5.11
ܥܘܫܢܐ prowess, strength 2.2.2, 2.2.3, 2.2.6
δύναμις ἀγωνιστική 2.2.2 — ἰσχύς 2.2.3, 2.2.6
بطش 2.2.2, 2.2.3
ܡܥܬܪ be rich 2.2.4. ܥܬܝܪܐ rich 5.5.10, 5.5.11. ܥܘܬܪܐ wealth 1.4.3, 2.2.2, 2.2.4, 2.3.8, 2.4.8, 5.1.4, 5.4.6, 5.4.8, 5.4.10, 5.5.1, 5.5.11
πλούσιος 5.5.10, 5.5.11. πλουτεῖν 2.2.4. πλοῦτος 1.4.3, 2.2.2, 2.2.4, 2.4.8, 5.4.6, 5.4.10, 5.5.1, 5.5.11 — ὑπάρχοντα 5.4.8 — χρήματα 2.3.8, 5.1.4
ثروة 5.4.8 — غناء 5.5.11. أغنياء 5.5.10. استغناء 2.2.4 — مال 2.2.2, 2.4.8, 5.4.10, 5.5.11 — متنعمون 5.1.4 — يسار 1.4.3, 2.2.2, 2.2.4, 2.3.8, 2.4.8, 5.4.6, 5.5.1

ܦܐܢܩܪܛܝܣܛܝܩܝܐ of the pancratium 2.2.7
παγκρατιαστικός 2.2.7
ܦܐܪܐܒܘܠܝ parabole 6.2.1
παραβολή 6.2.1
مثل 6.2.1

ܦܓܥܬܐ coincidences 3.3.5
  συμπτώματα 3.3.5
ܦܘܕܐ error, fault 4.5.4, 5.1.6, 5.2.5, 7.2.5, 7.4.3
  ἁμαρτάνειν 5.2.5. ἁμαρτία 7.2.5 — ἀτυχήματα? 4.5.4
  غلط 5.1.6, 7.2.5, 7.4.3
ܦܗܘܢ paean 7.5.5
  παιάν 7.5.5
  فادون 7.5.5
ܦܘܐܝܛܐ poet 2.4.7, 4.3.7, 5.1.8, 5.3.4, 5.4.11, 6.4.1, 7.1.2, 7.1.3, 7.1.4, 7.2.2, 7.3.3, 7.5.1, 7.5.3, 7.7.5, 7.8.2, 7.9.3. ܦܘܐܝܛܝܩܐ poetry, poetics 1.1.1, 1.4.2, 7.1.1, 7.1.2, 7.2.2, 7.2.3, 7.3.1, 7.3.4, 7.3.5, 7.5.title.
ܦܘܐܝܛܝܩܝܐ poetic 6.3.3, 7.1.4, 7.2.3, 7.3.5, 7.5.5, 7.6.1. ܦܘܐܝܛܝܩܝܘܬܐ poetic 7.1.4
  ποίημα 7.5.5. ποίησις 7.1.4, 7.2.3, 7.3.3, 7.5.3. ποιητής 2.4.7, 4.3.7, 5.1.8, 5.3.4, 5.4.11, 6.4.1, 7.1.2, 7.1.3, 7.5.1, 7.6.1, 7.7.5, 7.8.2.
  ποιητική 7.1.1, 7.1.4, 7.2.3. ποιητικόν 7.3.1, 7.3.4, 7.3.5
  شعر 7.1.1, 7.1.2, 7.1.4, 7.2.3, 7.3.1, 7.3.3, 7.3.4, 7.3.5, 7.5.title, 7.5.5.
  شاعر 7.1.2, 7.1.3, 7.1.4, 7.5.1, 7.5.3, 7.7.5, 7.8.2, 7.9.3. شعري 6.3.3.
  شعرية 1.4.2, 7.2.2, 7.2.3
ܠܦܘܓܪܦܐ to the written 7.8.1
  γράφειν/γραφική 7.8.1
  كتابة 7.8.1
ܦܘܠܝܛܝܐܣ constitutions 2.4.9. ܦܘܠܝܛܝܩܘܣ politics 1.5.4. ܦܘܠܝܛܝܩܐ political 1.7.4, 2.1.2, 7.1.2. ܦܘܠܝܛܐ politician (?) 6.6.3
  πολιτεία 6.6.3. πολιτεῖαι 2.4.9. πολιτική 1.5.4, 2.1.2. πολιτικοί 7.1.2. πολιτικά 1.7.4
  سياسة 2.1.2. سياسيات 1.7.4. سواس المدن 7.1.2 — صناعة مدنية 1.5.4
ܦܘܪܡܘܣ phormos 5.3.5
  φορμός 5.3.5
ܦܘܪܣܐ devices (of rhetoric) 1.3.4, 1.3.5
  حيل 1.3.4, 1.3.5
ܦܘܚܡܐ comparison 7.2.4 — accent 7.4.3
  παρ' ἄλληλα 7.2.4
  قايس 7.2.4
ܦܚܝܠܘܬܐ worthlessness 3.1.2
  μικροπρέπεια 3.1.2
  سفالة 3.1.2
ܦܓܢܐ rustics 7.7.1
  سقات الجمهور 7.7.1
ܦܝܠܘܣܘܦܘܬܐ philosophy 5.1.4, 6.2.4. ܦܝܠܘܣܘܦܐ philosophers 3.3.3, 6.5.3, 6.5.5. ܡܕܒܪ ܦܝܠܘܣܘܦܘܬܐ to philosophise 6.5.8

φιλοσοφεῖν 6.5.8. φιλοσοφία 5.1.4, 6.2.4. φιλόσοφοι 3.3.3, 6.5.3, 6.5.5
تعليم 5.1.4 — فلسفة 6.2.4. يتفلسف 6.5.8

ܦܝܣ persuade, argue persuasively, argue, make supplication; *passive* persuaded, know 1.1.1, 1.4.2, 1.4.5, 1.5.1, 1.5.2, 1.6.4, 2.4.3, 5.5.13, 6.2.4, 6.3.3, 6.3.4, 6.5.6, 6.6.4, 7.2.5, 7.8.2, 7.8.4. ܐܬܦܝܣ persuaded, obey 1.4.4, 2.4.3, 4.6.5, 5.5.13, 7.5.2, 7.9.11. ܦܝܣܐ persuasion 1.3.1, 1.4.1, 1.5.1, 1.6.2, 2.4.2, 4.6.5, 5.5.13, 7.1.2, 7.4.4. ܡܦܝܣܐ persuasive 1.6.2, 6.3.1, 6.5.7, 6.5.10, 7.1.1, 7.8.3, 7.8.5. ܡܦܝܣܢܐ persuasive 1.1.3, 1.2.4, 1.3.4, 1.4.5, 1.5.1, 1.6.1, 6.2.4, 7.8.5. ܠܐ ܡܦܝܣܢܐ not persuasive 7.5.4. ܡܦܝܣܢܝܐ persuasive 1.3.3, 1.4.3, 5.5.13, 6.6.4. ܡܦܝܣܢܘܬܐ persuasion 2.2.1
πείθειν 1.4.1, 1.4.2, 1.4.4, 5.5.13. πείθεσθαι 4.6.5. πιθανός 1.5.1, 1.6.2, 5.5.13, 6.2.4, 6.5.10, 7.1.1, 7.5.2, 7.8.5. ἀπίθανον 7.5.4. πιθανώτερα 1.4.3
استدراجية 1.3.4 — قبل 6.6.4 — تقرير 1.4.4 — قنع (IV) 1.4.2, 2.4.2, 6.3.3, 6.3.4. قناعة 7.5.2. إقناع 1.1.1, 1.3.1, 1.4.1, 1.4.2, 1.4.3, 1.4.5, 1.5.1, 1.5.2, 1.6.1, 1.6.2, 1.6.4, 2.2.1, 4.6.5, 5.5.13, 6.2.4, 6.5.7, 7.1.1, 7.1.2, 7.4.4, 7.8.2, 7.8.3, 7.8.4. إقناعية 5.5.13, 6.3.1. مقنع 1.2.4, 1.4.5, 1.5.1, 1.6.2, 6.2.4, 7.8.5 — موعظة 1.1.3

ܦܠܐܬܐ allegories 6.3.4
أمثال 6.3.4

ܡܦܠܓ divided 2.4.6. ܦܘ̈ܠܓܐ divisions 7.6.2, 7.6.3. ܡܢ ܦܘܠܓܐ (species of) from division 6.5.4. ܡܦܠܓܢܐ dividing 7.6.3
διαιρεῖν 2.4.6. διῃρημένη 7.6.3. διαίρεσις 7.6.2. ἐκ διαιρέσεως 6.5.4
جزأ 2.4.6 — اقسام 7.6.3. من القسمة 6.5.4. مقسم 7.6.3 — تفاصيل 7.6.2

ܦܠܝܪܘܦܘܪܐ excuse 1.5.3, 2.3.7
عذر 2.3.7. اعتذار 1.5.3

ܦܘܢܝܐ response, answer 7.10.title, 7.10.1, 7.10.2
ἀποκρίνεσθαι 7.10.1. ἀπόκρισις 7.10.2
جواب 7.10.1, 7.10.2

ܦܢܛܣܝܐ phantasia 4.3.2, 4.3.5
φαντασία 4.3.2, 4.3.5
تخيل 4.3.2, 4.3.5

ܦܣܐ lot 2.4.9, 6.2.2
κληροῦν 6.2.2. κλήρῳ 2.4.9
قرعة 2.4.9, 6.2.2

ܦܣܘ̈ܩܐ sections 7.5.5. ܦܣܘܩܐ (*pāsoqā*) 'stop' 7.4.3
فصول 7.5.5

ܡܦܨܚ creates (more) enjoyment 6.4.1
μουσικωτέρους 6.4.1
إفكه 6.4.1

احتال 1.5.3, 7.2.4. حيل 1.4.4, 4.3.6, 7.9.4. احتيال 1.5.2 — صرف وكد
4.3.5 — لطف 1.5.2

ܦܪܥ repay 2.3.6, 2.3.7. ܦܘܪܥܢܐ repayment 2.3.7, 2.3.8. response 7.4.1. ܦܘܪܥܢ ܫܘܟܠܐ repayment 2.3.6

ἀποδιδόναι 7.4.1 — τιμωρία 2.3.7

جواب 7.4.1 — رد 2.3.6, 2.3.7 — كفأ 2.3.7. مكافأة 2.3.6-8

ܡܦܪܫܢܐ separating 7.6.1. ܦܘܪܫܢܐ separation 2.4.6. ܦܪܝܫܘܬܐ superiority 3.1.1, 3.1.2

διαιρεῖσθαι 7.6.1. διαίρεσις 2.4.6 — μεγαλοπρέπεια 3.1.1, 3.1.2

مفصلة 2.4.6 — تقطع 7.6.1 — مروءة 3.1.1, 3.1.2

ܦܫܝܛܐ simple, simple minded 1.4.1, 1.6.3, 5.2.1, 7.1.3, 7.7.5 — prosaic 7.2.1 — general 4.6.1, 6.3.4. ܦܫܝܛܐܝܬ simply 2.4.5, 7.7.5 — generally, in general 4.6.2, 5.2.3, 6.6.4, 6.7.2

ἅπας 5.2.3 — ἁπλοῦς 1.6.3, 7.7.5. ἁπλῶς 2.4.5, 4.6.2, 6.6.4 — εὐήθη 7.1.3 — κοίνος 4.6.1 — μᾶλλον ὡς ἐπὶ τὸ πολύ 6.7.2 — σώφρων 5.2.1 — ψιλοί 7.2.1

جمهور 1.4.1 — سلماء الصدور 5.2.1 — مشتركة 4.6.1 — إطلاق 7.7.5. مطلقا 2.4.5. مطلقة 6.3.4 — مفردة 7.7.5 — في الأكثر 6.7.2 — كلي 4.6.2 — منثورة 7.2.1 — وحده 7.1.3

ܦܬܝܐ breadth 2.2.7

πλάστος 2.2.7

ܨܒܐ will, wish 5.1.8, 5.2.1, 5.3.6, 6.1.3, 6.5.7, 6.6.3, 7.8.4. ܡܨܛܒܝܢܐ 5.3.6. ܨܒܝܢܐ will, intention, purpose, choice 1.6.2, 3.3.5, 4.5.2, 4.6.5, 5.1.4, 5.1.6, 5.5.1, 5.5.7, 6.5.11, 7.5.3, 7.9.8. ܒܨܒܝܢܐ willingly, intentionally, voluntarily 1.4.5, 3.4.1, 4.1.1, 4.1.2. ܨܒܝܢܝܐ voluntary (*negative* involuntary) 1.5.1, 2.2.9, 2.4.3, 3.3.5, 3.4.1, 4.2.1, 7.9.8. of motive 6.5.4. ܨܒܝܢܐܝܬ voluntarily 4.2.4

βούλεσθαι 5.1.4, 5.1.8, 5.2.1, 6.1.3, 6.5.7, 7.8.4. βούλησις 4.2.1, 5.5.1 — ἑκούσιον 4.6.5, 5.1.6. ἑκών 4.1.1, 4.1.2, 4.2.4, 4.5.2 — θέλειν 6.6.3 — προαίρεσις 1.4.5, 3.3.5, 7.9.8

أمل 5.1.4 — اختيار 7.9.8. اختيارية 3.3.5, 6.5.11 — أراد 5.3.6. إرادة 4.2.1, 5.3.6, 6.1.3. إرادي 1.5.1, 2.2.9, 2.4.3. مراد 7.5.3. لارتياد 4.2.4 — بسعي 3.4.1 — شاء 6.6.3. مشيئة 1.4.5, 3.3.5, 3.4.1, 4.1.1, 4.5.2 — قصد 3.3.5, 5.1.6, 5.3.6. قصد 4.1.1, 4.2.1. مقصود 3.3.5 — هوى 5.2.1, 5.5.1 — وجه 6.5.4

ܡܨܒܬܢܐ ornamenting 7.9.4

κόσμος 7.9.4

مزين 7.9.4

ܨܕܘܐ irony 5.1.5, 7.10.2

ἡλικία 2.2.6, 5.4.3, 5.4.8, 5.5.1, 5.5.4
سن 5.4.8. أسنان 5.4.3, 5.5.1 — أقرانهم 5.5.4

ܩܘܡܘܕܝܬܐ comic 7.3.5
κωμῳδοποιοί 7.3.5

ܩܛܐܓܘܪܝܐ category 1.5.1
مقولة 1.5.1

(ܩܛܓܪ, see also under ܩܛܪܓ) ܩܛܝܓܪܢܐ accuser 7.9.11. ܩܛܝܓܪܢܘܬܐ prosecution, accusation 1.8.1, 5.3.6, 7.9.10
κατηγορεῖν 7.9.10. κατηγορία 1.8.1, 5.3.6
شاكي 7.9.11. شكاية 1.8.1, 5.3.6 — مشاجرات 7.9.10

ܩܘܛܠܐ populace, mob, people 1.6.2, 1.6.3, 2.2.2, 2.2.5, 2.3.3, 2.3.4, 2.4.5, 5.1.7, 6.3.4, 6.3.5, 6.4.1, 6.6.4, 7.3.3
δῆμος 5.1.7 — οἱ πολλοί 2.2.5
جمهور 1.6.2, 1.6.3, 2.2.2, 2.2.5, 2.3.3, 2.3.4, 2.4.5, 5.1.7, 6.3.4, 6.3.5, 6.4.1, 6.6.4, 7.3.3

ܩ̈ܛܐܦܛܝܩܝܬܐ affirmatives 1.6.3
موجبتان 1.6.3

ܩܛܪ̈ܐ contracts 1.5.2. ܩܛܝܪܐ compulsion, necessity 1.2.1, 4.4.4, 5.3.6. ܩܛܝܪܐ compelled 4.2.1, 4.2.3
ἀνάγκη 4.4.4 — βία 4.2.1, 4.2.3 — συγγραφαί 1.5.2 — συναναγκάζεσθαι 5.3.6
الزخم 1.2.1 — قسر 4.2.1, 5.3.6 — تقريرات 1.5.2 — استكراهي 4.2.1 — وجب 4.2.3 — مستولية 4.4.4

(ܩܛܪܓ, see also under ܩܛܓܪ) ܩܛܪܓ accuse, impeach, prosecute 1.2.2, 1.8.1, 1.8.2, 2.4.3, 4.5.7, 4.6.3, 6.5.10-12, 6.6.4, 7.9.5, 7.9.6, 7.9.9. ܩܘܛܪܓܐ charge, indictment, prosecution 4.2.1, 7.9.10, 7.9.11. ܡܩܛܪ̈ܓܢܐ accusers 6.5.12 — ܡܢ ܣܘܬܠ ܗܘ ܕܡܬܩܛܪܓ from the refutation of what is affirmed 6.5.6
δίκη 7.9.11 — κατηγορεῖν 1.2.2, 1.8.1, 2.4.3, 4.5.7, 6.5.6, 6.5.10-12, 7.9.6 — φεύγειν 6.6.4
محمولات 6.5.6 — خصم 6.5.12. خصومة 7.9.11 — ذم 2.4.3 — شكا 1.8.1. شاكي 7.9.9. شكاية 1.2.2, 1.8.2, 6.5.10, 7.9.6. مشكوة 4.2.1, 7.9.10

ܩܝܢܕܘܢܘܣ danger, risk, peril 4.3.2, 4.3.5, 4.3.6, 4.6.3, 5.2.4, 5.2.7. ܩܝܢܕܘܢܝܣܛܐܝܬ dangerously 3.3.3
κίνδυνος 4.3.6, 4.6.3, 5.2.4, 5.2.7. κινδυνευτικός 3.3.3
خطر 4.3.2 — مكاره 4.3.6 — هول 5.2.4 — مخوف 5.2.7

ܠܐ ܩܝܬܪܘܕܝܬܐ lyreless 7.5.1
ἄλυρον 7.5.1
غير مزهرية 7.5.1

ܩܠܝܠܘܬܐ speed 2.2.6, 2.2.7
τάχος 2.2.6, 2.2.7

ܒܪܬ ܡܠܐ word 7.1.1-4, 7.2.4, 7.4.4, 7.5.1, 7.5.2, 7.6.1, 7.8.2. wording 7.5.4, 7.8.1. ܒ̈ܢܬ ܡ̈ܠܐ words 7.title, 7.1.1, 7.1.4, 7.2.3, 7.3.title, 7.3.1, 7.3.2, 7.3.4, 7.3.5, 7.4.2, 7.5.2, 7.7.5. ܒܪܬ ܡܠܬܢܝܬܐ verbal 7.8.3. ܒܒܪܬ ܡܠܐ verbally 6.6.1. ܒ̈ܢܬ ܡ̈ܠܐ ܕܣܝ̈ܡܢ words laid down 7.3.3

λέξις 7.1.1, 7.1.3, 7.1.4, 7.3.1, 7.3.4, 7.5.2, 7.5.4, 7.6.1, 7.8.1, 7.8.2. παρὰ τὴν λέξιν 6.6.1 — ὀνόματα 7.1.4, 7.2.3, 7.4.2, 7.5.1 — ἐπίθετα 7.3.3

لفظ 7.1.1, 7.1.3, 7.2.4, 7.5.1, 7.5.2, 7.5.4, 7.6.1, 7.8.2. بسبب اللفظ 6.6.1. ألفاظ 7.title, 7.1.2, 7.1.4, 7.2.3, 7.3.1, 7.3.5, 7.4.2, 7.5.2. لفظة 7.7.5, 7.8.2. لفظى 7.8.3— ألفاظ موضوعة 7.3.3 — إسم 7.4.4 — كلام 7.1.4

ܡܠܝܠܘܬܐ avarice 3.1.2

ἀνελευθερία 3.1.2

دناءة 3.1.2

ܩܠ̈ܝܡܐ climes 1.3.2

اقاليم 1.3.2

ܩܠܣ praise 1.2.2, 1.8.1-3, 2.3.8, 2.4.7, 3.1.1, 3.2.1, 3.2.4, 3.3.title, 3.3.3, 3.4.1, 3.4.3, 4.5.3, 5.3.2, 6.4.2, 6.4.3, 6.6.1, 7.2.4, 7.2.6, 7.8.4, 7.9.2, 7.9.4, 7.9.5, 7.9.7, 7.9.9. ܡܩܠܣ praiseworthy, admired 1.4.2, 5.1.6, 7.2.5. ܡܩܠܣܢܐ praising, of praise, encomiastic 1.8.1, 3.3.2, 7.8.1. ܩܘܠܣܐ praise, laudation, encomium 1.5.3, 2.2.9, 2.3.2, 2.3.6, 3.2.1, 3.3.1, 3.3.4, 3.3.5, 3.4.1-3, 4.4.3, 4.5.3, 5.1.1, 5.5.5, 6.3.5, 6.5.10, 6.5.13, 7.5.1, 7.5.3, 7.9.2, 7.9.3, 7.9.7, 7.9.11. ܪܚܡ̈ܝ ܩܘܠܣܐ lovers of praise 5.5.10. ܡܬܩܠܣܢܐ praiseworthy 3.4.1. ܡܬܩܠܣܢܝܬܐ praiseworthy 3.2.1, 3.3.5

ἐγκωμιάζειν 2.4.7, 6.6.1. ἐγκώμιον 3.4.3, 7.9.7 — ἐπαινεῖν 1.8.1-3, 2.2.9, 3.1.1, 3.3.3, 3.3.5, 3.4.1, 5.3.2, 6.4.2, 6.4.3, 7.9.5, 7.9.7, 7.9.9. ἐπαινετόν 2.3.6, 2.3.8. ἔπαινος 1.8.1, 3.3.1, 3.3.3, 3.3.5, 3.4.1, 3.4.3, 4.4.3, 4.5.3, 6.5.13, 7.5.3, 7.9.3, 7.9.7, 7.9.11 — κοσμεῖν 7.2.4

ثناء 2.3.6. محبون للثناء 5.5.10 — حمد 1.8.3, 3.3.5, 7.8.4, 7.9.2. حمدة 5.5.5 — شريف 7.2.5 — فخر 4.4.3 — فخم 7.2.4 — مدح 1.2.2, 1.4.2, 1.5.3, 1.8.1-3, 2.2.9, 2.3.2, 3.1.1, 3.2.1, 3.2.4, 3.3.1-5, 3.4.1-3, 4.5.3, 5.1.1, 5.3.2, 6.3.5, 6.4.2, 6.6.1, 7.2.6, 7.5.3, 7.9.3-5, 7.9.7, 7.9.9, 7.9.11. مدحية 7.8.1. مديحية 7.5.1

ܡܚܙܝܐ soothsayer 6.5.4

Μαντίας 6.5.4

ܩܢܘܢܝܐ canonical 6.4.2

قوانين 6.4.2

ܡܕܚܠ fear 5.4.3

φοβεῖσθαι 5.4.3

خوف 5.4.3

ܡܩܘܣܡܘ beautify 7.1.3

κοσμεῖν 7.1.3 (AR 04a34)

تفخيم ? 7.1.3

ܡܦ̈ܣܩܐ contracted, abridged 7.5.6, 7.8.5. ܡܦܣܩܘܬܐ abridgement 7.9.1, 7.9.2

βραχεῖαι 7.5.6 — σύντομος 7.8.5 — ἀφαιρεῖν 7.9.1, 7.9.2

قصر 7.5.6 — اضمارات 7.8.5 — توديع 7.9.1 — يوجز 7.9.2

ܦܪ̈ܝܪܐ frigid, frigidities 7.3.title, 7.3.1, 7.3.4, 7.3.5

ψυχρόν 7.3.1, 7.3.4, 7.3.5

بارد 7.3.1, 7.3.4, 7.3.5

ܦܪܫ disclose, make explicit, put openly 7.2.5, 7.7.4, 7.9.4, 7.9.5, 7.10.2.

ܦܪܝܫܐ 7.1.4, 7.2.3, 7.2.5, 7.8.3, 7.8.4, 7.8.5. ܡܦܪܫܐ distinct 7.6.1.

ܦܪܝܫܘܬܐ open expression 7.5.1

δῆλον 7.2.5, 7.8.3 — καθαρά 7.8.4 — ποιεῖν πρὸ ὀμμάτων? 7.2.5 — σαφηνίζειν 7.2.3. σαφής 7.1.4, 7.8.5

يدل 7.8.3 — مشهور 7.1.4, 7.8.5 — تصريح ,صرح 7.5.1, 7.7.4, 7.9.4, 7.9.5, 7.10.2 — مفصل 7.6.1

ܡܬܡܪܦܘܬܐ, ܡܬܬܡܪܦ domination, become dominating 5.1.3

ἐπηρεασμός 5.1.3

عنت 5.1.3

ܡܣܝܒܘܬ ܩܕܡܘܬܐ old age 5.4.1

πρεσβύτεροι 5.4.1

أسن 5.4.1

ܪܒ, ܪܒܐ, ܪܒܬܐ major term, major premiss 1.3.7, 1.6.1, 1.6.4, 1.7.2, 1.7.3 — ܪܒܘܬܐ stature, size 2.2.3, 2.2.7, 2.2.9 — ܪܘܪܒܐ great 2.1.title — ܪܘܪܘܒܐ greatness, amplification, exaggeration, magnification 3.4.3, 6.1.title, 6.1.1, 6.1.3, 6.7.3, 7.8.1, 7.8.5. ܡܪܘܪܒܢܘܬܐ amplifying 3.4.2. ܡܪܒܐ amplification 7.10.3 — ܛܒܘܬ ܬܪܒܝܬܐ good upbringing 7.9.7

αὐξάνειν, αὔξειν, αὔξησις 3.4.3, 6.1.1, 6.7.3, 7.10.3. αὐξητικά 3.4.2 — μέγεθος 2.2.3, 2.2.7, 2.2.9, 6.1.3 — μεγαλοπρεπής 7.8.5 — ὑπερβολαί? 7.8.1 — παιδεία 7.9.7

جسامة 2.2.3, 2.2.9 — عظام 2.1.title. معظمة 3.4.2. تعظيم 3.4.3, 6.1.3, 7.8.1, 7.10.3 — التعظيم والتفخيم 7.8.5 — كبرى 1.3.7, 1.6.1, 1.7.2. تكبير 6.1.1, 6.7.3

ܪܓ desire 4.3.1, 5.1.4, 5.2.2, 5.4.8, 5.5.1, 5.5.4, 5.5.6, 5.5.7, 6.1.2, 6.1.3, 7.1.2, 7.9.5. ܪܓܝܓܐ desirable, desired, desire 3.3.2, 4.2.2, 4.3.1, 4.3.2, 4.3.3, 5.4.9, 5.5.1, 5.5.6, 6.5.7. ܪܓܬܐ desire, lust 2.4.4, 4.1.2, 4.2.1, 4.2.2, 4.2.3, 4.3.1, 5.1.4, 5.5.1, 5.5.6, 5.5.7, 7.5.3, 7.9.5. ܪܓܬܢܐ appetitive 4.2.1. ܪ̈ܘܓܬܢܐ lustful 4.2.3

βουλέσθαι 5.2.2 — ἐπιθυμεῖν 4.3.1, 5.1.4, 5.5.1, 5.5.6, 6.1.2, 6.1.3. ἐπιθυμία 2.4.4, 4.2.1, 4.2.2, 4.3.1, 4.3.3, 5.5.1, 5.5.6, 5.5.7, 6.1.2 — θυμός 4.2.3 — ὀρέγεσθαι 5.4.8, 6.1.3 — πάθος 5.1.4

يؤثرو 5.1.4 — أرب 7.5.3 — أنس 5.2.2 — يحبون 5.5.4 — اشتهى 4.3.1, 4.3.3, 6.1.3. شهوة 4.1.2, 4.2.1, 4.3.3, 5.1.4, 5.5.1, 5.5.6. شهو 5.5.6. شهوانى 4.2.1, 4.2.3. اشتهاء 2.4.4 — إشتاق 6.1.2, 6.1.3. شوق 4.3.1, 5.5.6, 5.5.7, 7.1.2 — مغتلم 4.2.2 — لذات ,لذة 4.2.2, 4.2.3, 6.5.7 — نزع 4.3.1, 5.4.8

ܪܓܙ be angry 5.1.3, 5.1.4, 5.1.5, 5.1.7, 5.1.8, 5.5.4, 6.3.5, 6.6.2. ܡܪܓܙܐ, ܡܪܓܙܢܐ cause anger, incite anger 5.1.5, 5.1.7. ܡܪܓܙܢܘܬܐ being angry, provocation 5.1.6, 7.9.4. ܡܬܪܓܙܢܐ object of anger, angered by 5.1.1, 5.1.2. ܪܘܓܙܐ anger 4.3.2, 5.1.title, 5.1.1, 5.1.2, 5.1.5, 5.1.6, 5.1.7, 5.1.8, 5.2.3, 5.2.7, 5.5.1, 5.5.3, 6.3.2, 7.5.3. ܪܓܘܙܬܢܐ angry, irascible 3.3.2, 4.2.2, 4.2.3, 5.1.1, 5.4.1, 5.5.2

θυμός 4.3.2. θυμικοί 5.5.2. θυμοῦσθαι 5.1.6. θυμώδεις 5.5.3 — μηνίειν 6.6.2 — ὀργή 4.2.3, 5.1.1, 5.1.2, 5.1.5, 5.1.6, 5.1.7, 5.1.8, 5.2.3, 5.2.7, 5.4.1, 5.5.1, 6.3.2, 7.5.3. ὀργίζειν 7.9.4. ὀργίζεσθαι 4.3.2, 5.1.4, 5.1.5, 5.1.6, 5.1.7, 5.1.8. ὀργιζόμενος 5.1.3, 6.3.5. ὀργίλος 3.3.2, 4.2.2, 5.1.1

مشتعل 6.3.5 — غضب 5.1.5, 5.1.6, 5.1.7, 5.1.8. مغضب 5.1.1, 5.1.3, 5.1.5. مغضوب 5.1.1, 5.1.2. غضب 4.3.2, 5.1.1, 5.1.2, 5.1.5, 5.1.7, 5.2.3, 5.2.7, 5.5.1, 5.5.2, 5.5.3, 5.5.4. غضوب 4.2.2. غضاب 3.3.2, 5.4.1

ܪ̈ܓܫܐ senses 4.3.1, 7.4.4. ܪܓܫܬܐ sensation 4.3.1, 4.3.2, 4.3.6, 7.4.4. ܪܓܫܢܝܬܐ sensual 4.3.2. ܡܪܓܫܢܘܬܐ sensing 4.3.1, 4.3.2, 4.3.6. ܡܬܪܓܫܢܘܬܐ perceptible 7.2.5

αἰσθάνεσθαι 4.3.2. αἴσθεσθαι 7.4.4. αἴσθησις 4.3.2, 7.2.5. αἰσθητός 4.3.1

حس 4.3.1, 4.3.2, 7.4.4. إحساس 4.3.6. حواس 7.4.4. محسوس 4.3.1. محسوسية 7.2.5 — وهم 4.3.6

ܪ̈ܕܝܐ well informed 5.4.1, 7.8.4. ܠܐ ܪ̈ܕܝܐ ignorant 7.2.2

πεπαιδευμένοι 5.4.1

متأدبون 5.4.1 — خواص 7.8.4 — مغبونون 7.2.2

ܪܗܛܐ running 2.2.6. race 2.2.7

δρόμος 2.2.6. δρομικός 2.2.7

ܪܗܛܪܐ, ܪܗܛܘܪ orator, rhetor *passim*. ܪܗܛܪܘܬܐ, ܪܛܘܪܝܩܐ, ܪܗܛܘܪܝܩܐ rhetoric, oratory *passim*. ܪܗܛܪܝܐ, ܪܛܘܪܝܩܝܐ rhetorical *passim*. ܡܡܠܠܐ ܪܗܛܪܝܐ rhetorical speech, rhetorical discourse 7.3.3, 7.5.5

ῥήτωρ 5.4.11, 6.5.4, 7.1.1, 7.1.2, 7.8.4. ῥητορική 1.2.1, 1.4.1, 1.4.2, 1.4.3, 1.5.1, 1.5.4, 1.5.5, 1.6.1, 1.6.2, 1.7.4, 1.8.1, 1.8.2, 2.1.2, 7.1.1, 7.1.2. ῥητορικός 1.7.4, 6.2.4, 6.6.4, 7.2.3 — λόγος 7.2.3, 7.3.3, 7.3.5, 7.5.5 — συμβουλεύων 2.3.1

خطيب *passim*. خطابة *passim*. خطابي *passim*. خاطب 1.8.2, 6.4.2, 7.10.1. مخاطب 3.3.4, 7.1.1 — ريطورية 1.5.1 — تشاجر 1.3.1 — مشير 2.1.5 — قائل 1.7.3 — متكلم 5.2.3, 6.3.7. كلام خطابي 7.3.3, 7.3.5. كلام 7.5.5 — مادح 3.3.4

ܪܚܡ to love 6.3.2, 6.3.6. ܪܚܡܐ friend, lover 5.2.1, 5.2.2, 6.1.2, 6.3.2. ܣܓܝܐܘܬ ܪܚܡܐ many friends 5.2.5. ܪܚܡܬܐ friendship 2.2.2, 5.2.1, 5.2.3. ܪܚܡܘܬܐ friendship, love 5.1.1, 5.1.7, 5.2.title, 5.2.3, 5.3.6, 7.5.3. ܙܕܩܝ ܪܚܡܘܬܐ dues of love 5.1.4. ܪܚܡܬ ܚܒܪܐ love of comrades 2.4.4. ܪܚܡܬ ܢܟܣܐ love of riches 2.4.4

ἐρᾶν 5.1.4 — ἐραστής 6.3.2 — φιλεῖν 6.3.2, 6.3.6. φιλία 2.2.2, 5.1.1, 5.2.1, 5.2.3, 7.5.3. φίλος 5.2.1, 5.2.2, 6.1.2 — πολυφιλία 5.2.5 — φιλεταιρία 2.4.4 — φιλοχρηματία 2.4.4

حب 6.3.6. محبة 2.2.2, 5.2.3 — محبة الأنسان 2.4.4 — محبة المال 2.4.4 — صديق 5.2.1, 5.2.2, 6.1.2. صداقة 5.1.1, 5.2.title, 5.2.1 — حق من الصداقة 5.1.4 — قربة 5.3.6 — كثافة الرفقة 5.2.5

ܪܗܛܘܪ, ܪܗܛܘܪܝܐ, ܪܗܛܘܪܝܩܐ see ܪܝܛܘܪܐ etc.

ܪܝܫܐ ܕܟܢܫܐ ruler of the assembly 1.8.2. ܪܝܫܢܘܬܐ authority 2.4.9, 5.4.11. ܠܐ ܪܝܫܢܘܬܐ anarchy 2.1.7

ἐκκλησιαστής 1.8.2

الرئيس المدبر لأمر الجماعة 1.8.2. رياسة 5.4.11 — لم قانون 2.1.7

ܡܪܟܒ composed, compound 6.7.2, 7.3.1. ܪܘܟܒܐ arrangement, combination, composition, construction 1.6.3, 1.7.1, 2.1.7, 2.4.6, 6.6.2, 6.6.4, 7.7.5. ܡܣܟܠܢܘܬ ܪܘܟܒܐ faulting the composition 6.7.3. ܬܪܟܒܐ combination 1.7.2

ἀσυλλόγιστον 6.7.3 — διπλᾶ 7.3.1 — ἐποικοδομεῖν 2.4.6

تأليف 1.7.1. مؤلف 6.7.2. رداءة التأليف 6.7.3 — ترتيب/مرتبة 1.6.3 — انعقد 1.7.2 — تركيب 2.1.7, 2.4.6, 7.7.5. مركبة 7.3.1

ܪܢܐ modulation 7.4.3, 7.8.3. ܐܕܫܐ ܕܪܢܝܐ sorts of modulation 7.4.3

τόνος 7.8.3

تثقيل 7.4.3 — نغمة 7.8.3

ܪܡܙܐ riddle 6.3.3, 7.2.5. ܪܡܝܙ enigmatic, allusive 6.3.4, 7.10.2. ܪܡܝܙܐܝܬ by suggestion 7.8.3

αἴνιγμα 7.2.5. αἰνιγματώδη 6.3.3

رمز 6.3.3 — اشارة 7.2.5, 7.8.3 — تعريض 7.10.2

ܡܬܪܥܝܢܘܬܐ enthymeme 1.3.4, 1.3.5, 1.3.7, 1.6.1, 1.6.2, 1.7.1-4, 1.8.4, 6.2.1, 6.2.4, 6.3.1, 6.3.2, 6.4.1, 6.4.3, 6.5.title, 6.5.1, 6.5.12, 6.5.14, 6.6.title, 6.6.1, 6.6.4, 6.7.2, 6.7.3, 7.1.2, 7.9.10, 7.10.1. ܡܚܫܒܬܐ ܡܬܪܥܝܢܝܬܐ enthymematic thought 6.3.6

ἐνθύμημα 1.3.7, 1.6.1, 1.7.1, 1.7.4, 1.8.4, 6.2.1, 6.2.4, 6.3.1, 6.3.2, 6.4.1, 6.4.3, 6.5.1, 6.5.12, 6.5.14, 6.6.1, 6.6.4, 6.7.2, 6.7.3, 7.9.10, 7.10.1. ἐνθυμηματικός 1.3.4 — προαίρεσις 6.3.6

ضمير 1.3.4, 1.3.7, 1.6.1, 1.6.2, 1.7.1, 1.7.2, 1.7.3, 6.2.4, 6.3.2, 6.4.1, 6.6.title, 6.6.1, 6.7.2, 6.7.3, 7.9.10, 7.10.1 — في الضمير 6.3.6 — تفكير 1.3.7, 1.7.1, 1.8.4, 6.2.1, 6.2.4, 6.3.1, 6.5.1, 6.7.2

ܡܬܪܥܝ appeased 5.2.2. ܐܬܪܥܝ think 6.3.2. ܪܥܝܢܐ intellect, opinion, thought, conception 5.1.1, 5.5.1, 5.5.11, 6.4.1, 6.7.2, 6.7.3 — maxim 6.2.1,

6.3.title, 6.3.1, 6.3.2, 6.3.3, 6.3.4, 6.3.5, 6.3.7. ܪܥܝܢܝܐ gnomic 6.3.1, 6.3.6, 6.3.7. ܬܪܥܝܬܐ mind, intention, purpose 4.5.5, 4.6.9, 5.1.2, 5.2.5, 5.5.1, 7.3.2, 7.9.4, 7.9.6. ܒܬܪܥܝܬܐ ܚܪܝܦܬܐ according to fine understanding 6.7.2. ܬܪܥܝܬܢܝܬܐ intellectual 3.1.2

γνώμη 6.3.1, 6.3.2, 6.3.3, 6.3.5, 6.3.7. γνώμη τῇ ἀρίστῃ 6.7.2 — ἕξεις 5.5.1 — εὐκατάλλακτοι 5.2.2 — διάνοια 4.6.9, 5.1.2, 7.3.2. διανοίας 3.1.2 — προαίρεσις 4.5.5 — φρονεῖν 6.3.2

رأى 3.1.2, 5.5.1, 5.5.11, 6.2.1, 6.3.1, 6.3.2, 6.3.3, 6.3.4, 6.3.5, 6.7.2. رأيي 6.3.1, 6.3.6, 6.3.7 — ظنون 6.4.1 — عقل 6.7.2 — قلب 7.9.4 — قول 6.7.3 — نية 4.5.5, 4.6.9, 5.2.5, 7.9.6 — همم 5.5.1

ܪܦܝܘܬܐ softness 5.3.2

μαλακία 5.3.2

انفعالات 5.3.2

ܪܘܩܕܢܐ rhapsody 7.1.3. ܠܐ ܪܘܩܕܢܝܬܐ non-dancing 7.5.1

ῥαψῳδία 7.1.3 — ἄχορον/ἄχορδον 7.5.1

ܪܚܡܘܬ ܠܚܒܪܘܬܐ kindness 2.2.2

أنعام 2.2.2

ܪܘܫܡܐ indication 6.7.2, 6.7.3, 7.1.4, 7.3.1 — sketch 7.8.4, 7.9.1, 7.9.7 — ܪܘܫܡܗܘܢ their (visual) indication 7.8.1

σημεῖον 6.7.2, 6.7.3, 7.1.4 — σκιαγραφία 7.8.4

رسم 6.7.2, 6.7.3, 7.3.1, 7.8.4, 7.9.1, 7.9.7 — علامة 7.1.4

ܪܘܫܥܐ impiety 4.6.8

ἀσεβής 4.6.8

حنث 4.6.8

ܪܬܡܐ accent 7.5.5, 7.5.6, 7.6.1. ܪܬܡܢܐ accented 7.5.5, 7.5.6. ܫܦܝܪܬ ܪܬܡܐ well accented 7.5.6

ῥυθμός 7.5.5. εὔρυθμος 7.5.6

نبرة 7.5.5, 7.5.6, 7.6.1

ܫܐܝܠ tropical 3.3.title, 3.3.1, 3.3.5. metaphorical 7.2.1, 7.2.6, 7.3.5, 7.7.1, 7.7.4. ܫܐܝܠܬܐ (ܡ̈ܠܐ) metaphors 7.2.3, 7.3.4, 7.7.1. ܫܐܝܠܘܬܐ metaphor 6.5.13, 7.2.title, 7.2.1, 7.2.2, 7.2.4, 7.2.5, 7.3.5, 7.4.2, 7.5.1, 7.7.2, 7.7.3, 7.7.5, 7.8.1, 7.8.4. ܫܐܝܠܐܝܬ secondarily 2.3.3 — ܫܘܐܠܐ interrogation 7.10.title, 7.10.1, 7.10.2

τὰ κύκλῳ 3.3.5 — μεταφορά 7.2.3, 7.2.4, 7.2.5, 7.3.4, 7.3.5, 7.5.1, 7.7.1-5 — ἐρώτησις 7.10.1 — ἀμφίβολα 7.10.2

استعارة 6.5.13, 7.2.1, 7.2.2, 7.2.3, 7.2.4, 7.2.6, 7.3.4, 7.3.5, 7.4.2, 7.5.1, 7.7.1, 7.7.2, 7.7.3, 7.7.5, 7.8.1, 7.8.4. استعاري 7.2.6, 7.7.1 — مجازية 7.7.4 — لا حقيقية 2.3.3 — سؤال 7.10.title, 7.10.1. سائل 7.10.2

ܫܒܚ praise, honour, glorify, commend, give credit 1.6.2, 3.2.1, 3.3.4, 3.3.5, 4.4.4, 4.6.8, 5.3.2, 5.3.3, 5.3.4, 5.4.8, 5.5.7, 6.3.5, 6.4.3, 6.5.3, 6.5.8, 6.5.11, 7.9.4, 7.9.7, 7.9.11. ܡܫܒܚܝܢ hold opinions 6.3.7. ܡܫܒܚܐ praised, praiseworthy, honoured, glorious, laudatory 3.1.1, 3.1.2, 3.3.2, 3.3.3, 3.4.2, 5.3.3 — reputable 1.3.7, 1.6.2, 1.6.3, 6.2.1, 6.4.2, 6.7.2, 7.9.11. ܡܫܒܚܘܬܐ reputation 1.6.3. ܡܫܬܒܚܢܐ, ܡܫܬܒܚܢܐ reputable 1.6.2, 1.6.3, 1.7.1, 1.8.4, 2.4.5. ܠܐ ܡܫܬܒܚܢܘܬܐ not being honoured 5.3.1, 5.3.3. ܫܘܒܚܐ praise, honour, glory, reputation 2.2.2, 2.2.5, 2.3.6, 2.4.8, 3.2.2, 4.1.2, 4.3.5, 5.1.2, 5.4.8, 5.4.10, 7.1.3 — opinion 5.5.5, 6.3.7

δοκοῦντα 6.4.2, 6.7.2. δόξα 2.2.2, 2.2.5, 2.4.8, 3.2.2, 5.3.3, 5.3.4, 5.4.8, 6.3.7, 6.5.3, 7.1.3. ἀδοξία 5.3.1, 5.3.3. οὐκ ἀδοξεῖν 5.3.4. ἔνδοξον 1.3.7, 1.6.2, 1.6.3. ἔνδοξοι 3.4.2. εὐδοκιμεῖν 4.4.4, 7.9.11. εὐδοξία 2.2.5, 4.3.5 — ἐγκωμιάζειν 3.3.5 — ἐπαινεῖν 5.3.2. ἐπαινετόν 3.1.1. ἔπαινος 3.3.3 — ἐπιείκεια 6.5.8 — δι' ἀρετήν 4.6.8 — λόγον ἔχειν 5.3.3 — προϋπολαμβάνοντες 6.3.7 — τιμᾶσθαι 5.4.8. τιμή 3.3.4, 4.1.2 — φιλοδοξεῖν 5.4.8

يثني 7.9.4 — تجلوها 3.3.2 — حكم 5.5.5 — حمد 3.3.5, 4.4.4, 6.3.7. حمد 1.6.3, 2.4.8, 3.1.2, 5.4.10. فوات الحمد 5.3.1, 5.3.3. إحماد 7.1.3. محمود 1.3.7, 1.6.2, 3.1.1, 6.2.1. محمودة 1.3.7, 1.6.2, 1.6.3, 1.7.1, 1.8.4, 2.4.5, 6.3.5, 6.7.2, 7.9.11 — مستخف 5.3.4 — اخلاقة 3.4.2 — مرتبة 5.4.8 — شرف 3.3.4 — مشهور 6.4.2 — تعجب 5.3.3 — معروف 6.4.2, 7.9.7 — لم يزل معظما 5.3.4 — فضيلة 4.6.8, 5.3.2 — كرامة 4.1.2, 4.3.5. إكرام 3.2.1 — مجد 2.2.2, 3.2.2 — مدح 2.3.6, 5.3.3. مادح 3.3.3. بمدح 7.9.7 — نباهة 2.2.5 — وجه 4.3.5

ܫܘܒܩܢܐ pardon, forgiveness, releasing 4.4.7, 4.5.4, 4.5.5, 4.5.6, 4.5.8, 5.1.6, 6.3.5

συγγιγνώσκειν 4.5.5. συγγνώμη 4.4.7, 4.5.4

صفح 4.4.7, 4.5.5 — مغفرة 4.5.5. مستغفر 4.5.5, 4.5.6, 5.1.6

(ܫܓܫ) see under (ܫܓܐ)

ܫܓܘܫܝܐ agitation 5.2.4

ταραχή 5.2.4

اختلاط 5.2.4

ܡܫܕܟܐ calms 5.1.7. ܡܫܬܕܟܐ calmed 5.1.5, 5.1.6

πρᾶοι 5.1.7. πραΰνεσθαι 5.1.5, 5.1.6

يسكن 5.1.7 — فتور 5.1.5. يفتر 5.1.6

ܫܘܝܘܬ ܫܡܐ homonymy 6.6.1, 7.2.3. ܫܘܝ̈ ܫܡܐ homonymous 7.2.5 — ܫܘܝ̈ ܓܢܣܐ of the same genus 7.3.5

ὁμωνυμία 6.6.1, 7.2.3 — ὁμογενῆ 7.3.5

لفظ مشترك 6.6.1. مشاركة في الإسم 7.2.5 — متفقات 7.2.3 — متجانسون 7.3.5

ܫܘܚܘܬܐ growth 2.4.7

αὐτοφυές 2.4.7

(ܫܚܐ) ܫܚܠܦ change, make different 7.2.2, 7.9.7. ܫܘܚܠܦܐ transference 7.2.title, 7.7.1, 7.7.2, 7.7.3, 7.7.5, 7.8.3, 7.8.5, 7.9.7. ܡܫܬܚܠܦܢܐ transference 7.3.5. ܡܫܬܚܠܦܢܘܬܐ transference 7.2.4, 7.2.5, 7.5.1

μεταβάλλειν 7.8.3 — μετατιθέναι 7.9.7 — μεταφέρειν 7.2.5, 7.3.5, 7.7.3. μεταφορά 7.2.4, 7.5.1, 7.7.2, 7.7.3, 7.7.5 — στρέφειν 7.9.7

معدول 7.5.1 — غير 7.2.2. تغيير 7.2.4, 7.7.5, 7.9.7. تغييرات 7.7.1, 7.7.2, 7.7.3, 7.8.3, 7.8.5 — تقلب 7.9.7

ܫܢܕܐ tortures 1.5.2, 4.6.1, 4.6.7

βάσανοι 1.5.2, 4.6.1, 4.6.7

عذاب 4.6.1 — تقريرات 1.5.2 — تنكيل 4.6.7

ܫܦܡ punish 5.1.6. ܫܘܦܡܐ punishment 5.1.2, 5.1.6

κολάζειν 5.1.6. κόλασις 5.1.6 — τιμωρία 5.1.2

عقوبة 5.1.2

ܫܦܝܥܘܬܐ liberality 3.1.1, 3.1.2

ἐλευθεριότης 3.1.1, 3.1.2

سخاء 3.1.1, 3.1.2

ܫܦܪ, ܫܦܝܪ fine, beautiful, noble, honourable 1.8.3, 2.2.9, 2.3.3, 3.1.1, 3.1.2, 3.2.1, 3.2.4, 3.3.3, 3.3.4, 3.3.5, 5.5.7, 5.5.8, 7.9.8 — appropriate 1.4.1, 2.2.3, 7.7.2, 7.7.3. ܡܫܬܦܪܝܢ are appropriate 7.7.4 — ܫܦܝܪܐ well 6.5.1. ܠܐ ܫܦܝܪ̈ not pleasing 7.3.3. ܫܘܦܪܐ beauty, attractiveness 1.2.1, 2.2.2, 2.2.3, 2.2.9, 5.4.6, 5.4.10, 6.1.1. ܫܦܝܪܘܬܐ beauty, fineness 4.3.6, 6.1.1 — ܫܘܦܪܕܢܐ flatterer 5.3.2

ἀπρεπέστερα 7.3.3 — ἀστεῖον 7.7.2, 7.7.3, 7.7.4 — εὖ 4.3.6 — κάλλος 2.2.2, 2.2.3, 2.2.9, 5.4.6, 5.4.10. καλόν 1.8.3, 2.3.3, 3.1.1, 3.2.1, 3.2.4, 3.3.3, 3.3.4, 5.5.7, 5.5.8, 6.1.1, 7.9.8. καλῶς 6.5.1 — κολακεία 5.3.2

مآثر 3.3.4 — جمال 2.2.2, 2.2.3, 2.2.9, 5.4.6, 5.4.10. جميل 1.8.3, 2.3.3, 3.1.1, 3.1.2, 3.3.5, 5.5.7, 5.5.8, 7.9.8 — أجود 6.1.1 — تحسن 7.7.2. لا تحسن 7.3.3. حسن 4.3.6, 6.1.1. حسنا 6.5.1. حسنة 4.3.6, 7.7.3. إحسان 3.2.1 — ممادح 3.2.4 — متملق 5.3.2

ܫܪܝܪ true, certain 1.3.7, 1.4.1, 1.7.1. 5.2.1, 5.3.4, 5.5.8, 6.3.2, 6.5.6, 6.7.3, 7.1.3, 7.2.2, 7.7.4. ܫܪܪ, ܐܫܪ establish, affirm, authenticate 1.1.2, 1.3.1, 1.4.1, 1.4.2, 1.4.3, 2.3.1, 4.6.3, 4.6.9, 5.2.3, 5.2.5, 6.3.5, 6.4.3, 6.5.4, 6.7.1, 6.7.3, 7.2.3, 7.8.5, 7.9.1, 7.9.4, 7.9.6, 7.9.8, 7.9.9, 7.9.11. ܡܫܪ is sure, is true, is certain 1.7.2, 5.2.7, 6.7.2, 6.7.3, 7.7.4. ܫܪܪܐ truth 1.3.7, 1.4.5, 2.1.2, 4.6.2, 5.1.4, 6.5.4, 6.5.13, 6.7.3, 7.5.3, 7.9.11. ܫܪܝܪܘܬܐ truth 1.5.4. ܫܘܪܪܐ establishment, confirmation, verification 1.3.1, 1.3.2, 1.3.3, 1.4.5, 1.5.3, 1.6.title, 1.6.1, 3.4.3, 6.2.4, 6.4.3, 6.5.14, 7.9.7, 7.9.10, 7.10.1. ܡܫܪܪܢܐ establishing, affirming, confirming 1.8.4, 5.3.6, 6.7.3, 7.9.1, 7.9.9. ܡܫܪܪܢܘܬܐ confirmation 6.5.1

ἀλήθεια 1.3.7, 2.1.2, 5.3.4. ἀληθές 1.3.7, 1.4.1, 1.5.3, 6.5.4, 7.5.3, 7.7.4 — ἀποδεικνύναι 5.2.3, 6.4.3, 7.9.1. ἀποδεικτικός 6.5.1, 6.5.14,

7.9.9. ἀπόδειξις 3.4.3, 6.2.4, 7.9.9, 7.9.10 — δεικνύναι 1.5.3, 1.6.1, 1.8.4, 6.4.3, 6.7.3, 7.10.1. δεικτικός 6.5.1, 6.5.14 — διώρικεν 1.3.1 — οἴεσθαι 5.2.7 — σαφῶς 6.5.13 — ὑπάρχειν 6.7.3

أكد 4.6.9, 5.2.3, 7.2.3, 7.9.7 — أمر 1.3.1 — برهانات 3.4.3 — تبين 7.9.1 — ثبت 1.3.1, 1.4.2, 5.2.5, 6.5.4, 6.7.1, 7.9.1, 7.9.6. إثبات 1.3.3, 1.4.5, 1.8.4, 4.6.3, 6.4.3, 7.9.11, 7.10.1. تثبيت 1.5.3, 1.6.title, 1.6.1, 6.5.1, 6.5.14 — حجة مقنعة 2.3.1 — حق 1.3.7, 1.4.5, 6.7.2. حقة 5.3.6. بالحقيقة 5.3.4. تحقيق 2.1.2. تحقق 6.2.4 — حكم 1.3.2 — يخلد 7.8.5 — صحح 6.7.3, 7.9.9. صحة 6.7.3, 7.1.3, 7.5.3. صحيحة 6.7.3, 7.2.2. مصحح 1.4.1, 6.2.4. تصحيح 7.9.8 — صدق 1.7.1, 5.2.1, 6.5.6, 6.7.2, 6.7.3, 7.7.4. صادق 1.3.7, 1.4.1. التصديق 7.9.4 — قر 5.2.3, 5.2.5 — قاس 1.4.2 — لزم 1.7.2 — نظر 1.3.1

ܫܘܪܝܐ beginning 2.4.3, 6.1.1, 7.5.5, 7.6.3. ܫܪܝܐ dissolution 6.7.1, 6.7.2. ܫܪܝܬܐ joint 7.4.3, 7.6.2. ܕܠܐ ܫܪܝܬܐ without a joint 7.6.2

ἀρχή 2.4.3, 6.1.1, 7.5.5, 7.6.3 — λύσις 6.7.1, 6.7.2 — ἐπιζευγνύναι 7.4.3 — κῶλα 7.6.2 — ἀφελής 7.6.2

مبدأ 2.4.3, 7.6.3. ابتداء 6.1.1. مبتدئة 7.5.5 — مناقضة 6.7.1 — رباطات 7.4.3 — توصل 7.6.2

ܫܪܝܚܘܬܐ wantonness 3.1.2. ܫܪ̈ܝܚܐ intemperate 4.2.3

ἀκολασία 3.1.2. ἀκόλαστοι 4.2.3

فجور 3.1.2. فجار 4.2.3

ܫܪ̈ܥܬܐ failings 5.3.3

ἁμαρτίαι 5.3.3

عثرات 5.3.3

ܬܐܡ̈ܬܐ 'twins' 7.6.1, 7.6.2. (ܝܚܝܕܝܬܐ) ܬܐܡܬܐ (solitary) 'twin' 7.6.2. ܬܐܡ̈ܝܐ doubling 7.6.3

ἀντίστροφοι 7.6.1 ? — μονόκωλον 7.6.2

مصاريع 7.6.1, 7.6.2. مصراع واحد 7.6.2. مصارعات 7.6.3

ܬܒܥ request, seek 4.5.5, 6.3.4. ܐܬܬܒܥ be punished 4.4.1, 4.4.3. ܬܒܥܐ, ܬܒܥܬܐ punishment 4.4.1, 4.6.8. ܬܒܘܥܐ avenger 4.6.7, 4.6.8. ܡܬܬܒܥܢܐ culprit 4.6.8

δίκην δοῦναι 4.4.1 — ζημία 4.4.1 — τιμωρεῖσθαι 4.4.3

عقوبة 4.4.3 — نكير 4.4.1

ܬܘܗ̈ܝܐ pauses 7.6.1

παύεσθαι 7.6.1 (AR 09b21) ?

ܬܪܝܘܬܐ indignation 3.1.2

ܬܚܘܡܐ definition 1.5.title, 4.1.title, 6.5.3, 7.3.1, 7.4.4. ܬܘܚܡܐ definition 6.4.2. regulation 6.6.2. ܗܘ ܕܣܝܡ ܡܬܚܡܢܐ defined subject 1.5.1. ܠܐ ܡܬܚܡ̈ܢܐ undefined 7.10.2. ܠܐ ܡܬܚܡܢܘܬܐ non-limitation 6.6.4

ἔλλειψις τοῦ πότε καὶ πῶς 6.6.4 — λόγος 7.4.4 — ὁρισμός 6.5.3. ὡρισμένοι 6.4.2 —διαιρεῖν 7.10.2 — ὑποκείμενον 1.5.1 — ἔρωτες 6.6.2 (cf. Commentary on 6.6.2)

حد 1.5.title, 6.5.3 — إطراح الشرائط 6.6.4 — مضبوطة 6.4.2 — جنس معين 1.5.1 — أقاويل 7.4.4 — مقام 7.3.1 — مهملات 7.10.2

ܬܚܬܝܬܐ (ܢܝܫܐ) lower sign 7.4.3

ܡܬܬܟܠ has confidence 5.2.7. ܬܟܠܢܘܬܐ confidence 4.4.1

شجع 5.2.7

ܬܫܥܝܬܐ narrative, narration 1.2.3, 1.3.4, 7.1.3, 7.9.1, 7.9.2, 7.9.3, 7.9.7, 7.9.8, 7.9.9 — ܕܩܠܝܠ ܠܬܢܝܐ 7.6.1 easy to learn

διήγησις 1.3.4, 7.9.1, 7.9.2, 7.9.7, 7.9.8, 7.9.9 — εὐμαθής 7.6.1

اقتصاص 1.2.3, 7.9.1, 7.9.2, 7.9.3, 7.9.7, 7.9.8, 7.9.9. قصصية 7.1.3 — سهل حفظ 7.6.1

ܬܢܝ contract 4.5.1, 4.6.1, 4.6.5, 4.6.6

συνθήκη 4.5.1, 4.6.1, 4.6.5, 4.6.6

عقد 4.6.1 — عهد 4.6.5, 4.6.6

ܪܫܡ ܛܘܦܣܐ prototype 4.3.6

μεμιμημένον (προτοτύπων) 4.3.6

ما حوكي 4.3.6

ܬܪܓܡ speak in public 6.5.6. ܡܬܪܓܡ make an exposition 1.3.6. ܬܘܪܓܡܐ exposition 1.1.3, 1.3.5, 1.3.6. discourses 7.2.1. public speech 6.5.6. public speaking 6.5.7. ܠܐ ܬܘܪܓܡܢܝܬܐ non-expository 1.3.5

δημηγορεῖν 6.5.6 — λόγοι 7.2.1

مفسر 1.3.6. تفسير 1.3.5, 1.3.6 — أأقوال 7.2.1 — تكلم في المحافل 6.5.6 — الناطق في المحافل 6.5.6

ܣܓܝ ܬܪ̈ܥܐ many-gated 7.5.1

πολύθυροι 7.5.1

كثير الأبواب 7.5.1

ܬܪܝܨܬܐ upright 4.4.6 — ܠܡܬܪܨܘ to correct 5.2.5 — ܡܬܪܨܢܐ correcting 6.5.10

δίκαια 4.4.6 — ἐπανορθώσασθαι 5.2.5 — διορθοῦν 6.5.10

# GREEK - SYRIAC
# ARISTOTLE - BAR HEBRAEUS
(Cf. Introduction, pp. 43-45)

ἀγαθός ܛܒܐ — ܡܝܬܪ ἀγαθόν ܡܘܬܪ

ἄγεσθαι ܢܓܕ

ἄγραφος ܠܐ ܟܬܝܒܐ

ἀγροικία ܒܥܪܐ

ἀγρός ܐܓܘܪܣܐ

ἀγών, ἀγωνιᾶν, ἀγωνίζεσθαι, ἀγωνιστική ܐܓܘܢܐ, ܐܓܘܢܐ ܥܒܕ, ܐܓܘܢܣܛܐ, ܐܓܘܢܣܛܝܩܘܬܐ ἀγῶνες ܡܬܟܬܫ̈ܢܐ ἀγωνιστική, δύναμις ἀγωνιστική ܬܟܬܘܫܐ, ܬܟܬܘܫܢܐ

ᾅδης ܫܝܘܠ

ἀδιάφθοροι ܒܪܝܡ, ܒܪܝܐ

ἀδικεῖν, ἀδικεῖσθαι, ἀδικούμενοι, ἀδίκημα, ἀδικία, ἄδικος, ἀδίκως ܛܠܡ, ܛܠܘܡܐ, ܛܠܘܡܘܬܐ, ܐܬܛܠܡ, ܛܠܝ̈ܡܐ, ܛܠܘܡ, ܛܠܘܡܐ, ܛܠܘܡܘܬܐ, ܛܠܘܡܐ ἀδικεῖν, ἀδικεῖσθαι, ἀδικήματα, ἀδικία, ἄδικος ܐܥܘܠ, ܡܬܥܘܠ, ܥܘܠ, ܥܘܠܐ , ܥܘܠܐ, ܬܥܘܠܐ, ܥܘܠܘܬܐ ἀδικεῖσθαι ܣܟܠܘܬܐ

ἄδικος? ܣܟܠܐ

ἀδοξεῖν ܒܣܪ — ܠܐ ܡܫܬܒܚܢܘܬܐ — ܩܠܐ οὐκ ἀδοξεῖν ܫܒܚ

ἀδύνατον ܠܐ ܡܬܡܨܝܢܐ, ܠܐ ܡܬܡܨܝܢܘܬܐ

ἀηδές ܠܝܬ ܡܢ ܗܢܝܘܬܐ

ἀθληταί ܐܬܠܝܛ̈ܐ ἆθλα ܐܬܠܘܣܐ

αἰδώς ܒܗܬ — ܒܗܬܬܐ

αἰθήρ ܐܬܝܪ

αἴνιγμα, αἰνιγματώδη ܪܡܙܐ

αἱρετόν ܓܒܝܐ, ܓܒܝܘܬܐ αἱρετά ܡܬܓܒܐ

αἰσθάνεσθαι, αἴσθεσθαι, αἴσθησις, αἰσθητός ܪܓܫ, ܪܓܫܬܐ, ܪܓܫܘܬܐ, ܡܪܓܫܢܘܬܐ, ܡܬܪܓܫܢܘܬܐ αἴσθησις ܚܘܫܐ

αἰσχρός ܒܣܪ αἰσχρόν ܒܨܝܪܐ — ܣܢܝܐ — ܢܟܝܪܐ

αἰσχύνεσθαι, αἰσχυντηλά, αἰσχρά, αἰσχυντικά, αἰσχύνη, ἀναίσχυντοι ܒܗܬ, ܡܒܗܬܢܐ, ܡܒܗܬܢܘܬܐ, ܡ̈ܒܗܬܢܝܬܐ, ܒܗܬܬܐ, ܒܗܬܬܢܘܬܐ, ܒ̈ܗܬܬܢܐ αἰσχύνεσθαι ܟܪܝ

αἰσχυντηλοί ܚܣܝܕܐ, ܡܬܚܣܕܝܢ

αἰτία, αἴτιον, αἴτιος ܥܠܬܐ παρὰ τὸ ἀναίτιον ὡς αἴτιον ܥܠܬܐ ܠܐ ܚܫܝܒܬ ܐܝܟ ܥܠܬܐ

ἄκαιρος ܥܘܕܒܐ ܕܒܢܝܐ — ܕܠܚܡܐ

ἀκμή, ἀκμάζοντες ܚܘܪܐ ἀκμάζοντος ܚܠܝܡܐ

ἀκολασία, ἀκόλαστοι ܦܪܝܥܘܬܐ, ܦܪ̈ܝܥܐ

ἐκ τοῦ ἀκολουθοῦντος ܡܢ ܢ̈ܩܘܦܐ

ἀκόντια ܫܠܦܬܐ (conjecture, MSS. ܫܠܝܬܐ)

ἄκος ܚܒܪ

ἀκρασία ܡܪ̈ܝܕܐ

ἀκρίβεια ἀκριβής ἀκριβεστάτη ἀκριβῶς ܚܬܝܬ ἀκριβολογητέον ܚܬܝܬܘܬ ܡܫܟܠܐ

ἀλαζονεία ܫܘܬܪܐ

ἀλήθεια ܫܪܝܪ, ܫܪܪܐ ἀληθές ܫܪܝܪ, ܫܪܪ, ܫܪܐ, ܫܪܪܐ

ἐκ τῶν πρὸς ἄλληλα (ܠܘܬ) ܡܢ ܗܠܝܢ ܕܠܘܬ ܚܕ̈ܕܐ παρ' ἄλληλα ܦܘܚܡܐ

ἄλυρον ܠܐ ܡܬܪܘܕܢܘܬܐ

ἁμαρτάνειν, ἁμάρτημα, ἁμαρτήματα ܣܟܠܐ, ܣܟܠܘܬܐ, ܣ̈ܟܠܗܐ ἁμαρτάνειν, ἁμαρτία ܦܘܕܐ ἁμαρτίαι ܡܪ̈ܝܕܐ — ܫܪ̈ܒܬܐ ἐκ τῶν ἁμαρτηθέντων ܚܛܗܐ

ἀμφίβολα ܥܘܐܠܐ

ἀμφισβητῶν, ἀμφισβητεῖν ܡܬܕܠܝܢܐ ἀμφισβητῶν ܡܬܬܕܝܢܘܬܐ, ܕܝܢܐ ἀμφισβητεῖν, ἀμφισβήτησις ܕܝܢܐ, ܬܕܝܢܐ

ἀνάγειν ܠܡܣܩܘܬܐ

ἀναγκαζόμενοι ܚܒܝܨܐ

ἀνάγκη, ἀναγκαῖον, ἀναγκάζειν ܐܠܝܨܐ, ܐܘܠܝܨܐ ἀναγκαῖον, ἀνάγκη, ἐξ ἀνάγκης ܐܢܘܣܐ, ܐܢܘܣܐܝܬ, ܐܢܘܣܝܐ ἀναγκαῖα ܩ̈ܠܝܠܬܐ ἀνάγκη ܦܠܛܪܐ

ἀναισχυντία ܠܚܣܕܘܬܐ

ἀνάλογον ܡܫܘܚܬܢܐ — ܡܫܘܚܘܬܐ ἐκ τοῦ ἀνάλογον συμβαίνειν ܕܡܫܘܚܘܬ ܕܠܘܩܒܠܐ

ἀναμιμνήσκειν, ἀνάμνησις ܡܥܗܕܘ, ܥܘܗܕܢܐ

ἀνανδρία ܠܐ ܓܢܒܪܘܬܐ

ἀναπηρία ܦܟܝܪܘܬܐ

ἀνασκευάζειν ܒܛܠ

ἀνδρεῖος, ἀνδρειότεροι, ἀνδρωδέστεροι, ἀνδρεία ܠܒܝܒܐ, ܠܒܝܒܐܝܬ, ܠܒܝܒܘܬܐ

ἀνελευθερία ܥܠܘܛܘܬܐ

ἀνομολογούμενα ܡܫܚܪ̈ܬܐ — ܦܫܪ̈ܬܐ

ἀντίδικος ܒܥܠܕܝܢܐ

ἀντίθεσις ܐܢܛܝܬܣܝܣ ἀντικεῖσθαι ܚܣܝܐ ἀντικεῖσθαι, ἀντίθεσις ܕܠܘܩܒܠܐ, ܕܠܘܩ̈ܒܠܝܐ, ܣܘܩܒܠܐ

ἀντιλέγοντες ܒܥܠܕܝܢܐ

ἀντιπαραβολή ܐܢܛܝܦܪܐܒܘܠ

ἀντίστροφοι? ܐܬܦ̈ܢܝܬܐ

ἀντισυλλογίζεσθαι ܐܢܛܝܣܘܠܣ

ἀξία, ἀξίωμα ܐܟܣܝܐ

ἀξιόπιστος ܫܘܐ ܠܡܬܗܝܡܢܘ

ἅπας, ἁπλοῦς, ἁπλῶς ܦܫܝܛܐ, ܦܫܝܛܐܝܬ

(οὐκ) ἄπειρον ܡܣܬܝܟܐ ἄπειρον ܠܐ ܡܣܬܝܟܢ ἀπειρία ܠܐ ܡܣܬܝܟܢܘܬܐ

ἀπίθανον ܠܐ ܡܬܦܝܣܢܐ

ἄπιστοι ܠܐ ܩܒܠ

ἀποδεικνύναι ܫܪܪ, ܐܫܪ ἀποδεικτικός ܫܘܪܪܐ, ܡܫܪܪܢܐ, ܡܫܪܪܢܘܬܐ ἀπόδειξις ܫܘܪܪܐ, ܡܫܪܪܢܐ ἀποδεικνύναι ܚܘܝ ἀπόδειξις ܐܦܘܕܝܩܛܝܩܐ — ܬܚܘܝܬܐ

ἀποδέχομαι ܩܒܠ

ἀποδιδῶσιν? ܚܣܝܐ

ἀποκρίνεσθαι, ἀπόκρισις ܦܢܝܐ

ἀπολογεῖσθαι ܡܦܩܐ ἀπολογεῖσθαι, ἀπολογούμενος, ἀπολογία ܪܘܚܐ ܢܦܩ, ܪܘܚܐ ܡܦܩ

ἀπολογία ? ܐܦܣܒܐ

ἀπολύεσθαι ܪܘܚܐ ܢܦܩ

ἀποτρέπειν ܟܠܐ

ἀποτροπή ܥܘܪܩܐ

ἀπόφανσις ܦܪܘܛܣܝܣ

ἀποδιδόναι ܦܪܥ

ἀπρεπέστερα ܠܐ ܦܝܫ̈ܢ

ἀρετή ܡܝܬܪ, ܡܝܬܪ̈ܬܐ, ܡܝܬܪܘܬܐ δι' ἀρετήν ܥܒܕ ἀρετή ܚܝܠܐ

ἀριθμός ܡܢܝܢܐ

ἀριστεύειν ܐܬܝܪܘ

ἀριστοκρατία ܐܪܝܣܛܘܩܪܛܝܐ

ἄριστος ܡܝܬܪ

ἁρμονία ܐܪܡܘܢܝܐ

ἁρμόττειν ܦܐܐ, ܠܐܩ ἁρμόττοντα ܕܦܐܝܐ τὸ ἁρμόττον ܕܘܠܐ

ἄρρυθμος ܡܫܘܚܐ ἄρρυθμον ܐܪܘܬܡܘܢ μήτε ἄρρυθμον ܕܠܐ ܡܫܘܚܐ ܐܪܡܘܢܝܐ

ἀρχαί ܦܪܘܛܘܡܣ ἀρχή ܫܘܪܝܐ

ἀσαφές ܟܣܝܘܬܐ

ἀσεβεῖν ܐܥܘܠ ἀσεβής ܪܘܫܥܐ

ἀστεῖον ܫܦܪ, ܫܦܝܪ, ܡܬܦܪܓ

ἀσυλλόγιστον ܡܟܢܫܢܐ — ܪܘܫܡܐ ܕܡܟܢܫܢܘܬܐ

ἀσύνδετος ܐܣܪܐ ܫܘܬܦܘܬ, ܐܣܝܪܘܬܐ ܠܐ ܐܠܐ ܒܪܬ

ἄτεχνοι ܐܘܡܢܘܬܐ (ܕܠܐ)

ἀτιμία ܨܥܪ ἀτιμότατον ܠܐ ܡܝܩܪܐ ἀτιμάζειν, ἀτίμητος ܫܘܛ, ܫܘܛܐ, ܫܘܛܘܬܐ, ܡܫܛܛܐ

ἀτυχήματα? ܫܘܪܥܐ ἀτυχήματα? ܦܘܕܐ

αὐγή ܐܘܓ

αὐξάνειν, αὔξειν, αὔξησις, αὐξητικά ܪܘܒܝܐ, ܡܪܒܝܢܘܬܐ, ܡܪܒܝܐ αὔξειν ܡܪܒܐ, ܡܪܒܝܢܐ, ܡܪܒܝܢܘܬܐ αὔξησις ܡܣܓܐ

αὐτάρκεια ܡܣܬܐ

αὐτοδίδακτος ܝܠܦ ܡܢ ܢܦܫܗ

αὐτοκράτωρ ܐܘܛܘܩܪܛܘܪ

αὐτόχθονες ܒܢܝܐ

αὐτοφυές ܟܝܢܘܬܐ

ἀφαιρεῖν ܦܣܩܘܬܐ ἀφαιρεῖσθαι ܫܩܠ

ἀφελής ܕܠܐ ܫܪܝܪܘܬܐ

ἀφροδίσια ܐܦܪܘܕܝܣܝܘܬܐ

ἄφρονες ܫܛܝܐ

ἄχορδον ܠܐ ܡܬܢܝܬܐ

ἄχορον/ἄχορδον ܠܐ ܪܩܕܘܬܐ

βάθος ܥܘܡܩܐ

βαρείᾳ ܐܪܝܐ (cf. Commentary on 7.7.1)

βάσανοι ܫܢܕܐ

βασιλεία ܕܘܒܪܐ — ܕܘܒܪܐ ܡܠܟܝܐ

βελτίων ܝܬܪ — ܟܐܢ, ܟܐܢܐ βελτίων, βέλτιστος ܡܝܬܪ, ܡܝܬܖ̈ܬܐ

βία ܐܢܢܩܐ — ܐܠܝܨܘܬܐ — ܩܛܝܪܐ

βίος ܚܝܐ

βλαβερόν ܚܒܠ βλαβερόν, βλάβαι ܗܢܩ, ܡܗܢܩ, ܗܢܝܩܘܬܐ

βλάπτειν ܗܢܩ

βοήθεια ܥܘܕܪܢ

βοηθεῖν ܥܕܪ

βουλεύειν, βουλεύεσθαι ܡܠܟ, ܡܠܟܐ, ܡܠܘܟܐ, ܡܠܘܟܢܐ βούλεσθαι,
βούλησις ܨܒܐ, ܨܒܝܢܐ βουλέσθαι ܪܓ

βραχεῖαι, βραχύκωλοι ܟܪܝܐ βραχεῖαι ܦܣܝ̈ܩܬܐ

γελοῖον ܓܚܘܟܬܐ γέλως ܓܘܚܟܐ γέλως/γελοῖος ܡܗܠܠܘܬܐ, ܡܗܠܝܠܘܬܐ,
ܬܗܠܠܬܐ

γένος ܓܢܣܐ γένος ܦܘܡܐ γένη ܐܕܫ̈ܐ διὰ τῶν γενῶν ܓܢܣܝܢ

γέρων, γῆρας ܣܒܐ, ܣܝܒܘܬܐ

γεωμετρία, γεωμετρεῖν ܓܐܘܡܛܪܝܐ, ܓܐܘܡܛܪܝܐ

γλῶτται ܐܡܫܟܐ — ܡܫܚܠܦܬܐ ܠܐ ܝܕܝܥܢ, ܢܘܟܪ̈ܝܐ ܠܫܢ̈ܐ

γνώμη, γνωμολογεῖν ܓܢܘܡ, ܓܢܘܡܠܘܓܝܐ, ܓܢܘܡܠܘܓܝܣܐ γνώμη
ܗܘܢܐ — ܪܥܝܢܐ γνώμη τῇ ἀρίστῃ ܫܦܝܪܬܐ ܒܬܪܥܝܬܐ

γυμνάζεσθαι ܕܘܪܫܐ

γεγραμμένος, ܟܬܝܒܐ γραφική ܟܬܒܘܬܐ, ܡܟܬܒܢܘܬܐ γραφικοί ܟ̈ܬܒܐ
γραφικωτάτη ܟܬܝܒܐ γράφειν/γραφική ܠܓܪܐܦܝܩܐ

δαιμόνιον ܫܐܕܐ

δαίμων ܓܕܐ

δαπάνη ܕܐܦܐܢ

δεῖ ܘܠܐ

δεικνύναι ܫܘܪܪܐ, ܫܪܪ, ܫܪܪܐ, ܡܫܪܪ δεικτικός ܫܘܪܪܐ, ܡܫܪܪܢܘܬܐ δεικτικόν
ܡܚܘܝܐ, ܡܚܘܝܢܘܬܐ

δειλία ܕܚܝܠܬܐ, ܕܚܠܘܬܐ, ܕܚܠܬܢܘܬܐ δειλοί ܕܚܠܬܢܝܢ

δεινόν ܕܚܝܠܬܐ

δεῖσθαι, δέησις ܦܝܣ, ܦܘܝܣܐ

δηλοῦν ܡܘܕܥܢܐ, ܡܘܕܥ — ܪܡܙ, ܪܡܙܐ

δημαγωγός ܕܝܡܐܓܘܓܘܣ

δημηγορεῖν, δημηγορία, δημηγορικός, δημηγορικώτατα ܡܠܠ, ܡܠܬܐ, ܡܡܠܠܐ, ܡܡܠܠܢܐ δημηγορεῖν ܐܬܪܛܪ, ܐܬܪܛܪܘܬܐ

δημοκρατία ܕܝܡܘܩܪܛܝܐ ܕܝܡܘܩܪܛܝܘܬܐ

δῆμος ܩܘܛܢܐ

δημόσιαι ܓܠܝܢ

διαβάλλειν, διαβολή ܐܟܠܩܪܨܝ, ܐܟܠܩܪܨܐ, ܡܐܟܠܩܪܨܐ

διάθεσις ܕܝܐܬܣܝܣ

διαιρεῖν ܡܬܦܠܓ διῃρημένη, διαίρεσις ܦܘܠܓܐ, ܡܬܦܠܓܢܐ ἐκ διαιρέσεως ܡܢ ܦܘܠܓܐ διαίρεσις ܦܘܪܫܐ διαιρεῖσθαι ܡܦܪ̈ܫܢܐ διαιρεῖν ܠܐ ܡܬܦܠܓܢܐ

διακεῖσθαι ܣܒܪ

διαλεκτική διαλεκτικός ܕܝܐܠܩܛܝܩܐ ܕܝܐܠܩܛܝܩܘܣ ܕܝܐܠܩܛܝܩܝܐ

διάλεκτος ܕܝܐܠܩܛܘܣ

διάνοια ܣܘܟܠܐ διάνοια, διανοίας ܬܪܥܝܬܐ, ܬܪܥܝܬܘܬܐ

διαπτυχαί ܕܝܐܦܛܘ̈ܟܐ

διατιθέναι ܢܛܘܪܘܬܐ

διαφέρειν ܢܓܕ

διήγησις ܬܫܥܝܐ

διθυραμβοποιοί ܕܝܬܘܪܐܡܒܘܢ

δικάζειν ܕܝܢܐ, ܕܝܢܐ ܡܓܙܪ δικάζεσθαι/διατριβαί ܬܘܓܪܐ δικαζόμενος ܕܝܢܐ, ܡܬܕܝܢܘܬܐ

δίκαιος ܙܕܝܩܐ, ܙܕܝܩܐ — ܟܐܢ, ܟܐܢܐ, ܟܐܢܐܝܬ, ܟܐܢܘܬܐ δίκαια ܬܪ̈ܝܨܬܐ δικαίως ܒܟܐܢܐ — ܟܐܢܐܝܬ

δικαιοσύνη ܙܕܝܩܘܬܐ — ܟܐܢܘܬܐ

δικανικός, δικανικά ܕܝܩܐܢܝܩܐ, ܕܝܩܢܝ̈ܩܐ, ܕܝ̈ܩܐܢܝܩܐ, ܕܝܩܢܝܩܐ δικανική ܟܐܢ, ܟܐܢܐ δικανικά ܕܝܢܐ, ܡܬܕܝܢܘܬܐ δικανικός, δικανικώτερα ܡܠܝܠܐ

δικαστήριον ܟܢܘܫܬܐ — ܕܝܢܐ, ܒܝܬ ܕܝܢܐ

δικαστής ܡܕܝܢܢܐ ܡܬܕܝܢܐ — ܕܝܢܐ

δίκη ܩܛܝܓܘܪܝܐ — ܬܒܥܬ ܕܝܢܐ, ܕܝܢܐ δίκην δοῦναι ܬܬܒܥ

διορθοῦν ܡܬܪܝܨܐ

διπλᾶ, διπλῆ ܥܦܝ̈ܦܐ, ܥܦܝ̈ܦܬܐ διπλᾶ ܡܥܦܦ

διώρικεν ܓܙܪ, ܐܓܙܪ

δίωσις ܕܝܘܣܝܣ

δόξα ܣܒܪ — ܫܒܚ, ܫܘܒܚܐ πρὸς δόξαν ܣܒܪ

δοκεῖν ܐܬܚܙܝ — ܚܫܒ — ܐܣܬܒܪ — ܣܒܪ δοκοῦντα ܡܣܬܒܪܢܐ

δράκων ܕܪܐܩܘܢ

δρόμος, δρομικός ܪܗܛܐ

δύναμις, δύνασθαι ܚܝܠܐ δυνάμεις ܫܠܝܛܘܬܐ δύναμις τῶν λόγων ܐܘܪܓܢܘܢ ܕܡ̈ܠܐ δύνασθαι, δυνατόν ܡܨܐ, ܡܬܡܨܝܢܐ δυνατόν ܡܫܟܚܢܐ δύναμις ἀγωνιστική ܟܘܫܪܐ

δυσέριδες ܚܪܝܢܐ

δωρητοί ܐܘܪܝܐ

ἐγκωμιάζειν, ἐγκώμιον ܩܠܣ, ܩܘܠܣܐ ἐγκωμιάζειν ܫܒܚ

ἐθίζεσθαι, εἰθισμένον, ἔθος ܥܝܕܐ, ܥܝܕܝܐ

ἔθνος ܥܡܐ

εἶδος ܐܕܫܐ εἴδη ܙܢܐ

εἰδότες ܝܕܥܬܐ

εἰκός, εἰκότα, εἰκότως ܙܕܩܐܝܬ, ܙܕܩܝܐ, ܙܕܩ̈ܘܬܐ

εἰκών, εἰκόνες ܕܡܘܬܐ ܐܝܩܘܢܐ, ܕܡܘ̈ܬܐ ܘܐܝܩ̈ܘܢܐ

εἰρομένη/ σύνδεσμος? ܡܫܬܠܡܢܐ

εἰρωνεία ܡܕܘܐ

εἷς κύριος ܚܕܢܝܘܬ ܪܝܫܢܘܬܐ

(οὐκ) εἰωθός ܠܡܥܝܕܐ

εἰωθότα, εἰωθυῖα ܡܥܝܕܐ

καθ' ἕκαστον ܡܬܝܢܐ

ἐκκλησιαστής ܪܝܫܐ ܕܥܕܬܐ

ἑκούσιον, ἑκών ܨܒܝܢܐ, ܡܨܒܝܢܐ, ܨܒܝܢܝܐ, ܨܒܝܢܐܝܬ

ἐκτός, τὰ ἐκτὸς/ἔξω ܒܪܐ

ἐλάχιστα ܡܙܥܪܐ

ἐλεγτικός, ἔλεγχος ܟܘܢܝܐ, ܡܟܘܢܢܐ, ܡܟܘܢܘܬܐ, ܡܬܟܘܢܢܐ—ܡܟܘܫܘܬܐ

ἐλεεῖν, ἐλεεινόν, ἔλεος ܪܚܡ, ܡܪܚܡ, ܪܚܡܘܬܐ

ἐλευθεριότης ܚܐܪܘܬܐ

ἔλλειψις τοῦ πότε καὶ πῶς ܠܐ ܡܬܚܡܢܘܬܐ

ἑλληνίζειν ܗܕܪܐ, ܗܕܝܪܘܬܐ

ἐλπίζειν, ἐλπίς ܣܒܪܐ ;ܣܟܝ, ܣܒܪܐ ܣܟܝܘܬ ἐλπίζειν ܡܣܒܪܐ, ܣܒܪܐ

ἐναντία ܐܢܛܝܦܘܦܣܝܣ ἐναντίος ܕܠܩܘܒܠܐ, ܕܠܩܘ̈ܒܠܐ, ܣܩܘܒܠܝܐ ἐναντίοι ܒܥܠܕܒܒܐ

ἐνδεεῖς ܣܢܝܩܘܬܐ

ἐνδέχεσθαι, ἐνδεχόμενον ܡܨܐ, ܡܬܡܨܝܢܐ

ἔνδοξα ܫܒܝܪ ἔνδοξον, ἔνδοξοι ܡܫܒܚܐ

ἐνέργεια/ἐνεργοῦντα ܡܥܒܕܢܘܬܐ

ἔνθεον ܢܒܝܐ

ἐνθύμημα, ἐνθυμηματικός ܡܬܪܥܝܢܘܬܐ

ἔνια ܡܢܬܐ

ἔνστασις ܐܢܣܛܣܝܣ

ἔντεχνος ܐܘܡܢܝܐ

ἐντιμότης/ἐντιμότερα ܪܚܝܡ ܐܝܩܪܐ

ἐξαλλάττειν ܚܘܠܦܐ

ἐξελέγχειν ? ܡܟܣܢܘܬܐ

ἕξις, τῆς ἕξεως ܐܟܣܝܣ, ܐܟܣܝܣܘܬܐ ἕξεις ܩܢܝܐ ἕξεις ܩܢ̈ܝܢܐ ἕξις?
ܐܘܡܢܘܬܐ

ἐοικέναι ܕܡܐ

ἐπαγγέλλεσθαι ܡܬܒܣܪ

ἐπάγγελμα ܗܦܓܓܠܡܐ

ἐπαγωγή ܗܦܓܘܓܐ

ἐπαινεῖν, ἐπαινετόν, ἔπαινος ܩܠܣ, ܩܠܣܐ, ܡܬܩܠܣܢܐ, ܡܬܩܠܣܢܘܬܐ
ἐπαινεῖν ܫܒܚ ἐπαινετόν, ἔπαινος ܡܫܒܚܐ

ἐπάνοδος ܐܦܐܢܘܕܘܣ — ܦܢܝܐ

ἐπανορθώσασθαι ܠܡܬܪܨܘ

ἔπεσθαι ܢܩܦܐ

ἐπηρεασμός ܡܨܥܪܢܘܬܐ, ܡܬܬܪܦ

ἐπίγραμμα ܕܢܝܐ — ܟܬܒܬܐ

ἐπιδεικνύναι, ἐπιδεικτικός ܡܚܘܝܢܐ, ܡܚܘܝܢܐ ἐπιδεικτική ܡܬܚܘܝܢܐ

ἐπιεικεῖς ܡܟܝܟܐ, ܡܟܝܟܐ ܦܐܝܬ ἐπιεικές, ἐπιείκεια ܡܟܝܟܐ ἐπιείκεια
ܫܒܩ

ἐπιζευγνύναι ܙܘܓܬܐ

ἐπίθετα ܐܦܝܬܛܐ — ܬܘܣܦܬܐ ܕܥܠ ܫܡ̈ܐ, ܬܘܣ̈ܦܬܐ ܕܥܠ ܫܡ̈ܐ, ܬܘܣ̈ܦܬܐ,
ܡܬܬܘܣ̈ܦܢܝܬܐ, ܡܬܬܘܣ̈ܦܢܝܬܐ

ἐπιθυμεῖν ܡܬܐܒܐ ἐπιθυμεῖν, ἐπιθυμία ܪܓܝ, ܪܓܝܓܐ, ܪܓܬܐ, ܪܓܝܓܬܐ

ἐπίλογος ܚܘܬܡܐ, ܚܬܡ ܡܐܡܪܐ

ἐπιμέλεια? ܢܛܝܪܘܬܐ

ἐπιστῆμαι ܝܕܥܬܐ

ἐπιτρέπειν ܡܦܪܣ

ἐποικοδομεῖν ܪܘܒܒܐ

τὸ παρὰ τὸ ἑπόμενον ܛܥܝܘܬ ܕܢܩ̈ܦܐ

ἐποποιοί ܐܦܝ

ἐρᾶν ܙܕܩ ܪܚܡܘܬܐ

ἐραστής ܪܚܡܐ

οἱ ἐριστικοί, ἐριστική ܗܪܣܛܝܩܝܐ, ܗܪܣܛܝܩܝܬܐ

ἐρώμενοι ܫܒܝܪ

ἔρως, ἔρωτες ܐܪܘܣ, ܐܪܘ̈ܛܗܣ— ܬܘܚܡܐ (cf. Commentary on 6.6.2)

ἐρώτησις ܫܘܐܠܐ

ἑταιρεία ܚܒܪܘܬܐ

εὐγένεια ܫܦܝܪܘܬ ܓܢܣܐ εὐγένεια εὐγενεῖς ܛܘܗܡܐ, ܛܒܘܬ ܛܘܗܡܐ, ܫܦܝܪܘܬ ܛܘܗܡܐ, ܛܘܗܡܐ ܫܦܝܪ

εὐγηρία, εὔγηρως ܛܒܐ ܣܒܘܬܐ, ܫܦܝܪ ܣܒܘܬܐ

εὐδαιμονία ܗܢܝܘܬܐ

εὐδαιμονισμός ܛܝܒܘܬܐ

εὐδοκιμεῖν ܗܘܝ — ܫܒܗܪ — ܫܒܚ

εὐδοξία ܫܘܒܚܐ

εὔελπις, εὐέλπιδες ܫܦܝܪ̈ ܣܒܪܐ, ܫܦܝܪܘܬ ܣܒܪܐ

εὐεργετεῖν, εὐεργετηκότες ܫܦܝܪܘܬ ܣܘܥܪܢܘܬܐ/ܣܘܥܪܢܐ, ܥܒܕ ܛܒ̈ܬܐ, ܥܒܕ̈ ܫܦܝܪ̈ܬܐ

εὐεργετήματα ܛܝܒܘܬܐ

εὐήθεις ܫܢܝ̈ܐ ܛܒ̈ܐ εὐήθη ܦܫܝܛܐ

εὐημερία ܦܘܪܓܢܐ

εὐθύς ܡܚܕܐ

εὐκαίρως ܙܒܢܐ ܒܗܢܐ

εὐκατάλλακτοι ܡܬܪܥܝܢ

εὐλόγιστοι ܫܦܝܪ̈ ܣܒܪܐ

εὐμάθεια ܝܘܠܦܢܐ εὐμαθής ܕܠܝܠ ܠܬܢܝܐ

εὐμνημόνευτον ܡܗܕܝܢܘܬܐ

εὔνοια, εὔνους ܐܘܐ ܒܪܝܢܘܬܐ

εὐνομούμεναις ܦܪܝܣ

εὔπιστοι ܕܠܝܠܝܢ ܠܡܗܝܡܢܘ

εὐπραγία/εὐπραξία, εὖ πράττειν ܡܨܠܚ, ܡܨܠܚܢܘܬܐ εὐπραξία ܫܦܝܪܘܬ ܣܘܥܪ̈ܢܘܬܐ

εὔρυθμος ܫܦܝܪܬ ܪܬܡܐ

εὐσεβής ܙܕܝܩܐ

εὐσχήμων ܫܦܝܪܘܬ ܐܣܟܡܐ

εὐτεκνία ܗܢܝܘܬ ܒܢܝܐ

εὐτυχία ܓܕܝܐ, ܓܕܝܘܬܐ εὐτυχίαι ܟܗܝܢܘܬܐ
εὐφραίνειν ܗܢܝ
ἐφεξῆς ܣܕܪܐ ܙܘ̈ܕܝ, ܒܣܕܪܐ
ἐχθρός, ἔχθρα ܒܥܠܕܒܒܐ ἐχθροί ܣܢܐܐ

ζῆλος, ζηλοῦν, ζηλοῦσθαι, ζηλωτικοί, ζηλωτοί, ζηλωτά ܛܢ, ܛܢܢܐ,
ܛܢܢܘ̈ܬܐ, ܛܢܢܬܢܐ, ܛܢܢܐ ζηλοῦν ܐܬܛܢܢܘ
ζημία ܚܘܣܪܢܐ— ܬܒܥܬܐ ζημία/τιμωρία ܦܘܪܥܢܐ

ἡγεμόνες ܗܓܡܘ̈ܢܐ
ἥδεσθαι, ἡδεώς, ἡδονή, ἡδύς ܗܢܝ, ܗܢܝܐܝܬ, ܗܢܝܐܘܬܐ, ܐܗܢܝ ἡδεῖς
συνδιαγαγεῖν καὶ συνδιημερεῦσαι ܚܒܝܒܐ ,ܗ̈ܢܝܐ
ἠθικά ܐܬܝܩܐ ἠθικοί ܒܥܝܬܪ ἠθική ܥܝܕܝܐ
ἦθος ܐܥܝܕܘܬܐ—ܥܝܕܐ—ܥ̈ܝܕܐ, ܥܝܕܝܐ ἤθη ܥ̈ܝܕܐ ἤθη? ܫܝܢܘܬܐ
ἡλικία ܐܪܥܐ—ܩܘܡܬܐ, ܩܘܡܬܐ ܒܢ̈ܝ
ἡμίθεοι ܐܠܗܬܐ
ἡμιωβέλια ܙ̈ܘܙܐ
ἡρῷος ܗܪܘܐܝܐ
ἧττον ܒܨܝܪܐ μᾶλλον καὶ ἧττον ܘܒܨܝܪܐ ܝܬܝܪܐ, ܘܒܨܝܪܐܝܬ ܕܝܬܝܪܐܝܬ ,ܗܝ

θαρραλέοι, θαρραλέον, θαρρεῖν, θάρσος ܡܠܒܒ, ܡܬܠܒܒ, ܠܒܝܒܐܝܬ,
ܠܒܝܒܘܬܐ
θαυμάζειν ܐܬܕܡܪ—ܬܕܡܘܪܬܐ
θέλειν ܨܒܐ
θεοί ܣܠܡܐ ܒܪܐ
θεωρός ܚܙ̈ܝܐ
θυμός ܚܡܬܐ, ܚܡܬܢܐ, ܚ̈ܡܬܢܐ θυμός ܪܘܓܙܐ, ܪ̈ܘܓܙܬܢܐ θυμός, θυμικοί,
θυμοῦσθαι, θυμώδεις ܪܘܓܙܐ, ܪܘܓܙܬܢܐ

ἴαμβος, ἰαμβεῖα ܐܝܡܒܘ
ἴδιος ܕܝܠܢܐܝܬ, ܕܝܠܗ ἰδίας ܒܝܬܝܐ
ἰδιώτης, ἰδιωτικοί ܗܕܝܘܛܐ, ܗܕ̈ܝܘܛܐ

ἱέρεια ܐܪܝܐ ܟܘܡܪܬܐ (cf. Commentary on 6.5.6)
ἱερός ܐܝܗܪܘܢ
ἰσχύς ܚܝܠܐ—ܚܘܣܢܐ—ܚܣܝܢܐ

καθαρά ܦܪܝܫܐ
καθόλου ܟܠܢܝܐ, ܒܟܠ, ܠܟܠ
κακία ܒܝܫ κακός, κακία, κακοπραγεῖν, κακοπραγίαι ܒܝܫ, ܒܝܫܘܬܐ
κακῶς ποιεῖν ܒܐܫ κακοήθεις ܒܝܫܝ ܥܝܕܐ
κάλλος, καλόν, καλῶς ܫܦܪ, ܫܦܝܪ, ܫܘܦܪܐ, ܫܦܝܪܘܬܐ καλῶς ܫܦܝܪܐ
καλόν ܝܐܝܐ—ܡܝܬܪ—ܡܥܠܝܘܬܐ καλῶς/ὀρθῶς ܫܘܝܬ καλῶς ἔχειν
ܒܐܝܡ, ܒܐܝܐ
καταφρονεῖν, καταφρόνησις ܡܒܣܐ, ܡܒܣܪ, ܡܒܣܪܢܘܬܐ, ܡܬܬܒܣܪܢܐ
κατηγορεῖν, κατηγορία ܩܛܝܓܘܪܝܘܬܐ κατηγορεῖν ܩܛܓܪ κατηγορεῖν,
κατηγορία ܡܟܠ, ܡܟܠܢܐ
κατορθοῦν ܬܪܨ
κέρδος ܝܘܬܪܢ, ܡܘܬܪܢ
κίνδυνος ܩܝܢܕܘܢܘܣ κινδυνευτικός ܩܝܢܕܘܢܘܣܐܝܬ
κληροῦν, κλήρῳ ܦܣܐ
κοινός ܓܘܢܝ, ܓܘܢܐ κοινῇ ܓܘܢܐܝܬ κοίνος ܦܝܫܓܐ
κολάζειν, κόλασις ܫܢܩ, ܫܢܩܐ
κολακεία ܫܘܦܪܕܢܐ
κοσμεῖν ܦܠܣ — ܡܣܡܣܘ
κόσμος ܡܓܒܬܐ
κρείττων ܡܝܬܪ
κρίνειν, κρίσις, κριτής ܕܘܢ, ܕܝܢܐ
κύκλος ܐܣܦܪܐ
τὰ κύκλῳ ܐܚܠ
κύρια ܐܘܛܘܩܣܝܢܐ
κύριοι, κύριαι ܡܪ̈ܝܐ, ܡܪܘܬܐ
μεγάλας θεοῦ κύων ܟܠܒܐ ܕܓܢܒܪܐ
κῶλα ܫܪܝܬܐ
κωμῳδοποιοί ܩܘܡܘܕܝܬܐ

λέξις ܠܟܣܝܣ (ܠܐܟܣܝܣ, ܠܗܟܣܝܣ), ܠܟܣܝ̈ܩܢܐ, ܠܟܣܝܩܢܘܬܐ — ܡܡܠܠܐ — ܒܪܬ ܩܠܐ, ܒܪ̈ܬ ܩ̈ܠܐ παρὰ τὴν λέξιν ܒܒܪܬ ܩܠܐ

ληστaί ܠ̈ܣܛܝܐ

λῆψις ܝܘܬܪܢ

λογικοί, λογιστική ܡܠܝܠܘܬܐ, ܡܠܝܠܐ λογισμός, διὰ λογισμόν, λογιστική ܚܘܫܒܢܐ ܚܘܫܒܢܝܐ

λόγος ܪܗܛܘܪܝܐ ܡܡܠܠܐ — ܬܚܘܡܐ — ܬܘܪܓܡܐ μετὰ λόγου ܗܘܢܐ λόγον ἔχειν ܚܫܒ παρὰ λόγον ܕܠܐ

λύπη, λυπηρόν ܥܝܩܘܬܐ — ܟܪܝܘܬܐ, ܡܟܪܝܢܘܬܐ

λύσις ܫܪܝܐ

λυσιτελεῖν ܝܘܬܪܢ

μαθηματικοί ܡܬܡ̈ܛܝܩܐ ποιεῖν μάθησιν ܐܠܦ

μακαρισμός ܛܘܒܢܘܬܐ

μακρά, ܐܪܝܟܐ — ܡ̈ܬܝܚܢ

μαλακία ܪܦܝܘܬܐ

μάλιστα , ἔτι μᾶλλον ܡܠܝܛܐ

μᾶλλον καὶ ἧττον ܝܬܝܪܐ ܘܒܨܝܪܐ, ܝܬܝܪܐܝܬ ܘܒܨܝܪܐܝܬ, ܗܝ ܕܝܬܝܪܐܝܬ μᾶλλον ὡς ἐπὶ τὸ πολύ ܣܓܝܐܐܝܬ

Μαντίας ܡܢܛܝܐ

μαρτυρία, μάρτυς ܣܗܕܐ, ܣܗܕܘܬܐ

μεγαλοπρέπεια ܦܪܘܫܘܬܐ μεγαλοπρεπής ܪܘܪܒܐ

μεγαλοψυχία ܪܒܘܬ ܢܦܫܐ μεγαλόψυχος ܪܒ ܢܦܫܐ

μέγεθος ܪܒܘܬܐ, ܪܘܪܒܐ — ܪܒܘܬ ܠܢܦܫܐ

μέθοδος ܡܬܘܕܘܣ

μεῖζον ܡܪܘܪܒܐ, ܡܪܘܪܒܢܘܬܐ

μειοῦν ܐܒܨܪ

μεμιμημένον ܡܕܡܝܢܘܬܐ μιμήματα, μιμητικώτατον ܕܡܐ

μέρη ܐܕܫܐ κατὰ μέρος ܡܬܢܝܐ

μέσον, μετρίως ܡܨܥܝܐ

μεταβάλλειν ܫܘܚܠܦܐ

οἱ μεταξύ ܡܨܥ̈ܝܐ

μετατιθέναι ܫܚܠܦ

μεταφέρειν ܫܘܚܠܦܐ, ܡܫܬܚܠܦܐ, ܡܫܬܚܠܦܢܘܬܐ

μεταφορά ܫܐܠ, ܫܐ̈ܝܠܬܐ (ܡ̈ܠܐ), ܫܐܝܠܘܬܐ — ܫܘܚܠܦܐ, ܡܫܬܚܠܦܢܘܬܐ

μετρεῖται, μέτρον ܡܫܘܚܬܐ, ܡܫܘܚܬܢܐ μήτε ἔμμετρον ܕܠܐ ܡܫܘܚܬܐ
μῆκος ܐܘܪܟܐ
μηνίειν ܪܓܙ
μικρόν ܙܥܪܐ
μικροπρέπεια ܦܠܓܘܬܐ
μικρότης ܙܥܘܪܐ
μικροψυχία ܙܥܘܪܘܬ ܢܦܫܐ μικρόψυχοι ܙܥܘܪ̈ܝ ܢܦܫܐ
μιμεῖσθαι ܡܬܚܫܢܐ
μισεῖν, μῖσος ܣܢܐ, ܣܢܐܬܐ
μνημονεύειν, μνημονευτά ܡܬܥܗܕ, ܡܥܗܕܢܐ
μοναρχία ܠܚܘܕܝܐ ܕܒܘܪܐ, ܕܒܪܢܘܬܐ ܝܚܝܕܝܘܬܐ
μονόκωλον ܐܬܪܬܐ ܝܚܝܕܝܬܐ
μουσικωτέρους ܡܙܡܪܝܢ
μοχθηρία, μοχθηρός ܒܝܫ
μυθολογεῖν ܡܘܬܘܠܘܓܝܐܣ

ναοποιοί ܥܒ̈ܕܝ, ܢܘ̈ܣܐ
νεμεσᾶν, νεμέσασχ' ܫܠܡܐ ܫܠܡ νεμεσᾶν ܡܬܚܣܡܝܢ νεμεσᾶν, νεμεσητικοί ܡܬܚܠܦܪ
νέος ܛܠܝܐ νεώτατος ܛܠܝܐ, ܛܠܝܘܬܐ νεότης ܛܠܝܘܬܐ
νίκη ܙܟܘܬܐ
νομίζειν ܚܫܒ — ܣܒܪ
νόμισμα ܕ̈ܝܢܪܐ
νόμος ܢܡܘܣܐ παρὰ τὸν νόμον ܠܐ ܢܡܘܣܝܬܐ ὑπὸ τοῦ νόμου κειμένην ܣܝܡܘܬ ܢܡܘܣܐ νομοθεσία ܣܝܡܘܬ ܢܡܘܣܐ νομοθέτης ܣܐܡ ܢܡܘܣܐ νομοθετεῖν ܢܡܘ̈ܣܝܐ τίθεσθαι νόμους ܣܐܡ ܢܡܘܣܐ
νοῦς ܣܘܟܠܐ

ξένος, ξενική, ξενικόν ܐܟܣܢܝܐ ξενικόν ܟܘܪܢܝܬܐ

οἴεσθαι ܗܓܐ — ܣܒܪ, ܣܒܪܐ — ܣܒܪ οἰήσεται ἀξίους ܚܫܒ
οἰκεῖον, οἰκειότης ܕܝܠܝ
ἐξ οἵων ܠܘܗܢܐ

ὀλιγωρεῖν ܫܘܛ ὀλιγωρία ܒܨܝܪܘܬ ܢܦܫܐ
τὸ ὅλον, ὅλως ܟܠܗ, ܟܠܐܝܬ
ὀλυμπιονίκῃ ܐܠܘܡܦܝܘܠܝܩܘܣ ὀλυμπιονίκης ܐܠܘܡܦܝܘܢܝܩܘܣ
ὁμιλία ܟܢܫܐ
πρὸ ὀμμάτων ܩܕܡ ܥܝ̈ܢܐ ποιεῖν πρὸ ὀμμάτων? ܨܝܪ
ὀμνύναι, ὀμόσας ܝܡܐ
ὁμογενῆ ܫܘ̈ܝ ܓܢܣܐ
οἱ ὅμοιοι, τὸ ὅμοιον ܕܡܝܐ, ܕܡܝܘܬܐ
ὁμολογεῖν ܡܘܕܐ, ܡܬܘܕܐ ὁμολογούμενα ܡܬܘܕܝܢܐ ὁμολογεῖν ܡܫܪܝܘܬܐ
ὁμωνυμία ܐܘܡܘܢܘܡܝܐ — ܫܘܝܘܬ ܫܡܐ
ὄνομα ܫܡܐ ὀνόματα ܒܪܬ ܡܠܐ, ܒ̈ܪܬ ܡ̈ܠܐ ὀνόματα καὶ ῥήματα ܫ̈ܡܗܐ ܘܡܐܡܪ̈ܐ ὀνόματα ἐπίθετα ܫ̈ܡܗܐ ܡܬܬܘܣܦ̈ܢܐ ἀπὸ τοῦ ὀνόματος ܡܢ ܦܐܪܘܢܘܡܐ
ὀξείᾳ ܐܘܟܣܝܐ
ὀργή, ὀργίζειν, ὀργίζεσθαι, ὀργιζόμενος, ὀργίλος ܪܓܙ, ܡܪܓܙܐ, ܡܪܓܙܢܐ, ܡܪܓܙܢܘܬܐ, ܡܬܪܓܙܢܐ, ܪܘܓܙܐ, ܪܓܝܙܘܬܐ ὀρέγεσθαι ܪܓ ὀργή ܚܡܬܐ ܚܡܬܢܐ, ܚܡܬܢ̈ܐ
ὄρεξις ܐܘܪܥܬܐ, ܘܐܪܥܐ
ὀρθαί—καλῶς/ὀρθῶς ܫܬܬ
ὁρισμός, ὡρισμένοι ܬܚܘܡܐ, ܬܚܘܡܐ
ὅρκος ܡܘܡܬܐ
οὐσίᾳ ܟܝܢܐ
ὄχλος ܟ̈ܢܫܐ ὄχλοι ܟܢܫ̈ܐ
ὄψις ܡܬܚܙܝܢܘܬܐ

παγκρατιαστικός ܦܐܢܩܪܛܝܣܛܝܩܐ
παιάν ܦܐܘܢ
παιδεία ܝܘܠܦܢ ܣܦܪܘܬܐ πεπαιδευμένοι ܪ̈ܕܝܐ
πάθος see πάσχειν πάθος
παῖς ܛܠܝܐ
πάντων ܕܟܠ
παραβολή ܦܪܐܒܘܠ
παράδειγμα ܐܘܚܐ, ܚܘܝܬܐ — ܦܪܕܝܓܡܐ
παρὰ λόγον ܕܠܐ

παραλογισμός (cf. πρόλογος) ܦܪܠܘܓܝܣܡܘܣ
  παραλογισμός/παραλογίζεσθαι ܦܪܠܘܓܝܛܝܩܐ
παραλογιστικόν ܣܘܦܣܛܐ
παραφυές ܐܒܒܐ
παροιμία ܡܬܠܐ
πάσχειν, πάθος, πάθη, παθήματα, παθητική, παθητικῶς, παθητικὸν ποιεῖν, πάθη καταστῆσαι/ ἄγειν ܚܫ, ܚܫܘܫܐ, ܚܫܐ, ܚܫ̈ܐ, ܚܫܘܫܘܬܐ, ܚܫܝܫܐ, ܚܫܝܫܢܐ πάθος ܪܓܬܐ
παύεσθαι ? ܬܘܗ̈ܐ
πείθειν ܦܝܣ, ܐܬܦܝܣ, ܦܝܣܐ πείθεσθαι ܐܬܦܝܣ
πένταθλος ܐܬܠܘܢܐ ܚܡܫ
περιέχοντα ܟܠܗܘܢ
περίοδοι, ἐν περιόδοις ܟܘܪ̈ܟܐ, ܟܘܪܟܐ
πεφυκός ܟܝܢܐ
πιθανός ܦܝܣܐ, ܦܝܣܢܐ, ܡܦܝܣܢܐ, ܡܦܝܣܢܝܐ πιθανώτερα ܡܦܝܣܢܝܐ
  πιθανά ܡܗܝܡܢܘܬܐ
πίστις, πιστεύειν ܗܝܡܢ, ܗܝܡܢܘܬܐ πιστός ܗܝܡܢ
πλάστος ܦܬܐ πεπλάσθαι ܓܒܠܐ
πλούσιος, πλουτεῖν, πλοῦτος ܥܬܝܪ, ܐܬܥܬܪ, ܥܘܬܪܐ
ποίημα ܦܘܐܝܛܝܩܝܐ ποίησις, ποιητής, ποιητική, ποιητικόν ܦܘܐܝܛܐ, ܦܘܐܝܛܝܩܐ, ܦܘܐܝܛܝܩܝܐ, ܦܘܐܝܛܝܩܘܬܐ ποιητικόν ܥܒܘܕܐ
πολιτεία ܦܘܠܝܛܝܐ πολιτεῖαι ܦܘܠܝܛܝܐܣ πολιτική, πολιτικοί, πολιτικά ܦܘܠܝܛܝܩܘܢ, ܦܘܠܝܛܝܩܝܐ πολῖται, πολιτεῖαι ܡܕܝܢ̈ܝܐ, ܡܕܝܢܝܘܬܐ
  πολιτική ܣܐܡ ܢܡܘܣܐ
οἱ πολλοί ܣܓܝܐܐ
πολύθυροι ܣܓܝ ܬܪ̈ܥܐ
πολυτεκνία ܣܓܝܐܘܬ ܒܢ̈ܝܐ
πολυφιλία ܣܓܝܐܘܬ ܪ̈ܚܡܐ
πολυωρεῖσθαι ܐܝܩܪ
πονηρία, πονηρός ܒܝܫ
πορίζειν ܦܪܣ ποριστaί ܦܪܘܣܐ ;ܥܬܝܪ
πρᾶγμα ܨܒܘ
πραγματευθῆναι ܦܪܓܡܛܘܬܐ
πρᾶοι, πραΰνεσθαι ܡܟܝܟܐ, ܐܬܡܟܟ
πραότης ܢܝܚܘܬܐ
πράττειν ܥܒܕ

πρέπον ܫܠܝܡܘܬܐ πρέπουσα/ἁρμόττειν ,ܦܐܝ

πρεσβύτεροι ܣܒܐ— ܣܒܘܬܐ ܬܘܣܦܬ

προάγειν/ἀνάγειν ܢܓܕܘܬܐ

προαίρεσις ܓܒܝܐ, ܓܒܝܢܐ, ܓܒܝܝܐ — ܡܬܪܥܝܢܐ ܣܘܟܠܐ — ܬܪܥܝܬܐ

προαιρούμενοι ܓܒܝܐ

πρόβλημα ܦܪܘܒܠܡܐ

προεπιπλήττειν ܚܪܝܐ

προοίμιον ܦܪܘܡܝܢ, ܦܪܘܡܝܘܢ προοιμιάζεσθαι ܦܪܘܡܝܢ,
 ܦܪܘܘܡܝܐܣܘܬܐ

πρόσθεσις? ܒܘܝܐ

προσθῆκαι ܡܒܙܪ̈ܐ

πρότασις ܦܪܘܛܐܣܝܣ

(προτοτύπων) ܪܫ ܛܘܦܣܐ

προτρέπειν, προτροπή ܠܒܛ, ܡܠܒܛܢܐ προτρέπειν ܡܠܟ, ܡܠܟܢܐ

προϋπολαμβάνοντες ܣܒܝܪܐ

πτώσεις ܦ̈ܬܠܬܐ

ῥαψῳδία ܪܦܣܘܕܝܐ

ῥήτωρ, ῥητορική, ῥητορικός ܪܗܛܪܐ, ܪܛܘܪ, ܪܗܛܪܘܬܐ, ܪܛܘܪܝܩܐ,
 ܪܗܛܘܪܝܩܐ, ܪܗܛܪܐ, ܪܛܘܪܝܩܝܐ

ῥυθμός ܡܫܘܚܬܐ — ܪܬܡܐ

σαλάκωνες ܣܐܠܩܘܢܣ

σαφηνίζειν, σαφής ܦܪܝܫܐ σαφῶς ܙܪܝܪܐ

σεμνός, σεμνοτέρα ܢܟܦܘܬܐ, ܡܢܟܦܐ, ܡܢܟܦܢܘܬܐ

σημεῖον ܐܬܐ — ܪܘܫܡܐ — ܫܘܕܥܐ

σκιαγραφία ܪܘܫܡܐ

σκοπός, σκοπεῖν ܢܝܫܐ

σόλοικοι ܣܘܠܘܩܘ

σοφιστής ܣܘܦܝܣܛܐ

σοφός δοξόσοφοι, σοφώτερον/παρασοφίζεσθαι, σοφία ܚܟܝܡ,
 ܚܟܡܬܐ

σπουδαῖος ܡܝܬܪ, ܡܝܬܪܘܬܐ σπουδαῖον ὑπολαμβάνεσθαι ܠܡܫܒܚܘܬܐ
σπουδή ܚܦܛ
στέρησεις ܓܠܝܙ̈ܘܬܐ
στοιχεῖον ܐܣܛܘܟܣܐ στοιχεῖα ܐܬ̈ܘܬܐ
στρατευόμενος ܐܣܛܪܛܝܛܐ στρατηγία ܐܣܛܪܛܝܓܘܬܐ
στρατηγός ܗܕܝܪܐ
στρέφειν ܥܓܠ, ܥܘܓܠܐ
συγγενές, συγγένεια ܐܚܝ̈ܢܐ, ܐܚܝܢܘܬܐ
συγγιγνώσκειν, συγγνώμη ܫܘܒܩܢܐ
συγγραφαί ܣܦܪ̈ܐ
συζῆν ܚܝܐ
συλλογίζεσθαι ܣܘܠܘܓܝܣܡܘܬܐ, ܣܘܠܘܓܝܣܡܬܢܐ, ܣܘܠܘܓܝܣܛܝܩܘܬܐ, ܣܠܓܣ
συλλογισμός ܣܘܠܘܓܝܣܡܘܣ, ܣܘܠܘܓܝܣܛܝܩܘܬܐ, ܣܘܠܘܓܝܣܛܝܩܐܝܬ
συλλογίζεσθαι/ συμπεραινόμενον ܡܟܢܫ
συμβαίνειν, διὰ τὸ συμβεβηκός ܓܕܫ, ܓܕܫܐ συμβεβηκότα πάθη ܚܫ̈ܐ
ܓܕ̈ܫܐ. ἐκ τοῦ τὸ συμβαῖνον … ἐξ ὧν συμβαίνει ܦܘܩܐ ܕܢܦܩܘܬ
ܠܕܠܩܘܒܠܐ
συμβουλεύειν, συμβουλευτικόν, συμβουλή ܡܠܟ, ܡܠܟܐ, ܡܠܟܘܐ, ܡܠܟܢܐ,
ܡܠܟܢܘܬܐ, ܡܬܡܠܟܢܐ, ܡܬܡܠܟܢܘܬܐ συμβουλή/ σύμβολον ܫܘܘܕܝܐ
συμπέρασμα ܣܘܡܦܪܣܡܐ — ܡܟܢܫܢܘܬܐ συλλογίζεσθαι/
συμπεραινόμενον ܡܟܢܫ
συμπτώματα ܦܓ̈ܥܬܐ
συμφέρειν, συμφέρον, (ἀ)σύμφορα ܦܩܚ, ܦܩܚܐ συμφέρον ܝܘܬܪܢ,
ܡܘܬܪ
συνάγειν ܐܬ̈ܟܢܫ
συναναγκάζεσθαι ܩܛܝܪܐ — ܐܢܢܩܐ
σύνδεσμος ܐܣܘܪ, ܐܣܘܪܐ σύνδεσμος/εἰρομένη? ܡܠܟܫܬܐ
συνηγορῶν ܣܢܐܓܪܘܬܐ
συνήθεια, τὸ σύνηθες ܥܝܕܐ, ܡܥܝܕܐ
συνθήκη ܬܢܝ
συντιθέναι ܡܪܟܒܐ
συντομία ܡܦܣܩܘܬܐ σύντομος ܦܣܝ̈ܩܐ
συνώνυμα ܫܡܐ ܫܘܐܝܘܬ
σχῆμα ܐܣܟܡܐ
σῶμα ܦܓܪܐ

σωφρονεῖν, σωφρονικοί, σώφρονες, σωφρόνως, σωφροσύνη ܢܬܢܟܦ, ܢܟܦ,
ܢܟܦܐܝܬ, ܢܟܦܘܬܐ σώφρων ܦܟܝܗܐ

τάξις, τάττειν/τάξαι ܛܘܟܣܐ, ܡܛܟܣܢܘܬܐ
ταπεινή, ταπεινοῦν ܡܟܝܟܐ ταπεινή ܡܟܝܟܘܬܐ
ταραχή ܫܓܝܫܘܬܐ
τάχος ܙܪܝܙܘܬܐ — ܩܠܝܠܘܬܐ
τεκμήριον ܫܘܕܥܐ
τέλος ܣܟܐ τέλος, τελευτή ܫܘܠܡܐ
τετράγωνον ܛܛܪܓܘܢܘܢ
τέχνη ܐܘܡܢܐܝܬ, ܐܘܡܢܘܬܐ — τέχναι τῶν λογῶν ܐܘܡܢܝܢ ܕܡ̈ܠܐ — τεχνῖται
ܐܘܡܢܐ τέχνη ܛܟܢܐ
τεχνικώτατοι ܚܪ̈ܝܦܐ
τεχνολογεῖν ܡܡ̈ܠܠܐ ܡܐܘܡܢܝܢ
τιμᾶν, τιμή, τιμήματα, τίμιον, τιμιώτατος ܝܩܪ, ܝܩܝܪܐ, ܡܝܩܪܐ, ܡܝܩܪ,
ܡܝܩܪܢܘܬܐ, ܐܬܝܩܪ, ܐܝܩܪܐ τιμᾶσθαι, τιμή ܫܒܚ, ܫܘܒܚܐ
τιμωρία/ ζημία ܚܘܣܪܢܐ τιμωρία, τιμωρεῖσθαι, τιμωρήσασθαι ܢܩܡܬܐ,
ܐܬܢܩܡ τιμωρία ܦܘܪܥܢܐ — ܫܘܢܩܐ τιμωρεῖσθαι ܢܬܬܒܥ
τόνος ܪܢܐ τόνοι ܢ̈ܥܡܬܐ
τόπος ܐܬܪܐ
τραγικόν ܐܛܪܓܘܕܝܩܘܬܐ τραγῳδίαι ܛܪܐܓܘܕܝܣ
τρόπος ܙܢܐ — ܠܐ ܫܬܬܘܬܐ
τροχαῖος ܛܪܘܟܐܘܣ
τυραννίς, τύραννος, ܛܘܪܢܐ, ܛܪܘܢܐ, ܛܪܘܢܢܐ τυραννίς ܡܪܘܕܘܬܐ
τύχη ܓܕܫܐ, ܓܕܢܐ, ܓܕܝܢܐ, ܓܕܝܢܘܬܐ τύχη, διὰ τύχην, ἀπὸ τύχης ܓܕܫ,
ܓܕܫܐ

ὕβρεις ܨܥܪܐ ὑβρίζειν, ὕβρις, ὑβρισταί ܨܥܪ, ܨܥܝܪܐ, ܨܥܪܐ, ܡܨܥܪܢܐ,
ܡܨܥܪܢܘܬܐ
ὑγίεια ὑγιεινόν ὑγιαίνειν ὑγιασθῆναι ܚܘܠܡܢܐ, ܡܚܠܡܢܐ, ܐܬܚܠܡ
ὑπάρχειν ܫܪܪ ὑπάρχοντα ܩܢܝܢܐ
ὑπερβολαί? ܝܘܬܪܢܐ ὑπερβολαί? ܪܘܪܒܐ
ὑπερευδαιμονεῖν ܓܕܢܐ
ὑπερέχειν ܡܬܝܪ

ὑποθήκη, ὑποτίθεσθαι ܡܠܟܐ
ὑποκείμενον ܡܬܣܝܡܢܐ ܗܘ ܕܣܝܡ
ὑποκορισμός ܦܘܓܪܐ
ὑπόκρισις, ὑποκριταί, ὑποκριτικά, ὑποκριτικωτάτη ܒܐܦ̈ܐ ܢܣܒ, ܢܣܒܬ
ܐܦ̈ܐ, ܡܣܒ ܒܐܦ̈ܐ ὑπόκρισις ܕܡܘܬܐ ὑποκριτική ܐܘܦܘܩܪܝܛܝܩܐ
ὑπολαμβάνειν ܚܫܒ — ܣܒܪ
ὑπουργεῖν ܡܫܡܫܢܘܬܐ

φαίνεσθαι, φαινόμενος ܡܬܚܙܝܐ, ܡܬܚܙܝܢܐ — ܣܒܪ, ܣܒܪܐ, ܡܣܬܒܪܢܘܬܐ
φαντασία ܡܬܚܠܡ, ܡܬܚܠܡܢܘܬܐ, ܡܬܚܠܡܢܘܬܐ — ܦܢܛܣܝܐ
φαῦλον ܒܝܫ φαῦλα ποιεῖν ܐܒܐܫ
φεύγειν ܥܪܩ
φθονεῖν φθονεῖσθαι φθονερός φθόνος ܚܣܡ, ܚܣܡ, ܚܣܡܢܐ,
ܐܬܚܣܡ, ܚܣܡܐ
φιλανθρωπία ܪܚܡܬ ܐܢܫܘܬܐ
φιλεῖν ܪܚܡ φιλία ܪܚܡܬܐ, ܪܚܡܘܬܐ φίλος ܪܚܡܐ
φιλεταιρία ܪܚܡܬ ܚܒܪܐ
φιλόγελως ܓܚܘܟܐ, ܓܚܟܐ
φιλοδοξεῖν ܫܘܒܚܐ
φιλόθεοι ܪ̈ܚܡܝ ܐܠܗܐ
φιλόλογοι ܪ̈ܚܡܝ ܡ̈ܠܐ
φιλοσοφεῖν ܡܕܒܪ. ܦܝܠܘܣܘܦܘܬܐ φιλοσοφία ܦܝܠܘܣܘܦܘܬܐ φιλόσοφοι
ܦ̈ܝܠܘܣܘܦܐ
φιλοτιμεῖσθαι ܐܝܩܪܐ φιλότιμος, φιλοτιμότερος ܪܚܡ ܐܝܩܪܐ, ܐܝܩܪܐ
φιλοχρηματία ܪܚܡܬ ܢܟ̈ܣܐ
φοβεῖσθαι, φοβερόν, φόβος ܕܚܠ, ܕܚܝܠܬܐ, ܕܚܝܠܘܬܐ, ܕܚܠܬܢܘܬܐ
φοβεῖσθαι ܩܦܠ
φορμός ܦܘܪܡܘܣ
φρήν ܡܕܥܐ
φρονεῖν ܐܬܪܥܐ
φρόνησις, φρόνιμοι, φρονιμώτεροι ܚܟܝ̈ܡܐ, ܚܟܝ̈ܡܬܢ, ܚܟܝܡܘܬܐ
φρόνιμοι ܡܗܝܪ
φυσικά ܟܝܢܐ φύσις, φύσει, διὰ φύσιν, κατὰ φύσιν ܟܝܢܐ, ܟܝܢܐ
φωνή ܩܠܐ

χάρις ܛܝܒܘܬܐ
χειμών ܣܬܘܗ̈ܝ
χρεία ܣܢܝܩܘܬܐ
χρήματα ܥܘܬܪܐ
χρήσιμος, χρῆσις ܝܘܬܪܢ   χρήσιμον ܒܪ

ψέγειν, ψόγος ܠܣܐ, ܡܠܣܢܐ, ܠܘܣܐ
ψευδομαρτυροῦντες ܣܗ̈ܕܐ ܕܫܘܩܪܐ
ψεῦδος, ψεύδεσθαι ܕܓܠ
ψιλοί ܦܫܝܛܐ
ψυχρόν ܩܪܝܪܐ

ὠφέλεια ܝܘܬܪܢ
ὠφέλιμον ܡܘܬܪ, ܡܘܬܪܘ, ܡܘܬܪܢ, ܝܘܬܪܢ

# ARABIC-SYRIAC
# IBN SĪNĀ - BAR HEBRAEUS
(Cf. Introduction, pp. 43-45)

ܥܒܘ̈ܕ ܐܒܗܘܬܐ ذوو الأبوة
ܥܒܘ̈ܕ مآثر — ܥܠܬܐ آثر — ܐܬܪ, ܡܥܠܬܢܐ يؤثرو, يؤثر
ܡܣܒ ܒܐܦ̈ܐ, ܢܣܒܬ ܒܐܦ̈ܐ, ܢܣܒ ܒܐܦ̈ܐ أخذ الوجه, أخذ بالوجوه — ܐܚܕ. أخذ
ܫܘܠܡ ܬܘܪܓܡܐ, ܫܘܠܡܐ آخر الخطبة, آخر
ܒܥܠܗ, أخوي
ܪ̈ܕܝܐ متأدبون — ܡܬܪܕܝܢܘܬܐ تأدب
ܐܟܝܢ مؤذيات
ܐܟܣ أذيات
ܗܢܟܝܢܐ, ܡܗܢܟܝܢ, ܗܢܟܝܢ — ܢܟܠ آذي, أذى
ܢܟܠܬܐ أرب
ܐܣܛܘܟܣܝܐ, ܐܣܛܘܟܣܐ اسطقس
ܐܣܛܘܟܣܐ, أصل — ܫܪܝܪܘܬ ܪܥܝܢܐ, ܫܪܝܪܘܬܐ أصالة الرأي, أصالة العقل
ܐܣܛܘܟܣܝܐ
ܐܛܪܘܓܘܕܝܐ اطراغودية
ܐܬܐܪܘܡܐܡܢ افمن
ܐܦܝ افى
ܩܠܝܡܐ اقاليم
ܐܫܪܪ, ܫܪܪ — ܫܪ — ܡܫܪܪܘܬܐ أكد
رداءة, مؤلف, تأليف — ܐܘܝܘܬܐ, ܐܘܐ, ܡܫܝܢܘܬܐ ألفة، ثقة بمؤالفته وصداقته
ܡܫܝܢܘܬ ܪܘܚܐ, ܪܘܚܐ, ܡܪܟܒ التأليف
ܡܚܫܢܢܐ, ܡܚܫܢܐ الميات, إحداث الألم
ܪܚܡܝ ܐܠܗܐ محبون لله
ܢܒܝܐ — ܣܓܝܡ إمام — ܐܡܡ. أيمة
ܠܚܫܒܐ أمور خطابية — ܥܘܕܪ̈ܢܐ أمارات — ܥܘܪ̈ܪܐ أمر
أمل — ܣܘܟܝܐ, ܡܣܟܝܢܐ مؤمل, تأميل, أمل — ܥܒܘ̈ܕ؛ ܣܟܝܐ, ܣܟܝܐ تأميل, أمل
ܡܣܟܝܢܐ
ܐܡܝܢ̈ܐ أمين — ܗܝܡܢ, ܐܬܗܝܡܢܘܬ أمن
— ܚܘܒ عند الناس — ܪܚܡܬ ܐܢܫܘܬܐ محبة للناس — ܒܢܝܢܫܘܬܐ — ܢܚ أنس
ܐܢܫܘܬܐ استئناس
ܠܒܐ أولى — ܐܣܛܘܟܣܝܐ, ܐܣܛܘܟܣܐ أول — ܡܐܢܝܘܬܐ آلة
ܐܝܡܒܝܩܐ, ܐܝܡܒܝܩܘ أيامبيقى

بجل ܝܩܪ
بخت ܓܕܐ, ܒܥܠܓܕܐ, ܓܕܢܐ, ܓܕܝܐ ܓܕܝܘܬܐ
مبدأ ,مبادئ ܥܠܬܐ — ܫܘܪܝܐ ابتداء ,مبدأ مبتدئة ܡܫܪܝܢܐ — في بادئ الرأي ܡܢ ܪܫܐ
بدل ܚܘܠܦܐ — تبديل ܫܘܚܠܦܐ
بر ܙܕܝܩܘܬܐ
بريء ܕܠܐ ܬܠܘܡ — براء ܒܪܝܘܬܐ
بارد ܩܪܝܪܐ
برهان ,برهانية ,ܐܦܘܕܝܩܛܝܩܝܐ, ܐܦܘܕܝܩܛܝܩܐ — برهانات ܬܚܘܝܬܐ,
ܡܚܘܝܢܘܬܐ — برهانات ܫܪܪܐ
بسالة ܐܬܠܝܛܘܬܐ — ܓܢܒܪܘܬܐ
استبشع ܐܣܬܢܝ
بصير ܚܣܝܪܐ — ܡܕܥܐ — بصيرة ܒܝܢܐ — بصيرة ومعرفة ,مستبصر ܣܟܘܠ,
ܣܘܟܠܘܬܐ — مبصرة ܡܬܚܙܝܢܘܬܐ
بطش ܚܘܣܢܐ
ابطال ܒܘܛܠܐ — يحتج في إبطال ܒܛܠ
بعد ܒܥܝܕܘܬܐ
بغض ܣܢܐ, ܣܢܐܬܐ
ينبغي ܐܠܝܨܐ — ܙܕܩܐ
بلد ܐܬܪܐ
بله ,أبله ܒܪܝܪܐ, ܒܪܝܪܘܬܐ
إم بنك ܒܘܡܣܢܐ
مبهمة ܠܚܡܘܬܐ
أبواب ܬܪܥܐ — كثير الأبواب ܣܓܝ ܬܪܥܐ
بيعة ? ܐܣܛܪܛܝܐ
اللسان والبيان ܕܠܫܢܐ ܐܘܪܚܐ — تبين ܡܦܪܫܢܐ

تمام ܫܘܡܠܝܐ

ثأر ܬܒܥܬܐ — إدراك الثأر ܢܩܡܬܐ
ثبت ,إثبات ,تثبيت تثبيت ܫܪܪ, ܫܪܪܐ, ܡܫܪܪܢܐ, ܫܘܪܪܬܐ — إثبات ,تثبيت ܐܚܝܕ,
ܚܘܝܐ, ܚܘܝܘܬܐ, ܡܚܘܝܢܘܬܐ
ثروة ܥܘܬܪܐ
تثقيل ܝܩܪܐ
ثناء ,محبون للثناء ܩܠܣܐ, ܡܩܠܣܐ — ܪܚܡ ܩܘܠܣܐ يشني ܫܒܚ

إجبار ܐܠܨܢܐ
جبن ,يجبنون ܕܚܠܬܐ, ܕܚܠܬܢܘܬܐ, ܕܚܠܬܢܘܬܐ, ܕܚܠܬܢܝܢ
جد ,جدية ,مجدودون ܓܕܐ, ܓܕܝܐ
جدل ,جدلي ܕܝܠܩܛܝܩܐ, ܕܝܠܩܛܝܩܘܣ, ܕܝܠܩܛܝܩܐ — جدلي ܡܪܕܝܠܩܛܝܩܐ

جذب ܢܓܕ
جريء ܠܒܝܒܘܬܐ
جزأ ܡܬܦܠܓ — جزئي ،جزئية ܡܢܬܢܝܐ, ܡܢܬܢܝܬܐ
بالجزاف ܐܟܡܐ
جسامة ܪܒܘܬܐ, ܪܒܘܬ ܓܘܫܡܐ
يجعل ܡܫܘܐ
جل ܡܘܪܒ — تجلوها ܡܡܪܡܝܢܐ — جلالة ܐܝܩܪܐ — أجل ܒܪܝܡܬ
جلد ܚܝܠܬܢܘܬܐ — ܡܣܝܒܪܢܐ
مجلس القضاء, مجالس ܡܘܬܒܐ, ܟܢܫܐ,
جمع ܟܢܫܐ — ܟܢܘܫܬܐ الجماعية — ܡܕܝܢܝܬܐ اجتماعية ܕܡܕܒܪܢܘܬܐ
جميل ܟܠܝܐ — ܟܠ — جمال ,جميل ܫܦܝܪ, ܫܦܝܪܐ, ܫܘܦܪܐ — بالجملة ܟܠܢܝܐܝܬ — إجمال
ܟܢܫܐ
جمهو ܗܘܠܝܐ — جمهور ܣܓܝܐܐ — ܥܡܐ — ܟܢܫܐ — سقات الجمهور
ܦܫܝܛܐ
اجتناب ܪܚܩܐ
جنس ܓܢܣܐ متجانسون ܓܢܣܝܐ ܫܘܝ ܓܢܣܐ
جناية ܣܟܠܘܬܐ
اجتهاد ܐܬܟܫܦ
جاهل ܗܕܝܘܛܐ, ܗܕܝܘܛܐ
أجاب ? ܦܢܝ — جواب ܦܘܢܝܐ — ܦܘܢܩܐ
أجود ܫܦܝܪܘܬܐ
جار ܫܒܒܐ — جار ,جور ,مجور ,جائر ܥܘܠ, ܥܘܠܡܢܘܬܐ, ܥܘܠܐ — جائر ,جور ,جار
ܥܘܠܐ, ܥܘܠܬܢܘܬܐ, ܥܘܠ, ܥܘܠܐ, ܥܘܠܐ, ܥܘܠܬܐ
مجازية ܫܐܝܠ
لا يجيدون ܗܕܝܘܛܐ, ܗܕܝܘܛܐ

حب، محبة ,رحم ܪܚܡ, ܪܚܡܬܐ — محبة الإنسان ܪܚܡܬ ܐܢܫܐ — محبة المال ܪܚܡܬ ܟܣܦܐ
— يحبون ܪܚܡ — تحبب ܐܘܝܘܬܐ
زكاء الحتد, المحتد زكاء ܛܘܗܡܐ, ܫܦܝܪ ܛܘܗܡܐ
حجة ܐܦܘܕܝܩܣܝܣ — ܥܠܬܐ — ܥܠܠܐ — حجة مقنعة ܦܘ — حجج ,احتجاج ܡܥܢܐ
حد ܬܚܘܡܐ
إحداث ,حداثة ܚܕܬܐ, ܚܕܬܘܬܐ
حذاب ܩܕܡ
حرفة — ܐܘܡܢܘܬܐ — حروف ܐܬܘܬܐ — ܡܥܒܕܢܘܬܐ, ܡܣܬܪܗܒܐ, ܡܥܒܕܢܐ منحرف ,محرفة ,تحريف
ܐܘܡܢܐ, ܐܘܡܢܘܬܐ
حركة ܙܘܥܐ
حزن ܟܪܝܘܬܐ
حس ,إحساس ,حواس ,محسوس ,محسوسية ܪܓܫܐ, ܪܓܫܬܐ, ܪܓܫܢܘܬܐ, ܡܬܪܓܫܢܘܬܐ,
ܡܬܪܓܫܢܘܬܐ
حسب ܠܦܘܬ ܗܘ, ܠܦܘܬ ܗܘ ܕ

حسد, يحسد, محسود, استحسد, حاسد, حسد, تحسيد ܚܣܡ, ܚܣܡ, ܡܚܣܡܢܘܬܐ,
ܚܣܡܐ, ܚܣܡܐ, ܐܬܚܣܡ
حسن, حسن السيرة ܦܐܝܐ — حسن السيرة ܟܐܢ — حسن ܠܬܐܡ — تحسن, لا تحسن,
حسن, حسنا, حسنة, إحسان ܫܦܪ, ܫܦܝܪ, ܫܦܝܪܢ ܠܐ, ܫܘܦܪܐ, ܫܦܝܪܘܬܐ, ܫܦܝܪܐ
— أحسن ܝܬܝܪ ܡܫܦܪ — أحسن حال ܡܦܠܚܢܘܬܐ
محصور ܡܚܣܢܐ
حصيف ܚܟܝܡ
حاصل ܕܐܦܐܝܢ — محصلون ܚܪܝܦܐ
سهل حفظ ܠܡܬܢܛܪܘ ܕܠܝܠ
تكلم فى المحافل ܬܪܓܡ — الناطق في المحافل ܬܪܓܡܢܐ
حق, حققة, حقيقة, بالحقيقة, تحقيق, تحقق ܫܪܪ, ܫܪܪ, ܫܪܝܪܐ, ܫܪܝܪܘܬܐ, ܫܪܝܪܐ — ܡܫܪܪܐ حقيقة,
حقيقى, حقيقى, لم حقيقى, تحقيق ܫܬܐܬ, ܫܬܐܬܐ ܠܐ, ܫܬܐܝܬ, ܫܬܐܘܬܐ —
حقيقية, بالحقيقة ܫܪܝܪܬܐ, ܡܫܪܪܐܝܬ — لا حقيقية ܐܫܠܝܬ — حقوق ܬܘܪ̈ܝ
— مستحق ܐܫܘܐ
استحقار, حقارة, تحقير تحقير ܫܝܛܘܬܐ, ܫܝܛܘܬܐ — حقيرة ܫܝܛܐ — تحقير ܐܪܝܘ
حكيم, حكمة, الحكمة أهل الاجتهاد ܚܟܝܡ, ܚܟܡܬܐ, ܚܟܡܬܐ — ܚܟܡ ܥܬܝܪ — حكم, حكم,
حاكم ܕܝܢ̈, ܡܬܕܝܢܢܐ, ܡܬܕܝܢܢܘܬܐ, ܕܝܢܐ, ܕܝܢܐ ܕܝܢ ܡܦܪ — حكم ܐܘܪܚܐ —
ܫܘܠܛܢܐ
محاكاة, محاكيات, تحاكي ܕܡܝܐ, ܕܘܡܝܐ, ܕܡܘܬܐ — ܡܕܡܝܢܘܬܐ ما حوكي ܡܬܕܡܝܢܐ ܐܝܟ —
حكاية ܡܬܠܐ
حل ܫܪܝܬ
حلف ܝܡܐ
حلم, تحلام, حليم ܢܝܚܐ, ܢܝܚܘܬܐ — حلم ܚܠܡܐ
حمد, حمدة, ملح, إحماد, فوات الحمد, حمد, حمد ܫܒܚ, ܫܘܒܚܐ, ܫܘܒܚܐ — ܡܫܒܚ ܠܐ,
ܡܫܒܚ, ܡܫܒܚܐ, ܡܫܒܚܘܬܐ, ܡܫܬܒܚܢܐ, ܡܫܬܒܚܢܐ, ܡܫܬܒܚܢܘܬܐ,
محمودات — ܡܫܒܚ ܝܬܝܪ — محمودة ܗܒܢ محمود — ܡܫܒܚ حمد — ܫܒܚܐ
مشهورات محمودة ܠܡܫܒܚܐ
حمقى ܫܛܝܐ
حمل ܫܩܠ — محمولات ܠܡܬܡܠܠܘ ܕܡܬܡܠܠܢ ܗܘ ܒܥܠ ܡܢ
حمى, حمية ܠܐܚܪܐ — حمية ܚܡܬܐ, ܠܥ
حنث ܥܒܘܪܐ
محنكون ܡܠܝܠܐ
حاجة ܣܢܝܩܘܬܐ, ܣܘܢܩܐ
محاورة ܚܘܪܐ — محاورات ܡܬܚܘܪܢܐ
حال, حالة ܡܬܗܦܟܢܘܬܐ — صلاح الحال, حسن الحال ܡܦܠܚܢܘܬܐ, ܦܠܚܘܬܐ ܡܦܠܚܢܘܬܐ —
احتال, ܠܚܝܠܐܝܬ, ܠܚܝܠܐ حيلة — ܢܟܠܐ حول — ܡܦܠܚܢܘܬܐ أحسن حال
احتيال, حيل ܦܘܪܫ, ܦܘܪܣܐ, ܦܘܪܣܐ ܫܟܚ
حى, حيى, استحى, استحياء ܒܗܬܐ, ܒܗܬܬܐ ܒܗܬܬܐ, ܒܗܬܐ ܠܐ,
غير — ܒܗܬܐ ܐ استحياء, حياء — ܒܗܬܬܐ, ܒܗܬܬܘܬܐ, ܒܗܬܬܐ
استحياء ܒܗܬܬܘܬܐ
حيث ܡܬܬܘܦܣ

ܚܬܡ ܡܐܡܪܐ, ܚܬܡܬܐ خاتمة
ܒܗܬܬܐ خجل
ܒܪܝܐ خارجية 2.2.2, 5.4.6. خارجة
ܒܗܬ مخازي
ܥܠܝܠܘܬܐ الخسة — ܒܛܠ خسيسة
ܟܣܪܘܢܝܐ خسروانيات
— ܕܝܠܝ, ܕܝܠܢܐܝܬ, ܕܝܠܝܘܬܐ, ܕܝܠܝܬܐ تخصيص, مخصصة, خاصة, خاص, خص
خواص — ܕ̈ܝܠܝܐ خواص — ܒܕܝܠܗ, ما هو خاص — ܡܕܝܠܐ مخصصات, يخصص
ܡܠܚܫܠܐ خصوصا — ܡܠܝܠܐ
ܢܡܘܣܐ خصلة
خصومات — ܡܬܚܪܝܢܐ, ܡܬܚܪܝܐ خصومة, خصم — ܒܥܠܕܒܒܐ خصم
ܡܬܚܪܝܢܐ خصومة — ܡܬܬܕܝܢܢܘܬܐ, ܡܬܬܕܝܢܢܐ
ܕܝܠܝܬ خاصية, خاصي
ܣܟܠܘܬܐ خطيئة — ܒܣܟܠܘ, ܚܛܐ خطأ — ܣܟܠܬܐ, ܣܟܠܐ خطأ
ܪܗܛܘܪܝܩܐ, ܪܗܛܘܪܘܬܐ, ܪܗܛܘܪ, ܪܗܛܘܪܐ مخاطب, خاطب, خطابي, خطابة, خطيب
ܗܡܘܢܐ خطباء — ܐܡܪ ܡܠܐ خطابة — ܪܗܛܘܪܝܩܝ, ܪܗܛܘܪܐ, ܪܗܛܘܪܝܩܝܐ
ܒܪ ܡܡܠܠܐ, ܡܡܠܠܐ مخاطبة, مخاطب —
ܩܢܕܘܢܘܣ خطر
ܣܢܘܢܝܬܐ خطاطيف
ܠܐ مستخف — ܡܬܒܣܪܢܐ, ܒܣܝܪܘܬܐ, ܡܒܣܪ الذي يستخف به, استخفاف
ܒܨܝܪ
ܒܛܠ إخفاق
ܢܟܠ خالب
ܙܪܪ يخلد
ܦܫܝܫܐ متخلخل
ܡܚܠܛܘܬܐ اختلاط — ܚܘܠܛܢܝܐ خلطية
ܡܫܚܠܦܢܐ خليفة — ܡܫܡܠܝܢܐ خليفة
— ܒܥܝܕܝܢ, ܥܝܕܐ ܒܝܫܐ, ܥ̈ܝܕܐ, ܒܥܝܕܐ متخلق, خلقي, سيئة أخلاقهم, إخلاق, خلق
ܐܝܬܝܩܐ, خلقيات, خلقية, أخلاق — ܕܐܝܬܝܩܘܣ خلق — ܐܣܟܡܐ خلق
ܡܣܟܡܢܐ أخلاقة — ܡܥܝܕ خلقي — ܐܝܬܝܩܝܐ
ܩܢܕܘܢܘܣ مخوف — ܕܚܠ خوف — ܕܚܠܬܐ, ܕܚܝܠ مخوف, خوف
— ܓܒܝܘܬܐ, ܓܒܝܐ مختار, اختيار — ܡܬܒܚܪܘܬܐ خير — ܛܒܘܬܐ, ܛܒܐ خير
ܕܒܪ سياسة الأخيار — ܛܪܝܨܘܬܐ الاخيار — ܓܒܝܢܐ اختيارية, اختيار
ܛܪܝܨܘܬܐ
ܡܦܢܛܣܝܢܐ, ܦܢܛܣܝܐ, ܦܢܛܣܝܢܐ, ܦܢܛܣܝܐ, ܐܬܦܢܛܣ, ܡܦܢܛܣ تخييل, تخيل, خيل
ܦܢܛܣܝܐ تخيل — ܡܬܦܢܛܣܢܘܬܐ, ܡܦܢܛܣܢܐ, ܡܦܢܛܣܢܘܬܐ

ܦܘܪܢܣܐ دبر
— ܡܦܣܩܢܐ استدراجية — ܕܪܓܘܬܐ, ܕܪܓܐ, ܕܪܓ, ܕܪܓ استدراج, استدراجية, استدراج, يستدرج
ܐܣܟܡܣܡܐ درجة — ܕܪܘܓܝܐ تدرج

ܒܥܘܬܐ داعية ,دعوى — ܕܝܢܐ ,ܕܘ̈ܢ دعوي
ܙܘ̈ܙܐ درهم
ܢܨܐ ܪܘܕܦܐ مدافعة
ܐܬܐ دليل — ܡܘܕܥܢܐ, ܫܘܕܥܐ, ܪܡܙܐ ܫܘܕܥܐ, ܡܘܕܥܢܘܬܐ, ܡܘܕܥ ܕ دلالة ,دليل ,دل
ܢܚܘܐ يدل — ܬܚܘܝܬܐ, ܬܚܘܝܬܐ دلالات —
ܡܠܘܛܘܬܐ دناءة
ܒܪܝܡܐ دهاة
ܐܡܝܢܐ أدوم
ܕܝܡܘܩܪܛܝܐ ديمقراطية

ܡܥܗܕܢܘܬܐ, ܥܘܗܕܢܐ, ܥܗܕܘ, ܡܬܥܗܕ تذكير ,ذكر ,ذكر
ذم — ܡܬܚܣܕܢܘܬܐ, ܚܣܕܐ, ܚܣܕ مذموم ,ذم — ܥܕܠܐ, ܡܥܕܠܐ, ܥܕܠ ܐܢܫ مذمة ,ذم
ܫܪܝܪܐ مذمة — ܥܕܠܐ — ܡܛܪܛ
ܐܡܘܢܐ مذهب
ܐܘܣܝܐ ذاتية — ܟܝܢܝܐ ܟܝܢܐ ذات
ܛܥܝܢܐ ذائعات

ܪܝܫܢܘܬܐ, ܪܝܫܐ ܕܥܕܬܐ رياسة ,الرئيس المدبر لأمر الجماعة — ܡܕܒܪܢܐ رؤساء
ܬܪܥܝܬܐ, ܪܥܝܢܐ, ܪܥܝܢܐ رأيى , رأى — ܡܪܐ مرآيه , رأى كلام رأي ,رأى
ܡܬܚܙܝܢܐ مري — ܒܡܡܠܠܘܬܐ ܒܡܡܠܠܢܐ, ܒܡܡܠܠ
ܡܪܒܝܢܐ ربان
ܐܣܝܪ, ܐܣܝܪܐ, ترك الرباطات ,عن رباطات ,لا رباطات , روابط , رباطات
ܫܪܝܬܐ رباطات — ܫܘܒܩܬ ܐܣܝܪܐ, ܒܬܪ ܩܠܐ ܠܐ ܐܣܝܪܬܐ
ܡܪܒܥܢܝܬ ܦܐܬ̈ܐ مربع الجوانب
ترتيب .7.9.10 على الترتيب ,على النسق والترتيب — ܡܛܟܣܐܝܬ, ܛܟܣܐ, ܛܟܣܐ ترتيب
ܫܘܕܝܐ مرتبة — ܪܘܒܒܐ ترتيب/مرتبة — ܡܕܪܓܘܬܐ, ܕܪܓܐ, ܕܪܓܐ ܕܪܓܐ
ܡܣܒܪܐ رجاء — ܡܣܒܪܐ رجا
ܦܢܝ ܦܬܓܡܐ, ܦܢܝ رد
ܫܘܚܠܦ ܫܡܐ ܫܘܚܠܦ ترادف
ܒܨܝܪܘܬܐ رذيلة — ܒܨܝܪܘܬܐ رذيلة — ܒܨܝܪ ,ܒܨܝܪ رذيلة ,يرذل
ܐܓܪܬܐ رسائل
ܪܘܫܡܐ — ܪܫܡܐ رسم
ܒܠܒܒ ܣܒܝܐ عن رضى
ܥܠܘܝܘܬܐ ترافع
ܫܘܬܐܣ ܪܘܒܐ كثافة الرفقة
ܪܘܟܒܐ, ܡܪܟܒ مركبة ,تركيب
ܪܡܙܐ رمز
ܡܬܟܒܫܢܘܬܐ رنق
— ܨܒܝܢܘܬ, ܨܒܝܢܐ, ܒܨܒܝܢܐ, ܨܒܝܢܐ, ܡܨܒܝܢܐ, ܨܒܐ لإرتياد ,مراد ,إرادي ,أراد
ܡܨܛܒܝܢܐ, ܨܒܐ إرادة , راد

ܕܘܪܫܐ ارتياض
ܡܬܒܗܠܢܘܬܐ روعة
ܩܕܡ قدم برؤية — ܚܙܝܐ رؤية — ܡܚܫܒܬܐ, ܚܘܫܒܢܐ, ܚܘܫܒܐ عن روية ,رؤية
ܡܬܚܙܝܢ
ܪܝܛܘܪܝܩܐ ريطورية

ܐܣܛܪܛܝܠܐ ? زحف
ܐܪܝܛܡ الزخم
ܫܘܕܥܐ ܙܒܢܝܐ دل على زمان
ܠܐ ܡܙܗܪܘܕܝܬܐ غير مزهرية — ܐܦܪܘܕܝܛܝܣܝܬܐ إلي الزهرة
ܢܬܒܗܪ زهو
ܝܬܪ زيادة المنفعة
ܡܨܒܬܐ مزين

ܫܘܐܠܐ سائل , سؤال
ܥܠܬܐ, ܥܠܬܐ سبب
ܡܩܬܪ سبق
ܫܦܝܥܘܬܐ سخاء
ܛܘܒܢܘܬܐ سعادة — ܛܘܒܬܢܘܬܐ, ܛܘܒܬܢܐ, ܛܘܒܢܐ سعادة ,سعيد
ܒܝܨܝܦܐ بسعي
ܡܣܟܢܘܬܐ سفالة
ܐܪܝܣܛܘܩܪܛܝܐ سياسة سقراطية
ܡܫܪܐ يسكن
ܚܠܝܨܘܬܐ سلب
ܡܬܬܕܪܢܝܐ مسلمة — ܦܫܝܛܐ سلماء الصدور
ܡܒܝܐܘ تسلية
ܫܡܗܐ, ܫܡܗܐ ܘܡܠܡܠܐ, ܫܡܝܐ أسماء موضوعة ,الأسماء والكلم ,إسم
ܒܪܬ ܩܠܐ إسم — ܫܡܗܐ, ܡܬܬܫܡܗܢܐ
— ܫܢܝܢܘܬܐ ܢܣܡܐ أمر وضع السنن ,ܢܣܡܐ ܫܢܬܐ سنة ,ܫܐܡ ܢܣܡܐ سان وشارع
ܩܪܝܬ ܫܢܝܬܐ أسن ,ܫܢܝܬܐ أسنان ,سن
سياسة — ܡܕܒܪܢܐ إساءة — ܒܝܫܬܐ مساوئ — ܒܝܫ, ܒܝܫܬܐ مسيئون ,سوء
سواس المدن ,سياسيات ,سياسة — ܡܕܒܪܢܘܬܐ, ܡܕܒܪܢܐ سياسات — ܕܒܘܪܐ
ܦܘܠܝܛܝܩܐ
ܣܘܦܣܛܝܩܐ, ܣܘܦܣܛܐ سوفسطائية ,سوفسطيقي
ܡܫܚܬܢܐ ܫܘܝܐ متساويات

ܒܘܪܐ ܕܥܠܝܡܘܬܐ شباب
ܗܕܪܝܘܬܐ, ܗܕܪܐ إشباع

شبيه , تشبه ,تشبيه ,تجري تشبيه — ܕ.ܕܘܡܝܐ, ܕ.ܕܡܐ تشبيه ܐܝܟ تشبيه ܡܬܕܡܐ
ܕ.ܕܡܝܐ, ܕ.ܕܘܡܝܐ ܕܘܡܝܐ — شبهة ܐܪܥܐ

شتم ,شتامون ,شتيمة ܚܣܕ ,ܚܣܕ ,ܚܣܕܐ ,ܡܚܣܕܢܐ ,ܡܚܣܕܢܘܬܐ

تشاجر ܪܗܛܘܬܐ — مشاجر ܒܥܠܕܒܒܐ — تشاجرية ,مشاجر ,مشاجرات,
مشاجرية — ܐ.ܬܚܪܝܢܐ, ܐ.ܬܚܪܝܢܘܬܐ, ܬܚܪܝܢܐ.ܕ, ܬܚܪܝܢܘܬܐ.ܕ متشاجرون
— ܛܠܒܪܐ مشاجرة — ܕ.ܚܪܐ مشاجرة — ܡܚܪܬܢܐ, ܡܚܪܬܐ, ܚܪܝܐ ܢܚܪܐ مشاجرية
ܛܠܝܒܪܘܬܐ مشاجرات

شجع ܡܬܬܠܒܒ — شجع ,شجاع ,شجاعة ,شجاعية ,شجاعة لا ܠܒܝܒܐ ,ܠܒܝܒܐܝܬ,
ܡܬܠܒܒ, ܡܠܒܒ مشجعات ,شجاعة ,شجع — ܠܐ ܠܒܝܒܘܬܐ ,ܠܒܝܒܘܬܐ
ܠܒܝܒܘܬܐ ,ܠܒܝܒܐܝܬ

شحة/شحبة ? ܚܣܝܐ

تشديد ,شدائد ܐܘܠܨܢܐ

شر — ܒܝܫ شرارة ܓܘܠܐ

شرط — ܬ̈ܢܝܐ — ܬܢܝܘܬܐ إطراح الشرائط ܠܐ ܡܬܬܢܝܢܘܬܐ

شرع, متعد الشرعة ,شريعة ,شارع ,متعرض شرع ,وضل الشريعة ܢܡܘܣܐ ,ܕܢܡܘܣܐ,
ܣܐܡ سان وشارع ܣܝܡܘܬ ܢܡܘܣܐ. ܣܐܡ ܢܡܘܣܐ, ܠܐ ܢܡܘܣܘܬܐ,
ܢܡܘܣܐ

شرف ܥܒܕ — شرف ܡܥܠܝܘܬܐ — شرف ܦܪܨܘܦܐ ܡܥܠܝܘܬ — شريف ܡܥܠܝ —
اشرف ܡܥܠܝ — رياسة شريفة ܐܪܝܫܢܘܬܐ ܛܘܦܪܬ

مشتركة ܐܟܘܬ ܫܡܐ — ܫܘܬܦܐ — ܚܫܝܐ — لفظ مشترك ,مشاركة في الإسم ܫܡܐ
ܫܘܬܦܘܬ, ܫܡܐ ܫܘܬܦ

شعر , شاعر ,شعري ,شعرية ܦܘܐܝܛܐ, ܦܘܐܝܛܝܩܐ, ܦܘܐܝܛܝܩܝܐ, ܦܘܐܝܛܝܩܘܬܐ
— أشعار ܡܫܘܚܬܐ

الشعري ܣܝܪܘܣ

مشتعل ܝܩܕ

مشاغبة ܗܪܛܝܩܘܬܐ

تشفح ܣܝܣ

شفقة ܚܪܐ, ܚܪܘܬܐ

اشتقاق الإسم ܡܢ ܦܪܐܘܡܝܐ

شكر ܡܘܕܐ

شكل , حسن الأشكال ܐܣܟܡܐ, ܐܣܟܡܐ ܫܦܝܪܘܬ — مشاكلة ܐܣܟܝܡܐ

شكا ,شاكي ,شكاية ,شاكي ,شكاية مشكوة ܩܒܠ, ܩܒܠܬܐ — ܩܒܠܬܐ شكاية ,شاكي ܡܩܒܠܢܐ,
شاكي ,شكا — ܡܩܒܠܢܐ, ܡܩܒܠܢܐ, ܡܩܒܠ شكاية ,شاكي ,شكا — ܡܩܒܠܢܘܬܐ
شكاية ܐܩܛܝܓܘܪܐ, ܩܛܝܓܘܪܐ, ܡܩܛܝܓܘܪܐ — شكاية ܩܒܠܬܐ

شنعة ,مستشنعة ܨܢܝܥܬܐ, ܨܢܝܥܘܬܐ

تشاهد ܚܣܝܐ — شاهد ,شهود الزور ,شهادة ܣܗܕܐ, ܣܗܕܐ ܕܓܠܐ, ܣܗܕܐ, ܣܗܕܘܬܐ
— شهادة ܐܣܗܕ — مشهود ܡܣܬܗܕܢܐ — مشهود ܠܣܗܕܘܬܐ

شهرة ,محمودة مشهورات ܝܕܝܥܐ — ܠܝܕܝܥܐ مشهور — ܡܫܡܗܐ مشهور ܦܪܝܣܐ

اشتهى ,شهوة ,شهو ,شهواني ,اشتهاء ܪܓ, ܪܓܬܐ, ܪܓܬܢܐ, ܪܓܝܓܘܬܐ, ܪܓܝܓܐ —
ܡܬܐܒ مشتهى

اشارة ܪܡܙܐ, ܐܪܡܙܬ — ܪܡܙ أشار, مشير, مشورة, مشورى, مشاورية, مشاورة, مشاورون
— ܡܬܡܠܟܢܘܬܐ, ܡܬܡܠܟܢܐ, ܡܠܟܢܘܬܐ, ܡܠܟܢܐ, ܡܠܟܐ, ܡܠܟ
مشورة ܡܠܟܐ — ܡܠܟ مشورة — مشير ܪܡܙܢܐ
إشتاق, شوق ܪܓܝ, ܪܓܝܓܐ, ܪܓܬܐ — ܪܓܓ شوق ܫܘܩܐ, ܐܫܬܘܩܘܬܐ
شاء, مشيئة ܨܒܐ, ܨܒܝܢܐ, ܨܒܝܢܐ — ܨܒܐ شىء ܨܒܘ
شيبة , شيبة حسنة ܣܝܒܘܬܐ ܛܒܬܐ, ܣܝܒܘܬܐ
شيخ, مشايخ, شيخوخة ܣܒܐ, ܣܝܒܘܬܐ

صبا, صبى ܛܠܝܐ
صحح, صحة, صحيحة, صحيح, مصحح, تصحيح ܫܪܝܪ, ܫܪܪ, ܐܫܪ, ܫܪܪ, ܫܪܪܐ, ܫܘܪܪܐ,
ܡܫܪܪܢܐ — ܫܪܝܪܬܐ صحيح ܚܠܝܡܬ — ܚܠܡ صح, صحة, مصحح ܡܚܠܡܢܐ, ܚܠܝܡܘܬܐ, ܐܬܚܠܡ
صحبة ܫܘܬܦܘܬܐ
صخابون ܩܥܝܐ
تصدير ܦܘܪܣܡܐ ܕܦܘܠܚܢܐ — ܦܘܪܣ صدر, يصدر, تصدير ܦܘܪܣܝܢ, ܦܘܪܣܐ ܡܣܬܝܒܘܬܐ —
صدر ܡܫܬܡܗ ܡܠܬܐ ܒܡܫܬܐ
سرعة التصديق , يقع التصديق , وجب تضديقا ,إيقاع التصديق , تصديق ,صدق,
صديق — ܫܪܝܪ صادقة — ܡܗܝܡܢܘܬܐ, ܗܝܡܢ جانب التصديق ,تلقى تصديق
صداقة ,حق من الصداقة ܪܚܡܐ, ܪܚܡܬܐ, ܪܚܡܘܬܐ, ܪܚܡܘܬܐ ܪܚܡܐ — صدق,
صادق ,التصديق ܫܪܝܪ, ܫܪܪ, ܫܪܪ
صرح ,تصريح ܦܪܣ, ܦܪܣܝܐ
مصارعة ܐܬܟܬܫ ܡܠܬܐ — ܡܨܠܐ مصاريع ,مصراع واحد ,مصارعات ܐܬܟܬܫܘܬܐ,
ܐܬܟܬܫܢܐ, ܐܬܟܬܫܘܬܐ ( ܡܬܢܨܝܢܘܬܐ)
صرف وكد — ܦܢܐ تصاريف ܬܘܠܡܐ
استصعب ܐܬܥܣܩ
تصغير ܡܙܥܪ — ܙܥܘܪܐ تصغير ,تصغير النفس صغر ܙܥܘܪܐ — يستصغار
ܥܣܩ
صفح ܐܬܟܢܝܐ
تصلح ܠܬܩܢ — صلاح ܐܬܬܩܢܐ صلاح الحال — ܬܘܩܢܐ مصالح ,مصلحة
صالح — ܡܬܩܢܐ ܬܘܩܢܐ ܕܦܬܓܡܐ وضع مصالح — ܛܒܐ مصلحة — ܬܩܢ
ܐܬܬܩܢ
صلف ܫܘܪܥܐ — صلفون ܫܘܪܥܢܐ
صناعة , صناعية ܐܘܡܢܐ, ܐܘܡܢܐ, ܐܘܡܢܘܬܐ, ܐܘܡܢܘܬܐ, ܐܘܡܢܐ — صنع,
صناعة ܛܒܐ — صنائع ܡܥܒܕܐ
أصناف ܙܢܐ
صواب ,صائب — ܓܡܝܪ إصابة ܫܘܝ
صوت ܩܠܐ

ضبط ܐܚܝܕܬܐ — مضبوطة ܐܬܚܝܕ
ضد, متضاد ܣܩܘܒܠܝܐ, ܣܩܘܒܠܝܐ, ܣܩܘܒܠܝܘܬܐ

,باضطرار ,مضطر ,ضروريات — ܣܢܝܩܝܐ ,ܡܣܢܩ ,ܣܢܝܩ ضار ,ضرر ,ضر
بالاضطرار ,بالضرورة ,ضرورة ,ضروري — ܐܠܝܨܐ اضطراريات ,باضطرارية
ܚܒܠܬܐ مضرة — ܢܟܐ مضرة — ܐܘܠܨܢܐ ,ܐܘܠܨܢܐܝܬ ,ܐܘܠܨܢܐ
ܐܪܙܒܐ ضربون ,ضرب
ܡܚܝܠܘܬ ܬܪܥܝܬܐ ضعف رأي
ܥܘܦܦܬܐ ,ܥܘܦܦܐ مضعفات ,مضاعفة
ܡܦܩܢܐ اضمارات — ܗܘܢܐ ܡܬܪܥܝܢܐ ,ܡܬܪܥܝܢܘܬܐ في الضمير ,ضمير
ܡܢ ܗܠܝܢ ܕܠܘܬ ܡܕܡ من المتضايفات

ܟܝܢܐ ,ܟܝܢܐ طبيعة ,طبع
ܒܥܝܐ مطلوب — ܒܥܘܬܐ مطلوب
مطلق — ܦܫܝܛܐܝܬ ,ܦܫܝܛܐ ,ܦܫܝܛܐ مطلقة ,مطلقا ,إطلاق — ܡܫܬܦܫܛܢܐ ,ܠܚܘܕ إطلاق ,يطلق
ܚܠܝܠܐ — ܚܒܫ
ܡܬܘܪܟ طول — ܐܪܝܟܐ طويل ,طول

,ܛܠܝܡܐ ,ܐܬܛܠܡ ,ܛܠܘܡܘܬܐ ,ܛܠܘܡܐ ,ܡܛܠܡ ظلامة ,ظلم ,ظالم ,متظلم ,مظلوم ,ظلم
ܥܘܠܐ ,ܐܥܘܠ — ܡܥܠܘܬܐ ظلم — ܛܠܘܡܐ ,ܛܠܘܡܘܬܐ ,ܛܠܘܡܬܐ ,ܛܠܡ
,ܫܦܝܪܘܬ ܣܒܪܐ ,ܫܦܝܪ ܣܒܪܐ ,ܣܒܪܐ ,ܣܒܪ ظنية ,حسن الظن ,ظن ,ظن
ظنون — ܡܣܬܒܪܢܘܬܐ ,ܡܣܬܒܪܢܐܝܬ ,ܡܣܬܒܪܢܐ ,ܡܣܒܪܢܘܬܐ
ܪܥܝܢܐ
ܡܬܚܘܝܢܐ ,ܡܬܚܙܝܢܐ ظاهر ,ظهر

اعتبار المعادلة — ܣܘܟܠܝܐ — ܡܫܘܚܬܐ اعتبار — ܚܘܫܒܐ — ܠܚܘܫܒ عبارة
ܫܘܝܘܬ ܕܡܫܘܚܬܐ
ܥܣܪܝܬܐ عشرات
ܬܗܪܘܬܐ متعجب — ܬܗ عجب — ܬܡܗ — ܐܬܕܡܪ تعجب
لا حدود — ܡܣܝܟܘܬܐ ,ܕܠܐ ܡܣܝܟܐ ܐܪܝܬܡܛܝܩܝܐ عددي ,لا عدد ايقاعي — ܡܢܝܢ عد
ܠܐ ܡܬܡܢܝܢ
— ܙܕܝܩܘܬܐ ,ܙܕܝܩܐ عدلاء ,عدل — ܟܐܢܐܝܬ ,ܟܐܢܘܬܐ ,ܟܐܢ عادلون ,عدلاء ,عدل
معادلة — ܡܫܚܠܦܐ — ܡܬܚܫܚܢܐ معتدل — ܡܫܘܚܬܐ عدل — ܡܫܚܠܦܢܘܬܐ معدول
— ܕܡܫܘܚܬ ܕܠܩܘܒܠܐ ,ܡܫܘܚܬܐ ܡܫܘܚܬܐ الوزن والمعادلة ,معتدل — ܐܬܟܠܗܝܐ
ܫܘܝܘܬ ܕܡܫܘܚܬܐ اعتبار المعادلة
ܗܐܟܐ عدو — ܒܥܠܕܒܒܐ عداوة ,عدو
ܦܠܝܓܘܬܐ اعتذار ,عذر — ܡܦܩ ܒܪܘܚܐ ,ܢܦܩ ܪܘܚܐ معذرة ,اعتذار ,عتذر
معارض — ܐܣܬܪܩܐ تعريضه — ܪܡܙܐ تعريض — ܒܥܙܐ ,ܒܥܙ عرضية ,عرض
ܕܠܩܘܒܠܐ
— ܝܕܘܥܘܬܐ معرفة — ܡܬܝܕܥ ,ܐܫܬܘܕܥ متعرف — ܡܝܕܥܢܐ ,ܝܕܝܥ معروف
ܗܘܟܠܐ معرفة — ܝܕܥܬܐ معرفة
ܪܒ ܢܦܫܐ عز

معاسر ܕܝܠܐ
الألذاء فى عشرتهم ܚܒܝܒܐ, ܗܢܝܐ
عصيف ܥܨܝܦܐ
عطوف, معطف ܥܛܘܦܐ, ܥܛܝܦܐ
عظام, معظمة, تعظيم, التعظيم والتفخيم ܪܘܪܒܐ, ܪܘܪܒܘܬܐ, ܡܪܘܪܒܢܘܬܐ, ܡܪܘܪܒܐ —
  عظم, معظم, تعظيم ܡܪܘܪܒ, ܡܪܘܪܒܐ, ܡܪܘܪܒܢܘܬܐ — لم يزل معظما ܥܡܝܪ
عفة, عفية, عفاف, أعفاء ܢܟܦܘܬܐ, ܢܟܦܐܝܬ, ܢܟܦ, ܐܬܢܟܦ
عقوبة ܥܘܢܫܐ عقوبة ܦܘܪܥܢܐ — ܢܬܬܦܪܥ عقوبة
عقد, ܩܛܪ — انعقد ܐܬܩܛܪ
عقل, عقلية ܗܘܢܐ, ܗܘܢܝܐ — عقلية, تعقل, عقلاء ܣܟܘܠ, ܣܘܟܠܬܐ, ܣܘܟܠܬܐ
  — عقل ܥܝܪܘܬܐ ܒܬܪܥܝܬܐ — عقلاء ܚܪܝܦܐ
علة ܥܠܬܐ أخذ ما ليس علة بعلة ܥܠܬܐ ܐܝܟ ܥܠܬܐ ܠܐ ܢܣܒܘܬ
علم, عالم ܝܕܥܬܐ, ܝܕܘܥܐ — علمي, علوم, علماء ܣܟܘܠ, ܣܘܟܠܬܐ, ܣܘܟܠܬܐ —
  تعاليم ܡܠܦܢܐ — تعلم ܪܘܫܡܐ — علامة ܫܘܕܥܐ — علامة ܐܬܐ
  تعليم ܦܠܣܘܦܘܬܐ — ܡܬܡܠܦܢܐ
مستعلى ܕܠܐ, ܕܘܝ
عام ܐܘܚܕܢܐ — عامة, عامي ܥܡܡܝܐ, ܥܡܡܐ — عامي ܥܠܡܐ — عامي
  ܗܕܝܘܛܐ, ܗܕܝܘܛܘܬܐ
عمود ܥܡܘܕܐ
معاملات ܡܣܒܪܢܘܬܐ — عامل ܡܫܡܠܝܢܐ
عنت ܡܬܬܦܪܘܥ, ܦܘܪܥܢܘܬܐ
عنفوان التشييخ ܥܘܕܪܐ ܕܥܡܘܡܝܬܐ
عناية ܒܪܐ, ܒܝܘܬܐ — معنى ܣܥܪܐ — ܣܘܥܪܢܐ
عهد, ܬܘܝ
يعود ܡܥܕܩ — غير عودى ܐܠ ܡܬܥܝܕܢܘܬܐ — عادة, عادات, عادي, اعتياد, اعتيادية,
  معتاد ܥܝܕܐ, ܥܝܕܝܐ, ܡܥܝܕܐ, ܡܥܝܕܢܐ
استعارة, استعاري ܫܐܝܠܐ, ܫܐܝܠܬܐ (ܡܠܬܐ), ܫܐܝܠܘܬܐ
عون ܥܕܪ — اعوان ܡܥܕܪܢܐ
جنس معين ܚܢܐ ܡܬܬܫܡܫܐ ܕܗܘܐ ܗܘ — نصب العين, بحذاء العين ܒܥܝܢܐ ܩܕܡ

مغبونون ܠܐ ܕܝܢܐ
غريب ܢܘܟܪܝܘܬܐ — غريبة, غرباء، غرابة ܐܟܣܢܝܐ — غريب ܢܘܟܪܝܐ ܠܫܢܐ —
  لغة غريبة ܢܘܟܪܝܘܬܐ ܠܐ ܡܬܝܕܥܢܐ ܠܫܢܐ
غريزي ܟܝܢܐ
غرض ܢܝܫܐ
غضب, غضبي ܚܡܬܐ, ܚܡܝܡܐ — غضب, مغضب, مغضوب, غضب, غضوب,
  غضاب ܪܓܙ, ܪܘܓܙܐ, ܡܪܓܙܐ, ܡܪܓܙܢܘܬܐ, ܡܬܪܓܙܢܐ, ܪܓܝܙܐ, ܪܓܘܙܬܢܐ
مغفرة, مستغفر ܫܘܒܩܢܐ
مغافص ? ܦܠܓ
غلب, غلبة ܙܟܘܬܐ — سياسة تغلبية ܦܘܠܝܛܝܐ
غلط ܦܘܕܐ — مغالطة, مغالطية ܣܘܦܝܣܛܝܩܐ, ܣܘܦܝܣܛܝܩܐ, ܣܘܦܝܣܛܝܩܝܐ

ܛܠܝܐ غلام — ܪܒܝܬܐ مغتلم
ܥܬܝܪܐ, ܡܥܬܪ, ܐܬܥܬܪ استغناء, أغنياء, غناء
ܫܘܠܡܐ غاية
ܛܢܢܐ غيرة, غير — ܫܚܠܦ, ܫܘܚܠܦܐ, ܡܫܬܚܠܦܐ, تغييرات, تغيير, غير
ܡܫܬܚܠܦܢܘܬܐ
ܚܡܬܐ غيظ

ܦܐܕܘܢ فادون
ܡܫܬܗܝܬܐ فتور
ܛܘܪܕܐ فتنة أو وقوع هرج
ܙܢܝܘܬܐ, ܙܢܝܐ فجار, فجور
ܫܢܝܐ فاحشة
ܩܘܠܣܐ — ܐܪܡܐ فخر
ܣܠܩ فخم — ܪܘܪܒܐ التعظيم والتفخيم — تفخيم ? ܡܣܩܡܣܩ
ܦܪܝܫܐܝܬ مفردة
ܬܘܪܓܡܐ تفسير, مفسر
ܦܫܝܩܬܐ فصيح
ܦܘܪܫܐ مفصلة — ܡܦܪܫܐ مفصل — ܦܣܘܠܐ تفاصيل — ܦܣܘܩܐ فصول
ܒܗܬ افتضح — ܒܗܬܬܐ, ܡܒܗܬܢܘܬܐ افتضاح, فضيحة, فضائح, فاضحات
فاضلون, فضائل, فضيلة, تفضل — ܡܝܬܪܘܬܐ, ܡܝܬܪ, ܐܬܝܬܪ أفضل, فضل, فضيلة, فاضل
فضيلة, فاضل — ܡܫܒܚܬܐ فضائل — ܥܒܕ فضيلة — ܡܠܐ فضيلة — ܛܒܬܐ
ܚܘܒ تفضيل — ܚܐܡ
ܟܝܢܐ فطرة
فعل جميل, حسن الفعال, جمال الفعل — ܡܥܒܕܢܘܬܐ فعل — ܣܥܘܪܘܬܐ فعل
افحل — ܩܕܝܫ, ܦܠܝܚܘܬܐ, ܦܠܝܚܘܬ ܫܘܚܠܦܘܬܐ/ܫܘܚܠܦܐ, ܦܠܝܚܘܬ ܫܘܚܠܦܘܬܐ
ܣܥܘܪܘܬܐ, ܣܥܝܪܐ, ܣܥܪܐ, ܣܥܪ انفعالى, انفعالات, انفعال — ܚܫܐ لا فعل — ܚܫܝܫܐ
ܪܘܫܘܬܐ انفعالات — ܚܫܐ انفعال — ܡܚܫܢܐ
ܩܘܡ فقراء — ܡܣܟܢܐܝܬ فقط, ܡܣܟܢ
فكرة — ܡܬܚܫܒܢܘܬܐ, ܚܘܫܒܐ, ܚܫܒ تفكير, بروية وفكرة, فكرى, فكر
ܬܪܥܝܬܐ تفكير — ܡܬܪܥܝܢ
ܡܦܟܗ إفكه
ܡܠܒܒ أفلح
ܦܝܠܘܣܘܦܘܬܐ, ܦܝܠܘܣܘܦܐ, ܦܝܠܣܦ يتفلسف, فلسفة
ܣܟܠ تفهيم, مفهمة
ܦܘܫ فوض — ܡܫܠܡܢܐ مفاوضة
ܫܘܝܘܬܐ, ܫܘܝ — ܫܘܝܐ, ܫܘܝ اتفاق, انفاقي
ܥܕܪ قائدتها — ܝܘܬܪܢܐ يفيد سمتا

ܥܒܐ قبح — ܣܢܝܐ قبيح, قبح — ܣܢܝ قبيح ܣܢܝܘܬܐ

قبل ܩܒܠ — قبيلة ܫܪܒܬܐ — قبيلة ܠܘܩܘܒܠܐ — مقابلة ܩܘܒܠܐ — متقابل, مقابلة
ܕܠܘܩܒܠܐ, ܕܠܘܩܘܒܠܐ, ܕܠܘܩܒܠܘܬܐ

مقابلة, متقابلات, ܐܢܛܝܩܝܡܢܐ, ܐܢܛܝܬܝܣܝܣ

قدر ܕܘ̈ܕ — ܡܫܚ — قدر ܚܝܠ, ܚܝܠܐ — قدرة ܚܝܠܐ ܡܨܝܐ — قدير, الاقتدار
ܚܝܠܐ

مقدمة ܦܪܘܛܣܝܣ

قر ܫܪܪ — تقرير ܐܬܛܝܣܝܣ — تقريرات ܩܛܓܪܝܐ — ܐܫܪܪܐ

استقراء ܗܦܓܘܓܐ

قربة ܩܪܝܒܘܬܐ — قرابة ܐܚܝܢܘܬܐ — شديد التقريب ܚܬܝܬ

قرعة ܦܣܐ

يقرن ܡܩܪܢܘܬܐ — أقرانهم ܒܢܝ ܩܘܡܬܗܘܢ

بالواجب والقسط ܟܐܢ

اقسام, من القسمة, مقسم ܦܘܠܓܐ, ܡܢ ܦܘܠܓܐ, ܡܬܦܠܓܢܐ — قسر ܩܛܝܪܐ,
ܩܛܝܪܐ — قسم ܡܢܬܐ

قاس ܩܫܐ

قصصية, اقتصاص ܬܫܥܝܬܐ

قصد, قصد, مقصود ܡܢܝܫܐ, ܡܢܝܫܢܐ, ܡܢܝܫܢܝܐ — قصدى, مقصود ܢܝܫܐ

قصر, قصير ܟܪܝܐ — قصر ܡܟܪܝܘܬܐ

قضيب ܫܒܛܐ (conjecture, MSS. ܫܒܝܠܐ)

قاضي, قضاء ܡܬܬܕܝܢܢܐ, ܡܬܬܕܝܢܢܘܬܐ, ܕܝܢܐ — قضية ܦܪܘܛܣܝܣ

تقطع ܡܬܦܣܩܢܐ

الأقل والأكثر, الأقل والأكثر من ܝܬܝܪܐ ܘܒܨܝܪܐ, ܝܬܝܪܐܝܬ ܘܒܨܝܪܐܝܬ, ܕܝܬܝܪܐܝܬ, ܗܘ, ܡܢ —
القلة ܒܨܝܪܘܬܐ

قلب ܬܗܦܘܟܝܬܐ — تقلب ܗܦܟ

قنع (IV), قناعة, إقناع, إقناعية, مقنع ܦܝܣ, ܐܬܦܝܣ, ܦܝܣܐ, ܡܦܝܣܐ, ܡܦܝܣܢܐ,
ܡܦܝܣܢܝܐ, ܡܦܝܣܢܘܬܐ — قنع ܡܬܦܝܣܢܘܬܐ

قوانين ܩܢܘܢܐ — لم قانون ܠܐ ܢܡܘܣܝܬܐ — تقنينه لقوانين ܒܩܢܘܢܐ ܡܩܢܢ

قيل ܡܬܐܡܪ — قول ܐܡܝܪܐ — أقاويل ܡܐܡܪܐ — أقوال ܬܫܥܝܬܐ — قائل
ܐܡܘܪܐ — مقولة ܡܠܬܐ ܐܡܝܪܬܐ

قوم ܩܝܡܐ — قائمون ܩܝܡܝܢ — مقاومة ܩܘܡ ܠܘܩܒܠܐ — ܩܘܡܬܐ — مقام
ܩܘܡܬܐ

قوة ܚܝܠܐ — ܡܬܚܝܠܢܘܬܐ — تقوي ܐܚܝܠ

قاس ܫܪܪ — قايس ܦܣܩܐ — قاس, قياس, قياسية ܣܘܠܘܓܝܣܡܘܣ,
ܣܘܠܘܓܝܣܛܝܩܐ, ܣܘܠܘܓܝܣܡܐ, ܣܘܠܘܓܝܣܛܝܩܘܬܐ, ܣܘܠܘܓܝܣܛܝܩܐ,
ܣܘܠܘܓܝܣܛܝܩܐܝܬ, ܡܣܠܓܣ

كبر ܣܓܝܐ, ܣܓܝܐܘܬܐ — كبرى ܪܒ, ܪܒܐ, ܪܒܘܬܐ — تكبير ܪܘܪܒܐ

مكتوبة, مكتوبة, غير مكتوب, كتابة, كتاب ܟܬܒܐ, ܟܬܝܒܐ, ܠܐ ܟܬܝܒܐ, ܟܬܒܢܐ,
ܟܬܒܢܘܬܐ, ܡܟܬܒܢܘܬܐ, ܟܬܒܢܝܘܬܐ — كتابة ܡܟܬܒܢܘܬܐ — كتابة ܓܪܡܡܛܝܩܐ

الأقل والأكثر ܝܬܝܪܐ ܘܒܨܝܪܐ, ܝܬܝܪܐܝܬ ܘܒܨܝܪܐܝܬ, ܕܝܬܝܪܐܝܬ, ܗܘ — كثيرة يوهم ܡܣܒܪܐ
— في الأكثر ܣܓܝܐܐܝܬ

ܕܓܠ كاذبة ,مكذب ,كذب
ܝܩܪ, أكرم ,كرم ,راغبون فى كرامة ,مؤثر للكرامة ,محب الكرامة ,كرامة ,مكرمون ,كرم
ܪܚܡ ܐܝܩܪܐ, ܐܬܝܩܪ, ܡܝܩܪܢܘܬܐ, ܠܐ ܡܝܩܪܐ, ܡܝܩܪ, ܡܝܩܪܐ, ܝܩܪ, ܝܩܝܪܐ
أكرم ,كريم — ܪܚܡܬ ܐܝܩܪܐ الكرامة — ܫܘܒܚܐ, ܫܒܚ إكرام ,كرامة — ܐܝܩܪܐ
ܡܝܩܪ
ܕܚܠ مكروه — ܡܬܚܝܪܐ استكراهي
ܐܣܦܝܪܐ كرة
ܦܪܥ ܦܘܪܥܢ ܛܝܒܘܬܐ, ܦܘܪܥܢܐ, ܦܪܥ مكافأة ,كفأ
كلية — ܟܠܝܐ, ܟܠܢܝܐܝܬ, ܟܠ, ܕܟܠ ,ܠܟܠ ,ܒܟܠ ,ܒܟܠܗ كلية ,كليا ,كلي ,في الكل ,كل
ܟܠܢ — كلي ܦܣܝܩܐܝܬ
ܡܬܛܠܦܢܐ متكلفة مجاوز
تكلم فى — ܡܡܠܠܐ ܪܗܛܪܐ, ܪܗܛܪܘܬܐ, ܪܗܛܪܐ كلام ,كلام خطابي , متكلم
ܒܪ ܡܠܐ كلام — ܐܬܪܛܢ المحافل
ܟܡܝܘܬܐ كمية
ܫܬܐܣܬܐ كنه
ܐܝܟܢܝܘܬܐ — ܐܝܟܢܝܘܬܐ كيفية

ܒܪܝܪܘܬܐ فضيل لب ,أصالة لبه ,ثقة بلبه ,لب
ܡܚܙܝܢܐ لاحظ
ܗܢܝ, ܗܢܝܢܘܬܐ, ܗܢܝܢܘܬܐ, ܗܢܝܐ التذاذ ,لم يلتذ ,يلتذ ,لذة ,لذات ,لذيذ ,لذ
التذاذ — ܪܓܝܓܬܐ, ܪܓܬܐ, ܪܓܝܓܐ ألذاذ ,لذة — ܐܝܟ ܕܠܐ ܡܢ ܗܢܝܢܘܬܐ
ܦܘܪܓܝܐ
ܡܢ ܬܘܩܦܐ لوازم — ܡܩܪ لزم
ܐܘܪܓܢܘ ܕܠܫܢܐ اللسان والبيان
ܠܘܩܛܝܐ لص
ܢܛܠ تلطف — ܦܘܪܣܐ لطف
ܐܠܘܡܐ إلزام
ܠܚܘܕܝܗ ܠܐ ܡܥܕܪܬܐ ,لحوديه لغة غريبة ,لغات
لفظي ,لفظة ,ألفاظ ,بسبب اللفظ ,لفظ — ܠܚܘܕܝܐܝܬ, ܠܚܘܕܝܐܝܬ, ܠܚܘܕܝܗ لفظي ,لفظ
ܒܬܪ ܡܠܐ ,ܒܬܪ ܡܠܐ ,ܒܬܪ ܡܠܝܐ ,ܒܬܪ ܡܠܐ ألفاظ موضوعة
ܥܬܝܪܘܬ ܠܫܢܐ غناء كثير فى اللفظ — ܡܡܠܠܐ لفظ — ܕܣܝܡܢ

أمثال — ܡܬܠܐ مثال — ܕܡܘܬܐ بالمثل — ܦܐܪܐܒܘܠܝ — ܡܬܠܐ مثل
ܦܪܕܝܓܡܐ تمثيل — ܡܬܠܬܐ — ܡܬܠܐ أمثال — ܡܬܠܢܘܬܐ
ܫܘܒܚܐ مجد
ܗܘܠܐ مواد
ܡܫܒܚܢܘܬܐ, ܡܫܒܚܢܘܬܐ, ܫܘܒܚܐ, ܡܫܒܚܐ, ܡܫܒܚ, ܫܒܚ مديحية , مدحية ,مدح —
مادح — ܡܫܒܚܢܐ مادح — ܫܒܚ مدح — ܫܘܒܚܐ, ܫܒܚ بمدح ,مادح ,مدح
ܫܒܚ ممادح — ܪܗܛܪܐ

مدينة ܟܪܟܐ — مدنية, مدينيات ܡܕܝܢܝܐ, ܡ̈ܕܝܢܝܐ, ܡܕܝܢܝܘܬܐ — سواس المدن, صناعة مدنية
ܦܘܠܝܛܝܩܐ, ܦܘܠܝܛܝܩܘܣ

مروءة ܦܪܘܨܘܬܐ

مماراة ܚܪܝܢܐ

مزاح ܓܘܚܟܐ — ܓܚܟ

مكاره ܡܣܪܩܘܬܗ

تمكن ܡܟܝܢܐ — ممكن, امكانى, غير ممكن, لا تمكن ܐܝܟܐ, ܡܬܟܝܢ ܐܦܠܐ, ܐܝܟܢ,
— ܠܐ ܡܬܡܨܝܢܘܬܐ, ܡܬܡܨܝܢܘܬܐ, ܡܬܡܨܝܢܘܬܐ, ܠܐ ܡܬܡܨܝܢܐ, ܡܬܡܨܝܢܐ
ممكنة ܡܨܝܢܐ

إملاء ܡܡܠܬܐ

ملح ܡܠܚ

متملق ܡܦܪܦܪܢܐ

ملك, سياسة الملك ܡܠܟ, ܡܠܟܐ ܕܡܕܒܪܐ — الملك ܡܠܟܐ — ملكة ܐܚܝܕܐ,
ܐܚܝܕܘܬܐ

منع ܟܠܐ

مال ܡܘܬܪܐ

ميل ܨܠܐ — لا ميل ܠܐ ܨܠܐ

نبرة ܪܬܡܐ, ܪܬܡܢܐ

نباهة ܥܘܡܩܐ

نبي ܢܒܝܐ

ينتج, منتج, منتجة ܡܝܠܕܢܐ, ܡܝܠܕܢܘܬܐ, ܡ̈ܬܝܠܕܢ — نتيجة ܣܘܢܦܪܣܡܐ —
مستنتجة ܣܘܠܘܓܝܣܛܝܩܘܬܐ

منشورة ܦܪܝܣܛܐ

نجح, إنجاح ܡܨܠܚܘܬܐ

نحيزة ܚܝܠܐ

نوادر ܠܐ ܫܟܝܚܐ

نزع ܢܓܕ — منزعة ܦܘܪܫܢܐ — منازعة ܐܓܘܢܐ — منازعون ܐܬܠܝܛܐ

نسب, الأنساب ܓܢܣܐ, ܓܢܣܐ ܫܪܒܬܐ, ܓܢܣܐ ܥܩܪܐ — نسب ܚܣܝܐ —
مناسب ܐܚܝܢܘܬܐ — ܢܐܚܝܢܐ مناسب ܐܚܝܢܘܬܐ — مناسبة ܐܚܝܢܐ ܕܟܝܢܐ ܥܩܪ̈ܐ

نصيحة ܡܠܟܐ

نصرة ܥܘܕܪܢܐ — ܡܥܕܪܢܐ ناصر ܐܥܕܪ

تنصل ܢܦܩ ܪܘܫܢܐ

منطق, منطقي ܡܠܠܘܬܐ, ܡܠܠܢܐ — منطق ܠܘܓܝܩܐ — الناطق في المحافل
ܪܗܛܘܪܐ

نظر ܥܘܝܪܐ — نظار ܚܙܝܐ — نظائر ܦܠܐܬܐ

نظام ܛܟܣܐ, ܛܟܣܐ, ܡܛܟܣܘܬܐ

متنعمون ܒܘܬܪܐ — أنعام ܒܥܝܪܐ ܠܐ ܡܠܠܐ — ܡܬܦܢܩܘܬܐ ܠܒܣܡܘܬܐ

نغم ܢܥܡܬܐ — ܢܥܡܬܐ نغمة ܪܢܐ

منافر, منافرية ܣܢܝܢܐ, ܡܣܢܝܢܐ — ܡܣܢܝܢܐ منافرة ܡܣܬܠܩܐ

صغر النفس, صغار الأنفس ܙܥܘܪܘܬ ܢܦܫܐ, ܙܥܘܪ̈ܝ ܢܦܫܐ — كبر نفس ܪܒܘܬ ܢܦܫܐ

استنفع ,انتفع ,منافع ,منفعة ,أنفع ,نافع ,نفع ,نفع — ܦܘܫܚܐ ,ܦܘܫܚ نافع ,منفعة ,نفع
منافع — ܥܕܪ نفع — ܝܘܬܪܢ, ܡܘܬܪܢܘܬܐ, ܡܘܬܪܢ, ܡܘܬܪ, ܘܡܘܬܪ, ܡܝܬܪ
ܦܘܪܣܐ حين أنفع — ܠܚܡܐ
ܡܣܒ ܒܐܦܐ نفاق
ܒܨܝܪܐ نقيصة
ܣܬܪܐ مناقضة — ܕܠܘܩܒܠܐ نقيض — ܐܢܛܝܦܐܣܝܣ, ܐܢܛܝܩܝܡܢܐ نقيض
ܡܬܦܪܥܢܐ, ܬܦܪܥ, ܡܬܦܪܥ, ܘܦܪܥ تنقيم ,مناقمة ,ناقم ,نقم
ܟܣ منكر — ܬܟܣܐ نكير
ܫܘܕܪܐ تنكيل
ܠܗܛ انتهب
ܠܐ ܡܣܬܝܟܘܬܐ لا نهاية
ܐܕܫܐ نوع
ܡܕܥܐ — ܬܪܥܝܬܐ نية

ܒܘܣܡܐ هجائية ,هجاء
ܢܝܫܐ هدف
ܠܘܪܚܐ فتنة أو وقوع هرج
ܬܗܠܠܬܐ, ܡܗܠܠܢܘܬܐ, ܡܗܠܠܘܬܐ استهزاء
ܓܘܕܐ — ܬܗܠܠܬܐ, ܡܗܠܠܢܘܬܐ, ܡܗܠܠܘܬܐ — ܒܘܣܡܐ, ܒܣܝܡܐ هزل
كبير ,كبر الهمة — ܬܪܥܝܬܐ همم — ܒܛܝܠܘܬܐ, ܡܒܛܠ, ܒܛܠ اهتمام ,مهتم ,اهتم ,هم
ܪܒ ܢܦܫܐ, ܪܒܘܬ ܢܦܫܐ الهمة
ܠܐ ܡܬܚܫܒܢܐ مهملات
ܓܐܘܡܛܪܝܐ, ܓܐܘܡܛܪܝܢܐ مهندس ,هندسة
ܫܘܪܕܐ هول
هوان — ܡܒܣܪܘܬܐ, ܡܬܒܣܪܢܐ, ܡܒܣܪܐ استهانة ,مستهان — ܡܒܣܝܪܐ هون
ܫܝܛܘܬܐ, ܫܘܛ استهانة
ܗܪܓ ܡܢ ܢܦܫܐ عن أهواء — ܫܒ هوى — ܪܓܝܓܐ, ܪܓܬܐ هوى
ܕܡܘܬܐ هيئة

موبخ — ܡܬܟܘܢܐ, ܡܟܘܢܘܬܐ, ܡܟܘܢܐ, ܟܘܢܐ, ܟܘܢ توبيخ ,موبخ ,وبخ
ܡܟܘܢܘܬܐ توبيخ — ܒܠܘܒܒܐ
ܐܘܢܘܬܐ ثقة بمؤالفته وصداقته
— ܡܬܒܥܝܢܐ وجب — ܐܠܨܐ ,ܐܠܝܨܐ واجبات ,وجب — ܐܠܝܨܐ واجب ,وجب
— ܒܥܝܢ بالواجب والقسط — ܙܕܩܐܝܬ, ܡܙܕܩ, ܙܕܩܐ, ܙܕܩܐ واجبة ,واجبات ,واجب
ܡܬܒܥܝܢܘܬܐ موجبتان
ܐܝܬܝܢܐ موجودات
ܒܦܣܝܩܬܐ إيجاز — ܦܣܝܩܘܬܐ يوجز
ܕܐܦܐܦܐ لها وجهان — ܐܕܫܐ وجوه — ܥܘܒܕܐ — ܪܓܝܓܐ — ܢܝܫܐ وجه
ܝܚܝܕܘܬ, ܕܘܒܪܐ ܚܕܝܐ ܠܚܘܕܝܗ وحدانية الرياسة ,سياسة وحدانية — ܦܫܝܛܐ وحده
ܪܝܫܘܬܐ

ܡܦܫܩܘܬܐ توديع

ܡܫܘܚܬܢܐ, ܕܠܐ ܡܫܘܚܬܐ, ܡܫܘܚܬܐ لا وزن, موزون, وزن

ܡܨܥܝܐ, (ܬܫܘܡܬܐ) ܡܨܥܝ ܡܨܥܝܐ المتوسطون, متوسط, المتوسط الموثوق, أوساط, واسطة
ܡܨ̈ܥܝܐ, ܡܨܥܝܐ, ܡܨܥܝܢܘܬܐ

ܡܢܗ يفيد سمتا — ܐܣܡܬܐ سمت

ܨܘܡܗܐ صفة

ܐܚܝܕܘܬܐ وصلة — ܕܚܒܝܐ موصلات, موصول — ܡܬܢܩܦܢܐ تصل — ܐܢܩܦ يصل
ܥܢܩܬܐ توصل —

ܐܬܬܪܐ موضع — ܣܝܡܐ ܕܣܝܡܘܬ ܠܕܠܩܘܒܠܐ وضع حكم بأزاء, ܒܬܪ ܩܠܐ ܕܣܝܡ, ܒܬܪ ܩܠܐ ܣܝܡܬܐ إسم/لفظ موضوع, ألفاظ موضوعة, أسماء موضوعة
ܡܬܬܣܝܡܢܐ, ܫܡ̈ܗܐ ܡܬܬܣܝܡܢܐ

ܡܦܝܣܢܘܬܐ موعظة

ܐܫܘܘܡܝܘܬܐ اتفاق الإسم — ܫܘܝܘܬ ܫܡܐ متفقات — ܫܘܐ وفق

ܙܒܢܐ ܒܗܢܐ ܙܒܢܐ وقت

ܒܡܥܒܕܢܘܬܐ وقاحة

ܡܬܬܩܪܝܢܐ يقر

ܒܢܝܐ ? موقع — ܐܪܡܘܢܝܩܝܐ ايقاعي — ܒܕܥ وقع

ܡܬܝܠܕܘܬ ܕܒ̈ܢܝܐ, ܒܡܘܠܕܘܬ ܒ̈ܢܝܐ حال الأولاد

— ܕܒܢܝܐ متولون لسياسة — ܫܠܝܛ — ܡܘܬܪ أولى — ܐܬܡܫܠܛܢܘܬܐ أولياء
ܡܫܠܛܢܝܬܐ مستولية

ܐܣܬܒܪܐ إيهام — ܡܬܚܫܒܢܘܬܐ — ܪܢܝܐ — ܣܒܪ وهم

ܒܘܬܪܐ يسار

ܗܝܡܢ يقن

ܡܡܝܢܬܐ يمين

# BIBLIOGRAPHY
OF WORKS CITED IN INTRODUCTION AND COMMENTARY

## Ancient and Medieval Authors

ANTONY OF TAGRIT, *The Fifth Book of the Rhetoric of Antony of Tagrit*, ed./tr. J. W. Watt (*Corpus Scriptorum Christianorum Orientalium* 480/481), (Louvain, 1986)

——, *Antony of Tagrit's Rhetoric Book One: Introduction, Partial Translation, and Commentary* by P. E. Eskenasy (Unpublished Dissertation, Harvard University, 1991); includes facsimile reproduction of MS. *Harvard, Houghton Syriac 25*, foll. 5v-55v

ARISTOTLE, *Aristote, "Rhétorique"*, ed./tr. M. Dufour and A. Wartelle, 3 vols. (Paris, 1960-1973)

——, *Aristotelis Ars Rhetorica*, ed. R. Kassel (Berlin and New York, 1976)

——, *Aristotle's* Ars Rhetorica, *The Arabic Version. A new edition with Commentary and Glossary*, by M. C. Lyons, 2 vols. (vol. 1 Introduction, Text, Commentary——vol. 2 Glossary), (Cambridge, 1982) [Abbreviated ARar]

——, *Aristotle* On Rhetoric. *A Theory of Civic Discourse, newly translated with Introduction, Notes, and Appendixes* by G. A. Kennedy (New York and Oxford, 1991)

BAR HEBRAEUS, *Gregorii Barhebraei Chronicon ecclesiasticum*, ed./tr. J. B. Abbeloos and T. J. Lamy, vols. I-II and III (Louvain, 1872-1874 and 1877)

——, *Gregorii Barhebraei Chronicon syriacum*, ed. P. Bedjan (Paris, 1890)

——, *Nomocanon Gregorii Barhebraei*, ed. P. Bedjan (Paris and Leipzig, 1898)

——, 'Une lettre de Bar Hébréus au Catholicos Denḥā Ier, ed./tr. J.-B. Chabot, *Journal asiatique*, ser. 9, vol. 11 (1898), 75-128

——, *Bar Hebraeus' Book of the Dove*, tr. A. J. Wensinck (Leiden, 1919)

——, *Ta'rīkh mukhtaṣar al-duwal*, ed. A. Ṣālḥānī (Beirut, 1890)

——, *The Book of Splendours* (*Ktābā d-Ṣemḥē*), ed. A. Moberg, *Le livre des splendeurs. La grande grammaire de Grégoire Barhebraeus* (Lund, 1922), tr. A. Moberg, *Das Buch der Strahlen. Die grössere Grammatik des Barhebräus* (Leipzig) I (1913), II (1907)

BAR SHAKKO, *Dialogues*, partial ed./tr. l'abbé [J. P. P.] Martin, *De la Métrique chez les Syriens* (*Abhandlungen für die Kunde des Morgenlandes, Band 7, Nr. 2*), (Leipzig, 1879)

AL-FĀRĀBĪ, *Falsafat Arisṭūṭālīs*, ed. M. Mahdi (Beirut, 1961)

——, *Philosophy of Plato and Aristotle*, tr. M. Mahdi (1962, rev. ed. Ithaca, New York, 2001)

——, *Deux ouvrages inédits sur la réthorique*: I. *K. al-Khaṭāba*, ed./ tr. J. Langhade; II. *Didascalia in rethoricam Aristotelis ex glosa Alpharabi*, ed. M. Grignaschi (Beirut, 1971)

IBN ABĪ UṢAIBI'A, *'Uyūn al-Anbā' fī Ṭabaqāt al-Aṭibbā'*, ed. A. Müller (Cairo/Königsberg, 1882/4)
IBN AL-NADĪM, *Kitāb al-Fihrist*, ed. G. Flügel (Leipzig, 1871); tr. B. Dodge, *The Fihrist of al-Nadīm*, 2 vols. (New York, 1970)
IBN RUSHD, *Averroès (Ibn Rušd). Commentaire moyen à la Rhétorique d'Aristote, Édition critique du texte arabe et traduction française* par M. Aouad, 3 vols. (vol. 1 Introduction–vol. 2 Edition and Translation–vol. 3 Commentary), (Paris, 2002) [Abbreviated IR Aouad]
IBN SĪNĀ, *Kitāb al-Majmū' aw al-Ḥikma al-'Arūḍiyya: fi ma'ānī Kitāb Rīṭūrīqa*, ed. M. S. Salem (Cairo, 1953)
——, *Al-Shifā', al-Mantiq VIII——al-Khaṭāba* (*La Logique VIII——Rhétorique)*, ed. M. S. Salem (Cairo, 1954) [Abbreviated IS]; German translation of chapter one in Würsch, *Avicennas Bearbeitungen der aristotelischen Rhetorik*, 140-174 (with commentary 175-212)
JOHN THE DEACON, ed. H. Rabe, 'Aus Rhetoren Handschriften: 5. Des Diakonen und Logotheten Johannes Kommentar zu Hermogenes Περὶ μεθόδου δεινότητος', *Rheinisches Museum* 63 (1908), 127-151

## Modern Authors

AOUAD, M., 'Les fondements de la *Rhétorique* d'Aristote reconsidérés par Fārābī, ou le concept de point de vue immédiat et commun', *Arabic Sciences and Philosophy* 2 (1992), 133-180
——, 'La *Rhétorique*. Tradition syriaque et arabe', in *Dictionnaire des philosophes antiques: I*, ed. R. Goulet (Paris, 1994), 455-472 and 'Compléments', in *Dictionnaire des philosophes antiques: Supplément* (Paris, 2003), 219-223
——, *Averroès (Ibn Rušd). Commentaire moyen à la Rhétorique d'Aristote. Édition critique du texte arabe et traduction française*, 3 vols. (Paris, 2002) [Abbreviated Aouad]
AOUAD, M, and RASHED, M, 'Commentateurs "satisfaisants" et "non satisfaisants" de la *Rhétorique* selon Averroès', in G. Endress and J. A. Aertsen (eds.), *Averroès and the Aristotelian Tradition* (Leiden, 1999), 83-124
ASSEMANI, S. E., *Bibliothecae Mediceae Laurentianae et Palatinae codicum manuscriptorum orientalium catalogus* (Florence, 1742)
BARSOUM, Ignatius Aphram I, *The Scattered Pearls. A History of Syriac Literature and Sciences*. Translated and edited by M. Moosa (Piscataway, NJ, 2003)
BAUMSTARK, A., *Geschichte der syrischen Literatur* (Bonn, 1922)
BENDRAT, J., 'Der Dialog über die Rhetorik des Jacob Bar Shakko', in *Paul de Lagarde und die syrische Kirchengeschichte*, ed. Göttinger Arbeitskreis für syrische Kirchengeschichte (Göttingen, 1968), 19-26
BLACK, D. L., *Logic and Aristotle's* Rhetoric *and* Poetics *in Medieval Arabic Philosophy* (Leiden, 1990)
BROCK, S., 'The Syriac Commentary Tradition', in C. Burnett (ed.), *Glosses and Commentaries on Aristotelian Logical Texts: The Syriac, Arabic and Medieval Latin Traditions* (London, 1993), 3-18

——, 'Two Letters of the Patriarch Timothy from the Late Eighth Century on Translations from Greek', *Arabic Sciences and Philosophy* 9 (1999), 233-246

BROCKELMANN, C., *Lexicon Syriacum*, 2nd. ed. (Halle, 1928) [Abbreviated *BrLex*]

BUTTERWORTH, C. E., 'The Rhetorician and his Relationship to the Community: Three Accounts of Aristotle's Rhetoric', in M. E. Marmura (ed.), *Islamic Theology and Philosophy* (New York, 1984), 111-136

COAKLEY, J. F., 'A Catalogue of the Syriac MSS. in the John Rylands Library', *Bulletin of the John Rylands University Library of Manchester* 75 (1993), 105-207

DODGE, B. (tr.), *The Fihrist of al-Nadīm*, 2 vols. (New York, 1970)

DROSSAART LULOFS, H. J., and POORTMAN, E. L. J., *Nicolaus Damascenus, De plantis. Five Translations* (*Aristoteles Semitico-Latinus* 4) (Amsterdam/Oxford/New York, 1989)

ENDRESS, G., 'The Circle of al-Kindī: Early Arabic Translations from the Greek and the Rise of Islamic Philosophy', in G. Endress and R. Kruk (eds.), *The Ancient Tradition in Christian and Islamic Hellenism: Studies on the Transmission of Greek Philosophy and Sciences dedicated to H. J. Drossaart Lulofs on his ninetieth birthday* (Leiden, 1997), 43-76

ENDRESS, G and GUTAS, D, *A Greek and Arabic Lexicon (Handbuch der Orientalistik*, I.xi*)*, (Leiden, 1992–)

FIEY, J. -M., 'Esquisse d'une bibliographie de Bar Hébraeus (+ 1286)', *Parole de l'Orient* 13 (1986), 279-312

FLÜGEL, G. (ed.), *Kitāb al-Fihrist* (Leipzig, 1871)

FURLANI, G., 'La psicologia di Barhebreo secondo il libro *La crema della Sapienza*', *Rivista degli studi orientali* 13 (1931-1932), 24-52

——, 'Di tre scritti in lingua siriaca di Barhebreo sull' anima', *Rivista degli studi orientali* 14 (1934), 284-308

GOLDZIHER, I., 'Matth. VII. 5 in der muhammedanischen Literatur', *Zeitschrift der Deutschen Morgenländischen Gesellschaft* 31 (1877), 765-767

GOULET, R., 'La *Poétique*', in *Dictionnaire des philosophes antiques I*, ed. R. Goulet (Paris, 1994), 448-451

GRIMALDI, W. M. A, *Aristotle*, Rhetoric*: A Commentary*, 2 vols. (New York, 1980-1988)

GUTAS, D., 'Paul the Persian on the Classification of the Parts of Aristotle's Philosophy: a Milestone between Alexandria and Baġdād', *Der Islam* 60 (1983), 231-267

——, *Avicenna and the Aristotelian Tradition* (Leiden, 1988)

——, 'Aspects of Literary Form and Genre in Arabic Logical Works', in C. Burnett (ed.), *Glosses and Commentaries on Aristotelian Logical Texts: The Syriac, Arabic and Medieval Latin Traditions* (London, 1993), 29-76

HADOT, P., 'Philosophie, dialectique, rhétorique dans l'Antiquité', *Studia Philosophica* 39 (1980), 139-166

HEINRICHS, W, *Arabische Dichtung und griechische Poetik* (Beirut, 1969)

——, 'Die antike Verknüpfung von phantasia und Dichtung bei den Arabern', *Zeitschrift der Deutschen Morgenländischen Gesellschaft* 128 (1978), 252-298

——, review of Lyons, Aristotle's *Ars Rhetorica*, in *Zeitschrift für Geschichte der Arabisch-Islamischen Wissenschaften* 1 (1984), 312-316

HUGONNARD-ROCHE, 'L'*Organon*. Tradition syriaque et arabe', in *Dictionnaire des philosophes antiques: I*, ed. R. Goulet (Paris, 1994), 502-528

——, 'La *Poétique*. Tradition syriaque et arabe: (Compléments)', in *Dictionnaire des philosophes antiques: Supplément* (Paris, 2003), 208-218

JANDER, K., *Oratorum et rhetorum graecorum fragmenta nuper reperta* (Bonn, 1913)

JANSSENS, F., 'Bar Hebraeus' *Book of the Pupils of the Eye*', *American Journal of Semitic Languages and Literatures* 47 (1930/1), 26-49, 94-134; 48 (1932), 209-263; 52 (1935), 1-21

JOOSSE, N. P. G., 'Bar Hebraeus' ܟܬܒܐ ܕܚܐܘܬ ܚܟܡܬܐ (*Butyrum Sapientiae*). A Description of the Extant Manuscripts', *Le Muséon* 112 (1999), 417-458

——, *A Syriac Encyclopaedia of Aristotelian Philosophy: Barhebraeus (13th c.),* Butyrum sapientiae, *Books of Ethics, Economy and Politics (Aristoteles Semitico-Latinus* 16*)* (Leiden and Boston, 2004)

KENNEDY, G. A., *Greek Rhetoric under Christian Emperors* (Princeton, 1983)

—— (tr.), *Aristotle* On Rhetoric. *A Theory of Civic Discourse* (New York and Oxford, 1991)

VAN LANTSCHOOT, N., *Inventaire des manuscrits syriaques des fonds Vatican (490-631), Barberini oriental et Neofiti (Studi e Testi* 243*)*, (Rome, 1965)

LYONS, M. C., *Aristotle's* Ars Rhetorica, *The Arabic Version. A new edition, with Commentary and Glossary*, 2 vols. (Cambridge, 1982) [Abbreviated Lyons]

MACOMBER, W. F., 'New Finds of Syriac Manuscripts in the Middle East', in W. Voigt (ed.), *XVII. Deutscher Orientalistentag (Würzburg)*, (Wiesbaden, 1969), II, 473-482

MARGOLIOUTH, D., *Analecta Orientalia ad Poeticam Aristoteleam* (London, 1887)

MARGOLIOUTH, G., *Descriptive List of Syriac and Karshuni MSS. in the British Museum Acquired since 1873* (London, 1899)

MEYERHOF, M., 'Von Alexandrien nach Bagdad', *Sitzungsberichte der Preussischen Akademie der Wissenschaften, Phil.-hist. Kl.* 23 (1930), 389-429

MORAUX, P., *Les listes anciennes des ouvrages d'Aristote* (Louvain, 1951)

NÖLDEKE, TH., *Kurzgefasste syrische Grammatik* (Leipzig, 1898, repr. with appendix by A. Schall, Darmstadt, 1966); *A Compendious Syriac Grammar*, tr. J. A. Crichton (London, 1904)

PANOUSSI, E., 'The Unique Arabic Manuscript of Aristotle's *Ars Rhetorica* and its two Editions published to date by 'Abdurrahman Badawi and by M[alcolm] C. Lyons', in S. J. al-Din Ashtinani, H. Matsubara, T. Iwami, and A. Matsumoto, *Consciousness and Reality. Studies in Memory of Toshihiko Izutsu* (Tokyo, 1998), 233-250

PAULY-WISSOWA, *Realencyclopädie der classischen Altertumswissenschaft* (Stuttgart/München, 1893–)

PAYNE SMITH, R., *Thesuarus Syriacus*, 2 vols. (Oxford, 1879-1901), and *Supplement*, by J. P. Margoliouth (Oxford, 1927) [Abbreviated *ThesSyr*]

PETERS, F. E., *Aristotle and the Arabs* (New York and London, 1968)

REININK, G. J., 'Severus Sebokts Brief an den Periodeutes Jonan: Einige Fragen zur aristotelischen Logik', in R. Lavenant (ed.), *III Symposium Syriacum 1980 (Orientalia Christiana Analecta* 221*)*, (Rome, 1983), 97-107

RIAD, E., *Studies in the Syriac Preface (Studia Semitica Upsaliensia* 11*)*, (Uppsala, 1988)

ROSENTHAL, F., *The Classical Heritage in Islam* (London, 1975)

SCHER, A., 'Notice sur les manuscrits syriaques et arabes conservés dans la bibliothèque de l'évêché chaldéen de Mardin', *Revue des bibliothèques* 18 (1908), 64-95

SCHOELER, G., 'Averroes' Rückwendung zu Aristoteles: die "Kurzen" und die "Mittleren Kommentare zum Organon",' *Bibliotheca Orientalis* 37 (1980), 294-301

SCHRIER, O. J., 'The Syriac and Arabic Versions of Aristotle's *Poetics*', in G. Endress and R. Kruk (eds.), *The Ancient Tradition in Christian and Islamic Hellenism: Studies on the Transmission of Greek Philosophy and Sciences dedicated to H. J. Drossaart Lulofs on his ninetieth birthday* (Leiden, 1997), 259-278

SEGAL, J. B., *The Diacritical Point and the Accents in Syriac* (London, 1953)

STROHMAIER, G., 'Ḥunain ibn Isḥāq - an Arab Scholar Translating into Syriac', *Aram* 3 (1991), 163-170

STROTHMANN, W., 'Die Schrift des Anton von Tagrit über die Rhetorik', in *Paul de Lagarde und die syrische Kirchengeschichte*, ed. Göttinger Arbeitskreis für syrische Kirchengeschichte (Göttingen, 1968), 199-216

TAKAHASHI, H., *Aristotelian Meteorology in Syriac. Barhebraeus,* Butyrum Sapientiae, *Books of Mineralogy and Meteorology* (*Aristoteles Semitico-Latinus* 15), (Leiden and Boston, 2004)

——, *Bar 'Ebroyo (Barhebraeus): A Bio-Bibliography* (Piscataway, N.J., forthcoming)

TEULE, H. G. B, '"La Critique du prince". Quelques aspects d'une philosophie politique dans l'œuvre de Barhebraeus', in G. J. Reinink and A. C. Kluglist (eds.), *After Bardaisan. Studies on Continuity and Change in Syriac Christianity in Honour of Professor Han J. W. Drijvers (Orientalia Lovaniensia Analecta 89)*, (Leuven, 1999), 287-294

——, 'Gregory Barhebraeus and his Time: The Syrian Renaissance', *Journal of the Canadian Society for Syriac Studies* 3 (2003), 21-43

——, 'The Syriac Translation of Avicenna's *kitāb al-ishārāt wa t-tanbihāt*', in J. J. van Ginkel, H. L. Murre-Van den Berg, and T. M. van Lint (eds.), *Redefining Christian Identity. Cultural Interaction in the Middle East since the Rise of Islam (Orientalia Lovaniensia Analecta 134)*, (Leuven, forthcoming)

WALZER, R., 'Zur Traditionsgeschichte der aristotelischen Poetik', *Studi italieni di filologia classica*, N.S. 11 (1934), 5-14; reprinted in idem, *Greek into Arabic* (Oxford, 1962), 129-136

——, 'Aspects of Islamic Political Thought: al-Fārābī and Ibn Xaldūn', *Oriens* 16 (1963), 40-60

WATT, J. W., 'The Syriac Reception of Platonic and Aristotelian Rhetoric', *Aram* 5 (1993), 579-601

——, 'Grammar, Rhetoric, and the Enkyklios Paideia in Syriac', *Zeitschrift der Deutschen Morgenländischen Gesellschaft* 143 (1993), 45-71

——, 'Syriac Rhetorical Theory and the Syriac Tradition of Aristotle's *Rhetoric*', in W. W. Fortenbaugh and D. C. Mirhady (eds.), *Peripatetic Rhetoric after Aristotle (Rutgers University Studies in Classical Humanities 6)*, (New Brunswick and London, 1994), 243-260

——, 'From Themistius to al-Fārābī: Platonic Political Philosophy and Aristotle's *Rhetoric* in the East', *Rhetorica* 13 (1995), 17-41

——, 'The Strategy of the Baghdad Philosophers. The Aristotelian Tradition as a Common Motif in Christian and Islamic Thought', in J. J. van Ginkel, H. L. Murre-Van den Berg, and T. M. van Lint (eds.), *Redefining Christian Identity. Cultural Interaction in the Middle East since the Rise of Islam (Orientalia Lovaniensia Analecta 134)*, (Leuven, forthcoming)

WÜRSCH, R., *Avicennas Bearbeitungen der aristotelischen Rhetorik: ein Beitrag zum Fortleben antiken Bildungsgutes in der islamischen Welt (Islamkundliche Untersuchungen* 146*)*, (Berlin, 1991) [Abbreviated Würsch]

ZIMMERMANN, F. W., *Al-Fārābī's Commentary and Short Treatise on Aristotle's* De Interpretatione (Oxford, 1981)

ZONTA, M., *Fonti greche e orientali dell'* Economia *di Bar-Hebraeus nell' opera "La Crema della Scienza"* (Naples, 1992)

——, 'Structure and Sources of Bar-Hebraeus' "Practical Philosophy" in *The Cream of Science*', in R. Lavenant (ed.), *Symposium Syriacum VII* (*Orientalia Christiana Analecta* 256), (Rome, 1998), 279-292

# CONCORDANCE OF PASSAGES

| *Aristotle* | *Ibn Sīnā* | *Bar Hebraeus* |
|---|---|---|
| | 1.1 (1.5-2.13) | 1.1.1 |
| | 1.1 (2.14-3.11) | 1.1.2 |
| | 1.1 (3.12-16;5.8-14;6.8) | 1.1.3 |
| 1.1.54a1-3 | 1.2 (6.11-7.12) | 1.2.1 |
| 1.1.54a3-11 | 1.2 (7.16-8.8) | 1.2.2 |
| 1.1 54a11-18 | 1.2 (8.9-15;12.5-14) | 1.2.3 |
| 1.1 54a18-26 | 1.2 (12.15-13.6) | 1.2.4 |
| 1.1 54a26-31 | 1.3 (13.9-14.9) | 1.3.1 |
| 1.1 54a31-b4 | 1.3 (14.9-15.15) | 1.3.2 |
| 1.1 54b5-16 | 1.3 (16.8-17.9) | 1.3.3 |
| 1.1 54b16-22 | 1.3 (17.10-18.6) | 1.3.4 |
| 1.1 54b22-28 | 1.3 (18.6-19.3) | 1.3.5 |
| 1.1 54b28-55a3 | 1.3 (19.5-8;20.12-15;20.2-7) | 1.3.6 |
| 1.1 55a3-18 | 1.3 (21.3-21.15) | 1.3.7 |
| 1.1 55a20-29 | 1.4 (22.3-23.7) | 1.4.1 |
| 1.1 55a29-36 | 1.4 (23.8-24.8) | 1.4.2 |
| 1.1 55a36-b7 | 1.4 (24.9-25.5) | 1.4.3 |
| 1.1 55b10-14 | 1.4 (25.8-25.13) | 1.4.4 |
| 1.1 55b15-21 | 1.4 (25.14-27.9) | 1.4.5 |
| 1.2 55b25-35 | 1.5 (28.11-30.2) | 1.5.1 |
| 1.2 55b35-56a1 | 1.5 (32.4-33.5) | 1.5.2 |
| 1.2 56a1-25 | 1.5 (33.6-34.5) | 1.5.3 |
| 1.2 56a25-35 | 1.5 (34.9-34.15) | 1.5.4 |
| 1.2 56a28-30 | 1.5 (35.6-35.9) | 1.5.5 |
| 1.2 56a35-b24 | 1.6 (35.12-36.5;37.6-14) | 1.6.1 |
| 1.2 56b26-57a1 | 1.6 (38.15;39.4-40.4) | 1.6.2 |
| 1.2 57a1-13 | 1.6 (41.7-12;42.2-14) | 1.6.3 |
| 1.2 57a13-19;22 - 57b1 | 1.6 (42.14-43.7) | 1.6.4 |
| 1.2 57a19-b3 | 1.6 (43.10-44.5; 45.1-4) | 1.7.1 |

| | | |
|---|---|---|
| 1.2 57b3-25; cf.AnPr 2.27 | 1.6 (44.12-16;8-12;45.4-8) | 1.7.2 |
| 1.2 57b25-58a2 | 1.7 (45.11-47.9) | 1.7.3 |
| 1.2 58a2-35 | 1.7 (47.12-49.4) | 1.7.4 |
| 1.3 58b6-20 | 2.1 (53.5-54.5; 54.18-55.1) | 1.8.1 |
| 1.3 58a37-b6;20-29 | 2.1 (55.2-6; 9-14) | 1.8.2 |
| 1.3 58b29-59a6 | 2.1 (55.14-56.6) | 1.8.3 |
| 1.3 59a6-29 | 2.1 (56.6-57.3) | 1.8.4 |
| 1.4 59a30-b2; 5 60b4-5 | 2.1 (57.7-58.3) | 2.1.1 |
| 1.4 59b2-23 | 2.1 (58.3-10) | 2.1.2 |
| 1.4 59b23-33 | 2.1 (58.11-59.4) | 2.1.3 |
| 1.4 59b33-60a6 | 2.1 (59.5-60.6) | 2.1.4 |
| 1.4 60a6-11 | 2.1 (60.7-14) | 2.1.5 |
| 1.4 60a12-17 | 2.1 (60.14-61.7) | 2.1.6 |
| 1.4 60a17-37 | 2.1 (61.8-15; 64.4) | 2.1.7 |
| 1.4 60a20-21,37-38; 8 65b29-66a2 | 2.1 (62.1-63.10) | 2.1.8 |
| 1.5 60b4-14 | 2.2 (64.11-65.7) | 2.2.1 |
| 1.5 60b14-31 | 2.2 (65.8-66.1) | 2.2.2 |
| 1.5 60b31-61a12 | 2.2 (66.2-67.1) | 2.2.3 |
| 1.5 61a12-25 | 2.2 (67.2-67.8) | 2.2.4 |
| 1.5 61a25-61b2 | 2.2 (67.9-68.7) | 2.2.5 |
| 1.5 61b3-18 | 2.2 (68.8-68.10) | 2.2.6 |
| 1.5 61b18-26 | 2.2 (68.10-68.14) | 2.2.7 |
| 1.5 61b26-28; 35-39 | 2.2 (69.1-69.2) | 2.2.8 |
| 1.5 61b39-62a14 | 2.2 (69.3-69.13) | 2.2.9 |
| 1.6 62a17-27 | 2.2 (69.14-70.3) | 2.3.1 |
| 1.6 62a27-34; cf. 63a5 | 2.2 (70.4 -71.4) | 2.3.2 |
| 1.6 62a34-62b9 | 2.2 (71.5-72.3) | 2.3.3 |
| 1.6 62b23-33 | 2.2 (72.3-72.9) | 2.3.4 |
| 1.6 62b33-63a10 | 2.2 (72.9-72.16) | 2.3.5 |
| 1.6 63a10-19 | 2.2 (72.16-73.13) | 2.3.6 |
| 1.6 63a19-33 | 2.2 (73.14-75.4) | 2.3.7 |
| 1.6 63a33-63b4 | 2.2 (75.4-75.15) | 2.3.8 |
| 1.7 63b5-33; cf. 64b26 | 2.3 (76.3-77.2) | 2.4.1 |
| 1.7 63b33-64a9 | 2.3 (77.3-77.16) | 2.4.2 |
| 1.7 64a10-23 | 2.3 (77.16-78.8) | 2.4.3 |
| 1.7 64a23-64b7 | 2.3 (78.9-79.5) | 2.4.4 |
| 1.7 64b7-65a9 | 2.3 (79.5-80.9) | 2.4.5 |
| 1.7 65a10-24 | 2.3 (80.9-81.5) | 2.4.6 |
| 1.7 65a24-30 | 2.3 (81.5) | 2.4.7 |

| | | |
|---|---|---|
| 1.7 65a30-65b19 | 2.3 (81.5-82.10) | 2.4.8 |
| 1.7 65b19-8 66a2; 12; 17-22 | 2.3 (82.11-83.10) | 2.4.9 |
| 1.9 66a23-24; 28- 66b9 | 2.4 (84.3-84.11) | 3.1.1 |
| 1.9 66b9-22 | 2.4 (84.12-85.6) | 3.1.2 |
| 1.9 66b22-67a6 | 2.4 (85.7-86.15) | 3.2.1 |
| 1.9 67a6-18 | 2.4 (86.16-87.14) | 3.2.2 |
| | 2.4 (87.14-88.6) | 3.2.3 |
| 1.9 67a18-32 | 2.4 (88.6-88.12) | 3.2.4 |
| 1.9 67a32-36 | 2.4 (88.13-89.1) | 3.3.1 |
| 1.9 67a37-b3 | 2.4 (89.1-89.4) | 3.3.2 |
| 1.9 67b3-12 | 2.4 (89.5-89.12) | 3.3.3 |
| 1.9 67b12-20 | 2.4 (89.12-90.5) | 3.3.4 |
| 1.9 67b21-36 | 2.4 (90.6-91.6) | 3.3.5 |
| 1.9 67b36-68a10 | 2.4 (91.7-91.17) | 3.4.1 |
| 1.9 68a10-22 | 2.4 (92.1-92.14) | 3.4.2 |
| 1.9 68a22-24;26-37 | 2.4 (92.15-93.1) | 3.4.3 |
| 1.10 68b1-10 | 2.5 (93.14-94.14) | 4.1.1 |
| 1.10 68b10-26 | 2.5 (94.14-96.1) | 4.1.2 |
| 1.10 68b26-69a7 | 2.5 (96.2-97.3) | 4.2.1 |
| 1.10 69a7-31 | 2.5 (97.3-97.16) | 4.2.2 |
| 1.10 69a32-b14 | 2.5 (98.1-99.3) | 4.2.3 |
| 1.10 69b14-32 | 2.5 (99.3-99.11) | 4.2.4 |
| 1.11 69b33-70a27 | 2.6 (99.14-100.10) | 4.3.1 |
| 1.11 70a27-b14 | 2.6 (100.10-101.6) | 4.3.2 |
| 1.11 70b14-29 | 2.6 (101.6-101.12) | 4.3.3 |
| 1.11 70b29-71a8 | 2.6 (101.12-102.5) | 4.3.4 |
| 1.11 71a8-24 | 2.6 (102.5-103.2) | 4.3.5 |
| 1.11 71a24-b12 | 2.6 (103.2-104.3) | 4.3.6 |
| 1.11 71b12-72a3 | 2.6 (104.3-104.9) | 4.3.7 |
| 1.12 72a4-28 | 2.7 (104.14-105.15) | 4.4.1 |
| 1.12 72a28-36 | 2.7 (105.15-106.11) | 4.4.2 |
| 1.12 72a36-b16 | 2.7 (106.9-107.6) | 4.4.3 |
| 1.12 72b16-73a4 | 2.7 (107.6-108.15) | 4.4.4 |
| 1.12 73a4-21 | 2.7 (108.15-109.16) | 4.4.5 |
| 1.12 73a21-27 | 2.7 (109.16-110.8) | 4.4.6 |
| 1.12 73a27-37 | 2.7 (110.8-14) | 4.4.7 |
| 1.13 73b1-18 | 2.8 (111.4-6) | 4.5.1 |
| 1.13 73b18-29; 39-74a18 | 2.8 (111.6-112.5) | 4.5.2 |
| 1.13 74a18-33 | 2.8 (112.5-113.10) | 4.5.3 |

| | | |
|---|---|---|
| 1.13 74a33-b9 | 2.8 (113.10-114.12) | 4.5.4 |
| 1.13 74b10-15 | 2.8 (114.13-115.4) | 4.5.5 |
| 1.13 74b15-23 | 2.8 (115.4-11) | 4.5.6 |
| 1.14 74b24-30 | 2.8 (115.12-116.15) | 4.5.7 |
| 1.14 74b30-75a21 | 2.8 (116.16-117.7) | 4.5.8 |
| 1.15 75a22-b8 | 2.9 (117.10-118.13) | 4.6.1 |
| 1.15 75b8-26 | 2.9 (119.1-15) | 4.6.2 |
| 1.15 75b26-76a11 | 2.9 (120.1-9) | 4.6.3 |
| 1.15 76a12-33 | 2.9 (120.9-121.11) | 4.6.4 |
| 1.15 76a33-b19 | 2.9 (121.12-122.14) | 4.6.5 |
| 1.15 76b19-31 | 2.9 (122.14-123.16) | 4.6.6 |
| 1.15 76b31-77a7 | 2.9 (124.1-13) | 4.6.7 |
| 1.15 77a7-20 | 2.9 (124.14-125.8) | 4.6.8 |
| 1.15 77a20-b11 | 2.9 (125.9-126.13) | 4.6.9 |
| | | |
| 2.1 77b16-78a30 | 3.1 (129.3-130.8) | 5.1.1 |
| 2.2 78a31-b13 | 3.1 (130.9-16) | 5.1.2 |
| 2.2 78b13-34 | 3.1 (130.16-131.9) | 5.1.3 |
| 2.2 78b34-79b4 | 3.1 (131.10-132.12) | 5.1.4 |
| 2.2 79b4 - 3 80a7 | 3.1 (132.13-133.11) | 5.1.5 |
| 2.3 80a7-33 | 3.1 (133.11-134.9) | 5.1.6 |
| 2.3 80a34-b16 | 3.1 (134.9-135.2) | 5.1.7 |
| 2.3 80b16-29 | 3.1 (135.2-8) | 5.1.8 |
| 2.4 80b34-81a25 | 3.2 (135.11-136.9) | 5.2.1 |
| 2.4 81a25-b33 | 3.2 (136.9-137.12) | 5.2.2 |
| 2.4 81b33-82a7; 16-19 | 3.2 (137.13-138.4) | 5.2.3 |
| 2.5 82a21-b3; 10-12 | 3.2 (138.5-139.2) | 5.2.4 |
| 2.5 82b13-26; 35-83a14 | 3.2 (139.2-14) | 5.2.5 |
| 2.5 83a14-25 | 3.2 (139.15-140.15) | 5.2.6 |
| 2.5 83a25-b11 | 3.2 (140.15-141.13) | 5.2.7 |
| 2.6 83b12-30 | 3.3 (142.3-12) | 5.3.1 |
| 2.6 83b30-84a23 | 3.3 (142.12-143.10) | 5.3.2 |
| 2.6 84a23-b1;5-11;19-36 | 3.3 (143.10-144.15) | 5.3.3 |
| 2.6 84b11-27;32-33;85a9-13 | 3.3 (144.15-145.6) | 5.3.4 |
| 2.6 85a13 - 7 85a34 | 3.3 (145.7-146.5) | 5.3.5 |
| 2.7 85a34-b11 | 3.3 (146.6-147.7) | 5.3.6 |
| 2.8 85b11-86a4 | 3.4 (147.11-148.13) | 5.4.1 |
| 2.8 86a4-24 | 3.4 (148.14-149.7) | 5.4.2 |
| 2.8 86a24 - 9 86b16 | 3.4 (149.7-150.8) | 5.4.3 |

| | | |
|---|---|---|
| 2.9 86b16-25 | 3.4 (150.13-151.8) | 5.4.4 |
| 2.9 86b25-87a5 | 3.4 (151.8-14) | 5.4.5 |
| 2.9 87a5-32 | 3.4 (151.15-152.12) | 5.4.6 |
| 2.9 87a32-b20 | 3.4 (152.12-153.5) | 5.4.7 |
| 2.10 87b21-88a9 | 3.4 (153.5-16) | 5.4.8 |
| 2.10 88a9-28 | 3.4 (154.1-11) | 5.4.9 |
| 2.11 88a29-b14 | 3.4 (154.12-155.4) | 5.4.10 |
| 2.11 88b14-30 | 3.4 (155.4-14) | 5.4.11 |
| 2.12 88b31-89a9 | 3.5 (156.1-157.1) | 5.5.1 |
| 2.12 89a9-25 | 3.5 (157.1-9) | 5.5.2 |
| 2.12 89a25-36 | 3.5 (157.9-158.6) | 5.5.3 |
| 2.12 89a36-b12 | 3.5 (158.7-18) | 5.5.4 |
| 2.13 89b13-24 | 3.5 (159.1-10) | 5.5.5 |
| 2.13 89b24-35 | 3.5 (159.11-160.2) | 5.5.6 |
| 2.13 89b35-90a16 | 3.5 (160.2-15) | 5.5.7 |
| 2.13 90a16 - 14 90b13 | 3.5 (160.16-161.16) | 5.5.8 |
| 2.15 90b14-31 | 3.5 (162.1-8) | 5.5.9 |
| 2.16 90b32-91a12 | 3.5 (162.9-16) | 5.5.10 |
| 2.16 91a14 - 17 91a30 | 3.5 (162.17-163.11) | 5.5.11 |
| 2.17 91a30-b7 | 3.5 (163.12-15) | 5.5.12 |
| 2.18 91b8-27 | 3.5 (163.16-164.8) | 5.5.13 |
| 2.18 91b28 - 19 92a23 | 3.6 (164.11-165.10) | 6.1.1 |
| 2.19 92a23-b14 | 3.6 (165.10-166.3) | 6.1.2 |
| 2.19 92b14-93a21 | 3.6 (166.4-167.6) | 6.1.3 |
| 2.20 93a22-30 | 3.6 (167.7-14) | 6.2.1 |
| 2.20 93a30-b23 | 3.6 (167.15-168.10) | 6.2.2 |
| 2.20 93b23-94a2 | 3.6 (168.11-169.6) | 6.2.3 |
| 2.20 94a2-18 | 3.6 (169.7-170.5) | 6.2.4 |
| 2.21 94a21-b6 | 3.6 (170.9-171.1) | 6.3.1 |
| 2.21 94b7-25 | 3.6 (171.1-9) | 6.3.2 |
| 2.21 94b25-95a2 | 3.6 (172.11-173.4) | 6.3.3 |
| 2.21 95a2-17 | 3.6 (173.5-174.1) | 6.3.4 |
| 2.21 95a17-24 | 3.6 (174.1-13) | 6.3.5 |
| 2.21 95a24-32 | 3.6 (174.13-175.7) | 6.3.6 |
| 2.21 95b1-19 | 3.6 (175.8-17) | 6.3.7 |
| 2.22 95b22-31 | 3.7 (176.4-177.8) | 6.4.1 |
| 2.22 95b29-96a23 | 3.7 (177.8-178.13) | 6.4.2 |
| 2.22 96a33-b22 | 3.7 (178.14-179.4) | 6.4.3 |
| 2.22 96b22 - 2.23 97a29 | 3.7 (179.5-12) | 6.5.1 |

| | | |
|---|---|---|
| 2.23 97a29-b20 | 3.7 (179.12-180.4) | 6.5.2 |
| 2.23 97b20-98a28 | 3.7 (180.5-181.4) | 6.5.3 |
| 2.23 98a29-b9 | 3.7 (181.4-7) | 6.5.4 |
| 2.23 98b9-29 | 3.7 (181.8-9) | 6.5.5 |
| 2.23 99a6-25 | 3.7 (181.9-182.2) | 6.5.6 |
| 2.23 99a25-32 | 3.7 (182.3-12) | 6.5.7 |
| 2.23 99a32-b13 | 3.7 (182.12-183.15) | 6.5.8 |
| 2.23 99b13-30 | 3.7 (183.15-184.9) | 6.5.9 |
| 2.23 99b30-00a14 | 3.7 (184.9-16) | 6.5.10 |
| 2.23 00a14-35 | 3.7 (184.16-185.10) | 6.5.11 |
| 2.23 00a35-b16 | 3.7 (185.10-186.15) | 6.5.12 |
| 2.23 00b16-25 | 3.7 (186.15-187.2) | 6.5.13 |
| 2.23 00b25-33 | 3.7 (187.2-7) | 6.5.14 |
| 2.24 00b34-01b9 | 3.8 (187.11-188.16) | 6.6.1 |
| 2.24 01b9-20 | 3.8 (189.1-11) | 6.6.2 |
| 2.24 01b20-34 | 3.8 (189.11-190.5) | 6.6.3 |
| 2.24 01b34-02a8;17-29 | 3.8 (190.5-191.1) | 6.6.4 |
| 2.25 02a30-37; b4-12 | 3.8 (191.2-16) | 6.7.1 |
| 2.25 02b12-03a2 | 3.8 (191.17-192.17) | 6.7.2 |
| 2.25 03a2 - 26 03a33 | 3.8 (192.18-193.16) | 6.7.3 |
| | | |
| 3.1 03b6-32 (cf. 04a10-12; 17-19) | 4.1 (197.3-198.4) | 7.1.1 |
| 3.1 03b32-04a18 | 4.1 (199.2-200.12) | 7.1.2 |
| 3.1 04a18-27 | 4.1 (200.12-201.5) | 7.1.3 |
| 3.1 04a27 - 3.2 04b8 | 4.1 (201.9-202.17) | 7.1.4 |
| 3.2 04b8-18 | 4.1 (203.1-10) | 7.2.1 |
| 3.2 04b18-26 | 4.1 (203.10-204.6) | 7.2.2 |
| 3.2 04b26-05a8 | 4.1 (204.7-205.5) | 7.2.3 |
| 3.2 05a8-26 | 4.1 (205.6-206.3) | 7.2.4 |
| 3.2 05a26-b19 | 4.1 (206.3-208.5) | 7.2.5 |
| 3.2 05b19-33 | 4.1 (208.5-209.9) | 7.2.6 |
| 3.3 05b34-06a6 | 4.1 (209.10-17) | 7.3.1 |
| 3.3 06a6-10 | 4.1 (210.1-4) | 7.3.2 |
| 3.3 06a10-14 | 4.1 (210.5-211.5) | 7.3.3 |
| 3.3 06a14-b4 | 4.1 (211.5-212.3) | 7.3.4 |
| 3.3 06b4 - 4 06b26;07a1-3;14-17 | 4.1 (212.4-16) | 7.3.5 |
| 3.5 07a19-30 | 4.2 (213.5-214.7) | 7.4.1 |
| 3.5 07a30-b6 | 4.2 (214.9-215.5) | 7.4.2 |
| 3.5 07b6-19 | 4.2 (215.5-216.1) | 7.4.3 |

| | | |
|---|---|---|
| 3.5 07b19 - 6 07b31 | 4.2 (216.1-217.6) | 7.4.4 |
| 3.6 07b31-08a9 | 4.2 (217.7-218.16) | 7.5.1 |
| 3.7 08a10-25; 32-36 | 4.2 (219.1-220.13) | 7.5.2 |
| 3.7 08a36-b20 | 4.2 (220.14-221.14) | 7.5.3 |
| 3.8 08b21-28 | 4.2 (221.15-222.12) | 7.5.4 |
| 3.8 08b28-09a13 | 4.2 (222.12-224.8) | 7.5.5 |
| 3.8 09a13-23; 08b30-32 | 4.2 (224.11-225.12) | 7.5.6 |
| 3.9 09a24-b9; cf. 10a22-28 | 4.3 (226.6-227.3) | 7.6.1 |
| 3.9 09b13-32 | 4.3 (227.3-228.1) | 7.6.2 |
| 3.9 09b32-10b5 | 4.3 (228.1-10) | 7.6.3 |
| 3.10 10b10-35 | 4.3 (228.10-229.10) | 7.7.1 |
| 3.10 10b35-11a4; 31-b23; 11 11b23-28; cf. 10b17-18 | 4.3 (229.10-230.5) | 7.7.2 |
| 3.11 11b31-12a12; 17-23; 12b10-11 | 4.3 (230.6-231.1) | 7.7.3 |
| 3.11 12b1-32 | 4.3 (231.1-9) | 7.7.4 |
| 3.11 12b32-13a28 | 4.3 (231.10-232.2) | 7.7.5 |
| 3.11 13a28 - 12 13b8 | 4.3 (232.2-16) | 7.8.1 |
| 3.12 13b8-21 | 4.3 (233.1-10) | 7.8.2 |
| 3.12 13b21-14a1 | 4.3 (233.10-234.5) | 7.8.3 |
| 3.12 14a1-17 | 4.3 (234.6-235.11) | 7.8.4 |
| 3.12 14a17-29 | 4.3 (235.11-236.6) | 7.8.5 |
| 3.13 14a30-36 | 4.4 (236.11-237.2) | 7.9.1 |
| 3.13 14a36-b7; cf. 14 15a23 | 4.4 (237.2-10) | 7.9.2 |
| 3.13 14b7-12; 14 14b19-21; 29 - 15a10; 23-24 | 4.4 (237.10-238.8) | 7.9.3 |
| 3.14 15a24-b10; cf. 15b37-38 | 4.4 (238.9-239.6) | 7.9.4 |
| 3.14 15b10-16a3 | 4.4 (239.7-240.2) | 7.9.5 |
| 3.15 16a4-b15 | 4.4 (240.3-241.2) | 7.9.6 |
| 3.16 16b16-29; 1.9 67b26-68a10 | 4.4 (241.3-242.8) | 7.9.7 |
| 3.16 16b32-17a36 | 4.4 (242.8-243.5) | 7.9.8 |
| 3.16 17a36 - 17 17b38 | 4.4 (243.5-244.3) | 7.9.9 |
| 3.17 17b38-18a32 | 4.4 (244.4-15) | 7.9.10 |
| 3.17 18a39-b33; cf. 18a27-33 | 4.4 (244.15-245.10) | 7.9.11 |
| 3.18 18b39-19a19 | 4.5 (245.15-246.15) | 7.10.1 |
| 3.18 19a19-b9 | 4.5 (246.15-247.9) | 7.10.2 |
| 3.19 19b10-20b3 | 4.5 (247.10-15) | 7.10.3 |

# ARISTOTELES SEMITICO-LATINUS

*Founded by*
H.J. Drossaart Lulofs

*General Editors*
H. Daiber
R. Kruk

* *Volumes 1 to 4 are available directly from the Royal Netherlands Academy of Arts and Sciences, P.O. Box 19121, 1000 GC Amsterdam, The Netherlands / edita@bureau.knaw.nl*

*1. Ḥunain ibn Isḥâq.– *Ein kompendium der aristotelischen Meteorologie in der Fassung des Ḥunain ibn Isḥâq.* Hrsg. mit Übers., Komm.und Einl. von H. Daiber. 1975. (viii, 117 [18 Arabic t.] pp., 4 [facs.] pl.). ISBN 07 20 48302 6
*2. Aristotle.– *The Arabic version of Aristotle's Parts of Animals. Books* XI-XIV *of the Kitāb al-Ḥayawān.* Critical ed. with introd. and sel. glossary by R. Kruk. 1979 (96 [4 fasc.], 156 Arabic t. pp.). ISBN 07 20 48467 7
*3. Gätje, H. *Das Kapitel über das Begehren aus dem Mittleren Kommentar des Averroes zur Schrift über die Seele.* [Mit Text u. Übers.] 1985. (viii, 100 [10 Arabic t.] pp.). ISBN 04 44 85640 4
*4. Nicolaus Damascenus, *De Plantis.* Five translations. Ed. with introd. by H.J. Drossaart Lulofs and E.L.J. Poortman. 1989. (xvi, 732 [incl. Syriac, Arabic, Hebrew, Latin, Greek t. and num. fasc.] pp.). ISBN 04 44 85703 6
5. Aristotle. *De Animalibus. Michael Scot's Arabic-Latin translation.* Three parts.
Part 1. Books I-X : History of Animals. Ed. by A.M.I. van Oppenraaij. *In Preparation.*
Part 2. Books XI-XIV : Parts of Animals. Ed. by A.M.I. van Oppenraaij. 1998. ISBN 90 04 11070 4
Part 3. Books XV-XIX : Generation of Animals. Ed. by A.M.I. van Oppenraaij. With a Greek index to *De Generatione Animalium* by H.J. Drossaart Lulofs. 1992. (xxvi, 504 [243 Latin p.] pp.). ISBN 90 04 09603 5
6. Aristotle's *De Anima* translated into Hebrew by Zeraḥyah ben Isaac ben Shealtiel Ḥen. Ed. by G. Bos. 1993. ISBN 90 04 09937 9
7. Lettinck, P. *Aristotle's* Physics *and its reception in the Arabic world.* With an edition of the unpublished parts of Ibn Bājja's *Commentary on the Physics.* 1994. ISBN 90 04 09960 3
8. Fontaine, R.. *Otot ha-Shamayim.* Samuel Ibn Tibbon's Hebrew version of Aristotle's *Meteorology.* A critical edition, with introduction, translation, and index. 1995. ISBN 90 04 10258 2
9. Aristoteles' *De Anima. Eine verlorene spätantike Paraphrase in arabischer und persischer Überlieferung.* Arabischer Text nebst Kommentar, quellengeschichtlichen Studien und Glossaren. Hrsg. von R. Arnzen. 1998. ISBN 90 04 10699 5
10. Lettinck P. *Aristotle's* Meteorology *and its reception in the Arab world.* With an Edition and Translation of Ibn Suwār's *Treatise on Meteorological Phenomena* and Ibn Bājja's *Commentary on the Meteorology.* 1999. ISBN 90 04 10933 1

11. Filius L.S. (ed.). *The Problemata Physica attributed to Aristotle.* The Arabic Version of Ḥunain ibn Isḥāq and the Hebrew Version of Moses ibn Tibbon. 1999. ISBN 90 04 11483 1
12. Schoonheim, P.L. *Aristotle's* Meteorology *in the Arabico-Latin Tradition.* A Critical Edition of the Texts, with Introduction and Indices. 2000. ISBN 90 04 11760 1
13. Poortman, E.L.J. *Petrus de Alvernia, Sententia super librum 'De vegetabilibus et plantis.* 2003. ISBN 90 04 11766 0
14. Gutman, O. *Pseudo-Avicenna, Liber Celi et Mundi.* A Critical Edition with Introduction. 2003. ISBN 90 04 13228 7
15. Takahashi, H. *Aristotelian Meteorology in Syriac.* Barhebraeus, *Butyrum Sapientiae,* Books of Mineralogy and Meteorology. 2004. ISBN 90 04 13031 4
16. Joosse, P. *A Syriac Encyclopaedia of Aristotelian Philosophy. Barhebraeus (13th c.),* Butyrum sapientiae, *Books of Ethics, Economy and Politics.* 2004. ISBN 90 04 14133 2
17. Akasoy, A.A. and A. Fidora. *The Arabic Version of The* Nicomachean Ethics. With an Introduction and Annotated Translation by Douglas M. Dunlop. 2005. ISBN 90 04 14647 4
18. Watt, J.W. with assistance of Daniel Isaac, Julian Faultless, and Ayman Shihadeh. *Aristotelian Rhetoric in Syriac.* Barhebraeus, *Butyrum Sapientiae,* Book of Rhetoric. 2005. ISBN 90 04 14517 6

*In Preparation*

Aristotle. *Historia Animalium. The Arabic translation commonly ascribed to Yaḥyā ibn al-Biṭrīq.* Ed. with introd. by L.S. Filius, J. den Heijer and J.N. Mattock.

Aristotle. *Poetica. The Syriac fragments.* Ed. by O. Schrier.

Aristotle. *Parva Naturalia. The Arabic translation.* Ed. by H. Daiber.

Aristoteles. *De Cælo. Die arabische Übersetzung.* Hrsg. von G. Endress.

Aristotle. *De Cælo. Gerard of Cremona's Arabic-Latin translation.* Ed. by A.M.I. van Oppenraaij.

Aristotle. *Physica. Gerard of Cremona's Arabic-Latin translation.* Ed. by D. Konstan.

Pedro Gallego. *De Animalibus. A Latin compendium of Aristotle's* De Animalibus. Ed. by A.M.I. van Oppenraaij.